TEXAS CRIMINAL LAWYER'S HANDBOOK

BY ROBERT K. GILL

HIGHLIGHTS

This new edition of ***Texas Criminal Lawyer's Handbook*** will keep you on the cutting edge of Texas criminal law, practice and procedure, with new and updated coverage of a broad range of issues, including:

SEARCH AND SEIZURE

- Investigatory vehicle stops: insurance investigations; warrants
- Misstatements, errors and omissions in affidavits
- Blood draws
- Appellate review of motions to suppress

RIGHT TO COUNSEL/EFFECTIVE ASSISTANCE OF COUNSEL

- How to make a McCoy complaint
- Defendant's request for an appeal

CONFESSIONS

- Invocation and waiver of right to attorney
- Suppression under Art. 38.23

DOUBLE JEOPARDY

- Dual-sovereignty (Gamble v. United States, 587 U.S. ___ (2019))
- Multiple punishments in successive trials
- Retrials after mistrials
- Probation revocation proceedings

EVIDENCE

- Cell phone data and GPS tracking
- Body worn cameras (new!)
- Expert witness qualifications
- Doctrine of forfeiture by wrongdoing

PRETRIAL MOTIONS

- Indictments and informations
- Allegations not required (attempted offense v. consummated offense)
- Sufficiency
- Grounds for challenge
- Guilty pleas: requirements for voluntary plea; involuntary pleas

TRIAL ISSUES

- Trial court considerations in deciding whether Batson violation occurred
- The parole charge (new!)
- Due process – prosecutorial conduct: suppression of evidence (new!)
- Defenses and justifications: self-defense; character evidence; mental status
- Pronouncing the verdict (new!)

And More!

James Publishing

James Publishing, Inc.
3505 Cadillac Avenue, Suite P-101
Costa Mesa, CA 92626

You can also visit us on the Internet!
www.jamespublishing.com

How To Access Your Digital Forms

Included with your copy of this book is access to all its forms in digital format. So you can easily open and modify the forms, **we have replaced our jamesforms.com website and our old CDs with a convenient ZIP file of Word documents.**

Access is easy.
If you purchased this title on jamespublishing.com, a link to download the ZIP file should have already been delivered to your email inbox. Be sure to add customer-service@jamespublishing.com to your safe sender list so this message doesn't land in a spam folder. You can also access the download link at any time by **logging in at jamespublishing.com and clicking My Account** in the upper right-hand corner.

No account yet? No problem.
If you do not yet have a jamespublishing.com account, or you are having trouble, please contact customer support at **1-866-725-2637** or customer-service@jamespublishing.com. We will get you setup right away.

How to unzip the file:
Once you download the ZIP file, you need to extract the files onto your system. Typically, files are downloaded into your Downloads folder unless another directory was specified. Follow these steps to unzip:

1. **Double-click the ZIP file**. In Windows XP or newer and Mac OS X, you can double-click the ZIP file and it will open in a new window. You can then copy the contents to another folder. OS X will create a new folder next to the ZIP file when you double-click it, but may not open it automatically.

2. **Right-click thc ZIP file**. In Windows you can right-click the ZIP file and select *Extract All...* or *Extract Here*. Extract All will allow you to set a path for the extracted folder to go, and Extract Here will decompress the folder and leave it in the same location as the ZIP file.

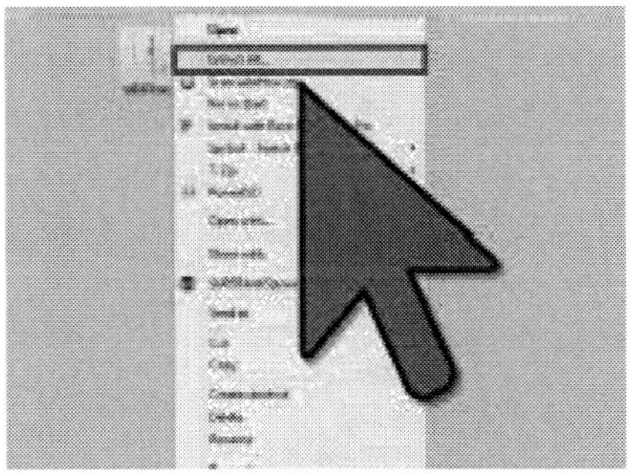

Can I share my digital forms with others?
No. Our forms are copyrighted, and they are licensed to a single individual book purchaser for his or her use only. It is unfair to our book authors if their forms are freely distributed, so please honor their hard work by not sharing their forms. Thank you for understanding.

(This page intentionally left blank.)

TEXAS CRIMINAL LAWYER'S HANDBOOK

VOLUME 1

by

Mark G. Daniel

Robert K. Gill

James Publishing

ISBN 978-1-949517-52-1

We view the publication of this work as the beginning of a dialogue with our readers. Periodic revisions to it will give us the opportunity to incorporate your suggested changes. Call us at (866) 72-JAMES or send your comments to:

Revision Editor
James Publishing, Inc.
3505 Cadillac Ave., Suite P-101
Costa Mesa, CA 92626

Managing Editor: Lisa Dunne
Typesetting: Nancy Russell

Revision 15, 09/14
Revision 16, 09/15
Revision 17, 09/16
Revision 18, 09/17
Revision 19, 09/18
Revision 20, 09/19

ABOUT THE AUTHORS

BOB GILL is a criminal defense attorney with the firm of Gill and Brissette in Fort Worth, Texas. He previously served as judge of the 213th District Court of Tarrant County, presiding over felony criminal cases for more than fourteen years. While on the bench, Judge Gill served Tarrant County as presiding criminal judge, juvenile board chairman, and twice served as the local administrative judge. Before and after his time on the bench, Judge Gill served as an assistant criminal district attorney in Tarrant County for a combined seventeen years.

Judge Gill has been Board Certified in Criminal Law by the Texas Board of Legal Specialization since 1988. He is a member of the State Bar of Texas, the Tarrant County Bar Association and the Tarrant County Criminal Defense Lawyers Association. He has written and lectured extensively on criminal law topics.

MARK G. DANIEL practices with the Fort Worth office of Evans, Gandy, Daniel & Moore. A former Assistant District Attorney in Tarrant County, Mr. Daniel has been in private practice since 1983, devoting his practice of criminal defense at the trial court level.

Mr. Daniel is past president of the Tarrant County Criminal Defense Lawyers Association (1991) and the Texas Criminal Defense Lawyers Association (2002-2003). He served as President of the Tarrant County Bar Association for the 2006-2007 bar year.

Mr. Daniel is Board Certified in criminal law by the Texas Board of Legal Specialization and the National Board of Trial Advocacy. He is also a frequent author and speaker on criminal law topics including defending capital murder cases, pre-trial motions, cross-examination, forfeitures, expert witnesses, privileges and punishment hearings.

(This page intentionally left blank.)

CONSTITUTIONAL RIGHTS

CONSTITUTIONAL PROVISIONS

Arrests

Search & Seizure

U.S. Constitution, 4th Amendment: "The right of the people to be secure in their persons, houses, papers, and effects, against unreasonable searches and seizures, shall not be violated, and no Warrants shall issue, but upon probable cause, supported by Oath or affirmation, and particularly describing the place to be searched, and the persons or things to be seized.

Texas Constitution, Art. 1, Sec. 9: "The people shall be secure in their persons, houses, papers, and possessions, from all unreasonable seizures or searches, and no warrant to search any place, or to seize any person or thing, shall issue without describing them as near as may be, nor without probable cause, supported by oath or affirmation."

See also, CCP Art. 1.06.

Confessions

Self-Incrimination

U.S. Constitution, 5th Amendment: "No person ... shall be compelled in any criminal case to be a witness against himself, nor be deprived of life, liberty, or property, without due process of law[.]"

Texas Constitution, Art. 1, Sec. 10: "[... The accused] ... shall not be compelled to give evidence against himself ..."

Confrontation

Right to Counsel

Speedy and Public Trial

U.S. Constitution, 6th Amendment: "In all criminal prosecutions, the accused shall enjoy the right to a speedy and public trial, by an impartial jury of the State and district wherein the crime shall have been committed ... and to be informed of the nature and cause of the accusation; to be confronted with the witnesses against him; to have compulsory process for obtaining Witnesses in his favor, and to have the assistance of counsel for his defence."

Texas Constitution, Art. 1, Sec. 10: "In all criminal prosecutions the accused shall have a speedy public trial by an impartial jury. He ... shall have the right of being heard by himself or counsel, or both, shall be confronted by the witnesses against him and shall have compulsory process for obtaining witnesses in his favor..."

See also, CCP Art. 1.05

Due Process of Law

Equal Protection of the Law

U.S. Constitution, 14th Amendment, Sec. 1: "No state shall make or enforce any law which shall abridge the privileges or immunities of citizens of the United States; nor shall any State deprive any person of life, liberty, or property, without due process of law; nor deny to any person within its jurisdiction the equal protection of the laws."

Texas Constitution, Art. 1, Sec. 19: "No citizen of this State shall be deprived of life, liberty, property, privileges or immunities, or in any manner disfranchised, except by the due course of the law of the land."

See also, CCP Art. 1.04.

U.S. Constitution, 5th Amendment: "... No person shall ... be deprived of life, liberty, or property without due process of law..."

Jeopardy

U.S. Constitution, 5th Amendment: "... [n]or shall any person be subject for the same offence to be twice put in jeopardy of life or limb."

Texas Constitution, Art. 1, Sec. 14: "No person, for the same offense, shall be twice put in jeopardy of life or liberty, nor shall a person be again put upon trial for the same offense, after a verdict of not guilty in a court of competent jurisdiction."

See also, CCP Arts. 1.10 and 1.11.

Freedom of Press

Freedom of Speech

Freedom of Religion

U.S. Constitution, 1st Amendment: "Congress shall make no law respecting an establishment of religion, or prohibiting the free exercise thereof; or abridging the freedom of speech, or of the press; or the right of the people peaceably to assemble, and to petition the Government for a redress of grievances."

Texas Constitution, Art. 1, Sec. 8: "Every person shall be at liberty to speak, write or publish his opinion on any subject, being responsible for the abuse of that privilege; and no law shall ever be passed curtailing the liberty of speech or of the press. In prosecutions for the publication of papers, investigating the conduct of officers, or men in public capacity, or when the matter published is proper for public information, the truth thereof may be given in evidence. And in all indictments for libels, the jury shall have the right to determine the law and the facts, under the direction of the court, as in other cases."

Texas Constitution, Art. 1, Sec. 5: "No person shall be disqualified to give evidence in any of the Courts of this State on account of his religious opinions, or for the want of any religious belief, but all oaths or affirmations shall be administered in the mode most binding upon the conscience, and shall be taken subject to the pains and penalties of perjury."

See also, CCP Arts. 1.16 and 1.17

Cruel and Unusual Punishments

U.S. Constitution, 8th Amendment: "Excessive bail shall not be required, nor excessive fines imposed, nor cruel and unusual punishments inflicted."

Texas Constitution, Art. 1, Sec. 3: "Excessive bail shall not be required, nor excessive fines imposed, nor cruel and unusual punishments inflicted."

See also, CCP Art 1.09.

TABLE OF CONTENTS

VOLUME 1

VOLUME 2

(This page intentionally left blank.)

EXPANDED TABLE OF CONTENTS

CHAPTER 1. ARRESTS

CHAPTER 2. SEARCH AND SEIZURE: PROPERTY

CHAPTER 3. SEARCH AND SEIZURE: PERSONS

CHAPTER 4. RIGHT TO COUNSEL AND EFFECTIVE ASSISTANCE OF COUNSEL

CHAPTER 5. SELF-INCRIMINATION

CHAPTER 6. CONFESSIONS

CHAPTER 7. RULES OF STATUTORY AND LEGAL INTERPRETATION

CHAPTER 8. DOUBLE JEOPARDY

CHAPTER 9. BAIL AND BOND ISSUES

CHAPTER 10. [RESERVED]

CHAPTER 11. EXAMINING TRIALS AND GRAND JURY HEARINGS

CHAPTER 12. PRETRIAL MOTIONS

CHAPTER 13. DISCOVERY

CHAPTER 14. JURY SELECTION AND VOIR DIRE

CHAPTER 15. TRIAL ISSUES

CHAPTER 16. EVIDENCE

CHAPTER 17. CHILD SEXUAL ABUSE

CHAPTER 18. SEX OFFENDER REGISTRATION

CHAPTER 19. PRESERVATION OF ERROR

CHAPTER 20. PUNISHMENT PHASE

CHAPTER 21. POST-TRIAL ISSUES

CHAPTER 22. EXPUNCTIONS AND NON-DISCLOSURES

(This page intentionally left blank.)

Chapter 1

ARRESTS

Table of Contents

§1:10 What Is an Arrest

CCP Art. 15.22. When a person is arrested

> *A person is arrested when he has been actually placed under restraint or taken into custody by an officer or person executing a warrant of arrest, or by an officer or person arresting without a warrant.*

An arrest occurs when a person's liberty of movement is restricted or restrained. Amores v. State, 816 S.W.2d 417 (Tex. Crim. App. 1991).

A person is seized for constitutional purposes, when under all of the circumstances, a reasonable person would believe that he is not free to leave. Nottingham v. State, 908 S.W.2d 585 (Tex.App.—Austin 1995).

A person is seized, *i.e.*, arrested, only when he has been restrained by means of physical force or when he has submitted to a show of authority. California v. Hodari, 499 U.S. 621, 111 S.Ct. 1547, 113 L.Ed.2d 690 (1991); Medford v. State, 13 S.W.3d 769 (Tex. Crim. App. 2000).

In determining whether a private citizen's actions constituted an arrest, the test is whether there has been such a display of authority that a reasonable person would believe that he was not free to leave. McGuire v. State, 847 S.W.2d 684 (Tex.App.—Houston [1st Dist.] 1993).

The police officer's subjective intent is one factor to be considered in determining whether a suspect is in custody. Miller v. State, 815 S.W.2d 805 (Tex.App.—Austin 1991, *pet. ref'd*).

The fact that a suspect has accompanied a police officer to a station does not amount to a showing that he is in custody or under arrest. Anderson v. State, 932 S.W.2d 502 (Tex. Crim. App. 1996).

The handcuffing of a suspect does not always mean that he is under arrest. Rhodes v. State, 945 S.W.2d 115 (Tex. Crim. App. 1997).

A person who is temporarily handcuffed and detained, but then released, has been seized and detained under the Fourth Amendment, but has not necessarily been arrested. State v. Sheppard, 271 S.W.3d 281 (Tex. Crim. App. 2008).

§1:20 Warrantless Arrests

§1:21 Probable Cause Requirement

It is state law and not federal law that governs the legality of state arrests; so long as the state law does not violate federal constitutional protections against unreasonable searches and seizures. Amores v. State, 816 S.W.2d 407 (Tex. Crim. App. 1991).

There is no federal constitutional requirement that a warrant be obtained as a pre-requisite to the validity of an arrest in a public place even if there was adequate time to obtain one, so long as probable cause exists. U.S. v. Watson, 423 U.S. 411, 96 S.Ct. 820, 46 L.Ed.2d 598 (1976).

A peace officer may arrest an offender without a warrant only if there is probable cause for the arrest. Hafford v. State, 828 S.W.2d 275 (Tex. App.—Fort Worth 1992, *pet. ref'd*).

Where officers find contraband during a Terry stop that establishes probable cause that the defendant has committed an offense within view of officers, the defendant can be arrested without a warrant. Griffin v. State, 215 S.W.3d 403 (Tex. Crim. App. 2006).

These exceptions to the warrant requirement are strictly construed. Dejarnette v. State, 732 S.W.2d 346 (Tex. Crim. App. 1987); Holland v. State, 788 S.W.2d 112 (Tex.App.—Dallas 1990).

Probable cause for a warrantless arrest requires that the officer have a reasonable belief that, based on facts and circumstances within the officer's personal knowledge, or of which the officer has reasonably trustworthy information, an offense has been committed. Torres v. State, 182 S.W.3d 899 (Tex. Crim. App. 2005).

Under the collective knowledge doctrine, when several officers are cooperating, their cumulative information may be considered in assessing reasonable suspicion or probable cause. State v. Martinez, 569 S.W.3d 621, 626 (Tex. Crim. App. 2019) citing State v. Duran, 396 S.W.3d 563, 569 n.12 (Tex. Crim. App. 2013).

Evidence of communication between officers is not always a necessary requirement to apply the collective knowledge doctrine. The sum of the information known to the cooperating officers—their cumulative information—should be considered in assessing probable cause. State v. Martinez, 569 S.W.3d at 627.

Probable cause is a fluid concept that cannot be readily, or even usefully, reduced to a neat set of legal rules. Baldwin v. State, 278 S.W.3d 367 (Tex. Crim. App. 2009).

Though the concept evades precise definition, it involves a reasonable ground for belief of guilt that is particularized with respect to the person to be searched or seized. Probable cause is a greater level of suspicion than reasonable suspicion and requires information that is more substantial in quality or content and a greater reliability with respect to the source of information. Probable cause is a relatively high level of suspicion, though it falls far short of a preponderance of the evidence standard. Baldwin.

Probable cause is dependent upon both the content of information possessed by police and its degree of reliability. The information used to establish probable cause must be more reliable than that used to establish reasonable suspicion. Hall v. State, 297 S.W.3d 294 (Tex. Crim. App. 2009) (holding that the state presented absolutely no evidence to show that the use of LIDAR technology to measure speed supplies was reasonably trustworthy information or that the trial judge took judicial notice of this fact).

The probable cause required for a valid warrantless arrest is the same as that required to make an arrest under an arrest warrant. Delgado v. State, 718 S.W.2d 718 (Tex. Crim. App. 1986).

A hunch, suspicion, or good-faith perception is not enough alone to satisfy the probable cause burden. Stull v. State, 772 S.W.2d 449 (Tex. Crim. App. 1989). The events perceived by the police officer must be out of the ordinary, suspicious and tie a suspect with a criminal act. Under the right circumstances, innocent activity can provide the basis for a showing of probable cause. Stull.

The constitutional validity of a warrantless arrest or search can only be decided in terms of the concrete factual situation presented by each case.

The "totality of the circumstances" test is applicable in determining whether probable cause to make a warrantless arrest exists. Amores v. State, 816 S.W.2d 407 (Tex. Crim. App. 1991); Illinois v. Gates, 462 U.S. 213, 103 S.Ct. 2317, 76 L.Ed.2d 527 (1983).

In the process of analyzing a warrantless arrest, it is the combination of factors that constitute a reasonable conclusion that there is probable cause to make an arrest without a warrant:

- Information that a crime has been committed
- Knowledge by the arresting officers of the facts of the crime
- Observations of the arresting officers
- Arresting officers' basis for believing that a suspect would take flight if not placed in custody

Allridge v. State, 850 S.W.2d 471 (Tex. Crim. App. 1991).

To determine if probable cause to make a warrantless arrest exists, the courts should analyze the objective facts known to the peace officer at the time of the arrest. Rosalez v. State, 875 S.W.2d 705 (Tex.App.—Dallas 1993, *pet. ref'd*).

A trial court is allowed to draw inferences from the testimony in determining whether probable cause exists. Banda v. State, 890 S.W.2d 42 (Tex. Crim. App. 1994) (where the trial court inferred that the defendant must have appeared drunk in public because he went from one private place to another; a journey which required that he appear in a public place).

The inferences drawn by the trial court must be reasonably based on the evidence, and must be non-conclusory. Amador v. State, 275 S.W.3d 872 (Tex. Crim. App. 2009).

There are several factors that can help to indicate that a suspect may be committing, or have just committed, an offense, or that the suspect may be attempting to escape from the commission of the offense. These factors include furtive movements and gestures, flight at the approach of strangers or law officers, the place where a suspect is found and the direction in which he is traveling, and being on a public street instead of in a private residence. Pyles, *supra*.

A peace officer may arrest, for a single offense, all persons as to whom probable cause exists to believe have committed that offense. Maryland v. Pringle, 540 U.S. 366, 124 S.Ct. 795, 157 L.Ed.2d 769 (2003).

A peace officer's subjective conclusions and later acquired knowledge should not be a part of the reviewing court's analysis. Rosalez, *supra*; Torres v. State, 868 S.W.2d 798 (Tex. Crim. App. 1993).

The initial burden of proof on a motion to suppress evidence on the basis of a Fourth Amendment violation rests with the defendant. Torres v. State, 182 S.W.3d 899 (Tex. Crim. App. 2005) (citing Russell v. State, 717 S.W.2d 7 (Tex. Crim. App. 1986)).

The defendant meets this burden by demonstrating that the arrest occurred without a warrant. Torres. Thereafter, the burden shifts to the state to prove the reasonableness of the warrantless arrest. Torres.

The state may satisfy this burden by showing that one of the statutory exceptions to the warrant requirement is met. Torres. The state's proof must consist of specific, articulable facts; mere opinions and conclusions will not suffice to show probable cause. Ford v. State, 158 S.W.3d 488 (Tex. Crim. App. 2005).

PRACTICE TIP: Defense counsel should seek to have the state stipulate that the arrest was made without a warrant for purposes of a motion to suppress hearing.

Under the appellate standard of review on Fourth Amendment claims (including probable cause analysis), an appellate court is to afford almost total deference to the trial court's determination of historical facts, and of application-of-law-to-fact issues that turn on credibility and demeanor, while reviewing de novo other application-of-law-to-fact issues. The prevailing party at the trial level has the benefit of deference on factual findings made in its favor. However, whether the facts, as determined by the trial court, add up to reasonable suspicion or probable cause is a question to be reviewed de novo. State v. Ford, 537 S.W.3d 19, 23 (Tex. Crim. App. 2017).

§1:21.1 Establishing Probable Cause

Hearsay is admissible in establishing probable cause for a warrantless arrest. Rance v. State, 815 S.W.2d 633 (Tex. Crim. App. 1991).

Probable cause can be based on a police officer's prior personal knowledge coupled with personally observed behavior. Beverly v. State, 792 S.W.2d 103 (Tex. Crim. App. 1990).

Activities that are not overtly criminal may be sufficient to constitute probable cause to believe that an offense had or was about to occur when coupled with a peace officer's prior knowledge. Guzman v. State, 955 S.W.2d 85 (Tex. Crim. App. 1997).

An investigating officer's hunch, suspicion or good faith perception is not sufficient, alone, to constitute probable cause for an arrest. The perceived events must be out of the ordinary, suspicious and tie a suspect with a criminal act. Stull v. State, 772 S.W.2d 449 (Tex. Crim. App. 1989).

Innocent activity, however, can provide the basis for a showing of probable cause. Illinois v. Gates, 462 U.S. 213, 103 S.Ct. 2317, 76 L.Ed.2d 527 (1983).

An officer may rely on reasonably trustworthy information provided by another person in making the overall probable cause assessment. Beverly, *supra*.

The test for probable cause in the case of police broadcasts is the information known to the officer who made the broadcast request. Crane v. State, 786 S.W.2d 338 (Tex. Crim. App. 1990). The requesting officer need not relate all of the relevant facts, but only such information as is necessary for the arresting officer to know who is wanted. Crane.

While police officers have the right to act on the basis of teletype dispatches and to assume that the requesting officer has sufficient probable cause to justify the arrest, the detention is not insulated from challenge where the record fails to establish that the issuing officer had probable cause. Amores v. State, 816 S.W.2d 407 (Tex. Crim. App. 1991).

PRACTICE TIP: Whenever the state seeks to establish probable cause for a warrantless arrest, attack all sources of information in an attempt to discredit or minimize the information. This typically can be accomplished by cross-examination seeking to eliminate all of the actions observed as constituting criminal activity.

Probable cause is not established where the officer supplying the information as to the commission of the offense cannot recall important underlying facts and his recalled description didn't match the description of the actual perpetrator. Rance, *supra.*

§1:21.2 Temporary Detentions Based on Reasonable Suspicion

Circumstances short of probable cause for an arrest may justify a temporary detention for purposes of further investigation. Ebarb v. State, 598 S.W.2d 842 (Tex. Crim. App. 1979).

In Davis v. State, 947 S.W.2d 240 (Tex. Crim. App. 1997), the court defined "reasonable suspicion" as requiring "that there is something out of the ordinary occurring and some indication that the unusual activity is related to crime."

The reasonableness of an investigatory detention must be examined in terms of totality of the circumstances and will be justified when the detaining officer has specific articulable facts that, taken together with rational inferences from those facts, lead the officer to conclude that the person is, has been, or will soon be engaged in criminal activity. Woods v. State, 956 S.W.2d 33 (Tex. Crim. App. 1997). Woods discards the "as consistent with innocent activity as with criminal activity" construct previously employed by reviewing courts.

Even in the absence of bad faith, a detention based on a mere hunch is illegal, and there must be "reasonable suspicion" by the police officer that some activity out of the ordinary is occurring or has occurred, some suggestion to connect the detained person with the unusual activity, and some indication that the activity is related to crime. Gurrola v. State, 877 S.W.2d 300 (Tex. Crim. App. 1994).

The reasonable suspicion standard is an objective standard that disregards any subjective intent of the officer making the stop and looks solely to whether an objective basis for the stop exists. Ford v. State, 158 S.W.3d 488 (Tex. Crim. App. 2005).

A mere opinion or conclusory statement will not suffice to establish reasonable suspicion; specific, articulable facts must be presented by the state or a court has no means to assess whether the opinion or conclusion was objectively reasonable. Ford.

Where the defendant is detained for violation of a traffic statute that makes the assessment of the violation a subjective determination on the part of the officer, specific articulable facts must be presented to the trial court to justify the detention. Ford (the defendant was detained for the offense of following too closely).

However, where the traffic violation for which the defendant is detained does not contain any subjective component, the officer's testimony that the defendant committed the violation is sufficient without testimony as to the underlying details of the violation. Castro v. State, 227 S.W.3d 737, 742 (Tex. Crim. App. 2007) (the defendant was detained for failing to signal a lane change).

During an investigative detention, a police officer may question a suspicious person on his identity, his reason for his presence in the area, and make similar reasonable inquiries of a truly investigatory nature. Alvarado v. State, 894 S.W.2d 869 (Tex. App.—El Paso 1995, *pet ref'd*).

A police officer may briefly stop a suspicious individual in order to determine his identity or to maintain the status quo momentarily while obtaining more information. Gurrola v. State, 877 S.W.2d 300 (Tex. Crim. App. 1994). The high crime reputation of an area where defendants were seen could not alone serve as basis for an investigative stop. Gurrola.

An individual has a right to refuse to answer the questions of a police officer and walk away unless the police officer has reasonable suspicion of criminal activity. Gurrola.

Mere flight alone does not justify an investigative detention. Gurrola.

An alleged traffic violation of failure to maintain a single lane does not amount to a reasonable suspicion where the state fails to also show that the movement to another lane could not be made safely under Transportation Code §545.060 (a). Hernandez v. State, 983 S.W.2d 867 (Tex.App.—Austin 1998).

PRACTICE TIP: Whenever the state relies on a traffic code violation as probable cause or reasonable suspicion for a traffic stop, read the applicable code section to ascertain whether they have proven all of the elements of the violation.

Where the initial detention is unlawful, any evidence seized subsequent to such detention is inadmissible. Gurrola, *supra*.

PRACTICE TIP: Always attack the initial detention and its basis in an attempt to suppress fruits gained from the detention.

Once a police officer makes a *bona fide* stop or arrest for a traffic offense, he can make an additional arrest for any other offense unexpectedly discovered while investigating or questioning the motorist. Hernandez v. State, 867 S.W.2d 900 (Tex.App.—Texarkana 1993, *no pet.*); Bachick v. State, 30 S.W.3d 549 (Tex.App.—Fort Worth 2000, *pet. ref'd*).

A computer check of the information provided by the detained individual is an integral part of the detention of an individual, but cannot be used as a means to unreasonably prolong the stop beyond a permissible period. Kothe v. State, 152 S.W.3d 54 (Tex. Crim. App. 2004).

§1:21.3 Exclusionary Rule

CCP Art. 38.23 Evidence Not To Be Used

> *(a) No evidence obtained by any officer or other person in violation of any provisions of the Constitution or laws of the State of Texas, or of the Constitution or laws of the United States of America, shall be admitted in evidence against the accused on the trial of any criminal case. In any case where the legal evidence raises an issue hereunder, the jury shall be instructed that if it believes, or has a reasonable doubt, that the evidence was obtained in violation of the provisions of this Article, then and in such event, the jury shall disregard any such evidence so obtained.*
>
> *(b) It is an exception to the provisions of Subsection (a) of this Article that the evidence was obtained by a law enforcement officer acting in objective good faith reliance upon a warrant issued by a neutral magistrate based on probable cause.*

The primary purpose of the exclusionary rule is to deter police activity that could not have been reasonably believed to be lawful by the officers committing the conduct. Drago v. State, 553 S.W.2d 375 (Tex. Crim. App. 1977).

Not every violation of a "law" of Texas, however, will invoke the exclusionary rule. Roy v. State, 608 S.W.2d 645 (Tex. Crim. App. [Panel Op.] 1980).

The federal exclusionary rule is a judicially created remedy designed to safeguard against future violations of Fourth Amendment rights through the rule's general deterrent effect. Arizona v. Evans, 514 U.S. 1, 115 S.Ct. 1185, 131 L.Ed.2d 34 (1995).

The issue of exclusion is separate from whether the Fourth Amendment has been violated. Arizona v. Evans.

The Fourth Amendment exclusionary rule does not apply to police mistakes leading to an unlawful search that are the result of isolated negligence attenuated from the search, rather than systemic error or reckless disregard of constitutional requirements. Herring v. U.S., 555 U.S. 135, 129 S.Ct. 695, 172 L.Ed.2d 496 (2009).

Art. 38.23(a) may not be invoked for statutory violations unrelated to the purpose of the exclusionary rule. Lane v. State, 951 S.W.2d 242 (Tex. App.—Austin 1997, *no pet.*); Carroll v. State, 911 S.W.2d 210 (Tex.App.—Austin 1995, *no pet.*).

Where there is nothing in the record to indicate that the objectionable evidence was obtained as a result of the alleged statutory violation, exclusion is not required. Stockton v. State, 756 S.W.2d 873 (Tex.App.—Austin 1988, *no pet.*).

Where a police officer who observes a defendant commit a traffic violation in his jurisdiction but then stops the defendant in another jurisdiction fails to notify the other jurisdiction's officers of the defendant's arrest on DWI charges arising out of the stop, the exclusionary rule is not implicated because the violation is not related to the purpose of the rule. Bachick v. State, 30 S.W.3d 549 (Tex. App.—Fort Worth 2000, *pet. ref'd*).

The purpose of a pre-trial motion is to address preliminary matters, not the merits of the case itself; thus a motion to suppress cannot be used to test the propriety of an arrest in an evading arrest case because the issue goes to an element of the case. Woods v. State, 153 S.W.3d 413 (Tex. Crim. App. 2005).

§1:30 Authority for Warrantless Arrests

§1:31 CCP Art. 14.01. Offense Within View

(a) A peace officer or any other person, may, without a warrant, arrest an offender when the offense is committed in his presence or within his view, if the offense is one classed as a felony or as an offense against the public peace.

(b) A peace officer may arrest an offender without a warrant for any offense committed in his presence or within his view.

Note that Subsection (a) allows an arrest by both peace officers and private citizens; but requires that the conduct witnessed be a felony or breach of the peace.

Subsection (b) authorizes arrest by peace officers only, but the peace officer can arrest for any offense and is not limited to felonies and breaches of the peace.

See also, CCP Art. 14.03 (d) and (g) that also authorize a peace officer to make a warrantless arrest outside of his jurisdiction for certain conduct.

§1:31.1 Warrantless Arrests by Peace Officers

A peace officer may arrest an offender without a warrant for any offense committed in his presence or in his view. Woodard v. State, 341 S.W.3d 404 (Tex. Crim. App. 2011).

The ultimate question under Article 14.01(b) is whether at that moment the facts and circumstances within the officer's knowledge and of which he had reasonably trustworthy information were sufficient to warrant a prudent man in believing that the arrested person had committed or was committing an offense. Woodard.

Probable cause for a warrantless arrest under Art. 14.01(b) may be based on an officer's prior knowledge and personal observations. Woodard.

An officer may rely on reasonably trustworthy information provided by another person in making the overall probable cause determination. Thus, all of the information to support probable cause does not have to be within an officer's personal knowledge. Woodard.

Under the collective knowledge doctrine, when several officers are cooperating, their cumulative information may be considered in assessing reasonable suspicion or probable cause. State v. Martinez, 569 S.W.3d 621, 626 (Tex. Crim. App. 2019) (citing State v. Duran, 396 S.W.3d 563, 569 n.12 (Tex. Crim. App. 2013)).

Evidence of communication between officers is not always a necessary requirement to apply the collective knowledge doctrine. The sum of the information known to the cooperating officers—their cumulative information—should be considered in assessing probable cause. State v. Martinez, 569 S.W.3d at 627.

CCP Art. 14.01 does not require that a police officer observing the commission of the offense be the actual arresting officer, as long as the observing officer effectively participated in the arrest and was aware of its circumstances. Astran v. State, 799 S.W.2d 761 (Tex. Crim. App. 1990).

This is true even where the officer making the actual stop was outside of his jurisdiction as long as the officer making the observation of illegal conduct was within his jurisdiction. Armendariz v. State, 123 S.W.3d 401 (Tex. Crim. App. 2003).

Unless officers can trace the smell of burning marijuana to a particular individual, the smell alone does not constitute probable cause for an arrest. State v. Steelman, 93 S.W.3d 102 (Tex. Crim. App. 2002).

§1:31.2 Who Is a Peace Officer

§1:31.2.1 Statutory Law

CCP Art. 2.12. Who are peace officers

The following are peace officers:

(1) sheriffs, their deputies, and those reserve deputies who hold a permanent

peace officer license issued under Chapter 1701, Occupations Code;

(2) constables, deputy constables, and those reserve deputy constables who hold a permanent peace officer license issued under Chapter 1701, Occupations Code;

(3) marshals or police officers of an incorporated city, town, or village, and those reserve municipal police officers who hold a permanent peace officer license issued under Chapter 1701, Occupations Code;

(4) rangers, officers, and members of the reserve officers corps commissioned by the Public Safety Commission and the Director of the Department of Public Safety;

(5) investigators of the district attorneys', criminal district attorneys', and county attorneys' offices;

(6) law enforcement agents of the Texas Alcoholic Beverage Commission;

(7) each member of an arson investigating unit commissioned by a city, a county, or the state;

(8) officers commissioned under Section 37.081, Education Code, or Subchapter E, Chapter 51, Education Code;

(9) officers commissioned by the General Services Commission;

(10) law enforcement officers commissioned by the Parks and Wildlife Commission;

(11) airport police officers commissioned by a city with a population of more than 1.18 million located primarily in a county with a population of 2 million or more that operates an airport that serves commercial air carriers;

(12) airport security personnel commissioned as peace officers by the governing body of any political subdivision of this state, other than a city described by Subdivision (11), that operates an airport that serves commercial air carriers;

(13) municipal park and recreational patrolmen and security officers;

(14) security officers and investigators commissioned as peace officers by the comptroller;

(15) officers commissioned by a water control and improvement district under Section 49.216, Water Code;

(16) officers commissioned by a board of trustees under Chapter 54, Transportation Code;

(17) investigators commissioned by the Texas Medical Board;

(18) officers commissioned by:

(A) the board of managers of the Dallas County Hospital District, the Tarrant County Hospital District, the Bexar County Hospital District, or the El Paso County Hospital District under Section 281.057, Health and Safety Code; and

(B) the board of directors of the Ector County Hospital District under Section 1024.117, Special District Local Laws Code;

(19) county park rangers commissioned under Subchapter E, Chapter 351, Local Government Code;

(20) investigators employed by the Texas Racing Commission;

(21) officers commissioned under Chapter 554, Occupations Code;

(22) officers commissioned by the governing body of a metropolitan rapid transit authority under Section 451.108, Transportation Code, or by a regional transportation authority under Section 452.110, Transportation Code;

(23) investigators commissioned by the attorney general under Section 402.009, Government Code;

(24) security officers and investigators commissioned as peace officers under Chapter 466, Government Code;

(25) officers appointed by an appellate court under Subchapter F, Chapter 53, Government Code;

(26) officers commissioned by the state fire marshal under Chapter 417, Government Code;

(27) an investigator commissioned by the commissioner of insurance under Section 701.104, Insurance Code;

(28) apprehension specialists and inspectors general commissioned by the Texas Juvenile Justice Department as officers under Sections 242.102 and 243.052, Human Resources Code;

(29) officers appointed by the inspector general of the Texas Department of Criminal Justice under Section 493.019, Government Code;

(30) investigators commissioned by the Commission on Law Enforcement Officer Standards and Education under Section 1701.160, Occupations Code;

(31) commission investigators commissioned by the Texas Private Security Board under Section 1702.061(f), Occupations Code;

(32) the fire marshal and any officers, inspectors, or investigators commissioned by an emergency services district under Chapter 775, Health and Safety Code;

(33) officers commissioned by the State Board of Dental Examiners under Section 254.013, Occupations Code, subject to the limitations imposed by that section;

(34) investigators commissioned by the Texas Juvenile Justice Department as officers under Section 221.011 , Human Resources Code; and

(35) the fire marshal and any related officers, inspectors, or investigators commissioned by a county under Subchapter B, Chapter 352, Local Government Code.

CCP Art. 2.122. Special Investigators

(a) The following named criminal investigators of the United States shall not be deemed peace officers, but shall have the powers of arrest, search, and seizure under the laws of this state as to felony offenses only:

(1) Special Agents of the Federal Bureau of Investigation;

(2) Special Agents of the Secret Service;

(3) Special Agents of the United States Immigration and Customs Enforcement;

(4) Special Agents of the Bureau of Alcohol, Tobacco, Firearms and Explosives;

(5) Special Agents of the United States Drug Enforcement Administration;

(6) Inspectors of the United States Postal Inspection Service;

(7) Special Agents of the Criminal Investigation Division of the Internal Revenue Service;

(8) Civilian Special Agents of the United States Naval Criminal Investigative Service;

(9) Marshals and Deputy Marshals of the United States Marshals Service;

(10) Special Agents of the United States Department of State, Bureau of Diplomatic Security;

(11) Special Agents of the Treasury Inspector General for Tax Administration;

(12) Special Agents of the Office of Inspector General of the United States Social Security Administration;

(13) Special Agents of the Office of Inspector General of the United States Department of Veterans Affairs; and

(14) a police officer with the Office of Security and Law Enforcement of the United States Department of Veterans Affairs.

(b) A person designated as a special policeman by the Federal Protective Services division of the General Services Administration under 40 U.S.C. Section 318 or 318d is not a peace officer but has the powers of arrest and search and seizure as to any offense under the laws of this state.

(c) A Customs and Border Protection Officer or Border Patrol Agent of the United States Customs and Border Protection or an immigration enforcement agent or deportation officer of the Department of Homeland Security is not a peace officer under the laws of this state but, on the premises of a port facility designated by the commissioner of the United States Customs and Border Protection as a port of entry for arrival in the United States by land transportation from the United Mexican States into the State of Texas or at a permanent established border patrol traffic check point, has the authority to detain a person pending transfer without unnecessary delay to a peace officer if the agent or officer has probable cause to believe that the person has engaged in conduct that is a violation of Section 49.02, 49.04, 49.07, or 49.08, Penal Code, regardless of whether the violation may be disposed of in a criminal proceeding or a juvenile justice proceeding.

(d) A commissioned law enforcement officer of the National Park Service is not a peace officer under the laws of this state, except that the officer has the powers of arrest, search, and seizure as to any offense under the laws of this state committed within the boundaries of a national park or national recreation area. In this subsection, "national park or national recreation area" means a national park or national recreation area included in the National Park System as defined by 16 U.S.C. Section 1c(a).

(e) A Special Agent or Law Enforcement Officer of the United States Forest Service is not a peace officer under the laws of this state, except that the agent or officer has the powers of arrest, search, and seizure as to any offense under the laws of this state committed within the National Forest System. In this subsection, "National Forest System" has the meaning assigned by 16 U.S.C. Section 1609.

(f) Security personnel working at a commercial nuclear power plant, including contract security personnel, trained and qualified under a security plan approved by the United States Nuclear Regulatory Commission, are not peace officers under the laws of

this state, except that such personnel have the powers of arrest, search, and seizure, including the powers under Section 9.51, Penal Code, while in the performance of their duties on the premises of a commercial nuclear power plant site or under agreements entered into with local law enforcement regarding areas surrounding the plant site.

(g) In addition to the powers of arrest, search, and seizure under Subsection (a), a Special Agent of the Secret Service protecting a person described by 18 U.S.C. Section 3056(a) or investigating a threat against a person described by 18 U.S.C. Section 3056(a) has the powers of arrest, search, and seizure as to:

(1) misdemeanor offenses under the laws of this state; and

(2) any criminal offense under federal law.

§1:31.2.2 Case Law

No difference exists for purposes of CCP Art. 14.01 in the authority granted to city police, deputy constables, and municipal park patrolmen. Love v. State, 687 S.W.2d 469 (Tex.App.—Houston [1st Dist.] 1985, *pet. ref'd*).

With the exception of the circumstances outlined in CCP Art. 14.03 (d) and (g), a peace officer has no authority to make arrests outside of his jurisdiction except to the extent those powers are granted to private citizens. Perkins v. State, 812 S.W.2d 326 (Tex. Crim. App. 1991).

PRACTICE TIP: A careful reading of the statute giving certain peace officers authority is necessary to determine the extent of their jurisdiction. Elliot v. State, 879 S.W.2d 381 (Tex.App.—Waco 1994, pet. ref'd) (interpreting Tex.Rev. Civ.Stat.Ann. Art. 1118x giving authority to metropolitan transit police).

A peace officer's statutory authority to arrest offenders under Art. 14.01 does not grant peace officers statewide authority to make such arrests. Reichaert v. State, 830 S.W.2d 348 (Tex.App.—San Antonio 1992, *pet. ref'd*).

A park ranger employed by a municipality has the authority to make warrantless arrests, subject to the limitations placed on him by park board trustees. Garza v. State, 822 S.W.2d 174 (Tex.App.—San Antonio 1991).

A campus police officer on duty at Southwest Texas State University who sees a motorist speeding on a street between two land areas of the campus has jurisdictional authority to stop and arrest such person and subsequently file DWI charges. Territorial jurisdiction is granted under Education Code §51.201 and 51.203 and CCP Arts. 2.12 (8) and 14.01. State v. Carroll, 855 S.W.2d 128 (Tex. App.—Austin 1993).

A campus police officer acting outside of his jurisdiction is not acting as a peace officer under the Code of Criminal Procedure. Preston v. State, 700 S.W.2d 227 (Tex. Crim. App. 1985).

A prosecuting attorney's investigator possesses county-wide jurisdiction to make arrests in the county in which the prosecuting attorney holds office; and has no authority to make traffic arrests outside that jurisdiction. Dominguez v. State, 924 S.W.2d 950 (Tex.App.—El Paso 1996).

Under *Tex. Code Crim. Pro.* art.2.122, designated federal officers, even though not deemed peace officers in the State of Texas, have the powers of arrest, search, and seizure as to felony, as opposed to misde-meanor, offenses. However, the provisions of Art. 14.03 do not apply to the actions of these officers. *Guerra v. State*, 432 S.W.3d 905, 911 (Tex. Crim. App. 2014).

The doctrine of "hot pursuit," provides that if a peace officer initiates pursuit of an offender in his jurisdiction he may then continue the pursuit into another jurisdiction. Preston, *supra*.

§1:31.3 Warrantless Arrests by Private Citizens

Article 14.01 permits private citizens to make arrests of those observed committing crimes against the public peace. Garner v. State, 779 S.W.2d 498 (Tex.App.—Fort Worth 1989, *pet.*

ref'd). Just as for peace officers, in order for a private citizen to make a valid arrest under this article, he must witness enough of the offense to form probable cause. Garner.

The right of a private citizen to make an arrest under Article 14.01 is limited to the time the offense is committed or while there is a continuing danger of a recommission. Turner v. State, 901 S.W.2d 767 (Tex.App.—Houston [14th Dist.] 1995, *pet. ref'd*). A private citizen cannot, after witnessing an offense, later pursue and validly arrest an offender. Turner, *supra*.

The right of a private citizen to make an arrest under this article also is limited to certain types of offenses; those that are classified as felonies and those that constitute a breach of the peace. Perkins v. State, 771 S.W.2d 195 (Tex.App.—Houston [1st Dist.] 1989, pet. granted, affirmed at 812 S.W.2d 326).

A security guard can validly make an arrest under this article as a private citizen. Turner, *supra*.

In making arrests under this article, private citizens must act in accordance with the law or fruits of the arrest are inadmissible in a subsequent trial under CCP Art. 38.23. State v. Johnson, 939 S.W.2d 586 (Tex. Crim. App. 1996).

PRACTICE TIP: Challenge the probable cause for warrantless arrests by citizens the same as a challenge of the probable cause for warrantless arrests by peace officers.

§1:31.4 Acts Constituting a Breach of Peace

Whether a particular act is a breach of the peace is decided on a case-by-case basis. Turner v. State, 901 S.W.2d 767 (Tex.App.—Houston [14th Dist.] 1995, *pet. ref'd*).

The following have been found to constitute a breach of the peace:

- Disorderly conduct by yelling and screaming. Brown v. State, 594 S.W.2d 86 (Tex. Crim. App. 1980)
- Carrying a concealed weapon. Smith v. State, 813 S.W.2d 599 (Tex.App.—Houston [14th Dist.] 1991, *pet. ref'd*)
- Drug transactions. Delgado v. State, 718 S.W.2d 718 (Tex. Crim. App. 1986)
- Public intoxication. Simpson v. State, 886 S.W.2d 449 (Tex.App.—Houston [1st Dist.] 1994, *pet. ref'd*)
- DWI. Romo v. State, 577 S.W.2d 251 (Tex. Crim. App. 1979); Cooper v. State, 961 S.W.2d 229 (Tex.App.—Houston [1st Dist.] 1997, *pet. ref'd*)
- Dangerous driving. Valencia v. State, 820 S.W.2d 397 (Tex.App.—Houston [14th Dist.] 1991, *pet. ref'd*); Ruiz v. State, 907 S.W.2d 600 (Tex.App.—Corpus Christi 1995)
- Assaults on peace officers. Harrison v. State, 445 S.W.2d 216 (Tex. Crim. App. 1969)
- Burglary. Perez v. State, 548 S.W.2d 47 (Tex. Crim. App. 1977)
- Shoplifting. Mungia v. State, 911 S.W.2d 164 (Tex.App.—Corpus Christi 1995)
- Throwing a bottle of beer on another person. Knot v. State, 853 S.W.2d 802 (Tex.App.—Amarillo 1993)
- Excessive acceleration. Collins v. State, 829 S.W.2d 894 (Tex.App.—Dallas 1992)

§1:31.5 Acts Not Constituting Breach of Peace

The following circumstances have been found to not constitute a breach of the peace:

- The offensive middle finger gesture (where it was found that the gesture did not tend to incite an immediate breach of the peace). State v. Rivenburgh, 933 S.W.2d 698 (Tex.App.—San Antonio 1996)

- Ordinary traffic law violations. Reichaert v. State, 830 S.W.2d 348 (Tex.App.—San Antonio 1992, *pet. ref'd*)

§1:32 CCP Art. 14.02. Within View of Magistrate

A peace officer may arrest, without warrant, when a felony or breach of the peace has been committed in the presence or within the view of a magistrate, and such magistrate verbally orders the arrest of the offender.

§1:33 CCP Art. 14.03. Authority of Peace Officers

(a) Any peace officer may arrest, without warrant:

(1) persons found in suspicious places and under circumstances which reasonably show that such persons have been guilty of some felony, violation of Title 9, Chapter 42, Penal Code, breach of the peace, or offense under §49.02, Penal Code, or threaten, or are about to commit some offense against the laws;

(2) persons who the peace officer has probable cause to believe have committed an assault resulting in bodily injury to another person and the peace officer has probable cause to believe that there is danger of further bodily injury to that person;

(3) persons who the peace officer has probable cause to believe have committed an offense defined by §25.07, Penal Code (violation of Protective Order), or by §38.112, Penal Code (violation of Protective Order issued on basis of sexual assault), if the offense is not committed in the presence of the peace officer;

(4) persons who the peace officer has probable cause to believe have committed an offense involving family violence;

(5) persons who the peace officer has probable cause to believe have prevented or interfered with an individual's ability to place a telephone call in an emergency, as defined by §42.062(d), Penal Code, if the offense is not committed in the presence of the peace officer; or

(6) a person who makes a statement to the peace officer that would be admissible against the person under Article 38.21 and establishes probable cause to believe that the person has committed a felony.

(b) A peace officer shall arrest, without a warrant, a person the peace officer has probable cause to believe has committed an offense under §25.07, Penal Code (violation of Protective Order), or §38.112, Penal Code (violation of Protective Order issued on basis of sexual assault), if the offense is committed in the presence of the peace officer.

(c) If reasonably necessary to verify an allegation of a violation of a protective order or of the commission of an offense involving family violence, a peace officer shall remain at the scene of the investigation to verify the allegation and to prevent the further commission of the violation or of family violence.

(d) A peace officer who is outside his jurisdiction may arrest, without warrant, a person who commits an offense within the officer's presence or view, if the offense is a felony, a violation of Chapter 42 or 49, Penal Code, or a breach of the peace. A peace officer making an arrest under this subsection shall, as soon as practicable after making the arrest, notify a law enforcement agency having jurisdiction

where the arrest was made. The law enforcement agency shall then take custody of the person committing the offense and take the person before a magistrate in compliance with Article 14.06 of this code.

(e) The justification for conduct provided under §9.21, Penal Code, applies to a peace officer when the peace officer is performing a duty required by this article.

(f) In this article, "family violence" has the meaning assigned by §71.004, Family Code.

(g)(1) A peace officer listed in Subdivision (1), (2), or (5), Article 2.12, who is licensed under Chapter 1701, Occupations Code, and is outside of the officer's jurisdiction may arrest without a warrant a person who commits any offense within the officer's presence or view, other than a violation of Subtitle C, Title 7, Transportation Code.

(2) A peace officer listed in Subdivision (3), Article 2.12, who is licensed under Chapter 1701, Occupations Code, and is outside of the officer's jurisdiction may arrest without a warrant a person who commits any offense within the officer's presence or view, except that an officer described in this subdivision who is outside of that officer's jurisdiction may arrest a person for a violation of Subtitle C, Title 7, Transportation Code, only if the offense is committed in the county or counties in which the municipality employing the peace officer is located.

(3) A peace officer making an arrest under this subsection shall as soon as practicable after making the arrest notify a law enforcement agency having jurisdiction where the arrest was made. The law enforcement agency shall then take custody of:

(A) the person committing the offense and take the person before a magistrate in compliance with Article 14.06; and

(B) any property seized during or after the arrest as if the property had been seized by a peace officer of that law enforcement agency.

See also, CCP Art. 14.01 when researching arrests for offenses committed in the presence of a peace officer.

Under Art. 14.03 subsections (d) and (g) a city police officer may arrest a suspect for DWI outside of his jurisdiction. Brother v. State, 166 S.W.3d 255 (Tex. Crim. App. 2005).

§1:33.1 Suspect's Commission of Offense

There are several factors that can help to indicate that a suspect may be committing, or have just committed, an offense, or that the suspect may be attempting to escape from the commission of the offense. These factors include furtive movements and gestures, flight at the approach of strangers or law officers, the place where a suspect is found and the direction in which he is traveling, and being on a public street instead of in a private residence. Pyles v. State, 755 S.W.2d 98 (Tex. Crim. App. 1988).

In addition, factors must indicate that a reasonable and prudent person would be justified in believing the suspect would take flight if not placed in custody. Pyles, *supra*.

§1:33.2 Suspect Found in Suspicious Place

The test under Article 14.03(a)(1) is a totality of the circumstances test. First, probable cause that the defendant committed a crime must be found. Second, the defendant must be found in a suspicious place. Dyar v. State, 125 S.W.3d 460 (Tex. Crim. App. 2003).

Rarely is any place considered to be a suspicious place per se. Muniz v. State, 851 S.W.2d 238 (Tex. Crim. App. 1993). Additional facts and reasonable inferences therefrom, however, may justifiably render a place suspicious from a police officer's perspective. Muniz (where facts and circumstances conduced to make the closet in which the defendant was hiding a suspicious place).

The determination of whether a place is a "suspicious place" is a highly fact-specific analysis. Dyar.

The time between the crime and the apprehension of the suspect in a suspicious place is an important factor. Dyar.

Any "place" may become suspicious when a person at that location and the accompanying circumstances raise a reasonable belief that the person has committed a crime and exigent circumstances call for immediate action or detention by police. Swain v. State, 181 S.W.3d 359 (Tex. Crim. App. 2005) (where the defendant was arrested at a residential treatment home because officers believed that he was a flight risk).

§1:33.2.1 Places Found to Be Suspicious

Under the facts and circumstances of a particular case, the following have been found to be suspicious places:

Dwelling places:

- A closet where the defendant was hiding. Muniz v. State, 851 S.W.2d 238 (Tex. Crim. App. 1993)
- An apartment where a murder occurred. Johnson v. State, 722 S.W.2d 417 (Tex. Crim. App. 1986)
- Defendant's house (where there was a dead body in the yard). Douglas v. State, 679 S.W.2d 790 (Tex.App.—Fort Worth 1984)
- Defendant's house where there is a stolen vehicle in the yard. Mitchell v. State, 756 S.W.2d 71. (Tex.App.—Texarkana 1988)
- Defendant's apartment. Wilson v. State, 722 S.W.2d 3 (Tex.App.—Dallas 1986)
- Defendant's garage. Crowley v. State, 842 S.W.2d 701 (Tex.App.—Houston [1st Dist.] 1992, *pet. ref'd*)

Vehicle:

- Defendant's car when found in vicinity of a shooting. Flores v. State, 895 S.W.2d 435 (Tex.App.—San Antonio 1995); Cornejo v. State, 917 S.W.2d 480 (Tex. App.—Houston [14th Dist.] 1996, *pet. ref'd*)
- The defendant's car. Hamel v. State, 582 S.W.2d 424 (Tex. Crim. App. [Panel Op.] 1979)

General locations:

- Apartment complex parking lot. Rysiejko v. State, 782 S.W.2d 529 (Tex. App.—Houston [14th Dist.] 1989, *pet. ref'd*)
- A high crime area. Thompson v. State, 533 S.W.2d 825 (Tex. Crim. App. 1976)
- Murder crime scene. Johnson v. State, 722 S.W.2d 417 (Tex. Crim. App. 1986); Douglas v. State, 679 S.W.2d 790 (Tex.App.—Fort Worth 1984, *no pet.*)
- Scene of an automobile accident outside of a bar. Cooper v. State, 961 S.W.2d 229 (Tex.App.—Houston [1st Dist.] 1997, *pet. ref'd*)
- A hiding place near a shoplifting scene. Blackmon v. State, 644 S.W.2d 738 (Tex. Crim. App. 1983)
- The street. Thomas v. State, 681 S.W.2d 672 (Tex. App.—Houston [14th Dist.] 1984, *pet. ref'd*)
- A hospital. Dyar v. State, 125 S.W.3d 460 (Tex. Crim. App. 2003)
- Any scene where the activity is as consistent with lawful activity as with

unlawful activity. Amores v. State, 816 S.W.2d 407 (Tex. Crim. App. 1991)

- Defendant's house where he was fleeing a DWI accident. Gallups v. State, 151 S.W.3d 196 (Tex. Crim. App. 2004)

§1:33.2.2 Places Found Not to Be Suspicious

Under the facts and circumstances of a particular case, the following have been found not to be suspicious places:

- An automobile (where the facts and circumstances did not demonstrate that the driver was intoxicated). Segura v. State, 826 S.W.2d 178 (Tex.App.—Dallas 1992, *pet. ref'd*)
- Defendant's apartment. Holland v. State, 788 S.W.2d 112 (Tex.App.—Dallas 1990)
- Apartment complex parking lot. Amores v. State, 816 S.W.2d 407 (Tex. Crim. App. 1991)
- Yard of another person's residence. Hoag v. State, 728 S.W.2d 375 (Tex. Crim. App. 1987)

§1:33.3 Assaults and Threats of Future Violence

A police officer is justified in arresting a suspect without an arrest warrant under CCP Art. 14.03 (a)(2) if he observes injuries on a victim, the victim tells the officer she fears the defendant will assault her again, and the defendant is found in close proximity to the victim (here only one block away). Romero v. State, 709 S.W.2d 53 (Tex.App.—Fort Worth 1986).

The assault does not have to occur in front of a peace officer in order for an arrest under this article to be valid as long as sufficient facts are related by a credible person. Damian v. State, 776 S.W.2d 659 (Tex.App.—Houston [14th Dist.] 1989, *pet. ref'd*).

The suspect does not have to be on the scene at the time of the arrest in order for the arrest to be valid. McClatchy v. State, 758 S.W.2d 328 (Tex. App.—Houston [14th Dist.] 1988).

Where police found a note purportedly written by the defendant admitting to murdering members of his family a warrantless arrest was authorized under CCP Art. 14.03(a)(4). Jackson v. State, 33 S.W.3d 828 (Tex. Crim. App. 2000).

§1:33.4 Authority of Peace Officers

A peace officer employed as a city police officer does not have authority to stop a person for a traffic offense in another city, even in the same county. State v. Kurtz, 152 S.W.3d 72 (Tex. Crim. App. 2004) (this also applies to most other peace officers under Art. 2.12 C.C.P.).

Legislative amendment has now given a peace officer listed in Subdivision (3), Article 2.12, who is licensed under Chapter 1701, Occupations Code, authority to arrest a person for a violation of Subtitle C, Title 7, Transportation Code, if the offense is committed in the county or counties in which the municipality employing the peace officer is located. Tex. Code Crim. Pro. art. 14.03(g)(2); York v. State, 342 S.W.3d 528, 535 (Tex. Crim. App. 2011).

Under Art. 14.03(g), the officer's reasonable suspicion must be limited to whether the suspect is committing, or had committed, an offense in the officer's presence or view. York.

§1:34 CCP Art. 14.04. When Felony Has Been Committed

> *Where it is shown by satisfactory proof to a peace officer, upon the representation of a credible person, that a felony has been committed, and that the offender is about to escape, so that there is no time to procure a warrant, such peace officer may, without warrant, pursue and arrest the accused.*

This rule breaks down into four elements:

- Person who gives the information to the police must be credible
- Offense under investigation must be a felony

- Offender must be about to escape
- There must be no time to procure an arrest warrant.

Crane v. State, 786 S.W.2d 338 (Tex. Crim. App. 1990).

This rule has been restated to require:

- Police officer to have satisfactory proof that a felony was committed
- Satisfactory proof that the person to be arrested is the offender
- Evidence that the offender is about to escape such that there is no time to procure a warrant

Dejarnette v. State, 732 S.W.2d 346 (Tex. Crim. App. 1987).

Whether there is satisfactory proof that a crime has been committed and the suspect is responsible is decided by looking at the totality of the circumstances. Hughes v. State, 24 S.W.3d 883 (Tex. Crim. App. 2000).

TIP TO THE PROSECUTION: Always establish the facts and circumstances indicating that the person providing the information is to be considered credible.

Article 14.04 must be strictly construed in the suspect's favor. Dowthitt v. State, 931 S.W.2d 244 (Tex. Crim. App. 1996).

§1:34.1 Credibility of Information

An identified private citizen whose only contact with the police results from witnessing a criminal act is inherently credible. Nelson v. State, 855 S.W.2d 26 (Tex.App.—El Paso 1993); Esco v. State, 668 S.W.2d 358 (Tex. Crim. App. 1982).

A police officer witnessing an offense is a credible person under this article. Dejarnette v. State, 732 S.W.2d 346 (Tex. Crim. App. 1987).

The test for probable cause in the case of police broadcasts is the information known to the officer who made the broadcast request. Crane v. State, 786 S.W.2d 338 (Tex. Crim. App. 1990).

Police broadcasts, based on probable cause, reporting a felony and a description of the suspect satisfy the requirements for arrest under CCP Art. 14.04. The requesting officer need not relate all of the relevant facts, but only such information as is necessary for the arresting officer to know who is wanted. Crane, *supra*.

§1:34.2 Escape of Suspect

In order to justify a warrantless arrest under Article 14.04, officers must have some evidence amounting to satisfactory proof that the offender is about to escape. Dowthitt v. State, 931 S.W.2d 244 (Tex. Crim. App. 1996). This article does not require a showing that the offender is in fact escaping; it merely requires a showing by satisfactory proof that the offender is about to escape such that there is no time to procure a warrant. Crane v. State, 786 S.W.2d 338 (Tex. Crim. App. 1990).

This requirement is obviously met where the suspect has previously fled or otherwise evidences an intention to flee. Dowthitt, *supra*. Attempts to elude police are another important factor in determining that the suspect was about to escape. Pyles v. State, 755 S.W.2d 98 (Tex. Crim. App. 1988). Fleeing from arresting officers in an automobile at a high rate of speed is satisfactory proof that the offender was about to escape. Crane, *supra*.

Where police link the occupants of a vehicle to a crime moments after its commission, it is unreasonable to expect them to break their pursuit to obtain a warrant in hopes of encountering the suspects at a later time. Hughes v. State, 24 S.W.3d 833 (Tex. Crim. App. 2000).

Merely going from one place to another is not escaping for purposes of this article. Stanton v. State, 743 S.W.2d 233 (Tex. Crim. App. 1988).

However, where the suspect is a passenger on a public bus going across state lines and offering the suspect many disembarking points, a warrantless arrest is justified based on exigent circumstances. Winters v. State, 897 S.W.2d 938 (Tex.App.—Beaumont 1995).

The proximity in time between the offense and the arrest help support a finding that the offender was about to escape. Allridge v. State, 850 S.W.2d 471 (Tex. Crim. App. 1991). Proximity to the crime scene is an important factor in determining whether the offender is about to escape. Dejarnette v. State, 732 S.W.2d 346 (Tex. Crim. App. 1987).

The proximity in time of the pursuit to the crime or its discovery is a factor which must be considered relative to other factors showing imminent escape in determining whether a warrantless arrest is justified on the ground that the suspect is about to escape. Dejarnette, *supra*. Whether the suspect has been confronted by police is a circumstance to be considered in determining whether escape is imminent; however, it is not sufficient in itself to constitute satisfactory proof of escape. Dejarnette.

The fact that the suspect knows that police are making inquiries about him or seeking him is an important factor in determining whether the suspect was about to escape. King v. State, 631 S.W.2d 486 (Tex. Crim. App. 1982).

However, this article does not permit a warrantless arrest in situations in which peace officers fear that the suspect will learn of his wanted status in the future. Maixner v. State, 753 S.W.2d 151 (Tex. Crim. App. 1988); Redd v. State, 712 S.W.2d 615 (Tex.App.—Houston [1st Dist.] 1986, *pet. ref'd*).

Where the suspect knows that the police are looking for him and nevertheless remains in the area, there is no evidence that the suspect is about to escape. Bell v. State, 724 S.W.2d 780 (Tex. Crim. App. 1986).

Another important factor is whether the police had questioned or apprehended any of the defendant's cohorts. Stanton v. State, 743 S.W.2d 233 (Tex. Crim. App. 1988).

§1:34.3 Insufficient Time to Procure Warrant

This article does not require proof that there was, in fact, no time to procure a warrant. Rysiejko v. State, 782 S.W.2d 529 (Tex.App.—Houston [14th Dist.] 1989, *pet. ref'd*).

Where the evidence showed that it would take one to two hours to procure a warrant, there was insufficient time under this article. Laca v. State, 893 S.W.2d 171 (Tex.App.—El Paso 1995). Where the evidence showed that it would take at least four hours to procure a warrant, there was insufficient time under this article. Proctor v. State, 871 S.W.2d 225 (Tex.App.—Eastland 1993, *pet. ref'd*).

Where evidence provided to police by a robbery victim was that the defendants were leaving for California that same day, exigent circumstances justified their warrantless arrest. Fry v. State, 639 S.W.2d 463 (Tex. Crim. App. 1982).

§1:34.4 Satisfactory Proof of Escape

In order for an arrest to be justified on the ground that the suspect is about to escape, there must be some evidence amounting to satisfactory proof, either related by a credible person to a peace officer or observed by the officer himself, indicating that the defendant is about to escape such that there is no time to procure an arrest warrant. Dejarnette v. State, 732 S.W.2d 346 (Tex. Crim. App. 1987).

"Satisfactory proof" for purposes of the warrantless arrest statutes means a factual showing equal to constitutional probable cause. Amores v. State, 816 S.W.2d 407 (Tex. Crim. App. 1991); Laca v. State, 893 S.W.2d 171 (Tex.App.—El Paso 1995).

An observing peace officer will be considered a "credible person" for purposes of this statute. Dejarnette, *supra*.

§1:35 Preventing Consequences of Theft Under CCP Art. 18.16

CCP Art. 18.16. Preventing consequences of theft

> *Any person has a right to prevent the consequences of theft by seizing any personal property that has been stolen and bringing it, with the person suspected of committing the theft, if that person can be taken, before a magistrate for examination, or delivering the property and the person suspected of committing the theft to a peace officer for that purpose. To justify a seizure under this article, there must be reasonable ground to believe the property is stolen, and the seizure must be openly made and the proceedings had without delay.*

This article authorizes a private citizen to make a warrantless arrest of a thief where the stolen property is found in the thief's possession.

Douglas v. State, 695 S.W.2d 817 (Tex.App.—Waco 1985).

This includes store employees who witness the defendant committing theft from the store. Simpson v. State, 815 S.W.2d 900 (Tex.App.—Fort Worth 1991).

The legality of an arrest under this article depends upon whether the party making the arrest and seizure had a "reasonable ground" or "probable cause" to believe that the property seized had been stolen and that the party arrested was the thief. Douglas, *supra*.

The alleged stolen property must be located before the arrest of the offender in order to justify the arrest under this article. Bernal v. State, 647 S.W.2d 699 (Tex.App.—San Antonio 1982).

The evidence must demonstrate that the defendant was the person who stole the property. Mitchell v. State, 756 S.W.2d 71 (Tex.App.—Texarkana 1988). The thief's admission that he had stolen the property supplies the "reasonable ground" or "probable cause" for the arrest. Douglas, *supra*.

Where the stolen property is found in the pocket of the defendant there is "reasonable ground" or "probable cause" to arrest him. Burkett v. State, 760 S.W.2d 345 (Tex.App.—Houston [1st Dist.] 1988).

The person making the arrest under this article may use the force authorized by CCP Art. 15.24, which provides that all reasonable means are permitted to effect an arrest, but that no greater force shall be used than is necessary. Simpson, *supra*.

§1:36 Rights of Police Officers Making Warrantless Arrests

CCP Art. 14.05. Rights of officer

In each case enumerated where arrests may be lawfully made without warrant, the officer or person making the arrest is justified in adopting all the measures which he might adopt in cases of arrest under warrant, except that an officer making an arrest without a warrant may not enter a residence to make the arrest unless:

(1) a person who resides in the residence consents to the entry; or

(2) exigent circumstances require that the officer making the arrest enter the residence without the consent of a resident or without a warrant.

Warrantless home arrests violate the Fourth Amendment absent probable cause and exigent circumstances. Payton v. New York, 445 U.S. 573, 100 S.Ct. 1371, 63 L.Ed.2d 639 (1980); Kirk v. Louisiana, 536 U.S. 635, 122 S.Ct. 2458, 153 L.Ed.2d 599 (2002); Winter v. State, 902 S.W.2d 571 (Tex.App.—Houston [1st Dist.] 1995).

If the premises to be searched to effectuate an arrest is the suspect's own residence, federal law is satisfied if there is a valid arrest warrant for the suspect. Exigent circumstances will allow officers to enter the residence to effectuate a warrantless arrest. Payton, *supra*.

CCP Art. 14.051. Arrest by peace officer from other jurisdiction

(a) A peace officer commissioned and authorized by another state to make arrests for felonies who is in fresh pursuit of a person for the purpose of arresting that person for a felony may continue the pursuit into this state and arrest the person.

(b) In this article, "fresh pursuit" means a pursuit without unreasonable delay by a peace officer of a person the officer reasonably suspects has committed a felony.

§1:36.1 Fresh ("Hot") Pursuit

The doctrine of "hot pursuit," provides that if a peace officer initiates pursuit of an offender in his jurisdiction he may then continue the pursuit into another jurisdiction. Preston v. State, 700 S.W.2d 227 (Tex. Crim. App. 1985).

A police officer may pursue and arrest a defendant outside his jurisdiction under the "hot pursuit" doctrine where the defendant's initial detention and subsequent arrest was lawfully initiated on the ground of suspicion. Yeager v. State, 104 S.W.3d 103 (Tex. Crim. App. 2003).

A "hot pursuit" is a continuous pursuit by police of a suspect without any break in the police effort to apprehend or in the subject's effort to escape. Jimenez v. State, 750 S.W.2d 798 (Tex.App.—El Paso 1988).

Exigent circumstances exist when the police are in "hot pursuit" of a suspect and can justify a warrantless entry of a residence in order to effectuate the arrest. U.S. v. Santana, 427 U.S. 38, 96 S.Ct. 2406, 49 L.Ed.2d 300 (1976). A suspect may not defeat an arrest that has been set in motion in a public place by escaping to a private place. Santana.

A retreat into an open garage during a police pursuit does not trigger the Fourth Amendment because there is no expectation of privacy in the open garage such as there may be in an actual house. Carter v. State, 824 S.W.2d 767 (Tex.App.—Waco 1992).

Police cannot use the "hot pursuit" doctrine to justify the warrantless arrest of persons suspected of "minor offenses" (such as non-jailable offenses) because exigent circumstances do not exist in this situation. Welsh v. Wisconsin, 466 U.S. 740, 104 S.Ct. 2091, 80 L.Ed.2d 732 (1984).

Possession of a handgun is not the type of "minor offense" contemplated by the Supreme Court in Welsh. Waddy v. State, 880 S.W.2d 458 (Tex.App.—Houston [14th Dist.] 1994, *pet. ref'd*). "Minor offense" as contemplated in Welsh does not equate with "misdemeanor." Waddy, *supra.*

A police officer's attempt to terminate a high-speed car chase that threatens the lives of innocent bystanders does not violate the Fourth Amendment, even when it places the fleeing motorist at risk of serious injury or death. Scott v. Harris, 550 U.S. 372, 127 S.Ct. 1769, 167 L.Ed.2d 686 (2007).

§1:40 Pretext Arrests

A pretextual seizure, in the most general sense, is one that is effectuated for an ulterior (*i.e.*, pretextual) motive. Crittenden v. State, 899 S.W.2d 668 (Tex. Crim. App. 1995).

In Garcia v. State, 827 S.W.2d 937 (Tex. Crim. App. 1992), the Court overruled Black v. State, 739 S.W.2d 240 (Tex. Crim. App. 1987), and held that for Fourth Amendment purposes, the validity of an arrest or stop must be determined solely by analyzing objectively the facts surrounding the event; and that such arrest or stop does not violate the Fourth Amendment simply because the police had an ulterior motive for making it or did not follow standard police procedure in doing so.

See discussion also, in Hamilton v. State, 831 S.W.2d 326 (Tex. Crim. App. 1992), where the Court held that an issue of pretext stop is not raised simply because the police validly stop a vehicle for a traffic violation when they have a more generalized suspicion that the driver of the vehicle was involved in a separate crime. The court also stated that if there is not, in fact, a pretext in the arrest, the defendant is not entitled to a jury charge under CCP Art. 38.23.

In Crittenden v. State, *supra*, the court addressed the pretext arrest doctrine in the context of Texas Constitution Art. I, §9. They held that the rule of Garcia, *supra*, should apply under the Texas Constitution as it did under the U.S. Constitution. Accordingly, under the U.S. and Texas Constitutions, if an officer has an objectively valid reason for a stop, no inquiry will be made as to his subjective motive for the stop. Under an objective approach, a seizing officer's subjective motivation in effectuating a seizure is deemed irrelevant to the determination of whether the seizure was reasonable. This, of course, is nothing more than the complete abandonment of any sort of pretext doctrine; because an officer's subjective intent in effectuating a seizure is irrelevant, there can never be an illegal pretext for a seizure.

The U.S. Supreme Court also recently has applied the objective test to claims of pretextual searches. Whren v. U.S., 517 U.S. 806, 116 S.Ct. 1769, 135 L.Ed.2d 89 (1996).

§1:50 Sources of Probable Cause

§1:51 Information Gained From Victims

Any person purporting to be a crime victim or witness may be presumed reliable; though the police must remain alert to the existence of any circumstances that would make that presumption inoperative in a particular case. Mungia v. State, 911 S.W.2d 164 (Tex.App.—Corpus Christi 1995).

Where a crime victim, who is a private citizen, reports the commission of a criminal offense, and whose only contact with law enforcement authorities is a result of having been victimized at the hands of another, the credibility and reliability of the information is inherent. Nelson v. State, 855 S.W.2d 26 (Tex.App.—El Paso 1993); Esco v. State, 668 S.W.2d 358 (Tex. Crim. App. 1982); Carter v. State, 713 S.W.2d 442 (Tex.App.—Fort Worth 1986).

§1:52 Information Gained From Ordinary Citizens

Where the reasonable suspicion for a police stop is related to the police from a known citizen-informant, the resulting stop is valid. Brother v. State, 166 S.W.3d 255 (Tex. Crim. App. 2005).

An identified private citizen whose only contact with the police results from witnessing a criminal act is inherently credible. Nelson v. State, 855 S.W.2d 26 (Tex.App.—El Paso 1993); Esco v. State, 668 S.W.2d 358 (Tex. Crim. App. 1982); Cornejo v. State, 917 S.W.2d 480 (Tex.App.—Houston [14th Dist.] 1996, *pet. ref'd*).

An affidavit based on the knowledge of a police officer or a person with no criminal record requires no corroboration. Marquez v. State, 725 S.W.2d 217 (Tex. Crim. App. 1987).

When a probable cause affidavit specifies a named informant as supplying the information upon which probable cause is based, the affidavit is sufficient if it is sufficiently detailed to suggest direct knowledge on the informant's part. Matamoros v. State, 901 S.W.2d 470 (Tex. Crim. App. 1995).

§1:53 Information Gained From Police Officers

A police officer can be a "credible person" for purposes of the warrantless arrest statutes. Laca v. State, 893 S.W.2d 171 (Tex.App.—El Paso 1995); Dejarnette v. State, 732 S.W.2d 346 (Tex. Crim. App. 1987).

An affidavit based on the knowledge of a police officer or a person with no criminal record requires no corroboration. Marquez v. State, 725 S.W.2d 217 (Tex. Crim. App. 1987).

§1:54 Information Gained From Informers

In making a warrantless arrest, officers may rely on information received from an informant if that information is reasonably corroborated by other matters within the officer's knowledge or by the officer's subsequent investigation. Draper v. U.S., 358 U.S. 307, 70 S.Ct. 329, 3 L.Ed.2d 327 (1959); Guzman v. State, 955 S.W.2d 85 (Tex. Crim. App. 1997).

Generally the search warrant affidavit must satisfy the two-pronged Aguilar-Spinelli test: (1) the informant obtained the relevant information in a reliable manner; and (2) the informant was reliable. Elardo v. State, 163 S.W.3d 760 (Tex.App.—Texarkana 2005, *pet. ref'd*).

However, under the subsequent Gates test, because the focus of the inquiry is whether the statements are sufficiently reliable for a finding of probable cause, a deficiency in one of the two factors of reliability of the informant may not be fatal if the totality of the circumstances indicates reliability. Elardo.

For example, the circumstances of a "controlled buy" of narcotics, standing alone, may be sufficient to reasonably confirm an informant's information and support the issuance of a probable cause warrant. Sadler v. State, 905 S.W.2d 21 (Tex.App.—San Antonio 1995, *no pet.*).

Requiring independent police corroboration—as a per se rule—is contrary to Gates and other precedent for two reasons. First, Gates criticizes per se rules for the determination of probable cause. Second, independent police corroboration has never been treated as a *per se* requirement in each and every case. Dixon v. State, 206 S.W.3d 613 (Tex. Crim. App. 2006).

An informant who had previously given accurate information and whose information given about the instant crime corresponded with the known facts of the offense will be considered credible. Guzman, *supra*.

Where an informant has provided reliable information in the past, arrives at the time and place she stated she would and is accompanied by an individual matching the description she had earlier given police, the police have sufficient corroborating evidence to justify a Terry stop. Carmouche v.

State, 10 S.W.3d 323 (Tex. Crim. App. 2000). See also Griffin v. State, 215 S.W.3d 403 (Tex. Crim. App. 2006) (the confidential informant's information was corroborated by police observations that the defendant was where the informant said he would be, was nervous and had a past involving drug activity).

A mere assertion or conclusion that an informer is credible, without more, is insufficient to establish credibility. Eisenhauer v. State, 678 S.W.2d 947 (Tex. Crim. App. 1984).

There is no requirement that police informants be infallible. Illinois v. Gates, 462 U.S. 213, 103 S.Ct. 2317, 76 L.Ed.2d 527 (1983).

The number of previous occasions where the informant has proven to have been correct is an important consideration in judging his reliability. Dixon.

An informant's first-hand observation of criminal activity provides a strong basis for the informant's knowledge of the facts he relays. Dixon.

The conclusory phrase "reliable source" is insufficient to establish the informant's reliability. Elardo.

The failure to undertake an independent verification of an informant's tip can undermine the reliability of the tip, especially where the informant is being used for the first time. Davis v. State, 144 S.W.3d 192 (Tex.App.—Fort Worth 2004, *pet. ref'd*) (*op. on reh'g*).

§1:55 Information Gained From Anonymous Tips

An anonymous caller is one who does not provide any identification information to officers or to dispatch, does not follow the suspect's vehicle, and is not present at the scene before the stop. Martinez v. State, 348 S.W.3d 919, 924 (Tex. Crim. App. 2011).

While an anonymous tip or telephone call may justify the initiation of an investigation, it alone will rarely establish the level of suspicion required to justify a detention. *See* Alabama v. White, 496 U.S. 325, 110 S.Ct. 2412, 110 L.Ed.2d 301 (1990); Davis v. State, 989 S.W.2d 859 (Tex.App.—Austin 1999, *pet. ref'd*).

An anonymous tip may, however, be sufficient if it contains sufficient "indicia of reliability" or if some aspects of it are sufficiently corroborated. White; Davis.

Corroboration by a police officer means, in light of the circumstances, he confirms enough facts so that he may reasonably conclude that the information provided is reliable and a detention is justified. White; State v. Sailo, 910 S.W.2d 184 (Tex.App.—Fort Worth 1995, *pet. ref'd*).

Where police arrive on the scene described in an anonymous tip and make a number of independent observations supporting the tip there can be sufficient corroboration of the tip to support a finding of reasonable suspicion. Furr v. State, 499 S.W.3d 872, 880 (Tex. Crim. App. 2016).

An officer's prior knowledge and experience, and his corroboration of the details of the tip, may be considered in giving the anonymous tip the weight it deserves. White; Stewart v. State, 22 S.W.3d 646 (Tex.App.—Austin 2000, *pet. ref'd*).

Mere corroboration of details easily obtainable at the time the information is provided will not support a finding of probable cause nor furnish the basis for reasonable suspicion. White; Davis.

The following are significant in determining whether reasonable suspicion exists for a temporary detention based upon information from an unknown tipster: (1) accurately predicting future behavior of third parties, (2) corroboration of a detail linking the accused to the stated criminal activity, and (3) a particularized and objective reason to suspect the accused. Glenn v. State, 967 S.W.2d 467 (Tex.App.—Amarillo 1998, *pet. dism'd. improv. granted*).

Other factors include whether the tip is specific and precise, and whether the tip was given by an informant who had firsthand information of the facts related. Sailo.

Before an anonymous tip constitutes reasonable suspicion it must be reliable in its assertion of illegal conduct, not just in its tendency to identify a determinate person. Florida v. J.L., 529 U.S. 266, 120 S.Ct. 1375, 146 L.Ed.2d 254 (2000).

An anonymous 911 call can furnish adequate reasonable suspicion for a stop where it contains sufficient indicia of reliability where the caller reported that the suspect ran the caller off the road; thereby establishing that the caller was a personal witness to criminal activity. *Prado Navarette v.*

California, 572 U.S. 572, 134 S.Ct. 1683, 188 L.Ed.2d 680 (2014).

The reliability of a tip can be heightened to the point where an officer is justified in making a detention when an informant places himself in a position to be easily identified and held responsible for the information provided. Hawes v. State, 125 S.W.3d 535 (Tex.App.—Houston [1st Dist.] 2002, *no pet.*); State v. Fudge, 42 S.W.3d 226 (Tex.App. —Austin 2001, *no pet.*).

Where an anonymous tip is fairly detailed in its description of the suspect, going so far as to give his name and predict his future actions, and is then independently verified by a police investigation, it can furnish a substantial basis under the totality of the circumstances test for a warrantless arrest of the suspect. Eisenhauer v. State, 678 S.W.2d 947 (Tex. Crim. App. 1984).

An anonymous tip that a described person is carrying a firearm is not sufficient to justify a Terry stop. Florida v. J.L.

The totality of the circumstances is the standard applied when determining the reasonableness of an investigative stop. Woods v. State, 956 S.W.2d 33 (Tex. Crim. App. 1997).

Anonymous tips can be considered as circumstances corroborative of an informant's tip. Illinois v. Gates, 462 U.S. 213, 103 S.Ct. 2317, 76 L.Ed.2d 527 (1983).

§1:60 Suppressing Warrantless Arrest

If a defendant is illegally arrested, the fruits of the arrest must be suppressed unless intervening circumstances or events between the arrest and interrogation relieve the taint of the illegal procedure. Gordon v. State, 801 S.W.2d 899 (Tex. Crim. App. 1990).

PRACTICE TIP: The defendant has the right to a jury charge under CCP Article 38.23 asking the jury to resolve factual disputes over whether evidence was illegally obtained, and therefore, inadmissible. Brochu v. State, 927 S.W.2d 745 (Tex.App.—Houston [14 Dist.] 1996).

The initial burden of proof is on a defendant when he seeks to suppress evidence. Russell v. State, 717 S.W.2d 7 (Tex. Crim. App.1986); Young v. State, 283 S.W.3d 854 (Tex. Crim. App. No. 75,352, April 22, 2009). As the movant in the motion to suppress evidence, a defendant must produce evidence that defeats the presumption of proper police conduct. Russell, Young.

Once the presumption is defeated, the burden shifts to the State to either produce evidence of a warrant or prove the reasonableness of the arrest. Young.

PRACTICE TIP: In conducting a motion to suppress hearing with arrest issues, take extra care to have the record reflect exactly the point in time when the actual arrest occurred.

It is within the trial court's discretion to grant the State's request to reopen a motion-to-suppress hearing to supplement the record with additional testimony, outside the jury's presence, even over the objection of the defendant. Black v. State, 362 S.W.3d 626 (Tex. Crim. App. 2012).

§1:61 Art. 38.23 Jury Charge

In order to be entitled to a jury charge under CCP Art. 38.23 regarding the legality of the obtaining of evidence: 1) a defendant must request an instruction based on a specific historical fact or facts; 2) there must be some affirmative evidence that puts the existence of that fact or facts into question; and 3) the disputed fact must be one that affects the determination of the legal issue. Madden v. State, 242 S.W.3d 504 (Tex. Crim. App. 2007).

Under CCP Art. 38.23, the defendant is entitled to a jury charge where there has been a factual issue raised as to whether the warrantless arrest was supported by adequate probable cause. The charge should instruct the jury that they should suppress the fruits of the arrest if they find it to be illegal. Coleman v. State, 45 S.W.3d 175 (Tex. App.—Houston [1st Dist.] 2001, *pet. ref'd*); Stone v. State, 703 S.W.2d 652 (Tex. Crim. App. 1986).

A defendant is not entitled to an article 38.23 instruction if the jury's verdict disposes of the issue that he asserts as the factual issue entitling him to the instruction. Porter v. State, 255 S.W.3d 234 (Tex. App.—Waco 2008, pet.ref'd)(where the jury's finding that the defendant was guilty of evading arrest or detention disposed of his issue that his detention was illegal); Wilkerson v. State, 933 S.W.2d 276 (Tex. App.—Houston [1st Dist.] 1996, pet.ref'd)(where the jury's finding that the defendant was guilty of delivery of drugs disposed of his issue that the police officer was lying and no drug transaction had occurred).

When a citizen is legally authorized to make a citizen's arrest, and when he effectuates that arrest in a reasonable manner—a manner that a peace officer, standing in the citizen's shoes, could have legally done under the Fourth Amendment—and without significantly increasing the risk of danger and harm to the public welfare, the fact that the citizen violated traffic laws in order to make the arrest will not implicate Article 38.23. Miles v. State, 241 S.W.3d 28 (Tex. Crim. App. 2007).

The Fourth Amendment does not apply to the actions of private individuals, and reading Article 38.23 to apply the Fourth Amendment to private individuals would lead to an absurdity. Ruiz v. State, ___ S.W.3d ___ at *2 (PD-1348-17, 2019 WL 2814867, Tex. Crim. App. July 3, 2019).

A defendant who moves for suppression under Art. 38.23 due to the violation of a statute has the burden of producing evidence of a statutory violation. Only when this burden is met does the State bear a burden to prove compliance. State v. Robinson, 334 S.W.3d 776, 779 (Tex. Crim. App. 2011).

Searches conducted in objectively reasonable reliance on binding appellate precedent are not subject to the Fourth Amendment exclusionary rule. Davis v. U.S., 564 U.S. ___, 131 S.Ct. 2419, 180 L.Ed.2d 285 (2011).

PRACTICE TIP: Although Texas has the statutory exclusionary rule contained in Art. 38.23, the State can use the Davis case to argue that the evidence was not "obtained" in violation of the law where legal precedent at the time of police conduct allowed the police action.

§1:70 Arrests Under Warrant

§1:71 What Is an Arrest Warrant

CCP Art. 15.01. Warrant of arrest

A "warrant of arrest" is a written order from a magistrate, directed to a peace officer or some other person specially named, commanding him to take the body of the person accused of an offense, to be dealt with according to law.

Texas courts have jurisdiction to issue warrants with statewide authority regardless of where venue lies. Emerson v. Borland, 927 S.W.2d 709 (Tex. App.—Austin 1996).

§1:72 What an Arrest Warrant Requires

CCP Art. 15.02. Requisites of warrant

It issues in the name of "The State of Texas," and shall be sufficient, without regard to form, if it have these substantial requisites:

1. It must specify the name of the person whose arrest is ordered, if it be known, if unknown, then some reasonably definite description must be given of him.

2. It must state that the person is accused of some offense against the laws of the State, naming the offense.

3. It must be signed by the magistrate, and his office be named in the body of the warrant, or in connection with his signature.

§1:72.1 Probable Cause Requirement

An arrest warrant affidavit must provide the issuing magistrate with sufficient information to support an independent judgment that probable cause exists for the issuance of the warrant. McFarland v. State, 928 S.W.2d 482 (Tex. Crim. App. 1996).

The affidavit must show probable cause that an offense was committed and that the person named in the warrant committed it. Bell v. State,

747 S.W.2d 898 (Tex.App.—Fort Worth 1988, *pet. ref'd*). The arrest warrant affidavit must set out the sources of the affiant's information. Evans v. State, 530 S.W.2d 932 (Tex. Crim. App. 1975).

The sufficiency of an affidavit for an arrest warrant is determined by a review of the "four corners" of the document. Gibbs v. State, 819 S.W.2d 821 (Tex. Crim. App.1991).

The applicable standard for the sufficiency of the affidavit is the totality of the circumstances test. Whaley v. State, 686 S.W.2d 950 (Tex. Crim. App. 1985); Belton v. State, 900 S.W.2d 886 (Tex. App.—El Paso 1995); Illinois v. Gates, 462 U.S. 213, 103 S.Ct. 2317, 76 L.Ed.2d 527 (1983).

A warrant affidavit should be interpreted in a common sense and realistic manner. The reviewing magistrate is permitted to draw reasonable inferences from the facts supporting the averments. Gibbs, *supra*.

Where the arrest warrant is valid, evidence seized or gained pursuant to the arrest will be validly admitted at trial. Gibbs.

PRACTICE TIP: Carefully examine the arrest warrant and supporting affidavit to look for ways in which they or the underlying facts supporting probable cause can be attacked.

The information contained in the arrest warrant affidavit can be based on either the direct personal observations of the affiant or on hearsay. Belton v. State, 900 S.W.2d 886 (Tex.App.—El Paso 1995). Hearsay within hearsay will support the issuance of an arrest warrant as long as the underlying circumstances indicate that there is a substantial basis for crediting the hearsay at each level. State v. Martin, 833 S.W.2d 129 (Tex. Crim. App. 1992).

A complaint supporting a municipal warrant for failure to appear must provide probable cause for an arrest by alleging why the act is unlawful and how the affiant came to have the knowledge. Gordon v. State, 801 S.W.2d 899 (Tex. Crim. App. 1990).

A capias is only valid when issued from a court with proper jurisdiction after a neutral magistrate has made a determination of probable cause. Green v. State, 78 S.W.3d 604 (Tex.App.—Fort Worth 2002).

§1:72.2 Accusation of Criminal Conduct

The arrest warrant affidavit must connect the defendant with the commission of the offense. Williams v. State, 787 S.W.2d 181 (Tex.App.—Beaumont 1990, *pet. ref'd*); Hankins v. State, 132 S.W.3d 380 (Tex. Crim. App. 2004)

An abbreviation of the penal code offense with which the defendant is charged will suffice under CCP Art. 15.02. Jones v. State, 568 S.W.2d 847 (Tex. Crim. App. 1978).

§1:72.3 Signing by a Magistrate

Where there was probable cause shown for the arrest of the defendant, an arrest was proper even though the warrant inadvertently was not signed until after the defendant was in the custody of the police. Dunn v. State, 951 S.W.2d 478 (Tex. Crim. App. 1997).

There is no requirement that an arrest warrant contain the time of its issuance. Belton v. State, 900 S.W.2d 886 (Tex.App.—El Paso 1995).

A printed recitation reading "Magistrate of Harris County" under the signature of the magistrate sufficiently named the office of the magistrate for purposes of this article. McMahon v. State, 630 S.W.2d 730 (Tex.App.—Houston [14th Dist.] 1982, *pet. ref'd*).

A typographical error indicating that the arrest warrant was signed into effect one year prior to the commission of the offense did not invalidate the arrest warrant. Rougeau v. State, 738 S.W.2d 651 (Tex. Crim. App. 1987).

§1:73 Who May Issue Arrest Warrants

CCP Art. 15.03. Magistrate may issue warrant or summons

(a) A magistrate may issue a warrant of arrest or a summons:

1. In any case in which he is by law authorized to order verbally the arrest of an offender;

2. When any person shall make oath before the magistrate that another has committed some offense against the laws of the State; and

3. In any case named in this Code where he is specially authorized to issue warrants of arrest.

(b) A summons may be issued in any case where a warrant may be issued, and shall be in the same form as the warrant except that it shall summon the defendant to appear before a magistrate at a stated time and place. The summons shall be served upon a defendant by delivering a copy to him personally, or by leaving it at his dwelling house or usual place of abode with some person of suitable age and discretion then residing therein or by mailing it to the defendant's last known address. If a defendant fails to appear in response to the summons a warrant shall be issued.

(c) For purposes of Subdivision 2, Subsection (a), a person may appear before the magistrate in person or the person's image may be presented to the magistrate through an electronic broadcast system.

(d) A recording of the communication between the person and the magistrate must be made if the person's image is presented through an electronic broadcast system under Subsection (c). If the defendant is charged with the offense, the recording must be preserved until:

(1) the defendant is acquitted of the offense; or

(2) all appeals relating to the offense have been exhausted.

(e) The counsel for the defendant may obtain a copy of the recording on payment of an amount reasonably necessary to cover the costs of reproducing the recording.

(f) In this article, "electronic broadcast system" means a two-way electronic communication of image and sound between a person and magistrate and includes secure Internet videoconferencing.

See CCP Art. 2.09 for a list of officers who qualify as magistrates.

§1:74 Suppressing Arrest

The initial burden of proof is on a defendant when he seeks to suppress evidence. Russell v. State, 717 S.W.2d 7 (Tex. Crim. App.1986). As the movant in the motion to suppress evidence, a defendant must produce evidence that defeats the presumption of proper police conduct. Russell; State v. Martinez, 569 S.W.3d 621, 624-5 (Tex. Crim. App. 2019).

If a defendant establishes 1) that a search or seizure occurred and 2) that no warrant was obtained, the burden of proof shifts to the State. Russell; Martinez.

Where the state produces the warrant and it is valid on its face, the defendant then has the burden of going forward to establish the invalidity of the warrant on some ground. Belton v. State, 900 S.W.2d 886 (Tex.App.—El Paso 1995); Rumsey v. State, 675 S.W.2d 517 (Tex. Crim. App. 1984).

TIP TO THE PROSECUTION: Always have a copy of the arrest warrant and affidavit prepared for introduction into evidence for the viewing of the court if the defense challenges the probable cause for the arrest.

PRACTICE TIP: The burden is on the defendant to ensure that the arrest warrant and affidavit are included in the record for appeal. Rumsey, supra.

The arrest warrant need not be physically present at the scene of the arrest in order for the arrest to be valid where the warrant was issued by the court by the time of the arrest. Clark v. State, 929 S.W.2d 5 (Tex. Crim. App. 1996).

A search incident to the execution of an invalid arrest warrant is constitutionally impermissible. Rumsey, *supra*.

An arrest pursuant to an invalid arrest warrant will be upheld if officers held another valid arrest warrant at the time of the arrest. Janecka v. State, 739 S.W.2d 813 (Tex. Crim. App. 1987).

If a defendant is illegally arrested, the fruits of the arrest must be suppressed unless intervening circumstances or events between the arrest and interrogation relieve the taint of the illegal procedure. Gordon v. State, 801 S.W.2d 899 (Tex. Crim. App. 1990).

PRACTICE TIP: The defendant has the right to a jury charge under CCP Article 38.23 asking the jury to resolve factual disputes over whether evidence was illegally obtained, and therefore, inadmissible. Brochu v. State, 927 S.W.2d 745 (Tex. App.—Houston [14th Dist.] 1996).

The Rules of Evidence do not apply to suppression hearings. This is because former Rule 1101(d)(4) that previously dictated to the contrary no longer exists. Granados v. State, 85 S.W.3d 217 (Tex. Crim. App. 2002).

Therefore, Rule 702 is not applicable at a suppression hearing. Hall v. State, 297 S.W.3d 294 (Tex. Crim. App. 2009).

In a pre-trial motion to suppress hearing, a trial court may rely upon any relevant, reliable, and credible information, even though it may be unsworn hearsay (in this case a police report found to be sufficiently reliable). The language of CCP Art. 28.01 is permissive, not restrictive, and allows reports to be used. Ford v. State, 305 S.W.3d 530 (Tex. Crim. App. 2009).

If the defendant takes the stand at trial he may be impeached with his suppression hearing testimony if he testifies contrary. Nelson v. State, 607 S.W.2d 554 (Tex. Crim. App. 1980).

Upon the request of the losing party on a motion to suppress evidence, the trial court shall state its essential findings. By "essential findings," it is meant that the trial court must make findings of fact and conclusions of law adequate to provide an appellate court with a basis upon which to review the trial court's application of the law to the facts. State v. Cullen, 195 S.W.3d 696 (Tex. Crim. App. No. 984-05, June 28, 2006).

PRACTICE TIP: TRCP 297, cited in Cullen, provides that the trial court shall file its findings of fact and conclusions of law within twenty days after a timely request is filed. It further provides that the court shall cause a copy of its findings and conclusions to be mailed to each party in the suit. The findings and conclusions need to be recorded in some way, whether written out and filed by the trial court, or stated on the record at the hearing.

It is within the trial court's discretion to grant the State's request to reopen a motion-to-suppress hearing to supplement the record with additional testimony, outside the jury's presence, even over the objection of the defendant. Black v. State, 362 S.W.3d 626 (Tex. Crim. App. 2012).

Where the trial court's written findings and conclusions of law are ambiguous and lack a credibility determination, an appellate court can remand the case for supplemental findings. State v. Mendoza, 365 S.W.3d 666 (Tex. Crim. App. 2012).

§1:75 Suppressing Arrest Warrant

§1:75.1 Objections to Arrest Warrant

Objections to the use of the fruits of an arrest warrant at trial are as follows:

- Affidavit for the arrest warrant does not set forth probable cause for the search [McFarland v. State, 928 S.W.2d 482 (Tex. Crim. App. 1996)]
- Affidavit for the arrest warrant is not properly sworn to by the affiant [CCP Art. 15.03.]

- Warrant is improper because it is based on an improperly dated affidavit [CCP Art. 15.03.]
- Warrant itself is improperly dated [Belton v. State, 900 S.W.2d 886 (Tex. App.—El Paso 1995, *pet. ref'd*)]
- Information in the affidavit attributed to a confidential informant is not sufficiently corroborated [Guzman v. State, 955 S.W.2d 85 (Tex. Crim. App. 1997)]
- Affidavit contains no recitation as to how the affiant learned the information he relates [Evans v. State, 530 S.W.2d 932 (Tex. Crim. App. 1975)]
- Affidavit contains no recitation as to how the informant came by the information he relates [Matamoros v. State, 901 S.W.2d 470 (Tex. Crim. App. 1995)]
- Information within the affidavit is stale and no longer states probable cause [Guerra v. State, 860 S.W.2d 609 (Tex. App.—Corpus Christi 1993, *no pet.*)]
- Information in the affidavit was obtained through illegal means [CCP Art. 38.23.]
- Affiant is not reliable [Johnson v. State, 803 S.W.2d 272 (Tex. Crim. App. 1990)]
- Hearsay within the affidavit is not properly credited at each level [State v. Martin, 833 S.W.2d 129 (Tex. Crim. App. 1992)]
- Affiant has intentionally misrepresented the facts in the affidavit [Hass v. State, 790 S.W.2d 609 (Tex. Crim. App. 1990)]
- Person signing the warrant is not a proper magistrate under the Code of Criminal Procedure [CCP Art. 2.09.]
- Magistrate issuing the warrant was not neutral and detached as required [CCP Art. 15.02.]
- Officers executing the warrant do not have proper jurisdiction [Britt v. State, 768 S.W.2d 514 (Tex.App.—Fort Worth 1989, *no pet.*)] CCP Art. 2.12.

§1:75.2 Going Behind Affidavit and Warrant

If an affirmative misrepresentation is knowingly included in a probable cause affidavit and is material and necessary to establishing the probable cause, the warrant is rendered invalid under the Fourth Amendment. Franks v. Delaware, 438 U.S. 154, 98 S.Ct. 2674, 57 L.Ed.2d 667 (1978); Hass v. State, 790 S.W.2d 609 (Tex. Crim. App. 1990).

The burden is on the defendant to show by a preponderance of the evidence that a falsehood in the affidavit was made knowingly, intentionally, or with reckless disregard for the truth. Janecka v. State, 937 S.W.2d 456 (Tex. Crim. App. 1996).

Where the defendant makes a substantial preliminary showing that a false statement knowingly and intentionally, or with reckless disregard for the truth, was included by the affiant in the warrant affidavit; and if the allegedly false statement is necessary to the finding of probable cause, the Fourth Amendment requires that a hearing be held at the defendant's request. Dancy v. State, 728 S.W.2d 772 (Tex. Crim. App. 1987).

In the event that at that hearing the allegation of perjury or reckless disregard is established by the defendant by a preponderance of the evidence, and, with the affidavit's false material set to one side, the affidavit's remaining content is insufficient to establish probable cause, the search warrant must be voided and the fruits of the search excluded to the same extent as if probable cause was lacking on the face of the affidavit. Dancy, *supra*.

Unconstitutionally defective portions of a search warrant do not necessarily invalidate the entire warrant or taint all of the evidence seized pursuant to the warrant. If only certain portions of a search warrant are invalid, only the evidence gathered pursuant to the offending portions is tainted. Massey v. State, 933 S.W2d 141 (Tex. Crim. App. 1996). The Texas Court of Criminal Appeals has not extended the Franks rationale to omissions as well as false statements. Massey.

PRACTICE TIP: When complaining of invalid portions of an arrest warrant, the defendant must identify the allegedly invalid portions of the warrant. In failing to identify how he was harmed by the complained of portion of the affidavit, the defendant will have failed to preserve his claim for review. Massey, supra.

Mere conclusory statements alleging lack of probable cause, defects in the warrant and procurement of evidence by illegal means are insufficient to make a substantial preliminary showing as required by Franks. Dancy, *supra.*

Under Franks, in order to be entitled to an evidentiary hearing on the allegations concerning the veracity of the affidavit, the defendant must:

- Allege deliberate falsehood or reckless disregard for the truth by the affiant, specifically pointing out the portion of the affidavit claimed to be false. Allegations of negligence or innocent mistake are insufficient, and the allegations must be more than conclusory.
- Accompany these allegations with an offer of proof stating the supporting reasons. Affidavits or otherwise reliable statements of witnesses should be furnished. If not, the absence of written support of the allegations must be satisfactorily explained.
- Show that when the portion of the affidavit alleged to be false is excised from the affidavit, the remaining content is insufficient to support issuance of the warrant.

Dancy, *supra.*

§1:75.3 Article 38.23 Jury Charge

Under CCP Art. 38.23, the defendant is entitled to a jury charge where there has been a factual issue raised as to whether the arrest warrant was supported by adequate probable cause. The charge should instruct the jury that they should suppress the fruits of the arrest if they find it to be illegal. Coleman v. State, 45 S.W.3d 175 (Tex.App.—Houston [1st Dist.] 2001, *pet. ref'd*); Stone v. State, 703 S.W.2d 652 (Tex. Crim. App. 1986).

A defendant who moves for suppression under Art. 38.23 due to the violation of a statute has the burden of producing evidence of a statutory violation. Only when this burden is met does the State bear a burden to prove compliance. State v. Robinson, 334 S.W.3d 776, 779 (Tex. Crim. App. 2011).

§1:76 Making Arrest

The Fourth Amendment does not forbid a full custodial warrantless arrest for a minor criminal offense such as a misdemeanor punishable by fine only. Atwater v. City of Lago Vista, 534 U.S. 318, 121 S.Ct. 1536 (2001).

CCP Art. 15.16. How warrant is executed

(a) The officer or person executing a warrant of arrest shall without unnecessary delay take the person or have him taken before the magistrate who issued the warrant or before the magistrate named in the warrant, if the magistrate is in the same county where the person is arrested. If the issuing or named magistrate is in another county, the person arrested shall without unnecessary delay be taken before some magistrate in the county in which he was arrested.

(b) Notwithstanding Subsection (a), to provide more expeditiously to the person arrested the warnings described by Article 15.17, the officer or person executing the arrest warrant may as permitted by that article take the person arrested before a magistrate in a county other than the county of arrest.

CCP Art. 15.17. Duties of arresting officer and magistrate

(a) In each case enumerated in this Code, the person making the arrest or the person having custody of the person arrested shall without unnecessary delay, but not later than 48 hours after the person is arrested, take the person arrested or have him taken before some magistrate of the county where

the accused was arrested or, to provide more expeditiously to the person arrested the warnings described by this article, before a magistrate in any other county of this state. The arrested person may be taken before the magistrate in person or the image of the arrested person may be presented to the magistrate by means of an electronic broadcast system. The magistrate shall inform in clear language the person arrested, either in person or through the electronic broadcast system, of the accusation against him and of any affidavit filed therewith, of his right to retain counsel, of his right to remain silent, of his right to have an attorney present during any interview with peace officers or attorneys representing the state, of his right to terminate the interview at any time, and of his right to have an examining trial. The magistrate shall also inform the person arrested of the person's right to request the appointment of counsel if the person cannot afford counsel. The magistrate shall inform the person arrested of the procedures for requesting appointment of counsel. If the person does not speak and understand the English language or is deaf, the magistrate shall inform the person in a manner consistent with Articles 38.30 and 38.31, as appropriate. The magistrate shall ensure that reasonable assistance in completing the necessary forms for requesting appointment of counsel is provided to the person at the same time. If the person arrested is indigent and requests appointment of counsel and if the magistrate is authorized under Article 26.04 to appoint counsel for indigent defendants in the county, the magistrate shall appoint counsel in accordance with Article 1.051. If the magistrate is not authorized to appoint counsel, the magistrate shall without unnecessary delay, but not later than 24 hours after the person arrested requests appointment of counsel, transmit, or cause to be transmitted to the court or to the courts' designee authorized under Article 26.04 to appoint counsel in the county, the forms requesting the appointment of counsel. The magistrate shall also inform the person arrested that he is not required to make a statement and that any statement made by him may be used against him. The magistrate shall allow the person arrested reasonable time and opportunity to consult counsel and shall, after determining whether the person is currently on bail for a separate criminal offense, admit the person arrested to bail if allowed by law. A recording of the communication between the arrested person and the magistrate shall be made. The recording shall be preserved until the earlier of the following dates: (1) the date on which the pretrial hearing ends; or (2) the 91st day after the date on which the recording is made if the person is charged with a misdemeanor or the 120th day after the date on which the recording is made if the person is charged with a felony. The counsel for the defendant may obtain a copy of the recording on payment of a reasonable amount to cover costs of reproduction. For purposes of this subsection, "electronic broadcast system" means a two-way electronic communication of image and sound between the arrested person and the magistrate and includes secure Internet videoconferencing.

(b) After an accused charged with a misdemeanor punishable by fine only is taken before a magistrate under Subsection (a) and the magistrate has identified the accused with certainty, the magistrate may release the accused without bond and order the accused to appear at a later date for arraignment in the applicable justice court or municipal court. The order must state in writing the time, date, and place of the arraignment, and the magistrate must sign the order. The accused shall receive a copy of the order on release. If an accused fails to appear as required by the order, the judge of the court in which the accused is required to appear shall issue a warrant for the arrest of

the accused. If the accused is arrested and brought before the judge, the judge may admit the accused to bail, and in admitting the accused to bail, the judge should set as the amount of bail an amount double that generally set for the offense for which the accused was arrested. This subsection does not apply to an accused who has previously been convicted of a felony or a misdemeanor other than a misdemeanor punishable by fine only.

(c) When a deaf accused is taken before a magistrate under this article or Article 14.06 of this Code, an interpreter appointed by the magistrate qualified and sworn as provided in Article 38.31 of this Code shall interpret the warning required by those articles in a language that the accused can understand, including but not limited to sign language.

(d) If a magistrate determines that a person brought before the magistrate after an arrest authorized by Article 14.051 of this code was arrested unlawfully, the magistrate shall release the person from custody. If the magistrate determines that the arrest was lawful, the person arrested is considered a fugitive from justice for the purposes of Article 51.13 of this code, and the disposition of the person is controlled by that article.

(e) In each case in which a person arrested is taken before a magistrate as required by Subsection (a), a record shall be made of: (1) the magistrate informing the person of the person's right to request appointment of counsel; (2) the magistrate asking the person whether the person wants to request appointment of counsel; and (3) whether the person requested appointment of counsel.

(f) A record required under Subsection (e) may consist of written forms, electronic recordings, or other documentation as authorized by procedures adopted in the county under Article 26.04(a).

(g) If a person charged with an offense punishable as a misdemeanor appears before a magistrate in compliance with a citation issued under Article 14.06(b) or (c), the magistrate shall perform the duties imposed by this article in the same manner as if the person had been arrested and brought before the magistrate by a peace officer. After the magistrate performs the duties imposed by this article, the magistrate except for good cause shown may release the person on personal bond. If a person who was issued a citation under Article 14.06(c) fails to appear as required by that citation, the magistrate before whom the person is required to appear shall issue a warrant for the arrest of the accused.

The failure to take the defendant before a magistrate after his arrest will not vitiate later fruits unless there was a causal connection between the failure to take the defendant before the magistrate and the later fruits. Ex parte Stansbery, 702 S.W.2d 643 (Tex. Crim. App. 1986).

A magistrate has no legal duty to inform defendants of the significance of signing a confession. Robinson v. State, 851 S.W.2d 216 (Tex. Crim. App. 1991).

CCP Art. 15.23. Time of arrest
An arrest may be made on any day or at any time of the day or night.

CCP Art. 15.24. What force may be used
In making an arrest, all reasonable means are permitted to be used to effect it. No greater force, however, shall be resorted to than is necessary to secure the arrest and detention of the accused.

See Penal Code §9.51, which sets out a justification for the use of force and deadly force in certain situations to effectuate an arrest or to prevent an escape.

CCP Art. 15.25. May break door

In case of felony, the officer may break down the door of any house for the purpose of making an arrest, if he be refused admittance after giving notice of his authority and purpose.

A felony arrest warrant gives peace officers the authority to enter the suspect's house to search for him. Brochu v. State, 927 S.W.2d 745 (Tex.App.—Houston [14th Dist.] 1996).

Under the Fourth Amendment, an arrest warrant issued upon a showing of probable cause carries with it the limited authority to enter a dwelling in which the suspect lives when there is reason to believe the suspect is in the dwelling. Payton v. New York, 445 U.S. 573, 100 S.Ct. 1371, 63 L.Ed.2d 639 (1980); Green v. State, 78 S.W.3d 604 (Tex.App.—Fort Worth 2002).Peace officers must be armed with a search warrant if they are seeking to arrest a suspect in the home of a third person, absent consent or exigent circumstances. Steagald v. U.S., 451 U.S. 204, 101 S.Ct. 1642, 68 L.Ed.2d 38 (1981); Hudson v. State, 662 S.W.2d 957 (Tex. Crim. App. 1984). CCP Art. 18.12(11) authorizes the issuance of search warrants for "persons."

Where police officers have an articulable fear for the safety of the occupants of a dwelling where the suspect is located, sufficient exigent circumstances have been shown. Fearance v. State, 771 S.W.2d 486 (Tex. Crim. App. 1988).

The Fourth Amendment incorporates the common law requirement that police officers entering a dwelling must knock on the door and announce their identity and purpose before attempting forcible entry. However, countervailing law enforcement interests militate against a rigid rule of enforcement of this principle. Wilson v. Arkansas, 514 U.S. 927, 115 S.Ct. 1914, 131 L.Ed.2d 976 (1995).

Thus, in order to justify a "no-knock" entry, the police must have a reasonable suspicion that knocking and announcing their presence, under the particular circumstances, would be dangerous or futile, or that it would inhibit the effective investigation of the crime by, for example, allowing the destruction of evidence. Richards v. Wisconsin, 520 U.S. 385, 117 S.Ct. 1416, 137 L.Ed.2d 615 (1997).

CCP Art. 15.26. Authority to arrest must be made known

In executing a warrant of arrest, it shall always be made known to the accused under what authority the arrest is made. The warrant shall be executed by the arrest of the defendant. The officer need not have the warrant in his possession at the time of the arrest, provided the warrant was issued under the provisions of this Code, but upon request he shall show the warrant to the defendant as soon as possible. If the officer does not have the warrant in his possession at the time of arrest he shall then inform the defendant of the offense charged and of the fact that a warrant has been issued. The arrest warrant, and any affidavit presented to the magistrate in support of the issuance of the warrant, is public information, and beginning immediately when the warrant is executed the magistrate's clerk shall make a copy of the warrant and the affidavit available for public inspection in the clerk's office during normal business hours. A person may request the clerk to provide copies of the warrant and affidavit on payment of the cost of providing the copies.

PRACTICE TIP: Be familiar with local police department regulations regarding the amount of force authorized in connection with effectuating an arrest and/or executing a search warrant.

(This page intentionally left blank.)

Chapter 2

SEARCH AND SEIZURE: PROPERTY

Table of Contents

§2:10 Constitutional and Statutory Provisions

U.S. Constitution, Fourth Amendment: The right of the people to be secure in their persons, houses, papers, and effects, against unreasonable searches or seizures, shall not be violated, and no warrants shall issue but upon probable cause, supported by oath or affirmation, and particularly describing the place to be searched, and the persons or things to be seized.

Texas Constitution, Art. 1 §9: The people shall be secure in their persons, houses, papers, and possessions, from all unreasonable seizures or searches, and no warrant to search any place, or to seize any person or thing, shall issue without describing them as near as may be, nor without probable cause, supported by oath or affirmation.

U.S. Constitution, Fourteenth Amendment: ...nor shall any State deprive any person of life, liberty, or property, without due process of law; nor deny to any person within its jurisdiction the equal protection of the laws.

CCP Art. 1.06. Searches and seizures: The people shall be secure in their persons, houses, papers and possessions from all unreasonable seizures or searches. No warrant to search any place or to seize any person or thing shall issue without describing them as near as may be, nor without probable cause supported by oath or affirmation.

Searches conducted outside the judicial process without prior approval by judge or magistrate are per se unreasonable under the Fourth Amendment; subject only to a few specifically established and well-delineated exceptions. Coolidge v. New Hampshire, 403 U.S. 443, 91 S.Ct. 2022, 29 L.Ed.2d 564 (1971).

The Fourth Amendment does not prohibit all seizures; but only those that are unreasonable. United States v. Brignoni-Ponce, 422 U.S. 873, 95 S.Ct. 2574, 45 L.Ed.2d 607 (1975).

In determining whether a "suspicionless search" is reasonable under the Fourth Amendment, the public interest must be balanced against the individual's right to personal security in light of three factors:

- State interest involved
- Level of intrusion on the individual's privacy
- Effectiveness of the procedure used in its stated goal

Brown v. Texas, 443 U.S. 47, 99 S.Ct. 2637, 61 L.Ed.2d 357 (1979). State v. Sanchez, 856 S.W.2d 166 (Tex. Crim. App. 1993).

For example, the supervision of probationers is a special need of the state that is recognized to permit a degree of infringement upon privacy (such as warrantless searches of probationers' homes) that would not be constitutional if applied to the public at large. Griffin v. Wisconsin, 483 U.S. 868, 107 S.Ct. 3164, 97 L.Ed.2d 709 (1987).

Texas law recognizes that the balancing test is two-pronged; weighing the State's interest against the level of intrusion on the individual. Schenekl v. State, 30 S.W.3d 412 (Tex. Crim. App. 2000). This test applies to both random stops and checkpoints. Schenekl.

The Fourth Amendment requires that a seizure be based on specific, objective facts indicating that society's legitimate interests require a seizure of a particular individual, or that the seizure be carried out pursuant to a plan embodying explicit, neutral limitations on the conduct of individual officers in the field. Webb v. State, 739 S.W.2d 802 (Tex. Crim. App. 1987).

§2:20 Search and Seizure—General Concepts

A Fourth Amendment claim may be based on a trespass theory of search (one's personal effects have been trespassed), or a privacy theory of search (one's expectation of privacy was breached). State v. Rodriguez, 521 S.W.3d 1 (Tex. Crim. App. 2017); State v. Martinez, 570 S.W.3d 278, 283 (Tex. Crim. App. 2019).

§2:21 Reasonable Expectation of Privacy

§2:21.1 In General

The touchstone of Fourth Amendment analysis is whether a person has a constitutionally protected reasonable expectation of privacy. Katz v. United States, 389 U.S. 347, 88 S.Ct. 507, 19 L.Ed.2d 576 (1967); Richardson v. State, 865 S.W.2d 944 (Tex. Crim. App. 1993).

This analysis has two parts: 1) whether the individual seeking the protection has manifested a subjective expectation of privacy in the object of the challenged search; and 2) whether society is willing to recognize that expectation as reasonable. Smith v. Maryland, 442 U.S. 735, 99 S.Ct. 2577, 61 L.Ed.2d 220 (1979); State v. Martinez, 570 S.W.3d 278, 283 (Tex. Crim. App. 2019).

In analyzing under the second prong of the above formula, it should be kept in mind that the test of legitimacy is not whether the individual chooses to conceal assertedly private activity; but instead whether the government's intrusion infringes upon the personal and societal values protected by the Fourth Amendment. Oliver v. United States, 466 U.S. 170, 104 S.Ct. 1735, 80 L.Ed.2d 214 (1984).

Legitimizing of expectations of privacy by law must have a source outside of the Fourth Amendment, either by reference to concepts of real or personal property law or to understandings that are recognized and permitted by society. One of the main rights attaching to property is the right to exclude others, and one who owns or lawfully possesses or controls property will in all likelihood have a legitimate expectation of privacy by virtue of this right to exclude. Rakas v. Illinois, 439 U.S. 128, 99 S.Ct. 421, 58 L.Ed.2d 387 (1978).

The burden of establishing a legitimate expectation of privacy is upon the defendant. Villarreal v. State, 935 S.W.2d 134 (Tex. Crim. App. 1996).

The analysis of biological samples, such as blood, is a search that infringes upon privacy interests subject to the Fourth Amendment. State v. Martinez, 570 S.W.3d at 290.

There is a Fourth Amendment privacy interest in blood that has already been drawn for medical purposes. In cases where a defendant has not abandoned his blood, he will have a subjective expectation of privacy in his blood. In this circumstance, the State's subsequent testing of the blood is a Fourth Amendment search separate and apart from the seizure of the blood by the State. Where no exception to the warrant requirement applied, the State was required to obtain a warrant before testing Appellee's blood. State v. Martinez, 570 S.W.3d at 292.

The Fourth Amendment protects businesses as well as private homes; and protects against government administrative inspections as well as police searches. Marshall v. Barlow's, Inc., 436 U.S. 307, 98 S.Ct. 1816, 56 L.Ed.2d 305 (1978).

However, the expectation of privacy in commercial property is different from and less than that in a private residence. Minnesota v. Carter, 525 U.S. 83, 119 S.Ct. 469, 142 L.Ed.2d 373 (1998).

Where there is a lesser expectation of privacy, the Fourth Amendment's protections are correspondingly less stringent. Rakas v. Illinois, 439 U.S. 128, 99 S.Ct. 421, 58 L.Ed.2d 387 (1978) (automobile searches).

PRACTICE TIP: When trying to suppress the fruits of an allegedly improper search or seizure, object under Article I, §9 of the Texas Constitution and under the Fourth and Fourteenth Amendments to the U.S. Constitution, as well as statutory grounds to avoid waiving any issue for appeal.

§2:21.2 Where Reasonable Expectation Exists

An individual maintains a legitimate expectation of privacy in the record of his physical movements as captured by cell phone service providers through cell site location information (CSLI) data gathering. Carpenter v. United States, 585 U.S. ___, 138 S.Ct. 2206, 2217, 201 L.Ed.2d 507 (2018).

A person has a reasonable expectation of privacy in his body and searches for evidence from within his body; and such searches are subject to Fourth Amendment constraints. Schmerber v. California, 384 U.S. 757, 86 S.Ct. 1826, 16 L.Ed.2d 908 (1966); McBride v. State, 840 S.W.2d 111 (Tex. App.—Austin 1992, *pet. ref'd*).

A person has a reasonable expectation in being free from an unreasonably prolonged detention. Kothe v. State, 152 S.W.3d 54 (Tex. Crim. App. 2004).

A compelled surgical intrusion into an individual's body for evidence implicates expectations of privacy and security of such magnitude that the intrusion may be unreasonable even if likely to produce evidence of a crime. Winston v. Lee, 470 U.S. 753, 105 S.Ct. 1611, 84 L.Ed.2d 662 (1985).

Absent consent, surgical invasion to obtain evidence requires a valid search warrant obtained in compliance with the Texas Code of Criminal Procedure. McBride, *supra.*

Invasions of the body of an accused to obtain evidence may, under certain circumstances, comply with due process and constitute a reasonable search and seizure, if done pursuant to probable cause and after issuance of a warrant, by medical personnel using proper medical procedures and if done without brutality that "shocks the conscience." Schmerber v. California, 384 U.S. at 757-60, 86 S.Ct. at 1826-30, 16 L.Ed.2d at 908-14; Oviedo v. State, 767 S.W.2d 214, 217 (Tex.App.—Corpus Christi 1989, *no pet.*).

A person has a legitimate expectation of privacy in a blood sample given to hospital personnel for purposes of medical treatment. State v. Comeaux, 818 S.W.2d 46 (Tex. Crim. App. 1991).

However, whatever interests society may have in recognizing a privacy right in a person's body or in safeguarding the privacy of medical records, they are not sufficiently strong to require protection of blood-alcohol test results from tests taken by hospital personnel solely for medical purposes after a traffic accident. State v. Hardy, 963 S.W.2d 516 (Tex. Crim. App. 1997).

A person has a reasonable expectation of privacy in his home and the area immediately surrounding it (curtilage). Florida v. Jardines, 569 U.S. ___, 133 S.Ct. 1409, 1414-5, 185 L.Ed.2d 495 (2013).

This is true under HIPPA, also. State v. Huse, 491 S.W.3d 833, 843 (Tex. Crim. App. 2016).

There is a reasonable expectation of privacy in words spoken into a telephone receiver in a public telephone booth. Katz v. United States, 389 U.S. 347, 88 S.Ct. 507, 19 L.Ed.2d 576 (1967).

Under the Texas Constitution, there is a reasonable expectation of privacy in telephone numbers dialed; such that the use of a pen register may constitute a search. Richardson v. State, 865 S.W.2d 944 (Tex. Crim. App. 1993).

There is a reasonable expectation of privacy in letters and other sealed packages. U. S. v. Jacobsen, 466 U.S. 109, 104 S.Ct. 1652, 80 L.Ed.2d 85 (1984).

However, when the postal service delivers a defendant's letter to the addressee, it is delivered over the defendant's claim to any reasonable expectation of privacy in the letter. Garcia v. State, 960 S.W.2d 329 (Tex.App.—Corpus Christi 1997, *no pet.*).

A defendant has a reasonable expectation of privacy in a "glory hole booth" where it has a door and seven-foot high walls showing that the management expected patrons to have privacy in the booth. Liebman v. State, 652 S.W.2d 942 (Tex. Crim. App. 1983).

A defendant has a reasonable expectation of privacy in a public restroom stall that he occupies with the door shut. Cook v. State, 762 S.W.2d 714 (Tex.App.—Houston [1st Dist.] 1988, *pet. ref'd*).

A person has a reasonable expectation of privacy in her dorm room even after it has been searched by private citizens. A subsequent entry and search by law enforcement that does not fall within any recognized exception to the warrant requirement violates the Fourth Amendment. State v. Rodriguez, 521 S.W.3d 1 (Tex. Crim. App. 2017).

A person has a reasonable expectation of privacy in a home in which he is a legitimate guest. Minnesota v. Olson, 495 U.S. 91, 110 S.Ct. 1684, 109 L.Ed.2d 85 (1990).

The Fourth Amendment does not prohibit the obtaining of information, such as bank account documents, revealed to a third party and conveyed by him to government authorities. U.S. v. Miller, 425 U.S. 435, 96 S.Ct. 1619, 48 L.Ed.2d 71 (1976).

A prisoner has no reasonable expectation of privacy in his jail cell. Hudson v. Palmer, 468 U.S. 517, 104 S.Ct. 3194, 82 L.Ed.2d 393 (1984).

A person has a legitimate expectation of privacy in the contents of his cell phone because of its ability to store large amounts of private data both in the cell phone itself and by accessing remote services. State v. Granville, 423 S.W.3d 399, 408 (Tex. Crim. App. 2014).

Although a person may have a reasonable and legitimate expectation of privacy in the contents of his cell phone, he may lose that expectation under some circumstances, such as if he abandons his cell phone, lends it to others to use, or gives his consent to its search. State v. Granville, 423 S.W.3d at 409.

A citizen does not lose his reasonable expectation of privacy in the contents of his cell phone merely because that cell phone is being stored in a jail property room. State v. Granville, 423 S.W.3d at 416.

A warrant is generally required before searching a cell phone that is seized incident to arrest. Riley v. California, 573 U.S. 373, 134 S.Ct. 2473, 189 L.Ed.2d 430 (2014).

An individual may have a reasonable expectation of privacy in the recording device (black box) in his vehicle. Kirsch v. State, 276 S.W.3d 579, 587-8 (Tex. App.—Houston [1st Dist. 2008], pet. granted, aff'd at 306 S.W.3d 738 (Tex. Cr. App. 2010). See Texas Transportation Code §547.615.

The definition of "oral communication" found in Article 18.20 of the Code of Criminal Procedure incorporates the reasonable expectation of privacy test as set out in Katz and Berger. Long v. State, 535 S.W.3d 511, 538 (Tex. Crim. App. 2017).

PRACTICE TIP: In order to prove his reasonable expectation of privacy in the place searched, a defendant should attempt to demonstrate a proprietary interest in the place. If he has no proprietary interest in the place, he should try to demonstrate other connections such as a proprietary interest in items at the place searched or that he is a legitimate guest at the premises.

§2:21.3 Where No Reasonable Expectation Exists

A student does not have a reasonable expectation of privacy in a school locker where the locker is school property that remains under the control of school authorities, where the lockers have built-in combination locks and the assistant principal has a key that opens all of the lockers, and where students at the school are given student handbooks detailing locker policy specifying that the lockers shall remain under the jurisdiction of the school and are subject to search at any time reasonable cause exists. Shoemaker v. State, 971 S.W.2d 178 (Tex.App.—Beaumont 1998, *no pet.*).

However, whatever interests society may have in recognizing a privacy right in a person's body or in safeguarding the privacy of medical records, they are not sufficiently strong to require protection of blood-alcohol test results from tests taken by hospital personnel solely for medical purposes after a traffic accident. State v. Hardy, 963 S.W.2d 516 (Tex. Crim. App. 1997).

A defendant does not have a legitimate expectation of privacy in the clothing seized from him at a jail after his lawful arrest. Threadgill v. State, 146 S.W.3d 654 (Tex. Crim. App. 2004).

This is true under HIPPA, also. State v. Huse, 491 S.W.3d 833, 843 (Tex. Crim. App. 2016).

Once the term of a guest's occupancy of a motel room expires, the guest loses his exclusive right to privacy in the room. The property manager at that point has the right to enter the room, may consent to a search of the room, and may seize all items found. Brimage v. State, 918 S.W.2d 466 (Tex. Crim. App. 1996).

A temporary guest in a motel room does not have a subjective expectation of privacy that society is prepared to recognize as objectively reasonable. Ex parte Moore, 395 S.W.3d 152, 161 (Tex. Crim. App. 2013).

Defendants have no reasonable expectation of privacy in an apartment when they are present for a drug transaction, had never been there before and had no real connection to the residence. Minnesota v. Carter, 525 U.S. 83, 119 S.Ct. 469, 142 L.Ed.2d 373 (1998).

Persons travelling in automobiles on public thoroughfares have no reasonable expectation of privacy in their movements from one place to another. United States v. Knotts, 460 U.S. 276, 103 S.Ct. 1081, 75 L.Ed.2d 55 (1983).

A defendant has no reasonable expectation of privacy in personal items that are being held by the owner of a car repossession company in a shed under the owner's control. Kutzner v. State, 994 S.W.2d 180 (Tex. Crim. App. 1999).

Under the Fourth Amendment, there is no reasonable expectation of privacy in the installation and use of a pen register to record the numbers dialed from a particular telephone. Smith v. Maryland, 442 U.S. 735, 99 S.Ct. 2577, 61 L.Ed.2d 220 (1979).

However, under the Texas Constitution there is a reasonable expectation of privacy in telephone numbers dialed so that the use of a pen register may constitute a search. Richardson v. State, 865 S.W.2d 944 (Tex. Crim. App. 1993).

There is no reasonable expectation of privacy for activities conducted out-of-doors in fields, except in the area immediately surrounding the home. Oliver v. United States, 466 U.S. 170, 104 S.Ct. 1735, 80 L.Ed.2d 214 (1984).

The Fourth Amendment protections against unreasonable search and seizure do not extend to an individual who is growing marijuana in the curtilage of his home where the police observe the plants by aerial surveillance, because it is unreasonable for the individual to think he has constitutional protection under these circumstances. California v. Ciraolo, 476 U.S. 207, 106 S.Ct. 1809, 90 L.Ed.2d 210 (1986).

There is no reasonable expectation of privacy in garbage that has been placed in bags for collection outside the curtilage of the home. California v. Greenwood, 486 U.S. 35, 108 S.Ct. 1625, 100 L.Ed.2d 30 (1988).

A defendant has no reasonable expectation of privacy in abandoned trash even if it is within the curtilage of his home; and thus, a warrantless search is permitted. Levario v. State, 964 S.W.2d 290 (Tex.App.—El Paso 1997, *no pet.*).

A defendant does not enjoy an expectation of privacy in that which may be viewed by looking through his garage window. Bower v. State, 769 S.W.2d 887 (Tex. Crim. App. 1989).

Society does not recognize as reasonable an expectation of privacy in the information encoded in a gift card's magnetic stripe. U.S. v. Turner, 839 F.3d 429 (5th Cir. 2016).

§2:21.4 Intrusion Upon Property Principle

The Supreme Court recently enunciated that standing to contest a search or seizure may be predicated upon a theory of intrusion upon property. Under this theory, a Fourth Amendment claim may be based on a trespass theory of search; that is, that one's own personal effects have been trespassed. State v. Huse, 491 S.W.3d 833, 840 (Tex. Crim. App. 2016); Ford v. State, 477 S.W.3d 321, 328 (Tex. Crim. App. 2015) (both citing United States v. Jones, 565 U.S. 400, 132 S.Ct. 1945, 181 L.Ed.2d 911 (2012)).

§2:21.5 Private Party Search Doctrine

Under the private party search doctrine an individual's reasonable expectation of privacy does not apply in a Fourth Amendment analysis because the Fourth Amendment's warrant requirement applies only to government agents, not private citizens. State v. Rodriguez, 521 S.W.3d 1 (Tex. Crim. App. 2017).

The Fourth Amendment does not apply to the actions of private individuals, and reading Article 38.23 to apply the Fourth Amendment to private individuals would lead to an absurdity. Ruiz v. State, ___ S.W.3d ___ at *2 (PD-1348-17, 2019 WL 2814867, Tex. Crim. App. July 3, 2019).

PRACTICE TIP: Private party searches are subject to exclusion by a jury under Tex. Code Crim. Pro. art. 38.23 if there is a violation of the law involved, such as a theft or burglary.

§2:22 Exclusionary Rule

CCP Art. 38.23. Evidence not to be used

> *(a) No evidence obtained by an officer or other person in violation of any provisions of the Constitution or laws of the State of Texas, or of the Constitution or laws of the United States of America, shall be admitted in evidence against the accused on the trial of any criminal case. In any case where the legal evidence raises an issue hereunder, the jury shall be instructed that if it believes, or has a reasonable doubt, that the evidence was obtained in violation of*

the provisions of this Article, then and in such event, the jury shall disregard any such evidence so obtained.

(b) It is an exception to the provisions of Subsection (a) of this Article that the evidence was obtained by a law enforcement officer acting in objective good faith reliance upon a warrant issued by a neutral magistrate based on probable cause.

CCP Art. 38.23 is a statutorily created exclusionary rule and is much more inclusive than the federal exclusionary rule.

The state exclusionary rule excludes evidence obtained in violation of the U.S. Constitution, the Texas Constitution or Texas law. State v. Toone, 872 S.W.2d 750 (Tex. Crim. App. 1994).

PRACTICE TIP: When seeking to exclude evidence based on an unreasonable search or seizure, cite both Texas and Federal exclusionary rules. Rules not cited will be deemed waived for later appellate argument. Toone, supra. Counsel should also request a separate ruling on each constitutional and statutory ground.

The federal exclusionary rule is a judicially created rule aimed at deterring illegal searches and seizures. Pennsylvania Board of Probation and Parole v. Scott, 524 U.S. 357, 118 S.Ct. 2014, 141 L.Ed.2d 344 (1998).

Under federal exclusionary principles, whether the exclusionary sanction is appropriately imposed in a particular case is an issue separate from the question whether the Fourth Amendment rights of the party seeking to invoke the rule were violated by police conduct. Hudson v. Michigan, 547 U.S. 586, 126 S.Ct. 2159, 165 L.Ed.2d 56 (2006).

Evidence is not "fruit of the poisonous tree" simply because it would not have come to light, but for the illegal actions of the police. Hudson v. Michigan, (citing Segura v. United States, 468 U.S. 796 (1984)).

Criminal offenses occurring after illegal actions by law enforcement officers and not causally connected to the officers' conduct are not suppressible under the exclusionary rule. State v. Iduarte, 268 S.W.3d 544 (Tex. Crim. App. 2008) (defendant was charged with pointing a gun at an officer who lacked probable cause to enter the defendant's apartment).

The exclusionary rule prohibits introduction into evidence of tangible materials seized during an unlawful search, and of testimony concerning knowledge acquired during an unlawful search. Beyond that, the exclusionary rule also prohibits the introduction of derivative evidence, both tangible and testimonial, that is the product of the primary evidence, or that is otherwise acquired as an indirect result of the unlawful search, up to the point at which the connection with the unlawful search becomes so attenuated as to dissipate the taint. Murray v. United States, 108 S.Ct. 2529 (1988).

The use of evidence obtained in violation of the Fourth Amendment does not itself violate the federal constitution. U.S. v. Leon, 468 U.S. 897, 104 S.Ct. 3405, 82 L.Ed.2d 677 (1984).

The federal exclusionary rule only applies to criminal trials and therefore, does not apply to parole revocation hearings. Pennsylvania Board of Probation and Parole v. Scott, *supra*.

Under Texas law, Art. 38.23 applies the protections afforded by the Fourth Amendment and Art. I, §9 of the Texas Constitution to probationers and parolees. Tamez v. State, 534 S.W.2d 686 (Tex. Crim. App. 1976).

The Court of Criminal Appeals has held that CCP Art. 38.23 applies to evidence illegally obtained by private citizens (in a case where decedent's sons illegally entered defendant's home and seized evidence over a three-day period). State v. Johnson, 939 S.W.2d 586 (Tex. Crim. App. 1996).

Where a private individual is lawfully on a premises and takes objects to turn over to the police, and there is no evidence that the objects were taken for the purpose of depriving their owner of them but rather for the purposes of a criminal investigation, Art. 38.22 is not violated by their admission into evidence. Cobb v. Texas, 85 S.W.3d 258 (Tex. Crim. App. 2002).

In some instances, this is true even where the individuals enter the premises unlawfully in order to gather the evidence. Jenschke v. State, 147

S.W.3d 398 (Tex. Crim. App. 2004) (automobile burglary).

Similarly, Art. 38.23 will not bar admission of evidence where the defendant has no legal right to possess the evidence. Carlson v. State, 355 S.W.3d 78 (Tex.App.—Houston [1st Dist.] 2011, *pet. ref'd*) (child pornography containing images of the complainant).

Under federal law, the exclusionary rule does not apply to searches or arrests that are based on clerical errors by court clerks (such as not recalling warrants where the underlying charges have been quashed). Arizona v. Evans, 514 U.S. 1, 115 S.Ct. 1185, 131 L.Ed.2d 34 (1995).

The Fourth Amendment exclusionary rule does not apply to police mistakes leading to an unlawful search that are the result of isolated negligence attenuated from the search, rather than systemic error or reckless disregard of constitutional requirements. Herring v. U.S., 555 U.S. 135, 129 S.Ct. 695, 172 L.Ed.2d 496 (2009).

The Texas exclusionary rule does not exclude the fruits of a search conducted pursuant to an arrest warrant that should have been recalled from the computer system by law enforcement personnel. White v. State, 989 S.W.2d 108 (Tex.App.—San Antonio 1999).

The Supreme Court has recognized several exceptions to the exclusionary rule. Three of these exceptions involve the causal relationship between the unconstitutional act and the discovery of evidence. First, the independent source doctrine allows trial courts to admit evidence obtained in an unlawful search if officers independently acquired it from a separate, independent source. Second, the inevitable discovery doctrine allows for the admission of evidence that would have been discovered even without the unconstitutional source. Third, is the attenuation doctrine: Evidence is admissible when the connection between unconstitutional police conduct and the evidence is remote or has been interrupted by some intervening circumstance, so that the interest protected by the constitutional guarantee that has been violated would not be served by suppression of the evidence obtained. Utah v. Strieff, 579 U.S. ___, 136 S.Ct. 2056, 2061, 195 L.Ed.2d 400 (2016).

The good faith exception applies when an officer conducts a search in objectively reasonable reliance on the constitutionality of a statute that subsequently is declared unconstitutional. Illinois v. Krull, 480 U.S. 340, 107 S.Ct. 1160, 94 L.Ed.2d 364 (1987).

§2:22.1 Use of Evidence for Impeachment Purposes

Evidence obtained in violation of the Fourth Amendment may be used to impeach the defendant's trial testimony. The impeachment evidence need not squarely contradict the defendant's testimony on direct examination so long as it contradicts his testimony on cross-examination and the cross-examination questions would have been suggested to a reasonably competent cross-examiner. Manns v. State, 122 S.W.3d 171 (Tex. Crim. App. 2003).

Proper impeachment evidence includes physical evidence. Manns.

§2:23 Attenuation Doctrine

Attenuation can occur when the causal connection between the illegal police conduct and the discovery of the evidence is remote. Hudson v. Michigan, 547 U.S. 586, 126 S.Ct. 2159, 165 L.Ed.2d 56 (2006).

Attenuation also occurs when, even given a direct causal connection, the interest protected by the constitutional guarantee that has been violated would not be served by suppression of the evidence obtained. Hudson v. Michigan.

The attenuation doctrine is applicable to the CCP Art. 38.23 prohibition against evidence obtained in violation of the law because evidence sufficiently attenuated (or separated) from the violation of the law is not considered to be obtained therefrom. Johnson v. State, 871 S.W.2d 744 (Tex. Crim. App. 1994).

Thus, the attenuation doctrine is not an exception to Art. 38.23, but rather is a method of determining whether evidence was obtained in violation of the law. Johnson, *supra*.

The factors generally considered in assessing whether the taint of an unlawful arrest or search has been sufficiently attenuated to allow the admission of non-testimonial evidence in question are:

- Temporal proximity of the arrest and the evidence

- Presence of intervening circumstances
- Purpose and flagrancy of the official misconduct

Brown v. Illinois, 422 U.S. 590, 95 S.Ct. 2254, 45 L.Ed.2d 416 (1975); Dowthitt v. State, 931 S.W.2d 244 (Tex. Crim. App.1996); Utah v. Strieff, 579 U.S. ___, 136 S.Ct. 2056, 2061-2, 195 L.Ed.2d 400 (2016).

Attenuating factors can dissipate the taint of a defendant's illegal arrest from any derivative evidence that may have been obtained as a result of it. Thornton v. State, 145 S.W.3d 228 (Tex. Crim. App. 2004) (where passage of time and further offenses dissipated the taint of earlier DNA comparison testing).

The voluntary commission by the accused of another offense after an unlawful arrest generally operates as an intervening circumstance that purges any taint flowing from the unlawful arrest. Holmes, *supra*.

The clearest indications of attenuation should be required where police conduct is the most flagrantly abusive. Bell v. State, 724 S.W.2d 780 (Tex. Crim. App. 1986).

§2:24 Standing to Object to Search and Seizure

A defendant seeking to challenge a search or seizure bears the burden of proving that he had a legitimate expectation of privacy in the premises or thing searched or seized. Rawlings v. Kentucky, 448 U.S. 98, 100 S.Ct. 2565, 65 L.Ed.2d 633 (1980); Handy v. State, 189 S.W.3d 296 (Tex. Crim. App. 2006).

> **PRACTICE TIP:** It is critical for the defendant prove standing in all suppression situations. Where the defendant fails to prove that he has standing, this lack of proof may be used by appellate courts to uphold a search even where the state has not met its burden to show the reasonableness of the search. A boilerplate motion will not suffice as proof. Handy.

A defendant's privacy interest in the premises searched is a substantive element of his Fourth Amendment claim. It is the defendant's burden to establish this requisite privacy interest. Rakas v. Illinois, 439 U.S. 128, 99 S.Ct. 421, 58 L.Ed.2d 387 (1978); Kothe v. State, 152 S.W.3d 54, 59 (Tex. Crim. App. 2004).

To carry this burden, the accused must normally prove: (a) that by his conduct, he exhibited an actual subjective expectation of privacy, *i.e.*, a genuine intention to preserve something as private; and (b) that circumstances existed under which society was prepared to recognize his subjective expectation as objectively reasonable. Villarreal v. State, 935 S.W.2d 134 (Tex. Crim. App. 1996) citing Smith v. Maryland, 442 U.S. 735, 740, 99 S.Ct. 2577, 2580, 61 L.Ed.2d 220 (1979); Matthews v. State, 431 S.W.3d 596, 606 (Tex. Crim. App. 2014).

Questions of whether a defendant has standing to contest a search are subjected to a totality of the circumstances analysis. Villarreal.

Standing to object to a search or seizure is dependent upon the facts developed in the case. Rakas.

Defendants charged with crimes of possession may only claim the benefits of the exclusionary rule if their own Fourth Amendment rights have in fact been violated. U.S. v. Salvucci, 448 U.S. 83, 100 S.Ct. 2547, 65 L.Ed.2d 619 (1980).

In order to invoke the protections of CCP Art. 38.23 a defendant must prove that he has standing to complain of some violation of his rights. Chavez v. State, 9 S.W.3d 817 (Tex. Crim. App. 2000).

Certain factors should be considered in making the determination whether an accused has "standing" to challenge a search or seizure. These factors include whether:

- Alleged aggrieved person has a property or possessory interest in the thing seized or the place searched
- Alleged aggrieved person was legitimately on the premises
- Alleged aggrieved person had complete dominion or control and the right to exclude others
- Prior to the search, alleged aggrieved person took normal precautions customarily taken by those seeking privacy

- Property was put to some private use
- Claim of privacy is consistent with historical notions of privacy

U.S. v. Salvucci, supra; Matthews v. State, 431 S.W.3d 596, 607 (Tex. Crim. App. 2014).

Standing to assert Fourth Amendment rights can be established in three ways:

- Accused is lawfully present at the premises during the search
- Item seized is an essential element of the offense
- Accused has either proprietary or possessory interest in the place searched

Johnson v. State, 583 S.W.2d 399 (Tex. Crim. App. 1979); Garcia v. State, 960 S.W.2d 329 (Tex. App.—Corpus Christi 1997, *no pet.*).

A prosecutor may, without legal contradiction, simultaneously maintain that a defendant criminally possessed the seized goods but was not subject to a Fourth Amendment deprivation by the illegal seizure. U.S. v. Salvucci, *supra.*

A defendant contesting a search may, without legal contradiction, claim a reasonable expectation of privacy in the area or place searched without asserting any possessory interest in the thing seized. Chapa v. State, 729 S.W.2d 723 (Tex. Crim. App. 1987, fn1).

A defendant fails to establish a legitimate privacy interest in the premises searched, so as to afford standing to challenge a search, where he concedes he has no possessory or proprietary interest in the premises. Calloway v. State, 743 S.W.2d 645 (Tex. Crim. App. 1988).

Occupants of an automobile have to show a property or possessory interest in the vehicle or its contents in order to have standing to contest a search of the vehicle. Rakas v. Illinois, *supra.*

The state can raise for the first time on appeal the issue of the defendant's lack of standing to object. State v. Klima, 934 S.W.2d 109 (Tex. Crim. App. 1996).

§2:24.1 Defendants Who Have Standing

A legitimate overnight guest has standing to contest a search of the residence because he has a reasonable expectation of privacy therein. Luna v. State, 268 S.W.3d 594 (Tex. Crim. App. 2008).

A legitimate overnight guest has standing to challenge the legality of police entry of his host's home to arrest him. Minnesota v. Olson, 495 U.S. 91, 110 S.Ct. 1684, 109 L.Ed.2d 85 (1990).

A guest who has legitimately registered as a lodger has a "reasonable expectation of privacy" in a motel room. Moberg v. State, 810 S.W.2d 190 (Tex. Crim. App. 1991).

A fare-paying customer in a taxicab has a legitimate expectation of privacy in; and therefore, standing to challenge the search of, the area under the front seat of the taxicab. Chapa v. State, 729 S.W.2d 723 (Tex. Crim. App. 1987).

A defendant has standing to contest the search of a rental car that he has legitimately borrowed from the lessee, even though he is not listed as an authorized driver on the rental agreement. Parker v. State, 182 S.W.3d 923 (Tex. Crim. App. 2006).

The mere fact that a driver in lawful possession or control of a rental car is not listed on the rental agreement will not defeat his or her otherwise reasonable expectation of privacy. Byrd v. United States, 584 U.S.___, 138 S.Ct. 1518, 1531, 200 L.Ed.2d 805 (2018).

A passenger in a vehicle has standing to contest a stop of the vehicle because his Fourth Amendment rights have been infringed. Lewis v. State, 664 S.W.2d 345 (Tex. Crim. App. 1984).

If the initial stop of the vehicle was unlawful, the defendant then has standing to question the admissibility of the fruits of the search of the vehicle. Dominguez v. State, 924 S.W.2d 950 (Tex. App.—El Paso 1996, *no pet.*).

A defendant who testifies that he had legitimately borrowed an automobile from its legal owner has established a reasonable expectation of privacy in that automobile. Wilson v. State, 692 S.W.2d 661 (Tex. Crim. App. 1984); Matthews v. State, 431 S.W.3d 506, 610 (Tex. Crim. App. 2014).

However, if the defendant abandons the vehicle, he give up his expectation of privacy in it. Matthews, 431 S.W.3d at 610.

A defendant has standing to object to an unreasonable search of his office as well as of his home. Mancusi v. DeForte, 392 U.S. 364, 88 S.Ct.

2120, 20 L.Ed.2d 1154 (1968).

Because an individual has a right to be free from an unreasonably prolonged detention he has standing to contest the search of a companion during the prolonged detention. Kothe v. State, 152 S.W.3d 54 (Tex. Crim. App. 2004).

A defendant may have a reasonable expectation of privacy in a place where he keeps some of his property, even though he does not have an ownership interest in the premises. State v. Betts, 397 S.W.3d 198, 204 (Tex. Crim. App. 2013) (where the defendant had a reasonable expectation of privacy in his aunt's backyard where he kept his dogs).

§2:24.2 Defendants Who Do Not Have Standing

Once a person has been asked to leave a premises by one with authority to exclude him, and where that person has a reasonable opportunity to gather his personal effects prior to leaving, any expectation of privacy that he maintains in the premises is no longer one which society would view as reasonable. Granados v. State, 85 S.W.3d 217 (Tex. Crim. App. 2002).

A guest in a hotel or motel loses his reasonable expectation of privacy and consequently any standing to object to any search of the premises once the rental or occupancy period has terminated. Voelkel v. State, 717 S.W.2d 314 (Tex. Crim. App. 1986).

A defendant has no standing to complain of a Terry-frisk of a companion. Voelkel. A defendant has no standing to complain of the search of a passenger of the vehicle that he is driving because the Fourth Amendment confers no such third-party standing. Busby v. State, 990 S.W.2d 263 (Tex. Crim. App. 1999).

A passenger in a vehicle generally does not have standing to complain of a search of that vehicle. Jones v. State, 119 S.W.3d 766 (Tex. Crim. App. 2003).

A defendant lacks standing to contest the search of a stolen vehicle because he has no expectation of privacy that society is prepared to recognize as reasonable. Busby; Jackson v. State, 745 S.W.2d 4 (Tex. Crim. App. 1988).

This lack of standing applies also to a leased vehicle that is held past the agreed lease period. Hughes v. State, 897 S.W.2d 285 (Tex. Crim. App. 1994).

In the absence of any evidence showing that a defendant has a legitimate expectation of privacy in the vehicle searched, he does not have standing to contest its search. Flores v. State, 871 S.W.2d 714 (Tex. Crim. App. 1993).

While under some situations, an overnight guest may have standing to contest a search, there are factors which militate against such a claim. These include:

- Fact that the guest had no property at the location
- Lack of evidence that the guest had dominion or control over the premises
- Lack of evidence that the guest had plans to stay overnight

Villarreal v. State, 935 S.W.2d 134 (Tex. Crim. App. 1996).

Under the facts of this case, the defendant did not have standing to contest a search of a house where he was a non-overnight guest because his subjective expectation of privacy was one that society was prepared to recognize as objectively reasonable under the circumstances. Villarreal.

TIP TO THE PROSECUTION: The state should never presume the validity of standing simply because the defendant seeks suppression of evidence. Each factual situation should be reviewed on its merits and proper objections lodged.

§2:24.3 Abandoned Property

When an accused abandons property, he no longer has standing to complain of alleged police misconduct in the seizure of the property. McDuff v. State, 939 S.W.2d 607 (Tex. Crim. App. 1997).

Abandonment consists of two components: 1) the defendant must intend to abandon the property; and 2) the decision to abandon the property must be voluntary and not result from police misconduct. Swearingen v. State, 101 S.W.3d 89 (Tex. Crim.

App. 2003); Matthews v. State, 431 S.W.3d 596, 608-9 (Tex. Crim. App. 2014).

Abandonment is primarily a question of intent to be inferred from words spoken, acts done, and other objective facts and relevant circumstances, with the issue not being in the strict property-right sense, but rather whether the accused had voluntarily discarded, left behind, or otherwise relinquished his interest in the property so that he could no longer retain a reasonable expectation of privacy with regard to it at the time of the search. McDuff, *supra*.

Where police confiscate abandoned property independent of police misconduct, there is no seizure under the Fourth Amendment. McDuff, *supra*.

If an accused abandons property in response to unlawful police misconduct, the abandonment will not be considered a voluntary or independent act and thus the protections of the Fourth Amendment will apply. Hawkins v. State, 758 S.W.2d 255 (Tex. Crim. App. 1988).

Where the defendant abandoned property as a result of an improper police investigative detention, the evidence is inadmissible at trial. Hawkins; Gordon v. State, 4 S.W.3d 32 (Tex.App.—El Paso No. 8-98-0173-CR, June 17, 1999).

Where the evidence shows that the defendant pushed the auto in question with another auto (indicating that he had another mode of transportation), the car stayed in place for six days until the lot owners had it towed, and the defendant was located in another state during this time; the court found the vehicle had been abandoned. McDuff, *supra*.

Where a defendant tells police officers that the bag on the bus seat next to him is not his, he has abandoned it and has no standing to complain of a subsequent seizure and search of the bag in the absence of police misconduct giving rise to the abandonment. Velasquez v. State, 994 S.W.2d 676 (Tex. Crim. App. No. 1099-98, June 16, 1999).

§2:25 What Constitutes a "Search"

One well-recognized exception to the warrant requirement applies when the exigencies of the situation make the needs of law enforcement so compelling that a warrantless search is objectively reasonable under the Fourth Amendment. Kentucky v. King, 563 U.S. ___, 131 S.Ct. 1849, 179 L.Ed.2d 865 (2011).

The need to prevent the imminent destruction of evidence has long been recognized as a sufficient justification for a warrantless search. Kentucky v. King.

The exigent circumstances rule justifies a warrantless search when the conduct of the police preceding the exigency is reasonable in the same sense. Kentucky v. King.

Where the police did not create the exigency by engaging or threatening to engage in conduct that violates the Fourth Amendment, warrantless entry to prevent the destruction of evidence is reasonable and thus allowed. Kentucky v. King.

A search occurs when an expectation of privacy that society is prepared to consider reasonable is infringed. U. S. v. Jacobsen, 466 U.S. 109, 104 S.Ct. 1652, 80 L.Ed.2d 85 (1984); Richardson v. State, 865 S.W.2d 944 (Tex. Crim. App. 1993).

A search requires some action to discover concealed information. State v. Walden, 838 S.W.2d 342 (Tex.App.—Houston [1st Dist.] 1992, *no pet.*).

Police monitoring of a beeper placed into a private residence by surreptitious means is a search as contemplated by the Fourth Amendment. U.S. v. Karo, 468 U.S. 705, 104 S.Ct. 3296, 82 L.Ed.2d 530 (1984).

Where a government placed beeper reveals nothing more about its location than could have been gained by visual surveillance, there is no search; and therefore, no Fourth Amendment violation. U.S. v. Knotts, 460 U.S. 276, 103 S.Ct. 1081, 75 L.Ed.2d 55 (1983).

Where a police officer opened a closed box, viewed the contents and concluded that controlled substances were present, a search has occurred. Reynolds v. State, 781 S.W.2d 351 (Tex.App.—Houston [1st Dist.] 1989, *pet. ref'd*).

The use of a pen register may constitute a search under Art. 1 §9 of the Texas Constitution. Richardson, *supra*.

The purchase of an obscene magazine by a police officer in a retail store is not a search. Kramer v. State, 818 S.W.2d 923 (Tex.App.—Houston [14th Dist.] 1991, *pet. ref'd*).

The taking of a defendant's blood from his body is a search for Fourth Amendment purposes. Davis v. State, 831 S.W.2d 426 (Tex.App.—Austin 1992, *pet. ref'd*).

Requiring a defendant to produce handwriting samples is not a search. Ayala v. State, 657 S.W.2d 910 (Tex.App.—Austin 1983, *no pet.*).

The viewing of defendant's marijuana plants from a helicopter at an altitude of 350 to 400 feet is not a search. Moss v. State, 878 S.W.2d 632 (Tex. App.—San Antonio 1994, *pet. ref'd*).

The use of a dog to sniff a person's luggage, which is in a public place, is not a search. Strout v. State, 688 S.W.2d 188 (Tex.App.—Amarillo 1985, *no pet.*).

A sniff of the outside of an automobile by a trained canine is not a search within the meaning of the Fourth Amendment. United States v. Place, 462 U.S. 696, 103 S.Ct. 2637, 77 L.Ed.2d 110 (1983); Mohmed v. State, 977 S.W.2d 624 (Tex.App.—Fort Worth 1998, *pet. ref'd*).

Using a drug-sniffing dog on a homeowner's porch to investigate the contents of a home and its immediate surroundings is a search within the meaning of the Fourth Amendment. Florida v. Jardines, 569 U.S. ___, 133 S.Ct. 1409, 1417-18, 185 L.Ed.2d 495 (2013).

In order to invoke the protections of CCP Art. 38.23 a defendant must prove that he has standing to complain of some violation of his rights. Chavez v. State, 9 S.W.3d 817 (Tex. Crim. App. 2000).

The use of high-tech devices not in public use, such as heat detecting equipment, to examine a home from the outside is a search and unreasonable without a search warrant. Kyllo v. U.S., 533 U.S. 27, 121 S.Ct. 2038, 150 L.Ed.2d 94 (2001).

The Government's installation of a GPS device on a target's vehicle, and its use of that device to monitor the vehicle's movements, constitutes a search under the Fourth Amendment. U.S. v. Jones, 565 U.S ___, 132 S.Ct. 945, 181 L.Ed.2d 911 (2012) (where the court did not reach the issue of whether the search was reasonable).

The government conducts a search when it attaches a device to a person's body, without consent, for the purpose of tracking that individual's movements. Grady v. N. Carolina, 575 U.S. ___, 135 S. Ct. 1368, 1370, 191 L.Ed.2d 459 (2015)(where a satellite-based monitor was attached to a sex-offender). The Court did not decide the reasonableness of the search which will depend on the totality of the circumstances, including the nature and purpose of the search and the extent to which the search intrudes upon reasonable privacy expectations.

§2:26 What Constitutes a "Seizure"

A seizure of property occurs when there is some meaningful interference with an individual's possessory interest in that property. U. S. v. Jacobsen, 466 U.S. 109, 104 S.Ct. 1652, 80 L.Ed.2d 85, 104 S Ct 1652 (1984).

A brief detention of property is permitted on the basis of a reasonable, articulable suspicion that it contains contraband or evidence of criminal activity. Smith v. Ohio, 494 U.S. 541, 110 S.Ct. 1288, 108 L.Ed.2d 464 (1990).

To determine the constitutionality of an evidence seizure the courts balance the nature and the quality of the intrusion of the individual's Fourth Amendment interests against the importance of the governmental interests alleged to justify the intrusion. Hereford v. State, 339 S.W.3d 111 (Tex. Crim. App. 2011), *citing* Tennessee v. Garner, 471 US. 1, 105 S. Ct. 1694, 85 L.Ed.2d 1 (1985).

Through this balancing test, the Fourth Amendment analysis measures, under the totality of the circumstances, the objective reasonableness of a seizure. This reasonableness test goes further than merely evaluating when and where a seizure is made; it also accounts for the manner in which the seizure is carried out. The objective test is applied on a case-by-case basis; no bright line determines when a governmental intrusion becomes constitutionally impermissible. Hereford (where it was found to be unreasonable to use a Taser several times on an individual to recover cocaine from his mouth).

While societal needs justify some limitations on an individual's personal interests and condone minor intrusions of privacy and security, excessive encroachments are contrary to the protections afforded by the Fourth Amendment. Generally, officers may use only that amount of force that is necessary to effect the purpose of the stop or to overcome force used against the officer. Law enforcement may not use whatever means are available to seize evidence, regardless of reasonableness. If the means chosen are unreasonable, the evidence obtained by such means must be suppressed. Hereford.

Using these standards, the proper inquiry is whether, given the facts supported by the record, the force that was used to seize the evidence was objectively reasonable. On a claim of excessive force, the objectively reasonable standard ignores the underlying intent or motivation of the acting police officer. Evidence of the officer's subjective intent or motivation may be used only to assess the credibility of the officer's claims about what information was or was not available at the time of the incident in question. Hereford.

§2:27 Probable Cause for Searches

A search or seizure must be supported by probable cause; and must be made pursuant to a warrant or conducted pursuant to exigent circumstances that dispense with the requirement for a warrant. Schmerber v. California, 384 U.S. 757, 86 S.Ct. 1826, 16 L.Ed.2d 908 (1966); Amores v. State, 816 S.W.2d 407 (Tex. Crim. App. 1991); Estrada v. State, 154 S.W.3d 604 (Tex. Crim. App. 2005).

A search prior to the establishment of probable cause can never be considered valid. State v. Ballard, 987 S.W.2d 889 (Tex. Crim. App. 1999).

Probable cause exists where the facts and circumstances within the officer's knowledge and of which he has reasonably trustworthy information are sufficient in themselves to warrant a man of reasonable caution in the belief that a particular person has committed or is committing an offense. Amores, *supra*.

Probable cause to search exists when reasonably trustworthy facts and circumstances within the knowledge of the officer on the scene would lead a man of reasonable prudence to believe that the instrumentality of a crime or evidence of a crime will be found. McNairy v. State, 835 S.W.2d 101 (Tex. Crim. App. 1991).

The "totality of the circumstances" test applies in Texas for determining probable cause for a warrantless search and seizure. Eisenhauer v. State, 754 S.W.2d 159 (Tex. Crim. App.1988); Illinois v. Gates, 462 U.S. 213, 103 S.Ct. 2317, 76 L.Ed.2d 527 (1983).

Under the Gates test, the "veracity" and "basis of knowledge" prongs of Aguilar v. Texas for assessing the usefulness of an informant's tips are not independent. They are better understood as relevant considerations in the totality-of-the-circumstances analysis that traditionally has guided probable-cause determinations: a deficiency in one may be compensated for by a strong showing as to the other. Gates; Dixon v. State, 206 S.W.3d 613 (Tex. Crim. App. 2006).

The burden is on the State to prove the existence of probable cause to justify a warrantless arrest or search. Amores, *supra*; Coolidge v. New Hampshire, 403 U.S. 443, 91 S.Ct. 2022, 29 L.Ed.2d 564 (1971).

Hearsay is admissible on the issue of probable cause to arrest or search or to show consent to search. Juarez v. State, 758 S.W.2d 772 (Tex. Crim. App. 1988); McVickers v. State, 874 S.W.2d 662 (Tex. Crim. App. 1993).

Only the officer(s) who obtained the evidence that is the subject of the suppression motion can testify as to the underlying reason(s) for engaging in the conduct that produced the evidence. Campbell v. State, 910 S.W.2d 475, (Tex. Crim. App. 1995).

The standard for probable cause in applications for warrants to search and seize First Amendment materials is no higher than the standard existing for search and seizure of other items. New York v. P.J. Video, Inc., 475 U.S. 868, 106 S.Ct. 1610, 89 L.Ed.2d 871 (1986).

§2:28 Good Faith Exception

CCP Art. 38.23(b) contains a good faith exception applicable to peace officers acting upon a warrant issued upon a showing of probable cause. Gordon v. State, 801 S.W.2d 899 (Tex. Crim. App. 1990).

This provision is applicable to evidence seized after September 1, 1987. Gordon, *supra*.

Since Art. 38.23 requires that the officer be acting upon a warrant issued upon a showing of probable cause, the exception is applicable only in cases of technical law violations. Gordon, *supra*.

Where the record establishes that the defendant was arrested by officers acting in objective good faith reliance upon a warrant based on probable cause and issued by a neutral magistrate the arrest will be justified under the good faith exception even though the magistrate inadvertently did not sign the arrest warrant. Dunn v. State, 951 S.W.2d 478 (Tex. Crim. App. 1997).

The Federal constitution will not preclude a holding that evidence seized by officers acting in good faith and with due diligence should be admitted at trial as an exception to the exclusionary rule. United States v. Leon, 468 U.S. 897, 104 S.Ct. 3405, 82 L.Ed.2d 677 (1984).

The Fourth Amendment exclusionary rule does not apply to police mistakes leading to an unlawful search that are the result of isolated negligence attenuated from the search, rather than systemic error or reckless disregard of constitutional requirements. Herring v. U.S., 555 U.S. 135, 129 S.Ct. 695, 172 L.Ed.2d 496 (2009).

Searches conducted in objectively reasonable reliance on binding appellate precedent are not subject to the Fourth Amendment exclusionary rule. Davis v. U.S., 564 U.S. ___, 131 S.Ct. 2419, 180 L.Ed.2d 285 (2011).

In an intersection of the good faith exception with the fruit of the poisonous tree doctrine, the court finds that the good faith exception will apply when the prior law enforcement conduct that uncovered the evidence used in the affidavit for the search warrant was close enough to the line of validity that an objectively reasonable officer preparing the affidavit or executing the warrant would believe that the information supporting the warrant was not tainted by unconstitutional conduct. McClintock v. State, 541 S.W.3d 63, (Tex. Crim. App. 2017).

PRACTICE TIP: Although Texas has the statutory exclusionary rule contained in Art. 38.23, the State can use the Davis case to argue that the evidence was not "obtained" in violation of the law where legal precedent at the time of police conduct allowed the police action.

The state may raise the good faith exception to the exclusionary rule for the first time on discretionary review. McClintock v. State, 444 S.W.3d 15, 20 (Tex. Crim. App. 2014).

§2:29 Independent Source Doctrine

The federal independent source doctrine, which excepts from the exclusionary rule evidence initially observed during an unlawful search but later obtained lawfully through independent means, is applicable in Texas as it poses no conflict with Article 38.23 of the Texas Code of Criminal Procedure, the statutory exclusionary rule in Texas that requires suppression of evidence obtained in violation of the law. Wehrenberg v. State, 416 S.W.3d 458, 461 (Tex. Crim. App. 2013). At its core, the independent source doctrine provides that evidence derived from or obtained from a lawful source, separate and apart from any illegal conduct by law enforcement, is not subject to exclusion. Wehrenberg, 416 S.W.3d at 465; citing *Nix v. Williams*, 467 U.S. 431, 443, 104 S.Ct. 2501, 81 L.Ed.2d 377 (1984). Evidence obtained pursuant to an independent source, much like evidence for which a prior taint has been attenuated, is not obtained in violation of the law and is thus not subject to suppression under Art. 38.23. Wehrenberg, 416 S.W.3d at 468.

The independent source doctrine is broad enough to encompass both (1) evidence observed and obtained for the first time during an independent lawful search following a previous instance of unlawful police conduct, and (2) evidence observed in plain view during an initial unlawful entry, but later obtained independently from activities untainted by the initial illegality. Wehrenberg, 416 S.W.3d at 466-7.

Where police officers obtain a valid search warrant from information gained independently of that gained from an earlier illegal entry of a premises, the fruits gained by the serving of the valid warrant will be admissible in a subsequent trial under the Fourth Amendment. Murray v. United States, 487 U.S. 533, 108 S.Ct. 2529, 101 L.Ed.2d 472 (1988).

Under the "silver platter" doctrine evidence lawfully obtained by federal officers acting under a valid federal search warrant is admissible in state criminal proceedings. State v. Toone, 823 S.W.2d 744 (Tex.App.—Dallas 1992, *pet. granted, affirmed at* 872 S.W.2d 750).

§2:30 Inevitable Discovery Exception

The inevitable discovery doctrine allows the admission of evidence that police would have discovered by means wholly independent of any constitutional violation. Nix v. Williams, 467 U.S. 431, 104 S.Ct. 2501, 81 L.Ed.2d 377 (1984). This doctrine is recognized under federal law as an exception to the federal exclusionary rule. Nix v. Williams, *supra*.

The inevitable discovery doctrine does not apply to the Texas exclusionary rule codified in CCP Art. 38.23. State v. Daugherty, 931 S.W.2d 268 (Tex. Crim. App. 1996), citing Garcia v. State, 829 S.W.2d 796 (Tex. Crim. App. 1992, plurality op.).

PRACTICE TIP: Based on the cases cited above, if the state is trying to rely on the inevitable discovery doctrine to justify a search or seizure it is imperative that defense counsel object and preserve error on state grounds citing Art. I, §9 of the Texas Constitution and CCP Art. 38.23.

§2:40 Exceptions to Warrant Requirement

Both the Fourth Amendment to the United States Constitution as well as Art. I, §9 of the Texas Constitution forbid unreasonable searches and seizures. Warrantless searches are per se unreasonable unless they fall under one of a few exceptions. Brimage v. State, 918 S.W.2d 466 (Tex. Crim. App. 1996).

Established exceptions to the warrant requirement include the consent exception, the exigency exception, the automobile exception, the search-incident-to-arrest exception, and the special-needs exception. State v. Rodriguez, 521 S.W.3d 1 (Tex. Crim. App. 2017). There are several basic exceptions to the Fourth Amendment and Art. I, §9 warrant requirement: 1) consensual searches; 2) plain view searches; and 3) searches conducted under exigent circumstances. Spears v. State, 801 S.W.2d 571 (Tex. App.—Fort Worth 1990, *pet. ref'd*).

The exigent circumstances exception has several components:

- Searches conducted under an emergency exception
- Searches conducted to prevent the destruction of evidence or contraband
- Searches conducted to prevent officers and others from persons reasonably believed to be armed and dangerous

Spears, *supra*.

No amount of probable cause can justify a warrantless search where the State has not met its burden of showing exigent circumstances. Coolidge v. New Hampshire, 403 U.S. 443, 91 S.Ct. 2022, 29 L.Ed.2d 564 (1971).

The scope of a warrantless search is limited to the purpose that made its initiation permissible. Chimel v. California, 395 U.S. 752, 89 S.Ct. 2034, 23 L.Ed.2d 685 (1969).

The State bears the burden of establishing that a warrantless search falls under one of these exceptions. State v. Rodriguez, 521 S.W.3d 1 (Tex. Crim. App. 2017).

§2:41 Consents to Search

Searches that occur by way of voluntary consent are an exception to the warrant requirement. Schneckloth v. Bustamonte, 412 U.S. 218, 93 S.Ct. 2014, 36 L.Ed.2d 854 (1973); Valtierra v. State, 310 S.W.3d 442 (Tex. Crim. App. 2010).

Free and voluntary consent to search a premises by one in control of the premises is sufficient to sustain lawful search. Garcia v. State, 887 S.W.2d 846 (Tex. Crim. App. 1994).

Under Texas law a consent to search must be established by clear and convincing evidence. State v. Ibarra, 953 S.W.2d 242 (Tex. Crim. App. 1997); Valtierra v. State, 310 S.W.3d 442 (Tex. Crim. App. 2010).

Under the Fourth Amendment a consent to search must be established by a preponderance of the evidence. United States v. Matlock, 415 U.S. 164, 94 S.Ct. 988, 39 L.Ed.2d 242 (1974).

PRACTICE TIP: Counsel should always object to a consent to search by citing Art. 1, sec. 9 of the Texas Constitution because it affords more protection in this area than the United States Constitution. Montanez v. State, 195 S.W.3d 101 (Tex. Crim. App. 2006).

The burden requires the prosecution to show that the consent was positive and unequivocal, and there was no duress or coercion. Juarez v. State, 758 S.W.2.d 772 (Tex. Crim. App. 1988).

The Fourth and Fourteenth Amendments require that a consent not be coerced, by explicit or implicit means, by implied threat or covert force. Meekins v. State, 340 S.W.3d 454 (Tex. Crim. App. 2011).

The question of whether a consent to search was voluntary is a question of fact to be determined from the totality of all the circumstances. Ohio v. Robinette, 519 U.S. 33, 117 S.Ct. 417, 136 L.Ed.2d 347 (1996); Meekins, *supra*.

Several factors are to be examined in order to determine whether an accused freely and voluntarily consented:

- Whether, and to what extent, officers exhibited a show of force
- If the actions of the arresting officers can be classified as flagrant misconduct
- Whether the police threatened to obtain a search warrant if the detainee did not acquiesce, or otherwise claimed a right to search
- If the police first gave the accused Miranda warnings
- Whether the arrest was made in order to obtain consent
- If the accused knew that he could refuse to allow a search
- Whether consent was first offered by the accused or was in response to a police request
- Accused's education, intelligence, and physical condition
- Proximity of the consent to the arrest, since an intervening time period can provide a degree of attenuation of the taint

Dawson v. State, 868 S.W.2d 363 (Tex.App.—Dallas 1993, *pet. ref'd*).

Factors to be considered in evaluating whether consent was voluntary include: whether the accused was advised of his constitutional rights, the length of the detention, whether the questioning was repetitive or prolonged, whether the accused was aware that he could decline to answer the questions, and what kind of psychological impact the questioning had on the accused. Tucker v. State, 369 S.W.3d 179, 185 (Tex. Crim. App. 2012) citing Schneckloth, 412 U.S. at 226–27.

Testimony that a person gave consent after being warned of the right to refuse consent is some evidence that the consent was voluntary. Martinez v. State, 17 S.W.3d 677 (Tex. Crim. App. 2000).

The standard for measuring the scope of a suspect's consent under the Fourth Amendment is that of objective reasonableness; *i.e.*, what would the typical reasonable person have understood by the exchange between the officer and the suspect. Florida v. Jimeno, 500 U.S. 248, 111 S.Ct. 1801, 114 L.Ed.2d 297 (1991); Valtierra.

Consent cannot be established by showing a mere acquiescence to a claim of lawful authority. Johnson v. State, 803 S.W.2d 272 (Tex. Crim. App. 1990).

The ultimate question is whether the person's will has been overborne and his capacity for self-determination critically impaired, such that his consent to search must have been involuntary. Meekins.

The Fourth Amendment does not require as a condition to the giving of a voluntary consent that a defendant who is lawfully detained be first informed that he is free to go. Ohio v. Robinette, *supra*.

Law-enforcement officers are prohibited from using physical or mental compulsion to obtain consent, but statements made by law-enforcement officers to suspects must be analyzed under the totality of the circumstances. Fienen v. State, 390 S.W.3d 328, 335 (Tex. Crim. App. 2012).

Consents to search that are the product of official intimidation or harassment are not free and voluntary under the Fourth Amendment. Florida v. Bostick, 501 U.S. 429, 111 S.Ct. 2382, 115 L.Ed.2d 389 (1991).

The fact that a person is under arrest does not, in and of itself, prevent a free and voluntary consent from being given. Custody is merely one of the factors to be considered. United States v. Watson, 423 U.S. 411, 96 S.Ct. 820, 46 L.Ed.2d 598 (1976); Juarez, *supra.*

Consent is not rendered involuntary merely because the accused is under arrest, at least when the officers' guns are not drawn. Johnson v. State, 68 S.W.3d. 644 (Tex. Crim. App. 2002) (where it was held the defendant's consent to search was voluntary even though the defendant was handcuffed and arrested, no Miranda warnings were given, and no consent to search form was signed, because the officers' guns were not drawn, the officers were in appellant's house pursuant to a valid arrest warrant, and the initial protective sweep was legal).

Consent to search may be implied from the circumstances, such as when a citizen (later to become the defendant) calls police and claims a third person committed a crime on his premises. Under these circumstances, he consents to a crime scene search of his premises. Brown v. State, 856 S.W.2d 177 (Tex. Crim. App. 1993).

Although consent must be positive, it may be given orally or by action, or shown by circumstantial evidence. Valtierra.

Even when he is the perpetrator of the offense, when a homeowner makes a 911 call and requests immediate assistance because of an emergency, he is indicating his consent to (1) the arrival and entry of the responding officers to resolve that emergency, and (2) absent any evidence of the revocation of that consent, an objectively reasonable limited investigation by the responding officers into the emergency that the homeowner reported. Johnson v. State, 226 S.W.3d 439 (Tex. Crim. App. 2007).

A person's consent to search can be communicated to law enforcement in a variety of ways, including by words, action, or circumstantial evidence showing implied consent. Meekins.

Law enforcement may leave and re-enter the premises under the consent as long as they are engaged in objectively reasonable conduct under the circumstances. Johnson.

Valid consent may be implied under certain circumstances such as the defendant's application for a driver's license and implied consent to submit to breath testing for alcohol. South Dakota v. Neville, 459 U.S. 553, 103 S.Ct. 916, 74 L.Ed.2d 748 (1983).

Where the defendant invites undercover police into his home for purposes of carrying on illegal business, he has impliedly consented to their entry to conduct law enforcement business. Lewis v. United States, 385 U.S. 206, 87 S.Ct. 424, 17 L.Ed.2d 312 (1966).

The permissible scope of the search is generally defined by its expressed object. Florida v. Jimeno, *supra* (where the defendant's general consent allowed officers to search containers within the defendant's car that could have held narcotics); Valtierra (where officers were allowed to search the defendant's apartment for a runaway girl).

The standard for measuring the scope of consent "is that of 'objective' reasonableness" or what the ordinary reasonable person would have understood under the same circumstances. Florida v. Jimeno; State v. Weaver, 349 S.W.3d 521 (Tex. Crim. App. 2011).

A person is free to limit the scope of the consent that he gives, but a person's silence in the face of an officer's further actions may imply consent to that further action. Furthermore, if the consent to search is entirely open-ended, a reasonable person would have no cause to believe that the search will be limited in some way. Florida v. Jimeno; Valtierra; Johnson.

Officers are free to pursue the expressed object of the search unless and until the suspect places an explicit limitation on the scope of the search. Florida v. Jimeno, *supra*; Cardenas v. State, 857 S.W.2d 707 (Tex.App.—Houston [14th Dist.] 1993, *pet. ref'd*).

Hearsay is admissible on the issue of probable cause to arrest or search or to show consent to search. Juarez, *supra*; United States v. Matlock, *supra.*

A finding of voluntary consent is reviewed on appeal only for an abuse of discretion. The operative inquiry is whether the evidence presented at the suppression hearing fairly supports the trial court's finding of voluntary consent by clear and convincing evidence. Johnson.

A court reviewing the totality of the circumstances of a particular police-citizen interaction does so without regard for the subjective thoughts or intents of either the officer or the citizen. State v. Weaver.

§2:41.1 Third Person Consent

A third party can consent to a search to the detriment of another's privacy interest if the third party has actual authority over the place or thing to be searched. The third party may, in his own right, give valid consent when he and the absent, non-consenting person share common authority over the premises or property. Hubert v. State, 312 S.W.3d . 554 (Tex. Crim. App. 2010).

Common authority is shown by mutual use of the property by persons generally having joint access or control for most purposes. Therefore, it is reasonable to recognize that any of the co-inhabitants have the right to permit the inspection in his own right and that the others have assumed the risk that one of their number might permit the common area to be searched. Hubert.

Actual authority is not necessarily a prerequisite for a valid consensual search, however. When an officer reasonably, though erroneously, believes that a third party purporting to provide consent has actual authority over the place or thing to be searched, apparent authority exists and the purported consent from the third party can serve to make the search reasonable. Hubert.

The State has the burden to show that the person who consented to the search had actual or apparent authority to consent. To meet its burden, the State must provide evidence that a third party either had mutual access to and control over the place that was searched, or that the officers conducting the search reasonably believed that the facts provided to them by a third party would have been legally sufficient to justify a search as reasonable. Under the Fourth Amendment, the State must show by a preponderance of the evidence that it was reasonable for the officers to proceed on the information they had. Hubert.

Under the "common authority" test, where the defendant lives with a parent or other close relative, and the relative consents to a search of the defendant's bedroom, most courts presume that the relative has sufficient common authority over the bedroom to authorize the consent to search. The defendant may, however, overcome this presumption by presenting evidence that the defendant had exclusive possession of the searched premises. Hubert.

Several courts have applied a different test and a different presumption. Mainly, these courts have followed the view that, when two autonomous adults jointly occupy a dwelling and have separate bedrooms, each occupant generally has a higher expectation of privacy in his or her own bedroom. Absent some showing that one occupant has exercised control, retained control, or come to an understanding with other occupants that control will be shared over the others' bedrooms, these courts start from the presumption that an occupant exercises sole control over his own bedroom and has no joint access to others' bedrooms. The State can overcome this presumption by presenting facts that would support a finding that the third party who consented to the search of another's bedroom did, in fact, exercise some control over the bedroom. Hubert.

The Fourth Amendment does not prohibit a minor child from consenting to entry when the record shows the officer's belief in the child's authority to consent is reasonable under the facts known to the officer. Limon v. State, 340 S.W.3d 753 (Tex. Crim. App. 2011).

When the prosecution seeks to justify a warrantless search by proof of voluntary consent, it may show that consent was obtained from a third party who possessed common authority over or other sufficient relationship to the premises or effects sought to be inspected. United States v. Matlock, 415 U.S. 164, 94 S.Ct. 988, 39 L.Ed.2d 242 (1974); Boyle v. State, 820 S.W.2d 122 (Tex. Crim. App. 1989).

However, when a co-occupant is physically present and objects to the police entering the premises, the entry and search is unreasonable and invalid as to him. Georgia v. Randolph, 547 U.S. 103, 126 S.Ct. 1515, 164 L.Ed.2d 208 (2006).

An occupant who is absent due to a lawful detention or arrest stands in the same shoes as an occupant who is absent for any other reason and a third person who is present at the residence can give effective consent to search. Fernandez v. California, 571 U.S. ___, 134 S.Ct. 1126, 1134, 188, L.Ed.2d 25 (2014).

The holding in Georgia v. Randolph which allows a co-tenant who is present at the time of a premises search to refuse consent over the consent of another co-tenant does not apply to vehicular searches. State v. Copeland, 399 S.W.3d 159, 167

(Tex. Crim. App. 2013).

Common authority is mutual use of the property by persons generally having joint access or control for most purposes. Illinois v. Rodriguez, 497 U.S. 177, 110 S.Ct. 2793, 111 L.Ed.2d 148 (1990); Patrick v. State, 906 S.W.2d 481 (Tex. Crim. App. 1995).

The state has the burden to prove that the person giving the consent had common authority over the premises searched. Illinois v. Rodriguez, *supra*; Welch v. State, 93 S.W.3d 50 (Tex. Crim. App. 2002).

Under federal law, police may search a premises based on the consent of a third person who they apparently believed had common authority over the premises where the person did not in fact have such authority. Illinois v. Rodriguez, *supra*.

Common authority is not to be implied from the mere property interest that a third party has in the property. Matlock, *supra*; Boyle, *supra*.

A legal property interest is not sufficient or necessary because common authority derives from the mutual use of the property by persons generally having joint access or control for most purposes. Such mutual use leads to the conclusion that the third party has the right to permit inspection of the property in his own right and that the others have assumed the risk that one of their number might permit the common area to be searched. Matlock, *supra*; Boyle, *supra*.

An employee of a trucking firm who is operating a vehicle in the scope of his employment has authority to consent to a search of the vehicle. Maxwell v. State, 73 S.W.3d 278 (Tex. Crim. App. 2002).

A hotel clerk cannot validly consent to the search of a room that has been rented to a customer. Stoner v. California, 376 U.S. 483, 84 S.Ct. 889, 11 L.Ed.2d 856 (1964).

A landlord typically cannot validly consent to the search of a house that he has rented to another. Chapman v. United States, 365 U.S. 610, 81 S.Ct. 776, 5 L.Ed.2d 828 (1961)

A guest in a hotel room is protected against unreasonable searches and seizures, and the general requirement for a search warrant is not suspended merely because of the guest status of the occupant of the room. Moberg v. State, 810 S.W.2d 190 (Tex. Crim. App. 1991). Even where the defendant is present at the scene and does not consent to a search, a third-party consent is valid if the third party has mutual access and control over the property searched and if it can be said that the defendant assumed the risk that the third party would consent to a search. Welch v. State, 93 S.W.3d 50 (Tex. Crim. App. 2002) (upon her arrest, the defendant had handed over control of her car to a passenger).

Hearsay is admissible to show third party consent to search. Campbell v. State, 910 S.W.2d 475 (Tex. Crim. App. 1995).

Whether a third party had actual authority to consent to a search of another's property and whether an officer was reasonable in finding that a third party had apparent authority to consent are mixed questions of law and fact that reviewing courts should examine *de novo*. Hubert.

On appeal, determinations of actual and apparent authority are reviewed *de novo* as mixed questions of law and fact. Limon.

§2:41.2 Consents Following an Illegal Arrest

Notwithstanding an illegal arrest, consent to search, freely and voluntarily given, is still one of the recognized exceptions to the requirement of both a warrant and probable cause for a valid search. Juarez, *supra*.

When attempting to establish that there was voluntary consent after an illegal stop, the prosecution has a heavier burden to carry than when the consent is given after a permissible stop. Juarez, *supra*.

When seeking to use a consent to search obtained after an illegal stop, the prosecution must prove a voluntary consent to search and must also establish the existence of intervening factors which prove that the consent was sufficiently attenuated from an illegal stop or arrest. Juarez, *supra*. In other words, the prosecution must prove that the consent to search was obtained by means sufficiently distinguishable from the primary taint of the illegal arrest and was not a product of the illegal arrest. Juarez, *supra*.

Before it can be determined that evidence

derived from a warrantless but consensual search following an illegal arrest is admissible, it must first be found, by clear and convincing evidence, not only that the consent was voluntarily rendered, but also that due consideration was given to:

- Proximity of the consent to the arrest
- Whether the seizure brought about police observation of the particular object which they sought consent to search
- Whether the illegal seizure was "flagrant police misconduct"
- Whether the consent was volunteered rather than requested by the detaining officers
- Whether the arrestee was made fully aware of the fact that he could decline to consent and thus prevent an immediate search of the car or residence
- Whether the police purpose underlying the illegality was to obtain the consent

Boyle v. State, 820 S.W.2d 122 (Tex. Crim. App. 1989). *See also*, Juarez, *supra*, citing Brown v. Illinois, 422 U.S. 590, 95 S.Ct. 2254, 45 L.Ed.2d 416 (1975).

This test does not require that each of the factors set forth be resolved in favor of the prosecution. Juarez, *supra*.

Before it can be determined that evidence derived from a warrantless but consensual search following an illegal arrest is admissible, it must first be found, by clear and convincing evidence, not only that the consent was voluntarily rendered, but also that due consideration of the additional factors listed above militates in favor of the conclusion that the taint otherwise inherent in the illegality of the arrest has dissipated. Brick v. State, 738 S.W.2d 676 (Tex. Crim. App. 1987).

§2:41.3 Valid Consents

Even though a protective sweep of the defendant's home was illegal, the taint of the illegal search can be sufficiently attenuated by a voluntary consent that the defendant gave to police officers. The repeated giving of Miranda warnings and the reasonableness of the police officers are important factors in determining if the taint has been attenuated. Reasor v. State, 12 S.W.3d 813 (Tex. Crim. App. 2000).

The owner of a tractor-trailer rig may have sufficient common authority over and relationship to the vehicle in order to validly consent to a search of it. Boyle v. State, 820 S.W.2d 122 (Tex. Crim. App. 1989).

Where the evidence is clear that a landlord had an express oral agreement with the defendant-renter that the landlord could enter whenever he wished and that he could continue to use the premises by storing his property inside, the landlord had common authority over the property; and could therefore, validly consent to its search. Garcia v. State, 887 S.W.2d 846 (Tex. Crim. App. 1994).

Where the defendant's girlfriend testified that she, not the defendant, had signed the apartment lease and that she was responsible for one-half of the utility bills; where she returned to the apartment several times during the investigation to retrieve personal property; and where she informed investigators that she and the defendant were living together, the facts justified a finding that she had common authority over the apartment and could validly consent to its search. Patrick v. State, 906 S.W.2d 481 (Tex. Crim. App. 1995).

Where the defendant's mother had the only key to his room and entered at will, she had sufficient common authority over the room to consent to its search even though the defendant paid rent for the room and had installed the lock on the door. Grays v. State, 905 S.W.2d 54 (Tex.App.—Amarillo 1995, *no pet.*).

The owner of a car repossession company can give police the authority to look over a defendant's property which is being stored in the repossession company's shed. Kutzner v. State, 994 S.W.2d 180 (Tex. Crim. App. 1999).

Where two persons have joint control over an item (such as a duffel bag), either person can give valid consent to search it, and the fruits of the search are admissible against either. Frazier v. Cupp, 394 U.S. 731, 89 S.Ct. 1420, 22 L.Ed.2d 684 (1969).

The word "apparent" as it appears in Penal Code section 1.07(11) means assent in fact that, while not communicated expressly, is no less "clear and manifest to the understanding" for not having been explicitly verbalized. Baird v. State, 398 S.W.3d 220, 229 (Tex. Crim. App. 2013) (where the issue was whether defendant's house guest had apparent consent to access his computer).

§2:41.4 Invalid Consents

A landlord cannot validly consent to the search of a house he has rented to another. Chapman v. United States, 365 U.S. 610, 81 S.Ct. 776, 5 L.Ed.2d 828 (1961).

A night hotel clerk cannot validly consent to a search of a customer's room, even though by renting the room the renter impliedly consents to entry by maids, janitors and repairmen. Stoner v. California, 376 U.S. 483, 84 S.Ct. 889, 11 L.Ed.2d 856 (1964).

Where police officers invalidly detained the defendant and then threatened to bring in a drug-sniffing dog if the defendant did not consent to a search, the resulting consent was found to be involuntary. Mitchell v. State, 831 S.W.2d 829 (Tex.App.—Houston [1st Dist.] 1992, *pet. ref'd*).

Where the facts showed that the defendant resided in a room in his parents' home to which he had the only key to the padlock, that no one was allowed in the defendant's room and that his father (the homeowner) was allowed in the room only when the defendant was there, the father had insufficient control over the room in order to effectively consent to a search of the room. Becknell v. State, 720 S.W.2d 526 (Tex. Crim. App. 1986).

Where the defendant's estranged wife had moved out of the residence and filed for a divorce, she did not have authority to consent to warrantless searches of the residence because the defendant's right of personal privacy was superior to his estranged wife's community property interest in the residence. May v. State, 780 S.W.2d 866 (Tex. App.—Dallas 1989).

Where an employee has been issued a private locker by her employer on which she has placed a lock to which management does not have a key, it is reasonable to expect that her belongings will be stored without being subject to search, unless she has been placed on notice of the possibility of such a search. Under these facts, management has no authority to consent to a search of the locker. Dawson v. State, 868 S.W.2d 363 (Tex.App.—Dallas 1993, *pet. ref'd*).

Where the facts showed that the consenting party was in the defendant's home as a baby-sitter, lived on the same tract of land as the defendant in a separate house and had limited access to the defendant's house but was not permitted access to the area in which the search occurred, the record is insufficient to show that she had sufficient common authority over the premises to validly consent to its search. Riordan v. State, 905 S.W.2d 765 (Tex. App.—Austin 1995, *no pet.*).

§2:42 Plain View Doctrine

The plain view doctrine is an exception to the warrant requirement, which permits an officer to seize what he views in plain sight or open view if he is lawfully on the premises. Coolidge v. New Hampshire, 403 U.S. 443, 91 S.Ct. 2022, 29 L.Ed.2d 564 (1971); DeLao v. State, 550 S.W.2d 289 (Tex. Crim. App. 1977).

A seizure of an object is lawful under the plain view exception if three requirements are met. First, law enforcement officials must lawfully be where the object can be plainly viewed. Second, the incriminating character of the object in plain view must be immediately apparent to the officials. And third, the officials must have the right to access the object. Keehn v. State, 279 S.W.3d 330 (Tex. Crim. App. 2009).

The second prong, above, does not require the officer to "know" that certain items are evidence of a crime. Joseph, *supra*, (citing Texas v. Brown, 460 U.S. 730, 103 S.Ct. 1535, 75 L.Ed.2d 502 (1983)).

However, there must be probable cause to believe the property is associated with some criminal activity. Joseph, *supra*, (citing Arizona v. Hicks, 480 U.S. 321, 107 S.Ct. 1149, 94 L.Ed.2d 347 (1987)).

Where police officers had knowledge that the defendant had shot several people and fled in a vehicle described in a certain way, they were justified in seizing a gun found in plain view in a vehicle matching the description given by the witnesses. Martinez v. State, 17 S.W.3d 677 (Tex. Crim. App. No. 73,131, May 17, 2000).

Plain view, in the absence of exigent circumstances, can never justify a search and seizure without a warrant when law enforcement officials have no lawful right to access an object. Keehn; State v. Betts, 397 S.W.3d 198, 207 (Tex. Crim. App. 2013) (where officers could see malnourished dogs in the curtilage of a house from the street but had no warrant or exigency that would allow them to enter the property).

The seizure of contraband seen in plain view is constitutionally permissible under the emergency doctrine. Shepherd v. State, 273 S.W.3d 681 (Tex. Crim. App. 2008).

The automobile exception to the warrant requirement can justify a warrantless seizure when officers see contraband in plain view. Keehn.

It is not necessary that the discovery of incriminating evidence be inadvertent. Horton v. California, 496 U.S. 128, 110 S.Ct. 2301, 110 L.Ed.2d 112 (1990); State v. Haley, 811 S.W.2d 597 (Tex. Crim. App. 1991).

Probable cause for purposes of plain view seizures means that the facts available to the officer would warrant a man of reasonable caution to believe that certain items may be contraband, stolen property or useful as evidence of a crime. Texas v. Brown, *supra*.

For example, where an officer views what is apparently marijuana during a routine traffic stop, the officer is justified in seizing the marijuana. Walter v. State, 28 S.W.3d 538 (Tex. Crim. App. 2000).

So long as probable cause to believe that items found in plain view constitute contraband arises while police are still lawfully on the premises, and any further investigation into the nature of those items does not entail an additional and unjustified search of, or unduly prolonged police presence on, the premises, the seizure of those items is permissible under the Fourth Amendment. Dobbs v. State, 323 S.W.3d 184 (Tex. Crim. App. 2010) (where officers made further inquiry regarding golf clubs located in defendant's home during a narcotics search).

Unless it involves a greater search of the premises than that which is initially authorized, or in some other manner invades a legitimate privacy interest, a "further investigation" need not *itself* be justified by probable cause before it can permissibly supply the probable cause to support a plain-view seizure of contraband. Dobbs.

The seizure of property in plain view involves no invasion of privacy and is presumptively reasonable, assuming that there is probable cause to associate the activity with criminal activity. Payton v. New York, 445 U.S. 573, 100 S.Ct. 1371, 63 L.Ed.2d 639 (1980).

Where officers validly pursued a murder suspect into his apartment to make a warrantless arrest, they were justified in seizing evidence found in plain view in the apartment. Warden, Maryland Penitentiary v. Hayden, 387 U.S. 294, 87 S.Ct. 1642, 18 L.Ed.2d 782 (1967); Fearance v. State, 771 S.W.2d 486 (Tex. Crim. App. 1988).

An object coming into view during a search incident to an arrest that is appropriately limited in scope under existing law may be seized without warrant. Chimel v. California, 395 U.S. 752, 89 S.Ct. 2034, 23 L.Ed.2d 685 (1969).

The fact that a police officer is interested in an item of evidence and fully expects to find it in the course of a search would not invalidate its seizure if the search is confined in area and duration by the terms of the warrant or valid exception to the warrant requirement. Horton v. California, *supra*.

The plain view doctrine cannot justify the picking up or moving of the potential evidence in order to discover its evidentiary value. Such action constitutes a seizure for purposes of the Fourth Amendment and probable cause to believe that the item was contraband is necessary in order to support either a search or a seizure. Arizona v. Hicks, 480 U.S. 321, 107 S.Ct. 1149, 94 L.Ed.2d 347 (1987).

When a person has been lawfully arrested, the arresting officer may legally accompany him to his residence to obtain identification, and what the officer then observes in plain view may be seized. Washington v. Chrisman, 455 U.S. 1, 102 S.Ct. 812, 70 L.Ed.2d 778 (1982).

An officer may rely on his training and experience to draw inferences and make deductions that might well elude an untrained person. Texas v. Brown, *supra*.

For example, where an officer observes a tiny bit of plastic in the crease around the gas cap of an auto that he has stopped for a traffic violation, he may rely on his experience to suspect that the area contains narcotics, open the gas cap and inspect inside. Lopez v. State, 223 S.W.3d 408 (Tex. App.—Amarillo 2006, *no pet*).

The deployment of a flashlight at night in order to observe objects within plain view is not a search for purposes of determining probable cause. Texas v. Brown.

§2:43 Plain Touch Doctrine

Under the "plain touch" doctrine, contraband detected through the sense of touch during a pat-down search may be admissible where its evidentiary value is immediately apparent. Minnesota v. Dickerson, 508 U.S. 366, 113 S.Ct. 2130, 124 L.Ed.2d 334 (1993); Strickland v. State, 923 S.W.2d 617 (Tex.App.—Houston (1st Dist.) 1995, *no pet.*).

If the officer conducting the pat-down search has to squeeze, slide or otherwise manipulate the contents of the area being searched, the officer has exceeded the bounds of the pat-down search and evidence obtained is inadmissible. Minnesota v. Dickerson, *supra*; Strickland, *supra*.

The seizure of an item whose identity is already known occasions no further invasion of privacy. Graham v. State, 893 S.W.2d 4 (Tex.App.—Dallas 1994); Garcia v. State, 967 S.W.2d 902 (Tex. App.—Austin 1998, *no pet.*).

§2:44 The Community Caretaking Functions of Police Officers

The Supreme Court has established three doctrines as exceptions to the warrant requirement when a police officer acts pursuant to his or her community caretaking functions: 1) the Cady doctrine; 2) the emergency doctrine (not to be confused with the exigent circumstances doctrine); and 3) the automobile impoundment/inventory doctrine. Laney v. State, 117 S.W.3d 854 (Tex. Crim. App. 2003).

§2:44.1 The Cady Doctrine Community Caretaking Function

The Supreme Court has recognized a community caretaking function of law enforcement as a reasonable exception to the Fourth Amendment's warrant requirement. Cady v. Dombrowski, 413 U.S. 433, 93 S.Ct. 2523, 37 L. Ed. 2d 706 (1973).

Texas also recognizes the existence of the community caretaking function, but emphasizes its narrow applicability. Wright v. State, 7 S.W.3d 148 (Tex. Crim. App. 1999) (stopping of automobile on a public roadway). Only in the most unusual circumstances will warrantless searches of private, fixed property, or stops of persons located thereon, be justified under the community caretaking function, given the greater expectation of privacy inherent with respect to residences and other private real property. Wright.

As part of his duty to "serve and protect," a police officer may stop and assist an individual whom a reasonable person—given the totality of the circumstances—would believe is in need of help. In determining whether a police officer acted reasonably in stopping an individual to determine if he needs assistance, the following factors are relevant to said determination:

- Nature and level of the distress exhibited by the individual
- Location of the individual
- Whether or not the individual was alone and/or had access to assistance independent of that offered by the officer
- What extent the individual — if not assisted — presented a danger to himself or others

Wright.

The community caretaking function can justify the traffic stop of a vehicle where a reasonable person would believe that the passenger was in need of help. Byram v. State, 510 S.W.3d 918, 925 (Tex. Crim. App. 2017).

A police officer may not properly invoke his community caretaking function if he is primarily motivated by a non-community caretaking purpose Wright.

Where a law enforcement officer reasonably believes under the totality of the circumstances that an individual is in need of help, he may properly exercise his community caretaking function by seizing the individual. Gonzales v. State, 369 S.W.3d 851, 856-57 (Tex. Crim. App. 2012).

Where the officer's belief that the defendant was in need of assistance is unreasonable under the four factors enunciated in Wright, the seizure of the defendant is unreasonable under the Fourth Amendment. Corbin v. State, 85 S.W.3d 272 (Tex.

Crim. App. 2002) (where the defendant's car merely crossed the side stripe of the road for less than one second and his driving was otherwise unremarkable).

The Fourth Amendment does not bar police from warrantless entries and searches when they reasonably believe that a person is in need of immediate aid. Janicek v. State, 634 S.W.2d 687 (Tex. Crim. App. 1982).

§2:44.2 Emergency Doctrine (Exigent Circumstances)

The Emergency Doctrine (also known as the Exigent Circumstances Doctrine) has been formulated to allow immediate warrantless searches, which would otherwise be illegal, where there is reasonable cause to believe that, absent an immediate search, serious bodily harm or death may result. Brimage v. State, 918 S.W.2d 466 (Tex. Crim. App. 1994).

An objective standard of reasonableness is used in determining whether a warrantless search is justified under the Emergency Doctrine. This objective standard of reasonableness used in evaluating the police's conduct takes into account the facts and circumstances known to the police at the time of the search. Colburn v. State, 966 S.W.2d 511 (Tex. Crim. App. 1998); Garcia v. State, 827 S.W.2d 937 (Tex. Crim. App. 1992).

Under the Emergency Aid Doctrine, a police officer may enter and search a private residence without a warrant for the limited purpose of protecting or preserving life or avoiding serious injury when it is objectively reasonable. Laney v. State, 117 S.W.3d 854 (Tex. Crim. App. 2003).

Police may enter a home without a warrant when they have an objectively reasonable basis for believing that an occupant is seriously injured or imminently threatened with such injury. Brigham City v. Stuart, 547 U.S. 398, 126 S.Ct. 1943, 164 L.Ed.2d 650 (2006); 175 L.Ed.2d 410.

Where police have probable cause to suspect that a burglary is in progress in a residence, they may enter without a warrant for the purpose of searching for suspects, and protecting the residents and contents of the home. Barocio v. State, 158 S.W.3d 498 (Tex. Crim. App. 2005).

When police come upon the scene of a homicide they may make a prompt warrantless search of the area to see if there are other victims or if a killer is still on the premises. Mincey v. Arizona, 437 U.S. 385, 98 S.Ct. 2408, 57 L.Ed.2d 290 (1978); Brimage, *supra*.

The police may seize any evidence that is in plain view during the course of their legitimate emergency activities. Mincey v. Arizona, *supra*; citing Michigan v. Tyler, 436 U.S. 499, 98 S.Ct. 1942, 56 L.Ed.2d 486 (1978); Brimage, *supra*; Shepherd v. State, 273 S.W.3d 681 (Tex. Crim. App. 2008).

Once police officers are legitimately inside a residence under the Emergency Doctrine, they are justified in opening closed areas to search for an injured or dead person. Brimage, *supra*. A search of a vehicle trunk in the garage of the residence legitimately entered is lawful under the Emergency Doctrine. Brimage, citing United States v. Ross, 456 U.S. 798, 102 S.Ct. 2157, 72 L.Ed.2d 572 (1982).

However, where the emergency situation terminates and the police have no other legitimate reason to be on the premises, the plain view exception to the warrant requirement is no longer applicable. Miller v. State, 393 S.W.3d 255 (Tex. Crim. App. 2012).

The lawfulness of an emergency search terminates once the emergency ends. Miller, 393 S.W.3d at 265.

Fire fighters do not need a warrant or consent to enter a burning building. Michigan v. Clifford, 464 U.S. 287, 104 S.Ct. 641, 78 L.Ed.2d 477 (1984); Michigan v. Tyler, 436 U.S. 499, 98 S.Ct. 1942, 56 L.Ed.2d 486 (1978). Furthermore, firefighters can remain in a damaged building or residence for the purpose of determining the origin of the fire. Michigan v. Tyler, 436 U.S. at 510, 98 S.Ct. at 1950; see also Clifford, 464 U.S. at 293 & n. 4, 104 S.Ct. at 647 & n. 4. The determination of what constitutes a reasonable time to investigate varies according the circumstances of a particular fire. Michigan v. Tyler, 436 U.S. at 510 n. 6, 98 S.Ct. at 1950 n. 6; Tata v. State, 446 S.W.3d 456, 467 (Tex. App.—Houston [1st Dist.] 2014, pet.ref'd). Once in a building for this purpose, firefighters may seize evidence of arson that is in plain view. Michigan v. Tyler, 436 U.S. at 509, 98 S.Ct. at 1950; Tata v. State, 446 S.W.3d at 467.

Furthermore, law enforcement officers may enter premises to seize contraband that was found in plain view by firefighters or other emergency personnel, at least if the exigency is continuing, and the emergency personnel are still lawfully present. Martin v. State, ___ S.W.3d ___, *4 (02-18-00333-CR, 2019 WL 2134662, Tex. App.—Fort Worth May 16, 2019, no pet.).

Officers may search the pockets of an unconscious person for identification, medical history and weapons. Tijerina v. State, 578 S.W.2d 415 (Tex. Crim. App. 1979); Perez v. State, 514 S.W.2d 748 (Tex. Crim. App. 1974).

Even though the search incident to arrest exception does not apply to cell phones, other case-specific exceptions may still justify a warrantless search of a particular phone. One well-recognized exception applies when the exigencies of the situation make the needs of law enforcement so compelling that a warrantless search is objectively reasonable under the Fourth Amendment. Such exigencies could include the need to prevent the imminent destruction of evidence in individual cases, to pursue a fleeing suspect, and to assist persons who are seriously injured or are threatened with imminent injury. Riley v. California, 573 U.S. 373, 134 S.Ct. 2473, 2494, 189 L.Ed. 430 (2014).

§2:44.3 The Automobile Impoundment/Inventory Doctrine

The automobile impoundment/inventory doctrine is a subdivision of law enforcement's community caretaking function. Laney v. State, 117 S.W.3d 854 (Tex. Crim. App. 2003). *See further* §2:56.6.

§2:44.4 Crime Scene Exception

There is no crime scene exception to the warrant requirement that would allow a warrantless search of everything found within a crime scene after the area is secured. Flippo v. West Virginia, 528 U.S. 11, 120 S.Ct. 7, 145 L. Ed. 2d 16 (1999).

However, even when he is the perpetrator of the offense, when a homeowner makes a 911 call and requests immediate assistance because of an emergency, he is indicating his consent to (1) the arrival and entry of the responding officers to resolve that emergency and, (2) absent any evidence of the revocation of that consent, an objectively reasonable limited investigation by the responding officers into the emergency that the homeowner reported. Johnson v. State, 226 S.W.3d 439 (Tex. Crim. App. 2007).

§2:44.5 Special Needs Exception

Under the special needs exception, a warrantless search is reasonable when special needs, beyond the normal need for law enforcement, make the warrant and probable-cause requirement impracticable. State v. Rodriguez, 521 S.W.3d 1 (Tex. Crim. App. 2017). Searches of students by school authorities is an example of a special needs search. See New Jersey v. T.L.O., 469 U.S. 325, 105 S.Ct. 733, 83 L.Ed.2d 720 (1985).

§2:45 Prevention of Destruction of Evidence

One well-recognized exception to the warrant requirement applies when the exigencies of the situation make the needs of law enforcement so compelling that a warrantless search is objectively reasonable under the Fourth Amendment. Kentucky v. King, 563 U.S. 452, 131 S.Ct. 1849, 1856, 179 L.Ed.2d 865 (2011).

The need to prevent the imminent destruction of evidence has long been recognized as a sufficient justification for a warrantless search. Kentucky v. King, 131 S.Ct. at 1856.

The exigent circumstances rule justifies a warrantless search when the conduct of the police preceding the exigency is reasonable in the same sense. Kentucky v. King, 131 S.Ct. at 1858.

Where the police did not create the exigency by engaging or threatening to engage in conduct that violates the Fourth Amendment, warrantless entry to prevent the destruction of evidence is reasonable and thus allowed. Kentucky v. King, 131 S.Ct. at 1858.

The ultimate test to be applied is whether police had a reasonable belief that the contraband was about to be removed or destroyed. Turrubiate v. State, 399 S.W.3d 147, 152 (Tex. Crim. App. 2013).

The courts can also consider whether the occupants knew the police were "on their trail" and whether the evidence was readily destructible to aid in their assessment of the entire record in determining whether the officer reasonably believed that the removal or destruction of evidence was imminent. Turrubiate, 399 S.W.3d at 153.

The courts will not presume that the occupants of a residence who are aware of the presence of police and are in possession of contraband will destroy the contraband. Before a warrantless entry is justified, the record must show proof of imminent destruction based on affirmative conduct by those in possession of narcotics in the particular case. Turrubiate, 399 S.W.3d at 152-3.

McNairy, *supra*; Covarrubia v. State, 902 S.W.2d 549 (Tex.App.—Houston [1st Dist.] 1995, *no pet.*).

Where police have probable cause to search a residence and a good reason to believe that the defendant/resident would destroy evidence if allowed to enter the residence unaccompanied, the police can detain the defendant/resident and prevent him from entering the residence while they await the issuance of a search warrant. Illinois v. McArthur, 531 U.S. 326, 121 S.Ct. 946, 148 L.Ed.2d 838 (2001).

The smell of burning marijuana coming from a residence, among other factors, can support an officer's reasonable belief that exigent circumstances justify a warrantless entry of the residence to prevent the destruction of evidence. Estrada v. State, 154 S.W.3d 604 (Tex. Crim. App. 2005).

However, the courts require some evidence of exigency beyond mere knowledge of police presence and an odor of illegal narcotics. There must be some evidence of attempted or actual destruction of evidence based on an occupant's movement in response to the police knock. Turrubiate, 399 S.W.3d at 153.

Even though the search incident to arrest exception does not apply to cell phones, other case-specific exceptions may still justify a warrantless search of a particular phone. One well-recognized exception applies when the exigencies of the situation make the needs of law enforcement so compelling that a warrantless search is objectively reasonable under the Fourth Amendment. Such exigencies could include the need to prevent the imminent destruction of evidence in individual cases, to pursue a fleeing suspect, and to assist persons who are seriously injured or are threatened with imminent injury. Riley v. California, 573 U.S. 373, 134 S.Ct. 2473, 189 L.Ed.2d 430 (2014).

§2:46 Searches of Places and Things Incident to Arrest

Under both the Fourth Amendment to the United States Constitution and under Art. I §9 of the Texas Constitution, searches of a person and the area within his immediate control are excepted from the requirement of a warrant when incident to the lawful arrest of such person and otherwise proper in scope. United States v. Robinson, 414 U.S. 218, 94 S.Ct. 467, 38 L.Ed.2d 427 (1973); Carrasco v. State, 712 S.W.2d 120 (Tex. Crim. App. 1986).

A search can be validly conducted as a search incident to arrest only if it is substantially contemporaneous with the arrest and is confined to the immediate vicinity of the arrest. Stoner v. California, 376 U.S. 483, 84 S.Ct. 889 (1964).

Police are not authorized to conduct a vehicle search incident to a recent occupant's arrest after the arrestee has been secured and cannot access the interior of the vehicle. Arizona v. Gant, 556 U.S. ___, 129 S.Ct. 1710, 173 L.Ed.2d 485 (2009) (limiting the rule of New York v. Belton, 453 U.S. 454, 101 S.Ct. 2860, 69 L.Ed.2d 768 (1981)).

Circumstances unique to the automobile context justify a search incident to arrest when it is reasonable to believe that evidence of the offense of arrest might be found in the vehicle. Arizona v. Gant (citing Thornton v. United States, 541 U. S. 615, 124 S.Ct. 2127, 158 L.Ed.2d 905 (2004)).

If an arrestee is not an occupant or recent occupant of a vehicle, the validity of the search is examined under a Chimel analysis; *i.e.*, was the search limited to the area within the immediate control of the arrestee. State v. Kelly, 963 S.W.2d 866 (Tex.App.—San Antonio 1998, *no pet.*).

In determining whether the arrestee was a recent occupant of a vehicle at the time of his arrest, several factors should be examined:

- Arrestee's temporal and spatial proximity to his vehicle
- Whether there is evidence of flight
- Whether there is an indication that the arrestee quickly exited his vehicle in an attempt to avoid police contact

These factors should be balanced against law enforcement's need to search the vehicle for protective purposes. Kelly, *supra*.

The police may also examine the contents of any containers found within the passenger compartment; whether the container is open or closed. State v. Mercado, 944 S.W.2d 42 (Tex.App.—El Paso 1997).

The search will be upheld even where the container searched is such that it could hold neither a weapon nor evidence of the criminal conduct for which the suspect was arrested. United States v. Robinson, 414 U.S. 218, 94 S.Ct. 467, 38 L.Ed.2d 427 (1973).

Where the arrest occurs in a motel room, the entire motel room and any closed containers therein may be searched incident to arrest. Voelkel v. State, 717 S.W.2d 314 (Tex. Crim. App. 1986).

Where the police have probable cause to arrest a defendant for violating a parking statute that allows for an arrest for a violation, they may search a bag found on the floorboard of the driver's side of the vehicle as a search incident to arrest, even though the search incident to the arrest preceded formal custodial arrest by a few moments. Williams v. State, 726 S.W.2d 99 (Tex. Crim. App. 1986).

As part of a search incident to a valid arrest, a police officer is authorized to search the electronic contents of a cell phone recovered from the area within the arrestee's immediate control. U.S. v. Curtis, 635 F.3d. 704 C.A.5 (Tex. Crim. App. 2011), *citing* U. S. v. Finley, 477 F.3d 250, 259 (5th Cir.), cert. denied, 549 U.S. 1353 (2007).

If an arrest is made pursuant to an unconstitutional statute or ordinance, the arrest itself is unlawful, and under the exclusionary rule the evidence seized at such arrest must be excluded. Howard v. State, 617 S.W.2d 191 (Tex. Crim. App. 1979).

Where a search and seizure is based upon an arrest without warrant, the validity of the search and seizure depends on the probable cause for the arrest, and without probable cause for the arrest, the fruits of the search are inadmissible. Rios v. United States, 364 U.S. 253, 80 S.Ct. 1431, 4 L.Ed.2d 1688 (1960).

A search incident to arrest must be confined to the immediate vicinity of the arrest, and where an arrest takes place outside a dwelling, a search of the inside of the dwelling cannot be justified as incidental to the arrest. Vale v. Louisiana, 399 U.S. 30, 90 S.Ct. 1969, 26 L.Ed.2d 409 (1970).

A warrant is generally required before searching a cell phone that is seized incident to arrest. Riley v. California, ___ U.S. ___, 134 S.Ct. 2473, 189 L.Ed.2d 430 (2014).

§2:47 Protective (Cursory) Searches

"A protective sweep is a quick and limited search of a premises, incident to an arrest and conducted to protect the safety of police officers or others." Maryland v. Buie, 494 U.S. 325, 110 S.Ct. 1093, 108 L.Ed.2d 276 (1990). *See also*, Reasor v. State, 12 S.W.3d 813 (Tex. Crim. App. 2000).

A cursory safety check is a recognized exception to the warrant requirement. Mitchell v. State, 756 S.W.2d 71 (Tex.App.—Texarkana 1988, *no pet.*).

As an incident to the arrest in a dwelling, officers can, as a precautionary matter and without probable cause or reasonable suspicion, look in closets and other spaces immediately adjoining the place of arrest from which an attack could be immediately launched. Maryland v. Buie, *supra.*

Beyond that, however, there must be articulable facts which, taken together with the rational inferences from those facts, would warrant a reasonably prudent officer in believing that the area to be swept harbors an individual posing a danger to those on the arrest scene. Maryland v. Buie, *supra*; Mitchell, *supra.*

An objectively reasonable and prudent police officer possessing such articulable facts may also make a brief sweep of the premises to look for possible victims or someone who may pose a danger to officers during their investigation. State v. Sheppard, 271 S.W.3d 281 (Tex. Crim. App. 2008).

When conducting an in-home arrest, a police officer may sweep the house only if he possesses an objectively reasonable belief, based on specific and articulable facts, that a person in that area poses a danger to that police officer or to other people in the area. This sweep must stay within the appropriate scope and may last long enough to dispel the reasonable suspicion of danger. Reasor, *supra.* Where no police officer expresses his belief that any third persons were inside the residence to be searched, and where no police officer articulated his belief that a third person inside the home was attempting to jeopardize either his or the public's safety, the protective search cannot be upheld. Reasor.

The Court of Criminal Appeals has recognized that an officer may conduct a cursory search of a hotel room for the purpose of securing the premises where a reasonable need is present, and may seize evidence discovered in plain view. Vuong v. State, 830 S.W.2d 929 (Tex. Crim. App.1992)

A search of a passenger compartment of an automobile, limited to those areas in which a weapon may be hidden, is permissible if an officer has a reasonable belief based on specific and articulable facts, which taken together with reasonable inferences drawn from those facts, that the subject is dangerous and may gain immediate control of weapons. The test to be employed is whether a reasonable and prudent man in the circumstances would be warranted in believing that his safety or that of others was in danger. Michigan v. Long, 463 U.S. 1032, 103 S.Ct. 3469, 77 L.Ed.2d 1201 (1983); State v. Nolan, 808 S.W.2d 556 (Tex. App.—Austin 1991, *no pet.*).

Where the circumstances surrounding the arrest of the defendant show ongoing criminal conduct, possession of weapons and numerous persons in and out of a residence, police were justified in conducting a search of a room next to the defendant for the pistol that allegedly was used by the defendant in the crime under investigation. Nichols v. State, 501 S.W.2d 107 (Tex. Crim. App. 1973)

The fact that another of the team of robbers under investigation was unapprehended justified the arresting officer in believing that his self-protection warranted looking through the open doorway of a bedroom adjoining the location of the arrest of the defendant, and supported the seizure of a pistol observed in an open nightstand drawer. Jones v. State, 565 S.W.2d 934 (Tex. Crim. App. 1978).

The burden is on the government to demonstrate an exigency. Vale v. Louisiana, 399 U.S. 30, 90 S.Ct. 1969, 26 L.Ed.2d 409 (1970); Mitchell, *supra*.

§2:48 Warrantless Entry of Residence Under Hot Pursuit

Absent probable cause and exigent circumstances, warrantless arrests in the home are prohibited by the Fourth Amendment. Payton v. New York, 445 U.S. 573, 100 S.Ct. 1371, 63 L.Ed.2d 639 (1980); Kirk v. Louisiana, 536 U.S. 635, 122 S.Ct. 2458, 153 L.Ed.2d 599 (2002).

However, "[i]f there is sufficient evidence of a citizen's participation in a felony to persuade a judicial officer that his arrest is justified, it is constitutionally reasonable to require him to open his doors to the officers of the law." Payton, *supra*.

A warrantless intrusion into a residence may be justified by hot pursuit of a fleeing felon, imminent destruction of evidence, the need to prevent a suspect's escape, or the risk of danger to police and other persons around the dwelling. Welsh v. Wisconsin, 466 U.S. 740, 104 S.Ct. 2091, 80 L.Ed.2d 732 (1984). The hot pursuit doctrine will not be applicable unless there is a continuous and immediate pursuit of an individual from the scene of a crime. Welsh v. Wisconsin.

A defendant cannot thwart an otherwise proper arrest that has been set in motion in a public place by retreating into her home. Here, the police had probable cause to arrest the defendant for an offense committed in the doorway of her home (a public place), and the need to act quickly to prevent the destruction of narcotics evidence supplied the exigency necessary to invoke the hot pursuit doctrine. U.S. v. Santana, 427 U.S. 38, 96 S.Ct. 2406, 49 L.Ed.2d 300 (1976).

Where probable cause exists to believe that an armed robber had entered a house a few minutes before, police are entitled to make a warrantless entry to arrest the robber and search for weapons. Warden, Maryland Penitentiary v. Hayden, 387 U.S. 294, 87 S.Ct. 1642, 18 L.Ed.2d 782 (1967).

Exigent circumstances justified the entry into an apartment by an officer to make a warrantless arrest of a suspect whom he believed had committed murder during a residential burglary earlier in the evening. The officer was aware that the suspect subsequently attempted to enter a second residence and the officer heard a woman's voice inside the apartment, which he did not know was the defendant's residence. Fearance v. State, 771 S.W.2d 486 (Tex. Crim. App. 1988).

Exigent circumstances did not justify the warrantless entry into an upstairs duplex for the purposes of the arrest of an overnight guest where police knew that the suspect was in the upstairs duplex with no suggestion of danger to other occupants of the duplex and it was evident that the suspect was going nowhere. Minnesota v. Olson, 495 U.S. 91, 110 S.Ct. 1684, 109 L.Ed.2d 85 (1990).

§2:49 Water Safety Checks

Parks and Wildlife Code §31.124, which allows an officer to stop and board a boat without probable cause or reasonable suspicion to conduct a water safety check, is constitutional. Schenekl v. State, 30 S.W.3d 412 (Tex. Crim. App. 2000).

§2:50 Searches of Particular Places

§2:51 Curtilage

"Curtilage" is a common law concept referring to the area immediately adjacent to the home to which the intimate activity of home life extends. Oliver v. United States, 466 U.S. 170, 104 S.Ct. 1735, 80 L.Ed.2d 214 (1984); White v. State, 890 S.W.2d 131 (Tex.App.—Texarkana 1994).

A person has a reasonable expectation of privacy in the curtilage of his home. Florida v. Jardines, 569 U.S. 1, 133 S.Ct. 1409, 1414-15, 185 L.Ed.2d 495 (2013).

The question of whether a particular area should be considered the curtilage of a dwelling depends on four factors:

- Proximity of the area claimed to be curtilage to the home
- Whether the area is within an enclosure surrounding the home
- Nature of the uses to which the area is put
- Steps taken by the resident to protect the area from observation by passersby

U. S. v. Dunn, 480 U.S. 294, 107 S.Ct. 1134, 94 L.Ed.2d 326 (1987).

The Fourth Amendment protections against unreasonable search and seizure do not extend to an individual who is growing marijuana in the curtilage of his home where the police observe the plants by aerial surveillance. California v. Ciraolo, 476 U.S. 207, 106 S.Ct. 1809, 90 L.Ed.2d 210 (1986).

Police observation from an altitude of 400 feet of a greenhouse containing marijuana which was located within the curtilage of the defendant's home was not a "search" as contemplated by the Fourth Amendment. Florida v. Riley, 488 U.S. 445, 109 S.Ct. 693, 102 L.Ed.2d 835 (1989); Moss v. State, 878 S.W.2d 632 (Tex.App.—San Antonio 1994, *pet. ref'd*).

Where the defendant owned the land on which a carport was situated and not only maintained control over the use of the carport, but established an expectation of privacy by placing personal belongings in the carport, she established a reasonable expectation of privacy in the curtilage such that a resulting warrantless search was unreasonable. Kann v. State, 694 S.W.2d 156 (Tex. App.—Dallas 1985, *pet. ref'd*).

Evidence obtained by the state as result of a criminal trespass on the defendant's property is inadmissible and subject to suppression. State v. Hobbs, 824 S.W.2d 317 (Tex.App.—San Antonio 1992, *pet. ref'd*).

An officers' conduct in bringing a trained drug-detection dog up to the threshold or area immediately outside of a front door for the purpose of conducting a canine-narcotics sniff was an unlicensed physical intrusion onto the curtilage of the home that constituted a search in violation of the Fourth Amendment. State v. Rendon, 477 S.W.3d 805, 808 (Tex. Crim. App. 2015) (where officers' physically intruded upon the curtilage of appellee's home in a manner that exceeded the scope of any express or implied license).

§2:52 Open Fields

The term "open fields" may include any unoccupied or undeveloped area outside of the curtilage. An open field need be neither open nor a field as those terms are used in common speech. Oliver v. United States, 466 U.S. 170, 104 S.Ct. 1735, 80 L.Ed.2d 214 (1984); White v. State, 890 S.W.2d 131 (Tex.App.—Texarkana 1994); Moss v. State, 878 S.W.2d 632 (Tex.App.—San Antonio 1994, *pet. ref'd*).

The protection of the Fourth Amendment against unreasonable searches and seizures does not extend to open fields. Oliver, *supra*; Barton v. State, 962 S.W.2d 132 (Tex.App.—Beaumont 1998, *pet. ref'd*).

§2:53 School Searches

The Fourth Amendment's prohibition against unreasonable searches and seizures applies to searches conducted by public school officials. New Jersey v. T.L.O., 469 U.S. 325, 105 S.Ct. 733, 83 L.Ed.2d 720 (1985); Coronado v. State, 835 S.W.2d 636 (Tex. Crim. App. 1992).

School officials need not obtain a warrant before searching a student who is under their authority. New Jersey v. T.L.O., *supra*; Coronado, *supra*.

However, the Fourth Amendment commands that all searches and seizures be reasonable. Therefore, the legality of a search of a public school student depends on the reasonableness, under all of the circumstances, of the search. New Jersey v. T.L.O., *supra*; Coronado, *supra*.

A two-prong test applies to determine the reasonableness of the search. First, a court must determine whether the search was justified at its inception. Second, a court must determine whether the search, as actually conducted, was reasonably related in scope to the circumstances which justified the interference in the first place. New Jersey v. T.L.O., *supra*; Coronado, *supra*; Shoemaker v. State, 971 S.W.2d 178 (Tex.App.—Beaumont 1998, *no pet.*).

In order to be reasonable, the content of the suspicion in the knowledge of the school official must match the degree of the intrusion on the person of the student. Safford United School District #1 v. Redding, 557 U.S. 364, 129 S.Ct. 2633, 174 L.Ed.2d 354 (2009).

A search of a student by a teacher or school official is justified at its inception when there are reasonable grounds for suspecting that the search will turn up evidence that the student has violated, or is violating, either the law or the rules of the school. New Jersey v. T.L.O., *supra*; Coronado, *supra*.

A search was clearly justified from its inception and related in scope to the circumstances justifying the search where the defendant was a likely suspect in a theft, where it was clear that the defendant knew of the locality of the stolen items, where the defendant was properly given her Miranda warnings and she voluntarily consented to the search. Shoemaker, *supra*.

A search is permissible in its scope when the measures adopted and used are reasonably related to the objectives of the search and are not excessively intrusive in light of the age and sex of the student, and the nature of the infraction. New Jersey v. T.L.O., *supra*; Coronado, *supra*.

Where the school officials had reasonable grounds for suspecting that their searches would produce evidence that the students were violating school rules, and the searches were reasonable and not excessively intrusive in light of the nature of the infraction, the searches will be upheld. Irby v. State, 751 S.W.2d 670 (Tex.App.—Eastland 1988, *no pet.*); Coffman v. State, 782 S.W.2d 249 (Tex.App.—Houston [14th Dist.] 1989, *no pet.)*; Goldberg v. State, 95 S.W.3d 345 (Tex.App.—Houston [1st Dist.] 2002, *pet. ref'd*).

§2:54 Administrative Searches

Warrantless inspections of commercial premises in certain highly regulated industries may be valid exceptions to the Fourth Amendment warrant requirement if three criteria are met. First, there must be a substantial government interest that informs the regulatory scheme pursuant to which the inspection or warrantless search is made. Second, the warrantless inspection must be necessary to further the regulatory scheme. Third, the statutory provision must provide a constitutionally adequate substitute for a warrant so as to limit properly the discretion of the officers performing the inspection. New York v. Burger, 482 U.S. 691, 107 S.Ct. 2636, 96 L.Ed.2d 601 (1987); Santikos v. State, 836 S.W.2d 631 (Tex. Crim. App. 1992).

The statute must carefully limit the inspection in time, place, and scope. Santikos, *supra*.

In order for the regulatory statute to be an adequate substitute for a warrant, it must meet escalating standards. Initially, the statute has to be sufficient in its content to give the owner of the regulated business notice that the search is authorized by law. Further, the statute must detail the scope of the search. Also, and of particular significance, the statute "must limit the discretion of the officers." Crosby, *supra*.

The owner of a closely regulated industry, such as one involving liquor, is considered to have a reduced expectation of privacy in the premises. Crosby v. State, 750 S.W.2d 768 (Tex. Crim. App. 1987).

However, where the regulated industry has private quarters on the premises in which individuals demonstrate a reasonable expectation of privacy, the administrative statute will not allow their inspection without a warrant. Crosby, *supra* (where officers searched the defendant's private dressing room where he had posted a sentry).

Where the inspecting officer exceeds the scope of a legitimate search pursuant to an administrative statute authorizing such a search there results in a violation of the Fourth Amendment and Art. I, §9 of the Texas Constitution. Crosby, *supra*.

T.A.B.C. §101.04 authorizes warrantless searches of premises holding liquor licenses and permits. Searches under this provision are reasonable where the state demonstrates:

- Substantial government interest that informs the regulatory scheme pursuant to which the inspection is made
- That the warrantless inspection is necessary to further the regulatory scheme
- That the inspection program, in terms of certainty and regularity of its application, provides a constitutionally adequate substitute for a warrant

McDonald v. State, 778 S.W.2d 88 (Tex. Crim. App. 1989).

Tex. Health & Safety Code §483.074 authorizes the warrantless seizure of dangerous drugs by a health investigator lawfully inspecting premises pursuant to the Texas Food, Drug, and Cosmetic Act. State v. Haley, 811 S.W.2d 597 (Tex. Crim. App. 1991).

Parks and Wildlife officers may board a boat to look for water safety equipment as a valid administrative search under Texas Wildlife Code §31.124 and any evidence they find in plain view (such as the intoxication of the boat's driver) is admissible at trial. Schenekl v. State, 30 S.W.3d 412 (Tex. Crim. App. 2000).

A prisoner has no reasonable expectation of privacy in his jail cell. Hudson v. Palmer, 468 U.S. 517, 104 S.Ct. 3194, 82 L.Ed.2d 393 (1984).

The Fourth Amendment does not prohibit a police officer from conducting a suspicionless search of a parolee (where the parolee has agreed to such as a condition of his release). Samson v. California, U.S. 843, 126 S.Ct. 2193, 165 L.Ed.2d 250 (2006).

Where an employer's search of an employee's alphanumeric pager was motivated by a legitimate work-related purpose and was not excessive in scope, the search will be found reasonable under the Fourth Amendment. City of Ontario, Cal. v. Quon, 560 U.S. 746, 130 S.Ct. 2619, 177 L.Ed.2d 216 (2010).

§2:55 Border and Border Checkpoint Searches

§2:55.1 Border Searches

The border search doctrine is an exception to the Fourth Amendment requirement of probable cause. Aycock v. State, 863 S.W.2d 183 (Tex.App.—Houston [14th Dist.] 1993, *pet. ref'd*).

It is within the power of the federal government to exclude aliens from the country, and this power can be effectuated by routine inspections and searches of individuals or conveyances seeking to cross the borders of the United States. Almeida-Sanchez v. United States, 413 U.S. 266, 93 S.Ct. 2535, 37 L.Ed.2d 596 (1973).

Persons entering and leaving the country may be examined as to their belongings and effects without violating the Fourth Amendment. California Bankers Assoc. v. Shultz, 416 U.S. 21, 94 S.Ct. 1494, 39 L.Ed.2d 812 (1974); Aycock, *supra*.

The Texas Constitution does not guarantee an individual any greater rights at the border against unreasonable searches and seizures than does the United States Constitution. Aycock, *supra*. Under Texas law, border searches apply with equal force to both entering and exiting travelers. Aycock.

Routine searches of the persons and effects of persons seeking to enter the country are not subject to any requirement of reasonable suspicion, probable cause, or warrant. United States v. Montoya de Hernandez, 473 U.S. 531, 105 S.Ct. 3304, 87 L.Ed.2d 381 (1985).

Routine border searches are authorized on no suspicion, and non-routine searches are authorized on suspicion alone. Further, border searches require no warrant to ensure their validity. Aycock, *supra*. A customs search at an international airport of both persons and luggage has been held to be the equivalent of a border search, conducted at the functional equivalence of the border. Aycock.

The detention of a traveler at the border, beyond the scope of a routine customs search and inspection, is justified at its inception if customs agents, considering all the facts surrounding the traveler and her trip, reasonably suspect that the traveler is smuggling contraband in her alimentary canal. Montoya de Hernandez, *supra*. Furthermore, a sixteen-hour detention necessary to determine the alimentary canal contents is not an unreasonably lengthy detention that is based on sufficient facts. Montoya de Hernandez.

International border searches of automobiles do not require reasonable suspicion. The government can make an inspection at the border without suspicion including removal, disassembly and reassembly of a vehicle gas tank. U.S. v. Flores-Montano, 541 U.S. 149, 124 S.Ct. 1582, 158 L.Ed.2d 311 (2004).

§2:55.2 Border Checkpoint Searches

Searches at checkpoints located at points removed from the border are constitutional only if justified by consent or probable cause to search. United States v. Ortiz, 422 U.S. 891, 95 S.Ct. 2585, 45 L.Ed.2d 623 (1975).

The Supreme Court listed several factors to be taken into consideration when deciding whether reasonable suspicion exists for the stop of a vehicle in a roving border patrol situation:

- Characteristics of the area in which the officer encounters the vehicle
- Proximity to the border
- Usual patterns of traffic on the particular road
- Officer's previous experience in detecting illegal entry and smuggling
- Information on recent illegal border crossings in the area
- Driver's behavior, such as erratic driving or obvious attempts to evade officers
- Physical aspects of the vehicle and the vehicle's load
- Extraordinary number of passengers, their behavior, or persons trying to hide

United States v. Brignoni-Ponce, *infra*; Saenz, *supra*.

The totality of the circumstances test applies to determine whether reasonable suspicion exists for a roving patrol stop conducted at a point removed from the border. United States v. Brignoni-Ponce, 422 U.S. 873, 95 S.Ct. 2574, 45 L.Ed.2d 607 (1975); Saenz v. State, 842 S.W.2d 286 (Tex. Crim. App. 1992).

The factors must be analyzed on a case-by-case basis to determine if there is reasonable suspicion for the initial detention. Saenz v. State, 842 S.W.2d 286 (Tex. Crim. App.1992).

When an officer who is on roving patrol makes observations which lead him reasonably to suspect that a particular vehicle may contain aliens who are illegally in the country, he may stop the car briefly and investigate the circumstances that provoke suspicion even though the facts may not amount to the probable cause required for an arrest. United States v. Brignoni-Ponce, *supra*; Saenz, *supra*.

The officer may question the driver and passengers about their citizenship and immigration status, and he may ask them to explain suspicious circumstances, but any further detention or search must be based on consent or probable cause. United States v. Brignoni-Ponce, *supra*; Saenz, *supra*; United States v. Cortez, 449 U.S. 411, 101 S.Ct. 690, 66 L.Ed.2d 621 (1981).

The nervous appearance of a driver of an older vehicle, driving down a certain highway without other articulable facts that create reasonable suspicion is insufficient to justify a warrantless stop of the vehicle. Loesch v. State, 921 S.W.2d 405 (Tex.App.—Corpus Christi 1996, *no pet.*).

The fact that the defendant was in a ranching area and did not appear to be a rancher, that the car appeared to be riding low, that the defendant-driver appeared nervous, that the vehicle was moving slowly and that the vehicle was registered in another county did not give rise to a reasonable suspicion and allow the defendant's detention. Sanchez v. State, 931 S.W.2d 331 (Tex.App.—San Antonio 1996, *pet. ref'd*).

Automotive travelers may be stopped at fixed checkpoints near the border without individualized suspicion even if the stop is based largely on ethnicity. United States v. Martinez-Fuerte, 428

U.S. 543, 96 S.Ct. 3074, 49 L.Ed.2d 1116 (1976); Gutierrez v. State, 22 S.W.3d 75 (Tex.App.—Corpus Christi 2000, *no pet.*).

Whatever the permissible scope of intrusiveness of a routine border search might be, searches of this kind may in certain circumstances take place not only at the border itself, but at its functional equivalents as well. For example, searches at an established station near the border, at a point marking the confluence of two or more roads that extend from the border, might be functional equivalents of border searches, and a search of the passengers and cargo of an airplane arriving at an airport after a nonstop flight from Mexico would clearly be the functional equivalent of a border search. Almeida-Sanchez v. United States, *supra*.

A search occurring at some distance inland from the border by U.S. Customs officers was justified where the agents had reason to believe that the vehicle or person was carrying contraband. Guadian v. State, 420 S.W.2d 949 (Tex. Crim. App.1967); Aycock, *supra*.

§2:56 Motor Vehicle Seizures and Searches

§2:56.1 In General

The stopping of a vehicle constitutes a "seizure" for Fourth Amendment purposes. Colorado v. Bannister, 449 U.S. 1, 101 S.Ct. 42, 65 L.Ed.2d 1 (1980); State v. Sanchez, 856 S.W.2d 166 (Tex. Crim. App. 1993).

During a traffic stop, any passengers in the vehicle are also "seized" and may challenge the constitutionality of the stop. Brendlin v. California, 551 U.S. 249, 127 S.Ct. 2400, 168 L.Ed.2d 132 (2007).

A police stop exceeding the time needed to handle the matter for which the stop was made violates the Constitution's shield against unreasonable seizures. A seizure justified only by a police-observed traffic violation, therefore, becomes unlawful if it is prolonged beyond the time reasonably required to complete the mission of issuing a ticket for the violation. Rodriguez v. United States, ___ U.S. ___, 135 S. Ct. 1609, 1612, 191 L.Ed.2d 492 (2015).

One of the exceptions to the Fourth Amendment warrant requirement exists where an automobile or other vehicle is stopped and the police have probable cause to believe it contains evidence of a crime. Colorado v. Bannister, *supra*; Neal v. State, 256 S.W.3d 264 (Tex. Crim. App. 2008).

The automobile exception also is an exception to the warrant requirement under Art. I, §9 of the Texas Constitution. Aitch v. State, 879 S.W.2d 167 (Tex.App.—Houston [14th Dist.] 1994, *pet. ref'd*).

This is because the ready mobility of a vehicle creates an exigency and because an individual has a reduced expectation of privacy in a vehicle due to its being subject to pervasive [government] regulation. Keehn v. State, 279 S.W.3d 330 (Tex. Crim. App. 2009).

The automobile exception does not require exigent circumstances. Neal.

Police officers may, without a warrant, seize a vehicle if they have probable cause to believe the vehicle itself, as opposed to its contents, is contraband. Florida v. White, 526 U.S. 559, 119 S.Ct. 1555, 143 L.Ed.2d 748 (1999); Lagaite v. State, 995 S.W.2d 860 (Tex.App.—Houston [1st Dist.] 1999 *pet. ref'd*).

Under the automobile exception, an officer may conduct a warrantless search of a motor vehicle if the officer has probable cause to believe the vehicle contains evidence of a crime. Chambers v. Maroney, 399 U.S. 42, 90 S.Ct. 1975, 26 L.Ed.2d 419 (1970); Amos v. State, 819 S.W.2d 156 (Tex. Crim. App. 1991).

If probable cause justifies the search of a lawfully stopped vehicle, it justifies the search of every part of the vehicle and its contents that may conceal the object of the search. Barnes v. State, 424 S.W.3d 218, 225 (Tex. App.—Amarillo 2014, *no pet.*); citing United States v. Ross, 456 U.S. 798, 825, 102 S.Ct. 2157, 72 L.Ed.2d 572 (1982).

In the context of the automobile exception to the warrant requirement, furtive gestures alone are not a sufficient basis for probable cause. While furtive movements are valid indicia of mens rea, they must be coupled with reliable information or other suspicious circumstances that directly, not just vaguely, connect the suspect to the evidence of crime, to constitute probable cause. Marcopoulos v. State, 538 S.W.3d 596, 600 (Tex. Crim. App. 2017).

A sniff of the outside of an automobile by a trained canine is not a search within the meaning of the Fourth Amendment. Illinois v. Caballes, 543 U.S. 405, 125 S.Ct. 834, 160 L.Ed.2d 842 (2005); United States v. Place, 462 U.S. 696, 103 S.Ct. 2637, 77 L.Ed.2d 110 (1983); Mohmed v. State, 977 S.W.2d 624 (Tex.App.—Fort Worth 1998, *pet. ref'd*).

Police are not authorized to conduct a vehicle search incident to a recent occupant's arrest after the arrestee has been secured and cannot access the interior of the vehicle. Arizona v. Gant, 556 U.S. 332, 129 S.Ct. 1710, 173 L.Ed.2d 485 (2009) (limiting the rule of New York v. Belton, 453 U.S. 454, 101 S.Ct. 2860, 69 L.Ed.2d 768 (1981)).

Circumstances unique to the automobile context justify a search incident to arrest when it is reasonable to believe that evidence of the offense of arrest might be found in the vehicle. Arizona v. Gant (citing Thornton v. United States, 541 U. S. 615, 124 S.Ct. 2127, 158 L.Ed.2d 905 (2004)).

The automobile exception to the Fourth Amendment of the United States Constitution does not require the existence of exigent circumstances in addition to probable cause in order to allow police to search the vehicle. Maryland v. Dyson, 527 U.S. 465, 119 S.Ct. 2013, 144 L. Ed. 2d 442 (1999). Colorado v. Bannister, *supra*; State v. Guzman, 959 S.W.2d 631 (Tex. Crim. App. 1998).

The totality of the circumstances test applies to determine whether sufficient probable cause exists for the warrantless search of a vehicle. Angulo v. State, 727 S.W.2d 276 (Tex. Crim. App. 1987).

If a car is readily mobile and probable cause exists to believe it contains contraband, the Fourth Amendment permits police to search the vehicle without more, even where its owners are arrested away from the vehicle. Pennsylvania v. Labron, 518 U.S. 938, 116 S.Ct. 2485, 135 L.Ed.2d 1031 (1996).

The automobile exception extends to all types of motor vehicles, including motor homes. The requisite factor for implementation of the automobile exception is the inherent mobility of a vehicle. Powell v. State, 898 S.W.2d 821 (Tex. Crim. App. 1994).

Where the vehicle that the police wish to search is located on private property and the defendant is not apprehended near the vehicle, the police must generally obtain a warrant in order to conduct the search. Coolidge v. New Hampshire, 403 U.S. 443, 91 S.Ct. 2022, 29 L.Ed.2d 564 (1971).

The automobile exception does not permit an officer without a warrant to enter a home or its curtilage in order to search a vehicle therein. Collins v. Virginia, 584 U.S. ___, 138 S.Ct. 1663, 1671, 201 L.Ed.2d 9 (2018).

Where police officers have probable cause to search an automobile at the scene where it was stopped, they can constitutionally do so later at the station house without first obtaining a warrant. Texas v. White, 423 U.S. 67, 96 S.Ct. 304, 46 L.Ed.2d 209 (1975); Guzman, *supra*.

A vehicle lawfully in police custody may be searched on the basis of probable cause to believe that it contains contraband, and there is no requirement of exigent circumstances to justify such a warrantless search. United States v. Johns, 469 U.S. 478, 105 S.Ct. 881, 83 L.Ed.2d 890 (1985); Guzman, *supra*.

The search does not have to be undertaken immediately after impounding the vehicle, and a search conducted three days after the impoundment of the vehicle is not unreasonable. United States v. Johns, *supra*.

Where the police have probable cause to arrest a defendant for violating a parking statute which allows for an arrest for a violation, they may search a bag found on the floorboard of the driver's side of the vehicle as a search incident to arrest, even though the search incident to the arrest preceded formal custodial arrest by few moments. Williams v. State, 726 S.W.2d 99 (Tex. Crim. App. 1986).

One has a lesser expectation of privacy in a vehicle than in a business or dwelling. California v. Carney, 471 U.S. 386, 105 S.Ct. 2066, 85 L.Ed.2d 406 (1985).

A search warrant authorizing the search of a particular premises allows the concurrent search of vehicles that are on the premises at the time of the issuance of the warrant. Hughes v. State, 843 S.W.2d 591 (Tex. Crim. App. 1992).

A vehicle not on the premises at the time of the issuance of the warrant, and which is not specifically named in the warrant, cannot be searched if it arrives on the premises at a later time. State v. Barnett, 788 S.W.2d 572 (Tex. Crim. App. 1990).

Where police find contraband in the passenger compartment of a vehicle, they then have probable cause to suspect that the trunk may contain contraband and are allowed to search. Osban v. State, 726 S.W.2d 107 (Tex. Crim. App. 1986).

Police who have probable cause may examine the exterior of an automobile located in a public place, and may go so far as to take exterior paint samples from it. Cardwell v. Lewis, 417 U.S. 583, 94 S.Ct. 2464, 41 L.Ed.2d 325 (1974).

Police may search all portions of a vehicle for which they have probable cause to search. Cardenas v. State, 857 S.W.2d 707 (Tex.App.—Houston [14th Dist.] 1993, *pet. ref'd*) (where the search extended to a secret compartment in the defendant's trunk).

The holding in Georgia v. Randolph which allows a co-tenant who is present at the time of a premises search to refuse consent over the consent of another co-tenant does not apply to vehicular searches. State v. Copeland, 399 S.W.3d 159, 167 (Tex. Crim. App. 2013).

The Fourth Amendment permits police officers to approach bus passengers at random to ask questions and to request their consent to searches, provided a reasonable person would understand that he or she is free to refuse. Florida v. Bostick.

It is not required under the Fourth Amendment that the police officers inform the bus passengers of their right to refuse for a consent to search to be valid. U.S. v. Drayton, 536 U.S. 194, 122 S.Ct. 2105, 153 L.Ed.2d 242 (2002).

§2:56.2 Investigatory Vehicle Stops

§2:56.2.1 In General

Officers may stop vehicles for investigative purposes where they have specific articulable facts which, considering the officer's experience and his inferences from those facts, would reasonably warrant an intrusion on the freedom of the citizen stopped for such an investigation. Reyes v. State, 910 S.W.2d 585 (Tex.App.—Amarillo 1995, *pet. ref'd*); Cardenas v. State, 857 S.W.2d 707 (Tex. App.—Houston [14th Dist.] 1993, *pet. ref'd*).

A police stop exceeding the time needed to handle the matter for which the stop was made violates the Constitution's shield against unreasonable seizures. A seizure justified only by a police-observed traffic violation, therefore, becomes unlawful if it is prolonged beyond the time reasonably required to complete the mission of issuing a ticket for the violation. Rodriguez v. United States, ___ U.S. ___, 135 S. Ct. 1609, 1612, 191 L.Ed.2d 492 (2015).

In a case where the combined logical force of circumstances when examined together conduce to establish reasonable suspicion that a vehicle may contain contraband, the traffic stop can be extended to allow for additional investigation. Ramirez-Tamayo v. State, 537 S.W.3d 29, 39 (Tex. Crim. App. 2017)(where the circumstances included a new-model rental car with what appeared to be inoperable windows despite the absence of any visible damage to the car, the presence of unusually strong odors suspected of masking the scent of contraband, the location of the stop being along an interstate highway, and an abnormally nervous driver permitted a reasonable inference that appellant was engaging in illegal activity).

While reasonable suspicion does not authorize an unduly prolonged detention and investigation, employing a trained drug dog to perform an open-air search by walking around the car is a reasonable method of confirming or dispelling the reasonable suspicion that a vehicle contains drugs. Ramirez-Tamayo v. State, 537 S.W.3d at 39.

The temporary detention of an automobile to allow an olfactory inspection by a police dog trained to detect the odor of illegal drugs is not offensive to the Fourth Amendment when based on a reasonable suspicion that the automobile contains narcotics. Mohmed v. State, 977 S.W.2d 624 (Tex. App.—Fort Worth 1998).

The odor of marijuana emanating from a vehicle is sufficient to support a reasonable suspicion. Davis v. State, 947 S.W.2d 240 (Tex. Crim. App. 1997); Mohmed v. State, 977 S.W.2d 624 (Tex.App.—Fort Worth 1998).

An anonymous tip, sufficiently corroborated by police observations and reliably predicting future behavior, may justify an investigatory detention. Alabama v. White, 496 U.S. 325, 110 S.Ct. 2412, 110 L.Ed.2d 301 (1990).

However, where an anonymous informer never stated that he had personal knowledge of the facts of his report and no additional facts within the report indicated any special or personal knowledge on the part of the informer, the anonymous tip is insufficient to support probable cause for an automobile search. Rojas v. State, 797 S.W.2d 41 (Tex. Crim. App. 1990).

When officers make a valid traffic stop, they are entitled to take sufficient measures to guarantee their safety, which includes ordering drivers out of their cars. Pennsylvania v. Mimms, 434 U.S. 106, 98 S.Ct. 330, 54 L.Ed.2d 331 (1977); Goodwin v. State, 799 S.W.2d 719 (Tex. Crim. App. 1990).

§2:56.2.2 Incidental Searches

Police are not authorized to conduct a vehicle search incident to a recent occupant's arrest after the arrestee has been secured and cannot access the interior of the vehicle. Arizona v. Gant, 556 U.S. 332, 129 S.Ct. 1710, 173 L.Ed.2d 485 (2009) (limiting the rule of New York v. Belton, 453 U.S. 454, 101 S.Ct. 2860, 69 L.Ed.2d 768 (1981)).

Circumstances unique to the automobile context justify a search incident to arrest when it is reasonable to believe that evidence of the offense of arrest might be found in the vehicle. Arizona v. Gant (citing Thornton v. United States, 541 U. S. 615, 124 S.Ct. 2127, 158 L.Ed.2d 905 (2004)).

Where an individual in a vehicle has been placed under arrest for an offense and another offense is discovered during the arrest, as long as there is probable cause to arrest for the newly-discovered offense, and the search occurs close in time to the defendant's formal arrest, an officer may conduct a search incident to arrest on the basis of an offense discovered after formal arrest for a different crime. State v. Sanchez, 538 S.W.3d 545, 551 (Tex. Crim. App. 2017).

If an arrestee is not an occupant or recent occupant of a vehicle, the validity of the search is examined under a Chimel analysis, *i.e.*, was the search limited to the area within the immediate control of the arrestee. State v. Kelly, 963 S.W.2d 866 (Tex.App.—San Antonio 1998, *no pet.*).

In determining whether the arrestee was a recent occupant of a vehicle at the time of his arrest, several factors should be examined:

- Arrestee's temporal and spatial proximity to his vehicle
- Whether there is evidence of flight
- Whether there is an indication that the arrestee quickly exited his vehicle in an attempt to avoid police contact

These factors should be balanced against law enforcement's need to search the vehicle for protective purposes. Kelly, *supra*.

The police may also examine the contents of any containers found within the passenger compartment, whether the container is open or closed during a search incident to arrest; State v. Mercado, 944 S.W.2d 42 (Tex.App.—El Paso 1997).

The search will be upheld even where the container searched is such that it could hold neither a weapon nor evidence of the criminal conduct for which the suspect was arrested. United States v. Robinson, 414 U.S. 218, 94 S.Ct. 467, 38 L.Ed.2d 427 (1973).

When police make an investigative traffic stop, an officer may conduct a protective search of the detainee's automobile when the officer has a reasonable belief, based on specific and articulable facts, that the detainee may pose a danger to the officer or to others. Michigan v. Long, 463 U.S. 1032, 103 S.Ct. 3469, 77 L.Ed.2d 1201 (1983); Goodwin, *supra*.

Persons travelling by bus, train or automobile have the same Fourth Amendment rights as everyone else. Florida v. Bostick, 501 U.S. 429, 111 S.Ct. 2382, 115 L.Ed.2d 389 (1991).

Generally, a routine traffic stop does not place a person in custody for Miranda purposes. But a traffic stop may escalate from a non-custodial detention into a custodial detention when formal arrest ensues or a detainee's freedom of movement is restrained to the degree associated with a formal arrest. Appellate courts evaluate whether a person has been detained to the degree associated with arrest on a case-by-case basis. In making the custody determination, the primary question is whether a reasonable person would perceive the detention to be a restraint on his movement comparable to formal arrest, given all the objective circumstances. State v. Ortiz, 382 S.W.3d 367, 372 (Tex. Crim. App. 2012).

In evaluating whether a reasonable person would believe his freedom has been restrained to the degree of formal arrest, the appellate courts look only to the objective factors surrounding the detention. The subjective beliefs of the detaining officer are not included in the calculation of whether a suspect is in custody. But if the officer manifests his belief to the detainee that he is a suspect, then that officer's subjective belief becomes relevant to the determination of whether a reasonable person in the detainee's position would believe he is in custody. Conversely, any undisclosed subjective belief of the suspect that he is guilty of an offense should not be taken into consideration—the reasonable person standard presupposes an innocent person. State v. Ortiz, 382 S.W.3d at 372-73.

Generally, a routine traffic stop does not place a person in custody for Miranda purposes. But a traffic stop may escalate from a non-custodial detention into a custodial detention when formal arrest ensues or a detainee's freedom of movement is restrained to the degree associated with a formal arrest. Appellate courts evaluate whether a person has been detained to the degree associated with arrest on a case-by-case basis. In making the custody determination, the primary question is whether a reasonable person would perceive the detention to be a restraint on his movement comparable to formal arrest, given all the objective circumstances. State v. Ortiz, 382 S.W.3d 367, 372 (Tex. Crim. App. 2012).

In evaluating whether a reasonable person would believe his freedom has been restrained to the degree of formal arrest, the appellate courts look only to the objective factors surrounding the detention. The subjective beliefs of the detaining officer are not included in the calculation of whether a suspect is in custody. But if the officer manifests his belief to the detainee that he is a suspect, then that officer's subjective belief becomes relevant to the determination of whether a reasonable person in the detainee's position would believe he is in custody. Conversely, any undisclosed subjective belief of the suspect that he is guilty of an offense should not be taken into consideration—the reasonable person standard presupposes an innocent person. State v. Ortiz, 382 S.W.3d at 372-73.

§2:56.2.3 Traffic Violations

Even if a vehicle's tires touch the fog line, a momentary touch of the fog line, without any other indicator of criminal activity, is generally not enough to justify the stop of the vehicle for driving on an improved shoulder under Transportation Code section 545.058(a). State v. Cortez, 543 S.W.3d 198, 206 (Tex. Crim. App. 2018).

Section 545.058(a) provides for permissible reasons for a person to drive on the improved shoulder under seven listed circumstances. State v. Cortez, 543 S.W.3d at 207.

Courts have a duty to strictly construe criminal statutes outside the penal code with any doubt resolved in favor of the accused to avoid a constitutional violation. State v. Cortez, 543 S.W.3d at 206.

§2:56.2.4 Insurance Investigations

Investigatory stops based solely on an "unconfirmed" return from a state vehicle insurance database turn on the testimony regarding the reliability of the database. State v. Binkley, 541 S.W.3d 923, 930 (Tex. App.—Fort Worth 2018, no pet.); Contreras v. State, 309 S.W.3d 168 (Tex. App.—Amarillo 2010, pet.ref'd).

§2:56.2.5 Warrants For The Vehicle

Once an officer discovers that the owner of a vehicle has an outstanding arrest warrant, he needs only reasonable suspicion that the owner is in the vehicle. It is fair to infer that the registered owner of a vehicle is in the vehicle absent information that defeats the inference. United States v. Pyles, 904 F.3d. 422, 424-5 (6th Cir. 2018).

§2:56.3 Roadblocks and License Checkpoints

The United States Supreme Court has upheld DWI roadblocks on Fourth Amendment grounds where there is a systematic, statewide administrative scheme with guidelines set by an advisory committee. Michigan Dept. of State Police v. Sitz, 496 U.S. 144, 110 S.Ct. 2481, 110 L.Ed.2d 412, (1990).

Until a governing body in Texas authorizes a constitutional statewide procedure for DWI roadblocks, such roadblocks are unreasonable and unconstitutional under the Fourth Amendment of the U.S. Constitution. Holt v. State, 887 S.W.2d 16 (Tex. Crim. App. 1994).

In the absence of evidence of authoritatively

standardized procedures followed in operating the subject roadblock in order to serve its stated purpose and minimize the officers' discretion, and in the absence of testimony or empirical evidence demonstrating the effectiveness of the roadblock, a roadblock is an unreasonable seizure under the Fourth Amendment. State v. Sanchez, 856 S.W.2d 166 (Tex. Crim. App. 1993).

A checkpoint to verify drivers' licenses and vehicle registration is permissible, but a checkpoint whose primary purpose is to detect evidence of ordinary criminal wrongdoing is not. Lujan v. State, 331 S.W.3d 768 (Tex. Crim. App. 2011).

If the primary purpose of the checkpoint is lawful—a license check as opposed to general law enforcement—police can act on other information that arises at the stop. The checkpoint's primary purpose of license and insurance verification does not prohibit police from considering other unrelated offenses that they discover during the stop. Lujan.

The trial court's ruling on a motion to suppress evidence obtained at a license checkpoint is reviewed for abuse of discretion. The trial court is given almost complete deference in its determination of historical facts, especially when based on an assessment of credibility and demeanor. The same deference is given to the trial court with respect to its rulings on the application of the law to questions of fact if resolution of those questions depends on an evaluation of credibility and demeanor. Mixed questions of law and fact that do not turn on credibility and demeanor are reviewed *de novo.* When the trial court does not make express findings of fact, the reviewing court must view the evidence in the light most favorable to the trial court's ruling and should assume the trial court made implicit findings of fact that support its ruling as long as those findings are supported by the record. Lujan.

Where a checkpoint program's (such as a program to interdict illegal drugs) primary purpose is indistinguishable from the general interest in crime control, it violates the Fourth Amendment because the program's purpose does not fall into one of the previously recognized exceptions to the general rule that a seizure must be accompanied by some level of individualized suspicion. City of Indianapolis v. Edmond, 531 U.S. 32, 121 S.Ct. 447, 148 L.Ed.2d 333 (2000).

Random, roving patrol driver's license checkpoints conducted without adequate administrative policy have been found to be too intrusive under the Fourth Amendment to justify their minimal effectiveness. Delaware v. Prouse, 440 U.S. 648, 99 S.Ct. 1391, 59 L.Ed.2d 660 (1979).

States may develop methods for spot checks of motor vehicles that involve less intrusion or that do not involve unconstrained exercise of discretion, such as questioning of all oncoming traffic at roadblock-type stops. Delaware v. Prouse, *supra*.

The Fourth Amendment requires that a seizure be based on:

- Specific evidence of an existing violation
- Showing that "reasonable legislative or administrative standards for conducting an inspection are satisfied," or
- Showing that the "search is carried out pursuant to a plan containing specific neutral criteria."

Webb v. State, 695 S.W.2d 676 (Tex.App.—Dallas 1985) affirmed at 739 S.W.2d 802 (Tex. Crim. App. 1987).

A driver's license checkpoint that is a mere subterfuge for a DWI roadblock because of its proximity to bars is improper under the Fourth Amendment without proper neutral safeguards. Webb v. State, 739 S.W.2d 802 (Tex. Crim. App. 1987).

A police action is not a roadblock where police are merely observing automobiles in a congested area and ticketing any traffic offenses they observe; even where the intent of the police is by heavy ticketing to cut down use of the road in question. State v. Skiles, 938 S.W.2d 447 (Tex. Crim. App. 1997) (where the area in question was one where teens "cruised").

The Edmond-type presumptive rule of unconstitutionality does not apply to checkpoints conducted for the purpose of gathering information from the public about a crime in all likelihood committed by others. Illinois v. Lidster, 540 U.S. 419, 124 S.Ct. 885, 157 L.Ed.2d 843 (2004) (where the Court went on to find that the checkpoint in question was reasonable under its particular facts).

§2:56.4 Checking Identification Numbers

Because of the important role played by the vehicle identification number (VIN) in the pervasive governmental regulation of the automobile and the efforts by the Federal Government to ensure that the VIN is placed in plain view, there is no reasonable expectation of privacy in the VIN. New York v. Class, 475 U.S. 106, 106 S.Ct. 960, 89 L.Ed.2d 81(1986).

Inspections of motor vehicles performed by police officers, who are entitled to be on the property where the vehicles are located, which in no way damage the vehicles and are limited to determining the correct identification numbers of the vehicles, are not searches within the meaning of the Fourth Amendment. Alternatively, if such inspections constitute a Fourth Amendment search, then no search warrant is necessary because such inspections are reasonable and do not violate anyone's Fourth Amendment rights. Wood v. State, 632 S.W.2d 734 (Tex. Crim. App. 1982).

Where a police officer on a traffic stop had to reach into the passenger compartment of the vehicle to move papers which were obscuring the VIN, the search was found to be sufficiently unintrusive so as to be constitutionally permissible in light of the lack of a reasonable expectation of privacy in the VIN and the fact that the officers observed respondent commit two traffic violations. New York v. Class, *supra*.

Police officers are not authorized to enter a vehicle to obtain a dashboard-mounted VIN when the VIN is visible from outside the automobile. If the VIN is in the plain view of someone outside the vehicle, there is no justification for governmental intrusion into the passenger compartment to see it. New York v. Class, *supra.*

§2:56.5 Searches of Persons During Stop of Automobile

When officers make a valid traffic stop, they are entitled to take sufficient measures to guarantee their safety, which includes ordering drivers out of their cars. Pennsylvania v. Mimms, 434 U.S. 106, 98 S.Ct. 330, 54 L.Ed.2d 331 (1977); Goodwin v. State, 799 S.W.2d 719 (Tex. Crim. App. 1990).

During a traffic stop the officer may request certain information from a driver, such as the driver's license, vehicle registration, and proof of insurance, and run a computer check on that information. Lerma v. State, 543 S.W.3d 184, 190 (Tex. Crim. App. 2018).

An officer is also permitted to ask drivers and passengers about matters unrelated to the purpose of the stop, so long as the questioning does not measurably extend the duration of the stop. Lerma v. State, 543 S.W.3d at 190.

There is no per se rule that an officer must immediately conduct a computer check on the driver's information before questioning the occupants of the vehicle. Once the computer check is completed, and the officer knows that the driver has a current valid license, no outstanding warrants, and the car is not stolen, the traffic stop investigation is fully resolved. However, if an officer develops reasonable suspicion that the driver or an occupant of the vehicle is involved in criminal activity the officer may continue questioning the individual regardless of whether the official tasks of a traffic stop have come to an end. Lerma v. State, 543 S.W.3d at 190-1.

During the course of a detention, an officer may, in certain circumstances, conduct a pat-down search of an individual to determine whether the person is carrying a weapon. In order to justify a pat-down, the officer must reasonably believe that the suspect is armed and dangerous, such that the officer can point to specific and articulable facts which reasonably lead him to conclude that the suspect might possess a weapon. Reasonable suspicion in this context is based on an objective assessment of the officer's actions in light of the facts and circumstances surrounding the detention. Lerma v. State, 543 S.W.3d at 191.

Police are not authorized to conduct a vehicle search incident to a recent occupant's arrest after the arrestee has been secured and cannot access the interior of the vehicle. Arizona v. Gant, 556 U.S. ___, 129 S.Ct. 1710, 173 L.Ed.2d 485 (2009) (limiting the rule of New York v. Belton, 453 U.S. 454, 101 S.Ct. 2860, 69 L.Ed.2d 768 (1981)).

Circumstances unique to the automobile context justify a search incident to arrest when it is reasonable to believe that evidence of the offense of arrest might be found in the vehicle. Arizona v. Gant (citing Thornton v. United States, 541 U. S.

615, 124 S.Ct. 2127, 158 L.Ed.2d 905 (2004)).

However, if the officer stops a person for speeding and issues a citation rather than making a full custodial arrest, he is not permitted to make a full search of the vehicle. Knowles v. Iowa, 525 U.S. 113, 119 S.Ct. 484, 142 L.Ed.2d 492 (1998).

Where police have probable cause to believe that a vehicle contains contraband, they may search the entire vehicle including the belongings of passengers that are capable of containing the object of the probable cause. Wyoming v. Houghton, 526 U.S. 295, 119 S.Ct. 1297, 143 L.Ed.2d 408 (1999).

If an arrestee is not an occupant or recent occupant of a vehicle, the validity of the search is examined under a Chimel analysis; *i.e.*, was the search limited to the area within the immediate control of the arrestee. State v. Kelly, 963 S.W.2d 866 (Tex.App.—San Antonio 1998, *no pet.*).

An investigative detention during the course of a traffic stop, in which the subject is not free to leave, is a seizure for purposes of the Fourth Amendment, and the appellate court must analyze the stop under the reasonableness standard. Whren v. United States, 517 U.S. 806, 116 S.Ct. 1769, 135 L.Ed.2d 89 (1996); Love v. State, 252 S.W.3d 684 (Tex.App.—Texarkana 2008, *pet. ref'd*).

Both the initial detention and the duration of the detention must be reasonable in order for the fruits of a search to be admissible. Love.

The reasonableness of the duration of the detention will be looked at on a case-by-case basis. The propriety of the stop's duration is judged by assessing whether the police diligently pursued a means of investigation that was likely to quickly dispel or confirm their suspicions. Love.

Where an officer has reasonable grounds to believe that he is in danger of bodily injury at the hands of the occupants of a vehicle, a limited search is permissible solely for his own protection. Satterwhite, *supra*.

In determining whether the arrestee was a recent occupant of a vehicle at the time of his arrest, several factors should be examined:

- Arrestee's temporal and spatial proximity to his vehicle
- Whether there is evidence of flight
- Whether there is an indication that the arrestee quickly exited his vehicle in an attempt to avoid police contact

These factors should be balanced against law enforcement's need to search the vehicle for protective purposes. Kelly, *supra*.

The police may also examine the contents of any containers found within the passenger compartment; whether the container is open or closed. State v. Mercado, 944 S.W.2d 42 (Tex. App.—El Paso 1997, *no pet.*).

The search will be upheld even where the container searched is such that it could hold neither a weapon nor evidence of the criminal conduct for which the suspect was arrested. United States v. Robinson, 414 U.S. 218, 94 S.Ct. 467, 38 L.Ed.2d 427 (1973).

When police make an investigative traffic stop, an officer may conduct a protective search of the detainee's automobile when the officer has a reasonable belief, based on specific and articulable facts, that the detainee may pose a danger to the officer or to others. Michigan v. Long, 463 U.S. 1032, 103 S.Ct. 3469, 77 L.Ed.2d 1201 (1983); Goodwin, *supra*.

Persons travelling by bus, train or automobile have the same Fourth Amendment rights as everyone else. Florida v. Bostick, 501 U.S. 429, 111 S.Ct. 2382, 115 L.Ed.2d 389 (1991).

§2:56.6 Vehicle Inventory Searches

An inventory is permissible under both the Fourth Amendment of the United States Constitution and Article I §9 of the Texas Constitution if conducted pursuant to a lawful impoundment. South Dakota v. Opperman, 428 U.S. 364, 96 S.Ct. 3092, 49 L.Ed.2d 1000 (1976); Benavides v. State, 600 S.W.2d 809 (Tex. Crim. App. 1980); Lagaite v. State, 995 S.W.2d 860 (Tex.App.—Houston [1st Dist.] 1999, *pet. ref'd*).

For an impoundment of a vehicle to be lawful, it must be reasonable under the Fourth Amendment. Roberts v. State, 444 S.W.3d 770, 774 (Tex. App.—Fort Worth 2014, pet.filed).

Impoundment of a car may be lawful under many circumstances. Reasonable cause for impoundment may exist when:

- Vehicle has been used in the commission of a crime [Gauldin v. State, 683 S.W.2d 411 (Tex. Crim. App. 1984)]
- Unattended vehicle is abandoned, illegally parked, or otherwise endangering other traffic [Opperman, *supra*; Benavides, *supra*.]
- Driver is incapacitated and unable to remove the vehicle [Colorado v. Bertine, 479 U.S. 367, 107 S.Ct. 738, 93 L.Ed.2d 739 (1987); Boughton v. State, 643 S.W.2d 147 (Tex.App.—Fort Worth 1982, *no pet.*)]
- Driver is removed from his automobile, placed under custodial arrest, and his property cannot be protected by any means other than impoundment. [Daniels v. State, 600 S.W.2d 813 (Tex. Crim. App. 1980); Lagaite, *supra*.]

Impoundment of a vehicle is authorized if there is a reasonable connection between the crime and the vehicle, such as where the defendant used the vehicle shortly after the crime or used the vehicle to obtain the vehicle used in the crime. Wynne v. State, 676 S.W.2d 650 (Tex.App.—Fort Worth 1984); Lagaite, *supra*.

The court of criminal appeals has observed that there are many circumstances under which law enforcement may reasonably impound an automobile, including (1) the driver's arrest when the arrest is reasonably connected to the vehicle; (2) statutory authorization; (3) vehicle abandonment or a vehicle that is hazardous and presents a danger to the public; (4) a reasonable belief that the vehicle is stolen; (5) vehicle removal from an accident scene; and (6) parking violations. Roberts, 444 S.W.3d at 776.

When vehicles are impounded, local police departments generally follow a routine practice of securing and inventorying the automobiles' contents. These procedures were developed in response to three distinct needs: 1) the protection of the owner's property while it remains in police custody; 2) the protection of the police against claims or disputes over lost or stolen property; and 3) the protection of the police from potential danger. South Dakota v. Opperman, *supra*; Autran v. State, 887 S.W.2d 31 (Tex. Crim. App. 1994) (plurality opinion).

A vehicle inventory search may be conducted without a warrant if a standard inventory protocol is followed, the search is not a pretext for an investigation and if the scope of the search is reasonable. State v. Giles, 867 S.W.2d 105 (Tex. App.—El Paso 1993, *pet. ref'd*).

The court of criminal appeals has long held that an inventory search must not deviate from police department policy. Roberts, 444 S.W.3d at 778. The burden of proving a proper inventory is on the State. Roberts v. State, 444 S.W.3d 770, 774 (Tex. App.—Fort Worth 2014, pet.filed).

There is no requirement that an officer obtain a search warrant to conduct an inventory if the inventory is part of a bona fide routine administrative caretaking function of the police. Autran, *supra*.

An inventory search cannot be justified if there are reasonable alternatives to impounding the vehicle. Gords v. State, 824 S.W.2d 785 (Tex.App.—Dallas 1992, *pet. ref'd*).

Nothing prohibits the exercise of police discretion in deciding whether to impound a vehicle or to leave it locked in a public place, so long as that discretion is exercised according to standard criteria and on the basis of something other than suspicion of evidence of criminal activity. Colorado v. Bertine, *supra*.

Where the state satisfies its burden concerning an inventory through the testimony of police officers that an inventory policy existed and that the policy was followed, there is no need to introduce a written inventory into evidence. Stephen.

Officers may inventory a vehicle trunk as a means of protection against possible future claims of theft of property by the police from the trunk. Williams v. State, 621 S.W.2d 613 (Tex. Crim. App. 1981); Stephen, *supra*.

However, the mere arrest of a defendant cannot be construed to authorize the seizure of his automobile when the arrest took place two or more blocks away from the automobile. Benavides, *supra*.

In order to validly inventory vehicle contents and use fruits of the inventory in court, police should develop a policy to govern the conducting of the inventory. Absent such a policy, the search is not sufficiently regulated to satisfy the Fourth Amendment and the fruits of such inventories are properly suppressed. Florida v. Wells, 495 U.S. 1, 110 S.Ct. 1632, 109 L.Ed.2d 1 (1990).

A police officer may be allowed sufficient latitude to determine whether a particular container should or should not be opened in light of the nature of the search and characteristics of the container itself if this discretion is made a part of the department's vehicle inventory policy. Florida v. Wells, *supra.*

The discovery of contraband in one area of a vehicle during a valid inventory procedure establishes probable cause for a warrantless search of the remainder of the vehicle. Michigan v. Thomas, 458 U.S. 259, 102 S.Ct. 3079, 73 L.Ed.2d 750 (1982).

§2:56.7 Containers in Vehicles

The police may search an automobile and the containers within it where they have probable cause to believe contraband or evidence is contained. California v. Acevedo, 500 U.S. 565, 111 S.Ct. 1982, 114 L.Ed.2d 619 (1991).

Where police make an arrest of a vehicle occupant after a valid traffic stop, they may examine the contents of any open or closed container found within the passenger compartment. New York v. Belton, 453 U.S. 454, 101 S.Ct. 2860, 69 L.Ed.2d 768 (1981); Goodwin v. State, 799 S.W.2d 719 (Tex. Crim. App. 1990).

Probable cause to believe that a container placed in the trunk of a taxi contains contraband or evidence does not justify a search of the entire cab. United States v. Ross, 456 U.S. 798, 102 S.Ct. 2157, 72 L.Ed.2d 572 (1982).

Art. 1, §9 of the Texas Constitution provides a privacy interest in closed containers which is not overcome by the general policy considerations underlying an inventory, and provides greater protection than the Fourth Amendment. Autran, *supra.*

Officers may search a closed or locked container, but may not rely upon the inventory exception to conduct such a warrantless search. Autran.

The courts of appeals are split over whether to follow the plurality opinion in Autran. Several have declined to follow Autran. *See*, Hatcher v. State, 916 S.W.2d 643 (Tex.App.—Texarkana, *pet. ref'd*); Trujillo v. State, 952 S.W.2d 879 (Tex.App.—Dallas 1997, *no pet.*); Wells v. State, 968 S.W.2d 483 (Tex. App.—Eastland 1998, *pet. ref'd*). At least one court of appeals has followed Autran. State v. Lawson, 886 S.W.2d 554 (Tex.App.—Fort Worth 1994, *pet. ref'd*).

If the police acting on a valid consent to search wish to search closed containers within an automobile, they may do so without separately requesting permission to search each individual container. Florida v. Jimeno, 500 U.S. 248, 111 S.Ct. 1801, 114 L.Ed.2d 297 (1991).

However, the suspect may explicitly delineate the scope of the search, and exclude certain containers from his consent. Florida v. Jimeno, *supra.*

The scope of a warrantless search of an automobile is not defined by the nature of the container in which the contraband is secreted. Rather, it is defined by the object of the search and the places in which there is probable cause to believe that it may be found. United States v. Ross, *supra.*

A warrantless search of an automobile can include a search of a container or package found inside the car when the search of the vehicle was supported by probable cause. United States v. Ross.

When the police do not have probable cause to search the entire vehicle as in Ross, but rather have probable cause to search only a container of some type in the vehicle, and the vehicle is in police custody, the police must obtain a warrant before searching the container. United States v. Chadwick, 433 U.S. 1, 97 S.Ct. 2476, 53 L.Ed.2d 538 (1977).

§2:56.8 GPS Devices

The Government's installation of a GPS device on a target's vehicle, and its use of that device to monitor the vehicle's movements, constitutes a search under the Fourth Amendment. *U.S. v. Jones*, 565 U.S. 400, 132 S.Ct. 945, 181 L.Ed.2d 911 (2012) (where Court did not reach the issue of whether the search was reasonable); *see also U.S. v. Katzin*, 732 F.3d 187, 198 (3rd Cir. (Pa.) 2013); State v. Jackson, 464 S.W.3d 724, 730 (Tex. Crim. App. 2015).

§2:57 Homes

Before law enforcement can enter a home without a warrant, they need probable cause and exigent circumstances. Parker v. State, 206 S.W.3d 593 (Tex. Crim. App. 2006).

The well-established probable cause standard that applies to a warrantless entry or search of a specific location is that "[p]robable cause to search exists when reasonably trustworthy facts and circumstances within the knowledge of the officer on the scene would lead a man of reasonable prudence to believe that the instrumentality of a crime or evidence of a crime will be found." Estrada v. State, 154 S.W.3d 604 (Tex. Crim. App. 2005); Parker.

Exigent circumstances, those which justify an immediate need to enter a residence without first obtaining a search warrant, must also exist. Estrada; Parker.

There are three categories of exigent circumstances that justify a warrantless intrusion by police officers: (1) providing aid or assistance to persons whom law enforcement reasonably believes are in need of assistance; (2) protecting police officers from persons whom they reasonably believe to be present, armed, and dangerous; and (3) preventing the destruction of evidence or contraband. McNairy v. State, 835 S.W.2d 101 (Tex. Crim. App. 1991); Gutierrez v. State, 221 S.W.3d 680 (Tex. Crim. App. 2007).

Probable cause is the accumulation of facts which, when viewed in their totality, would lead a reasonable police officer to conclude, with a fair probability, that a crime has been committed or is being committed by someone. Parker.

The determination of whether an officer has probable cause and exigent circumstances to enter a person's home without a warrant is a factual one based on the sum of all the information known to the officer at the time of entry. Parker (citing Estrada and State v. Steelman, 93 S.W.3d 102 (Tex. Crim. App. 2002)).

A reviewing court should analyze each piece of evidence as part of the totality of information, as it relates to both the probable cause and the exigent circumstances determinations. Parker.

Using a drug-sniffing dog on a homeowner's porch to investigate the contents of a home and its immediate surroundings is a search within the meaning of the Fourth Amendment. Florida v. Jardines, 569 U.S. 1, 133 S.Ct. 1409, 1417-18, 185 L.Ed.2d 495 (2013).

Using a drug-sniffing dog on a homeowner's porch to investigate the contents of a home and its immediate surroundings is a search within the meaning of the Fourth Amendment. Florida v. Jardines, 569 U.S. 1, 133 S.Ct. 1409, 1417-18, 185 L.Ed.2d 495 (2013).

The automobile exception does not permit an officer without a warrant to enter a home or its curtilage in order to search a vehicle therein. Collins v. Virginia, 584 U.S. ___, 138 S.Ct. 1663, 167, 201 L.Ed.2d 9 (2018).

§2:58 Searches by Dogs

A probable-cause hearing focusing on a dog's alert should proceed much like any other. The court should allow the parties to make their best case, consistent with the usual rules of criminal procedure. And the court should then evaluate the proffered evidence to decide what all the circumstances demonstrate. If the State has produced proof from controlled settings that a dog performs reliably in detecting drugs, and the defendant has not contested that showing, then the court should find probable cause. If, in contrast, the defendant has challenged the State's case (by disputing the reliability of the dog overall or of a particular alert), then the court should weigh the competing evidence. Florida v. Harris, 568 U.S. 237, 133 S.Ct. 1050, 1058, 185 L.Ed.2d 61 (2013).

Training records can suffice to establish a dog's reliability in detecting drugs. Florida v. Harris, 133 S.Ct. at 1059.

Using a drug-sniffing dog on a homeowner's porch to investigate the contents of a home and its immediate surroundings is a search within the meaning of the Fourth Amendment. Florida v. Jardines, 569 U.S. 1, 133 S.Ct. 1409, 1417-18, 185 L.Ed.2d 495 (2013).

Scent-discrimination lineups, whether conducted with individuals or inanimate objects, are separate and distinct from dog-scent tracking evidence. Even the briefest review of the scientific principles underlying dog scenting reveals that, contrary to the conclusions of many courts, there are significant scientific differences among the various uses of scenting: tracking, narcotics detection, and scent lineups. Winfrey v. State, 323 S.W.3d 875 (Tex. Crim. App. 2010).

Scent-discrimination lineups, when used alone or as primary evidence, are legally insufficient to support a conviction. Winfrey v. State, 393 S.W.3d 763, 772-73 (Tex. Crim. App. 2013).

A sniff of the outside of an automobile by a trained canine is not a search within the meaning of the Fourth Amendment. Illinois v. Caballes, 543 U.S. 405, 125 S.Ct. 834, 160 L.Ed.2d 842 (2005); United States v. Place, 462 U.S. 696, 103 S.Ct. 2637, 77 L.Ed.2d 110 (1983); Mohmed v. State, 977 S.W.2d 624 (Tex.App.—Fort Worth 1998, pet. ref'd).

In order to properly conduct a canine search, officers must legitimately be in the place where the search is conducted. State v. Weaver, 349 S.W.3d 521, 532 (Tex. Crim. App. 2011)(where the search exceeded the scope of consent).

In reviewing the sufficiency of a search warrant affidavit, if a canine search is found to be illegal and the remainder of the affidavit does not state sufficient probable cause, the resulting search is illegal. McClintock v. State, 444 S.W.3d 15, 19 (Tex. Crim. App. 2014).

For a case where there was sufficient probable cause contained in the affidavit after recitations involving an illegal canine search were omitted see State v. Phu Le, 463 S.W.3d 872 (Tex. Crim. App. 2015).

§2:59 Searches for Stored Communications

On March 23, 2018, the Clarifying Lawful Overseas Use of Data Act (CLOUD Act) became effective. The CLOUD Act amends the Stored Communications Act, 18 U. S. C. §2701 et seq., by adding the following provision:

"A [service provider] shall comply with the obligations of this chapter to preserve, backup, or disclose the contents of a wire or electronic communication and any record or other information pertaining to a customer or subscriber within such provider's possession, custody, or control, regardless of whether such communication, record, or other information is located within or outside of the United States." CLOUD Act §103(a)(1). See U.S. v. Microsoft Corporation, 584 U.S. ___, 138 S.Ct. 1186, 1187-8, 200 L.Ed.2d 610 (2018).

§2:60 Motions to Suppress Evidence

CCP Art. 28.01 §(1)(6) provides that ". . . [w]hen a hearing on the motion to suppress evidence is granted, the court may determine the merits of said motion on the motions themselves, or upon opposing affidavits, or upon oral testimony, subject to the discretion of the court. . ."

PRACTICE TIP: When witnesses are unavailable to appear for a hearing on a motion to suppress, an affidavit can provide sufficient evidence on which the court may base its determination.

Defense counsel may either file a pretrial motion to suppress evidence or wait until the trial on the merits and object when the alleged unlawfully obtained evidence is offered. The trial court has the option of either hearing a motion to suppress the evidence prior to trial or waiting until the defendant's counsel makes an objection at the trial on the merits when the alleged unlawfully obtained evidence is offered. Roberts v. State, 545 S.W.2d 157, 158 (Tex. Crim. App. 1977).

The question of whether to hold a hearing on a pretrial motion to suppress evidence rests within the discretion of the trial court. Calloway v. State, 743 S.W.2d 645 (Tex. Crim. App. 1988).

The court may elect to determine the merits of a motion to suppress evidence only during the trial upon the merits when proper objection is then lodged, rather than at a pretrial hearing. Calloway, *supra*.

Even if a pretrial motion to suppress is called to the attention of the trial court, no error is presented if the trial court, in its discretion, declines to hear the same. Calloway, *supra*. While the court is not required to hear any pretrial motion to suppress evidence, the accused retains his right to raise any appropriate objection at trial. Calloway.

A defendant making a motion that evidence seized from him be suppressed bears the initial burden of proof, also known as the burden of production. Russell v. State, 717 S.W.2d 7 (Tex. Crim. App. 1986); Ford v. State, 158 S.W.3d 488 (Tex. Crim. App. 2005).

The defendant has the burden to produce evidence establishing: (1) that a search or seizure occurred; and (2) that the search or seizure occurred without a warrant or without valid consent. Alvarado v. State, 894 S.W.2d 869 (Tex.App.—El Paso 1995, *pet. ref'd*); Ford v. State, 158 S.W.3d 488 (Tex. Crim. App. 2005).

Once the defendant has produced this evidence, then the burden shifts to the State to show:

- Search or seizure was pursuant to a valid warrant, in which case the state must produce both the warrant and the supporting affidavit
- If the search or arrest was effected without a warrant, the state must prove the reasonableness of the search or seizure
- If the search is allegedly consensual, the state must establish that the defendant's consent was freely and voluntarily given

Alvarado, *supra.*

Where the state produces both a warrant and an affidavit, the burden shifts back to the defendant to show that the warrant is invalid. Russell, *supra.* Where the state cannot produce a valid warrant and affidavit it must justify the search on other grounds. Russell.

TIP TO THE BENCH: The decision of when to hold a motion to suppress is within the discretion of the trial court. The hearing can be held pre-trial or when an objection is made to the admission of evidence. Calloway v. State, 743 S.W.2d 645 (Tex. Crim. App. 1988).

The decision whether to hold the hearing outside the presence of the jury also rests in the discretion of the trial court subject to the interests of justice. Texas Rules of Evidence Rule 104.

It is within the trial court's discretion to grant the State's request to reopen a motion-to-suppress hearing to supplement the record with additional testimony, outside the jury's presence, even over the objection of the defendant. Black v. State, 362 S.W.3d 626 (Tex. Crim. App. 2012).

Upon the request of the losing party on a motion to suppress evidence, the trial court shall state its essential findings. By "essential findings," it is meant that the trial court must make findings of fact and conclusions of law adequate to provide an appellate court with a basis upon which to review the trial court's application of the law to the facts. State v. Cullen, 195 S.W.3d 696 (Tex. Crim. App. 2006).

PRACTICE TIP: TRCP 297, cited in Cullen, provides that the trial court shall file its findings of fact and conclusions of law within twenty days after a timely request is filed. It further provides that the court shall cause a copy of its findings and conclusions to be mailed to each party in the suit. The findings and conclusions need to be recorded in some way, whether written out and filed by the trial court, or stated on the record at the hearing. A trial court's ruling on a motion to suppress evidence is reviewed on appeal under a bifurcated standard of review. Carmouche v. State, 10 S.W.3d 323 (Tex. Crim. App. 2000).

The appeals court gives almost total deference to the trial court's rulings on questions of historical fact and application of law to fact questions that turn on an evaluation of credibility and demeanor. However, a trial court's rulings on mixed questions of law and fact are reviewed de novo when they do not turn on the credibility and demeanor of the witnesses. Johnson v. State, 68 S.W.3d 644 (Tex. Crim. App. 2002).

Where the trial court's written findings and conclusions of law are ambiguous and lack a credibility determination, an appellate court can remand the case for supplemental findings. State v. Mendoza, 365 S.W.3d 666 (Tex. Crim. App. 2012).

§2:61 Form: Motion to Suppress Physical Evidence (Search Without Warrant)

See our companion book *Texas Criminal Forms* (James Publishing) Form 2-2.

§2:62 Art. 38.23 Jury Charge

Article 38.23 provides that evidence obtained in violation of the Constitution or laws of the United States or Texas may not be admitted in a criminal case. The statute also provides that a jury instruction should be submitted if a fact issue is raised about whether such a violation has occurred. The jury instruction requires the jury to disregard evidence that it finds was obtained in violation of the United States or Texas Constitution or laws. Hamal v. State, 390 S.W.3d 302 (Tex. Crim. App. 2012); Robinson v. State, 377 S.W.3d 712 (Tex. Crim. App. 2012).

To be entitled to an Article 38.23 jury instruction, three predicates must be met: (1) the evidence heard by the jury must raise an issue of fact; (2) the evidence on that fact must be affirmatively contested; and (3) the contested factual issue must be material to the lawfulness of the challenged conduct. Hamal, 390 S.W.3d at 306; Robinson, 377 S.W.3d at 719.

When a disputed, material issue of fact is successfully raised, the terms of the statute are mandatory, and the jury must be instructed accordingly. Evidence to justify an Article 38.23(a) instruction can derive from any source, no matter whether strong, weak, contradicted, unimpeached, or unbelievable. But it must, in any event, raise a *factual* dispute about how the evidence was obtained. Where the issue raised by the evidence at trial does *not* involve controverted historical facts, but only the proper application of the law to undisputed facts, that issue is properly left to the determination of the trial court. Robinson, 377 S.W.3d at 719.

Under CCP Art. 38.23, the defendant is entitled to a jury charge where there has been a factual issue raised as to whether the warrantless search was supported by adequate probable cause. The charge should instruct the jury that they should suppress the fruits of the search if they find it to be illegal. Coleman v. State, 45 S.W.3d 175 (Tex. App.—Houston [1st Dist.] 2001, *pet. ref'd*); Stone v. State, 703 S.W.2d 652 (Tex. Crim. App. 1986).

A defendant who moves for suppression under Art. 38.23 due to the violation of a statute has the burden of producing evidence of a statutory violation. Only when this burden is met does the State bear a burden to prove compliance. State v. Robinson, 334 S.W.3d 776, 779 (Tex. Crim. App. 2011).

Searches conducted in objectively reasonable reliance on binding appellate precedent are not subject to the Fourth Amendment exclusionary rule. Davis v. U.S., 564 U.S. 229, 131 S.Ct. 2419, 180 L.Ed.2d 285 (2011).

But neither the Fourth Amendment exclusionary rule nor Article 38.23(a) of the Code of Criminal Procedure, requires the suppression of evidence that was not "obtained" as a result of some illegality. State v. Jackson, 464 S.W.3d 724, 731 (Tex. Crim. App. 2015).

Not every but/for product of police illegality will constitute evidence "obtained" from that illegality for either federal or state exclusionary rule purposes; evidence is not subject to suppression, in other words, "simply because it would not have come to light but for the illegal actions of the police. State v. Jackson, 464 S.W.3d at 731.

The temporal proximity of the arrest and confession, the presence of intervening circumstances, and, particularly, the purpose and flagrancy of the official misconduct" all must be considered. State v. Jackson, 464 S.W.3d at 731 (where the court found that independent observation of defendant's speeding attenuated the taint of illegal GPS tracking of his vehicle).

PRACTICE TIP: Although Texas has the statutory exclusionary rule contained in Art. 38.23, the State can use the Davis case to argue that the evidence was not "obtained" in violation of the law where legal precedent at the time of police conduct allowed the police action.

§2:70 Searches Conducted With Warrant

§2:71 Applicable Statutes

CCP Art. 18.01. Search warrant

> *(a) A "search warrant" is a written order, issued by a magistrate and directed to a peace officer, commanding him to search for any property or thing and to seize the same and bring it before such magistrate or commanding him to search for and photograph a child and to deliver to the magistrate any of the film exposed pursuant to the order.*
>
> *(b) No search warrant shall issue for any purpose in this state unless sufficient facts are first presented to satisfy the issuing magistrate that probable cause does in fact exist for its issuance. A*

sworn affidavit setting forth substantial facts establishing probable cause shall be filed in every instance in which a search warrant is requested. Except as provided by Article 18.011, the affidavit is public information if executed, and the magistrate's clerk shall make a copy of the affidavit available for public inspection in the clerk's office during normal business hours.

(b-1)(1) For purposes of this article, a magistrate may consider information communicated by telephone or other reliable electronic means in determining whether to issue a search warrant. The magistrate may examine an applicant for a search warrant and any person on whose testimony the application is based. The applicant or other person must be placed under oath before the examination.

(2) If an applicant for a search warrant attests to the contents of an affidavit submitted by reliable electronic means, the magistrate must acknowledge the attestation in writing on the affidavit. If the magistrate considers additional testimony or exhibits, the magistrate must:

(A) ensure that the testimony is recorded verbatim by an electronic recording device, by a court reporter, or in writing;

(B) ensure that any recording or reporter's notes are transcribed and that the transcription is certified as accurate and is preserved;

(C) sign, certify the accuracy of, and preserve any other written record; and

(D) ensure that the exhibits are preserved.

(3) An applicant for a search warrant who submits information as authorized by this subsection must prepare a proposed duplicate original of the warrant and must read or otherwise transmit its contents verbatim to the magistrate. A magistrate must enter into an original search warrant the contents of a proposed duplicate original that are read to the magistrate. If the applicant transmits the contents by reliable electronic means, the transmission received by the magistrate may serve as the original search warrant.

(4) The magistrate may modify a search warrant that is submitted as described by Subdivision (3). If the magistrate modifies the warrant, the magistrate must:

(A) transmit the modified version to the applicant by reliable electronic means; or

(B) file the modified original and direct the applicant to modify the proposed duplicate original accordingly.

(5) A magistrate who issues a search warrant for which information is provided by telephone or reliable electronic means must:

(A) sign the original documents;

(B) enter the date and time of issuance on the warrant; and

(C) transmit the warrant by reliable electronic means to the applicant or direct the applicant to sign the judge's name and enter the date and time on the duplicate original.

(6) Evidence obtained pursuant to a search warrant for which information was provided in accordance with this subsection is not subject to suppression on the ground that issuing the warrant in compliance with this subsection was unreasonable under the circumstances, absent a finding of bad faith.

(c) A search warrant may not be issued under Article 18.02(10) unless

the sworn affidavit required by Subsection (b) sets forth sufficient facts to establish probable cause: (1) that a specific offense has been committed, (2) that the specifically described property or items that are to be searched for or seized constitute evidence of that offense or evidence that a particular person committed that offense, and (3) that the property or items constituting evidence to be searched for or seized are located at or on the particular person, place, or thing to be searched. Except as provided by Subsections (d), (i), and (j), only a judge of a municipal court of record or a county court who is an attorney licensed by the State of Texas, a statutory county court judge, a district court judge, a judge of the Court of Criminal Appeals, including the presiding judge, a justice of the Supreme Court of Texas, including the chief justice, or a magistrate with jurisdiction over criminal cases serving a district court may issue warrants under Article 18.02(10).

(d) Only the specifically described property or items set forth in a search warrant issued under Subdivision (10) of Article 18.02 of this code or property, items or contraband enumerated in Subdivisions (1) through (9) or in Subdivision (12) of Article 18.02 of this code may be seized. A subsequent search warrant may be issued pursuant to Subdivision (10) of Article 18.02 of this code to search the same person, place, or thing subjected to a prior search under Subdivision (10) of Article 18.02 of this code only if the subsequent search warrant is issued by a judge of a district court, a court of appeals, the court of criminal appeals, or the supreme court.

(e) A search warrant may not be issued under Subdivision (10) of Article 18.02 of this code to search for and seize property or items that are not described in Subdivisions (1) through (9) of that article and that are located in an office of a newspaper, news magazine, television station, or radio station, and in no event may property or items not described in Subdivisions (1) through (9) of that article be legally seized in any search pursuant to a search warrant of an office of a newspaper, news magazine, television station, or radio station.

(f) A search warrant may not be issued pursuant to Article 18.021 of this code unless the sworn affidavit required by Subsection (b) of this article sets forth sufficient facts to establish probable cause:

(1) that a specific offense has been committed;

(2) that a specifically described person has been a victim of the offense;

(3) that evidence of the offense or evidence that a particular person committed the offense can be detected by photographic means; and

(4) that the person to be searched for and photographed is located at the particular place to be searched.

(g) A search warrant may not be issued under Subdivision (12), Article 18.02, of this code unless the sworn affidavit required by Subsection (b) of this article sets forth sufficient facts to establish probable cause that a specific felony offense has been committed and that the specifically described property or items that are to be searched for or seized constitute contraband as defined in Article 59.01 of this code and are located at or on the particular person, place, or thing to be searched.

(h) Except as provided by Subsection (i) of this article, a warrant under Subdivision (12), Article 18.02 of this code may only be issued by:

(1) a judge of a municipal court of record who is an attorney licensed by the state;

(2) a judge of a county court who is an attorney licensed by the state; or

(3) a judge of a statutory county court, district court, the court of criminal appeals, or the supreme court.

(i) In a county that does not have a judge of a municipal court of record who is an attorney licensed by the state, a county court judge who is an attorney licensed by the state, or a statutory county court judge, any magistrate may issue a search warrant under Subdivision (10) or Subdivision (12) of Article 18.02 of this code. This subsection is not applicable to a subsequent search warrant under Subdivision (10) of Article 18.02 of this code.

(j) Any magistrate who is an attorney licensed by this state may issue a search warrant under Article 18.02(10) to collect a blood specimen from a person who:

(1) is arrested for an offense under Section 49.04, 49.045, 49.05, 49.06, 49.065, 49.07, or 49.08, Penal Code; and

(2) refuses to submit to a breath or blood alcohol test.

Art. 18.02. GROUNDS FOR ISSUANCE.

(a) A search warrant may be issued to search for and seize:

(1) property acquired by theft or in any other manner which makes its acquisition a penal offense;

(2) property specially designed, made, or adapted for or commonly used in the commission of an offense;

(3) arms and munitions kept or prepared for the purposes of insurrection or riot;

(4) weapons prohibited by the Penal Code;

(5) gambling devices or equipment, altered gambling equipment, or gambling paraphernalia;

(6) obscene materials kept or prepared for commercial distribution or exhibition, subject to the additional rules set forth by law;

(7) a drug, controlled substance, immediate precursor, chemical precursor, or other controlled substance property, including an apparatus or paraphernalia kept, prepared, or manufactured in violation of the laws of this state;

(8) any property the possession of which is prohibited by law;

(9) implements or instruments used in the commission of a crime;

(10) property or items, except the personal writings by the accused, constituting evidence of an offense or constituting evidence tending to show that a particular person committed an offense;

(11) persons;

(12) contraband subject to forfeiture under Chapter 59 of this code; or

(13) electronic customer data held in electronic storage, including the contents of and records and other information related to a wire communication or electronic communication held in electronic storage; or

(14) a cellular telephone or other wireless communications device, subject to Article 18.0215.

(b) For purposes of Subsection (a)(13), "electronic communication," "electronic storage," and "wire communication" have the meanings assigned by Article 18.20, and "electronic customer data" has the meaning assigned by Article 18.21.

CCP Art. 18.03. Search warrant may order arrest

If the facts presented to the magistrate under Article 18.02 of this chapter also establish the existence of probable cause that a person has committed some offense under the laws of this state, the search warrant may, in addition, order the arrest of such person.

Art. 18.04. Contents of Warrant

A search warrant issued under this chapter shall be sufficient if it contains the following requisites:

(1) that it run in the name of "The State of Texas";

(2) that it identify, as near as may be, that which is to be seized and name or describe, as near as may be, the person, place, or thing to be searched;

(3) that it command any peace officer of the proper county to search forthwith the person, place, or thing named; [and]

(4) that it be dated and signed by the magistrate; and

(5) that the magistrate's name appear in clearly legible handwriting or in typewritten form with the magistrate's signature.

Tex. Code Crim. Pro. Art. 18.065. EXECUTION OF WARRANT ISSUED BY DISTRICT JUDGE FOR DNA SPECIMEN.

(a) A warrant issued by the judge of a district court under Article 18.02(10) to collect a DNA specimen from a person for the purpose of connecting that person to an offense may be executed in any county in this state.

(b) This article does not apply to a warrant issued by a justice of the peace, judge, or other magistrate other than a judge of a district court.

A search warrant is defined in CCP Art. 18.01 as "a written order, issued by a magistrate and directed to a peace officer." State v. Toone, 872 S.W.2d 750 (Tex. Crim. App. 1994).

The Fourth Amendment imposes three requirements for searches and seizures conducted pursuant to a warrant:

- Warrant must be issued by a neutral and detached magistrate
- Officers seeking a search warrant must demonstrate to the magistrate probable cause to believe that the evidence sought is pertinent to the case
- Warrant must particularly describe the thing(s) to be seized as well as the place to be searched

Dalia v. United States, 441 U.S. 238, 99 S.Ct.1682, 60 L.Ed.2d 177 (1979).

A search warrant may not be procured lawfully by the use of illegally obtained information. Brown v. State, 605 S.W.2d 572 (Tex. Crim. App. 1980).

Where police officers obtain a valid search warrant from information gained independently of that gained from an earlier illegal entry of a premises, the fruits gained by the serving of the valid warrant will be admissible in a subsequent trial under the Fourth Amendment. Murray v. United States, 487 U.S. 533, 108 S.Ct. 2529, 101 L.Ed.2d 472 (1988).

Plain view evidence (evidence connected with a crime that does not consist of fruits, instrumentalities, or contraband) can be properly seized when found during the execution of a search warrant, even if it is not specifically named in the warrant. Joseph v. State, 807 S.W.2d 303 (Tex. Crim. App. 1991).

If the state has obtained a valid search warrant it does not need the suspect's consent to search. Therefore, the implied consent law does not offer greater protection than the Fourth Amendment, and police may obtain a search warrant for a DWI suspect's blood. Beeman v. State, 86 S.W.3d 613 (Tex. Crim. App. 2002).

TIP TO THE PROSECUTION: A judge may seal a search warrant affidavit for 31 days (with one 30-day extension) if the state shows a compelling state interest in insuring the safety of an individual or guarding wiretap information. See Tex Code Crim. Pro. art. 18.011.

When a trial court is determining probable cause to support the issuance of a search warrant, there are no credibility determinations to be made; rather, the trial court is constrained to the four corners of the affidavit. State v. McLain, 337 S.W.3d 268 (Tex. Crim. App. 2011).

Accordingly, when an appellate court reviews a magistrate's decision to issue a warrant, it applies a highly deferential standard because of the constitutional preference for searches to be conducted pursuant to a warrant as opposed to a warrantless search. As long as the magistrate had a substantial basis for concluding that probable cause existed, the appellate court will uphold the magistrate's probable cause determination. McLain.

Property seized under a warrant will not be excluded from evidence unless there is a causal connection between an unlawful seizure and the subsequent search of the property. State v. Powell, 306 S.W.3d 761 (Tex. Crim. App. 2010).

§2:72 Who May Issue Search Warrants

CCP Art. 18.01 specifies that search warrants shall be issued by a "magistrate."

CCP Art. 2.09 specifies what persons are considered to be magistrates under Texas law.

CCP Art. 18.01 (c) specifies that an evidentiary search warrant under CCP Art. 18.02 (10) can only be issued by judges of statutory county courts, district courts, the Court of Criminal Appeals, the Supreme Court; and by a judge of a municipal court or county court who is an attorney licensed by the state.

CCP Art. 18.01 (d) specifies that subsequent evidentiary search warrants can only be issued by a judge of a district court, the court of appeals, the court of criminal appeals or the supreme court.

A district judge may sign search warrants for execution in any county in the state. Green v. State, 880 S.W.2d 198 (Tex.App.—Texarkana 1994, *no pet.*).

A search warrant may not be issued by a statutory county court judge for execution in a different county. Sanchez v. State, 365 S.W.3d 681 (Tex. Crim. App. 2012).

The good faith exception to the exclusionary rule as contained in CCP Art. 38.23 (b) will allow the admission of evidence seized under an unsigned warrant where the warrant contained probable cause and was unsigned because of a magistrate's oversight. Dunn v. State, 951 S.W.2d 478 (Tex. Crim. App. 1997).

§2:73 Requirements of Affidavit

The Code of Criminal Procedure does not limit the class of individuals who can file an affidavit for a search warrant. The affidavit may be filed by anyone, including a peace officer whose jurisdiction does not include the premises to be searched. Dickey v. State, 816 S.W.2d 832 (Tex. App.—Eastland 1991, *no pet.*).

Affidavits for search warrants must be tested and interpreted by magistrates and courts in a common sense and realistic fashion. United States v. Ventresca, 380 U.S. 102, 85 S.Ct. 741, 13 L.Ed.2d 684 (1965); Barnes v. State, 876 S.W.2d 316 (Tex. Crim. App. 1994).

A magistrate is permitted to draw reasonable inferences from the facts and circumstances alleged in the affidavit. Ramos v. State, 934 S.W.2d 358 (Tex. Crim. App. 1996).

Courts must interpret affidavits and warrants in

a common sense and realistic fashion and avoid hypertechnical analysis. Davis v. State, 202 S.W.3d 149 (Tex. Crim. App. 2006).

Where failures in the affidavit result in a failure to allege how the conduct cited could result in a violation of the law, the affidavit fails to set forth probable cause. Hall v. State, 795 S.W.2d 195 (Tex. Crim. App. 1990) (where the affidavit failed to show how the defendant's possession of a rifle would constitute a crime on his part).

The affidavit is important because it serves as a mechanism by which a responsible public officer's integrity is ensured by making the affiant legally responsible for any statements of fact relied upon by the magistrate who issues the warrant. Reese v. State, 712 S.W.2d 131 (Tex. Crim. App. 1986), *supra*.

A document must be sworn to before it can be said to constitute an affidavit. This is generally done in the "jurat," which is not in and of itself a part of the affidavit. Reese v. State.

An affidavit is sufficient where it is sworn to in front of a notary public rather than the magistrate who issued the warrant. Hughes v. State, 334 S.W.3d 379 (Tex.App.—Amarillo, 2011, *no pet.*).

An oath for an affidavit may be administered over the telephone and will support a search warrant and the related seizure of evidence. Clay v. State, 382 S.W.3d 465, 470 (Tex.App.—Waco, 2012, *no pet.*) (where the affidavit was then faxed to the judge).

The failure to sign a search warrant affidavit does not, by itself, invalidate the warrant if other evidence proves that the affiant personally swore to the truth of the facts in the affidavit before the issuing magistrate. Smith v. State, 207 S.W.3d 787 (Tex. Crim. App. 2006).

When the jurat is facially defective, the fact that it was properly sworn to may be shown by other evidence. Reese v. State.

A warrant may incorporate an affidavit by reference even when they are not on the same instrument, but two instruments stapled together. Reese. Where the warrant incorporates the affidavit by reference and thus creates a single document containing both instruments, the contents of both documents will be examined to determine if both are sufficient under law. Reese.

Generally, incorporating the appendices to an affidavit by reference would be preferred. Barnes v. State, 876 S.W.2d 316 (Tex. Crim. App. 1994). However, where the evidence at the suppression hearing shows that the issuing magistrate essentially considered the attached appendices as part and parcel of the warrant affidavit, the appendices are physically attached to the affidavit, and the matter contained therein is an obvious continuation of that paragraph of the affidavit setting forth the basis for probable cause, the attachments will be considered part of the affidavit. Barnes.

§2:74 Probable Cause Requirement

CCP Art. 18.01 specifies that a sworn affidavit setting forth substantial facts establishing probable cause shall be filed in every instance in which a search warrant is requested.

Under both the Fourth Amendment and Art. I, §9 of the Texas Constitution, an arrest or search warrant may only be issued upon a showing of probable cause, supported by oath or affirmation. Reese v. State, 712 S.W.2d 131 (Tex. Crim. App. 1986).

An affidavit in support of a search warrant must allege substantial facts establishing probable cause to believe that the items in question would be found at the identified place. State v. McLain, 337 S.W.3d 268 (Tex. Crim. App. 2011).

Probable cause sufficient to support a search warrant exists if the facts contained within the four corners of the affidavit and the reasonable inferences drawn therefrom justify the magistrate's conclusion that the object of the search is probably on the premises at the time of issuance. McLain.

The "totality of the circumstances" test applies to analysis for the determination of probable cause for search warrants under the Fourth Amendment. Illinois v. Gates, 462 U.S. 213, 103 S.Ct. 2317, 76 L.Ed.2d 527 (1983); Bower v. State, 769 S.W.2d 887 (Tex. Crim. App. 1989). The same test also applies to search warrant analysis under Art. I, §9 of the Texas Constitution. Bower.

Probable cause exists when, under the totality of the circumstances, there is a fair probability that contraband or evidence of a crime will be found at the specified location. It is a flexible and non-demanding standard. McLain.

A magistrate's decision to issue a search warrant will be upheld on appeal where the magistrate had a substantial basis for concluding that a search would uncover evidence of wrongdoing. On appeal the magistrate's decision is reviewed under this deferential standard of review, rather than *de novo*, because of the Fourth Amendment's strong preference for searches conducted pursuant to a warrant. Illinois v. Gates, *supra*; Moreno v. State, 415 S.W.3d 284 (Tex. Crim. App. 2013).

The adoption of the Gates test does not dispense with the necessity of examining the traditional "two prongs" of an affidavit to determine if they set forth probable cause. Rather, it removes their talismanic quality and requires an examination of the affidavit as a whole. Hall v. State, 795 S.W.2d 195 (Tex. Crim. App. 1990).

As a practical matter, one must approach the probable cause analysis of an affidavit in the same manner as under the Aguilar test. However, the final step in the analysis is now to demonstrate how the failures in the affidavit affect the overall reliability of the probable cause determination. Illinois v. Gates, *supra*.

The reliability of the affiant and his sources of information are part of the totality of the circumstances that a magistrate should evaluate in making a probable cause determination. Jaben v. United States, 381 U.S. 214, 85 S.Ct. 1365, 14 L.Ed.2d 345 (1965); Johnson v. State, 803 S.W.2d 272 (Tex. Crim. App. 1990).

Texas allows hearsay on hearsay to form the evidentiary basis for a warrant, so long as there is a substantial basis for crediting the hearsay at each level. Hall, *supra*.

A warrant is not invalid merely because the officer failed to state the obvious in the affidavit. Lagrone v. State, 742 S.W.2d 659 (Tex. Crim. App.1987).

A magistrate is entitled to recognize that a police officer is qualified to make certain observations related to the scope of his employment. Davis v. State, 202 S.W.3d 149 (Tex. Crim. App. 2006) (where the affidavit recited that a patrol officer recognized "the strong chemical odor he has associated with the manufacture of methamphetamine").

Neither federal nor Texas law defines precisely what degree of probability will suffice to establish probable cause, but that probability cannot be based on mere conclusory statements of an affiant's belief. An affiant must present an affidavit that allows the magistrate to independently determine probable cause, and the magistrate's actions cannot be a mere ratification of the bare conclusions of others. Rodriguez v. State, 232 S.W.3d 55. 61 (Tex. Crim. App. 2007).

Reviewing courts must give great deference to the magistrate's probable-cause determination. McLain.

§2:75 Sources of Information Recited in Affidavit

A magistrate is entitled to rely on source information supplied by an average citizen without corroboration since, unlike many police informants, they are much less likely to produce false or untrustworthy information. Jaben v. United States, 381 U.S. 214, 85 S.Ct. 1365, 14 L.Ed.2d 345 (1965); Johnson v. State, 803 S.W.2d 272 (Tex. Crim. App. 1990); Marquez v. State, 725 S.W.2d 217 (Tex. Crim. App. 1987).

The above rule applies to law enforcement officers. The magistrate may rely on the affidavit of a police officer based on his knowledge or the knowledge of other officers. Jaben v. United States, *supra*; Marquez, *supra*.

A reviewing magistrate may rely on the affidavit of a police officer based on his knowledge or the knowledge of other officers because they are plainly a reliable basis for a warrant. United States v. Ventresca, 380 U.S. 102, 85 S.Ct. 741, 13 L.Ed.2d 684 (1965); Johnson, *supra*.

The reliability of the affiant and his sources of information are part of the totality of the circumstances that a magistrate should evaluate in making a probable cause determination. Jaben v. United States, 381 U.S. 214, 85 S.Ct. 1365, 14 L.Ed.2d 345 (1965); Johnson v. State, 803 S.W.2d 272 (Tex. Crim. App. 1990).

When a probable cause affidavit specifies a named informant as supplying the information upon which probable cause is based, the affidavit must be sufficiently detailed to suggest direct knowledge on the informant's part. Wilkerson v. State, 726 S.W.2d 542 (Tex. Crim. App. 1986); Matamoros v. State, 901 S.W.2d 470 (Tex. Crim. App. 1995).

The issue in cases where a search warrant affidavit relies on information supplied by a confidential informant is whether the magistrate had a substantial basis for crediting the informant's hearsay. State v. Duarte, 389 S.W.3d 349 (Tex. Crim. App. 2012).

Tips from anonymous or first-time confidential informants of unknown reliability must be coupled with facts from which an inference may be drawn that the informant is credible or that his information is reliable. State v. Duarte, at 358.

A first-time informant's hearsay can be credited: if the tip is corroborated; if it is a statement against penal interest; if it is consistent with information provided by other informants; if it is a detailed first-hand observation; or if it is coupled with an accurate prediction of the subject's future behavior. State v. Duarte, at 358-59.

An informant's tip should be corroborated through the independent investigation of the police or through other sources of information. Trevino v. State, 875 S.W.2d 373 (Tex.App.—Corpus Christi 1994, *no pet.*).

Relying on information received from an informant is acceptable so long as the informant's statement is reasonably corroborated by other matters within the officer's knowledge. Knight v. State, 814 S.W.2d 545 (Tex.App.—Houston [1st Dist.] 1991, *no pet.*).

However, when a probable cause affidavit specifies a named informant as supplying the information upon which probable cause is based, the affidavit is sufficient if it includes enough detail to suggest direct knowledge on the informant's part. In this situation, the issuing magistrate does not have to rely upon a presumption of reliability (as in the case of an unnamed or confidential informant), but is able to assess the named informant's reliability based upon the details provided. State v. Elrod, 538 S.W.3d 551, 561-2 (Tex. Crim. App. 2017).

The affidavit is not rendered insufficient merely because it alleges an informant has reported that a substance he has seen is heroin, marijuana, or other contraband without showing the informant's qualifications to recognize the substance. Capistran v. State, 759 S.W.2d 121 (Tex. Crim. App.1988); Carroll v. State, 911 S.W.2d 210 (Tex.App.—Austin 1995, *no pet.*).

The observations of police officers can be an important factor in deciding if sufficient probable cause is stated in the search warrant affidavit. Moreno v. State, 415 S.W.3d 284, 287 (Tex. Crim. App. 2013).

Where law enforcement officers are able to corroborate the information given by an anonymous informant, a magistrate is justified in concluding that the anonymous informant had some familiarity with the defendant's affairs. Where the magistrate could reasonably infer that the anonymous informer had some familiarity with the defendant and his affairs, the magistrate could further, and reasonably, conclude that the informer's tip, although perhaps insufficient in itself to establish probable cause to search, was nevertheless a circumstance to be considered, along with all of the other circumstances, in the determination of whether probable cause existed. Flores v. State, 319 S.W.3d 697 (Tex. Crim. App. 2010).

Corroboration of public facts alone will not suffice to establish the reliability of an anonymous informant whose credibility is unknown. Knight, *supra.*

For further information on the legal requirements for corroboration of sources of probable cause information, *see* §§1:51-1:55.

§2:76 Age of Information Recited in Affidavit

The facts stated in a search affidavit must be so closely related to the time of the issuance of the warrant that a finding of probable cause is justified. State v. McLain, 337 S.W.3d 268 (Tex. Crim. App. 2011).

Where the totality of the circumstances contained within the four corners of the affidavit lead to a reasonable inference that the observations stated in the affidavit occurred on the same date that the offense was alleged to have occurred, there can be adequate information stated to support a finding of probable cause. State v. Jordan, 342 S.W.3d 565 (Tex. Crim. App. 2011).

Under the totality-of-the-circumstances standard set out in Jordan, a search warrant affidavit in a DWI case is not sufficient to show probable cause where there could have been a 25-hour gap between the time the officer first stopped the defendant and the time he obtained a search warrant for the defendant's blood. Crider v. State, 352 S.W.3d 704 (Tex. Crim. App. 2011).

There is no set time limit on how old information contained in an affidavit may be. Bower v. State, 769 S.W.2d 887 (Tex. Crim. App. 1989).

The proper method to determine whether the facts supporting a search warrant have become stale is to examine, in light of the criminal activity involved, the time elapsing between the occurrence of the events set out in the affidavit and the time the search warrant was issued. Rowell v. State, 14 S.W.3d 806 (Tex.App.—Houston [1st Dist.] 2000), *aff'd*, 66 S.W.3d 279 (Tex. Crim. App. 2001).

Mechanically counting days is of little assistance in the determination of staleness; rather, common sense and reasonableness must prevail, with considerable deference given to the magistrate's judgment. State v. Toone, 823 S.W.2d 744 (Tex. App.—Dallas 1992, *pet. granted, affirmed at* 872 S.W.2d 750).

Facts attested to in an affidavit supporting a search warrant must have occurred recently enough to justify a finding of probable cause at the time of issuance. Guerra v. State, 860 S.W.2d 609 (Tex. App.—Corpus Christi 1993, *no pet.*).

An affidavit that stated that an informant had observed the suspect in possession of marijuana at the named location "within the past seventy-two hours," has been found to be sufficient. Capistran v. State, 759 S.W.2d 121 (Tex. Crim. App. 1988).

Where the evidence showed that the information relied on was furnished to police between November 7 and November 10, and the warrant issued on November 13, the information relied on was not too "stale." Hafford v. State, 989 S.W.2d 439 (Tex. App.—Houston [1st Dist.] No. 1-98-0503-CR March 25, 1999).

In cases where the search warrant affidavit indicates an on-going offense or course of conduct, the passage of time between observation and warrant is a less significant factor. Morris v. State, 62 S.W.3d 817 (Tex.App.—Waco 2001, *no pet.*), Jones v. State, 364 S.W.3d 854 (Tex. Crim. App. 2012).

§2:77 Description of Place to Be Searched

One of the specific commands of the Fourth Amendment is that no warrant shall issue except one "particularly describing the place to be searched." Long v. State, 132 S.W.3d 443 (Tex. Crim. App. 2004).

The constitutional objectives of requiring a "particular" description of the place to be searched include: 1) ensuring that the officer searches the right place; 2) confirming that probable cause is, in fact, established for the place described in the warrant; 3) limiting the officer's discretion and narrowing the scope of his search; 4) minimizing the danger of mistakenly searching the person or property of an innocent bystander or property owner; and 5) informing the owner of the officer's authority to search that specific location. Long; Bonds v. State, 403 S.W.2d 867, 874-5 (Tex. Crim. App. 2013).

If a search warrant/affidavit authorizes the search of a residence and its "premises," then officers may generally search outlying structures within the curtilage of that residence. Long.

However, a warrant to enter a nearby business establishment that is open to the public does not give officers authority to enter the proprietor's home absent separate probable cause and authority to enter the home. Long.

A search warrant is considered sufficient if it identifies, as near as may be, that which is to be seized and names or describes, as near as may be, the person, place, or thing to be searched. CCP Art. 18.04; Rios v. State, 901 S.W.2d 704 (Tex.App.—San Antonio 1995, *no pet.*).

The test for sufficiency of the description of the place to be searched is whether the officer executing the warrant could, with reasonable effort, locate the premises and distinguish it from others in the community. Bonds, 403 S.W.3d at 875. and if the deficiencies, if any, in the description do not give rise to a reasonable probability that mistaken execution will take place at an unintended site. Olivas v. State, 631 S.W.2d 553 (Tex.App.—El Paso 1982, *no pet.*).

The particularity requirement is related to the probable cause requirement in that it enables the magistrate to determine whether probable cause exists for the requested search. However, the Fourth Amendment does not require perfection in the warrant's description of the place to be searched. Bonds, 403 S.W.3d at 875.

A warrant may be invalid upon its issuance because its description of the place to be searched or the person or things to be seized is insufficient on its face. Alternatively, it may prove insufficiently particular as a result of subsequently discovered facts. Bonds, 403 S.W.3d at 875.

The description must also protect innocent parties from a reasonable probability of a mistaken execution of a defective warrant. Bridges v. State, 574 S.W.2d 560 (Tex. Crim. App. 1978).

The primary objectives of the descriptive averment are to:

- Direct the executing officer to the place to be searched
- Confirm that probable cause has focused on the place named in the warrant
- Limit the officer's discretion and narrow the scope of his search
- Minimize the danger of mistakenly executing the warrant on the unintended property of an innocent owner or resident
- Apprize the owner or resident of the officer's authority to search his premises

Taylor v. State, 974 S.W.2d 851 (Tex.App.—Houston [14th Dist.] 1998, *no pet.*).

Where a warrant describes a multi-unit dwelling, the description must contain sufficient guidelines to apprise the officers executing the warrant of the particular unit to be searched. Morales v. State, 640 S.W.2d 273 (Tex. Crim. App. 1982); Jones v. State, 914 S.W.2d 675 (Tex.App.—Amarillo 1996, *no pet.*).

Where the affidavit in support of a search warrant describes the location of the property to be searched in such descriptive detail as to give a reasonably prudent law enforcement officer affirmative confidence in continuing the execution of the warrant, the affidavit overrides any incorrect numerical address. State v. James, 848 S.W.2d 258 (Tex.App.—Beaumont 1993, *no pet.*).

The identity of the person named as the occupant of the apartment controls over any misstated apartment number. Mansell v. State, 756 S.W.2d 95 (Tex.App.—San Antonio 1988, *pet. ref'd*).

The description contained in the affidavit limits and controls the description contained in the warrant. Madrid v. State, 595 S.W.2d 106 (Tex. Crim. App. 1979); Rios, *supra.*

When the affidavit is made a part of the warrant, the description of the premises contained in the affidavit can be used to aid the description found in the warrant. Phoenix v. State, 488 S.W.2d 759 (Tex. Crim. App.1972); Rios, *supra.*

However, technical discrepancies in the descriptive portions of a search warrant will not automatically void a warrant. Bridges, *supra.*

Where a warrant issues to search a fixed premises, a particular description of vehicles in the affidavit is necessary to search the vehicles at the premises. State v. Barnett, 788 S.W.2d 572 (Tex. Crim. App. 1990).

An automobile not on the premises to be searched at the time of the issuance of the search warrant cannot be searched under the authority of the search warrant as issued. Barnett, *supra.*

The affidavit need not set out separate probable cause recitations to search the described vehicles; it is enough that the affidavit set out probable cause to search the premises at which the vehicles are located. Hughes v. State, 843 S.W.2d 591 (Tex. Crim. App. 1992).

§2:78 Description of Owner or Occupant of Premises

A search warrant is considered sufficient if it identifies, as near as may be, that which is to be seized and names or describes, as near as may be, the person, place, or thing to be searched. CCP Art. 18.04. Rios v. State, 901 S.W.2d 704 (Tex.App.—San Antonio 1995, *no pet.*).

The identity of the person named as the occupant of the apartment controls over any misstated apartment number. Jones v. State, 914 S.W.2d 675 (Tex.App.—Amarillo 1996, *no pet.*).

It is not necessary to include the name of the offender in the search warrant. Walthall v. State, 594 S.W.2d 74 (Tex. Crim. App. 1980). If the name of the offender is unknown, it is sufficient to describe him in the affidavit and warrant. Walthall.

If the identity of the offender is unknown, it is sufficient to aver that the premises are in control of "parties unknown to the affiant." Walthall.

§2:79 Description of Property to Be Seized

The Fourth Amendment requires that those searches deemed necessary should be as limited as possible. The specific evil that limitation targets is not that of intrusion per se, but of a general, exploratory rummaging in a person's belongings. The Fourth Amendment is intended to preclude general warrants by requiring a particular description of the things to be seized. United States v. Blake, 868 F.3d 960, 973 (Eleventh Circuit, 2017)(where the court found that a warrant for Facebook data was overbroad, by not being limited to a particular time period and communications with particular classes of persons).

A search warrant is considered sufficient if it identifies, as near as may be, that which is to be seized and names or describes, as near as may be, the person, place, or thing to be searched. CCP Art. 18.04. Rios v. State, 901 S.W.2d 704 (Tex.App.—San Antonio 1995, *no pet.*).

An item to be searched for with a search warrant must be described as nearly as may be possible. Gonzalez v. State, 577 S.W.2d 226 (Tex. Crim. App. 1979). The requirements for a sufficiently particular description can vary according to the thing being described. Gonzalez.

A warrant may be sufficient with only a generic description, if more specific description of the thing to be seized is unavailable. Winkfield v. State, 792 S.W.2d 727 (Tex.App.—Corpus Christi 1990, *pet. ref'd*).

Where a search warrant affidavit mentioned a safe as part of the basis for probable cause, police were allowed to seize the safe under the warrant even though it was not listed among the items to be seized. State v. Powell, 306 S.W.3d 761 (Tex. Crim. App. 2010).

Furthermore, assuming that the seizure of the safe by the police violated the defendant's Fourth Amendment possessory rights in the safe, there was no causal connection between any unlawful seizure of the safe and the otherwise lawful search of the safe resulting in the acquisition of the illegal property. In other words, the otherwise lawful search of the safes was "wholly unrelated" to any prior unlawful seizure of the safe because the police were going to search the safe even if they had not seized it. Powell.

The generic description " intoxicating liquors" is sufficiently particular for a warrant for alcoholic beverages. Gonzales v. State, *supra*. The description, "drugs or dangerous drugs . . . unlawfully kept and possessed," is sufficiently particular to allow a valid search warrant to issue. Gonzales.

An affidavit that is global in its description of the property to be seized, that is too encompassing and general, is defective and invalid. This is especially true where the things to be seized are books, records, cards, letters, receipts, lists, pictures etc. Stanford v. Texas, 379 U.S. 476, 85 S.Ct. 506, 13 L.Ed.2d 431 (1965) (where the description ". . . books, records, pamphlets, cards, receipts, lists, memoranda, pictures, recordings and other written instruments concerning the Communist Party in Texas" was found to be unconstitutionally intolerable). *See also*, Walthall v. State, 594 S.W.2d 74 (Tex. Crim. App. 1980).

The phrase, "all items of personal property commonly used in the commission of a criminal offense," is too broad and general to validly authorize a search. Walthall.

Blood is an item that may lawfully be seized under the authority of a search warrant under CCP Art 18.02 (10). Flores v. State, 871 S.W.2d 714 (Tex. Crim. App. 1993).

Under CCP Art. 18.02 (10) a warrant may lawfully issue ordering a person to give blood, saliva, and hair samples for testing and evidentiary comparison. Longoria v. State, 636 S.W.2d 521 (Tex. Crim. App. 1982).

§2:80 Misrepresentations in Affidavit

If an affirmative misrepresentation is knowingly included in a probable cause affidavit, and is material and necessary to establishing the probable cause, the warrant is rendered invalid under the Fourth Amendment. Franks v. Delaware, 438 U.S. 154, 98 S.Ct. 2674, 57 L.Ed.2d 667 (1978); Massey v. State, 933 S.W.2d 141 (Tex. Crim. App. 1996).

The burden is on the defendant to show by a

preponderance of the evidence that a falsehood in the affidavit was made knowingly, intentionally, or with reckless disregard for the truth. Janecka v. State, 937 S.W.2d 456 (Tex. Crim. App. 1996).

Where the defendant makes a substantial preliminary showing that a false statement made knowingly and intentionally, or with reckless disregard for the truth, was included by the affiant in the warrant affidavit, and if the allegedly false statement is necessary to the finding of probable cause, the Fourth Amendment requires that a hearing be held at the defendant's request. Dancy v. State, 728 S.W.2d 772 (Tex. Crim. App. 1987).

To mandate an evidentiary hearing, the challenger's attack must be more than conclusory and must be supported by more than a mere desire to cross-examine. There must be allegations of deliberate falsehood or of reckless disregard for the truth, and those allegations must be accompanied by an offer of proof. They should point out specifically the portion of the warrant affidavit that is claimed to be false, and they should be accompanied by a statement of supporting reasons. Affidavits or sworn or otherwise reliable statements of witnesses should be furnished, or their absence satisfactorily explained. Allegations of negligence or innocent mistake are insufficient. Cates v. State, 120 S.W.3d 352 (Tex. Crim. App. 2003).

The defendant must: (1) Allege deliberate falsehood or reckless disregard for the truth by the affiant, specifically pointing out the portion of the affidavit claimed to be false; (2) Accompany these allegations with an offer of proof stating the supporting reasons; and (3) Show that when the portion of the affidavit alleged to be false is excised from the affidavit, the remaining content is insufficient to support the issuance of the warrant. Ramsey v. State, 579 S.W.2d 920 (Tex. Crim. App. 1979); Cates.

Franks and Ramsey call for even more specific facts to be alleged than other more typical issues raised at a suppression hearing. Harris v. State, 227 S.W.3d 83 (Tex. Crim. App. 2007).

The first prong of the Franks/Ramsey test can be satisfied by alleging a deliberate falsehood by the affiant, specifically pointing out those portions of the affidavit claimed to be false, and identifying the specific reasons why this information is false in a motion. Cates.

Under the second prong of the Franks/Ramsey test, defense can make the required proof in a motion, in witness statements, or in an oral recitation as to the anticipated testimony of the witnesses. Cates.

The third prong can be met by examining the logical consequence of the defendant's proof under the first two prongs. Cates.

Nothing in our law requires the defendant to include a sworn affidavit in making a preliminary showing under Franks. Cates.

Mere conclusory statements in a pleading alleging lack of probable cause, defects in the search warrant and procurement of evidence by illegal means are insufficient to make a substantial preliminary showing as required by Franks. Dancy.

Unconstitutionally defective portions of a search warrant do not necessarily invalidate the entire warrant or taint all of the evidence seized pursuant to the warrant. If only certain portions of a search warrant are invalid, only the evidence gathered pursuant to the offending portions is tainted. Massey, *supra*.

A court reviewing a search warrant affidavit after false statements have been excised should not employ a heightened probable cause standard. Hyland v. State, ___ S.W.3d ___ at *4 (PD-0438-18, 2019 WL 2361502, June 5, 2019).

When portions of a search warrant affidavit have been excised, and a reviewing court re-examines the balance of the affidavit, the reviewing court should no longer give deference to the magistrate's initial probable cause determination—and should therefore abandon the usual substantial basis analysis—because the reviewing court is now examining a new, different affidavit. Hyland v. State, S.W.3d at *5.

In the event that the allegation of perjury or reckless disregard is established by the defendant by a preponderance of the evidence, and, with the affidavit's false material set to one side, the affidavit's remaining content is insufficient to establish probable cause, the search warrant must be voided and the fruits of the search excluded to the same extent as if probable cause was lacking on the face of the affidavit. Franks, *supra*; Dancy, *supra*.

PRACTICE TIP: When complaining of invalid portions of a search warrant, the defendant must identify the evidence seized pursuant to the allegedly invalid portions of the warrant. In failing to identify evidence that was seized pursuant to the complained of portion of the affidavit, the defendant will have failed to preserve the claim for review. Massey, supra.

A fabrication intended solely to obscure the identity of an informant for his or her protection is not the type of misrepresentation that offends the Fourth Amendment. Franks, *supra*; Janecka v. State, 937 S.W.2d 456 (Tex. Crim. App. 1996).

The Texas Court of Criminal Appeals has not extended the Franks rationale to omissions as well as false statements. Massey, *supra*.

Appellate courts review a trial court's decision on a Franks suppression issue under the same standard used for reviewing a probable cause deficiency, a mixed standard of review giving almost total deference to a trial court's rulings on questions of historical fact and application-of-law-to-fact questions that turn on an evaluation of credibility and demeanor while reviewing *de novo* application-of-law-to-fact questions that do not turn upon credibility and demeanor. Davis v. State, 144 S.W.3d 192 (Tex.App.—Fort Worth 2004, *pet. ref'd*) (*op. on reh'g*), citing Johnson v. State, 68 S.W.3d 644 (Tex. Crim. App. 2002).

§2:81 Misstatements, Errors and Omissions in Affidavits

A misstatement in an affidavit that is merely the result of simple negligence or inadvertence, as opposed to reckless disregard for the truth, will not render the warrant invalid based on it. Dancy v. State, 728 S.W.2d 772 (Tex. Crim. App. 1987).

Where the affiant omitted the criminal histories of his informants but corroborated their statements, and their statements were consistent with the peculiar facts of the offense as outlined in the affidavit and other evidence gathered during the investigation and discussed in the affidavit, the defendant was not able to show that the omissions were made intentionally or in reckless disregard of the truth, in an attempt to mislead the magistrate. Massey v. State, 933 S.W.2d 141 (Tex. Crim. App. 1996).

Where the officer-affiant recites information that was given to him incorrectly by his informant, he has not made the statement intentionally, knowingly or with reckless disregard for the truth. Jones v. State, 907 S.W.2d 850 (Tex.App.—Houston [1st Dist.] 1995).

Mere technical imprecision in the affidavit does not amount to a misrepresentation requiring the suppression of the warrant. Massey, *supra* (where the affidavit represented that injuries were caused to a certain body part of the victim while trial testimony showed that the injuries were in fact near that particular body part).

The Fourth Amendment's demand for a truthful showing of probable cause does not mean "truthful" in the sense that every fact recited in the warrant affidavit is necessarily correct, for probable cause may be founded upon hearsay and upon information received from informants, as well as upon information within the affiant's own knowledge that sometimes must be garnered hastily. It is to be "truthful" in the sense that the information put forth is believed or appropriately accepted by the affiant as true. Franks v. Delaware, 438 U.S. 154, 98 S.Ct. 2674, 57 L.Ed.2d 667 (1978).

Where the information material to the establishment of probable cause in the affidavit was substantially correct, there was no misrepresentation within the meaning of Franks. Janecka, *supra*.

An error in a search or arrest warrant, which the record shows is clearly a typographical error, is not the type of error that will vitiate the warrant. Rougeau v. State, 738 S.W.2d 651 (Tex. Crim. App. 1987) (where the typographical error showed the warrant to have been issued a year before the offense).

However, where the record reveals no evidence indicating that the date on the warrant is in error, the reviewing court will presume the warrant to be accurate. Green v. State, 799 S.W.2d 756 (Tex. Crim. App. 1990).

When a search warrant contains a typographical error in the description of the place to be searched and the warrant incorporates the supporting affidavit, which contains a correct description of the place to be searched, the trial court does not err in refusing to suppress the evidence seized during the search. Rios v. State, 901 S.W.2d 704 (Tex. App.—San Antonio 1995).

TIP TO THE PROSECUTION: Where the affidavit recites information which is a typographical error, it is mandatory to produce testimony at a hearing on a motion to suppress to establish the correct action and prove that the error was merely typographical.

Before a search may be justified on the basis of a partially tainted warrant affidavit, it must be clear that what remains after the tainted material has been excised still satisfies the probable cause standard. See McClintock v. State, 444 S.W.3d 15, 20 (Tex. Crim. App. 2014); Hyland v. State, ___ S.W.3d ___ at *6 (PD-0438-18, 2019 WL 2361502, June 5, 2019).

Ministerial violations of the search warrant statutes do not vitiate the search warrant in the absence of a showing of prejudice. Pecina v. State, 516 S.W.2d 401 (Tex. Crim. App. 1974); Roberts v. State, 963 S.W.2d 894 (Tex.App.—Texarkana 1998, *no pet.*).

§2:82 Search Warrants for Persons

CCP Art. 18.02(11) provides that a search warrant may issue for "persons."

The term "persons" in CCP Art. 18.02(11) refers to both the living and the dead. Ramos v. State, 934 S.W.2d 358 (Tex. Crim. App. 1996).

Officers must have a search warrant if they are seeking to arrest a suspect in the home of a third person, absent consent or exigent circumstances. Hudson v. State, 662 S.W.2d 957 (Tex. Crim. App. 1984); Steagald v. United States, 451 U.S. 204, 101 S.Ct. 1642, 68 L.Ed.2d 38 (1981).

A valid arrest warrant carries with it the implicit but limited authority to enter the residence of the person named in the warrant in order to execute that warrant. Payton v. New York, 445 U.S. 573, 100 S.Ct. 1371, 63 L.Ed.2d 639 (1980); Morgan v. State, 963 S.W.2d 201 (Tex.App.—Houston [14th Dist.] 1998).

Under Payton, officers executing an arrest warrant must have a reasonable belief that the suspect resides at the place to be entered and have reason to believe that the suspect is present at the time the warrant is executed. Morgan. If the suspect is a co-resident of the third party, then Steagald does not apply, and Payton allows both arrest of the subject of the arrest warrant and use of evidence found against the third party. Morgan.

§2:83 Evidentiary Search Warrants

Evidentiary search warrants are those which issue under CCP Art. 18.02(10) and allow searches for items ". . . constituting evidence of an offense or constituting evidence tending to show that a particular person committed an offense." Davis v. State, 831 S.W.2d 426 (Tex.App.—Austin 1992, *pet. ref'd*).

Mere evidence is evidence connected with a crime, but does not consist of fruits, instrumentalities, or contraband. Warden, Maryland Penitentiary v. Hayden, 387 U.S. 294, 87 S.Ct. 1642, 18 L.Ed.2d 782 (1967); Joseph v. State, 807 S.W.2d 303 (Tex. Crim. App. 1991).

Where a search warrant authorizes a search for evidence and also for instruments of the crime, the warrant is not an "evidentiary" warrant under Art. 18.02(10). State v. Young, 8 S.W.3d 695 (Tex. App.—Fort Worth 1999, *no pet.*).

Where the object of the search warrant is property that is prohibited by law, the seizure of the media in which the property is stored does not convert the warrant from a search warrant into an evidentiary search warrant. Elardo v. State, 163 S.W.3d 760 (Tex.App.—Texarkana 2005, *pet. ref'd*) (where the warrant authorized seizure of images of child pornography stored on computers and disks).

Under CCP Art. 18.01(c) an evidentiary search warrant may not be issued unless the sworn affidavit sets forth sufficient facts to establish probable cause that:

- A specific offense has been committed
- Specifically described property or items that are to be searched for or seized constitute evidence of that offense or evidence that a particular person committed that offense
- Property or items constituting evidence to be searched for or seized are located

at or on the particular person, place, or thing to be searched

Bower v. State, 769 S.W.2d 887 (Tex. Crim. App. 1989).

There must be a nexus between the item to be seized and the alleged criminal behavior. Warden v. Hayden, *supra.*

The scope of a search, during which "mere evidence" may be found, is restricted to the object of the search and the places in which there is probable cause to believe it may be found. United States v. Ross, 456 U.S. 798, 102 S.Ct. 2157, 72 L.Ed.2d 572 (1982).

Officers also may seize mere evidence when the objects discovered and seized are reasonably related to the offense under investigation and their discovery is made in the course of a good faith search conducted within the parameters of a valid search warrant. Warden v. Hayden, *supra*; Bower, *supra.*

Where the court can reasonably conclude that a defendant used the item in question to assist him in the commission of the offense, the item constitutes implements or instrumentalities of the crime and can be seized pursuant to a search warrant under CCP Art. 18.02(9). Howk v. State, 969 S.W.2d 46 (Tex.App.—Beaumont 1998, *no pet.*).

§2:84 Anticipatory Search Warrants

An "anticipatory search warrant" is a warrant based upon an affidavit showing probable cause that at some future time (but not presently) certain evidence of crime will be located at a specified place. State v. Toone, 872 S.W.2d 750 (Tex. Crim. App. 1994, fn. 1; citing Wayne R. Lafave, Search And Seizure §3.7 (c), at 94 (1987)). *See also,* Toone v. State, 823 S.W.2d 744 (Tex.App.—Dallas 1992); *see also* U.S. v. Grubbs, 547 U.S. 90, 126 S.Ct. 1494, 164 L.Ed.2d 195 (2006)

Anticipatory warrants are not different in principle from ordinary warrants. They require the magistrate to determine: (1) that it is now probable that (2) contraband, evidence of a crime or a fugitive *will* be on the described premises (3) when the warrant is executed. U.S. v. Grubbs.

For a conditioned anticipatory search warrant to comply with the Fourth Amendment's requirement of probable cause, two prerequisites of probability must be satisfied: it must be true not only that if the triggering condition occurs there is a fair probability that contraband or evidence of a crime will be found in a particular place, but also that there is probable cause to believe the triggering condition *will occur*. U.S. v. Grubbs.

The Fourth Amendment's particularity requirement does not include the conditions precedent to execution of a warrant; but rather requires only particular descriptions of the place to be searched and the person or things to be seized. U.S. v. Grubbs.

§2:85 Motions to Suppress Fruits of Search Warrant

Where the defendant challenges the probable cause for the arrest or search of the defendant and the state relies upon a warrant to establish the basis for the arrest or search, the state bears the burden of producing the warrant and affidavit for inspection by the court. Miller v. State, 736 S.W.2d 643 (Tex. Crim. App. 1987).

When a defendant challenges the validity of a search, and the State introduces a facially valid search warrant, the burden of proof is on the defendant to go forward with evidence to show the invalidity of the warrant. Johnson v. State, 803 S.W.2d 272 (Tex. Crim. App. 1990).

Where the state produces the warrant and affidavit for the inspection of the trial court, the burden to see that they are included in the record for appeal is on the defendant. Miller, *supra.*

PRACTICE TIP: Once the burden of proof shifts back to the defendant, be prepared to go forward with testimony in support of the motion. This could entail issuing subpoenas for law enforcement officers.

The Rules of Evidence do not apply to suppression hearings. This is because former Rule 1101(d)(4) that previously dictated to the contrary no longer exists. Granados v. State, 85 S.W.3d 217 (Tex. Crim. App. 2002).

Therefore, Rule 702 is not applicable at a suppression hearing. Hall v. State, 297 S.W.3d 294 (Tex. Crim. App. 2009).

In a pre-trial motion to suppress hearing, a trial court may rely upon any relevant, reliable, and credible information, even though it may be unsworn hearsay (in this case a police report found to be sufficiently reliable). The language of CCP Art. 28.01 is permissive, not restrictive, and allows for reports to be used. Ford v. State, 305 S.W.3d 530 (Tex. Crim. App. 2009).

If the defendant takes the stand at trial he may be impeached with his suppression hearing testimony if he testifies contrary. Nelson v. State, 607 S.W.2d 554 (Tex. Crim. App. 1980).

§2:85.1 Form: Motion to Suppress Physical Evidence (Search With Warrant)

See our companion book *Texas Criminal Forms* (James Publishing) Form 2-3.

§2:86 Subsequent Search Warrants

In 1995, CCP Art. 18.01(d) was amended to permit the issuance of subsequent search warrants. Furthermore, it allows application retroactive to warrants executed before the effective date of the act, which is not prohibited by the Texas Constitution. Ibarra v. State, 11 S.W.3d 189 (Tex. Crim. App. 1999).

A second search warrant may be conducted on a premises if the second warrant authorizes a search for items not specifically named in the first warrant. Ramos v. State, 934 S.W.2d 358 (Tex. Crim. App. 1996).

§2:90 Objections to Search Warrants

Objections to the use of the fruits of a search warrant at trial are as follows:

- Affidavit for the search warrant does not set forth probable cause for the search [CCP Art. 18.01; Reese v. State, 712 S.W.2d 131 (Tex. Crim. App. 1986]
- Affidavit for the search warrant is not properly sworn to by the affiant [CCP Art. 18.01; Reese v. State, 712 S.W.2d 131 (Tex. Crim. App. 1986)]
- Warrant is improper because it is based on an improperly dated affidavit [CCP Art. 18.04; Gonzales v. State, 577 S.W.2d 226(Tex. Crim. App. 1979)]
- Warrant itself is improperly dated [CCP Art. 18.04]
- Information in the affidavit attributed to a confidential informant is not sufficiently corroborated [CCP Art. 18.01; Trevino v. State, 875 S.W.2d 373 (Tex.App.—Corpus Christi 1994, *no pet.*)]
- Affidavit contains no recitation as to how the affiant learned the information he relates [Evans v. State, 530 S.W.2d 932 (Tex. Crim. App. 1975)]
- Affidavit contains no recitation as to how the informant came by the information he relates [Matamoros v. State, 901 S.W.2d 470 (Tex. Crim. App. 1995)]
- Information within the affidavit is stale and no longer states probable cause [Gonzales v. State, 577 S.W.2d 226(Tex. Crim. App. 1979)]
- Information in the affidavit was obtained through illegal means [CCP Art. 38.23; Brown v. State, 605 S.W.2d 572 (Tex. Crim. App. 1980)]
- Affiant is not reliable [Johnson v. State, 803 S.W.2d 272 (Tex. Crim. App. 1990)]
- Hearsay within the affidavit is not properly credited at each level [Hall v. State, 795 S.W.2d 195 (Tex. Crim. App. 1990)]
- Insufficient description of the place to be searched [CCP Art. 18.01; Rios v. State, 901 S.W.2d 704 (Tex.App.—San Antonio 1995, *no pet.*)]
- Insufficient description of the person in control of the premises [CCP Art. 18.04; Rios v. State, 901 S.W.2d 704 (Tex. App.—San Antonio 1995, *no pet.*)]
- Insufficient description of the property to be seized [CCP Art. 18.04; Rios v.

State, 901 S.W.2d 704 (Tex.App.—San Antonio 1995, *no pet.*)]

- Affiant has intentionally misrepresented the facts in the affidavit [Dancy v. State, 728 S.W.2d 772 (Tex. Crim. App. 1987)]
- Person signing the warrant is not a proper magistrate under the Code of Criminal Procedure [CCP Art. 2.09; CCP Art. 18.01]
- Magistrate issuing the warrant was not neutral and detached as required [CCP Art. 18.01]
- Officers executing the warrant do not have proper jurisdiction [CCP Art. 2.12; Britt v. State, 768 S.W.2d 514 (Tex. App.—Fort Worth 1989, *no pet.*)]
- Items seized under the warrant are not allowable under the Code of Criminal Procedure (such as the personal writings of the accused) [CCP Art. 18.02]
- Items seized exceeded the scope of the search warrant [CCP Art. 18.02]
- Places searched exceeded the scope of the search warrant [CCP Art. 18.01]
- Warrant does not run "In the name of the State of Texas" [CCP Art. 18.04]
- Premises searched was previously searched under a warrant for the same items [Ramos v. State, 934 S.W.2d 358 (Tex. Crim. App. 1996)]

Upon the request of the losing party on a motion to suppress evidence, the trial court shall state its essential findings. By "essential findings," it is meant that the trial court must make findings of fact and conclusions of law adequate to provide an appellate court with a basis upon which to review the trial court's application of the law to the facts. State v. Cullen, 195 S.W.3d 696 (Tex. Crim. App. 2006).

PRACTICE TIP: TRCP 297, cited in Cullen, provides that the trial court shall file its findings of fact and conclusions of law within twenty days after a timely request is filed. It further provides that the court shall cause a copy of its findings and conclusions to be mailed to each party in the suit. The findings and conclusions need to be recorded in some way, whether written out and filed by the trial court, or stated on the record at the hearing.

It is within the trial court's discretion to grant the State's request to reopen a motion-to-suppress hearing to supplement the record with additional testimony, outside the jury's presence, even over the objection of the defendant. Black v. State, 362 S.W.3d 626 (Tex. Crim. App. 2012).

Where the trial court's written findings and conclusions of law are ambiguous and lack a credibility determination, an appellate court can remand the case for supplemental findings. State v. Mendoza, 365 S.W.3d 666 (Tex. Crim. App. 2012).

§2:91 Article 38.23 Jury Charge

In order to be entitled to a jury charge under CCP Art. 38.23, regarding the legality of the obtaining of evidence: (1) a defendant must request an instruction based on a specific historical fact or facts; (2) there must be some affirmative evidence that puts the existence of that fact or facts into question; and (3) the disputed fact must be one that affects the determination of the legal issue. Madden v. State, 242 S.W.3d 504 (Tex. Crim. App. 2007).

Under CCP Art. 38.23, the defendant is entitled to a jury charge where there has been a factual issue raised as to whether the search warrant was supported by adequate probable cause. The charge should instruct the jury that they should suppress the fruits of the search if they find it to be illegal. Coleman v. State, 45 S.W.3d 175 (Tex.App.—Houston [1st Dist.] 2001, *pet. ref'd*); Stone v. State, 703 S.W.2d 652 (Tex. Crim. App. 1986).

A defendant is not entitled an article 38.23 instruction if the jury's verdict disposes of the issue that he asserts as the factual issue entitling him to the instruction. Porter v. State, 255 S.W.3d 234 (Tex. App.—Waco 2008, pet.ref'd)(where the jury's finding that the defendant was guilty of evading arrest or detention disposed of his issue that his detention was illegal); Wilkerson v. State, 933 S.W.2d 276 (Tex. App.—Houston [1st Dist.] 1996, pet.ref'd)(where the jury's finding that the defendant was guilty of delivery of drugs disposed of his issue that the police officer was lying and no drug transaction had occurred).

The Fourth Amendment does not apply to the actions of private individuals, and reading Article 38.23 to apply the Fourth Amendment to private individuals would lead to an absurdity. Ruiz v. State, ___ S.W.3d ___ at *2 (PD-1348-17, 2019 WL 2814867, Tex. Crim. App. July 3, 2019).

§2:100 Going Behind Affidavit and Warrant

If an affirmative misrepresentation is knowingly included in a probable cause affidavit and is material and necessary to establishing the probable cause, the warrant is rendered invalid under the Fourth Amendment. Franks v. Delaware, 438 U.S. 154, 98 S.Ct. 2674, 57 L.Ed.2d 667 (1978); Hass v. State, 790 S.W.2d 609 (Tex. Crim. App. 1990).

The burden is on the defendant to show by a preponderance of the evidence that a falsehood in the affidavit was made knowingly, intentionally, or with reckless disregard for the truth. Janecka v. State, 937 S.W.2d 456 (Tex. Crim. App. 1996).

An inconsistency between testimony adduced at trial and the language of a search warrant affidavit does not always rise to the level of intentional perjury or reckless disregard for the truth, but rather can be mere negligence. Hinojosa v. State, 4 S.W.3d 240 (Tex. Crim. App. 1999).

Where the defendant makes a substantial preliminary showing that a false statement knowingly and intentionally, or with reckless disregard for the truth, was included by the affiant in the warrant affidavit, and if the allegedly false statement is necessary to the finding of probable cause, the Fourth Amendment requires that a hearing be held at the defendant's request. Dancy v. State, 728 S.W.2d 772 (Tex. Crim. App. 1987).

In the event that at that hearing the allegation of perjury or reckless disregard is established by the defendant by a preponderance of the evidence, and, with the affidavit's false material set to one side, the affidavit's remaining content is insufficient to establish probable cause, the search warrant must be voided and the fruits of the search excluded to the same extent as if probable cause was lacking on the face of the affidavit Dancy.

Unconstitutionally defective portions of a search warrant do not necessarily invalidate the entire warrant or taint all of the evidence seized pursuant to the warrant. If only certain portions of a search warrant are invalid, only the evidence gathered pursuant to the offending portions is tainted. Massey v. State, 933 S.W.2d 141 (Tex. Crim. App. 1996).

PRACTICE TIP: Make a careful comparison between the evidence seizures supported by the warrant and the evidence actually seized.

PRACTICE TIP: When complaining of invalid portions of a search warrant, the defendant must identify the evidence seized pursuant to the allegedly invalid portions of the warrant. In failing to identify evidence that was seized pursuant to the complained of portion of the affidavit, the defendant will have failed to preserve his claim for review. Massey, supra.

The Texas Court of Criminal Appeals has not extended the Franks rationale to omissions as well as false statements. Massey, *supra*.

Mere conclusory statements alleging lack of probable cause, defects in the search warrant and procurement of evidence by illegal means are insufficient to make a substantial preliminary showing as required by Franks. Dancy, *supra*.

Under Franks, in order to be entitled to an evidentiary hearing on the allegations concerning the veracity of the affidavit, the defendant must:

- Allege deliberate falsehood or reckless disregard for the truth by the affiant, specifically pointing out the portion of the affidavit claimed to be false; allegations of negligence or innocent mistake are insufficient, and the allegations must be more than conclusory
- Accompany these allegations with an offer of proof stating the supporting reasons; affidavits or otherwise reliable statements of witnesses should be furnished, if not, the absence of written

support of the allegations must be satisfactorily explained

- Show that when the portion of the affidavit alleged to be false is excised from the affidavit, the remaining content is insufficient to support issuance of the warrant.

Dancy, *supra*.

§2:110 Searches and Seizures of Persons Incidental to Search Warrants

Officers executing a search warrant for contraband have the authority to detain the occupants of the premises while a proper search is conducted. Michigan v. Summers, 452 U.S. 692, 101 S.Ct. 2587, 69 L.Ed.2d 340 (1981); Muehler v. Mena, 544 U.S. 93, 125 S.Ct. 1465, 161 L.Ed.2d 299 (2005).

However, once an individual has left the immediate vicinity of premises to be searched, a detention must be justified by some other rationale. Bailey v. U.S., 568 U.S. 186, 133 S.Ct. 1031, 1043, 185 L.Ed.2d 19 (2013).

Inherent in *Summers* authorization to detain an occupant of the place to be searched is the authority to use reasonable force to effectuate the detention. Muehler v. Mena.

A person's mere presence on the scene of the execution of a search warrant, without more (such as being named in the search warrant or there being a reasonable Terry articulation of danger perceived by police) does not allow a search of that person incident to the execution of the warrant. Ybarra v. Illinois, 444 U.S. 85, 100 S.Ct. 338, 62 L.Ed.2d 238 (1979); Lippert v. State, 664 S.W.2d 712 (Tex. Crim. App. 1984).

Some factors that may allow officers to search a person present at the scene of the execution of a search warrant include: (1) flight, furtive gestures or sudden movements towards a pocket or other place where a weapon might be concealed; (2) threats or attempts to resist detention; (3) the commission or attempted commission of any criminal offense; (4) whether the detained person is under the influence of alcoholic beverages or drugs; (5) whether officers know of the prior criminal record of the person, including drug arrests or convictions; and (6) whether officers have any reasonable suspicion that the person is armed and dangerous. Lippert; Worthey v. State, 805 S.W.2d 435 (Tex. Crim. App. 1991).

Any search of those occupants or others on the premises must meet the standards of Ybarra v. Illinois and Terry v. Ohio. Michigan v. Summers, *supra*, at 695-96 n. 4; Lippert, *supra*.

§2:120 Execution of Search Warrants

CCP Art. 18.06. Execution of warrants

> *(a) A peace officer to whom a search warrant is delivered shall execute the warrant without delay and forthwith return the warrant to the proper magistrate. A search warrant issued under Section 5A, Article 18.21, must be executed in the manner provided by that section not later than the 11th day after the date of issuance. In all other cases, a search warrant must be executed within three days from the time of its issuance. A warrant issued under this chapter shall be executed within a shorter period if so directed in the warrant by the magistrate.*
>
> *(b) On searching the place ordered to be searched, the officer executing the warrant shall present a copy of the warrant to the owner of the place, if he is present. If the owner of the place is not present but a person who is present is in possession of the place, the officer shall present a copy of the warrant to the person. Before the officer takes property from the place, he shall prepare a written inventory of the property to be taken. He shall legibly endorse his name on the inventory and present a copy of the inventory to the owner or other person in possession of the property. If neither the owner nor a person in possession of the property is present when the officer executes the warrant, the officer shall leave a copy of the warrant and the inventory at the place.*

CCP Art. 18.07. Days Allowed for Warrant to Run

(a) The period allowed for the execution of a search warrant, exclusive of the day of its issuance and of the day of its execution, is:

(1) 15 whole days if the warrant is issued solely to search for and seize specimens from a specific person for DNA analysis and comparison, including blood and saliva samples;

(2) 10 whole days if the warrant is issued under Section 5A, Article 18.21; or

(3) three whole days if the warrant is issued for a purpose other than that described by Subdivision (1) or (2).

(b) The magistrate issuing a search warrant under this chapter shall endorse on the search warrant the date and hour of its issuance.

(c) If a warrant is issued to search for and seize data or information contained in or on a computer, disk drive, flash drive, cellular telephone, or other electronic, communication, or data storage device, the warrant is considered to have been executed within the time allowed under Subsection (a) if the device was seized before the expiration of the time allowed. Notwithstanding any other law, any data or information contained in or on a device seized may be recovered and analyzed after the expiration of the time allowed under Subsection (a).

Police are required under the Fourth Amendment to knock and announce their presence and purpose before executing a search warrant. Wilson v. Arkansas, 514 U.S. 927, 115 S.Ct. 1914, 131 L.Ed.2d 976 (1995).

However, under the Fourth Amendment, in most cases a mere violation of the "knock and announce" rule will not result in exclusion of any evidence obtained. This is because the purpose of the rule is to protect surprised citizens from violence associated with acts of self-defense, to give individuals an opportunity to comply with the law and avoid the destruction of property associated with a forcible entry, and to allow residents the elements of privacy and dignity in being able to prepare themselves for the entry of the police, rather than to prevent the government from seeing or taking evidence described in a warrant. Hudson v. Michigan, 547 U.S. 586, 126 S.Ct. 2159, 165 L.Ed.2d 56 (2006); Wright v. State, 253 S.W.3d 287 (Tex. Crim. App. 2008)

Where the police reasonably believe that a prior announcement will place them or the evidence in peril, the knock and announce rule can be dispensed with by the issuing magistrate upon a recitation in the affidavit for search warrant. Wilson v. Arkansas, *supra.*

The officers must demonstrate in the affidavit by reasonable suspicion that knocking and announcing their presence and purpose would be dangerous, futile or inhibit the effective investigation of the crime (for example, by allowing the destruction of evidence). Richards v. Wisconsin, 520 U.S. 385, 117 S.Ct. 1416, 137 L.Ed.2d 615 (1997).

Even where the warrant is silent about the manner of the execution of the warrant, if circumstances support a reasonable inference of exigency when officers arrive at the door, they can go straight in. Richards v. Wisconsin.

A reviewing court must determine whether the facts and circumstances of a particular entry justify dispensing with the knock and announce requirement. Richards v. Wisconsin.

The burden of proof is on the state to justify dispensing with the knock and announce requirement. Ballard v. State, 104 S.W.3d 372 (Tex.App.—Beaumont 2003, *pet. ref'd*).

The showing required is not high, but must be case-specific. Richards v. Wisconsin.

The state's proof must at least indicate an unequivocal knowledge on the part of the authorities of the particular exigent circumstance(s) asserted. Ballard; U.S. v. Stewart, 867 F.2d 581 (10th Cir. 1989).

For example, mere knowledge that there is a handgun on the premises is not enough. Ballard.

The mere assumption that those in possession of controlled substances are normally in possession of firearms is insufficient as a matter of law to relieve authorities of their historical duty to knock and announce their presence. Price v. State, 93 S.W.3d 358 (Tex.App.—Houston [14th Dist.] 2002, *pet. ref'd*).

However, where the police had reliable knowledge that the occupants of a dwelling to be searched had weapons in their possession, had prior weapons charges, and were capable of aggressive, violent behavior on slight provocation, a no-knock and announce entry was justified. Marsh v. State, 115 S.W.3d 709 (Tex.App.—Austin 2003, *pet. ref'd*).

The state cannot rely on mere overgeneralizations to support a no-knock entry. Richards v. Wisconsin; Ballard.

Although the experienced officer may surmise that a party is likely to dispose of evidence when faced with the execution of the search warrant, such suspicions do not create an exigency to justify an unannounced entry. The mere fact that drugs are involved does not give the police probable cause to believe that evidence will be destroyed so as to justify an unannounced entry. Price.

To avail themselves of this exception to the knock-and-announce rule, officers must reasonably conclude that the resident has resolved to dispose of the evidence in the event of police intrusion. The police should have at least some specific facts as to the case at hand that would justify their apprehension. The specific facts can come in the form of the police seeing the defendant engaged in the act of destroying evidence, witnessing specific acts suggesting that destruction was imminent, or in the form of anecdotal evidence that the defendant had destroyed or attempted to destroy evidence upon a previous encounter with police. Price.

The state cannot justify a no-knock entry on the basis of a mere hunch or suspicion. U.S. v. Bates, 84 F.3d 790 (6th Cir. 1996).

Exigent circumstances will not be found if they are predicated upon the general fear of the officers executing the warrant. U.S. v. Becker, 23 F.3d 1537 1994).

Police in exigent circumstances can damage property so far as necessary for a no-knock entrance without demonstrating the suspected risk in any more detail than the law demands for an unannounced intrusion simply by lifting the latch. U.S. v. Ramirez, *infra*.

The fact that the person in control of the premises is a prison escapee with access to a large amount of weapons has been found to justify a no-knock entry of a premises. United States v. Ramirez, 523 U.S. 65, 118 S.Ct. 992, 140 L.Ed.2d 191 (1998).

In cases where officers have knocked and announced their presence, they may forcibly enter after a reasonable suspicion of exigency has ripened. U.S. v. Banks, 540 U.S. 31, 124 S.Ct. 521, 157 L.Ed.2d 343 (2003) (in this case officers were justified in entering 15-20 seconds after knocking and announcing).

The presence of an automobile on suspected premises, without more, does not give rise to search that automobile. State v. Barnett, 788 S.W.2d 572 (Tex. Crim. App. 1990).

When a search warrant is not executed within the time period provided by CCP Arts. 18.06 and 18.07 it becomes "functus officio," having no further official force or effect. It follows that any search whose legality depends on the warrant is unauthorized. Green v. State, 799 S.W.2d 756 (Tex. Crim. App. 1990).

Ministerial violations of the search warrant statute, such as not having an affidavit attached to the warrant served or not serving a copy of the warrant on the occupants of a premises, do not vitiate an otherwise valid search absent a showing of prejudice or harm to the defendant. Turner v. State, 886 S.W.2d 859 (Tex.App.—Beaumont 1994).

City police have county-wide jurisdiction to execute search warrants. Britt v. State, 768 S.W.2d 514 (Tex.App.—Fort Worth 1989, *no pet.*).

A home-rule municipal police force's jurisdiction for the execution of a valid search warrant is at least as broad as that of a general-law municipality, that is, at least countywide. $27,877.00 Current Money of U.S. v. State, 331 S.W.3d 110 (Tex. App.—Fort Worth, pet. filed).

Where at least one of the peace officers who participated in the execution of a search warrant and whose name was listed in the return had jurisdiction to conduct the search, the search is valid even if other participating officers do not have proper jurisdiction. Dickey v. State, 816 S.W.2d 832 (Tex.App.—Eastland 1991, *no pet.*).

A second search warrant may be conducted on a premises if the second warrant authorizes a search for items not specifically named in the first warrant. Ramos v. State, 934 S.W.2d 358 (Tex. Crim. App. 1996).

An officer may seize mere evidence of a crime even though such property is not particularly described in the search warrant when the objects discovered and seized are reasonably related to the offense in question, when the officer at the time of the seizure has a reasonable basis for drawing a connection between the observed objects and the crime which furnished the basis for the search warrant, and the discovery of such property is made in the course of a good faith search conducted within the perimeters of the search warrant. Warden v. Hayden, 387 U.S. 294, 87 S.Ct. 1642, 18 L.Ed.2d 782 (1967); Bower v. State, 769 S.W.2d 887 (Tex. Crim. App. 1989).

Warrants for electronic evidence that are in the hands of a third-party provider like Facebook are good for 10 full days. See Tex. Code Crim. Proc. Arts. 18.07(a)(2) and 18.21 section 5A. The officer has to execute the warrant no later than the 11th day after the warrant is issued. Execution means serving it on the third-party provider. See Tex. Code Crim. Proc. Art. 18.21 section 5A(g).

The provider has 15 business days to comply with the warrant after being served unless the warrant says otherwise due to an emergency situation. See Tex. Code Crim. Proc. Art. 18.21 section 5A(j).

§2:130 Search Warrant Returns

CCP Art. 38.23 does not apply to violations of CCP Art. 18.10 which prohibits the moving of evidence from a particular county before an order is issued because the moving of evidence to an unauthorized location after it has been legally obtained does not vitiate the status of such evidence as having been legally obtained. Martinez v. State, 17 S.W.3d 677 (Tex. Crim. App. No. 73,131, May 17, 2000).

(This page intentionally left blank.)

Chapter 3

SEARCH AND SEIZURE: PERSONS

Table of Contents

§3:10 What Constitutes "Search" of a Person

A search occurs when an expectation of privacy that society is prepared to consider as reasonable is infringed. U. S. v. Jacobsen, 466 U.S. 109, 104 S.Ct. 1652, 80 L.Ed.2d 85 (1984); Richardson v. State, 865 S.W.2d 944 (Tex. Crim. App. 1993).

A search in which the exclusionary rule may apply is one in which there is a quest for, a looking for, or a seeking out of that which offends against the law by law enforcement personnel or their agents. Vargas v. State, 542 S.W.2d 151 (Tex. Crim. App. 1976).

A stop and frisk is a search and seizure. Terry v. Ohio, 392 U.S. 1, 88 S.Ct. 1868, 20 L.Ed.2d 889 (1968); Davis v. State, 947 S.W.2d 240 (Tex. Crim. App. 1997).

The taking of a defendant's blood from his body is a search for Fourth Amendment purposes. Davis v. State, 831 S.W.2d 426 (Tex.App.—Austin 1992, *pet. ref'd.*).

Requiring a defendant to produce handwriting samples is not a search. Ayala v. State, 657 S.W.2d 910 (Tex.App.—Austin 1983, *no pet.*).

The use of a dog to sniff a person's luggage that is in a public place is not a search. United States v. Place, 462 U.S. 696, 103 S.Ct. 2637, 77 L.Ed.2d 110 (1983); Strout v. State, 688 S.W.2d 188 (Tex. App.—Amarillo 1985, *no pet.*).

The government conducts a search when it attaches a device to a person's body, without consent, for the purpose of tracking that individual's movements. Grady v. N. Carolina, 575 U.S. ___, 135 S. Ct. 1368, 1370, 191 L.Ed.2d 459 (2015) (where a satellite-based monitor was attached to a sex-offender). The Court did not decide the reasonableness of the search which will depend on the totality of the circumstances, including the nature and purpose of the search and the extent to which the search intrudes upon reasonable privacy expectations.

§3:20 What Constitutes "Seizure" of a Person

A seizure of the person occurs when one of the following has taken place:

- Physical force has been applied to the body of the suspect.
- The suspect has actually submitted to the officer's show of authority.

California v. Hodari, 499 U.S. 621, 111 S.Ct. 1547, 113 L.Ed.2d 690 (1991); Johnson v. State, 912 S.W.2d 227 (Tex. Crim. App. 1995).

That is, a seizure of the person within the meaning of the Fourth and Fourteenth Amendments occurs when the police conduct would have communicated to a reasonable person that he was not at liberty to ignore the police presence and go about his business. Florida v. Bostick, 501 U.S. 429, 111 S.Ct. 2382, 115 L.Ed.2d 389 (1991); Kaupp v. Texas, 538 U.S. 626, 123 S.Ct. 1834, 155 L.Ed.2d 814 (2003).

The same is true under CCP Art. 15.22 which codifies the definition of arrest. Medford v. State, 13 S.W.3d 769 (Tex. Crim. App. 2000).

This definition has also been adopted for cases to be decided under the Texas Constitution Art. I §9. Johnson, *supra.*

A "show of authority" occurs when actions of the police would cause a reasonable person to believe he or she is not free to leave. Hernandez v. State, 963 S.W.2d 921 (Tex.App.—San Antonio 1998, *no pet.*).

Examples of circumstances that may constitute a seizure, even where the person does not try to leave, include the following:

- The threatening presence of several officers.
- The display of a weapon by an officer.
- Some physical touching of the person of the citizen.
- The use of language or tone of voice of the officer indicating that compliance with the officer's request might be compelled.

California v. Hodari; Kaupp v. Texas 538 U.S. 626, 123 S.Ct. 1843, 155 L.Ed.2d 814 (2003).

However, a show of authority, without an application of physical force, to which a suspect yields, is not a seizure under the Fourth Amendment. California v. Hodari; Johnson.

Investigatory detentions and arrests are both seizures. Johnson, *supra*.

Article I, §9 of the Texas Constitution is consistent with the Fourth Amendment of the United States Constitution in determining whether police seizures, including Terry stops, are reasonable. Davis v. State, 829 S.W.2d 218 (Tex. Crim. App. 1992).

Under both the Fourth Amendment and Article I, §9, in either an arrest or investigative detention, the seizure of a citizen has not occurred until a reasonable person would believe he or she was not free to leave, and that person has yielded to the officer's show of authority or been physically forced to yield. California v. Hodari, *supra*; Johnson, *supra*.

The reasonable person standard presupposes an innocent person. Florida v. Bostick, 501 U.S. 429, 111 S.Ct. 2382, 115 L.Ed.2d 389 (1991); Anderson v. State, 932 S.W.2d 502 (Tex. Crim. App. 1996).

A "stop" to make an inquiry, on its own, does not show a seizure. Woodard v. State, 341 S.W.3d 404 (Tex. Crim. App. 2011).

In order to determine whether a particular encounter constitutes a seizure, a court must consider the totality of the circumstances surrounding the encounter to determine whether the police conduct would have communicated to a reasonable person that the person was not free to decline the officers' requests or otherwise terminate the encounter. Florida v. Bostick, *supra*; Johnson, *supra*.

An officer's subjective intent to arrest is irrelevant unless that intent is communicated to the suspect. United States v. Mendenhall, 446 U.S. 544, 100 S.Ct. 1870, 64 L.Ed.2d 497 (1980); Anderson, *supra*.

A "stop" to make an inquiry, on its own, does not show a seizure. Woodard v. State, 341 S.W.3d 404 (Tex. Crim. App. 2011).

A person who voluntarily accompanies investigating police officers to a certain location, knowing that he is a suspect, has not been seized for Fourth Amendment purposes. Anderson, *supra*.

A seizure may occur when a person stops his vehicle in response to a show of authority. United States v. Brignoni-Ponce, 422 U.S. 873, 95 S.Ct. 2574, 45 L.Ed.2d 607 (1975); Hernandez, *supra*; State v. Sanchez, 856 S.W.2d 166 (Tex. Crim. App. 1993).

However, where the defendant does not stop his vehicle in response to police commands, no seizure has occurred. Hernandez, *supra*.

A seizure that is lawful at its inception can violate the Fourth Amendment if its manner of execution unreasonably infringes interests protected by the Constitution. U.S. v. Jacobsen, 466 U.S. 109, 104 S.Ct. 1652, 80 L.Ed.2d 85 (1984); Illinois v. Caballes, 543 U.S. 405, 125 S.Ct. 834, 160 L.Ed.2d 842 (2005).

In Fourth Amendment terms, a traffic stop entails a seizure of the driver even though the purpose of the stop is limited and the resulting detention quite brief. Delaware v. Prouse, 440 U.S. 648, 99 S.Ct. 1391, 59 L.Ed.2d 660 (1979); Brendlin v. California, 551 U.S. 249, 127 S.Ct. 2400, 160 L.Ed.2d 132 (2007).

A traffic stop also results in the seizure of any passenger in the vehicle, and thus the passenger may challenge the constitutionality of the stop. Brendlin v. California.

An investigative detention during the course of a traffic stop, in which the subject is not free to leave, is a seizure for purposes of the Fourth Amendment, and the appellate court must analyze the stop under the reasonableness standard. Whren v. U.S., 517 U.S. 806, 116 S.Ct. 1769, 135 L.Ed.2d 89 (1996); Love v. State, 252 S.W.3d 684 (Tex.App.—Texarkana 2008, *pet. ref'd*).

When a defendant asserts a search and seizure violation under the Fourth Amendment, the defendant bears the burden of producing evidence to rebut the presumption of proper conduct by law enforcement. A defendant can satisfy this burden with evidence that the seizure occurred without a warrant. Woodard.

If the defendant satisfies the initial burden, the burden then shifts to the State to establish that the seizure was nevertheless reasonable under the applicable standard—either reasonable suspicion or probable cause. Woodard.

In the case of a citizen-police encounter the defendant has the burden to show that he was seized without a warrant, and until he does so the burden does not shift to the state. Woodard.

Generally, a routine traffic stop does not place a person in custody for Miranda purposes. But a traffic stop may escalate from a non-custodial detention into a custodial detention when formal arrest ensues or a detainee's freedom of movement is restrained to the degree associated with a formal arrest. Appellate courts evaluate whether a person has been detained to the degree associated with arrest on a case-by-case basis. In making the custody determination, the primary question is whether a reasonable person would perceive the detention to be a restraint on his movement comparable to formal arrest, given all the objective circumstances. State v. Ortiz, 382 S.W.3d 367, 372 (Tex. Crim. App. 2012).

In evaluating whether a reasonable person would believe his freedom has been restrained to the degree of formal arrest, the appellate courts look only to the objective factors surrounding the detention. The subjective beliefs of the detaining officer are not included in the calculation of whether a suspect is in custody. But if the officer manifests his belief to the detainee that he is a suspect, then that officer's subjective belief becomes relevant to the determination of whether a reasonable person in the detainee's position would believe he is in custody. Conversely, any undisclosed subjective belief of the suspect that he is guilty of an offense should not be taken into consideration—the reasonable person standard presupposes an innocent person. State v. Ortiz, 382 S.W.3d at 372-73.

§3:30 Degrees of Intrusion on Individuals

There are three general categories of police and citizen interactions. United States v. Mendenhall, 446 U.S. 544, 100 S.Ct. 1870, 64 L.Ed.2d 497 (1980); Crain v. State, 315 S.W.3d 43 (Tex. Crim. App. 2010).

- Stop and Talk (Mere Encounters) [§3:31]
- Investigative Detentions (Terry Stops) [§3:32]
- Arrests [§3:33]

In determining which category an interaction falls into, courts look at the totality of the circumstances. Crain.

§3:31 Stop and Talk (Mere Encounters)

The first category of police and citizen interactions is that of an encounter. Police officers do not violate the Fourth Amendment by merely approaching an individual in public to ask questions. Such an encounter does not require any justification on the part of the officer. United States v. Mendenhall, *supra*; Johnson v. State, 912 S.W.3d 227, 235 (Tex. Crim. App. 1995); State v. Garcia-Cantu, 253 S.W.3d 236 (Tex. Crim. App. 2008).

Consensual police-citizen encounters do not implicate Fourth Amendment protections. Woodard v. State, 341 S.W.3d 404 (Tex. Crim. App. 2011).

A seizure does not occur simply because a police officer approaches an individual and asks a few questions, so long as a reasonable person would feel free to disregard the police and go about his business. California v. Hodari, 499 U.S. 621, 111 S.Ct. 1547, 113 L.Ed.2d 690 (1991); Johnson, *supra*; State v. Velasquez, 982 S.W.2d 73 (Tex. App.—Houston [1st Dist.] 1998, *no pet*).

An encounter is a consensual interaction that the citizen is free to terminate at any time. Unlike an investigative detention and an arrest, an encounter is not considered a seizure that would trigger Fourth Amendment protection. Crain v. State, 315 S.W.3d 43 (Tex. Crim. App. 2010).

Law enforcement officers do not violate the Fourth Amendment by merely approaching an individual on the street or in another public place, by asking him if he is willing to answer some questions or asking some questions, or by offering in evidence his voluntary answers to such questions. State v. Castleberry, 332 S.W.3d 460 (Tex. Crim. App. 2011); Crain v. State, 315 S.W.3d 43 (Tex. Crim. App. 2010).

The crucial test is whether, taking into account the totality of the circumstances surrounding the encounter, the police conduct would have communicated to a reasonable person that he was not at liberty to ignore the police presence and go about his business. Florida v. Bostick, *supra*; Hunter v. State, 955 S.W.2d 102 (Tex. Crim. App. 1997); State v. Garcia-Cantu, 253 S.W.3d 236 (Tex. Crim. App. 2008).

Six factors are important to a determination of whether police have communicated to the defendant that he is not free to leave an encounter such that he is, in fact, detained:

- Whether the officer was in uniform
- Whether the officer exhibited a weapon
- Number of officers present
- Whether the officer suggested that he would obtain a warrant if the defendant did not comply
- Whether the officer told the defendant he believed the defendant was engaged in crime
- Whether the officer told the defendant that compliance was or was not required

Hunter, *supra*.

Even when the officer did not communicate to the citizen that the request for information may be ignored, the citizen's acquiescence to an official's request does not cause the encounter to lose its consensual nature. Woodard.

An encounter between a citizen and police officers is not rendered a detention simply by virtue of the facts that the officers involved asked for the citizen's identification and requested to search his bag during the course of the encounter. Florida v. Bostick, *supra*; Hunter, *supra*; State v. Castleberry.

The test is both objective and fact-specific; "the 'reasonable person' test presupposes an *innocent* person." Each citizen-police encounter must be factually evaluated on its own terms; there are no *per se* rules. Florida v. Bostick, 501 U.S. 429 (1991); State v. Garcia-Cantu, 253 S.W.3d 236 (Tex. Crim. App. 2008).

A consensual pat-down search does not elevate an encounter to the level of a detention. Henderson v. State, 965 S.W.2d 710 (Tex.App.—Houston [1st Dist.] 1998, *pet. ref'd*).

Even if the officer did not tell the citizen that the request for identification or information may be ignored, the fact that the citizen complied with the request does not negate the consensual nature of the encounter. State v. Castleberry.

The time, place, and surrounding circumstances must be taken into account, but the officer's conduct is the most important factor in determining whether a police-citizen interaction is a consensual encounter or a Fourth Amendment seizure. State v. Castleberry.

Officers may search the pockets of an unconscious person for identification, medical history and weapons. Tijerina v. State, 578 S.W.2d 415 (Tex. Crim. App. 1979); Perez v. State, 514 S.W.2d 748 (Tex. Crim. App. 1974).

Nothing in either the State or U.S. Constitutions prevents a police officer from knocking politely on any closed door. Cornealius v. State, 900 S.W.2d 731 (Tex. Crim. App. 1995).

Generally, however, when an officer through force or a showing of authority restrains a citizen's liberty, the encounter is no longer consensual. This is the point at which an encounter becomes a detention or arrest, both of which are seizures under the Fourth Amendment. Woodard.

A person's refusal to cooperate with a police request during a consensual encounter cannot, by itself, provide the basis for a detention. Wade v. State, 422 S.W.3d 661, 668 (Tex. Crim. App. 2013). In fact, neither nervousness nor a refusal to cooperate with an officer during a consensual encounter is sufficient, alone or in combination, to constitute the reasonable suspicion necessary to elevate a consensual encounter to a detention. Wade, 422 S.W.3d at 676.

In the case of a citizen-police encounter the defendant has the burden to show that he was seized without a warrant, and until he does so the burden does not shift to the state. Woodard.

§3:32 Investigative Detentions (Terry Stops)

The second category of citizen-police interaction is that of a temporary or investigative detention. This is a brief stop of a suspicious individual in order to determine his identity or to maintain the status quo momentarily while obtaining more information. Terry v. Ohio, 392 U.S. 1, 88 S.Ct. 1868, 20 L.Ed.2d 889 (1968).

An investigative detention, which implicates Fourth Amendment protections, occurs when a person yields to the police officer's show of authority under a reasonable belief that he is not free to leave. In determining whether the interaction constituted an encounter or a detention, courts focus on whether the officer conveyed a message that compliance with the officer's request was required—whether a reasonable person in the citizen's position would have felt free to decline the officer's requests or otherwise terminate the encounter. Johnson v. State, 414 S.W.3d 184, 193 (Tex. Crim. App. 2013).

When a court is conducting a determination of whether the interaction constituted an encounter or a detention, a court focuses on whether the officer conveyed a message that required compliance with the officer's request. The question is whether a reasonable person in the citizen's position would have felt free to decline the officer's requests or otherwise terminate the encounter. Crain v. State, 315 S.W.3d 43 (Tex. Crim. App. 2010).

When a suspect fails to yield to a show of physical force and there has been no actual use of physical force, then there is no seizure. State v. Castleberry, 332 S.W.3d 460 (Tex. Crim. App. 2011).

Examples of circumstances that might indicate a seizure would be the threatening presence of several officers, the display of a weapon by an officer, some physical touching of the person of the citizen, or the use of language or tone of voice indicating that compliance with the officer's request might be compelled. Crain *citing* U.S. v. Mendenhall, 446 U.S. 544, 100 S.Ct. 1870, 64 L.Ed.2d 497 (1980).

A defendant may be prosecuted for failing to identify himself during a valid Terry stop where the request for identification is reasonably related to the circumstances justifying the stop. Hiibel v. Sixth Judicial Dist. Court. of Nev., Humboldt Cty., 542 U.S. 177, 124 S.Ct. 2451, 159 L.Ed.2d 292 (2004).

The question of whether a citizen/police encounter is consensual or a Fourth Amendment de-tention is an issue of law and is subject to *de novo* review on appeal. Johnson v. State, 414 S.W.3d 184, 192 (Tex. Crim. App. 2013).

§3:32.1 Degree of Suspicion for Investigative Detention

There is no bright-line rule dictating when a consensual encounter becomes a detention. Furr v. State, 499 S.W.3d 872, 877 (Tex. Crim. App. 2016).

Under the Fourth Amendment, a warrantless detention of a person that amounts to less than a full-blown custodial arrest is permissible where the officer has a reasonable suspicion. Derichsweiler v. State, 348 S.W.3d 906 (Tex. Crim. App. 2011).

Under the Fourth Amendment, a temporary detention is justified when the detaining officer has specific articulable facts which, taken together with rational inferences from those facts, lead the officer to conclude that the person detained is, has been, or soon will be engaged in criminal activity. Terry v. Ohio, 392 U.S. 1, 30, 88 S.Ct. 1868, 20 L.Ed.2d 889 (1968); Derichsweiler.

The facts invoked to justify an investigative detention must support more than a mere hunch or good-faith intuition that criminal activity is afoot. Derichsweiler.

To support a reasonable suspicion, the articulable facts must show that some activity out of the ordinary has occurred, some suggestion to connect the detainee to the unusual activity, and some indication that the unusual activity is related to crime. Derichsweiler.

Unlike the case with probable cause to justify an arrest, it is not a *sine qua non* of reasonable suspicion that a detaining officer be able to pinpoint a particular penal infraction. Particularly with respect to information suggesting that a crime is *about* to occur, the requirement that there be some indication that the unusual activity is related to crime does not necessarily mean that the information must lead inexorably to the conclusion that a particular and identifiable penal code offense is imminent. It is enough to satisfy the lesser standard of reasonable suspicion that the information is sufficiently detailed and reliable—*i.e.*, it supports more than an inarticulate hunch or intuition—to suggest that *something* of an apparently criminal nature is brewing. Derichsweiler.

When reviewing an investigative detention under either state or federal law, it is accepted that law enforcement officers may stop and briefly detain persons suspected of criminal activity on less information than is constitutionally required for probable cause to arrest. Crockett v. State, 803 S.W.2d 308 (Tex. Crim. App.1991); Johnson, 912 S.W.2d 227 (Tex. Crim. App. 1995).

A peace officer has the right to detain a suspect for questioning in a criminal investigation if the detention is based on reasonable suspicion and restricted in obtrusiveness, time of detention, and scope of the investigation. United States v. Brignoni-Ponce, 422 U.S. 873, 95 S.Ct. 2574, 45 L.Ed.2d 607 (1975).

This standard is an objective one — there need only be an objective basis for the stop — the subjective intent of the officer conducting the stop is irrelevant. Derichsweiler.

Where the objective facts necessary to justify an investigative detention are obvious from the record, the investigating officer need not specifically testify to them in order for the detention to be upheld. State v. Sheppard, 271 S.W.3d 281 (Tex. Crim. App. 2008).

The reasonable suspicion determination is made by considering the totality of the circumstances. Derichsweiler.

The totality of the circumstances test allows the courts to consider additional content gleaned from the context of the officer's knowledge, and credits an officer's ability to make rational inferences from his observations and other known facts. State v. Kerwick, 393 S.W.3d 270, 275-76 (Tex. Crim. App. 2013).

In assessing whether reasonable suspicion exists, a reviewing court may take into account an officer's ability to draw on his own experience and specialized training to make inferences from and deductions about the cumulative information available to him that might well elude an untrained person. Ramirez-Tamayo v. State, 537 S.W.3d 29, 36 (Tex. Crim. App. 2017).

In conducting this totality of the circumstances determination, appellate courts use a bifurcated standard of review: (1) giving almost total deference to a trial court's determination of historical facts, and application of law to fact questions that turn on credibility and demeanor; and (2) reviewing *de novo* application of law to fact questions that do not turn upon credibility and demeanor. Derichsweiler.

The totality of the circumstances may all seem innocent enough in isolation, but if they combine to reasonably suggest the imminence of criminal conduct, an investigative detention is justified. The relevant inquiry is not whether particular conduct is innocent or criminal, but the degree of suspicion that attaches to particular non-criminal acts. Derichsweiler.

Moreover, the detaining officer need not be personally aware of every fact that objectively supports a reasonable suspicion to detain; rather, the cumulative information known to the cooperating officers at the time of the stop is to be considered in determining whether reasonable suspicion exists. A 911 police dispatcher is ordinarily regarded as a "cooperating officer" for purposes of making this determination. Derichsweiler.

A reasonable suspicion entails some minimal level of objective justification for making a stop, that is, something more than inchoate or unparticularized suspicion or hunch, but less than the level of suspicion required for probable cause. United States v. Sokolow, 490 U.S. 1, 109 S.Ct. 1581, 104 L.Ed.2d 1 (1989); Foster v. State, 326 S.W.3d 609 (Tex. Crim. App. 2010).

Even in the absence of bad faith, a detention based on a mere hunch is illegal, and there must be "reasonable suspicion" by the police officer that some activity out of the ordinary is occurring or has occurred, some suggestion to connect the detained person with the unusual activity, and some indication that the activity is related to crime. Gurrola v. State, 877 S.W.2d 300 (Tex. Crim. App. 1994).

Circumstances that will raise suspicion that illegal conduct is taking place need not be per se criminal. Rather, such circumstances may include any facts, which in some measure render the likelihood of the existence of criminal conduct greater than the likelihood that it does not exist. United States v. Sokolow, *supra*; Crockett, *supra*.

The reasonableness of an investigatory detention must be examined in terms of totality of the circumstances and will be justified when the detaining officer has specific articulable facts that, taken together with rational inferences from those facts, lead the officer to conclude that the person is, has been, or will soon be engaged in criminal activity. Woods v. State, 956 S.W.2d 33 (Tex. Crim. App. 1997). Woods discards the "as consistent with innocent activity as with criminal activity" construct previously employed by reviewing courts.

Even though Woods does away with the "as consistent with innocent activity as with criminal activity" construct, the reasonable suspicion standard still requires that there be something out of the ordinary occurring and some indication that the unusual activity is related to crime. Davis, *supra*; Viveros, *supra*.

Because reasonable suspicion is determined by the totality of the circumstances, the courts must look at all of the facts together to make the reasonable suspicion determination; facts that do not show reasonable suspicion in isolation may do so when combined with other facts. United States v. Brignoni-Ponce, 422 U.S. 873, 885 n. 10, 95 S.Ct. 2574, 2582 n.10, 45 L.Ed.2d 607 (1975); Loesch v. State, 958 S.W.2d 830 (Tex. Crim. App. 1997).

Sometimes it will be obvious that otherwise illegal conduct is justified by surrounding circumstances. But a defense would matter only if the facts establishing it were so obvious that an objective officer viewing the situation would be unreasonable in failing to realize that the person's conduct was allowed by law. A determination that reasonable suspicion exists need not rule out the possibility of innocent conduct. The reasonable suspicion standard accepts the risk that officers may stop innocent people. The mere possibility that an act is justified will not negate reasonable suspicion. Jaganathan v. State, 479 S.W.3d 244, 248 (Tex. Crim. App. 2015).

SEARCH AND SEIZURE: PERSONS

An officer may have an objectively reasonable basis to justify at least a temporary detention to investigate the cause of unusual driving, even if the erratic driving might ultimately have proven to derive from some other, innocent cause. The possibility of an innocent explanation does not deprive a detaining officer of the capacity to entertain reasonable suspicion of criminal conduct. Indeed, the principal function of an investigation is to resolve that very ambiguity and establish whether the activity is in fact legal or illegal. Leming v. State, P 493 S.W.3d 552, 564-5 (Tex. Crim. App. 2016 at *9).

Information gained from a confidential informant, coupled with relevant observations by police officers, can be sufficient reasonable suspicion to justify a Terry stop. Griffin v. State, 215 S.W.3d 403 (Tex. Crim. App. 2006).

To support reasonable suspicion, an anonymous tip requires some indicia that the caller is credible or that his information is reliable. Matthews v. State, 431 S.W.3d 596, 603 (Tex. Crim. App. 2014).

The fact that an area is a high crime area is among the relevant contextual considerations in a Terry analysis. Adams v. Williams, 407 U.S. 143, 92 S.Ct. 1921, 32 L. Ed. 2d 612 (1972).

Time of day and proximity to a bar district can be relevant factors that support reasonable suspicion. Foster, 326 S.W.3d at 613 (where the defendant was detained on suspicion of DWI at 1:30 a.m. a few blocks from Austin's Sixth Street bar district).

The flight of the defendant can serve to increase suspicion that he was engaged or about to be engaged in illegal activity. Matthews, 431 S.W.3d at 606.

The reasonable suspicion standard is an objective standard that disregards any subjective intent of the officer making the stop and looks solely to whether an objective basis for the stop exists. Ford v. State, 158 S.W.3d 488 (Tex. Crim. App. 2005).

A mere opinion or conclusory statement will not suffice to establish reasonable suspicion; specific, articulable facts must be presented by the state or a court has no means to assess whether the opinion or conclusion was objectively reasonable. Ford.

Where the defendant is detained for violation of a traffic statute that makes the assessment of the violation a subjective determination on the part of the officer, specific articulable facts must be presented to the trial court to justify the detention. Ford (the defendant was detained for the offense of following too closely).

However, where the traffic violation for which the defendant is detained does not contain any subjective component, the officer's testimony that the defendant committed the violation is sufficient without testimony as to the underlying details of the violation. Castro v. State, 227 S.W.3d 737 (Tex. Crim. App. 2007) (the defendant was detained for failing to signal a lane change).

In justifying a stop, the police officer can make rational inferences from the articulable facts based upon the officer's personal knowledge and experience. Davis v. State, 829 S.W.2d 218 (Tex. Crim. App. 1992).

Police may make an investigatory stop of an individual on the basis of a "wanted flyer" issued by another department, which was issued on the basis of articulable facts supporting a reasonable suspicion that the person wanted had committed an offense. United States v. Hensley, 469 U.S. 221, 105 S.Ct. 675, 83 L.Ed.2d 604 (1985). The stop made on the basis of the "wanted flyer" must be no more intrusive than would be permitted the police department issuing the "flyer." Hensley.

Flight from a show of authority may be a factor in support of a finding of reasonable suspicion that an individual is involved in criminal activity. Gilbert v. State, 874 S.W.2d 290 (Tex.App.—Houston [1st Dist.] 1994, *pet. ref'd*).

Unprovoked flight from a high crime area can support a finding of reasonable suspicion warranting a Terry stop. Illinois v. Wardlow, 528 U.S. 119, 120 S.Ct. 673, 145 L.Ed.2d 570 (2000).

PRACTICE TIP: Always challenge, by way of a motion to suppress, the initial detention and its legal and factual basis in an attempt to suppress fruits gained from the detention.

The fact that a person is handcuffed does not always mean that he is under arrest. Rhodes v. State, 945 S.W.2d 115 (Tex. Crim. App. 1997) (where an officer testified that during a car chase scenario he handcuffed the defendant for his safety and the safety of other officers, and during this time the defendant dropped drugs on the ground, the incident which formed the basis of the prosecution). See also, Mays v. State, 726 S.W.2d 937 (Tex. Crim. App. 1986).

This is true even where the officer handcuffed the defendant for officer's safety and placed him in the back seat of his patrol car for additional questioning. U.S. v. Sokolow; Balentine v. State, 71 S.W.3d 763 (Tex. Crim. App. 2002).

The burden is on the State to prove the existence of probable cause to justify a warrantless arrest or search. Coolidge v. New Hampshire, 403 U.S. 443, 91 S.Ct. 2022, 29 L.Ed.2d 564 (1971); Amores v. State, 816 S.W.2d 407 (Tex. Crim. App. 1991).

Where certain driving facts do not give rise to a reasonable suspicion of criminal activity, the stop of an automobile is unjustified and fruits of the stop should be suppressed. Viveros, *supra*.

An alleged traffic violation of failure to maintain a single lane does not amount to a reasonable suspicion where the state fails to show also that the movement to another lane could not be made safely under Transportation Code §545.060(a). Hernandez v. State, 978 S.W.2d 137 (Tex.App.—Austin 1998 *pet. ref'd*).

Before an officer can have reasonable suspicion to believe that a defendant committed the traffic offense of failing to obey a "Left Lane for Passing Only" sign, the officer must be aware of facts that support a reasonable inference that the defendant drove past the sign before being pulled over. Jaganathan v. State, 479 S.W.3d 244, 247 (Tex. Crim. App. 2015).

Since under *Transportation Code* sec. 545.060 it is an offense to change marked lanes when it is unsafe to do so; and also an independent offense to fail to remain entirely within a marked lane of traffic so long as it remains practical to do so, regardless of whether the deviation from the marked lane is, under the particular circumstances, unsafe; an officer has reasonable suspicion to detain a driver if either of these circumstances are observed. Leming v. State, 493 S.W.3d 552, 564-5 (Tex. Crim. App. 2016.

In some cases, a traffic control device or sign will be too far away from the location of the alleged traffic violation to support a finding of reasonable suspicion. Abney v. State, 394 S.W.3d 542, 550 (Tex. Crim. App. 2013) (where a "left lane for passing only" sign was at least 15 miles away).

Even if a vehicle's tires touch the fog line, a momentary touch of the fog line, without any other indicator of criminal activity, is generally not enough to justify the stop of the vehicle for driving on an improved shoulder under Transportation Code section 545.058(a). State v. Cortez, 543 S.W.3d 198, 206 (Tex. Crim. App. 2018).

Section 545.058(a) provides for permissible reasons for a person to drive on the improved shoulder under seven listed circumstances. State v. Cortez, 543 S.W.3d at 207.

Courts have a duty to strictly construe criminal statutes outside the penal code with any doubt resolved in favor of the accused to avoid a constitutional violation. State v. Cortez, 543 S.W.3d at 206.

PRACTICE TIP: Whenever the state relies on a traffic code violation as probable cause or reasonable suspicion for a traffic stop, read the applicable code section to ascertain whether they have proven all of the elements of the violation.

Where an initial detention is unlawful, any evidence obtained after the detention is inadmissible. Schwartz v. State, 635 S.W.2d 545 (Tex. Crim. App. 1982); Gurrola, *supra.*

Also, under the Fourth Amendment, a search or seizure may be permissible even though the officer's justification for the action includes a reasonable mistake of law. Heien v. North Carolina, 574 U.S. 54, 135 S.Ct. 530, 534, 190 L.Ed.2d 475 (2014) (where an officer stopped a vehicle because one of its two brake lights was out, but a court later determined that a single working brake light was all the law required).

§3:32.2 Scope of Detention

A police officer may briefly stop a suspicious individual in order to determine his identity or to maintain the status quo momentarily while obtaining more information. Gurrola v. State, 877 S.W.2d 300 (Tex. Crim. App. 1994); Hoag v. State, 728 S.W.2d 375 (Tex. Crim. App. 1987).

An individual has a right to refuse to answer the questions of a police officer and walk away unless the police officer has reasonable suspicion of criminal activity. Gurrola, *supra.*

There is no "bright line" time limit for Terry stops. The reasonableness of the detention depends on whether the police diligently pursued a means of investigation that was likely to dispel or confirm their suspicions quickly. U.S. v. Sharpe, 470 U.S. 675, 105 S.Ct. 1568, 84 L.Ed.2d 605 (1985); Balentine v. State, 71 S.W.3d 763 (Tex. Crim. App. 2002).

An investigative detention must be temporary and last no longer than is necessary to effectuate the purpose of the stop. Florida v. Royer, 460 U.S. 491, 103 S.Ct. 1319, 75 L.Ed.2d 229 (1983).

Where officers achieve the purpose of their initial detention (such as where they determine an accused in not intoxicated after a traffic stop), there must be articulable facts or rational inferences supporting a conclusion that the accused is engaged in further criminal activity in order to justify a continued detention. Davis v. State, 947 S.W.2d 240 (Tex. Crim. App. 1997).

Although the line of questioning must be reasonably related to the purpose of the contact, a police officer is permitted to broaden the line of questioning beyond the scope of the original subject matter if he or she notices additional suspicious factors. United States v. Sharpe; Glazner v. State, 175 S.W.3d 262 (Tex. Crim. App. 2005).

Where the record shows that officers pursued their investigation in a quick, diligent, and reasonable manner, a 45- to 60-minute delay while waiting for a drug-sniffing dog was not an unreasonable delay in the investigative detention. Glenn v. State, 967 S.W.2d 467 (Tex.App.—Amarillo 1998, *pet. dism'd as improv. granted*).

During an investigative detention, a police officer may question a suspicious person on his identity, his reason for his presence in the area, and make similar reasonable inquiries of a legitimate investigatory nature. Alvarado v. State, 894 S.W.2d 869 (Tex.App.—El Paso 1995, *pet. ref'd*).

However, once the reason for the initial detention has been accomplished, absent specific articulable facts showing that the suspect is engaged in further criminal activity, the suspect must be released. St. George v. State, 237 S.W.3d 720 (Tex. Crim. App. 2007).

A computer check of the information provided by the detained individual is an integral part of the detention of an individual, but cannot be used as a means to unreasonably prolong the stop beyond a permissible period. Kothe v. State, 152 S.W.3d 54 (Tex. Crim. App. 2004).

One reasonable method of confirming or dispelling the reasonable suspicion that a vehicle contains drugs is to have a trained drug dog perform an open air search by walking around the car. If the dog alerts, the presence of drugs is confirmed, and police may make a warrantless search Matthews v. State, 431 S.W.3d 596, 603-4 (Tex. Crim. App. 2014).

A 15- to 25-minute wait for a drug dog to arrive and perform an open air search is not a prolonged investigative detention under some circumstances. Matthews, 431 S.W.3d at 605.

§3:32.3 Invalid Investigatory Detentions (Terry Stops)

Where officers lack any reasonable suspicion to believe that the defendant was engaged in or had engaged in criminal conduct, an investigative stop is not permissible. Brown v. Texas, 443

U.S. 47, 99 S.Ct. 2637, 61 L.Ed.2d 357 (1979); Gurrola v. State, 877 S.W.2d 300 (Tex. Crim. App. 1994).

Once the reason for the initial detention has been accomplished, absent specific articulable facts showing that the suspect is engaged in further criminal activity, the suspect must be released. St. George v. State, 237 S.W.3d 720 (Tex. Crim. App. 2007).

In order for police to stop and frisk a subject, they must have a reasonable suspicion to believe that particular subject was engaged in or had engaged in criminal conduct, and his mere proximity to others so suspected does not permit the stop and frisk. Ybarra v. Illinois, 444 U.S. 85, 100 S.Ct. 338, 62 L.Ed.2d 238 (1979).

The high crime reputation of a certain geographical area will not alone serve as the basis for an investigative stop. Amorella v. State, 554 S.W.2d 700 (Tex. Crim. App. 1977); Gurrola, *supra*.

Mere flight alone does not justify an investigative detention where officers do not observe overt criminal activity. Gurrola; Salcido v. State, 758 S.W.2d 261 (Tex. Crim. App. 1988).

However, where an individual flees a high crime area without police provocation, it can constitute sufficient suspicious circumstances to arouse an officer's reasonable suspicion and justify a Terry stop. Illinois v. Wardlow, 528 U.S. 119, 120 S.Ct. 673, 145 L. Ed. 2d 570 (2000).

Nervous, evasive behavior is a pertinent factor in determining reasonable suspicion for a Terry stop. Illinois v. Wardlow; Balentine v. State, 71 S.W.3d 763 (Tex. Crim. App. 2002).

Four individuals engaged in an argument in a parking lot in the late afternoon is not so out of the ordinary as to give rise to the belief that they were engaged in criminal activity. Hawkins v. State, 758 S.W.2d 255 (Tex. Crim. App. 1988).

The detention of a suspect having an aggressive conversation in a residential parking lot in late afternoon, where the suspect did nothing more suspicious than walk away from a police officer was not based on reasonable suspicion. Gurrola, *supra*.

A narcotic officer's conclusion that travel from Houston to the city of Chicago, using cash to purchase tickets, looking around the train station lobby, speaking little with one's traveling companions, and becoming nervous when involuntarily detained in public by narcotics investigators does not support a sufficient inference of wrongdoing to justify an investigatory detention where there is no information in the record to support an inference that drug dealers engage in these behaviors on a more frequent basis than the general public. Crockett v. State, 803 S.W.2d 308 (Tex. Crim. App. 1991).

In order for an officer's detention of a suspect to have been reasonable, the suspect's conduct must have been sufficiently distinguishable from that of innocent people under the same circumstances as to clearly, if not conclusively, set him apart from innocent people. Montano v. State, 843 S.W.2d 579 (Tex. Crim. App. 1992).

In Montano, the officer's observations of the following conduct, even taken together, were not sufficient to justify a temporary detention:

- Defendant and his companion had appeared nervous and appeared to have been scanning the area for someone watching or following them;
- Defendant and his companion asked a question of an airline employee and then bypassed ticket counters before approaching a concourse;
- Defendant was wearing a heavy leather jacket even though it was a warm and sunny day;
- Defendant handed his bag to his companion before going through the magnetometer, whereupon the companion placed the defendant's bag on the conveyor to be x-rayed;
- When stopped, the defendant stated that they were traveling to San Antonio on Northwest Airlines (although the officers knew that Northwest Airlines did not have a flight to San Antonio at that hour); and
- Both suspects acted nervous throughout the detention.

An anonymous tip that a described person is carrying a firearm, without more, is not sufficient to justify a Terry stop because it provides no predictive information which would allow testing of the informant's knowledge and credibility, and because it contains no means to test the reliability of the assertion of illegality beyond the identity of the determinative person. Florida v. J.L., 529 U.S. 529, 120 S.Ct. 1375, 146 L. Ed. 2d 254 (2000).

An officer does not have sufficient reasonable suspicion to detain a suspect when the totality of his information is based upon observing the suspect walking with another person at 2 a.m. in an area known for narcotics activity and combined with the officer's unsubstantiated belief the suspect is a known criminal. Brodnex v. State, 485 S.W.3d 432, 438 (Tex. Crim. App. 2016).

Even though an investigatory detention may be unconstitutional, evidence seized as part of a search incident to arrest following the detention may be admissible where discovery of a valid arrest warrant attenuates the connection between the unlawful stop and the evidence seized incident to arrest. Utah v. Strieff, 579 U.S. ___, 136 S.Ct. 2056, 2064, 195 L.Ed.2d 400 (2016).

§3:32.4 Searches of Persons During Investigative Detentions (Terry Searches)

When an officer validly detains a person for investigation, even in the absence of probable cause, he can conduct a limited search of the outer clothing for weapons where he reasonably fears for his or her safety, or that of others. Terry v. Ohio, 392 U.S. 1, 88 S.Ct. 1868, 20 L.Ed.2d 889 (1968); Davis v. State, 829 S.W.2d 218 (Tex. Crim. App. 1992).

Whether a police frisk of the outside of a defendant's pocket for weapons is legal is judged under the objective standard of whether the facts available to the officer at the time of the frisk would warrant a reasonably cautious person to believe that the action taken was appropriate. Griffin v. State, 215 S.W.3d 403 (Tex. Crim. App. 2006).

Under the objective standard, the officer's testimony that he did not subjectively fear the defendant is not dispositive of whether the officer could legally frisk the defendant for weapons. Griffin.

The officer making the Terry search must have information leading him to reasonably believe that the defendant is armed and dangerous in order to conduct the search. Sibron v. State of New York, 392 U.S. 40, 88 S.Ct. 1889, 20 L.Ed.2d 917 (1968); Davis, *supra*. The purpose of a limited search after an investigatory stop is not to discover evidence of crime, but to allow the peace officer to pursue investigation without fear of violence. Davis.

A Terry search is not justified as a matter of routine. O'Hara v. State, 27 S.W.3d 548 (Tex. Crim. App. 2000).

However, it is objectively reasonable for police to believe that a seller of narcotics might be armed because concealed weapons are part and parcel of the drug trade, especially where the police knew that the seller had been arrested for the same offense just two days before and moved his hand toward his pocket during an investigative detention based on reasonable suspicion. Griffin.

An officer need not be absolutely certain that an individual is armed; the issue is whether a reasonably prudent person would justifiably believe he or others are in danger. O'Hara; Balentine v. State, 71 S.W.3d 763 (Tex. Crim. App. 2002).

Where law enforcement officers stopped the defendant pursuant to an articulable suspicion that he was trafficking in cocaine, they are justified in approaching him with caution, and under these circumstances it is not unreasonable for them to conduct a limited search for weapons because weapons and violence are frequently associated with drug transactions. Carmouche v. State, 10 S.W.3d 323 (Tex. Crim. App. 2000). *See also,* Illinois v. Wardlow, 528 U.S. 119, 120 S.Ct. 673, 145 L.Ed.2d 570 (2000).

Terry permits a search for only those weapons that could reasonably harm the police officer. If in the course of a pat-down frisk the officer satisfies himself that the suspect has no such weapons, the officer has no valid reason to further invade the suspect's right to be free of police intrusion absent probable cause to arrest. Lippert v. State, 664 S.W.2d 712, 721 (Tex. Crim. App. 1984); Davis, *supra*.

Where an officer frisks a suspect during an investigatory detention and finds a matchbox in the suspect's pocket, the officer is not permitted to search the matchbox without further articulation of why he believed the matchbox contained a weapon and why he feared the suspect could use it against him. Davis.

The discovery of what was suspected to be a pen or pencil in the suspect's pocket, and was later found to be a crack pipe, will not give rise to a reasonable suspicion of possession of a weapon. Thomas v. State, 853 S.W.2d 734 (Tex.App.—Houston [1st Dist.] 1993, *no pet.*).

Several factors should be considered in determining whether a weapons search is justified:

- Flight
- Inadvertent gestures and sudden movements toward a pocket where a weapon might be concealed
- Threats and attempts to resist detention
- Commission of a criminal offense
- Intoxication

Worthey v. State, 805 S.W.2d 435 (Tex. Crim. App. 1991); Lippert v. State, 664 S.W.2d 712 (Tex. Crim. App. 1984).

A pat-down is justified where the officer is alone, the stop occurs on a rural roadway and the defendant is wearing a "belt-knife." O'Hara, *supra*.

The defendant's inconsistent statements to the investigating officer are a factor that can justify an officer's suspicion that the defendant may be the type of person who would conceal a weapon. Balentine.

The fact that the police/citizen encounter occurs in a high crime, high drug area is a factor in an analysis as to whether a frisk for weapons was proper under the totality of the circumstances. Furr v. State, 499 S.W.3d 872, 881 (Tex. Crim. App. 2016).

It is reasonable for a police officer to search a defendant's purse where the officer told the defendant not to move her hand, yet she made a sudden move for her purse obstructing her hand and purse from the officer's view, and where the defendant could have easily retrieved a gun from the purse. Worthey, *supra*.

When during the course of a pat-down search an officer feels what he suspects to be a weapon, he can remove the item from the defendant to further investigate. When in the course of doing so the officer discovers that the item is not a weapon, it does not render the search unreasonable. The fruits of such a search are admissible in evidence against the defendant. Balentine.

Officers may use such force as is reasonably necessary to effect the goal of the stop, investigation, maintenance of the status quo, or officer safety. Terry v. Ohio, 392 U.S. 1, 88 S.Ct. 1868, 20 L.Ed.2d 889 (1968).

PRACTICE TIP: Cross-examination of the seizing officer during a motion to suppress evidence discovered during a "pat-down" search should clearly establish:

- Specific facts which indicated the unusual activity was related to crime
- Specific crime to which the activity was related
- At what specific point during the "pat-down" did the officer feel he could pursue his investigation without fear of violence
- How and why the object seized from the defendant could be believed to be a weapon.

Though an officer may ask a defendant to identify himself during a valid investigative detention, that does not automatically mean that the officer can search a defendant's person to obtain or confirm his identity. Consequently, the officer cannot reach into a defendant's pocket for his identification unless there exists some exception to the usual probable cause requirement. Baldwin v. State, 278 S.W.3d 367 (Tex. Crim. App. 2009).

§3:32.5 Plain Touch Doctrine

Under the "plain touch" doctrine, contraband detected through the sense of touch during a pat-down search may be admissible where its evidentiary value is immediately apparent. Minnesota v. Dickerson, 508 U.S. 366, 113 S.Ct. 2130, 124 L.Ed.2d 334 (1993); Strickland v. State, 923 S.W.2d 617 (Tex.App.—Houston [1st Dist.] 1995, *no pet.*).

If the officer conducting the pat-down search has to squeeze, slide or otherwise manipulate the contents of the area being searched, the officer has exceeded the bounds of the pat-down search and evidence obtained is inadmissible. Minnesota v. Dickerson, *supra*; Strickland, *supra*.

The seizure of an item whose identity is already known occasions no further invasion of privacy. Garcia v. State, 967 S.W.2d 902 (Tex.App.—Austin 1998, *no pet.*); Graham v. State, 893 S.W.2d 4 (Tex.App.—Dallas 1994, *no pet.*).

Since the evidentiary value of a matchbook is not immediately apparent from is plain feel, its seizure will not be upheld under the plain feel exception. Moore v. State, 855 S.W.2d 123 (Tex. App.—Tyler 1993, *no pet.*).

Where an object on the defendant's person felt like a pen or pencil to the officer conducting a frisk of the defendant, the plain feel exception does not allow its seizure. Thomas v. State, 853 S.W.2d 734 (Tex.App.—Houston [1st Dist.] 1993, *no pet.*).

Where the searching officer testified that he immediately recognized the incriminating nature of a cellophane baggie when he patted down the defendant's pocket during a Terry stop before further manipulating the object, the search was proper. In the matter of L.R., 975 S.W.2d 656 (Tex. App.—San Antonio 1998, *no writ*).

Where the officer frisking the defendant pursuant to a tip that the defendant possessed narcotics immediately recognized the bulge in the defendant's pocket as money, the scope of the search was reasonable and the testimony properly admitted. Carmouche v. State, 10 S.W.3d 323 (Tex. Crim. App. 2000).

Where a police officer immediately recognizes a container in the defendant's pocket that is the same type of container in which the defendant had previously been caught carrying contraband, the evidentiary value is immediately apparent and the object can be removed from the pocket. Griffin v. State, 215 S.W.3d 403 (Tex. Crim. App. 2006).

Where the incriminating character of a 35-millimeter film canister was not immediately apparent under the facts known to the officer making the search, the evidence obtained therefrom should be suppressed. Campbell v. State, 864 S.W.2d 223 (Tex.App.—Waco 1993, *pet. ref'd*).

When the conditions of the plain feel doctrine are not present, an officer conducting a valid investigative detention must have probable cause in order to conduct a search for non-weapon contraband or other evidence. Baldwin v. State, 278 S.W.3d 367 (Tex. Crim. App. 2009).

§3:33 Arrests

The third category of police-citizen interaction is that of an arrest. An arrest must be justified by probable cause to believe that the suspect has committed or is committing an offense. Amores v. State, 816 S.W.2d 407 (Tex. Crim. App. 1991).

A person who is temporarily handcuffed and detained, but then released, has been seized and detained under the Fourth Amendment, but he has not necessarily been arrested. State v. Sheppard, 271 S.W.3d 281 (Tex. Crim. App. 2008).

CCP Art. 15.22.

> *A person is arrested when he has been actually placed under restraint or taken into custody by an officer or person executing a warrant of arrest, or by an officer or person arresting without a warrant.*

Article 15.22 is of no help in determining whether that person has been subjected to a Fourth Amendment arrest or an investigatory detention. The statute, drafted long before *Terry v. Ohio*, has been called "legislatively obsolete" because it does not distinguish between custodial arrests and temporary detentions. Sheppard.

Whether a police/citizen encounter is categorized as an "arrest" or "detention" depends upon several factors, including the amount of force displayed, the duration of the detention, the efficiency of the investigative process and whether it is conducted at the original location or the person is transported to another location, the officer's expressed intent-that is, whether he told the detained person that he was under arrest or was being detained only for a temporary investigation, and any other relevant factors. If the degree of incapacitation appears more than necessary to simply safeguard the officers and assure the suspect's presence during a period of investigation, this suggests the detention is an arrest. Sheppard.

The test for probable cause for a warrantless arrest is whether at that moment the facts and circumstances within the officer's knowledge and of which he had reasonably trustworthy information were sufficient to warrant a prudent man in believing the arrested person had committed or

SEARCH AND SEIZURE: PERSONS

was committing an offense. Guzman v. State, 955 S.W.2d 85 (Tex. Crim. App. 1997).

§3:40 Searches of Persons Incident to Arrest

Under both the Fourth Amendment to the United States Constitution and under Art. I, §9 of the Texas Constitution, searches of a person and the area within his immediate control are excepted from the requirement of a warrant when incident to the lawful arrest of such person and otherwise proper in scope. United States v. Robinson, 414 U.S. 218, 94 S.Ct. 467, 38 L.Ed.2d 427 (1973); Busby v. State, 990 S.W.2d 263 (Tex. Crim. App. 1999); Carrasco v. State, 712 S.W.2d 120 (Tex. Crim. App. 1986).

Fourth Amendment jurisprudence prohibits unreasonable searches incident to arrest. McGee v. State, 105 S.W.3d 609 (Tex. Crim. App. 2003); Illinois v. Lafayette, 462 U.S. 640, 103 S.Ct. 2605, 77 L.Ed.2d 65 (1983).

The initial burden of proof is on a defendant when he seeks to suppress evidence obtained as a result of a warrantless arrest. Russell v. State, 717 S.W.2d 7 (Tex. Crim. App.1986); Young v. State, 283 S.W.3d 854 (Tex. Crim. App. 2009).

As the movant in the motion to suppress evidence, a defendant must produce evidence that defeats the presumption of proper police conduct. Russell; Young.

Once this is shown, the burden shifts to the State to either produce evidence of a warrant or prove the reasonableness of the arrest. Young.

There are two rationales for the search incident to arrest exception to the warrant requirement: 1) the need to disarm the suspect in order to take him into custody; and 2) the need to preserve evidence for later use at trial. Knowles v. Iowa, 525 U.S. 113, 119 S.Ct. 484, 142 L.Ed.2d 492 (1998).

A search can be validly conducted as a search incident to arrest only if it is substantially contemporaneous with the arrest and is confined to the immediate vicinity of the arrest. Stoner v. California, 376 U.S. 483, 84 S.Ct. 889, 11 L.Ed.2d 856 (1964).

When an arrest is made, it is reasonable for the arresting officer to search the arrestee's person and the area within his immediate control, meaning the area from within which he might gain possession of a weapon or destructible evidence. Chimel v. California, 395 U.S. 752, 89 S.Ct. 2034, 23 L.Ed.2d 685 (1969); Goodwin v. State, 799 S.W.2d 719 (Tex. Crim. App. 1990).

A search incident to a valid arrest needs no additional Fourth Amendment justification, and a full search of the person may be made, extending to all clothing worn and containers carried by the arrestee. United States v. Robinson, *supra*; Gustafson v. Florida, 414 U.S. 260, 94 S.Ct. 488, 38 L.Ed.2d 456 (1973).

The Fourth Amendment does not prohibit the search of a person incident to arrest based on probable cause where the person was placed under custodial arrest in violation of a state law that allows only the issuance of a summons for the offense. Virginia v. Moore, 553 U.S. 164, 128 S.Ct. 1598, 170 L.Ed.2d 559 (2008).

Searches and seizures that can be made on the spot at the time of the arrest may legally be conducted later when the accused arrives at the place of detention. United States v. Edwards, 415 U.S. 800, 94 S.Ct. 1234, 39 L.Ed.2d 771 (1974); Rogers v. State, 774 S.W.2d 247 (Tex. Crim. App. 1989).

In the context of a search incident to arrest, it is irrelevant that the arrest occurs immediately before or after the search as long as sufficient probable cause existed for the officers to arrest before the search was conducted. State v. Ballard, 987 S.W.2d 889 (Tex. Crim. App. 1999); State v. Ford, 537 S.W.3d 19, 24 (Tex. Crim. App. 2017). .

A search which precedes an arrest and which precipitates the arrest cannot be justified as a search incident to arrest. Smith v. Ohio, 494 U.S. 541, 110 S.Ct. 1288, 108 L.Ed.2d 464 (1990).

CCP Art. 38.23 does not require the exclusion of evidence that a crime was committed after an unlawful arrest. Donoho v. State, 39 S.W.3d 324 (Tex.App.—Fort Worth No. 2001) (where the defendant committed an aggravated assault on a peace officer after an arrest); State v. Mayorga, 901 S.W.2d 943 (Tex. Crim. App. 1995) (where the defendant resisted arrest after an illegal detention).

A police officer who validly searches a person incident to arrest, and who encounters something of a suspicious nature may continue to investigate the suspicious item. United States v. Robinson, *supra* (where a cigarette package was legally searched); Carrasco v. State, 712 S.W.2d 120 (Tex. Crim. App. 1986) (where a shoulder bag was searched).

The warrantless seizure of a suspect's clothing subsequent to a legal arrest, while in custody or detention, is permissible. United States v. Edwards, 415 U.S. 800, 94 S.Ct. 1234, 39 L.Ed.2d 771 (1974); Marquez v. State, 725 S.W.2d 217 (Tex. Crim. App. 1987); Oles v. State, 993 S.W.2d 103 (Tex. Crim. App. No. 0764-98, May 26, 1999) (even where the defendant has been in custody for eight days before the clothing is seized and it is seized for a different offense).

The wallet of a person arrested for traffic offenses may be validly searched as a search incident to arrest. Snyder v. State, 629 S.W.2d 930 (Tex. Crim. App. 1982).

Where there is probable cause, the limited intrusion to which a defendant is subjected when police scrape under his fingernails as part of a stationhouse detention is reasonable under the Fourth Amendment, given the potential for the ready destruction of the evidence. Cupp v. Murphy, 412 U.S. 291, 93 S.Ct. 2000, 36 L.Ed.2d 900 (1973).

Exigent circumstances can justify the warrantless swabbing of a defendant's penis to obtain DNA evidence based on the nature of the sexual assault offense, the strength of the probable cause, the relatively short amount of time between the assault and the search, the showing of a need to act before the DNA evidence could be damaged or destroyed, and the manner in which the search was conducted in a private room by a trained technician, under both the Fourth Amendment and Art. I, sec. 9 of the Texas Constitution. Ontiveros v. State, 240 S.W.3d 369 (Tex.App.—Austin 2007, *pet.ref'd*).

When officers make an arrest supported by probable cause to hold for a serious offense and they bring the suspect to the station to be detained in custody, taking and analyzing a cheek swab of the arrestee's DNA is, like fingerprinting and photographing, a legitimate police booking procedure that is reasonable under the Fourth Amendment. Maryland v. King, 569 U.S. ___, 133 S.Ct. 1958, 186 L.Ed. 2d 1 (2013).

In some circumstances a valid search incident to arrest can include a visual body cavity search. McGee.

A warrant is generally required before searching a cell phone that is seized incident to arrest. Riley v. California, ___ U.S. ___, ___ S.Ct. ___, ___ L.Ed.2d ___ (Nos. 13-132 and 13-212, 2014 WL 2864483, June 25, 2014).

§3:50 Searches of Persons During Stop of Automobile and Bus

When officers make a valid traffic stop, they are entitled to take sufficient measures to guarantee their safety, which includes ordering drivers out of their cars. Pennsylvania v. Mimms, 434 U.S. 106, 98 S.Ct. 330, 54 L.Ed.2d 331 (1977); Goodwin v. State, 799 S.W.2d 719 (Tex. Crim. App. 1990).

The Mimms rule applies to passengers as well as to drivers. That is, an officer making a traffic stop may also order passengers to get out of the car pending completion of the stop. Maryland v. Wilson, 519 U. S. 408, 117 S.Ct. 882, 137 L.Ed.2d 41 (1997).

A passenger is seized, just as the driver is, from the moment a car stopped by the police comes to a halt on the side of the road. A passenger therefore has standing to challenge a stop's constitutionality. Brendlin v. California, 551 U. S. 249, 127 S.Ct. 2400, 168 L.Ed.2d 132 (2007).

The temporary seizure of driver and passengers ordinarily continues, and remains reasonable, for the duration of the stop. Normally, the stop ends when the police have no further need to control the scene, and inform the driver and passengers they are free to leave. An officer's inquiries into matters unrelated to the justification for the traffic stop do not convert the encounter into something other than a lawful seizure, so long as those inquiries do not measurably extend the duration of the stop. Arizona v. Johnson, 555 U.S. 323, 129 S.Ct. 781, 172 L.Ed.2d 694 (2009) (citing Muehler v. Mena, 544 U. S. 93, 125 S.Ct. 1465, 161 L.Ed.2d 299 (2005)).

Officers who conduct routine traffic stops may perform a Terry frisk of a driver and any passengers upon reasonable suspicion that they may be armed and dangerous. Knowles v. Iowa, 525 U. S. 113, 119 S.Ct. 484, 142 L.Ed.2d 492 (1998).

Police are not authorized to conduct a vehicle search incident to a recent occupant's arrest after the arrestee has been secured and cannot access the interior of the vehicle. Arizona v. Gant, 556 U.S. 332, 129 S.Ct. 1710, 173 L.Ed.2d 485 (2009) (limiting the rule of New York v. Belton, 453 U.S. 454, 101 S.Ct. 2860, 69 L.Ed.2d 768 (1981)).

Circumstances unique to the automobile context justify a search incident to arrest when it is reasonable to believe that evidence of the offense of arrest might be found in the vehicle. Arizona v. Gant (citing Thornton v. United States, 541 U. S. 615, 124 S.Ct. 2127, 158 L.Ed.2d 905 (2004)).

However, if the officer stops a person for speeding and issues a citation rather than making a full custodial arrest, he is not permitted to make a full search of the vehicle. Knowles v. Iowa, 525 U.S. 113, 119 S.Ct. 484, 142 L.Ed.2d 492 (1998).

Where police have probable cause to believe that a vehicle contains contraband, they may search the entire vehicle including the belongings of passengers that are capable of containing the object of the probable cause. Wyoming v. Houghton, 526 U.S. 295, 119 S.Ct. 1297, 143 L.Ed.2d 408 (No. 1999).

If an arrestee is not an occupant or recent occupant of a vehicle, the validity of the search is examined under a Chimel analysis; *i.e.*, was the search limited to the area within the immediate control of the arrestee. State v. Kelly, 963 S.W.2d 866 (Tex.App.—San Antonio 1998, *no pet.*).

In determining whether the arrestee was a recent occupant of a vehicle at the time of his arrest, several factors should be examined:

- Arrestee's temporal and spatial proximity to his vehicle
- Whether there is evidence of flight
- Whether there is an indication that the arrestee quickly exited his vehicle in an attempt to avoid police contact

These factors should be balanced against law enforcement's need to search the vehicle for protective purposes. Kelly, *supra*; Satterwhite v. State, 726 S.W.2d 81 (Tex. Crim. App. 1986).

Where an officer has reasonable grounds to believe that he is in danger of bodily injury at the hands of the occupants of a vehicle, a limited search is permissible solely for his own protection. Satterwhite, *supra*.

Once a police officer makes a *bona fide* stop or arrest for a traffic offense, he can make an additional arrest for any other offense unexpectedly discovered while investigating or questioning the motorist. Bachick v. State, 30 S.W.3d 549 (Tex. App.—Fort Worth 2000, *pet. ref'd*); Hernandez v. State, 867 S.W.2d 900 (Tex.App.—Texarkana 1993, *no pet.*).

The Fourth Amendment permits police officers to approach bus passengers at random to ask questions and to request their consent to searches, provided a reasonable person would understand that he or she is free to refuse. Florida v. Bostick, 501 U.S. 429, 111 S.Ct. 2382, 115 L.Ed.2d 389 (1991).

It is not required under the Fourth Amendment that the police officers inform the bus passengers of their right to refuse for a consent to search to be valid. U.S. v. Drayton, 536 U.S. 194, 122 S.Ct. 2105, 153 L.Ed.2d 242 (2002). *See* Illinois v. Caballes, 543 U.S. 405, 125 S.Ct. 834, 160 L.Ed.2d 842 (2005).

§3:60 Searches of Persons Incidental to Search Warrants

Officers executing a search warrant for contraband have the authority to detain the occupants of the premises while a proper search is conducted. Michigan v. Summers, 452 U.S. 692, 101 S.Ct. 2587, 69 L.Ed.2d 340 (1981); Muehler v. Mena, 544 U.S. 93, 125 S.Ct. 1465, 161 L.Ed.2d 299 (2005).

However, once an individual has left the immediate vicinity of premises to be searched, a detention must be justified by some other rationale. Bailey v. U.S., 568 U.S. 186, 133 S.Ct. 1031, 1043, 185 L.Ed.2d 19 (2013).

A person's mere presence on the scene of the execution of a search warrant, without more (such as being named in the search warrant or there being a reasonable Terry articulation of danger perceived by police) does not allow a search of that person incident to the execution of the warrant. Ybarra v. Illinois, 444 U.S. 85, 100 S.Ct. 338, 62 L.Ed.2d 238 (1979); Lippert, *supra*; Samuel v. State, 895 S.W.2d 487 (Tex.

App.—Austin 1995); Gordon v. State, 4 S.W.3d 32 (Tex.App.—El Paso 1999, *no pet.*).

Where officers had a warrant to search for narcotics on the premises where the defendant was located, and upon seeing the narcotics team the defendant immediately began to run, the officers had reasonable suspicion to detain and frisk the defendant. Salazar v. State, 893 S.W.2d 138 (Tex. App.—Houston [1st Dist.] 1995, *pet. ref'd*).

§3:70 Inventory Searches of Persons

At the stationhouse, it is entirely proper for the police to remove and list or inventory property found on the person or in the possession of an arrested person who is to be jailed. A range of governmental interests supports an inventory process. Illinois v. Lafayette, 462 U.S. 640, 103 S.Ct. 2605, 77 L.Ed.2d 65 (1983); Nash v. State, 682 S.W.2d 338 (Tex.App.—Dallas 1984, *no pet.*).

It is not unreasonable for police, as part of the routine inventory procedure incident to incarcerating an arrested person, to search any container or article in his possession, in accordance with established inventory procedures. Illinois v. Lafayette, *supra.*

Examining all the items removed from the arrestee's person and listing them is justified as a reasonable administrative procedure to protect the police against false claims and to protect the arrestee against theft of property in police custody. Nash, *supra.*

Police are not required to obtain a warrant to seize, at the jail, the clothing of a defendant who is lawfully in custody as the result of a lawful arrest. United States v. Edwards, 415 U.S. 800, 806-07, 94 S.Ct. 1234, 1239, 39 L.Ed.2d 771 (1974); Oles v. State, 993 S.W.2d 103 (Tex. Crim. App. No. 0764-98, May 26, 1999); Contreras v. State, 838 S.W.2d 594 (Tex.App.—Corpus Christi 1992, *pet. ref'd*).

This is because the defendant harbors no reasonable expectation of privacy in his clothing that is in the custody of law enforcement officers. Oles, *supra.*

§3:71 Jail and Prison Searches

Deference must be given to the officials in charge of a jail or correctional facility to conduct the type of body search of detainees that they feel necessary unless there is substantial evidence demonstrating that their response to a situation is exaggerated. This can include strip-type searches of persons detained for minor offenses, as well as body cavity inspections. Florence v. Board of Chosen Freeholders of County of Burlington, 566 U.S. 318, 132 S.Ct. 1510, 182 L.Ed.2d 566 (2012).

Society is not prepared to recognize as legitimate any subjective expectation of privacy that a prisoner might have in his prison cell and, accordingly, the Fourth Amendment proscription against unreasonable searches does not apply within the confines of the prison cell. Hudson v. Palmer, 468 U.S. 517, 104 S.Ct. 3194, 82 L.Ed.2d 393 (1984).

§3:80 Searches of Persons at Airports, Bus and Train Stations

An encounter between a citizen and police officers is not rendered a detention simply by virtue of the facts that the officers involved asked for the citizen's identification and requested to search his bag during the course of the encounter. Hunter v. State, 955 S.W.2d 102 (Tex. Crim. App. 1997).

Six factors are important to a determination whether police have communicated to the defendant that he is not free to leave an encounter such that he is, in fact, detained:

- Whether the officer was in uniform
- Whether the officer exhibited a weapon
- Number of officers present
- Whether the officer suggested that he would obtain a warrant if the defendant did not comply
- Whether the officer told the defendant he believed the defendant was engaged in crime
- Whether the officer told the defendant that compliance was or was not required

Hunter, *supra.*

A consensual pat-down search does not elevate an encounter to the level of a detention. Henderson v. State, 965 S.W.2d 710 (Tex.App.—Houston [1st Dist.] 1998, *pet. ref'd*).

SEARCH AND SEIZURE: PERSONS

Where officers have specific and articulable facts that warrant a reasonable belief that a defendant's luggage contains drugs, they may seize the luggage briefly to pursue further investigation. United States v. Place, 462 U.S. 696, 103 S.Ct. 2637, 77 L.Ed.2d 110 (1983).

The seizure of luggage carries the same scope limitations as the seizure of a person where seized on less than probable cause. United States v. Place, *supra*. A 90-minute seizure of luggage based upon reasonable suspicion has been found to be unreasonable. United States v. Place.

Using a trained narcotics dog to sniff a defendant's luggage does not constitute a search for Fourth Amendment purposes. United States v. Place, *supra*; Strout v. State, 688 S.W.2d 188 (Tex. App.—Amarillo 1985, *no pet.*).

A narcotic officer's exploratory physical manipulation of a piece of luggage found near its owner is a violation of the Fourth Amendment. Bond v. U.S., 529 U.S. 334, 146 L. Ed. 2d 365 (2000).

Where a suspect denies ownership of a piece of luggage during an encounter with police, police may validly search the luggage without a warrant because there was a voluntary abandonment. Wooden v. State, 886 S.W.2d 385 (Tex.App.—Houston [1st Dist.] 1994, *no pet.*).

Where the defendant paid cash for round trip tickets out a roll of $20 bills, traveled under a name that did not match that under which his telephone number was listed, was headed to Miami, stayed in Miami only 48 hours, appeared nervous during the trip, and checked none of his luggage, sufficient reasonable suspicion existed to detain him for further investigation. United States v. Sokolow, 490 U.S. 1, 109 S.Ct. 1581, 104 L.Ed.2d 1 (1989).

The fact that a defendant arrived from Fort Lauderdale, arrived early in the morning, that he and his companion tried to conceal the fact that they were travelling together, and that he and his companion had no luggage was not sufficient to support a reasonable suspicion that he was committing a criminal offense. Reid v. Georgia, 448 U.S. 438, 100 S.Ct. 2752, 65 L.Ed.2d 890 (1980).

A narcotic officer's findings that travel from Houston to the city of Chicago, using cash to purchase tickets, looking around the train station lobby, speaking little with one's traveling companions, and becoming nervous when involuntarily detained in public by narcotics investigators does not support a sufficient inference of wrongdoing to justify an investigatory detention where there is no information in the record to support an inference that drug dealers engage in these behaviors on a more frequent basis than the general public. Crockett v. State, 803 S.W.2d 308 (Tex. Crim. App. 1991).

In order for an officer's detention of a suspect to have been reasonable, the suspect's conduct must have been sufficiently distinguishable from that of innocent people under the same circumstances as to clearly, if not conclusively, set him apart from innocent people. Montano v. State, 843 S.W.2d 579 (Tex. Crim. App. 1992).

Even taken together, the following officer's observations were not sufficient to justify a temporary detention:

- Defendant and his companion had appeared nervous and appeared to have been scanning the area for someone watching or following them
- Defendant and his companion asked a question of an airline employee and then bypassed ticket counters before approaching a concourse
- Defendant was wearing a heavy leather jacket even though it was a warm and sunny day
- Defendant handed his bag to his companion before going through the magnetometer, whereupon the companion placed the defendant's bag on the conveyor to be x-rayed
- When stopped, the defendant stated that they were traveling to San Antonio on Northwest Airlines (although the officers knew that Northwest Airlines did not have a flight to San Antonio at that hour)
- Both suspects acted nervous throughout the detention

Montano, *supra*.

§3:90 Invasive Body Searches

§3:90.1 Statutory Law

Tex. Code Crim. Pro. Art. 18.24. BODY CAVITY SEARCH DURING TRAFFIC STOP. (a) In this article, "body cavity search" means an inspection that is conducted of a person's anal or vaginal cavity in any manner, but the term does not include a pat-down.

(b) Notwithstanding any other law, a peace officer may not conduct a body cavity search of a person during a traffic stop unless the officer first obtains a search warrant pursuant to this chapter authorizing the body cavity search.

§3:90.2 Case Law

There are several different forms of intrusive searches: strip searches, visual body-cavity searches, and manual body-cavity searches. McGee v. State, 105 S.W.3d 609 (Tex. Crim. App. 2003).

The term "strip search" generally refers to an inspection of a naked person, without any scrutiny of the person's cavities. A "visual body-cavity search" includes a visual inspection of a person's anal or genital areas. A "manual body-cavity search" involves some degree of probing or touching a person's body cavities. McGee.

In deciding whether to admit evidence discovered during an intrusive search, courts must consider the scope of the particular intrusion, the manner in which it is conducted, the justification for initiating it, and the place in which it is conducted. McGee.

In reviewing a motion to suppress evidence taken from a defendant's body, six factors should be considered in determining the reasonableness of such bodily search and seizure:

- Existence of probable cause and a search warrant, absent exigent circumstances
- Extent to which the procedure threatens the safety or health of the individual
- Taking of all reasonable medical precautions and employment of no unusual or untested procedure
- Procedure was performed by a physician in a hospital according to accepted medical practices
- Search may be unjustifiable if it endangers the life or health of the accused
- Extent of intrusion upon the individual's dignitary interests, personal privacy, and bodily integrity

Winston v. Lee, 470 U.S. 753, 105 S.Ct. 1611, 84 L.Ed.2d 662 (1985); State v. Avila, 910 S.W.2d 505 (Tex.App.—El Paso 1994, *no pet.*).

The natural metabolization of alcohol in the bloodstream does not present a per se exigency that justifies an exception to the Fourth Amendment's warrant requirement for nonconsensual blood testing in all drunk-driving cases. Consistent with general Fourth Amendment principles, the exigency in the DWI/blood draw context must be determined case by case based on the totality of the circumstances. Missouri v. McNeely, 569 U.S. 141, 133 S. Ct. 1552, 185 L. Ed. 2d 696 (2013).

The taking of a defendant's blood from his body is a search for Fourth Amendment purposes. State v. Johnston, 336 S.W.3d 649 (Tex. Crim. App. 2011); citing Schmerber v. California, 384 U.S. 757, 86 S.Ct. 1826, 16 L.Ed.2d 908 (1966).

Where a hospital performs a diagnostic test to obtain evidence of a patient's criminal conduct for law enforcement, it is an unreasonable search if the patient has not consented to the procedure, because the interest of using the threat of criminal sanctions to deter pregnant women from using drugs cannot justify a departure from the general rule that an official nonconsensual search is unconstitutional if not authorized by a valid warrant. Ferguson v. Charleston, 532 U.S. 429, 111 S.Ct. 2382, 149 L.Ed.2d 205 (2001).

The taking of a defendant's urine is a search for Fourth Amendment purposes. Macias v. State, 649 S.W.2d 150 (Tex.App.—El Paso 1983, *no pet.*).

The taking of dental casts of a defendant is a type of relatively unintrusive identification evidence that is seizable without constitutional implication. Marquez v. State, 725 S.W.2d 217 (Tex. Crim. App. 1987).

Where police had probable cause to believe that the defendant has drugs in his mouth and would try to destroy the evidence, they were permitted to search his mouth for the drugs. Holmes v. State,

962 S.W.2d 663 (Tex.App.—Waco 1998, *pet. ref'd* untimely filed).

Where there is probable cause, the limited intrusion to which a defendant is subjected when police scrape under his fingernails as part of a stationhouse detention is reasonable under the Fourth Amendment given the potential for ready destruction of the evidence. Cupp v. Murphy, 412 U.S. 291, 93 S.Ct. 2000, 36 L.Ed.2d 900 (1973).

Exigent circumstances can justify the warrantless swabbing of a defendant's penis to obtain DNA evidence based on the nature of the sexual assault offense, the strength of the probable cause, the relatively short amount of time between the assault and the search, the showing of a need to act before the DNA evidence could be damaged or destroyed, and the manner in which the search was conducted in a private room by a trained technician, under both the Fourth Amendment and Art. I, sec. 9 of the Texas Constitution. Ontiveros v. State, 240 S.W.3d 369 (Tex.App.—Austin 2007, *pet.ref'd*).

Relatively unintrusive identification evidence, like fingerprints, line-ups, and handwriting exemplars, can be gathered without a warrant while a person is in custody after arrest, without violating the Fourth Amendment. Contreras v. State, 838 S.W.2d 594 (Tex.App.—Corpus Christi 1992, *pet. ref'd*); Mulder v. State, 707 S.W.2d 908, 914 (Tex. Crim. App. 1986)

Scent-discrimination lineups, whether conducted with individuals or inanimate objects, are separate and distinct from dog-scent tracking evidence. Even the briefest review of the scientific principles underlying dog scenting reveals that, contrary to the conclusions of many courts, there are significant scientific differences among the various uses of scenting: tracking, narcotics detection, and scent lineups. Winfrey v. State, 323 S.W.3d 875 (Tex. Crim. App. 2010).

Scent-discrimination lineups, when used alone or as primary evidence, are legally insufficient to support a conviction. Winfrey.

When officers make an arrest supported by probable cause to hold for a serious offense and they bring the suspect to the station to be detained in custody, taking and analyzing a cheek swab of the arrestee's DNA is, like fingerprinting and photographing, a legitimate police booking procedure that is reasonable under the Fourth Amendment. Maryland v. King, 569 U.S. ___, 133 S.Ct. 1958, 186 L.Ed. 2d 1 (2013).

§3:91 Blood Draws

A claim that the Fourth Amendment was violated may be based on a trespass theory of search, where one's own personal effects have been trespassed, or a privacy theory of search, where one's own expectation of privacy was breached. Under the privacy theory, a person has standing to contend that a search or seizure was unreasonable if (1) he has a subjective expectation of privacy in the place or object searched, and (2) society is prepared to recognize that expectation as reasonable or legitimate. State v. Martinez, 570 S.W.3d 278, 283 (Tex. Crim. App. 2019).

The withdrawal of blood from a person is considered a search under the Fourth Amendment. See Douds v. State, 434 S.W.3d 842 (Tex.App.—Houston [14th Dist.]2014, pet.granted).

The non-consensual taking of a blood sample for the purpose of determining the alcohol content of a semi-conscious suspect's blood can sometimes be justified by the exigency of the rapid dissipation of the alcohol. Aliff v. State, 627 S.W.2d 166 (Tex. Crim. App. 1982).

However, where the suspect is unconscious and cannot be given a breath test, the exigent circumstances rule almost always permits a blood test without a warrant. Mitchell v. Wisconsin, 588 U.S. ___, ___ S.Ct. ___, ___ L.Ed.2d ___ (No. 18-6210, 2019 WL 2619471, June 27, 2019).

The natural metabolization of alcohol in the bloodstream does not present a per se exigency that justifies an exception to the Fourth Amendment's warrant requirement for nonconsensual blood testing in all drunk-driving cases. Consistent with general Fourth Amendment principles, the exigency in the DWI/blood draw context must be determined case by case, based on the totality of the circumstances. Missouri v. McNeely, 569 U.S. 141, 133 S. Ct. 1552, 185 L. Ed. 2d 696 (2013).

The status of the case as a misdemeanor or felony does not affect the Fourth Amendment analysis under McNeely. See Douds v. State, 434 S.W.3d 842 (Tex.App.—Houston [14th Dist.]2014, pet.granted).

The defendant has the initial burden to produce evidence that the blood draw statute was violated and that the evidence should be excluded. If he meets that burden, the burden of proof then shifts to the state. State v. Robinson, 334 S.W.3d 776 (Tex. Crim. App. 2011).

Texas Transportation Code §724.012(b) does not constitute a valid exception to the Fourth Amendment's warrant requirement. State v. Anderson, 444 S.W.3d 895, 909 (Tex. App.—Beaumont, no pet.). This is a good case for general search of person issues and Supreme Court cases.

The analysis of biological samples, such as blood, is a search that infringes upon privacy interests subject to the Fourth Amendment. State v. Martinez, 570 S.W.3d 278, 290 (Tex. Crim. App. 2019).

There is a Fourth Amendment privacy interest in blood that has already been drawn for medical purposes. In cases where a defendant has not abandoned his blood, he will have a subjective expectation of privacy in his blood. In this circumstance, the State's subsequent testing of the blood is a Fourth Amendment search, separate and apart from the seizure of the blood by the State. Where no exception to the warrant requirement applied, the State was required to obtain a warrant before testing Appellee's blood. State v. Martinez, 570 S.W.3d at 292.

However, the State does not need a warrant to obtain the results of blood-alcohol testing performed by a hospital for medical purposes following a traffic accident. Huse v. State, 491 S.W.3d 833 (Tex. Crim. App. 2016).

The well-established exigent circumstances exception applies when the exigencies of the situation make the needs of law enforcement so compelling that a warrantless search is objectively reasonable under the Fourth Amendment. Under this exception, a law-enforcement officer may be justified in conducting a warrantless search to prevent the imminent destruction of evidence. State v. Garcia, 569 S.W.3d 142, 148 (Tex. Crim. App. 2018)(where the court found that the evidence did not support a finding of exigent circumstances).

Any exigent-circumstances review should be informed by the totality of the facts and circumstances available to the officer and analyzed under an objective standard of reasonableness. State v. Garcia, 569 S.W.3d at 148.

If an officer holds an objectively reasonable belief that an evidence-destroying medical treatment is about to take place, the Fourth Amendment does not command him to wait until the treatment is mere moments away before he may act. In such a situation, an officer is permitted to take all reasonable measures, up to and including initiating a warrantless blood draw, to preserve the integrity of important evidence. State v. Garcia, 569 S.W.3d at 159.

While prevention of the destruction of evidence can justify a warrantless search, this burden is difficult to sustain in a DWI warrantless blood draw case. Ordinary dissipation of alcohol in the blood and delays in getting a warrant probably will not justify the warrantless search. Anderson, 444 S.W.3d at 911.

The good faith exception found in Tex. Code Crim. Pro. art. 38.23(b) will not justify a warrantless blood draw because 38.23(b) requires that the officer relied in good faith on a warrant. Anderson, 444 S.W.3d at 912.

§3:100 Article 38.23 Jury Charge

Article 38.23 provides that evidence obtained in violation of the Constitution or laws of the United States or Texas may not be admitted in a criminal case. The statute also provides that a jury instruction should be submitted if a fact issue is raised about whether such a violation has occurred. The jury instruction requires the jury to disregard evidence that it finds was obtained in violation of the United States or Texas Constitution or laws. Hamal v. State, 390 S.W.3d 302 (Tex. Crim. App. 2012); Robinson v. State, 377 S.W.3d 712 (Tex. Crim. App. 2012).

To be entitled to an Article 38.23 jury instruction, three predicates must be met: (1) the evidence heard by the jury must raise an issue of fact; (2) the evidence on that fact must be affirmatively contested; and (3) the contested factual issue must be material to the lawfulness of the challenged conduct. Hamal, 390 S.W.3d at 306; Robinson, 377 S.W.3d at 719.

When a disputed, material issue of fact is successfully raised, the terms of the statute are mandatory, and the jury must be instructed accordingly. Evidence to justify an Article 38.23(a) instruction can derive from any source no matter whether strong, weak, contradicted, unimpeached, or unbelievable. But it must, in any event, raise a *factual* dispute about how the evidence was obtained. Where the issue raised by the evidence at trial does *not* involve controverted historical facts, but only the proper application of the law to undisputed facts, that issue is properly left to the determination of the trial court. Robinson, 377 S.W.3d at 719.

Under CCP Art. 38.23, the defendant is entitled to a jury charge where there has been a factual issue raised as to whether his detention was supported by adequate reasonable suspicion. The charge should instruct the jury that they should suppress the fruits of the detention and search if they find them to be illegal. Woods v. State, 956 S.W.2d 33 (Tex. Crim. App. 1997, *pet. ref'd*).

A defendant is not entitled to an article 38.23 instruction if the jury's verdict disposes of the issue that he asserts as the factual issue entitling him to the instruction. Porter v. State, 255 S.W.3d 234 (Tex. App.—Waco 2008, pet.ref'd)(where the jury's finding that the defendant was guilty of evading arrest or detention disposed of his issue that his detention was illegal); Wilkerson v. State, 933 S.W.2d 276 (Tex. App.—Houston [1st Dist.] 1996, pet.ref'd)(where the jury's finding that the defendant was guilty of delivery of drugs disposed of his issue that the police officer was lying and no drug transaction had occurred).

Upon the request of the losing party on a motion to suppress evidence, the trial court shall state its essential findings. By "essential findings," it is meant that the trial court must make findings of fact and conclusions of law adequate to provide an appellate court with a basis upon which to review the trial court's application of the law to the facts. State v. Cullen, 195 S.W.3d 696 (Tex. Crim. App. 2006).

PRACTICE TIP: TRCP 297, cited in Cullen, provides that the trial court shall file its findings of fact and conclusions of law within twenty days after a timely request is filed. It further provides that the court shall cause a copy of its findings and conclusions to be mailed to each party in the suit. The findings and conclusions need to be recorded in some way, whether written out and filed by the trial court, or stated on the record at the hearing.

The Fourth Amendment does not apply to the actions of private individuals, and reading Article 38.23 to apply the Fourth Amendment to private individuals would lead to an absurdity. Ruiz v. State, ___ S.W.3d ___ at *2 (PD-1348-17, 2019 WL 2814867, Tex. Crim. App. July 3, 2019).

A defendant who moves for suppression under Art. 38.23 due to the violation of a statute has the burden of producing evidence of a statutory violation. Only when this burden is met does the State bear a burden to prove compliance. State v. Robinson, 334 S.W.3d 776, 779 (Tex. Crim. App. 2011).

Searches conducted in objectively reasonable reliance on binding appellate precedent are not subject to the Fourth Amendment exclusionary rule. Davis v. U.S., 564 U.S. 229, 131 S.Ct. 2419, 180 L.Ed.2d 285 (2011).

PRACTICE TIP: Although Texas has the statutory exclusionary rule contained in Art. 38.23, the State can use the Davis case to argue that the evidence was not "obtained" in violation of the law where legal precedent at the time of police conduct allowed the police action.

§3:110 Challenging Searches of Person

Defense counsel may either file a pretrial motion to suppress evidence or wait until the trial on the merits and object when the alleged unlawfully obtained evidence is offered. The trial court has the option of either hearing a motion to suppress the evidence prior to trial or waiting until the defendant's counsel makes an objection at the trial on the merits when the alleged unlawfully obtained evidence is offered. Roberts v. State, 545 S.W.2d 157, 158 (Tex. Crim. App. 1977).

When a defendant asserts a search and seizure violation under the Fourth Amendment, the defendant bears the burden of producing evidence to rebut the presumption of proper conduct by law enforcement. Woodard v. State, 341 S.W.3d 404 (Tex. Crim. App. 2011).

A defendant can satisfy this burden with evidence that the seizure occurred without a warrant. Woodard.

If the defendant satisfies the initial burden, the burden then shifts to the State to establish that the seizure was nevertheless reasonable under the applicable standard—either reasonable suspicion or probable cause. Woodard.

It is within the trial court's discretion to grant the State's request to reopen a motion-to-suppress hearing to supplement the record with additional testimony, outside the jury's presence, even over the objection of the defendant. Black v. State, 362 S.W.3d 626 (Tex. Crim. App. 2012).

§3:111 Appellate Review of Motions to Suppress

When the defendant files a motion to suppress evidence on Fourth Amendment grounds, he has the initial burden of proving that a warrantless search occurred; if he succeeds, the burden shifts to the State to prove that a warrant requirement exception applies. In ruling on the motion, and upon request of the losing party, the trial judge is required to make findings of fact and conclusions of law expressing the basis for his ruling. Reviewing courts should afford almost total deference to the trial judge's findings on matters of historical fact, especially when those findings are based on an evaluation of credibility and demeanor. Applications of law to fact or mixed questions of law and fact are entitled to deference only if they turn on an evaluation of credibility and demeanor; otherwise, they are reviewed de novo. State v. Garcia, 569 S.W.3d 142, 148 (Tex. Crim. App. 2018).

A Fourth Amendment reasonableness inquiry should be informed by the facts that were available to the officer when he conducted the contested search. State v. Garcia, 569 S.W.3d at 150.

In assessing the reasonableness of an officer's actions, a reviewing court should take into account not only the facts known to the officer, but also the specific reasonable inferences which he is entitled to draw from the facts in light of his experience. State v. Garcia, 569 S.W.3d at 151.

Despite its fact-sensitive analysis, reasonableness is ultimately a question of substantive Fourth-Amendment law which should be reviewed de novo by an appeals court. State v. Garcia, 569 S.W.3d at 151-2.

When the trial court makes explicit fact findings, the appellate court determines whether the evidence (viewed in the light most favorable to the trial court's ruling) supports these fact findings. The reviewing court must defer to a trial judge's factual findings which, when read in their totality, reasonably support his legal conclusion—even if viewed piecemeal and in isolation, they might be considered ambiguous. We give the same non-technical, common-sense deference to the trial judge's individual factual findings as we do to the totality of those findings. State v. Garcia, 569 S.W.3d at 153.

The United States Supreme Court has expressly "decline[d] to hold that the seriousness of the offense under investigation itself creates exigent circumstances of the kind that under the Fourth Amendment justify a warrantless search." State v. Garcia, 569 S.W.3d at 153.

Chapter 4

RIGHT TO COUNSEL AND EFFECTIVE ASSISTANCE OF COUNSEL

Table of Contents

§4:10 Constitutional and Statutory Provisions

United States Constitution, Sixth Amendment: In all criminal prosecutions, the accused shall . . . have the assistance of counsel for his defense.

Texas Constitution, Art 1 §10 [H] e shall have the right of being heard by himself or counsel, or both.

CCP Art. 1.05. Rights Of Accused

In all criminal prosecutions the accused shall have a speedy public trial by an impartial jury. He shall have the right to demand the nature and cause of the accusation against him, and to have a copy thereof. He shall not be compelled to give evidence against himself. He shall have the right of being heard by himself, or counsel, or both; shall be confronted with the witnesses against him, and shall have compulsory process for obtaining witnesses in his favor. No person shall be held to answer for a felony unless on indictment of a grand jury.

CCP Art. 1.051

(a) A defendant in a criminal matter is entitled to be represented by counsel in an adversarial judicial proceeding. The right to be represented by counsel includes the right to consult in private with counsel sufficiently in advance of a proceeding to allow adequate preparation for the proceeding.

§4:20 Right to Counsel in General

The right to counsel exists under both the Fifth and Sixth amendments to the U.S. Constitution. McNeil v. Wisconsin, 501 U.S. 171, 111 S. Ct. 2204, 115 L.Ed.2d 158 (1991); Upton v. State, 853 S.W.2d 548 (Tex. Crim. App. 1993).

While there is a difference between the Fifth Amendment and Sixth Amendment rights to counsel, neither is superior or greater than the other. Patterson v. Illinois, 487 U.S. 285, 108 S. Ct. 2389, 101 L.Ed.2d 261 (1988).

The right to counsel attaches in any criminal trial the result of which is to deprive a defendant of his liberty, regardless of how petty the offense; and no person may be imprisoned where he was tried without counsel, unless he knowingly and intelligently waives counsel. Argersinger v. Hamlin, 407 U.S. 25, 92 S. Ct. 2006, 32 L.Ed.2d 530 (1972).

Neither Art. 1, §19 of the Texas Constitution (the state due course of law provision) or CCP Art. 1.05 confer a right to counsel independent of that guaranteed by Art. 1, §10 of the Texas Constitution. McCambridge v. State, 778 S.W.2d 70 (Tex. Crim. App. 1989).

A suspect also has the right to counsel under CCP Art. 38.22 when dealing with police in a custodial setting.

A juvenile is entitled to an attorney at all phases of the juvenile proceeding; except that the right to counsel at a detention hearing may be waived. Family Code §51.10.

The right to counsel at a critical stage of trial is a waivable-only right, but the same is not true of the right to prevent the admission of evidence obtained in violation of the right to counsel. Appellate courts have consistently held that a party forfeits a complaint that evidence was obtained in violation of the right to counsel if no objection is lodged at trial. Darcy v. State, 488 S. W.3d 325, 329-30 (Tex. Crim. App. 2016).

The Sixth Amendment guarantees to each criminal defendant the assistance of counsel for his defense. The Sixth Amendment, in granting to the accused personally the right to make his defense, speaks of the assistance of counsel, and an assistant, however expert, is still an assistant. McCoy v. Louisiana, 584 U.S. ___, 138 S.Ct. 1500, 1507-8, 200 L.Ed.2d 821 (2018).

Autonomy to decide that the objective of the defense is to assert innocence belongs in the category of decisions that are reserved for the client. McCoy v. Louisiana, 138 S.Ct. at 1508.

Consequently, a defendant has the right to insist that counsel refrain from admitting guilt, even when counsel's experienced-based view is that confessing guilt offers the defendant the best chance to avoid the death penalty. With individual liberty—and, in capital cases, life—at stake, it is the defendant's prerogative, not counsel's, to decide on the objective of his defense: to admit guilt in the hope of gaining mercy at the sentencing stage, or to maintain his innocence, leaving it to the State to prove his guilt beyond a reasonable doubt. McCoy v. Louisiana, 138 S.Ct. at 1508.

When a client expressly asserts that the objective of his defense is to maintain innocence of the charged criminal acts, his lawyer must abide by that objective and may not override it by conceding guilt. McCoy v. Louisiana, 138 S.Ct. at 1509.

Because a client's autonomy, not counsel's competence, is in issue in this situation, the courts do not apply ineffective-assistance-of-counsel jurisprudence. Violation of a defendant's Sixth Amendment-secured autonomy ranks as error of the kind appellate decisions have called structural; and when present, such an error is not subject to harmless-error review. McCoy v. Louisiana, 138 S.Ct. at 1510-11.

A defendant cannot simply remain silent before and during trial and raise a McCoy complaint for the first time after trial; however, a defendant faced with a McCoy issue should not be expected to object with the precision of an attorney. A defendant makes a McCoy complaint with sufficient clarity when he presents "express statements of [his] will to maintain innocence." Turner v. State, 570 S.W.3d 250, 276 (Tex. Crim. App. 2018).

§4:30 Fifth Amendment Right to Counsel

The Fifth Amendment guarantees that no person shall be compelled to be a witness against himself. Miranda v. Arizona, 384 U.S. 436, 86 S. Ct. 1602, 16 L.Ed.2d 694 (1966). A suspect undergoing custodial interrogation has the Fifth Amendment right to the assistance of counsel in his dealings with law enforcement agents. Miranda. This right includes both the right to consult with a lawyer prior to questioning, as well as the right to have a lawyer present during questioning. Miranda.

Persons charged with contempt of court and facing possible incarceration have a right to be represented by counsel at the contempt proceeding. Ex parte Gonzales, 945 S.W.2d 830 (Tex. Crim. App. 1997).

A defendant may forfeit his right to have counsel present during a psychiatric interview by the state if he demonstrates intent to present expert psychiatric testimony as to his future dangerousness. Lagrone v. State, 942 S.W.2d 602 (Tex. Crim. App. 1997).

§4:31 Invocation of Fifth Amendment Right to Counsel

If an accused clearly invokes his Fifth Amendment right to counsel during custodial interrogation by the police, all interrogation must cease, and any subsequent waiver of counsel, to be effective, must be the product of either accused-initiated communications with the police, or police-initiated with the accused in the presence of counsel. Edwards v. Arizona, 451 U.S. 477, 101 S. Ct. 1880, 68 L.Ed.2d 378 (1981); Upton v. State, 853 S.W.2d 548 (Tex. Crim. App. 1993).

Where an accused has made it known that he intends to deal with law enforcement only through counsel, counsel must be present at the time the accused is approached for further interrogation. Minnick v. Mississippi, 498 U.S. 146, 111 S. Ct. 486, 112 L.Ed.2d 489 (1990); Murphy v. State, 801 S.W.2d 917 (Tex. Crim. App. 1991).

If an accused expresses his desire to deal with the police only through counsel, he is not subject to further interrogation by authorities until counsel has been made available to him, unless the accused himself initiates further communications, exchanges, or conversations with the police. Smith v. State, 779 S.W.2d 417 (Tex. Crim. App. 1989); citing Edwards v. Arizona, 451 U.S. 477, 101 S. Ct. 1880, 68 L.Ed.2d 378 (1981).

An accused's invocation of his Sixth Amendment right to counsel during a judicial proceeding does not constitute an invocation of his Fifth Amendment right to counsel. McNeil v. Wisconsin, 501 U.S. 171, 111 S. Ct. 2204, 115 L.Ed.2d 158 (1991).

Once an accused has invoked his Fifth Amendment right to counsel, this right is invoked for interrogation on the specific crime for which he is suspected, as well as for any other crime and by any other interrogators. McNeil v. Wisconsin; Upton v. State, *supra*.

Whether or not an accused has sufficiently invoked his right to counsel is measured on a totality of the circumstances basis. Smith, *supra*.

Events occurring outside the presence of the suspect and entirely unknown to him can have no bearing on his capacity to comprehend and knowingly relinquish a constitutional right. Terrell v. State, 891 S.W.2d 307 (Tex.App.—El Paso 1994, *pet. ref'd*), citing Moran v. Burbine, 475 U.S. 412, 106 S. Ct. 1135, 89 L.Ed.2d 410 (1986).

Police conduct such as not informing the suspect that his family has retained an attorney for him is irrelevant to the inquiry into the effectiveness of the suspect's waiver of counsel, absent a showing that such conduct prevented the suspect from attaining awareness and comprehension of the information conveyed in the Miranda warnings and the consequences of abandoning those rights. Terrell, *supra*, citing Moran v. Burbine, *supra*.

A defendant's pre-Miranda invocation of his Fifth Amendment right is admissible against him at trial where he is not subjected to custodial interrogation and his Sixth Amendment rights have not yet attached. Griffith v. State, 55 S.W.3d 598 (Tex. Crim. App. 2001)(where the defendant invoked his rights when asked whether or not he would consent to a breath test in a DWI case).

§4:31.1 Equivocal Invocation of Fifth Amendment Right

If the accused's invocation of his right to counsel is equivocal, interrogation may continue for the limited purpose of discovering whether the accused wants to consult an attorney or proceed without an attorney. Lucas v. State, 791 S.W.2d 35 (Tex. Crim. App. 1989).

A request for counsel that is ambiguous in scope will be afforded a broad rather than a narrow interpretation. Smith v. State, 779 S.W.2d 417 (Tex. Crim. App. 1989), citing Connecticut v. Barrett, 479 U.S. 523, 107 S. Ct. 828, 93 L.Ed.2d 920 (1987); *see also*, Michigan v. Jackson, 475 U.S. 625, 106 S. Ct. 1404, 89 L.Ed.2d 631 (1986).

Further questioning of the suspect may be permitted for the limited purpose of clarifying an equivocal invocation of the right to counsel. Jamail v. State, 787 S.W.2d 372 (Tex. Crim. App. 1990); Smith v. State, *supra*.

However, where the invocation of the right to counsel is clear, a suspect's post-request responses to further interrogation may not be used to cast retrospective doubt on the clarity of the initial request itself. Smith v. State, *supra*, citing Smith v. Illinois, 469 U.S. 91, 105 S. Ct. 490, 83 L.Ed.2d 488 (1984).

§4:31.2 Sufficient Invocation of Right to Counsel

A formal or absolute demand for an attorney is not required to sufficiently invoke the right. All that is necessary is that the suspect indicate in some manner to authorities that he wishes to exercise his right. Ochoa v. State, 573 S.W.2d 796 (Tex. Crim. App. 1978).

Where a suspect simply asks for "his attorney," he has sufficiently invoked his right to counsel. Smith v. State, 779 S.W.2d 417 (Tex. Crim. App. 1989).

The statement, "I don't want to answer those questions without my lawyer," accompanied by statements such as "No answer" and "I don't want to answer that" are sufficient to invoke the right to counsel. Hicks v. State, 860 S.W.2d 419 (Tex. Crim. App. 1993).

Where the suspect surrendered to authorities in the presence of his attorney and advised them through his attorney that he did not wish to be questioned in the absence of counsel, he sufficiently invoked his right to counsel. Stone v. State, 612 S.W.2d 542 (Tex. Crim. App. 1981).

§4:31.3 Insufficient Invocation of Right to Counsel

A suspect's question, "[d]o I need to talk to a lawyer before I sign?" is not a sufficient invocation of the right to remain silent. Robinson v. State, 851 S.W.2d 216 (Tex. Crim. App. 1991).

A suspect's statement in a letter to a sheriff that, "I'm in here by myself and still can't talk to a lawyer on this," is not a sufficient invocation of the right to counsel. Lucas v. State, 791 S.W.2d 35 (Tex. Crim. App. 1989).

A suspect's statement that, "[m]aybe I should talk to someone," is not a sufficient invocation of the right to counsel. Dinkins v. State, 894 S.W.2d 330 (Tex. Crim. App. 1995).

A suspect's inquiry as to whether he would have a lawyer appointed to him upon reaching another city, when the inquiry dealt with charges pending in that other city is an insufficient invocation of the right to counsel. Collins v. State, 727 S.W.2d 565 (Tex. Crim. App. 1987).

The defendant's refusal to sign the bottom of a magistrate warning form does not constitute the invocation of the right to counsel. Jacobs v. State, 787 S.W.2d 397 (Tex. Crim. App. 1990).

Where the suspect merely told his brother and grandmother to contact his attorney, even when done in the presence of a law enforcement officer, he did not sufficiently personally invoke his right to an attorney. Casias v. State, 678 S.W.2d 140 (Tex. App.—Waco 1984, *no pet.*).

§4:31.4 Limited Invocation

Under certain narrow circumstances, interrogation may continue where an accused has invoked a limited right to counsel accompanied by an affirmative statement expressing his willingness to otherwise go forward with the interview. Hicks v. State, 860 S.W.2d 419 (Tex. Crim. App. 1993), citing Connecticut v. Barrett, 479 U.S. 523, 107 S. Ct. 828, 93 L.Ed.2d 920 (1987).

§4:31.5 Invocation of Right by Suspect's Attorney

The circumstances under which an attorney may invoke his client's Fifth Amendment rights are:

- Attorney-client relationship exists
- Attorney invokes the right after conferring with the client or in the client's presence
- Accused does nothing to contradict the attorney
- Officers agree not to question the accused in the attorney's absence

Janecka v. State, 739 S.W.2d 813 (Tex. Crim. App. 1987).

Counsel cannot invoke the Fifth Amendment rights of a criminal defendant who has not met with counsel, and who has not himself expressed a desire to invoke the right. Lucas v. State,791 S.W.2d 35 (Tex. Crim. App. 1989).

§4:31.6 Reinitiation of Communication by the Accused

A defendant who has invoked his Fifth Amendment right to counsel can later waive that right by reinitiating contact with law enforcement authorities. Hicks v. State, 860 S.W.2d 419 (Tex. Crim. App. 1993), citing Edwards v. Arizona, 451 U.S. 477, 101 S. Ct. 1880, 68 L.Ed.2d 378 (1981). *See also*, Baldree v. State, 784 S.W.2d 676 (Tex. Crim. App. 1989).

Even if the defendant validly invokes his right to an attorney, he can later waive the right by resuming conversations with officers of his own volition. Etheridge v. State, 903 S.W.2d 1 (Tex. Crim. App. 1994).

A valid waiver of the Fifth Amendment right will not be found by showing only that he responded to further police-initiated custodial interrogation. Hicks, *supra*, citing Edwards v. Arizona, *supra*.

The circumstances must show that the accused initiated the conversation by remarks which can be fairly said to represent a desire to open up a more generalized discussion relating directly or indirectly to the investigation. Oregon v. Bradshaw, 462 U.S. 1039, 103 S. Ct. 2830, 77 L.Ed.2d 405 (1983) (plurality opinion); Lucas v. State, 791 S.W.2d 35 (Tex. Crim. App. 1989).

Where after invoking his right to remain silent, a suspect asked a police officer, "[w]ell, what is going to happen to me now?" he was found to have reinitiated contact such that officers could begin interrogation. Oregon v. Bradshaw, *supra*.

A suspect's statement that, "I'm ready. I told you I would tell you about it if you would let me talk to [the attorney]," constituted a valid reinitiation of contact where the suspect had, in fact, talked to the attorney. Mays v. State, 726 S.W.2d 937 (Tex. Crim. App. 1986).

A suspect's post-invocation request for a polygraph examination is a sufficient reinitiation of contact to allow further interrogation. Wyrick v. Fields, 459 U.S. 42, 103 S. Ct. 394, 74 L.Ed.2d 214 (1982).

The question, "[h]ow is everyone in Georgia doing?" asked by the defendant to police officers investigating his case, constituted initiation of further communication with police following invocation of the Fifth Amendment by the defendant. Janecka v. State, 739 S.W.2d 813 (Tex. Crim. App. 1987).

§4:31.7 When Officers Can Reapproach Suspect

A circumstance under which officers may reapproach a suspect who has invoked his right to counsel is that in which officers reapproach to question about a different offense; provided that the suspect's original invocation must have been as to the specific offense under discussion at the time of the invocation. Arizona v. Roberson, 486 U.S. 675, 108 S. Ct. 2093, 100 L.Ed.2d 704 (1988).

Officers can reapproach a suspect who has invoked his Fifth Amendment protections when they seek to question him for a different offense. For Fifth Amendment purposes, the "same" offense does not mean "factually related" or "factually intertwined" offenses. Rather, the proper test to determine whether two offenses are the same or different for purposes of double jeopardy is that set forth in Blockburger v. United States: that where the same act or transaction constitutes a violation of two distinct statutory provisions the test to be applied to determine whether there are two offenses or only one, is whether each provision requires proof of a fact which the other does not. Cobb v. State, 85 S.W.3d 258 (Tex. Crim. App. 2002).

The same result is reached under the Texas Constitution. Cobb.

§4:32 Waiver of Fifth Amendment Right to Counsel

Statements made by an accused during police interrogation will be admissible if the prosecution establishes that he knowingly and intelligently waived his privilege against self-incrimination and his right to counsel. Miranda v. Arizona, 384 U.S. 436, 86 S. Ct. 1602, 16 L.Ed.2d 694 (1966).

The state has the burden of establishing a valid waiver of the Fifth Amendment right to counsel. Michigan v. Jackson, 475 U.S. 625, 106 S. Ct. 1404, 89 L.Ed.2d 631 (1986); Upton v. State, 853 S.W.2d 548 (Tex. Crim. App. 1993). A waiver is an intentional and knowing relinquishment of a known right. Miranda, *supra*.

A defendant may waive his Miranda and CCP Art. 38.22 rights provided the waiver is made voluntarily, knowingly, and intelligently. Jacobs v. State, 787 S.W.2d 397 (Tex. Crim. App. 1990), citing Moran v. Burbine, 475 U.S. 412, 106 S. Ct. 1135, 89 L.Ed.2d 410 (1986).

The suspect's waiver of his Miranda rights must be voluntary in the sense that it must be the product of a free and deliberate choice rather than a product of intimidation, coercion or deception. Moran.

Only if the totality of the circumstances surrounding the interrogation reveal both an uncoerced choice and the requisite level of comprehension may a court properly conclude that the Miranda and CCP Art. 38.22 rights have been waived. Jacobs, *supra*.

Whether a waiver is shown must depend in each case upon the particular facts and circumstances surrounding the case, including the background, experience, and conduct of the accused. Muniz v. State, 851 S.W.2d 238 (Tex. Crim. App. 1993), citing Johnson v. Zerbst, 304 U.S. 458, 58 S. Ct. 1019, 82 L.Ed.2d 1461 (1938).

However, the circumstances of the taking of the statement along with other writings and recitations can add up to the conclusion that the defendant executed a valid waiver of his rights. Garcia, *supra*.

"Knowing" in the context of waiver was defined as, "an intellectual, conscious understanding, by thought process and reason, of the releasing of, or absolute surrender of, a right, or of a constitutionally granted guarantee; and, the understanding of the effects of waiving such a right of a constitutionally granted guarantee." Combs v. State, 631 S.W.2d 534 (Tex.App.—Houston [1st Dist.] 1982), *reversed on other grounds,* 643 S.W.2d 709 (Tex. Crim. App. 1982).

The law does not necessarily require an explicit waiver. In some cases, a waiver can be inferred from the actions and words of the person interrogated. North Carolina v. Butler, 441 U.S. 369, 99 S. Ct. 1755, 60 L.Ed.2d 286 (1979).

The U.S. Constitution does not require that a criminal suspect must know and understand every possible consequence of a waiver of his Fifth Amendment privilege. Colorado v. Spring, 479 U.S. 564, 107 S. Ct. 851, 93 L.Ed.2d 954 (1987).

The suspect's advance knowledge of all possible subjects of questioning is not relevant to determining whether the suspect voluntarily, knowingly, and intelligently waived his Fifth Amendment rights. Colorado v. Spring, *supra*.

TIP TO THE PROSECUTION: For a written statement to unambiguously meet the waiver requirements of CCP Art. 38.22 Sec 2(b), the preferable practice is for the statement to contain the following language, near or adjacent to the signature of the individual giving the statement: "I knowingly, voluntarily and intelligently waived the rights described above before and during the making of this statement." Garcia v. State, 919 S.W.2d 370 (Tex. Crim. App. 1994).

§4:32.1 Valid Waivers

A voluntary, knowing, and intelligent waiver of the right to remain silent must be proven by a preponderance of the evidence. Robinson v. State, 851 S.W.2d 216 (Tex. Crim. App. 1991), citing Colorado v. Connelly, 479 U.S. 157, 107 S. Ct. 515, 93 L.Ed.2d 473 (1986).

If the prosecution shows that a suspect's decision not to rely on his Miranda rights was uncoerced, that he at all times knew he could stand mute and consult a lawyer, and that he was aware the State could use his statement against him, the State's burden of proof is met and waiver is shown as a matter of law. Robinson, *supra*, citing Moran v. Burbine, 475 U.S. 412, 106 S. Ct. 1135, 89 L.Ed.2d 410 (1986).

Under certain narrow circumstances, interrogation may continue where an accused has invoked a limited right to counsel accompanied by an affirmative statement expressing his willingness to otherwise go forward with the interview. Hicks v. State, 860 S.W.2d 419 (Tex. Crim. App. 1993), citing Connecticut v. Barrett, 479 U.S. 523, 107 S. Ct. 828, 93 L.Ed.2d 920 (1987).

Where a suspect invokes his right to counsel only as to a "formal" statement, interrogation may continue informally; and the suspect may later fully waive the right to counsel by informing law enforcement officers that he wishes to make a "formal" statement without benefit of counsel. Corwin v. State, 870 S.W.2d 23 (Tex. Crim. App. 1993).

A suspect's statement to officer that, "I'm ready. I told you I would tell you about it if you would let me talk to [the attorney]," was a sufficient waiver of his rights (and also constituted a reinitiation of contact with officers). Mays v. State, 726 S.W.2d 937 (Tex. Crim. App. 1986).

A defendant affirmatively waives his right to counsel by using words to the effect: "I ain't interested in a lawyer." Lucas v. State,791 S.W.2d 35 (Tex. Crim. App. 1989).

The phrase, "I do hereby voluntarily waive these rights," on each page of a written confession has been found to constitute a valid waiver. Cockrell v. State, 933 S.W.2d 73 (Tex. Crim. App. 1996).

Where the suspect at first invokes his right to counsel then voluntarily withdraws the invocation in the absence of interrogation, there is a valid waiver. Muniz v. State, 851 S.W.2d 238 (Tex. Crim. App. 1993) (where the defendant stated, "No, I will talk to him later" when the officer began to dial the attorney's telephone number).

§4:32.2 Invalid Waivers

The mere failure of the suspect to invoke his rights is not a valid waiver thereof. Miranda v. Arizona, 384 U.S. 436, 86 S. Ct. 1602, 16 L.Ed.2d 694 (1966). Waivers will not be presumed from silence. Miranda.

The fact that an incriminating statement was eventually made will not presume a valid waiver. Miranda.

Where a suspect did not expressly waive his rights and did not indicate that he had ceased to rely on an agreement with police to not question him in his attorney's absence, the resulting confession was involuntarily made. Stone v. State, 612 S.W.2d 542 (Tex. Crim. App. 1981).

Where the written confession of defendant does not contain any statement whatever to the effect that defendant, prior to making the statement, voluntarily, knowingly, and intelligently waived his rights, the confession should not have been admitted in evidence. Thibedeaux v. State, 729 S.W.2d 137 (Tex.App.—Beaumont 1987, *pet. ref'd*).

§4:40 Sixth Amendment Right to Counsel

The Sixth Amendment right to counsel attaches when adversary judicial criminal proceedings are initiated; whether by way of formal charge, preliminary hearing, indictment, information or arraignment. McNeil v. Wisconsin, 501 U.S. 171, 111 S. Ct. 2204, 115 L.Ed.2d 158 (1991); Green v. State, 872 S.W.2d 717 (Tex. Crim. App. 1994).

The Sixth Amendment right to counsel is global as to all charges arising out of the same offense. Upton v. State, 853 S.W.2d 548 (Tex. Crim. App. 1993) (where the defendant's Sixth Amendment rights had attached to a theft offense and police sought to question him about a murder related to the theft).

For Sixth Amendment purposes, the "same" offense does not mean "factually related" or "factually intertwined" offenses. Rather, the proper test to determine whether two offenses are the same or different for purposes of double jeopardy is that set forth in Blockburger v. United States: that where the same act or transaction constitutes a violation of two distinct statutory provisions the test to be applied to determine whether there are two offenses or only one, is whether each provision requires proof of a fact which the other does not. Texas v. Cobb, 532 U.S. 162, 121 S. Ct. 1335, 149 L.Ed.2d 321 (2001).

When an accused's Sixth Amendment right to counsel attaches he is entitled to the assistance of counsel at each critical stage of the prosecution, absent a valid waiver. Michigan v. Jackson, 475 U.S. 625, 106 S. Ct. 1404, 89 L.Ed.2d 631 (1986); Upton, *supra*.

Whether a particular proceeding is a critical stage generally turns on an assessment of the usefulness of counsel to the accused at that particular proceeding. Patterson v. Illinois, 487 U.S. 285, 108 S. Ct. 2389, 101 L.Ed.2d 261 (1988); Upton.

The question of when the Sixth Amendment right to counsel attaches is separate and distinct from the question of whether a certain proceeding is a critical stage. Michigan v. Jackson, *supra*; Upton.

The Sixth Amendment right to counsel is offense-specific; that is, it cannot be invoked as to future offenses. McNeil v. Wisconsin, *supra*.

However, where a defendant's Sixth Amendment rights have attached to a capital murder charge, his rights are violated when the state solicits a conversation between the defendant and an informant, and the conversation is then used in the punishment phase of the capital trial. Wesbrook v. State, 29 S.W.3d 103 (Tex. Crim. App. 2000); Manns v. State, 122 S.W.3d 171 (Tex. Crim. App. 2003).

Incriminating statements pertaining to pending charges are inadmissible at the trial of those charges, notwithstanding the fact that the police were also investigating other crimes, if in obtaining this evidence, the state violated the Sixth Amendment by knowingly circumventing the defendant's right to the assistance of counsel. Thompson v. State, 93 S.W.3d 16 (Tex. Crim. App. 2001).

The dismissal of pending charges does not always terminate the attorney-client relationship and the Sixth Amendment right to counsel; such as where the dismissal of charges was done to facilitate a continued investigation of the transaction in question. State v. Frye, 897 S.W.2d 324 (Tex. Crim. App. 1995).

The Sixth Amendment right to choose one's own counsel does not extend to the choice of someone who is not licensed to practice law, to someone who the defendant cannot afford or who declines to represent the defendant for another reason, or to an attorney who has a previous or ongoing relationship with another party. Wheat v. U.S., 486 U.S. 153, 108 S. Ct. 1692, 100 L.Ed.2d 140 (1988).

Where the trial court has erroneously deprived the defendant of his right to counsel of his choice, the defendant is entitled to a reversal of his conviction. U.S. v. Gonzalez-Lopez, 548 U.S. 140, 126 S. Ct. 2557, 165 L.Ed.2d 409 (2006).

Sixth Amendment concerns regarding a licensed, but suspended or disbarred attorney are reviewed on a case-by-case approach. The attorney is incompetent as a matter of law if it may be reasonably inferred from the reason for the disciplinary action that the attorney was incompetent to represent the defendant in the proceeding in question. Cantu v. State, 930 S.W.2d 594 (Tex. Crim. App. 1996).

§4:41 Invocation of Sixth Amendment Right to Counsel

The Sixth Amendment right to counsel automatically becomes effective at the inception of adversary judicial criminal proceedings. Fuller v. State, 829 S.W.2d 191 (Tex. Crim. App. 1992).

When an accused invokes his Fifth Amendment right to counsel, he has effectively invoked his Sixth Amendment right to counsel. McNeil v. Wisconsin, 501 U.S. 171, 111 S. Ct. 2204, 115 L.Ed.2d 158 (1991); Upton v. State, 853 S.W.2d 548 (Tex. Crim. App. 1993).

§4:42 Waiver of Sixth Amendment Right to Counsel

An accused can waive his Sixth Amendment right to counsel in the same manner as the Fifth Amendment right to counsel. Patterson v. Illinois, 487 U.S. 285, 108 S. Ct. 2389, 101 L.Ed.2d 261 (1988).

The prosecution has the burden of proving a voluntary, knowing, and intelligent relinquishment of the Sixth Amendment right to counsel. Michigan v. Harvey, 494 U.S. 344, 110 S. Ct. 1176, 108 L.Ed.2d 293 (1990); Michigan v. Jackson, 475 U.S. 625, 106 S. Ct. 1404, 89 L.Ed.2d 631 (1986); Upton v. State, 853 S.W.2d 548 (Tex. Crim. App. 1993).

The Miranda warnings are sufficient to make an accused aware of his Sixth Amendment right to counsel during police questioning. Patterson v. Illinois, *supra*; Michigan v. Harvey, *supra*.

When a suspect waives his right to counsel after receiving warnings equivalent to the Miranda warnings, that will generally suffice to establish a knowing and intelligent waiver of the Sixth Amendment right to counsel for the purpose of post-indictment questioning. Patterson v. Illinois, *supra*.

This is true even where the defendant has appeared in front of a magistrate and had counsel appointed for him. Montejo v. Louisiana, 556 U.S. ___, 129 S. Ct. 2079, 173 L.Ed.2d 955 (2009) (overruling Michigan v. Jackson, 475 U.S. 625, 106 S. Ct. 1404, 89 L.Ed.2d 631 (1986)).

The police may initiate interrogation only through notice to defense counsel once the Sixth Amendment right to counsel has attached and an attorney-client relationship has been established. Upton, *supra*; Holloway v. State, 780 S.W.2d 787 (Tex. Crim. App. 1989) (in a case decided based on Michigan v. Jackson, now overruled by Montejo v. Louisiana).

An accused cannot unilaterally waive his Sixth Amendment right to counsel once the right has attached and the attorney-client relationship has been established. Holloway, *supra* (in a case decided based on Michigan v. Jackson, now overruled by Montejo v. Louisiana).

Where the Sixth Amendment right to counsel has attached but the defendant is not yet represented by counsel, any subsequent waiver of the Sixth Amendment must be by accused-initiated communication or by police-initiated communication in the presence of counsel. Upton, *supra*; Fuller v. State, 829 S.W.2d 191 (Tex. Crim. App. 1992) (in a case decided based on Michigan v. Jackson, now overruled by Montejo v. Louisiana).

Once the Sixth Amendment right to counsel has attached and has been invoked, any subsequent waiver during a police-initiated custodial interview is ineffective. McNeil v. Wisconsin, *supra*; Upton.

The attachment of the Sixth Amendment right to counsel as to one offense does not affect police investigations as to offenses for which the right has not attached. Maine v. Moulton, 474 U.S. 159, 106 S. Ct. 477, 88 L.Ed.2d 481 (1985). However, information gathered by police investigators as to offenses for which the Sixth Amendment right has not attached cannot be used in the trial of offenses for which the right has attached and counsel has not been notified. Wesbrook v. State, 29 S.W.3d 103 (Tex. Crim. App. 2000) (where police used a jailhouse informant to gather information which was later used at defendant's capital murder trial).

Absent a valid waiver, a confession taken after the attachment of the Sixth Amendment right to counsel is inadmissible. Upton v. State, 853 S.W.2d 548 (Tex. Crim. App. 1993).

The failure of the defendant to request counsel at a preindictment hearing does not constitute a waiver of counsel for Sixth Amendment purposes. Green v. State, 872 S.W.2d 717 (Tex. Crim. App. 1994) (now overruled by Montejo v. Louisiana).

§4:42.1 Valid Waivers

Where an accused is read the Miranda rights before a post-indictment interview with law enforcement and no attorney-client relationship has been established, he can validly waive his Sixth Amendment rights in the same fashion as a Fifth Amendment waiver. Patterson v. Illinois, 487 U.S. 285, 108 S. Ct. 2389, 101 L.Ed.2d 261 (1988).

Where a defendant whose Sixth Amendment rights had attached through the filing of formal charges initiated the contact with police, which led to his giving of a confession, was repeatedly read his Miranda warnings and did not invoke any of his rights, he has given a waiver which is constitutionally acceptable under the Sixth Amendment. Fuller v. State, 829 S.W.2d 191 (Tex. Crim. App. 1992).

§4:42.2 Invalid Waivers

Where an accused invokes his right to counsel at a magistrate's warning and the state does not prove that he either rescinded his request for counsel or knowingly and intelligently waived his right, a resulting confession is inadmissible. Nehman v. State, 721 S.W.2d 319 (Tex. Crim. App. 1986).

A Sixth Amendment waiver is presumed invalid if secured pursuant to a police-initiated conversation. Michigan v. Jackson, 475 U.S. 625, 106 S. Ct. 1404, 89 L.Ed.2d 631 (1986).

The Sixth Amendment renders inadmissible in the prosecution's case-in-chief statements deliberately elicited from a defendant without an express waiver of the right to counsel. Maine v. Moulton, 474 U.S. 159, 106 S. Ct. 477, 88 L.Ed.2d 481 (1985).

A waiver of Sixth Amendment right to counsel is invalid if an attorney-client relationship has been established and the defendant is reapproached by law enforcement outside the presence of counsel. Upton v. State, 853 S.W.2d 548 (Tex. Crim. App. 1993); Holloway v. State, 780 S.W.2d 787 (Tex. Crim. App. 1989).

§4:43 Sixth Amendment Critical Stage Analysis

When an accused's Sixth Amendment right to counsel attaches to an offense for which adversarial proceedings have begun, he is entitled to the assistance of counsel at each "critical" stage of the prosecution, absent a valid waiver. Michigan v. Jackson, 494 U.S. 344, 110 S. Ct. 1176, 108 L.Ed.2d 293 (1990); Upton v. State, 853 S.W.2d 548 (Tex. Crim. App. 1993).

The determination of whether a particular proceeding is a "critical" stage generally turns on an assessment of the usefulness of counsel to the accused at that particular proceeding. Patterson v. Illinois, 487 U.S. 285, 108 S. Ct. 2389, 101 L.Ed.2d 261 (1988); Upton, *supra.*

Neither the U.S. Supreme Court nor the Court of Criminal Appeals has established a bright line rule for when adversarial proceedings have begun. U.S. v. Gouveia, 467 U.S. 180, 104 S. Ct. 2292, 81 L.Ed.2d 146 (1984); State v. Frye, 897 S.W.2d 324 (Tex. Crim. App. 1995).

Whether adversary proceedings have begun for purposes of Sixth Amendment analysis is not entirely a constitutional question, but largely a matter of local law. Moore v. Illinois, 434 U.S. 220, 98 S. Ct. 458, 54 L.Ed.2d 424 (1977); Fuller v. State, 829 S.W.2d 191 (Tex. Crim. App. 1992).

The factors that the courts examine to decide if a proceeding is a critical stage are: (1) whether the proceeding either (i) had a consequence adverse to the defendant as to the ultimate disposition of the charge which could have been avoided or mitigated if defendant had been rep-resented by counsel at that proceeding; or (ii) offered a potential opportunity for benefitting the defendant as to the ultimate disposition of the charge through rights that could have been exer-cised by counsel, and (2) whether the adverse consequence could have been avoided, or the lost opportunity regained, by action that subsequently provided counsel could have taken. Gilley v. State, 418 S.W.3d 114, 120 (Tex. Crim. App. 2014).

The right to counsel at a critical stage of the criminal proceedings must be affirmatively waived and cannot be forfeited by inaction alone. Gilley, 418 S.W.3d at 119, *citing Oliver v. State*, 872 S.W.2d 713, 716 (Tex. Crim. App. 1994).

§4:43.1 Photographic Identification

A post-indictment photo display used to test witness identification prior to trial is not a "critical" stage where the defendant is not present for the procedure. U.S. v. Ash, 413 U.S. 300, 93 S. Ct. 2568, 37 L.Ed.2d 619 (1973); Poullard v. State, 833 S.W.2d 273 (Tex.App.—Houston [1st Dist.] 1992, *pet. ref'd*).

§4:43.2 Police Lineup

There is no Sixth Amendment right to counsel at a pre-trial lineup where formal charges have not been filed against the defendant. Kirby v. Illinois, 406 U.S. 682, 92 S. Ct. 1877, 32 L.Ed.2d 411

(1972); McFarland v. State, 928 S.W.2d 482 (Tex. Crim. App. 1996).

However, there is a right to counsel at a pre-trial lineup where formal charges have been initiated against the defendant. Barnhill v. State, 657 S.W.2d 131 (Tex. Crim. App. 1983). A post-indictment lineup is a critical stage of prosecution. U.S. v. Wade, 388 U.S. 218, 87 S. Ct. 1926, 18 L.Ed.2d 1149 (1967).

§4:43.3 Handwriting and Voice Exemplars

The taking of handwriting exemplars before indictment and before appointment of counsel was not a "critical stage" of criminal proceedings. Gilbert v. California, 388 U.S. 263, 87 S. Ct. 1951, 18 L.Ed.2d 1178 (1967).

Since handwriting exemplars are non-testimonial in nature, the Sixth Amendment is not implicated where they are requested from the defendant. Giles v. State, 867 S.W.2d 105 (Tex.App.—El Paso 1993, *pet. ref'd*).

The taking of voice exemplars after the initiation of criminal proceedings is not a critical stage. Strong v. State, 805 S.W.2d 478 (Tex.App.—Tyler 1990, *pet. ref'd*).

§4:43.4 Dental Impressions

There is no Sixth Amendment right to counsel at the taking of dental impressions where the defendant is not yet formally charged. Spence v. State, 795 S.W.2d 743 (Tex. Crim. App.1990).

§4:43.5 Breath Tests and DWI Videotapes

Where police request a chemical test of a DWI suspect before the filing of formal charges, he has no right to consult with an attorney to decide whether to submit to the requested test. McCambridge v. State, 778 S.W.2d 70 (Tex. Crim. App. 1989).

A DWI videotape procedure conducted before the filing of charges is not a critical stage for Sixth Amendment analysis. Sontag v. State, 841 S.W.2d 889 (Tex.App.—Corpus Christi 1992, *pet. ref'd*).

§4:43.6 Confessions

Once adversarial judicial proceedings have been initiated, a confession is a critical stage. Nehman v. State, 721 S.W.2d 319 (Tex. Crim. App. 1986).

§4:43.7 Arrest

An arrest alone, whether with or without a warrant, does not trigger adversarial judicial proceedings. Green v. State, 872 S.W.2d 717 (Tex. Crim. App. 1994). The warning of a defendant of his rights by a magistrate pursuant to statute does not trigger the Sixth Amendment. Green.

§4:43.8 Arraignment

Where certain matters such as notice of the insanity defense, abatement, and motions to quash the indictment must be presented at arraignment, it is a critical stage entitling the defendant to the assistance of counsel. Hamilton v. Alabama, 368 U.S. 52, 82 S. Ct. 157, 7 L.Ed. 2d 114 (1961).

Under Texas law, a defendant's appearance before a magistrate under Tex. Code Crim. Pro. Art. 15.17 is a critical stage triggering the defendant's Sixth Amendment right to counsel. Rothgery v. Gillespie County, Texas, 554 U.S. 191, 128 S. Ct. 2578, 171 L.Ed.2d 366 (2008).

§4:43.9 Filing of Charges

The filing of charges triggers the Sixth Amendment right to counsel. Lucas v. State, 791 S.W.2d 35 (Tex. Crim. App. 1989); Janecka v. State, 739 S.W.2d 813 (Tex. Crim. App. 1987). The filing of a felony complaint triggers adversarial judicial proceedings. Barnhill v. State, 657 S.W.2d 131 (Tex. Crim. App. 1983).

Indictment triggers the Sixth Amendment right to counsel. Patterson v. Illinois, 487 U.S. 285, 108 S. Ct. 2389, 101 L.Ed.2d 261 (1988); DeBlanc v. State, 799 S.W.2d 701 (Tex. Crim. App. 1990).

The filing of a misdemeanor complaint triggers adversarial judicial proceedings. McCambridge v. State, 712 S.W.2d 499 (Tex. Crim. App. 1986).

§4:43.10 Examining Trials and Preliminary Hearings

Where a preliminary evidentiary hearing is held binding a defendant over to the grand jury, such a hearing is a critical stage of a criminal prosecution requiring the guiding hand of counsel "to protect the indigent accused against an erroneous or improper prosecution." Coleman v. Alabama, 399 U.S. 1, 26 L.Ed.2d 387, 90 S. Ct. 1999 (1970).

A preliminary hearing is not elevated to "critical stage" status merely by the filing of a complaint where the proceeding merely consisted of the defendant being warned of his rights and a probable cause determination being made. Green v. State, 872 S.W.2d 717 (Tex. Crim. App. 1994).

§4:43.11 Indigency Hearings

An indigency hearing is not a critical stage of the proceedings requiring the assistance of counsel. Johnson v. State, 894 S.W.2d 529 (Tex.App.—Austin 1995, *no pet.*).

§4:43.12 Psychiatric and Competency Examinations

A defendant's Sixth Amendment right to counsel is violated where defense counsel is not notified in advance that a psychiatric examination will encompass the issue of future dangerousness, in the absence of an affirmative waiver of the right to counsel. Estelle v. Smith, 451 U.S. 454, 101 S. Ct. 1866, 68 L.Ed.2d 359 (1981); Cook v. State, 741 S.W.2d 928 (Tex. Crim. App. 1987).

The right that counsel be notified does not encompass the right to have counsel actually present during the examination. Estelle v. Smith; Cook.

A competency examination is a critical stage for purposes of the Sixth Amendment, and a defendant is entitled to have counsel notified in advance of the examination, although there is no right to have the attorney present during the examination. Heflin v. State, 640 S.W.2d 58 (Tex.App.—Austin 1982, *pet. ref'd*).

§4:43.13 Trial

It is axiomatic that a defendant is entitled to counsel during the trial of his case. U.S. Constitution, Sixth Amendment; Texas Constitution, Art. I, §10; CCP Art. 1.051(a).

A defendant is entitled to the assistance of counsel during the voir dire process. Shipley v. State, 790 S.W.2d 604 (Tex. Crim. App. 1990).

The stage of trial at which evidence is presented is a critical stage. Medley v. State, 47 S.W.3d 17 (Tex.App.—Amarillo 2001, *pet. ref'd*).

§4:43.14 Revocation of Probation

A defendant is entitled to counsel at a probation revocation proceeding. CCP Art. 42.12 §21; Hatten v. State, 32 S.W.3d 868 (Tex.App.—Texarkana 2000, *pet. filed*).

§4:43.15 Contempt Proceedings

A contempt hearing is a critical stage entitling the accused to the assistance of counsel. Ex parte Gonzales, 945 S.W.2d 830 (Tex. Crim. App. 1997).

§4:43.16 Motions for New Trial

The time allotted by statute for the filing and hearing of a motion for new trial is a critical stage entitling the defendant to the assistance of counsel. Cooks v. State, 240 S.W.3d 906 (Tex. Crim. App. 2006).

§4:43.17 Appeals

A defendant is entitled to the assistance of counsel on his first appeal where the appeal is a matter of right under state law. Anders v. California, 386 U.S. 738, 87 S. Ct. 1397, 18 L.Ed.2d 493 (1967).

TIP TO THE BENCH: Where defendants, who have been represented by retained counsel at trial, are determined by the court to be indigent for the purposes of appeal, trial judges would be well advised to inquire and determine whether retained counsel expects to remain in the case, and make such inquiry and determination a part of the record. Such retained counsel should always request the permission of the court to withdraw before abandoning the case. Ward v. State, 740 S.W.2d 794 (Tex. Crim. App. 1987).

§4:43.18 Discretionary Review

A defendant has no constitutional right to counsel for pursuing discretionary review, even though a defendant has a right to prepare and file a petition for discretionary review. Ex parte Wilson, 956 S.W.2d 25 (Tex. Crim. App. 1997).

The State is under no federal constitutional obligation to provide counsel for indigent defendants to pursue discretionary appeals. Ross v. Moffitt, 417 U.S. 600, 94 S. Ct. 2437, 41 L.Ed.2d 341 (1974).

§4:43.19 Juvenile Proceedings

For right to counsel purposes, there is no material difference between adult and juvenile proceedings in which an adjudication of guilt is sought by prosecutors. In re Gault, 387 U.S. 1, 87 S. Ct. 1428, 18 L.Ed.2d 1149 (1967).

A juvenile is entitled to an attorney at all phases of the juvenile proceeding, except that the right to counsel at a detention hearing may be waived. Family Code §51.10.

A juvenile respondent has a right to counsel at a hearing held to determine if the juvenile court should waive its jurisdiction. A violation of this right is structural error and per se reversible. D.L.J., Jr. v. State, 981 S.W.2d 815 (Tex.App.—Houston [1st Dist.] 1998, *no pet.*).

A juvenile has no right to counsel at a psychological exam conducted for the neutral purpose of determining whether a juvenile should be transferred to criminal court, because the examination is statutorily required and counsel would serve no functional purpose. Hidalgo v. State, 983 S.W.2d 746 (Tex. Crim. App. 1999).

§4:43.20 Guilty Pleas

The entry of a guilty plea to a felony or misdemeanor criminal charge is a critical stage to which the Sixth Amendment right to counsel applies. Argersinger v. Hamlin, 407 U.S. 25, 92 S. Ct. 2006, 32 L.Ed. 2d 530 (1972); Iowa v. Tovar, 541 U.S. 77, 124 S. Ct. 1379, 158 L.Ed.2d 209 (2004).

§4:44 Remedy for Sixth Amendment Violations

When a Sixth Amendment violation has occurred, the trial court must identify and then neutralize the taint by tailoring relief appropriate in the circumstances to assure the defendant effective assistance of counsel and a fair trial. State v. Frye, 897 S.W.2d 324 (Tex. Crim. App. 1995).

A dismissal may be proper when a defendant suffers demonstrable prejudice, or a substantial threat thereof, and where the trial court is unable to identify and neutralize the taint by other means. Frye.

Where the state gathers evidence in violation of the Sixth Amendment and offers it in the punishment phase of a capital murder trial, the proper remedy is suppression of the evidence. Where the evidence is improperly admitted, the admission is subjected to harmless error analysis on appeal. Wesbrook v. State, 29 S.W.3d 103 (Tex. Crim. App. 2000); Thompson v. State, 93 S.W.3d 16 (Tex. Crim. App. 2001).

§4:50 Trial Court Duty to Appoint Counsel

§4:51 Statutory Provisions

Art. 1.051. Right to Representation by Counsel

> *(a) A defendant in a criminal matter is entitled to be represented by counsel in an adversarial judicial proceeding. The right to be represented by counsel includes the right to consult in private with counsel sufficiently in advance of a proceeding to allow adequate preparation for the proceeding.*

(b) For the purposes of this article and Articles 26.04 and 26.05 of this code, "indigent" means a person who is not financially able to employ counsel.

(c) An indigent defendant is entitled to have an attorney appointed to represent him in any adversary judicial proceeding that may result in punishment by confinement and in any other criminal proceeding if the court concludes that the interests of justice require representation. Except as otherwise provided by this subsection, if an indigent defendant is entitled to and requests appointed counsel and if adversarial judicial proceedings have been initiated against the defendant, a court or the courts' designee authorized under Article 26.04 to appoint counsel for indigent defendants in the county shall appoint counsel as soon as possible, but not later than the end of the third working day after the date on which the court or the courts' designee receives the defendant's request for appointment of counsel. In a county with a population of 250,000 or more, the court or the courts' designee shall appoint counsel as required by this subsection as soon as possible, but not later than the end of the first working day after the date on which the court or the courts' designee receives the defendant's request for appointment of counsel.

(d) An eligible indigent defendant is entitled to have the trial court appoint an attorney to represent him in the following appellate and postconviction habeas corpus matters:

(1) an appeal to a court of appeals;

(2) an appeal to the Court of Criminal Appeals if the appeal is made directly from the trial court or if a petition for discretionary review has been granted;

(3) a habeas corpus proceeding if the court concludes that the interests of justice require representation; and

(4) any other appellate proceeding if the court concludes that the interests of justice require representation.

(e) An appointed counsel is entitled to 10 days to prepare for a proceeding but may waive the preparation time with the consent of the defendant in writing or on the record in open court. If a nonindigent defendant appears without counsel at a proceeding after having been given a reasonable opportunity to retain counsel, the court, on 10 days' notice to the defendant of a dispositive setting, may proceed with the matter without securing a written waiver or appointing counsel. If an indigent defendant who has refused appointed counsel in order to retain private counsel appears without counsel after having been given an opportunity to retain counsel, the court, after giving the defendant a reasonable opportunity to request appointment of counsel or, if the defendant elects not to request appointment of counsel, after obtaining a waiver of the right to counsel pursuant to Subsections (f) and (g), may proceed with the matter on 10 days' notice to the defendant of a dispositive setting.

(f) A defendant may voluntarily and intelligently waive in writing the right to counsel. A waiver obtained in violation of Subsection (f-1) or (f-2) is presumed invalid.

(f-1) In any adversary judicial proceeding that may result in punishment by confinement, the attorney representing the state may not:

(1) initiate or encourage an attempt to obtain from a defendant who is not represented by counsel a waiver of the right to counsel; or

RIGHT TO COUNSEL, EFFECTIVE ASSISTANCE OF COUNSEL

(2) communicate with a defendant who has requested the appointment of counsel, unless the court or the court's designee authorized under Article 26.04 to appoint counsel for indigent defendants in the county has denied the request and, subsequent to the denial, the defendant:

(A) has been given a reasonable opportunity to retain and has failed to retain private counsel; or

(B) waives or has waived the opportunity to retain private counsel.

(f-2) In any adversary judicial proceeding that may result in punishment by confinement, the court may not direct or encourage the defendant to communicate with the attorney representing the state until the court advises the defendant of the right to counsel and the procedure for requesting appointed counsel and the defendant has been given a reasonable opportunity to request appointed counsel. If the defendant has requested appointed counsel, the court may not direct or encourage the defendant to communicate with the attorney representing the state unless the court or the court's designee authorized under Article 26.04 to appoint counsel for indigent defendants in the county has denied the request and, subsequent to the denial, the defendant:

(1) has been given a reasonable opportunity to retain and has failed to retain private counsel; or

(2) waives or has waived the opportunity to retain private counsel.

(g) If a defendant wishes to waive the right to counsel for purposes of entering a guilty plea or proceeding to trial, the court shall advise the defendant of the nature of the charges against the defendant and, if the defendant is proceeding to trial, the dangers and disadvantages of self-representation. If the court determines that the waiver is voluntarily and intelligently made, the court shall provide the defendant with a statement substantially in the following form, which, if signed by the defendant, shall be filed with and become part of the record of the proceedings:

"I have been advised this ______ day of __________, 2 ____, by the (name of court) Court of my right to representation by counsel in the case pending against me. I have been further advised that if I am unable to afford counsel, one will be appointed for me free of charge. Understanding my right to have counsel appointed for me free of charge if I am not financially able to employ counsel, I wish to waive that right and request the court to proceed with my case without an attorney being appointed for me. I hereby waive my right to counsel. (signature of defendant)"

(h) A defendant may withdraw a waiver of the right to counsel at any time but is not entitled to repeat a proceeding previously held or waived solely on the grounds of the subsequent appointment or retention of counsel. If the defendant withdraws a waiver, the trial court, in its discretion, may provide the appointed counsel 10 days to prepare.

(i) Except as otherwise provided by this subsection, if an indigent defendant is entitled to and requests appointed counsel and if adversarial judicial proceedings have not been initiated against the defendant, a court or the courts' designee authorized under Article 26.04 to appoint

counsel for indigent defendants in the county shall appoint counsel immediately following the expiration of three working days after the date on which the court or the courts' designee receives the defendant's request for appointment of counsel. If adversarial judicial proceedings are initiated against the defendant before the expiration of the three working days, the court or the courts' designee shall appoint counsel as provided by Subsection (c). In a county with a population of 250,000 or more, the court or the courts' designee shall appoint counsel as required by this subsection immediately following the expiration of one working day after the date on which the court or the courts' designee receives the defendant's request for appointment of counsel. If adversarial judicial proceedings are initiated against the defendant before the expiration of the one working day, the court or the courts' designee shall appoint counsel as provided by Subsection (c).

(j) Notwithstanding any other provision of this section, if an indigent defendant is released from custody prior to the appointment of counsel under this section, appointment of counsel is not required until the defendant's first court appearance or when adversarial judicial proceedings are initiated, whichever comes first.

(k) A court or the courts' designee may without unnecessary delay appoint new counsel to represent an indigent defendant for whom counsel is appointed under Subsection (c) or (i) if:

(1) the defendant is subsequently charged in the case with an offense different from the offense with which the defendant was initially charged; and

(2) good cause to appoint new counsel is stated on the record as required by Article 26.04(j) (2).

PRACTICE TIP: For the detailed procedures the trial court must follow to appoint counsel, see Tex. Code of Crim. Pro. article 26.04 for non-capital cases [see §4:53] and article 26.052 for capital cases.

§4:52 Right to Appointment of Counsel in General

A criminal defendant facing a possibility of imprisonment in misdemeanor cases is entitled to receive the benefit of "the guiding hand of counsel." Argersinger v. Hamlin, 407 U.S. 25, 92 S. Ct. 2006, 32 L.Ed.2d 530 (1972); CCP Art.1.051(c).

A defendant who faces a fine as the only possible punishment is entitled to appointed counsel only if the court concludes that the interest of justice require such representation. Bancroft v. State, 881 S.W.2d 838 (Tex.App.—Tyler 1994, *no pet.*); CCP Art.1.051(c).

Even if the punishment range includes jail time as a possibility, if only a fine is actually assessed the judgment is not void if the defendant was not represented by counsel. Price v. State, 866 S.W.2d 606 (Tex. Crim. App. 1993).

However, a defendant is entitled to appointed counsel if he could be assessed a probated sentence that includes the possibility of confinement if the probated sentence is revoked. Alabama v. Shelton, 535 U.S. 654, 122 S. Ct. 1704, 152 L.Ed.2d 888 (2002).

If an accused appears in court without counsel, the trial court has a duty to hold a hearing to determine if the accused is aware of his right to hire counsel, to determine whether he intends to do so, and if it appears the defendant has sufficient resources to do so, then the court need not appoint counsel. Ex parte Gonzales, 945 S.W.2d 830 (Tex. Crim. App. 1997); Oliver v. State, 872 S.W.2d 713 (Tex. Crim. App. 1994).

If the court determines that the defendant is indigent and the defendant does not validly waive his right to counsel, the court cannot conduct any adversarial hearing until counsel has been appointed for the defendant. Oliver.

The trial court is not required to appoint a particular lawyer who is agreeable to the defendant. Solis v. State, 792 S.W.2d 95 (Tex. Crim. App.

1990); Cain v. State, 976 S.W.2d 228 (Tex.App.—San Antonio 1998, *no pet.*).

Unless a defendant decides to represent himself or shows adequate cause for the appointment of new counsel, he must accept the lawyer appointed by the court. Carmell v. State, 963 S.W.2d 833 (Tex.App.—Fort Worth 1998, *pet. ref'd*), *rev'd on other grounds* 529 U.S. 513, 120 S. Ct. 1260, 146 L.Ed.2d 577 (2000); Garner v. State, 864 S.W.2d 92 (Tex.App.—Houston [14th Dist.] 1993, *pet. ref'd*).

A defendant's right to counsel is not violated by a trial court's *sua sponte* appointment of additional counsel where it is felt that retained counsel may require assistance. McFarland v. State, 928 S.W.2d 482 (Tex. Crim. App. 1996).

A defendant is entitled to counsel for purposes of direct appeal. CCP Art. 1.051. A defendant who faces punishment for contempt of court is entitled to appointed counsel if indigent. Ex parte Gonzales, 945 S.W.2d 830 (Tex. Crim. App. 1997).

Under Art. 26.052(e), a defendant is not entitled to the appointment of counsel until adversarial judicial proceedings are brought against him in that particular jurisdiction. Busby v. State, 253 S.W.3d 661 (Tex. Crim. App. 2008).

Article 2.07 of the Texas Code of Criminal Procedure sets out how attorneys pro tem are to be appointed and compensated. The statute provides for the appointment of either private attorneys or prosecutors from other jurisdictions within the state to take over for the recused or disqualified District or County Attorney. If the trial court appoints a prosecutor from another jurisdiction, that prosecutor gets paid for his or her regular prosecutorial job without any additional compensation. But, if the trial court appoints a private attorney, that person (or team, as in this case) is paid in the same amount and manner as an attorney representing an indigent defendant. The State of Texas Ex Rel. Brian W. Wice, Relator v. The Fifth Judicial District Court of Appeals, Respondent, ___ S.W.3d ___, *2 (Tex. Crim. App. No. WR-86,920-02, 2018 WL 6072183, November 21, 2018).

Article 26.05 states that the trial court shall authorize payment for appointed counsel (assuming that the trial court has not appointed a member of a public defender's office) according to a fee schedule adopted by formal action of the judges in a particular county and does not authorize payment outside of the schedule. The State Ex Rel. Wice, ___ S.W.3d at *2.

§4:52.1 Ten-Day Rule

Counsel appointed by the court for trial is entitled to a minimum of ten days preparation time. CCP Art. 1.051(e).

The ten-day preparation period applies to the actual preparation time and not the time of the formal appointment. Sheppard v. State, 634 S.W.2d 953 (Tex.App.—Fort Worth 1982, *no pet.*).

Where the defendant indicates that he wishes to proceed *pro se* and formerly hired counsel is then appointed stand-by counsel, it is not error to deny the defendant ten days preparation time. Johnson v. State, 653 S.W.2d 324 (Tex.App.—San Antonio 1983), *affirmed at* 760 S.W.2d (Tex. Crim. App. 1988).

A violation of the ten-day preparation time requirement is not subject to harmless error analysis on appeal. Marin v. State, 891 S.W.2d 267 (Tex. Crim. App. 1994).

§4:53 Establishing Indigence

CCP Art. 26.04. Procedures for Appointing Counsel.

> *(a) The judges of the county courts, statutory county courts, and district courts trying criminal cases in each county, by local rule, shall adopt and publish written countywide procedures for timely and fairly appointing counsel for an indigent defendant in the county arrested for, charged with, or taking an appeal from a conviction of a misdemeanor punishable by confinement or a felony. The procedures must be consistent with this article and Articles 1.051, 15.17, 26.05, and 26.052. A court shall appoint an attorney from a public appointment list using a system of rotation, unless the court appoints an attorney under Subsection (f), (f-1), (h), or (i). The court shall appoint attorneys from among the next five names on the appointment list in the order in which*

the attorneys' names appear on the list, unless the court makes a finding of good cause on the record for appointing an attorney out of order. An attorney who is not appointed in the order in which the attorney's name appears on the list shall remain next in order on the list.

(b) Procedures adopted under Subsection (a) shall:

(1) authorize only the judges of the county courts, statutory county courts, and district courts trying criminal cases in the county, or the judges' designee, to appoint counsel for indigent defendants in the county;

(2) apply to each appointment of counsel made by a judge or the judge's designee in the county;

(3) ensure that each indigent defendant in the county who is charged with a misdemeanor punishable by confinement or with a felony and who appears in court without counsel has an opportunity to confer with appointed counsel before the commencement of judicial proceedings;

(4) require appointments for defendants in capital cases in which the death penalty is sought to comply with any applicable requirements under Articles 11.071 and 26.052;

(5) ensure that each attorney appointed from a public appointment list to represent an indigent defendant perform the attorney's duty owed to the defendant in accordance with the adopted procedures, the requirements of this code, and applicable rules of ethics; and

(6) ensure that appointments are allocated among qualified attorneys in a manner that is fair, neutral, and nondiscriminatory.

(c) Whenever a court or the courts' designee authorized under Subsection (b) to appoint counsel for indigent defendants in the county determines for purposes of a criminal proceeding that a defendant charged with or appealing a conviction of a felony or a misdemeanor punishable by confinement is indigent or that the interests of justice require representation of a defendant in the proceeding, the court or the courts' designee shall appoint one or more practicing attorneys to represent the defendant in accordance with this subsection and the procedures adopted under Subsection (a). If the court or the courts' designee determines that the defendant does not speak and understand the English language or that the defendant is deaf, the court or the courts' designee shall make an effort to appoint an attorney who is capable of communicating in a language understood by the defendant.

(d) A public appointment list from which an attorney is appointed as required by Subsection (a) shall contain the names of qualified attorneys, each of whom:

(1) applies to be included on the list;

(2) meets the objective qualifications specified by the judges under Subsection (e);

(3) meets any applicable qualifications specified by the Texas Indigent Defense Commission; and

(4) is approved by a majority of the judges who established the appointment list under Subsection (e).

(e) In a county in which a court is required under Subsection (a) to appoint an attorney from a public appointment list:

(1) the judges of the county courts and statutory county courts trying misdemeanor cases in the county, by formal action:

(A) shall:

(i) establish a public appointment list of attorneys qualified to provide representation in the county in misdemeanor cases punishable by confinement; and

(ii) specify the objective qualifications necessary for an attorney to be included on the list; and

(B) may establish, if determined by the judges to be appropriate, more than one appointment list graduated according to the degree of seriousness of the offense, the attorneys' qualifications, and whether representation will be provided in trial court proceedings, appellate proceedings, or both; and

(2) the judges of the district courts trying felony cases in the county, by formal action:

(A) shall:

(i) establish a public appointment list of attorneys qualified to provide representation in felony cases in the county; and

(ii) specify the objective qualifications necessary for an attorney to be included on the list; and

(B) may establish, if determined by the judges to be appropriate, more than one appointment list graduated according to the degree of seriousness of the offense, the attorneys' qualifications, and whether representation will be provided in trial court proceedings, appellate proceedings, or both.

(f) In a county in which a public defender's office is created or designated under Article 26.044, the court or the court's designee may appoint that office to represent the defendant in accordance with guidelines established for the office.

(f-1) In a county in which a managed assigned counsel program is operated in accordance with Article 26.047, the managed assigned counsel program may appoint counsel to represent the defendant in accordance with the guidelines established for the program.

(g) A countywide alternative program for appointing counsel for indigent defendants in criminal cases is established by a formal action in which two-thirds of the judges of the courts designated under this subsection vote to establish the alternative program. An alternative program for appointing counsel in misdemeanor and felony cases may be established in the manner provided by this subsection by the judges of the county courts, statutory county courts, and district courts trying criminal cases in the county. An alternative program for appointing counsel in misdemeanor cases may be established in the manner provided by this subsection by the judges of the county courts and statutory county courts trying criminal cases in the county. An alternative program for appointing counsel in felony cases may be established in the manner provided by this subsection by the judges of the district courts trying criminal cases in the county. In a county in which an alternative program is established:

(1) the alternative program may:

(A) use a single method for appointing counsel or a combination of methods; and

(B) use a multicounty appointment list using a system of rotation; and

(2) the procedures adopted under Subsection (a) must ensure that:

(A) attorneys appointed using the alternative program to represent defendants in misdemeanor cases punishable by confinement:

(i) meet specified objective qualifications for that representation, which may be graduated according to the degree of seriousness of the offense and whether representation will be provided in trial court proceedings, appellate proceedings, or both; and

(ii) are approved by a majority of the judges of the county courts and statutory county courts trying misdemeanor cases in the county;

(B) attorneys appointed using the alternative program to represent defendants in felony cases:

(i) meet specified objective qualifications for that representation, which may be graduated according to the degree of seriousness of the offense and whether representation will be provided in trial court proceedings, appellate proceedings, or both; and

(ii) are approved by a majority of the judges of the district courts trying felony cases in the county;

(C) appointments for defendants in capital cases in which the death penalty is sought comply with the requirements of Article 26.052; and

(D) appointments are reasonably and impartially allocated among qualified attorneys.

(h) In a county in which an alternative program for appointing counsel is established as provided by Subsection (g) and is approved by the presiding judge of the administrative judicial region, a court or the courts' designee may appoint an attorney to represent an indigent defendant by using the alternative program. In establishing an alternative program under Subsection (g), the judges of the courts establishing the program may not, without the approval of the commissioner's court, obligate the county by contract or by the creation of new positions that cause an increase in expenditure of county funds.

(i) A court or the court's designee required under Subsection (c) to appoint an attorney to represent a defendant accused or convicted of a felony may appoint an attorney from any county located in the court's administrative judicial region.

(j) An attorney appointed under this article shall:

(1) make every reasonable effort to contact the defendant not later than the end of the first working day

after the date on which the attorney is appointed and to interview the defendant as soon as practicable after the attorney is appointed;

(2) represent the defendant until charges are dismissed, the defendant is acquitted, appeals are exhausted, or the attorney is permitted or ordered by the court to withdraw as counsel for the defendant after a finding of good cause is entered on the record; and

(3) with respect to a defendant not represented by other counsel, before withdrawing as counsel for the defendant after a trial or the entry of a plea of guilty:

(A) advise the defendant of the defendant's right to file a motion for new trial and a notice of appeal;

(B) if the defendant wishes to pursue either or both remedies described by Paragraph (A), assist the defendant in requesting the prompt appointment of replacement counsel; and

(C) if replacement counsel is not appointed promptly and the defendant wishes to pursue an appeal, file a timely notice of appeal.

(k) A court may replace an attorney who violates Subsection (j)(1) with other counsel. A majority of the judges of the county courts and statutory county courts or the district courts, as appropriate, trying criminal cases in the county may remove from consideration for appointment an attorney who intentionally or repeatedly violates Subsection (j)(1).

(l) Procedures adopted under Subsection (a) must include procedures and financial standards for determining whether a defendant is indigent. The procedures and standards shall apply to each defendant in the county equally, regardless of whether the defendant is in custody or has been released on bail.

(m) In determining whether a defendant is indigent, the court or the court's designee may consider the defendant's income, source of income, assets, property owned, outstanding obligations, necessary expenses, the number and ages of dependents, and spousal income that is available to the defendant. The court or the court's designee may not consider whether the defendant has posted or is capable of posting bail, except to the extent that it reflects the defendant's financial circumstances as measured by the considerations listed in this subsection.

(n) A defendant who requests a determination of indigency and appointment of counsel shall:

(1) complete under oath a questionnaire concerning his financial resources;

(2) respond under oath to an examination regarding his financial resources by the judge or magistrate responsible for determining whether the defendant is indigent; or

(3) complete the questionnaire and respond to examination by the judge or magistrate.

(o) Before making a determination of whether a defendant is indigent, the court shall request the defendant to sign under oath a statement substantially in the following form:

"On this ______________ day of ________________________, 20 _____, I have been advised by the (name of the court) Court of my right to representation by counsel in connection with the charge pending against me. I am without means to employ counsel of my own choosing and I hereby request

the court to appoint counsel for me. (Signature of the defendant.)"

(p) A defendant who is determined by the court to be indigent is presumed to remain indigent for the remainder of the proceedings in the case unless a material change in the defendant's financial circumstances occurs. If there is a material change in financial circumstances after a determination of indigency or nonindigency is made, the defendant, the defendant's counsel, or the attorney representing the state may move for reconsideration of the determination.

(q) A written or oral statement elicited under this article or evidence derived from the statement may not be used for any purpose, except to determine the defendant's indigency or to impeach the direct testimony of the defendant. This subsection does not prohibit prosecution of the defendant under Chapter 37, Penal Code.

(r) A court may not threaten to arrest or incarcerate a person solely because the person requests the assistance of counsel.

In the appointment of counsel context, a defendant is indigent if he is financially without the means to employ counsel of his own choosing. Whitehead v. State, 130 S.W.3d 866 (Tex. Crim. App. 2004).

The trial court may disbelieve an allegation of indigency if there is a reasonable, articulable basis for doing so, either because there is conflicting evidence or because the evidence submitted is in some manner suspect or determined by the court to be inadequate. Whitehead.

An inquiry into the reasonableness of a defendant's expenses and financial obligations is proper in order to adequately determine whether a defendant is capable of paying for or entitled to a free appellate record. Tuck v. State, 215 S.W.3d 411 (Tex. Crim. App. 2007).

The appointment of counsel statute does not give the trial court the option to rule upon an unsworn motion, and contains two different oath requirements. First, upon requesting a determination of indigence, the defendant must detail his financial resources under oath by completing a written questionnaire, by responding to examination by a judge or magistrate, or by both. Second, before a court determines that a defendant is indeed indigent, the defendant must sign a form oath, provided by statute, stating that he is without means to employ counsel. Whitehead.

A defendant is indigent for purposes of the appointment of appellate counsel if he is not financially able to employ counsel. Tex. Code Crim. Pro. Art. 1.051(b); McFatridge v. State, 309 S.W.3d 1 (Tex. Crim. App. 2010).

Determining indigency for purposes of appointing counsel and indigency for purposes of obtaining a free record are discrete inquiries, but the factors to be considered are the same. A defendant can be found indigent for one purpose without being found indigent for the other. McFatridge.

For the purpose of determining entitlement to a free appellate record, a defendant is considered indigent if he cannot pay or give security for the record. Whitehead.

The appellate rule authorizing a free appellate record contains an oath requirement. Rule 20.2 provides that a defendant, within the time for perfecting an appeal, may request a free record by motion and affidavit. Only sworn allegations are to be considered in determining whether a defendant is entitled to a free record. Whitehead.

There is a two-step process for determining whether a defendant is indigent for the purpose of obtaining a free record on appeal: 1) the defendant must make a *prima facie* showing of indigence; and 2) when the prima facie showing of indigence is made, the burden shifts to the state to show that the defendant is not in fact indigent. Whitehead.

The same standard should be used to determine whether to appoint counsel for appeal. Whitehead.

Unless there is some basis in the record to find the defendant's *prima facie* showing to be inaccurate or untrue, the trial court should accept it as sufficient to find him indigent.

The trial court need not appoint counsel until an accused demonstrates that he or she is indigent. Switzer v. State, 809 S.W.2d 781 (Tex.App.—Houston [14th Dist.] 1991, *no pet.*).

Relevant to both indigency determinations are the defendant's income, source of income, assets, property owned, outstanding obligations, necessary expenses, the number and ages of dependents, and spousal income that is available to the defendant. Each county should have guidelines and financial standards that it applies to determine whether a defendant is indigent for purposes of appointing counsel. McFatridge.

The burden is on the defendant to establish that he is indigent and entitled to appointed counsel. Bancroft v. State, 881 S.W.2d 838 (Tex.App.—Tyler 1994, *no pet.*).

If the court finds that the defendant is unable to employ counsel and has not abandoned his right to counsel, the court cannot hold adversarial proceedings until the defendant has had counsel appointed to represent him. Oliver v. State, 872 S.W.2d 713 (Tex. Crim. App. 1994).

§4:54 Assessing Costs for Court-Appointed Counsel

A claim of insufficient evidence to support a requirement that the defendant reimburse the county for attorney fees, as mandated by a clerk's bill of costs, presents a criminal law matter and is cognizable on a defendant's direct appeal. Armstrong v. State, 340 S.W.3d 759 (Tex. Crim. App. 2011).

Furthermore, a defendant is not required to object at the trial to court ordered reimbursement of appointed attorney fees in order to preserve appellate challenge to the sufficiency of evidence of his financial resources and ability to pay. Mayer v. State, 309 S.W.3d 552, 556 (Tex. Crim. App. 2010).

Court costs and attorney fees, as reflected in a certified bill of costs, need neither be orally pronounced nor incorporated by reference in the judgment to be effective. Armstrong.

In absence of a trial court order mandating reimbursement of appointed attorney fees and a finding that a previously indigent person has the funds to pay the costs, a district clerk lacks authority to assess attorney fees as part of a bill of costs. In re Daniel, 396 S.W.3d 545, 549 (Tex. Crim. App. 2013).

Where appellant has knowledge of the issue of court-assessed attorney fees and fails to appeal it from the original imposition of deferred adjudication, she procedurally defaults the issue for appeal after later adjudication. Riles v. State, 452 S.W.3d 333, 338 (Tex. Crim. App. 2015).

§4:55 Form for Court-Appointed Counsel

See our companion book *Texas Criminal Forms* (James Publishing) for the following sample forms:

- Form 4-6, Declaration in Support of Request for Court-Appointed Counsel.
- Form 4-7, Order Appointing Counsel for Trial.
- Form 4-10, Order Appointing Counsel for Appeal.

§4:60 Conflicts of Interest

Trial courts in the pretrial context must recognize a presumption in favor of a defendant's counsel of choice, but also that presumption may be overcome not only by a demonstration of actual conflict but by a showing of a serious potential for conflict. The evaluation of the facts and circumstances of each case under this standard must be left primarily to the informed judgment of the trial court. Bowen v. Carnes, 343 S.W.3d 805, 812 (Tex. Crim. App. 2011), citing Wheat v. U.S., 486 U.S. 153, 108 S.Ct. 1692, 100 L.Ed.2d 140 (1988).

When a trial court unreasonably or arbitrarily interferes with the defendant's right to choose counsel, its actions rise to the level of a constitutional violation. Therefore, courts must exercise caution in disqualifying defense attorneys, especially if less serious means would adequately protect the government's interests. Bowen v. Carnes; citing Wheat v. U.S.

An actual conflict of interest exists if counsel is required to make a choice between advancing his client's interest in a fair trial or advancing other interests (perhaps counsel's own) to the detriment of his client's interest. James v. State, 763 S.W.2d 776 (Tex. Crim. App. 1989); Acosta v. State, 233 S.W.3d 349 (Tex. Crim. App. 2007).

In order to meet the Strickland standard in a conflict of interest case, appellant must show first that defense counsel actively represented conflicting interests and that an actual conflict of interest adversely affected his lawyer's performance. If appellant demonstrates this, then the second prong of the Strickland test will be met because prejudice is presumed. Failure to make the required showing of a conflict of interest will defeat the ineffectiveness claim. Banda v. State, 890 S.W.2d 42 (Tex. Crim. App. 1994), *cert. denied*, 515 U.S. 1105, 115 S. Ct. 2253, 132 L.Ed.2d 260 (1995).

This standard applies where the conflict results from the lawyer advancing another's interest as well as where the lawyer is advancing his own interest. Acosta.

A conclusory allegation of a conflict of interest is insufficient to carry the defendant's burden to show a conflict. Stephenson v. State, 255 S.W.3d 652 (Tex.App.—Fort Worth, 2008, *pet. ref'd*).

Merely showing a potential for conflict does not meet the burden; the defendant must show that an actual conflict existed. Cuyler v. Sullivan, 446 U.S. 355, 100 S. Ct. 1708, 64 L.Ed.2d 333 (1980); Routier v. State, 112 S.W.3d 554 (Tex. Crim. App. 2003).

A defendant who fails to object at trial must demonstrate that an actual conflict of interest adversely affected his lawyer's performance. Cuyler, *supra*; Routier v. State, 112 S.W.3d 554 (Tex. Crim. App. 2003).

If one codefendant stands to gain significantly by counsel adducing probative evidence or plausible arguments that are damaging to another codefendant there is a conflict of interest present in counsel's joint representation. Foster v. State, 693 S.W.2d 412 (Tex. Crim. App. 1985).

Requiring or permitting a single attorney to represent codefendants does not always violate the constitutional guarantees to effective assistance of counsel, and the mere possibility of a conflict of interest is insufficient to impugn a criminal conviction. Holloway v. Arkansas, 435 U.S. 475, 98 S. Ct. 1173, 55 L.Ed.2d 426 (1978); Maya v. State, 932 S.W.2d 633 (Tex.App.—Houston [14th Dist.] 1996, *no pet.*).

However, whenever a trial court improperly requires joint representation over timely objection, reversal is automatic. Holloway v. Arkansas, *supra*; Amaya v. State, 677 S.W.2d 159 (Tex.App.—Houston [1st Dist.] 1984, *pet. ref'd*).

There are at least three significant potential conflicts of interest inherent in most cases of multiple representation. They are:

- A jointly represented defendant may be deprived of advantageous plea bargaining options which would be available to him if he were separately represented
- A jointly represented defendant may be harmed more than would a separately represented defendant by incriminating evidence admitted against a codefendant; specifically, a joint attorney may be unable to argue that one defendant is less guilty than the others, or that one defendant deserves less punishment than the others, whereas a separate attorney would be free to do so
- One attorney representing several defendants may be less able than a separate attorney would be to reduce harm arising from testimony by a codefendant and his witnesses which is inconsistent with testimony of the defendant and his witnesses

Amaya, *supra*.

An objection to joint representation can be made at any point during the trial as long as made as soon as the objection becomes known and as long as it is not done as a dilatory tactic. Objections made after trial are untimely. Lerma v. State, 679 S.W.2d 488 (Tex. Crim. App. 1982) (opinion on rehearing).

Where the record shows that the defendants were never warned by their trial attorney or by the court about a potential or actual conflict of interest, the defense attorney breached a legal duty to his clients and violated a professional responsibility. Ex parte Acosta, 672 S.W.2d 470 (Tex. Crim. App. 1984).

Absent an express, voluntary and knowing waiver, an actual conflict of interest that hinders the effectiveness of counsel will mandate a new trial. Maya v. State, 932 S.W.2d 633 (Tex.App.—Houston [14th Dist.] 1996, *no pet.*).

§4:61 Waiver of Conflicts of Interest

Because a criminal defendant has a limited constitutional right to employ counsel of choice, he inherently possesses the power to waive his right to conflict-free counsel. Wheat v. U.S., 486 U.S. 153, 108 S. Ct. 1692, 100 L.Ed.2d 140 (1988); Jones v. State, 728 S.W.2d 469 (Tex.App.—Houston [1st Dist.] 1987, *no pet.*).

A defendant waives his right to separate counsel when he insists upon joint representation after being advised of the possible risks and dangers thereof. No inquiry by the trial court is required to be initiated in the absence of any knowledge of any special circumstances where the defendant expressly waives the right to separate counsel. Jones.

However, the waiver of conflict-free counsel is no less significant than the waiver of counsel altogether. To be effective, the record must show the defendant is aware of the conflict of interest, realizes the consequences of continuing with such counsel, knows that he has the right to obtain other counsel, and then knowingly and voluntarily waives these rights. Ex parte Prejean, 625 S.W.2d 731 (Tex. Crim. App. 1981).

Where a court justifiably finds an actual conflict of interest, it may decline a proffer of waiver of that conflict, and insist that defendants be separately represented. Wheat, *supra*.

While a trial court has substantial latitude in refusing to accept such waivers, a presumption exists that a defendant is entitled to counsel of his choice and a trial court cannot infringe upon one's constitutional right to counsel unless there is an actual or serious potential for conflict. Wheat, *supra*; Maya v. State, 932 S.W.2d 633 (Tex.App.—Houston [14th Dist.] 1996, *no pet.*).

§4:62 Situations Where Conflict Is Presented

Where the defendant's attorney was retained by the defendant's employer and the attorney is influenced in his basic strategic decisions by the employer's interests, a conflict of interest is present. Wood v. Georgia, 450 U.S. 261, 101 S. Ct. 1097, 67 L.Ed.2d 220 (1981).

Counsel had an actual conflict of interest where he represented codefendants and called one codefendant to testify to the detriment of the other codefendant where he did not advise the defendants of the potential for the conflict of interest. Gonzales v. State, 605 S.W.2d 278 (Tex. Crim. App. 1980); Ex parte Parham, 611 S.W.2d 103 (Tex. Crim. App. 1981).

An attorney has an actual conflict of interest where arranges his trial strategy to favor one codefendant over the other. Pina v. State, 29 S.W.3d 315 (Tex.App.—El Paso 2000, *pet. ref'd*).

A disciplinary proceeding brought by a client against counsel creates an actual conflict of interest. However, counsel has the burden to include the allegations or facts of the disciplinary action in the record, otherwise the record will merely show a potential conflict of interest. Garner v. State, 864 S.W.2d 92 (Tex.App.—Houston [1st Dist.] 1993, *pet. ref'd*).

§4:63 Situations Where No Conflict Is Presented

A defense attorney does not have a conflict of interest where she defended herself against a possible later ineffective assistance of counsel allegation by putting on the record that she communicated a plea bargain offer to the defendant. Monreal v. State, 947 S.W.2d 559 (Tex. Crim. App. 1997).

Conflicts in personality and disagreements between counsel and client are not automatic grounds for new counsel. King v. State, 29 S.W.3d 556 (Tex. Crim. App. 2000).

Requiring or permitting a single attorney to represent codefendants is a not *per se* violative of constitutional guarantees of effective assistance of counsel. Almanzar v. State, 702 S.W.2d 653 (Tex. Crim. App. 1986).

A situation where the same attorney can ethically represent two codefendants is where the testimony of one codefendant is not adverse to that of the other codefendant(s). Almanzar.

When the defense strategy in a case was to show that neither defendant could have committed the crime because both were elsewhere at the time, both alibis were distinctly different as to place and did not depend on testimony of any same witness, neither defendant attempted to incriminate the other, and counsel for the defendants reiterated at the punishment phase the belief that both defendants were innocent, there was no demonstrated conflict of interest. James v. State, 763 S.W.2d 776 (Tex. Crim. App.1989).

Where a lawyer's representation of a testifying witness is complete, involved an offense that had nothing to do with the charges against the current client, and the previous client himself has waived any objection to the lawyer's continued representation of the current client, the record reveals no actual or serious potential for conflict of interest inherent in the lawyer cross-examining his former client. Bowen v. Carnes, 343 S.W.3d 805 (Tex. Crim. App. 2011).

The filing of a civil action against a court appointed attorney is not a per se conflict of interest which would warrant the disqualification of such attorney at the whim of the criminal defendant. Dunn v. State, 819 S.W.2d 510 (Tex. Crim. App. 1991); McKinny v. State, 76 S.W.3d 463 (Tex. App.—Houston [1st Dist.] 2002, *no pet.*).

§4:64 Duty of Trial Court

The trial court has a duty to investigate a conflict of interest presented by multiple representation only if the court knows or reasonably should know a particular conflict exists. Cuyler v. Sullivan, 446 U.S. 355, 100 S. Ct. 1708, 64 L.Ed.2d 333 (1980); Routier v. State, 112 S.W.3d 554 (Tex. Crim. App. 2003).

Where the trial court knows or reasonably should know of the existence of other types of conflict of interest it has a duty to further investigate. Wood v. Georgia, 450 U.S. 261, 101 S. Ct. 1097, 67 L.Ed.2d 220 (1981).

Where the trial court suspects or is informed of a potential conflict of interest, it may hold a hearing exploring the nature of the allegations without improperly requiring disclosure of the confidential communications of the accused. Holloway v. Arkansas, 435 U.S. 475, 98 S. Ct. 1173, 55 L.Ed.2d 426 (1978).

However, a trial court is not required to hold a hearing sua sponte on a defendant's motion for a change of counsel, and its failure to do so does not deny an accused his procedural or substantive due process rights. Garner v. State, 864 S.W.2d 92 (Tex. App.—Houston [1st Dist.] 1993, *pet. ref'd*).

Where a defendant does not allege a true conflict of interest, the trial court has no duty to *sua sponte* inquire into the attorney-client relationship. Malcolm v. State, 628 S.W.2d 790 (Tex. Crim. App. 1982).

In order to preserve error on a claim of conflict of interest in a multiple representation situation, the defendant must advance a valid basis for his claim. Calloway v. State, 699 S.W.2d 824 (Tex. Crim. App. 1985).

§4:65 Duty of Counsel

Where the record shows that the defendants were never warned by their trial attorney or by the court about a potential or actual conflict of interest, the defense attorney breached a legal duty to his clients and violated a professional responsibility. Ex parte Acosta, 672 S.W.2d 470 (Tex. Crim. App.1984).

PRACTICE TIP: See Texas Disciplinary Rules of Professional Conduct Rules 1.06-1.09 and 1.13 for further information on a lawyer's duty in a conflict of interest situation.

§4:66 Replacement or Withdrawal of Counsel

The burden is on the defendant to prove that he is entitled to a change of counsel and he must show that there is adequate cause for the change. Thomas v. State, 550 S.W.2d 60 (Tex. Crim. App. 1976); Childress v. State, 794 S.W.2d 119 (Tex.App.—Houston [1st Dist.] 1990, *pet. ref'd*).

A defendant does not establish adequate cause for the replacement of counsel merely by asserting disagreement and conflict between himself and his attorney. Cain v. State, 976 S.W.2d 228 (Tex. App.—San Antonio 1998, *no pet.*); Boston v. State, 965 S.W.2d 546 (Tex.App.—Houston [14th Dist.] 1997, *no pet.*).

Before an attorney may withdraw from the representation of a defendant, he must have the permission of the trial court. Ward v. State, 740 S.W.2d 794 (Tex. Crim. App. 1987).

A motion to withdraw as counsel is not self-proving. Whitehead v. State, 130 S.W.3d 866 (Tex. Crim. App. 2004).

PRACTICE TIP: After completion of a trial, retained counsel should always file a motion to withdraw unless counsel intends to represent the defendant on appeal. Whitehead.

The decision to allow counsel to withdraw from a case is within the sound discretion of the trial court. Green v. State, 840 S.W.2d 394 (Tex. Crim. App. 1992).

The question of whether or not to grant a motion for continuance to obtain different counsel is traditionally within the sound discretion of the trial judge. Rosales v. State, 841 S.W.2d 368 (Tex. Crim. App. 1992). There is no mechanical test for deciding when a denial of a motion for continuance to obtain different counsel is an abuse of discretion. Rosales.

Some of the factors to be considered by the trial court in whether to grant a continuance to a defendant to hire substitute counsel are:

- Length of the requested delay
- Whether lead counsel has an associate who is adequately prepared to try the case
- Whether other continuances have been requested and granted
- Balanced convenience or inconvenience to litigants, witnesses, opposing counsel and the court
- Whether the requested delay is for a legitimate reason, or whether it is dilatory and contrived
- Whether there are other unique factors present

Brown v. State, 630 S.W.2d 876 (Tex.App.—Fort Worth 1982, *no pet.*).

The right to counsel of one's choice is not absolute and may in some circumstances be forced to bow to the general interest in the prompt and efficient administration of justice. Rosales, *supra.*

A request for another lawyer cannot be made so as to obstruct the orderly procedure in the courts or to interfere with the fair administration of justice. Burgess v. State, 816 S.W.2d 424 (Tex. Crim. App. 1991).

Under CCP Art. 26.04 substitution of counsel must be approved by the trial court even once the case is on appeal. Enriquez v. State, 999 S.W.2d 906 (Tex.App.—Waco 1999, *no pet.*).

The trial court is under no duty to search for counsel until an attorney is found who is agreeable to the accused. Stearnes v. Clinton, 780 S.W.2d 216 (Tex. Crim. App. 1989).

A court-appointed attorney who replaces the preceding attorney on a case is entitled to ten days preparation time. CCP Art. 1.051(e). A violation of the ten-day preparation time requirement is not subject to harmless error analysis on appeal. Marin v. State, 891 S.W.2d 267 (Tex. Crim. App. 1994).

An objection is required to complain on appeal of an improper substitution of counsel. Springer v. State, 940 S.W.2d 322 (Tex.App.—Dallas 1997, *no pet.*).

The trial court must have a principled reason to replace appointed counsel over the objection of counsel and the defendant. Stotts v. Wisser, 894 S.W.2d 366 (Tex. Crim. App. 1995).

An attorney may not withdraw without the permission of the trial court. Wenzy v. State, 855 S.W.2d 47 (Tex.App.—Houston [14th Dist.] 1993, *pet. ref'd*).

§4:67 Disqualification of Counsel

There is a strong presumption in favor of a defendant's right to retain counsel of choice; however, this presumption may be overridden by other important considerations relating to the integrity of the judicial process and the fair and orderly administration of justice. Gonzalez v. State, 117 S.W.3d 831 (Tex. Crim. App. 2003).

In moving to disqualify appellant's counsel of choice, the government bears a heavy burden of establishing that disqualification is justified. Gonzalez.

However, when a trial court unreasonably or arbitrarily interferes with the defendant's right to choose counsel, its actions rise to the level of a constitutional violation. Gonzalez.

Counsel may be disqualified under the disciplinary rules when the opposing party can demonstrate actual prejudice resulting from opposing counsel's service in the dual role of advocate-witness. Gonzalez.

Allegations of one or more violations of the disciplinary rules or evidence showing only a possible future violation are not sufficient. In determining whether counsel should be disqualified because counsel is a potential witness, Texas courts use rule 3.08 of the Texas disciplinary rules of professional conduct as a guideline. The rule does not present the disqualification standard, but does provide considerations relevant to the determination. Gonzalez.

§4:70 Right to Self-Representation

§4:71 Statutory Provisions

CCP Art. 1.051. Right to Representation By Counsel

> *(f) (f) A defendant may voluntarily and intelligently waive in writing the right to counsel. A waiver obtained in violation of Subsection (f-1) or (f-2) is presumed invalid.*
>
> *(f-1) In any adversary judicial proceeding that may result in punishment by confinement, the attorney representing the state may not:*
>
> *(1) initiate or encourage an attempt to obtain from a defendant who is not represented by counsel a waiver of the right to counsel; or*
>
> *(2) communicate with a defendant who has requested the appointment of counsel, unless the court or the court's designee authorized under Article 26.04 to appoint counsel for indigent defendants in the county has denied the request and, subsequent to the denial, the defendant:*
>
> *(A) has been given a reasonable opportunity to retain and has failed to retain private counsel; or*
>
> *(B) waives or has waived the opportunity to retain private counsel.*
>
> *(f-2) In any adversary judicial proceeding that may result in punishment by confinement, the court may not direct or encourage the defendant to communicate with the attorney representing the state until the court advises the defendant of the right to counsel and the procedure for requesting appointed counsel and the defendant has been given a reasonable opportunity to request appointed counsel. If the defendant has requested appointed counsel, the court may not direct or encourage the defendant to communicate with the attorney representing the state unless the court or the court's designee authorized under Article 26.04 to appoint counsel for indigent defendants in the county has denied the request and, subsequent to the denial, the defendant:*
>
> *(1) has been given a reasonable opportunity to retain and has failed to retain private counsel; or*
>
> *(2) waives or has waived the opportunity to retain private counsel.*
>
> *(g) If a defendant wishes to waive the right to counsel for purposes of entering a guilty plea or proceeding to trial, the court shall advise the defendant of the nature of the charges against the defendant and, if the defendant is proceeding to trial, the dangers and disadvantages of self-representation. If*

the court determines that the waiver is voluntarily and intelligently made, the court shall provide the defendant with a statement substantially in the following form, which, if signed by the defendant, shall be filed with and become part of the record of the proceedings:

"I have been advised this ______ day of __________, 2 ____, by the (name of court) Court of my right to representation by counsel in the case pending against me. I have been further advised that if I am unable to afford counsel, one will be appointed for me free of charge. Understanding my right to have counsel appointed for me free of charge if I am not financially able to employ counsel, I wish to waive that right and request the court to proceed with my case without an attorney being appointed for me. I hereby waive my right to counsel. (signature of defendant)"

(h) A defendant may withdraw a waiver of the right to counsel at any time but is not entitled to repeat a proceeding previously held or waived solely on the grounds of the subsequent appointment or retention of counsel. If the defendant withdraws a waiver, the trial court, in its discretion, may provide the appointed counsel 10 days to prepare.

(i) Except as otherwise provided by this subsection, if an indigent defendant is entitled to and requests appointed counsel and if adversarial judicial proceedings have not been initiated against the defendant, a court or the courts' designee authorized under Article 26.04 to appoint counsel for indigent defendants in the county shall appoint counsel immediately following the expiration of three working days after the date on which the court or the courts' designee receives the defendant's request for appointment of counsel. If adversarial judicial proceedings are initiated against the defendant before the expiration of the three working days, the court or the courts' designee shall appoint counsel as provided by Subsection (c). In a county with a population of 250,000 or more, the court or the courts' designee shall appoint counsel as required by this subsection immediately following the expiration of one working day after the date on which the court or the courts' designee receives the defendant's request for appointment of counsel. If adversarial judicial proceedings are initiated against the defendant before the expiration of the one working day, the court or the courts' designee shall appoint counsel as provided by Subsection (c).

(j) Notwithstanding any other provision of this section, if an indigent defendant is released from custody prior to the appointment of counsel under this section, appointment of counsel is not required until the defendant's first court appearance or when adversarial judicial proceedings are initiated, whichever comes first.

(k) A court or the courts' designee may without unnecessary delay appoint new counsel to represent an indigent defendant for whom counsel is appointed under Subsection (c) or (i) if: (1) the defendant is subsequently charged in the case with an offense different from the offense with which the defendant was initially charged; and (2) good cause to appoint new counsel is stated on the record as required by Article 26.04(j)(2).

§4:72 In General

The Sixth Amendment to the U.S. Constitution and Article I, §10 of the Texas Constitution provide that a defendant in a criminal trial has the right to effective assistance of counsel.

However, this right to counsel may be waived, and the defendant may choose to represent himself at trial. Faretta v. California, 422 U.S. 806, 95 S. Ct. 2525, 45 L.Ed.2d 562 (1975).

The right to self-representation will not attach until it is clearly and unequivocally asserted. Ex parte Winton, 837 S.W.2d 134 (Tex. Crim. App. 1992); Cain v. State, 976 S.W.2d 228 (Tex.App.—San Antonio 1998, *no pet.*).

§4:73 Waiver of Right to Counsel

The Sixth Amendment to the United States Constitution and Article I, §10 of the Texas Constitution provide that a defendant in a criminal trial has the right to assistance of counsel. This right may be waived, and a defendant may choose to represent himself at trial. Faretta v. California, 422 U.S. 806, 95 S. Ct. 2525, 45 L.Ed.2d 562 (1975).

The constitutional right of self-representation does not arise from the accused's power to waive the assistance of counsel, but independently from the Sixth Amendment grant to the accused personally the right to defend. When a defendant asserts his *pro se* rights, analysis must center not on a waiver of counsel analysis, but on whether the defendant is aware of the dangers and disadvantages of self-representation. Thus, the focus of a trial court's admonitions to a defendant wishing to proceed *pro se* is on the knowing and intelligent assertion of the right to self-representation. Johnson v. State, 760 S.W.2d 277 (Tex. Crim. App. 1988).

A waiver of the right to counsel will not be lightly inferred, and the courts will indulge every reasonable presumption against the validity of such a waiver. Geeslin v. State, 600 S.W.2d 309 (Tex. Crim. App. [Panel Op.] 1980).

A waiver of counsel must be made competently, knowingly and intelligently, and voluntarily. Collier v. State, 959 S.W.2d 621 (Tex. Crim. App. 1997) (citing Godinez v. Moran, 509 U.S. 389, 113 S. Ct. 2680, 125 L.Ed.2d 321 (1993)), *cert. denied*, 525 U.S. 929 (1998).

Where the trial judge finds no evidence that the defendant's assertion of his Sixth Amendment right to self-representation was untimely, conditional, or that it would be disruptive or dilatory, then the defendant should be allowed to represent himself. Ex parte Winton, 837 S.W.2d 134 (Tex. Crim. App. 1992).

The decision to waive counsel and proceed pro se is made knowingly and intelligently in a case where the defendant is contesting his guilt, if it is made with a full understanding of the right to counsel, which is being abandoned, as well as the dangers and disadvantages of self-representation. Collier, *supra*; Blankenship v. State, 673 S.W.2d 578 (Tex. Crim. App. 1984).

The decision is made voluntarily if it is uncoerced. Collier. No formulaic questioning is required to establish a knowing and intelligent waiver. Blankenship. However, a trial court can make certain that an accused's professed waiver of counsel is understandingly and wisely made only from a penetrating and comprehensive examination of all circumstances surrounding the waiver. Blankenship.

The trial court's questioning should focus on the defendant's ability to knowingly and intelligently waive his right to counsel, rather than his legal experience. Funderburg v. State, 717 S.W.2d 637 (Tex. Crim. App. 1986).

The record must reflect that the trial court thoroughly admonished the defendant. Collier, *supra*.

In a case where the defendant is contesting his guilt, the record must be sufficient for a reviewing court to make an assessment that the defendant was made aware of the dangers and disadvantages of self-representation. Goffney v. State, 843 S.W.2d 583 (Tex. Crim. App. 1992); Johnson v. State, 760 S.W.2d 277 (Tex. Crim. App.1988).

In a case where a defendant appears without counsel and does not contest his guilt the sole issue is whether there was a knowing, voluntary and intelligent waiver of counsel. Johnson v. State, 614 S.W.2d 116 (Tex. Crim. App. 1981). The same is true where the defendant appears without counsel and enters a plea of true to allegations in a petition to revoke probation. Hatten v. State, 71 S.W.3d 332 (Tex. Crim. App. 2002).

Presuming waiver from a silent record is impermissible. The record must show, or there must be an allegation and evidence which show, that an accused was offered counsel but intelligently and understandingly rejected the offer. Carnley v. Cochran 369 U.S. 506, 8 L.Ed.2d 70, 82 S. Ct. 884 (1962).

It is not enough that the record show mere conclusions by the trial court that the defendant is aware of the dangers and disadvantages of self-representation. Goffney, *supra*. The presumption of regularity of a judgment will not suffice for the requirement of recorded admonishments. Goffney.

There is no federal constitutional right to self-representation on appeal. Martinez v. Court of Appeals, 528 U.S. 152, 120 S. Ct. 684, 145 L.Ed.2d 597 (2000).

If the defendant has stand-by counsel, it is not necessary that he be admonished by the trial court as to the dangers and disadvantages of self-representation. Walker v. State, 962 S.W.2d 124 (Tex.App.—Houston [1st Dist.] 1997, *pet. ref'd*).

To assess whether a waiver is effective, courts consider the totality of the circumstances. This means that courts must examine the particular facts and circumstances surrounding that case, including the background, experience, and conduct of the accused. Johnson v. Zerbst, 304 U.S. 458 (1938); Williams v. State, 252 S.W.3d 353 (Tex. Crim. App. 2008).

The Constitution permits judges to take a realistic account of the particular defendant's mental capacities by asking whether a defendant who seeks to conduct his own defense at trial is mentally competent to do so. That is to say the Constitution permits States to insist upon representation by counsel for those competent enough to stand trial but who still suffer from severe mental illness to the point where they are not competent to conduct trial proceedings by themselves. Indiana v. Edwards, 554 U.S. 164, 128 S. Ct. 23379, 171 L.Ed.2d 345 (2008); Chadwick v. State, 309 S.W.3d 558 (Tex. Crim. App. 2010).

When the record does not affirmatively show that the defendant was sufficiently admonished as required by Faretta, it is reversible error, not subject to a harm analysis. Goffney v. State, 843 S.W.2d 583 (Tex. Crim. App. 1992); Williams.

An insufficient admonishment regarding a defendant's right to appointed counsel is also not subject to harm analysis. Williams.

§4:74 Duty of the Trial Court

The constitutional right to counsel imposes on the trial judge the serious and weighty responsibility to determine whether there is a proper waiver thereof by the accused. Oliver v. State, 872 S.W.2d 713 (Tex. Crim. App. 1994).

In a case where the defendant contests his guilt, the record must affirmatively show that the defendant was made aware of the dangers and disadvantages of self-representation. Johnson v. State, 760 S.W.2d 277 (Tex. Crim. App. 1988); Faretta v. California, 422 U.S. 806, 95 S. Ct. 2525, 45 L.Ed.2d 562 (1975).

TIP TO THE BENCH: Trial courts should make a diligent inquiry into the reasons a defendant wants to represent himself. If it turns out that the true problem is a conflict of interest between the defendant and counsel, the trial court should make further inquiry into the basis of the conflict, and determine whether new counsel should be appointed or retained.

To decide whether a defendant's waiver is knowing and intelligent, the court must make an inquiry, evidenced by the record, which shows that the defendant has the intelligence to demonstrate a capacity to waive his right to counsel and the ability to appreciate the practical disadvantage he will confront in representing himself. George v. State, 9 S.W.3d 234 (Tex.App.—Texarkana 1999, *no pet.*).

It is not mandatory that the warnings be given in writing because this would have the effect of forcing counsel upon a defendant who refused to sign a written waiver. Burgess v. State, 816 S.W.2d 424 (Tex. Crim. App. 1991). However, the record must show that the defendant understands the consequences of his waiver. Goffney v. State, 843 S.W.2d 583 (Tex. Crim. App. 1992).

There are no formulaic questions that are to be put to a defendant wishing to represent himself. Johnson, *supra*.

In a case where a defendant appears without counsel and does not contest his guilt the record must only reflect that there was a knowing, voluntary and intelligent waiver of counsel. Johnson v. State, 614 S.W.2d 116 (Tex. Crim. App. 1981). The same is true where the defendant appears without counsel and enters a plea of true to allegations in a petition to revoke probation. Hatten v. State, 71 S.W.3d 332 (Tex. Crim. App. 2002).

In a case where the defendant intends to enter a guilty plea, the Sixth Amendment is satisfied when the trial court admonishes the defendant of the nature of the charges against him, of his right to be counseled regarding his plea, and of the range of allowable punishments attendant upon the guilty plea. Iowa v. Tovar, 541 U.S. 77, 124 S. Ct. 1379, 158 L.Ed.2d 209 (2004).

The failure to properly admonish a defendant on the dangers and disadvantages of self-representation is error involving fundamental constitutional systemic requirements and is categorically immune to a harmless error analysis. Faretta, *supra*.

Where the self-representation admonishments, although sufficient, were given after the defendant had participated in jury selection, they were untimely. Manley v. State, 23 S.W.3d 172 (Tex. App.—Waco 2000, *pet. ref'd*).

When advising a defendant about the dangers and disadvantages of self-representation, the trial judge must inform the defendant that there are technical rules of evidence and procedure, and he will not be granted any special consideration solely because he asserted his *pro se* rights. Johnson v. State, 760 S.W.2d 277 (Tex. Crim. App. 1988); Williams v. State, 252 S.W.3d 353 (Tex. Crim. App. 2008).

But a trial judge has no duty to inquire into an accused's age, education, background or previous mental history in every instance where an accused expresses a desire to represent himself. Goffney v. State, 843 S.W.2d 583 (Tex. Crim. App. 1992); Williams.

TIP TO THE BENCH: In Johnson v. State, supra, the Court went on to say that the effect of admonishments should reflect a knowledge by defendant of the dangers and disadvantages of self-representation, so that the record will establish that he knows what he is doing and his choice is made with eyes open. The defendant should be aware of the practical disadvantages and that there are technical rules of evidence and procedure, and that he will not be granted any special consideration solely because he asserted his pro se rights, and that he is about to embark on a risky course.

The right to represent one's self extends to the submission of a *pro se* brief on appeal where the defendant has been properly admonished. Ex parte Davis, 818 S.W.2d 64 (Tex. Crim. App. 1991).

A defendant who represented himself at trial cannot claim ineffective assistance of counsel in post-trial matters. Martin v. State, 630 S.W.2d 952 (Tex. Crim. App. 1982).

§4:74.1 Valid Waivers of Counsel

Where a defendant intelligently and knowingly waives his right to counsel and affirmatively asserts his right to self representation, it is error for the trial court to deny his right of self-representation even if the defendant knew little about trial procedure. Blankenship v. State, 673 S.W.2d 578 (Tex. Crim. App. 1984).

TIP TO THE BENCH: CCP Art. 1.051(g) provides that the court shall advise the defendant of the dangers and disadvantages of self-representation. It also provides that if the court finds that the defendant's waiver of counsel is voluntary, the defendant shall sign a statement (contained in the article) to that effect.

§4:74.2 Invalid Waivers of Counsel

The failure to request counsel at a pretrial hearing does not amount to a voluntary relinquishment or abandonment of the right to counsel. Before the court can find that the defendant has waived his right to counsel there must be a basis in the record for concluding that he knowingly, voluntarily, and intelligently relinquished or abandoned his right to assistance of counsel. Oliver v. State, 872 S.W.2d 713 (Tex. Crim. App.1994).

Presuming waiver from a silent record is impermissible. The record must show, or there must be an allegation and evidence which show, that an accused was offered counsel but intelligently and understandingly rejected the offer. Carnley v. Cochran 369 U.S. 506, 8 L.Ed.2d 70, 82 S. Ct. 884 (1962).

Where a defendant expresses dissatisfaction with appointed counsel and requests different counsel, this does not constitute a valid waiver of counsel or a request for self-representation. Renfro v. State, 586 S.W.2d 496 (Tex. Crim. App. 1979).

§4:74.3 Waiver of Waiver of Right to Counsel

A defendant may waive his right to represent himself once the right has been asserted. McKaskle v. Wiggins, 465 U.S. 168, 104 S. Ct. 944, 79 L.Ed.2d 122 (1984); Funderburg v. State, 717 S.W.2d 637 (Tex. Crim. App. 1986).

The defendant may withdraw the waiver of the right to counsel under CCP Art. 1.051(h) at any time. Walker v. State, 962 S.W.2d 124 (Tex.App.—Houston [1st Dist.] 1997, *pet. ref'd*).

However, a trial court may refuse to permit a defendant to withdraw his waiver where: 1) it will interfere with the orderly administration of the business of the court; 2) result in unnecessary delay or inconvenience to witnesses; or 3) prejudice the state. Medley v. State, 47 S.W.3d 17 (Tex.App.—Amarillo 2001, *pet. ref'd*).

While the record must reflect that a defendant waived his right to self-representation after it was asserted, it is not subject to the same stringent standards as the waiver of the right to counsel. Funderburg, *supra*. A waiver may be found if it reasonably appears to the court that the defendant has abandoned his initial request to represent himself. Funderburg.

§4:75 Failure of Non-Indigent Defendant to Retain Counsel

CCP Art. 1.051(e)

> *(e) An appointed counsel is entitled to 10 days to prepare for a proceeding but may waive the preparation time with the consent of the defendant in writing or on the record in open court. If a nonindigent defendant appears without counsel at a proceeding after having been given a reasonable opportunity to retain counsel, the court, on 10 days' notice to the defendant of a dispositive setting, may proceed with the matter without securing a written waiver or appointing counsel. If an indigent defendant who has refused appointed counsel in order to retain private counsel appears without counsel after having been given an opportunity to retain counsel, the court, after giving the defendant a reasonable opportunity to request appointment of counsel or, if the defendant elects not to request appointment of counsel, after obtaining a waiver of the right to counsel pursuant to Subsections (f) and (g), may proceed with the matter on 10 days' notice to the defendant of a dispositive setting.*

If the trial judge determines after a hearing that the defendant has sufficient funds to hire counsel, understands the importance of retaining counsel and has been given ample opportunity to hire counsel, the failure of the defendant to hire counsel may be regarded by the court as relinquishment of the right to counsel. Oliver v. State, 872 S.W.2d 713 (Tex. Crim. App.1994).

§4:76 Stand-By Counsel

The term "stand-by counsel" usually describes situations when, in response to a defendant's request for self-representation, the trial court instead allows the defendant's attorney to remain as counsel and be available to advise the defendant and participate in the case, or not, as requested by the defendant. Walker v. State, 962 S.W.2d 124 Tex.App.—Houston [1st Dist.] 1997, *pet. ref'd*).

An accused has no right to hybrid representation (self-representation and representation by counsel), although the trial court has the discretion to permit it. Scarbrough v. State, 777 S.W.2d 83 (Tex. Crim. App. 1989).

Accepting an offer of stand-by counsel that is later retracted does not waive a previously asserted right to self-representation. Scarbrough. If a trial court refuses to appoint stand-by counsel or withdraws an offer of stand-by counsel, a defendant must choose between two mutually exclusive rights: the right to self-representation without stand-by counsel or representation by counsel. Scarbrough.

A defendant's Sixth Amendment rights are not violated when a trial judge appoints stand-by counsel, even over the defendant's objection, to relieve the judge of the need to explain and enforce basic rules of courtroom protocol or to assist the defendant in overcoming routine obstacles that stand in the way of the defendant's achievement of his own clearly indicated goals. Participation by counsel to steer a defendant through the basic procedures of trial is permissible even in the unlikely event that it somewhat undermines the *pro se* defendant's appearance of control over his own defense. McKaskle v. Wiggins, 465 U.S. 168, 104 S. Ct. 944, 79 L.Ed.2d 122 (1984).

A defendant's Faretta rights impose some limits on the extent of stand-by counsel's unsolicited participation before the jury in two ways: 1) the *pro se* defendant is entitled to preserve control over the case he chooses to present to the jury; 2) participation by stand-by counsel without the defendant's consent should not be allowed to destroy the jury's perception that the defendant is representing himself. McKaskle. Participation by standby counsel outside the presence of the jury engages only the first of these two limitations. McKaskle.

Once a *pro se* defendant invites or agrees to any substantial participation by counsel, subsequent appearances by counsel must be presumed to be with the defendant's acquiescence, at least until the defendant expressly and unambiguously renews his request that stand-by counsel be silenced. McKaskle.

The trial court has every right to appoint counsel to a party already represented by counsel. McFarland v. State, 928 S.W.2d 482 (Tex. Crim. App. 1996).

The trial court should ensure that stand-by counsel has sufficient experience and familiarity with the case to continue as lead counsel if need be, or the trial court may be found to have abused its discretion. Brown v. State, 630 S.W.2d 876 (Tex. App.—Fort Worth 1982, *no pet.*).

§4:80 Right to Counsel at Administrative and Prison Hearings

Prison inmates do not have a right to retained or appointed counsel in disciplinary hearings because they are not criminal proceedings. Baxter v. Palmigiano, 425 U.S. 308, 96 S. Ct. 1551, 47 L.Ed. 2d 810 (1976).

Prison inmates are not constitutionally entitled to the appointment of lawyers while they are administratively segregated under suspicion of having committed a criminal offense where no adversary judicial proceedings have yet been initiated against them. U.S. v. Gouveia, 467 U.S. 180, 104 S. Ct. 2292, 81 L.Ed.2d 146 (1984).

Parolees are not absolutely entitled to counsel at parole revocation hearings; rather the decision is made on a case-by-case basis in the exercise of sound discretion by hearing authorities. In deciding if the defendant should have been afforded counsel, the courts look at such factors as the complexity of the facts, the defendant's ability to ask meaningful questions, understand the proceedings and present evidence; and whether the defendant was represented by counsel at a preliminary hearing. Ex parte Taylor, 957 S.W.2d 43 (Tex. Crim. App. 1997); Gagnon v. Scarpelli, 411 U.S. 778, 93 S. Ct. 1756, 36 L.Ed.2d 656 (1973).

§4:90 Right to Effective Assistance of Counsel

§4:91 In General

The defendant has the right to the effective assistance of counsel. U.S. Constitution, Sixth and Fourteenth Amendments; Texas Constitution, Art. I, §10.

Counsel's performance is evaluated based on the law in effect at the time of the trial. Vaughn v. State, 931 S.W.2d 564 (Tex. Crim. App. 1996). The test is to be applied at the time of trial, not through hindsight. Wilkerson v. State, 726 S.W.2d 542 (Tex. Crim. App. 1986), *cert. denied*, 480 U.S. 940, 107 S. Ct. 1590, 94 L.Ed.2d 779 (1987). The appellate courts will scrutinize counsel's representation on a highly deferential basis and make every effort to eliminate the distorting effects of hindsight. Thompson v. State, 9 S.W.3d 808 (Tex. Crim. App. 1999).

The assessment of whether a defendant received effective assistance of counsel must be made according to the facts of each case. Ex parte Scott, 581 S.W.2d 181 (Tex. Crim. App. 1979). The same standard applies in evaluating appointed and retained counsel. Cuyler v. Sullivan, 446 U.S. 355, 100 S. Ct. 1708, 64 L.Ed.2d 333 (1980).

A strategic choice made after thorough investigation is practically unassailable. A strategic choice made after less than thorough investigation is reasonable to the extent reasonable professional judgment supports the limitation. Strickland v. Washington, 466 U.S. 668, 104 S. Ct. 2052, 80 L.Ed.2d 674 (1984); Patrick v. State, 906 S.W.2d 481 (Tex. Crim. App. 1995).

Even where counsel's decisions open the door to the admission of extraneous offenses, if the appellate court deems the decision to be a legitimate, strategic or tactical one, the defendant will not be able to overcome the presumption that counsel employed sound trial strategy. Williams v. State, 301 S.W.3d 675 (Tex. Crim. App. 2009).

It can be ineffective assistance of counsel for counsel not to investigate whether a third party was the perpetrator of the offense. Ex parte Amezquita, 223 S.W.3d 363, 368 (Tex. Crim. App. 2006) (where the third party was in possession of the complainant's cell phone right after the commission of the offense).

Failing to perform a necessary function as counsel due to the lack of payment is not a strategic choice, it is an economic one, and can constitute deficient performance. Ex parte Briggs, 187 S.W.3d 458 (Tex. Crim. App. 2005) (where the attorney failed to investigate medical evidence).

This standard has never been interpreted to mean that the accused is entitled to errorless or perfect counsel. Bridge v. State, 726 S.W.2d 558 (Tex. Crim. App.1986).

In assessing counsel's effectiveness, the courts will not isolate or separate out one portion of trial counsel's performance. Ex parte Welborn, 785 S.W.2d 391 (Tex. Crim. App.1990).

Isolated instances in the record reflecting errors of commission or omission do not cause counsel to become ineffective, nor can ineffective assistance of counsel be established by isolating or separating out one portion of the trial counsel's performance for examination. Bridge, *supra*; Johnson v. State, 629 S.W.2d 731 (Tex. Crim. App.1981).

However, even if no one instance alone is sufficient proof of ineffective assistance of counsel, counsel's performance, as a whole, may compel such a finding. Welborn, *supra*; Winn v. State, 871 S.W.2d 756 (Tex.App.—Corpus Christi 1993, *no pet.*) (where counsel's representation fell below the objective standard of reasonableness required by Strickland because counsel failed to seek out witnesses who could have impeached the State's physical evidence, conducted a cursory voir dire examination, failed to preserve error, failed to object to inadmissible evidence, and offered a harmful videotape).

An applicant must show omissions or other mistakes made by counsel that amount to professional errors of a magnitude sufficient to raise a reasonable probability that the outcome of the trial would have been different but for the errors. Butler v. State, 716 S.W.2d 48 (Tex. Crim. App. 1986).

An error in trial strategy will be deemed inadequate representation only if counsel's actions are without any plausible basis. Jackson v. State, 877 S.W.2d 768 (Tex. Crim. App. 1994).

An appellate court looks to the totality of the representation and the particular circumstances of each case in evaluating the effectiveness of counsel. Ex Parte Felton, 815 S.W.2d 733 (Tex. Crim. App. 1991).

Appellate courts presume that trial counsel is better positioned than the appellate court to judge the pragmatism of the particular case, and that he made all significant decisions in the exercise of reasonable professional judgment. Jackson v. State, 877 S.W.2d 768 (Tex. Crim. App. 1994).

The Strickland standard applies to the punishment phase as well as the guilt-innocence phase of a criminal trial. Hernandez v. State, 988 S.W.2d 770 (Tex. Crim. App. 1999) (overruling Ex parte Duffy, 607 S.W.2d 507 (Tex. Crim. App. 1980)); Milburn v. State, 3 S.W.3d 919 (Tex. Crim. App. 1999).

Counsel may be found to have rendered ineffective assistance of counsel where she does not investigate the defendant's mental health history where there are indications that the defendant suffered from a mental illness. Ex parte LaHood, 401 S.W.3d 45, 52 (Tex. Crim. App. 2013).

Both the performance and prejudice prongs of the Strickland ineffectiveness inquiry are mixed questions of law and fact, but the prejudice prong often contains subsidiary questions of historical fact, some of which may turn upon the credibility and demeanor of witnesses. Appellate courts must show almost total deference to a trial court's findings of historical facts as well as mixed questions of law and fact that turn on an evaluation of credibility and demeanor. Riley v. State, 378 S.W.3d 453 (Tex. Crim. App. 2012).

Trial management is the lawyer's province: Counsel provides his or her assistance by making decisions such as what arguments to pursue, what evidentiary objections to raise, and what agreements to conclude regarding the admission of evidence. Some decisions, however, are reserved for the client—notably, whether to plead guilty, waive the right to a jury trial, testify in one's own behalf, and forgo an appeal. McCoy v. Louisiana, 584 U.S. ___, 138 S.Ct. 1500, 1508, 200 L.Ed.2d 821 (2018). *See also* Turner v. State, 570 S.W.3d 250, 274-5 (Tex. Crim. App. 2018).

Numerous choices affecting conduct of the trial do not require client consent, including the objections to make, the witnesses to call, and the arguments to advance. McCoy v. Louisiana, 138 S.Ct. at 1509.

Counsel, in any case, must still develop a trial strategy and discuss it with her client. McCoy v. Louisiana, 138 S.Ct. at 1509.

§4:92 Defendant's Burden

A defendant has the burden to prove a claim of ineffective assistance of counsel. The burden is by a preponderance of the evidence. Cox v. State, 389 S.W.3d 817 (Tex. Crim. App. 2012).

The defendant must overcome the presumption that, under the circumstances, the challenged action might be considered sound trial strategy. Jackson, *supra*.

To prevail, the defendant must show: 1) counsel's performance was deficient to the extent that counsel failed to function as the counsel guaranteed by the Sixth Amendment; and 2) there is a reasonable probability that, but for counsel's errors, the result of the proceeding would have been different. Strickland v. Washington, 466 U.S. 668, 104 S. Ct. 2052, 80 L.Ed.2d 674 (1984); Cox, S.W.3d at 819.

A reasonable probability is a probability sufficient to undermine confidence in the outcome of the case. Strickland, *supra*; Cox, S.W.3d at 819.

The "reasonable probability" standard under the second prong is not an "outcome-determinative" test; that is, a defendant need not show that it is more probable than not that the jury would have arrived at a different verdict had the errors not occurred. Strickland.

A probability may be reasonable even though it does not constitute a preponderance of the evidence. Snow v. State, 697 S.W.2d 663, 668 (Tex. App.—Houston [1st Dist].1985), *pet. dism'd* 794 S.W.2d 371 (Tex. Crim. App. 1987)

A verdict or conclusion only weakly supported by the record is more likely to have been affected by errors than one with overwhelming record support. Strickland, *supra*.

It is not sufficient to show that counsel's errors had some conceivable effect on the outcome of the proceedings. Dewberry v. State, 4 S.W.3d 735 (Tex. Crim. App. 1999). The issue is whether counsel's assistance was reasonable under all the circumstances and prevailing professional norms at the time of the alleged error. Mallet v. State, 9 S.W.3d 856 (Tex.App.—Fort Worth 2000, *no pet.*).

The Strickland prejudice prong applied today presents a more difficult burden than does the harm analysis under Rule 44.2 of the Texas Rules of Appellate Procedure. Ex parte Martinez, 330 S.W.3d 891 (Tex. Crim. App. 2011).

Where the defendant pleaded guilty, in order to satisfy the second prong of the test he must show that, but for counsel's errors, he would not have pleaded guilty but would have insisted on going to trial. Hill v. Lockhart, 474 U.S. 52, 106 S. Ct. 366, 88 L.Ed.2d 203, (1985); Ex parte Akhtab, 901 S.W.2d 488 (Tex. Crim. App. 1995).

When the trial court has properly admonished a defendant as to the consequences of his plea of guilty, there is a *prima facie* showing that the plea was made knowingly and voluntarily and the defendant has the burden of proof to show otherwise. Martinez v. State, 981 S.W.2d 195 (Tex. Crim. App. 1998).

Any allegation of ineffectiveness must be firmly founded in the record, and the record must affirmatively demonstrate the alleged ineffectiveness. McFarland v. State, 928 S.W.2d 824 (Tex. Crim. App. 1992).

Where the record is silent as to trial counsel's motivation for taking certain action, appellate courts will presume that the decisions made were made on reasonable professional judgment. Mallett v. State, 65 S.W.3d 59 (Tex. Crim. App. 2001); Prine v. State, 537 S.W.3d 113, 117 (Tex. Crim. App. 2017).

However, in situations where there can be no objectively reasonable trial strategy for counsel's performance, a finding of deficient performance can be made even on a silent record. Andrews v. State, 159 S.W.3d 98 (Tex. Crim. App. 2005) (where counsel failed to object to a detrimental misstatement of law made by the state during closing arguments).

However, when trial counsel fails to provide his reasoning for taking or not taking action, appellate courts will find counsel's performance deficient only if the conduct was so outrageous that no competent attorney would have engaged in it. It is the applicant's responsibility to overcome the strong presumption that counsel made a reasonable strategic decision. Ex parte Scott, 541 S.W.3d 104, 117 (Tex. Crim. App. 2017).

The defendant fails to carry his burden when the probability of a different result absent the alleged deficient conduct is not established. Carmona v. State, 941 S.W.2d 949 (Tex. Crim. App. 1997); Ex parte Cash, 178 S.W.3d 816 (Tex. Crim. App. 2005).

A vague, inarticulate sense that counsel could have provided a better defense is not a legal basis for finding counsel constitutionally incompetent. Bone v. State, 77 S.W.3d 828 (Tex. Crim. App. 2002).

The defendant cannot meet his burden to show ineffective assistance of counsel when the caselaw evaluating counsel's actions and decisions in that instance was nonexistent, not definitive, or was unsettled. Ex parte Bahena, 195 S.W.3d 704 (Tex. Crim. App. 2006). *See also* Ex parte Smith, 296 S.W.3d 78 (Tex. Crim. App. 2009) (same result where the proper construction of a statute remains unresolved).

Where the law on an issue is unsettled, a claim of ineffective assistance of counsel cannot be sustained. State v. Bennett, 415 S.W.3d 867, 869 (Tex. Crim. App. 2013) (where the issue was the applicable statute of limitations for the offense of aggravated assault).

If a defendant can demonstrate that defense counsel entirely failed to subject the prosecution's case to meaningful adversarial testing, so that there was a constructive denial of the assistance of counsel altogether, then prejudice, because it is so likely, is legally presumed. Cannon v. State, 252 S.W.3d 342 (Tex. Crim. App. 2008) *citing* United States v. Cronic, 466 U.S. 648 (1984).

§4:93 Duty of Counsel

In assessing competence, counsel is held accountable for knowledge, or the ability to attain knowledge, of relevant legal matters that are neither novel nor unsettled. Ex parte Welch, 981 S.W.2d 183 (Tex. Crim. App. 1998). Counsel has a duty to make a reasonable investigation of the facts or to make a reasonable decision that makes a particular investigation unnecessary. McFarland v. State, 928 S.W.2d 482 (Tex. Crim. App. 1996).

Once counsel has investigated the facts and developed a defensive theory, counsel has the obligation to present sufficient available evidence in support of that defensive theory. Butler v. State, 716 S.W.2d 48 (Tex. Crim. App. 1986); Shelton v. State, 841 S.W.2d 526 (Tex.App.—Fort Worth 1992, *no pet.*).

Counsel has a duty to seek out witnesses who will establish a defense for his client. Ex parte Duffy, 607 S.W.2d 507 (Tex. Crim. App. 1980). Consequently, counsel has the obligation to exercise due diligence in securing the testimony of prospective witnesses through the issuance of a subpoena. Drew v. State, 743 S.W.2d 207 n. 17 (Tex. Crim. App.1987) (citing Tex. Jur.3d, Vol. 25, Criminal Law, §3490, pp. 370- 371). This duty arises even when the witness promises to attend. Drew.

Counsel has a duty to see that necessary expert witnesses are available to the defendant for trial. If the defendant cannot afford the expert witnesses, counsel has three options: (1) Subpoena all of the experts who are involved in the case and introduce medical records through the experts and elicit their expert opinions; (2) If counsel is convinced that the defendant could not pay for experts to assist him in preparation for trial or to provide expert testimony, withdraw from the case explaining to the court that applicant was now indigent, prove that indigency and request appointment of new counsel; or (3) Remain as counsel, but request investigatory and expert witness fees from the trial court for a now-indigent client pursuant to Ake v. Oklahoma. Ex parte Briggs, 187 S.W.3d 458 (Tex. Crim. App. 2005).

Counsel has a duty to inform the defendant of a plea bargain offer extended by the state. Ex parte Lemke, 13 S.W.3d 791 (Tex. Crim. App. 2000). At least one appeals court also holds that counsel has a duty to inform the client about a plea bargain acceptance deadline. Turner v. State, 49 S.W.3d 461 (Tex.App.—Fort Worth 2001), *pet. dismissed* 118 S.W.3d 772 (2003).

Counsel has a duty to advise his client of the direct consequences of a guilty plea. However, he is under no duty to inform the client about collateral consequences such as use of the conviction for impeachment purposes, loss of employment, loss of voting rights, suspension of driving privileges, dishonorable discharge from the military and the loss of the right to bear firearms. Ex parte Morrow, 952 S.W.2d 530 (Tex. Crim. App. 1997).

Trial counsel has the duty to consult with and fully advise his client concerning the meaning and effect of a judgment rendered by a court. Ex parte Fontenot, 3 S.W.3d 32 (Tex. Crim. App. 1999); Ex parte Axel, 757 S.W.2d 369 (Tex. Crim. App. 1988).

Trial counsel has a duty to consult with and fully advise the defendant of his right to appeal from that judgment, the necessity of giving notice of appeal, taking other steps to pursue an appeal, as well as expressing his professional judgment as to possible grounds for appeal and their merit, and delineating the advantages and disadvantages of appeal. Fontenot; Axel.

If appellate counsel's action or inaction denies a defendant his opportunity to prepare and file a petition for discretionary review, that defendant has been denied his Sixth Amendment right to effective assistance of counsel. Ex parte Wilson, 956 S.W.2d 25 (Tex. Crim. App. 1997).

Counsel fulfills his obligation to inform the defendant that the defendant has a right to file a *pro se* petition for discretionary review where counsel advises the defendant of this fact in his initial appointment letter. Ex parte Lozada-Mendoza, 45 S.W.3d 107 (Tex. Crim. App. 2001).

§4:94 Raising Issue of Ineffective Counsel

The issue of ineffective assistance of counsel can be raised on a motion for new trial. Reyes v. State, 849 S.W.2d 812 (Tex. Crim. App. 1993).

The issue of ineffective assistance of counsel can be raised on a *habeas corpus* application — in fact, this method is preferable to direct appeal because of the ability of the applicant to offer additional evidence at a *habeas* hearing. Ex parte Torres, 943 S.W.2d 469 (Tex. Crim. App. 1997).

A claim of ineffective assistance of counsel has a slim chance of prevailing on direct appeal because the undeveloped record on appeal generally will be insufficient to allow the defendant to satisfy the two prongs of the Strickland test. Thompson v. State, 9 S.W.3d 808 (Tex. Crim. App. 1999).

Under the Sixth Amendment a defendant is not required to raise his ineffective assistance of counsel claim on direct appeal in order to raise it in a collateral attack on his conviction. Massaro v. U.S., 538 U.S. 500, 123 S. Ct. 1690, 155 L.Ed.2d 714 (2003).

The issue can be raised on a habeas application even where addressed on direct appeal if additional evidence can be adduced at the habeas hearing. Ex parte Torres, *supra*.

A defendant cannot make out a colorable habeas corpus claim of ineffective assistance of counsel where he instructed counsel to follow the particular strategy of which he later complains. Schriro v. Landrigan, 550 U.S. 465, 127 S.Ct. 1933, 167 L.Ed.2d 836 (2007).

It is error to deny the defendant an opportunity at a probation revocation hearing to develop the issue of ineffective assistance of counsel at the original trial or plea proceeding of the case. Carter v. State, 641 S.W.2d 557 (Tex. Crim. App. 1982).

A defendant may pursue a claim of ineffective assistance of counsel on an appeal of the punishment phase of an adjudication because it is unrelated to a claim regarding the propriety of the conviction. Kirtley v. State, 56 S.W.3d 48 (Tex. Crim. App. 2001).

A defendant's failure to raise claim of ineffective assistance of counsel in the trial court does not procedurally bar from him from raising it on direct appeal. Tex.R.App.P. 33.1(a); Robinson v. State, 16 S.W.3d 808 (Tex. Crim. App. 2000).

If called upon to testify on an accusation of ineffective assistance of counsel, an attorney cannot invoke the Fifth Amendment unless the conduct alleged involves a violation of the criminal law. Porchia v. State, 904 S.W.2d 147 (Tex.App.—Dallas 1995, *pet. ref'd*).

§4:95 Ineffective Counsel

It is possible that a single egregious error of omission or commission by appellant's counsel constitutes ineffective assistance. Jackson v. State, 766 S.W.2d 504 (Tex. Crim. App. 1985) (modified on other grounds on remand from U.S. Supreme Court, Jackson v. State, 766 S.W.2d 518 (Tex. Crim. App. 1988)).

However, even if no single instance is sufficient proof of ineffective assistance of counsel, counsel's performance, as a whole, may compel such a finding. Welborn, *supra*; Winn v. State, 871 S.W.2d 756 (Tex.App.—Corpus Christi 1993, *no pet.*) (where counsel's representation fell below the objective standard of reasonableness required by Strickland because counsel failed to seek out witnesses who could have impeached the State's physical evidence, conducted a cursory voir dire examination, failed to preserve error, failed to object to inadmissible evidence, and offered a harmful videotape).

A suspended or disbarred attorney is incompetent as a matter of law if the reasons for the discipline imposed reflect so poorly upon the attorney's competence that it may be reasonably inferred that the attorney was incompetent to represent the defendant. Cantu v. State, 930 S.W.2d 594 (Tex. Crim. App. 1996).

§4:95.1 Failure to Conduct Investigation

Counsel has an absolute duty to conduct a prompt investigation of the circumstances of the case and to explore all avenues likely to lead to facts relevant to the merits of the case. Ex parte Briggs, 187 S.W.3d 458 (Tex. Crim. App. 2005); Ex parte Niswanger, 335 S.W.3d 611, 615 (Tex. Crim. App. 2011).

In any ineffectiveness case, a particular decision not to investigate must be directly assessed for reasonableness in all the circumstances, applying a heavy measure of deference to counsel's judgments. Briggs.

In order for a defendant to demonstrate ineffective assistance for counsel's failure to conduct an investigation, he must show what counsel would have learned from the investigation. Mooney v. State, 817 S.W.2d 693 (Tex. Crim. App. 1991). He must further show that the consequence of the failure was that the only viable defense was not advanced. McFarland v. State, 928 S.W.2d 482 (Tex. Crim. App. 1996).

Where an attorney failed to conduct an investigation in a murder case he was ineffective when this fact was coupled with his lack of experience and lack of time allotted for preparation. Ybarra v. State, 629 S.W.2d 943 (Tex. Crim. App. 1982).

A failure of the attorney to investigate can render the defendant's guilty plea involuntary. Haynes v. State, 790 S.W.2d 824 (Tex.App.—Austin 1990, *no pet.*); Briggs.

The failure of trial counsel to prepare and because of the unpreparedness advising the defendant to waive a jury resulted in a finding of ineffective assistance of counsel. Ex parte Dunham, 650 S.W.2d 825 (Tex. Crim. App. 1983).

The failure of counsel in a death penalty case to conduct a complete investigation into the defendant's background is reasonable only when reasonable professional judgments support the limitations on the investigation. Wiggins v. Smith, 539 U.S. 510, 123 S. Ct. 2527, 156 L.Ed.2d 471 (2003); Ex parte Woods, 176 S.W.3d 224 (Tex. Crim. App. 2005).

Counsel is bound to make reasonable efforts to obtain and review material that counsel knows the prosecution will probably rely on as evidence of aggravation at the sentencing phase of trial. Rompilla v. Beard, 545 U.S. 374, 125 S. Ct. 2456, 162 L.Ed.2d 360 (2005).

Where there is evidence that the defendant may be mentally ill, in some cases counsel is ineffective for failing to investigate whether he was insane at the time of the offense. Ex Parte Imoudu v. State, 284 S.W.3d 866 (Tex. Crim. App. 2009).

Trial counsel can be found to have rendered ineffective assistance for failing to investigate the defendant's mental health history and failing to have him evaluated for competency. Ex parte Truong, 568 S.W.3d 690, 691 (Tex. Crim. App. 2018).

Failure to hire a forensic expert can be ineffective assistance of counsel where counsel does not have sufficient experience to conduct a proper investigation without the assistance of an expert. Ex parte Napper, 322 S.W.3d 202 (Tex. Crim. App. 2010).

Furthermore, defense counsel has an obligation to conduct an investigation that is diligent enough to reveal whether he needs the help of an expert in preparing for trial and cross-examining witnesses. This can be accomplished through a variety of investigative tools including: an informal pre-hiring consultation with an expert, consultation with knowledgeable defense attorneys, continuing legal education, use of a medical library, and use of the internet. Ex parte Napper.

In judging whether trial counsel has adequately challenged scientific evidence, the courts employ the rule of contemporary assessment of counsel's conduct which judges the reasonableness of counsel's conduct according to the standards and procedures in place at the time of counsel's conduct. Maryland v. Kulbicki, 577 U.S. ___, 136 S.Ct. 2, ___ L.Ed.3d ___ (2015).

§4:95.2 Failure to Conduct Discovery

In order for a defendant to demonstrate ineffective assistance for counsel's failure to conduct proper discovery, he must show that what counsel discovered would be useful to his defense. Allen v. State, 47 S.W.3d 47 (Tex.App.—Fort Worth 2001, *no pet.*). Counsel is not ineffective for failure to seek pretrial discovery of scientific testing results where the results of the testing turned out to be inconclusive. Allen.

In order for a defendant to demonstrate ineffective assistance of counsel where he alleges a failure to conduct discovery of the state's witnesses, he must show that favorable material would have been found. Thompson v. State, 915 S.W.2d 897 (Tex. App.—Houston [1st Dist.] 1996, *pet. ref'd*).

Because a defendant's constitutional right of confrontation includes the right to have trial proceedings conducted in a way that he can understand, counsel can be found to have rendered ineffective assistance of counsel where no motion for interpreter is urged. Ex parte Cockrell, 424 S.W.3d 543, 557 (Tex. Crim. App. 2014).

§4:95.3 Failure to Properly Carry Out Plea Bargaining

Defendants are entitled to effective counsel during the plea bargaining process. Ex parte Battle, 817 S.W.2d 81 (Tex. Crim. App. 1991).

A defendant is entitled to have his lawyer attempt to negotiate a plea bargain in an appropriate case. Mitchell v. State, 762 S.W.2d 916 (Tex.App.—San Antonio 1988, *pet. ref'd*).

A lawyer's performance falls below an objective standard of reasonableness where he fails to inform his client of a plea bargain acceptance deadline. Turner v. State, 49 S.W.3d 461 (Tex.App.—Fort Worth 2001, *pet. granted*).

To establish prejudice in a claim of ineffective assistance of counsel in which a defendant is not made aware of a plea-bargain offer, or rejects a plea-bargain because of bad legal advice, the applicant must show a reasonable probability that: (1) he would have accepted the earlier offer if counsel had not given ineffective assistance; (2) the prosecution would not have withdrawn the offer; and (3) the trial court would not have refused to accept the plea bargain. Ex parte Argent, 393 S.W.3d 781, 784 (Tex. Crim. App. 2013).

Counsel is not ineffective for failing to communicate a plea bargain offer where the negotiations did not progress to the point of an actual plea bargain offer. Harvey v. State, 97 S.W.3d 162 (Tex.App.—Houston [14th Dist.] 2002, *pet. ref'd*).

The defendant has the burden of proving that the results of the proceeding would have been different had the offer been communicated; i.e., that he would have accepted the offer had it been conveyed. Dickerson v. State, 87 S.W.3d 632 (Tex.App.—San Antonio 2002, *no pet.*); Missouri v. Frye, 566 U.S. 134, 132 S.Ct. 1399, 182 L.Ed.2d 379 (2012).

Counsel is not ineffective if the evidence shows that the defendant would not have taken the offer had it been communicated or where the offer was one the defendant had previously indicated an unwillingness to accept. Harvey.

Where defense counsel gives incorrect advice to the defendant during the plea process which results in the defendant rejecting the plea and going to trial, counsel may be found to have rendered ineffective assistance of counsel. If ineffective assistance was rendered, the remedy is for the courts to order specific performance of the original plea offer. Lafler v. Cooper, 566 U.S. 156, 132 S.Ct. 1376, 182 L.Ed.2d 398 (2012).

§4:95.4 Failure to Properly Advise on Guilty Pleas

In attacking a guilty plea on ineffective assistance grounds, a defendant must show counsel's alleged deficiencies caused the plea to be unknowing and involuntary. Rodriguez v. State, 899 S.W.2d 658 (Tex. Crim. App. 1995).

When a defendant challenges the voluntariness of a plea entered upon the advice of counsel, contending that his counsel was ineffective, the voluntariness of the plea depends on: (1) whether counsel's advice was within the range of competence demanded of attorneys in criminal cases and if not, (2) whether there is a reasonable probability that, but for counsel's errors, he would not have pleaded guilty and would have insisted on proceeding to trial. Ex parte Morrow, 952 S.W.2d 530 (Tex. Crim. App. 1997), citing Hill v. Lockhart, 474 U.S. 52, 106 S. Ct. 366, 88 L.Ed.2d 203, (1985).

Where the defendant was informed by his counsel that he could receive shock probation from the judge, even though he was not eligible, his plea of guilty was involuntary. Ex parte Kelly, 676 S.W.2d 132 (Tex. Crim. App. 1984).

Counsel is ineffective where the defendant is not informed of the deportation consequences of his guilty plea. Padilla v. Kentucky, 559 U.S. 356, 130 S. Ct. 1473, 176 L.Ed.2d 284 (2010).

A defendant can obtain post-conviction relief if he can show that he would not have accepted a plea had he known it would lead to deportation and also demonstrates a reasonable probability that, but for his counsel's errors, he would not have pleaded guilty and would have insisted on going to trial. Lee v. United States, 582 U.S. ___, 137 S.Ct. 1958, 1969, 198 L.Ed.2d 476 (2017).

The decision in Padilla v. Kentucky does not apply retroactively to a person whose conviction became final before it was decided. Chaidez v. U.S., 568 U.S. 342, 133 S.Ct. 1103, 185 L.Ed.2d 149 (2013); Ex parte De Los Reyes, 392 S.W.3d 675, 679 (Tex. Crim. App. 2013).

Padilla extends to circumstances where a defendant's guilty plea causes him to automatically lose legal immigration status (including temporary protected status) and become removable. Where a guilty plea causes a loss of status automatically rendering a defendant removable, the conviction has removal consequences and Padilla is triggered. Ex parte Aguilar, 537 S.W.3d 122, 127 (Tex. Crim. App. 2017).

Criminal law attorneys are generally not knowledgeable of specialized immigration law and may not understand the effect of a criminal conviction on a noncitizen. As such, appellate courts anticipate and expect, but do not demand, that criminal law attorneys will rely on their immigration-law counterparts when representing noncitizens. When a criminal defense attorney is advised by an immigration attorney and correctly relies on that advice, the advice and immigration-law knowledge is imputed to the criminal defense attorney and his performance is evaluated in light of that expertise. In such a case, if the advice is clear, explicit, and succinct, then plea counsel has a duty to provide correct advice. Ex parte Aguilar, 537 S.W.3d at 127-8.

Plea counsel will be found deficient for providing incorrect advice to a defendant despite clear and correct instructions from an immigration attorney, upon whom plea counsel assured the defendant he would rely. Ex parte Aguilar, 537 S.W.3d at 129.

An attorney is not ineffective for failing to object to the trial court's lack of admonishment to the defendant on the subject of deportation. Akhtab v. State, 901 S.W.2d 488 (Tex. Crim. App. 1995).

An attorney is ineffective where he fails to properly advise the defendant that his state and federal sentences would run consecutively, where the defendant demonstrated that he would not have pleaded guilty but for the erroneous advice. Ex parte Moody, 991 S.W.2d 856 (Tex. Crim. App. 1999).

Where counsel relates incorrect advice to the defendant regarding eligibility for parole, counsel will have performed deficiently because parole eligibility is easily determined based on the offense charged and the offense date. Ex parte Moussazadeh, 361 S.W.3d 684 (Tex. Crim. App. 2012) (where the court disavowed the prior test requiring that the defendant show that advice regarding parole eligibility formed an affirmative part or essential element of the plea agreement); Ex parte Evans, 537 S.W.3d 109 (Tex. Crim. App. 2017)(where counsel incorrectly advised the defendant that first-degree injury to a child is not an aggravated offense for parole purposes).

Advising a DWI defendant that she could receive deferred adjudication probation is ineffective assistance. Ex parte Stamnitz, 768 S.W.2d 461 (Tex.App.—Houston [1st Dist.] 1989, *no pet.*).

Where an attorney advised the defendant that she would serve no time in jail on her probated sentence, her plea was involuntary, not only because of misinformation by her attorney, but also because she had no notice that jail time could be required by the trial court as a condition of probation. Fielder v. State, 834 S.W.2d 509 (Tex.App.—Fort Worth 1992, *pet. ref'd*); Rodriguez v. State, 470 S.W.3d 823, 828 (Tex. Crim. App. 2015). However, even if the court requires the state to re-offer the original plea bargain offer, the judge is not required to approve it. Rodriguez v. State, 470 S.W.3d at 829.

Where defense counsel fails to advise the defendant of a valid defense to his charge and the defendant enters a guilty plea based on that advice, counsel can be found to have rendered ineffective assistance of counsel. Ex parte Lewis, 517 S.W.3d 917, 923 (Tex. Crim. App. 2017)(where the court found that counsel did not have an adequate command of the law applicable to the case).

§4:95.5 Failure to Properly Conduct Jury Selection

In order to prevail on a complaint of deficient jury selection performance, the defendant must show that had counsel made the proper choices that the outcome of the trial would have been different. Mitchell v. State, 989 S.W.2d 747 (Tex. Crim. App. 1999).

Where a defendant alleges that counsel was ineffective for failure to peremptorily strike a particular venireman, he must rebut the presumption of sound trial strategy. Cardenas v. State, 30 S.W.3d 384 (Tex. Crim. App. 2000).

Where the record does not contain the reason counsel failed to strike a venireman, the defendant will not prevail on his ineffective assistance claim. Delrio v. State, 840 S.W.2d 443 (Tex. Crim. App. 1992) (where counsel in a possession case failed to strike or challenge an ex-narcotics officer who knew the defendant and stated that he could not be impartial).

Just as in Delrio, where it was presumed that counsel made a tactical not to strike a juror who was actually biased, it will be presumed in the absence of evidence to the contrary that counsel made a tactical decision not to strike a juror with an implied bias. State v. Morales, 253 S.W.3d 686 (Tex. Crim. App. 2008).

If the exigencies of trial call upon trial counsel to make a difficult choice between exercising a scarce peremptory challenge to preserve improper denial of a challenge for cause for appeal, on the one hand, and exercising that peremptory challenge for some other purpose in order to secure a perceived advantage at trial, on the other, it does not violate the defendant's Sixth Amendment right to the effective assistance of counsel for trial counsel to opt for the latter. Morales.

Failing to ask any questions on voir dire and using peremptory challenges against veniremembers who have already been excused are not *per se* ineffective assistance of counsel, and where the record does not show counsel's reasons for these actions, the defendant cannot prevail on appeal. Goodspeed v. State, 187 S.W.3d 390 (Tex. Crim. App. 2005).

Where counsel misstates the law regarding cumulation of sentences during voir dire, counsel will not be found ineffective unless the record demonstrates that the jury relied on the misstatement of law. Cox v. State, 389 S.W.3d 817 (Tex. Crim. App. 2012).

§4:95.6 Failure to Interview and Present Witnesses

In order to establish ineffective assistance of counsel for the failure to seek out and interview witnesses, the defendant must demonstrate that the failure precluded him from presenting a viable defense. Ex parte Duffy, 607 S.W.2d 507 (Tex. Crim. App. 1980); Mallet v. State, 9 S.W.3d 856 (Tex.App.— Fort Worth 2000, *no pet.*). The record will not support a finding of ineffective assistance where there is no evidence that the defendant ever gave the names of the witnesses to the attorney or that they would have been willing and able to testify at trial. Mallet.

In order for a defendant to demonstrate ineffective assistance of counsel for failure to present witnesses, he must demonstrate that the testimony of the witnesses would have benefited him. Curry v. State, 861 S.W.2d 479 (Tex.App.—Fort Worth 1993, *pet. ref'd*); Kober v. State, 988 S.W.2d 230 (Tex. Crim. App. 1999).

The defendant's burden under the second prong of Strickland is to show that there is a reasonable probability that he would have been found not guilty if counsel had interviewed and presented the absent witness(es). Perez v. State, 310 S.W.3d 890 (Tex. Crim. App. 2010) (where the evidence the defendant claimed was alibi testimony wouldn't suffice for that purpose).

In evaluating the potential impact of an alibi witness, the appellate courts will also consider the relative strength of the state's case. Perez.

Where the evidence showed that witnesses would have testified that the defendant was not the perpetrator of the crime, counsel was ineffective for failure to interview them. Butler v. State, 716 S.W.2d 48 (Tex. Crim. App. 1986).

Where a defendant alleges that counsel was ineffective for failing to call his friends and relatives at punishment, he must show that their testimony would have affected the outcome of the case. Hoang v. State, 825 S.W.2d 729 (Tex.App.—Houston [1st Dist.] 1992, *pet. ref'd*).

Where counsel presented a codefendant as an alibi witness without asking questions which would have revealed that the codefendant had pleaded guilty to the case two days earlier, counsel was ineffective. Ex parte Hill, 863 S.W.2d 488 (Tex. Crim. App. 1993).

It may be considered reasonable trial strategy for counsel to not interview defense witnesses before trial where the failure to interview them was strategically done to bolster their credibility with the jury. Ahmadi v. State, 864 S.W.2d 776 (Tex. App.—Fort Worth 1993, *pet. ref'd*).

Defense counsel will not be ineffective for failure to call a particular expert witness where equivalent testimony was presented to the jury through another source. Ex parte Flores, 387 S.W.3d 626 (Tex. Crim. App. 2012).

Trial counsel can be found ineffective for failing to take reasonable steps to secure the testimony of a critical witness who is unable to travel to court, such as seeking to take the witness' deposition or pursuing a motion for continuance. Frangias v. State, 392 S.W.3d 642, 656-60 (Tex. Crim. App. 2013).

§4:95.7 Improper Handling of Evidentiary Matters

In order for a defendant to demonstrate ineffective assistance of counsel for failure to make an objection at trial, the defendant must identify the specific objection counsel should have made and cite authority that the objection would have been successful. Mallet v. State, 9 S.W.3d 856 (Tex. App.—Fort Worth 2000, *no pet.*); Ortiz v. State, 93 S.W.3d 79 (Tex. Crim. App. 2002).

Where all the record shows is that trial counsel failed to object where the state tried to introduce hearsay statements which were previously ruled inadmissible, the appellant has failed to rebut the presumption that this was a reasonable trial strategy decision. Thompson v. State, 9 S.W.3d 808 (Tex. Crim. App. 1999).

In order to demonstrate that counsel rendered ineffective assistance of counsel for failure to file a motion to suppress, the defendant must show that the motion would have been successful. Jackson v. State, 973 S.W.2d 954 (Tex. Crim. App. 1998).

Likewise, a defendant will not be prejudiced by his attorney's failure to object to the admission of evidence where a previous motion to suppress was properly overruled. Ex parte Moore, 395 S.W.3d 152, 161 (Tex. Crim. App. 2013).

Where defense counsel called the defendant as a witness and brought out a prior conviction for murder, which the state would have been unable to prove, his performance fell below an objective standard of reasonableness. Stone v. State, 17

S.W.3d 348 (Tex.App.—Corpus Christi 2000, *pet. ref'd*).

A court of appeals has found a defense attorney to have rendered ineffective assistance in a child abuse case where the attorney failed to request limiting instructions for extraneous offenses. Yzaguirre v. State, 938 S.W.2d 129 (Tex.App.—Amarillo 1996) *reversed at* 957 S.W.2d 38 (Tex. Crim. App. 1997) (where the concurring opinion hinted that counsel was ineffective for failing to require the state to designate the primary offense on which they were relying for conviction).

However, another court of appeals has found that counsel was not ineffective for failure to request a limiting instruction where the record was silent as to counsel's possible trial strategy. Gone v. State, 54 S.W.3d 27 (Tex.App.—Texarkana 2001, *pet. ref'd*).

Where counsel failed to minimize the possible harm by requesting an instruction limiting the jury's consideration of a prior conviction for impeachment purposes only, and did not object to the prosecutor's final argument in which he used the prior conviction to argue the defendant's propensity to kill counsel's performance fell below the objective standard of reasonableness under prevailing professional norms. Ramirez v. State, 873 S.W.2d 757 (Tex.App.—El Paso 1994, *pet. ref'd*).

Similarly, where counsel fails to object to a misstatement of law made by the state during closing argument, where the argument is detrimental to the defendant, and there can be no objectively reasonable trial strategy in failing to object, counsel's performance will be found to be deficient. Andrews v. State, 159 S.W.3d 98 (Tex. Crim. App. 2005).

Counsel is not ineffective where he fails to object to evidence that is admissible. Johnson v. State, 977 S.W.2d 725 (Tex.App.—Fort Worth 1998, *pet. ref'd*).

Counsel is not ineffective for failure to require the state to elect the primary offense which they intend to rely on to seek a conviction in a child abuse case where counsel already knew which act would be the primary offense for such purposes. Gone, *supra*.

In order to prevail on a claim that his attorney performed an inadequate cross-examination, a defendant must show that there is a reasonable probability that the result of his trial likely would have been different had his attorney conducted a more effective cross. Furthermore, because cross-examination is an art, not a science, it cannot be adequately judged in hindsight and it is very difficult for a defendant to rebut the presumption that counsel's conduct fell within the wide range of reasonable professional assistance. Ex parte McFarland, 163 S.W.3d 743 (Tex. Crim. App. 2005).

However, where trial counsel fails to confront a witness with a prior inconsistent statement that goes directly to the contested issue at trial (here the witness' identification of the defendant) counsel may be found to have rendered ineffective assistance. Ex parte Saenz, 491 S.W.3d 819, 833 (Tex. Crim. App. 2016).

Counsel's failure to allow the defendant to testify can amount to ineffective assistance and is reviewed under the Strickland standard. Johnson v. State, 169 S.W.3d 223 (Tex. Crim. App. 2005).

Under the facts of one case, counsel performed deficiently under the first prong of Strickland for eliciting testimony from the defendant at the guilt phase of his trial that the defendant was already incarcerated on two convictions that were pending on appeal. Robertson v. State, 187 S.W.3d 475 (Tex. Crim. App. 2006).

Defense counsel has not been shown to have performed deficiently in failing to object on Confrontation Clause grounds where the record does not contain counsel's reasons for failing to object and does not establish whether the witness could or would have testified if an objection had been lodged. Menefield v. State, 363 S.W.3d 591 (Tex. Crim. App. 2012).

Counsel can be found to have rendered ineffective assistance where he fails to object to the admission of the results of polygraph exams that support the prosecution's case. Ex parte Bryant, 448 S.W.3d 29, 41 (Tex. Cr. App. 2014).

Where the only reason given for not presenting evidence favorable to the defendant is that it would be difficult to edit and present, and there is no evidence that the decision was the result of a trial strategy, defense counsel will be found to have rendered ineffective assistance of counsel. Ex parte Overton, 444 S.W.3d 632, 637 (Tex. Crim. App. 2014).

§4:95.8 Improperly Handling Jury Charge

An attorney is ineffective for failing to request a defensive jury charge where it is clearly raised by the evidence. Vasquez v. State, 830 S.W.2d 948 (Tex. Crim. App. 1992).

The failure to request an accomplice witness charge where the case hinged on the testimony of an accomplice witness is ineffective assistance of counsel. Ex parte Zepeda, 819 S.W.2d 874 (Tex. Crim. App. 1991).

An attorney is not ineffective for failing to request an accomplice witness charge where there is no fact issue raised. Calixto v. State, 66 S.W.3d 505 (Tex.App.—Austin 2001, *pet. ref'd*).

Even though the fact issue may be raised, an attorney does not render ineffective assistance of counsel in failing to request an accomplice witness instruction where the instruction would have undermined counsel's strategy of claiming that the defendant was not involved in the offense. McKinny v. State, 76 S.W.3d 463 (Tex.App.—Houston [1st Dist.] 2002, *no pet.*).

An attorney is not ineffective for failure to request a jury charge that is not authorized by law. Robertson v. State, 852 S.W.2d 508 (Tex. Crim. App. 1993).

An attorney is not ineffective where he fails to request a particular instruction (a reasonable doubt instruction on extraneous offenses) where the defendant did not suffer egregious harm because of the omission of the charge (because the proof clearly showed that the defendant committed the extraneous offenses). Allen v. State, 47 S.W.3d 47 (Tex.App.—Fort Worth 2001, *no pet.*).

Defense counsel's failure to object to an improper parole charge will generally not be found to be ineffective where the record is silent as to the reason for the failure to object. Mata v. State, 226 S.W.3d 425 (Tex. Crim. App. 2007).

Although the lawyer's failure to request an accomplice witness charge was deficient performance, the defendant was not prejudiced here because other evidence was sufficient to corroborate the accomplice. Davis v. State, 278 S.W.3d 346 (Tex. Crim. App. 2009).

Counsel may not be objectively unreasonable in failing to request a mistake of fact instruction in a case where the culpable mental state for the offense requires the state to prove a lack of mistake. Okonkwo v. State, 398 S.W.3d 689 (Tex. Crim. App. 2013).

Ineffective assistance of counsel may be found where defense counsel fails to request an instruction on the medical care defense where some testimony raises the defense, even where other testimony negates the defense. Villa v. State, 417 S.W.3d 455, 464 (Tex. Crim. App. 2013).

§4:95.9 Improper Handling of Punishment Phase

The failure to file the requested punishment election can be ineffective assistance of counsel. Ex parte Walker, 794 S.W.2d 36 (Tex. Crim. App. 1990).

The prejudice prong, as it relates to the incorrect advice of counsel on probation eligibility, requires a showing that: (1) the defendant was initially eligible for probation; (2) counsel's advice was not given as a part of a valid trial strategy; (3) the defendant's election of the assessor of punishment was based upon his attorney's erroneous advice; and (4) the results of the proceeding would have been different had his attorney correctly informed him of the law. State v. Recer, 815 S.W.2d 730 (Tex. Crim. App. 1991).

A defendant meets the prejudice prong of his ineffective assistance of counsel claim by demonstrating that he would have opted for a jury if his attorney had correctly advised him that he was ineligible for probation from the trial court. He does not have to show that the likely outcome of the jury trial he waived would have been more favorable than the court trial he had. Miller v. State, 548 S.W.3d 497, 498 (Tex. Crim. App. 2018).

An attorney's inaccurate advice about the defendant's ineligibility for probation from a jury and his eligibility for probation from the judge was ineffective assistance of counsel in this case. Ex parte Canedo, 818 S.W.2d 814 (Tex. Crim. App. 1991).

The failure of trial counsel to sufficiently advise the defendant as to the consequences of electing to have the jury assess punishment amounted to ineffective assistance of counsel. Jackson v. State, 766 S.W.2d 504 (Tex. Crim. App. 1985).

Counsel is not ineffective at the punishment phase where the defendant was provided an opportunity to change his mind about his sentencing election and chose the court even though he knew that the court could not probate his sentence. Mapp v. State, 880 S.W.2d 144 (Tex.App.—Tyler 1994, *no pet.*).

Counsel can be found ineffective for failing to challenge the sufficiency of a habitual allegation. Ex parte Miller, 330 S.W.3d 610 (Tex. Crim. App., *op. on rehearing*) (where the proof did not show that the second offense was committed after the first offense became final).

The failure to challenge a void prior conviction used to enhance punishment will render counsel ineffective. Ex parte Felton, 815 S.W.2d 733 (Tex. Crim. App. 1991).

Where the defendant alleges that the attorney was ineffective for filing a defective application for probation, he must show evidence that the jury would have considered probation if he were eligible. Mallet v. State, 9 S.W.3d 856 (Tex. App.—Fort Worth 2000, *no pet.*); Trevino v. State, 752 S.W.2d 735 (Tex.App.—Eastland 1988), *pet. dismissed* 759 S.W.2d 142.

An attorney is ineffective where he fails to prove a defendant's eligibility for probation where the facts show that the jury would have considered it. Ware v. State, 875 S.W.2d 432 (Tex.App.—Waco 1994, *pet. ref'd*).

Counsel is ineffective where he fails to file an application for probation for a defendant who has lived out a deferred adjudication probation and has no other offenses on his record. Ex parte Welch, 981 S.W.2d 183 (Tex. Crim. App. 1998).

The failure to investigate a void alleged prior conviction is ineffective assistance. Ex parte Langley, 833 S.W.2d 141 (Tex. Crim. App. 1992).

Counsel may be found to have rendered ineffective assistance of counsel where she does not investigate the defendant's mental health history where there are indications that the defendant suffered from a mental illness. Ex parte LaHood, 401 S.W.3d 45, 52 (Tex. Crim. App. 2013)

The failure of counsel in a death penalty case to conduct a complete investigation into the defendant's background is reasonable only when reasonable professional judgments support the limitations on the investigation. Wiggins v. Smith, 539 U.S. 510, 123 S. Ct. 2527, 156 L.Ed.2d 471 (2003).

A failure to conduct a complete investigation into the defendant's background may be found reasonable when the defendant denies having been abused as a child and his family fails to cooperate with the investigation. Ex parte Martinez, 195 S.W.3d 713 (Tex. Crim. App. 2006).

In a death penalty case, counsel can be found ineffective for failure to present mitigating evidence. Ex parte Gonzales, 204 S.W.3d 391 (Tex. Crim. App. 2006) (counsel failed to present evidence of the defendant's abuse at the hands of his father and the effects that it had on him).

In a non-death case counsel can be found ineffective for failure to present character evidence where the record shows that the witnesses would have been able to offer mitigating testimony. Milburn v. State, 15 S.W.3d 267 (Tex.App.— Houston [14th Dist.] 2000, *pet. ref'd*); Shanklin v. State, 190 S.W.3d 154 (Tex.App.—Houston [1st Dist.] 2005, pet. dism'd); Ex parte Scott, 541 S.W.3d 104, (Tex. Crim. App. 2017)..

A defense attorney's decision not to present particular witnesses at the punishment stage may be a strategically sound decision if the attorney bases it on a determination that the testimony of the witnesses may be harmful, rather than helpful, to the defendant. However, a failure to uncover and present mitigating evidence cannot be justified as a tactical decision when defense counsel has not conducted a thorough investigation of the defendant's background. Shanklin.

Depending on the strength of the state's case, counsel could be found ineffective for failing to object to prejudicial testimony, failing to request pretrial notice of the state's expert witnesses and failing to call a witness in rebuttal. Ex parte Lane, 303 S.W.3d 702 (Tex. Crim. App. 2009).

An attorney can be ineffective where he fails to pursue information that would demonstrate that the defendant could not have committed an extraneous offense offered at punishment. Ex parte Rogers, 369 S.W.3d 858 (Tex. Crim. App. 2012).

Defense counsel's performance during penalty phase of capital murder trial, in presenting expert testimony that defendant was statistically more likely to act violently in the future because he was black, fell outside bounds of competent representation; counsel knew that psychologist's report reflected view that defendant's race disproportionately predisposed him to violent conduct where the principal point of dispute during penalty phase was whether defendant was likely to act violently in future. Counsel specifically elicited testimony about connection between defendant's race and likelihood of future violence, and put psychologist's expert report into evidence. Buck v. Davis, ___ U.S. ___, 137 S.Ct. 759, 197 L.Ed.2d 1 (2017).

Counsel is not ineffective for failing to object to the state's closing arguments when the state's arguments are proper. Ex parte Scott, 541 S.W.3d at 122.

§4:95.10 Probation Revocations

Counsel is ineffective for failure to recognize that a defendant's probation had expired such that a due diligence claim should have been pursued, where the defendant showed that the outcome of the probation revocation hearing would have been different. Torres v. State, 39 S.W.3d 631 (Tex. App.—Corpus Christi 2000, *no pet.*).

§4:95.11 Appellate Matters

Retained counsel must always give notice of appeal if requested to do so by the client, and the failure to do so is ineffective assistance of counsel. Ex parte Axel, 757 S.W.2d 369 (Tex. Crim. App. 1988).

Where a defendant has expressly requested an appeal, counsel performs deficiently by disregarding this instruction. Prejudice is presumed because it is a critical stage, and the defendant is not required to show any merits of his underlying claims. This is true even in a case such as this where the client has waived appeal during a plea. Garza v. Idaho, ___ U.S. ___, 139 S.Ct. 738, 203 L.Ed.2d 77 (2019).

Where the defendant has not conveyed his decision to appeal to the attorney, the attorney is not *per se* ineffective for failure to file a notice of appeal, and the Strickland standard will apply to the situation. Roe v. Flores-Ortega, 528 U.S. 470, 120 S. Ct. 1029, 145 L.Ed.2d 985 (2000).

In some instances, counsel will not be ineffective for a failure to raise sufficiency of evidence on appeal. Ex parte Flores, 387 S.W.3d 626 (Tex. Crim. App. 2012).

A defendant is not entitled to competent counsel on habeas corpus matters, and therefore, this is not a valid issue for a subsequent writ under CCP Art. 11.071. Ex parte Graves, 70 S.W.3d 103 (Tex. Crim. App. 2002).

In some instances, counsel will not be ineffective for a failure to raise sufficiency of evidence on appeal. Ex parte Flores, 387 S.W.3d 626 (Tex. Crim. App. 2012).

A post-conviction writ of habeas corpus is not available for claims of ineffective assistance of counsel in post-trial DNA testing proceedings where the defendant has not demonstrated that he is confined because of an error in those proceedings. Ex parte Baker, 185 S.W.3d 894 (Tex. Crim. App. 2006).

§4:95.12 Attorney-Client Relations

Where a defendant alleges that his counsel was ineffective for failure to meet with him, he must show that the proposed meetings would have benefited his defense. Perrett v. State, 871 S.W.2d 838 (Tex.App.—Houston [14th Dist.] 1994, *no pet.*).

Ineffective assistance of counsel may result from an attorney's conflict of interest. Strickland v. Washington, 466 U.S. 668, 692 (1984); Routier v. State, 112 S.W.3d 554 (Tex. Crim. App. 2003).

An actual conflict of interest exists when counsel is required to make a choice between advancing his client's interest in a fair trial or advancing other interests (perhaps his own) to the detriment of his client's interest. James v. State, 763 S.W.2d 776 (Tex. Crim. App. 1989); Routier.

When the defendant or his attorney brings a potential conflict of interest to the attention of the trial court, the trial court must investigate and determine whether the risk of the conflict of interest is too remote to warrant separate counsel. Holloway v. Arkansas, 435 U.S. 475 (1978); Routier.

If the defendant and his attorney fail to bring the potential conflict to the attention of the trial court and the appealing defendant relies on the argument that the trial court should have been aware of the conflict, the defendant cannot obtain a reversal on appeal unless he shows that his attorney was operating under an actual conflict of interest that adversely affected counsel's performance. No additional showing of harm or prejudice is required. Cuyler v. Sullivan, 446 U.S. 335 (1980); Routier.

Counsel's failure to obtain the defendant's consent to pursue a particular strategy doesn't automatically render his performance deficient. Florida v. Nixon, 543 U.S. 175, 125 S. Ct. 551, 160 L.Ed.2d 565 (2004).

Chapter 5

SELF-INCRIMINATION

Table of Contents

§5:10 Constitutional and Statutory Provisions

United States Constitution, 5th Amendment:

> *No person ... shall be compelled in any criminal case to be a witness against himself.*

Texas Constitution, Art. l, §10:

> *[T]he accused ... shall not be compelled to give evidence against himself.*

Texas Code of Criminal Procedure art. 1.05. Rights of Accused:

> *In all criminal prosecutions the accused shall have a speedy public trial by an impartial jury. He shall have the right to demand the nature and cause of the accusation against him and to have a copy thereof. He shall not be compelled to give evidence against himself. He shall have the right of being heard by himself, or counsel, or both; he shall be confronted with the witnesses against him and shall have compulsory process for obtaining witnesses in his favor. No person shall be held to answer for a felony unless on indictment of a grand jury.*

§5:20 Constitutional Protections

§5:21 General Points

It is a fundamental tenet of Texas and federal constitutional jurisprudence that every person has the right to avoid self-incrimination by exercising the privilege provided him by the Fifth Amendment and the Texas Constitution. Chapman v. State, 115 S.W.3d 1 (Tex. Crim. App. 2003).

The protection of the Fifth Amendment of the U.S. Constitution is extended to citizens as against invasion by the states under the Fourteenth Amendment. Murphy v. Waterfront Commission of New York Harbor, 378 U.S. 52, 84 S.Ct. 1594, 12 L.Ed.2d 678 (1964).

The Fifth Amendment privilege:

- Protects citizens against the compelled giving of testimonial evidence. Schmerber v. California, 384 U.S. 757, 86 S.Ct. 1826, 16 L.Ed.2d 908 (1966); Olson v. State, 484 S.W.2d 756 (Tex. Crim. App. 1972).
- Extends to compelled statements that lead to the discovery of incriminating evidence even though the statements themselves are not incriminatory and are not introduced into evidence. U.S. v. Hubbell, 530 U.S. 27, 120 S.Ct. 2037, 147 L.Ed.2d 24 (2000).
- Grants a witness immunity from the use of that compelled testimony in a subsequent criminal case. Chavez v. Martinez, 538 U.S. 760, 123 S.Ct. 1994, 155 L.Ed.2d 984 (2003).

§5:22 Comparison of Federal and State Protections

Art. 1, §10 of the Texas Constitution affords greater protection to a defendant than the Fifth Amendment with regard to the concept of pre-arrest silence. Heidelberg v. State, 144 S.W.3d 535 (Tex. Crim. App. 2004) (the Fifth Amendment protects only post-arrest silence while Art. 1, §10 protects both pre-and post-arrest silence).

The Texas Constitution, Art. I, §10, does not provide broader protection than the Fifth Amendment merely because of differences in language. Miffleton v. State, 777 S.W.2d 76 (Tex. Crim. App. 1989).

§5:23 Times When the Fifth Can Be Invoked

The Fifth Amendment privilege can be asserted in any proceeding, civil or criminal, administrative or judicial, investigatory or adjudicatory. Kastigar v. United States, 406 U.S. 441, 92 S.Ct. 1653, 32 L.Ed.2d 212 (1972); In re Gault, 387 U.S. 1, 87 S.Ct. 1428, 18 L.Ed.2d 527 (1967) (the protection extends equally to civil proceedings because the nature of the protection goes to the questions asked, not the proceeding itself); Chapman v. State, 115 S.W.3d 1 (Tex. Crim. App. 2003); Zani v. State, 701 S.W.2d 249 (Tex. Crim. App. 1985) (privilege can be asserted in any proceeding and protects against disclosures that the witness reasonably believes could be used in a criminal prosecution or could lead to other evidence that might be so used).

The privilege does not turn upon the type of proceeding, but upon the nature of the statement or admission and the exposure which it invites. Chapman *citing* Estelle v. Smith, 451 U.S. 454, 101 S.Ct. 1866, 68 L.Ed.2d 359 (1981).

The privilege also protects a grand jury witness from being compelled to give self-incriminating testimony. State v. Rutherford, 18 S.W.3d 666 (Tex. App.—San Antonio 1999, *pet. ref'd*).

A person who has been convicted of a crime, is in prison or on probation still has a right against self-incrimination concerning statements that would incriminate him for some other offense. Chapman.

§5:24 When the Fifth Is Applicable

The privilege extends to answers to questions that might provide a link in the chain of evidence to establish guilt, or have a tendency to establish guilt. Barcenes v. State, 940 S.W.2d 739 (Tex.App.—San Antonio 1997, *pet. ref'd*); Ohio v. Reiner, 532 U.S. 17, 121 S.Ct. 1252, 149 L.Ed.2d 158 (2001).

A witness may invoke the Fifth Amendment not only to answers that would themselves support a conviction, but also to those that would supply a link in the chain of evidence needed to prosecute the witness. For the privilege to apply, it need only be evident from the implications of the question that a responsive answer (or explanation why it cannot be answered) might be dangerous in that an injurious disclosure could result. Ohio v. Reiner, 532 U.S. 17, 121 S.Ct. 1252, 149 L.Ed.2d 158 (2001).

The Fifth Amendment privilege extends to compelled statements that lead to the discovery of incriminating evidence even though the statements themselves are not incriminatory and are not introduced into evidence. U.S. v. Hubbell, 530 U.S. 27, 120 S.Ct. 2037, 147 L.Ed.2d 24 (2000).

§5:25 When the Fifth Is Not Applicable—Falsehoods

The Fifth Amendment does not confer the right to lie under oath. Brogan v. United States, 522 U.S. 398, 118 S.Ct. 805, 139 L.Ed.2d 830 (1998); Butterfield v. State, 992 S.W.2d 448 (Tex. Crim. App. 1999).

Likewise, the Fifth Amendment does not confer a right to make a false entry in a governmental record. State v. Maitland, 993 S.W.2d 880 (Tex. App.—Fort Worth 1999, *no pet.*).

A defendant's (or witness's) false testimony can be the basis for a perjury charge, even where the defendant's (or witness's) Fifth Amendment rights were violated. Butterfield v. State, 992 S.W.2d 448 (Tex. Crim. App.1999) (the defendant gave false testimony about the location of his missing daughter).

Because the Fifth Amendment does not condone perjury, a grand jury witness who is later indicted for perjury before the grand jury is not entitled to suppression of the false testimony on the basis that no warning of his Fifth Amendment privilege to remain silent had been given. U.S. v. Wong, 431 U.S. 174, 97 S.Ct. 1823, 52 L.Ed.2d 231 (1977).

§5:26 When the Fifth Is Not Applicable—No Incrimination

The government may compel witnesses to testify when their incriminating statements (or evidence derived from those statements) cannot be used against the speaker in any criminal case. United States v. Balsys, 524 U.S. 666, 118 S.Ct. 2218, 141 L.Ed.2d 575 (1998); Kastigar v. United States, 406 U.S. 441, 92 S.Ct. 1653, 32 L.Ed.2d 212 (1972).

Furthermore, when the relevant limitations period for an offense has expired, the protection provided by the Fifth Amendment becomes moot and the privilege against self-incrimination no longer applies. Stogner v. California, 539 U.S. 607, 123 S.Ct. 2446, 156 L.Ed.2d 544 (2003).

After a co-defendant witness has been finally convicted or acquitted, that witness no longer has a Fifth Amendment privilege and his testimony becomes available to the parties. Anderson v. State, 717 S.W.2d 622 (Tex. Crim. App. 1986).

§5:27 When the Fifth Is Not Applicable—Waiver

Just as a defendant can fail to invoke his Fifth Amendment privilege, a defendant can also voluntarily forfeit his Fifth Amendment privilege if he freely chooses to take the stand and make incriminating statements. Minnesota v. Murphy, 465 U.S. 420, 427, 104 S.Ct. 1136, 79 L.Ed.2d 409 (1984); Johnson v. State, 357 S.W.3d 653 (Tex. Crim. App. 2012).

This is true even if not done knowingly and intelligently. Murphy, 465 U.S. at 427-28; Johnson.

If a witness voluntarily testifies to a part of the evidence, he waives his right against self-incrimination and cannot afterwards reassert his privilege. Stephens v. State, 59 S.W.3d 377 (Tex. App.—Houston [1st Dist.] 2001, *pet. ref'd*); Rogers v. United States, 340 U.S. 367, 71 S.Ct. 438, 95 L.Ed. 344 (1951).

A defendant does not waive his right to invoke the Fifth at the punishment phase by testifying at the guilt/innocence phase of the trial. Beathard v. State, 767 S.W.2d 423 (Tex. Crim. App. 1989).

§5:30 Invoking the Privilege

§5:31 Privilege Must Be Asserted

The privilege against compelled self-incrimination is not ordinarily self-executing. In all but a few specific situations, a criminal defendant must timely assert his privilege. Chapman v. State, 115 S.W.3d 1 (Tex. Crim. App. 2003); Johnson v. State, 357 S.W.3d 653 (Tex. Crim. App. 2012).

The Fifth Amendment does not preclude a witness from testifying voluntarily in matters that may incriminate him. If, therefore, he desires the protection of the privilege, he must claim it or he will not be considered to have been "compelled" within the meaning of the Amendment. Chapman *citing* Minnesota v. Murphy, 465 U.S. 420, 104 S.Ct. 1136, 79 L.Ed.2d 409 (1984); Johnson v. State, 357 S.W.3d 653 (Tex. Crim. App. 2012).

A trial court is relieved of the obligation to make further determination of whether the witness's assertion of the Fifth Amendment privilege is valid after learning that the witness's legal counsel advised the assertion of the privilege. Suarez v. State, 31 S.W.3d 323 (Tex.App.—San Antonio 2000, *no pet.*).

§5:32 Calling a Witness Who Will Assert the Privilege

A party generally may not call as a witness anyone who has indicated he will assert his privilege against self-incrimination. Anderson v. State, 717 S.W.2d 622 (Tex. Crim. App. 1986).

A defendant's right to compulsory process under the Sixth Amendment does not override a potential witness's Fifth Amendment privilege against self-incrimination. Barcenes v. State, 940 S.W.2d 739 (Tex.App.—San Antonio 1997, *pet. ref'd*).

PRACTICE TIP: If it is known that a witness intends to take the Fifth, the witness should be called outside the presence of the jury for this purpose. Bridge v. State, 726 S.W.2d 558 (Tex. Crim. App. 1986); Suarez v. State, 31 S.W.3d 323 (Tex. App.—San Antonio 2000, no pet.).

§5:40 Violation of Self-Incrimination Protection

§5:41 General Points

The Fifth Amendment protects citizens against the compelled giving of testimonial evidence. Schmerber v. California, 384 U.S. 757, 86 S.Ct. 1826, 16 L.Ed.2d 908 (1966); Olson v. State, 484 S.W.2d 756 (Tex. Crim. App. 1972).

Statements are compelled when required over the defendant's invocation of his Fifth Amendment rights. *See* Butterfield v. State, 992 S.W.2d 448 (Tex. Crim. App. 1999).

A claimant may be required to testify only if it clearly appears to the court that he is mistaken as to having a reasonable cause to apprehend danger from answering. Hoffman v. U. S., 341 U.S. 479, 71 S.Ct. 814, 95 L.Ed. 1118 (1951).

§5:42 Penalty Situation Threats

In the classic penalty situation, a person is threatened with punishment for relying upon his Fifth Amendment privilege. The key inquiry in this penalty situation is "whether the accused was deprived of his free choice to admit, to deny, or to refuse to answer." Chapman v. State, 115 S.W.3d 1 (Tex. Crim. App. 2003), *relying on* Minnesota v. Murphy, 465 U.S. 420, 104 S.Ct. 1136, 79 L.Ed.2d 409 (1984).

An example of a penalty situation is where a public employee (such as a police officer) is directed to answer questions pertaining to an investigation or face termination. Garrity v. New

Jersey, 385 U.S. 493, 87 S.Ct. 616, 17 L.Ed.2d 562 (1967).

A contrary example is a situation where a probationer is required to participate in a treatment program and be truthful with his probation officer. In this situation, the defendant is not penalized for invoking his Fifth Amendment privilege. The defendant still has the responsibility to assert his privilege if he fears that his answers may incriminate him. Chapman.

The critical inquiry is whether a state has gone beyond merely requiring a probationer to appear and speak on matters relevant to his probationary status or "whether [it goes] further and require[s] him to choose between making incriminating statements and jeopardizing his conditional liberty by remaining silent." Chapman; Minnesota v. Murphy.

In the classic penalty situation, a defendant need not affirmatively invoke his right to remain silent because in these situations the right is self-executing. Minnesota v. Murphy, 465 U.S. 420, 429-41, 104 S.Ct. 1136, 79 L.Ed.2d 409 (1984); Johnson v. State, 357 S.W.3d 653 (Tex. Crim. App. 2012).

§5:43 Lack of Knowing Waiver

A defendant's Fifth Amendment rights may be violated where he is required to answer questions in the absence of his Miranda rights and a knowing waiver thereof. *See* Estelle v. Smith, 451 U.S. 454, 101 S.Ct. 1866, 68 L.Ed.2d 359 (1981); Wilkens v. State, 847 S.W.2d 547 (Tex. Crim. App. 1992).

§5:50 Specific Situations

§5:51 Discovery During a Search

A defendant has no Fifth Amendment or Art. 1, Sec. 10 privilege against self-incrimination in the contents of her purse where the search is otherwise reasonable. *Woods v. State*, 970 S.W.2d 770 (Tex. App.—Austin 1998, *pet. ref'd*).

The seizure of personal business records of the defendant discovered while law enforcement was performing a search pursuant to a search warrant does not constitute compelled self-incrimination because the records were seized by law enforcement rather than being produced by the defendant. Andresen v. Maryland, 427 U.S. 463, 96 S.Ct. 2737, 49 L.Ed.2d 627 (1976); Goldberg v. State, 95 S.W.3d 345 (Tex.App.—Houston *pet. ref'd*).

§5:52 Documents—General Points

The Fifth Amendment does not independently proscribe the compelled production of every sort of incriminating evidence, but only applies when the accused is compelled to make a testimonial communication that is incriminating. Fisher v. United States, 425 U.S. 391, 96 S.Ct. 1569, 48 L.Ed.2d 39 (1976); Goldberg v. State, 95 S.W.3d 345 (Tex.App.—Houston *pet. ref'd*).

A party is privileged from producing the evidence but not from its production. Johnson v. United States, 228 U.S. 457, 33 S.Ct. 572, 57 L.Ed. 919 (1913); Goldberg (the defendant's notebook discovered during a school search was admitted against him).

This principle recognizes that the protection afforded by the Self-Incrimination Clause of the Fifth Amendment adheres basically to the person, not to information that may incriminate him. Couch v. United States, 409 U.S. 322, 93 S.Ct. 611, 34 L.Ed.2d 548 (1973); Goldberg.

All incriminating papers are not privileged. Only incriminating, *testimonial* communications are privileged. Cuadra v. State, 715 S.W.2d 723 (Tex. App.—Houston [14th Dist.] 1986, *pet. ref'd*).

Requiring the defendant to produce a document that is the basis of his prosecution in the presence of the jury violates his Fifth Amendment right to be free from self-incrimination. Phillips v. State, 480 S.W.2d 648 (Tex. Crim. App. 1972).

The privilege against self-incrimination also extends to documents that furnish a link in a chain of evidence needed to prosecute an accused. Hoffman v. United States, 341 U.S. 479, 71 S.Ct. 814, 95 L.Ed. 1118 (1951); Phillips.

§5:53 Documents—Voluntarily Prepared

The Fifth Amendment does not prohibit requiring a person to produce incriminating documents whose creation was not compelled. U.S. v. Hubbell, 530 U.S. 27, 120 S.Ct. 2037, 147 L.Ed.2d 24 (2000).

Where the original preparation of the papers sought by law enforcement was wholly voluntary, it is not compelled testimonial evidence. Fisher v. United States (an IRS summons required defendants to produce personal tax records prepared by their accountants).

If the party has voluntarily compiled the document, no compulsion is present and the contents of the document are not privileged, even where the document is a personal business record of the defendant. United States v. Doe, 465 U.S. 605, 104 S.Ct. 1237, 79 L.Ed.2d 552 (1984); Goldberg.

The privilege against self-incrimination cannot be invoked with respect to corporate records. Bellis v. United States, 417 U.S. 85, 94 S.Ct. 2179, 40 L.Ed.2d 678 (1974).

However, even though the contents of a document may not be privileged, the act of producing it may be. That is, the fact that the prosecution has subpoenaed the records from the defendant may have a testimonial and incriminatory effect because compliance with the subpoena tacitly concedes the existence of the document and their possession or control by the defendant. United States v. Doe, 465 U.S. 605, 104 S.Ct. 1237, 79 L.Ed.2d 552 (1984); Fisher v. United States, 425 U.S. 391, 96 S.Ct. 1569, 48 L.Ed.2d 39 (1976).

§5:54 Fingerprinting

Requiring the defendant to submit to the giving of his/her fingerprints does not violate the Fifth Amendment because the fingerprints of the defendant are non-testimonial evidence. U.S. v. Wade, 388 U.S. 218, 87 S.Ct. 1926, 18 L.Ed.2d 1149 (1967).

There is no constitutional right protecting the defendant from submitting to fingerprinting at the direction of the Court. Cassell v. State, 507 S.W.2d 228 (Tex. Crim. App. 1974).

However, fingerprints taken in violation of the Fourth Amendment are subject to suppression. Davis v. Mississippi, 394 U.S. 721, 89 S.Ct. 1394, 22 L.Ed.2d 676 (1969).

§5:55 Physical Characteristics

The Fifth Amendment does not prohibit requiring a person to exhibit physical characteristics. Pennsylvania v. Muniz, 496 U.S. 582, 110 S.Ct. 2638, 110 L.Ed.2d 528 (1990).

The Fifth Amendment typically offers no protection against compulsion to submit to fingerprinting, photographing, or measurements, to write or speak for identification, to appear in court, to stand, to assume a stance, to walk, or to make a particular gesture. Schmerber v. California, 384 U.S. 757, 86 S.Ct. 1826, 16 L.Ed.2d 908 (1966); Miffleton v. State, 777 S.W.2d 76 (Tex. Crim. App. 1989).

A lineup, under proper safeguards, does not compel self-incrimination. (Proper safeguards are presence of counsel and proper standards for conducting the lineup to assure non-suggestion of identity.) U.S. v. Wade.

There is no constitutional impediment, either as a search and seizure or concerning the privilege against self-incrimination, preventing the taking of dental impressions from a criminal defendant. Marquez v. State, 725 S.W.2d 217 (Tex. Crim. App. 1987), *citing* Patterson v. State, 509 S.W.2d 857 (Tex. Crim. App. 1974).

A hair sample, like handwriting and voice exemplars, is an identifying physical characteristic unprotected by the Fifth Amendment. Lopez v. State, 643 S.W.2d 431 (Tex.App.—Corpus Christi 1982, *no pet.*); United States v. Dionisio, 410 U.S. 1, 93 S.Ct. 764, 35 L.Ed.2d 67 (1973).

Admission of the visual portion of a videotaped sobriety test does not offend either the federal or Texas constitutional privileges against self-incrimination because such a videotape is not compelled testimony. Miffleton v. State, 777 S.W.2d 76 (Tex. Crim. App. 1989).

§5:56 Blood and Breath Tests

Because a breath test refusal is not a compelled self-incrimination, evidence that a defendant refused a breath test is admissible under the Texas implied consent law. Thomas v. State, 723 S.W.2d 696 (Tex. Crim. App. 1986).

Breath samples are not testimonial communication protected by the Fifth Amendment. Rodriguez v. State, 631 S.W.2d 515 (Tex. Crim. App.1982); Miffleton v. State, 777 S.W.2d 76 (Tex. Crim. App. 1989).

Police are not forbidden from seeking a suspect's breath sample because "[n]ot only does the breath testing decision not involve custodial interrogation, it does not involve the privilege against self-incrimination." McCambridge v. State, 712 S.W.2d 499 (Tex. Crim. App. 1986) (remanded on other grounds); Miffleton.

Forcibly extracting a blood sample from a driving while intoxicated suspect who refuses to consent upon the advice of counsel does not violate the Fifth Amendment. Schmerber v. California, 384 U.S. 757, 86 S.Ct. 1826, 16 L.Ed.2d 908 (1966) (a blood sample is not testimonial in nature, but rather constitutes real or physical evidence which does not violate the Fifth Amendment); Miffleton v. State, 777 S.W.2d 76 (Tex. Crim. App. 1989).

§5:57 Handwriting Samples

Compelling an accused to provide a handwriting exemplar does not constitute a violation of Article I, §10 of the Texas Constitution. Olson v. State, 484 S.W.2d 756 (Tex. Crim. App. 1972) (*opinion on motion for rehearing*).

It is likewise not a violation of the Fifth Amendment. Gilbert v. California, 388 U.S. 263, 87 S.Ct. 1951, 18 L.Ed.2d 1178 (1967).

PRACTICE TIP: Handwriting exemplars are useful in forgery and hot check cases to prove or disprove that a particular person wrote the instrument in question. See Tex. Code Crim. Pro. Art. 38.27 and Tex.R.Evid. 901(B) (2).

§5:58 Voice Exemplars

Voice exemplars are not, in and of themselves, testimonial evidence. Therefore, a defendant who offers an exemplar of his voice does not waive his Fifth Amendment privilege and subject himself to cross-examination. Williams v. State, 116 S.W.3d 788 (Tex. Crim. App. 2003).

Where a voice exemplar is to be used only for identification purposes, and not for its testimonial or communicative content, its compelled production is not a violation of the Fifth Amendment. U.S. v. Dionisio, 410 U.S. 1, 93 S.Ct. 764, 35 L.Ed.2d 67 (1973).

Compelling a defendant to read, before the jury, certain statements or words attributed to the assailant does not constitute compelling an accused to give evidence against himself in violation of Article I, section 10 of the Texas Constitution. Fuller v. State, 858 S.W.2d 528 (Tex. App.—Eastland 1993, *pet. ref'd*).

§5:59 Post-Conviction Rehabilitation Programs

A prison clinical rehabilitation program, which is acknowledged to bear a rational relation to a legitimate penological objective, does not violate the privilege against compelled self-incrimination when it requires inmates to complete a form accepting responsibility for their crimes and to detail their prior sexual activities if the adverse consequences an inmate faces for not participating are related to the program objectives and do not constitute atypical and significant hardships in relation to the ordinary incidents of prison life. McKune v. Lile, 536 U.S. 24, 122 S.Ct. 2017, 153 L.Ed.2d 47 (2002).

§5:70 Psychiatric and Psychological Examinations

§5:71 Statutory Provision

Tex. Code Crim. Pro. art. 46B.007. Admissibility of Statements and Certain Other Evidence

> *A statement made by a defendant during an examination or trial on the defendant's incompetency, the testimony of an expert based on that statement, and evidence obtained as a result of that statement may not be admitted in evidence against the defendant in any criminal proceeding, other than at:*
>
> *(1) a trial on the defendant's incompetency; or*
>
> *(2) any proceeding at which the defendant first introduces into evidence a statement, testimony, or evidence described by this article.*

§5:72 General Points

When the defendant initiates a psychiatric examination and based thereon presents psychiatric testimony on the issue of future dangerousness, the trial court may compel an examination of the defendant by an expert of the state's or court's choosing and the state may present rebuttal testimony of that expert based upon his examination of the defendant. Soria v. State, 933 S.W.2d 46 (Tex. Crim. App. 1996).

Where a defense expert who has examined the defendant testifies that the defendant lacked the requisite mental state to commit an offense, the prosecution may present psychiat¬ric evidence in rebuttal. Kansas v. Cheever, 571 U.S. ___, 134 S.Ct. 596, 187 L.Ed.2d 579 (2013)(where the defendant presented evidence that he did not have the requisite intent to commit the offense due to methamphetamine intoxication).

However, rebuttal testimony is limited to the issues raised by the defense expert. Soria; *see also* Buchanan v. Kentucky, 483 U.S. 402, 107 S.Ct. 2906, 97 L.Ed.2d 336 (1987) (the prosecution may rebut the defense's presentation with evidence from the defense-sponsored psychiatric reports); Wilkens v. State, 847 S.W.2d 547 (Tex. Crim. App. 1992), *cert. den.*, 507 U.S. 1005, 113 S.Ct. 1646, 123 L.Ed.2d 268 (1993) (raising the insanity defense and offering supporting evidence waives the defendant's Fifth Amendment rights as to the state's use of psychiatric rebuttal evidence); Hernandez v. State, 805 S.W.2d 409 (Tex. Crim. App. 1990), *cert. den.*, 500 U.S. 960, 111 S.Ct. 2275, 114 L.Ed.2d 726 (1991) (criminal defendants "open the door" to state-sponsored rebuttal on issue of competency by presenting defense-sponsored expert testimony).

Furthermore, a trial court may order a criminal defendant to submit to a state-sponsored psychiatric exam on future dangerousness when the defense demonstrates the intent to put on future dangerousness expert testimony based on an interview with the defendant. Lagrone v. State, 942 S.W.2d 602 (Tex. Crim. App. 1997).

The same may also be true where the defense intends to introduce expert testimony based on an interview with the defendant encompassing diminished capacity or mitigating evidence. Davis v. State, 313 S.W.3d 317 (Tex. Crim. App. 2010).

A defendant does not have the right to have counsel present during a psychiatric examination under either the Fifth or Sixth Amendment. Bennett v. State, 766 S.W.2d 227 (Tex. Crim. App.1989); Lagrone.

A defendant can waive his Fifth Amendment privilege by presenting the testimony of a mental health expert. Powell v. State, 742 S.W.2d 353 (Tex. Crim. App. 1987) (where the defendant pursued the insanity defense).

To be entitled to appellate review of the trial court's ruling that a Lagrone examination would not be limited to the same areas examined by the defense expert, a defendant is required to submit to the Lagrone examination and suffer any actual use by the state of the results of this examination. Hernandez v. State, 390 S.W.3d 310, 322 (Tex. Crim. App. 2012).

§5:73 Required Warning and Notice

Prior to an in-custody psychiatric examination ordered by the court to determine a defendant's competency to stand trial, the defendant must be warned that he has the right to remain silent, and that any statement he makes can be used against him at the sentencing proceeding. Estelle v. Smith, 451 U.S. 454, 101 S.Ct. 1866, 68 L.Ed.2d 359 (1981).

Furthermore, the defendant's Sixth Amendment right to counsel is violated where defense counsel is not notified in advance that the psychiatric examination will encompass the issue of future dangerousness. Estelle v. Smith; Ex parte Woods, 745 S.W.2d 21 (Tex. Crim. App. 1988).

Admission at the penalty stage of a capital felony trial of a psychiatrist's testimony on the crucial issue of future dangerousness violates the defendant's Fifth Amendment privilege against compelled self-incrimination because of the lack of appraisal of rights and a knowing waiver thereof. Estelle v. Smith; Wilkens v. State, 847 S.W.2d 547 (Tex. Crim. App.1992).

§5:80 Pre- and Post-Arrest Silence

The federal constitution protects post-arrest silence only after Miranda warnings have been given. Doyle v. Ohio, 426 U.S. 610, 96 S.Ct. 2240, 49 L.Ed.2d 91 (1976). Thus, the Fifth Amendment does not prohibit the state from using the defendant's un-Mirandized, post-arrest silence to impeach the defendant where he testifies at trial. Fletcher v.

Weir, 445 U.S. 603, 102 U.S. 1309, 71 L.Ed.2d 490 (1982).

However, the Texas Constitution protects a defendant's post-arrest silence even before such warnings have been administered. Heidelberg v. State, 144 S.W.3d 535 (Tex. Crim. App. 2004); Sanchez v. State, 707 S.W.2d 575 (Tex. Crim. App. 1986).

It is error for the trial court to admit an audio tape of the defendant invoking one of his constitutional rights after his Miranda rights had been read him and where the police proceeded to interrogate him. Hardie v. State, 807 S.W.2d 319 (Tex. Crim. App. 1991) (a violation of both the federal and state constitutions).

However, a defendant's pre-arrest, pre-Miranda invocation of his right to counsel is admissible in a DWI prosecution in the context of his refusal to submit to a breath test. Griffith v. State, 55 S.W.3d 598 (Tex. Crim. App. 2001).

Where a defendant has answered questions after having been read his Miranda warnings, he has waived his right to silence and the state can comment on his failure to answer certain questions. Schragin v. State, 378 S.W.3d 510, 519 (Tex. App.—Fort Worth 2012, *no pet.*).

If a post-arrest invocation of rights by the defendant is erroneously admitted, the appeals courts conduct a harm analysis under Tex. R. App. P. 44.2 because the error involved is constitutional in nature. Gray v. State, 986 S.W.2d 814 (Tex. App.—Beaumont 1999, *no pet.*).

Pre-arrest, pre-Miranda silence is not protected by the Fifth Amendment right against compelled self-incrimination, and prosecutors may comment on such silence regardless of whether a defendant testifies. Salinas v. State, 369 S.W.3d 176, 179 (Tex. Crim. App. 2012); Salinas v. Texas, 570 U.S. ___, 133 S.Ct. 2174, 186 L.Ed.2d 376 (2013).

The Fifth Amendment privilege generally is not self-executing, and anyone who desires its protection must claim it. Salinas v. Texas, 133 S.Ct. at 2181-2.

A defendant's pre-arrest, pre-Miranda silence can also be used to impeach his testimony. Jenkins v. Anderson, 447 U.S. 231, 100 S.Ct. 2124, 65 L.Ed.2d 86 (1980).

§5:90 Immunity Agreements

§5:91 Statutory Immunity Provisions

Several Texas statutes contain immunity agreements designed to require witness testimony in certain types of cases:

- Prostitution. A party to an offense of prostitution may be required to furnish evidence or testify about the offense. If a party is required to furnish evidence or testimony about the offense, he may not be prosecuted for that offense except for aggravated perjury. Tex. Penal Code §43.06.
- Gambling. A party to an offense of gambling may be required to furnish evidence or testify about the offense. If a party is required to furnish evidence or testimony about the offense, he may not be prosecuted for that offense except for aggravated perjury. Tex. Penal Code §47.08.
- Organized Crime. A party to an offense of engaging in organized criminal activity may be required to furnish evidence or testify about the offense. If a party is required to furnish evidence or testimony about the offense, he may not be prosecuted for that offense except for aggravated perjury or contempt. Tex. Penal Code §71.04.
- Hazing. In the prosecution of a hazing offense, the court may grant immunity from prosecution for the offense to each person who is subpoenaed to testify for the prosecution and who does testify for the prosecution. Those persons who report a hazing incident are immune from prosecution. Tex. Educ.Code §37.155.
- Legislative Witnesses. A witness called by either house or by a legislative committee does not have a privilege to refuse to testify to a fact or produce a document on the ground that the testimony or document may tend to disgrace the person or otherwise make the person infamous. However, if a person testifies or produces a document

while claiming that the testimony or document may incriminate him, the person may not be indicted or prosecuted for any transaction, matter, or thing about which the person truthfully testified or produced evidence. Tex. Gov't.Code §301.025.

The grant of immunity for testimony about organized crime (Texas Penal Code §71.04) is coextensive with the scope of self-incrimination as provided by the Texas Constitution and is therefore sufficient to compel testimony over a claim of the privilege. Absolute, complete or transactional immunity which accords full immunity from prosecution for the offense for which the compelled testimony relates affords the witness broader protection than does the self-incrimination privilege embodied in the Texas Constitution, and is therefore not required to be granted to the prospective witness. Ex parte Shorthouse, 640 S.W.2d 924 (Tex. Crim. App. 1982).

The grant of immunity for hazing (Tex.Educ. Code §37.155) is coextensive with the scope of the Fifth Amendment privilege. Therefore, the immunity grant in §37.155 is sufficient to remove any real or appreciable hazard of self-incrimination and to compel reporting over a claim of privilege. State v. Boyd, 38 S.W.3d 155 (Tex. Crim. App. 2001).

§5:92 Purpose and Policy

The logical corollary to a person's Fifth Amendment right to not incriminate himself is the concept of immunity. United States v. Apfelbaum, 445 U.S. 115, 100 S.Ct. 948, 63 L.Ed.2d 250 (1980); Butterfield v. State, 992 S.W.2d 448 (Tex. Crim. App. 1999).

Among the necessary and most important of the powers of the states as well as the federal government to assure the effective functioning of government in an ordered society is the broad power to compel residents to testify in court or before grand juries or agencies. Murphy v. Waterfront Commission, 378 U.S. 52, 84 S.Ct. 1594, 12 L.Ed.2d 678 (1964) (White, concurring); Smith v. State, 70 S.W.3d 848 (Tex. Crim. App. 2002) (Cochran, concurring).

The power to compel testimony, and the corresponding duty to testify, are embedded in the Sixth Amendment. Kastigar v. United States, 406 U.S. 441, 92 S.Ct. 1653, 32 L.Ed.2d 212 (1972); Smith (Cochran, concurring).

The doctrine of equitable immunity does not exist in Texas. Graham v. State, 994 S.W.2d 651 (Tex. Crim. App. 1999).

Where relator had been granted use and derivative use immunity during a hearing on his habeas writ alleging ineffective assistance of counsel, it was unclear whether he faced any substantial or real risk of further criminal liability; thus he was not entitled to a writ of prohibition to keep the state from calling him as a witness. In re Medina, 475 S.W.3d 291, 308 (Tex. Crim. App. 2015).

§5:93 Types of Immunity

Use *immunity* (or testimonial immunity) with *derivative use immunity* arises when a witness has been compelled to give evidence. Under this type of immunity, he may not refuse to answer on grounds of self-incrimination, but no testimony or other information compelled under the order (or any information directly or indirectly derived from such testimony or other information) may be used against the witness in any criminal case.

Transactional immunity provides that no charge may be brought or prosecuted against the witness as a consequence of his having testified relating to a particular transaction. A grant of use and derivative use immunity (also known as the *use plus use-fruits immunity*) is coextensive with the scope of the Fifth Amendment privilege against compelled self-incrimination, and therefore sufficient to compel testimony over this claim of privilege. Kastigar v. United States, 406 U.S. 441, 92 S.Ct. 1653, 32 L.Ed.2d 212 (1972); State v. Boyd, 38 S.W.3d 155 (Tex. Crim. App. 2001).

§5:94 Authority for Immunity Agreements

The authority to grant immunity derives from the authority of a prosecutor to dismiss prosecutions (Tex. Code Crim. Pro. art. 32.02), which directs that a dismissal made by the prosecutor must be approved by the trial court. Therefore, a prosecutor has no authority to grant immunity without court approval, because the approval of the court is essential to establish immunity. Smith v. State, 70 S.W.3d 848 (Tex. Crim. App. 2002).

The defendant is not entitled to grant a witness immunity, or to require a court to grant a witness immunity. Smith v. State, 708 S.W.2d 518 (Tex. App.—Houston [1st Dist.] 1986, *pet. ref'd*).

§5:95 Procedure

Because it is the prosecutor who initiates a dismissal and sets the reasons for the dismissal, it is the prosecutor who is responsible for crafting the conditions of an immunity agreement. The terms and conditions of an immunity agreement are wholly within the bargaining process of the parties involved in the contract, subject to the veto power of the court over their final agreement. Smith v. State, 70 S.W.3d 848 (Tex. Crim. App. 2002).

However, when a court has not approved a prosecutor's agreement to grant immunity from prosecution, there is no grant of immunity on which a defendant can rely. Graham v. State, 994 S.W.2d 651 (Tex. Crim. App. 1999).

Just as judicial approval is required for dismissal of charges under an immunity agreement, judicial approval is required for an immunity agreement that is made without any charges having been filed. Graham.

An order of dismissal based on an immunity agreement is not required to state that the dismissal was "with prejudice" in order to be enforceable. Furthermore, because a filing of the reasons for a grant of immunity is not required, the trial judge is not required to incorporate those reasons into the order of dismissal. Smith.

When a prosecutor offers a contract of immunity (and where the agreement has judicial approval), the witness will be exempt from prosecution if an honest and fair disclosure of the crime is given. Zani v. State, 701 S.W.2d 249 (Tex. Crim. App. 1985).

If a witness nevertheless refuses to testify after having been granted immunity, he can be punished with contempt. United States v. Mandujano, 425 U.S. 564, 96 S.Ct. 1768, 48 L.Ed.2d 212 (1976); Butterfield v. State, 992 S.W.2d 448 (Tex. Crim. App. 1999).

Supervision of the performance of an immunity agreement is the province of the prosecutor. Smith.

A person's grand jury testimony under a grant of immunity cannot constitutionally be used to impeach him when he is a defendant in a later criminal trial. New Jersey v. Portash, 440 U.S. 450, 99 S.Ct. 1292, 59 L.Ed.2d 501 (1979).

§5:96 Double Jurisdictional Immunity

Once an immunity agreement is consummated, all other prosecutorial entities (in Texas, the federal system, and other states) must abide by it, at least to the extent of use immunity. Murphy; Smith v. State, 70 S.W.3d 848 (Tex. Crim. App. 2002) (Cochran, concurring).

§5:100 Hearings on Preliminary Issues

Texas Rule of Evidence 104. Preliminary Questions

> *(d) Testimony by accused out of the hearing of the jury. The accused does not, by testifying upon a preliminary matter out of the hearing of the jury, subject himself to cross-examination as to other issues in the case.*

By testifying outside the presence of the jury on the question of the admissibility of evidence, the defendant does not subject himself to cross-examination on other matters. Cooper v. State, 769 S.W.2d 301 (Tex.App.—Houston [1st Dist.] 1989, *pet. ref'd*).

Testimony given for a limited purpose outside the presence of the jury is not admissible thereafter on the issue of guilt. Davis v. State, 961 S.W.2d 156 (Tex. Crim. App. 1998).

Under Rule 104(d) testimony given by a defendant outside the presence of the jury on a preliminary issue is not admissible in front of the jury at the punishment phase, even where the defendant testified at the guilt phase. Nelson v. State, 765 S.W.2d 401 (Tex. Crim. App. 1989).

Under the Fifth Amendment, testimony given by a defendant out of the presence of the jury on a preliminary search question is not admissible against him in the guilt/innocence phase of the trial. Simmons v. U.S., 390 U.S. 377, 384, 88 S.Ct. 967 L.Ed.2d 1247 (1968).

Chapter 6

CONFESSIONS

Table of Contents

§6:10 Constitutional and Statutory Provisions

§6:11 Fifth Amendment

> *U.S. Constitution, 5th Amendment: "No person... shall be compelled in any criminal case to be a witness against himself, nor be deprived of life, liberty, or property without due process of law..."*

The Fifth Amendment right to counsel is the right to interrogation counsel. Pecina v. State, 361 S.W.3d 68, 71 (Tex. Crim. App. 2012) (citing Montejo v. Louisiana, 556 U.S. 778, 129 S.Ct. 2079, 173 L.Ed.2d 955 (2009)).

The Fifth Amendment prohibits the government from compelling a criminal suspect to bear witness against himself. Pecina 361 S.W.3d at 74-5.

The Fifth Amendment right to interrogation counsel is triggered by the Miranda warnings that police must give before beginning any custodial questioning. Pecina, 361 S.W.3d at 75; Montejo.

The Fifth Amendment right to counsel applies to post-magistration custodial interrogation. Pecina, 361 S.W.3d at 77.

§6:12 Sixth Amendment

> *U.S. Constitution, 14th Amendment: "...nor shall any State deprive any person of life, liberty, or property without due process of law; nor deny to any person within its jurisdiction the equal protection of the laws."*

The Sixth Amendment right to counsel is the right to trial counsel. Pecina v. State, 361 S.W.3d 68, 77 (Tex. Crim. App. 2012) (citing Montejo v. Louisiana, 556 U.S. 778, 129 S.Ct. 2079, 173 L.Ed.2d 955 (2009)).

The Sixth Amendment right to trial counsel is triggered by judicial arraignment or magistration conducted under Code of Criminal Procedure Art. 15.17; and it guarantees a defendant the right to have counsel present at all critical stages of the criminal proceedings. Pecina, 361 S.W.3d at 77; Montejo.

Generally, an Article 15.17 initial appearance and magistration marks the initiation of adversarial judicial proceedings in Texas and plainly signals the attachment of a defendant's Sixth Amendment right to counsel. Pecina, 361 S.W.3d at 77.

Thus, a Sixth Amendment request for an attorney at an arraignment, initial appearance, or Article 15.17 hearing is a request for the guiding hand of counsel for all judicial criminal proceedings. Pecina, 361 S.W.3d at 78.

However, a defendant's invocation of his right to counsel at his arraignment or initial appearance says nothing about his possible invocation of his right to counsel during later police-initiated custodial interrogation. The magistration hearing is not an interrogation event. A defendant who has been arraigned may invoke his Sixth Amendment right to counsel for purposes of custodial interrogation when the police or other law enforcement agents approach him and give him his Miranda warnings. Pecina, 361 S.W.3d at 78.

This is because the Sixth Amendment right to counsel applies to post-magistration custodial interrogation. Pecina, 361 S.W.3d at 78.

After formal adversary proceedings have begun, the Sixth Amendment right to counsel applies in exactly the same way as the Fifth Amendment right applies to custodial interrogation. Thus, Miranda warnings serve the arrestee's interests in both the Fifth and Sixth Amendment rights to counsel during custodial interrogations conducted after a person has been formally charged. Pecina, 361 S.W.3d at 78.

The Sixth Amendment right to counsel is offense specific. It attaches only to an offense for which a prosecution has been initiated. Rubalcado v. State, 424 S.W.3d 560, 570 (Tex. Crim. App. 2014).

For Sixth Amendment right-to-counsel purposes offenses are considered separate if they would be considered separate under the *Blockburger* same-elements test, *i.e.* each statutory provision proscribing the respective charges requires proof of a fact that the other does not. Rubalcado, 424 S.W.3d at 570-1.

Offenses that have the same elements under the *Blockburger* test are nevertheless separate if they involve separate allowable units of prosecution. Rubalcado, 424 S.W.3d at 571.

To the extent that multiple incidents conform to the charges, they are subsumed by the charges for double-jeopardy purposes until and unless the State timely elects what specific offense is being charged. Rubalcado, 424 S.W.3d at 571.

The right to counsel may be violated by the elicitation of evidence of extraneous offenses if that evidence is used in the prosecution for which charges had been pending. Rubalcado, 424 S.W.3d at 571; *citing* Thompson v. State, 93 S.W.3d 16, 22 (Tex. Crim. App. 2001).

The State is responsible, in the Sixth Amendment context, for the knowledge of all of its actors. Thus, the State's knowledge that a defendant's Sixth Amendment rights have attached is imputed from one state actor to another. Rubalcado, 424 S.W.3d at 574.

§6:13 Texas Constitutional Provisions

Texas Constitution, Art. 1, §10. RIGHTS OF ACCUSED IN CRIMINAL PROSECUTIONS.

In all criminal prosecutions the accused shall have a speedy public trial by an impartial jury. He shall have the right to demand the nature and cause of the accusation against him, and to have a copy thereof. He shall not be compelled to give evidence against himself, and shall have the right of being heard by himself or counsel, or both, shall be confronted by the witnesses against him and shall have compulsory process for obtaining witnesses in his favor, except that when the witness resides out of the State and the offense charged is a violation of any of the anti-trust laws of this State, the defendant and the State shall have the right to produce and have the evidence admitted by deposition, under such rules and laws as the Legislature may hereafter provide; and no person shall be held to answer for a criminal offense, unless on an indictment of a grand jury, except in cases in which the punishment is by fine or imprisonment, otherwise than in the penitentiary, in cases of impeachment, and in cases arising in the army or navy, or in the militia, when in actual service in time of war or public danger.

Texas Constitution, Art.1, §19 DEPRIVATION OF LIFE, LIBERTY, ETC.; DUE COURSE OF LAW.

No citizen of this State shall be deprived of life, liberty, property, privileges or immunities, or in any manner disfranchised, except by the due course of the law of the land.

§6:14 Texas Statutory Provisions

Tex. Code Crim. Pro. Art. 2.32. ELECTRONIC RECORDING OF CUSTODIAL INTERROGATIONS.

(a) In this article:

(1) "Electronic recording" means an audiovisual electronic recording, or an audio recording if an audiovisual electronic recording is unavailable, that is authentic, accurate, and unaltered.

(2) "Law enforcement agency" means an agency of the state, or of a county, municipality, or other political subdivision of this state, that employs peace officers who, in the routine performance of the officers' duties, conduct custodial interrogations of persons suspected of committing criminal offenses.

(3) "Place of detention" means a police station or other building that is a place of operation for a law enforcement agency, including a municipal police department or county sheriff's department, and is owned or operated by the law enforcement agency for the purpose of detaining persons in connection with the suspected violation of a penal law.

The term does not include a courthouse.

(b) Unless good cause exists that makes electronic recording infeasible, a law enforcement agency shall make a complete and contemporaneous electronic recording of any custodial interrogation that occurs in a place of detention and is of a person suspected of committing or charged with the commission of an offense under:

(1) Section 19.02, Penal Code (murder);

(2) Section 19.03, Penal Code (capital murder);

(3) Section 20.03, Penal Code (kidnapping);

(4) Section 20.04, Penal Code (aggravated kidnapping);

(5) Section 20A.02, Penal Code (trafficking of persons);

(6) Section 20A.03, Penal Code (continuous trafficking of persons);

(7) Section 21.02, Penal Code (continuous sexual abuse of young child or children);

(8) Section 21.11, Penal Code (indecency with a child);

(9) Section 21.12, Penal Code (improper relationship between educator and student);

(10) Section 22.011, Penal Code (sexual assault);

(11) Section 22.021, Penal Code (aggravated sexual assault); or

(12) Section 43.25, Penal Code (sexual performance by a child).

(c) For purposes of Subsection (b), an electronic recording of a custodial interrogation is complete only if the recording:

(1) begins at or before the time the person being interrogated enters the area of the place of detention in which the custodial interrogation will take place or receives a warning described by Section 2(a), Article 38.22, whichever is earlier; and

(2) continues until the time the interrogation ceases.

(d) For purposes of Subsection (b), good cause that makes electronic recording infeasible includes the following:

(1) the person being interrogated refused to respond or cooperate in a custodial interrogation at which an electronic recording was being made, provided that:

(A) a contemporaneous recording of the refusal was made; or

(B) the peace officer or agent of the law enforcement agency conducting the interrogation attempted, in good faith, to record the person's refusal but the person was unwilling to have the refusal recorded, and the peace officer or agent contemporaneously, in writing, documented the refusal;

(2) the statement was not made as the result of a custo-

dial interrogation, including a statement that was made spontaneously by the accused and not in response to a question by a peace officer;

(3) the peace officer or agent of the law enforcement agency conducting the interrogation attempted, in good faith, to record the interrogation but the recording equipment did not function, the officer or agent inadvertently operated the equipment incorrectly, or the equipment malfunctioned or stopped operating without the knowledge of the officer or agent;

(4) exigent public safety concerns prevented or rendered infeasible the making of an electronic recording of the statement; or

(5) the peace officer or agent of the law enforcement agency conducting the interrogation reasonably believed at the time the interrogation commenced that the person being interrogated was not taken into custody for or being interrogated concerning the commission of an offense listed in Subsection (b).

(e) A recording of a custodial interrogation that complies with this article is exempt from public disclosure as provided by Section 552.108, Government Code.

CCP Art. 38.21. Statement

A statement of an accused may be used in evidence against him if it appears that the same was freely and voluntarily made without compulsion or persuasion, under the rules hereafter prescribed.

CCP Art. 38.22. When Statements May Be Used

§1. In this article, a written statement of an accused means:

(1) a statement made by the accused in his own handwriting; or

(2) a statement made in a language the accused can read or understand that:

(A) is signed by the accused; or

(B) bears the mark of the accused, if the accused is unable to write and the mark is witnessed by a person other than a peace officer.

§2. No written statement made by an accused as a result of custodial interrogation is admissible as evidence against him in any criminal proceeding unless it is shown on the face of the statement that:

(a) the accused, prior to making the statement, either received from a magistrate the warning provided in Article 15.17 of this code or received from the person to whom the statement is made a warning that:

(1) he has the right to remain silent and not make any statement at all and that any statement he makes may be used against him at his trial;

(2) any statement he makes may be used as evidence against him in court;

(3) he has the right to have a lawyer present to advise him prior to and during any questioning;

(4) if he is unable to employ a lawyer, he has the right to have a lawyer appointed to advise him prior to and during any questioning; and

(5) he has the right to terminate the interview at any time; and

(b) the accused, prior to and during the making of the statement, knowingly, intelligently, and voluntarily waived the rights set out in the warning prescribed by Subsection (a) of this section.

§3. (a) No oral or sign language statement of an accused made as a result of custodial interrogation shall be admissible against the accused in a criminal proceeding unless:

(1) an electronic recording, which may include motion picture, video tape, or other visual recording, is made of the statement;

(2) prior to the statement but during the recording the accused is given the warning in Subsection (a) of §2 above and the accused knowingly, intelligently, and voluntarily waives any rights set out in the warning;

(3) the recording device was capable of making an accurate recording, the operator was competent, and the recording is accurate and has not been altered;

(4) all voices on the recording are identified; and

(5) not later than the 20th day before the date of the proceeding, the attorney representing the defendant is provided with a true, complete, and accurate copy of all recordings of the defendant made under this article.

(b) Every electronic recording of any statement made by an accused during a custodial interrogation must be preserved until such time as the defendant's conviction for any offense relating thereto is final, all direct appeals therefrom are exhausted, or the prosecution of such offenses is barred by law.

(c) Subsection (a) of this section shall not apply to any statement which contains assertions of facts or circumstances that are found to be true and which conduce to establish the guilt of the accused, such as the finding of secreted or stolen property or the instrument with which he states the offense was committed.

(d) If the accused is a deaf person, the accused's statement under §2 or §3(a) of this article is not admissible against the accused unless the warning in §2 of this article is interpreted to the deaf person by an interpreter who is qualified and sworn as provided in Article 38.31 of this code.

(e) The courts of this state shall strictly construe Subsection (a) of this section and may not interpret Subsection (a) as making admissible a statement unless all requirements of the subsection have been satisfied by the state, except that:

(1) only voices that are material are identified; and

(2) the accused was given the warning in Subsection (a) of §2 above or its fully effective equivalent.

§4. When any statement, the admissibility of which is covered by this article, is sought to be used in connection with an official proceeding, any person who swears falsely to facts

and circumstances which, if true, would render the statement admissible under this article is presumed to have acted with intent to deceive and with knowledge of the statement's meaning for the purpose of prosecution for aggravated perjury under §37.03 of the Penal Code. No person prosecuted under this subsection shall be eligible for probation.

§5. Nothing in this article precludes the admission of a statement made by the accused in open court at his trial, before a grand jury, or at an examining trial in compliance with Articles 16.03 and 16.04 of this code, or of a statement that is the res gestae of the arrest or of the offense, or of a statement that does not stem from custodial interrogation, or of a voluntary statement, whether or not the result of custodial interrogation, that has a bearing upon the credibility of the accused as a witness, or of any other statement that may be admissible under law.

§6. In all cases where a question is raised as to the voluntariness of a statement of an accused, the court must make an independent finding in the absence of the jury as to whether the statement was made under voluntary conditions. If the statement has been found to have been voluntarily made and held admissible as a matter of law and fact by the court in a hearing in the absence of the jury, the court must enter an order stating its conclusion as to whether or not the statement was voluntarily made, along with the specific finding of facts upon which the conclusion was based, which order shall be filed among the papers of the cause. Such order shall not be exhibited to the jury nor the finding thereof made known to the jury in any manner. Upon the finding by the judge as a matter of law and fact that the statement was voluntarily made, evidence pertaining to such matter may be submitted to the jury and it shall be instructed that unless the jury believes beyond a reasonable doubt that the statement was voluntarily made, the jury shall not consider such statement for any purpose nor any evidence obtained as a result thereof. In any case where a motion to suppress the statement has been filed and evidence has been submitted to the court on this issue, the court within its discretion may reconsider such evidence in his finding that the statement was voluntarily made and the same evidence submitted to the court at the hearing on the motion to suppress shall be made a part of the record the same as if it were being presented at the time of trial. However, the state or the defendant shall be entitled to present any new evidence on the issue of the voluntariness of the statement prior to the court's final ruling and order stating its findings.

§7. When the issue is raised by the evidence, the trial judge shall appropriately instruct the jury, generally, on the law pertaining to such statement.

§8. Notwithstanding any other provision of this article, a written, oral, or sign language statement of an accused made as a result of a custodial interrogation is admissible against the accused in a criminal proceeding in this state if:

> *(a) the statement was obtained in another state and was obtained in compliance with the laws of that state or this state; or*
>
> *(b) the statement was obtained by a federal law enforcement officer in this state or another state and was obtained in compliance with the laws of the United States.*

§9. Notwithstanding any other provision of this article, no oral, sign language, or written statement that is made by a person accused of an offense listed in Article 2.32(b) and made as a result of a custodial interrogation occurring in a place of detention, as that term is defined by Article 2.32, is admissible against the accused in a criminal proceeding unless:

(1) an electronic recording was made of the statement, as required by Article 2.32(b); or

(2) the attorney representing the state offers proof satisfactory to the court that good cause, as described by Article 2.32(d), existed that made electronic recording of the custodial interrogation infeasible.

§6:20 Custody Analysis

The taking of a statement from an accused is not governed by Miranda or CCP Art. 38.22 unless the accused is in custody. *See* Miranda v. Arizona, 384 U.S. 436, 86 S.Ct. 1602, 16 L.Ed.2d 694 (1966); CCP Art. 38.22.

The custodial interrogation test is the proper test to be applied in deciding cases under the Fifth Amendment, but not under the Sixth Amendment, which should be analyzed in the context of the deliberate-elicitation test. Fellers v. U.S., 540 U.S. 519, 124 S.Ct. 1019, 157 L.Ed.2d 1016 (2004).

At trial, the defendant bears the initial burden of proving that a statement was the product of custodial interrogation. Gardner v. State, 306 S.W.3d 274 (Tex. Crim. App. 2009).

The State has no burden to show compliance with Miranda unless the record as a whole clearly establishes that the defendant's statement was the product of custodial interrogation by an agent for law enforcement. The defendant bears this initial burden and the mere filing of a motion to suppress does not carry the burden. Herrera v. State, 241 S.W.3d 520 (Tex. Crim. App. 2007).

Miranda and its prophylactic safeguards only apply to custodial statements. Wolfe v. State, 917 S.W.2d 270 (Tex. Crim. App. 1996).

A trial judge's ultimate "custody" determination presents a mixed question of law and fact. The appellate courts afford almost total deference to a trial judge's "custody" determination when the questions of historical fact turn on credibility and demeanor. Conversely, when the questions of historical fact do not turn on credibility and demeanor, appellate courts review a trial judge's "custody" determination *de novo*. Herrera.

§6:21 Custody for Fifth Amendment Purposes

§6:21.1 "Custodial Interrogation" Defined

Custodial interrogation for purposes of Miranda includes both express questioning and its functional equivalent; that is, words or actions that, given the officer's knowledge of any special susceptibilities of the suspect, the officer knows or reasonably should know are likely to have the force of a question on the accused, and therefore, be reasonably likely to elicit an incriminating response. Rhode Island v. Innis, 446 U.S. 291, 100 S.Ct. 1682, 64 L.Ed.2d 297 (1980) and Pennsylvania v. Muniz, 496 U.S. 582, 110 S.Ct. 2638, 110 L.Ed.2d 528 (1990).

This "should know" test is the general test for determining whether interrogation occurs. This test focuses primarily upon the perceptions of the suspect, rather than the intent of the police. State v. Cruz, 461 S.W.3d 531, 536-7 (Tex. Crim. App. 2015). In Rhode Island v. Innis, it was held that officers did not engage in interrogation of the defendant by carrying on a conversation in his presence regarding whether school kids would find and harm themselves with a weapon the defendant was suspected of hiding near the school grounds.

In Pennsylvania v. Muniz, *supra*, a distinction was drawn for Fifth Amendment purposes between questions which are intended to elicit a "testimonial" response and those which are not. A "testimonial" response is one that would place the suspect in the cruel trilemma of self-accusation, perjury, or contempt. *See also,* Gassaway v. State, 957 S.W.2d 48 (Tex. Crim. App. 1997).

Questions which cause an accused to communicate an express or implied assertion of fact or belief, such as asking an accused in a driving while intoxicated case if he knows the date of his sixth birthday, are testimonial in nature. Muniz. Questions which are of a routine booking nature, such as name, address, height, and weight, are permissible where not intended to elicit information for investigatory purposes. Muniz.

The physical characteristics of the defendant's speech such as slurring, are not testimonial in nature and therefore, not subject to Fifth Amendment protection. Muniz. Therefore, requiring the DWI suspect to read from a prepared text is not testimonial in nature and not custodial interrogation, even where the suspect has invoked his right to an attorney. Jones v. State, 795 S.W.2d 171 (Tex. Crim. App. 1990).

Requiring a DWI defendant to recite the alphabet and to count backwards tests his mental and physical faculties and is therefore non-testimonial in nature. Gassaway v. State, 957 S.W.2d 48 (Tex. Crim. App. 1997).

Custodial interrogation is questioning initiated by law enforcement officers after a person has been taken into custody or otherwise deprived of his freedom of action in any significant way. Miranda v. Arizona, 384 U.S. 436, 86 S.Ct. 1602, 16 L.Ed.2d 694 (1966); Herrera v. State, 241 S.W.3d 520 (Tex. Crim. App. 2007).

Unwarned statements obtained as a result of custodial interrogation may not be used as evidence by the State in a criminal proceeding during its case-in-chief. Miranda; Herrera.

"Custody" has the same meaning under CCP Art. 38.22 as it does under the Fifth Amendment. Wicker v. State, 740 S.W.2d 779 (Tex. Crim. App. 1987).

§6:21.2 The Functional Equivalent of Questioning

In a situation where police officers played upon a suspect's religious convictions by discussing, in his presence, the fact that the child/victim would not receive a proper Christian burial until the body was found, and the suspect led the police to the body as a result, it was held that the discussion was the functional equivalent of custodial interrogation and the suspect's statements were inadmissible. Brewer v. Williams, 430 U.S. 387, 97 S.Ct. 1232, 51 L.Ed.2d 424 (1977).

The fact that a police officer was stationed in an interview room when a recently detained murder suspect confessed the murder to his wife, did not elevate the situation to the functional equivalent of interrogation where the purpose for the presence of the officer was to protect the wife, even though the officers were aware of the possibility that the defendant would confess. Arizona v. Mauro, 481 U.S. 520, 107 S.Ct. 1931, 95 L.Ed.2d 458 (1987).

An example of a situation in which law enforcement officers engage in conduct that is likely to evoke an incriminating response is one in which they take a suspect for a polygraph examination and interview. McCrory v. State, 643 S.W.2d 725 (Tex. Crim. App. 1982).

§6:21.3 Custody Status Test

When considering whether a person is in custody for Miranda purposes, the courts apply a reasonable person standard; that is, a person is in custody only if, under the circumstances, a reasonable person would believe that his freedom of movement was restrained to the degree associated with a formal arrest. Dowthitt v. State, 931 S.W.2d 244 (Tex. Crim. App. 1996). The custody inquiry also includes an examination of all of the objective circumstances surrounding the questioning. Dowthitt.

Two discrete inquiries are essential to determine whether a person is in custody: 1) what were the circumstances surrounding the interrogation, and 2) given those circumstances, would a reasonable person have felt he or she was not at liberty to terminate the interrogation and leave? Thompson v. Keohane, 516 U.S. 99, 116 S.Ct. 457, 133 L.Ed.2d 383 (1995).

There are four general situations that may constitute custody:

- Suspect is physically deprived of freedom of action in any significant way
- Law enforcement officer tells the suspect that suspect cannot leave
- Law enforcement officers create a situation that would lead a reasonable person to believe that his or her freedom of movement has been significantly restricted
- There is probable cause to arrest and law enforcement officers do not tell the suspect that suspect is free to leave

Gardner v. State, 306 S.W.3d 274 (Tex. Crim. App. 2009).

Being the "focus" of an investigation does not necessarily render a person "in custody" for purposes of receiving Miranda warnings or those required under Article 38.22 of the Code of Criminal Procedure. Gardner v. State, 306 S.W.3d 274 (Tex. Crim. App. 2009).

Four factors have been recognized as useful in determining if a non-custodial encounter has escalated into a custodial encounter:

- Whether probable cause to arrest exists
- Subjective intent of the police to hold the suspect
- Subjective belief of a defendant as to the status of his freedom
- Whether or not the focus of the investigation has finally centered on the defendant

State v. Stevenson, 958 S.W.2d 824 (Tex. Crim. App. 1997).

These factors are relevant only to the extent they are manifested to the suspect through the words and actions of law enforcement officials; the custody determination is based entirely upon objective circumstances. Stevenson.

A noncustodial situation is not converted to one in which Miranda applies simply because even in the absence of any formal arrest or restraint on freedom of movement, the questioning took place in a coercive environment. Estrada v. State, 313 S.W.3d 274, 294 (Tex. Crim. App. 2010).

A suspect's age or experience is not relevant to the Miranda custody analysis. Yarborough v. Alvarado, 541 U.S. 652, 124 S.Ct. 2140, 158 L.Ed.3d 938 (2004).

However, where it was known to the interviewing officer at the time of police questioning that the interviewee was a juvenile, or would have been objectively apparent to a reasonable officer, the inclusion in the Miranda custody analysis of that fact is consistent with the objective nature of the custody test. While a child's age will not be a determinative, or even a significant, factor in every case, in some cases, it will prove an important factor in deciding if the child was in custody for Miranda purposes. J.D.B. v. North Carolina, 564 U.S. ___, 131 S.Ct. 2394, 2406, 180 L.Ed.2d 310 (2011).

CCP Art. 15.22 states that "[a] person is arrested when he has been actually placed under restraint or taken into custody by an officer or person executing a warrant of arrest, or by an officer or person arresting without a warrant." *See* Dancy v. State, 728 S.W.2d 772 (Tex. Crim. App. 1987).

The handcuffing of a suspect does not always mean that he is under arrest. Rhodes v. State, 945 S.W.2d 115 (Tex. Crim. App. 1997) (officer testified that, during a car chase incident, he handcuffed the defendant for his safety and the safety of other officers and, during this time, the defendant dropped to the ground the drugs which formed the basis of the prosecution). *See also*, Mays v. State, 726 S.W.2d 937 (Tex. Crim. App. 1986).

Incarceration does not always constitute "custody" for Miranda purposes when an inmate is questioned by law enforcement officials regarding an offense separate and distinct from the offense for which he was incarcerated. Herrera v. State, 241 S.W.3d 520 (Tex. Crim. App. 2007) (where the court found that the defendant who was incarcerated on an unrelated warrant was not in custody for purposes of interrogation on a separate offense).

In evaluating whether an incarcerated person is in "custody" for Miranda purposes, the following circumstances surrounding the interrogation should be considered: (1) the language used to summon the inmate; (2) the physical surroundings of the interrogation; (3) the extent to which the inmate is confronted with evidence of his or her guilt; (4) the additional pressure exerted to detain the inmate or the change in the surroundings of the inmate which results in an added imposition on the inmate's freedom of movement; and (5) the inmate's freedom to leave the scene and the purpose, place, and length of the questioning. Herrera.

When a prisoner is questioned, the determination of custody should focus on all of the features of the interrogation. Where the facts of the case are consistent with an environment in which a reasonable person would have felt free to terminate the interview and leave, a person serving time in a prison is not in custody for Miranda purposes. Howes v. Fields, 565 U.S. ___, 132 S.Ct. 1181, 182 L.Ed.2d 17 (2012).

§6:21.4 Subjective Intent of Police

The subjective intent of the police and the subjective belief of the defendant become a part of the analysis if the subjective intent of the police has been manifested in their words or actions. Dowthitt v. State, 931 S.W.2d 244 (Tex. Crim. App. 1996),

CONFESSIONS

citing Stansbury v. California, 511 U.S. 318, 114 S.Ct. 1526, 128 L.Ed.2d 293 (1994).

A police officer's unarticulated plan to take a motorist into custody following a traffic stop has no bearing on whether the motorist was in custody at a particular time. The relevant inquiry is how a reasonable man in the motorist's place would have understood the situation. Berkemer v. McCarty, 468 U.S. 420, 104 S.Ct. 3138, 82 L.Ed.2d 317 (1984).

An officer's unarticulated plan and subjective beliefs about what may have occurred have no bearing on whether or not appellant was in custody at a particular time. Ard v. State, 418 S.W.3d 256 (Tex. App.—Houston [14th Dist.] 2013, *no pet.*).

§6:21.5 Restriction on Movement

A person is in custody only if, under the circumstances, a reasonable person would believe that his or her freedom of movement was restrained to the degree associated with a formal arrest. Dowthitt, *supra*, citing Stansbury v. California, 511 U.S. 318, 114 S.Ct. 1526, 128 L.Ed.2d 293 (1994). The "reasonable person" standard presupposes an innocent person. Dowthitt, citing Florida v. Bostick, 501 U.S. 429, 111 S.Ct. 2382, 115 L.Ed.2d 389 (1991).

The restriction on the suspect's freedom of movement must amount to the degree associated with an arrest, as opposed to an investigative detention. Dowthitt, citing Stansbury.

The defendant was in custody for Miranda purposes where police officers blocked her car into a car wash stall and pointed a gun at her during questioning. Taylor v. State, 874 S.W.2d 362 (Tex. App.—Fort Worth 1994, *no pet.*).

§6:21.6 Probable Cause

Where the defendant was questioned for approximately 12 hours, during which time he admitted being present during the murders in question (which gave the police probable cause to arrest him), and during which time the police exercised control over him (accompanying him to the restroom and not allowing him to see his wife), the defendant was found to be in custody. Dowthitt v. State, 931 S.W.2d 244 (Tex. Crim. App. 1996).

If the defendant is trying to show that he was in custody because officers had probable cause to arrest him, he must show that the officers manifested that probable cause to him. Such manifestation can occur if the officers relate information substantiating probable cause to the suspect or the suspect relates such information to the officers. Furthermore, custody is established only if the manifestation of probable cause is combined with other circumstances which would lead a reasonable person to believe that he is under restraint to the degree associated with an arrest. Dowthitt, citing Stansbury v. California, 511 U.S. 318, 114 S.Ct. 1526, 128 L.Ed.2d 293 (1994).

§6:21.7 Location of Questioning

The fact that the questioning of the defendant took place at the police station does not in and of itself establish that the defendant was in custody. *See* Oregon v. Mathiason, 429 U.S. 492, 97 S.Ct. 711, 50 L.Ed.2d 714 (1977) (suspect came in voluntarily, was told he was not under arrest, participated in a 30-minute interview, and then left); Meek v. State, 790 S.W.2d 618 (Tex. Crim. App. 1990) (suspect came in voluntarily, was allowed to go to his car unhindered during the interview, and then left after the statements were taken); and Dancy v. State, 728 S.W.2d 772 (Tex. Crim. App. 1987) (suspect voluntarily accompanied officers to the station, answered questions, gave hair samples, and allowed officers to test his shoes, and arrest was not made until a later point).

Cases decided under Miranda have made clear that a "compelling atmosphere"—the phenomenon that marks a "custodial interrogation" and against which warnings are required—may develop beyond the confines of the station house. Orozco v. Texas, 394 U.S. 324, 89 S.Ct. 1095, 22 L.Ed.2d 311 (1969).

§6:21.8 Focus of Investigation

The fact that an investigation has focused on the defendant does not trigger the need for Miranda warnings in a non-custodial setting. Minnesota v. Murphy, 465 U.S. 420, 104 S.Ct. 1136, 79 L.Ed.2d 409 (1984).

The mere fact that a suspect has become the "focus" of the investigation, without more, does not convert a roadside stop into an arrest. State

v. Stevenson, 958 S.W.2d 824 (Tex. Crim. App. 1997). In order to amount to an arrest, enforcement officials must manifest to the suspect that he is the focus of the investigation. Stevenson.

Whether the defendant is the "focus of the investigation" for Miranda purposes involves questioning by law enforcement officers after the defendant has been taken into custody or otherwise deprived of his freedom of action in any significant way. Beckwith v. United States, 425 U.S. 341, 96 S.Ct. 1612, 48 L.Ed.2d 1 (1976).

§6:21.9 Traffic Stops

Generally, a routine traffic stop does not place a person in custody for Miranda purposes. But a traffic stop may escalate from a non-custodial detention into a custodial detention when formal arrest ensues or a detainee's freedom of movement is restrained to the degree associated with a formal arrest. Appellate courts evaluate whether a person has been detained to the degree associated with arrest on a case-by-case basis. In making the custody determination, the primary question is whether a reasonable person would perceive the detention to be a restraint on his movement comparable to formal arrest, given all the objective circumstances. State v. Ortiz, 382 S.W.3d 367, 372 (Tex. Crim. App. 2012).

In evaluating whether a reasonable person would believe his freedom has been restrained to the degree of formal arrest, the appellate courts look only to the objective factors surrounding the detention. The subjective beliefs of the detaining officer are not included in the calculation of whether a suspect is in custody. But if the officer manifests his belief to the detainee that he is a suspect, then that officer's subjective belief becomes relevant to the determination of whether a reasonable person in the detainee's position would believe he is in custody. Conversely, any undisclosed subjective belief of the suspect that he is guilty of an offense should not be taken into consideration—the reasonable person standard presupposes an innocent person. State v. Ortiz, 382 S.W.3d at 372-3.

§6:22 Admissible Custodial Statements

§6:22.1 Statements to State Caseworkers

Where a defendant is in custody of law enforcement but makes incriminating statements to civil child abuse caseworkers who are not acting as agents of law enforcement or pursuant to law enforcement practices, the statements are not the product of custodial interrogation and are admissible. Cantu v. State, 817 S.W.2d 74 (Tex. Crim. App. 1991); Paez v. State, 681 S.W.2d 34 (Tex. Crim. App. 1984); Berry v. State, 233 S.W.3d 847 (Tex. Crim. App. 2007).

However, where the investigator is acting for the express purpose of investigating allegations of child abuse and then turning the product over to the proper authority for prosecution, a custodial interview of the defendant will be found to be custodial interrogation. Cates v. State, 776 S.W.2d 170 (Tex. Crim. App. 1989).

Where a suspect is not in custody at the time he makes a statement to a caseworker, the resulting statement is not a product of custodial interrogation and is admissible even in the absence of Miranda compliance. Wicker v. State, 740 S.W.2d 779 (Tex. Crim. App. 1987).

§6:22.2 Questioning by Civilians

Custodial statements made to news reporters who are not acting as state agents are admissible at the defendant's subsequent trial. Escamilla v. State, 143 S.W.3d 814 (Tex. Crim. App. 2004).

§6:22.3 Spontaneous Oral Statements

Where a defendant in custody makes a spontaneous admission during the reading of Miranda rights to effect that he killed a jailer, the statement is admissible at trial. Hernandez v. State, 819 S.W.2d 806 (Tex. Crim. App. 1991).

Where a defendant in custody following the giving of Miranda warnings, observes his brother also in custody and states, "He didn't do it; I did it," the statement is admissible because it is not the product of interrogation. Richards v. State, 524 S.W.2d 67 (Tex. Crim. App. 1975).

Where a suspect made the unsolicited remark, "[y]ou have the right one; I am Pete," to arresting officers, the remark was admissible because it was not the product of custodial interrogation. Sosa v. State, 769 S.W.2d 909 (Tex. Crim. App. 1989).

Statements beyond the scope of an officer's custodial interrogation are admissible where the circumstances demonstrate that the officer's question was not leading or suggestive, that the suspect was excited or emotionally stimulated, and that the suspect had been informed of his Miranda rights. Etheridge v. State, 903 S.W.2d 1 (Tex. Crim. App. 1994) (where the suspect proceeded to admit his guilt after the officer asked if he knew why he was being arrested).

Where a defendant (who was in custody) made an admission in an exchange with the judge initiated by himself in the noncoercive atmosphere of open court with his lawyers present, it is not considered the result of "interrogation" in any sense of how that term is described in Miranda. Williams v. State, 270 S.W.3d 112 (Tex. Crim. App. 2008).

§6:22.4 General and Routine Questions

An inquiry of a driving-while-intoxicated suspect being transported by police to a police station as to whether or not he would take a breath test is not interrogation for Miranda purposes. Shepherd v. State, 915 S.W.2d 177 (Tex.App.—Fort Worth 1996, *pet. ref'd*).

General on-the-scene questioning as to the facts surrounding a crime or other general questioning of citizens in a fact-finding process is not affected by Miranda rules. Cannon v. State, 691 S.W.2d 664 (Tex. Crim. App. 1985).

A police officer's questions asked for the purpose of obtaining routine information such as name, address or social security number does not constitute custodial interrogation. Garner v. State, 779 S.W.2d 498 (Tex. App.—Fort Worth 1989, *pet. ref'd*).

Requiring a suspect to reveal his name during a valid Terry stop does not violate his Fifth Amendment rights where the disclosure does not implicate any articulable real and appreciable fear on the suspect's part that his name would be used to incriminate him or that it would furnish a link in the chain of evidence needed to prosecute him. Hiibel v. Sixth Judicial Dist. Court of Nev., Humboldt Cty., 542 U.S. 177, 124 S.Ct. 2451, 159 L.Ed.2d 292 (2004).

§6:22.5 Booking Questions

There is a routine booking question exception to Miranda that exempts from Miranda's coverage questions to secure the biographical data necessary to complete booking or pretrial services. Alford v. State, 358 S.W.3d 647 (Tex. Crim. App. 2012), *citing* Pennsylvania v. Muniz, 496 U.S. 582, 600-02, 110 S.Ct. 2638, 110 L.Ed.2d 528 (1990) (Brennan, J., *plurality op.*).

Questions that are asked for record-keeping purposes only and which are reasonably related to the police's administrative concerns fall outside the protections of Miranda. Alford; Pennsylvania v. Muniz.

Although termed a "booking" exception, this exception appears to be somewhat broader than booking and encompasses routine administrative processing associated with arrest or custody. The point of the exception is that questions that fall within the exception serve a legitimate administrative need. State v. Cruz, 461 S.W.3d 531, 537 (Tex. Crim. App. 2015).

To determine whether a particular question falls within the booking exception, courts ask whether the question reasonably relates to a legitimate administrative concern, applying an objective standard. State v. Cruz, 461 S.W.3d at 537.

If a question is a legitimate administrative question, then it does not matter whether the officer should know that the question is reasonably likely to elicit an incriminating response. That is, a legitimate administrative question is exempt from the "should know" test and is deemed not to be interrogation. State v. Cruz, 461 S.W.3d at 537.

Whether a question reasonably relates to an administrative concern must be ascertained by both the content of the question and the circumstances in which the question is asked. State v. Cruz, 461 S.W.3d at 540.

In deciding whether the questions are legitimate booking questions or a pretext for eliciting incriminating information the following factors can be considered:

- the nature of the questions, such as whether they seek merely identifying data necessary for booking;
- the context of the interrogation, such as whether the questions were asked during a non-investigative clerical booking process and pursuant to a standard booking form or questionnaire;
- the knowledge and intent of the government agent asking the questions;
- the relationship between the question asked and the crime the defendant was suspected of committing;
- the administrative need for the information sought;
- and any other indications that the questions were designed, at least in part, to elicit incriminating evidence and merely asked under the guise or pretext of seeking routine biographical information. State v. Cruz, 461 S.W.3d at 538.

A question that seeks to elicit biographical data may be deemed not interrogation under either of two theories. First, such a question may be deemed not interrogation because it does not meet the general test for interrogation, i.e., it does not meet the "should know" test. That is, a court could decide that a particular question about biographical data was so innocuous that its tendency to produce an incriminating response was not something the police officer should have known. Second a biographical question may be deemed not interrogation under the booking (or administrative) exception. That is, a court could decide that a particular question about biographical data was a routine administrative inquiry. State v. Cruz, 461 S.W.3d at 537-8.

The biographical nature of a question does not alone exempt it from being interrogation because such questions may constitute interrogation under the "should know" test. State v. Cruz, 461 S.W.3d at 538-9.

Questioning that seeks to elicit biographical data does not become interrogation simply because the identifying information may later aid law enforcement in conducting a criminal investigation. State v. Cruz, 461 S.W.3d at 539.

However, the elicitation of biographical data that has incriminating value in and of itself and which does not simply lead to other incriminating evidence can constitute interrogation. State v. Cruz, 461 S.W.3d at 539 (in this case, the suspect's name could be considered incriminating because he had previously given a false name; his cell phone number could be considered incriminating because it ultimately put him near the scene of the offense).

Routine booking questions are, by definition, questions normally attendant to arrest and custody and do not, by their very nature, involve the psychological intimidation that Miranda is designed to prevent. At the same time, they serve a legitimate administrative need. Alford, citing United States v. Doe, 878 F.2d 1546, 1551 (1st Cir. 1989).

Questions directed to the name, address, height, weight, eye color, date of birth, and current age of the arrestee are Miranda-exempt because these questions are reasonably related to the police's administrative concerns. Alford; Pennsylvania v. Muniz.

Questions regarding a suspect's name, address, weight, height, place of employment, and physical disabilities are normally attendant to arrest and custody. Townsend v. State, 813 S.W.2d 181, 186 (Tex.App.—Houston [14th Dist.] 1991, *pet. ref'd*)

Conversely, questions that do not reasonably relate to a legitimate administrative concern are not booking questions within the exception. Alford, citing Branch v. State, 932 S.W.2d 577, 581 (Tex. App.—Tyler 1995, *no pet.*) (asking defendant "where he had been going at the time he was pulled over, when and what he had last eaten, and whether he had drunk an alcoholic beverage... went beyond the scope of that normally attending arrest and custody and amounted to custodial interrogation").

In deciding the admissibility of a statement under the exception, a trial court must examine whether, under the totality of the circumstances, a question is reasonably related to a legitimate administrative concern. In deciding this, the trial court applies an objective standard. An appellate court generally reviews de novo the objective reasonableness of a question's stated administrative purpose, but defers to the trial court's resolution of disputed facts. Alford.

§6:22.6 Overheard Statements

Because society is not prepared to recognize a legitimate expectation of privacy in conversations between arrestees who are in custody in a county law enforcement building, statements made by the arrestees that are tape-recorded without their knowledge by law enforcement officers are admissible in the absence of any deliberate misrepresentations by law enforcement. State v. Scheineman, 77 S.W.3d 810 (Tex. Crim. App. 2002).

The fact that a police officer was stationed in an interview room when a recently detained murder defendant confessed the murder to his wife did not elevate the situation to the functional equivalent of interrogation where the purpose for the presence of the officer was to protect the wife, even though the officers were aware of the possibility that the defendant would confess. Arizona v. Mauro, 481 U.S. 520, 107 S.Ct. 1931, 95 L.Ed.2d 458 (1987).

The contents of a telephone conversation between a defendant in custody and his mother are admissible because they are not the product of custodial interrogation. Autry v. State, 626 S.W.2d 758 (Tex. Crim. App. 1982).

§6:22.7 Public Safety Exception

The Miranda warnings are not necessary even if the suspect is in custody where the interrogation is necessary to ensure the safety of the public or the officer. New York v. Quarles, 467 U.S. 649, 104 S.Ct. 2626, 81 L.Ed.2d 550 (1984), Bryant v. State, 816 S.W.2d 554 (Tex.App.—Fort Worth 1991, *no pet.*).

§6:22.8 Custodial Statements for Impeachment Purposes

CCP Art. 38.22 §5 allows the admission of "a *voluntary* oral statement, whether or not the result of custodial interrogation that has a bearing upon the credibility of the accused as a witness." *See* Roberts v. State, 672 S.W.2d 570 (Tex.App.—Fort Worth 1984); Girndt v. State, 623 S.W.2d 930 (Tex. Crim. App. 1981); Appling v. State, 904 S.W.2d 912 (Tex.App.—Corpus Christi 1995, *pet. ref'd*).

The use of oral statements for impeachment under CCP Art. 38.22 §5 does not require the statement to have been recorded in accordance with §3. Jones v. State, 859 S.W.2d 537 (Tex.App.—Houston [1st Dist.] 1993, *pet. ref'd*).

TIP TO THE PROSECUTION: Always interview police officers who had contact with the defendant to learn of any statements made by the defendant that were not recorded in writing or on audiotape. These statements can be admitted to impeach the defendant's trial testimony.

TIP TO THE DEFENSE: If the state seeks to offer a custodial statement of the defendant as impeachment evidence, request a hearing outside the presence of the jury to determine its voluntariness.

Prior inconsistent custodial statements can be used to impeach the testimony of an accused even though the statements were inadmissible in the state's case-in-chief because of a failure to comply with Miranda as long as the evidence satisfies legal standards for trustworthiness. Harris v. New York, 401 U.S. 222, 91 S.Ct. 643, 28 L.Ed.2d 1 (1971); Lykins v. State, 784 S.W.2d 32 (Tex. Crim. App. 1989); Baker v. State, 956 S.W.2d 19 (Tex. Crim. App. 1997).

Likewise, the Sixth Amendment does not forbid the use of statements taken in violation where they are offered for impeachment purposes only. This is because the constitutional violation occurs at the time the statement is elicited, not when it is offered at trial for impeachment purposes. Kansas v. Ventris, 556 U.S. ___, 129 S.Ct. 1841, 173 L.Ed.2d 801 (2009).

Miranda and the Fifth Amendment do not prohibit impeachment of a testifying defendant with statements he made in custody after the administration of the warnings. Anderson v. Charles, 447 U.S. 404, 100 S.Ct. 2180, 65 L.Ed.2d 222 (1980).

The failure to administer the Miranda warnings creates a presumption of compulsion and consequently, unwarned statements that are otherwise voluntary within the meaning of the Fifth Amendment must be excluded from evidence under Miranda; but the presumption, though not rebuttable for purposes of the state's case-in-chief, does not require that the statements and their fruits be discarded as inherently tainted. Oregon v. Elstad, 470 U.S. 298, 105 S.Ct. 1285, 84 L.Ed.2d 222 (1985).

However, even though U.S. constitutional grounds may not prohibit the use of an illegally obtained confession, its use may be prohibited under CCP Art. 38.23 which prohibits the use of evidence obtained in violation of the laws of the State of Texas. Robbins v. State, 696 S.W.2d 689 (Tex.App.—Dallas 1985).

Statements made by a defendant during plea bargain negotiations are not later admissible against him for impeachment purposes. Wayne v. State, 756 S.W.2d 724 (Tex. Crim. App. 1988).

Even if the confession is used for impeachment, failure to make a determination of voluntariness outside the presence of the jury, when requested, is reversible error. Madden v. State, 691 S.W.2d 688 (Tex. Crim. App. 1985).

If the prosecution violates a defendant's Fifth Amendment rights by introducing an inadmissible confession at trial compelling the defendant to testify in rebuttal, the use of the compelled testimony is prohibited at a retrial. Harrison v. U.S., 392 U.S. 219, 88 S.Ct. 2008, 20 L.Ed.2d 1047 (1968).

§6:23 Interrogation in Non-Custodial Setting

Where a defendant is not under arrest or in custody, his voluntary statement made without threat, promise, or persuasion, is admissible in evidence against him. Miranda v. Arizona, 384 U.S. 436, 86 S.Ct. 1602, 16 L.Ed.2d 694 (1966); CCP Art. 38.22 §5.

The Texas statutory warning is not a prerequisite to the admission of a voluntary statement that does not stem from custodial interrogation. CCP Art. 38.22 §5.

The U.S. Supreme Court has held that the Miranda warning is not a pre-requisite to admissibility of a confession or statement made while not under custodial interrogation. Beckwith v. U.S., 425 U.S. 341, 96 S.Ct. 1612, 48 L.Ed.2d 1 (1976).

Even though a non-custodial statement will not be excluded for a failure to comply with the prophylactic warning requirements of Miranda and CCP Art. 38.22, the procedures surrounding the giving of the statement are still subject to due process and due course of law scrutiny. Wolfe v. State, 917 S.W.2d 270 (Tex. Crim. App. 1996).

Miranda is not implicated where a suspect who is not under arrest voluntarily appears at a police station and is allowed to leave unhindered after a brief interview. California v. Beheler, 463 U.S. 1121, 103 S.Ct. 3517, 77 L.Ed.2d 1275 (1983).

When a defendant is not in custody, law enforcement officers are not required to scrupulously honor his invocation of rights, even where the defendant has been read his rights. Estrada v. State, 313 S.W.3d 274 (Tex. Crim. App. 2010).

Where the initial detention of a defendant is lawful and not unreasonably prolonged, no additional Fourth Amendment justification is necessary for law enforcement officers to ask questions of the defendant. Muehler v. Mena, 544 U.S. ___, 125 S.Ct. 1465, 161 L.Ed.2d 299 (2005).

§6:24 Admissible Non-Custodial Statements

§6:24.1 Statements to Probation Officers

The Fifth and Fourteenth Amendments do not prohibit the introduction of evidence of a defendant's admissions to a probation officer made during a non-custodial monthly report. A probationer's responsibility to provide truthful answers to the probation officer's questions does not convert voluntary statements into compelled ones. Minnesota v. Murphy, 465 U.S. 420, 104 S.Ct. 1136, 79 L.Ed.2d 409 (1984).

The fact that a probationer is ordered as a condition of supervision to submit to a polygraph examination does not elevate the polygraph interview to a custodial situation. Marcum v. State, 983 S.W.2d 762 (Tex.App.—Houston [14th Dist.] 1998, *pet. ref'd*).

Where the defendant has no outstanding warrants and no probable cause to arrest him exists, admissions made to his probation officer during monthly reports are admissible. Payne v. State,

579 S.W.2d 932 (Tex. Crim. App. 1979); Holmes v. State, 752 S.W.2d 700 (Tex.App.—Waco 1988, *no pet.*).

However, where the defendant is being detained by the probation officer prior to his arrest on a probation revocation warrant, any statement made to the probation officer which is the product of interrogation should be suppressed. Creeks v. State, 542 S.W.2d 849 (Tex. Crim. App. 1976).

§6:24.2 Statements to State Caseworkers

An interview conducted by a state social caseworker investigating whether or not to instigate proceedings to terminate the parent-child relationship is not custodial interrogation. Davis v. State, 687 S.W.2d 78 (Tex. App.—Dallas 1985, *pet. ref'd*); Wicker v. State, 740 S.W.2d 779 (Tex. Crim. App. 1987).

However, where the caseworker is acting as an agent of law enforcement, the Miranda warnings are a necessary predicate to any interview of the defendant. Wilkerson v. State, 173 S.W.3d 521 (Tex. Crim. App. 2005).

§6:24.3 Traffic Stops

Where a person detained on a routine traffic stop is not subjected to restraints comparable to those associated with a formal arrest, he is not in custody for Miranda purposes. Therefore, questions asked by police during the traffic stop are not custodial interrogation. Berkemer v. McCarty, 468 U.S. 420, 104 S.Ct. 3138, 82 L.Ed.2d 317 (1984). *See also,* State v. Stevenson, 958 S.W.2d 824 (Tex. Crim. App. 1997).

The request of a motorist to perform a roadside balancing test at a location visible to passing motorists, without more, does not elevate the traffic stop to a custodial interrogation. Pennsylvania v. Bruder, 488 U.S. 9, 109 S.Ct. 205, 102 L.Ed.2d 172 (1988).

§6:25 Agency Relationship

§6:25.1 Statements to Inmates

Where law enforcement agents use a civilian to deliberately elicit incriminating statements from a defendant, the defendant's Sixth Amendment right to counsel has been violated. Massiah v. U.S., 377 U.S. 201, 84 S.Ct. 1199, 12 L.Ed.2d 246 (1964).

Three factors are examined to determine if the defendant's statement was deliberately elicited: (1) whether the inmate was acting under instructions as a paid informant for law enforcement; (2) whether the inmate was ostensibly no more than a fellow inmate of the defendant; and (3) whether the defendant was in custody and under indictment at the time he was engaged in conversation by the fellow inmate. U.S. v. Henry, 447 U.S. 264, 100 S.Ct. 2183, 65 L.Ed.2d 115 (1980).

Deliberate elicitation simply involves some conduct designed to obtain incriminating state-ments. Such conduct has not occurred if the informant is merely a passive listening post who relates any statements the defendant makes of his own volition. Rubalcado v. State, 424 S.W.3d 560, 576 (Tex. Crim. App. 2014).

The person claiming that there is an agency relationship between the interrogator and police has the burden of proving it. Wilkerson v. State, 173 S.W.3d 521, 529 (Tex. Crim. App. 2005).

The law does not presume an agency relationship between foreign and U.S. police. Alvarado v. State, 853 S.W.2d 17 (Tex. Crim. App. 1991). The agency relationship may be express or implied from the actions of the parties. Alvarado.

Where there is no evidence that U.S. police had any involvement with the apprehension or interrogation of the suspect other than informing foreign authorities that the suspect had crossed the border, the agency relationship was not shown to have existed. Alvarado.

A prisoner's confession to a fellow inmate who was acting as a government agent and where the confession is made as a result of a promise by the agent to protect the prisoner/defendant from fellow inmates is deemed to be coerced, and therefore inadmissible under the Fourteenth Amendment. Arizona v. Fulminante, 499 U.S. 279, 111 S.Ct. 1246, 113 L.Ed.2d 302 (1991).

However, any information obtained by the inmate before he enters into an agreement with the State is free of any Sixth Amendment concerns. Wesbrook v. State, 29 S.W.3d 103, (Tex. Crim. App. 2000) (*plurality op.*); Thompson v. State, 93 S.W.3d 16 (Tex. Crim. App. 2001).

Where an inmate who was a government agent did not take any action that would have constituted the functional equivalent of interrogation, there is no Sixth Amendment violation. Kuhlmann v. Wilson, 477 U.S. 436, 106 S.Ct. 2616, 91 L.Ed.2d 364 (1986).

Likewise, there is no Sixth Amendment violation where the inmate was not found to be a government agent. Manns v. State, 122 S.W.3d 171 (Tex. Crim. App. 2003).

A letter from a defendant in jail to someone outside of jail is not custodial interrogation; therefore, a letter admitting a crime is admissible. Hightower v. State, 629 S.W.2d 920 (Tex. Crim. App. 1982).

Evidence obtained through the use of a government agent can be found to be harmless error at trial. Wesbrook.

§6:25.2 Statements to Private Citizens

The person claiming that there is an agency relationship between a private citizen and law enforcement has the burden of proving it. Wilkerson v. State, 173 S.W.3d 521, 529 (Tex. Crim. App. 2005).

To determine whether an agency relationship exists between a private citizen and law enforcement, courts will look to the following factors: (1) the relationship between the private citizen and law enforcement; (2) the purpose of the citizen's interview with the defendant; and (3) whether a reasonable person in the defendant's position could have believed that the interviewer was a law enforcement agent. Elizondo v. State, 382 S.W.3d 389 (Tex. Crim. App. 2012) (where the court found that a loss-prevention officer was not an agent of law enforcement).

§6:30 Magistration and Sufficiency of Miranda Warnings

§6:31 Statutory Law

CCPArt. 2.09. Who Are Magistrates

> *Each of the following officers is a magistrate within the meaning of this Code: The justices of the Supreme Court, the judges of the Court of Criminal Appeals, the justices of the Courts of Appeals, the judges of the District Court, the magistrates appointed by the judges of the district courts of Bexar County, Dallas County, or Tarrant County that give preference to criminal cases, the criminal law hearing officers for Harris County appointed under Subchapter L, Chapter 54, Government Code, the criminal law hearing officers for Cameron County appointed under Subchapter BB, Chapter 54, Government Code, the magistrates or associate judges appointed by the judges of the district courts of Lubbock County, Nolan County, or Webb County, the magistrates appointed by the judges of the criminal district courts of Dallas County or Tarrant County, the associate judges appointed by the judges of the district courts and the county courts at law that give preference to criminal cases in Jefferson County, the associate judges appointed by the judges of the district courts and the statutory county courts of Brazos County, Nueces County, or Williamson County, the magistrates appointed by the judges of the district courts and statutory county courts that give preference to criminal cases in Travis County, the criminal magistrates appointed by the Brazoria County Commissioners Court, the criminal magistrates appointed by the Burnet County Commissioners Court, the criminal magistrates appointed by the Burnet County Commissioners Court, the county judges, the judges of the county courts at law, judges of the county criminal courts, the judges of statutory probate courts, the associate judges appointed by the judges of the statutory probate courts under Chapter 54A , Government Code, the associate judges appointed by the judge of a district court under Chapter 54A, Government Code, the magistrates appointed under Subchapter JJ, Chapter 54, Government Code, as added by H.B. No. 2132, Acts of the 82nd Legislature, Regular Session, 2011, the justices of the peace, and the mayors and recorders and the judges of the municipal courts of incorporated cities or towns.*

CCP Art. 14.06. Must Take Offender Before Magistrate

(a) Except as otherwise provided by this article, in each case enumerated in this Code, the person making the arrest or the person having custody of the person arrested shall take the person arrested or have him taken without unnecessary delay, but not later than 48 hours after the person is arrested, before the magistrate who may have ordered the arrest, before some magistrate of the county where the arrest was made without an order, or, to provide more expeditiously to the person arrested the warnings described by Article 15.17 of this Code, before a magistrate in any other county of this state. The magistrate shall immediately perform the duties described in Article 15.17 of this Code.

(b) A peace officer who is charging a person, including a child, with committing an offense that is a Class C misdemeanor, other than an offense under Section 49.02, Penal Code, may, instead of taking the person before a magistrate, issue a citation to the person that contains written notice of the time and place the person must appear before a magistrate, the name and address of the person charged, the offense charged, and the following admonishment, in boldfaced or underlined type or in capital letters:

"If you are convicted of a misdemeanor offense involving violence where you are or were a spouse, intimate partner, parent, or guardian of the victim or are or were involved in another, similar relationship with the victim, it may be unlawful for you to possess or purchase a firearm, including a handgun or long gun, or ammunition, pursuant to federal law under 18 U.S.C. Section 922(g)(9) or Section 46.04(b), Texas Penal Code. If you have any questions whether these laws make it illegal for you to possess or purchase a firearm, you should consult an attorney."

(c) If the person resides in the county where the offense occurred, a peace officer who is charging a person with committing an offense that is a Class A or B misdemeanor may, instead of taking the person before a magistrate, issue a citation to the person that contains written notice of the time and place the person must appear before a magistrate of this state as described by Subsection (a), the name and address of the person charged, and the offense charged.

(d) Subsection (c) applies only to a person charged with committing an offense under:

(1) Section 481.121, Health and Safety Code, if the offense is punishable under Subsection (b)(1) or (2) of that section;

(1-a) Section 481.1161, Health and Safety Code, if the offense is punishable under Subsection (b)(1) or (2) of that section;

(2) Section 28.03, Penal Code, if the offense is punishable under Subsection (b)(2) of that section;

(3) Section 28.08, Penal Code, if the offense is punishable under Subsection (b)(1) of that section;

(4) Section 31.03, Penal Code, if the offense is punishable under Subsection (e)(2)(A) of that section;

(5) Section 31.04, Penal Code, if the offense is punishable under Subsection (e)(2) of that section;

(6) Section 38.114, Penal Code, if the offense is punishable as a Class B misdemeanor; or

(7) Section 521.457, Transportation Code.

CCP Art. 15.17. Duties of Arresting Officer and Magistrate

(a) In each case enumerated in this Code, the person making the arrest or the person having custody of the person arrested shall without unnecessary delay, but not later than 48 hours after the person is arrested, take the person arrested or have him taken before some magistrate of the county where the accused was arrested or, to provide more expeditiously to the person arrested the warnings described by this article, before a magistrate in any other county of this state. The arrested person may be taken before the magistrate in person or the image of the arrested person may be presented to the magistrate by means of an electronic broadcast system. The magistrate shall inform in clear language the person arrested, either in person or through the electronic broadcast system, of the accusation against him and of any affidavit filed therewith, of his right to retain counsel, of his right to remain silent, of his right to have an attorney present during any interview with peace officers or attorneys representing the state, of his right to terminate the interview at any time, and of his right to have an examining trial. The magistrate shall also inform the person arrested of the person's right to request the appointment of counsel if the person cannot afford counsel. The magistrate shall inform the person arrested of the procedures for requesting appointment of counsel. If the person does not speak and understand the English language or is deaf, the magistrate shall inform the person in a manner consistent with Articles 38.30 and 38.31, as appropriate. The magistrate shall ensure that reasonable assistance in completing the necessary forms for requesting appointment of counsel is provided to the person at the same time. If the person arrested is indigent and requests appointment of counsel and if the magistrate is authorized under Article 26.04 to appoint counsel for indigent defendants in the county, the magistrate shall appoint counsel in accordance with Article 1.051. If the magistrate is not authorized to appoint counsel, the magistrate shall without unnecessary delay, but not later than 24 hours after the person arrested requests appointment of counsel, transmit, or cause to be transmitted to the court or to the court's designee authorized under Article 26.04 to appoint counsel in the county, the forms requesting the appointment of counsel. The magistrate shall also inform the person arrested that he is not required to make a statement and that any statement made by him may be used against him. The magistrate shall allow the person arrested reasonable time and opportunity to consult counsel and shall, after determining whether the person is currently on bail for a separate criminal offense, admit the person arrested to bail if allowed by law. A recording of the communication between the arrested person and the magistrate shall be made. The recording shall be preserved until the earlier of the following dates: (1) the date on which the pretrial hearing ends; or (2) the 91st day after the date on which the recording is made if the person is charged with a misdemeanor or the 120th day after the date on which the recording is made if the person is charged with a felony. The counsel for the defendant may obtain a copy of the recording on payment of a reasonable amount to cover costs of reproduction. For purposes of this subsection, "electronic broadcast system" means a two-way electronic communication of image and sound between the arrested person and the magistrate and includes secure Internet videoconferencing.

(b) After an accused charged with a misdemeanor punishable by fine only is taken before a magistrate under Subsection (a) and the magistrate has identified the accused with certainty, the magistrate may release the accused without bond and order the accused to appear at a later date for arraignment in the applicable justice court or municipal court. The order must state in writing the time, date, and place of

the arraignment, and the magistrate must sign the order. The accused shall receive a copy of the order on release. If an accused fails to appear as required by the order, the judge of the court in which the accused is required to appear shall issue a warrant for the arrest of the accused. If the accused is arrested and brought before the judge, the judge may admit the accused to bail, and in admitting the accused to bail, the judge should set as the amount of bail an amount double that generally set for the offense for which the accused was arrested. This subsection does not apply to an accused who has previously been convicted of a felony or a misdemeanor other than a misdemeanor punishable by fine only.

(c) When a deaf accused is taken before a magistrate under this article or Article 14.06 of this Code, an interpreter appointed by the magistrate qualified and sworn as provided in Article 38.31 of this Code shall interpret the warning required by those articles in a language that the accused can understand, including but not limited to sign language.

(d) If a magistrate determines that a person brought before the magistrate after an arrest authorized by Article 14.051 of this code was arrested unlawfully, the magistrate shall release the person from custody. If the magistrate determines that the arrest was lawful, the person arrested is considered a fugitive from justice for the purposes of Article 51.13 of this Code, and the disposition of the person is controlled by that article.

(e) In each case in which a person arrested is taken before a magistrate as required by Subsection (a), a record shall be made of:

(1) the magistrate informing the person of the person's right to request appointment of counsel;

(2) the magistrate asking the person whether the person wants to request appointment of counsel; and

(3) whether the person requested appointment of counsel.

(f) A record required under Subsection (e) may consist of written forms, electronic recordings, or other documentation as authorized by procedures adopted in the county under Article 26.04(a).

(g) If a person charged with an offense punishable as a misdemeanor appears before a magistrate in compliance with a citation issued under Article 14.06(b) or (c), the magistrate shall perform the duties imposed by this article in the same manner as if the person had been arrested and brought before the magistrate by a peace officer. After the magistrate performs the duties imposed by this article, the magistrate except for good cause shown may release the person on personal bond. If a person who was issued a citation under Article 14.06(c) fails to appear as required by that citation, the magistrate before whom the person is required to appear shall issue a warrant for the arrest of the accused.

CCP Art. 15.16. How Warrant Is Executed

(a) The officer or person executing a warrant of arrest shall without unnecessary delay take the person or have him taken before the magistrate who issued the warrant or before the magistrate named in the warrant, if the magistrate is in the same county where the person is arrested. If the issuing or named magistrate is in another county, the person arrested shall without unnecessary delay be taken before some magistrate in the county in which he was arrested.

(b) Notwithstanding Subsection (a), to provide more expeditiously to the person arrested the warnings described by Article 15.17, the officer or person

executing the arrest warrant may as permitted by that article take the person arrested before a magistrate in a county other than the county of arrest.

§6:32 Delay in Taking Before Magistrate

CCP Art. 15.17(a) requires that the person making an arrest shall without unnecessary delay take the arrestee before a magistrate. Where a defendant is taken before a magistrate within 16 hours of his arrest the "without unnecessary delay" requirement is satisfied, even where there was a magistrate available at the time of the arrest. Jenkins v. State, 912 S.W.2d 793 (Tex. Crim. App. 1995).

Absent a showing of a causal connection between the failure to take an accused before a magistrate and the accused's confession, the validity of the confession is not affected. Boyd v. State, 811 S.W.2d 105 (Tex. Crim. App. 1991).

Where the record shows that the defendant voluntarily confessed within two hours of his arrest, there is no evidence of a causal connection between any CCP Art. 15.17 violation and the defendant's voluntary decision to confess. Jenkins.

It is well-settled that an unreasonable delay in bringing an arrestee before a magistrate will not invalidate an otherwise voluntary confession if the arrestee was properly advised of his Miranda rights prior to making the statement. Garcia v. State, 191 S.W.3d 870, 876 (Tex.App.—Houston [14th Dist.] 2006, *no pet.*).

Delay in taking a defendant before a magistrate will not invalidate a confession where the delay was due to reasonable investigative and processing procedures necessitated by the particular facts of the case. Cantu v. State, 842 S.W.2d 667, 680 (Tex. Crim. App. 1992).

§6:33 Sufficiency of Warnings

§6:33.1 In General

A defendant in custody has a right to certain procedural safeguards designed to effectively secure his privilege against self-incrimination. Miranda v. Arizona, 384 U.S. 436, 86 S.Ct. 1602, 16 L.Ed.2d 694 (1966).

In Texas, these procedural safeguards are codified as a set of warnings in CCP Art. 38.22 §§2 and 3. *See* Herrera v. State, 241 S.W.3d 520 (Tex. Crim. App. 2007).

The Miranda warnings and a valid waiver thereof are a constitutional predicate to the admission of a custodial statement in state and federal courts. Dickerson v. U.S., 530 U.S. 428, 120 S.Ct. 2326, 147 L.Ed.2d 405 (2000).

The Miranda warnings are not constitutionally mandated, but are procedural safeguards necessary to prevent governmental coercion. Alvarado v. State, 853 S.W.2d 17 (Tex. Crim. App. 1991).

In order for a subsequent, custodial confession to be admissible, it must be shown that the defendant was advised of his rights and given an opportunity to exercise them before any questioning by law enforcement officers. Miranda, and CCP Art. 38.22. In other words, the prophylactic requirements of Miranda and CCP Art. 38.22 are prerequisite to the admission of a custodial confession. Baker v. State, 956 S.W.2d 19 (Tex. Crim. App. 1997).

An accused held in custody must be given the required warnings prior to questioning. A failure to do so results in forfeiture of the use of any statement obtained during that interrogation by the prosecution during its case-in-chief. Jones v. State, 119 S.W.3d 766 (Tex. Crim. App. 2003) (where the resulting statement was admitted in the punishment phase of a capital murder trial and the constitutional error was found to be harmless beyond a reasonable doubt).

Two interrogation sessions separated by a gap in time can be considered part of a single interview for the purpose of Article 38.22 and Miranda; thus sufficient warnings given at the beginning of the first session will carry over and apply to the second session. Bible v. State, 162 S.W.3d 234 (Tex. Crim. App. 2005).

However, a break in the interrogation can sometimes require the giving of new warnings. Flemming v. State, 949 S.W.2d 876 (Tex.App.—Houston [14th Dist.] 1997, *no pet.*).

The failure to Mirandize the defendant before his initial interrogation will render later Miranda warnings ineffective and make a subsequent statement inadmissible. Martinez v. State, 272 S.W.3d 615 (Tex. Crim. App. 2009).

The prosecution bears the burden of proving admissibility when a Miranda violation is found. Martinez.

§6:33.2 Lack of Miranda Warnings

The failure to administer the Miranda warnings creates a presumption of compulsion and consequently, unwarned statements that are otherwise voluntary within the meaning of the Fifth Amendment must be excluded from evidence under Miranda; but the presumption, though not rebuttable for purposes of the state's case-in-chief, does not require that the statements and their fruits be discarded as inherently tainted. Oregon v. Elstad, 470 U.S. 298, 105 S.Ct. 1285, 84 L.Ed.2d 222 (1985); Baker v. State, 956 S.W.2d 19 (Tex. Crim. App. 1997).

The absence of Miranda warnings does not require the suppression of non-testimonial fruits of a defendant's statement where the statement was made voluntarily and was uncoerced. U.S. v. Patane, 542 U.S. 630, 124 S.Ct. 2620, 159 L.Ed.2d 667 (2004) (*plurality opinion*) (where the defendant was prosecuted for possessing a gun that was found as a result of his statement).

When a defendant is not in custody, law enforcement officers are not required to scrupulously honor his invocation of rights, even where the defendant has been read his rights. Estrada v. State, 313 S.W.3d 274 (Tex. Crim. App. 2010).

As a general rule, the Miranda warnings are not a prerequisite to the admission of a statement obtained in a foreign country by foreign officials. Alvarado. Despite the inapplicability of Miranda to confessions obtained by foreign officials, the confession will still be excluded if the circumstances surrounding the taking of the confession shock the conscience of the U.S. court. Alvarado.

§6:33.3 Incomplete or Inaccurate Warnings

The warnings are sufficient where they reasonably convey to a suspect his rights under Miranda. Florida v. Powell, 559 U.S. ___, 130 S.Ct. 1195, 175 L.Ed.2d 1009 (2010).

CCP Art. 38.22 warnings do not have to be given verbatim to the suspect in order for a resulting confession to be admissible. Where the warnings substantially comply with CCP Art. 38.22, the trial court does not err in admitting the confession. Cockrell v. State, 933 S.W.2d 73 (Tex. Crim. App. 1996) (suspect was warned that the statement could be used against him in "court" and that it could be used against him at "trail" instead of "trial"); Sosa v. State, 769 S.W.2d 909 (Tex. Crim. App. 1989).

Warning a suspect that he had a right to an attorney "prior to *or* during any questioning," sufficiently warned the suspect that he had a right to an attorney "prior to *and* during any questioning." Penry v. State, 691 S.W.2d 636 (Tex. Crim. App. 1985), citing California v. Prysock, 453 U.S. 355, 101 S.Ct. 2806, 69 L.Ed.2d 696 (1981) (emphasis added).

A warning to a suspect that, "anything I say may be used against me," is sufficient even though no reference is made to using the statement in court or at a trial. Williams v. State, 883 S.W.2d 317 (Tex. App.—Dallas 1994, *pet. ref'd*).

§6:33.4 Warnings for Written Statements

The warnings required to be given to a suspect in custody are contained in CCP Art. 38.22 §2 for written statements and in §3 for oral statements. The §2 warnings and a waiver thereof must appear on the face of any resulting written confession. Westley v. State, 754 S.W.2d 224 (Tex. Crim. App. 1988); Heiselbetz v. State, 906 S.W.2d 500 (Tex. Crim. App. 1995).

The warnings provided in CCP Art. 38.22 §2(a) are virtually identical to the Miranda warnings, with the exception that the warning that an accused "has the right to terminate the interview at any time" as set out in §2(a)(5) is not required by Miranda. Herrera v. State, 241 S.W.3d 520, 526 (Tex. Crim. App. 2007).

TIP TO THE PROSECUTION: Compose a form for the taking of a suspect's statement, which contains on its face the CCP Art. 38.22 warnings and a valid waiver thereof, and distribute it to all local police agencies for their use.

Where the statutory warnings are considered as being incorporated into the confession rather than appearing on its face, the facial warning requirement of CCP Art. 38.22 will be deemed satisfied. White v. State, 779 S.W.2d 809 (Tex. Crim. App. 1989).

The CCP Art. 38.22 §2(a) requirement that the warnings must be given by a magistrate or the person to whom the statement is made is satisfied so long as the officer taking the confession was present when the warnings were given. Dowthitt v. State, 931 S.W.2d 244 (Tex. Crim. App. 1996).

Because a written statement is not "obtained" until it is signed, giving the required warnings before the accused signs the statement meets the statutory requirements. Dowthitt, 931 S.W.2d at 258-9 (where the defendant was not in custody when he began giving the statement).

§6:33.5 Warnings for Oral Statements

Article 38.22, §3 of the Code of Criminal Procedure provides that no oral statement of an accused made as a result of custodial interrogation shall be admissible against the accused in a criminal proceeding unless (1) the statement was recorded and (2) prior to the statement but during the recording, the accused was warned of his rights and knowingly, intelligently, and voluntarily waived those rights. Joseph v. State, 309 S.W.3d 20, 23-4 (Tex. Crim. App. 2010).

The statute contains two distinct elements pertaining to a statement's admissibility: the defendant's receipt of the prescribed warning and his waiver of the rights set out in the warning. Joseph, 309 S.W.3d at 24.

The CCP Art. 38.22 §2(a) requirement that the warnings must be given by a magistrate or the person to whom the statement is made does not apply to oral confessions that are governed by §3. Dowthitt v. State, 931 S.W.2d 244, 258-9 (Tex. Crim. App. 1996).

§6:34 "Two-Step" Confessions

The failure to give Miranda warnings before an oral confession does not automatically render a subsequent written confession involuntary. Corwin v. State, 870 S.W.2d 23 (Tex. Crim. App. 1993); Oregon v. Elstad, 470 U.S. 298, 105 S.Ct. 1285, 84 L.Ed.2d 222 (1985).

In a custodial situation, the failure to give Miranda warnings before a first statement renders a second statement that repeats the substance of the first statement inadmissible; even where Miranda warnings are given before the second statement. Missouri v. Seibert, 542 U.S. ___, 124 S.Ct. 2601, 159 L.Ed.2d 643 (2004) (*plurality op.*).

The taint from a first confession can be sufficiently attenuated to allow admission of a subsequent confession where the defendant is brought before a magistrate for Miranda warnings and the further interrogation done by a second law enforcement officer. Sterling v. State, 800 S.W.2d 513 (Tex. Crim. App. 1990); Elstad. *See also*, Rodriguez v. State, 968 S.W.2d 554 (Tex.App—Houston [14th Dist.] 1998 *no pet.*).

Where questioning of the defendant that occurred pre-Miranda was inadvertent (rather than deliberate) and the defendant's post-Miranda statements were voluntary, the trial court does not err in allowing the admission of the post-Miranda statements by finding that there was not an illegal two-step interrogation. Carter v. State, 309 S.W.3d 31 (Tex. Crim. App. 2010).

The taint of an earlier inducement can be sufficiently attenuated even in the absence of a specific repudiation of the earlier inducement. Sterling. It is also not necessary to inform the suspect that his earlier, oral statement cannot be used against him in order for the subsequent written statement to be admissible. Elstad.

The question of whether the rationale of Elstad applies when a suspect makes incriminating statements after a knowing and voluntary waiver of his right to counsel notwithstanding earlier police questioning in violation of the Sixth Amendment has not yet been decided. Fellers v. U.S., 540 U.S. 519, 124 S.Ct. 1019, 157 L.Ed.2d 1016 (2004).

The appropriate remedy when a two-step interrogation technique has been impermissibly employed is the suppression of both the unwarned and the warned statements. Vasquez v. State, 483 S.W.3d 550, 555 (Tex. Crim. App. 2016).

A defendant's objection that he was subject to an impermissible two-step interrogation technique must be sufficiently specific for the trial court to understand the objection. Vasquez v. State, 483 S.W.3d at 556.

§6:35 Out-of-State Confessions

Under basic conflict-of-law principles, the law of the forum in which the judicial proceeding is held governs the admissibility of evidence. Therefore, CCP Art. 38.22 (being a procedural evidentiary rule), governs the admissibility of out-of-state confessions offered in Texas trials. Nonn v. State, 41 S.W.3d 677 (Tex. Crim. App. 2001).

Out-of-state confessions must pass a substantial compliance test rather than a strict compliance test in order to be admissible under CCP Art. 38.22 §2. Nonn v. State, 41 S.W.3d 677 (Tex. Crim. App. 2001).

However, oral statements offered under §5 of Art. 38.22 must strictly comply in order to be admissible because of a legislative mandate in §5. Nonn v. State, 41 S.W.3d 677 (Tex. Crim. App. 2001).

Out-of-state confessions made after September 1, 2001 will be governed by CCP Art. 38.22 §8 which reads as follows:

> ***§8.*** *Notwithstanding any other provision of this article, a written, oral, or sign language statement of an accused made as a result of a custodial interrogation is admissible against the accused in a criminal proceeding in this state if:*
>
> *(1) the statement was obtained in another state and was obtained in compliance with the laws of that state or this state; or*
>
> *(2) the statement was obtained by a federal law enforcement officer in this state or another state and was obtained in compliance with the laws of the United States.*

§6:40 Invocation and Waiver of Rights

§6:41 Invocation of Rights

The Supreme Court has held that the Miranda warnings and a valid waiver thereof are a constitutional predicate to the admission of a custodial statement in state and federal courts. Dickerson v. U.S., 530 U.S. 428, 120 S.Ct. 2326, 147 L.Ed.2d 405 (2000).

Although the Fifth Amendment right to interrogation counsel is triggered by the Miranda warnings that police must give before beginning any custodial questioning and the Sixth Amendment right to trial counsel is triggered by judicial arraignment or Article 15.17 magistration each right to counsel applies to post-magistration custodial interrogation, and each is invoked and waived in exactly the same manner—under the Fifth Amendment prophylactic Miranda rules. Pecina v. State, 361 S.W.3d 68, 71 (Tex. Crim. App. 2012).

The accused must unambiguously request counsel during a custodial interrogation; thus, he must articulate his desire to have counsel present sufficiently clearly that a reasonable police officer in the circumstances would understand the statement to be a request for an attorney. Pecina, 361 S.W.3d at 79 (citing Davis v. United States, 512 U.S. 452, 458-59, 114 S.Ct. 2350, 129 L.Ed.2d 362 (1994)).

The Supreme Court has held that, in deciding whether an accused actually invoked his right to counsel, reviewing courts must use an objective standard "[t]o avoid difficulties of proof and to provide guidance to officers conducting interrogations[.]" Pecina, 361 S.W.3d at 79 (citing Davis v. United States).

To protect the Fifth Amendment privilege against self-incrimination, the police may not continue or re-initiate custodial interrogation of a suspect who has previously requested assistance of counsel after the police informed him of his right to counsel at the beginning of a custodial interrogation. Pecina, 361 S.W.3d at 80.

When a defendant is not in custody, law enforcement officers are not required to scrupulously honor his invocation of rights, even where the defendant has been read his rights. Estrada v. State, 313 S.W.3d 274 (Tex. Crim. App. 2010).

In reviewing claims concerning Miranda violations and the admission of statements made as the result of custodial interrogation, appellate courts afford almost total deference to the trial court's rulings on questions of historical fact and on application of law to fact questions that turn upon credibility and demeanor while reviewing *de novo* the trial court's rulings on application of law to fact questions that do not turn upon credibility and demeanor. Pecina v. State, 361 S.W.3d at 79.

§6:42 Waiver of Rights

§6:42.1 Case Law on Waiver

§6:42.1.1 In General

Miranda and its prophylactic safeguards only apply to custodial statements. Wolfe v. State, 917 S.W.2d 270 (Tex. Crim. App. 1996).

Texas Code of Criminal Procedure Art. 38.22 §§ 2 and 3 provide that a defendant's custodial-interrogation statement is not admissible unless, prior to making the statement, he received the warnings provided in Art. 15.17 or Art. 38.22, §2(a) or Sec. 3(a) (which incorporate the requirements of Miranda), and he knowingly, intelligently, and voluntarily waived those rights. Oursbourn v. State, 259 S.W.3d 159, 171-2 (Tex. Crim. App. 2008).

A defendant may waive his Miranda and CCP Art. 38.22 rights provided the waiver is made voluntarily, knowingly, and intelligently. Jacobs v. State, 787 S.W.2d 397 (Tex. Crim. App. 1990), citing Moran v. Burbine, 475 U.S. 412, 106 S.Ct. 1135, 89 L.Ed.2d 410 (1986).

A waiver is an intentional and knowing relinquishment of a known right. Miranda v. Arizona, 384 U.S. 436, 86 S.Ct. 1602, 16 L.Ed.2d 694 (1966).

"Knowing" in the context of waiver is an intellectual, conscious understanding, by thought process and reason, of the releasing of, or absolute surrender of, a right, or of a constitutionally granted guarantee; and, the understanding of the effects of waiving such a right of a constitutionally granted guarantee. Combs v. State, 631 S.W.2d 534 (Tex. App.—Houston [1st Dist.] 1982), *rev'd on other grounds* 643 S.W.2d 709 (Tex. Crim. App. 1982).

It is the State's burden to establish a valid waiver of Miranda rights by a preponderance of the evidence. Leza v. State, 351 S.W.3d 344, 349 (Tex. Crim. App. 2011); Colorado v. Connelly, 479 U.S. 157, 168, 107 S.Ct. 515, 93 L.Ed.2d 473 (1986).

There are two facets to any inquiry with respect to the adequacy of a purported waiver of Miranda rights: First, the waiver must be voluntary in the sense that it was the product of a free and deliberate choice rather than intimidation, coercion, or deception. Second, the waiver must be made with a full awareness both of the nature of the right being abandoned and the consequences of the decision to abandon it. Leza, 351 S.W.3d at 349; Moran v. Burbine, 475 U.S. 412, 421, 106 S.Ct. 1135.

Only if the totality of the circumstances surrounding the interrogation reveals both an uncoerced choice and the requisite level of comprehension may a court properly conclude that the Miranda rights have been waived. Joseph v. State, 309 S.W.3d 20, 25 (Tex. Crim. App. 2010); Moran v. Burbine, 475 U.S. 412, 421, 106 S.Ct. 1135.

The totality-of-the-circumstances approach requires the consideration of "all the circumstances surrounding the interrogation," including the defendant's experience, background, and conduct. Joseph, 309 S.W.3d at 25.

It will suffice to render a waiver knowing and intelligent that the accused has been made aware, and fully comprehends, that he has the right to remain silent in the face of police interrogation and to discontinue the dialogue at any time, and that the consequence of his waiver is that his words may be used against him later in a court of law. Leza, 351 S.W.3d at 350.

A suspect's awareness of all the possible subjects of questioning in advance of interrogation is not relevant to determining whether the suspect voluntarily, knowingly, and intelligently waived his Fifth Amendment privilege under Miranda. Leza, 351 S.W.3d at 350; *citing* Colorado v. Spring, 479 U.S. 564, 574, 107 S.Ct. 851, 857, 93 L.Ed.2d 954 (1987).

Similarly, the failure to immediately inform a defendant of the subject of the interrogation impacts neither the voluntariness nor the knowing and intelligent nature of any waiver of his statutory rights—as a matter of law. Leza, 351 S.W.3d at 350.

The U.S. Constitution does not require that a criminal suspect knows and understands every possible consequence of a waiver of his Fifth Amendment privilege. Colorado v. Spring, 479 U.S. at 577, 107 S.Ct. at 859.

Only if the totality of the circumstances surrounding the interrogation reveal both an uncoerced choice and the requisite level of comprehension may a court properly conclude that the Miranda and CCP Art. 38.22 rights have been waived. Jacobs.

The mere failure of the suspect to invoke his rights is not a valid waiver thereof. Miranda v. Arizona.

Waivers will not be presumed from silence. Miranda v. Arizona, 384 U.S. at 475; Joseph v. State, 309 S.W.3d 20, 24 (Tex. Crim. App. 2010). The fact that an incriminating statement was eventually made will not presume a valid waiver. Miranda v. Arizona, 384 U.S. at 475; Joseph, 309 S.W.3d at 24.

§6:42.1.2 Implied Waivers

A suspect who has received and understood his Miranda warnings, and has not invoked his Miranda rights, implicitly waives the right to remain silent by making an uncoerced statement to the police. Berghuis v. Thompkins, 560 U.S. ___, 130 S.Ct. 2250, 176 L.Ed.2d 1098 (2010).

An implicit waiver of the right to remain silent is sufficient to admit a defendant's statement into evidence. An express waiver is not necessary. Berguis v. Thompkins.

Police are not required to obtain a waiver of the suspect's right to remain silent before interrogating the suspect. Berguis v. Thompkins.

Neither a written nor an oral express waiver is required. Joseph v. State, 309 S.W.3d 20, 24 (Tex. Crim. App. 2010).

In some cases, a waiver can be inferred from the actions and words of the person interrogated. North Carolina v. Butler, 441 U.S. 369, 373, 99 S.Ct. 1755, 60 L.Ed.2d 286 (1979); Joseph, 309 S.W.3d at 24.

Whether a waiver is shown must depend in each case upon the particular facts and circumstances surrounding the case, including the background, experience, and conduct of the accused. Muniz v. State, 851 S.W.2d 238 (Tex. Crim. App. 1993), *citing* Johnson v. Zerbst, 304 U.S. 458, 58 S.Ct. 1019, 82 L.Ed.2d 1461 (1938).

§6:42.1.3 Waivers in Written Statements

For a written statement to unambiguously meet the waiver requirements of CCP Art. 38.22 §2(b), the preferable practice is for the statement to contain the following language, near or adjacent to the signature of the individual giving the statement: "I knowingly, voluntarily and intelligently waived the rights described above before and during the making of this statement." Garcia v. State, 919 S.W.2d 370, 387 (Tex. Crim. App. 1994).

The phrase, "I do hereby voluntarily waive these rights," on each page of a written confession has been found to constitute a valid waiver. Cockrell v. State, 933 S.W.2d 73 (Tex. Crim. App. 1996).

Where a written confession of defendant does not contain any statement whatever to the effect that defendant, prior to making the statement, voluntarily, knowingly, and intelligently waived his rights, the confession should not be admitted in evidence. Thibedeaux v. State, 729 S.W.2d 137, 139 (Tex.App.—Beaumont 1987, *pet. ref'd*).

However, the circumstances of the taking of the statement along with other writings and recitations can add up to the conclusion that the defendant executed a valid waiver of his rights. Garcia, 919 S.W.2d at 387.

§6:42.2 Voluntariness of Waivers

§6:42.2.1 Voluntariness of Waivers Under Miranda

For purposes of the Fifth Amendment, waiver of the privilege against compelled self-incrimination during custodial questioning can be deemed involuntary only if it is a product of official coercion, intimidation, or deception. Leza v. State, 351 S.W.3d 344, 352 (Tex. Crim. App. 2011).

Where a defendant's drug intoxication is not due to any causative action on the part of the police, his assertion that his intoxication rendered his Miranda waiver involuntary is foreclosed as a matter of federal constitutional law because the Fifth Amendment privilege against self-incrimination is not concerned with moral and psychological pressures to confess emanating from sources other than official coercion. Leza, 351 S.W.3d at 350.

Drug intoxication can, however, be a factor that is relevant to determining whether a Miranda waiver was knowing and intelligent. Leza, 351 S.W.3d at 351.

On direct appeal, the courts measure the propriety of the trial court's ruling with respect to alleged Miranda violations under the totality of the circumstances, almost wholly deferring to the trial court on questions of historical fact and credibility, but reviewing *de novo* all questions of law and mixed questions of law and fact that do not turn on credibility determinations. Leza, 351 S.W.3d at 349.

§6:42.2.2 Voluntariness of Waivers Under Art. 38.22

A claim that a purported waiver of the state statutory rights enumerated in Article 38.22 is involuntary need not be predicated on police overreaching. Leza v. State, 351 S.W.3d 344, 349 (Tex. Crim. App. 2011) (citing Oursbourn v. State, 259 S.W.3d 159, 172 (Tex. Crim. App. 2008)).

Circumstances not attributable to the police that nevertheless adversely impact an accused's ability to resist reasonable police entreaties to waive his statutory rights, such as intoxication, are factors in the voluntariness inquiry, though they are usually not enough, by themselves, to render a statement inadmissible under Article 38.22. Leza, 351 S.W.3d at 352 (citing Oursbourn, 259 S.W.3d at 172).

Drug intoxication can be a factor that is relevant to determining whether a waiver of statutory rights under Art. 38.22 was made knowingly and intelligently. Leza, 351 S.W.3d at 351.

Claims of involuntariness under Art. 38.22 can be, but need not be, predicated on police overreaching. Claims of involuntariness that are not themselves relevant to due process claims could involve sweeping inquiries into the state of mind of a criminal defendant who has confessed. Oursbourn, 259 S.W.3d at 172.

§6:42.2.3 Jury Charge on the Voluntariness Issue

§6:42.2.3.1 Jury Charges and Miranda Issues

Due process and Miranda claims may warrant both general and specific voluntariness jury instructions; while Texas statutory claims warrant only a general voluntariness jury instruction. It is the defendant's responsibility to delineate which type of "involuntariness" he is claiming—a general (perhaps subjective) lack of voluntariness or a specific police-coerced lack of voluntariness—because the jury instruction is very different depending upon the type of claim. Oursbourn v. State, 259 S.W.3d 159, 174 (Tex. Crim. App. 2008).

A statement that is involuntary as a matter of constitutional law is also involuntary under Article 38.22, but the converse need not be true. Oursbourn, 259 S.W.3d at 169.

Because the failure of police to honor a defendant's rights under Miranda is not itself a constitutional violation, a defendant is not entitled to an Art. 38.23 charge when evidence at trial shows that the police did not comply with Miranda. Under these circumstances, the defendant is entitled to a charge under Art. 38.22. Contreras v. State, 312 S.W.3d 566 (Tex. Crim. App. 2010).

§6:42.2.3.2 Charging Art. 38.22 Issues

The obvious purpose of Art. 38.22, §7 is to authorize and require jury instructions regarding the warnings and safeguards for written and oral statements outlined in Article 38.22, §§2 and 3 (warnings on the right to remain silent, right to counsel, etc). Oursbourn v. State, 259 S.W.3d 159, 175 (Tex. Crim. App. 2008).

As with §6, the trial judge's §7 jury instructions are general ones that set out the pertinent law and legal requirements of §§2 and 3 (or, in an appropriate case, those of Article 15.17). Oursbourn, 259 S.W.3d at 176.

The §7 instruction sets out the requirements of 38.22, §2 or §3 and asks the jury to decide whether all of those requirements were met. Oursbourn, 259 S.W.3d at 173.

The issue to be decided is whether there was compliance with the statutory warnings set out in both Articles 15.17 (Duties of Arresting Officer and Magistrate) and 38.22, §§2 and 3, and the voluntariness of the defendant's waiver of these rights. For the issue to be raised by the evidence there must be a genuine factual dispute, just as is true under Article 38.23 issues. Oursbourn, 259 S.W.3d at 176.

The same procedures—including a hearing outside the presence of the jury and the entry of written findings—that apply to a general voluntariness challenge under §6, also apply to a challenge that is made to the sufficiency of warnings and voluntary waiver of the rights communicated by those warnings. Oursbourn, 259 S.W.3d at 176.

§6:43 Invocation and Waiver of Specific Rights

§6:43.1 Invocation and Waiver of Right to Remain Silent

§6:43.1.1 General Rules on Invocation of Right to Remain Silent

Persons subject to questioning by law enforcement officers have a right to remain silent. Miranda and CCP Art. 38.22. Before these persons are questioned they have a right to be warned that they have such right. Miranda and CCP Art. 38.22.

The failure of law enforcement to cut off questioning when a suspect invokes his right to remain silent renders any subsequent statement inadmissible. Dowthitt v. State, 931 S.W.2d 244 (Tex. Crim. App. 1996) (citing Michigan v. Mosley, 423 U.S. 96, 96 S.Ct. 321, 46 L.Ed.2d 313 (1975)).

The suspect's right to remain silent must be scrupulously honored. The failure to scrupulously honor this right will result in the suppression of a resulting confession. Michigan v. Mosley.

A law enforcement agent is not required to cease his questioning of a suspect unless the suspect's invocation of his right to remain silent is unambiguous. Dowthitt; citing Davis v. United States, 512 U.S. 452, 114 S.Ct. 2350, 129 L.Ed.2d 362 (1994); Berghuis v. Thompkins, 560 U.S. ___, 130 S.Ct. 2250, 176 L.Ed.2d 1098 (2010).

A law enforcement agent is not required to clarify ambiguous remarks, but may continue to question in order to do so. Dowthitt.

§6:43.1.2 Sufficient Invocation of Right to Remain Silent

Where a suspect tells an interrogating officer that he doesn't want to talk to him and doesn't want to talk about it anymore, he has sufficiently invoked his right to remain silent. Ramos v. State, 245 S.W.3d 410 (Tex. Crim. App. 2007).

A suspect's statement that he "didn't see how he could help himself by talking to [officers]," has been found to be a sufficient invocation of the right to remain silent. Murphy v. State, 766 S.W.2d 246 (Tex. Crim. App. 1989).

A suspect's statement to police when asked if he wished to discuss an offense that he "wanted a little time" to think about the matter, has been found to be a sufficient invocation of the right to remain silent. Phillips v. State, 701 S.W.2d 875 (Tex. Crim. App. 1985).

No magic word or phrase is necessary to invoke the right to remain silent. Prolonged silence and lack of cooperation with authorities will serve to invoke it. Watson v. State, 762 S.W.2d 591 (Tex. Crim. App. 1988).

Where the defendant concluded his handwritten statement with the phrase, "I have nothing else to say," he validly invoked his right to remain silent. Autry v. State, 626 S.W.2d 758 (Tex. Crim. App. 1982).

§6:43.1.3 Insufficient Invocation of Right to Remain Silent

A law enforcement agent is not required to cease questioning of a suspect unless the suspect's invocation of his right to remain silent is unambiguous. Dowthitt v. State, 931 S.W.2d 244 (Tex. Crim. App. 1996), citing Davis v. United States, 512 U.S. 452, 114 S.Ct. 2350, 129 L.Ed.2d 362 (1994).

A suspect's statement that "I can't say any more than that. I need to rest," is not an unambiguous invocation of the right to remain silent. Dowthitt.

A suspect's statement that "[m]aybe I should talk to someone," is not an unambiguous invocation of the right to remain silent. Dinkins v. State, 894 S.W.2d 330 (Tex. Crim. App. 1995).

§6:43.1.4 Valid Waivers of Right to Remain Silent

A voluntary, knowing, and intelligent waiver of the right to remain silent must be proven by a preponderance of the evidence. Robinson v. State, 851 S.W.2d 216 (Tex. Crim. App. 1991) (citing Colorado v. Connelly, 479 U.S. 157, 107 S.Ct. 515, 93 L.Ed.2d 473 (1986)).

§6:43.2 Invocation and Waiver of Right to Attorney

§6:43.2.1 Fifth Amendment Right to Attorney

The Fifth Amendment right to counsel is the right to interrogation counsel. Pecina v. State, 361 S.W.3d 68 (Tex. Crim. App. 2012) (citing Montejo v. Louisiana, 556 U.S. 778, 129 S.Ct. 2079, 173 L.Ed.2d 955 (2009)).

The Fifth Amendment right to interrogation counsel is triggered by the Miranda warnings that police must give before beginning any custodial questioning. Pecina; Montejo.

The Fifth Amendment right to counsel applies to post-magistration custodial interrogation. Pecina.

A suspect undergoing custodial interrogation has the right to the assistance of counsel in his dealings with law enforcement agents. This right includes both the right to consult with a lawyer prior to questioning, as well as the right to have a lawyer present during questioning. Miranda v. Arizona, 384 U.S. 436, 86 S.Ct. 1602, 16 L.Ed.2d 694 (1966); CCP Art. 38.22 §2.

A request for counsel that is ambiguous in scope will be afforded a broad rather than a narrow interpretation. Smith v. State, 779 S.W.2d 417 (Tex. Crim. App. 1989); citing Connecticut v. Barrett, 479 U.S. 523, 107 S.Ct. 828, 93 L.Ed.2d 920 (1987).

Further questioning of the suspect may be permitted for the limited purpose of clarifying an equivocal invocation of the right to counsel. Smith v. State; Jamail v. State, 787 S.W.2d 372 (Tex. Crim. App. 1990).

However, where the invocation of the right to counsel is clear, a suspect's post-request responses to further interrogation may not be used to cast retrospective doubt on the clarity of the initial request itself. Smith v. State, citing Smith v. Illinois, 469 U.S. 91, 105 S.Ct. 490, 83 L.Ed.2d 488 (1984).

A suspect who has expressed his desire to deal with the police only through counsel is not subject to further interrogation by the authorities until counsel has been made available to him, unless the accused himself initiates further communication, exchanges, or conversations with the police. Edwards v. Arizona, 451 U.S. 477, 484–485, 101 S.Ct. 1880, 1884–1885, 68 L.Ed.2d 378 (1981).

The Edwards rule holds true whether a contemplated reinterrogation concerns the same or a different offense, or whether the same or different law enforcement authorities are involved in the second investigation; under any scenario, the suspect's invocation of his Fifth Amendment rights bars any further interrogation. Arizona v. Roberson, 486 U.S. 675, 688, 108 S.Ct. 2093, 2101, 100 L.Ed.2d 704 (1988).

Once an accused has invoked his right to counsel, he may not be subjected to further interrogation until counsel is actually present, unless the accused himself initiates contact with the authorities. Murphy v. State, 801 S.W.2d 917 (Tex. Crim. App. 1991), citing Minnick v. Mississippi, 498 U.S. 46, 111 S.Ct. 486, 112 L.Ed.2d 489 (1990). This is true even where the accused has consulted with counsel in the interim. Murphy; Minnick.

Where a suspect has invoked his right to counsel, his rights are violated when police continue interrogation. Whether police reinitiation of contact with the suspect amounts to the functional equivalent of interrogation is judged on the basis of the definition of "interrogation" set out in Rhode Island v. Innis (446 U.S. 291, 100 S.Ct. 1682, 64 L.Ed.2d 297 (1980)). Moran v. State, 213 S.W.3d 917 (Tex. Crim. App. 2007).

This definition of "interrogation" focuses primarily upon the perceptions of the suspect, rather than the intent of the police. Moran (citing Innis).

Where the defendant omits mention of the actions of the police and gives another reason for his continued cooperation with police in his suppression motion testimony, these factors will support a finding that he did not subjectively feel that the police were further interrogating him. Moran.

Under certain narrow circumstances, interrogation may continue where an accused has invoked a limited right to counsel accompanied by an affirmative statement expressing his willingness to otherwise go forward with the interview. Hicks v. State, 860 S.W.2d 419 (Tex. Crim. App. 1993) (citing Connecticut v. Barrett).

A circumstance under which officers may reapproach a suspect who has invoked his right to counsel is that in which officers reapproach to question about a different offense, provided that the suspect's original invocation must have been only as to the specific offense under discussion at the time of the invocation. Arizona v. Roberson, 486 U.S. 675, 108 S.Ct. 2093, 100 L.Ed.2d 704 (1988).

Events occurring outside the presence of the suspect and entirely unknown to him can have no bearing on his capacity to comprehend and knowingly relinquish a constitutional right. Fuller v. State, 253 S.W.3d 220 (Tex. Crim. App. 2008).

Police conduct such as not informing the suspect that his family has retained an attorney for him is irrelevant to the inquiry into the effectiveness of the suspect's waiver of counsel, absent a showing that such conduct prevented the suspect from attaining awareness and comprehension of the information conveyed in the Miranda warnings and the consequences of abandoning those rights. Terrell v. State, 891 S.W.2d 307, 311 (Tex.App.—El Paso 1994, *pet. ref'd*) (citing Moran v Burbine).

One officer's knowledge that a defendant has requested counsel is imputed to every other state agent. Herron v. State, 86 S.W.3d 621, 628 (Tex. Crim. App. 2002) (citing Arizona v. Roberson, 486 U.S. 675, 687-88, 108 S.Ct. 2093, 100 L.Ed.2d 704 (1988)).

Whether a resumption of questioning after a refusal to talk is consistent with scrupulously honoring the right to remain silent depends on the facts of each case. Five factors are considered when examining whether rights were scrupulously honored:

- Whether the suspect was informed of the right to remain silent before the first questioning;
- Whether the suspect was informed of the right to remain silent before the subsequent questioning;
- The length of time between the first and subsequent questioning;
- If the subsequent questioning focused on a different crime; and
- Whether police scrupulously honored the suspect's initial invocation of the right to silence (resolution of this issue does not turn on an evaluation of credibility and demeanor). Michigan v. Mosley, 423 U.S. 96, 96 S.Ct. 321, 46 L.Ed.2d 313 (1975); Maestas; Maestas v. State, 987 S.W.2d 59 (Tex. Crim. App.1999); Herron v. State, 86 S.W.3d 621 (Tex. Crim. App. 2002).

§6:43.2.2 Sixth Amendment Right to Attorney

The Sixth Amendment right to counsel is the right to trial counsel. Pecina v. State, 361 S.W.3d 68 (Tex. Crim. App. 2012) (citing Montejo v. Louisiana, 556 U.S. 778, 129 S.Ct. 2079, 173 L.Ed.2d 955 (2009)).

The Sixth Amendment right to trial counsel is triggered by judicial arraignment or magistration conducted under Code of Criminal Procedure Art. 15.17; and it guarantees a defendant the right to have counsel present at all critical stages of the criminal proceedings. Pecina; Montejo.

Generally, an Article 15.17 initial appearance and magistration marks the initiation of adversarial judicial proceedings in Texas and plainly signals the attachment of a defendant's Sixth Amendment right to counsel. Pecina.

Thus, a Sixth Amendment request for an attorney at an arraignment, initial appearance, or Article 15.17 hearing is a request for the guiding hand of counsel for all judicial criminal proceedings. Pecina.

However, a defendant's invocation of his right to counsel at his arraignment or initial appearance says nothing about his possible invocation of his right to counsel during later police-initiated custodial interrogation. The magistration hearing is not an interrogation event. A defendant who has been arraigned may invoke his Sixth Amendment right to counsel for purposes of custodial interrogation when the police or other law enforcement agents approach him and give him his Miranda warnings. Pecina.

This is because the Sixth Amendment right to counsel applies to post-magistration custodial interrogation. Pecina.

After formal adversary proceedings have begun, the Sixth Amendment right to counsel applies in exactly the same way as the Fifth Amendment right applies to custodial interrogation. Thus, Miranda warnings serve the arrestee's interests in both the Fifth and Sixth Amendment rights to counsel during custodial interrogations conducted after a person has been formally charged. Pecina.

A defendant also has a right to counsel under the Sixth Amendment at any critical stage. *See* Montejo v. Louisiana, 556 U.S. ___, 129 S.Ct. 2079, 173 L.Ed.2d 955 (2009) (overruling Michigan v. Jackson, 475 U.S. 625, 106 S.Ct. 1404, 89 L.Ed.2d 631 (1986)).

The Sixth Amendment does not bar police-initiated interrogation of an accused who has previously asserted his right to counsel during a magistrate's warning. Montejo v. Louisiana; Hughen v. State, 297 S.W.3d 330 (Tex. Crim. App. 2009).

§6:43.2.3 Sixth Amendment Violations

Where a defendant has counsel representing him on a charge, before law enforcement can question him on a factually interwoven charge they are under an obligation to contact his attorney and gain his permission. State v. Frye, 897 S.W.2d 324 (Tex. Crim. App. 1995); Upton v. State, 853 S.W.2d 548 (Tex. Crim. App. 1993). Note: Both Frye and Upton were decided based on Michigan v. Jackson, 475 U.S. 625, 106 S.Ct. 1404, 89 L.Ed.2d 631 (1986) now overruled by Montejo v. Louisiana, 556 U.S. __ , 129 S.Ct. 2079, 173 L.Ed.2d 955 (2009).

If police initiate interrogation after a defendant's invocation of his right to counsel at any critical stage of the proceeding, any alleged waiver of his right to counsel is invalid under the Sixth Amendment. Montejo v. Louisiana.

The Sixth Amendment does not bar police-initiated interrogation of an accused who has previously asserted his right to counsel during a magistrate's warning where litigation has not reached a critical stage. Montejo v. Louisiana; Hughen v. State, 297 S.W.3d 330 (Tex. Crim. App. 2009).

The defendant can unilaterally waive his Sixth Amendment right to counsel where he initiates the communication with law enforcement. *See* Michigan v. Harvey, 494 U.S. 344, 110 S.Ct. 1176, 108 L.Ed.2d 293 (1990); Ripkowski v. State, 61 S.W.3d 378 (Tex. Crim. App. 2001); State v. Maldonado, 259 S.W.3d 184 (Tex. Crim. App. 2008). Note: Cases were decided based on Michigan v. Jackson, 475 U.S. 625, 106 S.Ct. 1404, 89 L.Ed.2d 631 (1986) (now overruled by Montejo v. Louisiana).

Where the police officer merely introduced himself to a defendant, and the defendant then presented the officer with a letter and said that he had been waiting to talk to somebody, the defendant was found to have initiated the communication with police. Maldonado.

An accused is denied the basic protections of the Sixth Amendment when there is used against him at his trial evidence of his own incriminating words deliberately elicited from him by law enforcement agents after he had been indicted and in the absence of counsel. Fellers v. U.S., 540 U.S. 519, 124 S.Ct. 1019, 157 L.Ed.2d 1016 (2004).

The deliberate-elicitation test is consistently applied in Sixth Amendment cases; as opposed to the custodial interrogation test applied in Fifth Amendment cases. Fellers.

The Sixth Amendment does not forbid the use of statements taken in violation where they are offered for impeachment purposes only. This is because the constitutional violation occurs at the time the statement is elicited, not when it is offered at trial for impeachment purposes. Kansas v. Ventris, 556 U.S. 586, 129 S.Ct. 1841, 173 L.Ed.2d 801 (2009).

Where the state recorded the defendant's telephone calls from jail to his attorney, a Sixth Amendment violation requiring dismissal of the indictment was not established absent evidence that the defendant was prejudiced by the State obtaining information which led to admissible evidence against the defendant or obtaining any information that would give the State a tactical advantage. Woodruff v. State, 330 S.W.3d 709 (Tex.App.—Texarkana, 2010, *pet. ref'd*).

§6:43.2.4 Sufficient Invocation of Right To Attorney

Whether or not an accused has sufficiently invoked his right to counsel is measured on a totality of the circumstances basis. Smith v. State, 779 S.W.2d 417 (Tex. Crim. App. 1989).

The phrase "I don't want to give up any right, though, if I don't got no lawyer," is an unequivocal invocation of right to counsel. State v. Gobert, 275 S.W.3d 888 (Tex. Crim. App. 2009).

Where a suspect simply asks for "his attorney," he has sufficiently invoked his right to counsel. Smith v. State, 779 S.W.2d 417 (Tex. Crim. App. 1989).

The statement "I don't want to answer those questions without my lawyer," accompanied by statements such as "No answer" and "I don't want to answer that," is sufficient to invoke the right to counsel. Hicks v. State, 860 S.W.2d 419 (Tex. Crim. App. 1993).

The phrase "I think I want a lawyer" is sufficient to invoke the right to counsel. Jones v. State, 742 S.W.2d 398 (Tex. Crim. App. 1982).

A formal or absolute demand for an attorney is not required to sufficiently invoke the right. All that is necessary is that the suspect indicates in some manner to authorities that he wishes to exercise his right. Ochoa v. State, 573 S.W.2d 796 (Tex. Crim. App. 1978).

Where the suspect surrenders to authorities in the presence of his attorney and advises them through his attorney that he did not wish to be questioned in the absence of counsel, he sufficiently invoked his right to counsel. Stone v. State, 612 S.W.2d 542 (Tex. Crim. App. 1981).

§6:43.2.5 Reinitiation of Contact by Accused

If an accused expresses his desire to deal with the police only through counsel, he is not subject to further interrogation by authorities until counsel has been made available to him; unless the accused himself initiates further communications, exchanges, or conversations with the police. Herron v. State, 86 S.W.3d 621, 628 (Tex. Crim. App. 2002); citing Edwards v. Arizona, 451 U.S. 477, 101 S.Ct. 1880, 68 L.Ed.2d 378 (1981).

Where the suspect has invoked his right to remain silent, he may only be reapproached in a manner that scrupulously honors his continuing right to cut off questioning. Murphy v. State, 766 S.W.2d 246 (Tex. Crim. App. 1989); citing Michigan v. Mosley, 423 U.S. 96, 96 S.Ct. 321, 46 L.Ed.2d 313 (1975).

A passage of time and the repeating of the suspect's Miranda rights are two factors in determining if the right to remain silent has been scrupulously honored. Murphy.

Where the police continue to question the suspect after the invocation of the right to remain silent in an effort to persuade him to change his mind, the right has not been scrupulously honored. Hearne v. State, 534 S.W.2d 703 (Tex. Crim. App. 1976). *See also*, Faulder v. State, 611 S.W.2d 630 (Tex. Crim. App. 1979); Dowthitt v. State, 931 S.W.2d 244 (Tex. Crim. App. 1996).

Even if the defendant validly invokes his right to an attorney, he can later waive the right by resuming conversations with officers of his own volition. Etheridge v. State, 903 S.W.2d 1 (Tex. Crim. App. 1994).

A defendant who has invoked his Fifth Amendment right to counsel can later waive that right by reinitiating contact with law enforcement authorities. Hicks v. State, 860 S.W.2d 419 (Tex. Crim. App. 1993); citing Edwards v. Arizona, 451 U.S. 477, 101 S.Ct. 1880, 68 L.Ed.2d 378 (1981). *See also*, Baldree v. State, 784 S.W.2d 676 (Tex. Crim. App. 1989).

When a suspect has invoked his right to counsel, but then voluntarily reinitiates conversation with the police and expressly waives his right to counsel, the Edwards rule has been satisfied and police are free to directly deal with the suspect until a subsequent invocation. Cross v. State, 144 S.W.3d 521 (Tex. Crim. App. 2004).

A valid waiver of the Fifth Amendment right will not be found by showing only that he responded to further police-initiated custodial interrogation. Hicks, citing Edwards v. Arizona.

The circumstances must show that the accused initiated the conversation by remarks which fairly can be said to represent a desire to open up a more generalized discussion relating directly or indirectly to the investigation. Oregon v. Bradshaw, 462 U.S. 1039, 103 S.Ct. 2830, 77 L.Ed.2d 405 (1983) (*plurality op.*). Where after invoking his right to remain silent, a suspect asked a police officer, "[w]ell, what is going to happen to me now?" he was found to have reinitiated contact such that officers could begin interrogation. Bradshaw.

A suspect's statement that, "I'm ready. I told you I would tell you about it if you would let me talk to [the attorney]," constituted a valid reinitiation of contact where the suspect had, in fact, talked to the attorney. Mays v. State, 726 S.W.2d 937 (Tex. Crim. App. 1986).

After reinitiating conversation with the police, the suspect must also validly waive the right to counsel. Oregon v. Bradshaw.

A suspect is deemed to have waived his previously-invoked right to counsel only when (1) the suspect himself initiates further communication with police, and (2) after he re-initiates communication with police, the suspect validly waives the right to counsel. Oregon v. Bradshaw.

Once communication is reinitiated, police are free to reinitiate any future communications and obtain any further statements as long as each statement is voluntarily made after the waiver of Miranda rights. Cross.

Federal constitutional law does not prohibit the police from clarifying whether a suspect wishes to waive his rights in a situation where the suspect has reinitiated contact with police after earlier invoking his rights. Marshall v. State, 210 S.W.3d 618 (Tex. Crim. App. 2006).

Where the police officer merely introduced himself to a defendant, and the defendant then presented the officer with a letter and said that he had been waiting to talk to somebody, the defendant was found to have initiated the communication with police. State v. Maldonado, 259 S.W.3d 184 (Tex. Crim. App. 2008).

A suspect's post-invocation request for a polygraph examination is a sufficient reinitiation of contact to allow further interrogation. Wyrick v. Fields, 459 U.S. 42, 103 S.Ct. 394, 74 L.Ed.2d 214 (1982).

The question, "[h]ow is everyone in Georgia doing?" asked by the defendant to police officers investigating his case, constituted initiation of further communication with police following invocation of the Fifth Amendment by the defendant. Janecka v. State, 739 S.W.2d 813 (Tex. Crim. App. 1987).

Where the defendant asked for counsel at his arraignment then was immediately asked if he wanted to speak to detectives, he did not unilaterally reinitiate communications with police as required by the Edwards rule. Pecina v. State, 268 S.W.3d 564 (Tex. Crim. App. 2008).

The Edwards rule is inapplicable where the defendant has experienced a break in Miranda custody for a period of at least 14 days before he is re-approached by law enforcement officers. Maryland v. Shatzer, 559 U.S. ___, 130 S.Ct. 1213, 175 L.Ed.2d 1045 (2010) (where the defendant's release into the general prison population constituted a "break in custody").

A circumstance under which officers may reapproach a suspect who has invoked his right to counsel is that in which officers reapproach to question about a different offense, provided that the suspect's original invocation must have been as to the specific offense under discussion at the time of the invocation. Arizona v. Roberson, 486 U.S. 675, 108 S.Ct. 2093, 100 L.Ed.2d 704 (1988).

§6:43.2.6 Insufficient Invocation of Right to Attorney

A suspect's question, "[d]o I need to talk to a lawyer before I sign?" is not a sufficient invocation of the right to remain silent. Robinson v. State, 851 S.W.2d 216 (Tex. Crim. App. 1991).

A suspect's statement in a letter to a sheriff that, "I'm here in by myself and still can't talk to a lawyer on this," is not a sufficient invocation of the right to counsel. Lucas v. State, 791 S.W.2d 35 (Tex. Crim. App. 1989).

A suspect's statement that, "[m]aybe I should talk to someone," is not a sufficient invocation of the right to counsel. Dinkins v. State, 894 S.W.2d 330 (Tex. Crim. App. 1995).

The defendant's statement, "I should have an attorney," was not an unambiguous request for an attorney under the totality of the circumstances. Davis v. State, 313 S.W.3d 317 (Tex. Crim. App. 2010).

A suspect's inquiry as to whether he would have a lawyer appointed to him upon reaching another city, when the inquiry dealt with charges pending in that other city is an insufficient invocation of the right to counsel. Collins v. State, 727 S.W.2d 565 (Tex. Crim. App. 1987).

Where the suspect at first invokes his right to counsel then voluntarily withdraws the invocation in the absence of interrogation, there is a valid waiver. Muniz v. State, 851 S.W.2d 238 (Tex. Crim. App. 1993) (where defendant stated, "No, I will talk to him later" when the officer began to dial the attorney's telephone number).

The defendant's refusal to sign the bottom of a magistrate warning form does not constitute the invocation of the right to counsel. Jacobs v. State, 787 S.W.2d 397 (Tex. Crim. App. 1990).

Where the suspect merely told his brother and grandmother to contact his attorney, even when done in the presence of a law enforcement officer, he did not sufficiently personally invoke his right to an attorney. Casias v. State, 678 S.W.2d 140 (Tex. App.—Waco 1984, *no pet.*).

Likewise, a defendant's request of a friend to call the defendant's attorney is not a sufficient invocation of the right to counsel. Nichols v. State, 754 S.W.2d 185 (Tex. Crim. App. 1988).

§6:43.2.7 Invocation of Right by Suspect's Attorney

The circumstances under which an attorney may invoke a client's Fifth Amendment rights are:

- Attorney-client relationship exists
- Attorney invokes the right after conferring with the client or in the client's presence
- Accused does nothing to contradict the attorney, and
- Officers agree not to question the accused in the attorney's absence

Janecka v. State, 739 S.W.2d 813 (Tex. Crim. App. 1987).

Efforts by an attorney, occurring outside the presence of the defendant and entirely unknown to him, do not constitute an invocation of his right to counsel. Fuller v. State, 253 S.W.3d 220 (Tex. Crim. App. 2008) (citing Moran v. Burbine, 475 U.S. 412, 106 S.Ct. 1135, 89 L.Ed.2d 410 (1986)).

§6:43.2.8 Valid Waivers of Right to Attorney

A voluntary, knowing, and intelligent waiver of the right to remain silent must be proven by a preponderance of the evidence. Robinson v. State, 851 S.W.2d 216 (Tex. Crim. App. 1991) (citing Colorado v. Connelly, 479 U.S. 157, 107 S.Ct. 515, 93 L.Ed.2d 473 (1986)).

If the prosecution shows that a suspect's decision not to rely on his Miranda rights was not coerced, that he at all times knew he could stand mute and consult a lawyer, and that he was aware the State could use his statement against him, the State's burden of proof is met and waiver is shown as a matter of law. Robinson (citing Moran v. Burbine, 475 U.S. 412, 106 S.Ct. 1135, 89 L.Ed.2d 410 (1986)).

Under certain narrow circumstances, interrogation may continue where an accused has invoked a limited right to counsel accompanied by an affirmative statement expressing his willingness to otherwise go forward with the interview. Hicks v. State, 860 S.W.2d 419 (Tex. Crim. App. 1993) (citing Connecticut v. Barrett, 479 U.S. 523, 107 S.Ct. 828, 93 L.Ed.2d 920 (1987)).

Where a suspect invokes his right to counsel only as to a "formal" statement, interrogation may continue informally, and the suspect may later fully waive the right to counsel by informing law enforcement officers that he wishes to make a "formal" statement without benefit of counsel. Corwin v. State, 870 S.W.2d 23 (Tex. Crim. App. 1993).

A suspect's statement to officer that, "I'm ready. I told you I would tell you about it if you would let me talk to [the attorney]," was a sufficient waiver of his rights (and also constituted a reinitiation of contact with officers). Mays v. State, 726 S.W.2d 937 (Tex. Crim. App. 1986).

§6:43.2.9 Invalid Waivers of Right to Attorney

The mere failure of the suspect to invoke his rights is not a valid waiver thereof. Miranda v. Arizona, 384 U.S. 436, 86 S.Ct. 1602, 16 L.Ed.2d 694 (1966).

Waivers will not be presumed from silence. Miranda.

Where a suspect did not expressly waive his rights and did not indicate that he had ceased to rely on an agreement with police to not question him in his attorney's absence, a resulting confession was involuntarily made. Stone v. State, 612 S.W.2d 542 (Tex. Crim. App. 1981).

Where the written confession of defendant does not contain any statement whatever to the effect that defendant, prior to making the statement, voluntarily, knowingly, and intelligently waived his rights, the confession should not have been admitted in evidence. Thibedeaux v. State, 729 S.W.2d 137 (Tex.App.—Beaumont 1987, *pet. ref'd*).

§6:43.3 Right to Terminate Interrogation

§6:43.3.1 In General

A defendant has the right to terminate a custodial interrogation with law enforcement at any time. Miranda v. Arizona, 384 U.S. 436, 86 S.Ct. 1602, 16 L.Ed.2d 694 (1966); CCP Art. 38.22.

A suspect's invocation of the right to terminate the interrogation must be scrupulously honored. The failure to scrupulously honor this right will result in the suppression of a resulting confession. Michigan v. Mosley, 423 U.S. 96, 96 S.Ct. 321, 46 L.Ed.2d 313 (1975); Faulder v. State, 611 S.W.2d 630 (Tex. Crim. App. 1979).

Where a suspect has invoked his right to remain silent, he may only be re-approached in a manner that scrupulously honors his continuing right to cut off questioning. Murphy v. State, 766 S.W.2d 246 (Tex. Crim. App. 1989), citing Michigan v. Mosley.

Whether a resumption of questioning after a refusal to talk is consistent with scrupulously honoring the right to remain silent depends on the facts of each case. Five factors are considered when examining whether rights were scrupulously honored:

- Whether the suspect was informed of the right to remain silent before the first questioning;
- Whether the suspect was informed of the right to remain silent before the subsequent questioning;
- The length of time between the first and subsequent questioning;
- If the subsequent questioning focused on a different crime; and
- Whether police scrupulously honored the suspect's initial invocation of the right to silence (resolution of this issue does not turn on an evaluation of credibility and demeanor). Michigan v. Mosley, 423 U.S. 96, 96 S.Ct. 321, 46 L.Ed.2d 313 (1975); Maestas; Maestas v. State, 987 S.W.2d 59 (Tex. Crim. App.1999); Herron v. State, 86 S.W.3d 621 (Tex. Crim. App. 2002).

§6:43.4 Right to Contact Consulate

The Vienna Convention on Consular Relations grants a foreign national who has been arrested, imprisoned or taken into custody the right to contact his consulate and requires the arresting government authorities to inform the individual of this right "without delay." Vienna Convention, Art. 36(1)(b), 21 U.S.T. at 100-101; 595 U.N.T.S. at 292; Maldonado v. State, 998 S.W.2d 239 (Tex. Crim. App. 1999).

However, if the Vienna treaty is not followed in the case of a foreign national, CCP Art. 38.23 does not require the exclusion of a resulting confession because a treaty violation is not a "law" violation under CCP Art. 38.23. Rocha v. State, 16 S.W.3d 1 (Tex. Crim. App. 2000).

Several courts have held that the Vienna Convention does not create individually enforceable rights. Sorto v. State, 173 S.W.3d 469 (Tex. Crim. App. 2005).

In order to prevail on a Vienna Convention treaty violation claim, the defendant must show a causal connection between the violation and his resulting confession. Sorto.

Where the evidence shows that law enforcement officers faxed notice to the defendant's consulate within 48 hours of his arrest, the defendant has failed to show a deliberate delay under the treaty. Sorto.

Even if the Vienna Convention treaty creates a judicially enforceable right (which the Court assumed without deciding), suppression of a confession is not an appropriate remedy. Sanchez-Llamas v. Oregon, 548 U.S. 331, 126 S.Ct. 2669, 165 L.Ed.2d 557 (U.S. 2006); Sierra v. State, 218 S.W.3d 85 (Tex. Crim. App. 2007).

PRACTICE TIP: Sanchez-Llamas suggests using the failure of law enforcement to notify the defendant's national consulate as part of a broader attack on the voluntariness of the confession.

The International Court of Justice Avena decision and a subsequent presidential memorandum urging state enforcement of the Avena decision do not constitute binding federal law preempting Art. 11.071, §5 of the Texas Code of Criminal Procedure under the Supremacy Clause of the United States Constitution and neither qualify as a previously unavailable factual or legal basis under §5(a) (1). Ex parte Medellin, 223 S.W.3d 315 (Tex. Crim. App. 2006).

§6:50 Voluntariness of Confessions

Under Texas Code of Criminal Procedure Article 38.21, "A statement of an accused may be used in evidence against him if it appears that the same was freely and voluntarily made without compulsion or persuasion." Oursbourn v. State, 259 S.W.3d 159, 169 (Tex. Crim. App. 2008).

§6:51 In General

Article 38.22 of the Code of Criminal Procedure sets out the rules governing admissibility of a defendant's written and/or oral statement that is the product of custodial interrogation. Oursbourn v. State, 259 S.W.3d 159, 171 (Tex. Crim. App. 2008).

The prosecution is under no burden to prove a confession is voluntary until the defendant presents some evidence raising a question of voluntariness. Terrazas v. State, 4 S.W.3d 720 (Tex. Crim. App. 1999); Romero v. State, 800 S.W.2d 539 (Tex. Crim. App. 1990).

The prosecution must then prove voluntariness by a preponderance of the evidence, when the issue is litigated before the judge as to the admissibility of the statement. Terrazas; Romero.

The state need not rebut a defendant's assertions but only must only controvert them. Muniz v. State, 851 S.W.2d 238 (Tex. Crim. App. 1993).

Voluntariness is determined under a totality of the circumstances test, weighing the particular facts and circumstances of each specific case. Schneckloth v. Bustamonte, 412 U.S. 218, 93 S.Ct. 2041, 36 L.Ed.2d 854 (1973); Mason v. State, 116 S.W.3d 248 (Tex.App.—Houston [14th Dist.] 2003, *pet. ref'd*).

A confession is involuntary or coerced if the totality of the circumstances demonstrate that the confessor did not make the decision to confess of his own free will. Arizona v. Fulminante, 499 U.S. 279, 111 S.Ct. 1246, 113 L.Ed.2d 302 (1991). A finding of coercion need not be based on actual violence by a government agent, a credible threat is sufficient. Fulminante.

Claims of involuntariness under Article 38.22 can be, but need not be, predicated on police overreaching, and they could involve the sweeping inquiries into the state of mind of a criminal defendant who has confessed that are not of themselves relevant to due process claims. Oursbourn, 259 S.W.3d at 172.

The voluntariness determination must be made by the trial court without regard to the truth or falsity of the alleged confession. Rogers v. Richmond, 365 U.S. 524, 81 S.Ct. 735, 5 L.Ed.2d 760 (1961).

In order for a confession to be found voluntary, it does not have to be in the exact language of the defendant. In fact, it can be handwritten by the interrogating officer. Henson v. State, 794 S.W.2d 385 (Tex.App.—Dallas 1990, *pet. ref'd*).

A police officer telling a defendant in a non-custodial setting "what had to be" in her statement is not the type of practice that has been held to be so inherently coercive as to make a statement involuntary. Terrazas.

Circumstances relevant to determining if a confession was voluntarily made include:

- Length of the detention and interrogation
- Whether the defendant was permitted access to family or attorney
- Presence or absence of physical brutality

Lane v. State, 933 S.W.2d 504 (Tex. Crim. App. 1996).

The circumstances support the voluntariness of the confession where:

- Defendant initiated a chain of events leading to his interviews with police
- Defendant initiated numerous attempts to mislead police with false alibis
- Police action was not coercive because the interviews were low-keyed and non-confrontational
- Defendant was repeatedly "Mirandized"

Lane.

Under Articles 38.21 and 38.22, fact scenarios that can raise a state-law claim of involuntariness (even though they do not raise a federal constitutional claim) include the following: (1) the suspect was ill and on medication and that fact may have rendered his confession involuntary; (2) the suspect was mentally retarded and may not have "knowingly, intelligently, and voluntarily" waived his rights; (3) the suspect "lacked the mental capacity to understand his rights"; (4) the suspect was intoxicated, and he "did not know what he was signing and thought it was an accident report"; (5) the suspect was confronted by the brother-in-law of his murder victim and beaten; (6) the suspect was returned to the store he broke into for questioning by several persons armed with six-shooters. Oursbourn, 259 S.W.3d at 172-3.

Although the courts have held that youth, intoxication, mental retardation, and other disabilities are usually not enough, by themselves, to render a statement inadmissible under Article 38.22, they are factors that a jury, armed with a proper instruction, is entitled to consider. Oursbourn, 259 S.W.3d at 173.

A defendant may claim that his statement was not freely and voluntarily made and, thus, may not be used as evidence against him under several different theories: (1) Article 38.22, §6, General Voluntariness; (2) Miranda v. Arizona as expanded in Article 38.22, §§2 and 3 (the Texas Confession Statute); or (3) the Due Process Clause. It may be involuntary under one, two, or all three theories. The theory of involuntariness determines whether and what type of an instruction may be appropriate. Oursbourn, 259 S.W.3d at 169.

Where the voluntariness issue is submitted to the jury, the state's burden is to prove voluntariness beyond a reasonable doubt. Oursbourn, 259 S.W.3d at 175.

Under Texas statutory law, there are three types of jury instructions that relate to the taking of confessions: (1) a "general" Article 38.22, §6 voluntariness instruction; (2) a "general" Article 38.22, §7 warnings instruction (involving warnings given under §§2 and 3); and (3) a "specific" Article 38.23(a) exclusionary-rule instruction. Oursbourn, 259 S.W.3d at 173.

Obviously, the evidence must raise a voluntariness issue, and the defendant should request a jury instruction that relates to his theory of involuntariness. But if the defendant never presents a proposed jury instruction (or fails to object to the lack of one), any potential error in the charge is reviewed only for egregious harm under Almanza; Oursbourn, 259 S.W.3d at 174.

§6:52 Art. 38.22 §6 General Voluntariness Issues

Under Texas Code of Criminal Procedure Art. 38.22 §6, the voluntariness of any statement of an accused can be challenged whether the statement was made in or out of custody. Terrazas v. State, 4 S.W.3d 720 (Tex. Crim. App. 1999); Oursbourn v. State, 259 S.W.3d 159, 171 (Tex. Crim. App. 2008).

When evidence raises an issue of the voluntariness of a defendant's statement under Art. 38.22, the trial judge must give a general voluntariness instruction in the jury charge. Oursbourn, 259 S.W.3d at 175.

This is the sequence of events that seems to be contemplated by §6: (1) a party notifies the trial judge that there is an issue about the voluntariness of the confession (or the trial judge raises the issue on his own); (2) the trial judge holds a hearing outside the presence of the jury; (3) the trial judge decides whether the confession was voluntary; (4) if the trial judge decides that the confession was voluntary, it will be admitted, and a party may offer evidence before the jury suggesting that the confession was not in fact voluntary; (5) if such evidence is offered before the jury, the trial judge shall give the jury a voluntariness instruction. Oursbourn, 259 S.W.3d at 175.

Section 6 expressly dictates the content of that instruction to be as follows: "unless the jury believes beyond a reasonable doubt that the statement was voluntarily made, the jury shall not consider such statement for any purpose nor any evidence obtained as a result thereof." Because §6 contains its own jury-instruction provision, it is not governed by the jury-instruction provision found in §7. Oursbourn, 259 S.W.3d at 175.

An interpretation of §6 that requires some sort of litigation before it becomes law applicable to the case accords not only with the statutory language but also with common sense. The broad range of voluntariness issues covered by §6 could easily be implicated by evidence that would also be relevant for other purposes, and §6 does not even require the existence of a factual dispute that might at least obliquely alert the trial judge to the need for an instruction. The §6 requirement that voluntariness be litigated in some manner before a jury instruction becomes necessary ensures that the trial judge is on notice that the instruction is required. Oursbourn, 259 S.W.3d at 176.

Article 38.22, §6 is "the law applicable" to any case in which a question is raised and litigated as to the general voluntariness of a statement of an accused. Under that statute, the trial judge must then (1) make an independent determination that the statement was made under voluntary conditions; and then (2) instruct the jurors that they shall not consider the statement for any purpose unless they believe, beyond a reasonable doubt, that the statement was made voluntarily. Oursbourn, 259 S.W.3d at 180-1.

Article 38.22 is aimed at protecting suspects from police overreaching. Section 6 of that article also protects people from themselves because the sole focus of the section is upon whether the defendant voluntarily made the statement freely and voluntarily, without compulsion or persuasion. Or, in the case of a custodial-interrogation statement, whether the suspect "knowingly, intelligently, and voluntarily" waived the rights set out in Article 38.22 §2(a) or §(3)(a). These inquiries do not turn solely on police overreaching. The behavior of the police may or may not be a factor. A confession given under the duress of hallucinations, illness, medications, or even a private threat, for example, could be involuntary under Article 38.21 and the Texas confession statute. Oursbourn, 259 S.W.3d at 172.

Thus, a claim that a purported waiver of the statutory rights enumerated in Article 38.22 is involuntary need not be predicated on police overreaching. Leza v. State, 351 S.W.3d 344, 352 (Tex. Crim. App. 2011) (citing Oursbourn, 259 S.W.3d at 172).

Circumstances unattributable to the police that nevertheless adversely impact an accused's ability to resist reasonable police entreaties to waive his statutory rights, such as intoxication, are factors in the voluntariness inquiry, though they are usually not enough, by themselves, to render a statement inadmissible under Article 38.22. Leza, 351 S.W.3d at 352 (citing Oursbourn, 259 S.W.3d at 173).

The exclusion of expert witness testimony that is so general that it has little, if any, relevance to a jury's voluntariness determination is not an abuse of trial court discretion. Lucio v. State, 351 S.W.3d 878, 902 (Tex. Crim. App. 2011).

§6:53 Miranda and Art. 38.22 §§2 and 3 Voluntariness Issues

Sections 2 and 3 of Art. 38.22 apply to a defendant's custodial-interrogation statements and provide that a defendant's custodial-interrogation statement is not admissible unless, prior to making the statement, he received the warnings provided in Art. 15.17 or Art. 38.22, §2(a) or §3(a) (which incorporate the requirements of Miranda), and he knowingly, intelligently, and voluntarily waived those rights. Oursbourn v. State, 259 S.W.3d 159, 171-2 (Tex. Crim. App. 2008).

It is the State's burden to establish a valid waiver of Miranda rights by a preponderance of the evidence. Leza v. State, 351 S.W.3d 344 (Tex. Crim. App. 2011).

There are two facets to any inquiry with respect to the adequacy of a purported waiver of Miranda rights: First, the waiver must be voluntary in the sense that it was the product of a free and deliberate choice rather than intimidation, coercion, or deception. Second the waiver must be made with a full awareness both of the nature of the right being abandoned and the consequences of the decision to abandon it. Leza.

Before it may be said that a waiver of a Miranda right is involuntary, however, there must be some element of official intimidation, coercion, or deception. And, with respect to the requirement that the waiver also be knowing and intelligent, once it is determined that a suspect at all times knew he could stand mute, and that he was aware of the State's intention to use his statements to secure a conviction, the analysis is complete and the waiver is valid as a matter of law. Leza.

It will suffice to render a waiver knowing and intelligent, in other words, that the accused has been made aware, and fully comprehends, that he has the right to remain silent in the face of police interrogation and to discontinue the dialogue at any time, and that the consequence of his waiver is that his words may be used against him later in a court of law. Leza.

A suspect's awareness of all the possible subjects of questioning in advance of interrogation is not relevant to determining whether the suspect voluntarily, knowingly, and intelligently waived his Fifth Amendment privilege under Miranda. Leza (citing Colorado v. Spring, 479 U.S. 564, 577, 107 S.Ct. 851, 93 L.Ed.2d 954 (1987)).

Similarly, the failure to immediately inform a defendant of the subject of the interrogation impacts neither the voluntariness nor the knowing and intelligent nature of any waiver of his statutory rights—as a matter of law. Leza.

Where a defendant's drug intoxication is not due to any causative action on the part of the police, his assertion that his intoxication rendered his Miranda waiver involuntary is foreclosed as a matter of federal constitutional law because the Fifth Amendment privilege against self-incrimination is not concerned with moral and psychological pressures to confess emanating from sources other than official coercion. Leza.

Drug intoxication can, however, be a factor that is relevant to determining whether a Miranda waiver was knowing and intelligent. Leza.

Similarly, drug intoxication can be a factor that is relevant to determining whether a waiver of statutory rights under Art. 38.22 was knowing and intelligent. Leza.

The obvious purpose of Art. 38.22, §7 is to authorize and require jury instructions regarding the warnings and safeguards for written and oral statements outlined in Article 38.22, §2 & §3 (warnings on the right to remain silent, right to counsel, etc). Oursbourn, 259 S.W.3d at 175.

As with §6, the trial judge's §7 jury instructions are general ones that set out the pertinent law and legal requirements of §§2 and 3 (or, in an appropriate case, those of Article 15.17). Oursbourn, 259 S.W.3d at 176.

Due process and Miranda claims may warrant both general and specific voluntariness jury instructions; Texas statutory claims warrant only a general voluntariness jury instruction. It is the defendant's responsibility to delineate which type of "involuntariness" he is claiming—a general (perhaps subjective) lack of voluntariness or a specific police-coerced lack of voluntariness—because the jury instruction is very different depending upon the type of claim. Oursbourn, 259 S.W.3d at 174.

The §7 instruction sets out the requirements of 38.22, §2 or §3 and asks the jury to decide whether all of those requirements were met. Oursbourn, 259 S.W.3d at 173.

The issue to be decided is whether there was compliance with the statutory warnings set out in both Articles 15.17 (Duties of Arresting Officer and Magistrate) and 38.22, §§2 and 3, and the voluntariness of the defendant's waiver of the rights. For the issue to be raised by the evidence there must be a genuine factual dispute, just as is true under Article 38.23 issues. Oursbourn, 259 S.W.3d at 176.

The same procedures—including a hearing outside the presence of the jury and the entry of written findings—that apply to a general voluntariness challenge under §6, also apply to a challenge that is made to the sufficiency of warnings and voluntary waiver of the rights communicated by those warnings. Oursbourn, 259 S.W.3d at 176.

Claims of involuntariness under Art. 38.22 can be, but need not be, predicated on police overreaching. Claims of involuntariness that are not themselves relevant to due process claims could involve sweeping inquiries into the state of mind of a criminal defendant who has confessed. Oursbourn, 259 S.W.3d at 172.

A statement that is involuntary as a matter of constitutional law is also involuntary under Article 38.22, but the converse need not be true. Oursbourn, 259 S.W.3d at 169.

Miranda and its prophylactic safeguards only apply to custodial statements. Wolfe v. State, 917 S.W.2d 270 (Tex. Crim. App. 1996).

There is no violation of a defendant's Miranda rights that apply to custodial-interrogation statements unless there is police misconduct causally related to a waiver of rights. Oursbourn, 259 S.W.3d at 170.

Because the failure of police to honor a defendant's rights under Miranda is not itself a constitutional violation, a defendant is not entitled to an Art. 38.23 charge when evidence at trial shows that the police did not comply with Miranda. Under these circumstances, the defendant is entitled to a charge under Art. 38.22. Contreras v. State, 312 S.W.3d 566 (Tex. Crim. App. 2010).

The failure to administer the Miranda warnings creates a presumption of compulsion and consequently, unwarned statements that are otherwise voluntary within the meaning of the Fifth Amendment must be excluded from evidence under Miranda, but the presumption, though not rebuttable for purposes of the state's case-in-chief, does not require that the statements and their fruits be discarded as inherently tainted. Oregon v. Elstad, 470 U.S. 298, 105 S.Ct. 1285, 84 L.Ed.2d 222 (1985); Baker v. State, 956 S.W.2d 19 (Tex. Crim. App. 1997).

The absence of Miranda warnings does not require the suppression of non-testimonial fruits of a defendant's statement where the statement was made voluntarily and was uncoerced. U.S. v. Patane, 542 U.S. 630, 124 S.Ct. 2620, 159 L.Ed.2d 667 (2004) (*plurality op.*) (where the defendant was prosecuted for possessing a gun that was found as a result of his statement).

Despite the inapplicability of Miranda to confessions obtained by foreign officials, the confession will still be excluded if the circumstances surrounding the taking of the confession shock the conscience of the U.S. court. Alvarado v. State, 853 S.W.2d 17 (Tex. Crim. App. 1991).

On direct appeal, the courts measure the propriety of the trial court's ruling with respect to alleged Miranda violations under the totality of the circumstances, almost wholly deferring to the trial court on questions of historical fact and credibility, but reviewing *de novo* all questions of law and mixed questions of law and fact that do not turn on credibility determinations. Leza.

§6:54 Due Process Issues

Due process may warrant both general and specific voluntariness jury instructions. It is the defendant's responsibility to delineate which type of involuntariness he is claiming—a general (perhaps subjective) lack of voluntariness or a specific police-coerced lack of voluntariness—because the jury instruction is very different depending upon the type of claim. Oursbourn v. State, 259 S.W.3d 159, 174 (Tex. Crim. App. 2008).

A confession may be involuntary under the Due Process Clause only when there is police overreaching. Absent police misconduct causally related to the confession, there is simply no basis for concluding that any state actor has deprived a criminal defendant of due process of law. Oursbourn, 259 S.W.3d at 169-170.

Involuntary confessions offend due process only when they flow from improper conduct of law enforcement officials. Lane v. State, 933 S.W.2d 504 (Tex. Crim. App. 1996).

A statement is involuntary if there was official, coercive conduct of such a nature that any statement obtained thereby was unlikely to have been the product of an essentially free and unconstrained choice by its maker. Alvarado v. State, 912 S.W.2d 199 (Tex. Crim. App. 1995).

The test is whether the defendant's will was overborne by police coercion. Guardiola v. State, 20 S.W.3d 216 (Tex.App.—Houston [14th Dist.] 2000, *pet. ref'd*); Mason v. State, 116 S.W.3d 248 (Tex.App.—Houston [14th Dist.] 2003, *pet. ref'd*).

Coercive police activity is a necessary predicate to the finding that a confession is not voluntary within the meaning of the Due Process Clause of the Fourteenth Amendment. Colorado v. Connelly, 479 U.S. 157, 107 S.Ct. 515, 93 L.Ed.2d 473 (1986).

In determining whether police conduct is improper, the court should take into account police knowledge of the suspect's special weaknesses, including youth and low intelligence. Lane; Gallegos v. Colorado, 370 U.S. 49, 82 S.Ct. 1209, 8 L.Ed.2d 325 (1962).

Certain interrogation techniques, either in isolation or as applied to the unique characteristics of a particular suspect, will render a confession involuntary and thus, inadmissible. Miller v.

Fenton, 474 U.S. 104, 106 S.Ct. 445, 88 L.Ed.2d 410 (1985).

However, factors bearing on the characteristics of the accused are irrelevant in the absence of any state action that would support a finding of police misconduct or overreaching. Terrazas v. State, 4 S.W.3d 720 (Tex. Crim. App. 1999); Colorado v. Connelly.

Both physical and mental compulsion remove the voluntariness element from a defendant's decision to incriminate himself. Thomas v. State, 723 S.W.2d 696 (Tex. Crim. App. 1986).

Physical compulsion includes such obvious force as physical torture or extended deprivation of food and water. Thomas (citing U.S. v. Carignan, 342 U.S. 36, 72 S.Ct. 97, 96 L.Ed.2d 48 (1951)).

Mental compulsion includes the more subtle force associated with offering a defendant two choices, one of which results in a penalty, punishment or detriment from which the defendant is entitled to be free. Thomas (citing South Dakota v. Neville, 459 U.S. 553, 103 S.Ct. 916, 74 L.Ed.2d 748 (1983)).

Statements that have been found to be involuntary under Miranda or the Due Process Clause involve the crucial element of police overreaching and involve fact scenarios such as the following: (1) the suspect was subjected to a four-hour interrogation while incapacitated and sedated in an intensive-care unit; (2) the suspect, while on medication, was interrogated for over eighteen hours without food, medication, or sleep; (3) the police officers held a gun to the head of the wounded suspect to extract a confession; (4) the police interrogated the suspect intermittently for 16 days using coercive tactics while he was held incommunicado in a closed cell without windows and was given limited food; (5) the suspect was held for four days with inadequate food and medical attention until he confessed; (6) the suspect was subjected to five days of repeated questioning during which police employed coercive tactics; (7) the suspect was held incommunicado for three days with little food, and the confession was obtained when officers informed him that their chief was preparing to admit a lynch mob into the jail; (8) the suspect was questioned by relays of officers for 36 hours without an opportunity for sleep. Oursbourn, 259 S.W.3d at 170-1 (citing Colorado v. Connelly).

Also, a confession obtained under threat of removal from office of the defendants as police officers if they refused to answer (even though they were given a warning that anything they said would be used against them and that they could refuse to answer if it would tend to incriminate them) was coerced and invalid in a subsequent prosecution for conspiracy to obstruct administration of traffic laws. Garrity v. New Jersey, 385 U.S. 493, 87 S.Ct. 616, 17 L.Ed.2d 562 (1967).

As is evident from these fact scenarios, due process and Miranda claims of involuntariness generally do not require sweeping inquiries into the state of mind of a criminal defendant who has confessed. They involve an objective assessment of police behavior. The Constitution leaves voluntariness claims based on the defendant's state of mind to be resolved by state laws governing the admission of evidence. In Texas, that state law is Article 38.22, the Texas Confession Statute. Oursbourn, 259 S.W.3d at 171.

§6:55 Art. 38.23 Issues

Article 38.23 provides that evidence obtained in violation of the Constitution or laws of the United States or Texas may not be admitted in a criminal case. The statute also provides that a jury instruction should be submitted if a fact issue is raised about whether such a violation has occurred. The jury instruction requires the jury to disregard evidence that it finds was obtained in violation of the United States or Texas Constitution or laws. Hamal v. State, 390 S.W.3d 302 (Tex. Crim. App. 2012); Robinson v. State, 377 S.W.3d 712 (Tex. Crim. App. 2012).

To be entitled to an Article 38.23 jury instruction, three predicates must be met: (1) the evidence heard by the jury must raise an issue of fact; (2) the evidence on that fact must be affirmatively contested; and (3) the contested factual issue must be material to the lawfulness of the challenged conduct. Hamal, 390 S.W.3d at 306; Robinson, 377 S.W.3d at 719.

When a disputed, material issue of fact is successfully raised, the terms of the statute are mandatory, and the jury must be instructed accordingly. Evidence to justify an Article 38.23(a) instruction can derive from any source, no matter whether strong, weak, contradicted, unimpeached, or unbelievable. But it must, in any event, raise a *factual* dispute about how the evidence was obtained. Where the issue raised by the evidence at trial does *not* involve controverted historical facts, but only the proper application of the law to undisputed facts, that issue is properly left to the determination of the trial court. Robinson, 377 S.W.3d at 719.

If there is a disputed fact issue about whether an inherently coercive practice was employed—by either an officer or a private citizen—to wring a confession out of a suspect against his will, a specific exclusionary-rule instruction under Article 38.23 is appropriate. Oursbourn, 259 S.W.3d at 177.

The Article 38.23(a) "specific" instruction is fact-based: For example, "Do you believe that Officer Obie held a gun to the defendant's head to extract his statement? If so, do not consider the defendant's confession." Oursbourn, 259 S.W.3d at 173-4.

§6:56 Involuntary Confessions

If a confession is involuntarily obtained, it is error for either the confession or evidence obtained from it to be admitted at trial. Sossamon v. State, 816 S.W.2d 340 (Tex. Crim. App. 1991); citing Jackson v. Denno, 378 U.S. 368, 84 S.Ct. 1774, 12 L.Ed.2d 908 (1964); Baker v. State, 956 S.W.2d 19 (Tex. Crim. App. 1997).

There is no statutory exception in Art. 38.22 (as there is under Art. 38.23) allowing the admission of statements that constitute a crime committed after law enforcement officials violate Art. 38.22 while attempting to obtain evidence of a previously committed crime. Nguyen v. State, 292 S.W.3d 671 (Tex. Crim. App. 2009).

The express language of Art. 38.22 does not include an exception after a 38.22 violation for statements that are not confessional in nature, do not implicate the accused for the offense prosecuted, or constitute an offense. Nguyen.

§6:56.1 Factors Rendering a Confession Involuntary

§6:56.1.1 Promises

A promise will render a confession "involuntary" if it is:

- of some benefit to the accused
- positive
- made or sanctioned by a person in authority; and
- of such a character as would likely influence the accused to speak untruthfully

Smith v. State, 779 S.W.2d 417 (Tex. Crim. App. 1989); Long v. State, 823 S.W.2d 259 (Tex. Crim. App. 1991).

To determine if the promise of a benefit was likely to influence a suspect to speak untruthfully, courts must look to whether the circumstances surrounding the promise made the suspect inclined to admit a crime he did not commit. Sossamon v. State, 816 S.W.2d 340 (Tex. Crim. App. 1991).

A promise will not render a resulting confession inadmissible unless someone in authority makes the promise. Dixon v. State, 624 S.W.2d 373 (Tex. App.—Dallas 1981, *no pet.*) (promise by victim's mother to drop charges if the defendant confessed did not render the confession involuntary); Bordman v. State, 56 S.W.3d 63 (Tex.App.—Houston [14th Dist.] 2001, *pet. ref'd*) (where the defendant confessed to a church elder).

Promises made to the defendant before he became a suspect do not affect the voluntariness of a subsequent confession. Arnold v. State, 873 S.W.2d 27 (Tex. Crim. App. 1993).

A defendant does not have to show that his confession was false in order to prevail on the issue of whether a promise by law enforcement induced him to confess untruthfully. Martinez v. State, 127 S.W.3d 792 (Tex. Crim. App. 2004).

In situations where there was testimony that the defendant could have taken a police officer's statement to be a promise, the admission of the confession will be upheld where the appellate courts find there was no positive promise made to the defendant. Martinez.

A prediction about future events (such as a detective saying to the defendant that things will go better for you if you cooperate) is not the same as a promise because the prediction about future events depends on the actions of the defendant rather than the detective. Mason v. State, 116 S.W.3d 248 (Tex. App.—Houston [14th Dist.] 2003, *pet. ref'd*).

§6:56.1.1.1 Promises Not Affecting Voluntariness

A promise to allow a suspect to take a polygraph is not the type of promise that will induce a person to falsely inculpate himself. Smith v. State, 779 S.W.2d 417 (Tex. Crim. App. 1989).

Where a detective told the defendant that he would do what he could to help the defendant if he gave further information on another suspect's involvement in other crimes, the statements did not render the subsequent confession involuntary. Garcia v. State, 919 S.W.2d 370 (Tex. Crim. App. 1994).

Where a police officer made the general statement he would help the defendant if the defendant cooperated with him, the resulting confession was voluntary. Dykes v. State, 657 S.W.2d 796 (Tex. Crim. App. 1983).

Where the detective told the defendant that he would inform the district attorney as to his cooperation or lack of same, the resulting confession was voluntary. Sorola v. State, 674 S.W.2d 809 (Tex.App.—San Antonio 1984), affirmed at 693 S.W.2d 417 (Tex. Crim. App. 1985).

Promises to seek the appropriate charge based upon the facts and circumstances of the case do not render a subsequent confession involuntary. Jacobs v. State, 787 S.W.2d 397 (Tex. Crim. App. 1990); Freeman v. State, 723 S.W.2d 727 (Tex. Crim. App. 1986).

Where the promise made was for a benefit that the defendant should know would occur anyway as a matter of course, the promise will not render a subsequent confession involuntary. Jacobs (where the defendant was allowed a visit from his girlfriend).

A promise to contact charitable authorities on behalf of the defendant's family where the contact could have been made by anyone, including defendant's family, does not render a subsequent confession involuntary. Muniz v. State, 851 S.W.2d 238 (Tex. Crim. App. 1993).

A statement by a prosecutor to effect that the case seemed like a good death penalty case and that the state would do its best to get the death penalty is not a promise that would likely induce an accused to speak untruthfully. Long v. State, 823 S.W.2d 259 (Tex. Crim. App. 1991).

§6:56.1.1.2 Promises and Other Factors Affecting Voluntariness

Where a defendant was promised a reduction of time to be served in another case it was found to be likely to induce him to speak untruthfully and rendered the resulting confession involuntary. Sossamon v. State, 816 S.W.2d 340 (Tex. Crim. App. 1991).

If a suspect is told that things might go easier on him if he confesses, this will be an important factor in deciding against voluntariness. Sterling v. State, 800 S.W.2d 513 (Tex. Crim. App. 1990).

A confession made after a representation that the state would not seek the death penalty in exchange, is inadmissible. McMahon v. State, 582 S.W.2d 786 (Tex. Crim. App. 1978).

A promise to drop charges against the defendant's mother in exchange for his confession rendered the resulting confession involuntary. Walker v. State, 626 S.W.2d 777 (Tex. Crim. App. 1982).

§6:56.1.2 "For or Against"

A confession is not admissible if the uncontradicted evidence shows the person who obtained the confession informed the accused prior to the interrogation that his confession might be used "for or against" him. Dinkins v. State, 894 S.W.2d 330 (Tex. Crim. App. 1995).

A confession resulting from a law enforcement agent's pre-interrogation statement that it can be used "for or against" the defendant is inadmissible as a matter of law because it constitutes an improper inducement and because it does not comply with the statutory warnings in CCP Art. 38.22. Dunn v. State, 721 S.W.2d 325 (Tex. Crim. App. 1986) (*plurality opinion*).

Where the proper statutory warning is given and a suspect is told at a different time that a statement can be used "for or against" him, there is no statutory violation.

CONFESSIONS

The voluntariness of the statement may be affected, but it is not rendered automatically inadmissible. Nenno v. State, 970 S.W2d 549 (Tex. Crim. App. 1998).

The *per se* rule of inadmissibility as stated in Dinkins and Dunn does not apply to an officer's remarks which were made during the subsequent interrogation. Creager v. State, 952 S.W.2d 852 (Tex. Crim. App. 1997).

Where the representation that the confession can be used "for or against" the suspect occurs during the interrogation, the issue is one of voluntariness of the confession. Creager.

However, where there is a factual discrepancy as to whether such a representation was made, the trial judge is responsible for determining whether the confession is admissible. Dinkins.

Evidence that a defendant received an improper warning need not be wholly rebutted, but merely contradicted in order that a confession be admissible. Muniz v. State, 851 S.W.2d 238 (Tex. Crim. App. 1993).

§6:56.1.3 Intoxication

Intoxication is but one relevant factor in determining whether a suspect understood his rights. Ripkowski v. State, 61 S.W.3d 378 (Tex. Crim. App. 2001).

The fact that the person making the statement was intoxicated at the time he confessed is not alone sufficient to render the confession involuntary. Garcia v. State, 919 S.W.2d 370 (Tex. Crim. App. 1994).

In order for a resulting confession to be involuntary there must also be some evidence of police coercion. Ripkowski v. State, 61 S.W.3d 378 (Tex. Crim. App. 2001).

If the suspect is intoxicated to the point that he is incapable of making an independent, informed choice of free will, then his confession is involuntary. Nichols v. State, 754 S.W.2d 185 (Tex. Crim. App. 1988).

Where the record supported the conclusion that the defendant was not so intoxicated on cocaine as to render his confession involuntary the trial court's finding will be upheld. Jenkins v. State, 912 S.W.2d 793 (Tex. Crim. App. 1995).

§6:56.1.4 Pain and/or Torture

Where the record did not demonstrate that the defendant was in pain to the point he could not make an informed decision, his subsequent confession will be found voluntary. Jenkins v. State, 912 S.W.2d 793 (Tex. Crim. App. 1995).

A confession resulting from brutal torture was obtained in violation of the Due Process Clause. Brown v. Mississippi, 297 U.S. 278, 56 S.Ct. 461, 80 L.Ed. 682 (1936).

Where police officers held a gun to the head of the defendant to obtain a confession, the resulting confession was involuntarily obtained. Beecher v. Alabama, 389 U.S. 35, 88 S.Ct. 189, 19 L.Ed.2d 35 (1967).

§6:56.1.5 Deception or Misrepresentation

In determining the voluntariness of a defendant's written statement, police falsehoods are relevant. Mason v. State, 116 S.W.3d 248 (Tex.App.—Houston [14th Dist.] 2003, *pet. ref'd*); Frazier v. Cupp, 394 U.S. 731, 89 S.Ct. 1420, 22 L.Ed.2d 684 (1969).

Trickery or deception does not make a statement involuntary unless the method is calculated to produce an untruthful confession or is offensive to due process. Creager v. State, 952 S.W.2d 852 (Tex. Crim. App. 1997); Mason.

The effect of a lie must be analyzed in the context of all the circumstances of the interrogation. Mason.

Some types of police deception employed during custodial interrogation designed to elicit a confession from an accused are permissible. The focus is whether the behavior of the police was such as to overbear the will of the accused. Rogers v. Richmond, 365 U.S. 534, 81 S.Ct. 735, 5 L.Ed.2d 760 (1961).

Misrepresentations made by police to a suspect during an interrogation are a relevant factor in assessing whether the suspect's confession was voluntary, but they are insufficient to render an otherwise voluntary confession inadmissible. Green v. State, 934 S.W.2d 92 (Tex. Crim. App. 1996) (citing Frazier v. Cupp, 394 U.S. 731, 89 S.Ct. 1420, 22 L.Ed.2d 684 (1969)).

The misrepresentation must be viewed in the context of the totality of the circumstances. Green (citing Frazier v. Cupp).

Of the numerous types of police deception, a misrepresentation relating to an accused's connection to the crime is the least likely to render a confession involuntary. Green.

A police misrepresentation that they had an eyewitness to the murder for which the suspect was being interrogated did not rise to the level of coercion contemplated in Lynumn v. Illinois, 372 U.S. 528, 83 S.Ct. 917, 9 L.Ed.2d 922 (1963). Green.

It is not impermissible for the police to falsely tell the suspect that his accomplice had given a complete confession. Frazier v. Cupp.

It is not impermissible for police to falsely tell the suspect that the victim, on his deathbed, had identified the suspect as the perpetrator. Rodriquez v. State, 934 S.W.2d 881 (Tex.App.—Waco 1996, *no pet.*).

Article 38.23 of the Code of Criminal Procedure bars the admissibility of a confession where the interrogating officer fabricates documentary evidence in violation of Texas Penal Code §37.09 and uses it to persuade a suspect to confess. Wilson v. State, 311 S.W.3d 452 (Tex. Crim. App. 2010) (where the officer fabricated a forensic fingerprint report).

Other types of deception which are likely to lead to involuntary confessions are based on extrinsic considerations. Green.

For example, a threat to take away a suspect's welfare benefits and custody of her children was found to be inherently coercive because it did more than affect the suspect's belief concerning her actual guilt or innocence; it impaired her free choice, thereby casting doubt upon the reliability of the resulting confession. Lynumn v. Illinois.

It is impermissible for the police to falsely suggest that a close police officer friend of the suspect would lose his job if the suspect did not cooperate and confess. Spano v. New York, 360 U.S. 315, 79 S.Ct. 1202, 3 L.Ed.2d 1265 (1959).

Mere silence by law enforcement officials as to the subject matter of the interrogation is not "trickery" sufficient to invalidate a suspect's waiver of Miranda rights. Colorado v. Spring, 479 U.S. 564, 107 S.Ct. 851, 93 L.Ed.2d 954 (1987).

§6:56.1.6 Prolonged Interrogation; Lack of Food or Sleep

In order to make a voluntariness claim at trial where alleging a lack of sleep, a defendant must show that there is a connection between his lack of sleep and coercive government conduct. Either the police must have caused the defendant to go without sleep or they must have somehow exploited the lack of sleep to overbear the defendant's will. Contreras v. State, 312 S.W.3d 566, 575 (Tex. Crim. App. 2010).

Where the defendant successfully raises this issue, he will be entitled to an Art. 38.23 instruction in the jury charge. Contreras, 312 S.W.3d at 575.

Holding a defendant for a prolonged period without allowing him to call relatives or an attorney can also result in an involuntary confession. Contreras, 312 S.W.3d at 578.

A two-hour interrogation is not a sufficiently lengthy period to render a resulting confession involuntary. Contreras, 312 S.W.3d 579.

Lack of sleep for 16 hours will not alone render a suspect's confession involuntary. Barney v. State, 698 S.W.2d 114 (Tex. Crim. App. 1985).

Where the suspect's inability to eat or sleep was brought about by his conscience and not by the police, there is no official coercion and, therefore, a resulting confession is not involuntary. Chambers v. State, 866 S.W.2d 9 (Tex. Crim. App. 1993).

Questioning by relays of officers over a 36-hour period without adequate opportunity for sleep rendered a resulting confession involuntary. Ashcraft v. Tennessee, 322 U.S. 143, 64 S.Ct. 921, 88 L.Ed.2d 1192 (1944).

Where a defendant was held for four days without adequate food and medical attention, the resulting confession was involuntary. Reck v. Pate, 367 U.S. 433, 81 S.Ct. 1541, 6 L.Ed.2d 948 (1961).

Where a defendant was held for five days of repeated questioning during which police employed coercive tactics, a resulting confession was found to be involuntary. Culombe v. Connecticut, 367 U.S. 568, 81 S.Ct. 1860, 6 L.Ed.2d 1037 (1961).

Where a defendant was held incommunicado for three days with little food, and was informed by officers that the chief of police was ready to admit a lynch mob, the resulting confession was found to be involuntary. Payne v. Arkansas, 356 U.S. 560, 78 S.Ct. 844, 2 L.Ed.2d 975 (1958).

Where a defendant on medication was interrogated for over 18 hours without food or sleep, a resulting confession was found involuntary. Greenwald v. Wisconsin, 390 U.S. 519, 88 S.Ct. 1152, 20 L.Ed.2d 77 (1968).

Where a defendant was incapacitated and sedated in an intensive-care unit, a four-hour interrogation was found to render a subsequent confession involuntary. Mincey v. Arizona, 437 U.S. 385, 98 S.Ct. 2408, 57 L.Ed.2d 290 (1978).

§6:56.1.7 Force or Violence

A threat of violence made by a police officer in order to obtain a confession may render a resulting confession inadmissible; however, where no express or implied threat is made by police, a suspect's belief that a confession will relieve the danger will not render a subsequent confession inadmissible. Roberts v. State, 545 S.W.2d 157 (Tex. Crim. App. 1977).

A confession resulting from brutal torture has been obtained in violation of the Due Process Clause. Brown v. Mississippi, 297 U.S. 278, 56 S.Ct. 461, 80 L.Ed. 682 (1936); Connor v. State, 640 S.W.2d 374 (Tex.App.—1982), affirmed at 773 S.W.2d 13 (Tex. Crim. App. 1989).

Where police officers held a gun to the head of the defendant to obtain a confession, the resulting confession was involuntarily obtained. Beecher v. Alabama, 389 U.S. 35, 88 S.Ct. 189, 19 L.Ed.2d 35 (1967).

§6:56.1.8 Psychological Tactics

There is no *per se* rule against the use of psychological tactics in interrogations. Mason v. State, 116 S.W.3d 248 (Tex.App.—Houston [14th Dist.] 2003, *pet. ref'd*).

Interrogation tactics that include praying with and praying for the accused should be considered as a factor in the totality of the circumstances test of the voluntariness of a confession. Davis v. North Carolina, 384 U.S. 737, 86 S.Ct. 1761, 16 L.Ed.2d 895 (1966).

§6:56.1.9 Lack of Intellect or Mental Impairment

The totality of the circumstances standard for assessing the voluntariness of a confession given by a person of normal mentality is also the appropriate standard to apply when a confession is made by someone suffering from mental retardation and mental illness. Delao v. State, 235 S.W.3d 235 (Tex. Crim. App. 2007).

There is no requirement that a person be literate before his confession can be admissible. Westley v. State, 754 S.W.2d 224 (Tex. Crim. App. 1988).

Where the evidence shows that a suspect's lack of literacy did not prevent him from understanding the warnings and his rights, a resulting confession will be admissible. Westley.

In order for a defendant's mental condition to render a confession involuntary it must be shown in connection with official coercion. Walker v. State, 842 S.W.2d 301 (Tex.App.—Tyler 1992, *no pet.*).

A suspect's limited intelligence is a factor to be considered in a voluntariness analysis; but does not mandate a finding of involuntariness as a matter of law. King v. State, 831 S.W.2d 891 (Tex.App.—Houston [14th Dist.] 1992, *no pet.*).

A mental defect may be significant enough to render a confession inadmissible. Page v. State, 614 S.W.2d 819 (Tex. Crim. App. 1981).

Where the bulk of the evidence shows that the defendant had the basic reasoning skills necessary to understand his warnings, a resulting confession will be found voluntary. Penry v. State, 903 S.W.2d 715 (Tex. Crim. App. 1995).

Insanity will negate the admissibility of a confession where this weakness is exploited by coercive tactics. Blackburn v. Alabama, 361 U.S. 199, 80 S.Ct. 274, 4 L.Ed.2d 242 (1960).

Where a police physician administered a "truth-serum" drug to the defendant, the resulting confession was rendered involuntary. Townsend v. Sain, 372 U.S. 293, 83 S.Ct. 745, 9 L.Ed.2d 770 (1963).

Emotional confusion and debilitation of a suspect may call into question the voluntariness of a confession. Ballestero v. State, 640 S.W.2d 423 (Tex.App.—San Antonio 1982, *no pet.*).

§6:56.1.10 Language Barriers

An ability to understand the police officers, understand the oral and written warnings and to read the confession will defeat a claim of inability to sufficiently understand the English language. Farmah v. State, 789 S.W.2d 665 (Tex.App.—Houston [1st Dist.] 1990), overruled on other grounds 883 S.W.2d 674 (Tex. Crim. App. 1994).

Where the evidence shows that the law enforcement agents went to great lengths to translate everything several times to the defendant in order to ensure that he understood what he was doing, a trial court does not abuse its discretion in ruling the resulting confession voluntary. Montoya v. State, 810 S.W.2d 160 (Tex. Crim. App. 1989).

A statement dictated in Spanish but recorded in English is not rendered an involuntary oral confession where the Code of Criminal Procedure is otherwise followed. Mestiza v. State, 923 S.W.2d 720 (Tex.App.—Corpus Christi 1996, *no pet.*).

§6:56.1.11 Use of Grand Jury Subpoena

Where a defendant has invoked any of his Miranda or CCP Art. 38.22 rights, the use of a grand jury subpoena to bring him in for further questioning renders a subsequent confession involuntary. Guardiola v. State, 20 S.W.3d 216 (Tex.App.—Houston [14th Dist.] 2000 *pet. ref'd*).

§6:56.1.12 Threats Against Family Members

Threats against family members can result in an involuntary confession. Contreras v. State, 312 S.W.3d 566, 578 (Tex. Crim. App. 2010).

Threats to arrest a family member can result in an involuntary confession where police do not have probable cause to arrest the family member. Where they have sufficient probable cause, the threats will not vitiate the voluntariness of the confession. Contreras, 312 S.W.3d at 578.

§6:57 The Voluntariness Hearing

§6:57.1 In General

If, at any point during trial, an issue arises as to the voluntariness of a custodial statement made by the defendant, the trial court must hold a hearing on the issue. Jackson v. Denno, 378 U.S. 368, 84 S.Ct. 1774, 12 L.Ed.2d 908 (1964). The failure to hold a voluntariness hearing where the record indicates a voluntariness issue is reversible error. Hugley v. State, 505 S.W.2d 914 (Tex. Crim. App. 1974).

A voluntariness hearing must also be held where the defendant challenges a non-custodial statement made to a law enforcement officer. Terrazas v. State, 4 S.W.3d 720 (Tex. Crim. App. 1999).

Even if the confession is used for impeachment, failure to make a determination of voluntariness outside the presence of the jury, when requested, is reversible error. Madden v. State, 691 S.W.2d 688 (Tex. Crim. App. 1985). The voluntariness hearing must be held outside the presence of the jury. Rule 104(c) Texas Rules of Evidence. The trial court is not required to hold the voluntariness hearing pretrial but may do so at any time before the statement is presented to the jury. Ross v. State, 678 S.W.2d 491 (Tex. Crim. App. 1984).

As the movant in a motion to suppress a confession, the defendant has the burden to produce evidence that defeats the presumption of proper police conduct; thereby shifting the burden of proof to the state. Chavarria v. State, 876 S.W.2d 388 (Tex.App.—El Paso 1994). At a hearing to determine the voluntariness of a confession, the state need not rebut the defendant's assertions, but only controvert them. Muniz v. State, 851 S.W.2d 238 (Tex. Crim. App. 1993).

By taking the stand during the voluntariness hearing, the accused does not subject himself or herself to cross-examination as to other issues in the case. Rule 104(d) Texas Rules of Evidence.

The trial court may ask questions at the hearing in order to determine specific issues, as long as there is no indication that the court is not impartial. Richardson v. State, 632 S.W.2d 700 (Tex.App.—Fort Worth 1982).

TIP TO THE PROSECUTION: If, during the voluntariness hearing, the defendant presents testimony on a particular issue or develops the issue on cross-examination, present testimony controverting the defendant's assertions. The failure to do so will result in a finding at trial or on appeal that the confession should not be admitted.

The burden is on the defendant, as the moving party in a motion to suppress evidence obtained in violation of the law under Art. 38.23, to produce evidence demonstrating a causal connection between the alleged statutory violation and the resulting evidence. The burden then shifts to the state to either disprove the evidence the defendant has produced, or bring an attenuation-of-taint argument to demonstrate that the causal chain asserted by the defendant was in fact broken. Pham v. State, 175 S.W.3d 767 (Tex. Crim. App. 2005).

A defendant who moves for suppression under Art. 38.23 due to the violation of a statute has the burden of producing evidence of a statutory violation. Only when this burden is met does the State bear a burden to prove compliance. State v. Robinson, 334 S.W.3d 776, 779 (Tex. Crim. App. 2011).

The Rules of Evidence do not apply at suppression hearings. This is because former Rule 1101(d)(4) that previously dictated to the contrary no longer exists. Granados v. State, 85 S.W.3d 217 (Tex. Crim. App. 2002).

Therefore, Rule 702 is not applicable at a suppression hearing. Hall v. State, 297 S.W.3d 294 (Tex. Crim. App. 2009).

In a pre-trial motion to suppress hearing, a trial court may rely upon any relevant, reliable, and credible information, even though it may be unsworn hearsay (in this case a police report found to be sufficiently reliable). The language of CCP Art. 28.01 is permissive, not restrictive, and allows for reports to be used. Ford v. State, 305 S.W.3d 530 (Tex. Crim. App. 2009).

It is within the trial court's discretion to grant the State's request to reopen a motion-to-suppress hearing to supplement the record with additional testimony, outside the jury's presence, even over the objection of the defendant. Black v. State, 362 S.W.3d 626 (Tex. Crim. App. 2012).

Appellate courts review a trial court's ruling on a motion to suppress for an abuse of discretion and overturn that ruling only if it is outside the zone of reasonable disagreement. Martinez v. State, 348 S.W.3d 919, 922 (Tex. Crim. App. 2011). They conduct their review with two standards, giving almost total deference to a trial court's determination of historic facts and mixed questions of law and fact that rely on the credibility of a witness, but applying a *de novo* standard of review to pure questions of law and mixed questions that do not depend on credibility determinations. Martinez, 348 S.W.3d. at 922–23.

§6:57.2 Findings of Fact and Conclusions of Law

If the trial court finds beyond a reasonable doubt that the confession is voluntarily made and admissible as a matter of law and fact, the judge prepares and signs an order stating these findings. The order is filed among the papers of the cause. CCP Art. 38.22 §6.

TIP TO THE BENCH: Findings of fact and conclusions of law must be filed in the record before the record is filed in the appellate court (i.e., within 75 days of the verdict). Green v. State, 906 S.W.2d 937 (Tex. Crim. App.1995).

The requirement that the trial court file written findings of fact and conclusions of law applies to bench trials as well as jury trials. Wicker v. State, 740 S.W.2d 779 (Tex. Crim. App. 1987). The findings must be filed whether or not the defendant requests them, and if they are not filed the appeal will be abated for their preparation. Wicker; Urias v. State, 155 S.W.3d 141 (Tex. Crim. App. 2004).

Art. 38.22, sec. 6 clearly requires that the trial court make findings of fact and conclusions of law in all cases concerning voluntariness, whether or not requested by a party. The statute has no exceptions. Vasquez v. State, 411 S.W.3d 918, 920 (Tex. Crim. App. 2013).

A trial court satisfies the requirements of Art. 38.22 when it dictates its findings and conclusions to the court reporter, and they are transcribed and made a part of the statement of facts, filed with the district clerk, and made a part of the appellate record. Murphy v. State, 112 S.W.3d 592 (Tex. Crim. App. 2003).

As a constitutional matter, the trial court's conclusion as to the voluntariness of a confession must appear in the record with unmistakable clarity. Bonham v. State, 644 S.W.2d 5 (Tex. Crim. App. 1983).

TIP TO THE BENCH: When making written findings of fact and conclusions of law, it is the better practice to make an express finding on the issue of waiver of rights. Stanley v. State, 866 S.W.2d 306 (Tex. App.—Houston [14th Dist.] 1993).

The findings of fact and conclusions must be made by the judge who heard the testimony at the hearing and not by a succeeding judge. Garcia v. State, 15 S.W.3d 533 (Tex. Crim. App. 2000).

TIP TO THE BENCH: When writing findings of fact and conclusions of law regarding the voluntariness of a confession, the trial court is not obligated to outline testimony which does not support its conclusions. Guidry v. State, 12 S.W.3d 15 (Tex. Crim. App. 1999). However, the findings must be sufficiently detailed to enable the appellate court to determine the basis for the trial court's ruling and to assist the appellate court in determining the sufficiency of the evidence to support whatever unstated findings of fact were made by the fact finder. Guidry.

Where the trial court finds that the statement was not voluntary, CCP Art. 38.22 §6 does not require the entry of written findings of fact and conclusions of law. Terrazas v. State, 4 S.W.3d 720 (Tex. Crim. App. 1999).

PRACTICE TIP: Where a trial court has ruled a statement voluntary, be sure to request that the trial court enter written findings of fact and conclusions of law. The right to findings and conclusions is a statutory right which is forfeited by a party's failure to insist upon its implementation. Terrazas v. State, 4 S.W.3d 720 (Tex. Crim. App. 1999).

TIP TO THE BENCH: The findings of fact and conclusions of law must be made by the judge that heard the testimony. If that judge is unavailable for any reason to prepare them, the case must be abated for another voluntariness hearing. Garcia v. State, 15 S.W.3d 533 (Tex. Crim. App. 2000).

Where the trial court's written findings and conclusions of law are ambiguous and lack a credibility determination, an appellate court can remand the case for supplemental findings. State v. Mendoza, 365 S.W.3d 666. 673 (Tex. Crim. App. 2012).

§6:57.3 Voluntariness Issue to Jury

§6:57.3.1 Statutory Provisions

CCP Art. 38.22 §6

In all cases where a question is raised as to the voluntariness of a statement of an accused, the court must make an independent finding in the absence of the jury as to whether the statement was made under voluntary conditions. If the statement has been found to have been voluntarily made and held admissible as a matter of law and fact by the court in a hearing in the absence of the jury, the court must enter an order stating its conclusion as to whether or not the statement was voluntarily made, along with the specific finding of facts upon which the conclusion was based, which order shall be filed among the papers of the cause. Such order shall not be exhibited to the jury nor the finding thereof made known to the jury in any manner. Upon the finding by the judge as a matter of law and fact that the statement was voluntarily made, evidence pertaining to such matter may be submitted to the jury and it shall be instructed that unless the jury believes beyond a reasonable doubt that the statement was voluntarily made, the jury shall not consider such statement for any purpose nor any evidence obtained as a result thereof. In any case where a motion to suppress the statement has been filed and evidence has been submitted to the court on this issue, the court within its discretion may reconsider such evidence in its finding that the statement was voluntarily made and the same evidence submitted to the court at the hearing on the motion to suppress shall be made a part of the record the same as if it were being presented at the time of trial. However, the state or the defendant shall be entitled to present any new evidence on the issue of the voluntariness of the statement prior to the court's final ruling and order stating its findings.

CCP Art. 38.23. Evidence not to be used

(a) No evidence obtained by an officer or other person in violation of any provision of the Constitution or laws of the State of Texas, or of the Constitution or laws of the United States of America, shall be admitted in evidence against the accused on the trial of any criminal case. In any case where the legal evidence raises an issue hereunder, the jury shall be instructed that if it believes, or has a reasonable doubt, that the evidence was obtained in violation of the provisions of this Article, then and in such event, the jury shall disregard any such evidence so obtained.

(b) It is an exception to the provisions of Subsection (a) of this Article that the evidence was obtained by a law enforcement officer acting in objective good faith reliance upon a warrant issued by a neutral magistrate based on probable cause.

Art. 38.23 requires the exclusion of evidence where there is a causal connection between the legal violation and the obtaining of the evidence. Johnson v. State, 871 S.W.2d 744 (Tex. Crim. App. 1994)

§6:57.3.2 Application of Law

The issue of the voluntariness of a confession can be submitted to the jury under two different theories depending on the proof adduced at trial. If there is a factual dispute as to how the evidence was obtained, the jury should be instructed under art. 38.23. If the defense introduces evidence at trial from which a reasonable jury could conclude that the statement was not voluntary, a voluntariness charge under Art. 38.22 §6 is required. Vasquez v. State, 225 S.W.3d 541 (Tex. Crim. App. 2007).

When the evidence raises an issue of the voluntariness of a defendant's statement under Article 38.22, the trial judge must give a general voluntariness instruction under §§6 and 7 of that article because the law is applicable to the case. The law is applicable to the case because the statute requires an instruction in this situation. Oursbourn v. State, 259 S.W.3d 159, 165 (Tex. Crim. App. 2008).

However, when the defendant does not request this statutorily mandated instruction, the trial court's failure to include it is reviewed only for egregious harm under Almanza; Oursbourn.

The first step in deciding upon an appropriate jury instruction is identifying the theory of involuntariness because this will determine what type of instruction will be appropriate. Oursbourn, at 169.

Even though the trial court has a *sua sponte* duty to include an Art. 38.23 voluntariness instruction in the charge where raised by the evidence, it is incumbent on the defendant to explain to the trial court what he desires in the way of an instruction. Contreras v. State, 312 S.W.3d 566 (Tex. Crim. App. 2010).

Under Texas statutory law, there are three types of instructions that relate to the taking of confessions: (1) a general Article 38.22, §6, Voluntariness Instruction; (2) a general Article 38.22, §7, Warnings Instruction (involving warnings given under §§2 and 3; and (3) a specific Article 38.23(a), Exclusionary-Rule Instruction. Oursbourn, at 173.

In essence, the §6 general instruction asks the jury: "Do you believe, beyond a reasonable doubt, that the defendant's statement was voluntarily made? If it was not, do not consider the defendant's confession." The §7 instruction sets out the requirements of Art. 38.22, §2 or §3, and asks the jury to decide whether all of those requirements were met. The Article 38.23(a) specific instruction is fact-based: For example, "Do you believe that Officer Obie held a gun to the defendant's head to extract his statement? If so, do not consider the defendant's confession." Oursbourn, at 173.

Due process and Miranda claims may warrant both "general" and "specific" voluntariness instructions; Texas statutory claims warrant only a "general" voluntariness instruction. It is the defendant's responsibility to delineate which type of "involuntariness" he is claiming—a general (perhaps subjective) lack of voluntariness or a specific police-coerced lack of voluntariness—because the jury instruction is very different depending upon the type of claim. Oursbourn, at 174.

If the defendant never presents a proposed jury instruction (or fails to object to the lack of one), any potential error in the charge is reviewed only for "egregious harm" under Almanza. Oursbourn, at 174.

Article 38.22, §6 expressly dictates the content of that instruction to be as follows: "Unless the jury believes beyond a reasonable doubt that the statement was voluntarily made, the jury shall not consider such statement for any purpose nor any evidence obtained as a result thereof." Thus, Art. 38.22, §6 is "the law applicable" to any case in which a question is raised and litigated as to the general voluntariness of a statement of a defendant. Oursbourn, at 175.

Because §6 contains its own jury-instruction provision, it is not governed by the jury-instruction provision found in §7. The obvious purpose of §7 is to authorize and require jury instructions regarding the warnings and safeguards for written and oral statements outlined in Art. 38.22, §§2 and 3 (warnings on the right to remain silent, right to counsel, etc.). Oursbourn, at 175.

A §6 instruction becomes "law applicable to the case" only if the parties actually litigate a §6 voluntariness issue before the trial judge. If such litigation occurs (on the admissibility of evidence, for example), a jury instruction need not be specifically requested, although a request would still be necessary to obtain the most beneficial harm analysis under Almanza. Oursbourn, at 175.

If the defendant made his statement as the result of custodial interrogation, he is also entitled, when the issue is raised by the evidence, to have the jury decide whether he was adequately warned of his rights and knowingly and intelligently waived these rights. The phrase "the issue" in §7 refers to compliance with the statutory warnings set out in both Articles 15.17 (Duties of Arresting Officer and Magistrate) and 38.22, §§2 and 3, and the voluntariness of the defendant's waiver of the rights. For it to be "raised by the evidence" there must be a genuine factual dispute, just as is true under Article 38.23 issues. As with §6, the trial judge's §7 jury instructions are "general" ones that set out the pertinent law and legal requirements of §§2 and 3 (or, in an appropriate case, those of Article 15.17). Oursbourn, at 176.

Under Art. 38.23, a jury instruction is required only if there is a genuine dispute about a material fact. A defendant must establish three foundation requirements to trigger an Article 38.23 instruction: (1) the evidence heard by the jury must raise an issue of fact; (2) the evidence on that fact must be affirmatively contested; and (3) the contested factual issue must be material to the lawfulness of the challenged conduct in obtaining the statement claimed to be involuntary. The defendant must offer evidence that, if credited, would create a reasonable doubt as to a specific factual matter essential to the voluntariness of the statement. This factual dispute can be raised only by affirmative evidence, not by mere cross-examination questions or argument. Oursbourn, at 177.

If raised, Art. 38.23 is "the law applicable" to the case. Because such an instruction is statutorily mandated, the trial judge must include it in the jury instructions when the voluntariness of a defendant's statement is at issue. Oursbourn, at 181.

Because the failure of police to honor a defendant's rights under Miranda is not itself a constitutional violation, a defendant is not entitled to an Art. 38.23 charge when evidence at trial shows that police did not comply with Miranda. Contreras v. State, 312 S.W.3d 566 (Tex. Crim. App. 2010). Under these circumstances, the defendant is entitled to a charge under Art. 38.22.

At trial, the defendant should be permitted to show the circumstances under which the confession was allegedly made so that the jury may evaluate its reliability and credibility. Crane v. Kentucky, 476 U.S. 683, 106 S.Ct. 2142, 90 L.Ed.2d 636 (1986). The defendant may offer witnesses before the jury to establish an issue of non-voluntariness and it is error to refuse him this right. Ross v. State, 504 S.W.2d 862 (Tex. Crim. App. 1974).

However, where the defendant is claiming that his confession was involuntary because he requested a lawyer but does not claim that his confession was false or otherwise unreliable, the trial court does not err in refusing to allow him to put on testimony alleging that the police were not credible. Guidry v. State, 9 S.W.3d 133 (Tex. Crim. App. 1999).

Before the trial court is required to instruct the jury on the law pertaining to the voluntariness of confessions, some evidence must be presented to the jury that raises the issue. Butler v. State, 872 S.W.2d 227 (Tex. Crim. App. 1994).

Absent some positive evidence that the statement of the defendant was coerced by law enforcement, the trial court does not abuse its discretion in refusing an Art. 38.23 instruction. It is not enough that the jury may disbelieve certain testimony. Janecka v. State, 937 S.W.2d 456 (Tex. Crim. App. 1996); Perry v. State, 158 S.W.3d 438 (Tex. Crim. App. 2004).

Where there is no factual dispute regarding the necessary probable cause for the arrest of the defendant, he is not entitled to an Art. 38.23 instruction. Jackson v. State, 33 S.W.3d 828 (Tex. Crim. App. 2000); Wesbrook v. State, 29 S.W.3d 103 (Tex. Crim. App. 2000).

Even where there is evidence raising the issue of voluntariness, the defendant is not entitled to a specific instruction as to whether the statement met all technical and mechanical requirements, but rather is entitled to submission of an instruction surrounding the general issue of whether he was adequately warned. White v. State, 779 S.W.2d 809 (Tex. Crim. App. 1989); Bell v. State, 582 S.W.2d 800 (Tex. Crim. App. 1979); Dinkins v. State, 894 S.W.2d 330 (Tex. Crim. App. 1995).

An instruction which focuses on a particular factor that may render a statement involuntary is an impermissible comment on the weight of the evidence. Rocha v. State, 16 S.W.3d 1 (Tex. Crim. App. 2000); Gallo v. State, 239 S.W.3d 757 (Tex. Crim. App. 2007) (defendant claimed that mental retardation made his confession involuntary).

The trial court is allowed as necessary to give instruction to the jury clarifying the law surrounding the issue. Cockrell v. State, 933 S.W.2d 73 (Tex. Crim. App. 1996).

Where the defense raises the voluntariness issue in front of the jury, the state has the burden to prove voluntariness beyond a reasonable doubt. CCP Art. 38.22 §6.

TIP TO THE BENCH: For an example of the proper jury charge to be given on the voluntariness of a confession, see Mendoza v. State, 88 S.W.3d 236 (Tex. Crim. App. 2002).

§6:60 Illegal Arrests and Resulting Confessions

§6:61 In General

The primary taint of an illegal arrest bears so strongly on the will of a suspect that evidence (including confessions) obtained as a result of the illegality may not be used. Wong Sun v. U.S., 371 U.S. 471, 83 S.Ct. 407, 9 L.Ed.2d 441 (1963). This rationale applies under Texas law as CCP Art. 38.23 prohibits use of any evidence "obtained" in violation of the laws. Bell v. State, 724 S.W.2d 780 (Tex. Crim. App. 1986).

Where a defendant is illegally arrested and there is a causal connection between the arrest and a subsequent confession, the confession is inadmissible. De Bolt v. State, 604 S.W.2d 164 (Tex. Crim. App. 1980).

Where a suspect is illegally arrested and then confesses, the resulting confession is inadmissible unless the state can show that the taint of the illegal arrest was sufficiently attenuated to the point that the confession is sufficiently an act of free will. Gregg v. State, 667 S.W.2d 125 (Tex. Crim. App. 1984).

The "fruit of the poisonous tree" doctrine is not applicable where knowledge or possession of the evidence in question is obtained from a source independent of the state's wrongful act. Wicker v. State, 667 S.W.2d 137 (Tex. Crim. App. 1984), citing Costello v. U.S., 365 U.S. 265, 81 S.Ct. 534, 5 L.Ed.2d 551 (1961).

A confession should not be suppressed where the law violation committed by the police does not bear any relation to the purposes the law is to serve. New York v. Harris, 495 U.S. 14 (1990) (where the law violation had to do with an illegal warrantless in-home arrest of the defendant and the confession was later taken at the police station).

§6:62 Attenuation Analysis

A four-prong analysis is applied to determine if the taint of the illegal arrest is attenuated to the point that the confession should be admitted:

- Giving of Miranda warnings
- Temporal proximity of the arrest and the confession
- Presence of intervening circumstances
- Purpose and flagrancy of the official misconduct

Brown v. Illinois, 422 U.S. 590, 95 S.Ct. 2254, 45 L.Ed.2d 416 (1975); Monge v. State, 315 S.W.3d 35 (Tex. Crim. App. 2010).

Texas has adopted the Brown test for the purposes of analyzing the admissibility of confessions made following illegal arrests under state statutory law. Hankins v. State, 132 S.W.3d 380 (Tex. Crim. App. 2004).

The burden is on the defendant, as the moving party in a motion to suppress evidence obtained in violation of the law under Art. 38.23, to produce evidence demonstrating a causal connection between the alleged statutory violation and the resulting evidence. The burden then shifts to the state to either disprove the evidence the defendant has produced, or bring an attenuation-of-taint argument to demonstrate that the causal chain asserted by the defendant was in fact broken. Pham v. State, 175 S.W.3d 767 (Tex. Crim. App. 2005).

§6:62.1 Giving Miranda Warnings

The giving of Miranda warnings alone, even repeated Miranda warnings, are not enough to purge the taint of an otherwise illegal arrest. Bell (citing Taylor v. Alabama, 457 U.S. 687, 102 S.Ct. 2664, 73 L.Ed.2d 314 (1982)).

However, the giving of Miranda warnings can be an important factor when combined with other factors. Crutsinger v. State, 206 S.W.3d 607 (Tex. Crim. App. 2006).

The less flagrant the police misconduct surrounding the illegal arrest, the more important the giving of the Miranda warnings become as tending to attenuate the taint of the illegal arrest. Self v. State, 709 S.W.2d 662 (Tex. Crim. App. 1986); Little v. State, 758 S.W.2d 551 (Tex. Crim. App. 1988).

However, the giving of Miranda warnings before the confession is a Brown factor that weighs in favor of the state. Monge v. State, 315 S.W.3d 35 (Tex. Crim. App. 2010).

§6:62.2 Temporal Proximity

The temporal proximity of the arrest and the confession is generally not a strong determining factor *per se*. Bell v. State, 724 S.W.2d 780 (Tex. Crim. App. 1986). For examples of cases in which the time span between illegal arrest and the confession has been found too short to attenuate the taint, *see*:

- Ussery v. State, 651 S.W.2d 767 (Tex. Crim. App. 1983) (one and a half hours)
- Green v. State, 615 S.W.2d 700 (Tex. Crim. App. 1980) (about two hours)
- Beasley v. State, 674 S.W.2d 762 (Tex. Crim. App. 1982) (time period of two to three days apparently, from poorly developed record)

For examples of cases in which the time span between illegal arrest and the confession has been found sufficiently long to attenuate the taint, *see*:

- Dowdy v. State, 534 S.W.2d 336 (Tex. Crim. App. 1976) (three hours)
- Coleman v. State, 643 S.W.2d 947 (Tex. Crim. App. 1982) (five hours)
- Townsley v. State, 652 S.W.2d 791 (Tex. Crim. App. 1983) (24 hours)

- Gant v. State, 649 S.W.2d 30 (Tex. Crim. App. 1983) (29 hours)
- Alonzo v. State, 591 S.W.2d 842 (Tex. Crim. App. 1979) (two days)
- Crutsinger v. State, 206 S.W.3d 607 (Tex. Crim. App. 2006) (approximately one hour where there were significant intervening circumstances)

The examples referenced in the preceding lists demonstrate that the temporal proximity of the confession to the illegal arrest is analyzed on a case-by-case basis and is, at best, an ambiguous factor. Self v. State, 709 S.W.2d 662 (Tex. Crim. App. 1986).

However, a short period of time between the illegal arrest and the confession is a Brown factor that weighs in favor of the defendant. Monge v. State, 315 S.W.3d 35 (Tex. Crim. App. 2010).

§6:62.3 Intervening Circumstances

The importance of intervening circumstances to the analysis depends on the origin and nature of the intervening circumstances. Intervening circumstances that are themselves products of the illegal arrest militate strongly against the attenuation of the taint. Taylor v. Alabama, 457 U.S. 687, 102 S.Ct. 2664, 73 L.Ed.2d 314 (1982) (police obtained an arrest warrant during the interrogation but it was itself based on information obtained from the tainted interrogation).

Where the intervening circumstances are the product of police investigation independent of the illegal arrest, they militate in favor of attenuation of the taint. Townsley v. State, 652 S.W.2d 791 (Tex. Crim. App. 1983) (probable cause was obtained by examining the body of the deceased and by interviewing neighbors). The intervening circumstances do not have to actually occur after the illegal arrest, but rather must manifest themselves so as to significantly intervene and thus attenuate the taint of the illegal arrest. Foster v. State, 677 S.W.2d 507 (Tex. Crim. App. 1984). The state's burden to establish intervening circumstances that attenuate the taint is heavy. Foster. The defendant's status as a lawyer is an insufficient intervening circumstance. Foster.

Allowing the suspect to read the confession of a co-defendant during the interrogation is, alone, an insufficient intervening circumstance. Gregg v. State, 667 S.W.2d 125 (Tex. Crim. App. 1984). Merely allowing the suspect to drink coffee and talk with his alcohol program counselor during the interrogation are insufficient intervening circumstances to attenuate the taint of an illegal arrest. Ussery v. State, 651 S.W.2d 767 (Tex. Crim. App. 1983).

Confronting a suspect with evidence that is derived independently of the illegal arrest is a factor that weighs in favor of the state. Monge v. State, 315 S.W.3d 35 (Tex. Crim. App. 2010).

Sufficient intervening circumstances are present when five days elapse between the illegal arrest and the confession, and the suspect is allowed to consult with attorneys and family. Wicker v. State, 667 S.W.2d 137 (Tex. Crim. App. 1984).

An extremely important intervening circumstance is the release of the defendant from custody between the illegal arrest and the confession. Maixner v. State, 753 S.W.2d 151 (Tex. Crim. App. 1988).

Taking a defendant before a neutral magistrate is an important intervening circumstance. Hankins v. State, 132 S.W.3d 380 (Tex. Crim. App. 2004).

The fact that the defendant became emotional, stated that he had "messed up," and asked to speak to the detective is a product of the defendant's free will and an intervening circumstance which weighs heavily in favor of the state. Crutsinger v. State, 206 S.W.3d 607 (Tex. Crim. App. 2006).

§6:62.4 Police Misconduct

The fourth factor enunciated in Brown, that of police conduct, is one of the most important factors to be considered. Bell v. State, 724 S.W.2d 780 (Tex. Crim. App. 1986); and is perhaps the most important of the four factors. Self v. State, 709 S.W.2d 662 (Tex. Crim. App. 1986). *See* §6:82.

The proof of attenuation required should be the clearest where the police conduct is the most flagrant. Examples of flagrant police conduct include:

- Reliance on factors in making an arrest which were so lacking in indicia of probable cause as to render belief in its existence entirely unreasonable
- Arrest effectuated as a pretext for collateral objectives

- Arrest which is unnecessarily intrusive on personal privacy

Bell.

An arrest made solely on the basis of an unsubstantiated tip that identified the defendant only as an acquaintance of the murder victim is an example of flagrant police misconduct. Brown. An arrest made with probable cause but without the formality of an arrest warrant is an example of non-flagrant police conduct lacking the quality of purposefulness of an expedition for evidence indicative of flagrant misconduct. Maixner; Self.

Where the police had probable cause to obtain a warrant to arrest the defendant for an offense, although they arrested the defendant without a warrant for another offense, their conduct was found to be not purposeful or flagrant. Crutsinger v. State, 206 S.W.3d 607 (Tex. Crim. App. 2006); Monge v. State, 315 S.W.3d 35 (Tex. Crim. App. 2010).

§6:70 Oral Confessions

§6:71 Types

Oral confessions are admissible under several circumstances:

- Made in a non-custodial situation (CCP Art. 38.22 §5)
- Statement is electronically recorded and the proper predicate is laid under CCP Art. 38.22 §3
- Statement is made by the accused in open court at his trial, before a grand jury, or at an examining trial (CCP Art. 38.22 §5)
- Statement is res gestae of the arrest or of the offense (CCP Art. 38.22 §5)
- Statement has a bearing upon the credibility of the accused as a witness (CCP Art. 38.22 §5)
- Statement is admissible under law (CCP Art. 38.22 §5)
- Statement contains assertions of facts or circumstances that are found to be true and which conduce to establish the guilt of the accused, such as the finding of secreted or stolen property or the instrument with which he states the offense was committed (CCP Art. 38.22 §3(c))

§6:72 In General

A non-custodial oral statement is admissible as substantive evidence as well as for its impeachment value. Chambliss v. State, 647 S.W.2d 257 (Tex. Crim. App. 1983). The law surrounding the voluntariness of confessions applies to oral confessions to the same extent as written confessions. Boles v. Stevenson, 379 U.S. 43, 85 S.Ct. 174, 13 L.Ed.2d 109 (1964); Terrazas v. State, 4 S.W.3d 720 (Tex. Crim. App. 1999).

Where the voluntariness of an oral confession is questioned, a voluntariness hearing must be held. It is reversible error to not hold such a hearing. Moore v. State, 505 S.W.2d 887 (Tex. Crim. App. 1974).

A defendant can invoke the right to an attorney as to a written statement while waiving the right as to oral statements. Connecticut v. Barrett, 479 U.S. 523, 107 S.Ct. 828, 93 L.Ed.2d 920 (1987).

Illegally obtained oral confessions are not admissible in the punishment phase of capital murder trials. Rumbaugh v. State, 589 S.W.2d 414 (Tex. Crim. App. 1979).

When the State introduces a part of an oral confession that inculpates defendant, the court should allow the defendant to elicit from the state witness that part of the confession that exculpates defendant. Texas Rules of Evidence 107.

An oral confession is sufficient evidence to convict if the evidence otherwise proves the corpus delicti. Gordon v. State, 667 S.W.2d 544 (Tex. App.—Beaumont 1983, *pet. ref'd*).

TIP TO THE PROSECUTION: When presenting an oral confession to the jury, prepare a written transcript. This will allow the jury to better follow the wording of the confession and is permissible when accompanied by the proper instruction. Moore v. State, 882 S.W.2d 844 (Tex. Crim. App. 1994).

§6:72.1 Form: Motion to Reduce Oral Statements to Writing

See our companion book *Texas Criminal Forms* (James Publishing) Form 6-1.

§6:73 Admissibility

The requirements for the admissibility of oral statements are found in CCP Art. 38.22 §§3 and 5. Generally, the requirements for the admissibility for admission of oral statements are the same as that for written statements. However, there are some exceptions.

The oral confession statute does not require that a recorded statement contain an express verbal statement from an accused that he waives his rights prior to giving a statement. Barefield v. State, 784 S.W.2d 38 (Tex. Crim. App. 1989); Etheridge v. State, 903 S.W.2d 1 (Tex. Crim. App. 1994).

The CCP Art. 38.22 §2(a) requirement that the warnings must be given by a magistrate or the person to whom the statement is made does not apply to oral confessions, which are governed by §3. Dowthitt v. State, 931 S.W.2d 244 (Tex. Crim. App. 1996).

The plain language of Art. 38.22, §3(e) requires strict compliance with all portions of §3(a), which sets out the specific conditions that must be satisfied before such statements may be used as evidence against a defendant. Art. 38.22, §3(a)(1) makes no distinction between in-state and out-of-state oral statements, made as a result of custodial interrogation, which are not in compliance with its dictates; and therefore, Texas law will always govern admissibility. Davidson v. State, 25 S.W.3d 183 (Tex. Crim. App. 2000).

CCP Art. 38.22. When Statements May Be Used

> *§8. Notwithstanding any other provision of this article, a written, oral, or sign language statement of an accused made as a result of a custodial interrogation is admissible against the accused in a criminal proceeding in this state if:*
>
> *(1) the statement was obtained in another state and was obtained in compliance with the laws of that state or this state*
>
> *(2) the statement was obtained by a federal law enforcement officer in this state or another state and was obtained in compliance with the laws of the United States.*

Where a defendant is a juvenile at the time of the commission of an offense, the admissibility of the defendant's statement is decided under Title 3 of the Texas Family Code, not Article 38.22; and therefore Davidson is inapplicable. Vega v. State, 84 S.W.3d 613 (Tex. Crim. App. 2002).

§6:73.1 Assertions of Truth and Discovery of Evidence

CCP Art. 38.22 §3(c) allows admission of oral statements that contain assertions of fact or circumstances conducive to establishing the guilt of the accused and places no limitation on the manner in which the facts asserted are found to be true. Port v. State, 791 S.W.2d 103 (Tex. Crim. App. 1990). The examples set out in CCP Art. 38.22 §3(c) are illustrative only and are not a limitation on the admission of oral statements under this Section. Gunter v. State, 858 S.W.2d 430 (Tex. Crim. App. 1993).

The statement is admissible if some of the facts therein are found to be true after the statement is made. Port. Even if only one of the assertions contained within an oral statement is found to be true, the entire confession is admissible. Port; Gunter. There is no requirement that the defendant clearly admit commission of the crime in order for the entire confession to be admissible. Anderson v. State, 701 S.W.2d 868 (Tex. Crim. App. 1985).

In Port, the defendant's statement was found to be admissible because a subsequent autopsy corroborated his statement that he used a particular handgun to cause the death of the deceased; and the fact that the handgun was already in the custody of the police did not render the statement inadmissible.

In a case where the defendant orally confessed that he used a particular knife to commit a murder but it was never established that the particular knife could have been the murder weapon, the statement was found to be inadmissible. Romero v. State, 800 S.W.2d 539 (Tex. Crim. App. 1990).

Where the defendant's statement led to the discovery of the victim's body, the entire statement is admissible. Anderson.

The phrase "[f]ound to be true," as contained in Art. 38.22 §3(c), means facts about which the police were unaware at the time of the confession that are later, after the confession, found to be true. Dansby v. State, 931 S.W.2d 297 (Tex. Crim. App. 1996). The statute places no limitation on the manner in which the facts are found to be true. Gunter.

Statements that are nothing more than an assertion of guilt are not admissible under this section. Almanza v. State, 839 S.W.2d 817 (Tex. Crim. App. 1992) (defendant merely pointed to a piece of paper later found to contain heroin and stated that it was his "personal stuff").

Even where the most incriminating part of the defendant's long, continuous statement was given after the earlier statement that led to evidence which conduced to establish his guilt, the entire statement was nevertheless admissible. Marini v. State, 593 S.W.2d 709 (Tex. Crim. App. 1980).

The giving of the Miranda warnings is not a prerequisite to the admission of a statement admitted under this theory; even where the statement was made as the result of custodial interrogation. Perillo v. State, 758 S.W.2d 567 (Tex. Crim. App. 1988); Ex parte Stansbery, 702 S.W.2d 643 (Tex. Crim. App. 1986). However, at least one other court has held that a valid Miranda waiver is necessary to the admis-sion of a statement under this theory, where the statement was made while the suspect was in custody. Hutchison v. State, 424 S.W.3d 164, 182 (Tex. App.—Texarkana 2014, *no pet.*).

§6:73.2 Electronically Recorded Statements

Under Article 38.22, §3(a)(2) of the Code of Criminal Procedure, before an oral recorded statement may be admitted into evidence, the State must show, *inter alia,* that prior to the statement but during the recording the accused is given the warning in Subsection (a) of §2 above and the accused knowingly, intelligently, and voluntarily waives any rights set out in the warning. Leza v. State, 351 S.W.3d 344 (Tex. Crim. App. 2011).

Art. 38.22 §3(a)(5) prohibits the admission of a recorded oral statement if a copy of the statement is not provided to defense counsel at least twenty (20) days before the proceeding. For purposes of this section, "proceeding" means all steps between official accusation and final judgment. Thus, a copy must be served upon defense counsel at least twenty (20) days before voir dire in the case begins. Tigner v. State, 928 S.W.2d 540 (Tex. Crim. App. 1996). Transcripts of the electronic recording do not constitute copies of the recordings for purposes of the statute; the copy itself must be an electronic recording. Tigner.

The proceeding to which the 20-day requirement applies is the same proceeding at which the evidence is rendered inadmissible, when there is no compliance. Thus, failure to provide the recording twenty days before a pretrial hearing renders the oral confession inadmissible at the pretrial hearing. Sells v. State, 121 S.W.3d 748 (Tex. Crim. App. 2003).

The defendant must object at a pretrial hearing to preserve error in the state's failure to deliver to him copies of any electronically recorded confession at least twenty (20) days prior to a "proceeding." Lane v. State, 933 S.W.2d 504 (Tex. Crim. App. 1996) (plurality opinion). The statute requires only that the defendant have access to the tapes at least twenty (20) days before the proceeding, not that copies actually be delivered to him. Lane.

The practical remedy for the failure to comply with §3(a)(5) with regard to the pretrial hearing is a 20-day continuance of the hearing. Lane; Sells.

Since the legislature deleted the applicable provision in 1989, the oral confession statute does not require that the suspect be informed that his confession is being tape-recorded. Moore v. State, 882 S.W.2d 844 (Tex. Crim. App. 1994). A law enforcement officer's subjective reasoning for intentionally not informing a suspect of the fact that the confession is being recorded is no longer independently relevant to the admissibility of the oral confession. Moore.

A confession recorded without the knowledge of the suspect will not be found involuntary even though the detective ignored the suspect's specific request that the confession not be recorded, even where the suspect would not have made the confession had he known it was being recorded. Flemming v. State, 949 S.W.2d 876 (Tex.App.—Houston [14th Dist.] 1997).

Accidental alterations in the audiotape do not render it inadmissible if the alteration is sufficiently explained such that the reliability and trustworthiness of the recording are intact. Quinones v. State, 592 S.W.2d 933 (Tex. Crim. App. 1980).

Where brief interruptions in the tape recording occur accidentally, obscuring nothing of value in the dialogue, and there is adequate evidence to support the conclusion that the breaks were merely inadvertent and did not affect the overall reliability of the tape, the tape will be admissible. Maldonado v. State, 998 S.W.2d 239 (Tex. Crim. App. 1999).

Circumstantial evidence can be sufficient to establish the authenticity and voluntariness of a sound recording. Wallace v. State, 782 S.W.2d 854 (Tex. Crim. App. 1989).

An electronically recorded oral statement is not required to contain an express waiver of rights by the defendant before it can be admissible. Rocha v. State, 16 S.W.3d 1 (Tex. Crim. App. 2000).

A claim that certain portions of an audio recording of a defendant's statement to the police are inaudible does not mean that these portions of the court reporter's record are lost or destroyed for purposes of TEX.R.App.P. 34.6(f). Lucio v. State, 351 S.W.3d 878 (Tex. Crim. App. 2011).

For an example of a case where it was held that audio recordings that were incomplete and inaccurately represented a conversation between a peace officer and a defendant were inadmissible pursuant to article 38.22, section 3(a)(3) of the Code of Criminal Procedure see Flores v. State, (No. PD-1189-15, 2018 WL 2327162, May 23, 2018, unpublished).

§6:73.3 Statements Res Gestae of Arrest

Where a police officer was looking for someone who had just shot the deceased, had the defendant at gunpoint, and was told by the defendant, "I shot her," the statement was admissible as *res gestae* of the arrest under CCP Art. 38.22 §5. Bryant v. State, 816 S.W.2d 554 (Tex.App.—Fort Worth 1991, *no pet.*).

Under the above circumstances, the officer is not required to warn the defendant of his rights under Miranda before the statement can be admitted. Bryant (citing New York v. Quarles, 467 U.S. 649, 104 S.Ct. 2626, 81 L.Ed.2d 550 (1984)).

§6:74 Prior Testimony of the Defendant

Reading a portion of the defendant's grand jury testimony, which contained a confession to a crime, is permitted under CCP Art. 38.22 §5. Fuller v. State, 827 S.W.2d 919 (Tex. Crim. App. 1992).

§6:80 Corroboration of Extrajudicial Confessions

Under the common law, the corpus delicti rule concerns the usability in a criminal case of a confession made by the defendant outside of court. The old corpus-delicti usability rule has, however, been superceded by the due-process sufficiency of the evidence model set out in Jackson v. Virginia. Carrizales v. State, 414 S.W.3d 737, 742 (Tex. Crim. App. 2015); Nisbett v. State, 552 S.W.3d 244, 263 (Tex. Crim. App. 2018).

No criminal conviction can be based upon a defendant's extrajudicial confession unless the confession is corroborated by independent evidence tending to establish the *corpus delicti*. Fisher v. State, 851 S.W.2d 298 (Tex. Crim. App. 1993).

The *corpus delicti* rule requires that there be some independent evidence tending to show the essential nature of the charged crime. That is, there must be evidence that an offense was committed and that it was the result of criminal conduct rather than accident. Salazar v. State, 86 S.W.3d 640 (Tex. Crim. App. 2002). The rule does not require corroboration of every element and descriptive allegation in the indictment. Salazar.

The corpus delicti rule requires corroboration of two elements of a crime—"an injury or loss and a criminal agent"—but there need not be any independent evidence that the defendant was the criminal culprit. Bradford v. State, 515 S.W.3d 433, 437 (Tex. App.—Houston [14th Dist.] 2017, pet.ref'd).

The corpus delicti rule applies to admissions of incriminating facts that do not amount to a full confession of guilt. Bradford v. State, 515 S.W.3d at 437.

The corpus delicti rule will apply to crimes of omission as well as crimes of commission. Bradford v. State, 515 S.W.3d at 442 (where appellant was charged with the offense of failing to report child abuse).

In a capital murder case, the evidence must also establish the *corpus delicti* of the underlying offense making the murder a capital crime. Gribble v. State, 808 S.W.2d 65 (Tex. Crim. App. 1990) (*plurality op.*). The corroborating evidence need not, however, be sufficient by itself to establish the underlying offense. Gribble.

Texas criminal law recognizes a closely related crimes exception to the corpus delicti rule in cases with an extrajudicial confession, and it is implicated when the temporal connection between the offenses confessed to is sufficiently close that introduction of the confession does not violate the purposes of the corpus delicti rule. Miller v. State, 457 S.W.3d 919, 927 (Tex. Crim. App. 2015).

The closely related crime exception comes into play where an accused is charged with more than one crime, and the accused makes a statement related to all the crimes charged, but the prosecution is only able to establish the corpus delicti of one of the crimes charged. Under those circumstances where the relationship between the crimes is sufficiently close so that the introduction of the statement will not violate the purpose underlying the corpus delicti rule, the statement of the accused will be admissible as to all the crimes charged. Miller, 919 S.W.3d at 926.

The *corpus delicti* doctrine does not apply to extraneous offenses offered at the punishment phase of a capital murder trial. Bible v. State, 162 S.W.3d 234 (Tex. Crim. App. 2005).

However, an uncorroborated confession is sufficient evidence to revoke probation. Bush v. State, 506 S.W.2d 603 (Tex. Crim. App. 1974).

A judicial confession does not require corroboration. Dinnery v. State, 592 S.W.2d 343 (Tex. Crim. App. 1979).

§6:90 Juvenile Confessions

Family Code §51.09. Waiver of Rights

Unless a contrary intent clearly appears elsewhere in this title, any right granted to a child by this title or by the constitution or laws of this state or the United States may be waived in proceedings under this title if:

(1) the waiver is made by the child and the attorney for the child;

(2) the child and the attorney waiving the right are informed of and understand the right and the possible consequences of waiving it;

(3) the waiver is voluntary; and

(4) the waiver is made in writing or in court proceedings that are recorded.

Family Code §51.095. Admissibility of a Statement of a Child

(a) Notwithstanding Section 51.09, the statement of a child is admissible in evidence in any future proceeding concerning the matter about which the statement was given if:

(1) the statement is made in writing under a circumstance described by Subsection (d) and:

(A) the statement shows that the child has at some time before the making of the statement received from a magistrate a warning that:

(i) the child may remain silent and not make any statement at all and that any statement that the child makes may be used in evidence against the child;

(ii) the child has the right to have an attorney present to advise the

child either prior to any questioning or during the questioning;

(iii) if the child is unable to employ an attorney, the child has the right to have an attorney appointed to counsel with the child before or during any interviews with peace officers or attorneys representing the state; and

(iv) the child has the right to terminate the interview at any time;

(B) and:

(i) the statement must be signed in the presence of a magistrate by the child with no law enforcement officer or prosecuting attorney present, except that a magistrate may require a bailiff or a law enforcement officer if a bailiff is not available to be present if the magistrate determines that the presence of the bailiff or law enforcement officer is necessary for the personal safety of the magistrate or other court personnel, provided that the bailiff or law enforcement officer may not carry a weapon in the presence of the child; and

(ii) the magistrate must be fully convinced that the child understands the nature and contents of the statement and that the child is signing the same voluntarily, and if a statement is taken, the magistrate must sign a written statement verifying the foregoing requisites have been met;

(C) the child knowingly, intelligently, and voluntarily waives these rights before and during the making of the statement and signs the statement in the presence of a magistrate; and

(D) the magistrate certifies that the magistrate has examined the child independent of any law enforcement officer or prosecuting attorney, except as required to ensure the personal safety of the magistrate or other court personnel, and has determined that the child understands the nature and contents of the statement and has knowingly, intelligently, and voluntarily waived these rights;

(2) the statement is made orally and the child makes a statement of facts or circumstances that are found to be true and tend to establish the child's guilt, such as the finding of secreted or stolen property, or the instrument with which the child states the offense was committed;

(3) the statement was res gestae of the delinquent conduct or the conduct indicating a need for supervision or of the arrest;

(4) the statement is made:

(A) in open court at the child's adjudication hearing;

(B) before a grand jury considering a petition, under Section 53.045, that the child engaged in delinquent conduct; or

(C) at a preliminary hearing concerning the child held in compliance with this code,

other than at a detention hearing under Section 54.01; or

(5) subject to Subsection (f), the statement is made orally under a circumstance described by Subsection (d) and the statement is recorded by an electronic recording device, including a device that records images, and:

(A) before making the statement, the child is given the warning described by Subdivision (1)(A) by a magistrate, the warning is a part of the recording, and the child knowingly, intelligently, and voluntarily waives each right stated in the warning;

(B) the recording device is capable of making an accurate recording, the operator of the device is competent to use the device, the recording is accurate, and the recording has not been altered;

(C) each voice on the recording is identified; and

(D) not later than the 20th day before the date of the proceeding, the attorney representing the child is given a complete and accurate copy of each recording of the child made under this subdivision.

(b) This section and Section 51.09 do not preclude the admission of a statement made by the child if:

(1) the statement does not stem from interrogation of the child under a circumstance described by Subsection (d); or

(2) without regard to whether the statement stems from interrogation of the child under a circumstance described by Subsection (d), the statement is:

(A) voluntary and has a bearing on the credibility of the child as a witness; or

(B) recorded by an electronic recording device, including a device that records images, and is obtained:

(i) in another state in compliance with the laws of that state or this state; or

(ii) by a federal law enforcement officer in this state or another state in compliance with the laws of the United States.

(c) An electronic recording of a child's statement made under Subsection (a)(5) or (b)(2)(B) shall be preserved until all juvenile or criminal matters relating to any conduct referred to in the statement are final, including the exhaustion of all appeals, or barred from prosecution.

(d) Subsections (a)(1) and (a)(5) apply to the statement of a child made:

(1) while the child is in a detention facility or other place of confinement;

(2) while the child is in the custody of an officer; or

(3) during or after the interrogation of the child by an officer if the child is in the possession of the Department of Family and Protective Services and is suspected to have engaged in conduct that violates a penal law of this state.

(e) A juvenile law referee or master may perform the duties imposed on a magistrate under this section without the approval of the juvenile court if the

juvenile board of the county in which the statement of the child is made has authorized a referee or master to perform the duties of a magistrate under this section.

(f) A magistrate who provides the warnings required by Subsection (a)(5) for a recorded statement may at the time the warnings are provided request by speaking on the recording that the officer return the child and the recording to the magistrate at the conclusion of the process of questioning. The magistrate may then view the recording with the child or have the child view the recording to enable the magistrate to determine whether the child's statements were given voluntarily. The magistrate's determination of voluntariness shall be reduced to writing and signed and dated by the magistrate. If a magistrate uses the procedure described by this subsection, a child's statement is not admissible unless the magistrate determines that the statement was given voluntarily.

Family Code §51.17. Procedure and Evidence

(a) Except for the burden of proof to be borne by the state in adjudicating a child to be delinquent or in need of supervision under Section 54.03(f) or otherwise when in conflict with a provision of this title, the Texas Rules of Civil Procedure govern proceedings under this title.

(b) Discovery in a proceeding under this title is governed by the Code of Criminal Procedure and by case decisions in criminal cases.

(c) Except as otherwise provided by this title, the Texas Rules of Evidence apply to criminal cases and Articles 33.03 and 37.07 and Chapter 38, Code of Criminal Procedure, apply in a judicial proceeding under this title.

(d) When on the motion for appointment of an interpreter by a party or on the motion of the juvenile court, in any proceeding under this title, the court determines that the child, the child's parent or guardian, or a witness does not understand and speak English, an interpreter must be sworn to interpret for the person as provided by Article 38.30, Code of Criminal Procedure.

(e) In any proceeding under this title, if a party notifies the court that the child, the child's parent or guardian, or a witness is deaf, the court shall appoint a qualified interpreter to interpret the proceedings in any language, including sign language, that the deaf person can understand, as provided by Article 38.31, Code of Criminal Procedure.

(f) Any requirement under this title that a document contain a person's signature, including the signature of a judge or a clerk of the court, is satisfied if the document contains the signature of the person as captured on an electronic device or as a digital signature. Article 2.26, Code of Criminal Procedure, applies in a proceeding held under this title.

(g) Articles 21.07, 26.07, 26.08, 26.09, and 26.10, Code of Criminal Procedure, relating to the name of an adult defendant in a criminal case, apply to a child in a proceeding held under this title.

(h) Articles 57.01 and 57.02, Code of Criminal Procedure, relating to the use of a pseudonym by a victim in a criminal case, apply in a proceeding held under this title.

(i) Except as provided by Section 56.03(f), the state is not required to pay any cost or fee otherwise imposed for court proceedings in either the trial or appellate courts.

Family Code §52.02. Release or Delivery to Court

(a) Except as provided by Subsection (c), a person taking a child into custody, without unnecessary delay and without first taking the child to any place other than a juvenile processing office designated under Section 52.025, shall do one of the following:

(1) release the child to a parent, guardian, custodian of the child, or other responsible adult upon that person's promise to bring the child before the juvenile court as requested by the court;

(2) bring the child before the office or official designated by the juvenile board if there is probable cause to believe that the child engaged in delinquent conduct, conduct indicating a need for supervision, or conduct that violates a condition of probation imposed by the juvenile court;

(3) bring the child to a detention facility designated by the juvenile board;

(4) bring the child to a secure detention facility as provided by Section 51.12(j);

(5) bring the child to a medical facility if the child is believed to suffer from a serious physical condition or illness that requires prompt treatment;

(6) dispose of the case under Section 52.03; or

(7) if school is in session and the child is a student, bring the child to the school campus to which the child is assigned if the principal, the principal's designee, or a peace officer assigned to the campus agrees to assume responsibility for the child for the remainder of the school day.

(b) A person taking a child into custody shall promptly give notice of the person's action and a statement of the reason for taking the child into custody, to:

(1) the child's parent, guardian, or custodian; and

(2) the office or official designated by the juvenile board.

(c) A person who takes a child into custody and who has reasonable grounds to believe that the child has been operating a motor vehicle in a public place while having any detectable amount of alcohol in the child's system may, before complying with Subsection (a):

(1) take the child to a place to obtain a specimen of the child's breath or blood as provided by Chapter 724, Transportation Code; and

(2) perform intoxilyzer processing and videotaping of the child in an adult processing office of a law enforcement agency.

(d) Notwithstanding Section 51.09(a), a child taken into custody as provided by Subsection (c) may submit to the taking of a breath specimen or refuse to submit to the taking of a breath specimen without the concurrence of an attorney, but only if the request made of the child to give the specimen and the child's response to that request is videotaped. A videotape made under this subsection must be maintained until the disposition of any proceeding against the child relating to the arrest is final and be made available to an attorney representing the child during that period.

§6:91 In General

Although juvenile delinquency proceedings are considered civil proceedings, they are quasi-criminal in nature. In Re J.R., 907 S.W.2d 107 (Tex.App.—Austin 1995, *no writ*); C.E.J. v. State, 788 S.W.2d 849 (Tex.App.—Dallas 1990, *writ denied*); Smith v. Rankin, 661 S.W.2d 152 (Tex. App.—Houston [1st Dist.] 1983, *orig. proceeding*).

Numerous aspects of juvenile proceedings are governed by criminal procedural rules; including:

- State's burden of proof
- Presumption of innocence
- Right to trial by jury
- Privilege against self-incrimination
- Right to confrontation of witnesses
- Right to representation by counsel

Family Code §54.03; In Re J.R.; In Re M.A.G., 541 S.W.2d 899 (Tex. Civ. App. Corpus Christi 1976, *writ ref'd n.r.e.*); In Re R.C.S., 940 S.W.2d 750 (Tex.App.—El Paso 1997) (*op. denying rehearing*).

Where the defendant was a juvenile at the time of his arrest, the provisions of the Texas Family Code control issues regarding the admissibility of a confession (even where the defendant is later certified to stand trial as an adult). Roquemore v. State, 60 S.W.3d 862 (Tex. Crim. App. 2001). The appellate courts have established a policy of strict compliance with the Family Code. Roquemore.

Other than these matters, civil procedural rules apply. Family Code §51.17(a) & (b); In Re R.C.S.

Family Code §51.095 is the juvenile equivalent of CCP Art. 38.22.

Where a defendant is a juvenile at the time of the commission of an offense, the admissibility of the defendant's statement is decided under Title 3 of the Family Code, not Art. 38.22. Vega v. State, 84 S.W.3d 613 (Tex. Crim. App. 2002).

Where it was known to the interviewing officer at the time of police questioning that the interviewee was a juvenile, or would have been objectively apparent to a reasonable officer, the inclusion in the Miranda custody analysis of that fact is consistent with the objective nature of the custody test. While a child's age will not be a determinative, or even a significant, factor in every case, in some cases, it will prove an important factor in deciding if the child was in custody for Miranda purposes. J.D.B. v. North Carolina, 564 U.S. ___, 131 S.Ct. 2394, 2406, 180 L.Ed.2d 310 (2011).

Before the enactment of Family Code §51.17 the Family Code applied to all proceedings until transfer to adult court, such that the Family Code governed procedure surrounding the taking of confessions. Travis v. State, 921 S.W.2d 559 (Tex. App.—Beaumont 1996); Griffin v. State, 765 S.W.2d 422 (Tex. Crim. App. 1989).

Certain statements by juveniles are exempted from use by the state as confessions. Family Code §53.03(c) (statements made by a juvenile during an intake conference); Family Code §54.01 (statements made by a juvenile during a detention hearing).

Where the police had no reason to disbelieve the defendant's assertions that he was 17 years of age at the time he gave a confession, and it is later learned that the defendant was actually 15, the defendant has waived any error resulting from the police not complying with the Family Code rules for taking juvenile confessions. Childs v. State, 21 S.W.3d 631 (Tex.App.—Houston [14th Dist.] 2000, *pet. ref'd*).

§6:92 Custodial Statements

Before a police officer can take the custodial confession of a juvenile, a decision to further detain the juvenile must be made by the proper official designated by the juvenile court. Comer v. State, 776 S.W.2d 191 (Tex. Crim. App. 1989), citing Family Code §51.09(b)(1) (as it existed before the 1997 amendments).

Failure to take the juvenile before the proper authority before subjecting him to further custody will render a subsequent confession inadmissible. Comer.

Under the plain language of Family Code §52.02(b)(1), an officer must inform a child's parent of "the reason" for taking the child into custody. That is, police must provide a parent with the legal justification for the officer's action. However, the section does not require police to re-notify parents concerning their suspicions of criminal conduct or any other further suspicions. Hampton v. State, 86 S.W.3d 603 (Tex. Crim. App. 2002).

Family Code §52.02(a) has three requirements once a juvenile is taken into custody:

- the officer must do one of the six acts enumerated in the statute;
- without unnecessary delay; and

- without first taking the child to any place other than a juvenile processing office.

Roquemore v. State, 60 S.W.3d 862 (Tex. Crim. App. 2001) (where officers violated the statute by taking the juvenile to recover stolen property first).

PRACTICE TIP: Effective September 1, 2007, there are seven requirements an officer must fulfill under §52.02(a) upon taking a juvenile into custody. See §6:160, above.

Family Code §52.02(a) requires that after being warned by a magistrate that a juvenile suspect must be interrogated only in an area designated for such by a juvenile court. Le v. State, 993 S.W.2d 650 (Tex. Crim. App. 1999).

Under Family Code §51.09(d)(2), if a statement does not stem from a custodial interrogation, the statement is admissible. Roquemore.

Once a defendant produces evidence that §52.02(a) was violated, the burden then shifts to the state to show compliance with the statute. Roquemore.

Evidence obtained in violation of §52.02(a) should be excluded under CCP Art. 38.23 where there is a causal connection between the illegality and the evidence. Roquemore.

The burden is on the defendant, as the moving party in a motion to suppress evidence obtained in violation of the law under Art. 38.23, to produce evidence demonstrating a causal connection between the alleged statutory violation and the resulting evidence. The burden then shifts to the state to either disprove the evidence the defendant has produced, or bring an attenuation-of-taint argument to demonstrate that the causal chain asserted by the defendant was in fact broken. Pham v. State, 175 S.W.3d 767 (Tex. Crim. App. 2005).

Before a juvenile's statement will be excluded from evidence under CCP Art. 38.22 for a violation of the Family Code §52.02(b) that requires a detaining authority to notify the juvenile's parent, there must be a causal connection between the failure to notify the parent and the giving of the statement. Gonzales v. State, 67 S.W.3d 910 (Tex. Crim. App. 2002).

Where a juvenile's statement is taken in another state, a conflict-of-laws analysis is conducted to determine which state's laws govern the admissibility of the statement. Vega v. State, 84 S.W.3d 613 (Tex. Crim. App. 2002).

§6:93 Voluntariness

The state carries the burden of proving that a confession was given voluntarily under the due process clause; at least once accused has alleged it was not. Griffin v. State, 765 S.W.2d 422 (Tex. Crim. App. 1989). The voluntariness of a waiver of the right against self-incrimination and due process rights must be established by a preponderance of the evidence. Griffin.

The proper test in determining whether a juvenile has validly waived his privilege against self-incrimination is the totality of the circumstances test. Spears v. State, 801 S.W.2d 571 (Tex.App.—Fort Worth 1990). If the circumstances indicate that the juvenile defendant was threatened, coerced, promised something in exchange for his confession, or incapable of understanding his rights and warnings, the trial court must conclude the confession is involuntary. In re R.M., 880 S.W.2d 297 (Tex.App.—Fort Worth 1994).

A confession was found to be voluntary where on the day following the arrest the 16-year-old suspect was removed from the juvenile detention center to the police department, and after being warned of his rights by a magistrate was taken upstairs to a designated juvenile facility, but, on finding that facility unavailable, was removed to homicide division and was questioned while isolated from all adult offenders and was then taken back downstairs and warned of his rights a second time and then signed the confession in the magistrate's presence. Matthews v. State, 677 S.W.2d 282 (Tex.App.—Fort Worth 1984).

The fact that a juvenile's oral statement to police was not obtained in compliance with the Family Code did not render a subsequent written confession inadmissible in a criminal trial of the juvenile as an adult, where the subsequent written statement was given after the juvenile waived her Miranda rights; and where a second magistrate's warning was a significant intervening circumstance. Griffin. *See also*, In Re J.T.H., 779 S.W.2d 954 (Tex.App.—Austin 1989).

§6:94 Sufficiency of Warnings

Family Code §51.09 requires that a magistrate certify that the juvenile "knowingly, intelligently and voluntarily" waived his rights prior to accepting the juvenile's confession. In re R.M., 880 S.W.2d 297 (Tex.App.—Fort Worth 1994).

A warning which was given to a child following his detention in connection with a burglary, which expressly warned him of his right to counsel prior to or during interrogation and which contained the substantial equivalent of the Miranda language, was adequate to meet the Miranda requirements despite the fact that the child was not warned that an attorney would be appointed to represent him if he were too poor to employ an attorney himself. In re B.J.N., 667 S.W.2d 347 (Tex.App.—Amarillo 1984).

The juvenile warning statute does not require that the child's parent be informed of the juvenile's right to court-appointed counsel before a confession is given, nor does the statute require that a child's parent be present when the juvenile waives right to counsel. In re B.J.N.

A juvenile's statement that was written before the juvenile was given the statutory warnings by a magistrate, but not signed until after a magistrate gave the juvenile the warnings, where the magistrate informed the juvenile that he did not have to give a statement at all, the magistrate was convinced that the juvenile understood the nature and contents of the statement, and the juvenile signed it voluntarily, was admissible. Petree v. State, 778 S.W.2d 507 (Tex.App.—Dallas 1989).

The reading of the magistrate's warnings by someone other than the magistrate will not render a confession inadmissible where the magistrate was present during the reading of the warnings, made inquiry of the juvenile as to whether he understood them, and then magistrate then signed the required certification. In re S.D.W., 811 S.W.2d 739 (Tex. App.—Houston [1st Dist.] 1991).

Texas Family Code subsection 51.095(a)(1)(A) does not explicitly prohibit the presence of law-enforcement officers when a magistrate reads the required statutory rights to a juvenile. Herring v. State, 395 S.W.3d 161, 165 (Tex. Crim. App. 2013).

TIP TO THE PROSECUTION: Compose a form for the taking of a suspect's statement which contains on its face the Family Code §51.095 warnings and a valid waiver thereof, and distribute it to all local police agencies for their use.

Further revisions to chapter 6

6:22.8; 6:34; 6:35; 6:57

§6:95 Oral Statements

Where the oral confession of a juvenile led to the recovery of stolen property, the statement was admissible. Salazar v. State, 648 S.W.2d 421 (Tex. App.—3 1983). *See also*, Littlefield v. State, 720 S.W.2d 254 (Tex.App.—Beaumont 1986); Spears v. State, 801 S.W.2d 571 (Tex.App.—Fort Worth 1990).

If even one assertion in an oral statement is found to be true, the entire statement is admissible. S.D.J. v. State, 879 S.W.2d 370 (Tex.App.—Eastland 1994).

§6:100 Objections to Admissibility

§6:101 Requirement of Objection

Lodging an objection is required if the defendant wishes to complain against the admission of a confession. Ross v. State, 678 S.W.2d 491 (Tex. Crim. App. 1984); Harris v. State, 827 S.W.2d 949 (Tex. Crim. App. 1992); Wainwright v. Sykes, 433 U.S. 72, 97 S.Ct. 2497, 53 L.Ed.2d 594 (1977).

A defendant who objected to the admission of his confession under state law was not required to specifically object to its admission on a particular statutory ground in order to invoke the state exclusionary rule. He was only required to object to its admissibility on the ground that it was obtained through illegal search or seizure. Polk v. State, 738 S.W.2d 274 (Tex. Crim. App. 1987).

However, an objection to a technical aspect of the taking of the confession must be specific enough to apprise the trial court of the nature of the complaint. For example, an objection that a confession is not voluntary is not specific enough to preserve appeal on the issue of whether the confession is invalid because the suspect was informed that the confession could be used "for or against" him. Ramirez v. State, 815 S.W.2d 636 (Tex. Crim. App. 1991).

An objection as to an "improper predicate" is insufficient to preserve the issue. Walsh v. State, 658 S.W.2d 285 (Tex.App.—Fort Worth 1983).

The failure to object to a statement first used to impeach the defendant waives any error in its subsequent admission during the state's case in rebuttal. Ross.

Appellate courts review a trial court's ruling on a motion to suppress for an abuse of discretion and overturn that ruling only if it is outside the zone of reasonable disagreement. Martinez v. State, 348 S.W.3d 919, 922 (Tex.Crim.App.2011). They conduct their review with two standards, giving almost total deference to a trial court's determination of historic facts and mixed questions of law and fact that rely on the credibility of a witness, but applying a *de novo* standard of review to pure questions of law and mixed questions that do not depend on credibility determinations. Martinez, 348 S.W.3d. at 922–23.

§6:102 Nature of Objection

There are many different general objections which can be lodged to the admissibility of a confession, each with many separate subdivisions. Some of the general areas and their subdivisions are as follows.

§6:102.1 Lack of Voluntariness

- State has not proven voluntariness, generally (has not sustained its burden of proof). Terrazas v. State, 4 S.W.3d 720 (Tex. Crim. App. 1999).
- Confession was not taken in compliance with Miranda or CCP Art. 38.22. Wolfe v. State, 917 S.W.2d 270 (Tex. Crim. App. 1996).
- Due process or due course of law violation. Wolfe.
- Decision to confess was not made of the defendant's own free will. Lane v. State, 933 S.W.2d 504 (Tex. Crim. App. 1996).
- Mental or physical compulsion was employed. Colorado v. Connelly, 479 U.S. 157, 107 S.Ct. 515, 93 L.Ed.2d 473 (1986).
- Coercive police activity was employed. Connelly.
- Confession was involuntarily obtained. Ochoa v. State, 573 S.W.2d 796 (Tex. Crim. App. 1978).
- Confession is not the language of the defendant. Henson v. State, 794 S.W.2d 385 (Tex.App.—Dallas 1990, *pet. ref'd*).
- Promise made to the defendant by law enforcement officials rendered the confession involuntary. Sossamon v. State, 816 S.W.2d 340 (Tex. Crim. App. 1991).
- Defendant was told that the statement could be used "for or against" him. Dinkins v. State, 894 S.W.2d 330 (Tex. Crim. App. 1995).
- Defendant was intoxicated to the point that he was incapable of making an independent, informed choice of his free will. Nichols v. State, 754 S.W.2d 185 (Tex. Crim. App. 1988).
- Law enforcement officials inflicted pain on the defendant or tortured him such that his resulting confession was involuntary. Jenkins v. State, 912 S.W.2d 793 (Tex. Crim. App. 1995).
- Deception and/or misrepresentations by police rendered the confession involuntary. Green v. State, 934 S.W.2d 92 (Tex. Crim. App. 1996).
- Prolonged interrogation that rendered the confession involuntary. Barney v. State, 698 S.W.2d 114 (Tex. Crim. App. 1985).
- Defendant was deprived of food or sleep to the point that his resulting confession was rendered involuntary. Greenwald v. Wisconsin, 390 U.S. 519, 88 S.Ct. 1152, 20 L.Ed.2d 77 (1968).
- Confession was the product of force or violence such that it was involuntary. Roberts v. State, 545 S.W.2d 157 (Tex. Crim. App. 1977).

- Police employed prayer tactics which rendered the confession involuntary. Davis v. North Carolina, 384 U.S. 737, 86 S.Ct. 1761, 16 L.Ed.2d 895 (1966).
- Defendant's lack of intellect or his mental impairment was used through official coercion to render the confession involuntary. Walker v. State, 842 S.W.2d 301 (Tex.App.—Tyler 1992).
- Defendant was unable to understand English to the point that the resulting confession was rendered involuntary. Farmah v. State, 789 S.W.2d 665 (Tex. App.—Houston [1st Dist.] 1990).

§6:102.2 Inadequate Warnings

- Warnings did not comply with CCP Art. 38.22 or Miranda. Cockrell v. State, 933 S.W.2d 73 (Tex. Crim. App. 1996).
- Warnings do not appear on the face of the resulting written confession. Heiselbetz v. State, 906 S.W.2d 500 (Tex. Crim. App. 1995).
- Language of the warnings did not substantially comply with the wording of Miranda or CCP Art. 38.22. Cockrell.
- Warnings were not given by a magistrate. Dowthitt v. State, 931 S.W.2d 244 (Tex. Crim. App. 1996).
- Warnings were not given by the person to whom the statement was given. Dowthitt.
- Hiatus took place in interrogation and the warnings were not properly re-administered. Dowthitt.
- Foreign national defendant not warned of his right to contact his country consulate under the Vienna Convention on Consular Relations. Maldonado v. State, 998 S.W.2d 239 (Tex. Crim. App. 1999).

§6:102.3 Invalid Waiver

- Waiver was not voluntary, knowing or intelligent. Robinson v. State, 851 S.W.2d 216 (Tex. Crim. App. 1991).
- Waiver was not the product of a free and deliberate choice. Moran v. Burbine, 475 U.S. 412, 106 S.Ct. 1135, 89 L.Ed.2d 410 (1986).
- Waiver was the product of coercion. Robinson.
- Background of the accused was such that the waiver was involuntary. Colorado v. Spring, 479 U.S. 564, 107 S.Ct. 851, 93 L.Ed.2d 954 (1987).
- Written statement contains no waiver of rights. Garcia v. State, 919 S.W.2d 370 (Tex. Crim. App. 1994).

§6:102.4 Lack of Compliance With CCP Art. 38.22

- Warnings were insufficient under CCP Art. 38.22. Cockrell.
- Defendant invoked his right to counsel. Smith v. State, 779 S.W.2d 417 (Tex. Crim. App. 1989).
- Defendant invoked his right to remain silent. Dowthitt.
- Defendant invoked his right to terminate the interrogation. Michigan v. Mosley, 423 U.S. 96, 96 S.Ct. 321, 46 L.Ed.2d 313 (1975).
- Defendant invoked his right to a court-appointed attorney. Smith.
- Defendant was told that his statement could be used "for or against" him. Dinkins v. State, 894 S.W.2d 330 (Tex. Crim. App. 1995).

§6:103 Suppression Under Art. 38.23

A defendant who moves for suppression under Art. 38.23 due to the violation of a statute has the burden of producing evidence of a statutory violation. Only when this burden is met does the State bear a burden to prove compliance. State v. Robinson, 334 S.W.3d 776, 779 (Tex. Crim. App. 2011).

Searches conducted in objectively reasonable reliance on binding appellate precedent are not subject to the Fourth Amendment exclusionary rule. Davis v. U.S., 564 U.S. ___, 131 S.Ct. 2419, 2429, 180 L.Ed.2d 285 (2011).

PRACTICE TIP: Although Texas has the statutory exclusionary rule contained in Art. 38.23, the State can use the Davis case to argue that the evidence was not "obtained" in violation of the law where legal precedent at the time of police conduct allowed the police action.

The Fourth Amendment does not apply to the actions of private individuals, and reading Article 38.23 to apply the Fourth Amendment to private individuals would lead to an absurdity. Ruiz v. State, ___ S.W.3d ___ at *2 (PD-1348-17, 2019 WL 2814867, Tex. Crim. App. July 3, 2019).

It is within the trial court's discretion to grant the State's request to reopen a motion-to-suppress hearing to supplement the record with additional testimony, outside the jury's presence, even over the objection of the defendant. Black v. State, 362 S.W.3d 626 (Tex. Crim. App. 2012).

(This page intentionally left blank.)

Chapter 7

RULES OF STATUTORY AND LEGAL INTERPRETATION

Table of Contents

§7:10 Hierarchical Governance

§7:11 Case Law

A statute cannot be superseded by a rule. Igo v. State, 210 S.W.3d 645 (Tex. Crim. App. 2006) (appellate rule relating to new trials superseded by statute setting out harm analysis standard for jury charge error); Rent v. State, 982 S.W.2d 382 (Tex. Crim. App. 1998) (appellate rule relating to new trials superseded by statute relating to remands for new trials).

§7:20 Rules of Statutory and Rules Construction

§7:21 Basic Rules

§7:21.1 Statutory Construction

When discerning the meaning of a statute, the reviewing court should start its analysis by looking at the plain language of the statute in question. Ex parte Whiteside, 12 S.W.3d 819 (Tex. Crim. App. 2000).

Appellate courts are required to construe a statute in accordance with the plain meaning of its literal text unless the language of the statute is ambiguous or the plain meaning leads to absurd results. Boykin v. State, 818 S.W.2d 782 (Tex. Crim. App. 1991); Hampton v. State, 86 S.W.3d 603 (Tex. Crim. App. 2002).

Consequently, the courts focus on the text of the statute and interpret it in a literal manner, attempting to discern the fair, objective meaning of the text. Boykin.

It is the court's duty when interpreting the statute to give the ordinary and plain meaning to the language of the Legislature. Boykin.

Statutory construction is a question of law, and appellate courts review the record de novo. Ramos v. State, 303 S.W.3d 302, 306 (Tex.Crim.App.2009).

When the Legislature meets, after a particular statute has been judicially construed, without changing that statute, the courts will presume the Legislature intended the same construction should continue to be applied to that statute. Marin v. State, 891 S.W.2d 267 (Tex. Crim. App. 1994); Dyar v. State, 125 S.W.3d 460 (Tex. Crim. App. 2003).

In construing whether a statute is vague and/or overbroad, there is an elementary principle of statutory construction: a statute is interpreted in accordance with the plain meaning of its language unless the language is ambiguous or the plain meaning leads to absurd results. Boykin.

A statutory construction that would create a needless conflict between separate articles of the Code of Criminal Procedure is to be avoided, if at all possible. Joslin v. State, 722 S.W.2d 725 (Tex. App.—Dallas 1986), *vacated on other grounds*, 761 S.W.2d 376 (Tex. Crim. App. 1988).

In interpreting a prior law, the courts generally accord little weight to subsequent legislative enactments. Volosen v. State, 227 S.W.3d 77 (Tex. Crim. App. 2007) *citing* Ex parte Schroeter, 958 S.W.2d 811 (Tex. Crim. App. 1997).

The rule of *ejusdem generis* provides that where general words follow specific words in a statutory enumeration, the general words are construed to embrace only objects similar in nature to those objects enumerated by the preceding specific words. It is one of those canons of statutory construction that may prove useful in determining the plain meaning of statutory language: that plain meaning constituting the best indicator of legislative intent to which we are bound to give effect. Shipp v. State, 331 S.W.3d 433 (Tex. Crim. App. 2011).

§7:21.2 Rules Construction

The strictures that apply to statutory construction do not apply to an appellate court's construction of the Rules of Criminal Evidence. Ludwig v. State, 931 S.W.2d 239 (Tex. Crim. App. 1996).

Thus, appellate courts may consider extratextual sources to interpret a rule even if the plain language is unambiguous. Henderson v. State, 962 S.W.2d 544 (Tex. Crim. App. 1997).

§7:22 Statutory Intentions

§7:22.1 Statutory Law

Tex.Gov't.Code §311.021. Intention in Enactment of Statutes.

In enacting a statute, it is presumed that:

(1) compliance with the constitutions of this state and the United States is intended;

(2) the entire statute is intended to be effective;

(3) a just and reasonable result is intended;

(4) a result feasible of execution is intended; and

(5) public interest is favored over any private interest.

§7:22.2 Case Law

When interpreting statutes, the courts seek to effectuate the collective intent or purpose of the legislators who enacted the legislation. Boykin v. State, 818 S.W.2d 782 (Tex. Crim. App. 1991); Camacho v. State, 765 S.W.2d 431 (Tex. Crim. App. 1989).

Statutes are to be construed, if at all possible, so as to give effect to all of their parts, and so that no part is to be construed as void or redundant. Badgett v. State, 42 S.W.3d 136 (Tex. Crim. App. 2001).

It is presumed in the enactment of a statute that the entire statute and all words in the statute are intended to be effective, and the language therein will create a just and reasonable result. Tex Gov't Code §311.021; State v. Mancuso, 919 S.W.2d 86 (Tex. Crim. App. 1996).

A reviewing court must consider the statute's context and presume that the legislature not only intended that a particular sentence would work a just and reasonable result, but that the intended result would be feasible of execution. State ex rel. White v. Bradley, 956 S.W.2d 725 (Tex.App.—Fort Worth 1997), *rev'd on other grounds*, 990 S.W.2d 245 (Tex. 1999).

§7:23 Statute Construction Aids

§7:23.1 Statutory Law

Tex Gov't Code §311.023. Statute Construction Aids.

In construing a statute, whether or not the statute is considered ambiguous on its face, a court may consider among other matters the:

(1) object sought to be attained;

(2) circumstances under which the statute was enacted;

(3) legislative history;

(4) common law or former statutory provisions, including laws on the same or similar subjects;

(5) consequences of a particular construction;

(6) administrative construction of the statute; and

(7) title (caption), preamble, and emergency provision.

§7:23.2 Case Law

In conducting an extratextual inquiry, courts may consider, among other matters: 1) the object sought to be attained; 2) the circumstances under which the statute was enacted; 3) legislative history; 4) common law or former statutory provisions, including laws on the same or similar subjects; 5) the consequences of a particular construction; 6) administrative construction of the statute; and 7) the title (caption), preamble, and emergency provision. Tex Gov't Code §311.023; Jordan v. State, 36 S.W.3d 871 (Tex. Crim. App. 2001); Brown v. State, 943 S.W.2d 35 (Tex. Crim. App. 1997).

The courts can also consider previous executive interpretations of the statute in question. Hines v. State, 75 S.W.3d 444 (Tex. Crim. App. 2002).

The courts may also look to other offense provisions contained in the same statutory section. Long v. Texas, 931 S.W.2d 285 (Tex. Crim. App. 1996) (comparing stalking provision to other provisions contained in Penal Code §42.07).

In construing a statute, whether or not the statute is considered ambiguous on its face, a court may consider among other matters the consequences of a particular construction. Griego v. State, 853 S.W.2d 664 (Tex.App.—Houston [14th Dist.] 1993, *no pet.*)

§7:24 Irreconcilable Statutes and Amendments

§7:24.1 Statutory Law

Tex Gov't Code §311.025. Irreconcilable Statutes and Amendments.

(a) Except as provided by §311.031(d), if statutes enacted at the same or different sessions of the legislature are irreconcilable, the statute latest in date of enactment prevails.

(b) Except as provided by §311.031(d), if amendments to the same statute are enacted at the same session of the legislature, one amendment without reference to another, the amendments shall be harmonized, if possible, so that effect may be given to each. If the amendments are irreconcilable, the latest in date of enactment prevails.

(c) In determining whether amendments are irreconcilable, text that is reenacted because of the requirement of Article III, §36, of the Texas Constitution is not considered to be irreconcilable with additions or omissions in the same text made by another amendment. Unless clearly indicated to the contrary, an amendment that reenacts text in compliance with that constitutional requirement does not indicate legislative intent that the reenacted text prevail over changes in the same text made by another amendment, regardless of the relative dates of enactment.

(d) In this section, the date of enactment is the date on which the last legislative vote is taken on the bill enacting the statute.

(e) If the journals or other legislative records fail to disclose which of two or more bills in conflict is latest in date of enactment, the date of enactment of the respective bills is considered to be, in order of priority:

(1) the date on which the last presiding officer signed the bill;

(2) the date on which the governor signed the bill; or

(3) the date on which the bill became law by operation of law.

§7:24.2 Case Law

Statutes that have the same purpose or relate to the same subject are "in pari material," and must be construed together if possible. Petta v. State, 840 S.W.2d 721 (Tex.App.—Corpus Christi 1992, *pet. ref'd*).

Statutory provisions must first be irreconcilable before one of them will take precedence over the other. H & C Communications, Inc. v. Reed's Food International, Inc., 887 S.W.2d 475 (Tex.App.—San Antonio 1994, *no pet.*).

When a harmonious construction of statutes dealing with the same or similar subject matter is not possible, the more recent legislative enactment should prevail. State v. McKinney, 803 S.W.2d 374 (Tex.App.—Houston [14th Dist.] 1990, *no pet.*).

§7:30 Definitions of Words, Phrases and Terms

§7:31 Words and Phrases

§7:31.1 Statutory Law

CCP Art. 3.01. Words and Phrases.

All words, phrases and terms used in this Code are to be taken and understood in their usual acceptation in common language, except where specially defined.

§7:31.2 Case Law

In determining plain meaning, "[w]ords and phrases shall be read in context and construed according to the rules of grammar and usage." Tex Gov't Code §311.011(a); Dowthitt v. State, 931 S.W.2d 244 (Tex. Crim. App.1996).

Words and phrases are to be read in context and given their common, everyday meaning unless they have acquired technical or particular meaning. R.R.E. v. Glenn, 884 S.W.2d 189 (Tex.App.—Fort Worth 1994, *writ denied*).

The meaning of words and phrases used in a statute is a question of pure law; and the application of the scope of a statute to specific, undisputed historical facts is a mixed question of law and fact. Both of these matters are reviewed de novo at each appellate level. Hampton v. State, 86 S.W.3d 603 (Tex. Crim. App. 2002).

Words that are not statutorily defined are to be given their usual meanings and no specific jury instructions are required. Garcia v. State, 887 S.W.2d 846 (Tex. Crim. App.1994), *cert. denied*, 514 U.S. 1005, 115 S.Ct.1317, 131 L.Ed.2d 198 (1995).

Jurors are presumed to know and apply the common and ordinary meanings. Wheeler v. State, 35 S.W.3d 126 (Tex.App.—Texarkana 2000, *pet. ref'd*).

§7:32 Common and Technical Terms

§7:32.1 Statutory Law

Tex Gov't Code §311.011. Common and Technical Usage of Words.

> *(a) Words and phrases shall be read in context and construed according to the rules of grammar and common usage.*
>
> *(b) Words and phrases that have acquired a technical or particular meaning, whether by legislative definition or otherwise, shall be construed accordingly.*

§7:32.2 Case Law

Words and phrases are to be read in context and given their common, everyday meaning unless they have acquired technical or particular meaning. R.R.E. v. Glenn, 884 S.W.2d 189 (Tex.App.—Fort Worth 1994, *writ denied*).

The canons of construction dictate that words and phrases possessing a technical meaning are generally to be considered as having been used in their technical sense. This applies to those terms that have a known and established legal meaning, or which have acquired a peculiar and appropriate meaning in the law, as where the words used have a well-known common law meaning. However, in some cases justice is best served, and more consistently applied, if jurors are provided a precise, uniform definition to guide their determination of the particular circumstances at issue. Medford v. State, 13 S.W.3d 769 (Tex. Crim. App. 2000).

The legislature has obligated the courts to construe statutory words or phrases having technical or particular meaning, such as terms of art or science, in accordance with their technical meaning. State v. Howard, 908 S.W.2d 602 (Tex. App.—Amarillo 1995, *no pet.*).

§7:33 Interpretations of Certain Words

Tex Gov't Code §311.016. "May," "Shall," "Must," etc.

> *The following constructions apply unless the context in which the word or phrase appears necessarily requires a different construction or unless a different construction is expressly provided by statute:*
>
> *(1) "May" creates discretionary authority or grants permission or a power.*
>
> *(2) "Shall" imposes a duty.*
>
> *(3) "Must" creates or recognizes a condition precedent.*
>
> *(4) "Is entitled to" creates or recognizes a right.*
>
> *(5) "May not" imposes a prohibition and is synonymous with "shall not."*
>
> *(6) "Is not entitled to" negates a right.*
>
> *(7) "Is not required to" negates a duty or condition precedent.*

§7:40 Headings

Tex Gov't Code §311.024. Headings.

> *The heading of a title, subtitle, chapter, subchapter, or section does not limit or expand the meaning of a statute.*

§7:50 Prospective Operation of Statutes

Tex Gov't Code §311.022. Prospective Operation of Statutes.

> *A statute is presumed to be prospective in its operation unless expressly made retrospective.*

§7:60 Special or Local Provision Prevails Over General

§7:61 Statutory Law

Tex Gov't Code §311.026. Special or Local Provision Prevails Over General.

(a) If a general provision conflicts with a special or local provision, the provisions shall be construed, if possible, so that effect is given to both.

(b) If the conflict between the general provision and the special or local provision is irreconcilable, the special or local provision prevails as an exception to the general provision, unless the general provision is the later enactment and the manifest intent is that the general provision prevail.

§7:62 Case Law

If a general provision conflicts with a specific provision, the provisions shall be construed, if possible, so that effect is given to both. Tex Gov't Code §311.026(a); Dillehey v. State, 815 S.W.2d 623 (Tex. Crim. App. 1991).

If the statutes are unable to be reconciled, the specific statute will prevail as an exception to the general statute, unless the general statute is the later enactment and the manifest intent is that the general provision prevail. Tex Gov't Code §311.026(b); State v. Mancuso, 919 S.W.2d 86 (Tex. Crim. App. 1996).

If the definition of an offense does not prescribe a culpable mental state, a culpable mental state is nevertheless required unless the definition plainly dispenses with any mental element. Penal Code §6.02(b); Harvey v. State, 78 S.W.3d 368 (Tex. Crim. App. 2002).

§7:63 Doctrine of In Pari Materia

The rule of *in pari materia* is a principle of statutory interpretation, a means of divining and giving full effect to legislative intent. Two statutes that are *in pari materia* are to be construed together, each enactment in reference to the other, as though they were part of one and the same law. Any conflict between their provisions will be harmonized, if possible, and effect will be given to all the provisions of each act if they can be made to stand together and have concurrent efficacy. Mills v. State, 722 S.W.2d 411 (Tex. Crim. App. 1986).

Statutes may be said to be *in pari materia* when they relate to the same person or thing, to the same class of persons or things, or have the same purpose or object. Characterization of the object or purpose is more important than characterization of subject matter in determining whether different statutes are closely enough related to justify interpreting one in light of the other. Mills. *See also* Strickland v. State, 193 S.W.3d 662 (Tex.App.—Fort Worth 2006, *pet. ref'd*) (the doctrine of *in pari materia* applies if two statutes share a common purpose or object).

A defendant has a due process right to be prosecuted under a "special" statute that is *in pari materia* with a broader statute when these statutes irreconcilably conflict. Ex parte Smith, 185 S.W.3d 887 (Tex. Crim. App. 2006).

To determine whether two statutes share a common purpose, we consider whether the two statutes (1) are contained in the same legislative act, (2) require the same elements of proof, (3) involve different penalties, and (4) were clearly written to achieve the same objective. Strickland.

Because the doctrine of *in pari material* is applicable only to a comparison of statutes (passed by the same governmental body), the doctrine does not apply to a comparison between a statute and a court-made rule. State v. Vasilas, 253 S.W.3d 268 (Tex. Crim. App. 2008).

A defendant's *in pari materia* claim is generally not cognizable as a motion to quash because generally the indictment will be sufficient on its face. The claim is also not cognizable on a pre-trial writ of habeas corpus. A decision on an *in pari materia* claim would be premature before the state has had an opportunity to develop a complete factual record during a trial. Ex parte Smith.

Convictions in a single trial for the offenses of fraudulent use or possession of identifying information and failure to identify do not violate the doctrine of *in pari materia*. Jones v. State, 396 S.W.3d 558, 563 (Tex. Crim. App. 2013).

PRACTICE TIP: The in pari materia claim is cognizable at the jury charge stage of the trial, in the nature of a request for a lesser included offense in the charge. See Ex parte Smith.

§7:70 Construction of Penal Offenses

Penal Code §1.05. Construction of Code

> *(a) The rule that a penal statute is to be strictly construed does not apply to this code. The provisions of this code shall be construed according to the fair import of their terms, to promote justice and effect the objectives of the code.*
>
> *(b) Unless a different construction is required by the context, §§311.011, 311.012, 311.014, 311.015, and 311.021 through 311.032 of Chapter 311, Government Code (Code Construction Act), apply to the construction of this code.*
>
> *(c) In this code:*
>
> *(1) a reference to a title, chapter, or section without further identification is a reference to a title, chapter, or section of this code; and*
>
> *(2) a reference to a subchapter, subsection, subdivision, paragraph, or other numbered or lettered unit without further identification is a reference to a unit of the next-larger unit of this code in which the reference appears.*

§7:71 Applicability of Penal Code to Offenses Under Other Codes

Penal Code §1.03(b) controls the application of Penal Code provisions to criminal offenses defined outside the Penal Code. It directs the export of the provisions contained only in Titles 1, 2, and 3 of the Penal Code to criminal offenses defined outside the Penal Code and contemporaneously bars the import of extra-Penal Code offenses to offenses defined in Titles 4 through 11 of the Penal Code. The offenses defined in Title 4 of the Penal Code apply to offenses defined outside the Penal Code only where the Legislature has designated that Title 4 is applicable via legislative action like the amendments made to the Controlled Substances Act, the Simulated Controlled Substances Act, the Dangerous Drugs Act, the Abusable and Volatile Chemicals Act, and the Election Code. State v. Colyandro, 233 S.W.3d 870 (Tex. Crim. App. 2007).

§7:72 Construction of Offenses Outside Penal Code

Tex. Gov't Code §311.035. CONSTRUCTION OF STATUTE OR RULE INVOLVING CRIMINAL OFFENSE OR PENALTY.

> *(a) In this section, "actor" and "element of offense" have the meanings assigned by Section 1.07, Penal Code.*
>
> *(b) Except as provided by Subsection (c), a statute or rule that creates or defines a criminal offense or penalty shall be construed in favor of the actor if any part of the statute or rule is ambiguous on its face or as applied to the case, including:*
>
> *(1) an element of offense; or*
>
> *(2) the penalty to be imposed.*
>
> *(c) Subsection (b) does not apply to a criminal offense or penalty under the Penal Code or under the Texas Controlled Substances Act.*
>
> *(d) The ambiguity of a part of a statute or rule to which this section applies is a matter of law to be resolved by the judge.*

§7:80 Constitutionality of Statutes

§7:81 In General

In construing a statute, the courts begin with the presumption that it is constitutional. White v. State, 50 S.W.3d 31 (Tex.App.—Waco 2001, *pet. ref'd*).

The courts must uphold the statute if it can be afforded a reasonable construction that renders it constitutional and effectuates legislative intent. White.

In construing whether a law is vague and/or overbroad, the courts keep in mind the elementary principle of statutory construction: they interpret a statute in accordance with the plain meaning of its language unless the language is ambiguous or the plain meaning leads to absurd results. Sanchez v. State, 995 S.W.2d 677 (Tex. Crim. App. 1999).

There is no basis under Texas law for a trial court to conduct a pretrial evidentiary hearing to determine the "as applied" constitutionality of a state penal or criminal procedural statute or to make a pretrial declaratory judgment on same. St. ex rel. Lykos v. Fine, 330 S.W.3d 904 (Tex. Crim. App. 2011) (where the trial court sought to convene a hearing to determine the constitutionality of the Texas death penalty scheme).

§7:82 Basic Constitutional Principles

It is well-established that criminal laws must be sufficiently clear in at least three respects:

- A person of ordinary intelligence must be given a reasonable opportunity to know what is prohibited.
- The law must establish determinate guidelines for law enforcement.
- Where First Amendment freedoms are implicated, the law must be sufficiently definite to avoid chilling protected expression.

Grayned v. City of Rockford, 408 U.S. 104, 92 S.Ct.2294, 33 L.Ed.2d 222 (1972); Long v. Texas, 931 S.W.2d 285 (Tex. Crim. App. 1996).

Absent First Amendment considerations, the Due Process Clause requires that a law be specific enough to: (1) give a person of ordinary intelligence a reasonable opportunity to know what is prohibited, and (2) establish determinate guidelines for law enforcement. Long.

A statute will survive attack as being unconstitutionally vague provided it gives fair warning to the defendant as to what conduct it proscribes. New York v. Ferber, 458 U.S. 747, 102 S.Ct.3348, 73 L.Ed.2d 1113 (1982).

In order to mount a successful attack on the basis that a statute is facially unconstitutional, a defendant must show that there is no conceivable set of circumstances in which the statute is capable of a constitutional application. Briggs v. State, 789 S.W.2d 918 (Tex. Crim. App. 1990).

Constitutional errors may be waived by failure to object at trial. Briggs.

§7:83 First Amendment Considerations

When a statute is capable of reaching First Amendment freedoms, the doctrine of vagueness demands a greater degree of specificity than in other contexts. Long v. Texas, 931 S.W.2d 285 (Tex. Crim. App. 1996).

Greater specificity is required to preserve adequately the right of free expression because uncertain meanings inevitably lead citizens to steer far wider of the unlawful zone than if the boundaries of the forbidden areas were clearly marked. Grayned v. City of Rockford, 408 U.S. 104, 92 S.Ct.2294, 33 L.Ed.2d 222 (1972); Long. Moreover, when a vagueness challenge involves First Amendment considerations, a criminal law may be held facially invalid even though it may not be unconstitutional as applied to the defendant's conduct. Gooding v. Wilson, 405 U.S. 518, 92 S.Ct.1103, 31 L.Ed.2d 408 (1972); Long.

Where First Amendment freedoms are implicated, the law must be sufficiently definite to avoid chilling protected expression. Long.

Under the First Amendment, a statute may be subject to a facial challenge even though it may have some legitimate application. Long.

A defendant can challenge a statute on a First Amendment claim where the statute's deterrent effect on legitimate expression is both real and substantial, and the statute is not readily subject to a narrowing construction by the state courts. Young v. American Mini Theatres, Inc., 427 U.S. 50, 96 S.Ct.2440, 49 L.Ed.2d 310 (1976); White v. State, 50 S.W.3d 31 (Tex.App.—Waco 2001, *pet. ref'd*).

A statute places a real and substantial burden on protected speech when there is a realistic danger that the statute itself will significantly compromise recognized First Amendment protections of parties not before the court. Members of City Council

v. Taxpayers for Vincent, 466 U.S. 789, 104 S.Ct.2118, 80 L.Ed.2d 772 (1984); White.

Even if the statute substantially burdens these constitutional guarantees, the courts will not conclude that it is unconstitutionally vague if they can narrowly construe it in such a manner as to remove the seeming threat or deterrence to constitutionally protected expression. Broadrick v. Oklahoma, 413 U.S. 601, 93 S.Ct.2908, 37 L.Ed.2d 830 (1973); White.

A statute impermissibly compels a person's speech in violation of the First Amendment when the statute requires him "to be an instrument for fostering public adherence to an ideological point of view he finds unacceptable." Wooley v. Maynard, 430 U.S. 705, 97 S.Ct.1428, 51 L.Ed.2d 752 (1977); White.

§7:84 Due Process Claims

Absent First Amendment considerations, the Due Process Clause requires that a law be specific enough to: (1) give a person of ordinary intelligence a reasonable opportunity to know what is prohibited, and (2) establish determinate guidelines for law enforcement. Long v. Texas, 931 S.W.2d 285 (Tex. Crim. App. 1996).

It is a basic principle of due process that a statute is void for vagueness if its prohibitions are not clearly defined. The void-for-vagueness doctrine requires that a penal statute define the criminal offense with sufficient definiteness that ordinary people can understand what conduct is prohibited and in a manner that does not permit arbitrary and discriminatory enforcement. Although a statute is not impermissibly vague because it fails to define words or phrases, it is invalid if it fails to give a person of ordinary intelligence a reasonable opportunity to know what conduct is prohibited. Moreover, where a statute does not substantially implicate constitutionally protected conduct or speech, it is valid unless it is impermissibly vague in all applications. State v. Holcombe, 187 S.W.3d 496 (Tex.Crim.App.2006); Watson v. State, 369 S.W.3d 865, 870 (Tex. Crim. App. 2012).

Due process requires that a criminal statute give fair notice of that conduct which is criminally prohibited. Bynum v. State, 767 S.W.2d 769 (Tex. Crim. App. 1989).

Where a due process vagueness claim does not involve a First Amendment issue the courts will not address the merits of the defendant's claims unless he first makes a showing that the statute is unconstitutional as applied to him. Vuong v. State, 830 S.W.2d 929 (Tex. Crim. App. 1992).

Where no First Amendment rights are involved, the reviewing court need only examine the statute to determine whether it is impermissibly vague as applied to the defendant's specific conduct. Bynum.

The natural corollary to this principle is that a defendant to whom a statute clearly applies may not successfully challenge it for vagueness. Vuong.

Accordingly, it is the defendant's burden to establish that the statute is unconstitutional as applied to him; that it might be unconstitutional to others is not sufficient. Rodriguez v. State, 47 S.W.3d 86 (Tex.App.—Houston [14th Dist.] 2001, *no pet.*).

Absent a First Amendment claim, a facial challenge can be mounted successfully only if the statute is vague in all of its applications. Long v. Texas, 931 S.W.2d 285 (Tex. Crim. App. 1996).

§7:85 Specific Statutory Provisions

The absence of a "reasonable person" requirement is not necessarily fatal to a statute's constitutionality. Long v. State, 931 S.W.2d 285 (Tex. Crim. App. 1996).

In some situations an affirmative defense for constitutionally protected activity can save a statute from a constitutionality challenge. *See* Long.

A savings clause may give courts more latitude to place a narrowing construction upon a statute that would save it from a constitutionality challenge. Long.

§7:86 The Single Subject Rule

§7:86.1 Constitutional Provision

TEX. CONST. art. III, § 35

> *(a) No bill (except general appropriation bills, which may embrace the various subjects and accounts, for and on account of which moneys are appropriated) shall contain more than one subject.*

(b) The rules of procedure of each house shall require that the subject of each bill be expressed in its title in a manner that gives the legislature and the public reasonable notice of that subject. The legislature is solely responsible for determining compliance with the rule.

(c) A law, including a law enacted before the effective date of this subsection, may not be held void on the basis of an insufficient title.

§7:86.2 Case Law

Under TEX. CONST. art. III, § 35(a) a statute is facially unconstitutional where the bill in which it was enacted or amended contained more than one subject. Ex parte Jones, 440 S.W.3d 628, 629 (Tex. Crim. App. 2014) (where the court found that a 2011 amendment to *TEX. PENAL CODE* §38.04(b)(2)(A), the evading arrest statute, did not violate the single subject rule).

§7:90 Conflict of Laws Principles

Traditional conflict-of-law principles prescribe that issues that are strictly procedural in nature are governed by the laws of the forum state, whereas issues that are substantive in nature require an analysis of which state has the most significant relationship with the communication in question. Gonzalez v. State, 45 S.W.3d 101 (Tex. Crim. App. 2001) *citing* Restatement (Second) of Conflict of Laws §139 (1971).

A substantive right has been defined by the Texas Court of Criminal Appeals as a right to the equal enjoyment of fundamental rights, privileges, and immunities or a right that can be protected or enforced by law. Gonzalez.

A procedural right is a right that helps in the protection or enforcement of a substantive right. Gonzalez; Vega v. State, 84 S.W.3d 613 (Tex. Crim. App. 2002).

There are, under Texas conflict-of-law principles, several factors to consider in determining which jurisdiction has the most significant relationship to the case, including: (1) where the injury or unlawful conduct occurred; (2) the place where the relationship between the parties is the strongest; (3) the number and nature of contacts that the non-forum state has with the parties and with the transaction involved; (4) the relative materiality of the evidence that is sought to be excluded; and (5) the fairness to the parties. Gonzalez; Vega.

§7:100 Ex Post Facto Laws

There are four categories of ex post facto laws: (1) Every law that makes an action done before the passing of the law, and which was innocent when done, criminal; and punishes such action; (2) Every law that aggravates a crime, or makes it greater than it was, when committed; (3) Every law that changes the punishment, and inflicts a greater punishment, than the law annexed to the crime, when committed; (4) Every law that alters the legal rules of evidence, and receives less, or different, testimony, than the law required at the time of the commission of the offence, in order to convict the offender. Phillips v. State, 362 S.W.3d 606, 610 (Tex. Crim. App. 2011)(overruled on other grounds by Ex parte Heilman, 456 S.W.3d 159 (Tex. Crim. App. 2015)).

The Ex Post Facto Clause applies not only to laws that are facially retroactive, but also to laws that are applied retroactively. Phillips (overruled on other grounds by Ex parte Heilman, 456 S.W.3d 159 (Tex. Crim. App. 2015)).

The right to be free from ex post facto laws or the ex post facto application of a law is an absolute right—a first category Marin right and nnot be waived or forfeited. Phillips (overruled on other grounds by Ex parte Heilman, 456 S.W.3d 159 (Tex. Crim. App. 2015)).

A defendant can raise a claim for the first time on appeal that his convictions were barred by the Ex Post Facto Clause. Ieppert v. State, 908 S.W.2d 217 (Tex. Crim. App. 1995).

A statute of limitations may be changed or repealed without violating constitutional prohibitions against ex post facto laws in any case where a right to acquittal has not been absolutely acquired by the completion of the period of limitations. Phillips (overruled on other grounds by Ex parte Heilman, 456 S.W.3d 159 (Tex. Crim. App. 2015)).

However, a facially retroactive law that revives a previously time-barred offense violates the Ex Post Facto Clause. Phillips; (overruled on other grounds by Ex parte Heilman, 456 S.W.3d 159

(Tex. Crim. App. 2015)); Stogner v. California, 539 U.S. 607, 123 S.Ct. 2446 156 L.Ed.2d 544 (2003).

The Texas constitutional prohibition against a retroactive law has never been made applicable to statutes merely affecting matters of procedure that do not disturb vested substantive rights. Grimes v. State, 807 S.W.2d 582 (Tex. Crim. App. 1991).

Where a defendant asserts that a particular statute is an ex post facto law, the courts must determine: (1) whether the statute is being applied retroactively; and (2) whether its provisions constitute punishment for constitutional purposes. Rodriguez v. State, 93 S.W.3d 60 (Tex. Crim. App. 2002).

The question whether a statute constitutes punishment for constitutional purposes is answered by application of what is known as the "intent-effects" test. Rodriguez.

Under the "intent-effects" test, a reviewing court must first ask whether the legislature intended the statute to be a criminal punishment. Rodriguez.

Whether a particular punishment is criminal or civil is, at least initially, a matter of statutory construction. A court must first ask whether the legislature, in establishing the penalizing mechanism, indicated either expressly or impliedly a preference for one label or the other. Hudson v. United States, 522 U.S. 93, 118 S.Ct.488, L.Ed.2d 450 (1997); Rodriguez.

A reviewing court must afford a high level of deference to the legislature's stated aims in passing the statute. Hudson; Rodriguez.

Where the legislature manifests an expressly punitive intent, the inquiry is at an end and the statute is a violation of the ex post facto clause. Kennedy v. Mendoza-Martinez, 372 U.S. 144, 83 S.Ct.554, 9 L.Ed.2d 644 (1963); Rodriguez.

If the legislature intends to establish a civil remedy, a reviewing court then examines "whether the statutory scheme [is] so punitive either in purpose or effect as to transform what was clearly intended as a civil remedy into a criminal penalty." Hudson; Rodriguez.

The legislature's manifest intent will be rejected only where the party challenging the statute provides the clearest proof that the statute is actually criminally punitive in operation. Kansas v. Hendricks, 521 U.S. 346, 117 S.Ct.2072, 138 L.Ed.2d 501 (1997); Rodriguez.

To evaluate whether the effects of a statute are criminally punitive, courts generally consider:

- Whether the sanction involves an affirmative disability or restraint
- Whether it has traditionally been regarded as a punishment
- Whether it comes into play only on a finding of scienter
- Whether its operation will promote the traditional aims of punishment—retribution and deterrence
- Whether the behavior to which it applies is already a crime
- Whether an alternative purpose to which it may rationally be connected is assignable to it
- Whether it appears excessive in relation to the alternative purpose assigned

Kennedy v. Mendoza-Martinez, 372 U.S. 144, 83 S.Ct.554, 9 L.Ed.2d 644 (1963); Rodriguez.

A clear example of an ex post facto law is a law enacted after expiration of a previously applicable limitations period when it is applied to revive a previously time-barred prosecution. Stogner v. California, 539 U.S. 607, 123 S.Ct.2446, 156 L.Ed.2d 544 (2003).

The use of a successfully completed deferred adjudication to enhance the punishment for a later offense when the statute permitting such an enhancement did not exist at the time adjudication was deferred is an ex post facto violation. Scott v. State, 55 S.W.3d 593 (Tex. Crim. App. 2001).

Authorizing conviction of certain sexual offenses on the victim's testimony alone where corroborating evidence had previously been required is an ex post facto violation. Carmell v. Texas. 529 U.S. 513, 120 S.Ct. 1620, 146 L.Ed.2d 577 (2000).

§7:110 Separation of Powers

The separation of powers clause of Tex.Const., Art. II, §1, provides for the separation of powers of the three departments of Texas government: Judicial, Legislative, and Executive. Ex parte Davis, 947 S.W.2d 216 (Tex. Crim. App. 1996).

The separation of powers provision may be violated in either of two ways: 1) when one branch of government assumes, or is delegated, to whatever degree, a power that is more properly attached to another branch; or 2) when one branch unduly interferes with another branch so that the other branch cannot effectively exercise its constitutionally assigned powers. Ex parte Perry, 483 S.W.3d 884, 894-5 (Tex. Crim. App. 2016). A separation of powers claim is cognizable on pretrial habeas. Ex parte Perry, 483 S.W.3d at 895.

§7:120 Computation of Time

Tex.Gov't.Code §311.014. Computation of Time.

> *(a) In computing a period of days, the first day is excluded and the last day is included.*
>
> *(b) If the last day of any period is a Saturday, Sunday, or legal holiday, the period is extended to include the next day that is not a Saturday, Sunday, or legal holiday.*
>
> *(c) If a number of months is to be computed by counting the months from a particular day, the period ends on the same numerical day in the concluding month as the day of the month from which the computation is begun, unless there are not that many days in the concluding month, in which case the period ends on the last day of that month.*

§7:130 Doctrine of Stare Decisis

Under the doctrine of stare decisis, the courts hold that it is often better to be consistent than right. This doctrine promotes judicial efficiency and consistency, fosters reliance on judicial decisions, and contributes to the actual and perceived integrity of the judicial process. Bawcom v. State, 78 S.W.3d 360 (Tex. Crim. App. 2002).

However, overruling precedent is acceptable under certain circumstances. Some factors that support overruling precedent are: 1) when the original rule is flawed from the outset, 2) when older precedent conflicts with a newer decision that is found to be more soundly reasoned, and 3) when the rule consistently creates unjust results or places unnecessary burdens upon the system. Bawcom.

The achievement of harmony between criminal and civil precedent may also be considered in determining what rule to fashion. Awadelkariem v. State, 974 S.W.2d 721 (Tex. Crim. App. 1998).

In determining whether to retain or reject a particular rule of law, the courts may also consider whether justifications proffered for the rule have been undercut with the passage of time. Awadelkariem.

§7:140 Unpublished and Plurality Appellate Court Opinions

§7:141 Court of Appeals Unpublished Opinions

Tex.R.App.Pro. Rule 47.7. Unpublished Opinions

> *(a) Criminal Cases. Opinions and memorandum opinions not designated for publication by the court of appeals under these or prior rules have no precedential value but may be cited with the notation, "(not designated for publication)."*
>
> *(b) Civil Cases. Opinions and memorandum opinions designated "do not publish" under these rules by the courts of appeals prior to January 1, 2003 have no precedential value but may be cited with the notation, "(not designated for publication)." If an opinion or memorandum opinion issued on or after that date is erroneously designated "do not publish," the erroneous designation will not affect the precedential value of the decision.*

§7:142 Court of Criminal Appeals Unpublished Opinions

Tex.R.App.Pro. Rule 77.3. Unpublished Opinions

Unpublished opinions have no precedential value and must not be cited as authority by counsel or by a court.

§7:143 Plurality Opinions

Plurality opinions are not binding precedent. State v. Hardy, 963 S.W.2d 516 (Tex. Crim. App. 1997).

§7:150 Estoppel

A party may be estopped from asserting a claim that is inconsistent with that party's prior conduct. Arroyo v. State, 117 S.W.3d 795 (Tex. Crim. App. 2003) (the state turned over a rap sheet on a witness and later tried to assert that the defendant had not shown the witness to be the same person named in the rap sheet).

A defendant who requests and receives a jury charge on a lesser-included offense is estopped from complaining that his conviction of that lesser-included offense was barred by limitations. State v. Yount, 853 S.W.2d 6 (Tex. Crim. App. 1993).

A defendant, who affirmatively requests that the trial court not submit to the jury one of the special issues statutorily required for capital sentencing, is estopped from arguing on appeal that the trial court had erred in not submitting the special issue. Prystash v. State, 3 S.W.2d 522 (Tex. Crim. App. 1999).

A defendant who agrees to stipulate to a fact is estopped from complaining on appeal that the evidence is insufficient even where the stipulation is not formally introduced into evidence. Bryant v. State, 187 S.W.3d 397 (Tex. Crim. App. 2005).

Where the defendant's objection prevented the state from fulfilling its burden of proof at a suppression hearing, the defendant is prevented under the invited-error doctrine from asserting this ground on appeal. Vennus v. State, 282 S.W.3d 70 (Tex. Crim. App. 2009).

Where a defendant requests an improper lesser included charge or has some responsibility for its inclusion, he is estopped on appeal from complaining of its inclusion in the charge. Woodard v. State, 322 S.W.3d 648 (Tex. Crim. App. 2010).

A defendant who declines to have a witness attached and brought to court is estopped from arguing that her confrontation rights were violated on the grounds that the witness was absent from court. Woodall v. State, 336 S.W.3d 634 (Tex. Crim. App. 2011).

§7:160 Statutory Presumptions

§7:161 Statutory Law

Texas Penal Code § 2.05. Presumption

(a) Except as provided by Subsection (b), when this code or another penal law establishes a presumption with respect to any fact, it has the following consequences:

(1) if there is sufficient evidence of the facts that give rise to the presumption, the issue of the existence of the presumed fact must be submitted to the jury, unless the court is satisfied that the evidence as a whole clearly precludes a finding beyond a reasonable doubt of the presumed fact; and

(2) if the existence of the presumed fact is submitted to the jury, the court shall charge the jury, in terms of the presumption and the specific element to which it applies, as follows:

(A) that the facts giving rise to the presumption must be proven beyond a reasonable doubt;

(B) that if such facts are proven beyond a reasonable doubt the jury may find that the element of the offense sought to be presumed exists, but it is not bound to so find;

(C) that even though the jury may find the existence of such element, the state must prove beyond a reasonable doubt each of the other elements of the offense charged; and

(D) if the jury has a reasonable doubt as to the existence of a fact or facts giving rise to the presumption, the presumption fails and the jury shall not consider the presumption for any purpose.

(b) When this code or another penal law establishes a presumption in favor of the

defendant with respect to any fact, it has the following consequences:

(1) if there is sufficient evidence of the facts that give rise to the presumption, the issue of the existence of the presumed fact must be submitted to the jury unless the court is satisfied that the evidence as a whole clearly precludes a finding beyond a reasonable doubt of the presumed fact; and

(2) if the existence of the presumed fact is submitted to the jury, the court shall charge the jury, in terms of the presumption, that:

(A) the presumption applies unless the state proves beyond a reasonable doubt that the facts giving rise to the presumption do not exist;

(B) if the state fails to prove beyond a reasonable doubt that the facts giving rise to the presumption do not exist, the jury must find that the presumed fact exists;

(C) even though the jury may find that the presumed fact does not exist, the state must prove beyond a reasonable doubt each of the elements of the offense charged; and

(D) if the jury has a reasonable doubt as to whether the presumed fact exists, the presumption applies and the jury must consider the presumed fact to exist.

§7:162 Case Law

When charging the jury on a statutory presumption, the court must charge jurors that they may use the presumption to find the defendant guilty only if the State proves the facts giving rise to the presumption beyond a reasonable doubt. Hollander v. State, 414 S.W.3d 746, 753 (Tex. Crim. App. 2013).

(This page intentionally left blank.)

Chapter 8

DOUBLE JEOPARDY

DOUBLE JEOPARDY

Table of Contents

§8:10 Basic Double Jeopardy Principles

§8:11 Constitutional and Statutory Provisions

U.S. Constitution, Fifth Amendment: " ... nor shall any person be subject for the same offense to be twice put in jeopardy of life or limb."

Texas Constitution, Art. 1 §14: "No person, for the same offense, shall be twice put in jeopardy of life or liberty, nor shall a person be again put upon trial for the same offense, after a verdict of not guilty in a court of competent jurisdiction."

CCP Art. 1.10. JEOPARDY

"No person for the same offense shall be twice put in jeopardy of life or liberty; nor shall a person be again put upon trial for the same offense, after a verdict of not guilty in a court of competent jurisdiction."

The double jeopardy clause is a guarantee against being twice put to trial for the same offense. Abney v. U.S., 431 U.S. 651, 97 S.Ct. 2034, 52 L.Ed.2d 651 (1977); Phillips v. State, 787 S.W.2d 391 (Tex. Crim. App. 1990).

The Fifth Amendment guarantee against being placed in double jeopardy is applicable to the states through the Fourteenth Amendment. Benton v. Maryland, 395 U.S. 784, 89 S.Ct. 2056, 23 L.Ed.2d 707 (1969).

The Texas and United States Constitutions' double jeopardy provisions provide substantially identical protections. Ex parte Mitchell, 977 S.W.2d 575 (Tex. Crim. App. 1997), *cert. denied*, 525 U.S. 873 (1998).

The only exception is in cases where the prosecutor causes a mistrial. State v. Webb, 980 S.W.2d 924 (Tex.App.—Fort Worth 1998), *affirmed at* 12 S.W.3d 808 (Tex. Crim. App. 2000).

§8:12 Basic Double Jeopardy Protections

Both the United States and Texas Constitutional provisions speak of double jeopardy in terms of the same offense rather than the same transaction. Phillips v. State, 787 S.W.2d 391 (Tex. Crim. App. 1990).

Protection against double jeopardy consists of three separate constitutional protections:

- Against a second prosecution for the same offense after acquittal
- Against a second prosecution for the same offense after conviction
- Against multiple punishments for the same offense.

U.S. v. Halper, 490 U.S. 435, 109 S.Ct. 1892, 104 L.Ed.2d 487 (1989); Ex parte Stover, 946 S.W.2d 343 (Tex. Crim. App. 1997).

§8:13 Blockburger Test

Texas employs the Blockburger test for deciding when two offenses are the same for double jeopardy purposes. The applicable rule is that where the same act or transaction constitutes a violation of two distinct statutory provisions, the test to be applied to determine whether there are two offenses or only one, is whether each provision requires proof of a fact which the other does not. Blockburger v. U.S., 284 U.S. 299, 52 S.Ct. 180, 76 L.Ed.2d 306 (1932); U.S. v. Dixon, 509 U.S. 688, 113 S.Ct. 2849, 125 L.Ed.2d 556 (1993); Ervin v. State, 991 S.W.2d 804 (Tex. Crim. App. 1999).

If application of the Blockburger test reveals that the offenses have identical statutory elements or that one is a lesser included offense of the other, then the two offenses are the same for double jeopardy purposes. Granger v. State, 850 S.W.2d 513 (Tex. Crim. App. 1993).

In the multiple punishments context, the Blockburger test is simply a rule of statutory construction, which is useful in attempting to ascertain legislative intent. Hence, the Supreme Court has concluded that the Blockburger test cannot negate a clearly expressed legislative intent to impose multiple punishments. Missouri v. Hunter, 459 U.S. 359, 366, 103 S.Ct. 673, 74 L.Ed.2d 535 (1983); Ervin v. State, *supra*.

The Blockburger test's status as a rule of statutory construction raises an inverse conclusion as well: the Blockburger test cannot authorize two punishments where the legislature clearly intended only one. This raises the possibility that there exist other rules of statutory construction that may be employed to help ascertain whether a legislature intended multiple punishments. Ex parte Ervin, *supra*.

For double jeopardy purposes, the same offense means the identical criminal act, not the same offense by name. Ex parte Goodbread, 967 S.W.2d 859 (Tex. Crim. App. 1998).

As an illustration, successive prosecutions for possession of a pornographic photograph and also a pornographic videotape resulting from single incident of possession did not place a defendant in double jeopardy because each offense called for proof of an element which the other did not. Vineyard v. State, 958 S.W.2d 834 (Tex. Crim. App. 1998).

The offenses of assault on a public servant and resisting arrest are not the same offense for double jeopardy purposes because they are not the same offense under the Blockburger test. Ortega v. State, 171 S.W.3d 895 (Tex. Crim. App. 2005).

Since double jeopardy analysis is concerned with the actual offense, the state may not prosecute a defendant under a second indictment that merely substitutes the name of a victim for the phrase "unknown to the grand jury" which had been alleged in the first indictment. Ex parte Coleman, 940 S.W.2d 946 (Tex. Crim. App. 1996).

The Court of Criminal Appeals' opinion in Hall v. State, 225 S.W.3d 524 (Tex. Crim. App. 2007) dealing with lesser included offense analysis reiterated that the Blockburger test remains the applicable test for double jeopardy analysis. Ex parte Watson. 306 S.W.3d 259 (Tex. Crim. App. No. 294-08, May 6, 2009).

§8:14 Legislative Intent Test

When multiple offenses are prosecuted at a single trial, the Double Jeopardy Clause prevents the sentencing court from prescribing greater punishment than the legislature intended. Missouri v. Hunter, 459 U.S. 359, 366, 103 S.Ct. 673, 74 L.Ed.2d 535 (1983); Ervin v. State, 991 S.W.2d 804 (Tex. Crim. App. 1999).

A defendant suffers multiple punishments in violation of the Double Jeopardy Clause when he is convicted of more offenses than the legislature intended. Ball v. United States, 470 U.S. 856, 105 S.Ct. 1668, 84 L.Ed.2d 740 (1985); Ervin v. State, *supra*.

The Blockburger test is a useful tool for ascertaining legislative intent, but it is not the only tool. Other (nonexclusive) considerations relevant to determining whether the Legislature intended multiple punishments are: whether the offenses' provisions are contained within the same statutory section, whether the offenses are phrased in the alternative, whether the offenses are named similarly, whether the offenses have common punishment ranges, whether the offenses have a common focus (*i.e.,* whether the "gravamen" of the offense is the same) and whether that common focus tends to indicate a single instance of conduct, whether the elements that differ between the offenses can be considered the "same" under an imputed theory of liability which would result in the offenses being considered the same under Blockburger analysis (*i.e.,* a liberalized Blockburger standard utilizing imputed elements), and whether there is legislative history containing an articulation of an intent to treat the offenses as the same or different for double jeopardy purposes. Ervin v. State, *supra*.

For example, because the Legislature intended to make possession of each individual controlled substance within the same penalty group a separate and distinct offense, convictions for both heroin and cocaine possession are permitted under double jeopardy analysis even where they arise from a single incident of possession. Watson v. State, 900 S.W. 2d 60 (Tex. Crim. App. 1995).

§8:15 Allowable Units of Prosecution Analysis

The Double Jeopardy Clause is offended if a defendant is successively prosecuted for the same offense. The legislature defines whether offenses are the same. It does so by prescribing the allowable unit of prosecution, which is a distinguishable discrete act that is a separate violation of the statute. The discovery of the allowable unit of prosecution is a task of statutory construction. Sanabria v. United States, 437 U.S. 54, 98 S.Ct. 2170, 57 L.Ed.2d 43 (1978); Ex parte Hawkins, 6 S.W.3d 554 (Tex. Crim. App. 1999).

The "allowable units of prosecution" analysis

is undertaken in cases in which the convictions at issue arose from the same statutory provision. Ex parte Milner, 394 S.W.3d 502 (Tex. Crim. App. 2013) (where the defendant was successively prosecuted under the capital murder statute).

Absent an express statement defining the allowable unit of prosecution, the gravamen of an offense best describes the allowable unit of prosecution. Loving v. State, 401 S.W.3d 642, 647 (Tex. Crim. App. 2013).

The gravamen of an offense can be: (1) the result of the conduct; (2) the nature of the conduct; or (3) the circumstances surrounding the conduct. To determine the gravamen of a statutory provision, the appellate courts have used various tools, including a focus on grammar, and when examining the statute, focusing on sentence syntax and whether the statute refers to an item in the singular or plural (usually the direct object). Loving.

The unit of prosecution can be defined by the element of the offense requiring a completed act and that, if each statutory provision protects a victim from a different type of harm, there is evidence that the Legislature intended for each commission of a prohibited act to be punished separately. Loving.

Thefts from two separate people during the same transaction can both be prosecuted because they involve two separate violations of the theft statute; *i.e.*, two allowable units of prosecution. Inglehart v. State, 837 S.W.2d 122 (Tex. Crim. App. 1992).

The allowable unit of prosecution in a burglary is the unlawful entry; therefore, it offends the double jeopardy clause for a defendant to be convicted of a burglary against two separate complainants for a single entry. Ex parte Cavazos, 203 S.W.3d 333 (Tex. Crim. App. 2006).

Because the allowable unit of prosecution in an assaultive offense is each victim, each person threatened in a robbery case can be the subject of an individual prosecution. Ex parte Hawkins, 6 S.W.3d 554 (Tex. Crim. App. 1999) (*overruling* Ex parte Crosby, 703 S.W.2d 683 (Tex. Crim. App. 1986); Simmons v. State, 745 S.W.2d 348 (Tex. Crim. App. 1987); and Cook v. State, 840 S.W.2d 384 (Tex. Crim. App. 1992)).

A defendant can be prosecuted for each separate piece of child pornography in his possession because each is an allowable unit of prosecution. Vineyard v. State, 958 S.W.2d 834 (Tex. Crim. App. 1998).

Under this theory a defendant who commits unlawful acts while operating a motor vehicle may be convicted and punished for each person injured and/or murdered in violation of a single statute. Phillips v. State, 787 S.W.2d 391 (Tex. Crim. App. 1990).

The same is true for acts prosecuted under the official oppression statute. Haight v. State, 137 S.W.3d 48 (Tex. Crim. App. 2004).

However, in a capital murder prosecution where the aggravating element is the murder of multiple victims (Penal Code §19.03(a)(7)(A)), the allowable unit of prosecution is at minimum two victims so that a defendant is subjected to double jeopardy where he is subjected to more than one prosecution arising out of a single set of facts. Saenz v. State, 166 S.W.3d 270 (Tex. Crim. App. 2005); Ex parte Milner; 394 S.W.3d 508.

For the offense of making false statement to obtain property or credit contained in Penal Code sec. 32.32, the appropriate unit of prosecution for double jeopardy analysis is the "materially false or misleading statement," not the loan application. Each materially false or misleading statement constitutes a separate offense. Jones v. State, 323 S.W.3d 885 (Tex. Crim. App. 2010).

The clear language of §21.11(a)(2)(A) (indecency by exposure to a child) indicates that the exposure, not the number of children present, constitutes the unit of prosecution. Therefore, no matter how many children are present, a defendant can only be prosecuted for one indecent exposure to a child per exposure. Harris v. State, 359 S.W.3d 625 (Tex. Crim. App. 2011).

The text of the criminal-attempt statute does not define an allowable unit of prosecution, nor does it change the allowable unit of prosecution of the offense attempted. Given that a criminal attempt to commit an offense is simply an act amounting to more than mere preparation of the intended offense, criminal-attempt offenses acquire their allowable unit of prosecution from the offense attempted. Ex parte Milner, 394 S.W.3d 508-09.

Indecency with a child by exposure and indecency with a child by contact are separate and distinct offenses. Therefore, a conviction for each offense in a single trial is permissible under double jeopardy principles because the Legislature intended to allow separate punishments under these circumstances. Loving.

Even though aggravated assault on a public servant and intoxication assault are not the "same offense," they have the same allowable unit of prosecution (the injury of a single individual) and therefore a conviction in a single trial for each offense is prohibited under double jeopardy principles. Shelby v. State, 448 S.W.3d 431, 439 (Tex. Crim. App. 2014).

§8:16 Dual-Sovereignty

Under the dual-sovereignty doctrine, an individual may be tried and sentenced in both state and federal court for the same conduct because a crime under one sovereign's laws is not the same offense as a crime under the laws of another sovereign. Gamble v. United States, 587 U.S. ___, ___ S.Ct. ___, ___ L.Ed.2d ___ (No. 17-646, 2019 WL 2493923, June 17, 2019).

§8:20 Previous Jeopardy and Subsequent Prosecutions

Although the double jeopardy clause speaks of being twice placed in jeopardy of life or limb, it is also applicable to imprisonment and monetary penalties. Dept. of Revenue v. Kurth Ranch, 511 U.S. 767, 114 S.Ct. 1937, 128 L.Ed.2d 767 (1994); Ex parte Chappell, 959 S.W.2d 627 (Tex. Crim. App. 1998).

§8:21 When Jeopardy Attaches

Before the double jeopardy clause is invoked, an individual must have been placed in jeopardy for a particular offense. Ex parte George, 913 S.W.2d 523 (Tex. Crim. App. 1995).

In a jury trial, jeopardy attaches when the jury is sworn; Pierson v. State, 426 S.W.3d 763 (Tex. Crim. App. 2014); Martinez v. Illinois, 572 U.S. ___, 134 S.Ct. 2070, 188 L.Ed.2d 1112 (2014).

Jeopardy attaches in a trial to the court when the defendant pleads to the indictment. State v. Torres, 805 S.W.2d 418 (Tex. Crim. App. 1991).

Jeopardy attaches in a negotiated plea bargain proceeding when the trial judge accepts the plea bargain. Ortiz v. State, 933 S.W.2d 523 (Tex. Crim. App. 1996).

Where the state abandons or waives a count or paragraph of a charging instrument after jeopardy has attached, a retrial is barred on that count or paragraph. State v. Florio, 845 S.W.2d 849 (Tex. Crim. App. 1992). *See also* Brown v. State, 900 S.W.2d 805 (Tex.App.—San Antonio 1995, *pet. ref'd*).

If the State dismisses, waives, or abandons a charge after a jeopardy has attached (after a jury is impaneled and sworn in a jury trial), it is tantamount to an acquittal, as the State is barred from later litigating those allegations. If a charge is abandoned in this fashion, it should not be included in a judgment as a conviction. Duran v. State, 492 S.W.3d 741, 745 (Tex. Crim. App. 2016).

The prosecution must take affirmative steps on the record to validly waive, dismiss or abandon that portion of a charging instrument they wish to reserve for a possible later prosecution. The mere failure to read the applicable portions of the charging instrument to the trier of fact, without more, results in the attachment of jeopardy to those portions. Ex parte Preston, 833 S.W.2d 515 (Tex. Crim. App. 1992).

§8:22 When Jeopardy Does Not Attach

Jeopardy does not attach and bar retrial where the first conviction is void. Hoang v. State, 872 S.W.2d 694 (Tex. Crim. App. 1993) (where the first convictions were void because the defendant was a juvenile at the time of their commission and had not been certified by a juvenile court).

Jeopardy does not attach where a defendant is convicted under an unconstitutional statute. Lowry v. State, 671 S.W.2d 601 (Tex.App.—Dallas 1984), *affirmed in part, reversed in part* 692 S.W.2d 86 (Tex. Crim. App. 1985).

A fundamentally defective indictment does not confer jurisdiction on the trial court and therefore, jeopardy does not attach. Cook v. State, 902 S.W.2d 471 (Tex. Crim. App. 1995).

Jeopardy does not attach to counts or paragraphs that are abandoned before jeopardy attaches. Proctor v. State, 841 S.W.2d 1 (Tex. Crim. App. 1992).

Jeopardy does not attach to a trial if an appellate mandate has not yet issued in the case from a prior appeal. Ex parte Macias, 541 S.W.3d 782, 785-6 (Tex. Crim. App. 2017).

PRACTICE TIP: A writ of habeas corpus is the proper means to attack a trial court judgment that is jurisdictionally void. Ex parte Sanchez, 918 S.W.2d 526 (Tex. Crim. App. 1996).

§8:23 Previous Convictions and Subsequent Prosecutions

CCP Art. 28.13. Former Acquittal or Conviction

> *A former judgment of acquittal or conviction in a court of competent jurisdiction shall be a bar to any further prosecution for the same offense, but shall not bar a prosecution for any higher grade of offense over which said court had not jurisdiction, unless such judgment was had upon indictment or information, in which case the prosecution shall be barred for all grades of the offense.*

The double jeopardy clause protects against multiple prosecutions for the same offense. Jeffers v. U.S., 432 U.S. 137, 97 S.Ct. 2207, 53 L.Ed.2d 168 (1977); Ex parte Kopecky, 821 S.W.2d 957 (Tex. Crim. App. 1992).

For double jeopardy purposes, the same offense means the identical criminal act, not the same offense by name. Ex parte Goodbread, 967 S.W.2d 859 (Tex. Crim. App. 1998).

When it cannot be determined from the state's pleadings whether the offenses prosecuted are the same, the court must look to the proof offered at trial. Goodbread, *supra*.

When an indictment permits the state to obtain only one conviction, a defendant is not placed in jeopardy for more than one criminal act unless the State offers multiple instances of conduct in support of the indictment. Goodbread, *supra*.

If evidence of more than one offense is admitted and a conviction for either could be had under the indictment, and neither the state nor the court elects, a plea of former conviction is good upon a prosecution based upon one of said offenses, it being uncertain for which one the conviction was had. Goodbread, *supra*.

Consequently, where the state dismisses an indictment after jeopardy attaches without offering proof of any instance of conduct, only the act alleged in the indictment is jeopardy barred. Ex parte Goodman, 152 S.W.3d 67 (Tex. Crim. App. 2004) (this is true even though there were multiple instances of conduct that the state could have offered in support of the indictment).

In order to ensure that the state does not offer jeopardy barred proof at a subsequent trial, the trial court may require the state to prove, by a preponderance of the evidence, that it is not relying upon such proof. If the state is unable to so prove, then the trial court must select, from among the constituent acts that the state does prove, and strike from the jury's consideration, the one constituent act that most closely resembles the act alleged in the first indictment. Ex parte Goodman.

A double jeopardy violation occurs if the defendant is tried twice for the same offense in a single trial even if the sentences run concurrently. Ervin v. State, 991 S.W.2d 804 (Tex. Crim. App. 1999) (where the offenses were manslaughter and intoxication manslaughter).

§8:24 Greater Inclusive and Lesser Included Offenses

CCP Art. 37.14. Acquittal of Higher Offense as Jeopardy

> *"If a defendant, prosecuted for an offense which includes within it lesser offenses, be convicted of an offense lower than that for which he is indicted, and a new trial be granted him, or the judgment be arrested for any cause other than the want of jurisdiction, the verdict upon the first trial shall be considered an acquittal of the higher offense; but he may, upon a second trial, be convicted of the same offense of which he was before convicted, or any other inferior thereto."*

See also CCP Art. 28.13, above.

Greater inclusive and lesser included offenses are the same offense for jeopardy purposes. Brown v. Ohio, 432 U.S. 161, 97 S.Ct. 2221, 53 L.Ed.2d 187 (1977); Parrish v. State, 869 S.W.2d 352 (Tex. Crim. App. 1994).

Double jeopardy rules prohibit the State from obtaining a conviction for an offense when the defendant has previously been convicted of a lesser-included offense of that offense. Ex parte Amador 326 S.W.3d 202 (Tex. Crim. App. 2010).

Generally, if a defendant is acquitted of a greater offense, he cannot be tried for a lesser included offense. State v. Engelking, 817 S.W.2d 64 (Tex. Crim. App. 1991) (where there was insufficient evidence to prove the aggravating element of the greater offense).

However, where the state requests that the jury be instructed on the lesser included offense, or the court instructs on the lesser included offense without objection from the state, the defendant may be retried on the lesser charge where he has been acquitted on appeal of the greater charge by reason of insufficient evidence. Granger v. State, 850 S.W.2d 513 (Tex. Crim. App. 1993); Hampton v. State, 165 S.W.3d 691 (Tex. Crim. App. 2005).

An exception to the general rule that conviction of a lesser offense bars prosecution for a greater offense is where all the events necessary to the greater crime have not taken place at the time the prosecution for the lesser has begun. Brown v. Ohio, *supra*.

The Double Jeopardy Clause does not prohibit a retrial for a lesser included offense when the first trial was before the court and there was sufficient evidence on which the trial court could have found the defendant guilty of the lesser offense. Shute v. State, 877 S.W.2d 314 (Tex. Crim. App. 1994).

The double jeopardy clause also prohibits a subsequent prosecution where a defendant has been convicted or acquitted of an offense that "subsumes" another offense. Ex parte Pruitt, 233 S.W.3d 338 (Tex. Crim. App. 2007) (defendant's acquittal of aggravated sexual assault of a child by penetration barred a subsequent prosecution for aggravated sexual assault of a child by genital-to-genital contact).

§8:25 Previous Acquittals and Subsequent Prosecutions

CCP Art. 1.11 Acquittal a Bar

> *An acquittal of the defendant exempts him from a second trial or a second prosecution for the same offense, however irregular the proceedings may have been; but if the defendant shall have been acquitted upon trial in a court having no jurisdiction of the offense, he may be prosecuted again in a court having jurisdiction.*

See also CCP Art. 28.13, above.

An acquittal of charges bars retrial of the same charges on double jeopardy principles. Smalis v. Pennsylvania, 476 U.S. 140, 106 S.Ct. 1745, 90 L.Ed.2d 116 (1986); Ex parte Kopecky, 821 S.W.2d 957 (Tex. Crim. App. 1992).

A jury verdict that necessarily decides a critical issue of ultimate fact in a defendant's favor protects him from prosecution for any charge for which that is an essential element. Yeager v. U.S., 557 U.S. ___, 129 S.Ct. 2360, 174 L.Ed.2d 78 (2009).

An instructed verdict is the functional equivalent of an acquittal for double jeopardy purposes. Smalis v. Pennsylvania, *supra*; Ex parte Coleman, 940 S.W.2d 946 (Tex. Crim. App. 1996).

This is true even where the state has refused to present evidence during the trial. Martinez v. Illinois, 572 U.S. ___, 134 S.Ct. 2070, ___ L.Ed.2d ___ (2014).

Whether the acquittal is based on a jury verdict of not guilty or on a ruling by the court that the evidence is insufficient to convict, any further prosecution, including an appeal by the prosecution that would lead to a second trial, is prohibited by the double jeopardy clause. State v. Blackshere, 344 S.W.3d 400 (Tex. Crim. App. 2011).

Where a court acquits a defendant of a charge during trial and trial proceeds on other charges, the court cannot reinstate the acquitted charge in the absence of statutory authority to do so. Smith v. Massachusetts, 543 U.S. 462, 125 S.Ct. 1129, 160 L.Ed.2d 914 (2005).

Where the trial court grants a motion for new trial based on insufficient evidence the state is barred from retrying the defendant on the same charge. Moore v. State, 749 S.W.2d 54 (Tex. Crim. App. 1988).

An acquittal bars retrial even where the charging instrument was defective. *See* Studer v. State, 799 S.W.2d 263 (Tex. Crim. App. 1990) (a defective charging instrument confers jurisdiction on the trial court).

Even an erroneous acquittal (such as where the trial court misconstrues a statute or erroneously adds an extra element to the proof required) will serve as a jeopardy bar to a subsequent trial. Evans v. Michigan, 568 U.S. ___, 133 S.Ct. 1069, 1073, 185 L.Ed.2d 124 (2013).

A defendant who has been acquitted under an indictment alleging an offense against a particular victim can be retried for the same course of conduct if the subsequent indictment alleges a different victim. Bailey v. State, 87 S.W.3d 122 (Tex. Crim. App. 2002).

Where the trial court dismisses an indictment on the State's motion after jeopardy attaches, then the Double Jeopardy Clause prohibits the State from reprosecuting the defendant for the offense for which he had been placed in jeopardy of conviction. Proctor v. State, 841 S.W.2d 1 (Tex. Crim. App. 1992).

Where the state has not elected a primary act for conviction, any acts that were offered as proof, and would allow a conviction under the allegations of the indictment at that trial, are jeopardy-barred at a subsequent trial. Ex parte Pruitt, 233 S.W.3d 338 (Tex. Crim. App. 2007).

Where a defendant has been acquitted of capital murder in the course of burglary, a subsequent prosecution for the underlying burglary is jeopardy-barred, but a prosecution for aggravated assault on the same facts is not. Ex parte Castillo, 469 S.W.3d 165, 172 (Tex. Crim. App. 2015).

§8:30 Multiple Punishments

A multiple punishments double jeopardy claim can arise in two contexts: (1) the lesser-included offense context, in which the same conduct is punished twice -- once for the basic conduct, and a second time for that same conduct plus more (for example, attempted assault of Y and assault of Y; assault of X and aggravated assault of X); and (2) punishing the same criminal act twice under two distinct statutes when the legislature intended the conduct to be punished only once (for example, causing a single death by committing both intoxication manslaughter and involuntary manslaughter). Langs v. State, 183 S.W.3d 680 (Tex. Crim. App. 2006).

§8:31 Multiple Punishments in Single Trial

When multiple offenses are prosecuted at a single trial, the Double Jeopardy Clause prevents the sentencing court from prescribing greater punishment than the legislature intended. Missouri v. Hunter, 459 U.S. 359, 103 S.Ct. 673, 74 L.Ed.2d 535 (1983); Ervin v. State, 991 S.W.2d 804 (Tex. Crim. App. 1999).

A defendant suffers multiple punishments in violation of the Double Jeopardy Clause when he is convicted of more offenses than the legislature intended. Ball v. United States, 470 U.S. 856, 105 S.Ct. 1668, 84 L.Ed.2d 740 (1985); Ervin v. State, *supra.*

The Blockburger case addresses two multiple-punishment issues: the "continuous action vs. separate and distinct acts" issue, and the "one act violates separate distinct statutes" issue. Aekins v. State, 447 S.W.3d 270, 277 (Tex. Crim. App. 2014).

The first part of the Blockburger test asks whether each criminal act is a separate and distinct one, separated by time. If the offense is a single continuous act, with a single impulse, in which several different statutory provisions are necessarily violated along that continuum, the offenses merge together. This is variously called "the merger doctrine," "the single impulse doctrine," or, here in Texas, "the doctrine of subsumed acts." If more than one statutory offense is necessarily committed by that single criminal act and impulse, then the offenses merge and the defendant may be punished only once. Aekins, 447 S.W.3d at 274-5.

Where two acts are the products of separate impulses, even though they may occur closely together in time, the defendant can be convicted of each act in a single trial. Aekins, 447 S.W.3d at 283.

Cumulative punishment, consistent with the double jeopardy clause, may be imposed where separate offenses occur in the same transaction, as long as each conviction requires proof of an additional element that the other does not. Blockburger v. U.S., 284 U.S. 299, 52 S.Ct. 180, 76 L.Ed.2d 306 (1932); Phillips v. State, 787 S.W.2d 391 (Tex. Crim. App. 1990).

In certain limited circumstances, the Blockburger "same elements" test is not the sole test for analyzing a multiple-punishment claim. Because legislative intent, rather than the presence or absence of the "same elements" is the ultimate inquiry, the "same elements" test, although the usual method for discerning legislative intent, cannot authorize two punishments where the legislature clearly intended only one, nor, conversely, negate a clearly expressed legislative intent to impose multiple punishments. Ervin.

Under Ervin, additional non-exclusive factors should be examined to determine if two offenses are the same in the context of multiple punishment: whether offenses are in the same statutory section; whether the offenses are phrased in the alternative; whether the offenses are named similarly; whether the offenses have common punishment ranges; whether the offenses have a common focus; whether the common focus tends to indicate a single instance of conduct; whether the elements that differ between the two offenses can be considered the same under an imputed theory of liability that would result in the offenses being considered the same under Blockburger; and whether there is legislative history containing an articulation of an intent to treat the offenses as the same or different for double-jeopardy purposes. Ervin; Bigon v. State, 252 S.W.3d 360 (Tex. Crim. App. 2008).

A multiple-punishments double-jeopardy violtion may arise either in the context of lesser-included offenses (when the same conduct is punished under both a greater and a lesser-included statutory offense) or when the same criminal act is punished under two distinct statutory provisions, but the legislature intended only one punishment. Aekins v. State, 447 S.W.3d at 274.

A multiple punishments claim can arise in a lesser-included offense context, in which the same conduct is punished twice under two distinct statutes when the legislature intended the conduct to be punished only once. Langs v. State, 183 S.W.3d 680 (Tex. Crim. App. 2006).

The double jeopardy clause does not bar cumulative punishments imposed in a single proceeding. Ohio v. Johnson, 467 U.S. 493, 104 S.Ct. 2536, 81 L.Ed.2d 425 (1984); Phillips, *supra.*

Manslaughter and intoxication manslaughter are the same offense for double jeopardy purposes when they involve the same victim, and imposing convictions for both in this situation violates the Double Jeopardy Clause. A double jeopardy violation occurs even when, as in this case, the sentences are concurrent. Ball v. United States, *supra*; Ervin v. State, *supra.*

Convictions for both felony murder and intoxication manslaughter in the same trial, which arise from a single offense, can violate the double jeopardy clause. Bigon.

An offer to sell drugs and the possession of drugs with intent to complete that particular sale are one offense for double jeopardy purposes because they are both part of the same criminal "impulse." Lopez v. State, 108 S.W.3d 293 (Tex. Crim. App. 2003).

Multiple punishments for possession with intent to deliver and manufacturing a controlled substance for a single quantity of controlled substance violate double jeopardy because the legislature has established that both offenses are alternative means of punishing a single offense in the continuum of drug distribution. Weinn v. State, 326 S.W.3d 189 (Tex. Crim. App. 2010).

Attempted capital murder (attempting to cause the death of a peace officer) and aggravated robbery offenses arising out of the same transaction against the same victim can each be prosecuted in a single trial because the legislature has determined that each be a separate offense. Cervantes v. State, 815 S.W.2d 569 (Tex. Crim. App. 1991); *see also* Garrett v. United States, 471 U.S. 773, 105 S.Ct. 2407, 85 L.Ed.2d 764 (1985).

However, a defendant cannot be prosecuted for both felony murder with aggravated robbery as the underlying offense and aggravated robbery because the aggravated robbery is a lesser included offense of the felony murder as charged and the legislature has not expressed an intention that multiple punishments should be allowed in this context. Littrell v. State, 271 S.W.3d 273 (Tex. Crim. App. 2008).

A defendant can be prosecuted for injury to a child and any other penal code offense in the same trial because the legislature has authorized multiple punishments within the injury to a child statute, Texas Penal Code §22.04(h). Desormeaux v. State, 362 S.W.3d 233 (Tex.App.—Beaumont 2012, *no pet.*).

It is permissible for a jury to convict a defendant for both the offense of capital murder and the separate offense of engaging in organized criminal activity by committing capital murder as a member of a criminal street gang, and punish the defendant for both where they are prosecuted in a single trial, even where these two are the same offense under the Blockburger test. Garza v. State, 213 S.W.3d 338 (Tex. Crim. App. 2007).

Under the pleadings in this particular case, the offense of criminal solicitation was subsumed within the proof necessary to establish the intent to commit capital murder under the attempted capital murder indictment. Consequently, under the pleadings in this case, attempted capital murder and solicitation of capital murder are the same offense under the Blockburger test. Bien v. State, 550 S.W.3d 180, 187 (Tex. Crim. App. 2018).

Because of the "fundamental nature of the double jeopardy protections, a double jeopardy claim may be raised for the first time on appeal or even for the first time on collateral attack" if two conditions are met: (1) "the undisputed facts show the double jeopardy violation is clearly apparent on the face of the record"; and (2) "when enforcement of the usual rules of procedural default serves no legitimate state interest. Gonzalez v. State, 8 S.W.3d 640 (Tex. Crim. App. 2000).

When offenses, one of which could give rise to a multiple-punishment double-jeopardy violation, are listed disjunctively in a jury charge, the burden is upon the defendant to preserve, in some fashion a double jeopardy objection at or before the time the charge is submitted to the jury, or else the record is insufficient to meet the burden under Gonzalez. Langs v. State, 183 S.W.3d 680 (Tex. Crim. App. 2006).

Serious bodily injury committed against the same victim at the same time should be considered the same offense for purposes of the double-jeopardy prohibition against multiple punishments regardless of whether that injury to that victim resulted from the actor's act, his omission, or by a combination of his act and omission. Villaneuva v. State, 227 S.W.3d 744 (Tex. Crim. App. 2007) (the defendant had been prosecuted for both injury to a child by act and injury to a child by omission).

There is no double jeopardy violation when a defendant is convicted of both aggravated sexual assault by penetration of the vagina and aggravated sexual assault by penetration of the anus occurring in the same transaction because the legislature intended for these to be separate offenses. Gonzales v. State, 304 S.W.3d 838 (Tex. Crim. App. 2010).

The principles of double jeopardy prohibit the State from obtaining a conviction for indecency with a child and aggravated sexual assault of a child based on a single act of molestation because indecency with a child is a lesser-included offense of aggravated sexual assault of a child when both offenses are predicated on the same act. Evans v. State, 299 S.W.3d 138 (Tex. Crim. App. 2009).

Convictions in a single trial for aggravated robbery and aggravated assault are double jeopardy violations where the aggravated assault as plead is a lesser-included offense of aggravated robbery. Ex parte Denton, 399 S.W.3d 540, 547 (Tex. Crim. App. 2013).

However, depending on how the offenses are charged a defendant can be convicted of both aggravated robbery and aggravated assault in a single trial because a "units of prosecution" analysis can show that the legislature intended to allow multiple punishments. Garfias v. State, 424 S.W.3d 54, 61 (Tex. Crim. App. 2014).

Convictions in a single trial for aggravated robbery by threats and aggravated robbery by causing bodily injury against the same victim violates the Double Jeopardy clause. Cooper v. State, 430 S.W.3d 426, 434 (Tex. Crim. App. 2014).

The legislature's intent was to permit one punishment where continuous sexual abuse is alleged against a single victim within a specified time frame. This intent extends to the continuous sexual abuse statute's enumerated predicate offenses and to criminal attempts to commit those predicate offenses. Price v. State, 434 S.W.3d 601, 610 (Tex. Crim. App. 2014).

Because felony DWI and intoxication assault do

not have the same type of focus, the same actual focus or gravamen, and they do not have the same unit of prosecution convictions for each in the same trial does not violate double jeopardy principles. Ex parte Benson, 459 S.W.3d 67, 89 (Tex. Crim. App. 2015).

The Texas Legislature's intent in sexual assault cases is to punish each discrete assault. Separate criminal acts committed during a single sexual encounter may be punished separately, but a criminal act (such as exposure or contact) that is committed as part of a continuing sexual assault that results in one complete, ultimate act of penetration may not be punished along with that complete, ultimate act. Steps along the way to one sexual assault merge into the completed act. Aekins v. State, 447 S.W.3d 270, 277-8 (Tex. Crim. App. 2014).

A person who commits more than one sexual act against the same person may be convicted and punished for each separate and discrete act, even if those acts were committed in close temporal proximity. The key is that one act ends before another act begins and is thus, motivated by a separate impulse. This is true for acts violating not only different statutes, but different subsections of a single statute, and even different discretely prohibited acts within the same subsections. Aekins, 447 S.W.3d at 278.

When evaluating multiple convictions for sexual offenses in the double jeopardy context the following rules apply: (1) when a single exposure or contact offense is incident to and subsumed by a penetration offense, the offenses are the same for double-jeopardy purposes, and (2) the Texas Legislature has not manifested its intent to allow multiple punishments for those same offenses, so (3) multiple convictions for those same offenses violate double-jeopardy principles. Aekins, 447 S.W.3d at 279.

In other words, where two crimes are such that the one cannot be committed without necessarily committing the other, then they stand in the relationship of greater and lesser offenses, and the defendant cannot be convicted or punished for both. Aekins, 447 S.W.3d at 280.

The Legislature intended only one conviction for one completed sexual assault. This means that multiple convictions for exposure, contact and penetration for one complete, ultimate sexual assault violates the Double Jeopardy Clause. Patterson v. State, 152 S.W.3d 88, 91-2 (Tex. Crim. App. 2004).

Separate convictions for sexual assault based on defendant's contact of victim's sexual organ with his mouth and penetration of victim's sexual organ with his mouth and/or tongue arising out of same criminal act violate the prohibition against double jeopardy. Aekins, 447 S.W.3d at 281.

A person can be convicted of indecency by exposure and indecency by contact in a single trial because even though these acts are criminalized in the same statute, they require two distinct acts. Loving v. State, 401 S.W.3d 642, 646-9 (Tex. Crim. App. 2013).

The indecency with a child statute criminalizes three separate contact acts—touching of the (1) anus, (2) breast, or (3) genitals. A person who touches a child's anus, breast, and genitals may be convicted of three offenses because each touching is a separate act. Pizzo v. State, 235 S.W.3d 711, 719 (Tex. Crim. App. 2007).

A single count alleging sexual contact is not subsumed by a count alleging penetration where there is evidence of multiple incidents of both contact and penetration which could have formed the basis for each count. Maldonado v. State, 461 S.W.3d 144, 150 (Tex. Crim. App. 2015).

The legislature intended that both theories of indecency with a child (exposure and fondling) may be pled and punished even when the exposure precedes the contact and even when both acts occur within the same transaction when the evidence presented actually supports conviction and punishment under each theory of the offense. Speights v. State, 464 S.W.3d 719, 724 (Tex. Crim. App. 2015).

A sexually violent predator civil-commitment order violation is a circumstances-surrounding-the-conduct crime. A violation arises only by the circumstance that the person has been adjudicated a sexually violent predator who has been civilly committed. It is the circumstance coupled with the conduct that results in a criminal offense. Therefore, a person can only be convicted of a single violation of the order in a single trial. Stevenson v. State, 499 S.W.3d 842, 851 (Tex. Crim. App. 2016).

See also sec. 17:72

§8:32 Multiple Punishments in Successive Trials

A defendant waives his double jeopardy claim as to multiple prosecutions when his motion to sever is granted. Jeffers v. United States, 432 U.S. 137, 97 S.Ct. 2207, 53 L.Ed.2d 168 (1977); Gongora v. State, 916 S.W.2d 570 (Tex.App.—Houston [1st Dist.] 1996, *pet. ref'd*); Currier v. Virginia, 585 U.S. ___, 138 S.Ct. 2144, 201 L.Ed.2d 650 (2018).

A defendant ordinarily may not be punished or tried twice for a greater-inclusive and a lesser-included offense without violating double jeopardy because lesser-included offenses typically do not pass muster under the *Blockburger* test because the elements of the lesser offense are wholly subsumed by the elements of the greater offense. Ex parte Chaddock, 369 S.W.3d 880, 882-3 (Tex. Crim. App. 2012).

An exception to this rule is where the legislature has specifically authorized cumulative punishment under two statutes in a single prosecution. Ex parte Chaddock, at page 2, citing Missouri v. Hunter, 459 U.S. 359, 103 S.Ct. 673, 74 L.Ed.2d 535 (1983).

The Hunter rule, while applicable in a multiple punishment single trial context, is not applicable in the successive prosecution context; and therefore, any statute that purports to authorize a second conviction for a lesser included offense in a successive trial operates unconstitutionally. Ex parte Chaddock, at page 4.

Under the dual-sovereignty doctrine, an individual may be tried and sentenced in both state and federal court for the same conduct because a crime under the laws of one sovereign is not the same offense as a crime under the laws of another sovereign. Gamble v. United States, 587 U.S. ___, ___ S.Ct. ___, ___ L.Ed.2d ___ (No. 17-646, 2019 WL 2493923, June 17, 2019).

§8:40 Retrials and Double Jeopardy Clause

§8:41 Retrials After Mistrials

A mistrial is a device used to halt trial proceedings when the error is so prejudicial that expenditure of further time and expense would be wasteful or futile. A trial court may properly exercise its discretion to declare a mistrial if an impartial verdict cannot be reached, or if a verdict of conviction could be reached but would have to be reversed on appeal due to an obvious procedural error. Ladd v. State, 3 S.W.3d 547 (Tex. Crim. App. 1999).

Despite the general prohibition against jeopardy-barred trials, there are two exceptions when a criminal defendant may be tried a second time without violating double-jeopardy principles if the prosecution ends prematurely as the result of a mistrial: (1) if the criminal defendant consents to retrial or (2) there was a manifest necessity to grant a mistrial. Pierson v. State, 426 S.W.3d 763 (Tex. Crim. App. 2014).

The consent of the defendant to the mistrial must appear in the record as a deliberate relinquishment on the defendant's part—an exercise of her primary control—if it is to be relied upon as a reason to allow the State to re-prosecute her. Consent need not be expressed, but may be implied from the totality of circumstances attendant to a declaration of mistrial. Ex parte Garrels, 559 S.W.3d 517, 523 (Tex. Crim. App. 2018).

The initial burden is on the defendant to go forth with evidence in support of the allegation of former jeopardy. In order to satisfy this prima facie burden, the defendant need only establish that she was tried for the same offense after a mistrial. Once the defendant makes this initial showing, the burden shifts to the State to prove that appellant consented to the order terminating her first trial. Ex parte Garrels, 559 S.W.3d at 524.

Where a jury is unable to reach a decision in a case (and the foreman does not sign a verdict form), the Double Jeopardy clause does not bar a second trial. Blueford v. Arkansas, 566 U.S. ___, 132 S.Ct. 2044, 182 L.Ed.2d 937 (2012).

A jury note indicating that the jury has acquitted of a particular charge is not an informal verdict of acquittal under Texas law where it lacks the "finality necessary to amount to an acquittal" as required under Blueford v. Arkansas. Traylor v. State, 567 S.W.3d 741, 748 (Tex. Crim. App. 2018).

The asking of an improper question will seldom call for a mistrial because in most cases an instruction to disregard will cure any harm. A mistrial is only required where the improper question is clearly prejudicial to the defendant and is of such character that an instruction to disregard will not cure the impression made on the minds of the jurors.

Ladd, *supra.*

The determination of whether a given error necessitates a mistrial must be made on the facts of the particular case on trial. Ladd, *supra.*

§8:42 Manifest Necessity

As a general rule, the prohibition against double jeopardy will prevent a retrial if the defendant is placed in jeopardy and the jury is discharged without the defendant's consent. Green v. United States, 355 U.S. 184, 78 S.Ct. 221, 2 L.Ed.2d 199 (1957); Alvarez v. State, 864 S.W.2d 64 (Tex. Crim. App. 1993).

However, a retrial is not jeopardy barred if the mistrial was based on manifest necessity. Oregon v. Kennedy, 456 U.S. 667, 102 S.Ct. 2083, 72 L.Ed.2d 416 (1982); Alvarez, *supra.*

Manifest necessity exists when the circumstances render it impossible to arrive at a fair verdict, when it is impossible to continue with trial, or when the verdict would be automatically reversed on appeal because of trial error. Hill v. State, 90 S.W.3d 308 (Tex. Crim. App. 2002).

The initial burden of proving a double jeopardy violation is on the defendant. He meets that burden by proving that he was tried for the same offense after a mistrial. The burden then shifts to the state to prove manifest necessity for the mistrial. Hill; Pierson v. State, 426 S.W.3d 763 (Tex. Crim. App. 2014).

Before granting a mistrial on grounds of manifest necessity, a trial court must determine whether alternative courses of action are available and, if so, choose one that is less drastic than a mistrial. Ex parte Brown v. State, 907 S.W.2d 835 (Tex. Crim. App.1995). The trial court's objective in those circumstances is to choose the alternative that best preserves the defendant's right to have the trial completed before the jury that has already been seated. Brown, *supra.*

Where a trial judge grants a mistrial despite the available option of less drastic alternatives, there is no manifest necessity prompting the decision and a retrial is barred by double jeopardy. Ex parte Little, 887 S.W.2d 62 (Tex. Crim. App. 1994).

The Fifth Amendment is not offended by a successive prosecution for the same offense when the earlier proceeding was terminated at the defendant's request, unless the attorney representing the government deliberately set out to provoke the defendant's motion for mistrial. Oregon v. Kennedy, 456 U.S. 667, 102 S.Ct. 2083, 72 L.Ed.2d 416 (1982); Bauder v. State, 921 S.W.2d 696 (Tex. Crim. App. 1996).

Manifest necessity issues decided under the Texas Constitution will also be decided using the Oregon v. Kennedy standard. Ex parte Lewis, 219 S.W.3d 335 (Tex. Crim. App. 2007) (overruling Bauder II, (974 S.W.2d 729 (Tex. Crim. App. 1998) and its progeny, including Ex parte Peterson, 117 S.W.3d 804 (Tex. Crim. App. 2003) and State v. Lee, 15 S.W.3d 921 (Tex. Crim. App. 2000)).

In determining whether the prosecutorial misconduct warranted a mistrial, the court should balance three factors: (1) the severity of the misconduct (the magnitude of the prejudicial effect of the prosecutor's remarks), (2) the measures adopted to cure the misconduct (the efficacy of any cautionary instruction by the judge), and (3) the certainty of conviction absent the misconduct (the strength of the evidence supporting the conviction). Mosley v. State, 983 S.W.2d 249 (Tex. Crim. App. 1998), *cert. denied*, 526 U.S. 1070, 143 L. Ed. 2d 550, 119 S.Ct. 1466 (1999); Ramon v. State, 159 S.W.3d 927 (Tex. Crim. App. 2004).

TIP TO THE BENCH: Although it is not legally required, a trial judge is well-advised to set out his factual findings on the record in support of his ruling on a double jeopardy motion. Ex parte Lewis.

Manifest necessity exists where leaving a juror on the jury makes it impossible for the jury to arrive at a fair verdict Parrish v. State, 38 S.W.3d 831 (Tex.App.—Houston [14th Dist.] 2001, *pet. ref'd*).

Where a mistrial granted at the defendant's request was not mandated under the facts of the case and an instruction to disregard would have been sufficient, a future prosecution for the same offense is not jeopardy barred because the request for mistrial could not have been prompted by the state's deliberate or reckless misconduct. Ex parte Primrose, 950 S.W.2d 775 (Tex.App.—Fort Worth 1997, *pet. ref'd*) (i.e., the first prong of the Kennedy analysis is a threshold determination).

Where a defendant is harmed by the state's failure to reveal exculpatory evidence and a mistrial has been declared, a retrial may be barred by double jeopardy. Ex parte Masonheimer, 220 S.W.3d 494 (Tex. Crim. App. 2007).

There is manifest necessity for a mistrial where the jury is unable to reach a verdict and the trial court has employed less drastic alternatives such as issuing an Allen charge, allowing the jury more time to deliberate and verifying the jury's deliberation status. Ex parte Perusquia, 336 S.W.3d 270 (Tex.App.—San Antonio 2010, *pet. ref'd*).

Manifest necessity for a retrial can exist where the original mistrial was caused by an improper question asked by defense counsel and an instruction to disregard was not a viable alternative to the granting of the mistrial. Pierson v. State, 426 S.W.3d 763 (Tex. Crim. App. 2014).

The trial court's ruling on an issue of manifest necessity is reviewed on an abuse of discretion standard with the appellate court assessing the objective facts in the light most favorable to the trial judge's ruling. Ex parte Wheeler, 203 S.W.3d 317 (Tex. Crim. App. 2006).

§8:43 Retrials Following Appeals

Underlying the application of double jeopardy principles to instances where convictions have been reversed on appeal is the concept of continuing jeopardy. Continuing jeopardy means, in effect, an accused may be retried after his conviction has been reversed on appeal because the proceedings against him never stopped. Montana v. Hall, 481 U.S. 400, 107 S.Ct. 1825, 95 L.Ed.2d 354 (1987); Ex parte Mitchell, 977 S.W.2d 575 (Tex. Crim. App. 1997).

The double jeopardy clause does not bar retrial where the defendant has managed through appeal or some other procedure to have his conviction set aside because of reversible error. United States v. Dinitz, 424 U.S. 600, 96 S.Ct. 1075, 47 L.Ed.2d 267 (1976); Granger v. State, 850 S.W.2d 513 (Tex. Crim. App. 1993).

A retrial is barred on double jeopardy grounds after appeal if there is legally insufficient evidence to support the conviction. Burks v. United States, 437 U.S. 1, 98 S.Ct. 2141, 57 L.Ed.2d 1 (1978); Granger, *supra*.

However, where the conviction is set aside due to factually insufficient evidence the double jeopardy clause does not prohibit retrial of the defendant on the same charges. Tibbs v. Florida, 457 U.S. 31, 102 S.Ct. 2211, 72 L.Ed.2d 652 (1982).

The double jeopardy clause of the Texas Constitution does not bar retrial of an accused whose conviction for the same offense has been reversed on appeal, or as the result of a post-conviction writ of habeas corpus proceeding, due to prosecutorial misconduct. Ex parte Davis, 957 S.W.2d 9 (Tex. Crim. App. 1997); Ex parte Mitchell, *supra*.

A capital murder case that was reversed on the defendant's appeal can be retried where the jury originally deadlocked on the punishment issues and a life sentence was imposed by the trial judge as mandated by law in that situation. Sattazahn v. Pennsylvania, 537 U.S. 101, 123 S.Ct. 732, 154 L.Ed.2d 588 (2003).

The issue-preclusion component of the Double Jeopardy Clause does not bar the Government from retrying defendants after a jury has returned irreconcilably inconsistent verdicts of conviction and acquittal, and the convictions are later vacated for legal error unrelated to the inconsistency. Bravo-Fernandez v. U.S., 580 U.S. ___, 137 S.Ct. 352, 362-3, 196 L.Ed.2d 242 (2016).

§8:50 Raising Double Jeopardy Claims

§8:51 Habeas Corpus Writs

A pretrial writ of habeas corpus is usually the procedural vehicle by which a defendant should raise a successive prosecution for the same offense double jeopardy claim. Ex parte Robinson, 641 S.W.2d 552 (Tex. Crim. App. 1982); Abney v. U.S., 431 U.S. 651, 97 S.Ct. 2034, 52 L.Ed.2d 651 (1977); Apolinar v. State, 820 S.W.2d 792 (Tex. Crim. App.1991).

§8:52 Special Pleas

CCP Art. 27.05. Defendant's Special Plea

> *"A defendant's only special plea is that he has already been prosecuted for the same or a different offense arising out*

DOUBLE JEOPARDY

of the same criminal episode that was or should have been consolidated into one trial, and that the former prosecution:

1. resulted in acquittal;

2. resulted in conviction;

3. was improperly terminated; or

4. was terminated by a final order or judgment for the defendant that has not been reversed, set aside, or vacated and that necessarily required a determination inconsistent with a fact that must be established to secure conviction in the subsequent prosecution."

The statutorily prescribed procedure utilized on a special plea mandates that the defendant's claim in the special plea shall not be determined before the trial on the merits. *See* CCP Art. 27.07.

Trial courts are required to submit the special plea to the trier of fact unless, assuming all the facts alleged in the plea to be true, the special plea does not present a legally sufficient former jeopardy claim. Arredondo v. State, 582 S.W.2d 457 (Tex. Crim. App. 1979).

§8:53 On Appeal

In order to raise the issue of a double jeopardy violation on appeal, the record must explicitly show the violation. Gonzalez v. State, 8 S.W.3d 640 (Tex. Crim. App. 2000) (where the record merely reflected a general verdict of guilty from an indictment alleging several offenses).

§8:60 Remedy for Double Jeopardy Violations

Where a defendant files a pretrial habeas writ claiming a double jeopardy violation and the appeals courts find such a violation, the case will be remanded to the trial court with instructions to dismiss the pending prosecution. State v. Engelking, 817 S.W.2d 64 (Tex. Crim. App. 1991).

If a defendant has been found guilty in one trial of two offenses that are determined to be the same for double jeopardy purposes, the most serious punishment test is used to determine which offense to dismiss and which to retain. That test requires retaining the offense with the most serious punishment and vacating any remaining offenses that are the same for double jeopardy purposes. Landers v. State, 957 S.W.2d 558 (Tex. Crim. App.1997).

§8:70 Double Jeopardy and Sentencing Proceedings

Double jeopardy analysis is inapplicable to non-capital sentencing proceedings. Monge v. California, 524 U.S. 721, 118 S.Ct. 2246, 141 L.Ed.2d 615 (1998); Bell v. State, 994 S.W.2d 173 (Tex. Crim. App. 1999).

Use of unadjudicated offenses at the punishment phase of a trial does not bar their later prosecution. Witte v. U.S., 515 U.S. 389, 115 S.Ct. 2199, 132 L.Ed.2d 351 (1995); Ex parte Broxton, 888 S.W.2d 23 (Tex. Crim. App. 1994).

Where the trial court pronounces a statutorily authorized sentence, any attempt to alter the sentence after the day of the original sentencing violates the defendant's double jeopardy rights. Harris v. State, 153 S.W.3d 394 (Tex. Crim. App. 2005).

The Double Jeopardy Clause does not preclude retrial on a prior conviction allegation in the noncapital sentencing context where in the original proceeding the trial judge pronounced an illegal sentence that was based on a misinterpretation of the law. Wooldridge v. State, 237 S.W.3d 714 (Tex. Crim. App. 2007).

§8:80 Administrative Hearings and Double Jeopardy

§8:81 Administrative License Revocation Proceedings

The Texas Department of Public Safety and a district attorney are not same parties for collateral estoppel purposes, and therefore, a district attorney is not prohibited from relitigating an adverse finding in a prior administrative proceeding for revocation of a driver's license in a subsequent criminal prosecution for DWI. Reynolds v. State, 4 S.W.3d 15 (Tex. Crim. App. 1999); State v. Brabson, 976 S.W.2d 859 (Tex. Crim. App. 1998).

Furthermore, collateral estoppel principles do not prohibit our Legislature from expressly providing that the determination of an administrative judge in a civil administrative proceeding to revoke a person's driver's license does not preclude litigation of the same or similar facts in a criminal prosecution. Reynolds, *supra.*

An administrative driver's license suspension does not constitute punishment for purposes of the Double Jeopardy Clause of the Fifth Amendment, and therefore, a subsequent prosecution for driving while intoxicated does not implicate the protection under the Double Jeopardy Clause against multiple punishments for the same offense. Tharp v. State, 935 S.W.2d 157 (Tex. Crim. App.1996).

This is true even though under Blockburger analysis, the Court of Criminal Appeals has found that a driver's license suspension under Tex. Rev. Civ. Stat. Art. 6687b-1, §2(a) and the offense of Driving While Intoxicated under P.C. §49.01 are the same offense for double jeopardy purposes. Voisinet v. State, 935 S.W.2d 424 (Tex. Crim. App. 1996).

§8:82 Probation Revocation Proceedings

The result of a hearing on a motion to revoke probation is neither a conviction nor acquittal for purposes of double jeopardy analysis. Salinas v. State, 1 S.W.3d 700 (Tex.App.—Amarillo 1999, *pet. ref'd*). This is because they are administrative proceedings rather than criminal trials. Cobb v. State, 851 S.W.2d 871 (Tex. Crim. App.1993).

Because jeopardy does not attach in revocation proceedings for any criminal offense that is alleged as a violation of the terms of community supervision, double jeopardy principles cannot properly apply to bar a subsequent prosecution under these circumstances. State v. Waters, 560 S.W.3d 651, 658 (Tex. Crim. App. 2018).

The double jeopardy clauses of the U.S. and Texas constitutions are not offended by the use in a subsequent trial of a new offense allegation that was used successfully or unsuccessfully to revoke a probation. Chambers v. State, 700 S.W.2d 597 (Tex. Crim. App. 1985).

Even though no amendment is allowed once evidence has been taken in a revocation hearing, the state is not prevented by statute or double jeopardy principles from dismissing the petition and filing a subsequent motion. Johnson v. State, 633 S.W.2d 687 (Tex.App.—Amarillo 1982, *pet. ref'd*).

A dismissal of a new offense by the state does not preclude the state from seeking revocation by proof of the conduct that was the basis of the new offense. Ex parte Moffett, 542 S.W.2d 184 (Tex. Crim. App. 1976).

§8:83 Parole Revocation Proceedings

A determination by a hearing examiner of insufficient evidence to revoke parole does not operate to collaterally estop prosecution in state district court. Ex parte Daniel, 781 S.W.2d 412 (Tex.App.— Houston [1st Dist.] 1989 *pet. ref'd*); Salinas v. State, 1 S.W.3d 700 (Tex.App.—Amarillo 1999, *pet. ref'd*).

§8:84 Jail Disciplinary Proceedings

Administrative sanctions such as jail discipline are not criminal punishment for double jeopardy purposes when they are not grossly unrelated to the remedial interests of the sanctioning body. Ex parte Hernandez, 953 S.W.2d 275 (Tex. Crim. App. 1997).

§8:90 Prosecutions by Separate Sovereigns

A defendant may be prosecuted in both federal and state court for the same offense. Bartkus v. Illinois, 351 U.S. 121, 79 S.Ct. 676, 3 L.Ed.2d 684 (1956); Ex parte Gary, 895 S.W.2d 465 (Tex. App.—Amarillo 1995, *pet. ref'd*).

Two separate states can prosecute a defendant for the same offense. Heath v. Alabama, 474 U.S. 82, 106 S.Ct. 433, 88 L.Ed.2d 387 (1985).

§8:100 Civil Penalties and Double Jeopardy

The mere assessment of a drug tax against a defendant is not a punishment for the purposes of the double jeopardy clause. Ex parte Chappell, 959 S.W.2d 627 (Tex. Crim. App. 1998).

In fact, absent full payment of the drug tax or

an arrangement with the collecting authority for payment of the amount due, there is no punishment for double jeopardy purposes. Ex parte Ward, 964 S.W.2d 617 (Tex. Crim. App. 1998).

Furthermore, the attachment of a tax lien against a defendant's property without an attempt to enforce the lien is not punishment for double jeopardy purposes. Ex parte Ward, *supra*.

However, a criminal conviction for possession of drugs is punishment for double jeopardy purposes when an assessment is later made and collection sought for a drug tax for the same drugs. Dept. of Revenue v. Kurth Ranch, 511 U.S. 767, 114 S.Ct. 1937, 128 L.Ed.2d 767 (1994).

§8:110 Double Jeopardy and Contempt Proceedings

It is well established that a contempt conviction is criminal if it punishes for past violations, and civil if it attempts to coerce future action. Ex parte Williams, 799 S.W.2d 304 (Tex. Crim. App. 1990).

Double jeopardy principles generally do not apply to an order assessing solely coercive confinement when a contemnor can obtain release by purging contempt. Yates v. United States, 355 U.S. 66, 78 S.Ct. 128, 2 L.Ed.2d 95 (1957); Ex parte Jones, 36 S.W.3d 139 (Tex.App.—Houston [1st Dist.] 2000, *pet. ref'd*).

Where a defendant has already been prosecuted for criminal contempt of court for an act, a subsequent criminal prosecution is barred by the Double Jeopardy Clause of the U.S. Constitution. U.S. v. Dixon, 509 U.S. 688, 113 S.Ct. 2849, 125 L.Ed.2d 556 (1993); Ex parte Rhodes, 974 S.W.2d 735 (Tex. Crim. App. 1998).

§8:115 Double Jeopardy and Protective Orders

Code of Criminal Procedure Art. 17.292 is not criminally punitive and therefore jeopardy does not attach following the issuance of a protective order under that section. Ex parte Necessary, 333 S.W.3d 782 (Tex.App.—Houston [1st Dist.], 2010, *no pet.*).

§8:120 Basic Collateral Estoppel Principles

The collateral estoppel doctrine provides that when an issue of ultimate fact has been determined by a valid and final judgment, that issue cannot again be litigated between the same parties in any future lawsuit. Ashe v. Swenson, 397 U.S. 436, 90 S.Ct. 1189, 25 L.Ed.2d 469 (1970); Headrick v. State, 988 S.W.2d 226 (Tex. Crim. App. 1999).

Collateral estoppel bars any retrial of specific and discrete facts that have been fully and fairly adjudicated. Ex parte Watkins, 73 S.W.3d 264 (Tex. Crim. App. Nos. 1460-01 and 1461-01, April 3, 2002).

The mere possibility that a fact may have been determined in a former trial is insufficient to bar relitigation of that same fact in a second trial. In applying the doctrine of collateral estoppel, courts must first determine whether the jury determined a specific fact, and if so, how broad in terms of time, space and content was the scope of its finding. Watkins.

In deciding whether a party is collaterally estopped from litigating an issue, a reviewing court must examine the record of a prior proceeding, taking into account the pleadings, evidence, charge, and other relevant matters, and conclude whether a rational jury could have grounded its verdict upon an issue other than that which the defendant seeks to foreclose from consideration. Ashe v. Swenson, *supra*; Ex parte Mathes, 830 S.W.2d 596 (Tex. Crim. App. 1992); State v. Sauceda, 980 S.W.2d 642 (Tex. Crim. App. 1998).

The doctrine of collateral estoppel does not depend on slight differences in statutory language or an alternate "manner and means." Rather, it depends on the scope of a specific factual finding in a particular case. Ex parte Taylor, 101 S.W.3d 434 (Tex. Crim. App. 2002) (the state was estopped from retrying the defendant for intoxication manslaughter by reason of marijuana intoxication, where a jury had previously acquitted him of intoxication manslaughter by reason of alcohol intoxication arising out of the same incident).

Collateral estoppel deals only with specific factual determinations, not legal claims or legal conclusions. State v. Stevens, 235 S.W.3d 736 (Tex. Crim. App. 2007) (citing Guajardo v. State, 109 S.W.3d 456 (Tex. Crim. App. 2003)).

Courts must determine exactly what facts were necessarily decided in the first proceeding and whether those necessarily decided facts constitute essential elements of the offense in the second trial. Ex parte Taylor.

Mere issues of the admissibility of evidence are not elements essential to proving the commission of an offense; therefore, where a court has granted a defendant's motion to suppress, that issue can be relitigated in another case arising from the same transaction. Murphy v. State, 239 S.W.3d 791 (Tex. Crim. App. 2007).

That is, the State is not barred by the Double Jeopardy Clause from relitigating a suppression issue that was not an ultimate fact in the first prosecution and was not an ultimate fact in the second prosecution. York v. State, 342 S.W.3d 528 (Tex. Crim. App. 2011).

Collateral estoppel operates only if the very fact or point in issue in the second case was determined in the prior proceeding. It must be precisely the same issue in both cases. Thus, issue preclusion is limited to cases where the legal and factual situations are identical. Collateral estoppel may apply to a phase, an issue of fact, or congeries of fact, depending on the particular circumstances. Ex parte Taylor.

On the other hand, issue preclusion cannot be defeated simply by advancing new or different evidence to support the same issue already litigated. Ex parte Taylor.

An exception to the application of traditional double jeopardy analysis may exist where the additional facts necessary to sustain a charge have not occurred or have not been discovered despite the exercise of due diligence. *See* Ashe v. Swenson, *supra* (Brennan, J., concurring); Ex parte Mathes, *supra* (fn.4).

A conviction that is reversed on appeal cannot be used to bar a subsequent prosecution on collateral estoppel principles. Garcia v. State, 768 S.W.2d 726 (Tex. Crim. App. 1987).

§8:130 Collateral Estoppel in Punishment Proceedings

The state is barred from relitigating the issue of "sudden passion" in a subsequent trial where a jury has found against the state on this issue in a previous trial of an offense arising out of the same criminal transaction. Ex parte Watkins, 73 S.W.3d 264 (Tex. Crim. App. 2002).

Where a jury returns a verdict finding against the state on a special issue in a death penalty case, the state is collaterally estopped from seeking the death penalty in the trial of a case involving a second victim of the same offense. Ex parte Mathes, 830 S.W.2d 596 (Tex. Crim. App. 1992).

However, where a jury merely is unable to answer a special issue, the state is not foreclosed from litigating it in a second proceeding because the issue has not been finally determined against the state. Padgett v. State, 717 S.W.2d 55 (Tex. Crim. App. 1986).

§8:140 Collateral Estoppel and Probation Revocation Proceedings

Collateral estoppel does not apply to bar a subsequent criminal prosecution following a trial judge's finding of "not true" at a revocation hearing. State v. Waters, 560 S.W.3d 651, 663 (Tex. Crim. App. 2018) (overruling Ex parte Tarver, 725 S.W.2d 195 (Tex. Crim. App. 1986) and Wafer v. State, 58 S.W.3d 158 (Tex. App.—Amarillo 2001)).

An acquittal of a new offense will not bar subsequent prosecution of the allegation in a motion to revoke probation. Ex parte Tarver, 725 S.W.2d 195, 200 (Tex. Crim. App. 1986).

§8:150 Raising Collateral Estoppel Claims

It is appropriate for a defendant to apply for a pretrial writ of habeas corpus where the claims concern collateral estoppel and constitutional double jeopardy violations. Ex parte Robinson, 641 S.W.2d 552 (Tex. Crim. App. 1982); Ex parte Watkins, 73 S.W.3d 264 (Tex. Crim. App. 2002).

Collateral estoppel claims not alleging constitutional double jeopardy violations are not cognizable on application for pretrial writ of habeas corpus. This is because there is an adequate remedy at law by way of direct appeal. Headrick v. State, 988 S.W.2d 226 (Tex. Crim. App. 1999) (where the defendant sought to assert collateral estoppel based on an administrative judge's decision).

In order to obtain appellate review of a collateral estoppel claim, a defendant must introduce a record of the first proceeding in the second proceeding and include that record on appeal. Guajardo v. State, 109 S.W.3d 456 (Tex. Crim. App. 2003).

Chapter 9

BAIL AND BOND ISSUES

Table of Contents

§9:10 Right to Bail

§9:11 Statutory and Constitutional Law

CCP Art. 1.07. Right to bail

> *All prisoners shall be bailable unless for capital offenses when the proof is evident. This provision shall not be so construed as to prevent bail after indictment found upon examination of the evidence, in such manner as may be prescribed by law.*

CCP Art. 1.09. Cruelty forbidden

> *Excessive bail shall not be required, nor excessive fines imposed, nor cruel or unusual punishment inflicted.*

CCP Art. 17.38. Rules applicable to all cases of bail

> *The rules in this Chapter respecting bail are applicable to all such undertakings when entered into in the course of a criminal action, whether before or after an indictment, in every case where authority is given to any court, judge, magistrate, or other officer, to require bail of a person accused of an offense, or of a witness in a criminal action.*

Texas Constitution Art.1 §11. Bail

> *§11. All prisoners shall be bailable by sufficient sureties, unless for capital offenses, when the proof is evident; but this provision shall not be so construed as to prevent bail after indictment found upon examination of the evidence, in such manner as may be prescribed by law.*

Texas Constitution Art. 1, §13. Excessive bail or fines; cruel and unusual punishment; remedy by due course of law

> *§13. Excessive bail shall not be required, nor excessive fines imposed, nor cruel or unusual punishment inflicted. All courts shall be open, and every person for an injury done him, in his lands, goods, person or reputation, shall have remedy by due course of law.*

§9:12 In General

With narrow exceptions, Article I, §11 of the Texas Constitution provides all prisoners a right to bail pending trial. Smith v. State, 829 S.W.2d 885 (Tex.App.—Houston [1st Dist.] 1992, *pet. ref'd*).

A defendant has a liberty interest in bail, which requires the protection of the due process clause of the Fourteenth Amendment. Smith v. State, 993 S.W.2d 408 (Tex.App.—Houston [14th Dist.] 1999, *pet. ref'd*); Robinson v. State, 700 S.W.2d 710 (Tex. App.—Houston [14th Dist.] 1985, *no pet.*).

The primary purpose of bond is to ensure the defendant's presence in court at all proceedings. Estrada v. State, 594 S.W.2d 445 (Tex. Crim. App. [Panel Op.] 1980). The decision regarding a proper bail amount lies within the sound discretion of the trial court. Ex parte Brown, 959 S.W.2d 369 (Tex.App.—Fort Worth 1998, *no pet.*); Ex parte Green, 940 S.W.2d 799 (Tex.App.—El Paso 1997, *no pet.*). There is no precise standard for reviewing bail bond settings. Ex parte Watson, 940 S.W.2d 733 (Tex.App.—Texarkana 1997, *no pet.*); Ex parte Pemberton, 577 S.W.2d 266 (Tex. Crim. App. [Panel Op.] 1979).

The trial court does not have inherent authority to impose conditions on a defendant's pre-trial bond that are not authorized by statute; and further, Art. 17.15 does not implicitly authorize other conditions not expressly stated. Ex parte Tucker, 977 S.W.2d 713 (Tex.App.—Fort Worth 1998, *pet. dism'd*).

Absent legislative intent to the contrary, a trial court has inherent power in misdemeanor and felony appeals to impose conditions on bail that directly or indirectly relate to the purpose of assuring the defendant's continued appearance. Dallas v. State, 983 S.W.2d 276 (Tex. Crim. App. 1998). It is not necessary that the bond condition in question relate directly to securing the defendant's presence in court. Estrada, *supra*. It is sufficient if the condition indirectly increases the likelihood that the defendant will appear. Rodriguez v. State, 744 S.W.2d 361 (Tex.App.—Corpus Christi 1988, *no pet.*); Estrada.

Determining the "reasonableness" of a bail condition must be done in light of its purpose, to assure the presence of the defendant. Valenciano v.

State, 720 S.W.2d 523 (Tex. Crim. App. 1986). In each individual case where conditions are imposed, those conditions must strike a balance between society's interest in assuring that the defendant will appear if and when his conviction becomes final and the defendant's interest in remaining free pending appeal. Valenciano.

The trial court's decision on pretrial bond conditions is reviewable under an abuse of discretion standard. Miller v. State, 855 S.W.2d 92 (Tex.App.—Houston [14th Dist.] 1993, *pet. ref'd*).

A trial court does not have the discretion to set a differential bail bond amount depending upon whether a cash bond or a surety bond is used. Professional Bondsmen of Texas v. Carey, 762 S.W.2d 691 (Tex.App.—Amarillo 1988, *no pet.*). The trial court does not have the authority to require a cash bond or surety bond to the exclusion of the other. Carey; Ex parte Deaton, 582 S.W.2d 151 (Tex. Crim. App.1979).

The practice of a grand jury recommending the amount of bail is not supported in the statutes and is not a commendable practice. Ex parte Dueitt, 529 S.W.2d 531 (Tex. Crim. App. 1975).

A defendant whose adjudication of guilt has been deferred is entitled to bail pending an adjudication hearing. Gutierrez v. State, 927 S.W.2d 783 (Tex.App.—Houston [14th Dist.] 1996, *no pet.*); Ex parte Laday, 594 S.W.2d 102 (Tex. Crim. App. 1980).

If a trial court makes a finding favorable to a convicted person under CCP Art. 64.04, the trial court may release the person on bail after a hearing. V.A.C.C.P Art. 17.48.

§9:13 Form: Sample Application for Writ of Habeas Corpus

See our companion book *Texas Criminal Forms* (James Publishing) Form 9-2.

§9:20 Defendant's Burden to Object to Improper Bond Conditions

The party complaining of the bond condition has the burden of demonstrating that the trial court abused its discretion by imposing an excessive condition of bond. Ex parte Rubac, 611 S.W.2d 848 (Tex. Crim. App. [Panel Op.] 1981).

A defendant must object to a bond condition when it is imposed or he fails to preserve error for appeal. Smith v. State, 993 S.W.2d 408 (Tex. App.—Houston [14th Dist.] 1999, *pet. ref'd*); Ex parte Sotelo, 878 S.W.2d 179 (Tex.App.—Fort Worth 1993, *pet. ref'd*). Additionally, in the *habeas corpus* context, a defendant's failure to object to the conditions at the time that they were imposed also prevents him from challenging the constitutionality of the conditions via a post-conviction collateral attack. Smith.

While the failure to object to the imposition of conditions of a bond waives the right to complain of constitutional error, a *habeas* applicant may assert a complaint concerning the reasonableness of the conditions arising from an order revoking bond. Smith.

A defendant may at any time litigate the reasonableness of a bond condition by way of a *habeas corpus* action. A bail condition that places an improper infringement on a defendant's freedom of action is within the scope of *habeas corpus* relief because it is a restraint. Valenciano v. State, 720 S.W.2d 523 (Tex. Crim. App. 1986).

Where the record reflects that the defendant did not object to the trial court's action, did not develop a record, and did not obtain an adverse ruling, he has waived appeal of the trial court's decision to not set an appeal bond. Hill v. State, 902 S.W.2d 57 (Tex.App.—Houston [1st Dist.] 1995).

§9:30 Fixing Amount of Bail

CCP Art. 17.15 Rules for Fixing Amount of Bail

> *The amount of bail to be required in any case is to be regulated by the court, judge, magistrate or officer taking the bail; they are to be governed in the exercise of this discretion by the Constitution and by the following rules:*
>
> *1. The bail shall be sufficiently high to give reasonable assurance that the undertaking will be complied with.*
>
> *2. The power to require bail is not to be so used as to make it an instrument of oppression.*

BAIL AND BOND ISSUES

3. The nature of the offense and the circumstances under which it was committed are to be considered.

4. The ability to make bail is to be regarded, and proof may be taken upon this point.

5. The future safety of a victim of the alleged offense and the community shall be considered.

CCP Art. 56.02. Crime victims' rights

(a) A victim, guardian of a victim, or close relative of a deceased victim is entitled to the following rights within the criminal justice system:

... (2) the right to have the magistrate take the safety of the victim or his family into consideration as an element in fixing the amount of bail for the accused;

The decision regarding a proper bail amount lies within the sound discretion of the trial court. Ex parte Brown, 959 S.W.2d 369 (Tex.App.—Fort Worth 1998, *no pet.*); Ex parte Green, 940 S.W.2d 799 (Tex.App.—El Paso 1997, *no pet.*).

The amount of bail must be high enough to give reasonable assurance that the accused will appear as required, but the amount should not be oppressively high. Ex parte McDonald, 852 S.W.2d 730 (Tex.App.—San Antonio 1993, *no pet.*).

In addition to the considerations set forth in Arts. 17.15 and 56.02, other factors may be considered by the trial court in setting bail, such as:

- Accused's work record, family and community ties, length of residency, prior criminal record, if any, and conformity with the conditions of any previous bond
- Existence of outstanding bonds, if any
- Alleged aggravated circumstances involved in the offense

Smith v. State, 829 S.W.2d 885 (Tex.App.—Houston [1st Dist.] 1992, *pet. ref'd*).

TIP TO THE STATE: When the state presents no evidence on a particular enumerated factor in Art. 17.15 or when it presents evidence that is indecipherable, the courts will assume they consider these factors unworthy of attention. Ex parte Prelow, 929 S.W.2d 54 (Tex.App.—San Antonio 1996, no pet.).

A court of appeals has no jurisdiction to hear interlocutory appeals regarding excessive bail or the denial of bail because there is no constitutional or statutory authority granting this authority. Ragston v. State, 424 S.W.3d 49, 52 (Tex. Crim. App. 2014).

§9:31 Existence of Outstanding Bonds

The existence of other bonds may be taken into consideration when setting bond. Ex parte Watson, 940 S.W.2d 733 (Tex.App.—Texarkana 1997, *no pet.*); Nguyen v. State, 881 S.W.2d 141 (Tex. App.—Houston [1st Dist.] 1994, *no pet.*).

CCP Art. 15.17 requires a magistrate setting bail to determine whether the person is currently on bail for a separate criminal offense; and implies that if the person is on bail for another offense, bail should not be set on the current case.

§9:32 Conformity With Previous Bonds

The trial court may also consider the fact that the accused has previously failed to appear in court while on bail. Ex parte Poindexter, 511 S.W.2d 529 (Tex. Crim. App. 1974).

§9:33 Defendant's Criminal Record

Prior felony convictions and the potential punishment in the case for which bond is being set are two considerations. Ex parte Runo, 535 S.W.2d 188 (Tex. Crim. App.1976).

§9:34 Circumstances of Offense

The amount of bail also must be based on the nature of the offense and the circumstances under which it was committed. Ex parte Brown, 959 S.W.2d 369 (Tex.App.—Fort Worth 1998, *no pet.*); Ex parte

Davila, 623 S.W.2d 408 (Tex. Crim. App. [Panel Op.] 1981).

§9:35 Ability to Make Existing Bond Amount

In seeking to reduce the amount of bail ordered by the trial court, the defendant has the burden to show that the amount is excessive. Ex parte Watson, 940 S.W.2d 733 (Tex.App.—Texarkana 1997, *no pet.*); Ex parte Rubac, 611 S.W.2d 848 (Tex. Crim. App. [Panel Op.] 1981). The defendant must show that he has attempted and failed to make bail in the amount fixed. Ex parte Welch, 729 S.W.2d 306 (Tex.App.—Dallas 1987, *no pet.*); Ex parte Sellers, 516 S.W.2d 665 (Tex. Crim. App. 1974).

The defendant's ability to make bail is a relevant factor, but is not dispositive. Esquivel v. State, 922 S.W.2d 601 (Tex.App.—San Antonio 1996, *no pet.*). A defendant's mere inability meet the bond set by the trial court does not automatically render the bail excessive. Ex parte Brown, 959 S.W.2d 369 (Tex.App.—Fort Worth 1998, *no pet.*).

Like indigence, the ability of a bail bondsman to post bond should not be a controlling factor for the fixing of bail by the trial court. Wright v. State, 976 S.W.2d 815 (Tex.App.—Houston [1st Dist.] 1998, *no pet.*).

§9:36 Future Safety of Victim

The court also should consider the future safety of the victim of the alleged offense and the community at large. Ex parte Wood, 952 S.W.2d 41 (Tex.App.—San Antonio 1997, *no pet.*). The Court of Criminal Appeals has stated that under Art. 17.15(5) the "victim of the alleged offense" includes only the complainant in the charged offense. Ludwig v. State, 812 S.W.2d 323 (Tex. Crim. App. 1991).

§9:37 Threats and Actions of Defendant

Where the accused has made threats that he "will not be tried" or is otherwise not disposed to regard the obligation of ordinary bonds, the fixing of a higher bond is justifiable. Wright v. State, 976 S.W.2d 815 (Tex.App.—Houston [1st Dist.] 1998, *no pet.*).

Higher bonds are justified where defendant:

- Attempted to obtain fake identification to flee the country
- Committed the offense as part of a plan to escape punishment for another, more serious charge
- Has funds to post a lower bond and is likely to obtain considerably more assets that could be used to accomplish the goal of fleeing the jurisdiction

Wright.

§9:38 Cases on Pretrial Bond Amounts

The Court of Criminal Appeals has yet to condone a bail amount even approaching seven figures, even in a capital case. Ludwig v. State, 812 S.W.2d 323 (Tex. Crim. App. 1991) ($1,000,000 bond was found to be excessive and bond was reduced to $50,000). Where a defendant was alleged to have committed a premeditated retaliation-murder, a $150,000 bond was not unreasonable despite his youthful age and ties to the community. Ex parte Prelow, 929 S.W.2d 54 (Tex.App.—San Antonio 1996, *no pet.*).

A bond of $500,000 was reduced to $100,000 in cases involving murder and injury to a child where the facts surrounding the offenses were not developed at the *habeas* hearing. Smithwick v. State, 880 S.W.2d 510 (Tex.App.—San Antonio 1994, *no pet.*). A bond was reduced in a capital murder case from $1,000,000 to $75,000 where the facts surrounding the offense were not developed at the *habeas* hearing. Ex parte McDonald, 852 S.W.2d 730 (Tex.App.—San Antonio 1993, *no pet.*).

Where a defendant had no criminal record, had ties to the community even though he was not a Texas resident and was returning to California when he was arrested, $60,000 in bonds for three serious felonies was found to be proper. Nguyen v. State, 881 S.W.2d 141 (Tex.App.—Houston [1st Dist.] 1994, *no pet.*). Where a defendant did not show an inability to post a higher bond, exhibited continued illegal activity and had threatened to flee, a $200,000 bond was not excessive in four charges of failure to remit gasoline taxes. Wisenbaker v. State, 782 S.W.2d 534 (Tex.App.—Houston [14th Dist.] 1989, *no pet.*).

$100,000 was not an excessive amount of bail where the defendant was charged in an assault and murder case involving a child and had no ties to the community. O'Neill v. State, 635 S.W.2d 166 (Tex. App.—Houston [1st Dist.] 1982, *no pet.*). Bail of $350,000 in capital murder case and $100,000 in an unrelated aggravated murder case was reduced to $50,000 and $20,000 respectively where the defendant presented several mitigating factors at the bond hearing. Ex parte Wood, 952 S.W.2d 41 (Tex.App.—San Antonio 1997, *no pet.*).

A $250,000 bond for an unemployed armed robbery defendant was reduced to $50,000. Ex parte Ivey, 594 S.W.2d 98 (Tex. Crim. App. 1980). A $100,000 bond for an indigent capital murder defendant who admitted driving the get-away car was reduced to $20,000. Ex parte Vasquez, 558 S.W.2d 477 (Tex. Crim. App. 1977).

§9:40 Specific Bond Conditions

Art. 17.40 gives trial judges the authority to impose conditions on a defendant's bond that are not specifically authorized by statute.

> *CCP Art. 17.40. Conditions related to victim or community safety*
>
> *(a) To secure a defendant's attendance at trial, a magistrate may impose any reasonable condition of bond related to the safety of a victim of the alleged offense or to the safety of the community.*
>
> *(b) At a hearing limited to determining whether the defendant violated a condition of bond imposed under Subsection (a), the magistrate may revoke the defendant's bond only if the magistrate finds by a preponderance of the evidence that the violation occurred.*

§9:41 Statutorily Authorized Bond Conditions

§9:41.1 Ignition Interlock Devices

> *CCP Art. 17.441. Conditions requiring motor vehicle ignition interlock*
>
> *(a) Except as provided by Subsection (b), a magistrate shall require on release that a defendant charged with a subsequent offense under §§49.04-49.06, Penal Code, or an offense under §49.07 or 49.08 of that code:*
>
> *(1) have installed on the motor vehicle owned by the defendant or on the vehicle most regularly driven by the defendant, a device that uses a deep-lung breath analysis mechanism to make impractical the operation of a motor vehicle if ethyl alcohol is detected in the breath of the operator; and*
>
> *(2) not operate any motor vehicle unless the vehicle is equipped with that device.*
>
> *(b) The magistrate may not require the installation of the device if the magistrate finds that to require the device would not be in the best interest of justice.*
>
> *(c) If the defendant is required to have the device installed, the magistrate shall require that the defendant have the device installed on the appropriate motor vehicle, at the defendant's expense, before the 30th day after the date the defendant is released on bond.*
>
> *(d) The magistrate may designate an appropriate agency to verify the installation of the device and to monitor the device. If the magistrate designates an agency under this subsection, in each month during which the agency verifies the installation of the device or provides a monitoring service the defendant shall pay a fee to the designated agency in the amount set by the magistrate. The defendant shall pay the initial fee at the time the agency verifies the installation of the device. In each subsequent month during which the defendant is required to pay a fee the defendant shall pay the fee on the first occasion in that month that the agency provides a monitoring service. The magistrate shall set the fee in an amount not to exceed $10 as determined by the county auditor, or by the commissioners court of the county if the county does not have a county auditor, to be sufficient to cover*

the cost incurred by the designated agency in conducting the verification or providing the monitoring service, as applicable in that county.

By conducting a hearing and then determining that the installation of the interlock device was appropriate, the trial court complied with Art. 17.441. Ex parte Elliott, 950 S.W.2d 714 (Tex. App.—Fort Worth 1997, *pet. ref'd*). After the court has determined that the defendant has been previously convicted of DWI and that installation of the device was in the best interest of justice, Art. 17.441 requires installation of the device. Elliot.

Because subsection (b) of Art. 17.441 affords the trial court the discretion to find that the interest of justice mandates against the installation of an interlock device, it does not violate the separation of powers provision and is not unconstitutional. Elliot. The requirement of an interlock device, which is a less severe infringement on the privilege of driving an automobile, does not constitute punishment and is not oppressive. Elliot.

§9:41.2 Conditions Related to Victim or Community Safety

CCP Art. 17.40. Conditions Related to Victim or Community Safety

(a) To secure a defendant's attendance at trial, a magistrate may impose any reasonable condition of bond related to the safety of a victim of the alleged offense or to the safety of the community.

(b) At a hearing limited to determining whether the defendant violated a condition of bond imposed under Subsection (a), the magistrate may revoke the defendant's bond only if the magistrate finds by a preponderance of the evidence that the violation occurred. If the magistrate finds that the violation occurred, the magistrate shall revoke the defendant's bond and order that the defendant be immediately returned to custody. Once the defendant is placed in custody, the revocation of the defendant's bond discharges the sureties on the bond, if any, from any future liability on the bond. A discharge under this subsection from any future liability on the bond does not discharge any surety from liability for previous forfeitures on the bond.

In a case where the defendant was convicted of aggravated assault, a bond condition that the defendant stay away from and not communicate with the victim was found to be reasonable because it was rationally related to the purpose of assuring that the defendant commit no further acts of violence, which in turn increased the likelihood that he would appear in court when ordered. Rodriguez v. State, 744 S.W.2d 361 (Tex.App.—Corpus Christi 1988, *no pet.*).

§9:41.3 Conditions Where Child Is Alleged Victim

CCP Art. 17.41. Condition Where Child Alleged Victim

(a) This article applies to a defendant charged with an offense under any of the following provisions of the Penal Code, if committed against a child younger than 14 years of age:

(1) Chapter 21 (Sexual Offenses) or 22 (Assaultive Offenses);

(2) Section 25.02 (Prohibited Sexual Conduct); or

(3) Section 43.25 (Sexual Performance by a Child).

(b) Subject to Subsections (c) and (d), a magistrate shall require as a condition of bond for a defendant charged with an offense described by Subsection (a) that the defendant not:

(1) directly communicate with the alleged victim of the offense; or

(2) go near a residence, school, or other location, as specifically described in the bond, frequented by the alleged victim.

(c) A magistrate who imposes a condition of bond under this article may

grant the defendant supervised access to the alleged victim.

(d) To the extent that a condition imposed under this article conflicts with an existing court order granting possession of or access to a child, the condition imposed under this article prevails for a period specified by the magistrate, not to exceed 90 days.

§9:41.4 Home Curfew and Electronic Monitoring

CCP Art. 17.43. Home curfew and electronic monitoring as condition

(a) A magistrate may require as a condition of release on personal bond that the defendant submit to home curfew and electronic monitoring under the supervision of an agency designated by the magistrate.

(b) Cost of monitoring may be assessed as court costs or ordered paid directly by the defendant as a condition of bond.

CCP Art. 17.44. Home confinement, electronic monitoring, and drug testing as condition

(a) A magistrate may require as a condition of release on bond that the defendant submit to:

(1) home confinement and electronic monitoring under the supervision of an agency designated by the magistrate; or

(2) testing on a weekly basis for the presence of a controlled substance in the defendant's body.

(b) In this article, "controlled substance" has the meaning assigned by §481.002, Health and Safety Code.

(c) The magistrate may revoke the bond and order the defendant arrested if the defendant:

(1) violates a condition of home confinement and electronic monitoring;

(2) refuses to submit to a test for controlled substances or submits to a test for controlled substances and the test indicates the presence of a controlled substance in the defendant's body; or

(3) fails to pay the costs of monitoring or testing for controlled substances, if payment is ordered under Subsection (e) as a condition of bond and the magistrate determines that the defendant is not indigent and is financially able to make the payments as ordered.

(d) The community justice assistance division of the Texas Department of Criminal Justice may provide grants to counties to implement electronic monitoring programs authorized by this article.

(e) The cost of electronic monitoring or testing for controlled substances under this article may be assessed as court costs or ordered paid directly by the defendant as a condition of bond.

Electronic monitoring is allowed as a condition of bond by CCP Art. 17.44. Grady v. State, 962 S.W.2d 128 (Tex.App.—Houston [1st Dist.] 1997, *pet. ref'd*). Requiring a defendant to wear an electronic monitor and to observe curfew conditions are not unreasonable appeal bond conditions because they increase the likelihood of defendant's appearance in court. Smith v. State, 993 S.W.2d 408 (Tex.App.—Houston [14th Dist.] 1999, *pet. ref'd*); Ly v. State, 908 S.W.2d 598 (Tex. App.—Houston [1st Dist.] 1995, *no pet.*).

Requiring the defendant to submit to electronic monitoring and to pay associated fees is a valid condition of appeal bond. Speth v. State, 939 S.W.2d 969 (Tex.App.—Houston [14th Dist.] 1997, *no pet.*)

§9:41.5 Drug Testing

CCP Art. 17.44. Home confinement, electronic monitoring, and drug testing as condition

(a) A magistrate may require as a condition of release on bond that the defendant submit to:

(1) home confinement and electronic monitoring under the supervision of an agency designated by the magistrate; or

(2) testing on a weekly basis for the presence of a controlled substance in the defendant's body.

(b) In this article, "controlled substance" has the meaning assigned by §481.002, Health and Safety Code.

(c) If a defendant violates a condition of home confinement and electronic monitoring, refuses to submit to a test for controlled substances, or submits to a test for controlled substances and the test indicates the presence of a controlled substance in the defendant's body, the magistrate may revoke the bond and order the defendant arrested.

(d) The community justice assistance division of the Texas Department of Criminal Justice may provide grants to counties to implement electronic monitoring programs authorized by this article.

(e) The cost of electronic monitoring or testing for controlled substances under this article may be assessed as court costs or ordered paid directly by the defendant as a condition of bond.

In a case where the defendant was convicted of possession of heroin, a condition of his appeal bond that required him to submit to urine testing and attend drug counseling was found to be reasonable because the defendant's continued abstinence from heroin was rationally related to his appearance in court when necessary. Estrada v. State, 594 S.W.2d 445 (Tex. Crim. App. [Panel Op.] 1980).

Random urinalysis is allowed as a condition of bond by CCP Art. 17.44. Grady v. State, 962 S.W.2d 128 (Tex.App.—Houston [1st Dist.] 1997, *pet. ref'd*).

§9:41.6 Conditions Requiring AIDS and HIV Instruction

CCP Art. 17.45. Conditions requiring AIDS and HIV instruction

A magistrate may require as a condition of bond that a defendant charged with an offense under §43.02, Penal Code, receive counseling or education, or both, relating to acquired immune deficiency syndrome or human immunodeficiency virus.

§9:41.7 Conditions for Defendant Charged With Stalking

CCP Art. 17.46. Conditions for a defendant charged with stalking

(a) A magistrate may require as a condition of release on bond that a defendant charged with an offense under §42.072, Penal Code, may not:

(1) communicate directly or indirectly with the victim; or

(2) go to or near the residence, place of employment, or business of the victim or to or near a school, day-care facility, or similar facility where a dependent child of the victim is in attendance.

(b) If the magistrate requires the prohibition contained in Subsection (a)(2) of this article as a condition of release on bond, the magistrate shall specifically describe the prohibited locations and the minimum distances, if any, that the defendant must maintain from the locations.

§9:41.8 Submission of DNA Specimen

A magistrate shall require, as a condition of release of a defendant described by Gov. Code §411.1471(a) (basically all sex offenders), that the defendant provide to a law enforcement agency one or more specimens for the purpose of creating a DNA record. V.A.C.C.P Art. 17.47.

BAIL AND BOND ISSUES

§9:41.9 Conditions in Family Violence Cases

Tex. Code Crim. Pro. Art. 17.49. Conditions for Defendant Charged With Offense Involving Family Violence

(a) In this article:

(1) "Family violence" has the meaning assigned by Section 71.004, Family Code.

(2) "Global positioning monitoring system" means a system that electronically determines and reports the location of an individual through the use of a transmitter or similar device carried or worn by the individual that transmits latitude and longitude data to a monitoring entity through global positioning satellite technology. The term does not include a system that contains or operates global positioning system technology, radio frequency identification technology, or any other similar technology that is implanted in or otherwise invades or violates the individual's body.

(b) A magistrate may require as a condition of release on bond that a defendant charged with an offense involving family violence:

(1) refrain from going to or near a residence, school, place of employment, or other location, as specifically described in the bond, frequented by an alleged victim of the offense;

(2) carry or wear a global positioning monitoring system device and, except as provided by Subsection (h), pay the costs associated with operating that system in relation to the defendant; or

(3) except as provided by Subsection (h), if the alleged victim of the offense consents after receiving the information described by Subsection (d), pay the costs associated with providing the victim with an electronic receptor device that:

(A) is capable of receiving the global positioning monitoring system information from the device carried or worn by the defendant; and

(B) notifies the victim if the defendant is at or near a location that the defendant has been ordered to refrain from going to or near under Subdivision (1).

(c) Before imposing a condition described by Subsection (b)(1), a magistrate must afford an alleged victim an opportunity to provide the magistrate with a list of areas from which the victim would like the defendant excluded and shall consider the victim's request, if any, in determining the locations the defendant will be ordered to refrain from going to or near. If the magistrate imposes a condition described by Subsection (b)(1), the magistrate shall specifically describe the locations that the defendant has been ordered to refrain from going to or near and the minimum distances, if any, that the defendant must maintain from those locations.

(d) Before imposing a condition described by Subsection (b)(3), a magistrate must provide to an alleged victim information regarding:

(1) the victim's right to participate in a global positioning monitoring system or to refuse to participate in that system and the procedure for requesting that the magistrate terminate the victim's participation;

(2) the manner in which the global positioning monitoring system technology functions and the risks and limitations of that technology, and the extent to which the system

will track and record the victim's location and movements;

(3) any locations that the defendant is ordered to refrain from going to or near and the minimum distances, if any, that the defendant must maintain from those locations;

(4) any sanctions that the court may impose on the defendant for violating a condition of bond imposed under this article;

(5) the procedure that the victim is to follow, and support services available to assist the victim, if the defendant violates a condition of bond or if the global positioning monitoring system equipment fails;

(6) community services available to assist the victim in obtaining shelter, counseling, education, child care, legal representation, and other assistance available to address the consequences of family violence; and

(7) the fact that the victim's communications with the court concerning the global positioning monitoring system and any restrictions to be imposed on the defendant's movements are not confidential.

(e) In addition to the information described by Subsection (d), a magistrate shall provide to an alleged victim who participates in a global positioning monitoring system under this article the name and telephone number of an appropriate person employed by a local law enforcement agency whom the victim may call to request immediate assistance if the defendant violates a condition of bond imposed under this article.

(f) In determining whether to order a defendant's participation in a global positioning monitoring system under this article, the magistrate shall consider the likelihood that the defendant's participation will deter the defendant from seeking to kill, physically injure, stalk, or otherwise threaten the alleged victim before trial.

(g) An alleged victim may request that the magistrate terminate the victim's participation in a global positioning monitoring system at any time. The magistrate may not impose sanctions on the victim for requesting termination of the victim's participation in or refusing to participate in a global positioning monitoring system under this article.

(h) If the magistrate determines that a defendant is indigent, the magistrate may, based on a sliding scale established by local rule, require the defendant to pay costs under Subsection (b)(2) or (3) in an amount that is less than the full amount of the costs associated with operating the global positioning monitoring system in relation to the defendant or providing the victim with an electronic receptor device.

(i) If an indigent defendant pays to an entity that operates a global positioning monitoring system the partial amount ordered by a magistrate under Subsection (h), the entity shall accept the partial amount as payment in full. The county in which the magistrate who enters an order under Subsection (h) is located is not responsible for payment of any costs associated with operating the global positioning monitoring system in relation to an indigent defendant.

(j) A magistrate that imposes a condition described by Subsection (b)(1) or (2) shall order the entity that operates the global positioning monitoring system to notify the court and the appropriate local law enforcement agency if a defendant violates a condition of bond imposed under this article.

(k) A magistrate that imposes a condition described by Subsection (b) may only allow or require the defendant to execute or be released under a type of bond that is authorized by this chapter.

BAIL AND BOND ISSUES

(l) This article does not limit the authority of a magistrate to impose any other reasonable conditions of bond or enter any orders of protection under other applicable statutes.

§9:42 Pretrial Bond Conditions (Upheld)

Where the defendant was on bond for DWI and was found to have previously been convicted of DWI a condition that he install an interlock device on his vehicle was found to be reasonable because by assuring that the defendant not violate the law, the condition went to assuring his presence in court when required. Ex parte Elliott, 950 S.W.2d 714 (Tex.App.—Fort Worth 1997, *pet. ref'd*).

§9:43 Pretrial Bond Conditions (Not Upheld)

Requiring a defendant to satisfy a civil judgment in a sister court as a condition of bond is improper because it bears no rational relationship to the objective of securing the defendant's appearance before the trial court. Smith v. State, 829 S.W.2d 885 (Tex.App.—Houston [1st Dist.] 1992, *pet. ref'd*).

The trial court lacks the authority to require the defendant to appear with an attorney as a term and condition of pretrial bond. Meador v. State, 780 S.W.2d 836 (Tex.App.—Houston [14th Dist.] 1989, *no pet.*).

§9:44 Forms and Motions

See our companion book *Texas Criminal Forms* (James Publishing):

- Form 9-7.1 Written Objection To Bond Conditions
- Form 9-7.2 Defendant's Motion to Modify Bond Conditions
- Form 9-8 Habeas Corpus Petition for Relief From Unreasonable Bond Condition

§9:50 Increasing Bond Amounts

It is within the trial court's discretion to increase the bail set. Meador v. State, 780 S.W.2d 836 (Tex.App.—Houston [14th Dist.] 1989, *no pet.*). A reviewing court will not disturb the trial court's decision to increase bail unless it finds that the trial court has abused its discretion. Miller v. State, 855 S.W.2d 92 (Tex.App.—Houston [14th Dist.] 1993, *pet. ref'd*). No precise standard exists for determining what constitutes "good and sufficient cause" under Art. 17.09; and therefore, each case must be reviewed on an individual basis. Miller.

Where the accused has made threats that he "will not be tried" or is not otherwise disposed to regard the obligation of ordinary bonds, a higher bond is justified. Wright v. State, 976 S.W.2d 815 (Tex.App.—Houston [1st Dist.] 1998).

Higher bonds are justified where the defendant:

- Attempted to obtain fake identification to flee the country
- Committed the offense as part of a plan to escape punishment for another, more serious charge
- Has funds to post a lower bond and is likely to obtain considerably more assets that could be used to accomplish the goal of fleeing the jurisdiction

Wright.

§9:60 Denial of Bond

CCP Art. 17.152. Denial of Bail for Violation of Certain Court Orders or Conditions of Bond in a Family Violence Case

(a) In this article, "family violence" has the meaning assigned by Section 71.004, Family Code.

(b) Except as otherwise provided by Subsection (d), a person who commits an offense under Section 25.07, Penal Code, related to a violation of a condition of bond set in a family violence case and whose bail in the case under Section 25.07, Penal Code, or in the family violence case is revoked or forfeited for a violation of a condition of bond, may be taken into custody and, pending trial or other court proceedings, denied release on bail if, following a hearing, a judge or magistrate determines by a preponderance of the evidence that the person violated a condition of bond related to:

BAIL AND BOND ISSUES

(1) the safety of the victim of the offense under Section 25.07, Penal Code, or the family violence case, as applicable; or

(2) the safety of the community.

(c) Except as otherwise provided by Subsection (d), a person who commits an offense under Section 25.07, Penal Code, other than an offense related to a violation of a condition of bond set in a family violence case, may be taken into custody and, pending trial or other court proceedings, denied release on bail if, following a hearing, a judge or magistrate determines by a preponderance of the evidence that the person committed the offense.

(d) A person who commits an offense under Section 25.07(a) (3), Penal Code, may be held without bail under Subsection (b) or (c), as applicable, only if, following a hearing, the judge or magistrate determines by a preponderance of the evidence that the person went to or near the place described in the order or condition of bond with the intent to commit or threaten to commit:

(1) family violence; or

(2) an act in furtherance of an offense under Section 42.072, Penal Code.

(e) In determining whether to deny release on bail under this article, the judge or magistrate may consider:

(1) the order or condition of bond;

(2) the nature and circumstances of the alleged offense;

(3) the relationship between the accused and the victim, including the history of that relationship;

(4) any criminal history of the accused; and

(5) any other facts or circumstances relevant to a determination of whether the accused poses an imminent threat of future family violence.

(f) A person arrested for committing an offense under Section 25.07, Penal Code, shall without unnecessary delay and after reasonable notice is given to the attorney representing the state, but not later than 48 hours after the person is arrested, be taken before a magistrate in accordance with Article 15.17. At that time, the magistrate shall conduct the hearing and make the determination required by this article.

Tex. Code Crim Pro. Art. 17.153. Denial of Bail for Violation of Condition of Bond Where Child Alleged Victim

(a) This article applies to a defendant charged with a felony offense under any of the following provisions of the Penal Code, if committed against a child younger than 14 years of age:

(1) Chapter 21 (Sexual Offenses);

(2) Section 25.02 (Prohibited Sexual Conduct); or

(3) Section 43.25 (Sexual Performance by a Child).

(b) A defendant described by Subsection (a) who violates a condition of bond set under Article 17.41 and whose bail in the case is revoked for the violation may be taken into custody and denied release on bail pending trial if, following a hearing, a judge or magistrate determines by a preponderance of the evidence that the defendant violated a condition of bond related to the safety of the victim of the offense or the safety of the community. If the magistrate finds that the violation occurred, the magistrate may revoke the defendant's bond and order that the defendant be immediately returned to custody. Once the defendant is placed in custody, the revocation of the defendant's bond discharges the

> *sureties on the bond, if any, from any future liability on the bond. A discharge under this subsection from any future liability on the bond does not discharge any surety from liability for previous forfeitures on the bond.*

Due process requires the trial court to provide a defendant with reasonable notice that it intends to deny bail pending appeal and to allow a defendant a meaningful opportunity to be heard. Smith v. State, 993 S.W.2d 408 (Tex.App.—Houston [14th Dist.] 1999, *pet. ref'd*).

A defendant who is serving a sentence in another state and has been returned to Texas through the Interstate Agreement on Detainers is not eligible for bail. Mills v. State, 626 S.W.2d 583 (Tex. App.—Amarillo 1981, *pet. ref'd*).

CCP Art. 15.17 requires a magistrate setting bail to determine whether the person is currently on bail for a separate criminal offense; and implies that if the person is on bail for another offense, bail should not be set on the current case.

§9:70 Revocation of Bond

A trial court is permitted to revoke bail on a finding by a preponderance of the evidence of a violation of a valid bond condition. CCP Art. 44.04(c); Smith v. State, 993 S.W.2d 408 (Tex.App.—Houston [14th Dist.] 1999, *pet. ref'd*). Due process protections of notice and a reasonable opportunity to be heard attach to an appeal bond revocation proceeding. Smith. The statute does require presentation of evidence and that the revocation be based on that evidence. Smith.

Bail pending appeal of a conviction may be revoked for the commission of a subsequent offense, even in the absence of a specific condition that no additional offense be committed while on such bail. Oldham v. State, 743 S.W.2d 734 (Tex. App.—Fort Worth 1987, *pet. ref'd*).

A defendant's pretrial bond cannot be revoked if his failure to appear for trial is involuntary due to confinement in a jail or penitentiary. Fernandez v. State, 516 S.W.2d 677 (Tex. Crim. App. 1974).

The trial court may forfeit the bond of a defendant if he does not appear within a reasonable time after his name is called; but the defendant's slight tardiness is not enough to permit forfeiture of his bond. Meador v. State, 780 S.W.2d 836 (Tex. App.—Houston [14th Dist.] 1989, *no pet.*).

§9:80 Personal Bonds

CCP Art. 17.03. Personal bond

> *(a) Except as provided by Subsection (b) of this article, a magistrate may, in the magistrate's discretion, release the defendant on his personal bond without sureties or other security.*
>
> *(b) Only the court before whom the case is pending may release on personal bond a defendant who:*
>
> *(1) is charged with an offense under the following sections of the Penal Code:*
>
> *(A) Section 19.03 (Capital Murder);*
>
> *(B) Section 20.04 (Aggravated Kidnapping);*
>
> *(C) Section 22.021 (Aggravated Sexual Assault);*
>
> *(D) Section 22.03 (Deadly Assault on Law Enforcement or Corrections Officer, Member or Employee of Board of Pardons and Paroles, or Court Participant);*
>
> *(E) Section 22.04 (Injury to a Child, Elderly Individual, or Disabled Individual);*
>
> *(F) Section 29.03 (Aggravated Robbery);*
>
> *(G) Section 30.02 (Burglary);*
>
> *(H) Section 71.02 (Engaging in Organized Criminal Activity);*
>
> *(I) Section 21.02 (Continuous Sexual Abuse of Young Child or Children); or*

(J) Section 20A.03 (Continuous Trafficking of Persons);

(2) is charged with a felony under Chapter 481, Health and Safety Code, or Section 485.033, Health and Safety Code, punishable by imprisonment for a minimum term or by a maximum fine that is more than a minimum term or maximum fine for a first degree felony; or

(3) does not submit to testing for the presence of a controlled substance in the defendant's body as requested by the court or magistrate under Subsection (c) of this article or submits to testing and the test shows evidence of the presence of a controlled substance in the defendant's body.

(c) When setting a personal bond under this chapter, on reasonable belief by the investigating or arresting law enforcement agent or magistrate of the presence of a controlled substance in the defendant's body or on the finding of drug or alcohol abuse related to the offense for which the defendant is charged, the court or a magistrate shall require as a condition of personal bond that the defendant submit to testing for alcohol or a controlled substance in the defendant's body and participate in an alcohol or drug abuse treatment or education program if such a condition will serve to reasonably assure the appearance of the defendant for trial.

(d) The state may not use the results of any test conducted under this chapter in any criminal proceeding arising out of the offense for which the defendant is charged.

(e) Costs of testing may be assessed as court costs or ordered paid directly by the defendant as a condition of bond.

(f) In this article, "controlled substance" has the meaning assigned by Section 481.002, Health and Safety Code.

(g) The court may order that a personal bond fee assessed under Section 17.42 be:

(1) paid before the defendant is released;

(2) paid as a condition of bond;

(3) paid as court costs;

(4) reduced as otherwise provided for by statute; or

(5) waived.

CCP Art. 17.031. Release on personal bond

(a) Any magistrate in this state may release a defendant eligible for release on personal bond under Article 17.03 of this code on his personal bond where the complaint and warrant for arrest does not originate in the county wherein the accused is arrested if the magistrate would have had jurisdiction over the matter had the complaint arisen within the county wherein the magistrate presides. The personal bond may not be revoked by the judge of the court issuing the warrant for arrest except for good cause shown.

(b) If there is a personal bond office in the county from which the warrant for arrest was issued, the court releasing a defendant on his personal bond will forward a copy of the personal bond to the personal bond office in that county.

The granting of a personal bond is a matter within the discretion of the court before whom the case is pending. Ex parte Trillo, 540 S.W.2d 728 (Tex. Crim. App. 1976), *overruled on other grounds*; Aguilar v. State, 621 S.W.2d 781 (Tex. Crim. App. 1981). There will be some situations where a personal bond will not be appropriately within the discretion of a trial court, and a personal bond should not be granted. Trillo.

A person who is arrested without a warrant must be released on a personal bond after 24 hours if arrested for a misdemeanor, and after 48 hours if arrested for a felony, if he cannot obtain a surety bond or post bond himself. CCP Art. 17.033.

§9:90 Release of Certain Mentally Ill Defendants

CCP Art. 17.032. Release on Personal Bond of Certain Mentally Ill Defendants

> *(a) In this article, "violent offense" means an offense under the following sections of the Penal Code:*
>
> *(1) Section 19.02 (murder);*
>
> *(2) Section 19.03 (capital murder);*
>
> *(3) Section 20.03 (kidnapping);*
>
> *(4) Section 20.04 (aggravated kidnapping);*
>
> *(5) Section 21.11 (indecency with a child);*
>
> *(6) Section 22.01(a)(1) (assault), if the offense involved family violence as defined by Section 71.004, Family Code;*
>
> *(7) Section 22.011 (sexual assault);*
>
> *(8) Section 22.02 (aggravated assault);*
>
> *(9) Section 22.021 (aggravated sexual assault);*
>
> *(10) Section 22.04 (injury to a child, elderly individual, or disabled individual);*
>
> *(11) Section 29.03 (aggravated robbery);*
>
> *(12) Section 21.02 (continuous sexual abuse of young child or children); or*
>
> *(13) Section 20A.03 (continuous trafficking of persons).*
>
> *(b) Notwithstanding Article 17.03(b), or a bond schedule adopted or a standing order entered by a judge, a magistrate shall release a defendant on personal bond unless good cause is shown otherwise if:*
>
> *(1) the defendant is not charged with and has not been previously convicted of a violent offense;*
>
> *(2) the defendant is examined by the local mental health authority, local intellectual and developmental disability authority, or another qualified mental health or intellectual disability expert under Article 16.22;*
>
> *(3) the applicable expert, in a written assessment submitted to the magistrate under Article 16.22:*
>
> *(A) concludes that the defendant has a mental illness or is a person with an intellectual disability and is nonetheless competent to stand trial; and*
>
> *(B) recommends mental health treatment or intellectual disability services for the defendant, as applicable;*
>
> *(4) the magistrate determines, in consultation with the local mental health authority or local intellectual and developmental disability authority, that appropriate community-based mental health or intellectual disability services for the defendant are available in accordance with Section 534.053 or 534.103, Health and Safety Code, or through another mental health or intellectual disability services provider; and*
>
> *(5) the magistrate finds, after considering all the circumstances, a pretrial risk assessment, if applicable, and any other credible information provided by the attorney representing the state or the defendant, that release on personal bond would reasonably ensure the defendant's appearance in court as required and the safety of the*

BAIL AND BOND ISSUES

community and the victim of the alleged offense.

(c) The magistrate, unless good cause is shown for not requiring treatment, shall require as a condition of release on personal bond under this article that the defendant submit to outpatient or inpatient mental health treatment or intellectual disability services as recommended by the local mental health authority, local intellectual and developmental disability authority, or another qualified mental health or intellectual disability expert if the defendant's:

(1) mental illness or intellectual disability is chronic in nature; or

(2) ability to function independently will continue to deteriorate if the defendant is not treated.

(d) In addition to a condition of release imposed under Subsection (c), the magistrate may require the defendant to comply with other conditions that are reasonably necessary to ensure the defendant's appearance in court as required and the safety of the community and the victim of the alleged offense.

(e) In this article, a person is considered to have been convicted of an offense if:

(1) a sentence is imposed;

(2) the person is placed on community supervision or receives deferred adjudication; or

(3) the court defers final disposition of the case.

§9:100 Regulation of Bail Bond Sureties

For questions regarding the rules which bail bond sureties are required to follow and the statutes regulating county bail bond board activity, *see* Texas Occupations Code Chapter 1704.

§9:110 Release of Defendant Because of Delay

CCP Art. 17.151. Release because of delay

§1. A defendant who is detained in jail pending trial of an accusation against him must be released either on personal bond or by reducing the amount of bail required, if the state is not ready for trial of the criminal action for which he is being detained within:

(1) 90 days from the commencement of his detention if he is accused of a felony;

(2) 30 days from the commencement of his detention if he is accused of a misdemeanor punishable by a sentence of imprisonment in jail for more than 180 days;

(3) 15 days from the commencement of his detention if he is accused of a misdemeanor punishable by a sentence of imprisonment for 180 days or less; or

(4) five days from the commencement of his detention if he is accused of a misdemeanor punishable by a fine only.

§2. The provisions of this article do not apply to a defendant who is:

(1) serving a sentence of imprisonment for another offense while the defendant is serving that sentence;

(2) being detained pending trial of another accusation against the defendant as to which the applicable period has not yet elapsed;

(3) incompetent to stand trial, during the period of the defendant's incompetence; or

(4) being detained for a violation of the conditions of a previous release related to the safety of a victim of the alleged offense or to the safety of the community under this article.

§9:111 In General

Art. 17.151 provides, in relevant part, that a defendant accused of a felony who is detained in jail pending trial must be released, either on personal bond or by reducing the amount of bail required, if the State is not ready for trial within ninety days from the commencement of detention if he is accused of a felony. Ex parte Watson, 940 S.W.2d 733 (Tex.App.—Texarkana 1997, *no pet.*). The article further provides that the provisions do not apply to a defendant who is being detained pending trial of another accusation against him as to which the applicable period has not yet elapsed. Watson.

Article 17.151 does not violate separation of powers, and is not an impermissible encroachment upon prosecutorial discretion. Ex parte Gill, 413 S.W.3d 425, 432 (Tex. Crim. App. 2013); Jones v. State, 803 S.W.2d 712 (Tex. Crim. App. 1991).

The constitutional rule that a defendant being held on a charge of capital murder is not entitled to bail when the proof is evident is subject to the provisions of Art. 17.151. Beckcom v. State, 938 S.W.2d 780 (Tex.App.—Corpus Christi 1997, *no pet.*); Jones.

§9:112 Application of Time Limit

The time limit does not begin when the defendant is charged, but rather when he is actually detained. Balawajder v. State, 759 S.W.2d 504 (Tex.App.—Fort Worth 1988, *pet. ref'd*). The time period under the article does not begin to run until a defendant is certified as an adult and transferred to a criminal court. Ex parte Brosky, 863 S.W.2d 775 (Tex. App.—Fort Worth 1993, *no pet.*).

The state cannot defeat the operation of Art. 17.151 by filing another charge arising out of the same incident against the defendant to keep him in jail after the 90th day of his detention. Beckcom v. State, 938 S.W.2d 780 (Tex.App.—Corpus Christi 1997, *no pet.*). Where a subsequent indictment is for the same offense arising out of the same transaction for which the defendant was originally arrested, announcements of ready by the state carry forward to the new indictment. Behrend v. State, 729 S.W.2d 717 (Tex. Crim. App. 1987).

Article 17.151 contains no provisions excluding certain periods from the statutory time limit to accommodate exceptional circumstances. Rowe v. State, 853 S.W.2d 58 (Tex. Crim. App. 1993); Jones v. State, 803 S.W.2d 712 (Tex. Crim. App. 1991). A defendant's request to testify before the grand jury does not serve to remove him from the protections of Art. 17.151. Rowe.

§9:113 Readiness of State

When a defendant complains that the state was not ready within the statutory time period, the state has the burden to make a *prima facie* showing that it was. Jones v. State, 803 S.W.2d 712 (Tex. Crim. App. 1991). The State may satisfy its burden either by announcing ready within the allotted time or by announcing retroactively that it had been ready within the allotted time. Jones. The state's announcement, "the State is ready now, as it has been at all times," is sufficient to make a *prima facie* case of readiness within the statutory time limit. Applewhite v. State, 872 S.W.2d 32 (Tex. App.—Houston [1st Dist.] 1994, *no pet.*).

A prosecutor's statement at the writ hearing that, "the State has been ready for trial," was not sufficiently definite to show that the state was ready within the designated time. Jones.

The question of the state's "readiness" within the statutory limits refers to the preparedness of the prosecution for trial. Behrend v. State, 729 S.W.2d 717 (Tex. Crim. App. 1987). The concept of "ready" does not demand that the state have a perfect indictment. Behrend. In fact, where there is no showing of bad faith, the state may be prepared for trial even though the indictment that forms the basis for the prosecution of the offense is so defective as to be void. Behrend.

However, the state cannot be ready for trial under Art. 17.151 when no indictment has been returned. Kernahan v. State, 657 S.W.2d 433 (Tex. Crim. App. 1983).

Where the state enumerates before the court sufficient evidence to go to trial it has satisfied its obligation to show that it was ready for trial within the required time frame. Ex parte Watson, 940 S.W.2d 733 (Tex.App.—Texarkana 1997, *no pet.*).

Once the state makes a *prima facie* showing of readiness, it is up to the defendant to rebut it. Barfield v. State, 586 S.W.2d 538 (Tex. Crim. App. 1979). In the absence of a sufficient rebuttal by the defendant, the trial court has the discretion to find the State was timely ready for trial. Ex parte Brosky, 863 S.W.2d 775 (Tex.App.—Fort Worth 1993, *no pet.*).

Evidence to rebut the *prima facie* showing can be from any source, including cross-examination of those responsible for preparing the state's case; and may consist of, among other things, a demonstration that the state did not have a key witness or piece of evidence available by the last day of the applicable time limit. Applewhite, *supra*; Jones, *supra*.

PRACTICE TIP: An Art. 17.151 hearing can and should afford an opportunity to question and cross-examine the prosecutor concerning witness interviews and trial preparation.

To show the state's unreadiness, more than the mere fact that a witness had not been subpoenaed during the 90-day period must be shown. Applewhite, *supra*; Jones, *supra*.

A request by the state for a continuance does not constitute lack of readiness for purposes of Art. 17.151. Ex parte Stearnes, 761 S.W.2d 388 (Tex. App.—Amarillo 1988, *pet. ref'd*).

§9:114 Amount of Bond Set

Art. 17.151 states the accused must be released either on personal bond or by reducing the amount of bail required bond. Where the record reveals that the defendant cannot make any bond, the trial court is required to release him on a personal bond. Rowe v. State, 853 S.W.2d 581 (Tex. Crim. App. 1993).

Article 17.151 precludes a trial judge from considering factors other than the state's readiness for trial, such as the safety of the victim or the community, in determining whether an accused is entitled to release under that section. Ex parte Gill, 413 S.W.3d 425, 430 (Tex. Crim. App. 2013).

§9:115 Burden of Party Seeking Relief

The burden is on the party seeking review to see that a sufficient record is presented to show error requiring reversal. Tex.R.App.P. 50(d); Applewhite v. State, 872 S.W.2d 32 (Tex.App.—Houston [1st Dist.] 1994, *no pet.*).

A defendant's vague references to his inability to make bond are insufficient to require personal bond under Art. 17.151. Balawajder v. State, 759 S.W.2d 504 (Tex.App.—Fort Worth 1988, *pet. ref'd*).

§9:120 Bond in Family Violence Cases

CCP Art. 17.291. Further detention of certain persons

(a) In this article:

(1) "family violence has the meaning assigned to that phrase by §71.004, Family Code; and

(2) "magistrate" has the meaning assigned to it by Article 2.09 of this code.

(b) Article 17.29 does not apply when a person has been arrested or held without a warrant in the prevention of family violence if there is probable cause to believe the violence will continue if the person is immediately released. The head of the agency arresting or holding such a person may hold the person for a period of not more than four hours after bond has been posted. This detention period may be extended for an additional period not to exceed 48 hours, but only if authorized in a writing directed to the person having custody of the detained person by a magistrate who concludes that:

(1) the violence would continue if the person is release; and

(2) if the additional period exceeds 24 hours, probable cause exists to believe that the person committed

the instant offense and that, during the 10-year period preceding the date of the instant offense, the person has been arrested:

(a) on more than one occasion for an offense involving family violence; or

(b) for any other offense, if a deadly weapon, as defined by §1.07, Penal Code, was used or exhibited during commission of the offense or during immediate flight after commission of the offense.

CCP Art. 17.292. Magistrate's Order for Emergency Protection

(a) At a defendant's appearance before a magistrate after arrest for an offense involving family violence or an offense under Section 22.011, 22.021, or 42.072, Penal Code, the magistrate may issue an order for emergency protection on the magistrate's own motion or on the request of:

(1) the victim of the offense;

(2) the guardian of the victim;

(3) a peace officer; or

(4) the attorney representing the state.

(b) At a defendant's appearance before a magistrate after arrest for an offense involving family violence, the magistrate shall issue an order for emergency protection if the arrest is for an offense that also involves:

(1) serious bodily injury to the victim; or

(2) the use or exhibition of a deadly weapon during the commission of an assault.

(c) The magistrate in the order for emergency protection may prohibit the arrested party from:

(c-1) In addition to the conditions described by Subsection (c), the magistrate in the order for emergency protection may impose a condition described by Article 17.49(b) in the manner provided by that article, including ordering a defendant's participation in a global positioning monitoring system or allowing participation in the system by an alleged victim or other person protected under the order.

(1) committing:

(A) family violence or an assault on the person protected under the order; or

(B) an act in furtherance of an offense under Section 42.072, Penal Code;

(2) communicating:

(A) directly with a member of the family or household or with the person protected under the order in a threatening or harassing manner; or

(B) a threat through any person to a member of the family or household or to the person protected under the order;

(3) going to or near:

(A) the residence, place of employment, or business of a member of the family or household or of the person protected under the order; or

(B) the residence, child care facility, or school where a child protected under the order resides or attends; or

(4) possessing a firearm, unless

the person is a peace officer, as defined by Section 1.07, Penal Code, actively engaged in employment as a sworn, full-time paid employee of a state agency or political subdivision.

(d) The victim of the offense need not be present when the order for emergency protection is issued.

(e) In the order for emergency protection, the magistrate shall specifically describe the prohibited locations and the minimum distances, if any, that the party must maintain, unless the magistrate determines for the safety of the person or persons protected by the order that specific descriptions of the locations should be omitted.

(f) To the extent that a condition imposed by an order for emergency protection issued under this article conflicts with an existing court order granting possession of or access to a child, the condition imposed under this article prevails for the duration of the order for emergency protection.

(f-1) To the extent that a condition imposed by an order issued under this article conflicts with a condition imposed by an order subsequently issued under Chapter 85, Subtitle B, Title 4, Family Code, or under Title 1 or Title 5, Family Code, the condition imposed by the order issued under the Family Code prevails.

(f-2) To the extent that a condition imposed by an order issued under this article conflicts with a condition imposed by an order subsequently issued under Chapter 83, Subtitle B, Title 4, Family Code, the condition imposed by the order issued under this article prevails unless the court issuing the order under Chapter 83, Family Code:

(1) is informed of the existence of the order issued under this article; and

(2) makes a finding in the order issued under Chapter 83, Family Code, that the court is superseding the order issued under this article.

(g) An order for emergency protection issued under this article must contain the following statements printed in bold-face type or in capital letters:

"A VIOLATION OF THIS ORDER BY COMMISSION OF AN ACT PROHIBITED BY THE ORDER MAY BE PUNISHABLE BY A FINE OF AS MUCH AS $4,000 OR BY CONFINEMENT IN JAIL FOR AS LONG AS ONE YEAR OR BY BOTH. AN ACT THAT RESULTS IN FAMILY VIOLENCE OR A STALKING OFFENSE MAY BE PROSECUTED AS A SEPARATE MISDEMEANOR OR FELONY OFFENSE. IF THE ACT IS PROSECUTED AS A SEPARATE FELONY OFFENSE, IT IS PUNISHABLE BY CONFINEMENT IN PRISON FOR AT LEAST TWO YEARS. THE POSSESSION OF A FIREARM BY A PERSON, OTHER THAN A PEACE OFFICER, AS DEFINED BY SECTION 1.07, PENAL CODE, ACTIVELY ENGAGED IN EMPLOYMENT AS A SWORN, FULL-TIME PAID EMPLOYEE OF A STATE AGENCY OR POLITICAL SUBDIVISION, WHO IS SUBJECT TO THIS ORDER MAY BE PROSECUTED AS A SEPARATE OFFENSE PUNISHABLE BY CONFINEMENT OR IMPRISONMENT.

"NO PERSON, INCLUDING A PERSON WHO IS PROTECTED BY THIS ORDER, MAY GIVE PERMISSION TO ANYONE TO IGNORE OR VIOLATE ANY PROVISION OF THIS ORDER. DURING THE TIME IN WHICH THIS ORDER IS VALID, EVERY PROVISION OF THIS ORDER IS IN FULL FORCE AND EFFECT UNLESS A COURT CHANGES THE ORDER."

(h) The magistrate issuing an order for emergency protection under this article shall send a copy of the order to the chief of police in the municipality where the member of the family or household or individual protected by the order resides, if the person resides in a municipality, or to the sheriff of the county where the person resides, if the person does not reside in a municipality. If the victim of the offense is not present when the order is issued, the magistrate issuing the order shall order an appropriate peace officer to make a good faith effort to notify, within 24 hours, the victim that the order has been issued by calling the victim's residence and place of employment. The clerk of the court shall send a copy of the order to the victim.

(i) If an order for emergency protection issued under this article prohibits a person from going to or near a child care facility or school, the magistrate shall send a copy of the order to the child care facility or school.

(j) An order for emergency protection issued under this article is effective on issuance, and the defendant shall be served a copy of the order by the magistrate or the magistrate's designee in person or electronically. The magistrate shall make a separate record of the service in written or electronic format. An order for emergency protection issued under Subsection (a) or (b)(1) of this article remains in effect up to the 61st day but not less than 31 days after the date of issuance. An order for emergency protection issued under Subsection (b)(2) of this article remains in effect up to the 91st day but not less than 61 days after the date of issuance. After notice to each affected party and a hearing, the issuing court may modify all or part of an order issued under this article if the court finds that:

(1) the order as originally issued is unworkable;

(2) the modification will not place the victim of the offense at greater risk than did the original order; and

(3) the modification will not in any way endanger a person protected under the order.

(k) To ensure that an officer responding to a call is aware of the existence and terms of an order for emergency protection issued under this article, each municipal police department and sheriff shall establish a procedure within the department or office to provide adequate information or access to information for peace officers of the names of persons protected by an order for emergency protection issued under this article and of persons to whom the order is directed. The police department or sheriff may enter an order for emergency protection issued under this article in the department's or office's record of outstanding warrants as notice that the order has been issued and is in effect.

(l) In the order for emergency protection, the magistrate shall suspend a license to carry a concealed handgun issued under Subchapter H, Chapter 411, Government Code, that is held by the defendant.

(m) In this article:

(1) "Family," "family violence," and "household" have the meanings assigned by Chapter 71, Family Code.

(2) "Firearm" has the meaning assigned by Chapter 46, Penal Code.

(n) On motion, notice, and hearing, or on agreement of the parties, an order for emergency protection issued under this article may be transferred to the court assuming jurisdiction over the criminal act giving rise to the issuance of the emergency order for protection. On transfer, the criminal court may modify all or part of an order issued under this subsection in the same manner and under the same standards as the issuing court under Subsection (j).

§9:130 Appeal Bonds

§9:131 Applicable Statutes

CCP Art. 44.04. Bond pending appeal

(a) Pending the determination of any motion for new trial or the appeal from any misdemeanor conviction, the defendant is entitled to be released on reasonable bail.

(b) The defendant may not be released on bail pending the appeal from any felony conviction where the punishment equals or exceeds 10 years confinement or where the defendant has been convicted of an offense listed under Section 3g(a)(1), Article 42.12, but shall immediately be placed in custody and the bail discharged.

(c) Pending the appeal from any felony conviction other than a conviction described in Subsection (b) of this section, the trial court may deny bail and commit the defendant to custody if there then exists good cause to believe that the defendant would not appear when his conviction became final or is likely to commit another offense while on bail, permit the defendant to remain at large on the existing bail, or, if not then on bail, admit him to reasonable bail until his conviction becomes final. The court may impose reasonable conditions on bail pending the finality of his conviction. On a finding by the court on a preponderance of the evidence of a violation of a condition, the court may revoke the bail.

(d) After conviction, either pending determination of any motion for a new trial or pending final determination of the appeal, the court in which trial was had may increase or decrease the amount of bail, as it deems proper, either upon its own motion or the motion of the State or of the defendant.

(e) Any bail entered into after conviction and the sureties on the bail must be approved by the court where trial was had. Bail is sufficient if it substantially meets the requirements of this code and may be entered into and given at any term of court.

(f) In no event shall the defendant and the sureties on his bond be released from their liability on such bond or bonds until the defendant is placed in the custody of the sheriff.

(g) The right of appeal to the Court of Appeals of this state is expressly accorded the defendant for a review of any judgment or order made hereunder, and said appeal shall be given preference by the appellate court.

(h) If a conviction is reversed by a decision of a Court of Appeals, the defendant, if in custody, is entitled to release on reasonable bail, regardless of the length of term of imprisonment, pending final determination of an appeal by the state or the defendant on a motion for discretionary review. If the defendant requests bail before a petition for discretionary review has been filed, the Court of Appeals shall determine the amount of bail. If the defendant requests bail after a petition for discretionary review has been filed, the Court of Criminal Appeals shall determine the amount of bail. The sureties on the bail must be approved by the court where the trial was had. The defendant's right to release under this subsection attaches immediately on the issuance of the Court of Appeals' final ruling as defined by Tex. Crim. App.R. 209(c).

§9:132 Granting of Bail During Appeal

PRACTICE TIP: Art. 44.04 was changed considerably effective September 1, 1999. The prior law provided that a defendant was eligible for appeal bond unless his sentence was over 15 years. The law in effect for cases where a bond motion is made after September 1, 1999 is that a defendant is not eligible for appeal bond if his sentence is 10 years or

BAIL AND BOND ISSUES

more or if he receives any sentence for an article 42.12 §3(g) offense. Note that the language of subsection (b) is very broad and may require confinement while on appeal even if the defendant receives a probated sentence for any 3(g) offense.

The September 1, 1999 amendment to Art. 44.04 applies to any bond request made after that effective date. Cortez v. State, 36 S.W.3d 216 (Tex. App.—Houston [14th Dist.] 2001, *pet. filed*); Ex parte Cole, 43 S.W.3d 713 (Tex.App.—Fort Worth 2001, *no pet.*). The amendment does not violate the *ex post facto* or due process clauses of the Texas Constitution. Cortez.

A person who is sentenced to ten years' imprisonment, but who is placed under community supervision, is entitled to bond pending appeal under Art. 44.04(b). Lebo v. State, 90 S.W.3d 324 (Tex. Crim. App. 2002).

If a defendant is eligible for bail while on appeal, the trial court may continue him on his existing bond or admit him to a reasonable bail until his conviction becomes final. Art. 44.04(c). Ex parte Zigmond, 933 S.W.2d 666 (Tex.App.—San Antonio 1996, *no pet.*). The trial court may increase or decrease the amount of the bail, either on its own motion or on motion of the state. Art. 44.04(d).

Once the trial court determines that a person is eligible for appeal bond, the bail to be set must be reasonable. Perez v. State, 897 S.W.2d 893 (Tex. App.—San Antonio 1995, *no pet.*).

The factors listed in Art. 17.15 should be considered in setting the amount of the appeal bond:

- Bail shall be sufficiently high to give reasonable assurance that the undertaking will be complied with
- Power to require bail is not to be so used as to make it an instrument of oppression
- Nature of the offense and the circumstances under which it was committed are to be considered
- Ability to make bail is to be regarded, and proof may be taken upon this point
- Future safety of a victim of the alleged offense and the community shall be considered

Perez.

The burden is on the person seeking a reduction to show that the bail set is excessive. Ex parte Rubac, 611 S.W.2d 848 (Tex. Crim. App. 1981). While an accused's ability to make bail may be considered, it is not dispositive. Perez; Ex parte Rodriguez, 595 S.W.2d 549 (Tex. Crim. App. 1980).

The following factors should be considered in reviewing the reasonableness of the amount of bail on appeal:

- Punishment assessed
- Nature of the offense
- Appellant's work record, family ties, and length of residency
- Ability to make bond
- Prior criminal record of appellant
- Existence of other outstanding bonds
- Appellant's conformity with previous bond conditions

Jackson v. State, 810 S.W.2d 3 (Tex.App.—Houston [14th Dist.] 1991, *no pet.*); Ex parte Davila, 623 S.W.2d 408 (Tex. Crim. App. 1981).

§9:133 Conditions of Appeal Bond

Art. 44.04(c) authorizes a trial court to set reasonable conditions of bail pending appeal, including pending disposition of a petition for discretionary review filed by the state after an incarcerated defendant's conviction is reversed by a court of appeals and after the Court of Criminal Appeals has set the amount of bail pursuant to art. 44.04(h). Leonard v. State, 376 S.W.3d 886, 890 (Tex. App.—Fort Worth 2012, *pet.ref'd*).

Determining the reasonableness of a bail condition must be done in light of its primary purpose, to assure the defendant's presence in court. In each individual case, when conditions are imposed, those conditions must strike a balance between society's interest in assuring the defendant's appearance, if and when his conviction becomes final, and the defendant's interest in remaining free pending appeal. Cuellar.

Against the interest of a defendant to remain free pending appeal must be balanced the interest of society in enforcing the penal laws. Chief among these, in the cases of those who have been convicted of felonies, is to insure the public safety through:

- the deterrent influence of the penalties provided;
- the rehabilitation of those convicted of violations; and
- such punishment as may be necessary to prevent likely recurrence of criminal behavior. It is reasonable for a condition on bail pending appeal to have the purpose of protecting the public safety.

Ex parte Anderer, 61 S.W.3d 398 (Tex. Crim. App. 2001).

Even though Art. 44.04 does not address misdemeanor cases, a trial court has inherent power in misdemeanor appeals to impose conditions on bail that directly or indirectly relate to the purpose of assuring the defendant's continued appearance. Dallas v. State, 983 S.W.2d 276 (Tex. Crim. App. 1998).

TIP TO THE BENCH: While Art. 44.04(c) may not require the conditions to be in writing, the better practice would be to reduce any conditions imposed on bail to writing and cause a copy of the same to be served on the defendant and a copy attached to the bond. Rodriguez v. State, 744 S.W.2d 361 (Tex.App.—Corpus Christi 1988).

§9:134 Appeal Bond Conditions (Upheld)

An appeal bond condition that a defendant on bond for a criminally negligent homicide conviction who was also involved in another injury accident before trial not operate a motor vehicle while free on bail is reasonable because it has the purpose of protecting the public safety. Ex parte Anderer, 61 S.W.3d 398 (Tex. Crim. App. 2001).

In a case where the defendant was convicted of possession of heroin, a condition of his appeal bond that required him to submit to urine testing and attend drug counseling was found to be reasonable because the defendant's continued abstinence from heroin was rationally related to his appearance in court when necessary. Estrada v. State, 594 S.W.2d 445 (Tex. Crim. App. [Panel Op.] 1980).

In a case where the defendant was convicted of aggravated assault, a bond condition that he stay away from and not communicate with the victim was found to be reasonable because it was rationally related to the purpose of assuring that the defendant commit no further acts of violence, which in turn increased the likelihood that he would appear in court when ordered. Rodriguez v. State, 744 S.W.2d 361 (Tex.App.—Corpus Christi 1988, *no pet.*).

Electronic monitoring and random urinalysis are allowed as conditions of bond by CCP Art. 17.44. Grady v. State, 962 S.W.2d 128 (Tex.App.—Houston [1st Dist.] 1997, *pet. ref'd*). Requiring a defendant to wear an electronic monitor and to observe curfew conditions is not unreasonable because they increase the likelihood of his appearance in court. Smith v. State, 993 S.W.2d 408 (Tex.App.—Houston [14th Dist.] 1999, *pet. ref'd*); Ly v. State, 908 S.W.2d 598 (Tex.App.—Houston [1st Dist.] 1995, *no pet.*).

A condition prohibiting a defendant from associating with persons with whom he was associated in the commission of crime is not an unreasonable appeal bond condition because it increases the likelihood of his appearance in court. Smith; Rodriguez v. State, 744 S.W.2d 361 (Tex. App.—Corpus Christi 1988, *no pet.*) Appeal bond conditions that closely resemble conditions of probation will be upheld where they increase the likelihood of the defendant's appearance in court. Easton v. Rains, 866 S.W.2d 656 (Tex.App.—Houston [1st Dist.] 1993).

§9:135 Appeal Bond Conditions (Not Upheld)

A condition that a defendant not operate a motor vehicle while on appeal bond has been found unreasonable in a criminally negligent homicide case because it fails to advance the purpose of assuring appellant's presence in court when and if his conviction becomes final. Anderer v. State, 7 S.W.3d 245 (Tex.App.—Houston [14th Dist.] 1999, *pet. filed*).

A condition requiring the defendant to abandon his family residence as a condition of an appeal bond where he had been convicted of indecency with a child is unreasonable because it impinges on his freedom without forwarding society's interest in assuring his presence in any way. Valenciano v. State, 720 S.W.2d 523 (Tex. Crim. App. 1986).

In a misdemeanor case, the trial court has no authority to require attendance at Alcoholics Anonymous meetings as a condition of appeal bond. Grady v. State, 962 S.W.2d 128 (Tex.App.—Houston [1st Dist.] 1997, *pet. ref'd*).

In a misdemeanor cruelty to animals case, the trial court abused its discretion in prohibiting the defendant from engaging in the business of training and kenneling dogs as a condition of appeal bond. This condition is not relevant to securing appellant's appearance in court. Dallas v. State, 983 S.W.2d 276 (Tex. Crim. App. 1998).

Requiring a defendant to pay $44.50 in court costs as a condition of appeal bond was an abuse of discretion because it was not reasonably related to ensuring the defendant's appearance in court. Easton v. Rains, 866 S.W.2d 656 (Tex.App.—Houston [1st Dist.] 1993). A trial court abuses its discretion in ordering a payment into the registry of the court where the payment is earmarked for purposes other than securing the defendant's presence when his conviction is affirmed. Cuellar v. State, 985 S.W.2d 656 (Tex.App.—Houston [1st Dist.] 1999, *no pet.*).

A condition of bond that the defendant post the fact of his conviction on his web page was found to not serve the purpose of the defendant avoiding future criminal activity because there was no evidence presented that he used the Internet to commit the offense which was being appealed. Cuellar.

A condition prohibiting a defendant from working as a chiropractor for the duration of his appeal from a conviction for aggravated assault on a police officer is an invalid condition of appeal bond. Speth v. State, 939 S.W.2d 769 (Tex.App.—Houston [14th Dist.] 1997, *no pet.*).

A condition that a defendant submit to twice-weekly urinalysis at his expense as a condition of his appeal bond is unreasonable where the offense is not drug related and there is no showing at trial that the defendant has been involved with controlled substances in any way. Ex parte Sotelo, 878 S.W.2d 179 (Tex.App.—Fort Worth 1993, *pet. ref'd*). However, the same condition became reasonable when it was shown that the defendant tested positive for controlled substances while on the bond. Sotelo.

§9:136 Denial of Bail on Appeal

If the trial court has good cause to believe that the defendant would not appear when his conviction becomes final or that he is likely to commit another offense while on bail, bail may be denied. CCP Art. 44.04(c).

The evidence is sufficient to show that the defendant would be likely to commit another offense where defendant violated the terms of a previous probation, violated the terms of a work release program while in jail and vandalized automobiles after being indicted for the offense on appeal. Short v. State, 923 S.W.2d 168 (Tex.App.—Fort Worth 1996, *no pet.*).

The trial court may consider the nature of the underlying offense in reaching its decision to deny appeal bond. Ex parte Mendiola, 961 S.W.2d 625 (Tex.App.—San Antonio 1998, *no pet.*).

Where the testimony shows that the defendant had molested several children, the trial court did not abuse its discretion in refusing appeal bond on the basis that the defendant was likely to commit future offenses. Mendiola.

Where the state showed that the defendant had on a great number of occasions engaged in the same type of assaultive behavior as that for which he was found guilty by the jury, the evidence was sufficient to support the trial court's implied finding that there was good cause to believe that the defendant was likely to commit another offense while on appeal. Ex parte Castaneda, 739 S.W.2d 456 (Tex.App.—Corpus Christi 1987, *no pet.*).

Where the record reflects that the defendant did not object to the trial court's action, did not develop a record, and did not obtain an adverse ruling, he has waived appeal of the trial court's decision to not set an appeal bond. Hill v. State, 902 S.W.2d 57 (Tex.App.—Houston [1st Dist.] 1995, *pet. ref'd*).

§9:137 Revocation of Appeal Bond

If the trial court finds by a preponderance of the evidence that the defendant has violated a condition of the appeal bond it may revoke the bond. CCP Art. 44.04(c).

A computer-generated printout showing that the defendant violated the terms of his electronic monitoring agreement was sufficient to prove by a preponderance of the evidence that the defendant had violated the condition imposed upon him by the appeal bond. Ly v. State, 908 S.W.2d 598 (Tex. App.—Houston [1st Dist.] 1995, *no pet.*).

If a court finds that the defendant is likely to commit another offense while on bond, the court may revoke the bond even though no specific conditions were placed upon the defendant at the time of making bond. Oldham v. State, 743 S.W.2d 734 (Tex.App.—Fort Worth 1987, *pet. ref'd*); Ex Parte Le Blanc, 615 S.W.2d 724 (Tex. Crim. App. 1981).

Proof that a defendant committed an offense while on bail has been held sufficient to sustain an appeal bond revocation. Oldham; Putnam v. State, 582 S.W.2d 146 (Tex. Crim. App. 1979).

§9:138 Bail When Case Reversed

For the applicable statute *see* CCP Art. 44.04(h) in §9:131 above.

Where a conviction is reversed and the court of appeals is called upon to set bail pending a petition for discretionary review, it shall consider the factors set out in CCP Art. 17.15, but shall give primary consideration to the following three factors: 1) the fact that the conviction has been overturned; 2) the state's ability, if any, to retry the defendant; and 3) the likelihood that the decision of the court of appeals will be overturned on discretionary review. The length of the sentence is no longer a factor. Aviles v. State, 26 S.W.3d 696 (Tex.App.—Houston [14th Dist.] 2000, *pet. ref'd*).

§9:140 Constitutional Provisions

Texas Constitution Art.1 §11. Bail

> *§11. All prisoners shall be bailable by sufficient sureties, unless for capital offenses, when the proof is evident; but this provision shall not be so construed as to prevent bail after indictment found upon examination of the evidence, in such manner as may be prescribed by law.*

Texas Constitution. Art. I, §11a.

> *(a) Any person (1) accused of a felony less than capital in this State, who has been theretofore twice convicted of a felony, the second conviction being subsequent to the first, both in point of time of commission of the offense and conviction therefor, (2) accused of a felony less than capital in this State, committed while on bail for a prior felony for which he has been indicted, (3) accused of a felony less than capital in this State involving the use of a deadly weapon after being convicted of a prior felony, or (4) accused of a violent or sexual offense committed while under the supervision of a criminal justice agency of the State or a political subdivision of the State for a prior felony, after a hearing, and upon evidence substantially showing the guilt of the accused of the offense in (1) or (3) above, of the offense committed while on bail in (2) above, or of the offense in (4) above committed while under the supervision of a criminal justice agency of the State or a political subdivision of the State for a prior felony, may be denied bail pending trial, by a district judge in this State, if said order denying bail pending trial is issued within seven calendar days subsequent to the time of incarceration of the accused; provided, however, that if the accused is not accorded a trial upon the accusation under (1) or (3) above, the accusation and indictment used under (2) above, or the accusation or indictment used under (4) above within sixty (60) days from the time of his incarceration upon the accusation, the order denying bail shall be automatically set aside, unless a continuance is obtained upon the motion or request of the accused; provided, further, that the right of appeal to the Court of Criminal Appeals of this State*

is expressly accorded the accused for a review of any judgment or order made hereunder, and said appeal shall be given preference by the Court of Criminal Appeals.

(b) In this section:

(1) "Violent offense" means:

(A) murder;

(B) aggravated assault, if the accused used or exhibited a deadly weapon during the commission of the assault;

(C) aggravated kidnapping; or

(D) aggravated robbery.

(2) "Sexual offense" means:

(A) aggravated sexual assault;

(B) sexual assault; or

(C) indecency with a child.

§9:141 Denial of Bail in Capital Cases

The judge may deny bail in capital cases where the proof is evident. Angleton v. State, 955 S.W.2d 655 (Tex.App.—Houston [14th Dist.] 1997), *rev'd on other grounds,* 971 S.W.2d 65 (Tex. Crim. App. 1999). *See also,* CCP Art. 16.15.

The term "proof is evident" means the evidence is clear and strong, leading a well-guarded and dispassionate judgment to the conclusions that:

- Offense of capital murder has been committed
- Accused is the guilty party
- Jury will both convict the accused and will return findings requiring a death sentence

Angleton; Ex parte Graves, 853 S.W.2d 701 (Tex.App.—Houston [1st Dist.] 1993, *pet. ref'd*); Beck v. State, 648 S.W.2d 7 (Tex. Crim. App. 1983). The burden of proof is on the state to show that the proof is evident. Angleton; Beck.

The "substantial showing" burden of the accused's guilt at the bail hearing is far less than the trial burden of beyond a reasonable doubt. Angleton; Lee v. State, 683 S.W.2d 8 (Tex. Crim. App. 1985).

The state must also establish that the jury will assess the death penalty. Angleton; Ex parte Collum, 841 S.W.2d 960 (Tex.App.—Fort Worth 1992, *no pet.*).

§9:142 Denial of Bail in Other Cases

Texas Constitution Art. 1, §11a allows a defendant to be held without bond for a limited period where he commits a second criminal offense after being indicted and making bond for a first offense. Pharris v. State, 165 S.W.3d 681 (Tex. Crim. App. 2005).

To hold a person without bond, when that person is accused of a non-capital felony committed while on bail for a prior felony for which he has been indicted, the following sequence of events must occur: (1) A defendant must be indicted for a felony and be out of jail on bond; (2) A defendant must be then accused of committing, while on that bond, a felony less than capital in this state; (3) The defendant must be arrested on the accusation in 2; and (4) A district judge must hold a hearing wherein the state must show substantial evidence of the defendant's guilt for the felony in 2 and the district judge must enter an order denying bond, all within seven days of the defendant's arrest in 2. Pharris.

The state bears the burden of affirmatively showing compliance with the limits and safeguards of §11a. Pharris.

The appellate courts interpret §11a as favoring a defendant's access to bail, and strictly construe all of its provisions in favor of bail. Pharris.

Where denying bail under Art. I, §11(a) of the state constitution, the trial court must enter its order within seven (7) calendar days of the defendant's incarceration. Criner v. State, 878 S.W.2d 162 (Tex. Crim. App. 1994).

If the trial judge enters an order denying bail under Art. I, §11a, the defendant must be accorded a trial within sixty (60) days from his incarceration. Criner; Holloway v. State, 781 S.W.2d 605 (Tex. Crim. App.1989). If the accused is not brought to trial within sixty days, the trial judge's order denying bail is automatically set aside. Criner.

The rule that a defendant being held on a charge of capital murder is not entitled to bail when the proof is evident is subject to the provisions of CCP Art. 17.151. Beckcom v. State, 938 S.W.2d 780 (Tex.App.—Corpus Christi 1997, *no pet.*); Ex parte Jones v. State, 803 S.W.2d 712 (Tex. Crim. App. 1991).

§9:143 Form: Sample Motion to Deny Bail

See our companion book *Texas Criminal Forms* (James Publishing) for the following sample forms:

- Form 9-14.

§9:150 Bond for Post-Trial Habeas Corpus Applicants

§9:151 Statutory Law

CCP Art. 11.65. Bond for certain applicants

(a) This article applies to an applicant for a writ of habeas corpus seeking relief from the judgment in a criminal case, other than an applicant seeking relief from a judgment imposing a penalty of death.

(b) On making proposed findings of fact and conclusions of law jointly stipulated to by the applicant and the state, or on approving proposed findings of fact and conclusions of law made by an attorney or magistrate appointed by the court to perform that duty and jointly stipulated to by the applicant and the state, the convicting court may order the release of the applicant on bond, subject to conditions imposed by the convicting court, until the applicant is denied relief, remanded to custody, or ordered released.

(c) For the purposes of this chapter, an applicant released on bond under this article remains restrained in his liberty.

(d) Article 44.04(b) does not apply to the release of an applicant on bond under this article.

BAIL AND BOND ISSUES

Chapter 10

[RESERVED]

(This page intentionally left blank.)

[RESERVED]

Chapter 11

EXAMINING TRIALS AND GRAND JURY HEARINGS

Table of Contents

I. EXAMINING TRIALS

§11:10 In General

An examining trial is a hearing before a magistrate for the purpose of determining: (1) whether the state has probable cause to hold the defendant under the felony accusation, and the amount of bail which the defendant shall be required to post; or (2) whether the defendant shall be discharged. CCP Arts. 16.01 and 16.17; Taylor v. State, 671 S.W.2d 535 (Tex.App.—Houston [1st Dist.] 1983).

The return of an indictment terminates the accused's right to an examining trial. White v. State, 576 S.W.2d 843 (Tex. Crim. App. 1979); De Leon v. State, 758 S.W.2d 621 (Tex.App.—Houston [14th Dist.] 1988).

Failure to enter an order finding probable cause to hold the defendant within 48 hours of the hearing operates as a discharge of the accused. CCP Art. 16.17.

In cases where a juvenile has been certified to stand trial as an adult, the juvenile may have an absolute right to an examining trial depending on the date of the offense. Rogers, *infra.*

Where the offense for which the juvenile was certified was committed before September 1, 1987, the accused juvenile has the right to an examining trial. The failure to conduct one renders an indictment void. Family Code §54.02(h); Ex parte Rogers, 578 S.W.2d 752 (Tex. Crim. App. 1979).

Where the offense was committed after September 1, 1987 but before January 1, 1996, the accused juvenile has the right to have the trial court consider whether good cause exists to conduct an examining trial. Family Code §54.02; CCP §16.01.

For offenses committed as a juvenile after January 1, 1996, there is no right to an examining trial prior to indictment. Family Code §54.02(h).

A certified juvenile can validly waive his right to an examining trial. Family Code §51.09(a); Ex parte Rogers, *supra.*

The magistrate conducting the examining trial generally has the duties to ensure that the accused has counsel, is properly warned, and that he knows that he has a right to make a voluntary statement. CCP Arts. 16.01 *et seq.*

The Code of Criminal procedure states that the same rules of evidence that govern final trials shall govern examining trials. CCP Art. 16.07. However, the Rules of Evidence state that the Rules are not applicable to hearings on justification for pretrial detention not involving bail. Texas Rules of Evidence 101(d)(1)(F).

PRACTICE TIP: Make all objections to the method of conducting the examining trial (such as lack of confrontation, lack of adequate cross-examination) at the examining trial itself or they are waived. Wilkins v. State, 818 S.W.2d 844 (Tex. App.—Houston [1st Dist.] 1991, pet. ref'd).

§11:20 Use of Witness Testimony at Trial

Before examining trial testimony can be used at a subsequent trial, it must be reduced to writing by or under the direction of the magistrate; and examined (and any corrections made) and signed by the witness. Then, it must be certified by the magistrate. CCP Art. 16.09. In lieu of this procedure, a statement of facts can be authenticated by the state and defense counsel, and approved by the presiding magistrate. *Id.*

However, defense counsel cannot unilaterally exclude examining trial testimony from a subsequent trial merely by failing to authenticate the statement of facts. Wilkins v. State, 818 S.W.2d 844 (Tex.App.—Houston [1st Dist.] 1991, *pet. ref'd*).

Where the above predicate is met, the use of the testimony is further governed by Texas Rules Of Evidence 804 relating to former testimony. In order to admit former testimony under this Rule, the proponent must show that the witness is unavailable. *See* §16:72.18 for discussion of Rule 804.

In order to introduce examining trial testimony in a subsequent trial, the State has the burden of establishing clearly and satisfactorily that:

- Testimony of its witness was given under oath;

- Testimony is competent;
- Accused on trial is the same accused who was present, as an accused, at the examining trial;
- Accused had adequate opportunity through counsel to cross-examine the witness.

Russell v. State, 604 S.W.2d 914 (Tex. Crim. App. 1980).

Whether the accused had an adequate opportunity to cross-examine the witness depends on the following:

- Factors which are material to the ultimate finding concerning probable cause;
- Limitations generally imposed by the magistrate as to the scope and depth of permitted cross-examination;
- Constraints deterring defense counsel from extending cross-examination into explorations of details;
- Reflections of a properly authenticated record of cross-examination as actually conducted;
- Intimations of ineffective assistance of counsel;
- Others that may appear from time to time to be significantly weighty.

Russell, *supra.*

§11:30 Use of Defendant Testimony at Trial

In order to use the examining trial testimony of the defendant at a subsequent trial, the state must show that:

- Defendant received the proper examining trial warnings under CCP Art. 16.03
- Defendant was given an opportunity to procure counsel or had counsel appointed under CCP Art. 16.01
- Testimony of the defendant is in the form of a voluntary statement, is reduced to writing, is signed by the defendant, and is properly certified and signed by the magistrate under CCP Art. 16.04
- The examining trial testimony of a defendant is admissible under Texas Rules of Evidence 801(e)(2) as an admission of party-opponent. *See* §16:72.4 for discussion of Rule 801 (e)(2).

§11:40 [Reserved]

II. GRAND JURY HEARINGS

§11:50 In General

The Rules of Evidence, except with respect to privileges, do not apply to grand jury proceedings. Texas Rules of Evidence 101 (d)(1)(B).

§11:60 Use of Defendant Testimony at Trial

The grand jury testimony of a defendant is admissible under Texas Rules of Evidence 801(e)(2) as an admission by a party-opponent where the proper additional predicate is met.

The predicate must show that an accused testifying before a grand jury has been informed of:

- Offense of which he is accused
- County where the offense is said to have been committed
- As nearly as may be the time of the commission of the offense

CCP Art. 20.17.

The accused then is required to be warned orally and in writing as follows:

- Your testimony before this grand jury is under oath
- Any material question that is answered falsely before this grand jury subjects you to being prosecuted for aggravated perjury
- You have the right to refuse to make answers to any question, the answer to which would incriminate you in any manner
- You have the right to have a lawyer present outside this chamber to advise you before making answers to questions you feel might incriminate you
- Any testimony you give may be used against you at any subsequent proceeding

- If you are unable to employ a lawyer, you have the right to have a lawyer appointed to advise you before making an answer to a question, the answer to which you feel might incriminate you

CCP Art. 20.17.

Substantial and not strict compliance with the introductory warnings of Art. 20.17 is all that is required for admissibility of an accused's grand jury testimony. The piecemeal development of the nature of the offense against the accused and the time and place of its commission, through the accused's responses to the questions posed by the prosecutor, is sufficient compliance with the statute. Andino v. State, 645 S.W.2d 615 (Tex. App.—Austin 1983).

The same is true of the formal warnings set out in CCP Art. 20.17(c). *Id.*

The accused must be given a reasonable opportunity to retain counsel or apply to the court for an appointed attorney and to consult with the attorney prior to appearing before the grand jury. CCP Art. 20.17.

Where an accused testifies before a grand jury without first being administered the statutory warning, his testimony may not be used as substantive evidence. Dillard v. State, 640 S.W.2d 85 (Tex.App.—Fort Worth 1982).

§11:70 Appearances Before and Secrecy of Proceedings

Since September 1, 1989, counsel for a person accused or suspected in connection with a grand jury proceeding may address the grand jury about the matter being reviewed. CCP Art. 20.04.

However, counsel may not appear in front of the grand jury to assist a witness or person suspected while that person testifies before the grand jury. CCP Arts. 20.011 and 20.04.

Pursuant to CCP Art. 20.02, the proceedings of the grand jury are deemed to be secret. Article 20.02 (b) provides that any grand juror, bailiff, interpreter, stenographer who discloses anything transpiring before the grand jury shall be subject to contempt. The punishment range for the contempt citation is up to a $500 fine, up to 30 days in jail or both fine and confinement.

Under CCP Art.20.02 (b), counsel for a defendant may petition a court to order disclosure of information made secret pursuant to grand jury proceedings (*i.e.*, a transcript of witness testimony). This can be done by disclosure of a recording or typewritten transcript. The petition must be filed in the district court in which the case is pending. In the event the attorney for the defendant discloses the transcript or information contained therein, the attorney is subject to a contempt citation as noted above.

CCP Art. 20.02 (c) requires that the attorney representing the state shall warn any person who receives information in the form of transcript from a grand jury of the duty to maintain secrecy of information contained therein. Violation of this article is punishable by a contempt citation as noted above.

A subpoena to appear before a grand jury is not a seizure under the Fourth Amendment. U.S. v. Dionisio, 410 U.S. 1, 93 S.Ct. 764, 35 L.Ed.2d 67 (1973).

§11:71 Unauthorized Questioning

Under CCP Art. 20.04 "[n]o person other than the attorney representing the State or a grand juror may question a witness before the grand jury." Mason v. State, 322 S.W.3d 251 (Tex. Crim. App. 2010).

Where an unauthorized person has questioned a witness before the grand jury, the proper subject of a harm analysis is the product of those proceedings: the charging decision. Appellate courts will consider whether the appellant's substantial rights were affected by the violation and whether the unauthorized questioning had a substantial and injurious effect or influence on the grand jury's decision to indict under TRAP 44.2(b). If the record as a whole does not show that the violation influenced the grand jury, or if there was just a "slight effect," then the trial court was correct to deny the motion to quash. Mason.

§11:80 Use of Witness Testimony at Trial

The subsequent admission of testimony of grand jury witnesses other than the defendant is governed by Texas Rule of Evidence 804 concerning former testimony. The witness must be unavailable under

Rule 804 (a) in order for the testimony to be admitted under this provision. Jones v. State, 843 S.W.2d 487 (Tex. Crim. App. 1992). *See* §16:72.18 for discussion of Rule 804.

§11:90 Impact of Selection Procedures

Courts are required to follow the means and methods provided by the legislature in selecting grand juries; and an arbitrary disregard of those statutes in the selection and organization of the grand jury vitiates and renders such grand jury without authority. Ex parte Becker, 459 S.W.2d 442 (Tex. Crim. App. 1970).

However, the Court of Criminal Appeals has held that, absent an allegation of fraud or injury resulting from the selection of the grand jurors, minor deviations from the statutory procedure do not rise to a level requiring reversal. Garcia v. State, 919 S.W.2d 370 (Tex. Crim. App. 1994); Gentry v. State, 770 S.W.2d 780 (Tex. Crim. App. 1988) (where there were allegations that the paperwork was not properly certified and that an oath to a clerk improperly given); Hicks v. State, 630 S.W.2d 829 (Tex.App.—Houston [1st Dist.] 1982 *pet. ref'd*) (where the district court used "loose" procedures); Cantu v. State, 842 S.W.2d 667 (Tex. Crim. App. 1992) (where there was a technical violation of the state nepotism statute).

A defendant must raise his challenge to the composition of the grand jury at his earliest opportunity. Ratcliff v. Estelle, 597 F.2d 474 (C.A.Tex. 1979). Ordinarily the earliest opportunity to contest the composition is when the grand jury is impaneled. Francis v. State, 636 S.W.2d 591 (Tex.App.—San Antonio 1982). If a defendant has an opportunity to challenge the array when it is impaneled and does not do so, he may not challenge it at a later date. Bird v. State, 692 S.W.2d 65 (Tex. Crim. App. 1985).

Where a defendant was indicted after the grand jury had been impaneled and had not had an opportunity to challenge the array under CCP Art. 19.27, he may do so by way of a pretrial motion to quash the indictment. Rodriguez v. State, 597 S.W.2d 917 (Tex. Crim. App. 1980); Romo v. State, 641 S.W.2d 390 (Tex.App.—Tyler 1982).

A challenge to the composition of the grand jury raised for the first time on appeal is untimely. Francis, *supra*.

A defendant's contention that the grand jury was improperly constituted because it included a convicted felon amounts to a contention that the indictment was not returned by a lawfully chosen or impaneled grand jury. Such a contention constitutes an objection to the form of the indictment. Caraway v. State, 911 S.W.2d 400 (Tex.App.—Texarkana 1995).

If the defendant does not object to a defect of form or substance in an indictment before trial on the merits commences, he waives the defect and may not complain of it on appeal or in any other post-conviction proceeding. State v. Yount, 853 S.W.2d 6 (Tex. Crim. App. 1993).

§11:100 Challenges to Indictment on Due Process/Equal Protection Grounds

It is a violation of the U.S. Constitution's equal protection clause for a defendant to be tried under an indictment issued by a grand jury from which persons of his race or color have been purposely excluded by the State. Hernandez v. Texas, 347 U.S. 475, 74 S.Ct. 667, 98 L.Ed.2d 866 (1954); Garcia v. State, 919 S.W.2d 370 (Tex. Crim. App. 1994); Cantu v. State, 842 S.W.2d 667 (Tex. Crim. App. 1992).

A criminal defendant has standing to challenge the system used to select his grand jury on the ground that it arbitrarily excludes from service the members of any race and therefore denies him due process of law, it not being necessary that the defendant show actual harm or bias. Peters v. Kiff, 407 U.S. 493, 92 S.Ct. 2163, 32 L.Ed.2d 83 (1972); Bird v. State, 692 S.W.2d 65 (Tex. Crim. App. 1985).

The gravamen of due process is that a fair cross-section of the community must be represented on grand juries. Taylor v. Louisiana, 419 U.S. 522, 95 S.Ct. 692, 42 L.Ed.2d 690 (1974).

The United States Supreme Court has set forth the elements of a prima facie case of discrimination in the selection of grand jurors. Castaneda v. Partida, 430 U.S. 482, 97 S.Ct. 1272, 51 L.Ed.2d 498 (1977). This standard has been followed in the Texas courts. Ovalle v. State, 13 S.W.3d 774 (Tex. Crim. App. 2000); Gutierrez v. State, 954 S.W.2d 86 (Tex.App.—San Antonio 1997).

Under Castaneda, the defendant must show that the selection system employed resulted in substantial under-representation of his race by establishing:

- Group is a recognizable, distinct class that has been singled out for different treatment under the laws
- Degree to which the group was under-represented by comparing the proportion of the group in the total population to the proportion called to serve as grand jurors over a significant period of time
- Selection process is either susceptible to abuse or is not racially neutral

Id.

Where the defendant is successful in making out a case of purposeful discrimination in the selection of his grand jury, the remedy is dismissal of the indictment. Flores v. State, 783 S.W.2d 793 (Tex. App.—El Paso 1990).

Once appellant establishes the under-representation of a class over a significant period of time by use of gross population statistics, he demonstrates a prima facie case of discriminatory purpose, and the State has the burden to rebut his case. Cerda v. State, 644 S.W.2d 875 (Tex.App.—Amarillo 1982).

Where the defendant fails to show the composition of the grand jury that indicted him, evidence showing the composition of the grand juries for preceding years is irrelevant. If the class to which a defendant belongs is fully represented on the indicting grand jury, the defendant suffers no injury and exclusion of members of the class from earlier grand juries is irrelevant to his case. Only if the defendant's class is substantially under-represented on the indicting grand jury does the make-up of prior grand juries become relevant to explain whether this under-representation on the indicting grand jury is a statistical accident or the result of purposeful discrimination. Espinoza v. State, 604 S.W.2d 908 (Tex. Crim. App. 1980).

§11:101 Recognizable Classes

Spanish-surnamed Americans of Mexican descent are recognized as a clearly identifiable class with a history of being subjected to discriminatory treatment. Hernandez v. Texas, 347 U.S. 475, 74 S.Ct. 667, 98 L.Ed. 866 (1954).

The 18-21 age group is not a discernible class for purposes of proportional representation analysis in the selection of grand juries. Curtis v. State, 573 S.W.2d 219 (Tex. Crim. App. 1978).

Persons over age sixty five are not a distinctive group for purposes of showing fair cross section violations. Weaver v. State, 823 S.W.2d 371 (Tex. App.—Dallas 1992, *pet. ref'd*).

Where the defendant fails to show the proportional representation of a discernible class within the total population of the county in question, he has failed to establish the first prong under Castaneda v. Partida. Ovalle v. State, 13 S.W.3d 774 (Tex. Crim. App. 2000). Burks v. State, 583 S.W.2d 389 (Tex. Crim. App. 1979).

Where the overwhelming preponderance of the evidence did not show that the defendant was a member of a discernible political class, he was unable to show that his grand jury was comprised in an unconstitutional manner. Carrillo v. State, 566 S.W.2d 902 (Tex. Crim. App. 1978).

§11:102 Degree of Under-Representation

The United States Supreme Court never has announced mathematical standards for the demonstration of a denial of constitutional due process and equal protection by the "systematic" exclusion of an identifiable class from jury service. Alexander v. Louisiana, 405 U.S. 625, 92 S.Ct. 1221, 31 L.Ed.2d 536 (1972).

The Court has, however, declared that under a racially non-neutral selection procedure a sufficiently large disparity over a significant period of time supports the presumption of unconstitutional purposeful discrimination raised by the statistical showing. Ovalle v. State, 13 S.W.3d 774 (Tex. Crim. App. 2000); Castaneda v. Partida, 430 U.S. 482, 97 S.Ct. 1272, 51 L.Ed.2d 498 (1977).

The court has held that disparities less than a mean disparity of 16.97% spanning eleven years, is significant enough to establish a prima facie case of discrimination against Mexican-Americans in grand jury selection. Cerda v. State, 644 S.W.2d 875 (Tex.App.—Amarillo 1982).

A disparity of only 1.35% between the percentage of grand jurors summoned and the percentage of Spanish-surnamed individuals in the available county population does not establish an equal protection violation in the discriminatory selection of grand jurors. Gutierrez v. State, 954 S.W.2d 86 (Tex.App.—San Antonio 1997).

Furthermore, a disparity of only 6.35% between the available population and those who actually served on the grand jury in the relevant year does not amount to an equal protection violation. Gutierrez.

Where the record below revealed that Hispanics constituted between 9.9% and 10.9% of the population of the relevant county at the time of indictment; and that during the three years prior to the indictment, Hispanics made up approximately 10.1% of the grand jurors impaneled, there was no systematic under-representation of Hispanics on the county's grand juries and the defendant has failed to satisfy the second prong of the Castaneda test. Cantu v. State, 842 S.W.2d 667 (Tex. Crim. App. 1992).

Where the record revealed that the discrepancy between the expected number and the actual number of Hispanics serving on the grand jury was less than three standard deviations, the defendant has failed to carry his burden. Ovalle, *supra*.

§11:103 Systems Susceptible to Abuse

The key-man system (*i.e.*, the grand jury commissioner system codified in CCP Art. 19.01) still employed in many counties for impaneling grand juries is susceptible to abuse as applied and its proof will satisfy the third prong of the Castaneda test. Carter v. Jury Comm'n., 396 U.S. 320, 90 S.Ct. 518, 24 L.Ed.2d 549 (1970).

§11:104 Second and Subsequent Grand Juries

In the absence of a constitutional or legislative prohibition, a district court acts within its authority in impaneling a second grand jury. State v. Broaddus, 3 S.W.3d 919 (Tex. Crim. App. 1999).

(This page intentionally left blank.)

Chapter 12

PRETRIAL MOTIONS

Table of Contents

§12:10 Filing and Litigating Pretrial Motions

Pretrial preparation and motion practice are the cornerstones to criminal litigation. Every pretrial motion that can advantage the defendant should be filed. However, numbers of motions alone do not equate into benefit for one's client. Evidence supporting the relief requested in the motion is always necessary to fully develop the statutory and constitutional relief sought. Relief should always be requested separately under the Texas and Federal Constitutions. Heitman v. State, 815 S.W.2d 681 (Tex. Crim. App. 1991); Muniz v. State, 852 S.W.2d 520 (Tex. Crim. App. 1993).

PRACTICE TIP: The Code of Criminal Procedure now requires clerks to accept electronic and digital multimedia evidence for filing from defendants where they allow filing of such matters by the prosecutor. See CCP Art. 2.21.

§12:11 Statutes

CCP Art. 27.11. Ten Days Allowed for Filed Pleadings

In all cases the defendant shall be allowed ten entire days, exclusive of all fractions of a day after his arrest, and during the term of the court, to file written pleadings.

CCP Art. 27.12. Time After Service

In cases where the defendant is entitled to be served with a copy of the indictment, he shall be allowed the ten days time mentioned in the preceding article to file written pleadings after such service.

CCP Art. 28.01. Pretrial

Section 1. The court may set any criminal case for a pretrial hearing before it is set for trial upon its merits, and direct the defendant and his attorney, if any of record, and the State's attorney, to appear before the court at the time and place stated in the court's order for a conference and hearing. The defendant must be present at the arraignment, and his presence is required during any pretrial proceeding. The pretrial hearing shall be to determine any of the following matters:

(1) Arraignment of the defendant, if such be necessary; and appointment of counsel to represent the defendant, if such be necessary;

(2) Pleadings of the defendant;

(3) Special pleas, if any;

(4) Exceptions to the form or substance of the indictment or information;

(5) Motions for continuance either by the State or defendant; provided that grounds for continuance not existing or not known at the time may be presented and considered at any time before the defendant announces ready for trial;

(6) Motions to suppress evidence; when a hearing on the motion to suppress evidence is granted, the court may determine the merits of said motion on the motions themselves, or upon opposing affidavits, or upon oral testimony, subject to the discretion of the court;

(7) Motions for change of venue by the State or the defendant; provided, however, that such motions for change of venue, if overruled at the pretrial hearing, may be renewed by the State or the defendant during the voir dire examination of the jury;

(8) Discovery;

(9) Entrapment; and

(10) Motion for appointment of interpreter.

Section 2. When a criminal case is set for such pretrial hearing, any such preliminary matters not raised or filed seven days before the hearing will not thereafter be allowed to be raised or filed, except by permission of the court for good cause shown; provided that the defendant shall have sufficient notice of such hearing to allow him not less than 10 days in which to raise or file such preliminary matters. The record made at such pretrial hearing, the rulings of the court and the exceptions and objections thereto shall become a part of the trial record of the case upon its merits.

Section 3. The notice mentioned in Section 2 above shall be sufficient if given in any one of the following ways:

(1) By announcement made by the court in open court in the presence of the defendant or his attorney of record;

(2) By personal service upon the defendant or his attorney of record;

(3) By mail to either the defendant or his attorney of record deposited by the clerk in the mail at least six days prior to the date set for hearing. If the defendant has no attorney of record, such notice shall be addressed to defendant at the address shown on his bond, if the bond shows such an address; and if not, it may be addressed to one of the sureties on his bond. If the envelope containing the notice is properly addressed, stamped and mailed, the state will not be required to show that it was received.

§12:12 Time Limits for Filing Pretrial Motions

Art. 28.01 §2 requires that all motions be filed seven days prior to the date set for a pretrial hearing so long as the defendant has been given ten days notice of the hearing date. Untimely motions will not thereafter be allowed to be raised or filed, except by permission of the court for good cause shown. Zone v. State, 84 S.W.3d 733 (Tex.App.—Houston [1st Dist.] 2002), affirmed at 118 S.W.3d 776 (Tex. Crim. App. 2003).

The seven-day time limitation under CCP Art. 28.01 Sec. 2 refers to the filing of pretrial motions, not affidavits filed in support of the motion. Zone.

Preliminary matters under Art. 28.01 include the appointment of counsel, pleadings of the defendant, any special pleas, exceptions to the form or substance of the indictment, motions for continuance, motions to suppress evidence, motions to change venue, discovery motions, entrapment issues, and motions for appointment of an interpreter. Zone.

pretrial motions of constitutional dimension may be filed any time prior to trial. A defendant's failure to file a motion of constitutional dimension under the time restrictions of Art. 28.01 does not constitute a waiver of the issue, and the trial court must grant the defendant a hearing. Foster v. State, 779 S.W.2d 845 (Tex. Crim. App. 1989) (defendant sought to pursue a motion for change of venue).

§12:12.1 Misdemeanors

Where no indictment is required, the defendant is allowed ten entire days after his arrest to file written pleadings. CCP Art. 27.11.

When the provisions of CCP Art. 27.11 are either formally or informally invoked, the statutory 10 days must be afforded the defendant. Refusal to grant such time will result in reversible error without the defendant being required to show harm. Ashcraft v. State, 900 S.W.2d 817 (Tex.App.—Corpus Christ 1983, *pet. ref'd*).

§12:12.2 Felonies

CCP Art. 27.12 provides that in felony cases, or anytime the prosecution must be by indictment, the defendant has 10 days from service of the indictment upon him to file written pleadings. Roberts v. State, 93 S.W.3d 528 (Tex.App.—Houston [14th Dist.] 2002, *pet. ref'd*).

Failure to request 10 days to file written pleadings waives any error. Young v. State, 752 S.W.2d. 235 (Tex.App.—Fort Worth 1988) *aff'd at* 796 S.W.2d 195 (Tex. Crim. App. 1990).

§12:13 Pretrial Hearings

The terms of CCP Art. 28.01 are not mandatory, and the question of whether to hold a hearing on a pretrial motion to suppress evidence rests within the sound discretion of the trial judge. Calloway v. State, 743 S.W.2d 645 (Tex. Crim. App. 1988); Morrison

v. State, 71 S.W.3d 821 (Tex.App.—Corpus Christi 2002, *no pet.*).

The trial court is not required by law to hold a pretrial hearing, and has the discretion to determine the merits of such motions as a motion *in limine* or a motion to suppress during the trial itself. Moore v. State, 700 S.W.2d 193 (Tex. Crim. App. 1985).

Article 28.01 requires formal notice of a pre-trial hearing only when the court designates a separate, pre-trial setting for the hearing—not when the judge elects for the hearing to take place on the trial setting itself. State v. Velasquez, 539 S.W.3d 289, 295 (Tex. Crim. App. 2018).

PRACTICE TIP: A technical decision should be made by trial counsel on whether to seek a hearing on a motion to suppress evidence or statement of the defendant, where counsel feels that there is a strong likelihood of a successful suppression. If the suppression issue is heard at a pretrial hearing and relief is granted, the state has a statutory right to appeal this finding if jeopardy has not attached if the counsel for the state can certify that the appeal is not taken for purposes of delay and that the evidence is of substantial importance. Counsel may want to urge the court to carry the motion and object during trial. Thus, the issue could be heard after the jury is seated and sworn and at which time jeopardy is attached. This procedure would effectively prevent a state's appeal of the court's order suppressing evidence.

§12:14 Form: Motion for Additional Pretrial Motions

See our companion book *Texas Criminal Forms* (James Publishing), Form 12-1, Motion to Allow Additional pretrial Motions.

§12:20 Expert Witness Assistance for Indigents

§12:21 Statutes

CCP Art. 26.05. Compensation of Counsel Appointed to Defend

(d) A counsel in a noncapital case, other than an attorney with a public defender's office, appointed to represent a defendant under this code shall be reimbursed for reasonable and necessary expenses, including expenses for investigation and for mental health and other experts. Expenses incurred with prior court approval shall be reimbursed in the same manner provided for capital cases by Articles 26.052(f) and (g), and expenses incurred without prior court approval shall be reimbursed in the manner provided for capital cases by Article 26.052(h).

CCP Art. 26.052. Appointment of Counsel in Death Penalty Case, Reimbursement of Investigative Expenses

(f) Appointed counsel may file with the trial court a pretrial *Ex parte confidential request for advance payment of expenses to investigate potential defenses. The request for expenses must state:*

(1) the type of investigation to be conducted;

(2) specific facts that suggest the investigation will result in admissible evidence; and

(3) an itemized list of anticipated expenses for each investigation.

(g) The court shall grant the request for advance payment of expenses in whole or in part if the request is reasonable. If the court denies in whole or in part the request for expenses, the court shall:

(1) state the reasons for the denial in writing;

(2) attach the denial to the confidential request; and

(3) submit the request and denial as a sealed exhibit to the record.

(h) Counsel may incur expenses without prior approval of the court. On presentation of a claim for reimbursement, the court shall order reimbursement of counsel for the expenses, if the expenses are reasonably necessary and reasonably incurred.

§12:22 Defendant Has a Right to an Expert

An indigent defendant has a right to a court-appointed expert under certain circumstances. Ake v. Oklahoma, 470 U.S. 68, 105 S.Ct. 1087, 84 L.Ed.2d 53 (1985); Robertson v. State, 21 S.W.3d 554 (Tex.App.—Waco 2000, *pet. ref'd*).

A defendant is not guaranteed the right to choose a particular expert witness; rather the defendant has the right to access a competent expert. Ake.

A defendant is also entitled to independent expert assistance, not an expert who is required to report to the court or prosecution. Taylor v. State, 939 S.W.2d 148 (Tex. Crim. App. 1996).

A defendant is entitled to an expert that can serve one or two objectives: (1) play a partisan role by providing the defendant with the means to challenge the state's case; or (2) testify in support of the defense theory, if the expert's opinion supports the theory. Taylor.

Ake clearly establishes that when its threshold criteria are met, a State must provide a mental health professional capable of performing a certain role: conducting an appropriate examination and assisting in evaluation, preparation, and presentation of the defense. Unless a defendant is assured the assistance of someone who can effectively perform these functions, he has not received the minimum to which Ake entitles him. McWilliams v. Dunn, ___ U.S. ___, 137 S.Ct. 1790, 1792, 198 L.Ed.2d 341 (2017).

Access to expert assistance means more than an examination by a neutral expert. It also means the appointment of an expert to provide technical assistance to the defendant, to help evaluate the strength of his defense, to offer expert diagnosis if it is favorable to the defense, and to identify the weaknesses in the state's case by testifying or preparing counsel to cross-examine the opposing expert. Rey.

In capital cases, the defendant does not have the right to receive funds for this purpose; rather counsel has the right to be reimbursed for reasonable expenses incurred with prior court approval. Cantu v. State, 939 S.W.2d 627 (Tex. Crim. App. 1997).

Ake applies to non-psychiatric experts. Rey v. State, 897 S.W.2d 333 (Tex. Crim. App. 1995).

A defendant is entitled to assistance from the following experts where he makes the proper showing:

- A chemist, where analysis of a purported controlled substance is central in the case. McBride v. State, 838 S.W.2d 248 (Tex. Crim. App. 1992).
- A mental health professional, where there is a viable insanity claim. De Freece v. State, 848 S.W.2d 150 (Tex. Crim. App. 1993).
- A pathologist, when manner of death would be a contested issue at trial. Rey v. State, 897 S.W.2d 333 (Tex. Crim. App. 1995).

However, a defendant is not entitled to expert assistance in the following situation:

- A jury selection consultant. Busby v. State, 990 S.W.2d 263 (Tex. Crim. App. 1999).
- A polygraph examiner in a post-trial investigation. Jackson v. State, 992 S.W.2d 469 (Tex. Crim. App. 1999).

Failure to provide an expert after the defendant has made the threshold showing of need constitutes structured error and is not subject to a harm analysis. Rey.

For additional cases pertaining to using and presenting expert witness assistance, *see* §16:60.

§12:23 Defendant Must Show Compelling Need

A defendant must show a compelling need for the assistance of an expert. Matchett v. State, 941 S.W.2d 922 (Tex. Crim. App.1996); Robertson v. State, 21 S.W.2d 554 (Tex.App.—Waco 2000, *pet. ref'd*).

It is crucial that a defendant seeking appointment

of an expert under Ake make a preliminary showing that the expert assistance is necessary to address a significant issue at trial. Moore v. State, 935 S.W.2d 124 (Tex. Crim. App. 1996); Robertson.

The defendant must show a particularized need for the expert assistance. Cantu v. State, 939 S.W.2d 627 (Tex. Crim. App. 1997).

To that extent, a defendant must offer more than undeveloped assertions that the requested assistance would be beneficial. Moore; Robertson.

A trial court must appoint an expert to assist the defendant if a three-part federal due process of law test is met:

- There exists a private interest that will be affected by the action of the state;
- Governmental interest will be affected if the safeguard is provided;
- Probable value of the additional safeguards and the risk of erroneous deprivation of the affected interest if those safeguards are not provided. Rey v. State, 897 S.W.2d 333 (Tex. Crim. App. 1995).

An indigent defendant upon proper request is entitled to make his threshold showing required to obtain expert assistance *ex parte*. Williams v. State, 958 S.W.2d 186 (Tex. Crim. App. 1997).

§12:24 Form: Motions

See our companion book *Texas Criminal Forms* (James Publishing):

- Form 13-31, Motion for Approval of Expert Witness Expenses.
- Form 13-32, Motion for Independent Forensic Testing.
- Form 13-33.1, Motion for Defendant's Access to Physical Evidence.
- Form 13-33.2, Motion for Forensic Identity Testing.

§12:30 Investigative Assistance for Indigents

§12:31 Statutes

CCP Art. 26.05. Compensation of Counsel Appointed to Defend

(d) A counsel in a noncapital case, other than an attorney with a public defender's office, appointed to represent a defendant under this code shall be reimbursed for reasonable and necessary expenses, including expenses for investigation and for mental health and other experts. Expenses incurred with prior court approval shall be reimbursed in the same manner provided for capital cases by Articles 26.052(f) and (g), and expenses incurred without prior court approval shall be reimbursed in the manner provided for capital cases by Article 26.052(h).

CCP Art. 26.052. Appointment of Counsel in Death Penalty Case, Reimbursement of Investigative Expenses

(f) Appointed counsel may file with the trial court a pretrial *Ex parte confidential request for advance payment of expenses to investigate potential defenses. The request for expenses must state:*

(1) the type of investigation to be conducted;

(2) specific facts that suggest the investigation will result in admissible evidence; and

(3) an itemized list of anticipated expenses for each investigation.

(g) The court shall grant the request for advance payment of expenses in whole or in part if the request is reasonable. If the court denies in whole or in part the request for expenses, the court shall:

(1) state the reasons for the denial in writing;

(2) attach the denial to the confidential request; and

(3) submit the request and denial as a sealed exhibit to the record.

> *(h) Counsel may incur expenses without prior approval of the court. On presentation of a claim for reimbursement, the court shall order reimbursement of counsel for the expenses, if the expenses are reasonably necessary and reasonably incurred.*

§12:32 Investigative Expenses Are Within the Discretion of the Court

The allowance of investigative expenses is a matter within the sound discretion of the trial court, and an abuse of that discretion will not be found absent a showing of harm. Castillo v. State, 739 S.W.2d 280 (Tex. Crim. App. 1987).

§12:33 Record Must Show Specific Need

The record must reflect some specific need for the funds, such as the need for a particular expert or witness, and in what manner the defendant will be harmed if the funds are not provided. Phillips v. State, 701 S.W.2d 875 (Tex. Crim. App. 1985).

§12:34 Counsel's Duty to Investigate Mitigation

Defense counsel's failure to investigate the basis of his client's mitigation defense can amount to ineffective assistance of counsel. In determining whether counsel conducted a reasonable investigation, an appellate court's initial inquiry is whether a reasonable investigation should have uncovered the mitigating evidence. Ex parte Gonzales, 204 S.W.3d 391 (Tex. Crim. App. 2006).

This is also true in a non-capital case. *See* Wiggins v. Smith, 539 U.S. 510, 123 S.Ct. 2527, 156 L.Ed.2d 471 (2003).

In a non-death case, counsel can be found ineffective for failure to present character evidence where the record shows that the witnesses would have been able to offer mitigating testimony. Milburn v. State, 15 S.W.3d 267 (Tex.App.—Houston [14th Dist.] 2000, pet. ref'd); Shanklin v. State, 190 S.W.3d 154 (Tex.App.—Houston [1st Dist.] 2005), *pet.dism'd* 211 S.W.3d 315 (Tex. Crim. App. 2007).

A defense attorney's decision not to present particular witnesses at the punishment stage may be a strategically sound decision if the attorney bases it on a determination that the testimony of the witnesses may be harmful, rather than helpful, to the defendant. However, a failure to uncover and present mitigating evidence cannot be justified as a tactical decision when defense counsel has not conducted a thorough investigation of the defendant's background. Shanklin.

If counsel makes a decision to not present potentially mitigating evidence after a full investigation because it could lead to the presentation of aggravating evidence against the defendant, the decision will most likely be upheld as objectively reasonable. Ex parte Woods, 176 S.W.3d 224 (Tex. Crim. App. 2005).

§12:35 Form: Motions

See our companion book *Texas Criminal Forms* (James Publishing):

- Form 13-34.1, Motion for Approval of Funds for Court-Appointed Investigator.
- Form 13-34.2, Motion for Approval of Mitigation Specialist Expenses.

§12:40 Recusal and Disqualification of Trial Judge

A Texas judge may be removed from presiding over a case for one of three reasons: he is constitutionally disqualified; he is subject to a statutory strike (as in civil cases); or he is subject to statutory disqualification or recusal under Texas Supreme Court rules. Gaal v. State, 332 S.W.3d 448 (Tex. Crim. App. 2011).

§12:41 Constitution and Statutes

Tex. Const. Art. 5, §11. Disqualification of Judges; Exchange of Districts; Holding Court for Other Judges

> *No judge shall sit in any case wherein the judge may be interested, or where either of the parties may be connected with the judge, either by affinity or consanguinity, within such a degree as may be prescribed by law, or when the judge shall have been counsel in*

the case. When the Supreme Court, the Court of Criminal Appeals, the Court of Appeals, or any member of any of those courts shall be thus disqualified to hear and determine any case or cases in said court, the same shall be certified to the Governor of the State, who shall immediately commission the requisite number of persons learned in the law for the trial and determination of such cause or causes. When a judge of the District Court is disqualified by any of the causes above stated, the parties may, by consent, appoint a proper person to try said case; or upon their failing to do so, a competent person may be appointed to try the same in the county where it is pending, in such manner as may be prescribed by law.

And the District Judges may exchange districts, or hold courts for each other when they may deem it expedient, and shall do so when required by law. This disqualification of judges of inferior tribunals shall be remedied and vacancies in their offices filled as may be prescribed by law.

CCP Art. 30.01. Causes Which Disqualify

No judge or justice of the peace shall sit in any case where he may be the party injured, or where he has been of counsel for the State or the accused, or where the accused or the party injured may be connected with him by consanguinity or affinity within the third degree, as determined under Chapter 573, Government Code.

CCP Art. 30.02. District Judge Disqualified

Whenever any case is pending in which the district judge or criminal district judge is disqualified from trying the case, no change of venue shall be made necessary thereby; but the judge presiding shall certify that fact to the presiding judge of the administrative judicial district in which the case is pending and the presiding judge of such administrative judicial district shall assign a judge to try such case in accordance with the provisions of Article 200a, V.A.C.S.

Tex. Gov't Code §21.005. Disqualification

A judge or a justice of the peace may not sit in a case if either of the parties is related to him by affinity or consanguinity within the third degree, as determined under Chapter 573.

Tex. R. Civ. Pro. 18a. Recusal or Disqualification of Judges

(a) At least 10 days before the date set for trial or other hearing in any court other than the Supreme Court, the Court of Criminal Appeals or the Court of Appeals, any party may file with the clerk of the court a motion stating grounds why the judge before whom the case is pending should not sit in the case. The grounds may include any disability of the judge to sit in the case. The motion shall be verified and must state with particularity the grounds why the judge before whom the case is pending should not sit. The motion shall be made on personal knowledge and shall set forth such facts as would be admissible in evidence provided that facts may be stated upon information and belief if the grounds of such belief are specifically stated.

(b) On the day the motion is filed, copies shall be served on all other parties or their counsel of record, together with a notice that movant expects the motion to be presented to the judge three days after the filing of such motion unless otherwise ordered by the judge. Any other party may file with the clerk an opposing or concurring statement at any time before the motion is heard.

(c) Prior to any further proceedings in the case, the judge shall either recuse himself or request the presiding judge of the administrative judicial district to assign a judge to hear such motion. If the judge recuses himself, he shall enter

an order of recusal and request the presiding judge of the administrative judicial district to assign another judge to sit, and shall make no further orders and shall take no further action in the case except for good cause stated in the order in which such action is taken.

(d) If the judge declines to recuse himself, he shall forward to the presiding judge of the administrative judicial district, in either original form or certified copy, an order of referral, the motion, and all opposing and concurring statements. Except for good cause stated in the order in which further action is taken, the judge shall make no further orders and shall take no further action in the case after filing of the motion and prior to a hearing on the motion. The presiding judge of the administrative judicial district shall immediately set a hearing before himself or some other judge designated by him, shall cause notice of such hearing to be given to all parties or their counsel, and shall make such other orders including orders on interim or ancillary relief in the pending cause as justice may require.

(e) If within 10 days of the date set for trial or other hearing a judge is assigned to a case, the motion shall be filed at the earliest practicable time prior to the commencement of the trial or other hearing.

(f) If the motion is denied, it may be reviewed for abuse of discretion on appeal from the final judgment. If the motion is granted, the order shall not be reviewable, and the presiding judge shall assign another judge to sit in the case.

(g) The Chief Justice of the Supreme Court may also appoint and assign judges in conformity with this rule and pursuant to statute.

(h) If a party files a motion to recuse under this rule and it is determined by the presiding judge or the judge designated by him at the hearing and on motion of the opposite party, that the motion to recuse is brought solely for the purpose of delay and without sufficient cause, the judge hearing the motion may, in the interest of justice, impose any sanction authorized by Rule 215(2)(b).

Tex. R. Civ. Pro. 18b. Grounds for Disqualification and Recusal of Judges

(1) Disqualification

Judges shall disqualify themselves in all proceedings in which:

(a) they have served as a lawyer in the matter in controversy, or a lawyer with whom they previously practiced law served during such association as a lawyer concerning the matter; or

(b) they know that, individually or as a fiduciary, they have an interest in the subject matter in controversy; or

(c) either of the parties may be related to them by affinity or consanguinity within the third degree.

(2) Recusal

A judge shall recuse himself in any proceeding in which:

(a) his impartiality might reasonably be questioned;

(b) he has a personal bias or prejudice concerning the subject matter or a party, or personal knowledge of disputed evidentiary facts concerning the proceeding;

(c) he or a lawyer with whom he previously practiced law has been a material witness concerning it;

(d) he participated as counsel, adviser or material witness in the matter in controversy, or expressed

an opinion concerning the merits of it, while acting as an attorney in government service;

(e) he knows that he, individually or as a fiduciary, or his spouse or minor child residing in his household, has a financial interest in the subject matter in controversy or in a party to the proceeding, or any other interest that could be substantially affected by the outcome of the proceeding;

(f) he or his spouse, or a person within the third degree of relationship to either of them, or the spouse of such a person:

(i) is a party to the proceeding, or an officer, director, or trustee of a party;

(ii) is known by the judge to have an interest that could be substantially affected by the outcome of the proceeding;

(iii) is to the judge's knowledge likely to be a material witness in the proceeding.

(g) he or his spouse, or a person within the first degree of relationship to either of them, or the spouse of such a person, is acting as a lawyer in the proceeding.

(3) A judge should inform himself about his personal and fiduciary financial interests, and make a reasonable effort to inform himself about the personal financial interests of his spouse and minor children residing in his household.

(4) In this rule:

(a) "proceeding" includes pretrial, *trial, or other stages of litigation;*

(b) the degree of relationship is calculated according to the civil law system;

(c) "fiduciary" includes such relationships as executor, administrator, trustee, and guardian;

(d) "financial interest" means ownership of a legal or equitable interest, however small, or a relationship as director, advisor, or other active participant in the affairs of a party, except that:

(i) ownership in a mutual or common investment fund that holds securities is not a "financial interest" in such securities unless the judge participates in the management of the fund;

(ii) an office in an educational, religious, charitable, fraternal, or civic organization is not a "financial interest" in securities held by the organization;

(iii) the proprietary interest of a policyholder in a mutual insurance company, of a depositor in a mutual savings association, or a similar proprietary interest, is a "financial interest" in the organization only if the outcome of the proceeding could substantially affect the value of the interest;

(iv) ownership of government securities is a "financial interest" in the issuer only if the outcome of the proceeding could substantially affect the value of the securities;

(v) an interest as a taxpayer or utility ratepayer, or any similar interest, is not a "financial interest" unless the outcome of the proceeding could substantially affect the liability of the judge or a person related to him within the third degree more than other judges.

(5) The parties to a proceeding may waive any ground for recusal after it is fully disclosed on the record.

(6) If a judge does not discover that he is recused under subparagraphs (2)(e) or (2)(f)(iii) until after he has devoted substantial time to the matter, he is not required to recuse himself if he or the person related to him divests himself of the interest that would otherwise require recusal.

§12:42 Difference Between Recusal and Disqualification

Generally, a motion to recuse seeks to prevent a judge from hearing a case because of a nonconstitutional reason, while grounds for disqualification are limited to those identified in the constitution. Gaal v. State, 332 S.W.3d 448 (Tex. Crim. App. 2011).

Judges may be removed from a particular case either because they are disqualified or because they are recused. The grounds and procedures for each type of removal are fundamentally different. *See* In re Union Pacific Resources Co., 969 S.W.2d 427 (Tex. 1998).

§12:43 Recusal of Trial Judge

§12:43.1 Application of Civil Rule

Rule 18b(2) of the Texas Rules of Civil Procedure sets out the law concerning recusal and includes instances in which a judge must step down from hearing a case for reasons other than the disqualifying grounds listed in the constitution. Rule 18b(2) states, in relevant part, that a "judge shall recuse himself in any proceeding in which: (a) his impartiality might reasonably be questioned; [or] (b) he has a personal bias or prejudice concerning the subject matter or a party, or personal knowledge of disputed evidentiary facts concerning the proceeding[.]" Gaal v. State, 332 S.W.3d 448 (Tex. Crim. App. 2011).

Tex.R.Civ.P. 18a applies to criminal cases absent any explicit or implicit legislative intent indicating otherwise. Arnold v. State, 853 S.W.2d 543 (Tex. Crim. App. 1993); Sanchez v. State, 926 S.W.2d 391 (Tex.App.—El Paso 1996, *pet. ref'd*).

Rule 18a also applies in habeas proceedings that occur before the trial court. Ex parte Sinegar, 324 S.W.3d 578 (Tex. Crim. App. 2010).

The Due Process Clause may sometimes demand recusal even when a judge has no actual bias. Recusal is required when, objectively speaking, the probability of actual bias on the part of the judge or decision maker is too high to be constitutionally tolerable. Rippo v. Baker, 580 U.S. ___, 137 S.Ct. 905, 907, 197 L.Ed.2d 167 (2017).

A judge's remarks during trial that are critical, disapproving, or hostile to counsel, the parties, or their cases, usually will not support a bias or partiality challenge, although they may do so if they reveal an opinion based on extrajudicial information, and they will require recusal if they reveal such a high degree of favoritism or antagonism as to make fair judgment impossible. On the other hand, expressions of impatience, dissatisfaction, annoyance, and even anger, that are within the bounds of what imperfect men and women may display, do not establish bias or partiality. Gaal.

Judicial bias or partiality derived from opinions formed by the judge on the basis of facts introduced or events occurring in the course of the proceedings may be grounds for a recusal motion where they evidence a deep-seated favoritism or antagonism that would make fair judgment impossible. Gaal.

Merely designating someone as a "friend" on Facebook does not show the degree or intensity of a judge's relationship with a person such that the judge's impartiality might reasonably be questioned, or that the judge has a personal bias or prejudice concerning the subject matter or a party to the extent requiring the judge to recuse himself. Youkers v. State, 400 S.W.3d 200, 206 (Tex. App.—Dallas 2013, *pet.ref'd*).

§12:43.2 Motion to Recuse

The procedural requisites for recusal in Rule 18a(a) are mandatory, and a party who fails to conform waives his right to complain of a judge's failure to recuse himself. Arnold v. State, 853 S.W.2d 543 (Tex. Crim. App. 1993)

Rule 18a has a 10-day notice provision. Unless the motion to recuse is filed at least 10 days before trial, it is not sufficient to trigger the provisions of Rule 18a. Arnold.

However, where the defendant does not know of the possible grounds for recusal until well into trial, the 10-day rule of Rule 18a does not apply. Martin v. State, 876 S.W.2d 396 (Tex.App.—Fort Worth 1994, *no pet.*).

A motion to recuse is the proper vehicle to challenge any alleged bias of the trial judge in the case. Sanchez v. State, 926 S.W.2d 391 (Tex. App.—El Paso 1996, *pet. ref'd*).

In order to recuse a judge, any party may file a motion stating grounds why the judge before whom the case is pending should not sit in the case. Tex.R.Civ.P. 18a(a).

The grounds must be stated with particularity. Vargas v. State, 883 S.W.2d 256 (Tex.App.—Corpus Christi 1994, *pet. ref'd*).

A motion to recuse must be verified in order to comply with Rule 18a. Vargas; Moorhead v. State, 972 S.W.2d 93 (Tex.App.—Texarkana 1998, *no pet.*).

Rule 18a(b) requires that, on the day the motion is filed, copies be served upon all other parties or their counsel of record and that the motion be accompanied by "a notice that the movant expects the motion to be presented to the judge three days after the filing of such motion unless otherwise ordered by the judge." Ex parte Sinegar, 324 S.W.3d 578 (Tex. Crim. App. 2010).

§12:43.3 Duty of the Trial Judge

When a recusal motion is filed, the trial judge against whom the motion is directed may properly make an initial decision of whether the motion is sufficient to invoke Rule 18a. *See* Arnold (no error in not referring motion to recuse not timely filed); McDuffie v. State, 854 S.W.2d 195 (Tex.App.—Beaumont 1993, *pet. ref'd*).

Once a sufficient motion to recuse has been filed, before proceeding further in the case, the judge must either recuse himself or request the presiding judge of the administrative judicial district to assign a judge to hear the motion under Tex. Gov't Code §74.059(c)(3). Sanchez.

If a recusal motion is timely filed and facially sufficient, a hearing must be held. Sanchez.

Where it is found that a party was erroneously denied the right to a hearing on their motion to recuse, the remedy is to abate the case back to the trial court so that such hearing can be held. Sanchez.

A judge should recuse himself where he has a financial interest in the outcome of a case, even though the interest is less than what would have been considered personal or direct at common law. Caperton et.al. v. A.T. Massey Coal Co. et.al., 556 U.S. ___, 129 S.Ct. 2252, 173 L.Ed.2d 1208 (2009) citing Tumey v. Ohio, 273 U. S. 510 (1927).

A judge who participated as counsel in an earlier proceeding of the same case should also recuse himself. Caperton et.al. v. A.T. Massey Coal Co. et.al. (citing In re Murchison, 349 U. S. 133, 75 S.Ct. 623, 99 L.Ed. 942 (1955)).

In addition to the above two reasons for recusal, there are objective standards that require recusal under the due process clause when the probability of actual bias on the part of the judge or decisionmaker is too high to be constitutionally tolerable. Caperton et.al. v. A.T. Massey Coal Co. et.al. (citing Withrow v. Larkin, 421 U. S. 35 (1975)).

A judge does not have authority to take any further action after signing a voluntary recusal order. Ex parte Thuesen, 546 S.W.3d 145, 147 (Tex. Crim. App. 2017).

Interim or ancillary orders made by a regional presiding judge regarding the recusal of a trial judge—or the reinstatement or modification of judicial authority following a recusal—must be made in writing, signed by the presiding judge, and entered of record in the case. Ex parte Thuesen, 546 S.W.3d at 156.

§12:43.4 Appeals

If the motion to recuse is denied, the standard for review is abuse of discretion, and the denial may be reviewed on appeal from the final judgment. Tex.R.Civ.P. 18a(f); Thomas v. Walker, 860 S.W.2d 579 (Tex.App.—Waco 1993, *no writ*).

§12:44 Form: Motions and Order

See our companion book *Texas Criminal Forms* (James Publishing):

- Form 15-7, Motion for Recusal of Trial Judge.

- Form 15-8, Motion Concurring in Motion to Recuse Trial Judge.
- Form 15-9, Order of Referral to Presiding Administrative Judge.

§12:45 Disqualification of Trial Judge

§12:45.1 Basis for Motion

The grounds for disqualification of a judge stated in the Texas Constitution and the Texas Code of Criminal Procedure are exclusive. McDuffie v. State, 854 S.W.2d 195 (Tex.App.—Beaumont 1993, *pet. ref'd*).

Under Tex. Const. Art. V, §11 where a party shows that the trial judge has a bias in the case that is of such a nature and to such an extent as to deny the party due process of law, the judge will be disqualified. McClenan v. State, 661 S.W.2d 108 (Tex. Crim. App. 1983); McDuffie.

§12:45.2 Movant's Burden

The movant on a motion to disqualify, alleging that the trial judge is biased, has the burden to provide facts sufficient to establish that a reasonable man, knowing all the circumstances involved, would harbor doubts as to the impartiality of the trial judge. Kemp v. State, 846 S.W.2d 289 (Tex. Crim. App. 1992).

A motion to disqualify the judge must be *prima facie* adequate and state proper grounds upon which disqualification can be based in order for the trial judge to proceed to the next step of disqualifying himself or referring the motion to an administrative judge for hearing. McClenan v. State, 661 S.W.2d 108 (Tex. Crim. App. 1983).

Furthermore, before alleged bias becomes sufficient to warrant the disqualification of a judge, the movant must show that the bias stems from an extrajudicial source and results in an opinion on the merits on some basis other than what the judge learned from his participation in the case. United States v. Grinnell Corp., 384 U.S. 563, 86 S.Ct. 1698, 16 L.Ed.2d 778 (1966); Kemp.

In a situation where the presiding judge is ineligible to preside over the case, the defendant must move to have the judge disqualified as soon as he knows or should have known that an error has occurred. Lackey v. State, 364 S.W.3d 837 (Tex. Crim. App. 2012) (where the defendant preserved error by filing a subsequent pretrial motion to set aside the ineligible judge's rulings).

§12:45.3 Grounds

The opening clause of CCP Art. 30.01 means that a trial court judge, in any particular criminal prosecution, may be the party injured, and is therefore disqualified from presiding, if the evidence shows that he was among the defendant's victims in the criminal transaction or episode at issue, such that a reasonable person would harbor doubts as to the judge's impartiality. Whitehead v. State, 273 S.W.3d 285 (Tex. Crim. App. 2008).

A trial judge's arbitrary refusal to consider the full range of punishment in a case is an instance where a party's due process rights would be abridged and the judge would be disqualified. McClenan v. State, 661 S.W.2d 108 (Tex. Crim. App. 1983).

The mere fact that a trial judge issued a defendant's search or arrest warrant does not establish bias against that defendant in a subsequent criminal proceeding. Kemp v. State, 846 S.W.2d 289 (Tex. Crim. App. 1992).

If a trial judge participated in any manner in the preparation and investigation of the case, he would be a counsel for the state and hence disqualified. Gamez v. State, 737 S.W.2d 315 (Tex. Crim. App. 1987).

Where a judge personally participated as a prosecutor in a hearing on the case and consented to the defendant's waiver of a right during the hearing, she is disqualified as having actively participated in the case. Metts v. State, 510 S.W.3d 1 (Tex. Crim. App. 2016).

A motion to disqualify should be handled under the same procedural requirements as is a motion to recuse. Stafford v. State, 948 S.W.2d 921, (Tex. App.—Texarkana 1997, *pet. ref'd*).

The proceeding imposing probation and the proceeding revoking probation are the same case for the purpose of the disqualification provisions, and a judge is statutorily and constitutionally disqualified from presiding over a revocation hearing if he had prosecuted the original action. Ex parte Miller, 696 S.W.2d 908 (Tex. Crim. App. 1985).

A trial judge is disqualified from acting where

he sua sponte obtained personal knowledge about contested facts and used that personal knowledge in ruling on a motion to suppress. Haworth v. State, 533 S.W.3d 484, 487 (Tex. App.—Corpus Christi 2017, *no pet.*).

§12:45.4 Appeal

The refusal of a defendant's motion to disqualify is reviewable only for abuse of discretion. Tex.R.Civ.P. 18a(f).

The failure to disqualify the trial judge is an issue that can be raised for the first time on appeal. Whitehead v. State, 273 S.W.3d 285 (Tex. Crim. App. 2008).

Thus, an appellate court should not reverse a trial judge whose ruling on the motion was within the zone of reasonable disagreement. Kemp v. State, 846 S.W.2d 289 (Tex. Crim. App. 1992).

Disqualification may be raised for the first time in a collateral attack on the judgment. *See* Lee v. State, 555 S.W.2d 121 (Tex. Crim. App. 1977); In re K.E.M., 89 S.W.3d 814 (Tex.App.—Corpus Christi 2002, *no pet.*).

However, disqualification cannot be raised on post-trial habeas where the defendant was aware of the grounds and could have made the challenge at the trial court or on appeal. Ex parte Richardson, 201 S.W.3d 712 (Tex. Crim. App. 2006).

§12:46 Objecting to Judicial Assignments

A defendant must object to a judicial assignment prior to trial. Wilson v. State, 977 S.W.2d 379 (Tex. Crim. App. 1998).

§12:47 Form: Motions and Order

See our companion book *Texas Criminal Forms* (James Publishing):

- Form 15-10, Motion for Disqualification of Trial Judge.
- Form 15-11, Motion Concurring in Motion for Disqualification of Trial Judge.
- Form 15-12, Order of Referral to Presiding Administrative Judge.

§12:50 Change of Venue

§12:51 Statutes

CCP Art. 27.15. Change of Venue to Plead Guilty

When in any county which is located in a judicial district composed of more than one county, a party is charged with a felony and the maximum punishment therefore shall not exceed 15 years, and the district court of said county is not in session, such party may, if he desires to plead guilty, or enter a plea of nolo contendere, make application to the district judge of such district for a change of venue to the county in which said court is in session, and said district judge may enter an order changing the venue of said cause to the county in which the court is then in session, and the defendant may plead guilty or enter a plea of nolo contendere to said charge in said court to which the venue has been changed.

CCP Art. 31.01. On Court's Own Motion

Whenever in any case of felony or misdemeanor punishable by confinement, the judge presiding shall be satisfied that a trial, alike fair and impartial to the accused and to the State, cannot, from any cause, be had in the county in which the case is pending, he may, upon his own motion, after due notice to accused and the State, and after hearing evidence thereon, order a change of venue to any county in the judicial district in which such county is located or in an adjoining district, stating in his order the grounds for such change of venue. The judge, upon his own motion, after 10 days notice to the parties or their counsel, may order a change of venue to any county beyond an adjoining district; provided, however, an order changing venue to a county beyond an adjoining district shall be grounds for reversal if, upon timely contest by the defendant, the record of the contest affirmatively shows that any county in his own and the adjoining district is not subject to the same conditions which required the transfer.

CCP Art. 31.02. State May Have

Whenever the district or county attorney shall represent in writing to the court before which any felony or misdemeanor case punishable by confinement, is pending, that, by reason of existing combinations or influences in favor of the accused, or on account of the lawless condition of affairs in the county, a fair and impartial trial as between the accused and the State cannot be safely and speedily had; or whenever he shall represent that the life of the prisoner, or of any witness, would be jeopardized by a trial in the county in which the case is pending, the judge shall hear proof in relation thereto, and if satisfied that such representation is well-founded and that the ends of public justice will be subserved thereby, he shall order a change of venue to any county in the judicial district in which such county is located or in an adjoining district.

CCP Art. 31.03. Granted on Motion of Defendant

(a) A change of venue may be granted in any felony or misdemeanor case punishable by confinement on the written motion of the defendant, supported by his own affidavit and the affidavit of at least two credible persons, residents of the county where the prosecution is instituted, for either of the following causes, the truth and sufficiency of which the court shall determine:

(1) That there exists in the county where the prosecution is commenced so great a prejudice against him that he cannot obtain a fair and impartial trial; and

(2) That there is a dangerous combination against him instigated by influential persons, by reason of which he cannot expect a fair trial.

An order changing venue to a county beyond an adjoining district shall be grounds for reversal, if upon timely contest by defendant, the record of the contest affirmatively shows that any county in his own and the adjoining district is not subject to the same conditions which required the transfer.

(b) For the convenience of parties and witnesses, and in the interest of justice, the court upon motion of the defendant and with the consent of the attorney for the state may transfer the proceeding as to him to another district.

(c) The court upon motion of the defendant and with the consent of the attorney for the state may transfer the proceedings to another district in those cases wherein the defendant stipulates that a plea of guilty will be entered.

CCP Art. 31.04. Motion May Be Controverted

The credibility of the persons making affidavit for change of venue, or their means of knowledge, may be attacked by the affidavit of a credible person. The issue thus formed shall be tried by the judge, and the motion granted or refused, as the law and facts shall warrant.

§12:52 Motion Filing Deadlines Do Not Apply

Because a change of venue is a question of constitutional dimension, the pretrial filing deadlines of Art. 28.01 do not apply to change of venue motions. Revia v. State, 649 S.W.2d 625 (Tex. Crim. App. 1983); Gutierrez v. State, 979 S.W.2d 659 (Tex. Crim. App. 1998).

A defendant may file his change of venue motion after a jury has been selected in his case. Bell v. State, 938 S.W.2d 35 (Tex. Crim. App. 1996).

§12:53 Court's Motion for Change of Venue

Under CCP Art. 31.01, whenever a judge is

satisfied that a trial, fair and impartial to the defendant and state, cannot, from any cause, be had in the county in which the case is pending, he may on his own motion, change venue. Brimage v. State, 918 S.W.2d 466 (Tex. Crim. App. 1996) (*op. on rehearing*).

Where the state has filed a motion alternatively asking the court to *sua sponte* change venue, the court's own motion is not required. Aranda v. State, 736 S.W.2d 702 (Tex. Crim. App. 1987).

It will be presumed on appeal that the trial court had a sufficient factual basis for changing venue on its own motion unless the defendant brings proof, formally or informally, to refute the court's finding that a fair trial cannot be had. Brimage.

§12:53.1 Procedure

Under CCP Art. 31.01, the trial court may transfer venue on its own motion where: (1) due notice is given to the state and defendant; (2) the court hears evidence on its motion; (3) venue is changed to any county in the judicial district in which the original county is located or to an adjoining district; (4) if due notice is given to both the state and defendant, venue may be changed to a county beyond the adjoining district; and (5) the court must state in its order the grounds why a fair and impartial trial cannot be had in the county. *See* Brimage v. State, 918 S.W.2d 466 (Tex. Crim. App. 1996) (*op. on rehearing*).

Change of venue beyond an adjoining district shall be grounds for reversal if the defendant, on timely contest, affirmatively shows on the record that any county in his own or the adjoining district is not subject to the same conditions which required the transfer. CCP Art. 31.01.

The purpose of CCP Art. 31.01 is to require a court, once satisfied that a fair trial cannot be had, to give notice to both parties of its intention to change venue and to hold a hearing allowing either party to offer evidence either in support of or against the court's proposed change of venue. The statute does not require the court to offer evidence in support of its own motion, but rather merely offer the parties a chance to be heard on the matter. The court is only required to state in its order the grounds for its decision to change venue. *See* Brimage.

CCP Arts. 31.01 to 31.03 only require that a requested change of venue hearing be held before the trial is completed. A trial court does not commit error by holding in abeyance a ruling in a motion to change venue until after jury selection. Smith v. State, 850 S.W.2d 275 (Tex.App.—Fort Worth 1993, pet. ref'd).

§12:54 State's Motion for Change of Venue

Whenever the prosecuting attorney shall represent in writing that, by reason of existing combinations or influences in favor of the defendant, or on account of the lawless condition of affairs in the county, a fair and impartial trial as between the defendant and the State cannot be fairly and speedily had, or whenever he shall represent that the life of the prisoner or any witness would be jeopardized by a trial in the original county, a change of venue may be had. CCP Art. 31.02.

§12:54.1 Procedure

The procedure for the state obtaining a change of venue is:

(1) Upon the filing of a written motion, the court shall hear proof in relation to the prosecutor's representations.

(2) The court must be satisfied that the prosecutor's representations are well-founded and that the ends of justice will be served by a change of venue.

(3) The court may change venue to any county in the judicial district in which the original county is located or to an adjoining district.

CCP Art. 31.02.

The trial court must conduct an evidentiary hearing on the state's motion before changing venue thereon. Garza v. State, 974 S.W.2d 251 (Tex.App.—San Antonio, *pet. ref'd*).

While the defendant is required to attach supporting affidavits to his motion for change of venue under Art. 31.03, the state is not required to attach such affidavits to its motion under Art. 31.02. Garza.

§12:54.2 Contesting State's Motion

The defendant may contest the state's written representations and should do so by controverting affidavit. CCP Art. 31.04.

§12:55 Defendant's Motion for Change of Venue

Under CCP Art. 31.03, a change of venue may be had on the written motion of the defendant supported by his affidavit and the affidavit of at least two credible persons who are residents of the county where the prosecution is instituted. *See* Willingham v. State, 897 S.W.2d 351 (Tex. Crim. App. 1995).

§12:55.1 Procedure

A trial court may grant a change of venue on the written motion of the defendant in any felony or misdemeanor case punishable by confinement. The motion must be supported by the defendant's own affidavit and the affidavits of two credible persons, residents of the county of prosecution, stating that there exists in the county of prosecution so great a prejudice against him that he cannot obtain a fair and impartial trial. Taylor v. State, 93 S.W.3d 487 (Tex.App.—Texarkana 2002, *pet. ref'd*).

The defendant's motion must be in writing, sworn to by the defendant, supported by affidavits, and timely filed with the court. Cover v. State, 913 S.W.2d 611 (Tex.App.—Tyler 1995, *pet. ref'd*).

§12:55.2 Defendant's Affidavits

The motion must be supported by the affidavit of two credible citizens of the county, otherwise it is defective. Cover v. State, 913 S.W.2d 611 (Tex. App.—Tyler 1995, *pet. ref'd*).

Failure to file the defendant's affidavit and at least two others is a fatal defect. Cover.

The defendant's attorney cannot serve as one of the defendant's affiants. DeLeon v. State, 758 S.W.2d 621 (Tex.App.—Houston [14th Dist.] 1988, *no pet.*).

There must be an assertion in the affidavits that the affiants are residents of the county. Norwood v. State, 486 S.W.2d 776 (Tex. Crim. App. 1972).

A trial court does not abuse its discretion where it denies a change of venue motion that does not contain the required two affidavits. Horner v. State, 129 S.W.3d 210 (Tex.App.—Corpus Christi 2004, pet. ref'd).

A defendant's affidavits must contain more than conclusory allegations that he has been prejudiced or that a dangerous combination is working to deny him a fair trial. Buntion v. State, 482 S.W.3d 58, 74 (Tex. Crim. App. 2016).

§12:55.3 Form: Motion and Affidavit

See our companion book *Texas Criminal Forms* (James Publishing):

- Form 12-7, Change of Venue Motion.
- Form 12-8, Change of Venue Affidavit.

§12:55.4 State's Controverting Affidavit

A controverting affidavit, pursuant to CCP Art. 31.04, is a notarized statement of the opinion of the compurgator that the opposing affiant is not credible, and/or that opposing affiant's means of knowledge are not sufficient. A controverting affidavit is not a witness' sworn statement of fact as to a matter at trial, as contemplated by Rule 602. Burks v. State, 876 S.W.2d 877 (Tex. Crim. App. 1994).

The credibility of the persons making the affidavits, or their means of knowledge, may be attacked by the affidavit of a credible person, which forms a factual issue to be determined by the trial court. Taylor v. State, 93 S.W.3d 487 (Tex. App.—Texarkana 2002, *pet. ref'd*).

Controverting affidavits must assert that the defendant's affiants are not credible and/or that their knowledge is insufficient. Janecka v. State, 937 S.W.2d 456 (Tex. Crim. App. 1996).

The purpose of the controverting affidavits required by Art. 31.04 is to provide a form of pleading which establishes that there is a factual dispute in need of resolution. Busby v. State, 990 S.W.2d 263 (Tex. Crim. App. 1999).

Personal knowledge is not required, and Tex.R.Evid. 602 does not apply to controverting affidavits. Busby.

If the state does not file a controverting affidavit or if the controverting affidavit fails on its face to meet these two requirements, the defendant is entitled to a change of venue as a matter of law. Janecka; Lundstrom v. State, 742 S.W.2d 279 (Tex. Crim. App. 1986); Taylor v. State, 93 S.W.3d 487 (Tex.App.—Texarkana 2002, pet. ref'd).

§12:55.5 Form: State's Controverting Motion and Affidavit

See our companion book *Texas Criminal Forms* (James Publishing):

- Form 12-9, State's Controverting Motion.
- Form 12-10, State's Controverting Affidavit.

§12:55.6 Grounds for Defendant's Motion

A defendant is entitled to a change of venue if he shows that there were community influences which could affect the answers on voir dire or the testimony of witnesses at trial, or that for any other reason a fair and impartial trial could not be had in the county where the offense was committed. Bell v. State, 938 S.W.2d 35 (Tex. Crim. App. 1996).

§12:55.6.1 Prejudice

Under CCP Art. 31.03(a)(1), a change of venue may be granted if the defendant establishes that there exists in the county where the prosecution is commenced so great a prejudice against him that he cannot obtain a fair and impartial trial. *See* Willingham v. State, 897 S.W.2d 351 (Tex. Crim. App. 1995).

To justify a change of venue based upon media attention, a defendant must show that the publicity was pervasive, prejudicial, and inflammatory. Widespread publicity by itself is not considered inherently prejudicial. Indeed, even extensive knowledge of the case or defendant in the community as a result of pretrial publicity is not sufficient if there is not also some showing of prejudicial or inflammatory coverage. Gonzalez v. State, 222 S.W.3d 446 (Tex. Crim. App. 2007); Buntion v. State, 482 S.W.3d 58, 71 (Tex. Crim. App. 2016).

In examining whether the pretrial publicity is prejudicial and inflammatory, a trial court may take three matters into consideration: (1) the nature of the publicity; (2) any evidence presented at a change of venue hearing; and (3) testimony received from venire members at voir dire. Gonzalez.

The mere existence of media attention or publicity is not enough, by itself, to merit a change of venue. Gonzalez.

A defendant must demonstrate an actual, identifiable prejudice attributable to pretrial publicity on the part of the community from which members of the jury will come. Willingham.

The mere fact of media attention and publicity do not automatically establish prejudice or require a change of venue; jurors do not have to be totally ignorant of the facts and issues of a particular case. Teague v. State, 864 S.W.2d 505 (Tex. Crim. App. 1993).

The trial court is within its discretion to believe prospective jurors' statements that they are not unduly influenced and could deliver a fair verdict. Freeman v. State, 340 S.W.3d 717 (Tex. Crim. App. 2011). News stories that are accurate and objective are generally not considered to be prejudicial or inflammatory. Buntion v. State, 482 S.W.3d 58, 74 (Tex. Crim. App. 2016).

Even a large number of venire members who have heard of the case, or who could not set aside their opinions about the case, does not establish that pretrial publicity has permeated the community to such an extent that it is impossible to seat a fair and impartial jury. Freeman.

Racial prejudice may be grounds for changing venue. McWilliams v. State, 496 S.W.2d 630 (Tex. Crim. App. 1973).

The movant has the burden of proof. Willingham.

The defendant must establish that whatever publicity existed permeated the community to such an extent that the veniremembers' initial opinion, if any, could not be set aside. Etheridge v. State, 903 S.W.2d 1 (Tex. Crim. App. 1994).

In deciding whether the trial court abused its discretion in denying a motion to change venue, the reviewing court determines whether there existed such a prejudice in the community that it is doubtful that the defendant received a fair trial by an impartial jury. Moore v. State, 935 S.W.2d 124 (Tex. Crim. App. 1996).

§12:55.6.2 Dangerous Combination

A change of venue is required if there exists a "dangerous combination" against the accused "instigated by influential person, by reason of which" the accused cannot expect a fair trial. CCP Art. 31.03(a)(2).

§12:55.7 Trial Court Must Hold a Hearing

When the defendant files a change of venue motion and affidavits, and the state files a controverting affidavit under Art. 31.04, the trial court must conduct a hearing to resolve the factual disputes raised by the affidavits. Garza v. State, 974 S.W.2d 251 (Tex.App.—San Antonio, *pet. ref'd*); Burks v. State, 876 S.W.2d 877 (Tex. Crim. App. 1994).

The trial court must conduct an evidentiary hearing on the state's motion before changing venue thereon. Garza v. State, 974 S.W.2d 251 (Tex.App.—San Antonio, *pet. ref'd*).

Arts. 31.01-.03 provide only for a requested change of venue hearing to be held before the trial is completed, and a trial court does not commit error by holding in abeyance a ruling on a motion to change venue until after jury selection. Smith v. State, 850 S.W.2d 275 (Tex.App.—Fort Worth 1993, *pet. ref'd).*

The trial court may withhold ruling on a change of venue motion until after the completion of voir dire, but prior to the defendant's plea to the indictment, to see if an impartial jury can be seated in the case. Foster v. State, 770 S.W.2d 845 (Tex. Crim. App. 1989).

The burden is on the movant to require the trial court to hear and rule on the motion for change of venue. Gutierrez v. State, 979 S.W.2d 659 (Tex. Crim. App. 1998).

A trial court may use the jury selection process to help gauge the community climate. Colone v. State, 573 S.W.3d 249, 257 (Tex. Crim. App. 2019).

A trial court can rescind an order changing venue where no steps have been taken to carry out or to comply with the order changing venue, and the record reflects that the order was improperly entered. Colone v. State, 573 S.W.3d at 256.

§12:55.8 Preserving Error

In order to preserve error where the court has refused to grant a requested change of venue, the defendant should exhaust all peremptory challenges, request additional challenges and show that he was forced to take an unacceptable juror. Stiehl v. State, 585 S.W.2d 716 (Tex. Crim. App. 1979).

§12:55.9 Appellate Review

A change of venue under this provision is within the discretion of the court, subject to review only upon a showing that such discretion was abused. Gonzalez v. State, 222 S.W.3d 446 (Tex. Crim. App. 2007); Colone v. State, 573 S.W.3d 249, 257 (Tex. Crim. App. 2019).

If the trial court's decision falls within the zone of reasonable disagreement, it will be upheld. Freeman v. State, 340 S.W.3d 717 (Tex. Crim. App. 2011).

§12:55.10 Changes of Venue by Consent

For the convenience of the parties and witnesses, and in the interest of justice, the court, upon motion of the defendant and with the consent of the attorney for the State, may transfer the proceeding as to him to another district. CCP Art. 31.03(b).

Similarly, by consent, a defendant may have the case transferred to another district where he stipulates that a plea of guilty will be entered. CCP Art. 31.03(c).

§12:60 Speedy Trial

§12:61 Constitution and Statutes

United States Constitution Amend. VI.

> *In all criminal prosecutions, the accused shall enjoy the right to a speedy and public trial by an impartial jury of the State and district wherein the crime shall have been committed ....*

Texas Constitution Art. 1, §10.

> *In all criminal prosecutions the accused shall have a speedy public trial by an impartial jury.*

CCP Art. 1.05. Rights of Accused

In all criminal prosecutions the accused shall have a speedy public trial by an impartial jury.

CCP Art. 28.061. Discharge for Delay

If a motion to set aside an indictment, information, or complaint for failure to provide a speedy trial is sustained, the court shall discharge the defendant. A discharge under this article is a bar to any further prosecution for the offense discharged and for any other offense arising out of the same transaction, other than an offense of a higher grade that the attorney representing the state and prosecuting the offense that was discharged does not have the primary duty to prosecute.

§12:62 Texas Speedy Trial Act

§12:62.1 Statutory Law

Texas Code Crim. Pro. Art. 32A.01. Trial Priorities

(a) Insofar as is practicable, the trial of a criminal action shall be given preference over trials of civil cases, and the trial of a criminal action against a defendant who is detained in jail pending trial of the action shall be given preference over trials of other criminal actions not described by Subsection (b) or (c).

(b) Unless extraordinary circumstances require otherwise, the trial of a criminal action in which the alleged victim is younger than 14 years of age shall be given preference over other matters before the court, whether civil or criminal.

(c) Except as provided by Subsection (b), the trial of a criminal action against a defendant who has been determined to be restored to competency under Article 46B.084 shall be given preference over other matters before the court, whether civil or criminal.

The Texas Speedy Trial Act as found in CCP Art. 32A.02 was declared unconstitutional as a violation of the separation of powers doctrine. Meshell v. State, 739 S.W.2d 246 (Tex. Crim. App. 1987).

§12:62.2 Case Law

§12:63 Constitutional Speedy Trial Motions

Speedy trial guarantees are designed to minimize the possibility of lengthy incarceration before trial, to reduce the lesser impairment of liberty imposed on an accused while released on bail and to shorten the disruption of life caused by arrest and the presence of unresolved criminal charges. United States v. Loud Hawk, 474 U.S. 302, 106 S.Ct. 648, 654, 88 L.Ed.2d 640 (1986).

Constitutional speedy trial motions focus on post-indictment delay. State v. Munoz, 991 S.W.2d 818 (Tex. Crim. App. 1999).

The Sixth Amendment's speedy trial guarantee protects the accused from arrest or indictment through trial, but does not apply once a defendant has been found guilty at trial or has pleaded guilty to criminal charges. Betterman v. Montana, 578 U.S. ___, 136 S.Ct. 1609, 1612, 194 L.Ed.2d 723 (2016).

§12:63.1 Factors for Examination

There are four factors to be examined in determining whether a defendant has been deprived of his constitutional right to a speedy trial:

- The length of the delay, measured from the time the defendant was accused;
- The government's reason for the delay;
- The efforts made by the defendant to obtain a speedy trial; and
- The prejudice to the defendant as a result of the delay.

Barker v. Wingo, 407 U.S. 514, 92 S.Ct. 2182, 33 L.Ed.2d 101 (1972); Cantu v. State, 253 S.W.3d 273, 280 (Tex. Crim. App. 2008)

This balancing test requires weighing case-by-case the conduct of both the prosecution and the defendant. No single factor is a necessary or sufficient condition to the finding of a speedy trial violation. The related factors must be considered together with such other circumstances as may be relevant. Barker; State v. Munoz, 991 S.W.2d 818 (Tex. Crim. App. 1999).

When reviewing an application of the *Barker* test, a reviewing court uses the same burden of proof allocation as in the context of a motion to suppress, giving almost total deference to historical findings of fact of the trial court that the record supports and drawing reasonable inferences from those facts necessary to support the trial court's findings. Appellate courts review *de novo* whether there was sufficient presumptive prejudice to proceed to a *Barker* analysis and the weighing of the Barker factors, which are legal questions. Gonzales v. State, 435 S.W.3d 801, 808-9 (Tex. Crim. App. 2014).

§12:63.2 Length of Delay

The length of delay is a triggering mechanism for analysis of the other factors. Until there is some delay which is presumptively prejudicial, there is no necessity for inquiry into the other factors that go into the balance. Presumptive prejudice does not necessarily indicate a statistical probability of prejudice; it simply marks the point at which courts deem the delay unreasonable enough to trigger the Barker inquiry. Doggett v. United States, 505 U.S. 647, 112 S.Ct. 2686, 120 L.Ed.2d 520 (1992) (f.n.1); State v. Munoz, 991 S.W.2d 818 (Tex. Crim. App. 1999).

To trigger a speedy trial analysis, an accused must allege that the interval between accusation and trial has crossed the threshold dividing ordinary prejudicial delay from presumptively prejudicial delay. If the accused makes this showing, the court must then consider, as one factor among several, the extent to which the delay stretches beyond the bare minimum needed to trigger judicial examination of the claim. Doggett, Munoz.

The length of the delay is measured from the time the accused is arrested or formally accused. Gonzales v. State, 435 S.W.3d 801, 809 (Tex. Crim. App. 2014) (finding that a 6-year delay created a presumptive prejudice and undertaking a full *Barker* evaluation).

When the length of delay stretches well beyond the bare minimum needed to trigger a full *Barker* analysis, the length of a delay weighs against the State, and the longer the delay, the more the defendant's prejudice is compounded. This is due to the presumption that pretrial delay has prejudiced the accused intensifies over time. Gonzales, 435 S.W.3d at 809.

In general, courts deem delay approaching one year to be unreasonable enough to trigger the Barker enquiry. Balderas v. State, 517 S.W.3d 756, 768 (Tex. Crim. App. 2016).

A delay of as little as fourteen months in bringing a defendant to trial is too long a delay where it was found that the defense witnesses' memories were dimming and the state did nothing to refute the prejudice. State v. Perkins, 911 S.W.2d 548 (Tex.App.—Fort Worth 1995, *no pet.*).

However, a delay of eight and one-half years may not result in prejudice to a defendant under another fact situation. Emery v. State, 881 S.W.2d 702 (Tex. Crim. App. 1994).

§12:63.3 Reason for Delay

The third Barker factor—the defendant's assertion of his right to a speedy trial—is entitled to strong evidentiary weight in determining whether the defendant has been deprived of that right. Balderas v. State, 517 S.W.3d 756, 768 (Tex. Crim. App. 2016).

The length of delay can be subdivided into justifiable and unjustifiable reasons for delay depending on the circumstances of the case. Unjustifiable reasons for delay count towards the length of delay, while justifiable reasons for delay do not. Gonzales v. State, 435 S.W.3d 801, 810 (Tex. Crim. App. 2014).

Different weights should be assigned to different reasons for the delay. A deliberate attempt to delay the trial should be weighed heavily against the government. A more neutral reason such as negligence or overcrowded courts should be weighed against the government less heavily. A valid reason for the delay should not be weighed against the government at all. A delay which is attributable in whole or in part to the defendant may even constitute a waiver of a speedy trial claim. Barker v. Wingo, 407 U.S. 514, 92 S.Ct. 2182, 33 L.Ed.2d 101 (1972); State v. Munoz, 991 S.W.2d 818 (Tex. Crim. App. 1999).

Deliberate delay intended to hamper the defense weighs heavily against the State, while more neutral reasons, such as negligence or overcrowded courts, weigh less heavily. Additionally, the courts consider whether the government or the criminal defendant is more to blame for the delay. Balderas v. State, 517 S.W.3d at 771.

Delay caused by good faith plea negotiations is not the result of negligence or a deliberate attempt to delay the trial. Barker, Munoz

A crowded court docket is not a valid reason for delay and must be counted against the State, although not heavily. Shaw v. State, 117 S.W.3d 883 (Tex. Crim. App. 2003).

§12:63.4 The Defendant's Efforts

A defendant must raise a speedy-trial claim in the trial court in order to preserve that issue for appellate review. Henson v. State, 407 S.W.3d 764, 768 (Tex. Crim. App. 2013).

Initially filing a motion to dismiss instead of a motion for a speedy trial weakens a defendant's speedy trial claim because it shows a desire to have no trial instead of a speedy trial. Parkerson v. State, 942 S.W.2d 789 (Tex.App.—Fort Worth 1997, *no pet.*).

Court-appointed counsel, just as retained counsel, act on behalf of their clients, and delays sought by counsel are ordinarily attributable to the defendant when conducting a Barker v. Wingo analysis. Vermont v. Brillon, 556 U.S. ___, 129 S.Ct. 1283, 173 L.Ed.2d 231 (2009).

§12:63.5 Prejudice

A defendant has the burden to make some showing of prejudice although a showing of actual prejudice is not required. When a defendant makes a *prima facie* showing of prejudice, the State carries the obligation of proving that the accused suffered no serious prejudice beyond that which ensued from the ordinary and inevitable delay. State v. Munoz, 991 S.W.2d 818 (Tex. Crim. App. 1999).

There is no speedy trial violation where the defendant fails in his burden to show that he was prejudiced because of the delay. Knox v. State, 934 S.W.2d 678 (Tex. Crim. App. 1996).

Prejudice to the defendant is assessed in the light of the interests that the speedy trial right is designed to protect. These interests are:

- Preventing oppressive pretrial incarceration;
- Minimizing anxiety and concern of the accused; and
- Limiting the possibility that the defense will be impaired.

Of these factors, the most serious is the last, because the inability of a defendant adequately to prepare his case skews the fairness of the entire system. Barker v. Wingo, 407 U.S. 514, 92 S.Ct. 2182, 33 L.Ed.2d 101 (1972); Munoz.

In certain instances, the length of delay may be so excessive that it presumptively compromises the reliability of a trial in ways that neither party can prove or identify. In such instances, the defendant is absolved from the requirement to demonstrate prejudice. Gonzales v. State, 435 S.W.3d 801, 812-3 (Tex. Crim. App. 2014).

Where prejudice has been presumed, the state has the burden to persuasively rebut it. Gonzales, 435 S.W.3d at 815.

§12:63.6 Necessary Proof

An unsworn motion to dismiss for denial of speedy trial rights is not self-proving and cannot serve as proof of any fact. Newman v. State, 331 S.W.3d 447 (Tex. Crim. App. 2011).

The defendant invoking his right to a speedy trial must make some showing of prejudice resulting from the delay. Chapman v. Evans, 744 S.W.2d 133 (Tex. Crim. App. 1988).

A defendant's assertion of his speedy trial right is entitled to strong evidentiary weight in determining whether he has been deprived of his right to a speedy trial. Clarke v. State, 928 S.W.2d 709 (Tex.App.—Fort Worth 1996, *pet. ref'd*).

The trial court as finder of fact on a speedy trial motion is empowered, on the basis of credibility and demeanor evaluations, to completely disregard a witness' testimony, even if that testimony is uncontroverted. Kelly v. State, 163 S.W.3d 722 (Tex. Crim. App. 2005) (citing State v. Ross, 32 S.W.3d 853 (Tex. Crim. App. 2000)).

The burden is on the defendant on appeal to present a sufficient record to show that his speedy trial motion should have been granted. Newman.

§12:63.7 Remedy Is Dismissal

CCP Art. 28.061. Discharge for Delay

> *If a motion to set aside an indictment, information, or complaint for failure to provide a speedy trial is sustained, the court shall discharge the defendant. A discharge under this article is a bar to any further prosecution for the offense discharged and for any other offense arising out of the same transaction, other than an offense of a higher grade that the attorney representing the state and prosecuting the offense that was discharged does not have the primary duty to prosecute.*

If a violation of the right to a speedy trial is established, the proper remedy is dismissal of the prosecution with prejudice. Strunk v. United States, 412 U.S. 434, 93 S.Ct. 2260, 37 L.Ed.2d 56 (1973); Shaw v. State, 117 S.W.3d 883 (Tex. Crim. App. 2003).

§12:63.8 Form: Motions

See our companion book *Texas Criminal Forms* (James Publishing):

- Form 12-11, Motion for Speedy Trial.
- Form 12-12, Motion to Dismiss for Denial of Constitutional Right to Speedy Trial.

12:63.9 Interstate Agreement on Detainers (IAD)

The Interstate Agreement on Detainers (IAD) is a compact between states (and some other jurisdictions) that enables a party state to obtain custody of an out-of-state prisoner for prosecution and imposes duties to ensure a prisoner's quick return to the sending state. Texas has codified the IAD in Code of Criminal Procedure art. 51.14. Hopper v. State, 520 S.W.3d 915, 924 (Tex. Crim. App. 2017). When analyzing speedy trial claims that arise in the context of the IAD, the courts use the Barker factors to analyze the claim. Hopper v. State, 520 S.W.3d at 924

§12:64 Defendant's Right to Speedy Indictment

§12:64.1 Statutes

CCP Art. 32.01. Defendant in Custody and No Indictment Presented

> *When a defendant has been detained in custody or held to bail for his appearance to answer any criminal accusation before the district court, the prosecution, unless otherwise ordered by the court, for good cause shown, supported by affidavit, shall be dismissed and the bail discharged, if indictment or information be not presented against such defendant on or before the last day of the next term of the court which is held after his commitment or admission to bail or on or before the 180th day after the date of commitment or admission to bail, whichever date is later.*

§12:64.2 Application of the Statute

Art. 32.01 prevents citizens from being left in jail or on bail for long periods of time without being indicted. The State must indict within the period set by Art. 32.01, show good cause for the delay, or suffer the dismissal of the charges. Ex parte Martin, 6 S.W.3d 52 (Tex. Crim. App. 1999).

Art. 32.01 is satisfied for all subsequent charges once the state obtains a timely indictment against the defendant for any offense arising out of the same criminal transaction or occurrence. Cameron v. State, 988 S.W.2d 835 (Tex.App.—San Antonio 1999, *pet. ref'd*).

The Barker balancing test has been adopted to determine when pretrial delay denies an accused of his right to a speedy trial under CCP Art. 32.01:

- The length of the delay.
- The reason for the delay.
- The prejudice to the accused.
- The accused's assertion of the right.

Martin.

A motion to dismiss for failure to provide speedy indictment must be filed and heard before indictment as it has no effect if it is presented after indictment. Brooks v. State, 990 S.W.2d 278, 285 (Tex. Crim. App. 1999).

A writ of habeas corpus alleging an Art.

32.01 violation is moot where the state indicts the defendant before the writ is heard. Ex parte Countryman, 226 S.W.3d 435 (Tex. Crim. App. 2007).

§12:64.3 The State's Burden

A showing of good cause to continue the prosecution is unnecessary unless and until the defendant seeks a dismissal pursuant to the statute. Thus, there is no reason for the state to file a good-cause affidavit before the defendant files his motion to dismiss. It is sufficient that the state files its responsive affidavit before the district court rules. Ex parte Mallares, 953 S.W.2d 759 (Tex.App.—Austin 1997, *no pet.*).

§12:64.4 Trial Court May Dismiss Case

Although a trial court generally does not have the power to dismiss a case unless the prosecutor requests it, a trial court does have this power under Art. 32.01. Ex parte Mann, 89 S.W.3d 296 (Tex. App.—Fort Worth 2002, *no pet.*).

§12:64.5 Defendant May Still Be Prosecuted

CCP Art. 28.061, barring further prosecution for a discharged offense, has been amended, and no longer applies to a discharge under Art. 32.01. Therefore, even if a defendant is entitled to discharge from custody under Art. 32.01, he is not free from subsequent prosecution. Ex parte Seidel, 39 S.W.3d 221 (Tex. Crim. App. 2001).

§12:64.6 Form: Motion and Waiver

See our companion book *Texas Criminal Forms* (James Publishing):

- Form 12-13, Motion to Dismiss for Denial of Speedy Indictment.
- Form 12-14, Waiver of Speedy Indictment.

§12:65 Mandamus to Enforce Speedy Trial Rights

§12:65.1 Defendant May Petition for Writ of Mandamus

A defendant who seeks a speedy trial may do so by way of a petition for writ of mandamus. Chapman v. Evans, 744 S.W.2d 133 (Tex. Crim. App. 1988).

To obtain relief through a writ of mandamus, the relator must establish that (1) the act he seeks to compel is ministerial, rather than discretionary, in nature and (2) no other adequate remedy at law is available. Engle v. Coker, 820 S.W.2d 247 (Tex. App.—Beaumont 1991, *no pet.*).

An act is ministerial if it constitutes a duty clearly fixed and required by law, without the exercise of discretion or judgment. Engle v. Coker.

§12:65.2 Mandamus Not Appropriate for Speedy Trial Dismissals

Mandamus is not the proper remedy for a defendant seeking dismissal of his charges based upon an alleged speedy trial violation because he has an adequate remedy at law, that being a motion to dismiss the indictment under CCP Art. 27.03. Smith v. Gohmert, 962 S.W.2d 590 (Tex. Crim. App. 1998).

§12:65.3 Form: Petition for Writ

See our companion book *Texas Criminal Forms* (James Publishing):

- Form 12-15, Petition for Writ of Mandamus.

§12:70 Joinder and Severance

§12:71 Joinder and Severance of Multiple Defendants

§12:71.1 Statutes

CCP Art. 36.09. Severance on Separate Indictments

> *Two or more defendants who are jointly or separately indicted or complained against for the same offense or any offense growing out of the same*

> *transaction may be, in the discretion of the court, tried jointly or separately as to one or more defendants; provided that in any event either defendant may testify for the other or on behalf of the state; and provided further, that in cases in which, upon timely motion to sever, and evidence introduced thereon, it is made known to the court that there is a previous admissible conviction against one defendant or that a joint trial would be prejudicial to any defendant, the court shall order a severance as to the defendant whose joint trial would prejudice the other defendant or defendants.*

CCP Art. 36.10. Order of Trial

> *If a severance is granted, the defendants may agree upon the order in which they are to be tried; but if they fail to agree, the court shall direct the order of the trial.*

§12:71.2 Joinder

Under Art. 36.09, the trial court has discretion to join two or more defendants for trial unless statutory grounds for severance exist. Aguilar v. State, 26 S.W.3d 901 (Tex. Crim. App. 2000).

There is a specific statute controlling the joinder of drug offenses into a single trial. It explicitly requires the state to file written notice of joinder. Tex. Health and Safety Code §481.132.

§12:71.3 Severance

Art. 36.09 imposes two basic requirements for showing entitlement to a severance: (1) that the motion for severance be timely, and (2) that at least one of two possible grounds for severance be alleged, with supporting evidence. Qualley v. State, 206 S.W.3d 624 (Tex. Crim. App. 2006) *citing* Zafiro v. United States, 506 U.S. 534, 113 S.Ct. 933, 122 L.Ed.2d 317 (1993).

§12:71.4 Grounds for Severance

The two grounds for severance are: (1) the co-defendant has a previous admissible conviction, and (2) a joint trial would prejudice the (moving) defendant. Qualley v. State, 206 S.W.3d 624 (Tex. Crim. App. 2006) (*citing* Zafiro v. United States, 506 U.S. 534, 113 S.Ct. 933, 122 L.Ed.2d 317 (1993)).

Absent evidence of prejudice to one defendant in a joint trial, or evidence that one of the defendants has a prior admissible conviction, a motion for severance is left to the trial court's discretion. Marsh v. State, 115 S.W.3d 709 (Tex.App.—Austin 2003, pet. ref'd).

In order to establish prejudice entitling him to a severance, a defendant must show a serious risk that a specific trial right would be compromised by a joint trial, or that a joint trial would prevent the jury from making a reliable judgment about guilt or innocence, and that the problem could not be adequately addressed by lesser curative measures, such as a limiting instruction. Prejudice must be analyzed with regard to each defendant. Prejudice may be shown for one defendant in a trial but not another. Qualley.

To establish prejudice on the basis of the right to have a codefendant testify as a witness, the moving party must demonstrate: (1) a bona fide need for the testimony; (2) the substance of the desired testimony; (3) its exculpatory nature and effect; and (4) evidence that the designated co-defendant will in fact testify at a separate trial. Lacy v. State, 901 S.W.2d 518 (Tex.App.—Tyler 1995, *no pet.*).

The "previous admissible conviction" portion of the statute acts only to shield a defendant from the introduction of the co-defendant's conviction. The idea is that a defendant without a conviction may suffer "guilt by association" from the jury's exposure to the co-defendant's previous crime. It is for this reason that severance on this basis is mandatory only when the moving defendant himself has no prior conviction that would be admissible at either the guilt or punishment stage of trial. Qualley.

Failure to grant a severance on this basis is harmless if the co-defendant's previous conviction was not in fact admitted at trial. Qualley.

Claims made under the "prejudice" clause of the statute are not subject to harmless error analysis. Qualley.

When an accused is not entitled to a severance as a matter of right, the denial of a severance motion by the trial court constitutes an abuse of discretion only when the movant satisfies the "heavy burden" of showing "clear prejudice." Mendoza v. State, 61 S.W.3d 418 (Tex.App.—San Antonio 2001) *aff'd at* 88 S.W.3d 236 (Tex. Crim. App. 2002).

An example of a curative measure that can be employed by the trial court in a joint trial is an instruction to the jury to use a confession only against the confessing codefendant and then redacting the confession to eliminate the other defendant's name and any reference to his existence to cure the prejudice caused by admission of a codefendant's statement. Chavez v. State, 6 S.W.3d 56 (Tex.App.—San Antonio 1999, pet. ref'd) *citing* Richardson v. Marsh, 481 U.S. 200, 211, 107 S.Ct. 1702, 95 L.Ed.2d 176 (1987).

§12:71.5 Timeliness of Motion

A motion to sever on the grounds of unfair prejudice under Art. 36.09 is timely if made at the first opportunity or as soon as the grounds for prejudice become apparent or should have become apparent, thus providing the trial court an opportunity to rule on the potentially prejudicial evidence at the time it is introduced. Aguilar v. State, 26 S.W.3d 901 (Tex. Crim. App. 2000).

To be timely, a motion for severance must be made before trial if the factual basis for seeking a severance was known prior to trial. Qualley v. State, 206 S.W.3d 624 (Tex. Crim. App. 2006).

A motion to sever on the grounds of unfair prejudice is untimely if counsel waits until the close of evidence to make the motion. Aguilar.

The mere allegation that prejudice will result is not evidence of, or a sufficient showing of, prejudice under Art. 36.09, particularly when the severance is discretionary with the trial judge. Mendoza v. State, 61 S.W.3d 418 (Tex.App.—San Antonio 2001) *aff'd at* 88 S.W.3d 236 (Tex. Crim. App. 2002).

If the motion to sever is not supported by evidence, its denial is not an abuse of discretion. Marsh v. State, 115 S.W.3d 709 (Tex.App.—Austin 2003, pet. ref'd); Davila v. State, 4 S.W.3d 844 (Tex.App.—Eastland 1999, *no pet.*).

§12:71.6 Form: Motions

See our companion book *Texas Criminal Forms* (James Publishing):

- Form 12-20, Motion for Severance of Defendants' Cases.
- Form 12-21, State's Motion to Consolidate.

§12:72 Joinder and Severance of Multiple Counts

§12:72.1 Statutes

Tex. Penal Code §3.01. Definition

In this chapter, "criminal episode" means the commission of two or more offenses, regardless of whether the harm is directed toward or inflicted upon more than one person or item of property, under the following circumstances:

(1) the offenses are committed pursuant to the same transaction or pursuant to two or more transactions that are connected or constitute a common scheme or plan; or

(2) the offenses are the repeated commission of the same or similar offenses.

Tex. Penal Code §3.02. Consolidation and Joinder of Prosecutions

(a) A defendant may be prosecuted in a single criminal action for all offenses arising out of the same criminal episode.

(b) When a single criminal action is based on more than one charging instrument within the jurisdiction of the trial court, the state shall file written notice of the action not less than 30 days prior to the trial.

(c) If a judgment of guilt is reversed, set aside, or vacated, and a new trial ordered, the state may not prosecute in a single criminal action in the new trial any offense not joined in the former prosecution unless evidence to establish probable guilt for that offense was not known to the appropriate prosecuting

official at the time the first prosecution commenced.

Tex. Penal Code §3.03. Sentences for Offenses Arising Out of Same Criminal Episode

(a) When the accused is found guilty of more than one offense arising out of the same criminal episode prosecuted in a single criminal action, a sentence for each offense for which he has been found guilty shall be pronounced. Except as provided by Subsection (b), the sentences shall run concurrently.

(b) If the accused is found guilty of more than one offense arising out of the same criminal episode, the sentences may run concurrently or consecutively if each sentence is for a conviction of:

(1) an offense:

(A) under Section 49.07 or 49.08, regardless of whether the accused is convicted of violations of the same section more than once or is convicted of violations of both sections; or

(B) for which a plea agreement was reached in a case in which the accused was charged with more than one offense listed in Paragraph (A), regardless of whether the accused is charged with violations of the same section more than once or is charged with violations of both sections;

(2) an offense:

(A) under Section 33.021 or an offense under Section 21.02, 21.11, 22.011, 22.021, 25.02, or 43.25 committed against a victim younger than 17 years of age at the time of the commission of the offense regardless of whether the accused is convicted of violations of the same section more than once or is convicted of violations of more than one section; or

(B) for which a plea agreement was reached in a case in which the accused was charged with more than one offense listed in Paragraph (A) committed against a victim younger than 17 years of age at the time of the commission of the offense regardless of whether the accused is charged with violations of the same section more than once or is charged with violations of more than one section;

(3) an offense:

(A) under Section 21.15 or 43.26, regardless of whether the accused is convicted of violations of the same section more than once or is convicted of violations of both sections; or

(B) for which a plea agreement was reached in a case in which the accused was charged with more than one offense listed in Paragraph (A), regardless of whether the accused is charged with violations of the same section more than once or is charged with violations of both sections;

(4) an offense for which the judgment in the case contains an affirmative finding under Article 42.0197, Code of Criminal Procedure; or

(5) an offense:

(A) under Section 20A.02 or 43.05, regardless of whether the accused is convicted of

violations of the same section more than once or is convicted of violations of both sections; or

(B) for which a plea agreement was reached in a case in which the accused was charged with more than one offense listed in Paragraph (A), regardless of whether the accused is charged with violations of the same section more than once or is charged with violations of both sections.

(b-1) Subsection (b)(4) does not apply to a defendant whose case was transferred to the court under Section 54.02, Family Code.

(6) an offense:

(A) under Section 22.04(a)(1) or (2) or Section 22.04(a-1)(1) or (2) that is punishable as a felony of the first degree, regardless of whether the accused is convicted of violations of the same section more than once or is convicted of violations of more than one section; or

(B) for which a plea agreement was reached in a case in which the accused was charged with more than one offense listed in Paragraph (A) and punishable as described by that paragraph, regardless of whether the accused is charged with violations of the same section more than once or is charged with violations of more than one section.

Tex. Penal Code §3.04. Severance

(a) Whenever two or more offenses have been consolidated or joined for trial under Section 3.02, the defendant shall have a right to a severance of the offenses.

(b) In the event of severance under this section, the provisions of Section 3.03 do not apply, and the court in its discretion may order the sentences to run either concurrently or consecutively.

(c) The right to severance under this section does not apply to a prosecution for offenses described by Section 3.03(b) unless the court determines that the defendant or the state would be unfairly prejudiced by a joinder of offenses, in which event the judge may order the offenses to be tried separately or may order other relief as justice requires.

CCP Art. 21.24. Joinder of Certain Offenses

(a) Two or more offenses may be joined in a single indictment, information, or complaint, with each offense stated in a separate count, if the offenses arise out of the same criminal episode, as defined in Chapter 3 of the Penal Code.

(b) A count may contain as many separate paragraphs charging the same offense as necessary, but no paragraph may charge more than one offense.

(c) A count is sufficient if any one of its paragraphs is sufficient. An indictment, information, or complaint is sufficient if any one of its counts is sufficient.

§12:72.2 Joinder of Counts

An indictment may contain as many separate paragraphs charging the same offense as is necessary to meet the contingencies of the evidence. Where an indictment charges different theories under which a defendant may have committed a single statutory offense, the defendant is not entitled to sever the paragraphs. Hathorn v. State, 848 S.W.2d 101 (Tex. Crim. App. 1992).

Reading the current versions of Art. 21.24(a) of the code of criminal procedure and section 3.01 of the penal code together, the State is authorized to join two or more offenses in a single indictment if the offenses are part of the same transaction or if the offenses are part of a common scheme or plan. Willeford v. State, 72 S.W.3d 820 (Tex.App.—Fort Worth 2002, pet. ref'd).

It is currently permissible for the State to allege multiple nonproperty offenses in the same indictment and obtain convictions on each offense. Willeford.

A defendant does not have the right to consolidate offenses committed in the same criminal episode under Texas Penal Code §3.02; consolidation is permissive, not mandatory. Nelson v. State, 864 S.W.2d 496 (Tex. Crim. App. 1993).

§12:72.3 Severance of Counts

A motion to sever offenses against a single defendant is a pleading of the defendant under CCP Arts. 27.02(8) & 28.01, and must be raised and heard prior to trial. Thornton v. State, 986 S.W.2d 615 (Tex. Crim. App. 1999).

A motion to sever is not self-proving, and must be accompanied by evidence or its denial is not an abuse of discretion. Mulder v. State, 707 S.W.2d 908 (Tex. Crim. App. 1986).

Where the indictment alleges two or more separate offenses, the defendant is entitled to a severance under Texas Penal Code §3.04(a). Graham v. State, 19 S.W.3d 851 (Tex. Crim. App. 2000).

A trial judge's failure to grant a mandatory severance under Penal C §3.04 is subject to a harm analysis, and the error is harmless if it did not adversely affect the defendant's substantial rights Scott v. State, 235 S.W.3d 255 (Tex. Crim. App. 2007).

Any error in failing to grant a severance is harmless where the evidence of each of the crimes would have been admissible in the trial of the others. Tovar v. State, 165 S.W.3d 785 (Tex.App.—San Antonio 2005, *no pet.*).

For further information pertaining to joinder and severance of counts, as well as requiring the state to elect a primary count for conviction purposes, *see* §17:10.

§12:72.4 Form: Motions and Supporting Brief

See our companion book *Texas Criminal Forms* (James Publishing):

- Form 12-18.1, Motion for Severance of Counts.
- Form 12-18.2, Motion for Severance of Defendant's Cases.
- Form 12-19, Brief in Support of Motion for Severance of Counts.

§12:80 Testifying Free From Impeachment by Prior Convictions

§12:81 Statutes and Rules

Tex. R. Evid. 609. Impeachment by Evidence of a Criminal Conviction

> ***(a) In General.*** *Evidence of a criminal conviction offered to attack a witness's character for truthfulness must be admitted if:*
>
> *(1) the crime was a felony or involved moral turpitude, regardless of punishment;*
>
> *(2) the probative value of the evidence outweighs its prejudicial effect to a party; and*
>
> *(3) it is elicited from the witness or established by public record.*
>
> ***(b) Limit on Using the Evidence After 10 Years.*** *This subdivision (b) applies if more than 10 years have passed since the witness's conviction or release from confinement for it, whichever is later. Evidence of the conviction is admissible only if its probative value, supported by specific facts and circumstances, substantially outweighs its prejudicial effect.*
>
> ***(c) Effect of a Pardon, Annulment, or Certificate of Rehabilitation.*** *Evidence of a conviction is not admissible if:*

(1) the conviction has been the subject of a pardon, annulment, certificate of rehabilitation, or other equivalent procedure based on a finding that the person has been rehabilitated, and the person has not been convicted of a later crime that was classified as a felony or involved moral turpitude, regardless of punishment;

(2) probation has been satisfactorily completed for the conviction, and the person has not been convicted of a later crime that was classified as a felony or involved moral turpitude, regardless of punishment; or

(3) the conviction has been the subject of a pardon, annulment, or other equivalent procedure based on a finding of innocence.

(d) Juvenile Adjudications. *Evidence of a juvenile adjudication is admissible under this rule only if:*

(1) the witness is a party in a proceeding conducted under title 3 of the Texas Family Code; or

(2) the United States or Texas Constitution requires that it be admitted.

(e) Pendency of an Appeal *A conviction for which an appeal is pending is not admissible under this rule.*

(f) Notice. *Evidence of a witness's conviction is not admissible under this rule if, after receiving from the adverse party a timely written request specifying the witness, the proponent of the conviction fails to provide sufficient written notice of intent to use the conviction. Notice is sufficient if it provides a fair opportunity to contest the use of such evidence.*

§12:82 General Points

Once a criminal defendant takes the witness stand, he is subject to the same rules as any other witness and may be impeached, contradicted, made to give evidence against himself, cross-examined on new matters, and treated in every respect as any other witness, except when there are overriding constitutional or statutory provisions. Juhasz v. State, 827 S.W.2d 327 (Tex.App.—Corpus Christi 1992, *pet. ref'd*).

The purpose of Rule 609 is to give an adverse party a fair opportunity to contest the use of a witness' convictions and to prevent ambush. Johnson v. State, 885 S.W.2d 578 (Tex.App.—Dallas 1994, *no pet.*).

When attacking the credibility of witnesses, evidence of prior criminal convictions shall be admitted only if the crime was a felony or involved moral turpitude, regardless of punishment, and the court determines that the probative value outweighs its prejudicial effects to a party. Rule 609(a); Delk v. State, 855 S.W.2d 700 (Tex. Crim. App. 1993).

PRACTICE TIP: If you want to keep the jury from hearing about a defendant's prior conviction, don't ask the defendant about convictions on direct examination. By testifying on direct examination regarding his prior convictions, a defendant will generally waive any error in the admission of his prior convictions. Perea v. State, 870 S.W.2d 314 (Tex. App.—Tyler 1994, no pet.).

§12:83 Test for Admissibility of Priors

In unambiguously plain language, Rule 609(a) provides that witness credibility may be attacked by admitting evidence that the witness previously has been convicted of a felony or crime of moral turpitude if the trial court determines that the probative value of admitting the evidence simply outweighs its prejudicial effect. Meadows v. State, 455 S.W.3d 166, 170 (Tex. Crim. App. 2015).

The trial court should conduct a balancing test to determine if the probative value of the prior convictions is outweighed by their prejudicial effect. Theus v. State, 845 S.W.2d 874 (Tex. Crim. App. 1992).

Although not exclusive, the following factors should be considered: (1) the prior conviction's impeachment value; (2) its temporal proximity to the crime on trial; (3) the similarity between the prior offenses and the present offense; (4) the importance of the defendant's testimony; and (5) the importance of the credibility issue. Theus.

If the prior offenses involved deceptive conduct instead of violence, and if they are recent, the first two factors will favor their admission because they affect credibility and they indicate a propensity for running afoul of the law. Theus.

If the prior offenses are similar to the one on trial, the third factor will militate against their admission because of the danger that the jury might convict on the basis of past conduct rather than on the facts of the case on trial. Edwards v. State, 883 S.W.2d 692 (Tex.App.—Texarkana 1994, *pet. ref'd*).

The effect of the fourth and fifth factors depends on the type of defense presented. Edwards.

The proponent of the evidence has the burden to demonstrate the admissibility of the evidence against the defendant. Dale v. State, 90 S.W.3d 826 (Tex.App.—San Antonio 2002, *pet. ref'd*).

The trial court has wide discretion in deciding the question of admissibility, and its decision will not be reversed unless it is shown that there was a clear abuse of that discretion. Theus.

PRACTICE TIP: Before pursuing a motion to testify free of impeachment by prior convictions, counsel should deliver a request to the state that they give notice under Rule 609 of any prior conviction they intend to use to impeach the defendant at trial. See Chapter 13, Discovery.

§12:84 Convictions More Than 10 Years Old

In unambiguous plain language, Rule 609(b) limits Rule 609(a) by providing that evidence of a prior conviction is inadmissible if more than 10 years has elapsed since the later date of conviction or release of the witness from the confinement imposed for that conviction unless the court determines, in the interest of justice that the probative value of the conviction supported by specific facts and circumstances substantially outweighs its prejudicial effect. Meadows v. State, 455 S.W.3d 166, 170 (Tex. Crim. App. 2015).

In deciding whether, in the interests of justice, the probative value of a remote conviction substantially outweighs its prejudicial effect, a court may consider all the relevant specific facts and circumstances, including whether intervening convictions dilute the prejudice of the remote conviction. Meadows, 455 S.W.3d at 170 (abrogating the "tacking doctrine").

§12:85 Forms: Motions and Supporting Brief

See our companion book *Texas Criminal Forms* (James Publishing):

- Form 12-23.1, Motion to Testify Free of Impeachment.
- Form 12-23.2, Motion to Have Prior Convictions Not Mentioned.
- Form 12-24, Brief in Support of Motion to Testify Free of Impeachment by Prior Convictions.

§12:90 Indictments and Informations

§12:91 Statutes

CCP Art. 21.01. "Indictment"

An "indictment" is the written statement of a grand jury accusing a person therein named of some act or omission which, by law, is declared to be an offense.

CCP Art. 21.02. Requisites of an Indictment

(a) An indictment, information, complaint, or other charging instrument or a related document in a criminal case may be filed in electronic form with a judge or clerk of the court authorized to receive the document.

(b) A judge or clerk of the court is authorized to receive for filing purposes an information, indictment, complaint,

or other charging instrument or a related document in electronic form in accordance with Subchapter I, Chapter 51, Government Code, if:

(1) the document complies with the requirements that would apply if the document were filed in hard-copy form;

(2) the clerk of the court has the means to electronically store the document for the statutory period of record retention;

(3) the judge or clerk of the court is able to reproduce the document in hard-copy form on demand; and

(4) the clerk of the court is able to display or otherwise make the document available in electronic form to the public at no charge.

(c) The person filing the document and the person receiving the document must complete the electronic filing as provided by Section 51.804, Government Code.

(d) Notwithstanding Section 51.806, Government Code, an indictment, information, complaint, or other charging instrument or a related document transmitted in electronic form is exempt from a requirement under this code that the pleading be endorsed by a natural person. The requirement of an oath under this code is satisfied if:

(1) all or part of the document was sworn to; and

(2) the electronic form states which parts of the document were sworn to and the name of the officer administering the oath.

(e) An electronically filed document described by this section may be amended or modified in compliance with Chapter 28 or other applicable law. The amended or modified document must reflect that the original document has been superseded.

(f) This section does not affect the application of Section 51.318, Government Code, Section 118.052(3), Local Government Code, or any other law permitting the collection of fees for the provision of services related to court documents.

CCP Art. 21.03. What Should Be Stated

Everything should be stated in an indictment which is necessary to be proved.

CCP Art. 21.04. The Certainty Required

The certainty required in an indictment is such as will enable the accused to plead the judgment that may be given upon it in bar of any prosecution for the same offense.

§12:92 Indictments in General

The Texas Constitution guarantees to defendants the right to indictment by a grand jury for all felony offenses. Riney v. State, 28 S.W.3d 561 (Tex. Crim. App. 2000); Cook v. State, 902 S.W.2d 471 (Tex. Crim. App. 1995).

An indictment is a written instrument presented to a court by a grand jury charging a person with the commission of an offense. Tex. Const. Art. V, §12(b); Riney.

Indictment by grand jury protects citizens against arbitrary accusations by the government. Riney.

An indictment is essential to vest the trial court with jurisdiction. Riney; Cook.

An indictment provides a defendant notice of the offense charged so that he may prepare, in advance of trial, an informed and effective defense. Riney; Garcia v. State, 981 S.W.2d 683, 685 (Tex. Crim. App.1998).

Alternate pleading of different methods of committing an offense may be charged in one indictment. Kitchens v. State, 823 S.W.2d 256 (Tex. Crim. App. 1991), *cert. denied*, 504 U.S. 958, 112 S.Ct. 2309, 119 L.Ed.2d 230 (1992).

In fact, the indictment may and should be

comprised of as many counts as necessary to meet all of the contingencies in the evidence. Hathorn v. State, 848 S.W.2d 101 (Tex. Crim. App. 1992).

The term "count" is used to charge the offense itself, and a "paragraph" is a portion of a count, which charges a method of committing the offense. The substance of the allegation determines its character as a "count" or a "paragraph," not the terminology used. Dalton v. State, 898 S.W.2d 424 (Tex.App.—Fort Worth 1995, *pet. ref'd*).

An indictment may contain as many separate paragraphs charging the same offense as necessary. CCP Art. 21.24(b).

TIP TO THE PROSECUTION: If the indictment contains an allegation of the commission of an offense and pleads several different methods of the commission of this offense, ask the trial court to submit the allegations to the jury combined into one application paragraph in order to alleviate proving each separate allegation to each member of the jury.

§12:92.1 Allegations Required

The indictment must plead the offense in plain and intelligible words. Everything should be stated in an indictment which is necessary to be proved. The certainty required in an indictment is such that will enable the accused to plead the judgment that may be given upon it in bar of any prosecution for the same offense. State v. Zuniga, 512 S.W.3d 902, 906 (Tex. Crim. App. 2017).

An indictment is sufficient if it charges the commission of the offense in ordinary and concise language in such a manner as to enable a person of common understanding to know what is meant, and with that degree of certainty that will give the defendant notice of the particular offense with which he is charged, and enable the court, on conviction, to pronounce the proper judgment. State v. Zuniga, 512 S.W.3d at 906.

The language of an indictment is sufficient where it tracks the language of the penal statute in question. State v. Zuniga, 512 S.W.3d at 907.

The face of the indictment must charge all the elements of the offense in plain and intelligible words, such that a person of common understanding would know what is meant. State v. Mays, 967 S.W.2d 404 (Tex. Crim. App. 1998).

When a statutory term or element is defined by a statute, the charging instrument does not need to allege the definition of the term or element. Typically the definition of terms and elements are regarded as evidentiary matters. State v. Zuniga, 512 S.W.3d at 907.

However, in some cases, a charging instrument that tracks the statutory language may be insufficient to provide a defendant with adequate notice. This is so when the statutory language fails to be completely descriptive. For example, a statute which uses an undefined term of indeterminate or variable meaning requires more specific pleading in order to notify the defendant of the nature of the charges against him. Likewise, when a statute defines the manner or means of commission in several alternative ways, an indictment will fail for lack of specificity if it neglects to identify which of the statutory means it addresses. In such cases, more particularity is required to provide adequate notice. State v. Zuniga, 512 S.W.3d at 907.

Appellate courts to engage in a two-step analysis when analyzing whether a charging instrument provides adequate notice. First, the reviewing court must identify the elements of the offense. Next, it must consider whether the statutory language is sufficiently descriptive of the charged offense. State v. Jarreau, 512 S.W.3d 352, 354-5 (Tex. Crim. App. 2017).

Tex. Penal Code §1.07(a)(22) defines the elements of the offense to be the forbidden conduct, the required culpability, any required result, and the negation of any exception to the offense. Gray v. State, 152 S.W.3d 125 (Tex. Crim. App. 2004).

An indictment is constitutionally valid when it alleges the essential elements of the offense and charges a defendant with that offense. Duron v. State, 956 S.W.2d 547 (Tex. Crim. App. 1997).

An indictment must allege on its face the facts necessary (1) to show that the offense was committed; (2) to bar a subsequent prosecution for the same offense; and (3) to give the defendant notice of precisely what he is charged with. Weatherby v. State, 61 S.W.3d 733 (Tex.App.—

Fort Worth 2001, *pet. ref'd*).

The indictment must plead the culpable mental state for the offense. Dinkins v. State, 894 S.W.2d 330 (Tex. Crim. App. 1995).

When recklessness is an element of the offense, the charging instrument must allege the circumstances of the act which indicate that the defendant acted in a reckless manner. State v. Rodriguez, 339 S.W.3d 680 (Tex. Crim. App. 2011).

§12:92.2 Allegations Not Required

The elements of constituent offenses need not be pleaded. Robinson v. State, 596 S.W.2d 130 (Tex. Crim. App. 1980). Therefore, an indictment for attempt is not fundamentally defective for the failure to allege the constituent elements of the offense attempted. Epps v. State, 811 S.W.2d 237 (Tex.App.—Dallas 1991, *no pet.*); *see also* In re J.B.M., 157 S.W.3d 823 (Tex.App.—Fort Worth 2005, *no writ*).

Likewise, the state is not required to allege the constituent elements of an offense constituting the aggravating element of a capital murder indictment. Dinkins.

An indictment charging a consummated offense must properly charge all of the elements of that offense, but an indictment charging an attempted offense is not fundamentally defective for failure to allege the constituent elements of the offense attempted. Wood v. State, 560 S.W.3d 162, 168 (Tex. Crim. App. 2018).

The law of parties (under either a Penal Code §7.02(a) or (b) theory) need not be pled in the indictment. Vodochodsky v. State, 158 S.W.3d 502 (Tex. Crim. App. 2005).

In an aggregated theft case, under Texas Penal Code §31.09, the indictment need only allege aggregation, and each separate theft need not be specifically alleged. Kellar v. State, 108 S.W.3d 311 (Tex. Crim. App. 2003).

Allegations that are not essential to constitute the offense and that might be entirely omitted without affecting the charge against the defendant and without detriment to the indictment are treated as mere surplusage, and they may be entirely disregarded. Hernandez v. State, 903 S.W.2d (Tex. App.—Fort Worth 1995, *pet. ref'd*).

Unnecessary words or allegations in an indictment that are descriptive of statutorily required language must be proved by state as alleged. Hernandez.

The definitions of "intoxicated" in Texas Penal Code §49.01(2) are evidentiary and therefore do not need to be alleged in a charging instrument. Therefore, a trial court should not quash a DWI information charging a defendant with DWI due to the state's failure to allege the definition of "intoxicated" that it intends to prove at trial. State v. Barbernell, 257 S.W.3d 248 (Tex. Crim. App. No. 0867-07, July 2, 2008).

Generally, the State need not plead with additional specificity those matters which are statutorily defined in the alternative where the matter is not an act or omission of the defendant. State v. Jarreau, 512 S.W.3d 352, 354 (Tex. Crim. App. 2017).

An indictment charging delivery of a dangerous drug does not have to allege the nature of the dangerous drug as a device or a drug because that is not a manner or means of delivery and does not describe, concern, involve or go to the act of delivery. State v. Jarreau, 512 S.W.3d 352, 356 (Tex. Crim. App. 2017).

In an indictment alleging tampering with evidence, the specific identity of the tampered-with evidence is not an element of the offense. However, more specificity may be required in the indictment in order to provide the defendant with adequate notice of the charged conduct. State v. Zuniga, 512 S.W.3d 902, 909 (Tex. Crim. App. 2017).

§12:92.3 Sufficiency

The sufficiency of an indictment is a question of law reviewed on a *de novo* basis on appeal. State v. Moff, 154 S.W.3d 599 (Tex. Crim. App. 2004).

An indictment or information is sufficient under the Texas Constitution if it accuses the defendant of a crime with enough clarity and specificity to identify the penal statute under which the state intends to prosecute. Duron v. State, 956 S.W.2d 547 (Tex. Crim. App. 1997) (even though the indictment charging the defendant with indecency with a child alleged innocent conduct).

Tex. Code Crim. Pro. article 21.02 sets out what is required to make an indictment "sufficient." If an indictment does not comply with article 21.02, it is considered to be defective. Jenkins v. State, ___ S.W.3d ___ at *5 2018 WL 6332219, overruling Cook v. State, 902 S.W.2d 471 (Tex. Crim. App. 1995).

However, it has been well-settled since 1985 that a defect in an indictment may not prevent it from qualifying as an indictment under article V, section 12(b) of the Texas Constitution. An indictment can be defective, but still be an indictment that vests the court with jurisdiction. In fact, in Duron v. State, the court of criminal appeals held that in order for a defect to render the instrument a non-indictment, the defect must make it impossible for the defendant to know the offense with which he had been charged. Jenkins, ___ S.W.3d at *5.

Thus, with regard to the requirements under the constitutional definition of indictment—that it must (1) charge a person, and (2) charge the commission of an offense—the proper test is whether the face of the charging instrument is clear enough to give an appellant adequate notice of the charge against him. If this is not the case, the indictment is void. Jenkins, ___ S.W.3d at *5.

The face of the indictment can sufficiently put the defendant on notice that he is the defendant referred to in the indictment. Jenkins, ___ S.W.3d at *5.

Texas law requires the defendant to object to any error in the indictment before the day of trial and certainly before the jury is empaneled or any error of sufficiency is waived. Jenkins, ___ S.W.3d at *6.

An indictment is generally sufficient as long as it tracks the language of a penal statute that itself satisfies the constitutional requirement of notice. Lawrence v. State, 240 S.W.3d 912 (Tex. Crim. App. 2007).

Before a felony trial court has subject matter jurisdiction over an indictment, it must put the defendant on notice that the charging of a felony offense was intended. Kirkpatrick v. State, 279 S.W.3d 324 (Tex. Crim. App. 2008).

Where an indictment fails to provide sufficient notice to inform the accused of the specific acts for which he was charged, the trial court does not err in quashing the indictment. State v. Moff (where any of a large number of transactions could have been relied on by the state for conviction).

A statute is void for vagueness if it fails to define the criminal offense with sufficient definiteness so that ordinary people can understand what conduct is prohibited and in a manner that does not permit arbitrary and discriminatory enforcement. Lawrence.

If a statute does not substantially implicate constitutionally protected conduct or speech, it is valid unless it is impermissibly vague in all applications or as applied to the defendant. Lawrence.

When reviewing a trial court's decision to deny a motion to quash an indictment, an appellate court applies a *de novo* standard of review. Lawrence.

§12:92.4 Variance

A variance occurs when there is a discrepancy between the allegations in the charging instrument and the proof at trial. In a variance situation, the state has proven the defendant guilty of a crime, but has proven its commission in a manner that varies from the allegations in the charging instrument. Gollihar v. State, 46 S.W.3d 243 (Tex. Crim. App. 2001).

The widely-accepted rule, regardless of whether viewing variance as a sufficiency of the evidence problem or as a notice-related problem, is that a variance that is not prejudicial to a defendant's substantial rights is immaterial. In determining whether a defendant's substantial rights have been prejudiced in this context, two questions are generally asked: 1) whether the indictment, as written, informed the defendant of the charge against him sufficiently to allow him to prepare an adequate defense at trial; and 2) whether prosecution under the deficiently drafted indictment would subject the defendant to the risk of being prosecuted later for the same crime. Gollihar.

The Texas "immaterial variance" law as set out in Gollihar does not apply to the specific statutory elements alleged in the indictment. Cada v. State, 334 S.W.3d 766 (Tex. Crim. App. 2011) (a retaliation case where there was a variance between the pleading of the element of "a witness" and proof of the element of "an informant"); Byrd v. State, 336 S.W.3d 242 (Tex. Crim. App. 2011)(a theft case where there was a variance between the pleading of the injured party as "Mike Morales," and the proof which showed the injured party to be "Wal-Mart").

Allegations in an indictment that are not a statutory element or an integral part of an essential element of the offense charged fall under the immaterial variance rule of Gollihar. Fuller 73 S.W.3d 250, 254 (Tex. Crim. App. 2002) (a slight variance between the indictment and proof of the complainant's name is not a material variance).

Variances can be classified into three categories, depending upon the type of allegation that the State has pled in its charging instrument but failed to prove at trial. First, a variance involving statutory language that defines the offense always renders the evidence legally insufficient to support the conviction (i.e., such variances are always material). Second, a variance involving a non-statutory allegation that describes an "allowable unit of prosecution" element of the offense may or may not render the evidence legally insufficient, depending upon whether the variance is material (i.e., such variances are sometimes material). Finally, other types of variances involving immaterial non-statutory allegations do not render the evidence legally insufficient. Johnson v. State, 364 S.W.3d 292 (Tex. Crim. App. 2012) (where the precise act or nature of conduct was inconsequential because aggravated assault by causing serious bodily injury is a result-oriented offense). *See also* Ramos v. State, 407 S.W.3d 265, 269 (Tex. Crim. App. 2013).

§12:92.5 Number of Convictions Authorized

An indictment cannot authorize more convictions than there are counts. When the court's charge authorizes convictions on more than one paragraph per count, the trial judge has the responsibility of structuring the judgment to show only one conviction per count. Martinez v. State, 225 S.W.3d 550 (Tex. Crim. App. 2007).

§12:92.6 Election of Primary Act Relied on for Conviction

See §17:11 for a complete analysis of the case law on this subject.

§12:92.7 Duplicity

"Duplicity" is the technical fault of uniting two or more distinct and separate offenses in the same count of an indictment. Lebo v. State, 100 S.W.3d 417 (Tex.App.—San Antonio 2002, *pet. ref'd*).

The rule against duplicitous indictments is based on the proposition that a defendant must receive fair notice of the charge against which he must defend. Lebo.

An indictment that conjunctively alleges more than one culpable mental state in the commission of an offense is not duplicitous. Lebo.

§12:93 Challenges to Charging Instruments

§12:93.1 Statutes

CCP Art. 1.14. Waiver of Rights

(a) The defendant in a criminal prosecution for any offense may waive any rights secured him by law except that a defendant in a capital felony case may waive the right of trial by jury only in the manner permitted by Article 1.13(b) of this code.

(b) If the defendant does not object to a defect, error, or irregularity of form or substance in an indictment or information before the date on which the trial on the merits commences, he waives and forfeits the right to object to the defect, error, or irregularity and he may not raise the objection on appeal or in any other post-conviction proceeding. Nothing in this article prohibits a trial court from requiring that an objection to an indictment or information be made at an earlier time in compliance with Article 28.01 of this code.

CCP Art. 21.23.

The rules with respect to allegations in an indictment and the certainty required apply also to information.

CCP Art. 27.03. Motion to Set Aside Indictment

In addition to any other grounds authorized by law, a motion to set aside an indictment or information may be based on the following:

(1) That it appears by the records of the court that the indictment was not found by at least nine grand jurors, or that the information was not based upon a valid complaint;

(2) That some person not authorized by law was present when the grand jury was deliberating upon the accusation against the defendant, or was voting upon the same; and

(3) That the grand jury was illegally impaneled; provided, however, in order to raise such question on motion to set aside the indictment, the defendant must show that he did not have an opportunity to challenge the array at the time the grand jury was impaneled.

CCP Art. 27.04. Motion Tried by Judge

An issue of fact arising upon a motion to set aside an indictment or information shall be tried by the judge without a jury.

CCP Art. 27.08. Exception to Substance of Indictment

There is no exception to the substance of an indictment or information except:

(1) That it does not appear therefrom that an offense against the law was committed by the defendant;

(2) That it appears from the face thereof that a prosecution for the offense is barred by a lapse of time, or that the offense was committed after the finding of the indictment;

(3) That it contains matter which is a legal defense or bar to the prosecution; and

(4) That it shows upon its face that the court trying the case has no jurisdiction thereof.

CCP Art. 27.09. Exception to Form of Indictment

Exceptions to the form of an indictment or information may be taken for the following causes only:

(1) That it does not appear to have been presented in the proper court as required by law;

(2) The want of any requisite prescribed by Articles 21.02 and 21.21.

(3) That it was not returned by a lawfully chosen or empaneled grand jury.

CCP Art. 27.10. Written Pleadings

All motions to set aside an indictment or information and all special pleas and exceptions shall be in writing.

CCP Art. 28.04. Quashing Charge in Misdemeanor

If the motion to set aside or the exception to an indictment or information is sustained, the defendant in a misdemeanor case shall be discharged, but may be again prosecuted within the time allowed by law.

CCP Art. 28.05. Quashing Indictment in Felony

If the motion to set aside or the exception to the indictment in cases of felony be sustained, the defendant shall not therefore be discharged, but may immediately be recommitted by order of the court, upon motion of the State's attorney or without motion; and proceedings may afterward be had against him as if no prosecution had ever been commenced.

§12:93.2 Motion Must Be Filed and Heard Before Trial Date

Motions raising defects in charging instruments must be filed and heard before the scheduled trial date or the motion is waived. The burden is on the defendant to see that this is done. State v. Turner, 898 S.W.2d 303 (Tex. Crim. App. 1995).

Similarly, the defendant must object to a misdemeanor complaint before trial or the issue is waived. Ramirez v. State, 105 S.W.3d 628 (Tex. Crim. App. 2003).

A defendant must raise a claim that the indictment is defective on the grounds that it alleges the manner and means of committing the offense in the disjunctive prior to trial or the claim is forfeited. Swain v. State, 181 S.W.3d 359 (Tex. Crim. App. 2005).

Since the 1985 amendments to Texas Constitution Art. 5, §12(b), any variance between complaint and information, or any defect in the complaint must now be raised pretrial or the claim is waived. The matter cannot be validly raised for the first time on appeal since the mere filing of the complaint vests the trial court with jurisdiction. This amendment did not change the case law interpreting sufficiency of charging instruments, but only mandates that challenges be raised pretrial under Art. 28.10. Aguilar v. State, 846 S.W.2d 318 (Tex. Crim. App. 1993).

Substance exceptions to charging instruments must be raised before trial or the accused forfeits his right to raise objections on appeal or by collateral attack. While omitting an element of an indictment is a defect of substance in an indictment, the instrument does not cease to be an indictment despite the omission of that element. Studer v. State, 799 S.W.2d 263 (Tex. Crim. App. 1990).

A defendant may not raise for the first time on appeal a facial challenge to the constitutionality of a statute. This must be done in the trial court. Karenev v. State, 281 S.W.3d 428 (Tex. Crim. App. 2009).

§12:93.3 Grounds for Challenge

§12:93.3.1 General Challenges

The Texas and United States Constitutions grant a criminal defendant the right to fair notice of the specific charged offense. To provide this fair notice, the charging instrument must convey sufficient information to allow the accused to prepare a defense. In most cases, a charging instrument that tracks the relevant statutory text will provide adequate notice to the accused. State v. Ross, 573 S.W.3d 817, 820 (Tex. Crim. App. 2019).

However, tracking the language of the statute may be insufficient if the statutory language is not completely descriptive of an offense. State v. Ross, 573 S.W.3d at 820.

For example, if the prohibited conduct is statutorily defined to include more than one manner or means of commission, then the State must, upon timely request, allege the particular manner or means it seeks to establish. State v. Ross, 573 S.W.3d at 820.

An indictment can be challenged on the ground that the underlying statute is unconstitutional by not giving fair notice to the defendant of what conduct is criminally prohibited; in other words, that the statute is vague. Bynum v. State, 767 S.W.2d 769 (Tex. Crim. App. 1989).

Indictments based on statutes that regulate speech can be challenged on the ground that the underlying statute is overbroad. Bynum.

Under the First Amendment, a statute may be subject to a facial challenge even though it may have some legitimate application, but absent the First Amendment, a facial challenge could be mounted successfully only if the statute were vague in all of its applications. Sanchez v. State, 995 S.W.2d 677 (Tex. Crim. App. 1999).

For example, a North Carolina statute making it a felony for a registered sex offender to gain access to a number of websites, including commonplace social media websites like Facebook and Twitter, was found to be an impermissible restriction of the First Amendment's Free Speech Clause, applicable to the States under the Due Process Clause of the Fourteenth Amendment. Packingham v. North Carolina, 582 U.S. ___, 137 S.Ct. 1730, 1737, 198 L.Ed.2d 273 (2017).

In situations where a law reaches a substantial amount of constitutionally protected conduct, a facial challenge can be made to the statute even when it conceivably could have some valid applications. State v. Markovich, 77 S.W.3d 274 (Tex. Crim. App. 2002).

To be vague in all of its applications, a statute must necessarily be vague as to the litigant. If the statute is not vague as to the litigant, a Due Process challenge must necessarily fail. A person who engages in some conduct that is clearly proscribed cannot complain of the vagueness of the law as applied to the conduct of others. Sanchez.

Whenever recklessness enters into or is a part

or element of any offense, or it is charged that the defendant acted recklessly in the commission of an offense, the charging instrument must allege, with reasonable certainty, the act or acts relied upon to constitute recklessness or it is subject to a pretrial motion to quash. Smith v. State, 309 S.W.3d 10 (Tex. Crim. App. 2010).

The explication of the act or acts constituting recklessness may be the same as those that constitute the prohibited conduct, but they may also require additional pleading. Smith (explaining that an information charging indecent exposure would require a further allegation that the actor's exposition was done in a reckless manner).

An indictment that fails to allege all of the elements of a statutory offense can be challenged by way of a motion to quash. Grant v. State, 970 S.W.2d 22 (Tex. Crim. App. 1998).

Where the state adds a paragraph to the indictment seeking to toll the statute of limitations, such language must be challenged pretrial via a motion to quash the indictment or a motion to dismiss. This challenge cannot be made in a pretrial writ of habeas corpus where the deficiencies in such allegations are reparable. Ex parte Smith, 178 S.W.3d 797 (Tex. Crim. App. 2005).

When an indictment shows on its face that prosecution is absolutely barred by the statute of limitations and that pleading is not reparable, a defendant may seek relief from further prosecution via a pretrial writ of habeas corpus. Ex parte Smith.

For offenses such as murder with no statute of limitations, a defendant may establish a Fifth Amendment due-process violation where a prosecution has been significantly delayed by proving both prejudice and that an intentional delay was designed to give the state a tactical advantage. State v. Krizan-Wilson, 354 S.W.3d 808 (Tex. Crim. App. 2011).

A defendant's "in pari materia" claim is generally not cognizable as a motion to quash because generally the indictment will be sufficient on its face. The claim is also not cognizable on a pretrial writ of habeas corpus. Ex parte Smith, 185 S.W.3d 887 (Tex. Crim. App. 2006).

An indictment will not be found insufficient and therefore be quashed pretrial on the basis of insufficient evidence to support it. State v. Rosenbaum, 910 S.W.2d 934 (Tex. Crim. App. 1994).

A decision to quash an indictment for lack of certainty in the indictment's allegations is within the sound discretion of the trial court. State v. Draper, 940 S.W.2d 824 (Tex.App.—Austin 1997, *no pet.*).

The sufficiency of a charging instrument presents a question of law. An appellate court therefore reviews a trial judge's ruling on a motion to quash de novo. State v. Ross, 573 S.W.3d at 820.

The trial court did not abuse its discretion in holding a pretrial evidentiary hearing on Hill's motion to dismiss alleging a prosecutorial misconduct and vindictive prosecution. Under the plain language of Article 28.01, the trial court judge had the discretion to hold an evidentiary hearing on Hill's motion to quash and dismiss. State of Texas v. Hill, 499 S.W.3d 853 (Tex. Crim. App. 2016).

§12:93.3.2 Constitutional Challenges

§12:93.3.2.1 Overbreadth Challenges

The First Amendment provides in relevant part that "Congress shall make no law ... abridging the freedom of speech." U.S. Const. amend. I. As a general matter, the First Amendment means that government has no power to restrict expression because of its message, its ideas, its subject matter, or its content. Ashcroft v. Am. Civil Liberties Union, 535 U.S. 564, 573, 122 S.Ct. 1700, 152 L.Ed.2d 771 (2002); Wagner v. State, 539 S.W.3d 298, 310 (Tex. Crim. App. 2017).

Ordinarily, a facial challenge to the constitutionality of a statute can succeed only when it is shown that the statute is unconstitutional in all of its applications. State v. Johnson, 475 S.W.3d 860, 864 (Tex. Crim. App. 2015); Wagner v. State, 539 S.W.3d at 310.

The First Amendment overbreadth doctrine provides an exception to this rule, whereby a litigant may succeed in challenging a law that regulates speech if a substantial number of its applications are unconstitutional, judged in relation to the statute's plainly legitimate sweep. Wash. State Grange v. Wash. State Republican Party, 552 U.S. 442, 449 n.6, 128 S.Ct. 1184, 170 L.Ed.2d 151 (2008); Wagner v. State, 539 S.W.3d at 310.

Thus, the overbreadth doctrine prohibits the government from banning unprotected speech if a substantial amount of protected speech is prohibited or chilled in the process. Ashcroft v. Free Speech Coalition, 535 U.S. 234, 255, 122 S.Ct. 1389, 152 L.Ed.2d 403 (2002); Wagner v. State, 539 S.W.3d at 310.

The overbreadth doctrine is "strong medicine" to be employed with hesitation and only as a last resort. Ex parte Thompson, 442 S.W.3d 325, 349 (Tex. Crim. App. 2014); Wagner v. State, 539 S.W.3d at 310.

Penal Code Section 25.07(a)(2)(A) does not reach a substantial amount of constitutionally protected conduct, judged in relation to its plainly legitimate sweep. Wagner v. State, 539 S.W.3d at 310.

§12:93.3.2.2Vagueness Challenges

To pass constitutional muster, a law that imposes criminal liability must be sufficiently clear (1) to give a person of ordinary intelligence a reasonable opportunity to know what is prohibited and (2) to establish determinate guidelines for law enforcement. State v. Doyal, ___ S.W.3d ___ at *5 (PD-0254-18, 2019 WL 944022, February 27, 2019) (where the court concluded that § 551.143 of the Texas open meetings act is unconstitutionally vague on its face).

What renders a statute vague is the indeterminacy of precisely what the prohibited conduct is. State v. Doyal, ___ S.W.3d at *5.

It is a basic principle of due process that an enactment is void for vagueness if its prohibitions are not clearly defined. Grayned v. City of Rockford, 408 U.S. 104, 108–09, 92 S.Ct. 2294, 33 L.Ed.2d 222 (1972); Wagner v. State, 539 S.W.3d 298, 313 (Tex. Crim. App. 2017).

A statute which uses an undefined term of indeterminate or variable meaning requires more specific pleading in order to notify the defendant of the nature of the charges against him. State v. Ross, 573 S.W.3d 817, 820 (Tex. Crim. App. 2019).

A conviction fails to comport with due process if the statute under which it is obtained fails to provide a person of ordinary intelligence fair notice of what is prohibited, or is so standardless that it authorizes or encourages seriously discriminatory enforcement. United States v. Williams, 553 U.S. 285, 304, 128 S.Ct. 1830, 170 L.Ed.2d 650 (2008); Wagner v. State, 539 S.W.3d at 313.

Where a statute abuts upon sensitive areas of First Amendment freedoms, the doctrine of vagueness demands a greater degree of specificity than in other contexts. Long v. State, 931 S.W.2d 285, 287–88 (Tex. Crim. App. 1996); Wagner v. State, 539 S.W.3d at 313.

Greater specificity is required to preserve adequately the right of free expression because uncertain meanings inevitably lead citizens to steer far wider of the unlawful zone than if the boundaries of the forbidden areas were clearly marked. Long v. State, 931 S.W.2d at 288; Wagner v. State, 539 S.W.3d at 313-4.

But perfect clarity and precise guidance have never been required, even of regulations that restrict expressive activity. Holder v. Humanitarian Law Project, 561 U.S. 1, 19, 130 S.Ct. 2705, 177 L.Ed.2d 355 (2010); Wagner v. State, 539 S.W.3d at 314.

A statute is not unconstitutionally vague merely because the words or terms used are not specifically defined. Bynum v. State, 767 S.W.2d 769, 774 (Tex. Crim. App. 1989); see also State v. Holcombe, 187 S.W.3d 496, 499 (Tex. Crim. App. 2006); Wagner v. State, 539 S.W.3d at 314.

Rather, the words or phrase must be read in the context in which they are used, and ordinarily the statute must then be construed according to the rules of grammar and common usage. Bynum, 767 S.W.2d at 774; Wagner v. State, 539 S.W.3d at 314.

A statute satisfies vagueness requirements if the statutory language conveys sufficiently definite warning as to the proscribed conduct when measured by common understanding and practices. Jordan v. De George, 341 U.S. 223, 231–32, 71 S.Ct. 703, 95 L.Ed. 886 (1951); Wagner v. State, 539 S.W.3d at 314.

In general, in addressing a vagueness challenge, we will consider whether the statute is vague as applied to a defendant's conduct before considering whether the statute may be vague as applied to the conduct of others. Vill. of Hoffman Estates v. Flipside, Hoffman Estates, Inc., 455 U.S. 489, 495, 102 S.Ct. 1186, 71 L.Ed.2d 362 (1982); Wagner v. State, 539 S.W.3d at 314.

A plaintiff who engages in some conduct that is clearly proscribed cannot complain of the vagueness of the law as applied to the conduct of others. A court should therefore examine the complainant's conduct before analyzing other hypothetical applications of the law. Vill. of Hoffman Estates, 455 U.S. at 495, 102 S.Ct. 1186; Wagner v. State, 539 S.W.3d at 314.

In the context of a challenge to a statute that does not regulate protected speech, a court should uphold a vagueness challenge only if the statute is impermissibly vague in all of its applications. Vill. of Hoffman Estates, 455 U.S. at 494-5, 102 S.Ct. 1186; Wagner v. State, 539 S.W.3d at 314.

Applying the plain language of Section 25.07(a)(2)(A) to the facts of this case, we conclude that the statutory language is sufficiently clear to provide a person of ordinary intelligence a reasonable opportunity to know that appellant's course of conduct would be prohibited. Wagner v. State, 539 S.W.3d at 314.

More clarity is required of a criminal law when that law implicates First Amendment freedoms. State v. Doyal, ___ S.W.3d at *3.

The First Amendment is implicated when the government seeks to impose criminal sanctions on an elected official for communications made in his official capacity. State v. Doyal, ___ S.W.3d at *3.

A facial vagueness challenge to a statute that implicates First Amendment freedoms does not require a showing that there are no possible instances of conduct clearly falling within the statute's prohibitions. State v. Doyal, ___ S.W.3d at *4.

§12:93.4 Defendant's Burden

The defendant generally has the burden of proof on a motion to quash an indictment. Wheat v. State, 537 S.W.2d 20 (Tex. Crim. App. 1976); Farrar v. State, 95 S.W.3d 648 (Tex.App.—Eastland 2002, *no pet.*).

Where the defendant is challenging the constitutionality of a statute his burden is to show beyond a reasonable doubt that the statute is unconstitutional. Luquis v. State, 72 S.W.3d 355 (Tex. Crim. App. 2002).

In most instances, a defendant must make a pretrial objection to a substance defect in the information or indictment (usually by a motion to quash) or forfeit the right to complain about it on appeal. Smith v. State, 309 S.W.3d 10 (Tex. Crim. App. 2010).

The sufficiency of a charging instrument presents a question of law, the trial court's ruling on which is reviewed *de novo* by an appeals court. Smith.

§12:93.5 Form: Motions

See our companion book *Texas Criminal Forms* (James Publishing):

- Form 12-3, Motion to Quash Indictment.
- Form 12-4, Motion to Quash Indictment (Lack of Specificity of Deadly Weapon Allegation).

§12:94 Amendments to the Charging Instrument

§12:94.1 Statutes

CCP Art. 28.10. Amendment of Indictment or Information

(a) After notice to the defendant, a matter of form or substance in an indictment or information may be amended at any time before the date the trial on the merits commences. On the request of the defendant, the court shall allow the defendant not less than 10 days, or a shorter period if requested by the defendant, to respond to the amended indictment or information.

(b) A matter of form or substance in an indictment or information may also be amended after the trial on the merits commences if the defendant does not object.

(c) An indictment or information may not be amended over the defendant's objection as to form or substance if the amended indictment or information charges the defendant with an additional or different offense or if the substantial rights of the defendant are prejudiced.

CCP Art. 28.11. How Amended

All amendments of an indictment or information shall be made with the leave of the court and under its direction.

§12:94.2 What Is an Amendment

An amendment is an alteration to the face of the charging instrument which affects the substance of the charging instrument. Eastep v. State, 941 S.W.2d 130 (Tex. Crim. App. 1997) *overruled on other grounds in part by* Gollihar v. State, 46 S.W.3d 243 (Tex. Crim. App. 2001), *and* Riney v. State, 28 S.W.3d 561 (Tex. Crim. App. 2000).

The alteration of a cause number in an enhancement paragraph is an amendment. Sodipo v. State, 815 S.W.2d 551 (Tex. Crim. App. 1990); Eastep.

The alteration of a weapon in an aggravated assault indictment is an amendment. Hillin v. State, 808 S.W.2d 486 (Tex. Crim. App.1991); Eastep.

The addition of the manner and means of committing an offense is an amendment. Beebe v. State, 811 S.W.2d 604 (Tex. Crim. App.1991); Eastep.

The alteration of the alleged date is an amendment. Garcia v. State, 928 S.W.2d 666 (Tex. App.— Corpus Christi 1996, *no pet.*); Eastep.

The addition of a complainant is an amendment. McCoy v. State, 889 S.W.2d 354 (Tex.App.— Houston [14th Dist.] 1994, pet. ref'd); Eastep.

The alteration of the indictment from "two facsimile machines" to "one facsimile machine" is an amendment. Hilton v. State, 879 S.W.2d 74 (Tex.App.—Houston [14th Dist.] 1994, pet. ref'd); Eastep.

Deleting "delivery" and replacing it with "possession" is an amendment. Hinojosa v. State, 875 S.W.2d 339 (Tex.App.—Corpus Christi 1994, *no pet.*); Eastep.

A change of a name in an indictment pursuant to Art. 26.08 is not an amendment to that indictment under Art. 28.10. Kelley v. State, 823 S.W.2d 300 (Tex. Crim. App. 1992); Wynn v. State, 864 S.W.2d 539 (Tex. Crim. App. 1993).

However, the complete failure to allege the name of the defendant in the indictment renders that instrument not a valid charging instrument. Cook v. State, 902 S.W.2d 471 (Tex. Crim. App. 1995).

Alterations made solely to a separate written confession document are not sufficient to constitute an amendment to the indictment. Puente v. State, 320 S.W.3d 352 (Tex. Crim. App. 2010).

Because punishment enhancement allegations are not required to be plead in the indictment, the addition of an enhancement allegation by written motion does not constitute an amendment to the indictment. Brooks v. State, 957 S.W.2d 30 (Tex. Crim. App. 1997).

There are three situations where an alteration to the face of a charging instrument does not affect its substance, and, is therefore, an abandonment: (1) when it abandons one or more of the alternative means of committing an offense; (2) when it has the effect of reducing the prosecution to a lesser included offense; and (3) when it omits surplusage. Eastep.

Surplusage is unnecessary language not legally essential to constitute the offense alleged in the indictment. Eastep.

§12:94.3 Motion Must Be Filed Before Trial Date

A motion to amend a charging instrument must be made before the date that the trial commences. Sodipo v. State, 815 S.W.2d 551 (Tex. Crim. App. 1990).

Where an indictment is amended over the defendant's objection, the defendant is entitled to a 10-day continuance to prepare for trial. Rent v. State, 838 S.W.2d 548 (Tex. Crim. App. 1992).

Violations of Art. 28.10 are not subject to harm analysis. Brown v. State, 828 S.W.2d 762 (Tex. Crim. App. 1991); Eastep v. State, 941 S.W.2d 130 (Tex. Crim. App. 1997) *overruled on other grounds in part by* Gollihar v. State, 46 S.W.3d 243 (Tex. Crim. App. 2001), *and* Riney v. State, 28 S.W.3d 561 (Tex. Crim. App. 2000).

§12:94.4 Procedure to Amend

The mere granting of a motion to amend a charging instrument is not legally sufficient to constitute a valid amendment. Ward v. State, 829 S.W.2d 787 (Tex. Crim. App. 1992).

One way of validly amending a charging instrument is for the trial court to physically alter the indictment to reflect the amendment. Ward.

Another way to accomplish the amendment is for the prosecution to submit a photocopy of the original charging instrument that contains the amendment for the record. Riney v. State, 28 S.W.3d 561 (Tex. Crim. App. 2000); Perez v. State, 429 S.W.3d 639, 643 (Tex. Crim. App. 2014).

§12:94.5 Form: Motion to Amend

See our companion book *Texas Criminal Forms* (James Publishing):

- Form 12-6, Motion to Amend Indictment.

§12:95 Dismissal of Charging Instrument With Prejudice

A trial court has the power to dismiss a case without the state's consent when a defendant has been denied a right to a speedy trial, when there is a defect in the charging instrument, or pursuant to Art. 32.01, where a defendant is detained and no charging instrument is properly presented. State v. Johnson, 821 S.W.2d 609 (Tex. Crim. App. 1991).

Additionally, a charging instrument may be dismissed to remedy a violation of the Sixth Amendment right to counsel. State v. Frye, 897 S.W.2d 324 (Tex. Crim. App. 1995).

While a trial court may dismiss a charging instrument to remedy a constitutional violation, the dismissal of an indictment is a drastic measure only to be used in the most extraordinary circumstances. Frye.

Although a particular constitutional violation has not yet been recognized as a basis for a trial court to dismiss a charging instrument, this does not preclude a trial court from having authority to dismiss on that ground. State v. Terrazas, 962 S.W.2d 38 (Tex. Crim. App. 1998).

Where there is no constitutional violation, or where the defendant's rights were violated but dismissal of the indictment was not necessary to neutralize the taint of the unconstitutional action, the trial court abuses its discretion in dismissing the charging instrument without the consent of the state. Terrazas.

A trial court abuses its discretion in dismissing a charging instrument without the consent of the state to protect a defendant from retaliation in prison where no constitutional violation has occurred. State v. Mungia, 119 S.W.3d 814 (Tex. Crim. App. 2003).

§12:100 Statute of Limitations

§12:101 Statutes

Tex. Code Crim. Pro. Art. 12.01. Felonies

> *Except as provided in Article 12.03, felony indictments may be presented within these limits, and not afterward:*
>
> *(1) no limitation:*
>
> *(A) murder and manslaughter;*
>
> *(B) sexual assault under Section 22.011(a)(2), Penal Code, or aggravated sexual assault under Section 22.021(a)(1)(B), Penal Code;*
>
> *(C) sexual assault, if (i) during the investigation of the offense biological matter is collected and subjected to forensic DNA testing and the testing results show that the matter does not match the victim or any other person whose identity is readily ascertained; or (ii) probable cause exists to believe that the defendant has committed the same or similar sexual offense against five or more victims;*
>
> *(D) continuous sexual abuse of young child or children under Section 21.02, Penal Code;*
>
> *(E) indecency with a child under Section 21.11, Penal Code; or*
>
> *(F) an offense involving leaving the scene of an accident under Section 550.021, Transportation Code, if the accident resulted in the death of a person;*

(2) ten years from the date of the commission of the offense:

(A) theft of any estate, real, personal or mixed, by an executor, administrator, guardian or trustee, with intent to defraud any creditor, heir, legatee, ward, distributee, beneficiary or settlor of a trust interested in such estate;

(B) theft by a public servant of government property over which he exercises control in his official capacity;

(C) forgery or the uttering, using or passing of forged instruments;

(D) injury to an elderly or disabled individual punishable as a felony of the first degree under Section 22.04, Penal Code;

(E) sexual assault, except as provided by Subdivision (1); or

(F) arson;

(3) seven years from the date of the commission of the offense:

(A) misapplication of fiduciary property or property of a financial institution;

(B) securing execution of document by deception;

(C) a felony violation under Chapter 162, Tax Code;

(D) false statement to obtain property or credit under Section 32.32, Penal Code;

(E) money laundering;

(F) credit card or debit card abuse under Section 32.31, Penal Code; or

(G) fraudulent use or possession of identifying information under Section 32.51, Penal Code;

(4) five years from the date of the commission of the offense:

(A) theft or robbery;

(B) except as provided by Subdivision (5), kidnapping or burglary;

(C) injury to an elderly or disabled individual that is not punishable as a felony of the first degree under Section 22.04, Penal Code;

(D) abandoning or endangering a child; or

(E) insurance fraud;

(5) if the investigation of the offense shows that the victim is younger than 17 years of age at the time the offense is committed, 20 years from the 18th birthday of the victim of one of the following offenses:

(A) sexual performance by a child under Section 43.25, Penal Code;

(B) aggravated kidnapping under Section 20.04(a)(4), Penal Code, if the defendant committed the offense with the intent to violate or abuse the victim sexually; or

(C) burglary under Section 30.02, Penal Code, if the offense is punishable under Subsection (d) of that section and the defendant committed the offense with the intent to commit an offense described by Subdivision (1)(B) or (D) of this article or Paragraph (B) of this subdivision;

(6) ten years from the 18th birthday of the victim of the offense:

injury to a child under Section 22.04, Penal Code; or

(7) three years from the date of the commission of the offense: all other felonies.

CCP Art. 12.02. Misdemeanors

An indictment or information for any misdemeanor may be presented within two years from the date of the commission of the offense, and not afterward.

CCP Art. 12.03. Aggravated Offenses, Attempt, Conspiracy, Solicitation, Organized Criminal Activity

(a) The limitation period for criminal attempt is the same as that of the offense attempted.

(b) The limitation period for criminal conspiracy or organized criminal activity is the same as that of the most serious offense that is the object of the conspiracy or the organized criminal activity.

(c) The limitation period for criminal solicitation is the same as that of the felony solicited.

(d) Except as otherwise provided by this chapter, any offense that bears the title "aggravated" shall carry the same limitation period as the primary crime.

CCP Art. 12.04. Computation

The day on which the offense was committed and the day on which the indictment or information is presented shall be excluded from the computation of time.

CCP Art. 12.05. Absence From State and Time of Pendency of Indictment, etc., Not Computed

(a) The time during which the accused is absent from the state shall not be computed in the period of limitation;

(b) The time during the pendency of an indictment, information, or complaint shall not be computed in the period of limitation;

(c) The term "during the pendency," as used herein, means that period of time beginning with the day the indictment, information, or complaint is filed in a court of competent jurisdiction, and ending with the day such accusation is, by an order of a trial court having jurisdiction thereof, determined to be invalid for any reason.

CCP Art. 27.08. Exception to Substance of Indictment

There is no exception to the substance of an indictment or information except:

(1) That it does not appear therefrom that an offense against the law was committed by the defendant;

(2) That it appears from the face thereof that a prosecution for the offense is barred by a lapse of time, or that the offense was committed after the finding of the indictment;

(3) That it contains matter which is a legal defense or bar to the prosecution; and (4) That it shows upon its face that the court trying the case has no jurisdiction thereof.

§12:102 Purpose of the Statute of Limitations

The statute of limitations is an act of grace for the benefit of potential defendants, a voluntary surrendering by the people of their right to prosecute. Proctor v. State, 967 S.W.2d 840 (Tex. Crim. App. 1998).

This act of grace serves several objectives:

(1) it protects defendants from having to defend themselves against charges when the basic facts may—or may not—have become obscured by time; (2) it prevents prosecution of those who have been law-abiding for some years; and (3) it lessens the possibility of blackmail. Proctor.

§12:103 Computing the Limitations Period

The period of limitation for presentment of charging instruments begins with the day of commission of the offense and runs to the limits in terms of years respectively prescribed in Arts. 12.01, 12.02 and 12.03. Ex parte Matthews, 933 S.W.2d 134 (Tex. Crim. App. 1996).

For a single offense of aggregate theft, which is the combination of multiple offenses of theft arising from one scheme or continuing course of conduct, the statute of limitations does not begin to run until the date of the commission of the final incident of theft. King v. State, 17 S.W.3d 7 (Tex. App.—Houston [14th Dist.] 2000, *pet. ref'd*).

The statute of limitations for aggravated assault is governed by Tex. Code Crim. Pro. art. 12.03(d), not Article 12.01(7); thus the limitation period is the two year period of the primary crime of misdemeanor assault. The lesser-included offense with the greater limitation period does not control when the lesser-included offenses of the aggravated assault include both misdemeanor assault and a felony. State v. Schunior, 506 S.W.3d 29, 37 (Tex. Crim. App. 2016).

§12:104 Asserting the Statute of Limitations

Statute-of-limitations defenses that are based on facts (challenging a pleading that includes a tolling paragraph, explanatory averments, or even innuendo allegations, that suffice to show that the charged offense is not, at least on the face of the indictment, barred by limitations), are waived if not presented at or before the guilt phase of the trial, and cannot be presented in a pretrial writ. Phillips v. State, 362 S.W.3d 606 (Tex. Crim. App. 2011) (overruled on other grounds by Ex parte Heilman, 456 S.W.3d 159 (Tex. Crim. App. 2015)), *citing* Proctor v. State, 967 S.W.2d 840 (Tex. Crim. App. 1998).

Appeals courts will no longer unquestioningly distinguish between factual and pure-law limitations defenses. Instead, in circumstances lacking any legislative ex post facto violation—and especially when that occurs in the context of a good-faith, arm's length plea agreement—both are Marin category-three forfeitable rights, as under Proctor v. State. Ex parte Heilman, 456 S.W.3d 159 (Tex. Crim. App. 2015).

For offenses such as murder with no statute of limitations, a defendant may establish a Fifth Amendment due-process violation where a prosecution has been significantly delayed by proving both prejudice and that an intentional delay was designed to give the state a tactical advantage. State v. Krizan-Wilson, 354 S.W.3d 808 (Tex. Crim. App. 2011).

§12:104.1 Pretrial Procedure

Before trial, a defendant may assert the statute of limitations defense by filing a motion to dismiss under CCP Art. 27.08(2). Proctor v. State, 967 S.W.2d 840 (Tex. Crim. App. 1998).

The denial of a pretrial motion to dismiss on limitations grounds is not a final judgment from which an interlocutory appeal may be taken. Ahmad v. State, 158 S.W.3d 525 (Tex.App.—Fort Worth 2005, pet. ref'd).

If the state's pleading, on its face, shows that the offense charged is barred by limitations, then the defendant may challenge it by filing for habeas corpus relief. Ex parte Tamez, 38 S.W.3d 159 (Tex. Crim. App. 2001).

Denial of a pretrial writ of habeas corpus making the same ground would be appealable on an interlocutory basis. Ex parte Tamez.

§12:104.2 Procedure During Trial

At trial, the defendant may assert the defense by requesting a jury instruction on limitations if there is some evidence before the jury, from any source, that the prosecution is limitations-barred. If there is some such evidence and the defendant requests a jury instruction on the limitations defense, then the state must prove beyond a reasonable doubt that the prosecution is not limitations-barred. Proctor v. State, 967 S.W.2d 840 (Tex. Crim. App. 1998).

§12:105 Tolling Provisions

There are exceptions to the statute of limitations. One is that the time during the pendency of an indictment, information, or complaint shall not be computed in the period of limitation where the defendant was under indictment for the same conduct, same act, or same transaction. Hernandez v. State, 127 S.W.3d 768 (Tex. Crim. App. 2004); Ex parte Smith, 178 S.W.3d 797 (Tex. Crim. App. 2005).

The tolling provisions of Art. 12.05 operate as a constraint on the limitations defense. White v. State, 50 S.W.3d 31 (Tex.App.—Waco 2001, *pet. ref'd).*

A first indictment tolls the statute of limitations where both the first and subsequent indictments allege the same conduct, act or transaction, even where the offenses alleged are not contained in the same statute. Hernandez v. State, 127 S.W.3d 768 (Tex. Crim. App. 2004); Marks v. State, 560 S.W.3d 169, 170 (Tex. Crim. App. 2018).

However, a subsequent indictment is barred by the statute of limitations if it broadens or substantially amends the charges in the original indictment. Hernandez.

An information is sufficient to toll limitations in a felony case. Ex parte Ulloa, 514 S.W.3d 756, 760 (Tex. Crim. App. 2017).

If a previous indictment or other facts would toll the statute of limitations, the state must plead those facts in the indictment (or subsequent indictment) or the indictment is subject to a defense motion to dismiss. Tita v. State, 267 S.W.3d 33 (Tex. Crim. App. 2008).

A tolling paragraph need not be alleged with the same degree of particularity as we would expect of an allegation of the charged offense. Ex parte Smith; Freda v. State, 704 S.W.2d 41 (Tex. Crim. App. 1986).

Any purported defects of form and substance in the tolling paragraph relate to notice and must be brought to the trial court's attention before trial or they are waived under CCP Art. 1.14(b). They may and must be raised in a motion to quash or motion to dismiss the pleading. Ex parte Smith.

Purported defects in a tolling paragraph are forfeited unless raised in a pretrial motion to quash or dismiss, and such defects may not be raised in a pretrial writ because they do not deprive the trial court of its jurisdiction. Only when an indictment shows on its face that prosecution is absolutely barred by the statute of limitations and that pleading is not reparable, may a defendant seek relief from further prosecution via a pretrial writ of habeas corpus. Ex parte Smith.

A harm analysis under TRAP 44.2(b) is necessary when a trial court fails to grant a motion to quash an indictment that does not toll the statute of limitations. Mercier v. State, 322 S.W.3d 258 (Tex. Crim. App. 2010).

Before the court can charge the jury on the tolling provisions of CCP Art. 12.05, the record must contain sufficient evidence that a former indictment, information or complaint was pending in a court of competent jurisdiction for a sufficient length of time as to make the present charging instrument timely. White.

Presentment of an information charging official oppression vests a district court with jurisdiction over the offense and the defendant, making it a court of competent jurisdiction. State v. Drummond, 501 S.W.3d 78, 84 (Tex. Crim. App. 2016).

§12:106 Form: Motions Based on Statute of Limitations

See our companion book *Texas Criminal Forms* (James Publishing):

- Form 15-13.1, Motion to Dismiss Under Statute of Limitations.
- Form 15-13.2, Petition for Writ of Habeas Corpus Under Statute of Limitations.
- Form 15-14, Motion to Quash and Dismiss Indictment (Insufficient Tolling Allegation).
- Form 12-5, Brief in Support of Motion to Quash Indictment Based on Statute of Limitations.

§12:110 Identification Evidence

§12:111 Statutory Law

Tex. Code Crim. Pro. Art. 2.1386. Eyewitness identification protocols

(a) In this article, "law enforcement agency" means an agency of the state or an agency of a political subdivision of the state authorized by law to employ peace officers.

(b) The Texas Commission on Law Enforcement shall establish a comprehensive education and training program on eyewitness identification, including material regarding variables that affect a witness's vision and memory, practices for minimizing contamination, and effective eyewitness identification protocols.

(c) Each law enforcement agency shall require each peace officer who is employed by the agency and who performs eyewitness identification procedures to complete the education and training described by Subsection (b).

(Note: This requirement is satisfied by completion of Texas Commission on Law Enforcement (TCOLE) course number 3286).

Tex. Code Crim. Pro. Art. 38.20. PHOTOGRAPH AND LIVE LINEUP IDENTIFICATION PROCEDURES

Sec. 1. In this article, "institute" means the Bill Blackwood Law Enforcement Management Institute of Texas located at Sam Houston State University.

Sec. 2. This article applies only to a law enforcement agency of this state or of a county, municipality, or other political subdivision of this state that employs peace officers who conduct photograph or live lineup identification procedures in the routine performance of the officers' official duties.

Sec. 3. (a) Each law enforcement agency shall adopt, implement, and as necessary amend a detailed written policy regarding the administration of photograph and live lineup identification procedures in accordance with this article. A law enforcement agency may adopt:

(1) the model policy adopted under Subsection (b); or

(2) the agency's own policy that, at a minimum, conforms to the requirements of Subsection (c).

(b) The institute, in consultation with large, medium, and small law enforcement agencies and with law enforcement associations, scientific experts in eyewitness memory research, and appropriate organizations engaged in the development of law enforcement policy, shall develop, adopt, and disseminate to all law enforcement agencies in this state a model policy and associated training materials regarding the administration of photograph and live lineup identification procedures. The institute shall provide for a period of public comment before adopting the policy and materials.

(c) The model policy or any other policy adopted by a law enforcement agency under Subsection (a) must:

(1) be based on:

(A) credible field, academic, or laboratory research on eyewitness memory;

(B) relevant policies, guidelines, and best practices designed to reduce erroneous eyewitness identifications and to enhance the reliability and objectivity of eyewitness identifications; and

(C) other relevant information as appropriate; and

(2) address the following topics:

(A) the selection of photograph and live lineup filler photographs or participants;

(B) instructions given to a witness before conducting a photograph or live lineup identification procedure;

(C) the documentation and preservation of results of a photograph or live lineup identification procedure, including the documentation of witness statements, regardless of the outcome of the procedure;

(D) procedures for administering a photograph or live lineup identification procedure to an illiterate person or a person with limited English language proficiency;

(E) for a live lineup identification procedure, if practicable, procedures for assigning an administrator who is unaware of which member of the live lineup is the suspect in the case or alternative procedures designed to prevent opportunities to influence the witness;

(F) for a photograph identification procedure, procedures for assigning an administrator who is capable of administering a photograph array in a blind manner or in a manner consistent with other proven or supported best practices designed to prevent opportunities to influence the witness; and

(G) any other procedures or best practices supported by credible research or commonly accepted as a means to reduce erroneous eyewitness identifications and to enhance the objectivity and reliability of eyewitness identifications.

Sec. 4. (a) Not later than December 31 of each odd-numbered year, the institute shall review the model policy and training materials adopted under this article and shall modify the policy and materials as appropriate.

(b) Not later than September 1 of each even-numbered year, each law enforcement agency shall review its policy adopted under this article and shall modify that policy as appropriate.

Sec. 5. (a) Any evidence or expert testimony presented by the state or the defendant on the subject of eyewitness identification is admissible only subject to compliance with the Texas Rules of Evidence. Evidence of compliance with the model policy or any other policy adopted under this article or with the minimum requirements of this article is not a condition precedent to the admissibility of an out-of-court eyewitness identification.

(b) Notwithstanding Article 38.23 as that article relates to a violation of a state statute, a failure to conduct a photograph or live lineup identification procedure in substantial compliance with the model policy or any other policy adopted under this article or with the minimum requirements of this article does not bar the admission of eyewitness identification testimony in the courts of this state.

§12:112 General Points

An in-court identification is inadmissible when it has been tainted by an impermissibly suggestive pretrial identification procedure. Ibarra v. State, 11 S.W.3d 189 (Tex. Crim. App. 1999).

The test is whether, considering the totality of the circumstances, the identification procedure was so impermissibly suggestive as to give rise to a very substantial likelihood of irreparable misidentification. Simmons v. United States, 390 U.S. 377, 88 S.Ct. 967, 19 L.Ed.2d 1247 (1968); Loserth v. State, 963 S.W.2d 770 (Tex. Crim. App. 1998).

A pretrial identification procedure may be so suggestive and conducive to mistaken identification that subsequent use of that identification at trial would deny the accused due process of law. Brown v. State, 64 S.W.3d 94 (Tex.App.—Austin 2001, *no pet.*); Webb v. State, 760 S.W.2d 263 (Tex. Crim. App. 1988).

There is a Sixth Amendment right to counsel at a post-indictment identification procedure. Kirby v. Illinois, 406 U.S. 682, 92 S.Ct. 1877, 32 L.Ed.2d 411 (1972).

However, the right to counsel does not attach where the lineup was prior to indictment or other initiation of adversary judicial proceedings. *See* U.S. v. Gouveia, 467 U.S. 180, 81 L.Ed.2d 146, fn 5; Winn v. State, 503 S.W.2d 816 (Tex. Crim. App. 1974).

Aside from any question of right to counsel, it is recognized that some identification procedures conducted prior to trial may be so unnecessarily suggestive and conducive to irreparable mistaken identification as to deny due process of law. Stovall v. Denno, 388 U.S. 293, 18 L.Ed.2d 1199, 87 S.Ct. 1967 (1967).

Under Rule 801(e)(1)(c), bolstering is no longer a valid objection to testimony about identification made by another witness who testifies and is subject to cross-examination regarding her pretrial identifications. Smith v. State, 830 S.W.2d 328 (Tex.App.—Houston [14th Dist.] 1992, *no pet.*).

The Due Process Clause does not require a preliminary judicial inquiry into the reliability of an eyewitness identification when the identification was not procured under unnecessarily suggestive circumstances arranged by law enforcement. Perry v. New Hampshire, 565 U.S. ___, 132 S.Ct. 716, 181 L.Ed.2d 694 (2012).

§12:113 Reliability of Pretrial Identification Procedures

If the totality of the circumstances reveals no substantial likelihood of misidentification despite a suggestive pretrial procedure, subsequent identification testimony will be deemed reliable, reliability being the linchpin in determining the admissibility of identification testimony. Ibarra v. State, 11 S.W.3d 189 (Tex. Crim. App. 1999); Webb v. State, 760 S.W.2d 263 (Tex. Crim. App. 1988).

Suggestiveness may be created by the manner in which the pretrial identification procedure is conducted, for example, by police pointing out the suspect or suggesting that a suspect is included in the line-up or photo array. Ibarra; Barley v. State, 906 S.W.2d 27 (Tex. Crim. App. 1995).

Testimony is reliable if the totality of the circumstances reveals no substantial likelihood of misidentification despite a suggestive pretrial procedure. Brown v. State, 64 S.W.3d 94 (Tex. App.—Austin 2001, *no pet.*); Simmons v. United States, 390 U.S. 377, 384, 88 S.Ct. 967, 19 L.Ed.2d 1247 (1968).

The in-court identification testimony is admissible if the witness' ability to identify has an origin independent from the pretrial identification procedure. McFarland v. State, 928 S.W.2d 482 (Tex. Crim. App. 1996).

There are five non-exclusive factors used to assess the reliability of an identification procedure: (1) the opportunity of the witness to view the criminal at the time of the crime; (2) the witness' degree of attention; (3) the accuracy of the witness' prior description of the criminal; (4) the level of certainty demonstrated by the witness at the confrontation; and (5) the length of time between the crime and the confrontation. Loserth v. State, 963 S.W.2d 770 (Tex. Crim. App. 1998); Neil v. Biggers, 409 U.S. 188, 93 S.Ct. 375, 34 L.Ed.2d 401 (1972).

§12:114 Show-Up Identifications

The admission of evidence of a single suspect show-up identification without more does not violate due process. Garza v. State, 633 S.W.2d 508 (Tex. Crim. App. 1982); Neil v. Biggers, 409 U.S. 188, 93 S.Ct. 375, 34 L.Ed.2d 401 (1972).

Some suggestiveness is always present in a show-up identification and is balanced against: 1) the desirability of allowing the witness to view the suspect immediately after the commission of the offense while his memory is fresh and accurate; 2) the fact that the quick confirmation or denial of identification leads to the release of innocent suspects; and 3) the fact that the release of innocent suspects frees the police to continue the search for the perpetrator of the offense. Louis v. State, 825 S.W.2d 752 (Tex.App.—Houston [14th Dist.] 1992, *pet. ref'd*).

The pretrial procedure must be unnecessarily

suggestive and conducive to irreparable mistaken identification before it is objectionable. Garza.

Show-up identification procedures are analyzed under the totality of the circumstances. Garza; Louis.

The totality of the circumstances is analyzed using the following factors: (1) the opportunity to view; (2) the degree of attention; (3) the accuracy of the description; (4) the witness' level of certainty; and (5) the time between the crime and the confrontation. Garza; Louis.

§12:115 Photospread Identification Procedures

An in-court identification is inadmissible when it has been tainted by an impermissibly-suggestive pretrial photographic identification. Ibarra v. State, 11 S.W.3d 189 (Tex. Crim. App. 1999); Simmons v. United States, 390 U.S. 377, 88 S.Ct. 967, 19 L.Ed.2d 1247 (1968).

The test is whether, considering the totality of the circumstances, the photographic identification procedure was so impermissibly suggestive as to give rise to a very substantial likelihood of irreparable misidentification. Ibarra; Simmons.

Under the totality of the circumstances test, any suggestive conduct by law enforcement is weighed against evidence of the reliability of the photospread identification procedure. Luna v. State, 268 S.W.3d 594 (Tex. Crim. App. 2008).

Suggestiveness may be created by the manner in which the pretrial identification procedure is conducted, for example by police pointing out the suspect or suggesting that a suspect is included in the line-up or photo array. Barley v. State, 906 S.W.2d 27 (Tex. Crim. App. 1995); Rogers v. State, 774 S.W.2d 247 (Tex. Crim. App. 1989).

Suggestiveness may also arise where the witness is shown additional photographs or video of the defendant after an initial identification. Santos v. State, 116 S.W.3d 447 (Tex.App.—Houston [14th Dist.] 2003, pet. ref'd.).

Suggestiveness may also be created by the content of the line-up or photo array itself if the suspect is the only individual closely resembling the pre-procedure description. *See* Williams v. State, 675 S.W.2d 754 (Tex. Crim. App. 1984).

Furthermore, an individual procedure may be suggestive, or the cumulative effect of the procedures may be suggestive. Barley.

Every photographic lineup must contain individuals who fit the rough description of the suspect; however, it is not essential that all individuals be identical. Brown v. State, 64 S.W.3d 94 (Tex.App.—Austin 2001, *no pet.*)

There are numerous examples of what does and does not constitute impermissible suggestiveness. For example, a lineup that consists of five persons, two of whom have beards and are not physically close to the defendant in size and hair color, is not impermissibly suggestive. Turner v. State, 600 S.W.2d 927 (Tex. Crim. App. 1980); Brown.

The same holds true even if a defendant appears older than the other persons in the lineup. Williams v. State, 675 S.W.2d 754 (Tex. Crim. App. 1984); Brown.

A lineup is not impermissibly suggestive merely because the defendant is several inches taller than other persons in the lineup. Garcia v. State, 563 S.W.2d 925 (Tex. Crim. App. 1978).

On the other hand, a lineup will be impermissibly suggestive if the defendant was the only white male in the spread and the other pictures were of Mexican American males. Tapley v. State, 673 S.W.2d 284 (Tex.App.—San Antonio 1984, *pet. ref'd*); Brown.

Finally, the use of a lone photograph, without any of the traditional safeguards of a lineup, is inherently suspect. Loserth v. State, 985 S.W.2d 536 (Tex.App.—San Antonio 1998, *pet. ref'd*) (*op. on remand*); Brown.

§12:116 In-Court Identification Procedures

An in-court identification is inadmissible if it has been tainted by an impermissibly suggestive pretrial procedure. Ibarra v. State, 11 S.W.3d 189 (Tex. Crim. App. 1999).

The test is whether, considering the totality of the circumstances, the identification procedure was so impermissibly suggestive as to give rise to a very substantial likelihood of irreparable misidentification. Simmons v. United States, 390 U.S. 377, 88 S.Ct. 967, 19 L.Ed.2d 1247 (1968); Loserth v. State, 963 S.W.2d 770 (Tex. Crim. App. 1998); Barley v. State, 906 S.W.2d 27 (Tex. Crim. App. 1995).

A two-step analysis is used to determine the admissibility of an in-court identification: (1) whether the identification procedure was impermissibly suggestive; and (2) if the identification was the result of a suggestive procedure, whether or not it gives rise to a very substantial likelihood of irreparable misidentification, examining the totality of the circumstances. Delk v. State, 855 S.W.2d 700 (Tex. Crim. App. 1993).

The defendant has the burden to show the identification is unreliable by clear and convincing evidence. Delk; Bond v. State, 29 S.W.3d 169 (Tex. App.—Houston [14th Dist.], *pet. ref'd*).

If the defendant meets this burden, then the in-court identification is inadmissible unless the state can prove by clear and convincing evidence that the identification was of independent origin. Brown v. State, 64 S.W.3d 94 (Tex.App.—Austin 2001, *no pet.*); United States v. Wade, 388 U.S. 218, 240, 87 S.Ct. 1926, 18 L.Ed.2d 1149 (1967).

The following non-exhaustive factors are analyzed in determining the independent reliability of the identification weighing them against the corrupting effect of the suggestive identification itself: (1) the witness' opportunity to view the accused at the time of the crime; (2) the witness' degree of attention; (3) the accuracy of the witness' prior description of the criminal; (4) the level of certainty demonstrated at the pretrial confrontation; and (5) the time between the crime and the confrontation. Delk.

Additional factors that may be considered are: 1) any identification prior to the lineup of another person; 2) the identification by photograph of the defendant prior to the lineup; and 3) any failure to identify the defendant on a prior occasion. Santos v. State, 116 S.W.3d 447 (Tex.App.—Houston [14th Dist.] 2003, pet. ref'd).

The identification testimony will be admissible if the indicia of reliability outweigh the apparent corrupting effect of the unnecessarily suggestive pretrial occurrence. Delk.

The standard of review for a ruling on a motion to suppress an in-court identification procedure is for the appellate courts to afford almost total deference to a trial court's determination of the facts, especially when the trial court's findings are based on an evaluation of credibility and demeanor. They give the same amount of deference to mixed questions of law and fact if the resolution of those ultimate questions turns on an examination of credibility and demeanor. If mixed questions of law and fact do not relate to credibility and demeanor, then they review such determinations *de novo*. Guzman v. State, 955 S.W.2d 85 (Tex. Crim. App. 1997).

On appeal, in reviewing the trial judge's assessment of reliability, appellate courts consider the above seven factors, which are issues of historical fact, deferentially in a light favorable to the trial court's ruling. The courts then weigh them de novo against any corrupting effect of the suggestive pretrial identification procedure. The courts review the evidence adduced at the admissibility hearing as well as the evidence adduced at trial. Balderas v. State, 517 S.W.3d 756, 792 (Tex. Crim. App. 2016).

§12:117 Voice Identification Procedures

Voice is a competent means of identification if the witness had any previous acquaintance with the person identified. Wolf v. State, 674 S.W.2d 831 (Tex.App.—Corpus Christi 1984, *pet. ref'd*).

It is sufficient that the witness had heard such person's voice but once previous to the time in question. Norton v. State, 564 S.W.2d 614 (Tex. Crim. App. 1978); Williams v. State, 747 S.W.2d 812 (Tex.App.—Dallas 1986, *no pet.*).

Requiring the defendant to speak during a lineup or in court for purposes of identification does not violate his Fifth Amendment right against self-incrimination. United States v. Wade, 388 U.S. 218, 87 S.Ct. 1926, 18 L.Ed.2d 1149 (1967); Williams.

The same rule is applicable to challenges made under the Texas Constitution. *See* Olson v. State, 484 S.W.2d 756 (Tex. Crim. App.1969) (article I, section 10 of the Texas Constitution is no broader than the Fifth Amendment of the United States Constitution); Williams.

§12:118 Form: Motion to Suppress

See our companion book *Texas Criminal Forms* (James Publishing):

- Form 12-22, Motion to Suppress In-Court Identification.

§12:120 Invoking the Witness Rule

§12:121 Statutes

CCP Art. 36.03. Invocation of Rule

(a) Notwithstanding Rule 614, Texas Rules of Evidence, a court at the request of a party may order the exclusion of a witness who for the purposes of the prosecution is a victim, close relative of a deceased victim, or guardian of a victim only if the witness is to testify and the court determines that the testimony of the witness would be materially affected if the witness hears other testimony at the trial.

(b) On the objection of the opposing party, the court may require the party requesting exclusion of a witness under Subsection (a) to make an offer of proof to justify the exclusion.

(c) Subsection (a) does not limit the authority of the court on its own motion to exclude a witness or other person to maintain decorum in the courtroom.

(d) In this article:

(1) "Close relative of a deceased victim" and "guardian of a victim" have the meanings assigned by Article 56.01.

(2) "Victim" means a victim of any criminal offense.

(e) At the commencement of a trial, the court shall admonish each witness who is to testify as to those persons whom the court determines the witness may talk to about the case before the trial ends and those persons whom the witness may not talk to about the case. The court may punish as contempt a witness who violates the admonishment provided by the court.

CCP Art. 36.05. Not to Hear Testimony

Witnesses under rule shall be attended by an officer, and all their reasonable wants provided for, unless the court, in its discretion, directs that they be allowed to go at large; but in no case where the witnesses are under rule shall they be allowed to hear any testimony in the case.

CCP Art. 36.06. Instructed by the Court

Witnesses, when placed under rule, shall be instructed by the court that they are not to converse with each other or with any other person about the case, except by permission of the court, and that they are not to read any report of or comment upon the testimony in the case while under rule. The officer who attends the witnesses shall report to the court at once any violation of its instructions, and the party violating the same shall be punished for contempt of court.

Tex. R. Evid. 614. Excluding Witnesses

At a party's request, the court must order witnesses excluded so that they cannot hear other witnesses' testimony. Or the court may do so on its own. But this rule does not authorize excluding:

(a) a party who is a natural person and, in civil cases, that person's spouse;

(b) after being designated as the party's representative by its attorney:

(1) in a civil case, an officer or employee of a party that is not a natural person; or

(2) in a criminal case, a defendant that is not a natural person;

(c) a person whose presence a party shows to be essential to presenting the party's claim or defense; or

(d) the victim in a criminal case, unless the court determines that the victim's testimony would be materially affected by hearing other testimony at the trial.

§12:122 Purpose of the Rule

The Rule serves two purposes. First, it prevents witnesses from tailoring their testimony to fit that of other witnesses. Secondly, it enhances the jury's ability to detect falsehood by exposing inconsistencies in testimony. It prevents corroboration, contradiction, and the influencing of witnesses. White v. State, 958 S.W.2d 460 (Tex. App.—Waco 1997, *no pet.*).

The purpose of the Rule is to prevent the testimony from one witness to influence the testimony of other witnesses. Ladd v. State, 3 S.W.3d 547 (Tex. Crim. App. 1999).

§12:123 Witness Cannot Hear Testimony

The sequestration rules are not discretionary with the trial court. The court shall order the witnesses excluded at the request of a party or on its own motion. White v. State, 958 S.W.2d 460 (Tex.App.—Waco 1997, *no pet.*); Moore v. State, 882 S.W.2d 844 (Tex. Crim. App. 1994).

Once the Rule is invoked, unless a witness is excused from its requirements, he should not be allowed to hear any testimony in the case or talk to any other person about the case without the court's permission. Beasley v. State, 810 S.W.2d 838 (Tex. App.—Fort Worth 1991, *pet. ref'd*).

CCP Arts. 36.05 and 36.06 provide that witnesses placed under the Rule shall not "be allowed to hear any testimony" and are not permitted "to converse with each other or with any other person about the case." Russell v. State, 155 S.W.3d 176 (Tex. Crim. App. 2005).

CCP Art. 36.06 further provides that a witness cannot "read any report of or comment upon the testimony in the case." Russell.

Tex.R.Evid. 614 provides for prospective witnesses to be sworn and removed from the courtroom. Routier v. State, 112 S.W.3d 554 (Tex. Crim. App. 2003).

Under Art. 36.03 the trial court may exclude victims, their guardians, and close relatives of deceased victims if their testimony would be materially affected by hearing other testimony in the trial. CCP Art. 36.03.

§12:124 Exceptions to the Rule

Rule 614 does not authorize the court to exclude certain witnesses from the courtroom. In criminal cases, those witnesses are: (1) a defendant who is a natural person, the representative of a defendant that is not a natural person; (2) a person whose presence a party shows to be essential to the presentation of the party's case; and (3) a victim if the court does not determine that the victim's testimony would be materially affected by hearing other testimony. Russell v. State, 155 S.W.3d 176 (Tex. Crim. App. 2005).

The party seeking to exempt a witness under Rule 614 has the burden of showing that the claimed exception applies. White v. State, 958 S.W.2d 460 (Tex.App.—Waco 1997, *no pet.*); Moore v. State, 882 S.W.2d 844 (Tex. Crim. App. 1994).

There must be evidence in the record to support a finding exempting a witness from the Rule going beyond a mere comment from the court or party that the witness' presence is necessary. the presentation of the party's case. There must be evidence supporting a finding that the witness' presence in the courtroom has a critical importance to the party's case. White.

It is not enough that the reason for lifting the Rule was expediency. The party seeking an exception under Rule 614 has the burden of showing that one of the enumerated sections is met. Moore; Russell (where the state merely designated the witness as a case agent without further proof).

§12:124.1 Presence of the Victim

A sexual assault victim should have been excluded, as requested by defendant, from pretrial hearing on defense motion to suppress victim's in-court identification of defendant notwithstanding her right to "presence" conferred by Tex. Code Crim. Pro. Art. 56.02. Jimenez v. State, 787 S.W.2d 516 (Tex. Crim. App. 1990).

§12:124.2 Essential Witness

There is an exception to the "Rule" for an expert witness where it is demonstrated that such expert is a person whose presence could be essential to the case presentation, such as the situation where an expert's assistance to counsel is essential during testimony by the opponent's expert. Moore v. State, 882 S.W.2d 844 (Tex. Crim. App. 1994).

§12:124.3 Communication With Attorneys

Attorneys are permitted to discuss the testimony with witnesses who have been placed under the Rule. Archer v. State, 703 S.W.2d 664 (Tex. Crim. App. 1986).

§12:125 Violation of the Rule

There are basically two situations that arise under Rule 614 violations. One is when a party complains of the admission of evidence in violation of the Rule. In those cases, courts look at whether the complaining party objected and was harmed. The other situation that can arise under Rule 614 is when a witness is excluded from testifying. Routier v. State, 112 S.W.3d 554 (Tex. Crim. App. 2003).

Rule 614 contains no provision for sanctions for a violation. Routier.

§12:125.1 Disqualification of Witness for Rule Violation

When deciding whether to disqualify a witness from testifying under the Rule, the trial court must balance the interests of the state and the defendant, consider alternative sanctions, and consider the benefit and detriment arising from a disqualification in light of the nature and weight of the testimony to be offered. Webb v. State, 766 S.W.2d 236 (Tex. Crim. App. 1989); Routier.

A decision to disqualify a defense witness for violating the Rule must be balanced against the defendant's constitutional right to call witnesses on his behalf. Davis v. State, 872 S.W.2d 743 (Tex. Crim. App. 1994).

A court should look at two factors in deciding whether to allow the testimony of a witness who has violated the rule. First, the court should ascertain what kind of witness was involved. Second, the court should determine whether the witness actually conferred with or heard the testimony of another witness without court permission, and whether the witness' testimony will contradict the testimony of a witness he actually heard from the opposing side or corroborate the testimony of another witness he actually heard from the same side on an issue of fact bearing upon the issue of guilt or innocence. Minor v. State, 91 S.W.3d 824 (Tex.App.—Fort Worth 2002, *pet. ref'd*).

With respect to the first prong of this test, violations of the Rule involve two main categories of witnesses: 1) witnesses who have been sworn or listed as witnesses in the case and either hear testimony or discuss another's testimony; and 2) persons who were not intended to be witnesses and are not connected with the case-in-chief but who have, due to events during trial, become necessary witnesses. Minor.

If the witness was one who had no connection with either the state's case-in-chief or the defendant's case-in-chief and who, because of a lack of personal knowledge regarding the offense, was not likely to be called as a witness, then the court should allow the witness to testify. Minor.

A third factor in assessing harm is the nature or importance of the witness' testimony. The more important the witness' testimony, the more this militates for admission of the testimony. White v. State, 958 S.W.2d 460 (Tex.App.—Waco 1997, *no pet.*).

When deciding whether a witness for the defense should be prohibited from testifying because the witness was present in the courtroom during the trial, the court should determine: (1) if the rule was violated were there particular circumstances, other than the mere fact of the violation, which would tend to show the defendant or his counsel consented, procured or otherwise had knowledge of the witness' presence in the courtroom, together with knowledge of the content of that witness' testimony; and (2) if no particular circumstances exist to justify disqualification, is the excluded testimony crucial to the defense. Webb v. State, 766 S.W.2d 236 (Tex. Crim. App. 1989); Routier.

The testimony of an excluded witness can be crucial where it corroborates other evidence favorable to the defense that the jury would be more inclined to believe had the excluded testimony been admitted. Davis.

A witness' testimony can also be crucial where the witness' testimony is probative of an accomplice witness' credibility and the defense's theory of the case; where the witness also provides evidence of other witnesses' motives for testifying as they did; and where the excluded witness is the only witness who could corroborate the defendant's claim that another person had been involved in the offense. Webb.

A defense witness' testimony is probably not crucial where it merely contradicts neutral testimony provided by a state's witness. Routier.

§12:126 Appellate Review

If a party fails to make an adequate showing that the witness should be exempted under Rule 614, but the court nevertheless grants the exemption, the ruling is reviewed under an abuse of discretion standard. Martinez v. State, 867 S.W.2d 30 (Tex. Crim. App. 1993).

Violations of the Rule only constitute reversible error when they affect the substantial rights of the defendant under Tex.R.App.Proc. 44.2(b). Ladd v. State, 3 S.W.3d 547 (Tex. Crim. App. 1999).

§12:127 Form: Motions and Supporting Brief

See our companion book *Texas Criminal Forms* (James Publishing):

- Form 15-20, Motion Invoking the Rule.
- Form 15-21, Motion to Exclude Witness From the Rule.
- Form 15-22, Motion to Exclude Testimony of Witness Based on Violation of the Rule.
- Form 15-23, Defendant's Brief in Support of Motion to Exclude Testimony of Witness Based on Violation of the Rule.

§12:130 Entrapment

§12:131 Statutes

Tex. Penal Code §8.06. Entrapment

> *(a) It is a defense to prosecution that the actor engaged in the conduct charged because he was induced to do so by a law enforcement agent using persuasion or other means likely to cause persons to commit the offense. Conduct merely affording a person an opportunity to commit an offense does not constitute entrapment.*
>
> *(b) In this section "law enforcement agent" includes personnel of the state and local law enforcement agencies as well as of the United States and any person acting in accordance with instructions from such agents.*

§12:132 General Points

Entrapment is a defense to prosecution under Texas Penal Code §§2.03 and 8.06(a). State v. Taylor, 886 S.W.2d 262 (Tex. Crim. App. 1994).

To raise the issue of entrapment, the defendant has the burden to produce evidence of an inducement that was likely to cause persons not ready and willing to commit the crime to engage in the conduct charged. State v. Perez, 824 S.W.2d 223 (Tex.App.—Waco 1992, *pet. ref'd*).

In order for a defendant to raise a claim of entrapment, he must initially establish a *prima facie* showing of such a defense. Reese v. State, 877 S.W.2d 328 (Tex. Crim. App. 1994).

When a defendant raises the defense of entrapment at trial, he has the burden of producing evidence to establish every element of that defense. He must present a *prima facie* case that:

- he engaged in the conduct charged
- because he was induced to do so by a law enforcement agent
- who used persuasion or other means, and
- those means were likely to cause persons to commit the offense.

Once the defense makes a *prima facie* showing of each element, the state then has the burden of persuasion to disprove entrapment beyond a reasonable doubt. Hernandez v. State, 161 S.W.3d 491 (Tex. Crim. App. 2005).

§12:133 Pretrial Hearing

The entrapment defense is unique in that the legislature deliberately provided it may be tested and determined at a pretrial hearing pursuant to CCP Art. 28.01. State v. Taylor, 886 S.W.2d 262 (Tex. Crim. App. 1994).

A pretrial motion asserting entrapment as a matter of law is analogous to a motion for summary judgment in civil case in which, if there is no disputed fact issue, the movant is entitled to judgment as a matter of law. A defendant is entitled to dismissal of the charges under §8.06 in the pretrial hearing context only when he can establish entrapment as a matter of law with conflict-free, uncontradicted, uncontested or undisputed evidence. If the facts concerning entrapment are in dispute, there cannot be entrapment as a matter of law determined at the pretrial stage. It is the defendant, not the state, who must establish beyond a reasonable doubt that he was entrapped at the pretrial stage. At that stage, the state has no burden of proof except to raise a fact issue that a jury would be required to resolve. Hernandez v. State, 161 S.W.3d 491 (Tex. Crim. App. 2005).

A defendant's testimony which is not directly contradicted at a pretrial hearing may be disbelieved by the trial judge because as the sole trier of fact, the judge is not required to believe that testimony. Hernandez.

Because a pretrial determination of the defense of entrapment favorable to a defendant does not impact the charging instrument, but is, instead, a finding in the nature of an acquittal, the appropriate court order is one dismissing the prosecution with prejudice. The state cannot appeal this order under CCP Art. 44.01(a)(1). Taylor.

§12:134 Two-Prong Test for Entrapment

The test for entrapment under Texas Penal Code §8.06 is a two-prong test, involving subjective and objective elements. The first prong is a subjective test in which the defendant must show that he was in fact induced by law enforcement to engage in the illegal conduct. This subjective prong requires the defendant to show that he was induced to act because of police persuasion. The second prong is an objective test in which the defendant must show that the conduct that induced him to act would have induced an ordinary person. McGann v. State, 30 S.W.3d 540 (Tex.App.—Fort Worth 2000, *pet. ref'd*).

Under an objective test, once the defendant demonstrates that he was induced, the focus shifts to the police conduct itself. The question becomes whether the persuasion used by law enforcement was such as to cause an ordinarily law-abiding person of average resistance to commit the offense, not whether it was sufficient to cause the defendant to commit the offense. England v. State, 887 S.W.2d 902 (Tex. Crim. App. 1994).

Police conduct merely affording a person an opportunity to commit an offense does not constitute entrapment. Torres v. State, 980 S.W.2d 873 (Tex.App.—San Antonio 1998, *no pet.*).

In Texas, a defendant may not deny commission of an offense and assert entrapment as a defense. Barnes v. State, 70 S.W.3d 294 (Tex.App.—Fort Worth 2002, pet. ref'd).

The defendant need not plead guilty, but he cannot introduce positive evidence that he did not commit the act alleged. Barnes.

Normally, the factual issue of entrapment is a question for the jury unless as a matter the defendant has established beyond a reasonable doubt that he was entrapped. Where the evidence on the issue of entrapment is in conflict, the issue should be submitted to the jury. Melton v. State, 713 S.W.2d 107 (Tex. Crim. App. 1986).

When a definition or instruction on entrapment is given in the abstract portion of the charge, the application paragraph must list the specific conditions under which a jury authorized to acquit. Vega v. State, 394 S.W.3d 514, 520 (Tex. Crim. App. 2013).

§12:135 Form: Motion to Dismiss

See our companion book *Texas Criminal Forms* (James Publishing):

- Form 12-17, Motion to Dismiss Based on Entrapment.

§12:140 Motions in Limine

§12:141 General Points

A motion in limine is a method of raising objection to an area of inquiry prior to the matter reaching the ears of the jury through a posed question, jury argument, or other means. Norman v. State, 523 S.W.2d 669 (Tex. Crim. App. 1975).

As such, it is wider in scope and more effective than the sustaining of an objection made after the objectionable matter has been expressed. Norman.

A true motion in limine does not usually seek an immediate or definite ruling from the trial court. Rather, it seeks a ruling from the court to order the holding of a hearing outside the jury's presence before any mention is made of the evidence. Rawlings v. State, 874 S.W.2d 740 (Tex.App.—Fort Worth 1994, *no pet.*).

It seeks a ruling from the court for a hearing to be held outside the jury presence before any mention of the subject matter is made. Nunfio v. State, 808 S.W.3d 484 (Tex. Crim. App. 1991).

A motion in limine characteristically includes: (1) an objection to a general category of evidence; and (2) a request for an instruction that the proponent of that evidence approach the bench for a hearing on its admissibility before offering it. Rawlings.

A ruling on a motion in limine is merely preliminary because, in most cases, a trial judge is not in a position to rule on the admissibility of evidence before trial begins. Thus, the court's decision on the matter presented in the motion in limine is subject to reconsideration throughout the course of trial. Rawlings.

§12:142 Preservation of Error

The granting or denying of a motion in limine, without more, preserves nothing for appellate review. Fuller v. State, 253 S.W.3d 220 (Tex. Crim. App. 2008).

Instead, a defendant must object on the proper grounds at the time the evidence is offered at trial and must secure a ruling from the court. Snellen v. State, 923 S.W.2d 238 (Tex.App.—Texarkana 1996, pet. ref'd).

Furthermore, a trial court's ruling on a motion in limine is not within the scope of Tex.R.App.Proc. 52(b) (now Tex.R.App.Proc. 33.1), providing that when a court hears objections to offered evidence out of the presence of the jury and rules that the evidence shall be admissible, such objection shall be deemed to apply to such evidence as admitted before the jury without the necessity of repeating those objections. This is because Rule 52(b) requires a specific objection and a motion in limine is merely a general complaint seeking a hearing. Rawlings v. State, 874 S.W.2d 740 (Tex. App.—Fort Worth 1994, *no pet.*).

PRACTICE TIP: As a practical matter, counsel for a defendant should consider raising as many evidentiary complaints in the form of a motion in limine prior to trial as reasonably possible. If a hearing is secured on a motion in limine, the record should be adequately developed as to exactly what the character of the evidence is anticipated to be. Counsel should then formally object to this evidence and secure a ruling on the objection. This procedure will avoid the necessity of objecting in the presence of the jury and/or the jury being excused as the evidence is sought to be introduced at trial.

§12:143 Form: Motions in Limine

See our companion book *Texas Criminal Forms* (James Publishing):

- Form 15-17, Defendant's Motion in Limine.
- Form 15-18, State's Motion in Limine.

§12:150 Pretrial Habeas Corpus Writs

A claim is cognizable in a pretrial writ of habeas corpus if, resolved in the defendant's favor, it would deprive the trial court of the power to proceed and, therefore, result in the defendant's immediate release. State v. Weise, 55 S.W.3d 617 (Tex. Crim. App. 2001); Ex parte Smith, 185 S.W.3d 887 (Tex. Crim. App. 2006).

A defendant may raise certain issues in a pretrial writ of habeas corpus, which, if meritorious, would bar prosecution or conviction. Ex parte Smith, 178 S.W.3d 797 (Tex. Crim. App. 2005); Ex parte Smith, 185 S.W.3d 887 (Tex. Crim. App. 2006).

Overbreadth, a First Amendment doctrine that allows a facial challenge to a statute even though the statute might have some legitimate applications, is cognizable on pretrial habeas. Ex parte Ingram, 533 S.W.3d 887, 894 (Tex. Crim. App. 2017).

An *in pari materia* claim is not cognizable in a pretrial writ of habeas corpus. Ex parte Smith, 185 S.W.3d 887 (Tex. Crim. App. 2006).

A pretrial habeas writ generally may not be used to challenge the sufficiency of the indictment or to construe the meaning and application of the criminal statute defining the charged offense. A pretrial habeas may, however, be used to raise a claim that the statute under which an applicant is being prosecuted is unconstitutional on its face. Ex parte Zavala, 421 S.W.3d 227, 230-1 (Tex. App.—San Antonio 2013, *no pet.*).

Claims that revolve around anti-defensive issues—the mens rea, right to present a defense, and vagueness claims—are not cognizable on pretrial habeas. Ex parte Ingram, 533 S.W.3d at 894.

In order to pursue the remedy of pretrial habeas, a petitioner has to be restrained in his liberty. Being on bond and charged with an offense is sufficient restraint to make habeas application. Ex parte Zavala, 421 S.W.3d at 230.

§12:160 Competency of Defendant to Stand Trial

§12:161 Statutes

The law governing competency issues is at CCP Chapter 46B.

§12:162 Incompetent Person Is Not Subject to Trial

In both Texas and the federal system, it has long been accepted that a person whose mental condition is such that he lacks the capacity to understand the nature and object of the proceedings against him, to consult with counsel, and to assist in preparing his defense may not be subjected to a trial. Drope v. Missouri, 420 U.S. 162, 95 S.Ct. 896, 43 L.Ed.2d 103 (1975); McDaniel v. State, 98 S.W.3d 704 (Tex. Crim. App. 2003).

The conviction of an accused person while he is legally incompetent violates due process. Pate v. Robinson, 383 U.S. 375, 86 S.Ct. 836, 15 L.Ed.2d 815 (1966); McDaniel.

§12:163 Trial Court Must Inquire Into Competence

Thus, to protect a criminal defendant's constitutional rights, a trial court must inquire into the defendant's mental competence once the issue is sufficiently raised. Pate v. Robinson, 383 U.S. 375, 86 S.Ct. 836, 15 L.Ed.2d 815 (1966); McDaniel v. State, 98 S.W.3d 704 (Tex. Crim. App. 2003).

With respect to the evidentiary standard that must be met at the informal inquiry stage, a court must focus on three matters. First, the standard at the informal inquiry stage is whether there is "some evidence" of incompetency to stand trial. Art. 46B.004(c). The statute reads in full: "On suggestion that the defendant may be incompetent to stand trial, the court shall determine by informal inquiry whether there is some evidence from any source that would support a finding that the defendant may be incompetent to stand trial." Boyett v. State, 545 S.W.3d 556, 563-4 (Tex. Crim. App. 2018).

The statutory "some evidence" standard requires "more than none or a scintilla" of evidence that "rationally may lead to a conclusion of incompetency." Boyett v. State, 545 S.W.3d at 564.

Second, a trial court must consider only evidence of incompetency, and it must not weigh evidence of competency against the evidence of incompetency. In making this determination at the informal-inquiry stage, "a trial court must consider only that evidence tending to show incompetency" and "put aside all competing indications of competency." Boyett v. State, 545 S.W.3d at 564.

Third, some evidence must be presented at the informal inquiry stage to show that a defendant's mental illness is the source of his inability to participate in his own defense. There must be "some evidence from which it may rationally be inferred not only 1) that the defendant suffers some degree of debilitating mental illness, and that 2) he obstinately refuses to cooperate with counsel to his own apparent detriment, but also that 3) his mental illness is what fuels his obstinacy." Thus, it is not enough to present evidence of either a defendant's mental illness alone or his refusal to cooperate with counsel—rather, there must be some evidence indicating that the defendant's refusal to rationally engage with counsel is caused by his mental illness. Boyett v. State, 545 S.W.3d at 564.

Under CCP Art. 46B.003(a), "[a] person is incompetent to stand trial if the person does not have: (1) sufficient present ability to consult with the person's lawyer with a reasonable degree of rational understanding; or (2) a rational as well as factual understanding of the proceedings against the person." *See* McDaniel; Greene v. State, 225 S.W.3d 324 (Tex.App.—San Antonio 2007, *no pet.*).

Under Texas cases, the trial court must conduct a non-jury hearing, a Section 2 inquiry, on whether to hold a jury trial on the defendant's competency if evidence of the defendant's incompetency is brought to the attention of the court from any source. A Section 2 or competency inquiry is required only if the evidence brought to the judge's attention raises a bona fide doubt in the judge's mind about the defendant's competency to stand trial. Evidence is usually sufficient to create a bona fide doubt if it shows recent severe mental illness, at least moderate retardation, or truly bizarre acts by the defendant. McDaniel.

Bona fide doubt is still the proper standard under art. 46B.003 for determining whether a trial court should conduct a competency inquiry. If a trial judge has a *bona fide* doubt about the competency of the defendant, he or she shall conduct an informal inquiry to determine if there is evidence that would support a finding of incompetence. A *bona fide* doubt may exist if the defendant exhibits truly bizarre behavior or has a recent history of severe mental illness or at least moderate mental retardation. Montoya v. State, 291 S.W.3d 420 (Tex. Crim. App. 2009).

If sufficient evidence is presented to the court, the informal inquiry must be performed *sua sponte* if not requested by either party. Greene.

In making a determination whether some evidence exists that would support a finding that a defendant may be incompetent to stand trial, a trial court must consider only that evidence tending to show incompetency, putting aside all competing indications of competency, to find whether there is some evidence, a quantity more than none or a scintilla, that rationally may lead to a conclusion of incompetency. If so, then evidence exists to support a finding of incompetency, and the statutory scheme requires the trial court to conduct a formal competency trial. Turner v. State, 422 S.W.3d 676, 692-3 (Tex. Crim. App. 2013).

When such a bona fide doubt does exist, the court must conduct the Section 2 competency inquiry to determine whether there is some evidence to support a finding of incompetency, and, if so, to commence a Section 4 competency hearing. McDaniel.

The mere assertion in a motion that there is an issue as to the defendant's competency to stand trial, or a defendant's bare assertion that "I am incompetent," is not sufficient to raise a bona fide doubt as to the defendant's competency. McDaniel.

Prior hospitalization and treatment for depression do not *per se* warrant the trial court impaneling a separate jury to conduct a competency hearing. To raise the issue of competency by means of the defendant's past mental health history, there generally must be evidence of recent severe mental illness or bizarre acts by the defendant or of moderate retardation. Montoya.

§12:164 Competency Trial

The burden of proof at a competency hearing is on the defendant to prove he is incompetent by a preponderance of the evidence. Morris v. State, 214 S.W.3d 159 (Tex.App.—Beaumont 2007, *pet. filed*).

To prove incompetence, a defendant must prove he does not have a sufficient present ability to consult with his lawyer with a reasonable degree of rational understanding, or that he does not have a rational, as well as a factual, understanding of the proceedings against him. CCP Art. 46B.003(a); Morris.

Where there is a prior unvacated judgment of incompetency in evidence, the burden is on the state to prove the present competency of the defendant beyond a reasonable doubt. Bradford v. State, 172 S.W.3d 1 (Tex.App.—Fort Worth 2005, *no pet.*).

It is error to admit a defendant's statement from the incompetency examination, in violation of former CCP Art. 46.02, §3(g), for any purpose at the guilt/innocence phase of the trial. Mitten v. State, 145 S.W.3d 225 (Tex. Crim. App. 2004).

A jury trial on the issue of competency to stand trial is civil in nature. Williams v. State, 191 S.W.3d 242 (Tex.App.—Austin 2006, *no pet.*).

Procedural issues arising during competency trials are governed by the Rules of Civil Procedure. White v. State, 591 S.W.2d 851 (Tex. Crim. App. 1979).

Under the Rules of Civil Procedure, each side has six peremptory challenges in a competency trial. White.

The rules of evidence apply to hearings to determine a defendant's competency to stand trial. CCP Art. 46B.008.

A claim of amnesia generally will not render a defendant *per se* incompetent to stand trial. Morris v. State, 301 S.W.3d 281 (Tex. Crim. App. 2009).

This is because (1) amnesia is akin to missing evidence; (2) a contrary rule would unduly hamper the State's interest in the prosecution of violators of its criminal laws and jeopardize the safety and security of other citizens; and (3) amnesia can be easily feigned. Gonzales v. State, 313 S.W.3d 840 (Tex. Crim. App. 2010) *citing* Morris.

Also, amnesia does not necessarily affect a defendant's present ability to consult with his lawyer which is the test for competency. Owens v. State, 473 S.W.3d 812, 817 (Tex. Crim. App. 2015).

A trial judge is not required to conduct a competency hearing on his own initiative after hearing evidence that, due to alcohol or drug use, a defendant suffered amnesia with respect to events giving rise to the charged offense. Gonzales.

Should the formal competency trial result in a finding of competency, the trial court is not obliged to revisit the issue later absent a material change of circumstances suggesting that the defendant's mental status has deteriorated. However, especially when there has been a suggestion of incompetency but no formal adjudication of the issue, due process requires the trial court to remain ever vigilant for changes in circumstances that would make a formal adjudication appropriate. Turner v. State, 422 S.W.3d 676, 693 (Tex. Crim. App. 2013).

An appellate court measures the propriety of the competency verdict based on the evidence before the jury at the time of the verdict under the relevant legal standard set out in Art. 46B.003(a). Morris.

PRACTICE TIP: The incompetency statute no longer requires that a jury decide the competency issue if both sides are in agreement. CCP Art. 46B.005(c).

PRACTICE TIP: A defense attorney should be careful, if testifying at an incompetency hearing, not to reveal privileged attorney-client communications. The privilege can only be waived by the client.

§12:165 Appeal

When appealing a conviction on the merits, a defendant may appeal errors made in the incompetency-to-stand-trial hearing. Morris v. State, 214 S.W.3d 159 (Tex.App.—Beaumont 2007, *pet.filed*).

The trial court's order of competency to stand trial is not a final, appealable judgment. Lowe v. State, 999 S.W.2d 537 (Tex.App.—Houston [14th Dist.] 1999, *no pet.*).

Whether incompetency exists at the time of trial is left to the discretion of the trial judge; and this determination is reviewed on appeal under an abuse of discretion standard. Rice v. State, 991 S.W.2d 953 (Tex.App.—Fort Worth 1999, *pet. ref'd*).

The appropriate remedy when there is an error in competency proceedings is to abate the appeal and remand the cause to the trial court to determine the feasibility of a retrospective competency proceeding. Owens v. State, 473 S.W.3d 812, 816 (Tex. Crim. App. 2015). *See also* Turner v. State, 570 S.W.3d 250, 262 (Tex. Crim. App. 2018).

§12:166 Form: Motions and Agreed Judgments Regarding Competency

See our companion book *Texas Criminal Forms* (James Publishing):

- Form 15-3.1, Motion for Competency Examination.
- Form 15-3.2, Defendant's Motion to Vacate Judgment of Competency.
- Form 15-3.3, (State or Defendant's) Motion for Jury on Issue of Defendant's Competency.
- Form 15-3.4, Agreed Judgment of Incompetency to Stand Trial (Non-Violent).
- Form 15-3.5, Agreed Judgment of

Incompetency to Stand Trial (Violent).

- Form 15-3.6, Agreed Judgment of Indefinite Commitment.
- Form 15-3.7, Agreed Judgment of Mental Retardation.

§12:170 Guilty Pleas

§12:171 Statutes

CCP Art. 1.05. Rights of Accused

In all criminal prosecutions the accused shall have a speedy public trial by an impartial jury. He shall have the right to demand the nature and cause of the accusation against him, and to have a copy thereof. He shall not be compelled to give evidence against himself. He shall have the right of being heard by himself, or counsel, or both; shall be confronted with the witnesses against him, and shall have compulsory process for obtaining witnesses in his favor. No person shall be held to answer for a felony unless on indictment of a grand jury.

CCP Art. 1.13. Waiver of Trial by Jury

(a) The defendant in a criminal prosecution for any offense other than a capital felony case in which the state notifies the court and the defendant that it will seek the death penalty shall have the right, upon entering a plea, to waive the right of trial by jury, conditioned, however, that, except as provided by Article 27.19, the waiver must be made in person by the defendant in writing in open court with the consent and approval of the court, and the attorney representing the state. The consent and approval by the court shall be entered of record on the minutes of the court, and the consent and approval of the attorney representing the state shall be in writing, signed by that attorney, and filed in the papers of the cause before the defendant enters the defendant's plea.

(b) In a capital felony case in which the attorney representing the State notifies the court and the defendant that it will not seek the death penalty, the defendant may waive the right to trial by jury but only if the attorney representing the State, in writing and in open court, consents to the waiver.

(c) A defendant may agree to waive a jury trial regardless of whether the defendant is represented by an attorney at the time of making the waiver, but before a defendant charged with a felony who has no attorney can agree to waive the jury, the court must appoint an attorney to represent him.

CCP Art. 1.14. Waiver of Rights

(a) The defendant in a criminal prosecution for any offense may waive any rights secured him by law except that a defendant in a capital felony case may waive the right of trial by jury only in the manner permitted by Article 1.13(b) of this code.

(b) If the defendant does not object to a defect, error, or irregularity of form or substance in an indictment or information before the date on which the trial on the merits commences, he waives and forfeits the right to object to the defect, error, or irregularity and he may not raise the objection on appeal or in any other post-conviction proceeding. Nothing in this article prohibits a trial court from requiring that an objection to an indictment or information be made at an earlier time in compliance with Article 28.01 of this code.

CCP Art. 1.141. Waiver of Indictment for Noncapital Felony

A person represented by legal counsel may in open court or by written instrument voluntarily waive the right to be accused by indictment of any offense other than a capital felony. On waiver as provided in this article, the accused shall be charged by information.

CCP Art. 1.15. Jury in Felony

No person can be convicted of a felony except upon the verdict of a jury duly rendered and recorded, unless the defendant, upon entering a plea, has in open court in person waived his right of trial by jury in writing in accordance with Articles 1.13 and 1.14; provided, however, that it shall be necessary for the state to introduce evidence into the record showing the guilt of the defendant and said evidence shall be accepted by the court as the basis for its judgment and in no event shall a person charged be convicted upon his plea without sufficient evidence to support the same. The evidence may be stipulated if the defendant in such case consents in writing, in open court, to waive the appearance, confrontation, and cross-examination of witnesses, and further consents either to an oral stipulation of the evidence and testimony or to the introduction of testimony by affidavits, written statements of witnesses, and any other documentary evidence in support of the judgment of the court. Such waiver and consent must be approved by the court in writing, and be filed in the file of the papers of the cause.

CCP Art. 26.13. Plea of guilty

(a) Prior to accepting a plea of guilty or a plea of nolo contendere, the court shall admonish the defendant of:

(1) the range of the punishment attached to the offense;

(2) the fact that the recommendation of the prosecuting attorney as to punishment is not binding on the court. Provided that the court shall inquire as to the existence of a plea bargain agreement between the state and the defendant and, if an agreement exists, the court shall inform the defendant whether it will follow or reject the agreement in open court and before any finding on the plea. Should the court reject the agreement, the defendant shall be permitted to withdraw the defendant's plea of guilty or nolo contendere;

(3) the fact that if the punishment assessed does not exceed the punishment recommended by the prosecutor and agreed to by the defendant and the defendant's attorney, the trial court must give its permission to the defendant before the defendant may prosecute an appeal on any matter in the case except for those matters raised by written motions filed prior to trial;

(4) the fact that if the defendant is not a citizen of the United States of America, a plea of guilty or nolo contendere for the offense charged may result in deportation, the exclusion from admission to this country, or the denial of naturalization under federal law;

(5) the fact that the defendant will be required to meet the registration requirements of Chapter 62, if the defendant is convicted of or placed on deferred adjudication for an offense for which a person is subject to registration under that chapter; and

(6) the fact that if the defendant is placed on community supervision, after satisfactorily fulfilling the conditions of community supervision and on expiration of the period of community supervision, the court is authorized to release the defendant from the penalties and disabilities resulting from the offense as provided by Article 42A.701(f).

(b) No plea of guilty or plea of nolo contendere shall be accepted by the court unless it appears that the defendant is mentally competent and the plea is free and voluntary.

(c) In admonishing the defendant as herein provided, substantial compliance by the court is sufficient, unless the defendant affirmatively shows that he was not aware of the consequences of his plea and that he was misled or harmed by the admonishment of the court.

(d) The court may make the admonitions required by this article either orally or in writing. If the court makes the admonitions in writing, it must receive a statement signed by the defendant and the defendant's attorney that he understands the admonitions and is aware of the consequences of his plea. If the defendant is unable or refuses to sign the statement, the court shall make the admonitions orally.

(e) Before accepting a plea of guilty or a plea of nolo contendere, the court shall, as applicable in the case:

(1) inquire as to whether a victim impact statement has been returned to the attorney representing the state and ask for a copy of the statement if one has been returned; and

(2) inquire as to whether the attorney representing the state has given notice of the existence and terms of any plea bargain agreement to the victim, guardian of a victim, or close relative of a deceased victim, as those terms are defined by Article 56.01.

(f) The court must substantially comply with Subsection (e) of this article. The failure of the court to comply with Subsection (e) of this article is not grounds for the defendant to set aside the conviction, sentence, or plea.

(g) Before accepting a plea of guilty or a plea of nolo contendere and on the request of a victim of the offense, the court may assist the victim and the defendant in participating in a victim-offender mediation program.

(h) The court must substantially comply with Subsection (a)(5). The failure of the court to comply with Subsection (a)(5) is not a ground for the defendant to set aside the conviction, sentence, or plea.

(i) Notwithstanding this article, a court shall not order the state or any of its prosecuting attorneys to participate in mediation, dispute resolution, arbitration, or other similar procedures in relation to a criminal prosecution unless upon written consent of the state.

(h-1) The court must substantially comply with Subsection (a)(6). The failure of the court to comply with Subsection (a)(6) is not a ground for the defendant to set aside the conviction, sentence, or plea.

CCP Art. 26.14. Jury on Plea of Guilty

Where a defendant in a case of felony persists in pleading guilty or in entering a plea of nolo contendere, if the punishment is not absolutely fixed by law, a jury shall be impaneled to assess the punishment and evidence may be heard to enable them to decide thereupon, unless the defendant in accordance with Articles 1.13 or 37.07 shall have waived his right to trial by jury.

CCP Art. 27.02. Defendant's Pleadings

The pleadings and motions of the defendant shall be:

(1) A motion to set aside or an exception to an indictment or information for some matter of form or substance;

(2) A special plea as provided in Article 27.05 of this code;

(3) A plea of guilty;

(4) A plea of not guilty;

(5) A plea of nolo contendere, the legal effect of which shall be the same as that of a plea of guilty, except that such plea may not be used against the defendant as an admission in any civil suit based upon or growing out of the act upon which the criminal prosecution is based;

(6) An application for probation, if any;

(7) An election, if any, to have the jury assess the punishment if he is found guilty; and

(8) Any other motions or pleadings that are by law permitted to be filed.

CCP Art. 27.13. Plea of Guilty or Nolo Contendere in Felony

A plea of "guilty" or a plea of "nolo contendere" in a felony case must be made in open court by the defendant in person; and the proceedings shall be as provided in Articles 26.13, 26.14 and 27.02. If the plea is before the judge alone, same may be made in the same manner as is provided for by Articles 1.13 and 1.15.

CCP Art. 27.14. Plea of Guilty or Nolo Contendere in Misdemeanor

(a) A plea of "guilty" or a plea of "nolo contendere" in a misdemeanor case may be made either by the defendant or his counsel in open court; in such case, the defendant or his counsel may waive a jury, and the punishment may be assessed by the court either upon or without evidence, at the discretion of the court.

(b) A defendant charged with a misdemeanor for which the maximum possible punishment is by fine only may, in lieu of the method provided in Subsection (a) of this article, mail or deliver in person to the court a plea of "guilty" or a plea of "nolo contendere" and a waiver of jury trial. The defendant may also request in writing that the court notify the defendant, at the address stated in the request, of the amount of an appeal bond that the court will approve. If the court receives a plea and waiver before the time the defendant is scheduled to appear in court, the court shall dispose of the case without requiring a court appearance by the defendant. If the court receives a plea and waiver after the time the defendant is scheduled to appear in court but at least five business days before a scheduled trial date, the court shall dispose of the case without requiring a court appearance by the defendant. The court shall notify the defendant either in person or by certified mail, return receipt requested, of the amount of any fine assessed in the case and, if requested by the defendant, the amount of an appeal bond that the court will approve. The defendant shall pay any fine assessed or give an appeal bond in the amount stated in the notice before the 31st day after receiving the notice.

(c) In a misdemeanor case for which the maximum possible punishment is by fine only, payment of a fine or an amount accepted by the court constitutes a finding of guilty in open court as though a plea of nolo contendere had been entered by the defendant and constitutes a waiver of a jury trial in writing.

(d) If written notice of an offense for which maximum possible punishment is by fine only or of a violation relating to the manner, time, and place of parking has been prepared, delivered, and filed with the court and a legible duplicate copy has been given to the defendant, the written notice serves as a complaint to which the defendant may plead "guilty," "not guilty," or "nolo contendere." If the defendant pleads "not guilty" to the offense or fails to appear based on the written notice, a complaint shall be filed that conforms to the requirements of Chapter 45 of this code, and that complaint serves as an original complaint. A defendant may waive the filing of a sworn complaint and elect that the prosecution proceed on the written notice of the charged offense if the defendant agrees in writing with the prosecution, signs the agreement, and files it with the court.

(e)(1) Before accepting a plea of guilty or a plea of nolo contendere by a defendant charged with a misdemeanor involving family violence, as defined by Section 71.004, Family Code, the court

shall admonish the defendant by using the following statement:

"If you are convicted of a misdemeanor offense involving violence where you are or were a spouse, intimate partner, parent, or guardian of the victim or are or were involved in another, similar relationship with the victim, it may be unlawful for you to possess or purchase a firearm, including a handgun or long gun, or ammunition, pursuant to federal law under 18 U.S.C. Section 922(g)(9) or Section 46.04(b), Texas Penal Code. If you have any questions whether these laws make it illegal for you to possess or purchase a firearm, you should consult an attorney."

(2) The court may provide the admonishment under Subdivision (1) orally or in writing, except that if the defendant is charged with a misdemeanor punishable by fine only, the statement printed on a citation issued under Article 14.06(b) may serve as the court admonishment required by this subsection.

CCP Art. 27.15. Change of Venue to Plead Guilty

When in any county which is located in a judicial district composed of more than one county, a party is charged with a felony and the maximum punishment therefor shall not exceed fifteen years, and the district court of said county is not in session, such party may, if he desires to plead guilty, or enter a plea of nolo contendere, make application to the district judge of such district for a change of venue to the county in which said court is in session, and said district judge may enter an order changing the venue of said cause to the county in which the court is then in session, and the defendant may plead guilty or enter a plea of nolo contendere to said charge in said court to which the venue has been changed.

Tex. R. Evid. 410. Pleas, Plea Discussions, and Related Statements

(a) Prohibited Uses in Civil Cases. *In a civil case, evidence of the following is not admissible against the defendant who made the plea or was a participant in the plea discussions:*

(1) a guilty plea that was later withdrawn;

(2) a nolo contendere plea;

(3) a statement made during a proceeding on either of those pleas under Federal Rule of Criminal Procedure 11 or a comparable state procedure; or

(4) a statement made during plea discussions with an attorney for the prosecuting authority if the discussions did not result in a guilty plea or they resulted in a later-withdrawn guilty plea.

(b) Prohibited Uses in Criminal Cases. *In a criminal case, evidence of the following is not admissible against the defendant who made the plea or was a participant in the plea discussions:*

(1) a guilty plea that was later withdrawn;

(2) a nolo contendere plea that was later withdrawn;

(3) a statement made during a proceeding on either of those pleas under Federal Rule of Criminal Procedure 11 or a comparable state procedure; or

(4) a statement made during plea discussions with an attorney for the prosecuting authority if the discussions did not result in a guilty or nolo contendere plea or they resulted in a later-withdrawn guilty or nolo contendere plea.

(c) Exception. In a civil case, the court may admit a statement described in paragraph (a)(3) or (4) and in a criminal case, the court may admit a

statement described in paragraph (b) (3) or (4), when another statement made during the same plea or plea discussions has been introduced and in fairness the statements ought to be considered together.

§12:172 Waivers of Rights

A guilty plea is a waiver of several federal constitutional rights, including the protections against self-incrimination, the right to a speedy and public trial by jury, and the right to confrontation. Ex parte Barnaby, 475 S.W.3d 316, 322 (Tex. Crim. App. 2015).

These waivers must be not only voluntary but also a knowing, intelligent act done with sufficient awareness of the relevant circumstances and likely consequences. Ex parte Barnaby, 475 S.W.3d at 322.

A defendant must have sufficient awareness of the relevant circumstances, and must possess an understanding of the law in relation to the facts. To determine whether a defendant's awareness was sufficient at the time of his plea, a reviewing court looks to whether the plea was a voluntary and intelligent choice among the alternative courses of action open to the defendant. Ex parte Palmberg, 491 S.W.3d 804, 807 (Tex. Crim. App. 2015).

But a defendant need not have a comprehensive awareness of the specific impact that relinquishing his constitutional rights may have; sufficient awareness does not require complete knowledge of the prosecution's case. Ex parte Palmberg, b 491 S.W.3d 807 (where the court found that the defendant's plea was voluntary even where he did not know that the alleged controlled substance was consumed during presumptive testing).

The correct question for due process purposes is not whether the defendant knew every fact relevant to the prosecution of his case. Rather, the correct question is whether he was aware of sufficient facts—including an awareness that there are or may be facts that he does not *yet* know—to make an informed and voluntary plea. Ex parte Palmberg, 491 S.W.3d at 809; Ex parte Broussard, 517 S.W.3d 814, 817 (Tex. Crim. App. 2017).

§12:172.1 Right to Waive Trial by Jury

CCP Art. 1.13(a) provides that a defendant has the right, upon entering a plea, to waive the right of trial by jury. This can be done on the condition that such waiver must be made in person by the defendant in writing in open court, with the consent and approval of the court and the attorney representing the state. Johnson v. State, 72 S.W.3d 346 (Tex. Crim. App. 2002).

This is the rule in felony cases. Shaffer v. State, 769 S.W.2d 943 (Tex. Crim. App. 1989).

It is also the rule in misdemeanor cases. Josey v. State, 857 S.W.2d 815 (Tex.App.—Houston [14th Dist.] 1993, *no pet.*).

A defendant may withdraw his jury trial waiver if the withdrawal will not: 1) interfere with the orderly administration of the business of the court; 2) result in unnecessary delay or inconvenience to the witnesses; or 3) prejudice the state. The burden is on the defendant to establish these matters and the state can rebut the defendant's assertions. Green v. State, 36 S.W.3d 211 (Tex.App.—Houston [14th Dist.] 2001, *pet. ref'd*).

The defendant can withdraw his jury trial waiver only where he can show that the withdrawal will not cause adverse consequences to the state. Hobbs v. State, 298 S.W.3d 193 (Tex. Crim. App. 2009).

A defendant does not give up waivable rights unless he does so plainly, freely, and intelligently. If a defendant wants to relinquish a waivable right, he must expressly do so; i.e., he must intentionally relinquish or abandon a known right or privilege. Sometimes the waiver must be in writing; always, it must be on the record. The judge has an independent duty to implement such rights, absent an effective waiver. Marin v. State, 851 S.W.2d 275 (Tex. Crim. App. 1993).

When a defendant pleads guilty to a jury, the trial becomes unitary and the jury will always be called upon to assess punishment. A defendant cannot plead guilty to a jury and then be sentenced by a judge. In re The State of Texas ex rel. Jennifer Tharp, 393 S.W.3d 751, 755 (Tex. Crim. App. 2012).

§12:172.2 Plea Agreements

Because plea bargains are contractual agreements between the state and defendant, the appellate courts apply general contract-law principles. Ex parte Cox, 482 S.W.3d 112, 116 (Tex. Crim. App. 2016).

Although contractual concepts apply to plea bargains, such should not be strictly enforced to the detriment of due process. The terms of plea agreements, being contractual in nature, are left to the parties to determine and agree upon, and the courts will rarely disturb the terms of such agreements. Ex parte Cox, 482 S.W.3d at 116.

It is well established that, after the judge has accepted a plea bargain in open court, a defendant has a right to enforce the state's part of the plea bargain. Ex parte Cox, 482 S.W.3d at 116.

Where a plea bargain fails in whole or in part, the proper remedy is generally to return both parties to their original pre-plea positions. Ex parte Cox, 482 S.W.3d at 118.

This is also true in a case that has been charge-bargained. Thomas v. State, 516 S.W.3d 498, 504 (Tex. Crim. App. 2017).

A defendant may knowingly and intelligently waive his entire appeal as a part of a plea, even when sentencing is not agreed upon, where consideration is given by the State for that waiver. Ex parte Broadway, 301 S.W.3d 694 (Tex. Crim. App. 2009) (state gave up its right to a jury trial in consideration for the defendant waiving his appeal).

The State's relinquishment of its right to a jury trial is sufficient consideration to render a defendant's waiver of his right to appeal knowing and intelligent. Carson v. State, 559 S.W.3d 489, 496 (Tex. Crim. App. 2018).

In a charge-bargain case, T.R.A.P. Rule 25.2(a)(2) applies and the defendant can only appeal matters that were those matters that were raised by written motion filed and ruled on before trial or after getting the trial court's permission to appeal. Kennedy v. State, 297 S.W.3d 338 (Tex. Crim. App. 2009) (state agreed to forego prosecution of one charge in exchange for the defendant's plea to another charge).

The charge-bargain rules also apply where the defendant pleads guilty to one charge and the state agrees to plea in bar a second charge. Shankle v. State, 119 S.W.3d 808 (Tex. Crim. App. 2003).

§12:172.3 Form: Waivers

See our companion book *Texas Criminal Forms* (James Publishing):

- Form 15-1, Written Waiver of Jury Trial.
- Form 15-2, Waiver of Indictment.

§12:173 Guilty Plea Admonishments

§12:173.1 Admonishments Required

Compliance with the admonishments in CCP Art. 26.13 is mandatory. *See* Hughes v. State, 833 S.W.2d 137 (Tex. Crim. App. 1992); Elliott v. State, 874 S.W.2d 238 (Tex.App.—El Paso 1994, *no pet.*).

CCP Art. 26.13 requires the trial court to admonish the defendant of the direct consequences of his guilty plea before accepting the plea. The admonishments are:

- The punishment range;
- The fact that the state's recommendation is not binding on the court;
- The possibility of deportation; and
- The limited right to appeal.

Bessey v. State, 239 S.W.3d 809 (Tex. Crim. App. 2007).

The admonishments can be accomplished orally or in writing. Alvarez v. State, 63 S.W.3d 578 (Tex. App.—Fort Worth 2001, *no pet.*).

After September 1, 2007 courts are required to admonish defendants of the fact that it is unlawful for the defendant to possess or transfer a firearm or ammunition if the defendant is convicted of a misdemeanor involving family violence, as defined by Family Code Art. 26.13(a)(6) §71.004.

TIP TO THE BENCH: Where the defendant is a U.S. citizen, be sure that this fact is reflected in the record. A trial court that fails to admonish a defendant about the immigration consequences of his guilty plea, a silent record on citizenship, or a record that is insufficient to determine citizenship, establishes harm by the standard of Rule 44.2(b). Vannortrick v. State, 227 S.W.3d 706 (Tex. Crim. App. 2007).

§12:173.2 Admonishments Not Required

The trial court is not required to admonish a defendant of all consequences of a guilty plea; only those direct consequences that are punitive in nature or specifically enunciated by law. Mitschke v. State, 129 S.W.3d 130 (Tex. Crim. App. 2004).

The trial court is not required to admonish the defendant on any collateral consequences of the guilty plea. Collateral consequences of a guilty plea are those which are not definite consequences. Ex parte Morrow, 952 S.W.2d 530 (Tex. Crim. App. 1997).

The Code of Criminal Procedure does not require the trial court to admonish the defendant of the consequences of deferred adjudication before he enters an open plea of guilty or nolo contendere. Ray v. State, 919 S.W.2d 125 (Tex. Crim. App. 1996).

§12:173.3 Failure to Properly Admonish

For cases tried before CCP Art. 26.13 specifically required admonishment on the sex offender registration requirement, the failure to admonish the defendant is not reversible because the registration requirement, although a direct consequence, is not a punitive one. Mitschke v. State, 129 S.W.3d 130 (Tex. Crim. App. 2004).

The lack of CCP Art. 26.13 admonishments regarding citizenship is not grounds for relief unless the defendant shows harm. Ex parte Tovar, 901 S.W.2d 484 (Tex. Crim. App. 1995).

Similarly, where the trial court has failed to admonish a defendant who pleads guilty of the registration requirement for sex offenders, the defendant must show harm to prevail on appeal. Anderson v. State, 182 S.W.3d 914 (Tex. Crim. App. 2006); Bessey v. State, 239 S.W.3d 809 (Tex. Crim. App. 2007) (where the court reasoned that the defendant could not show harm because he had to serve 100 years before eligible for parole).

An attorney's performance was not found to be deficient where he failed to object to the lack of CCP Art. 26.13(a)(4) (citizenship) admonishment where the defendant failed to establish he was prejudiced by the omission. Ex parte Akhtab, 901 S.W.2d 488 (Tex. Crim. App. 1995) (where the court had not yet ruled on the effect of the trial court's failure to give a proper citizenship admonishment).

The trial court's failure to admonish a defendant concerning the deportation consequences of a plea of guilty is harmless where the record reflects that the defendant is a citizen of the U.S. Cain v. State, 947 S.W.2d 262 (Tex. Crim. App. 1997).

The admonishments under CCP Art. 26.13(a) are not constitutionally required because their purpose and function is to assist the trial court in making the determination that a guilty plea is knowingly and voluntarily entered. Aguirre-Mata v. State, 992 S.W.2d 495 (Tex. Crim. App. 1999).

§12:173.4 Appealing Improper Admonishments

Because the CCP Art. 26.13 admonishments are a waivable-only right, a defendant can raise the issue for the first time on appeal without having made an objection or raising the issue at trial. However, such an error is subject to a harm analysis. Bessey v. State, 239 S.W.3d 809 (Tex. Crim. App. 2007); Davison v. State, 405 S.W.3d 682, 687-8 (Tex. Crim. App. 2013).

Thus, a trial court commits nonconstitutional error when it fails to admonish a defendant on one of the statutorily required admonishments. Carranza v. State, 980 S.W.2d 653 (Tex. Crim. App. 1998).

The defendant has the burden of proof to show he was unaware of the consequences of his plea and that he was misled or harmed by the admonishment of the trial court. Carranza.

Generally, if a defendant is fully advised of the direct consequences of his plea, his ignorance of a collateral consequence does not render the plea involuntary. State v. Jimenez, 987 S.W.2d 886 (Tex. Crim. App. 1999).

§12:173.5 Form: Admonishments

See our companion book *Texas Criminal Forms* (James Publishing):

- Form 15-4, Written Plea Admonishments.

- Form 20-30, Written Admonishments of Revocation of Probation.

§12:174 Voluntariness of Plea

§12:174.1 Requirements for Voluntary Plea

A guilty plea constitutes a waiver of three constitutional rights: the right to a jury trial, the right to confront one's accusers, and the right not to incriminate oneself. Boykin v. Alabama, 395 U.S. 238, 89 S.Ct. 1709, 23 L.Ed.2d 274 (1969); Kniatt v. State, 206 S.W.3d 657 (Tex. Crim. App. 2006).

Accordingly, a guilty plea, to be consistent with due process of law, must be entered knowingly, intelligently, and voluntarily. Boykin; Kniatt.

To be voluntary, a guilty plea must be the expression of the defendant's own free will and must not be induced by threats, misrepresentations, or improper promises. Brady v. United States, 397 U.S. 742, 90 S.Ct. 1463, 25 L.Ed.2d 747 (1970); Kniatt.

A defendant may legitimately waive his appeal as a part of a plea bargain agreement. Blanco v. State, 18 S.W.3d 218 (Tex. Crim. App. 2000).

This is true even where the sentence is not agreed upon, but where consideration is given by the state for the waiver. Broadway v. State, 301 S.W.3d 694 (Tex. Crim. App. 2009).

A defendant's voluntary plea of no contest or guilty, which is intelligently made in light of the then-applicable law, cannot be invalidated because later judicial decisions indicate that the plea may have rested on a faulty premise. A knowing and intelligent guilty or no-contest plea does not require that all advice offered by the defendant's trial lawyer withstand retrospective examination in a post-conviction hearing. Briggs v. State, 560 S.W.3d 176, 190 (Tex. Crim. App. 2018).

Where the state and defendant agree that the state will not be bound by its recommendation if the defendant commits an offense between the date of his guilty plea and the sentencing hearing, and this agreement is approved by the trial court, it is an enforceable plea bargain agreement. When the defendant breaches this clause of the agreement, he is placed in the position of an open plea at his sentencing hearing. Moore v. State, 240 S.W.3d 248 (Tex. Crim. App. 2007).

A defendant must contemporaneously object to preserve error where the trial court intrudes into the plea-bargaining process. Moore v. State, 295 S.W.3d 329 (Tex. Crim. App. 2009).

PRACTICE TIP: An essential element of an enforceable plea bargain is that it be approved by the trial court. It is important to have the trial court approve the agreement on the record or by writing included in the record for a party to later enforce the terms of the agreement. Moore.

Because prosecutors have no federal constitutional duty to reveal impeaching or affirmative defense information prior to a defendant's guilty plea, a plea is not rendered involuntary where the information is not revealed. U.S. v. Ruiz, 536 U.S. 622, 122 S.Ct. 2450, 153 L.Ed.2d 586 (2002).

§12:174.2 Challenging Voluntariness of Plea

A defendant's sworn representation that his guilty plea is voluntary constitutes a formidable barrier in any subsequent collateral proceedings. Blackledge v. Allison, 431 U.S. 63, 97 S.Ct. 1621, 52 L.Ed.2d 136 (1977); Kniatt.

The voluntariness of a plea cannot be raised on direct appeal, but must be raised on a motion for new trial or on a *habeas corpus* petition. Cooper v. State, 45 S.W.3d 77 (Tex. Crim. App. 2001).

Where the record reflects that the trial court properly admonished the defendant, there is a *prima facie* showing that the plea was knowingly and voluntarily entered. Smith v. State, 857 S.W.2d 71 (Tex.App.—Dallas 1993, *pet. ref'd*).

The burden then shifts to the defendant to establish that he did not understand the consequences of his plea. Miller v. State, 879 S.W.2d 336 (Tex. App.—Houston [14th Dist.] 1994, *pet. ref'd*).

An applicant seeking habeas corpus relief on the basis of an involuntary guilty plea must prove his claim by a preponderance of the evidence. Ex parte Morrow, 952 S.W.2d 530 (Tex. Crim. App. 1997); Kniatt.

An applicant's delay in seeking habeas corpus relief may prejudice the credibility of his claim. Ex parte Young, 479 S.W.2d 45 (Tex. Crim. App. 1972); Kniatt.

The voluntary nature of a defendant's guilty plea can be shown in the record by the overwhelming evidence that the guilty plea was part of a strategy. Gardner v. State, 164 S.W.3d 393 (Tex. Crim. App. 2005).

A defendant's guilty plea may be found involuntary where defense counsel did not advise him of the possibility of removal from the U.S. because removal is nearly an automatic result for a broad class of noncitizen offenders. Padilla v. Kentucky, 559 U.S. 356, 130 S.Ct. 1473, 176 L.Ed.2d 284 (2010).

The collateral consequence of being committed as a sexually violent predator is a civil rather than punitive measure and not so automatic as to render a plea involuntary. Thomas v. State, 365 S.W.3d 537 (Tex.App.—Beaumont 2012, *no pet.*).

§12:174.3 Involuntary Pleas

Misrepresentations that may cause a plea to be involuntary can come from a variety of sources. While many claims allege erroneous advice or misinformation by defense counsel, misrepresentations can also come from the trial court, or the state. Ex parte Barnaby, 475 S.W.3d 316, 322 (Tex. Crim. App. 2015).

A complete failure to admonish a defendant as to the range of punishment he faces renders a plea involuntary without the defendant having to show harm. White v. State, 932 S.W.2d 593 (Tex.App.—Tyler 1995, pet. ref'd).

Improper admonishments do not render a plea involuntary unless the defendant carries his burden to plead and prove that he was harmed. Singleton v. State, 986 S.W.2d 645 (Tex.App.—El Paso 1998, *pet. ref'd*).

Where the statute under which the defendant was charged is unconstitutional and an improper admonishment resulted, the plea of guilty is not voluntarily or knowingly entered where the defendant shows harm. Ex parte Ward, 716 S.W.2d 529 (Tex. Crim. App. 1986).

Where counsel relates incorrect advice to the defendant regarding eligibility for parole, the defendant's resulting plea will be involuntary because parole eligibility is easily determined based on the offense charged and the offense date. Ex parte Moussazadeh, 361 S.W.3d 684 (Tex. Crim. App. 2012) (where the court disavowed the prior test requiring that the defendant show that advice regarding parole eligibility formed an affirmative part or essential element of the plea agreement).

Where the defendant pleads guilty, having been advised that he faces a certain range of punishment, the plea will be involuntary if, based on the indictment, he actually faced a lesser range of punishment. *See* Ex parte McDonald, 568 S.W.3d 688, 689 (Tex. Crim. App. 2018).

Where a defendant pleads guilty to a crime without having been informed of the elements of the crime, his plea is involuntary. Bradshaw v. Stumpf, 545 U.S. 175, 125 S.Ct. 2398, 162 L.Ed.2d 143 (2005).

False evidence can also cause a defendant to be misinformed. The key factor is whether a defendant has sufficient awareness of the relevant circumstances and likely consequences such that his plea is a knowing, intelligent act. If a defendant's knowledge of the relevant circumstances is lacking because of false evidence (instead of, for example, erroneous advice by counsel), his awareness is not sufficient for his plea to be voluntary. But a plea is not involuntary simply because a defendant does not correctly assess every relevant factor entering into his or her decision. Ex parte Barnaby, 475 S.W.3d at 322-3.

To prove a false-evidence habeas corpus claim, a claimant must first show that the evidence in his or her case was false and then that the false evidence was material. Ex parte Barnaby, 475 S.W.3d at 323.

The materiality of false evidence is measured by what impact that false evidence had on the defendant's decision to plead guilty. Ex parte Barnaby, 475 S.W.3d at 325 (where the court found that the value to the defendant of accepting his plea bargain on a drug case outweighed the value of knowing before his plea whether his laboratory report was false).

§12:175 Sufficiency of Pleas of Guilty

§12:175.1 Misdemeanor Cases

In misdemeanor cases before the court or jury, and in felony cases before a jury, the plea is sufficient to support the judgment. Brown v. State,

507 S.W.2d 235 (Tex. Crim. App. 1974); Lenox v. State, 56 S.W.3d 660 (Tex.App.—Texarkana 2001, *pet. ref'd*).

§12:175.2 Felony Cases

Article 1.15 requires substantiation of a guilty plea. By its plain terms it requires evidence in addition to, and independent of, the plea itself to establish the defendant's guilt. Menefee v. State, 287 S.W.3d 9 (Tex. Crim. App. No. 1530-08, July 1, 2009).

A judicial confession is generally sufficient to support a defendant's guilty plea. Dinnery v. State, 592 S.W.2d 343 (Tex. Crim. App. 1979); Honeycutt v. State, 82 S.W.3d 545 (Tex.App.—San Antonio 2002, pet. ref'd).

Under Art. 1.15, the evidence is sufficient to support a plea of guilty if it embraces every essential element of the offense charged. Stone v. State, 919 S.W.2d 424 (Tex. Crim. App. 1996).

Because a plea of guilty in Texas has to be supported by evidence, a valid plea of guilty or *nolo contendre* waives or forfeits the right to appeal a claim of error only when the judgment was rendered independent of, and not supported by, the error. Young v. State, 8 S.W.3d 656 (Tex. Crim. App. 2000) (overruling Helms v. State, 484 S.W.2d 924 (Tex. Crim. App. 1972)).

A defendant's assertion that the allegations in the indictment are true and correct is a judicial confession. Dinnery v. State, 592 S.W.2d 343 (Tex. Crim. App. 1979); Solis v. State, 945 S.W.2d 300 (Tex.App.—Houston [1st Dist.] 1997, *pet. ref'd*).

However, a defendant's sworn affirmation reaffirming his guilty plea to the charges in the indictment does not constitute a judicial confession and does not otherwise supply evidence, in whole or in part, sufficient to support the plea under Article 1.15. Menefee.

Where a guilty plea is entered in open court, it does not have to be orally made by the defendant in order to be voluntary and valid. Costilla v. State, 146 S.W.3d 213 (Tex. Crim. App. 2004).

In Ditto/Ervin v. State, 988 S.W.2d 236 (Tex. Crim. App. 1999), appellants pled guilty under a plea bargain that the state would recommend that the punishment not exceed 10 years confinement. Appellants filed applications for probation. In Ditto's case, the state specifically made no recommendation as to probation. Appellants received 10 years deferred from the judge, who admonished appellant that he was liable for up to 20 years confinement upon violation of probation. Both appellants were later adjudicated and sentenced to 20 years. The plea bargain with a cap of 10 years confinement was fulfilled when appellants were placed on deferred. The words of the statute are "[a]fter an adjudication of guilt, all proceedings ...continue as if the adjudication had not been deferred." After an adjudication of guilt, appellant was not in a position to withdraw his plea. The trial court properly sentenced appellant within the statutory limits for the charged offenses. Ditto/Ervin.

§12:176 Conditional Guilty Pleas

§12:176.1 Appeal Following Plea

Under Tex.R.App.Proc. 40(b)(1) (now Tex.R.App.Proc. 25.2), a defendant may plead guilty pursuant to a plea bargain and reserve for appeal the merits of the denial of written motions or issues on which the trial court had granted permission to appeal. Davis v. State, 870 S.W.2d 43 (Tex. Crim. App. 1994).

A defendant who had entered a guilty plea pursuant to a plea bargain may appeal all written pretrial motions on the grounds stated in the motions, regardless of the manner of proof at the guilty plea hearing. Ellis v. State, 705 S.W.2d 261 (Tex.App.—San Antonio 1986, *no pet.*). This applies to both felony and misdemeanor convictions. McGlynn v. State, 704 S.W.2d 18 (Tex. Crim. App. 1982).

A defendant may appeal the denial of a suppression motion despite the fact that he plead guilty and received a deferred adjudication. Dillehey v. State, 815 S.W.2d 623 (Tex. Crim. App. 1991).

§12:176.2 Deferred Sentencing

Where it is a condition of a plea bargain that if the defendant does not appear for a deferred sentencing date she will face the full range of punishment, the defendant has forfeited any complaint about the trial judge's participation in the plea negotiations and sentence may be pronounced anywhere within the punishment range. Hallmark v. State, 541 S.W.3d 167, 170-1 (Tex. Crim. App. 2017).

A proper objection must be lodged at the time of the plea in order to complain on appeal that the judge exceeded the plea bargain. Hallmark v. State, 541 S.W.3d at 170.

§12:177 Open Pleas of Guilty

Upon entering a plea of guilty in a non-capital felony case, a defendant is not entitled to a bifurcated trial—once the guilty plea is entered, the procedure becomes a "unitary trial" to determine the remaining issue of punishment. There does not exist a separate punishment phase. Appellant's written waiver of her Fifth Amendment right not to self-incriminate applied to the entire criminal adjudication proceeding including the assessment of punishment. Carroll v. State, 42 S.W.3d 129 (Tex. Crim. App. 2001).

When a defendant pleads guilty to a jury, the trial becomes unitary and the jury will always be called upon to assess punishment. A defendant cannot plead guilty to a jury and then be sentenced by a judge. In re The State of Texas ex rel. Jennifer Tharp, 393 S.W.3d 751, 755 (Tex. Crim. App. 2012).

When a defendant enters an open plea of guilty to an offense, he waives the right to appeal any non-jurisdictional defects, other than the voluntariness of his plea, which occurred before entry of the plea. Flowers v. State, 935 S.W.2d 131 (Tex. Crim. App. 1996).

However, a defendant who enters a plea of guilty to a jury without the benefit of a plea bargain waives or forfeits the right to appeal a claim of error only when the judgment was rendered independent of, and not supported by, the error. Young v. State, 8 S.W.3d 656 (Tex. Crim. App. 2000) (overruling Helms v. State, 484 S.W.2d 924 (Tex. Crim. App. 1972)).

Where a defendant pleads guilty without a punishment recommendation but the state agrees to plea in bar another offense, the sentence is considered to be a punishment recommended by the state and the defendant has no right to appeal. Shankle v. State, 119 S.W.3d 808 (Tex. Crim. App. 2003).

However, in a charge-bargain situation, a defendant may appeal matters that were raised by written motion filed and ruled on before trial. Kennedy v. State, 297 S.W.3d 338 (Tex. Crim. App. 2009).

Defendants who plead guilty without the benefit of a plea bargain (open plea) may raise claims of error occurring at or after the entry of the guilty plea. Jack v. State, 871 S.W.2d 741 (Tex. Crim. App. 1994).

Waivers of rights executed pursuant to CCP Art. 1.15 apply only to the guilt stage, and do not constitute a waiver of the right to confrontation and cross-examination at the punishment phase. Stringer v. State, 241 S.W.3d 52 (Tex. Crim. App. 2007).

§12:178 Pleas of Nolo Contendere

A plea of *nolo contendere* (no contest) has the same legal effect as a plea of guilty in a criminal case. Snyder v. State, 629 S.W.2d 930 (Tex. Crim. App. 1982).

However, a *nolo contendere* plea may not be used against the defendant as an admission in any civil suit based upon or growing out of the act upon which the criminal prosecution is based. Art. 27.02(5).

§12:178.1 Form: Waiver and Consent to Stipulate Evidence

See our companion book *Texas Criminal Forms* (James Publishing), Form 15-24.

§12:179 Withdrawal of Plea

CCP Art. 26.13(a)(2) provides that should the court reject any plea bargain agreement, the defendant shall be permitted to withdraw his plea of guilty or *nolo contendere*.

In a situation where the trial court does not accept a plea bargain, the burden is on the defendant to contemporaneously withdraw his guilty plea. Where the defendant does not move to withdraw his plea, the proceeding can be treated as an open plea by the trial court. Moore v. State, 295 S.W.3d 329 (Tex. Crim. App. 2009).

Where evidence inconsistent with guilt is

introduced, the defendant has a right upon timely request to change his guilty plea to a not guilty plea. However, the trial court has no duty to do it on its own motion. Mendez v. State, 138 S.W.3d 645 (Tex. Crim. App. 2004).

A defendant's punishment testimony given at a proceeding where he would be permitted to withdraw his plea of guilty is protected by Rule 410(3). Bowie v. State, 135 S.W.3d 55 (Tex. Crim. App. 2004).

The trial judge is not required to *sua sponte* withdraw the defendant's plea of guilty if he makes contrary statements in a presentence investigation; rather, the trial judge can find the defendant guilty, not guilty, or guilty of a lesser included offense. Solis v. State, 945 S.W.2d 300 (Tex.App.—Houston [1st Dist.] 1997, *pet. ref'd*).

A defendant may withdraw his jury trial waiver if the withdrawal will not: 1) interfere with the orderly administration of the business of the court; 2) result in unnecessary delay or inconvenience to the witnesses; or 3) prejudice the state. The burden is on the defendant to establish these matters and the state can rebut the defendant's assertions. Green v. State, 36 S.W.3d 211 (Tex.App.—Houston [14th Dist.] 2001, *no pet.*).

Tex.R.Evid. 410(1) makes withdrawn guilty and *nolo contendere* pleas inadmissible in a subsequent trial.

§12:180 Guilty Pleas in Absentia

Tex. Code Crim. Pro. Art. 27.19. Plea by Certain Defendants

(a) Notwithstanding any other provision of this code, a court shall accept a plea of guilty or nolo contendere from a defendant who is confined in a penal institution if the plea is made:

(1) in accordance with the procedure established by Article 27.18; or

(2) in writing, including a writing delivered by United States mail or secure electronic or facsimile transmission, before the appropriate court having jurisdiction in the county in which the penal institution is located, provided that:

(A) the defendant is notified by the court of original jurisdiction of the right to counsel and the procedures for requesting appointment of counsel, and is provided a reasonable opportunity to request a court-appointed lawyer; (B) if the defendant elects to proceed without counsel, the defendant must waive the right to counsel in accordance with Article 1.051;

(C) the defendant must waive the right to be present at the taking of the plea or to have counsel present, if the defendant has counsel; and

(D) if the defendant is charged with a felony, judgment and sentence are rendered in accordance with the conditions and the procedure established by Article 42.14(b).

(b) In this article, "penal institution" has the meaning assigned by Section 1.07, Penal Code.

(c) Before accepting a plea submitted under Subsection (a)(2), the court shall verify that the person submitting the plea is:

(1) the defendant named in the information or indictment; or

(2) a person with legal authority to act for the defendant named in the information or indictment.

Tex. Code Crim. Pro. Art. 42.14. In Absence of Defendant

(a) In a misdemeanor case, the judgment and sentence may be rendered in the absence of the defendant.

(b) In a felony case, the judgment and sentence may be rendered in the absence of the defendant only if:

(1) the defendant is confined in a penal institution;

(2) the defendant is not charged with a felony offense:

(A) that is listed in Section 3g(a)(1), Article 42.12; or

(B) for which it is alleged that:

(i) a deadly weapon was used or exhibited during the commission of the offense or during immediate flight from the commission of the offense; and

(ii) the defendant used or exhibited the deadly weapon or was a party to the offense and knew that a deadly weapon would be used or exhibited;

(3) the defendant in writing before the appropriate court having jurisdiction in the county in which the penal institution is located:

(A) waives the right to be present at the rendering of the judgment and sentence or to have counsel present;

(B) affirms that the defendant does not have anything to say as to why the sentence should not be pronounced and that there is no reason to prevent the sentence under Article 42.07;

(C) states that the defendant has entered into a written plea agreement with the attorney representing the state in the prosecution of the case; and

(D) requests the court to pronounce sentence in the case in accordance with the plea agreement;

(4) the defendant and the attorney representing the state in the prosecution of the case have entered into a written plea agreement that is made a part of the record in the case; and

(5) sentence is pronounced in accordance with the plea agreement.

(c) A judgment and sentence may be rendered under this article in the absence of the defendant only after the defendant is notified by the court of original jurisdiction of the right to counsel and the defendant requests counsel or waives the right to counsel in accordance with Article 1.051.

(d) In this article, "deadly weapon" and "penal institution" have the meanings assigned by Section 1.07, Penal Code.

(e) If a defendant enters a plea of guilty or nolo contendere under Article 27.19, the attorney representing the state may request at the time the plea is entered that the defendant submit a fingerprint of the defendant suitable for attachment to the judgment. On request for a fingerprint under this subsection, the county in which the defendant is confined shall obtain a fingerprint of the defendant and use first-class mail or other means acceptable to the attorney representing the state and the county to forward the fingerprint to the court accepting the plea.

§12:190 Pretrial DNA Testing In Capital Cases

§12:191 Statutory Law

Tex. Code Crim. Pro. Art. 38.43. Evidence Containing Biological Material

(a) In this article, "biological

evidence" means:

(1) the contents of a sexual assault examination kit; or

(2) any item that contains blood, semen, hair, saliva, skin tissue, fingernail scrapings, bone, bodily fluids, or any other identifiable biological material that was collected as part of an investigation of an alleged felony offense or conduct constituting a felony offense that might reasonably be used to:

(A) establish the identity of the person committing the offense or engaging in the conduct constituting the offense; or

(B) exclude a person from the group of persons who could have committed the offense or engaged in the conduct constituting the offense.

(b) This article applies to a governmental or public entity or an individual, including a law enforcement agency, prosecutor's office, court, public hospital, or crime laboratory, that is charged with the collection, storage, preservation, analysis, or retrieval of biological evidence.

(c) An entity or individual described by Subsection (b) shall ensure that biological evidence collected pursuant to an investigation or prosecution of a felony offense or conduct constituting a felony offense is retained and preserved:

(1) for not less than 40 years, or until the applicable statute of limitations has expired, if there is an unapprehended actor associated with the offense; or

(2) in a case in which a defendant has been convicted, placed on deferred adjudication community supervision, or adjudicated as having engaged in delinquent conduct and there are no additional unapprehended actors associated with the offense:

(A) until the inmate is executed, dies, or is released on parole, if the defendant is convicted of a capital felony;

(B) until the defendant dies, completes the defendant's sentence, or is released on parole or mandatory supervision, if the defendant is sentenced to a term of confinement or imprisonment in the Texas Department of Criminal Justice;

(C) until the defendant completes the defendant's term of community supervision, including deferred adjudication community supervision, if the defendant is placed on community supervision;

(D) until the defendant dies, completes the defendant's sentence, or is released on parole, mandatory supervision, or juvenile probation, if the defendant is committed to the Texas Juvenile Justice Department; or

(E) until the defendant completes the defendant's term of juvenile probation, including a term of community supervision upon transfer of supervision to a criminal court, if the defendant is placed on juvenile probation.

(d) The attorney representing the state, clerk, or other officer in possession of biological evidence described by Subsection (a) may destroy the evidence, but only if the attorney, clerk, or officer by mail notifies the defendant, the last attorney of record for the defendant, and the convicting court of the decision to destroy the evidence and a written objection is not

received by the attorney, clerk, or officer from the defendant, attorney of record, or court before the 91st day after the later of the following dates:

(1) the date on which the attorney representing the state, clerk, or other officer receives proof that the defendant received notice of the planned destruction of evidence; or

(2) the date on which notice of the planned destruction of evidence is mailed to the last attorney of record for the defendant.

(e) To the extent of any conflict, this article controls over Article 2.21.

(f) The Department of Public Safety shall adopt standards and rules authorizing a county with a population less than 100,000 to ensure the preservation of biological evidence by promptly delivering the evidence to the Department of Public Safety for storage in accordance with Section 411.053, Government Code, and department rules.

(g) The Department of Public Safety shall adopt standards and rules, consistent with best practices, relating to a person described by Subsection (b), that specify the manner of collection, storage, preservation, and retrieval of biological evidence.

(h) A person described by Subsection (b) may solicit and accept gifts, grants, donations, and contributions to support the collection, storage, preservation, retrieval, and destruction of biological evidence.

(i) Before a defendant is tried for a capital offense in which the state is seeking the death penalty, subject to Subsection (j), the state shall require either the Department of Public Safety through one of its laboratories or a laboratory accredited under Article 38.01 to perform DNA testing, in accordance with the laboratory's capabilities at the time the testing is performed, on any biological evidence that was collected as part of an investigation of the offense and is in the possession of the state. The laboratory that performs the DNA testing shall pay for all DNA testing performed in accordance with this subsection.

(j) As soon as practicable after the defendant is charged with a capital offense, or on a motion by the state or the defendant in a capital case, unless the state has affirmatively waived the death penalty in writing, the court shall order the state and the defendant to meet and confer about which biological materials collected as part of an investigation of the offense qualify as biological evidence that is required to be tested under Subsection (i). If the state and the defendant agree on which biological materials constitute biological evidence, the biological evidence shall be tested in accordance with Subsection (i). If the state and the defendant do not agree on which biological materials qualify as biological evidence, the state or the defendant may request the court to hold a hearing to determine the issue. On receipt of a request for a hearing under this subsection, the court shall set a date for the hearing and provide written notice of the hearing date to the state and the defendant. At the hearing, there is a rebuttable presumption that the biological material that the defendant requests to be tested constitutes biological evidence that is required to be tested under Subsection (i). This subsection does not in any way prohibit the state from testing biological evidence in the state's possession.

(k) If an item of biological evidence is destroyed or lost as a result of DNA testing performed under Subsection (i), the laboratory that tested the evidence must provide to the defendant any bench notes prepared by the laboratory that are related to the testing of the evidence and the results of that testing.

(l) The defendant's exclusive remedy for testing that was not performed as

required under Subsection (i) or (j) is to seek a writ of mandamus from the court of criminal appeals at any time on or before the date an application for a writ of habeas corpus is due to be filed in the defendant's case under Section 4(a), Article 11.071. An application for a writ of mandamus under this subsection does not toll any period of limitations applicable to a habeas petition under state or federal law. The defendant is entitled to only one application for a writ of mandamus under this subsection. At any time after the date an application for a writ of habeas corpus is filed in the defendant's case under Section 4(a), Article 11.071, the defendant may file one additional motion for forensic testing under Chapter 64.

(m) A defendant may have another laboratory accredited under Article 38.01perform additional testing of any biological evidence required to be tested under Subsection (i). On an ex parte showing of good cause to the court, a defendant may have a laboratory accredited under Article 38.01 perform testing of any biological material that is not required to be tested under Subsection (i). The defendant is responsible for the cost of any testing performed under this subsection.

§12:192 Case Law

Under 38.43, the trial court has, in the absence of agreement by the state and defendant, the discretion to determine when all necessary biological evidence has been tested. In re Luis Solis-Gonzalez, 489 S.W.3d 459, 462 (Tex. Crim. App. 2016).

(This page intentionally left blank.)

Chapter 13

DISCOVERY

Table of Contents

§13:10 The Basics of Discovery

§13:11 No General Right to Discovery

Criminal defendants do not have a general right to discover evidence in the state's possession, but they have been granted limited discovery by CCP Art. 39.14. Washington v. State, 856 S.W.2d 184 (Tex. Crim. App. 1993); Michaelwicz v. State, 186 S.W.3d 601 (Tex.App.—Austin 2006, pet. ref'd).

The prosecutor is not required to deliver his entire file to defense counsel, but only to disclose evidence favorable to the accused that, if suppressed, would deprive the defendant of a fair trial. Harm v. State, 183 S.W.3d 403 (Tex. Crim. App. 2006), *citing* United States v. Bagley, 473 U.S. 667, 105 S.Ct. 3375, 87 L.Ed.2d 481 (1985).

The state is under no duty to disclose neutral or inculpatory information to the defendant or to share all useful information with the defendant. The prosecution cannot be required to anticipate all possible defenses and provide the defendant with information to bolster those defenses. Michaelwicz.

PRACTICE TIP: The Code of Criminal Procedure now requires clerks to accept electronic and digital multimedia evidence for filing from defendants where they allow filing of such matters by the prosecutor. See CCP Art. 2.21.

§13:12 Scope of Statutory Discovery

§13:12.1 Statutory Law

CCP Art. 39.14. Discovery

(a) Subject to the restrictions provided by Section 264.408, Family Code, and Article 39.15 of this code, as soon as practicable after receiving a timely request from the defendant the state shall produce and permit the inspection and the electronic duplication, copying, and photographing, by or on behalf of the defendant, of any offense reports, any designated documents, papers, written or recorded statements of the defendant or a witness, including witness statements of law enforcement officers but not including the work product of counsel for the state in the case and their investigators and their notes or report, or any designated books, accounts, letters, photographs, or objects or other tangible things not otherwise privileged that constitute or contain evidence material to any matter involved in the action and that are in the possession, custody, or control of the state or any person under contract with the state. The state may provide to the defendant electronic duplicates of any documents or other information described by this article. The rights granted to the defendant under this article do not extend to written communications between the state and an agent, representative, or employee of the state. This article does not authorize the removal of the documents, items, or information from the possession of the state, and any inspection shall be in the presence of a representative of the state.

(b) On a party's request made not later than the 30th day before the date that jury selection in the trial is scheduled to begin or, in a trial without a jury, the presentation of evidence is scheduled to begin, the party receiving the request shall disclose to the requesting party the name and address of each person the disclosing party may use at trial to present evidence under Rules 702, 703, and 705, Texas Rules of Evidence. Except as otherwise provided by this subsection, the disclosure must be made in writing in hard copy form or by electronic means not later than the 20th day before the date that jury selection in the trial is scheduled to begin or, in a trial without a jury, the presentation of evidence is scheduled to begin. On motion of a party and on notice to the other parties, the court may order an earlier time at which one or more of the other parties must make the disclosure to the requesting party.

(c) If only a portion of the applicable document, item, or information is subject to discovery under this article,

the state is not required to produce or permit the inspection of the remaining portion that is not subject to discovery and may withhold or redact that portion. The state shall inform the defendant that a portion of the document, item, or information has been withheld or redacted. On request of the defendant, the court shall conduct a hearing to determine whether withholding or redaction is justified under this article or other law.

(d) In the case of a pro se defendant, if the court orders the state to produce and permit the inspection of a document, item, or information under this subsection, the state shall permit the pro se defendant to inspect and review the document, item, or information but is not required to allow electronic duplication as described by Subsection (a).

(e) Except as provided by Subsection (f), the defendant, the attorney representing the defendant, or an investigator, expert, consulting legal counsel, or other agent of the attorney representing the defendant may not disclose to a third party any documents, evidence, materials, or witness statements received from the state under this article unless:

(1) a court orders the disclosure upon a showing of good cause after notice and hearing after considering the security and privacy interests of any victim or witness; or

(2) the documents, evidence, materials, or witness statements have already been publicly disclosed.

(f) The attorney representing the defendant, or an investigator, expert, consulting legal counsel, or agent for the attorney representing the defendant, may allow a defendant, witness, or prospective witness to view the information provided under this article, but may not allow that person to have copies of the information provided, other than a copy of the witness's own statement. Before allowing that person to view a document or the witness statement of another under this subsection, the person possessing the information shall redact the address, telephone number, driver's license number, social security number, date of birth, and any bank account or other identifying numbers contained in the document or witness statement. For purposes of this section, the defendant may not be the agent for the attorney representing the defendant.

(g) Nothing in this section shall be interpreted to limit an attorney's ability to communicate regarding his or her case within the Texas Disciplinary Rules of Professional Conduct, except for the communication of information identifying any victim or witness, including name, except as provided in Subsections (e) and (f), address, telephone number, driver's license number, social security number, date of birth, and bank account information or any information that by reference would make it possible to identify a victim or a witness. Nothing in this subsection shall prohibit the disclosure of identifying information to an administrative, law enforcement, regulatory, or licensing agency for the purposes of making a good faith complaint.

(h) Notwithstanding any other provision of this article, the state shall disclose to the defendant any exculpatory, impeachment, or mitigating document, item, or information in the possession, custody, or control of the state that tends to negate the guilt of the defendant or would tend to reduce the punishment for the offense charged.

(i) The state shall electronically record or otherwise document any document, item, or other information provided to the defendant under this article.

(j) Before accepting a plea of guilty or nolo contendere, or before trial, each

party shall acknowledge in writing or on the record in open court the disclosure, receipt, and list of all documents, items, and information provided to the defendant under this article.

(k) If at any time before, during, or after trial the state discovers any additional document, item, or information required to be disclosed under Subsection (h), the state shall promptly disclose the existence of the document, item, or information to the defendant or the court.

(l) A court may order the defendant to pay costs related to discovery under this article, provided that costs may not exceed the charges prescribed by Subchapter F, Chapter 552, Government Code.

(m) To the extent of any conflict, this article prevails over Chapter 552, Government Code.

(n) This article does not prohibit the parties from agreeing to discovery and documentation requirements equal to or greater than those required under this article.

13:12.2 Case Law

The Texas Legislature intended Art. 39.14 to constitute a comprehensive pretrial discovery statute, and that criminal discovery orders must fall within the confines of that article's limited authorization. State ex rel. Wade v. Stephens, 724 S.W.2d 141 (Tex.App.—Dallas 1987, *no pet.*).

A corollary of this rule is that trial courts lack inherent authority to order pretrial discovery any greater than that authorized by Art. 39.14. Wade (where the court of appeals declared void a discovery order that was outside the trial court's statutory authority).

When Texas Code Criminal Procedure art. 39.14(f) says that a defendant may view but not obtain copies of discovery materials provided by the state that is exactly what it means. Also, the trial court does not have authority to override the statute and order that the defendant have copies. In re Matthew Powell, Lubbock County District Attorney v. Honorable Mark Hocker, County Court at Law Number One of Lubbock County, 516 S.W.3d 488, 495 (Tex. Crim. App. 2017).

The decision on what is discoverable is left to the discretion of the trial judge. McBride v. State, 838 S.W.2d 248 (Tex. Crim. App. 1992), *citing* Quinones v. State, 592 S.W.2d 933 (Tex. Crim. App. 1980).

Appellate courts will not disturb a trial judge's decision under Art. 39.14 absent an abuse of discretion. McBride.

However, the trial judge is required to permit discovery if the evidence sought is material to the defense of the accused. McBride.

The state has a continuing burden of disclosure once a motion for discovery has been granted. Crane v. State, 786 S.W.2d 338 (Tex. Crim. App. 1990).

It is the opinion of the Texas attorney general that the knowledge of an assistant criminal district attorney working in one division of an office is imputed to prosecutors in other sections of the office for purposes of art. 39.14. Tex. Atty. Gen. Op., No. KP-0213 (2018).

To the extent information provided to an assistant criminal district attorney acting in a civil capacity constitutes an item described by article 39.14(a) but is protected by the attorney-client privilege, the plain language of article (a) would exempt its disclosure to the defendant. However, a court would likely conclude that any exculpatory information meeting the requirements of article 39.14(h) obtained by such an attorney must be disclosed to the defendant, notwithstanding any attorney-client or other evidentiary privilege. Tex. Atty. Gen. Op., No. KP-0213 (2018).

To the extent that information obtained by an assistant criminal district attorney acting in a civil capacity is confidential under section 261.201 of the Family Code, any duty of disclosure in article 39.14(a) of the Code of Criminal Procedure would not be triggered except pursuant to court order obtained under subsection 261.201(b) or (c). A court would likely conclude that any exculpatory information obtained by an assistant criminal district attorney that meets the requirements of article 39.14(h) but that is made confidential by section 261.201 shall be disclosed only pursuant to court order obtained under subsection 261.201 (b) or (c). Tex. Atty. Gen. Op., No. KP-0213 (2018).

§13:13 Defendant's Burden

§13:13.1 General Points

Before a defendant is entitled to discovery, he must show: (1) good cause; (2) materiality; and (3) possession by the State of the information. Medina v. State, 986 S.W.2d 733 (Tex.App.—Amarillo 1999, *pet. ref'd*).

PRACTICE TIP: It is important to have the trial court rule on the motion for discovery and make specific orders because without the rulings, no error can be preserved. See Garcia v. State, 871 S.W.2d 279 (Tex.App.—El Paso 1994, no pet.).

§13:13.2 Defendant Must Show Good Cause

It is the defendant's burden to show that he has good cause under Art. 39.14 before the trial judge is required to permit discovery if the evidence sought is material to the defense of the accused. McBride v. State, 838 S.W.2d 248 (Tex. Crim. App. 1992); Oprean v. State, 201 S.W.3d 724 (Tex. Crim. App. 2006) (Cochran, J., concurring).

When a defendant has shown that the evidence he seeks is material, he has shown good cause. Quinones v. State, 592 S.W.2d 933 (Tex. Crim. App. 1980); McBride.

When a defendant has shown that the evidence he seeks is indispensable to the state's case, he has shown good cause. Bates v. State, 587 S.W.2d 121 (Tex. Crim. App. 1979); McBride.

§13:13.3 Defendant Must Show Materiality

The defendant must demonstrate that the information sought is material. Crane v. State, 786 S.W.2d 338 (Tex. Crim. App. 1990); Lagrone v. State, 942 S.W.2d 602 (Tex. Crim. App. 1997).

Evidence is material if there is a reasonable probability that, had the evidence been disclosed to the defense, the result of the proceeding would have been different. Harm v. State, 183 S.W.3d 403 (Tex. Crim. App. 2006), *citing* Ex parte Kimes, 872 S.W.2d 700 (Tex. Crim. App. 1993).

A reasonable probability is one that is sufficient to undermine confidence in the outcome of the trial. Harm; Ex parte Kimes.

Materiality is determined by examining the alleged error in the context of the entire record and overall strength of the state's case. Harm; Thomas v. State, 841 S.W.2d 399 (Tex. Crim. App. 1992).

The mere possibility that an item of undisclosed information might have helped the defendant or might have affected the outcome of the trial does not establish "materiality" in the constitutional sense. Crane.

§13:13.4 Defendant Must Show Possession by State

In order to show error on the trial court's refusal to order the state to turn over evidence, the defendant must show that the state possessed the evidence. Valdez v. State, 116 S.W.3d 94 (Tex. App.—Houston [14th Dist.] 2002, pet. ref'd).

Evidence held by agents of the state is considered in the possession of the state for discovery purposes. Johnston v. State, 917 S.W.2d 135 (Tex.App.—Fort Worth 1996, *pet. ref'd*).

§13:13.5 Defendant Must Be Specific

A motion for discovery must be specific; and if overly broad, will not support a later constitutional claim that evidence was withheld. State ex rel. Simmons v. Peca, 799 S.W.2d 426 (Tex.App.—El Paso 1990, *no pet.*); Thomas v. State, 511 S.W.2d 302 (Tex. Crim. App. 1974).

A general request for "all exculpatory evidence which the prosecution may have" is equivalent to no request at all. Villarreal v. State, 576 S.W.2d 51 (Tex. Crim. App. 1978).

Requests for "any favorable evidence," "statements of the prosecution witness which are favorable to the defendant," "all evidence favorable to the defendant material either to guilt or to punishment," are equivalent to no requests at all. Showery v. State, 690 S.W.2d 689 (Tex.App.—El Paso 1985, *pet. ref'd*).

Where a general request is made error only exists if there is a showing on appeal that undisclosed evidence exists which creates a reasonable doubt that did not otherwise exist. Green v. State, 587 S.W.2d 167 (Tex. Crim. App. 1979).

§13:13.6 Motion Must Be Timely Filed

Discovery matters are among those that must be litigated at a pre-trial hearing, if such is scheduled by the court. CCP Art. 28.01. *See* Scott v. State, 825 S.W.2d 521 (Tex.App.—Dallas 1992, *pet. ref'd*).

§13:14 Place and Time of Discovery

If discovery is allowed, the Defendant will have the right to inspect, copy or photograph the materials as authorized by the court, and the court's order shall specify the time, place and manner of such inspecting, copying or photocopying. No evidence, however, may be removed from the possession of the state and any inspection shall be in the presence of a representative of the state. Terrell v. State, 521 S.W.2d 618 (Tex. Crim. App. 1975).

In cases where it would be impractical to require the defense to conduct their examination of evidence at a state facility, the evidence or a copy thereof should be delivered to the defense for inspection. The state has a right to have their representative present during the examination of original material. Taylor v. State, 93 S.W.3d 487 (Tex.App.—Texarkana 2002, *pet. ref'd*) (where the evidence in question was a computer hard drive).

Because Art. 39.14 specifies that the trial court shall specify the manner in which the defense may be allowed to copy state's evidence, the trial court has the authority to order the state to make a copy of a DVD of the interview of the complainant at a child advocacy center in its possession. In re Dist. Attorney's Office of the 25th Judicial Dist., 358 S.W.3d 244, 245-6 (Tex. Crim. App. 2011).

Where no time is stated in the court's order for the delivery of discovery materials to the defendant, the state's disclosure is not untimely where it is provided immediately prior to the taking of testimony. Kirksey v. State, 132 S.W.3d 49 (Tex. App.—Beaumont 2004, *no pet.*).

§13:15 Open File Policy

An open-file policy generally satisfies the prosecution's duty to disclose exculpatory evidence. Harm v. State, 183 S.W.3d 403 (Tex. Crim. App. 2006).

However, an open file policy is not sufficient to comply with the notice requirements of Tex.R.Evid. 404(b) and other evidentiary rules that require specific notice of intent to introduce evidence. Buchanan v. State, 911 S.W.2d 11 (Tex. Crim. App. 1995).

§13:16 Form: General Motion for Discovery

See our companion book *Texas Criminal Forms* (James Publishing):

- Form 13-1, General Motion for Discovery.
- Form 13-1.2 Receipt for Discovery.
- Form 13-2.1 Motion for Discovery and Preservation of Specific Evidence.
- Form 13-2.2 Motion to Disclose Documents Signed or Made by Defendant.

- Form 13-2.3 Motion to Discover Search and Arrest Warrants.
- Form 13-2.4 Motion to Discover Evidence of Insanity, Incompetence or Diminished Mental Capacity of Defendant.
- Form 13-3.1 Motion Requesting the Prosecution to File a List of Physical Evidence.
- Form 13-3.2 Defendant's Motion to Designate Location of Physical Evidence.
- Form 13-4.1 Defendant's Motion for Duplicate Photographs.
- Form 13-4.2 Defendant's Motion for Duplicate Audio and Video Recordings.
- Form 13-4.3 Defendant's Motion to Produce Artistic and/or Photographic Likeness Created by Law Enforcement.
- Form 13-5 Defendant's Motion for Discovery and Preservation of Specific Evidence Relating to Canine Drug Search.

§13:20 Particular Types of Evidence

§13:21 Prosecution Witnesses

§13:21.1 Names of Prosecution Witnesses

The names of witnesses should be disclosed, upon proper motion by the defendant, if they will be used by the state at any stage in the trial. Richardson v. State, 744 S.W.2d 65 (Tex. Crim. App. 1987); Martinez v. State, 867 S.W.2d 30 (Tex. Crim. App. 1993).

The state is only required to reveal the names and addresses of the witnesses that it will actually call at trial. Beets v. State, 767 S.W.2d 711 (Tex. Crim. App. 1987).

If the trial judge allows a witness to testify who does not appear on the state's witness list, the courts will consider whether the prosecutor's actions constitute bad faith and whether the defendant could have reasonably anticipated the witness' testimony. Stoker v. State, 788 S.W.2d 1 (Tex. Crim. App. 1989); Martinez.

Reviewing courts have focused on three areas of inquiry in deciding whether the state acted in bad faith: (1) whether the defense shows that the state intended to deceive; (2) whether the state's notice left the defense adequate time to prepare; and (3) whether the state freely provided the defense with information (e.g., by maintaining an open files policy, by providing updated witness lists, or by promptly notifying the defense of new witnesses). Hardin v. State, 20 S.W.3d 84 (Tex. App.—Texarkana 2000, *pet. ref'd*); Martinez v. State, 131 S.W.3d 22 (Tex.App.—San Antonio 2003, *no pet.*).

In determining whether the defense could have anticipated the state's witness, reviewing courts also have examined three areas of inquiry: (1) the degree of surprise to the defendant; (2) the degree of disadvantage inherent in that surprise (e.g., the defendant was aware of what the witness would say, or the witness testified about cumulative or uncontested issues); (3) the degree to which the trial court was able to remedy that surprise (e.g., by granting the defense a recess, postponement, or continuance, or by ordering the State to provide the witness' criminal history). Martinez.

§13:21.1.1 Form: Defense Motion and State's Answer

See our companion book *Texas Criminal Forms* (James Publishing):

- Form 13-18, Motion to List State's Witnesses (All Persons Contacted).
- Form 13-19, State's Answer to Defendant's Motion to List Witnesses.

§13:21.2 Records of Prosecution Witnesses

§13:21.2.1 General Points

The prosecution must disclose criminal records of its witnesses if the defendant establishes:

- Good cause.
- Materiality.
- Possession by the state of the information.

Medina v. State, 986 S.W.2d 733 (Tex.App.—Amarillo 1999, *pet. ref'd*).

This rule also applies to juvenile records. Medina.

Where the defendant meets all the requirements of Art. 39.14 and shows that the requested criminal records of the state's witnesses exist and are within control of the state, it is error for the trial court to deny the request. Aguero v. State, 818 S.W.2d 128 (Tex.App.—San Antonio 1991, *pet. ref'd*).

Under the Fifth Amendment Due Process Clause (*see* Article I, §19, Texas Constitution), the arrest and conviction report of the State's witnesses constitutes impeachment evidence under Brady. U.S. v. Agurs, 427 U.S. 97, 96 S.Ct. 22392, 49 L.Ed.2d 342 (1976).

However, since such evidence serves only to impeach, a "specific" request must be made in order to invoke Brady. U.S. v. Agurs.

§13:21.2.2 Form: Motion

See our companion book *Texas Criminal Forms* (James Publishing):

- Form 13-20, Motion to Discover Criminal History of State's Witnesses.

§13:21.3 Prosecution Witness Statements

§13:21.3.1 Statute

Tex. R. Evid. 615. Producing a Witness's Statement in Criminal Cases

> ***(a) Motion to Produce.*** *After a witness other than the defendant testifies on direct examination, the court, on motion of a party who did not call the witness, must order an attorney for the state or the defendant and the defendant's attorney to produce, for the examination and use of the moving party, any statement of the witness that is in their possession and that relates to the subject matter of the witness's testimony.*
>
> ***(b) Producing the Entire Statement.*** *If the entire statement relates to the subject matter of the witness's testimony, the court must order that the statement be delivered to the moving party.*
>
> ***(c) Producing a Redacted Statement.*** *If the party who called the witness claims that the statement contains information that does not relate to the subject matter of the witness's testimony, the court must inspect the statement in camera. After excising any unrelated portions, the court must order delivery of the redacted statement to the moving party. If a party objects to an excision, the court must preserve the entire statement with the excised portion indicated, under seal, as part of the record.*
>
> ***(d) Recess to Examine a Statement.*** *Recess to Examine a Statement. On the moving party's request, the court must recess the proceedings to allow time for a party to examine the statement and prepare for its use.*
>
> ***(e) Sanction for Failure to Produce or Deliver a Statement.*** *If the party who called the witness disobeys an order to produce or deliver a statement, the court must strike the witness's testimony from the record. If an attorney for the state disobeys the order, the court must declare a mistrial if justice so requires.*
>
> ***(f) "Statement" Defined.*** *As used in this rule, a witness's "statement" means:*
>
> > *(1) a written statement that the witness makes and signs, or otherwise adopts or approves;*
> >
> > *(2) a substantially verbatim, contemporaneously recorded recital of the witness's oral statement that is contained in any recording or any transcription of a recording; or*
> >
> > *(3) the witness's statement to a grand jury, however taken or recorded, or a transcription of such a statement.*

§13:21.3.2 Prosecutor Must Produce Witness Statements

The plain language of Rule 615 requires a prosecutor to produce witness statements that are in the prosecutor's possession, after the witness testifies. Jenkins v. State, 912 S.W.2d 793 (Tex. Crim. App. 1995).

The party contesting production of a statement has the burden to show why the statement cannot be produced. Jenkins.

When a party seeks to invoke production of a prior statement of a witness under Rule 615, the following analysis should take place. First, the trial court should determine whether the writing or recording constitutes a "statement" as that term is defined under Rule 615(f). That determination falls within the sound discretion of the trial court. If the trial court concludes that the writing or recording is not a statement, then Rule 615 cannot mandate production. If, on the other hand, the trial court determines that the writing or recording is a "statement," then production is mandatory under Rule 615(a) if: (1) the statement is in the opposing party's possession, either actual or constructive; and (2) the statement relates to the subject matter concerning which the witness has testified. Proper application of this last requirement would prevent disclosure of mental impressions, personal beliefs, trial strategy, legal conclusions, or anything else that could not fairly be said to be the witness' own statement. In other words, if the trial court determines *in camera* that all or a portion of the statement would otherwise constitute "work product," then it would not "relate to the subject matter concerning which the witness has testified." Finally, if the trial court determines that portions of the statement do not relate to the subject matter of the witness' testimony, then Rule 615(c) mandates that those portions be excised from the writing or recording and the remainder produced for the movant. Jordan v. State, 897 S.W.2d 909 (Tex.App.—Fort Worth 1995, *no pet.)*.

An audio-taped interview, where it meets the definition of a statement in Rule 615, qualifies as a statement. Jordan.

The work product rule and attorney-client privilege cannot be asserted to prevent discovery under Rule 615(a) Tex.R.Evid. Mayfield v. State, 758 S.W.2d 371 (Tex.App.—Amarillo 1988, *no pet.*).

A report by an arresting officer detailing items found after an inventory of the defendant's car can be a statement under Rule 615. Cross v. State, 877 S.W.2d 25 (Tex.App.—Houston [1st Dist.] 1994, *pet. ref'd*).

§13:21.3.3 Other Documents Used by Witness

Tex. R. Evid. 612. Writing Used to Refresh a Witness's Memory

> ***(a) Scope.*** *This rule gives an adverse party certain options when a witness uses a writing to refresh memory:*
>
> *(1) while testifying;*
>
> *(2) before testifying, in civil cases, if the court decides that justice requires the party to have those options; or*
>
> *(3) before testifying, in criminal cases.*
>
> ***(b) Adverse Party's Options; Deleting Unrelated Matter.*** *An adverse party is entitled to have the writing produced at the hearing, to inspect it, to cross-examine the witness about it, and to introduce in evidence any portion that relates to the witness's testimony. If the producing party claims that the writing includes unrelated matter, the court must examine the writing in camera, delete any unrelated portion, and order that the rest be delivered to the adverse party. Any portion deleted over objection must be preserved for the record.*
>
> ***(c) Failure to Produce or Deliver the Writing.*** *If a writing is not produced or is not delivered as ordered, the court may issue any appropriate order. But if the prosecution does not comply in a criminal case, the court must strike the witness's testimony or—if justice so requires—declare a mistrial.*

§13:21.3.4 Form: Motion

See our companion book *Texas Criminal Forms* (James Publishing):

- Form 13-21, Motion to Produce Witnesses' Statements.

§13:21.4 Agreements Made With a Witness

§13:21.4.1 State Must Disclose Promises

A failure to disclose this information is a denial of the defendant's due process rights, in that it permits the jury to consider potentially biased information against the defendant without knowing of the bias or of the reason for the bias. Farris v. State, 676 S.W.2d 674 (Tex.App.—Houston [1st Dir.] 1984); *see* Giglio v. United States, 405 U.S. 150, 92 S.Ct. 763, 31 L.Ed.2d 104 (1972).

A plea-bargain agreement that calls for a witness to testify truthfully in another defendant's trial does not violate Rule 3.04 of the Texas State Bar Rules of Professional Conduct, or 18 U.S.C. §§201(b)(1)(A), 201(b)(3) (the federal anti-bribery statute). Castillo v. State, 221 S.W.3d 689 (Tex. Crim. App. 2007).

§13:21.4.2 Form: Motion

See our companion book *Texas Criminal Forms* (James Publishing):

- Form 13-27, Motion to Reveal Agreement with Witness.

§13:22 Photographs and Videorecordings

§13:22.1 Statutory Law

Tex. Code Crim. Pro. Art. 2.139. Video Recordings of Arrests For Intoxication Offenses. A person stopped or arrested on suspicion of an offense under Section 49.04, 49.045, 49.07, or 49.08, Penal Code, is entitled to receive from a law enforcement agency employing the peace officer who made the stop or arrest a copy of any video made by or at the direction of the officer that contains footage of:

(1) the stop;

(2) the arrest;

(3) the conduct of the person stopped during any interaction with the officer, including during the administration of a field sobriety test; or

(4) a procedure in which a specimen of the person's breath or blood is taken.

§13:22.2 Case Law

Photographs are only required to be made available to the defendant where they contain exculpatory evidence. Mize v. State, 754 S.W.2d 732 (Tex.App.—Corpus Christi 1988, *pet. ref'd*).

§13:23 Previous Testimony

§13:23.1 Grand Jury Testimony

§13:23.1.1 Defendant Must Show Special Reason or Particularized Need

CCP Art. 20.02 generally provides that grand jury proceedings are secret. In order to circumvent the traditional policy of grand jury secrecy, the defendant must show that either a special reason or particularized need exists before an inspection of the grand jury proceedings will be allowed. Bynum v. State, 767 S.W.2d 769 (Tex. Crim. App. 1989).

The totality of the circumstances must be examined when determining whether a particularized need exists. Bynum.

A particularized need includes impeachment of a witness, refreshing his recollection and testing his credibility. Dennis v. United States, 384 U.S. 885, 86 S.Ct. 1840, 16 L.Ed.2d 973 (1966).

A particularized need is not shown simply because the requested testimony pertains to a key prosecution witness, or because there is a "need" to locate inconsistencies in the witness' testimony. Bynum; Legate v. State, 52 S.W.3d 797 (Tex. App.—San Antonio 2001, *pet. ref'd*).

§13:23.1.2 Motion for Discovery of Grand Jury Testimony

See our companion book *Texas Criminal Forms* (James Publishing) Form 13-24.

§13:23.2 Previous Trial Testimony

§13:23.2.1 Defendant's Previous Trial Testimony

It is well-settled that an indigent defendant is entitled upon timely request to be furnished without cost, for use at a subsequent trial, a transcription of his earlier mistrial, if it is needed for an effective defense. Britt v. North Carolina, 404 U.S. 226, 92 S.Ct. 431, 30 L.Ed.2d 400, 403 (1971); Brooks v. State, 901 S.W.2d 742 (Tex.App.—Fort Worth 1995, *pet. ref'd*).

In such cases, the accused is presumed to have a need for the transcription of the court reporter's notes from his first trial. Armour v. State, 606 S.W.2d 891 (Tex. Crim. App. 1980).

Furthermore, the defendant does not bear the burden of showing a particularized need for the transcript, nor of showing that the alternatives to acquire the same evidence are inadequate. Brooks.

Where the state does not show that the defendant has no need for the witness testimony from his previous trial, harm to the defendant is presumed where the testimony is not provided. Brooks.

§13:23.2.2 Third-Party Trials

In the absence of a showing of some particularized need, the presumption of need should not be applied to transcriptions of third-party trials. McKibbon v. State, 749 S.W.2d 83 (Tex. Crim. App. 1988).

Rather, as to third-party trial, the defendant shall be required to demonstrate a specific need for the transcript. McKibbon.

Moreover, a simple request for the transcript, without more, is insufficient to show a particularized, specific need. McKibbon.

§13:23.2.3 Form: Motions

See our companion book *Texas Criminal Forms* (James Publishing):

- Form 13-25, Motion for Transcript of Defendant's Previous Trial.
- Form 13-26, Motion for Transcript of Co-Defendant's Trial.

§13:24 Discovering Informant Evidence

§13:24.1 Statute

§13:24.2 Defeating the State's Privilege to Withhold Informer's Identity

The State or the public entity involved in a prosecution has the privilege under Tex. R. Evid. 508(a) to withhold the name of any informer involved in a criminal prosecution. Virtually any public entity involved may claim the informer's privilege. Bodin v. State, 807 S.W.2d 313 (Tex. Crim. App. 1991).

The State's privilege, however, is not absolute. Three exceptions exist where:

1. The state has in some way voluntarily disclosed the identity of the informer. Tex. R. Evid. 508(c)(1).
2. The evidence shows that the informer may be able to give testimony essential to a fair determination of the guilt or innocence of the accused. Tex. R. Evid. 508(c)(2).
3. The court is not satisfied that the informer, who was relied upon to establish the legality of means by which evidence was obtained, is reliable or credible. Tex. R. Evid. 508(c)(3). Bodin.

If a public entity invokes the privilege and refuses to reveal the identity of the informant, it is incumbent on the defendant to file a motion asking that the trial court hold a hearing to determine if the prosecution should be allowed to persist in this refusal. Anderson v. State, 817 S.W.2d 69 (Tex. Crim. App. 1991).

PRACTICE TIP: File a motion to reveal the identity of an informer in every case where the state relies on information gathered from an informant. Even if the state is not ultimately required to reveal the identity, the hearing on the motion can be an excellent discovery device. It can also have the effect of inducing the state to dismiss the case or offer a favorable plea bargain.

A motion to reveal the identity of an informer should be filed in any case in which an informer is involved; its application is not limited to drug cases. Williams v. State, 62 S.W.3d 800 (Tex. App.—San Antonio 2001, *no pet.*) (defendant was charged with murder); Heard v. State, 995 S.W.2d 317 (Tex.App.—Corpus Christi 1999, *pet. ref'd*) (defendant was charged with murder).

Where the public entity validly invokes the privilege, the trial court shall give it an opportunity to show *in camera* facts relevant to determining whether the informer can give the testimony or whether the informer is reliable or credible. Tex. R. Evid. 508(c)(2) & (3).

It is left to the discretion of the trial court to determine when disclosure is warranted under this Rule. In order to show that the trial court erred in not ordering the disclosure, the defendant must show that the trial court abused its discretion. Stokes v. State, 978 S.W.2d 674 (Tex.App.—Eastland 1998, *pet. ref'd*).

Although the preferred method of conducting an *in camera* hearing under this Rule is to review affidavits, the trial court can require testimony if the affidavits will not satisfactorily resolve the matter. Tex. R. Evid. 508(c)(2).

TIP TO THE PROSECUTION: The burden is on the prosecution to request that the trial court hold an in camera hearing to determine the validity of the privilege. Hall v. State, 778 S.W.2d 473 (Tex. App.—Houston [14th Dist.] 1988, pet. ref'd).

TIP TO THE DEFENSE: If the trial court agrees to conduct an in camera hearing, be sure that the record contains the defense's request that the hearing be done on the record and preserved for appellate purposes.

§13:24.3 Defendant's Burden

Only where the defendant demonstrates to the trial court that there is, in fact, an informer is the trial court obligated to hold a hearing on the motion. Smith v. State, 781 S.W.2d 418 (Tex. App.—Houston [1st Dist.] 1989, *no pet.*).

The defendant must explain how the informer's testimony is relevant to his guilt or innocence. Tex. R. Evid. 508 does not contemplate this procedure for the punishment phase of a trial. Mills v. State, 847 S.W.2d 453 (Tex.App.—Eastland 1993, *pet. ref'd*).

The defendant has the burden to make a threshold showing that the informer's identity must be disclosed, and must do so by evidence stronger than mere conjecture or speculation. The mere filing of a motion to disclose the informer's identity is insufficient to make this threshold showing. Bodin v. State, 807 S.W.2d 313 (Tex. Crim. App. 1991).

The defendant's motion must go beyond mere cursory, conclusory allegations. Menefee v. State, 928 S.W.2d 274 (Tex.App.—Tyler 1996, *no pet.*).

Under Rule 508(c)(2), the defendant's burden is to show only that there is a reasonable probability that the informer can give testimony necessary to a fair determination of the issue of guilt or innocence. Anderson v. State, 817 S.W.2d 69 (Tex. Crim. App. 1991).

However, because the defendant may not actually know the nature of the informer's testimony, he or she is only required to make a plausible showing of how the informer's information may be important to merit an *in camera* hearing. A defendant is only required to make a plausible showing that the informer could give testimony necessary to a fair determination of guilt before the privilege is defeated and the identity must be revealed. Anderson; Bodin.

Upon review of such materials, the trial court should order disclosure only where the informer's potential testimony will significantly aid the defendant; mere conjecture or supposition about possible relevancy is insufficient. Bodin.

Where the evidence at the hearing on the motion to reveal the identity of the informer only shows that the police officers involved do not know if the informer can give testimony regarding the guilt or innocence of the defendant, the defendant has failed to carry his burden. Williams v. State,

62 S.W.3d 800 (Tex.App.—San Antonio 2001, *no pet.*).

Where the defendant has made the requisite "plausible showing" and the trial court fails to conduct an *in camera* hearing to determine whether the informer could, in fact, supply testimony necessary to a fair determination of guilt or innocence, the trial court has erred. Loving v. State, 882 S.W.2d 42 (Tex.App.—Houston [1st Dist.] 1994, *no pet.*).

If the trial court finds that there is a reasonable probability that the informer can give the testimony alleged, then the prosecution must reveal the identity of the informer or risk dismissal of the charges by the trial court. Edmond v. State, 911 S.W.2d 487 (Tex.App.—Texarkana 1995, *no pet.*).

Even if the trial court grants the motion and requires the state to reveal the name of the informant, the state has no duty to bring the informant to court. The defendant must issue a subpoena to secure the testimony of the informer. Ashorn v. State, 802 S.W.2d 888 (Tex.App.—Fort Worth 1991, *no pet.*).

§13:24.4 Challenging Reliability or Credibility of Informer

The Rule further provides that where the trial court is not satisfied that an informer, who is being relied on by the state to establish that evidence was legally obtained, is reliable and credible, the trial court may require that the identity of the informer be revealed by the state. Tex. R. Evid. 508(c)(3).

The trial court is not required to hold a hearing on this provision of the Rule where it is satisfied that the informer was credible or reliable. Hall v. State, 778 S.W.2d 473 (Tex.App.—Houston [14th Dist.] 1988, *pet. ref'd*).

TIP TO THE PROSECUTION: The burden is on the prosecution to request that the trial court hold an in camera hearing to determine the validity of the privilege. Hall.

§13:24.5 Mechanics of the Rule

Tex.R.Evid. 508(c)(2) creates a four-step process for resolving prosecution claims of privilege for informers:

1. The evidence must show that the informer may be able to give necessary evidence.
2. The prosecution must invoke the privilege.
3. The trial court must permit the prosecution to show *in camera* whether the witness can give the testimony.
4. If the court determines the informer can give the testimony, and the prosecution does not disclose the informer's identity, the charge must be dismissed.

Lary v. State, 15 S.W.3d 581 (Tex.App.—Amarillo 2000, *pet. ref'd*).

An informant's identity must be disclosed if he or she participated in the offense, was present at the time of the offense or arrest, or is otherwise shown to be a material witness to the transaction. Anderson v. State, 817 S.W.2d 69 (Tex. Crim. App. 1991).

If the informant is an eyewitness to an alleged offense, certainly the informant can give testimony necessary to a fair determination of the issues of guilt or innocence. Anderson.

Where the informer made a "covered buy" which served as the basis for a search warrant of the defendant's apartment, the informer's identity should have been revealed. Bodin v. State, 807 S.W.2d 313 (Tex. Crim. App. 1991).

§13:24.6 Form: Motions to Reveal Identity

See our companion book *Texas Criminal Forms* (James Publishing):

- Form 2-8, Motion to Reveal Identity of Informer (Testimony Relevant to Guilt or Innocence).
- Form 2-9, Motion to Reveal Identity of Informer (Challenge to Legality of Obtaining Evidence).

§13:25 Crime Stoppers Information

§13:25.1 Statutes

Tex. Gov't. Code §414.007. Confidentiality of Council Records

> *Council records relating to reports of criminal acts are confidential.*

Tex. Gov't. Code §414.008. Privileged Information

> *(a) Except as otherwise provided by this section, evidence of a communication between a person submitting a report of a criminal act to the council or a Crime Stoppers organization and the person who accepted the report on behalf of the council or organization is not admissible in a court or an administrative proceeding.*
>
> *(b) Records of the council or a Crime Stoppers organization concerning a report of criminal activity may not be compelled to be produced before a court or other tribunal except on a motion:*
>
> *(1) filed in a criminal trial court by a defendant who alleges that the records or report contains evidence that is exculpatory to the defendant in the trial of that offense; or*
>
> *(2) filed in a civil case by a plaintiff who alleges that denial of access to the records concerning the report of criminal activity abrogates any part of a cognizable common law cause of action, if the plaintiff is alleging abrogation:*
>
> *(A) was charged with or convicted of a criminal offense based at least partially on the report and the charges were dismissed, the plaintiff was acquitted, or the conviction was overturned, as applicable; and*
>
> *(B) in the motion establishes a prima facie case that the plaintiff's abrogated claim is based on injuries from the criminal charge or conviction caused by the wrongful acts of another performed in connection with the report.*
>
> *(c) On motion of a movant under Subsection (b), the court may subpoena the records or report. The court shall conduct an in camera inspection of materials produced under subpoena to determine whether the materials contain:*
>
> *(1) evidence that is exculpatory to the defendant; or*
>
> *(2) information necessary to a plaintiff as described by Subsection (b)(2).*
>
> *(d) If the court determines that the materials produced contain evidence that is exculpatory to the defendant or information necessary to a plaintiff as described by Subsection (b)(2), the court shall present the evidence to the movant in a form that does not disclose the identity of the person who was the source of the evidence, unless the state or federal constitution requires the disclosure of that person's identity. The court shall execute an affidavit accompanying the disclosed materials swearing that, in the opinion of the court, the materials disclosed represent the evidence the movant is entitled to receive under this section.*
>
> *(e) The court shall return to the council or Crime Stoppers organization the materials that are produced under this section but not disclosed to the movant. The council or Crime Stoppers organization shall store the materials at least until the first anniversary of the following appropriate date:*
>
> *(1) the date of expiration of the time for all direct appeals in a criminal case; or*
>
> *(2) the date a plaintiff's right to appeal in a civil case is exhausted.*

§13:25.2 Defendant Has a Right to Crime Stoppers Information

Although the above-quoted Crime Stoppers statutes state that Crime Stoppers information is confidential, a defendant has a constitutional right to production of crime stoppers information in possession of the local Crime Stoppers program, the Crime Stoppers Advisory Council or the District Attorney's office. Thomas v. State, 837 S.W.2d 106 (Tex. Crim. App. 1992).

Because exculpatory information contained within a crime stoppers report is Brady material, there is no burden on the defendant under the Fourteenth Amendment to specifically request the material. Crawford v. State, 892 S.W.2d 1 (Tex. Crim. App. 1994).

§13:25.3 Procedure; In-Camera Review

Both the State's and the defendant's interests can be served by requiring that Crime Stoppers information be inspected by the trial court *in camera*. Neither the attorneys for the State nor the defendant should be present. It will be the responsibility of the court to determine if the produced information contains *Brady* evidence. The court must, in its sound discretion, take steps to ensure that, to the extent possible, the information remains confidential. If information is deemed material at the time it is inspected or at any future stage of the trial, it must be released to the defendant pursuant to well-settled precedent. At the conclusion of the trial, the information shall be sealed and made part of the record. Thomas v. State, 837 S.W.2d 106 (Tex. Crim. App. 1992).

Under the procedure now set forth in the statute, a criminal defendant may file a motion asserting that the Crime Stoppers privileged report or information contains exculpatory material. Tex. Gov't. Code §414.008(b). The trial court may then subpoena the relevant records, review them *in camera*, determine whether they contain evidence exculpatory to the defendant, and present to the defendant any exculpatory information in a form not requiring the disclosure of the identity of the tipster unless required by the state or federal constitution. In Re Hinterlonge, 109 S.W.3d 611 (Tex.App.—Fort Worth 2003, *rehearing of motion for mandamus overruled*).

§13:25.4 Form: Motion and Supporting Brief

See our companion book *Texas Criminal Forms* (James Publishing):

- Form 13-7, Motion to Discover Crime Stoppers Information.
- Form 13-8, Defendant's Brief in Support of Motion to Discover Crime Stoppers Information.

§13:26 Victim and Defendant Statements

§13:26.1 Victim Impact Statements

§13:26.1.1 Statute

CCP Art. 56.03. Victim Impact Statement

> *(g) A victim impact statement is subject to discovery under Article 39.14 of this code before the testimony of the victim is taken only if the court determines that the statement contains exculpatory material.*

§13:26.1.2 Defendant's Right to the Statement

The defendant is entitled to discover exculpatory information contained in a victim impact statement given under Tex. Code of Crim. Pro. Art. 56.03. Jones v. State, 850 S.W.2d 223 (Tex.App.—Fort Worth 1993, *pet. ref'd*).

The victim impact statement is no different from any other statement given by a witness, and the defendant is entitled to inspect the victim impact statement after the testimony of the person giving it, for purposes of cross-examination. Enos v. State, 889 S.W.2d 303 (Tex. Crim. App. 1994).

§13:26.1.3 Defendant Must Request the Statement

The defendant has the burden to request the victim impact statement and make it part of the record for appeal. Harper v. State, 753 S.W.2d 516 (Tex.App.—Houston [1st Dist.] 1988, *pet. ref'd*).

§13:26.1.4 Form: Motion

See our companion book *Texas Criminal Forms* (James Publishing):

- Form 13-9, Motion to Discover Victim Impact Evidence.

§13:26.2 Defendant's Statement

§13:26.2.1 General Points

Under CCP Art. 38.22, admissions by the defendant to police should be disclosed to the defendant where he requests disclosure in a pretrial motion. Cruz v. State, 645 S.W.2d 498 (Tex. App.—San Antonio 1982), *affirmed at* 770 S.W.2d 778 (Tex. Crim. App. 1984).

Written statements of the defendant are discoverable. CCP Art. 39.14.

There is no harm in failing to disclose an inculpatory statement where the defendant filed no pretrial motion requesting such statements. Russeau v. State, 794 S.W.2d 816 (Tex.App.—Tyler 1990, *no pet.*).

A recorded oral statement of the defendant is not admissible unless the prosecution has provided defense counsel with a true, complete, and accurate copy of all recordings of the defendant. CCP Art. 38.22 §3(a)(5); Tigner v. State, 928 S.W.2d 540 (Tex. Crim. App. 1996).

PRACTICE TIP: The discovery of non-recorded oral statements is not provided for by statute. Defense counsel should try to discover such statements by way of a motion to reduce oral statements to writing.

§13:26.2.2 Form: Motion and Notice

See our companion book *Texas Criminal Forms* (James Publishing):

- Form 6-1, Motion to Reduce Oral Statements to Writing.
- Form 6-7, State's Notice of Intent to Offer Defendant's Electronically Recorded Oral Statement.

§13:26.3 Depositions of Elderly or Disabled Persons

Tex. Code Crim. Pro. Art. 39.025. Depositions of Elderly or Disabled Persons

(a) In this article:

(1) "Disabled person" means a person with a disability as defined by Section 3, Americans with Disabilities Act (42 U.S.C. 12102).

(2) "Elderly person" means a person 65 years of age or older.

(b) The court shall order the attorney representing the state to take the deposition of an elderly or disabled person who is the alleged victim of or witness to an offense not later than the 60th day after the date on which the state files an application to take the deposition under Article 39.02.

(c) The attorney representing the state and the defendant or the defendant's attorney may, by written agreement filed with the court, extend the deadline for the taking of the deposition.

(d) The court shall grant any request by the attorney representing the state to extend the deadline for the taking of the deposition if a reason for the request is the unavailability, health, or well-being of the victim or witness.

(e) The Texas Rules of Civil Procedure govern the taking of the deposition, except to the extent of any conflict with this code or applicable court rules adopted for criminal proceedings, in which event this code and the rules for criminal proceedings govern. The attorney representing the state and the defendant or defendant's attorney may agree to modify the rules applicable to the deposition by written agreement filed with the court before the taking of the deposition.

(f) If a defendant is unavailable to attend a deposition because the defendant is confined in a correctional

facility, the court shall issue any orders or warrants necessary to secure the defendant's presence at the deposition. The sheriff of the county in which a deposition under this subsection is to be taken shall provide a secure location for the taking of the deposition and sufficient law enforcement personnel to ensure the deposition is taken safely. The state's application to take a deposition or notice of deposition is not required to include the identity of any law enforcement agents the sheriff assigns to the deposition and may not serve as a basis for the defendant to object to the taking of the deposition.

(g) If a defendant is unavailable to attend a deposition for any reason other than confinement in a correctional facility, the defendant or defendant's attorney shall request a continuance from the court. The court may grant the continuance if the defendant or defendant's attorney demonstrates good cause for the continuance and that the request is not brought for the purpose of delay or avoidance. A defendant's failure to attend a deposition or request a continuance in accordance with this subsection constitutes a waiver of the defendant's right to be present at the deposition.

§13:27 Expert Witness Information

§13:27.1 General Points

§13:27.1.1 Statute

CCP Art. 39.14. Discovery

(b) On a party's request made not later than the 30th day before the date that jury selection in the trial is scheduled to begin or, in a trial without a jury, the presentation of evidence is scheduled to begin, the party receiving the request shall disclose to the requesting party the name and address of each person the disclosing party may use at trial to present evidence under Rules 702, 703, and 705, Texas Rules of Evidence. Except as otherwise provided by this subsection, the disclosure must be made in writing in hard copy form or by electronic means not later than the 20th day before the date that jury selection in the trial is scheduled to begin or, in a trial without a jury, the presentation of evidence is scheduled to begin. On motion of a party and on notice to the other parties, the court may order an earlier time at which one or more of the other parties must make the disclosure to the requesting party.

§13:27.1.2 Reciprocal Discovery

Texas has a reciprocal discovery rule for the exchange of expert witness information.

Art. 39.14(b) expressly authorizes the trial court to order any party to disclose the names of its expert witnesses to the other party upon motion or request, not just the state. Osbourn v. State, 59 S.W.3d 809 (Tex.App.—Austin 2001), *affirmed at* 92 S.W.3d 531 (Tex. Crim. App. 2002).

Apparently no showing of good cause is required, and thus, whether to issue an order is discretionary with the court. Osbourn.

§13:27.1.3 Procedure for Disclosure

The court shall specify the order, the time and manner in which the other party must make the disclosure to the moving party, but in specifying the time in which the other party shall make disclosure, the court shall require the other party to make the disclosure not later than the 20th day before the date the trial begins. Osbourn.

The matter of sanctions is not mentioned, including that of exclusion of the witness' testimony. Osbourn.

The statute is limited and applies only to evidence under Tex.R.Evid. 702, 703, and 705. Osbourn.

§13:27.1.4 Form: Motion and Witness Designation

See our companion book *Texas Criminal Forms* (James Publishing):

- Form 13-28, (State or Defendant's) Motion Requesting Disclosure of Expert Witnesses.
- Form 13-29, Designation of Expert Witness.

§13:27.2 Voir Dire Examination of Expert Witness

§13:27.2.1 Statute

Tex. R. Evid. 705(b) Voir Dire Examination of an Expert About the Underlying Facts or Data. Before an expert states an opinion or discloses the underlying facts or data, an adverse party in a civil case may—or in a criminal case must—be permitted to examine the expert about the underlying facts or data. This examination must take place outside the jury's hearing.

§13:27.2.2 Party Is Entitled to Voir Dire Expert Witness

Under Rule 705(b), a party is entitled, upon timely request, to conduct a voir dire examination directed to the underlying facts or data upon which the opinion of an opposing party's expert is based. Alba v. State, 905 S.W.2d 581 (Tex. Crim. App. 1995).

The trial court must allow this examination to be conducted prior to the expert giving his opinion and out of the hearing of the jury. Alba.

Affording a party the chance to voir dire, the expert witness gives the party the opportunity to determine the foundation of the expert's opinion without fear of eliciting damaging hearsay or other inadmissible evidence in the jury's presence. Goss v. State, 826 S.W.2d 162 (Tex. Crim. App. 1992).

A Rule 705(b) hearing may also supply counsel with sufficient ammunition to make a timely objection to the expert's testimony on the ground that it lacks a sufficient basis for admissibility. Goss.

§13:27.2.3 Timeliness of Request

The request to voir dire outside the jury's presence is timely if lodged at any point before the expert witness testifies as to the underlying facts and data. Harris v. State, 133 S.W.3d 760 (Tex. App.—Texarkana 2004, *pet. ref'd*).

§13:27.2.4 Preservation of Error

A request to voir dire an expert witness on the subject of his qualifications does not preserve error where the court did not allow voir dire on the underlying facts and data. Jenkins v. State, 912 S.W.2d 793 (Tex. Crim. App. 1993).

§13:27.2.5 Form: Motion

See our companion book *Texas Criminal Forms* (James Publishing):

- Form 13-30, Motion for Voir Dire of Expert Witness and for Pretrial Ruling on Admissibility of Expert Testimony.
- Form 13-30.2 Motion for Production of Statements, Reports, Writings and Underlying Data of Expert Witnesses
- Form 13-30.3 Motion for Production of Material Pertaining to Expert Witness

§13:28 Child Abuse Files

§13:28.1 Statutes

Tex.Fam.Code §261.201. Confidentiality and Disclosure of Information

40 Tex. Admin. Code §700.202. Definitions

40 Tex. Admin. Code §700.203. Access to Confidential Information Maintained by the Texas Department of Protective and Regulatory Services (TDPRS)

40 Tex. Admin. Code §700.204. Redaction of Records Prior to Release

40 Tex. Admin. Code §700.205. Procedures for Requesting Access to Confidential Information

40 Tex. Admin. Code §700.206. Videotapes, Audiotapes, and Photographs

40 Tex. Admin. Code §700.207. Charges for Copies of Records

§13:28.2 Discovery Procedures

A defendant is not entitled to obtain copies of Texas Department of Family and Protective Services (DFPS) records under Tex.Fam.Code §261.201 where the trial court has reviewed the records *in camera* and determined that the records would not be useful to the defendant in preparing or conducting his defense or his cross-examination of the witnesses, and where they do not show any prior allegation that was determined to be false. James v. State, 47 S.W.3d 710

(Tex.App.—Texarkana 2001, *no pet.*); *see also* Pennsylvania v. Ritchie, 480 U.S. 39, 107 S.Ct. 989, 94 L.Ed.2d 40 (1987).

PRACTICE TIP: Where the trial court has reviewed copies of DFPS records in camera to determine if they should be released to the defendant, always have the trial court place the records in the record of the case for later review by an appellate court in the event of an appeal. See James.

In the absence of a showing of necessity, the confidential nature of child abuse case reports should be maintained. Coachman v. State, 692 S.W.2d 940 (Tex.App.—Houston [1st Dist.] 1985, *pet. ref'd*).

A regulatory agency such as the Texas Department of Family and Protective Services (DFPS) waives its privilege against disclosure of materials made privileged by the Family Code where it discloses those materials to another state agency or individual. Patmore v. State, 831 S.W.2d 97 (Tex.App.—Eastland 1992, *no pet.*).

If the matter for which a privilege is sought has been disclosed to a third party, thus raising the question of waiver of the privilege, the party asserting the privilege has the burden of proving that no waiver has occurred. Patmore.

Because Art. 39.14 specifies that the trial court shall specify the manner in which the defense may be allowed to copy state's evidence, the trial court has the authority to order the state to make a copy of a DVD of the interview of the complainant at a child advocacy center in its possession. In re Dist. Attorney's Office of the 25th Judicial Dist., 358 S.W.3d 244, 245-6 (Tex. Crim. App. 2011).

§13:28.3 Form: Motion and Records Request

See our companion book *Texas Criminal Forms* (James Publishing):

- Form 17-28, Motion for Discovery of DFPS Records.
- Form 17-29, DFPS Records Request Form.

§13:29 Child Pornography

§13:29.1 Statutes

Art. 39.15. DISCOVERY OF EVIDENCE THAT CONSTITUTES CHILD PORNOGRAPHY.

(a) In the manner provided by this article, a court shall allow discovery under Article 39.14 of property or material:

(1) that constitutes child pornography, as described by Section 43.26(a)(1), Penal Code;

(2) the promotion or possession of which is prohibited under Section 43.261, Penal Code; or

(3) that is described by Section 2 or 5, Article 38.071, of this code.

(b) Property or material described by Subsection (a) must remain in the care, custody, or control of the court or the state as provided by Article 38.45.

(c) A court shall deny any request by a defendant to copy, photograph, duplicate, or otherwise reproduce any property or material described by Subsection (a), provided that the state makes the property or material reasonably available to the defendant.

(d) For purposes of Subsection (c), property or material is considered to be reasonably available to the defendant if, at a facility under the control of the state, the state provides ample opportunity for the inspection, viewing, and examination of the property or material by the defendant, the defendant's attorney, and any individual the defendant seeks to qualify to provide expert testimony at trial.

Art. 38.45. EVIDENCE THAT CONSTITUTES CHILD PORNOGRAPHY.

(a) During the course of a criminal hearing or proceeding, the court may

not make available or allow to be made available for copying or dissemination to the public property or material:

(1) that constitutes child pornography, as described by Section 43.26(a)(1), Penal Code;

(2) the promotion or possession of which is prohibited under Section 43.261, Penal Code; or

(3) that is described by Section 2 or 5, Article 38.071, of this code.

(b) The court shall place property or material described by Subsection (a) under seal of the court on conclusion of the criminal hearing or proceeding.

(c) The attorney representing the state shall be provided access to property or material described by Subsection (a). In the manner provided by Article 39.15, the defendant, the defendant's attorney, and any individual the defendant seeks to qualify to provide expert testimony at trial shall be provided access to property or material described by Subsection (a).

(d) A court that places property or material described by Subsection (a) under seal may issue an order lifting the seal on a finding that the order is in the best interest of the public.

§13:30 Right to Examination of Evidence by Independent Expert

§13:31 General Points

The burden is on the defendant to show good cause before a court must issue an order for production and inspection. Massey v. State, 933 S.W.2d 141, 153 (Tex.Crim.App.1996); Ehrke v. State, 459 S.W.3d 606, 611 (Tex. Crim. App. 2015).

There are two separate grounds under which a criminal defendant might qualify to inspect the state's evidence without having to meet his general discovery burden to show good cause: 1) that the evidence is material to the defense of the accused; and 2) that the evidence is indispensable to the state. Evidence is material to the accused if its omission would create a reasonable doubt that did not otherwise exist. Evidence is indispensable to the state when its exclusion from evidence would affect the essential proof that the defendant committed the crime. Ehrke, 459 S.W.3d at 611.

The right of inspection may be a qualified right when the evidence has been destroyed in the process of analysis. Norton v. State, 930 S.W.2d 101 (Tex. App.—Amarillo 1996, pet. ref 'd) McBride v. State, 838 S.W.2d 248 (Tex. Crim. App. 1992).

In the absence of materiality or indispensability, a defendant may have the additional burden of showing a significant issue of fact, which has been defined as a showing of a material issue sufficient to require the trial court to appoint an independent expert for an indigent defendant. Ehrke, 459 S.W.3d at 615.

In order to meet his burden to show good cause, a defendant should present affidavits or other evidence in support of his defensive theory; an explanation as to what his defensive theory is and why inspection of the evidence would be helpful in establishing that theory; or make a showing that there was a reason to question the state's evidence. The nature of the evidence and the importance and complexity of it may also have a direct bearing on whether the defendant is entitled to inspection. Ehrke, 459 S.W.3d at 615 *7.

However, while all defendants have an absolute right to inspect material and indispensable evidence against them, a defendant does not have an absolute right to a state-appointed expert. The indigent defendant has the additional burden of showing a significant issue of fact, which the Court defined as a showing of a material issue sufficient to require the trial court to appoint an independent expert. Ehrke, 459 S.W.3d at 615.

In order to be entitled to expert assistance for the inspection and analysis of evidence, the indigent must show: a reason to doubt the analysis by the state's expert; a reason to doubt that the evidence in question was other than claimed by the state; how an expert was needed to prepare his defense;information with regard to how important the scientific issue is in his case; or an explanation of how much help a defense expert could provide.

An indigent defendant should present affidavits or other evidence in support of his defensive theory;an explanation as to what his defensive theory is and why expert assistance would be helpful in establishing that theory; or he should make a showing that there was a reason to question the state's expert and proof. The nature of an expert's field and the importance and complexity of the issue may have a direct bearing on whether the appointment of an expert would be helpful. Ehrke, 459 S.W.3d at 615-6.

§13:32 Controlled Substances

A defendant has an absolute right to an independent chemical analysis of alleged contraband in possession cases. Pena v. State, 166 S.W.3d 274 (Tex.App.—Waco 2005, rev'd on other grounds at 191 S.W.3d 133, Tex. Crim. App. 2006) *citing* Terrell v. State, 521 S.W.2d 618 (Tex. Crim. App. 1975).

The indigent defendant has the additional burden of showing a significant issue of fact, which the Court defined as a showing of a material issue sufficient to require the trial court to appoint an independent expert. Ehrke, 459 S.W.3d at 615

§13:33 Tape Recordings

Original tape recordings should be produced and made available to counsel where they are indispensable to the state's case. Bates v. State, 587 S.W.2d 121 (Tex. Crim. App. 1979) (where the failure to allow inspection was not reversible error because the tapes were only one strand of incriminating evidence).

§13:34 Fingerprints

Latent fingerprints of the defendant should be produced. Hollowell v. State, 571 S.W.2d 179 (Tex. Crim. App. 1978) (where the failure to produce the defendant's fingerprints was harmless error under facts of the case). *See also* Helton v. State, 738 S.W.2d 734 (Tex.App.—Beaumont 1987, *pet. ref'd*).

§13:35 Ballistic Tests

The defendant should be allowed to conduct independent ballistic examinations on weapons where evidence is material to the prosecution. Quinones v. State, 592 S.W.2d 933 (Tex. Crim. App. 1980).

§13:36 Blood, Urine, Breath Test

Tex. Trans. Code § 724.018. Furnishing Information Concerning Test Results.

> *On the request of a person who has given a specimen at the request of a peace officer, full information concerning the analysis of the specimen shall be made available to the person or the person's attorney.*

Transportation Code §724.018 provides for discovery of these test results in cases arising under violations of the Motor Vehicle Act.

§13:37 Computer Hard Drive

Where a computer hard drive is indispensable to the state's case, the hard drive or an exact copy of it should be provided to the defense. Taylor v. State, 93 S.W.3d 487 (Tex.App.—Texarkana 2002, *pet. ref'd*).

§13:38 DNA Test Results

The results of DNA testing can be subject to a discovery order issued by the trial judge. Jackson v. State, 17 S.W.3d 664 (Tex. Crim. App. 2000).

§13:40 Failure to Provide Discovery

§13:41 Remedy

When a trial court grants a motion for discovery and the prosecution willfully fails to disclose the evidence ordered disclosed, the evidence will be suppressed. State v. LaRue, 152 S.W.2d 95 (Tex. Crim. App. 2004) (where the conduct was found to be not willful).

Evidence is willfully withheld if the act is done voluntarily and intentionally, with the specific intent to disobey the law. Dunklin v. State, 194 S.W.3d 14 (Tex.App.—Tyler 2006, *no pet.*) *citing* State v. LaRue, 108 S.W.3d 431, 434 (Tex.App.—Beaumont 2003), *aff'd*, 152 S.W.3d 95 (Tex. Crim. App. 2004).

The prosecutor's conduct will be found to be willful where it was a calculated effort to frustrate the defense. Oprean v. State, 201 S.W.3d 724 (Tex. Crim. App. 2006) (the prosecutor failed to turn over a videotape and then sandbagged her intent to introduce it at trial).

In order to establish a due process violation for the failure to comply with a discovery order, the defendant must: 1) show that he was prejudiced pre-trial; 2) show how the failure to comply substantially impaired his actual defensive posture at trial; and 3) explain how his defensive posture could have materially improved had he been alerted to the existence or significance of the evidence earlier. Francis v. State, 428 S.W.3d 850, 859 (Tex. Crim. App. 2014).

An appellate court will review a trial court's ruling to exclude evidence for willful prosecutorial defiance of a discovery order under an abuse-of-discretion standard, deferring to any trial-level ruling that falls within the zone of reasonable disagreement. An appellate court must pay almost absolute deference to the trial court's findings of fact based on determinations of credibility or demeanor. In the absence of any specific findings of fact from the trial court (either oral or written) spread on the record, a reviewing court must assume that the trial court resolved all fact issues in a way that is consistent with its ultimate ruling, so long as those presumed findings of fact are supported by the record. Francis, 428 S.W.3d at 855.

§13:42 Mandamus to Compel Discovery

Where the discovery in question is mandatory, rather than discretionary with the trial court, the courts of appeals have authority to issue a writ of mandamus to compel discovery in a criminal case. The defendant has the burden to show that there is no other adequate remedy and that he is seeking to compel a ministerial act. Dickens v. Ct. of Appeals, 727 S.W.2d 542 (Tex. Crim. App. 1987).

§13:50 Exculpatory and Mitigation Evidence

§13:51 Statutes

CCP Art. 2.01. Duties of District Attorneys

> *Each district attorney shall represent the State in all criminal cases in the district courts of his district and in appeals therefrom, except in cases where he has been, before his election, employed adversely. When any criminal proceeding is had before an examining court in his district or before a judge upon habeas corpus, and he is notified of the same, and is at the time within his district, he shall represent the State therein, unless prevented by other official duties. It shall be the primary duty of all prosecuting attorneys, including any special prosecutors, not to convict, but to see that justice is done. They shall not suppress facts or secrete witnesses capable of establishing the innocence of the accused.*

Tex. Disciplinary R. Prof'l. Conduct Rule 3.09. Special Responsibilities of a Prosecutor

> *The prosecutor in a criminal case shall:*
>
> *(a) refrain from prosecuting or threatening to prosecute a charge that the prosecutor knows is not supported by probable cause;*
>
> *(b) refrain from conducting or assisting in a custodial interrogation of an accused unless the prosecutor has made reasonable efforts to be assured that the accused has been advised of any right to, and the procedure for obtaining, counsel and has been given reasonable opportunity to obtain counsel;*
>
> *(c) not initiate or encourage efforts to obtain from an unrepresented accused a waiver of important pre-trial, trial or post-trial rights;*
>
> *(d) make timely disclosure to the defense of all evidence or information known to the prosecutor that tends to negate the guilt of the accused or mitigates the offense, and, in connection with sentencing, disclose to the defense and to the tribunal all unprivileged mitigating information known to the prosecutor, except when the prosecutor is relieved of this responsibility by a protective order of the tribunal; and*
>
> *(e) exercise reasonable care to prevent persons employed or controlled by the prosecutor in a criminal case*

from making an extrajudicial statement that the prosecutor would be prohibited from making under Rule 3.07.

§13:52 Duty of the State

It is axiomatic that the State has an affirmative duty to make available to an accused, in a timely manner, exculpatory evidence which is in its possession. Brady v. Maryland, 373 U.S. 83, 83 S.Ct. 1194, 10 L.Ed.2d 215 (1963); Ex parte Mitchell, 977 S.W.2d 575 (Tex. Crim. App. 1997).

The duty to disclose encompasses both impeachment and exculpatory evidence. Harm v. State, 183 S.W.3d 403 (Tex. Crim. App. 2006).

Brady has been extended to include the required revelation to an accused of material exculpatory evidence in the possession of police agencies and other parts of the prosecutorial team. Kyles v. Whitley, 514 U.S. 419, 115 S.Ct. 1555, 131 L.Ed.2d 490 (1995); Mitchell.

Even if the prosecutor was not personally aware of the evidence, the State is not relieved of its duty to disclose because "the State" includes, in addition to the prosecutor, other lawyers and employees in his office and members of law enforcement connected to the investigation and prosecution of the case. Ex parte Miles, 359 S.W.3d 647 (Tex. Crim. App. 2012), citing Kyles v. Whitley.

The duty to reveal material exculpatory evidence as dictated by Brady overrides the work-product privilege contained in Code of Criminal Procedure 39.14. Ex parte Miles.

The state's duty to reveal Brady material to the defense attaches when the information comes into the state's possession, whether or not the defense requested the information. Harm (citing Thomas v. State, 841 S.W.2d 399 (Tex. Crim. App. 1992)).

An open-file policy generally satisfies the prosecution's duty to disclose exculpatory evidence. Harm.

PRACTICE TIP: If a prosecutor is unsure whether certain evidence must be disclosed, the prosecutor should submit the evidence to the trial court for its consideration. See Thomas v. State, 841 S.W.2d 399 (Tex. Crim. App. 1992).

When police or prosecutors conceal significant exculpatory or impeaching material in the state's possession, it is ordinarily incumbent on the state to set the record straight when contrary evidence is presented at trial. Banks v. Dretke, 540 U.S. 668, 124 S.Ct. 1256, 157 L.Ed.2d 1166 (2004).

§13:53 Exculpatory, Mitigating or Impeaching

To succeed on a Brady claim, a defendant must show that the evidence withheld by the State was "favorable" to his case. Favorable evidence is that which, if disclosed and used effectively, may make the difference between conviction and acquittal. Pena v. State, 353 S.W.3d 797 (Tex. Crim. App. 2011).

Favorable evidence is any evidence that, if disclosed and used effectively, may make a difference between conviction and acquittal and includes both exculpatory and impeachment evidence. Harm v. State, 183 S.W.3d 403 (Tex. Crim. App. 2006) *citing* Thomas v. State, 841 S.W.2d 399 (Tex. Crim. App. 1992).

Exculpatory evidence may justify, excuse, or clear the defendant from fault, while impeachment evidence is that which disputes or contradicts other evidence. Harm; Thomas.

Under Brady, prosecutors must turn over impeachment evidence. Ex parte Richardson, 70 S.W.3d 865 (Tex. Crim. App. 2002).

Under Brady, nondisclosure of favorable evidence violates due process only if it is material to guilt or punishment. The mere possibility that an item of undisclosed information might have helped the defense, or might have affected the outcome of the trial, does not establish materiality in the constitutional sense. Pena.

Evidence is material if there is a reasonable probability that, had the evidence been disclosed to the defense, the result of the proceeding would have been different. Harm (*citing* Ex parte Kimes, 872 S.W.2d 700 (Tex. Crim. App. 1993)).

A reasonable probability is one that is sufficient to undermine confidence in the outcome of the trial. Harm; Ex parte Kimes.

Materiality is determined by examining the alleged error in the context of the entire record and overall strength of the state's case. Harm; Thomas.

In determining whether evidence not disclosed by prosecutors was material, in violation of Brady, the cumulative effect of all suppressed evidence favorable to the defendant should be considered, rather than considering each item of evidence individually. Kyles v. Whitley, 514 U.S. 419, 115 S.Ct. 1555, 131 L.Ed.2d 490 (1995).

Whether the right to Brady information extends to the pretrial stage of prosecution, however, is still an open question. Ex parte Palmberg, 491 S.W.3d 804, 814 (Tex. Crim. App. 2015 fn. 18).

§13:54 Specific Examples of Exculpatory Evidence

The prosecution has a duty to reveal impeaching information that shows that a state's witness was a paid police informant and to disclose information showing that a witness was intensively coached prior to testifying. Banks v. Dretke, 540 U.S. 668, 124 S.Ct. 1256, 157 L.Ed.2d 1166 (2004).

Evidence of a defendant's insanity or incompetency constitutes Brady material requiring disclosure. Ex Parte Lewis, 587 S.W.2d 170 (Tex. Crim. App. 1979); Nickerson v. State, 69 S.W.3d 661 (Tex.App.—Waco 2002, *pet. ref'd*) (evidence of insanity on videotape).

A log book kept by a former police officer showing that the state's star witness was not a truthful person has been found to be favorable evidence. Ex parte Richardson, 70 S.W.3d 865 (Tex. Crim. App. 2002).

An oral statement made by a witness who had previously given a written statement contained in the state's file should have been communicated to the defense where it contained favorable evidence. Flores v. State, 940 S.W.2d 189 (Tex.App.—San Antonio 1996, *no pet.*).

A witness' failure to identify the defendant in a pretrial photo lineup can be material exculpatory or mitigating evidence. Hall v. State, 283 S.W.3d 137 (Tex. Crim. App. 2009).

The state has a duty to reveal material admissible, such as audio recordings of conversations between the defendant and law enforcement. Pena v. State, 353 S.W.3d 797 (Tex. Crim. App. 2011) (where the recording would have impeached the officer's version of his conversation with the defendant).

Undisclosed police reports which identify other potential suspects in the offense can constitute other evidence that is favorable and material where the information can be used for impeachment purposes. Ex parte Miles, 359 S.W.3d 647 (Tex. Crim. App. 2012).

Evidence impeaching an eyewitness can be material where the State's other evidence is not strong enough to sustain confidence in the verdict. Smith v. Cain, 565 U.S. ___, 132 S.Ct. 627, 181 L.Ed.2d 571 (2012) (where the eyewitness was the only evidence linking the defendant to the crime).

Evidence of statements that case doubt on a witnesses' credibility (here statements of motive to "get" the defendant), evidence of a witnesses' attempts to procure a deal for testifying against a defendant and evidence that contradicts a witness' testimony are all examples of Brady material. Wearry v. Cain, 577 U.S. ___, 136 S.Ct. 1002, 1004, 194 L.Ed.2d 78 (2016).

§13:55 Inapplicability of Brady Rule

The Brady rule does not apply when the defendant was already aware of the information. Havard v. State, 800 S.W.2d 195 (Tex. Crim. App. 1989) (overruling an alleged Brady error involving the defendant's prior statement to police); Hayes v. State, 85 S.W.3d 809 (Tex. Crim. App. 2002) (there is no Brady violation where the defendant wrote the letter in question).

The Brady rule does not apply when the evidence in question is inadmissible. Ex parte Kimes, 872 S.W.2d 700 (Tex. Crim. App. 1993).

The state is not required to seek out exculpatory evidence independently on appellant's behalf, or furnish appellant with exculpatory or mitigating evidence that is fully accessible to appellant from other sources. Harm v. State, 183 S.W.3d 403 (Tex. Crim. App. 2006), *citing* Jackson v. State, 552 S.W.2d 798 (Tex. Crim. App. 1976).

Further, the prosecutor is not required to furnish the defendant with exculpatory and mitigating evidence which is equally and fully accessible to the defense. Pena v. State, 353 S.W.3d 797 (Tex. Crim. App. 2011).

Brady and its progeny do not require prosecuting authorities to disclose exculpatory information to defendants that the State does not have in its possession and that is not known to exist. Harm, *citing* Hafdahl v. State, 805 S.W.2d 396, 399 (Tex. Crim. App. 1990).

Where the evidence shows that the state did not come into the possession of the allegedly exculpatory information until after the defendant's trial, the Brady rule is not invoked. Ex parte Reed, 271 S.W.3d 698 (Tex. Crim. App. 2008).

§13:56 Establishing a Brady Violation

A defendant must satisfy three requirements to establish a Brady violation: (1) the state suppressed evidence; (2) the suppressed evidence is favorable to defendant; and (3) the suppressed evidence is material. Harm v. State, 183 S.W.3d 403 (Tex. Crim. App. 2006), *citing* Little v. State, 991 S.W.2d 864 (Tex. Crim. App.1999).

Additionally, we require that the evidence central to the Brady claim be admissible in court. Pena v. State, 353 S.W.3d 797 (Tex. Crim. App. 2011) (citing Ex parte Kimes, 872 S.W.2d 700, 703 (Tex. Crim. App.1993)); Ex parte Miles, 359 S.W.3d 647 (Tex. Crim. App. 2012).

Incorporated into the third prong, materiality, is a requirement that defendant must be prejudiced by the state's failure to disclose the favorable evidence. Harm, *citing* Banks v. Dretke, 540 U.S. 668, 124 S.Ct. 1256, 157 L.Ed.2d 1166 (2004).

Under Brady, the defendant bears the burden of showing that, in light of all the evidence, it is reasonably probable that the outcome of the trial would have been different had the prosecutor made a timely disclosure. Hampton v. State, 86 S.W.3d 603 (Tex. Crim. App. 2002).

The mere possibility that an item of undisclosed information might have helped the defense, or might have affected the outcome of the trial, does not establish "materiality" in the constitutional sense. Hampton.

It is irrelevant whether suppression of the favorable evidence was done willfully or inadvertently. Harm, *citing* Strickler v. Greene, 527 U.S. 263, 119 S.Ct. 1936, 144 L.Ed.2d 286 (1999).

If the defense has the opportunity to cross-examine concerning the allegedly exculpatory material and there is no showing the defense would have pursued a different trial strategy if he or she had known this information sooner, no Brady violation is shown. Taylor v. State, 93 S.W.3d 487 (Tex.App.—Texarkana 2002, *pet. ref'd*), *citing* Williams v. State, 995 S.W.2d 754 (Tex.App.—San Antonio 1999, *no pet.*).

At trial, evidence willfully withheld from disclosure under a discovery order should be excluded from evidence. Oprean v. State, 201 S.W.3d 724 (Tex. Crim. App. 2006).

When reviewing a trial judge's decision to admit evidence that the defense claims was withheld from discovery, an appellate court must determine whether the judge's decision was an abuse of discretion. Unless the trial judge's decision was outside the "zone of reasonable disagreement," an appellate court should uphold the ruling. When a trial judge makes findings of fact based on an evaluation of credibility and demeanor, an appellate court "should show almost total deference" to those findings. When the trial judge fails to enter written or oral findings of fact, an appellate court will "view the evidence in the light most favorable to the trial court's ruling and assume that the trial court made implicit findings of fact that support its ruling as long as those findings are supported by the record." Oprean.

On appeal where it is found that the state failed to divulge potentially exculpatory evidence (whether directly exculpatory or exculpatory as having impeachment value) and where the failure undermined confidence in the trial's outcome resulting in a violation of a defendant's due process right to a fair trial, the remedy prescribed is reversal of the conviction and remand to the trial court for further proceedings. Ex parte Mitchell, 977 S.W.2d 575 (Tex. Crim. App. 1997).

The failure to request a postponement or seek a continuance waives any error urged in an appeal on the basis of surprise or on the timeliness of notice. Martin v. State, 176 S.W.3d 887 (Tex.App.—Fort Worth 2005, *no pet.), citing* Lindley v. State, 635 S.W.2d 541, 544 (Tex. Crim. App. 1982).

§13:57 Form: Motion

See our companion book *Texas Criminal Forms* (James Publishing):

- Form 13-6, Motion to Produce Exculpatory and Mitigating Evidence.

§13:60 Other Discovery Tools

§13:61 Depositions of Witnesses

§13:61.1 Statutes

CCP Art. 39.02. Witness Depositions

> *Depositions of witnesses may be taken by either the state or the defendant. When a party desires to take the deposition of a witness, the party shall file with the clerk of the court in which the case is pending an affidavit stating the facts necessary to constitute a good reason for taking the* witness' *deposition and an application to take the deposition. On filing of the affidavit and application, and after notice to the opposing party, the court shall hear the application and determine if good reason exists for taking the deposition. The court shall base its determination and shall grant or deny the application on the facts made known at the hearing. This provision is limited to the purposes stated in Article 39.01.*

CCP Art. 39.03. Officers Who May Take the Deposition

> *Upon the filing of such an affidavit and application, the court shall appoint, order or designate one of the following persons before whom such deposition shall be taken:*
>
> 1. *A district judge.*
> 2. *A county judge.*
> 3. *A notary public.*
> 4. *A district clerk.*
> 5. *A county clerk.*
>
> *Such order shall specifically name such person and the time when and place where such deposition shall be taken. Failure of a witness to respond thereto, shall be punishable by contempt by the court. Such deposition shall be oral or written, as the court shall direct.*

§13:61.2 Defendant Must Show Good Reason

A defendant may take the deposition of a witness only upon a showing of good reason. May v. State, 738 S.W.2d 261 (Tex. Crim. App. 1987), *cert. den.*, 484 U.S. 872, 108 S.Ct. 206, 98 L.Ed.2d 158 (1987).

The defendant must show that the witness sought to be deposed possesses information critical to a significant factor at trial, or that such witness has information exclusively within that witness' knowledge. Janecka v. State, 937 S.W.2d 456 (Tex. Crim. App. 1996).

Before a trial court will be found to have abused its discretion in declining to permit depositions to be taken, there must be a showing the defendant was harmed by such action. James v. State, 546 S.W.2d 306 (Tex. Crim. App. 1977).

There is not an abuse of discretion in the denying of a motion to take a deposition where the witness testifies at trial, is subject to cross-examination by the defense, and the defendant does not otherwise show he or she was harmed by the trial court's action. Cooks v. State, 844 S.W.2d 697 (Tex. Crim. App. 1992).

CCP Art. 39.02 requires an affidavit, not a verified application. State ex. rel. Simmons v. Moore, 774 S.W.2d 711 (Tex.App.—El Paso 1989, *no pet.*).

§13:61.3 Form: Application to Take Deposition

See our companion book *Texas Criminal Forms* (James Publishing):

- Form 13-23.1, State or Defendant's Application to Take Deposition of Witness.

§13:62 Written Interrogatories

§13:62.1 Statute

CCP Art. 39.06. Written Interrogatories

> *When any such deposition is to be taken by written interrogatories, such written interrogatories shall be filed with the clerk of the court, and a copy of the same served on all other parties or their counsel for the length of time and in the manner required for service of interrogatories in civil action, and the same procedure shall also be followed with reference to cross-interrogatories as that prescribed in civil action.*

§13:62.2 Form: Application to Take Deposition by Written Interrogatories

See our companion book *Texas Criminal Forms* (James Publishing):

- Form 13-23.2, State or Defendant's Application to Take Deposition of Witness By Written Interrogatories.

§13:70 Exceptions to Discovery Rights

§13:71 Police Reports

Police and prosecution reports are not discoverable prior to trial. Michaelwicz v. State, 186 S.W.3d 601 (Tex.App.—Austin 2006, *pet. ref'd*).

Prosecutors are not required to disclose their investigative work. Michaelwicz.

A defendant has a right to have the court inspect a police report in camera to determine whether it contains any Brady material. Crawford v. State, 934 S.W.2d 744 (Tex.App.—Houston [1st Dist.] 1996, *pet. ref'd*).

§13:72 Medical Examiner's Report

Medical examiner's reports are not discoverable under Art. 39.14, since they are public records. Beeson v. State, 651 S.W.2d 944 (Tex.App.—Fort Worth 1983, *no pet.*).

Medical examiner records are subject to required public disclosure in accordance with Chapter 552, Government Code, except that a photograph or x-ray of a body taken during an autopsy is excepted from required public disclosure in accordance with Chapter 552, Government Code, but is subject to disclosure: (1) under a subpoena or authority of other law; or (2) if the photograph or x-ray is of the body of a person who died while in the custody of law enforcement. CCP Art. 49.25.

§13:73 Prior Jury Service

The state has no obligation under the discovery statutes to furnish its prior jury service information to the defense. Martin v. State, 577 S.W.2d 490 (Tex. Crim. App. 1979).

Prosecutors are not obligated to turn over juror information that is available to the defense on voir dire. Armstrong v. State, 897 S.W.2d 361 (Tex. Crim. App. 1995).

The defendant preserves no claim for appellate review where he does not follow the procedures required in the public records act. Etheridge v. State, 903 S.W.2d 1 (Tex. Crim. App. 1994).

PRACTICE TIP: The simplest method to obtaining prior jury service information is to simply ask the veniremen during voir dire. See Espinosa v. State, 653 S.W.2d 446 (Tex.App.—San Antonio 1982), aff'd, 669 S.W.2d 736 (Tex.Crim.App. 1984) (mandamus inappropriate remedy).

§13:80 Requests for Notice of Intention to Introduce Evidence

§13:81 General Points

The purpose of a notice requirement is to prevent surprise to the defendant and apprise him of the evidence the state plans to introduce at trial. Hernandez v. State, 176 S.W.3d 821 (Tex. Crim. App. 2005).

§13:81.1 Defendant Must Request Notice

Under Tex.R.Evid. 404(b) (and all other notice provisions since they reference Rule 404(b)), the defendant must file a timely "request for notice" in order to trigger the state's duty to provide notice under the particular provisions. Mitchell v. State, 982 S.W.2d 425 (Tex. Crim. App. 1998).

Merely filing the request in a discovery motion is not effective until ruled upon by the court. Espinosa v. State, 853 S.W.2d 36 (Tex. Crim. App. 1993).

§13:81.2 Request Must Be Timely

The defendant's request for notice must be timely; that is, notice must be requested in enough time to allow the state to comply in advance of trial. Chimney v. State, 6 S.W.3d 681 (Tex.App.—Waco 1999, *no pet.*).

For more information about timeliness of notice under this provision, *see* §15:113.

§13:81.3 Notice Must Be Timely

The rule requires "reasonable" notice. Hayden v. State, 66 S.W.3d 269 (Tex. Crim. App. 2001).

Generally, notice given at least 10 days in advance of trial is timely. Splawn v. State, 160 S.W.3d 103 (Tex.App.—Texarkana 2005, *pet. ref'd*).

However, the closer to trial the request for notice is made by the defense, the less notice is required by the state for admissibility. Self v. State, 860 S.W.2d 261 (Tex.App.—Fort Worth 1993, *pet. ref'd*) (five days notice reasonable where request made 19 days before trial).

Notice can be insufficient where defense counsel has insufficient time to investigate the subject of the notice. Webb v. State, 36 S.W.3d 164 (Tex. App.—Houston [14th Dist.] 2000, *pet. ref'd*).

Where the state's "notice" does not strictly state an intent to introduce the evidence (such as where the state merely delivers witness statements to the defense), the closer in time the delivery of the evidence is to the time of the request for notice, the more likely the "notice" will be found reasonable. Hayden.

An "open file" policy, by itself, is not sufficient to comply with the rule's notice requirement. Buchanan v. State, 911 S.W.2d 11 (Tex. Crim. App. 1995).

The Rule 404(b) notice provision is a rule of admissibility because Rule 404(b) literally conditions the admissibility of other crimes evidence on the state's compliance with the notice provision. Hernandez v. State, 176 S.W.3d 821 (Tex. Crim. App. 2005).

If an extraneous offense is admitted by the trial court in violation of the Rule 404(b) notice requirement, on appeal harm is analyzed on the basis of whether the defendant was surprised by the admission. Hernandez.

When erroneously admitted Rule 404(b) evidence is substantively admissible, the error is harmless unless (1) it substantially influenced the jury's verdict and (2) the defendant was surprised by the evidence. Hernandez; Allen v. State, 202 S.W.3d 364 (Tex.App.—Fort Worth 2006, *pet. ref'd*).

§13:82 Extraneous Offenses

§13:82.1 Statute

Tex. R. Evid. 404(b) Crimes, Wrongs, or Other Acts.

> *(1) Prohibited Uses. Evidence of a crime, wrong, or other act is not admissible to prove a person's character in order to show that on a particular occasion the person acted in accordance with the character.*
>
> *(2) Permitted Uses; Notice in Criminal Case. This evidence may be admissible for another purpose, such as proving motive, opportunity, intent, preparation, plan, knowledge, identity, absence of mistake, or lack of accident. On timely request by a defendant in a criminal case, the prosecutor must provide reasonable notice before trial that the prosecution intends to introduce such evidence—other than that arising in the same transaction—in its case-in-chief.*

§13:82.2 Evidence Rule Applies Only to Guilt Phase

Since Tex.R.Evid. 404(b) applies to the guilt phase of the trial, a request for 404(b) notice is only requesting notice for evidence sought to be admitted at that phase of the trial. Herring v. State, 752 S.W.2d 169 (Tex.App.—Houston [1st Dist.] 1988), *remanded on other grounds*, 758 S.W.2d 283 (Tex. Crim. App. 1988).

If an extraneous offense is admitted by the trial court in violation of the Rule 404(b) notice requirement, harm is analyzed on appeal on the basis of whether the defendant was surprised by its admission. Hernandez v. State, 176 S.W.3d 821 (Tex. Crim. App. 2005).

PRACTICE TIP: If the trial court allows admission of an extraneous offense in violation of the Rule 404(b) notice requirement, make a record of the surprise suffered by the defendant and his inability to contest, refute or mitigate the extraneous offense because of the lack of timely notice.

For more information about notice of extraneous offenses, *see* §15:113.

§13:82.3 Form: Request for Notice, Motion for Hearing, and Objection to Admissibility

See our companion book *Texas Criminal Forms* (James Publishing):

- Form 13-11.1, Request for Notice of State's Intention to Offer Extraneous Offenses Pursuant to Rule 404(b).
- Form 13-11.2, Motion for Pretrial Evidentiary Hearing on Admissibility of Extraneous Offenses.
- Form 13-11.3, Defendant's Written Objection to Admissibility of Extraneous Offenses, and Request for Findings of Fact and Conclusions of Law.
- Form 13-11.4 Defendant's Motion for Deadline on Notice of Extraneous Offenses

§13:83 Child Abuse Cases

§13:83.1 Statute

CCP Art. 38.37. Evidence of Extraneous Offenses or Acts

Section 3. On timely request by the defendant, the state shall give the defendant notice of the state's intent to introduce the case-in-chief evidence described by Section 2 in the same manner as the state is required to give notice under Rule 404(b), Texas Rules of Evidence.

Sec. 1. This article applies to a proceeding in the prosecution of a defendant for an offense, or an attempt or conspiracy to commit an offense, under the following provisions of the Penal Code:

(1) if committed against a child under 17 years of age:

(A) Chapter 21 (Sexual Offenses);

(B) Chapter 22 (Assaultive Offenses); or

(C) Section 25.02 (Prohibited Sexual Conduct); or

(2) if committed against a person younger than 18 years of age:

(A) Section 43.25 (Sexual Performance by a Child);

(B) Section 20A.02(a)(7) or (8); or

(C) Section 43.05(a)(2) (Compelling Prostitution) .

Sec. 2. Notwithstanding Rules 404 and 405, Texas Rules of Evidence, evidence of other crimes, wrongs, or acts committed by the defendant against the child who is the victim of the alleged offense shall be admitted for its bearing on relevant matters, including:

(1) the state of mind of the defendant and the child; and

(2) the previous and subsequent relationship between the defendant and the child.

Sec. 3. On timely request by the defendant, the state shall give the defendant notice of the state's intent to introduce in the case in chief evidence described by Section 2 in the same manner as the state is required to give notice under Rule 404(b), Texas Rules of Evidence.

Sec. 4. This article does not limit the admissibility of evidence of extraneous crimes, wrongs, or acts under any other applicable law.

§13:83.2 Defendant Must Request Notice

CCP Art. 38.37 provides that upon timely request, the state must give notice of its intent to introduce child abuse extraneous offense or bad act evidence. In order to be entitled to such notice, the defendant must make the proper request under the statute. McCoy v. State, 10 S.W.3d 50 (Tex.App.—Amarillo 1999, *no pet.*).

PRACTICE TIP: A request for notice should be filed in every case where evidence could possibly be admissible under Art. 38.37.

§13:83.3 Request Must Cite Art. 38.37

A request for notice of extraneous offenses under Rule 404(b) will not entitle the defendant to notice of extraneous offenses to be offered under Art. 38.37 and will not preserve error under Art. 38.37. Hitt v. State, 53 S.W.3d 697 (Tex.App.—Austin 2001, *pet. ref'd*).

For further information pertaining to the notice provision of CCP Art. 38.37, *see* §17:22.2.

§13:83.4 Form: Request for Notice

See our companion book *Texas Criminal Forms* (James Publishing):

- Form 13-12, Request for Notice of Extraneous Offenses in Child Abuse Case.

§13:84 Punishment Evidence

§13:84.1 Statute

CCP Art. 37.07. Verdict Must Be General; Separate Hearing on Proper Punishment

Section 3. Evidence of prior criminal record in all criminal cases after a finding of guilty.

(g) On timely request of the defendant, notice of intent to introduce evidence under this article shall be given in the same manner required by Rule 404(b), Texas Rules of Criminal Evidence. If the attorney representing the state intends to introduce an extraneous crime or bad act that has not resulted in a final conviction in a court of record or a probated or suspended sentence, notice of that intent is reasonable only if the notice includes the date on which and the county in which the alleged crime or bad act occurred and the name of the alleged victim of the crime or bad act. The requirement under this subsection that the attorney representing the state give notice applies only if the defendant makes a timely request to the attorney representing the state for the notice.

§13:84.2 Defendant Must Request Notice

CCP Art. 37.07 places the burden on the defendant to make the request for notice of the state. The state has no duty to provide notice until properly requested by the defendant to do so. Espinosa v. State, 853 S.W.2d 36 (Tex. Crim. App. 1993).

For cases on reasonableness and sufficiency of punishment phase notice, *see* §§20:28.3 and 20:28.4.

§13:84.3 Form: Request for Notice and Motion

See our companion book *Texas Criminal Forms* (James Publishing):

- Forms 13-10.1, Request for Notice of State's Intention to Introduce Punishment Evidence Pursuant to Art. 37.07.
- Form 13-10.2, Motion to Have Extraneous Offenses Not Mentioned.

§13:85 Impeachment Evidence

§13:85.1 Statute

Tex. R. Evid. 609(f) Notice. Evidence of a witness's conviction is not admissible under this rule if, after receiving from the adverse party a timely written request specifying the witness, the proponent of the conviction fails to provide sufficient written notice *of intent to use the conviction. Notice is sufficient if it provides a fair opportunity to contest the use of such evidence.*

§13:85.2 Party Must Request Notice

Tex.R.Evid. 609(f) precludes the use of prior convictions against a witness if the proponent of such evidence fails to give advance written notice of intent to use such evidence upon a timely written request. Brown v. State, 880 S.W.2d 249 (Tex. App.—El Paso 1994, *no pet.*).

Where the state does not give timely notice of its intent to use a prior conviction, it is error for the court to admit evidence of it. Bryant v. State, 997 S.W.2d 673 (Tex.App.—Texarkana 1999, *no pet.*).

PRACTICE TIP: Rule 609(f) is broadly written, applying to evidence of conviction of any witness, and to both the state and defense. Therefore, either party can take advantage of its provisions. If timely notice is not provided, the proponent cannot use the prior conviction information.

§13:85.3 Form: Request for Notice

See our companion book *Texas Criminal Forms* (James Publishing):

- Form 13-13, Request for Notice of State's Intention to Introduce Evidence of Impeachment.

§13:90 Public Information Act Requests

§13:91 Statutes

Tex. Gov't. Code §552.002. Definition of Public Information; Media Containing Public Information

> *(a) In this chapter, "public information" means information that is collected, assembled, or maintained under a law or ordinance or in connection with the transaction of official business:*
>
> *(1) by a governmental body; or*
>
> *(2) for a governmental body and the governmental body owns the information or has a right of access to it.*
>
> *(b) The media on which public information is recorded include:*
>
> *(1) paper;*
>
> *(2) film;*
>
> *(3) a magnetic, optical, or solid state device that can store an electronic signal;*
>
> *(4) tape;*
>
> *(5) Mylar;*
>
> *(6) linen;*
>
> *(7) silk; and*
>
> *(8) vellum.*
>
> *(c) The general forms in which the media containing public information exist include a book, paper, letter, document, printout, photograph, film, tape, microfiche, microfilm, photostat, sound recording, map, and drawing and a voice, data, or video representation held in computer memory.*

Tex. Gov't Code §552.0055. Subpoena Duces Tecum or Discovery Request

A subpoena duces tecum or a request for discovery that is issued in compliance with a statute or a rule of civil or criminal procedure is not considered to be a request for information under this chapter.

Tex. Gov't Code §552.022. Categories of Public Information; Examples

(a) Without limiting the amount or kind of information that is public information under this chapter, the following categories of information are public information and not excepted from required disclosure under this chapter unless they are expressly confidential under other law:

(1) a completed report, audit, evaluation, or investigation made of, for, or by a governmental body, except as provided by Section 552.108;

(2) the name, sex, ethnicity, salary, title, and dates of employment of each employee and officer of a governmental body;

(3) information in an account, voucher, or contract relating to the receipt or expenditure of public or other funds by a governmental body;

(4) the name of each official and the final record of voting on all proceedings in a governmental body;

(5) all working papers, research material, and information used to estimate the need for or expenditure of public funds or taxes by a governmental body, on completion of the estimate;

(6) the name, place of business, and the name of the municipality to which local sales and use taxes are credited, if any, for the named person, of a person reporting or paying sales and use taxes under Chapter 151, Tax Code;

(7) a description of an agency's central and field organizations, including:

(A) the established places at which the public may obtain information, submit information or requests, or obtain decisions;

(B) the employees from whom the public may obtain information, submit information or requests, or obtain decisions;

(C) in the case of a uniformed service, the members from whom the public may obtain information, submit information or requests, or obtain decisions; and

(D) the methods by which the public may obtain information, submit information or requests, or obtain decisions;

(8) a statement of the general course and method by which an agency's functions are channeled and determined, including the nature and requirements of all formal and informal policies and procedures;

(9) a rule of procedure, a description of forms available or the places at which forms may be obtained, and instructions relating to the scope and content of all papers, reports, or examinations;

(10) a substantive rule of general applicability adopted or issued by an agency as authorized by law, and a statement of general policy or interpretation of general applicability formulated and adopted by an agency;

(11) each amendment, revision, or repeal of information described by Subdivisions (7)-(10);

(12) final opinions, including concurring and dissenting opinions, and orders issued in the adjudication of cases;

(13) a policy statement or interpretation that has been adopted or issued by an agency;

(14) administrative staff manuals and instructions to staff that affect a member of the public;

(15) information regarded as open to the public under an agency's policies;

(16) information that is in a bill for attorneys' fees and that is not privileged under the attorney-client privilege;

(17) information that is also contained in a public court record; and

(18) a settlement agreement to which a governmental body is a party.

(b) A court in this state may not order a governmental body or an officer for public information to withhold from public inspection any category of public information described by Subsection (a) or to not produce the category of public information for inspection or duplication, unless the category of information is expressly made confidential under other law.

§13:92 Public Is Entitled to Information

The Texas Public Information Act's (TPIA) core provision provides that the public is entitled to information "collected, assembled, or maintained by a governmental body." City of San Antonio v. San Antonio Exp. News, 47 S.W.3d 556 (Tex. App.—San Antonio 2000, *review denied*).

However, there are statutory exceptions to this general principle that governmental information is public. These exceptions include:

- Information confidential by law (statute or judicial decision).
- Information within the informers' privilege.
- Certain personnel information (SSN's, home addresses, home phone numbers, and information relating to family of public employees).
- Information relating to litigation.
- Information relating to bidding.
- Information relating to location or price of property.
- Information within the attorney-client privilege.
- Certain law enforcement records which would interfere with the detection, investigation or prosecution of crime.
- Internal records of a law enforcement agency.
- Criminal history information.
- Trade secrets.
- Commercial or financial information privileged or confidential by law.
- Certain information relating to financial institutions or securities.
- Geological or geophysical information.
- Photographs of peace officers.
- Personal information relating to participants in neighborhood crime watch organizations.
- Crime victim compensation information.
- Family violence shelter center and sexual assault program information.
- Confidentiality of credit card, debit card, charge card and access device numbers.

- Government information related to security issues for computers.

Tex Gov't Code §§552.101-552.137.

§13:93 Statute Contains Specific Exceptions

The TPIA contains specific exceptions from compelled disclosure of information expressly made confidential by law, certain information relating to personnel files, and certain law-enforcement and prosecutors' records. City of San Antonio v. San Antonio Exp. News, 47 S.W.3d 556 (Tex.App.—San Antonio 2000, *review denied*).

The TPIA shall be liberally construed in favor of granting a request for information. City of San Antonio.

§13:94 Form: Request

See our companion book *Texas Criminal Forms* (James Publishing):

- Form 13-35, Public Information Act Letter Request

(This page intentionally left blank.)

CHAPTER 14

JURY SELECTION AND VOIR DIRE

Table of Contents

§14:10 Composition of Venire

§14:11 Statutory Law

CCP Art. 33.09. Jury drawn

Jury panels, including special venires, for the trial of criminal cases shall be selected and summoned (with return on summons) in the same manner as the selection of panels for the trial of civil cases except as otherwise provided in this Code.

CCP Art. 35.01. Jurors called

When a case is called for trial and the parties have announced ready for trial, the names of those summoned as jurors in the case shall be called. Those not present may be fined not exceeding fifty dollars. An attachment may issue on request of either party for any absent summoned juror, to have him brought forthwith before the court. A person who is summoned but not present, may upon an appearance, before the jury is qualified, be tried as to his qualifications and impaneled as a juror unless challenged, but no cause shall be unreasonably delayed on account of his absence.

CCP Art. 35.11. Preparation of list

The trial judge, on the demand of the defendant or his attorney, or of the State's counsel, shall cause a sufficient number of jurors from which a jury may be selected to try the case to be randomly selected from the members of the general panel drawn or assigned as jurors in the case. The clerk shall randomly select the jurors by a computer or other process of random selection and shall write or print the names, in the order selected, on the jury list from which the jury is to be selected to try the case. The clerk shall deliver a copy of the list to the State's counsel and to the defendant or his attorney.

CCP Art. 35.20. Names called in order

In selecting the jury from the persons summoned, the names of such persons shall be called in the order in which they appear upon the list furnished the defendant. Each juror shall be tried and passed upon separately. A person who has been summoned, but who is not present, may, upon his appearance before the jury is completed, be tried as to his qualifications and impaneled as a juror, unless challenged, but no cause shall be unreasonably delayed on account of such absence.

CCP Art. 35.26. Lists returned to clerk

(a) When the parties have made or declined to make their peremptory challenges, they shall deliver their lists to the clerk. Except as provided in Subsection (b) of this section, the clerk shall, if the case be in the district court, call off the first twelve names on the lists that have not been stricken. If the case be in the county court, he shall call off the first six names on the lists that have not been stricken. Those whose names are called shall be the jury.

(b) In a capital case in which the state seeks the death penalty, the court may direct that two alternate jurors be selected and that the first fourteen names not stricken be called off by the clerk. The last two names to be called are the alternate jurors.

For the technical aspects of the formation of the venire *see* Government Code Chapter 62. Within Chapter 62 are several methods counties are allowed to employ for the formation of jury venires.

§14:12 In General

The Sixth Amendment to the U.S. Constitution requires that a jury venire be drawn from a source fairly representative of the community. Taylor v. Louisiana, 419 U.S. 522, 95 S.Ct. 692, 42 L. Ed. 2d 690 (1975).

Article I, §10 of the Texas Constitution provides the same protection. Lacy v. State, 899 S.W.2d 284 (Tex.App.—Tyler 1995, *no pet.*).

However, there is no rule that requires that the petit jury actually chosen mirror the community and reflect the various distinctive groups in the population. Taylor v. Louisiana, *supra.*

A criminal defendant must make three showings to establish a *prima facie* violation of the Sixth Amendment's fair cross-section requirement. He or she must show: (1) that the group alleged to be excluded is a distinctive group in the community; (2) that the representation of this group in venires from which juries are selected is not fair and reasonable in relation to the number of such persons in the community; and (3) that this underrepresentation is due to systematic exclusion of the group in the jury-selection process. Berghuis v. Smith, 559 U.S. ___, 130 S.Ct. 1382, 176 L.Ed.2d 249 (2010), *citing* Duren v. Missouri, 439 U.S. 357, 99 S.Ct. 664, 58 L.Ed.2d 579 (1979).

A defendant is not entitled to a jury that includes minorities or is comprised of a proportional representation of races so long as the jury selection process was not subject to discrimination. Rousseau v. State, 855 S.W.2d 666 (Tex. Crim. App. 1993), *cert. denied,* 510 U.S. 919, 114 S.Ct. 313, 126 L. Ed. 2d 260 (1993); May v. State, 738 S.W.2d 261 (Tex. Crim. App. 1987), *cert. denied*, 484 U.S. 872, 108 S.Ct. 206, 98 L. Ed. 2d 158 (1987).

A defendant has no right to any particular individual serving on the jury. The defendant's only substantial right is that the jurors who do serve be qualified. Colone v. State, 573 S.W.3d 249, 261 (Tex. Crim. App. 2019).

The Sixth Amendment entitles every defendant to object to a venire that is not designed to represent a fair cross section of the community, whether or not the systematically excluded groups are groups to which the defendant belongs. Holland v. Illinois, 493 U.S. 474, 110 S.Ct. 803, 107 L. Ed. 2d 905 (1990).

A challenge to the array is the proper method of testing the composition of the jury venire. Callaway v. State, 818 S.W.2d 816 (Tex.App.—Amarillo 1991, *pet. ref'd*). *See* §14:13.

The burden of proof is on the movant to show that the juror selection process intentionally, systematically and arbitrarily excludes protected classes from jury service. Garcia v. State, 919 S.W.2d 370 (Tex. Crim. App. 1994).

PRACTICE TIP: In cases where the composition of the venire may be an issue, review the Commissioners Court minutes of the county in question to ascertain which composition plan the county is required to follow and to verify that it is properly enforced.

PRACTICE TIP: If it is anticipated that the composition of the venire may be an issue in a particular case, a party can by written application be present and observe the drawing of the names of prospective jurors and their placement on the jury lists. Government Code §62.005.

Where the trial court errs in some aspect of selecting and empaneling a venire, a defendant can only obtain a reversal by showing some type of harm. Cooks v. State, 844 S.W.2d 697 (Tex. Crim. App. 1992), *cert. denied*, 509 U.S. 927, 113 S.Ct. 3048, 125 L. Ed. 2d 732 (1993).

The Rules of Evidence apply to jury voir dire; thus any evidence offered in support of or opposing challenges for cause must be admissible under the Rules. Watson v. State, 917 S.W.2d 65 (Tex.App.—Fort Worth 1996, *pet. ref'd*).

§14:13 Challenges to Array

In Texas, challenges to the array are conducted under the authority of CCP Arts. 35.06 and 35.07.

CCP Art. 35.06. Challenge to array first heard

> *The court shall hear and determine a challenge to the array before interrogating those summoned as to their qualifications.*

CCP Art. 35.07. Challenge to the array

> *Each party may challenge the array only on the ground that the officer summoning the jury has willfully summoned jurors with a view to securing a conviction or an acquittal. All such challenges must be in writing setting forth distinctly the grounds of*

JURY SELECTION AND VOIR DIRE

> *such challenge. When made by the defendant, it must be supported by his affidavit or the affidavit of any credible person. When such challenge is made, the judge shall hear evidence and decide without delay whether or not the challenge shall be sustained.*

CCP Art. 35.08. When challenge is sustained

> *The array of jurors summoned shall be discharged if the challenge be sustained, and the court shall order other jurors to be summoned in their stead, and direct that the officer who summoned those so discharged, and on account of whose misconduct the challenge has been sustained shall not summon any other jurors in the case.*

CCP Art. 35.09. List of new venire

> *When a challenge to the array has been sustained, the defendant shall be entitled, as in the first instance, to service of a copy of the list of names of those summoned by order of the court.*

A challenge to the array is sometimes referred to as a motion to quash the venire. Callaway v. State, 818 S.W.2d 816 (Tex.App.—Amarillo 1991, *pet. ref'd*).

Art. 35.07 provides that a party may challenge an array only on the ground that the officer summoning the jury has willfully summoned jurors with a view to securing a conviction or acquittal. Cooks v. State, 844 S.W.2d 697 (Tex. Crim. App. 1992), *cert. denied*, 509 U.S. 927, 113 S.Ct. 3048, 125 L. Ed. 2d 732 (1993).

A trial court properly overrules the challenge to the array where the challenge alleges any ground other than that specifically authorized by Art. 35.07. Broussard v. State, 910 S.W.2d 952 (Tex. Crim. App. 1995).

A challenge to the array must be: (1) in writing, and (2) supported by affidavit. Garcia v. State, 919 S.W.2d 370 (Tex. Crim. App. 1994).

An instrument must be properly sworn to in order to properly be supported by affidavit. Esquivel v. State, 595 S.W.2d 516 (Tex. Crim. App. 1980), *cert. denied,* 449 U.S. 986, 101 S.Ct. 408, 66 L. Ed. 2d 251 (1980).

CCP Art. 35.06 unambiguously requires a challenge to the array to be made before the panel is qualified. Jackson v. State, 745 S.W.2d 4 (Tex. Crim. App. 1988), *cert. denied*, 487 U.S. 1241, 108 S.Ct. 2916, 101 L. Ed. 2d 947 (1988); Callaway, *supra*.

In order to prevail on a challenge to the array, a party must establish harm, *i.e.*, he must show that the method employed compromised the fairness of the trial. Lewis v. State, 815 S.W.2d 560 (Tex. Crim. App. 1991).

The burden of proof is on the party challenging the array to show that the array should be quashed. Garcia, *supra*.

In order to prevail, the defendant must produce evidence showing that the method employed systematically and arbitrarily excluded a cognizable protected class from selection. Garcia. This can generally be done through the use of statistical comparison between the population of the county at large and those summoned for jury service. Garcia.

A showing that the defendant was forced to accept an objectionable juror or was otherwise denied an impartial jury is required before reversal is merited. Callaway.

See §§11:100 through 11:103 of this book for further information on challenging the make-up of the venire.

§14:13.1 Form: Sample Motion/Challenge to Array

See our companion book *Texas Criminal Forms* (James Publishing) Form 14-1.

§14:14 Writs of Attachment

See CCP Art. 35.01 in §14:11.

In order to preserve error in the case of veniremembers who were summoned for jury duty but did not appear, the defendant must request writs of attachment for those veniremembers. Coleman v. State, 881 S.W.2d 344 (Tex. Crim. App. 1994), *cert.*

denied, 513 U.S. 1096, 115 S.Ct. 763, 130 L. Ed. 2d 660 (1995).

The statute for attaching veniremembers, CCP Art. 35.01 (*see* §14:11), is directory, not mandatory. Dowthitt v. State, 931 S.W.2d 244 (Tex. Crim. App. 1996). In the absence of governmental misconduct in summoning the venire, the failure to grant attachments is not reversible error unless the defendant shows injury. Dowthitt.

The defendant must show that because of the trial court's failure to issue the writ of attachment he was forced to accept an objectionable juror. Starks v. State, 776 S.W.2d 808 (Tex.App.—Fort Worth 1989, *pet. ref'd*).

In determining whether a defendant has been harmed by the trial court's failure to issue attachments for absent jurors, the term "objectionable juror" means "one against whom such cause for challenge exists as would likely affect his competency or his impartiality in the trial." Starks.

TIP TO THE BENCH: Persons who have been summoned for jury duty and who fail to appear are subject to a contempt action punishable by a fine of not less than $100 or more than $1,000. Government Code §62.041.

§14:14.1 Form: Motion for Attachment of Absent Jurors

See our companion book *Texas Criminal Forms* (James Publishing) Form 14-2 and 14-3.

§14:15 Juror Exemptions

CCP Art. 35.04. Claiming exemption

Any person summoned as a juror who is exempt by law from jury service may establish his exemption without appearing in person by filing a signed statement of the ground of his exemption with the clerk of the court at any time before the date upon which he is summoned to appear.

Government Code §62.106. Exemption From Jury Service

(a) A person qualified to serve as a petit juror may establish an exemption from jury service if the person:

(1) is over 70 years of age;

(2) has legal custody of a child younger than 12 years of age and the person's service on the jury requires leaving the child without adequate supervision;

(3) is a student of a public or private secondary school;

(4) is a person enrolled and in actual attendance at an institution of higher education;

(5) is an officer or an employee of the senate, the house of representatives, or any department, commission, board, office, or other agency in the legislative branch of state government;

(6) is summoned for service in a county with a population of at least 200,000, unless that county uses a jury plan under Section 62.011 and the period authorized under Section 62.011(b)(5) exceeds two years, and the person has served as a petit juror in the county during the 24-month period preceding the date the person is to appear for jury service;

(7) is the primary caretaker of a person who is an invalid unable to care for himself;

(8) except as provided by Subsection (b), is summoned for service in a county with a population of at least 250,000 and the person has served as a petit juror in the county during the three-year period preceding the date the person is to appear for jury service; or

(9) is a member of the United States military forces serving on active duty and deployed to a location away from the person's home station and out of the person's county of residence.

(b) Subsection (a)(8) does not apply if the jury wheel in the county has been reconstituted after the date the person served as a petit juror.

Government Code §62.106(1) which allows juror exemptions for persons over 70 years of age does not violate a defendant's rights to equal protection of the laws and to a fair cross section of the community under either the U.S. or Texas constitutions. Burks v. State, 876 S.W.2d 877 (Tex. Crim. App. 1997), *cert. denied,* 513 U.S. 1114, 115 S.Ct. 909, 130 L. Ed. 2d 791 (1994).

PRACTICE TIP: *In order to preserve error in the case of veniremembers who were summoned for jury duty but did not appear, the defendant must request writs of attachment for those veniremembers. Coleman v. State, 881 S.W.2d 344 (Tex. Crim. App. 1994), cert. denied, 513 U.S. 1096, 115 S.Ct. 763, 130 L. Ed. 2d 660 (1995).*

During jury selection, the trial court has the power to remove a prospective juror on the basis of an excuse, even if it is after the prospective juror has been questioned and accepted. The trial court retains this power in order to rectify problems created by such circumstances as, e.g., a venireperson's sudden realization that an excuse applies to her. Colone v. State, 573 S.W.3d 249, 261 (Tex. Crim. App. 2019).

§14:16 Additional Veniremembers

CCP Art. 34.02. Additional names drawn

In any criminal case in which the court deems that the veniremembers theretofore drawn will be insufficient for the trial of the case, or in any criminal case in which the venire has been exhausted by challenge or otherwise, the court shall order additional veniremembers in such numbers as the court may deem advisable, to be summoned as follows:

(a) In a jury wheel county, the names of those to be summoned shall be drawn from the jury wheel.

(b) In counties not using the jury wheel, the veniremembers shall be summoned by the sheriff.

Although there is not a specific statutory remedy where the court has an insufficient number of veniremembers to complete the selection of a jury, the court may call additional veniremembers from the central jury panel and proceed with the jury selection process. Broussard v. State, 910 S.W.2d 952 (Tex. Crim. App. 1995); Williams v. State, 631 S.W.2d 955 (Tex. Crim. App. 1982).

Where a juror becomes disabled before the swearing of the jury and there is an alternate juror available, the court also has the option of replacing the disabled juror with the alternate. Broussard.

§14:17 Number of Jurors

CCP Art. 33.01. Jury Size

(a) Except as provided by Subsection (b), in the district court, the jury shall consist of twelve qualified jurors. In the county court and inferior courts, the jury shall consist of six qualified jurors.

(b) In a trial involving a misdemeanor offense, a district court jury shall consist of six qualified jurors.

In a district court, a defendant can validly waive his right to be tried by twelve jurors and consent to a trial by a lesser number. Hatch v. State, 958 S.W.2d 813 (Tex. Crim. App. 1997) (where it was discovered that one of the jurors was not a U.S. citizen); Government Code §62.201.

In a county court, a defendant who has executed a valid written jury waiver may be tried by a jury of less than six jurors. Hanley v. State, 909 S.W.2d 117 (Tex.App.—Houston [14th Dist.] 1995, *no pet.*).

Texas statutory law provides two instances in which a trial can proceed with 11 jurors: (1) when the parties consent or (2) if a juror dies or the trial court finds that a juror has become disabled. Tex. Gov't Code Ann. § 62.201 (West 2013); Tex. Code Crim. Proc. Ann. art. 36.29(a) (West 2006 & Supp.2014); Stillwell v. State, 466 S.W.3d 908, 912 (Tex. App.—Fort Worth 2015, no pet.).

In the second instance, when a trial court finds that a juror has become disabled, consent is not necessary to proceed with the 11 jurors remaining on the panel. Stillwell v. State, 466 S.W.3d at 912.

§14:18 Alternate Jurors

CCP Art. 33.011. Alternate jurors

> *(a) In district courts, the judge may direct that not more than four jurors in addition to the regular jury be called and impaneled to sit as alternate jurors. In county courts, the judge may direct that not more than two jurors in addition to the regular jury be called and impaneled to sit as alternate jurors.*
>
> *(b) Alternate jurors in the order in which they are called shall replace jurors who, prior to the time the jury renders a verdict on the guilt or innocence of the defendant and, if applicable, the amount of punishment, become or are found to be unable or disqualified to perform their duties or are found by the court on agreement of the parties to have good cause for not performing their duties. Alternate jurors shall be drawn and selected in the same manner, shall have the same qualifications, shall be subject to the same examination and challenges, shall take the same oath, and shall have the same functions, powers, facilities, security, and privileges as regular jurors. An alternate juror who does not replace a regular juror shall be discharged after the jury has rendered a verdict on the guilt or innocence of the defendant and, if applicable, the amount of punishment.*

CCP Art. 35.26 Lists returned to clerk

> *(b) In a capital case in which the state seeks the death penalty, the court may direct that two alternate jurors be selected and that the first fourteen names not stricken be called off by the clerk. The last two names to be called are the alternate jurors.*

According to CCP Art. 35.15, the state and the defendant shall each be entitled to one peremptory challenge in addition to those otherwise allowed by law if one or two alternate jurors are to be impaneled. Each side is entitled to two peremptory challenges if three or four alternate jurors are to be impaneled. The additional peremptory challenges are to be used against an alternate juror only, and the other peremptory challenges allowed by law may not be used against an alternate juror.

In cases where a juror becomes ill before being sworn, the trial court may replace him with the next qualified member of the venire. Juarez v. State, 890 S.W.2d 184 (Tex.App.—Corpus Christi 1994, *no pet.*).

The same procedural rules that apply to the selection of regular jurors apply to the selection of alternate jurors. Cooks v. State, 844 S.W.2d 697 (Tex. Crim. App. 1992), *cert. denied*, 509 U.S. 927, 113 S.Ct. 3048, 125 L. Ed. 2d 732 (1993).

The trial court does not violate Texas Constitution, Art. V, Sec. 13, by allowing an alternate juror to remain in the jury room during deliberations, as long as the alternate juror does not vote with the 12 members of the jury. Trinidad v. State, 312 S.W.3d 23 (Tex. Crim. App. 2010).

§14:19 Disabled Jurors

CCP Art. 36.29. If a Juror Dies or Becomes Disabled

> *(a) Not less than twelve jurors can render and return a verdict in a felony case. It must be concurred in by each juror and signed by the foreman. Except as provided in Subsection (b), however, after the trial of any felony case begins and a juror dies or, as determined by the judge, becomes disabled from sitting at any time before the charge of the court is read to the jury, the remainder of the jury shall have the power to render the*

verdict; but when the verdict shall be rendered by less than the whole number, it shall be signed by every member of the jury concurring in it.

(b) If alternate jurors have been selected in a capital case in which the state seeks the death penalty and a juror dies or becomes disabled from sitting at any time before the charge of the court is read to the jury, the alternate juror whose name was called first under Article 35.26 of this code shall replace the dead or disabled juror. Likewise, if another juror dies or becomes disabled from sitting before the charge of the court is read to the jury, the other alternate juror shall replace the second juror to die or become disabled.

(c) After the charge of the court is read to the jury, if a juror becomes so sick as to prevent the continuance of the juror's duty and an alternate juror is not available, or if any accident of circumstance occurs to prevent the jury from being kept together under circumstances under which the law or the instructions of the court requires that the jury be kept together, the jury shall be discharged, except that on agreement on the record by the defendant, the defendant's counsel, and the attorney representing the state 11 members of a jury may render a verdict and, if punishment is to be assessed by the jury, assess punishment. If a verdict is rendered by less than the whole number of the jury, each member of the jury shall sign the verdict.

(d) After the jury has rendered a verdict on the guilt or innocence of the defendant and, if applicable, the amount of punishment, the court shall discharge an alternate juror who has not replaced a juror.

Where a juror becomes disabled, CCP Art. 36.29 thus allows a jury of less than 12 to render a verdict in a non-capital case but requires that an alternate replace a disabled juror in a death penalty case.

The language of CCP Art. 36.29 and the cases applying it make clear that the legislative intent was to limit its application to those cases where the juror was physically or mentally impaired in some way that hindered his ability to perform his duty as a juror. Brooks v. State, 990 S.W.2d 278 (Tex. Crim. App. 1999).

The determination as to whether a juror is disabled is within the discretion of the trial court. Absent an abuse of that discretion, no reversible error will be found. Brooks.

An CCP Art. 36.29 disability is not limited to physical disease; it can include a physical illness, mental condition or emotional state. Reyes v. State, 30 S.W.3d 409 (Tex. Crim. App. 2000).

The mere fact that the juror knows the defendant is not a disability except where that knowledge inhibits the juror from fully and fairly performing the functions of a juror. Reyes, (where the juror felt a fear of retaliation from the defendant).

A juror who simply disagrees with other jurors and who refuses to further deliberate for that reason is not disabled under sec. 36.29. Scales v. State, 380 S.W.3d 780, 786 (Tex. Crim. App. 2012).

Although there is not a specific statutory remedy where the court has an insufficient number of veniremembers to complete the selection and swearing of a jury, the court may call additional veniremembers from the central jury panel and proceed with the jury selection process. Broussard v. State, 910 S.W.2d 952 (Tex. Crim. App. 1995); Williams v. State, 631 S.W.2d 955 (Tex. Crim. App.1982).

Where a juror becomes disabled before the swearing of the jury and there is an alternate juror available, the court also has the option of replacing the disabled juror with the alternate. Broussard.

Where a juror has become disabled, the trial judge is required to consider and rule out less drastic alternatives, such as proceeding with a lesser number of jurors, before granting a mistrial. The judge must review the alternatives and choose the one which best preserves the defendant's right to have his trial completed before a particular tribunal. Hill v. State, 90 S.W.3d 308 (Tex. Crim. App. 2002).

Where the juror is not disabled, but merely disqualified, the defendant must waive his right to be tried by a jury of twelve before the trial may proceed to a verdict. Hatch v. State, 958 S.W.2d 813 (Tex. Crim. App. 1997); Government Code §62.201.

In a county court, a defendant who has executed a valid written jury waiver may be tried by a jury of less than six jurors. Hanley v. State, 909 S.W.2d 117 (Tex.App.—Houston [14th Dist.] 1995, *no pet.*).

There is no constitutional or statutory impediment to proceeding with less than six jurors in county court, so long as the defendant waives his right to trial by a complete jury under Article 1.14, and the State and the trial court are willing to consent to do so under Article 1.13(a). Ex parte Garza, 337 S.W.3d 903 (Tex. Crim. App. 2011).

TIP TO THE BENCH: When excusing a juror who has become disabled, the court must ensure that the record reflects the precise reason that the juror is being excused because the appellate courts cannot presume from a silent record that the juror was properly excused. See Scales v. State, 380 S.W.3d 780, 784 (Tex.Crim. App. 2012). Therefore, in order to support its judgment, the trial court must make a finding, sufficiently supported by the record, that the juror was disabled or unable to perform the duties of a juror.

While in a hearing to decide whether to excuse a juror the trial court is the sole fact-finder and judge of the credibility of the testifying jurors, the trial court's decision is subject to a review for abuse of discretion. Absent such an abuse, no reversible error will be found. Scales.

The improper dismissal of a juror under sec. 36.29 can constitute a violation of a defendant's right to a unanimous jury and subject the error to analysis under Texas Rule of Appellate Procedure 44.2(a). Scales v. State, 380 S.W.3d at 786.

§14:19.1 Sufficient Disability to Be Excused

- Intoxication has been found to disable a juror. Griffin v. State, 486 S.W.2d 948 (Tex. Crim. App. 1972).
- Flu has been found to constitute a sufficient disabling factor. Allen v. State, 536 S.W.2d 364 (Tex. Crim. App. 1976).
- Injuries from auto accidents can sufficiently disable a juror. Johnson v. State, 525 S.W.2d 170 (Tex. Crim. App. 1975).
- High blood pressure requiring hospitalization has been found to sufficiently disable a juror. Maciel v. State, 517 S.W.2d 789 (Tex. Crim. App. 1975).
- Death in the juror's family can constitute a sufficient disability. Wells v. State, 762 S.W.2d 673 (Tex.App.—Texarkana 1988, *pet. ref'd*).
- Finding that the juror was so concerned about his ability to support his family while on jury duty that he was unable to concentrate on the trial has been found to be a sufficient disability. Freeman v. State, 838 S.W.2d 772 (Tex.App.—Corpus Christi 1992, *pet. ref'd*).
- Juror who stated that he would be unable to concentrate on the trial due to time pressures associated with moving and starting a new job was found to be properly discharged on grounds that he was disabled. Ramos v. State, 934 S.W.2d 358 (Tex. Crim. App. 1996), *cert. denied*, 520 U.S. 1198, 117 S.Ct. 1556, 137 L. Ed. 2d 704 (1997).
- Inability to find childcare can constitute a sufficient basis for excusal. Edwards v. State, 981 S.W.2d 359 (Tex.App.—Texarkana 1998, *no pet.*).
- Juror's Alzheimer's disease which resulted in her inability to remember any details from her first day of jury service and her resulting emotional

distress have been found to be a sufficient basis for excusal. Timmons v. State, 952 S.W.2d 891 (Tex.App.—Dallas 1997, *no pet.*).

§14:19.2 Insufficient Disability to Be Excused

- Juror's arrest for carrying a handgun into the courthouse does not constitute a sufficient disablement under this article. Brooks v. State, 990 S.W.2d 278 (Tex. Crim. App. 1999).

- Alleged bias and prejudice are not a disability within meaning of this article. Bass v. State, 622 S.W.2d 101 (Tex. Crim. App. 1981), *cert. denied*, 456 U.S. 965, 102 S.Ct. 2046, 72 L. Ed. 2d 491 (1982).

- Juror is not disabled within the meaning of this article where it is discovered that he cannot consider the upper end of the range of punishment. Landrum v. State, 788 S.W.2d 577 (Tex. Crim. App. 1990).

- Juror is not disabled within the meaning of this article where it is discovered that he is not a U.S. citizen. Hatch v. State, 958 S.W.2d 813 (Tex. Crim. App. 1997).

Where the record only reveals that a juror has refused to further deliberate, there is insufficient evidence of disability to excuse the juror. Scales v. State, 380 S.W.3d 780, 786 (Tex. Crim. App. 2012).

§14:20 Juror Qualifications

Gov't Code §62.101. Jury Service

> *All individuals are competent petit jurors unless disqualified under this subchapter and are liable for jury service except as otherwise provided by this subchapter.*

Gov't Code §62.102. General Qualifications For Jury Service

> *A person is disqualified to serve as a petit juror unless the person:*
>
> *(1) is at least 18 years of age;*
>
> *(2) is a citizen of this state and of the county in which the person is to serve as a juror;*
>
> *(3) is qualified under the constitution and laws to vote in the county in which the person is to serve as a juror;*
>
> *(4) is of sound mind and good moral character;*
>
> *(5) is able to read and write;*
>
> *(6) has not served as a petit juror for six days during the preceding three months in the county court or during the preceding six months in the district court;*
>
> *(7) has not been convicted of misdemeanor theft or a felony; and*
>
> *(8) is not under indictment or other legal accusation of misdemeanor theft or a felony.*

Prospective jurors who cannot read and write are properly excused *sua sponte* by the trial court. Liveoak v. State, 717 S.W.2d 691 (Tex.App.—San Antonio 1986, *pet. ref'd*).

CCP Art. 33.02. Failure To Register

> *Failure to register to vote shall not disqualify any person from jury service.*

Texas Election Code §11.001. Eligibility to Vote

> *(a) Except as otherwise provided by law, to be eligible to vote in an election in this state, a person must:*
>
> *(1) be a qualified voter as defined by Section 11.002 on the day the person offers to vote;*

(2) be a resident of the territory covered by the election for the office or measure on which the person desires to vote; and

(3) satisfy all other requirements for voting prescribed by law for the particular election.

(b) For a person who resides on property located in more than one territory described by Subsection (a)(2), the person shall choose in which territory the residence of the person is located.

Sec. 11.002. Qualified Voter

In this code, "qualified voter" means a person who:

(1) is 18 years of age or older;

(2) is a United States citizen;

(3) has not been determined by a final judgment of a court exercising probate jurisdiction to be:

(A) totally mentally incapacitated; or

(B) partially mentally incapacitated without the right to vote;

(4) has not been finally convicted of a felony or, if so convicted, has:

(A) fully discharged the person's sentence, including any term of incarceration, parole, or supervision, or completed a period of probation ordered by any court; or

(B) been pardoned or otherwise released from the resulting disability to vote;

(5) is a resident of this state; and

(6) is a registered voter.

§14:21 Preliminary Testing of Qualifications

At the commencement of the voir dire procedure, and after any challenge to the array has been asserted, it is the responsibility of the trial judge to place the venire under oath according to CCP Art. 35.02, which sets out the statutory oath. CCP Art. 35.10.

After the venire is placed under oath, the trial judge must ask three questions of them to determine if they are qualified under the law. Those three questions are contained in CCP Art. 35.12.

CCP Art. 35.12. Mode of Testing

(a) In testing the qualification of a prospective juror after the juror has been sworn, the juror shall be asked by the court, or under its direction:

(1) Except for failure to register, are you a qualified voter in this county and state under the Constitution and laws of this state?

(2) Have you ever been convicted of theft or any felony?

(3) Are you under indictment or legal accusation for theft or any felony?

(b) In testing the qualifications of a prospective juror, with respect to whether the juror has been the subject of an order of nondisclosure or has a criminal history that includes information subject to that order, the juror may state only that the matter in question has been sealed.

TIP TO THE BENCH: It is advisable to phrase the last two questions to include theft accusations stemming from insufficient funds as a possible disqualifier because many veniremembers do not necessarily equate such an accusation with a theft offense. Therefore, many who legally fit the disqualification may not respond accurately to the question.

Depending on the answers to these questions veniremembers may be qualified, unqualified or absolutely disqualified. Green v. State, 764 S.W.2d 246 (Tex. Crim. App. 1989).

§14:30 Juror Disqualifications

Gov't Code §62.104. Disqualification for Legal Blindness

(a) A person who is legally blind is not disqualified to serve as a juror in a civil case solely because of his legal blindness except as provided by this section.

(b) A legally blind person is disqualified to serve as a juror in a civil case if, in the opinion of the court, his blindness renders him unfit to serve as a juror in that particular case.

(c) In this section, "legally blind" means having:

(1) no more than 20/200 of visual acuity in the better eye with correcting lenses; or

(2) visual acuity greater than 20/200, but with a limitation in the field of vision such that the widest diameter of the visual field subtends an angle no greater than 20 degrees.

Gov't Code §62.1041. Deaf or Hard of Hearing Juror

(a) A deaf or hard of hearing person is not disqualified to serve as a juror solely because of hearing loss except as provided by this section.

(b) A deaf or hard of hearing person is disqualified to serve as a juror if, in the opinion of the court, his hearing loss renders him unfit to serve as a juror in that particular case.

(c) A deaf or hard of hearing person serving as a juror shall be reasonably accommodated in accordance with the Americans with Disabilities Act (42 U.S.C. §12101 et seq.). An interpreter who is assisting a deaf or hard of hearing person serving as a juror may accompany the juror during all proceedings and deliberations in the case.

(d) If an interpreter is provided to a deaf or hard of hearing person serving as a juror in a district, county, or justice court, the county shall pay the cost of obtaining those services.

(e) A deaf or hard of hearing juror may request an auxiliary aid or service for a municipal court proceeding. The city shall honor the request unless the city can demonstrate that another effective means of communication exists. The city shall pay the cost unless the auxiliary aid or service will result in a fundamental alteration of the municipal court proceeding or in undue financial or administrative burdens.

(f) In this section, "deaf or hard of hearing" means having a hearing impairment, regardless of the existence of a speech impairment, that inhibits comprehension of an examination or proceeding or communication with others.

Gov't Code §62.105. Disqualification for Particular Jury

A person is disqualified to serve as a petit juror in a particular case if he:

(1) is a witness in the case;

(2) is interested, directly or indirectly, in the subject matter of the case;

(3) is related by consanguinity or affinity within the third degree, as determined under Chapter 573, to a party in the case;

> *(4) has a bias or prejudice in favor of or against a party in the case; or*
>
> *(5) has served as a petit juror in a former trial of the same case or in another case involving the same questions of fact.*

Where a venireman is *disqualified* from jury service, rather than absolutely disqualified, a party is required to challenge the venireman for cause to remove him from the jury. Mayo v. State, 4 S.W.3d 9 (Tex. Crim. App. 1999). This includes all reasons for challenge under Art. 35.16 that are not absolute disqualifications.

§14:31 What Constitutes Absolute Disqualification

CCP Art. 35.19. Absolute disqualification

> *No juror shall be impaneled when it appears that he is subject to the second, third or fourth cause of challenge in Article 35.16, though both parties may consent.*

A veniremember is absolutely disqualified if the veniremember:

- Has been convicted of theft or any felony
- Is under indictment or legal accusation for theft or any felony
- Is insane

CCP Art. 35.19 and 35.16(a)(2)(3)(4); Alvarado v. State, 822 S.W.2d 236 (Tex.App.—Houston [14th Dist.] 1991, *pet. ref'd*).

On the other hand, a disqualified veniremember is not absolutely disqualified under CCP Art. 35.19, but is subject to a challenge for cause under CCP Art. 35.16.

A trial judge has no authority on his own motion to excuse a prospective juror for cause under Art. 35.16. Warren v. State, 768 S.W.2d 300 (Tex. Crim. App. 1989); Green v. State, 764 S.W.2d 242 (Tex. Crim. App. 1989). However, the trial court may on its own motion excuse a prospective juror who is absolutely disqualified pursuant to CCP Art. 35.19. Warren.

Whether a venireman is absolutely disqualified is a question of fact for the trial court to determine. Hammond v. State, 799 S.W.2d 741 (Tex. Crim. App. 1990).

The language of CCP Art. 35.19 does not require indisputable certainty on the part of the trial court in making its determination on absolute disqualifications. Rather, Art. 35.19 provides that if it "appears" that the veniremember is absolutely disqualified, then he "shall not be empaneled[.]" Chambers v. State, 903 S.W.2d 21 (Tex. Crim. App. 1995). Thus, where it "appeared" that a veniremember was convicted of a federal felony which turned out to actually be a misdemeanor, the trial court's ruling that the he was absolutely disqualified was not overturned on appeal. Chambers.

Appellate courts apply an abuse of discretion standard when reviewing a trial court's ruling on an absolute disqualification. Chambers; Hammond v. State, 799 S.W.2d 741 (Tex. Crim. App. 1990), *cert. denied*, 501 U.S. 1259, 111 S.Ct. 2912, 115 L. Ed. 2d 1076 (1991).

The parties cannot waive Art. 35.19 disqualifications. Ex parte Smith, 817 S.W.2d 797 (Tex.App.—Amarillo 1991, *no pet.*).

However, failure to object to the impaneling of an absolutely disqualified venireman waives any error on appeal under art. 44.46 (see §14:33). Nelson v. State, 129 S.W.3d 108 (Tex. Crim. App. 2004).

There is some tension between the language of art. 35.19 stating that no absolutely disqualified venireman should be impaneled, and art. 44.46, which says that it is not error to impanel an absolutely disqualified venireman where the defendant does not object. It should be noted that under art. 44.46 the defendant can wait to make the objection at any time before the verdict is entered. Nelson.

TIP TO THE BENCH: If it is shown during voir dire that a venireman is absolutely disqualified, the court should not impanel that venireman unless the defendant affirmatively states that he has no objection. See Nelson.

The juror disqualifications under CCP Art. 35.16 which are not absolute disqualifications under Art. 35.19 are waivable under Art. 35.16. Mayo v. State, 4 S.W.3d 9 (Tex. Crim. App. 1999).

In the absence of other evidence, where the veniremember denies having a disqualifying conviction the trial court abuses its discretion in excusing him. Loughry v. State, 926 S.W.2d 382 (Tex.App.—Fort Worth 1996, *pet. ref'd*).

§14:31.1 Theft Convictions

A conviction for misdemeanor theft is an absolute disqualification. Holland v. State, 761 S.W.2d 307 (Tex. Crim. App. 1988), *cert. denied,* 489 U.S. 1091, 109 S.Ct. 1560, 103 L. Ed. 2d 863 (1989). A conviction for a Class C theft is sufficient for absolute disqualification. Pfeffer v. State, 683 S.W.2d 64 (Tex.App.—Amarillo 1984, *pet. ref'd*).

Even a theft conviction which occurred about twenty years before the jury service in question is sufficient for an absolute disqualification. Frame v. State, 615 S.W.2d 766 (Tex. Crim. App. 1981).

The statutory phrase "other legal accusation" corresponds with the legal definition of "accusation," specifically a formal criminal charge against an individual. Therefore, a civil pleading alleging conversion does not constitute a cause of challenge under Art. 35.19. Staley v. State, 887 S.W.2d 885 (Tex. Crim. App. 1994), *cert. denied,* 514 U.S. 1020, 115 S.Ct. 1366, 131 L. Ed. 2d 222 (1995).

Even where the veniremember cannot remember all of the salient facts of the alleged conviction, the trial court does not err in excusing him because where the record is silent, procedural rules are deemed to have been complied with. Enos v. State, 859 S.W.2d 594 (Tex.App.—Fort Worth 1993), *reversed on other grounds at* 889 S.W.2d 303 (Tex. Crim. App. 1994).

A juror who has previously been given a probated sentence is eligible for juror service after the probation has expired where he has been released from the disabilities of the probation. Payton v. State, 572 S.W.2d 677 (Tex. Crim. App. 1978).

In order to be qualified, a veniremember who has received a probated sentence for any disqualifying offense must have had the case physically dismissed and have been released from all legal disabilities by the court. Hoffman v. State, 922 S.W.2d 663 (Tex. App.—Waco 1996, *pet. ref'd*); Wolfe v. State, 917 S.W.2d 270 (Tex. Crim. App. 1996); CCP Art. 42.12; Smith v. State, 859 S.W.2d 463 (Tex.App.—Fort Worth 1993, *pet. ref'd*).

However, *see* R.R.E. v. Glenn, 884 S.W.2d 189 (Tex.App.—Fort Worth 1994) (a civil action) which holds that the full rights of convicted felons cannot be restored except by executive pardon because of the language of Art. XVI, §2 of the Texas Constitution.

A commutation does not remove the disqualification from serving on a jury. DeBlanc v. State, 799 S.W.2d 701 (Tex. Crim. App. 1990).

§14:31.2 Pending Theft Cases

A deferred adjudication probation is a pending case against a defendant. Brown v. State, 716 S.W.2d 939 (Tex. Crim. App. 1986).

Therefore, a deferred adjudication probation for theft is an absolute disqualification. Thomas v. State, 796 S.W.2d 196 (Tex. Crim. App. 1990). A pending theft charge requires disqualification whether or not the information charging the offense is sufficient under law. Thomas.

§14:31.3 Felony Convictions

A trial court does not abuse its discretion in disqualifying a juror where the record is unclear whether his federal tax conviction is a misdemeanor or a felony. Chambers v. State, 903 S.W.2d 21 (Tex. Crim. App. 1995).

§14:31.4 Pending Felony Cases

A deferred adjudication is deemed a pending case against a defendant, and therefore a veniremember on a deferred adjudication for felony cocaine possession results in the absolute disqualification of that veniremember. State v. Holloway, 886 S.W.2d 482 (Tex.App.—Houston [1st Dist.] 1994, *pet. ref'd*).

§14:31.5 Insanity

A veniremember will be properly excused for cause where he is disqualified because of insanity. Bass v. State, 622 S.W.2d 101 (Tex. Crim. App. 1981), *cert. denied,* 456 U.S. 965, 102 S.Ct. 2046,

72 L. Ed. 2d 491 (1982); Von Byrd v. State, 569 S.W.2d 883 (Tex. Crim. App. 1978).

§14:32 Disqualified Jurors

Jurors are disqualified if they fall into any of the following categories: 1) they are disqualified under Government Code §62.104 (*see* §14:30); 2) they are disqualified under Government Code §62.105 (*see* §14:30); or 3) they are disqualified under CCP Art. 35.16.

A deaf or hard of hearing person is disqualified under Government Code §62.1041 if in the opinion of the court the hearing loss renders him unfit to serve as a juror in that particular trial. Black v. State, 26 S.W.3d 895 (Tex. Crim. App. 2000). The disqualified venireman can be excused outside the presence of the state and defendant. Black.

Government Code, §573.023 specifies the manner of computing the degree of consanguinity between two persons and explicitly names the relationships that fall within the third degree for purposes of deciding if a juror is disqualified under Government Code §62.105(3). Ex parte Fierro, 79 S.W.3d 54 (Tex. Crim. App. 2002).

§14:33 Reversals Due to Disqualified Jurors

CCP Art. 44.46. Reversal of Conviction on the Basis of Service on Jury by a Disqualified Juror

> *A conviction in a criminal case may be reversed on appeal on the ground that a juror in the case was absolutely disqualified from service under Article 35.19 of this code only if:*
>
> > *(1) the defendant raises the disqualification before the verdict is entered; or*
> >
> > *(2) the disqualification was not discovered or brought to the attention of the trial court until after the verdict was entered and the defendant makes a showing of significant harm by the service of the disqualified juror.*

Where a statutorily disqualified juror has served on a jury in contravention of CCP Art. 35.16, Art. 44.46 is not in conflict with Texas Constitution Art. XVI, §2 which provides that, "Laws shall be made to exclude from office, serving on juries, and from the right of suffrage, those who may have been or shall hereafter be convicted of bribery, perjury, forgery, or other high crimes. This is because the phrase "high crimes" was found to be limited to criminal conduct that demonstrates the same type of moral corruption and dishonesty inherent in the offenses specified in the first part of the clause. Perez v. State, 11 S.W.3d 218 (Tex. Crim. App. 2000).

Art. 44.46(1) imposes an affirmative duty on the defendant to raise the issue of an absolutely disqualified juror before the verdict is entered. Where this is done, the defendant is entitled to a reversal of his conviction without a showing of harm. Nelson v. State, 129 S.W.3d 108 (Tex. Crim. App. 2004).

Where the disqualification was not discovered, and thus not brought to the attention of the trial court, until after the verdict was entered, a defendant may be granted a new trial only if the juror's service caused him "significant harm" under Art. 44.46(2). Ristoff v. State, 985 S.W.2d 623 (Tex.App.—Houston [1st Dist.] 1999, *no pet.*).

The defendant cannot call the juror in question during a motion for new trial hearing to establish harm. The testimony of a juror under Rule 606(b) is limited to harm resulting from an outside influence. White v. State, 225 S.W.3d 571 (Tex. Crim. App. 2007)

The defendant is entitled to a new trial only if he demonstrates that the disqualified juror's service caused him significant harm beyond the mere fact of conviction. Hernandez v. State, 952 S.W.2d 59 (Tex.App.—Austin 1997), *vacated on other grounds*, 957 S.W.2d 851 (Tex. Crim. App. 1998).

Where at the motion for new trial hearing the defendant made no attempt to show significant harm, he has failed to meet his burden. State v. Read, 965 S.W.2d 74 (Tex.App.—Austin 1998, *no pet*).

A defendant must object at trial that a juror was not a resident of the county of the trial or the objection is waived for appeal. Mayo v. State, 4 S.W.3d 9 (Tex. Crim. App. 1999). This is because a person who is not a resident of the county of trial is not absolutely disqualified from jury service under Art. 35.19.

Voir dire error in a non-capital case cannot be error affecting the punishment phase only under CCP Art. 44.29(b); therefore, the defendant has the right to begin a retrial in the guilt-innocence phase. Carson v. State, 6 S.W.3d 536 (Tex. Crim. App. 1999).

In capital cases, voir dire error that occurs in the context of a veniremember's inability to follow some facet of the law applying only at the punishment phase of trial constitutes "error affecting punishment only," and does not alone call for reversal of the conviction, but only a remand for a new punishment proceeding under CCP Art. 44.29(c). Clark v. State, 929 S.W.2d 5 (Tex. Crim. App. 1996); Ransom v. State, 920 S.W.2d 288 (Tex. Crim. App. 1996) (Opinion on State's motion for rehearing).

§14:40 Jury Shuffles

CCP Art. 35.11. Preparation of List

> *The trial judge, on the demand of the defendant or his attorney, or of the State's counsel, shall cause a sufficient number of jurors from which a jury may be selected to try the case to be randomly selected from the members of the general panel drawn or assigned as jurors in the case. The clerk shall randomly select the jurors by a computer or other process of random selection and shall write or print the names, in the order selected, on the jury list from which the jury is to be selected to try the case. The clerk shall deliver a copy of the list to the State's counsel and to the defendant or his attorney.*

§14:41 In General

The Texas Court of Criminal Appeals has mandated that consistent with the purpose of the statute—an assurance of the compilation of a random list of jurors—the jury shuffle is an "absolute right" available to either party. Jones v. State, 833 S.W.2d 118 (Tex. Crim. App. 1992), *cert. denied,* 507 U.S. 921, 113 S.Ct. 1285, 122 L. Ed. 2d 678 (1993).

Article 35.11 provides that a defendant is guaranteed that the jury panel will be shuffled once, at either his request or the State's. It does not mandate, however, that a defendant be allowed to reshuffle the panel after the State has caused the panel to be shuffled, absent some misconduct in the State's shuffle. Chappell v. State, 850 S.W.2d 508 (Tex. Crim. App. 1993).

A trial court's *sua sponte* shuffle of the jury list does not foreclose the defendant from requesting a second shuffle under Art. 35.11. Scott v. State, 805 S.W.2d 612 (Tex.App.—Austin 1991, *no pet.*); Wilkerson v. State, 681 S.W.2d 29 (Tex. Crim. App. 1984).

A defendant has a right to a "reshuffle" if the original shuffle was caused by someone other than the State, such as the trial judge or court personnel. Johnson v. State, 977 S.W.2d 137 (Tex. Crim. App. 1998). The defendant has a right to a "reshuffle" where the first shuffle was procedurally flawed. Johnson.

In a trial involving multiple defendants, the defense side of the table is not allowed more than one shake of the names of the members of the assigned jury panel. Latham v. State, 656 S.W.2d 478 (Tex. Crim. App. 1983).

An accused is not entitled to have a shuffle of all the names of the persons summoned for jury service during the week of his trial but is only entitled to have a shuffle of the names of those prospective jurors who make up the assigned jury panel from which will come the jury that will judge the facts of the accusation. Latham.

Where a clerk combines the jury questionnaires in a box, draws some slips out one at a time, but occasionally draws out a handful, and sometimes reshuffles the handful she had drawn, and where the top questionnaire is then removed until the list is complete, the statute has been complied with. McGee v. State, 909 S.W.2d 516 (Tex.App.—Tyler 1995, *pet. ref'd*).

§14:42 Timing of Motion

A motion to shuffle must be made before voir dire commences. Davis v. State, 782 S.W.2d 211

(Tex. Crim. App. 1989), *cert. denied,* 110.S.Ct. 2193, 495 U.S. 940, 109 L. Ed. 2d 520 (1990).

Voir dire in a non-capital case commences when the state begins its examination of the prospective jurors. Williams v. State, 719 S.W.2d 573 (Tex. Crim. App. 1986). In a capital case, the voir dire commences when the trial judge begins his examination of the panel. Yanez v. State, 677 S.W.2d 62 (Tex. Crim. App. 1984).

§14:43 Opportunity to View Venire

Compliance with CCP Art. 35.11 is had when counsel for either the state or the defendant is allowed the opportunity to view the venire seated in the courtroom in proper sequence and is thereafter allowed an opportunity to exercise his or her option to have the names shuffled. Williams v. State, 719 S.W.2d 573 (Tex. Crim. App. 1986).

There is no absolute right to shuffle the jury panel in circumstances where the defendant had the opportunity to view the original panel, declined to exercise his right to shuffle, and the shuffle at the State's request was done in the courtroom. Jones v. State, 833 S.W.2d 118 (Tex. Crim. App. 1992), *cert. denied,* 507 U.S. 921, 113 S.Ct. 1285, 122 L. Ed. 2d 678 (1993).

§14:44 Opportunity to View Jury Questionnaires

The trial court is not required to allow counsel to view jury questionnaires before they make their decision to shuffle. Davis v. State, 782 S.W.2d 211 (Tex. Crim. App. 1989), *cert. denied,* 110.S.Ct. 2193, 495 U.S. 940, 109 L. Ed. 2d 520 (1990).

However, the trial court is permitted to allow counsel to view the questionnaires before the decision to shuffle is made. Garza v. State, 7 S.W.3d 164 (Tex. Crim. App. 1999).

§14:45 Appellate Review

The trial court's denial of the defendant's legitimate request for a shuffle is subject to harmless error analysis on appeal. In order to merit reversal the defendant must probably show that someone unfit for jury service served on the jury or that the jury was constituted in a non-random manner. Ford v. State, 73 S.W.3d 923 (Tex. Crim. App. 2002) (where the error was found to be harmless).

Complaints about jury shuffle error must be preserved. Sanders v. State, 942 S.W.2d 3 (Tex. Crim. App. 1997); Powell v. State, 897 S.W.2d 307 (Tex. Crim. App. 1994). To prevail on appeal, a defendant must raise a specific objection about the jury shuffle at trial. James v. State, 772 S.W.2d 84 (Tex. Crim. App. 1989).

If CCP Art. 35.11 has not been followed, and a defendant requested the trial procedure about which he complains on appeal, appellate review of the impropriety is precluded. Valdez v. State, 472 S.W.2d 754 (Tex. Crim. App. 1971).

§14:46 Form: Sample Motion to Shuffle Venire

See our companion book *Texas Criminal Forms* (James Publishing) Form 14-6.

§14:50 Voir Dire Subject Matter

§14:51 Statutory Law

CCP Art. 35.17. Voir dire examination

> *1. When the court in its discretion so directs, except as provided in Section 2, the state and defendant shall conduct the voir dire examination of prospective jurors in the presence of the entire panel.*
>
> *2. In a capital felony case in which the State seeks the death penalty, the court shall propound to the entire panel of prospective jurors questions concerning the principles, as applicable to the case on trial, of reasonable doubt, burden of proof, return of indictment by grand jury, presumption of innocence, and opinion. Then, on demand of the State or defendant, either is entitled to examine each juror on voir dire individually and apart from the entire panel, and may further question the juror on the principles propounded by the court.*

§14:52 In General

The conduct of voir dire examination rests within the sound discretion of the trial court. Dowden v. State, 758 S.W.2d 264 (Tex. Crim. App. 1988).

The parties have broad latitude to question members of the venire. Battie v. State, 551 S.W.2d 401 (Tex. Crim. App. 1977), *cert. denied,* 434 U.S. 1041, 98 S.Ct. 782, 54 L. Ed. 2d 790 (1978).

Art. 1, §10 of the Texas Constitution guarantees a defendant the right to be heard by counsel. Such right includes the right of counsel to question members of the venire panel in order to intelligently exercise peremptory challenges. Ex parte McKay, 819 S.W.2d 478 (Tex. Crim. App. 1990); Jones v. State, 223 S.W.3d 379 (Tex. Crim. App. 2007)

Where the trial court disallows the defendant to ask a proper question on voir dire, it is a constitutional error. Jones.

Not all rulings limiting defense counsel's voir dire presentation are constitutional error as a *per se* violation of the right to counsel. Most rulings limiting voir dire will be subject to Rule 44.2(b) harm analysis. However, there may be instances when a judge's limitation on voir dire is so substantial as to warrant labeling the error as constitutional error subject to a Rule 44.2(a) harm analysis. Easley v. State, 424 S.W.3d 535, 538-9 (Tex. Crim. App. 2014).

Within reasonable limits, the trial court must allow the state and defense to explore attitudes that may render the veniremember challengeable for cause. Draughon v. State, 831 S.W.2d 331 (Tex. Crim. App. 1992), *cert. denied,* 509 U.S. 926, 113 S.Ct. 3045, 125 L. Ed. 2d 730 (1993).

It is proper for a party to ask questions designed to assess the relative desirability of the veniremember. Davis v. State, 894 S.W.2d 471 (Tex.App.—Fort Worth 1995, *no pet.*).

§14:52.1 Form: Sample Juror Questionnaire

See our companion book *Texas Criminal Forms* (James Publishing) Form 14-7.

§14:52.2 Form: Motion to Submit Jury Questionnaire

See our companion book *Texas Criminal Forms* (James Publishing) Form 14-9.1 and 14-9.2.

§14:53 Particular Inquiries Allowed

§14:53.1 Explanations of Law

During voir dire, a party may explain the law to the venire. Atkins v. State, 951 S.W.2d 787 (Tex. Crim. App. 1997) (remanded on rehearing for harm analysis).

The parties are permitted to discuss general principles of law applicable to the case during voir dire. Nevarez v. State, 832 S.W.2d 82 (Tex.App.—Waco 1992, *pet. ref'd*).

It is permissible for the parties to define terms as they are defined by law. Adanandus v. State, 866 S.W.2d 210 (Tex. Crim. App. 1993), *cert. denied,* 510 U.S. 1215, 114 S.Ct. 1338, 127 L. Ed. 2d 686 (1994).

The parties may question the venire as to any applicable lesser included offenses. Alfano v. State, 780 S.W.2d 494 (Tex.App.—Corpus Christi 1989, *no pet.*). The parties may explain to the jury that if a witness testifies he can be impeached with, among other things, prior convictions. Harris v. State, 656 S.W.2d 481 (Tex. Crim. App. 1983).

The trial court's refusal to allow a defendant to question a veniremember regarding his understanding of the term "reasonable doubt" constitutes reversible error in a non-capital case. Woolridge v. State, 827 S.W.2d 900 (Tex. Crim. App. 1992). The defendant has the right to examine a veniremember on a subject area even though the prosecutor has committed him to certain answers. White v. State, 629 S.W.2d 701 (Tex. Crim. App. 1981).

§14:53.1.1 Misstatements of Law

The right to ask proper questions does not include the right to misstate the law. Powell v. State, 897 S.W.2d 307 (Tex. Crim. App. 1994).

Defense counsel must accurately object when the state misinforms the venire during voir dire because if the point of error is different on appeal nothing will be presented for review. Sterling v. State, 800

S.W.2d 513 (Tex. Crim. App. 1990), *cert. denied,* 501 U.S. 1213, 111 S.Ct. 2816, 115 L. Ed. 2d 988 (1991).

The defendant must further show that he was somehow harmed by the remark before the case will be reversed on appeal. Jackson v. State, 822 S.W.2d 18 (Tex. Crim. App. 1990).

TIP TO THE PROSECUTION: If defense counsel misstates the law during voir dire, object on this ground. If the objection is sustained, ask the trial court to instruct the jury to disregard the misstatement of law. Etheridge v. State, 903 S.W.2d 1 (Tex. Crim. App. 1994).

A party should be allowed to ask the venire questions that seek to determine whether they understand that the standard of proof beyond a reasonable doubt constitutes a level of confidence under the law that is higher than both the preponderance of the evidence and the clear and convincing evidence standards. Fuller v. State, 363 S.W.3d 583 (Tex. Crim. App. 2012).

§14:53.2 Punishment Inquiries

The parties may inform the venire of the range of punishment applicable in the case. Estes v. State, 873 S.W.2d 771 (Tex.App.—Fort Worth 1994, *pet. ref'd*). This includes the range of punishment available for an enhanced offense. Estes.

A prosecutor may inform the venire of the range of punishment applicable if the state were to prove a prior conviction for enhancement purposes. Frausto v. State, 642 S.W.2d 506 (Tex. Crim. App. 1982). It is improper however, for the prosecutor to inform the venire of the particular allegations contained in the indictment of the defendant on trial. Frausto.

When the jury will set punishment in the case, it is error for the trial court to prohibit defendant's counsel from asking veniremembers questions relevant to punishment, testing their philosophy and feelings about punishment. Powell v. State, 631 S.W.2d 169 (Tex. Crim. App. 1982).

§14:53.3 Inquiries on Status of Victim or Witness

The defendant is allowed to discover a veniremember's views on the status of the victim in order that he may intelligently exercise his peremptory challenges. Maddux v. State, 862 S.W.2d 590 (Tex. Crim. App. 1993). Restrictions on a defendant's voir dire questioning designed to discover the veniremember's bias as to the victim's status as a child have been found improper. Cena v. State, 960 S.W.2d 804 (Tex.App.—El Paso 1997); Maddux.

The question "generally speaking, do you feel like you might have a problem convicting a defendant if the only eyewitness is a child" has been found to be a proper type of inquiry. Davis v. State, 894 S.W.2d 471 (Tex.App.—Fort Worth 1995, *no pet.*).

However, a veniremember is not challengeable for cause for an inability to consider the full range of punishment in a case involving a victim of a particular status where he can consider the full punishment range for the offense as set out by law. Sadler v. State, 977 S.W.2d 140 (Tex. Crim. App. 1998).

A defendant is allowed to explore the venire's ability to judge the credibility of police officer witnesses. Hernandez v. State, 508 S.W.2d 853 (Tex. Crim. App. 1974).

The trial court can disallow an inquiry of venire members as to whether they could be fair and impartial in a case in which the victim was nine years old because the inquiry is too broad and global. Barajas v. State, 93 S.W.3d 36 (Tex. Crim. App. 2002).

§14:53.4 Inquiries Into Status and Attitudes of Veniremembers

Counsel should be permitted to question veniremembers about their prior grand jury service. Gonzales v. State, 638 S.W.2d 132 (Tex.App.—Corpus Christi 1982, *no pet.*).

It is not error for the trial court to allow parties to question veniremembers about what verdict they reached during prior jury service. Whiting v. State, 943 S.W.2d 102 (Tex.App.—Houston [1st Dist.] 1997, *pet. ref'd*).

However, it also is not an abuse of discretion for a trial court to refuse to allow defense counsel to inquire of prospective jurors with prior jury service in criminal cases what verdict they reached in those cases. Bolden v. State, 634 S.W.2d 710 (Tex. Crim. App. 1982).

The defendant should be allowed to inquire as to the venire's feeling about moral issues where relevant to the case. Shipley v. State, 790 S.W.2d 604 (Tex. Crim. App. 1990) (where the issue was extra-marital affairs).

Although it is proper to question juror's views and sentiments on social and moral subjects generally, the courts do not permit a hypothetical case to be submitted, nor do they allow questions designed to bring out the juror's views on the case to be tried. Brown v. State, 674 S.W.2d 443 (Tex. App.—Dallas 1984), *affirmed at* 741 S.W.2d 453 (Tex. Crim. App. 1987).

The defense should be allowed to question the venire as to their attitudes about defendants who invoke the insanity defense where this is an issue in the case. Robinson v. State, 720 S.W.2d 808 (Tex. Crim. App. 1986).

The defendant should be allowed to explore any area of questioning which would reveal a possible bias against the defendant. Harrell v. State, 882 S.W.2d 65 (Tex.App.—Houston [14th Dist.] 1994, *pet. ref'd*).

§14:53.5 Inquiries Based on Situational Status of Witness

An inquiry whether the veniremember would be able to convict on the testimony of one eyewitness has been found to be a proper question. Orosco v. State, 827 S.W.2d 575 (Tex.App.—Fort Worth 1992, *pet. ref'd*), *cert. denied,* 506 U.S. 960, 113 S.Ct. 425, 121 L. Ed. 2d 347 (1992). An inquiry whether a veniremember would be able to convict a defendant without hearing directly from a confidential informant has been found to be a proper question. Payton v. State, 830 S.W.2d 722 (Tex.App.—Houston [14th Dist.] 1992, *no pet.*).

Also, whether a veniremember would be able to convict based upon a child-victim's videotaped testimony has been found to a proper inquiry. Newman v. State, 700 S.W.2d 307 (Tex.App.—Houston [1st Dist.] 1985), *reversed on other grounds at* 743 S.W.2d 641 (Tex. Crim. App. 1988).

§14:54 Means of Making Inquiry

§14:54.1 Type of Question Permitted

It is permissible to use hypothetical questions to explain the application of the law. Atkins v. State, 951 S.W.2d 787 (Tex. Crim. App. 1997); Cuevas v. State, 742 S.W.2d 331 (Tex. Crim. App. 1987).

It is also allowable to use a hypothetical regarding the victim's status as a child because it seeks to ascertain potential bias. Maddux v. State, 862 S.W.2d 590 (Tex. Crim. App. 1993) (where defense counsel sought to inquire if the venire could consider 5 years probation where the victim of the offense was a child). It is not proper to inquire how a veniremember would respond to particular circumstances presented in a hypothetical question. Cuevas.

Questions that are not clearly improper on some other basis can be asked for the purpose of intelligently exercising peremptory challenges subject to reasonable time limits imposed by the trial court. Barajas v. State, 93 S.W.3d 36 (Tex. Crim. App. 2002).

Questions phrased, "Can you be fair and impartial..." are overly broad and the trial court does not abuse its discretion in disallowing them. Barajas.

§14:55 Mechanics of Voir Dire

A trial court does not have to permit the parties to videotape the voir dire process. Curry v. State, 910 S.W.2d 490 (Tex. Crim. App. 1995).

§14:56 Preserving Error

§14:56.1 Preserving Error Where Proper Inquiry Disallowed

A trial court generally will not abuse its discretion unless it limits the appellant from asking a proper question concerning a proper area of inquiry. Allridge v. State, 762 S.W.2d 146 (Tex. Crim. App. 1988).

Where the trial court disallows the defendant to ask a proper question on voir dire, it is a constitutional error. Jones v. State, 223 S.W.3d 379 (Tex. Crim. App. 2007); Samaripas v. State, 454 S.W.3d 1 (Tex. Crim. App. 2014).

Where the trial court excludes a proper question during voir dire, the effect is subject to harmless error analysis. Gonzales v. State, 994 S.W.2d 170 (Tex. Crim. App. 1999).

Defense counsel must state a proper question in precise form. Jones v. State, 843 S.W.2d 487 (Tex. Crim. App. 1992), *cert. denied,* 507 U.S. 1035, 113 S.Ct. 1858, 123 L. Ed. 2d 479 (1993).

The record must reflect the precise question that counsel sought to ask. Caldwell v. State, 818 S.W.2d 790 (Tex. Crim. App. 1991), *cert. denied*, 503 U.S. 990, 112 S.Ct. 1684, 118 L. Ed. 2d 399 (1992).

Where the court disallows a proper inquiry, a defendant preserves error only if:

- Defendant exhausts all of his peremptory challenges
- Defendant requests more challenges
- Request is denied, and
- Defendant identifies an objectionable person seated on the jury on whom he would have exercised a peremptory challenge

Anson v. State, 959 S.W.2d 203 (Tex. Crim. App. 1997); Narvaiz v. State, 840 S.W.2d 415 (Tex. Crim. App. 1992), *cert. denied*, 507 U.S. 975, 113 S.Ct. 1422, 122 L. Ed. 2d 791 (1993).

There is no distinction between capital and non-capital cases for the purpose of the steps required to preserve error for the erroneous denial of proper questioning. Anson.

Defense counsel should object that the intelligent use of the defendant's peremptory challenges has been affected and that he has been deprived of the effective assistance of counsel. Sawyers v. State, 724 S.W.2d 24 (Tex. Crim. App. 1986).

When an appellant challenges a trial judge's limitation on the voir dire process, the reviewing court must analyze the claim under an abuse of discretion standard, the focus of which is whether the appellant proffered a proper question concerning a proper area of inquiry. Caldwell, *supra*.

Voir dire error in a non-capital case cannot be error affecting the punishment phase only under CCP Art. 44.29 (b); therefore, the defendant has the right to begin a retrial in the guilt-innocence phase. Carson v. State, 6 S.W.3d 536 (Tex. Crim. App. 1999).

Defense counsel's reply in the negative to whether there is an objection to the jury as selected at the conclusion of jury selection does not constitute a waiver of a previously preserved claim of error during voir dire proceedings. Stairhime v. State, 463 S.W.3d 902, 908 (Tex. Crim. App. 2015).

§14:56.2 Preserving Error for Improper Inquiry by State

Where the defendant claims that the state has been allowed to ask an improper voir dire question, he must contemporaneously object in order to preserve error. Boyd v. State, 811 S.W.2d 105 (Tex. Crim. App. 1991), *cert. denied,* 502 U.S. 971, 112 S.Ct. 448, 116 L. Ed. 2d 466 (1991).

The objection must be made as soon as the basis for the objection becomes apparent. Johnson v. State, 803 S.W.2d 272 (Tex. Crim. App. 1990), *cert. denied,* 501 U.S. 1259, 111 S.Ct. 2914, 15 L. Ed. 2d 1078 (1991). Objections made after the questions are answered do not preserve error for appeal. Russell v. State, 904 S.W.2d 191 (Tex.App.—Amarillo 1995, *pet. ref'd*).

If the defendant's objection is sustained, he must go further and request an instruction to disregard, and, if granted, seek a motion for mistrial in order to preserve the complaint for appeal. Holloway v. State, 695 S.W.2d 112 (Tex.App.—Fort Worth 1985), *aff'd*, 751 S.W.2d 866 (Tex. Crim. App. 1988).

Voir dire error in a non-capital case cannot be error affecting the punishment phase only under CCP Art. 44.29 (b); therefore, the defendant has the right to begin a retrial in the guilt-innocence phase. Carson v. State, 6 S.W.3d 536 (Tex. Crim. App. 1999).

§14:57 Restrictions on Voir Dire

§14:57.1 In General

The trial court has the power to impose reasonable restrictions on the conduct of voir dire. Marquez v. State, 725 S.W.2d 217 (Tex. Crim. App. 1987), *cert. denied*, 484 U.S. 872, 108 S.Ct. 201, 98 L. Ed. 2d 152 (1987). The exercise of that power is within the sound discretion of the trial judge. Marquez.

In making the determination whether the trial court abused its discretion in restricting the appellant's voir dire examination, the test is whether the question or questions sought to be asked are proper. If the question was proper and the defendant was prevented from asking it, then the defendant has been prevented from intelligently exercising his peremptory challenges. Faulder v. State, 745 S.W.2d 327 (Tex. Crim. App. 1987).

A proper question is one that seeks to discover a veniremember's views on an issue applicable to the case. Caldwell v. State, 818 S.W.2d 790 (Tex. Crim. App. 1991), *cert. denied*, 503 U.S. 990, 112 S.Ct. 1684, 118 L. Ed. 2d 399 (1992).

To be constitutionally compelled, it is not enough that a defendant's voir dire questions might be helpful. Rather, the trial court's failure to allow these questions must render the defendant's trial fundamentally unfair. Jacobs v. State, 560 S.W.3d 205, 211 (Tex. Crim. App. 2019) (where the defendant's question of the venire regarding whether they could be fair if they knew that the defendant had been previously convicted of a sexual offense was found to only marginally enhance his ability to explore their biases over the question he was permitted, which was in terms of conviction of an assaultive offense).

Not all rulings limiting defense counsel's voir dire presentation are constitutional error as a *per se* violation of the right to counsel. Most rulings limiting voir dire will be subject to Rule 44.2(b) harm analysis. However, there may be instances when a judge's limitation on voir dire is so substantial as to warrant labeling the error as constitutional error subject to a Rule 44.2(a) harm analysis. Easley v. State, 424 S.W.3d 535, 538-9 (Tex. Crim. App. 2014).

TIP TO THE BENCH: Although the trial judge is vested with the authority to impose reasonable restrictions on the accused's exercise of his voir dire examination, conducting a criminal trial promptly and expeditiously must never be undertaken at the risk of denying a party on trial a substantial right. Faulder.

It is improper for a trial judge to impose restrictions based on the mere possibility that an otherwise proper question might lengthen the voir dire process. The trial judge must first allow the question, and may later curtail similar questions if the voir dire process proves to be unduly lengthy. Battie v. State, 551 S.W.2d 401 (Tex. Crim. App. 1977), *cert. denied,* 434 U.S. 1041, 98 S.Ct. 782, 54 L. Ed. 2d 790 (1978).

TIP TO THE BENCH: Should a trial judge determine that either party is prolonging the voir dire process, the simple and effective remedy is to call the attorneys to the bench and instruct them to expedite the process. McCarter v. State, 837 S.W.2d 117 (Tex. Crim. App. 1992).

---

§14:57.2 Permissible Voir Dire Restrictions

§14:57.2.1 Questions and Areas Subject to Restriction

§14:57.2.1.1 Confusing, Repetitious, Broad and Vague Questions

A trial court may restrict confusing or misleading voir dire questions. Jones v. State, 850 S.W.2d 223 (Tex.App.—Fort Worth 1993, *pet. ref'd*). The trial court also has the power to terminate needlessly duplicitous or repetitious questioning. Allridge v. State, 762 S.W.2d 146 (Tex. Crim. App. 1988), *cert. denied*, 489 U.S. 1040, 109 S.Ct. 1176, 103 L. Ed. 2d 238 (1989).

If a prospective juror states his or her position clearly, unequivocally, and without reservation, the trial court does not err in refusing to permit further questioning. Guerra v. State, 771 S.W.2d 453 (Tex. Crim. App. 1988), *cert. denied,* 492 U.S. 925, 109 S.Ct. 3260, 106 L. Ed. 2d 606 (1989). However, defense counsel may not be precluded from the traditional voir dire examination simply because the questions asked are repetitious of those asked by the court and prosecutor. Mathis v. State, 576 S.W.2d 835 (Tex. Crim. App. 1979). This is because each party has the right to question potential jurors in their own individual manner to emphasize a point or uncover a hidden bias, and may not be forced to rely on other parties to ask similar questions. Williams v. State, 804 S.W.2d 95 (Tex. Crim. App. 1991).

A trial court does not abuse its discretion in restricting counsel from asking potential jurors broad, global question such as those about "their thoughts" on issues. Boyd v. State, 811 S.W.2d 105 (Tex. Crim. App. 1991), *cert. denied,* 502 U.S. 971, 112 S.Ct. 448, 116 L. Ed. 2d 466 (1991).

Likewise, vague questions about "what things" the veniremember thinks are important in determining the issues in the case, wholly unrelated to the case's procedural scheme, amount to a fishing expedition going beyond the scope of proper voir dire. Boyd.

Questions phrased, "Can you be fair and impartial..." are overly broad and the trial court does not abuse its discretion in disallowing them. Barajas v. State, 93 S.W.3d 36 (Tex. Crim. App. 2002).

TIP TO THE BENCH: The trial court can prevent global fishing expeditions on voir dire by requiring the parties to phrase their questions with the precision necessary to glean relevant information.

Examples of impermissibly global questions include questions asking a prospective capital juror's understanding of a life sentence or of parole, Boyd; and asking what cases would be appropriate for the death penalty, Allridge, *supra.*

Whether a veniremember would want to know certain legal parameters before deciding the issues in a case is not strictly relevant to a juror's duties or any issue in the case. What the jurors want to know is immaterial; the trial court will give jurors the proper information about the application of the law. Sells v. State, 121 S.W.3d 748 (Tex. Crim. App. 2003).

§14:57.2.1.2 Commitment Questions

A trial judge may limit a defendant's voir dire where a question commits a veniremember to a particular course of action based on a specific set of facts. Atkins v. State, 951 S.W.2d 787 (Tex. Crim. App. 1997); Dinkins v. State, 894 S.W.2d 330 (Tex. Crim. App. 1995); Standefer v. State, 59 S.W.3d 177 (Tex. Crim. App. 2001).

A commitment question is one that asks veniremen to resolve or refrain from resolving an issue a certain way after learning a particular fact. Standefer, *supra.*

A question may be proper if it seeks to discover a juror's views on an issue applicable to the case or to commit the juror to follow the law; however, if the question adds a fact in addition to those necessary to establish a challenge for cause it is an improper "commitment" question. Standefer, *supra.*

PRACTICE TIP: The Court of Criminal Appeals hints that questions that ask veniremen "could there be circumstances" are permissible because this wording does not ask a venireman to take or refrain from taking any action based on the parameters of the question. See Standefer.

A trial court may properly disallow hypothetical questions that are based on the facts of the case on trial. Coleman v. State, 881 S.W.2d 344 (Tex. Crim. App. 1994); Cuevas v. State, 742 S.W.2d 331 (Tex. Crim. App. 1987), *cert. denied,* 485 U.S. 1015, 108 S.Ct. 1488, 99 L. Ed. 2d 716 (1988).

A trial court may disallow the asking of open-ended questions designed so the veniremember could set the hypothetical parameters for their decision-making. Allridge v. State, 850 S.W.2d 471 (Tex. Crim. App. 1991), *cert. denied,* 510 U.S. 831, 114 S.Ct. 101, 126 L. Ed. 2d 68 (1993); Standefer v. State, 59 S.W.3d 177 (Tex. Crim. App. 2001).

TIP TO THE BENCH: This is a very tricky area for trial judges. The judge may have to call counsel to the bench to inquire as to the facts of the case before ruling on an objection of this nature.

The appropriate test for harm when the state is allowed to improperly commit jurors to a set of facts is the harmless error analysis set out in Rule 44.2(b) of the Texas Rules of Appellate Procedure. Sanchez v. State, 165 S.W.3d 707 (Tex. Crim. App. 2005).

§14:57.2.1.2.1 Improper Commitment Questions

The question "[d]o each of you feel as though you could evaluate a witness and his testimony and decide if he's being truthful without automatically dismissing his testimony because of some criminal history?" is a commitment question because it asks jurors to resolve witness credibility (issue) based on the knowledge that the witness has a criminal history (particular fact). Lydia v. State, 109 S.W.3d 495 (Tex. Crim. App. 2003).

For example, the inquiry "what ... is a case that is proper for the death penalty to be imposed is improper because it committed the veniremember to a particular fact situation. Boyd v. State, 811 S.W.2d 105 (Tex. Crim. App.1991), *cert. denied,* 502 U.S. 971, 112 S.Ct. 448, 116 L. Ed. 2d 466 (1991).

Asking veniremembers if they agree that a particular fact situation would be self-defense is improperly contracting with the venire. Montes v. State, 870 S.W.2d 643 (Tex.App.—El Paso 1994, *no pet.*).

A question asking if the venireman would be more likely, or less likely, generally, to view a defendant as a continuing threat to society, if the venireman knew he could not be paroled for a minimum of 40 years, is improper because it seeks to determine whether the venireman will give the parole instruction mitigating or aggravating effect in the context of the future dangerousness punishment issue. Sells v. State, 121 S.W.3d 748 (Tex. Crim. App. 2003).

The question "[w]ould you presume someone guilty if he or she refused a breath test on their refusal alone?" is an improper commitment question because the question asks whether the prospective juror would resolve the issue of guilt against the defendant if the juror learns a particular fact—that the defendant has refused a breath test. The facts in this question would not lead to a valid challenge for cause because a juror may permissibly presume guilt from such evidence. Standefer.

The question "[w]hat circumstances in your opinion warrant the imposition of the death penalty?" is an improper commitment question. It is an example of an open-ended question that is a commitment question because it asks the prospective juror to set the hypothetical parameters for his decision-making. An example of a proper question that seeks to uncover the same type of information is "Do you think there might be circumstances that would mitigate against the death penalty?" Allridge.

The question "[w]ould the minimum length of time a defendant could serve in prison before he could be paroled be something you would want to know in answering the special issues?" is an improper commitment question. The question relates to how a particular fact (in this case, the minimum amount of time a capital life defendant must be incarcerated before becoming eligible for parole) might influence jury deliberations. These types of questions implicate the strictures imposed by Standefer against commitment questions and by Barajas against ambiguous questions. The question is an attempt to commit the venire members to giving mitigating or aggravating effect to the minimum parole eligibility requirement. Additionally, this matter is not strictly relevant to a juror's duties or any issue in the case. What the jurors want to know is immaterial; the trial court will give jurors the proper information about the application of the law. Sells.

The question, "Do you believe disabilities of a defendant would be something you'd take into consideration?" is an improper commitment question in a capital case because jurors are not required to consider any particular type of evidence as mitigating. Davis v. State, 313 S.W.3d 317 (Tex. Crim. App. 2010).

§14:57.2.1.2.2 Proper Commitment Questions

The prosecutor used the "mercy killing" scenario as an example of an intentional murder in the context of questioning on the range of punishment for first degree murder. Then the prosecutor asked: If taking into consideration the wide range of circumstances which could constitute murder, could the venire member keep an open mind as to the full range of punishment? The questions were not improper commitment questions. They did not attempt to bind the venire member to resolve or refrain from resolving an issue (*i.e.*, the minimum punishment for an intentional murder) on the basis of one or more facts contained in the questions. Halprin v. State, 170 S.W.3d 111 (Tex. Crim. App. 2005).

The prosecutor gave a hypothetical example of a case involving the testimony of a single witness in an indecency with a child case and then asked: ". . . [a]ssume for me that you do believe her testimony beyond a reasonable doubt, you do believe her, and it meets all the elements of the charge, indecency with a child by contact, assume for me that you do believe her beyond a reasonable doubt, could you convict that hypothetical defendant of that charge or would you require some other witness or some other evidence?" The question is a proper commitment question because it leads to a valid challenge for cause without adding extra facts. Lee v. State, 206 S.W.3d 620 (Tex. Crim. App. 2006).

The state's inquiry whether the venire was more likely to believe a self-defense claim made by a woman was a proper commitment question because it could lead to a challenge for cause to a veniremember for having a bias for the female defendant. Braxton v. State, 226 S.W.3d 602 (Tex. App.—Houston [1st Dist.] 2007, *pet. dism'd*).

In a prosecution for tampering with a government record, the question "Do you believe there is anything wrong with putting false information in a police report?" was found to not be a commitment question. Jurors are required to follow the law that makes it a crime for a police officer to tamper with a government record. Asking the venire if they agree that the commission of such a crime is wrong does not commit them to resolve an issue of fact in a certain way. Rather, it inquires into the jurors' general beliefs as to the wrongness of conduct that the law has made a crime. Wingo v. State, 189 S.W.3d 270 (Tex. Crim. App. 2006).

§14:57.2.1.2.3 Non-Commitment Questions

In a case where defense counsel asked the venire if they could be fair and impartial in a case in which the victim was nine years old, it was found to not be a commitment question because it does not ask the prospective juror to resolve or refrain from resolving any issue. However, this "fair and impartial" question is a license to go fishing without providing any concrete information for the intelligent use of peremptory challenges or challenges for cause. Vague questions about "what things" the venire member thought were important in determining the issues in a case amounts to a fishing expedition going beyond the scope of proper voir dire. Barajas v. State, 93 S.W.3d 36 (Tex. Crim. App. 2002), *overruling* Nunfio v. State, 808 S.W.2d 482 (Tex. Crim. App. 1991), which had held that the question "If the victim is a nun, could you be fair and impartial?" was not a commitment question.

The prosecutor, in the context of the mitigation special issue, used mental retardation as an example of a factor that jurors might consider mitigating. The prosecutor then asked the prospective juror: Would he be able to keep an open mind to a life sentence with regard to the mitigation special issue even if he had already found that the defendant was guilty of killing a police officer and will be a future danger? The prosecutor did not improperly commit the prospective juror. The prosecution's question did not attempt to bind the juror to resolve or refrain from resolving an issue (*i.e.*, the mitigating evidence special issue) on the basis of one or more facts contained in the question. The totality of the voir dire record reflected that the prosecution explained that the prospective juror should have an open mind and consider all of the evidence in answering the mitigating evidence special issue. Halprin v. State, 170 S.W.3d 111 (Tex. Crim. App. 2005).

In a non-capital case the question, "what factors ... are important" in sentencing is not an improper commitment question because it does not ask the jurors how particular facts would influence their deliberations. It is an inquiry into the jurors' general philosophies and does not ask jurors to define situations in which they would impose a specific sentence. This question may be an improper commitment question in a death penalty case because sentencing for a capital felony has only two possible outcomes, life in prison without parole or the death penalty. Davis v. State, 349 S.W.3d 517 (Tex. Crim. App. 2010).

§14:57.2.1.3 Questions in Improper Form

A trial court also may restrict questions asked in improper form. Guerra v. State, 771 S.W.2d 453 (Tex. Crim. App. 1988), *cert. denied,* 492 U.S. 925, 109 S.Ct. 3260, 106 L. Ed. 2d 606 (1989).

More specifically, the trial court must be given some discretion to regulate the form of the question (*i.e.,* its semantics or phrasing), and to preclude those questions that the court might, in its discretion, find improperly constructed. Howard v. State, 941 S.W.2d 102 (Tex. Crim. App. 1996).

PRACTICE TIP: Where opposing counsel attempts to question without adequately explaining the law to the venire or individual veniremember, an objection to the "form of the question" is a valid objection and can be sustained by the trial court under Howard and Guerra.

Where the trial court sustains the state's objection to an improper commitment question but the defense is later allowed to question on the substance of the question, the trial court, by not placing an absolute limitation on the subject matter of the inquiry, has merely sustained an objection to the form of the original question. Hernandez v. State, 390 S.W.3d 310, 316 (Tex. Crim. App. 2012) (where the defense had sought to ask if the venireperson could consider a particular piece of evidence as mitigating).

Where the trial court in sustaining an objection based on the form of the question places no absolute limitation on the underlying substance of a defendant's voir dire question, it is incumbent upon defense counsel to rephrase an improperly phrased query or else waive the voir dire restriction. Trevino v. State, 815 S.W.2d 592 (Tex. Crim. App. 1991).

PRACTICE TIP: Where the trial court has sustained an objection that a question was in improper form, it is incumbent on the proffering party to rephrase the question or the point will be waived on appeal. Guerra.

§14:57.2.1.4 Preserving Error of Improper Question by State

In order to preserve error where the state has asked an improper question, the defendant must timely object and take all of the steps required to preserve error where the court has improperly denied one of his challenges for cause. Morrow v. State, 753 S.W.2d 372 (Tex. Crim. App. 1988).

§14:57.2.2 Subject Matter That May Be Restricted

§14:57.2.2.1 Inquiries on Incorrect Law

The trial court can prevent inquiries into subject matters that are no longer the law. Spence v. State, 795 S.W.2d 743 (Tex. Crim. App. 1990), *cert. denied*, 499 U.S. 932, 111 S.Ct. 1339, 113 L. Ed. 2d 271 (1991).

It is not error for the trial court to refuse to allow questioning on an area of law as to which there is to be no evidence presented at the trial. Jones v. State, 843 S.W.2d 487 (Tex. Crim. App. 1992), *cert. denied*, 507 U.S. 1035, 113 S.Ct. 1858, 123 L. Ed. 2d 479 (1993).

A trial court may restrict counsel's questioning on irrelevant matters. Boyd v. State, 811 S.W.2d 105 (Tex. Crim. App.1991), *cert. denied*, 502 U.S. 971, 112 S.Ct. 448, 116 L. Ed. 2d 466 (1991).

A trial court does not abuse its discretion in disallowing inquiries of veniremembers as to whether they could follow jury charge language that is not required by law. Hankins v. State, 132 S.W.3d 380 (Tex. Crim. App. 2004) (where the defendant sought to voir dire on the disapproved Geesa instruction).

§14:57.2.2.2 Definitions of Legally Undefined Terms

The trial court has the discretion to prohibit voir dire on a veniremember's understanding of the definition of undefined terms in the charge. Wheatfall v. State, 882 S.W.2d 829 (Tex. Crim. App. 1994). For example, a trial court does not abuse its discretion by refusing to permit counsel to question a veniremember regarding his definition of the term "probability." Lagrone v. State, 942 S.W.2d 602 (Tex. Crim. App. 1997), *cert.*

denied, 522 U.S. 917, 118 S.Ct. 305, 139 L. Ed. 2d 235 (1997).

A trial court does not abuse its discretion by refusing voir dire questioning on definitions of the terms "deliberately, probability, and criminal acts of violence" in a capital case. Milton v. State, 599 S.W.2d 824 (Tex. Crim. App. 1980), *cert. denied,* 451 U.S. 1031, 101 S.Ct. 3022, 69 L. Ed. 2d 400 (1981).

A trial court is, however, required under certain circumstances to allow the parties to question the venire as to their comprehension of certain terms as those terms are relevant to the issues in the case. Teague v. State, 864 S.W.2d 505 (Tex. Crim. App. 1993), *overruled on other grounds by* Robertson v. State, 871 S.W.2d 701 (Tex. Crim. App. 1993) (where the issue was the difference between the terms "intentionally" and "deliberately").

A trial court is on firmer ground limiting voir dire on the understanding of undefined terms in capital murder cases because in those cases voir dire examination can take an unreasonable length of time. Woolridge v. State, 827 S.W.2d 900 (Tex. Crim. App. 1992).

TIP TO THE BENCH: In situations such as a death penalty case, it can save a great deal of time on voir dire to encourage the parties to agree on a definition for terms not defined by law which are crucial to a veniremember's function as a juror.

It is error for the trial court to allow a party to limit the venire to its definition of a phrase not defined by law. Jackson v. State, 822 S.W.2d 18 (Tex. Crim. App. 1990), *cert. denied,* 509 U.S. 921, 113 S.Ct. 3034, 125 L. Ed. 2d 722 (1993).

§14:57.2.2.3 Factual Matters

It is permissible for the trial court to disallow questioning on whether members of the venire remembered specific aspects of a newspaper article. Faulder v. State, 745 S.W.2d 327 (Tex. Crim. App. 1987).

Questions about parole are properly disallowed in capital cases. Jones v. State, 982 S.W.2d 346 (Tex. Crim. App. 1998).

§14:57.3 Time Restrictions

§14:57.3.1 In General

The control of the voir dire examination is within the sound discretion of the trial judge, and it is well settled that the trial judge's discretionary authority extends to imposing reasonable limitations on the time for which counsel may question the jury panel. Caldwell v. State, 818 S.W.2d 790 (Tex. Crim. App. 1991), *cert. denied,* 503 U.S. 990, 112 S.Ct. 1684, 118 L. Ed. 2d 399 (1992).

Accordingly, a trial court's decision to limit questioning during voir dire may be reviewed only to determine whether such a restraint amounts to an abuse of discretion. Smith v. State, 703 S.W.2d 641 (Tex. Crim. App. 1985).

§14:57.3.2 Relevant Factors

Where the defendant is restricted while questioning the venire *collectively,* two factors are relevant in determining whether a trial court abused its discretion in limiting voir dire time: (1) whether the defendant's voir dire examination reveals an attempt to prolong the voir dire; for example, whether the questions were irrelevant, immaterial or unnecessarily repetitious; and (2) whether the questions that the defendant was not permitted to ask members of the venire were proper voir dire questions. De la Rosa v. State, 414 S.W.2d 668 (Tex. Crim. App. 1967).

Where the defendant is restricted while attempting to question veniremembers *individually,* three factors are relevant in determining whether a trial court abused its discretion in limiting voir dire time:

- Did defendant's voir dire examination reveal an attempt to prolong the voir dire; for example, were the questions irrelevant, immaterial or unnecessarily repetitious
- Were the questions that the defendant was not permitted to ask members of the venire proper voir dire questions
- Can defendant show that he was not permitted to examine jurors who served on the jury. Ratliff v. State, 690 S.W.2d 597 (Tex. Crim. App. 1985)

This test remains the same in the capital context, except that the third prong is whether the party was not permitted to ask proper questions of veniremembers who actually served on the jury. Etheridge v. State, 903 S.W.2d 1 (Tex. Crim. App. 1994).

Defense counsel does not unnecessarily prolong voir dire merely by addressing matters previously covered by the trial court or the state. Tobar v. State, 850 S.W.2d 182 (Tex. Crim. App. 1993); McCarter v. State, 837 S.W.2d 117 (Tex. Crim. App. 1992).

If the parties have made an agreement to be bound to a certain voir dire time limit, a reviewing court may consider the agreement as a factor in deciding if the trial judge impermissibly limited voir dire examination. Cantu v. State, 842 S.W.2d 667 (Tex. Crim. App. 1992), *cert. denied,* 509 U.S. 926, 113 S.Ct. 3046, 125 L. Ed. 2d 731 (1993).

§14:57.3.3 Preserving Error for Improper Time Restriction

Where the defendant has been restricted from asking additional voir dire questions, he must do several things to preserve error:

- Request additional time
- Inform the judge that counsel has additional subject matter on which to question the veniremember
- Present to the trial court a specific question counsel wishes to proffer
- Obtain an adverse ruling as to that request
- Exercise peremptory challenges on those veniremembers not questioned (and exhaust peremptory challenges); and
- Identify an objectionable juror who sat on the jury

Caldwell v. State, 818 S.W.2d 790 (Tex. Crim. App. 1991), *cert. denied*, 503 U.S. 990, 112 S.Ct. 1684, 118 L. Ed. 2d 399 (1992).

PRACTICE TIP: When conducting voir dire, have several proper questions written down and ready to proffer to the trial court in the event that the trial court attempts to terminate counsel's questioning prematurely.

TIP TO THE BENCH: Because of the unpredictability of veniremember's attitudes and the possible issues involved in a case, the imposition of an absolute time limit is a slippery slope. The trial court is advised to impose a flexible goal rather than an absolute time limit. Any proper question has the potential to lengthen the voir dire portion of a trial. Woolridge v. State, 827 S.W.2d 900 (Tex. Crim. App. 1992).

§14:57.3.4 Form for Additional Time

See our companion book *Texas Criminal Forms* (James Publishing) for the following sample form:

- Form 14-11 Motion for Additional Time to Conduct Voir Dire.

§14:60 Challenges for Cause

§14:61 Statutory Law

CCP Art. 35.16. Reasons for Challenge for Cause

(a) A challenge for cause is an objection made to a particular juror, alleging some fact which renders the juror incapable or unfit to serve on the jury. A challenge for cause may be made by either the state or the defense for any one of the following reasons:

(1) That the juror is not a qualified voter in the state and county under the Constitution and laws of the state; provided, however, the failure to register to vote shall not be a disqualification;

(2) That the juror has been convicted of misdemeanor theft or a felony;

(3) That the juror is under indictment or other legal accusation for misdemeanor theft or a felony;

(4) That the juror is insane;

(5) That the juror has such defect in the organs of feeling or hearing, or such bodily or mental defect or disease as to render the juror unfit for jury service, or that the juror is legally blind and the court in its discretion is not satisfied that the juror is fit for jury service in that particular case;

(6) That the juror is a witness in the case;

(7) That the juror served on the grand jury which found the indictment;

(8) That the juror served on a petit jury in a former trial of the same case;

(9) That the juror has a bias or prejudice in favor of or against the defendant;

(10) That from hearsay, or otherwise, there is established in the mind of the juror such a conclusion as to the guilt or innocence of the defendant as would influence the juror in finding a verdict. To ascertain whether this cause of challenge exists, the juror shall first be asked whether, in the juror's opinion, the conclusion so established will influence the juror's verdict. If the juror answers in the affirmative, the juror shall be discharged without further interrogation by either party or the court. If the juror answers in the negative, the juror shall be further examined as to how the juror's conclusion was formed, and the extent to which it will affect the juror's action; and, if it appears to have been formed from reading newspaper accounts, communications, statements or reports, or mere rumor or hearsay, and if the juror states that the juror feels able, notwithstanding such opinion, to render an impartial verdict upon the law and the evidence, the court, if satisfied that the juror is impartial and will render such verdict, may, in its discretion, admit the juror as competent to serve in such case. If the court, in its discretion, is not satisfied that the juror is impartial, the juror shall be discharged;

(11) That the juror cannot read or write.

No juror shall be impaneled when it appears that the juror is subject to the second, third or fourth grounds of challenge for cause set forth above, although both parties may consent. All other grounds for challenge may be waived by the party or parties in whose favor such grounds of challenge exist.

In this subsection, "legally blind" shall mean having not more than 20/200 of visual acuity in the better eye with correcting lenses, or visual acuity greater than 20/200 but with a limitation in the field of vision such that the widest diameter of the visual field subtends an angle no greater than 20 degrees.

(b) A challenge for cause may be made by the State for any of the following reasons:

(1) That the juror has conscientious scruples in regard to the infliction of the punishment of death for crime, in a capital case, where the State is seeking the death penalty;

(2) That he is related within the third degree of consanguinity or affinity, as determined under Chapter 573, Government Code, to the defendant; and

(3) That he has a bias or prejudice against any phase of the law upon which the State is entitled to rely for conviction or punishment.

(c) A challenge for cause may be made by the defense for any of the following reasons:

(1) That he is related within the third degree of consanguinity or affinity, as determined under Chapter 573, Government Code, to the person injured by the commission of the offense, or to any prosecutor in the case; and

(2) That he has a bias or prejudice against any of the law applicable to the case upon which the defense is entitled to rely, either as a defense to some phase of the offense for which the defendant is being prosecuted or as a mitigation thereof or of the punishment therefor.

CCP Art. 35.18. Other evidence on challenge

Upon a challenge for cause, the examination is not confined to the answers of the juror, but other evidence may be heard for or against the challenge.

CCP Art. 35.21. Judge to decide qualifications

The court is the judge, after proper examination, of the qualifications of a juror, and shall decide all challenges without delay and without argument thereupon.

§14:62 In General

A challenge for cause is an objection made to a juror for some legal reason that renders him unfit or incapable to serve on the jury. Castillo v. State, 913 S.W.2d 529 (Tex. Crim. App. 1995).

A party may properly challenge a veniremember for cause when he reveals that he will not be able to follow the applicable law in the case. The burden of demonstrating that a veniremember should be excused for cause rests with the party urging the excusal. Castillo. This must be done by a preponderance of the evidence. Fuller v. State, 829 S.W.2d 191 (Tex. Crim. App. 1992), *cert. denied,* 508 U.S. 941, 113 S.Ct. 2418, 124 L. Ed. 2d 640 (1993); Hernandez v. State, 757 S.W.2d 744 (Tex. Crim. App. 1988), *cert. denied,* 504 U.S. 974, 112 S.Ct. 2944 (1992), *overruled on other grounds*.

Before a veniremember can be challenged for cause, he must have the law explained to him and then state unequivocally that he cannot follow it. Chambers v. State, 903 S.W.2d 21 (Tex. Crim. App. 1995). A trial court will not be shown to have abused its discretion in failing to grant a challenge for cause where the law has not been fully explained to the veniremember. Chambers.

Similarly, a trial court does not abuse its discretion in overruling a challenge for cause where the defendant misinforms the veniremember of the applicable law. Garcia v. State, 887 S.W.2d 846 (Tex. Crim. App. 1994), *cert. denied*, 514 U.S. 1005, 115 S.Ct. 1317, 131 L. Ed. 2d 198 (1995).

PRACTICE TIP: Where a party has failed to inform the venire of the law before challenging a veniremember for cause for failure to follow the law, the opposing party should object that the question is not proper as to form. Howard v. State, 941 S.W.2d 102 (Tex. Crim. App. 1996).

Grounds for the exclusion of a veniremember may be shown by evidence other than the voir dire examination of the veniremember under Art. 35.18. Jernigan v. State, 661 S.W.2d 936 (Tex. Crim. App. 1983).

§14:63 Basis for Challenges for Cause

There are two opposing lines of cases pertaining to whether Art. 35.16 contains a comprehensive list of challenges for cause. Maldonado v. State, 998 S.W.2d 239 (Tex. Crim. App. 1999, fn.14).

One line of cases holds that Art. 35.16 which enumerates the reasons for challenges for cause is a complete list of challenges. Butler v. State, 830 S.W.2d 125 (Tex. Crim. App. 1992). The other line of cases holds that a challenge for cause may be predicated on facts that show that the prospective juror would be incapable or unfit to serve on the jury whether or not those facts fit within the enumerated factors of Art. 35.16. Mason v. State, 905 S.W.2d 570 (Tex. Crim. App. 1995), *cert.*

denied, 516 U.S. 1051, 116 S.Ct. 717, 133 L. Ed. 2d 670 (1996) (where the trial court excused a college freshman who stated he would be an unfit juror due to his preoccupation with school).

Regardless of which line of cases is now prevailing, and even under Mason, a trial court is not required to grant a challenge for cause not enumerated in CCP Art. 35.16. Rather, challenges not based upon a ground specifically enumerated in Art. 35.16 are addressed to the sound discretion of the trial judge. Mason; Maldonado. For example, where jury service could adversely affect the health of the veniremember the trial court has the discretion to excuse the veniremember. Goodwin v. State, 799 S.W.2d 719 (Tex. Crim. App. 1990), *cert. denied,* 501 U.S. 1259111 S.Ct. 2913, 115 L. Ed. 2d 1076 (1991).

A trial court will not abuse its discretion in failing to grant a challenge for cause based on a reason not expressly enumerated in CCP Art. 35.16. Maldonado.

There is also a doctrine of implied bias which states that since the Sixth Amendment promise of an impartial jury applies to the states, regardless of what Art. 35.16 provides, a state court would be bound to grant a challenge for cause if the failure to do so would result in a biased jury. Only extreme situations will justify a finding of implied bias, such as, perhaps, a situation where an assistant district attorney is on the venire of a case prosecuted by his office. State v. Morales, 253 S.W.3d 686 (Tex. Crim. App. 2008).

§14:64 Bias or Prejudice as Matter of Law

Where a party wishes to exclude a juror because of bias, it is the party seeking exclusion who must demonstrate, through questioning, that the potential juror lacks impartiality. Buntion, 482 S.W.3d 58, 84 (Tex. Crim. App. 2016).

If bias or prejudice is established as a matter of law, a challenge for cause must be granted by the trial court. Williams v. State, 773 S.W.2d 525 (Tex. Crim. App. 1988), *cert. denied,* 493 U.S. 900, 110 S.Ct. 257, 107 L. Ed. 2d 207 (1989).

Once a juror expressly admits his bias against a phase of law upon which both the State and defense are entitled to rely, a sufficient foundation has been laid to support a challenge for cause. Cardenas v. State, 325 S.W.3d 179 (Tex. Crim. App. 2010).

The opposing party or trial judge may then examine the juror further to ensure that he fully understands and appreciates the position that he is taking, but unless there is further clarification or vacillation by the juror, the trial judge must grant a challenge for cause if the juror persists in his position. Cardenas.

§14:64.1 Bias and Prejudice Defined

Bias is defined as an inclination toward one side of an issue rather than to the other, which leads to the natural inference that the veniremember will not act with impartiality. Anderson v. State, 633 S.W.2d 851 (Tex. Crim. App. 1982).

Bias against the law is the refusal to consider or apply the relevant law. It exists when a veniremember's beliefs or opinions would prevent or substantially impair the performance of his duties as a juror in accordance with his instructions and oath. Sadler v. State, 977 S.W.2d 140 (Tex. Crim. App. 1998).

Prejudice is defined as a pre-judgment. Anderson.

§14:64.2 Bias and Prejudice Established

The proper question to determine bias against the law is whether, in the proper case, where the facts justify it and the law allows it, the veniremember can fully and fairly apply the law as properly explained to him. Sadler v. State, 977 S.W.2d 140 (Tex. Crim. App. 1998).

Bias is established as a matter of law when a veniremember:

- Admits that he is biased for or against the defendant
- Admits or demonstrates prejudice toward a racial or ethnic class of which the defendant is a member
- Admits resentment towards the defendant because of some prior contact with the defendant
- Is related to the state's primary witness

Anderson v. State, 633 S.W.2d 851 (Tex. Crim. App. 1982).

A veniremember can also be found biased as a matter of law when he admits prejudice against persons who use intoxicating beverages in a case where the defendant is charged with an offense involving liquor. Morales v. State, 875 S.W.2d 724 (Tex.App.—Fort Worth 1994, *no pet.*).

A veniremember is biased as a matter of law when his answers conclusively establish bias. Banda v. State, 890 S.W.2d 42 (Tex. Crim. App. 1994), *cert. denied,* 515 U.S. 1105, 115 S.Ct. 2253, 132 L. Ed. 2d 260 (1995).

The standard for bias does not require that a juror's bias be proved with unmistakable clarity because many venire members simply cannot be asked enough questions to reach the point where their bias has been made unmistakably clear. Buntion v. State, 482 S.W.3d 58, 84 (Tex. Crim. App. 2016).

To establish that a challenge for cause is proper, the proponent of the challenge must show that the prospective juror understood the requirements of the law and could not overcome his prejudice well enough to follow the law. Buntion, 482 S.W.3d at 84.

Before a prospective juror may be excused for cause on this basis, the law must be explained to him, and he must be asked whether he can follow that law, regardless of his personal views. Buntion, 482 S.W.3d at 84.

When a veniremember is conclusively shown to be biased as a matter of law, he must be excused when challenged, even if he states that he can set aside his bias and provide a fair trial. Anderson.

§14:64.3 Bias and Prejudice Not Established

A veniremember is not biased as a matter of law when, despite an earlier *non-conclusive* adverse position, he states that he can follow the court's instructions and render a verdict according to the evidence. Adanandus v. State, 866 S.W.2d 210 (Tex. Crim. App. 1993), *cert. denied,* 510 U.S. 1215, 114 S.Ct. 1338, 127 L. Ed. 2d 686 (1994).

Under CCP Art. 35.16(a)(9) (challenge on the basis of bias or prejudice in favor of or against the defendant), it is not necessary to show a particular bias or prejudice in favor of or against the defendant. It is sufficient that the juror states that he cannot be a fair and impartial juror. Sosa v. State, 769 S.W.2d 909 (Tex. Crim. App.1989).

Bias is not conclusively established where the veniremember answers "I don't think so" when asked if he could follow the law. Moore v. State, 542 S.W.2d 664 (Tex. Crim. App. 1976), *cert. denied,* 431 U.S. 949, 97 S.Ct. 2666, 53 L. Ed. 2d 266 (1977).

Where the record contains conflicting statements by the veniremember, bias is not conclusively established. Banda v. State, 890 S.W.2d 42 (Tex. Crim. App. 1994), *cert. denied,* 515 U.S. 1105, 115 S.Ct. 2253, 132 L. Ed. 2d 260 (1995).

Showing that a potential juror is unable to articulate a set of facts upon which he could follow the law is not sufficient to establish bias as a matter of law. Hogue v. State, 711 S.W.2d 9 (Tex. Crim. App. 1986), *cert. denied,* 479 U.S. 922, 107 S.Ct. 329, 93 L. Ed. 2d 301 (1986).

A venire member's saying that he wants to hear evidence from the defense, and expects to hear such evidence, does not automatically disqualify him for having a bias or prejudice against the law placing the burden of proof on the State, or being unable to acquit the defendant unless the defense produced some evidence. Banda v. State, 890 S.W.2d 42, 57 (Tex. Crim. App. 1994).

§14:65 Substantial Impairment Test

When bias or prejudice is not established as a matter of law, the trial court has discretion to determine whether bias or prejudice actually exists to such a degree that the veniremember is disqualified. Little v. State, 758 S.W.2d 551 (Tex. Crim. App. 1988), *cert. denied,* 488 U.S. 934, 109 S.Ct. 328, 102 L. Ed. 2d 346 (1988).

The proper analysis to be used by the trial court to decide if a veniremember is challengeable for cause is whether his views would prevent or substantially impair his duty to act in accordance with the judge's instructions and the oath taken by the jury. Kemp v. State, 846 S.W.2d 289 (Tex. Crim. App. 1992), *cert. denied,* 508 U.S. 918, 113 S.Ct. 2361, 124 L. Ed. 2d 268 (1993).

The decision of a trial court regarding a challenge for cause will not be disturbed absent an abuse of discretion. Banda v. State, 890 S.W.2d 42 (Tex. Crim. App. 1994), *cert. denied,* 515 U.S. 1105,

115 S.Ct. 2253, 132 L. Ed. 2d 260 (1995). In other words, the judge's decision will be affirmed unless it is so clearly wrong as to lie outside the zone within which reasonable persons might disagree. Kemp.

In determining whether abuse of discretion exists in a situation where the trial court has denied a challenge for cause, the appellate court reviews all of the veniremember's answers to determine if they support the trial court's implied finding that the veniremember's views would not substantially impair the performance of his or her duties as a juror in accordance with the juror's oath. Post v. State, 936 S.W.2d 343 (Tex.App.—Fort Worth 1996, *pet. ref'd*). The trial court does not abuse its discretion in overruling a challenge for cause where the record shows that, although a potential juror initially expressed reservations about an area of the law, he ultimately testifies that he would follow the law. Cooks v. State, 844 S.W.2d 697 (Tex. Crim. App. 1992), *cert. denied,* 509 U.S. 927, 113 S.Ct. 3048, 125 L. Ed. 2d 732 (1993).

An isolated statement by a veniremember will not require that he be struck for cause when his testimony as a whole indicates that he was not biased. Cooks.

§14:66 Vacillating Veniremember

A vacillating veniremember is one who gives contradictory responses to those voir dire questions that test the veniremember's ability to follow the legal mandates set by the Legislature and by the holdings of the appellate courts. Howard v. State, 941 S.W.2d 102 (Tex. Crim. App. 1996).

Where the veniremember has vacillated between two positions or equivocated as to his views, appellate courts will give great deference to the decision of the trial court. This is because the trial court was in the best position to judge the veniremember's demeanor, tone and inflection of voice, hesitation or lack thereof, and body language. Banda v. State, 890 S.W.2d 42 (Tex. Crim. App. 1994), *cert. denied,* 515 U.S. 1105, 115 S.Ct. 2253, 132 L. Ed. 2d 260 (1995).

If a veniremember vacillates so that a trial court's ruling that the veniremember is subject to a challenge for cause can be supported by the record, then the trial court's ruling on the challenge will not be disturbed on appeal. Trevino v. State, 991 S.W.2d 849 (Tex. Crim. App. 1999); Green v. State, 840 S.W.2d 394 (Tex. Crim. App. 1992), *cert. denied,* 507 U.S. 1020, 113 S.Ct. 1819, 123 L. Ed. 2d 449 (1993), *disavowed on other grounds*.

Reviewing courts also give great deference to the trial court's ruling when the prospective juror's answers are unclear or contradictory. Maldonado v. State, 998 S.W.2d 239 (Tex. Crim. App. 1999); Colburn v. State, 966 S.W.2d 511 (Tex. Crim. App. 1998).

§14:67 Predicate for Challenge for Cause

Before a veniremember can be properly challenged for cause, the law must be fully explained to him. Jones v. State, 982 S.W.2d 386 (Tex. Crim. App. 1998), *cert. denied,* 120 S.Ct. 444, 145 L. Ed. 2d 362 (1999); Chambers v. State, 903 S.W.2d 21 (Tex. Crim. App. 1995). Once the law has been explained to the veniremember, he must be asked whether he can follow that law regardless of his personal views. Jones; Chambers.

If the veniremember states that he can follow the law regardless of his personal views, he is not challengeable for cause. Riley v. State, 889 S.W.2d 290 (Tex. Crim. App. 1993).

If the veniremember's views would substantially impair his ability to follow the law, then bias or prejudice exists to such a degree that the veniremember is disqualified. Little v. State, 758 S.W.2d 551 (Tex. Crim. App. 1988), *cert. denied,* 488 U.S. 934, 109 S.Ct. 328, 102 L. Ed. 2d 346 (1988).

§14:68 Areas of Proper Challenge for Cause

§14:68.1 Challenges for Cause by State or Defendant

The following are challenges for cause that can be made by either the state or the defendant. Unless otherwise noted, the defense would cite CCP Art. 35.16(c)(2) and the state would cite CCP Art. 35.16(b)(3) as statutory authority for their respective challenges for cause where veniremember:

- Unable to consider the minimum of the range of punishment—Nethery v.

State, 692 S.W.2d 686 (Tex. Crim. App. 1985); Cardenas v. State, 325 S.W.3d 179 (Tex. Crim. App. 2010).

- Unable to consider the full range of punishment—Banda v. State, 890 S.W.2d 42 (Tex. Crim. App. 1994), *cert. denied*, 515 U.S. 1105, 115 S.Ct. 2253, 132 L. Ed. 2d 260 (1995); Cardenas v. State, 325 S.W.3d 179 (Tex. Crim. App. 2010).
- Unable to consider the full range of punishment for a defendant who might be found guilty as a principle or as a party—Johnson v. State, 982 S.W.2d 403 (Tex. Crim. App. 1998); Cardenas v. State, 325 S.W.3d 179 (Tex. Crim. App. 2010).
- Unable to consider probation for a defendant who is eligible—Pierce v. State, 696 S.W.2d 899 (Tex. Crim. App. 1985), *cert. denied*, 496 U.S. 912, 110 S.Ct. 2603, 110 L. Ed. 2d 283 (1990); Cardenas v. State, 325 S.W.3d 179 (Tex. Crim. App. 2010).
- Unable to disregard an illegally obtained confession—Phillips v. State, 701 S.W.2d 875 (Tex. Crim. App. 1985)
- Holds the defendant's invocation of his Fifth Amendment rights against him—Guerra v. State, 771 S.W.2d 453 (Tex. Crim. App. 1988), *cert. denied*, 492 U.S. 925, 109 S.Ct. 3260, 106 L. Ed. 2d 606 (1989)
- Unable to hold the state to its burden of proof—Wheatfall v. State, 882 S.W.2d 829 (Tex. Crim. App. 1994)
- Served as a witness in the case at any phase of the trial—Wyle v. State, 777 S.W.2d 709 (Tex. Crim. App. 1989); CCP Art. 35.16(a)(6).
- Deafness would impair his service as a juror—Nobles v. State, 843 S.W.2d 503 (Tex. Crim. App. 1992); CCP Art. 35.16(a)(5)
- Low intelligence would affect his ability to serve as a juror—Burton v. State, 805 S.W.2d 564 (Tex.App.—Dallas 1991, *pet. ref'd*); CCP Art. 35.16(a)(5)
- Inability to read and write would affect his service as a juror—Allridge v. State, 850 S.W.2d 471 (Tex. Crim. App. 1991), *cert. denied*, 510 U.S. 831, 114 S.Ct. 101, 126 L. Ed. 2d 68 (1993); Flores v. State, 871 S.W.2d 714 (Tex. Crim. App. 1993); Stillwell v. State, 466 S.W.3d 908, 912 (Tex. App.—Fort Worth 2015, no pet.). CCP Art. 35.16(a)(11)
- Family situation would prevent her from making a decision in the case rendering her less than a fair and impartial juror—Sosa v. State, 769 S.W.2d 909 (Tex. Crim. App. 1989)
- Biased against a class of witnesses—Perry v. State, 864 S.W.2d 794 (Tex. App.—Fort Worth 1993, *no pet.*)
- Biased as a matter of law in favor of a class of witnesses, e.g., believes unequivocally that a police officer would never lie—Lane v. State, 822 S.W.2d 35 (Tex. Crim. App. 1991), *cert. denied*, 504 U.S. 920, 112 S.Ct. 1968, 118 L. Ed. 2d 568 (1992)
- Unable to consider circumstantial evidence—Narvaiz v. State, 840 S.W.2d 415 (Tex. Crim. App. 1992), *cert. denied*, 507 U.S. 975, 113 S.Ct. 1422, 122 L. Ed. 2d 791 (1993)
- Unable to presume the defendant innocent; challengeable for cause under Article 35.16(c)(2) for having a bias or prejudice against the law—Banda v. State, 890 S.W.2d 42 (Tex. Crim. App. 1994), *cert. denied*, 515 U.S. 1105, 115 S.Ct. 2253, 132 L. Ed. 2d 260 (1995)
- Under CCP Art. 35.16(a)(10), has established in mind a conclusion as to the guilt or innocence of the defendant as would influence him in his action in finding a verdict. However, a prospective juror is not challengeable for cause merely because he has heard news reports about the crime or the suspect. Heiselbetz v. State, 906 S.W.2d 500 (Tex. Crim. App. 1995); Macias v. State, 733 S.W.2d 192 (Tex. Crim. App. 1987), *cert. denied*, 484 U.S. 1079, 108 S.Ct. 1059, 98 L. Ed. 2d 1021 (1988)
- Unable to avoid consideration of a factor not properly before the jury (such as parole considerations in a death penalty case)—Felder v. State, 758 S.W.2d 760 (Tex. Crim. App. 1988), *cert. denied*, 440 U.S. 950, 99 S.Ct. 1433, 59 L. Ed. 2d 640 (1979).

- Under CCP Art. 35.16(a)(8), Cannot impartially judge the credibility of witnesses—Hernandez v. State, 563 S.W.2d 947 (Tex. Crim. App. 1978)
- Would consider the indictment as some evidence of guilt—Homan v. State, 662 S.W.2d 372 (Tex. Crim. App. 1984)
- Unable to return a not guilty verdict based upon a "technicality"—White v. State, 779 S.W.2d 809 (Tex. Crim. App. 1989) (where the veniremember stated that he would find the defendant guilty even if the state had not proven that the offense had occurred on or about the date alleged in indictment)
- Incapable of understanding the difference in the burdens of proof extant in the justice system—Staley v. State, 887 S.W.2d 885 (Tex. Crim. App. 1994), *cert. denied*, 514 U.S. 1020, 115 S.Ct. 1366, 131 L. Ed. 2d 222 (1995)
- Not willing or not able to state whether or not he could follow the law—Soria v. State, 933 S.W.2d 46 (Tex. Crim. App. 1996)
- Not a qualified voter in the county of the trial—Mayo v. State, 4 S.W.3d 9 (Tex. Crim. App. 1999); Gaona v. State, 733 S.W.2d 611 (Tex.App.—Corpus Christi 1987, *pet. ref'd*); CCP Art. 35.16(a)(1)
- Has been convicted of theft—Holland v. State, 761 S.W.2d 307 (Tex. Crim. App. 1988), *cert. denied,* 489 U.S. 1091, 109 S.Ct. 1560, 103 L. Ed. 2d 863 (1989); CCP Art. 35.16(a)(2)
- Has been convicted of a felony—Chambers v. State, 903 S.W.2d 21 (Tex. Crim. App. 1995); CCP Art. 35.16(a)(2)
- Under indictment or other legal accusation for theft—Brown v. State, 716 S.W.2d 939 (Tex. Crim. App. 1986); CCP Art. 35.16(a)(3).
- Under indictment or other legal accusation for a felony—State v. Holloway, 886 S.W.2d 482 (Tex. App.—Houston [1st Dist.] 1984, *pet. ref'd*); CCP Art.35.16(a)(3)
- Is insane—Von Byrd v. State, 569 S.W.2d 883 (Tex. Crim. App. 1978); CCP Art. 35.16(a)(4)• Served on the grand jury that found the indictment—CCP Art. 35.16(a)(7)
- Served on the petit jury in a former trial of the same case—CCP Art. 35.16(A)(8)

The following are based on grounds not specifically enumerated in CCP Art. 35.16, where veniremember:

- Would suffer adverse health affect—Goodwin v. State, 799 S.W.2d 719 (Tex. Crim. App. 1990), *cert. denied*, 501 U.S. 1259111 S.Ct. 2913, 115 L. Ed. 2d 1076 (1991)
- Not able to keep his mind on the trial such that his ability to serve effectively is impaired—Johnson v. State, 773 S.W.2d 322 (Tex. Crim. App. 1989), affirmed at 509 U.S. 350, 113 S.Ct. 2658, 125 L. Ed. 2d 290 (1993)
- Distracted by business or economic reasons to the extent that ability to serve would be impaired—Allridge v. State, 850 S.W.2d 471 (Tex. Crim. App. 1991), *cert. denied*, 510 U.S. 831, 114 S.Ct. 101, 126 L. Ed. 2d 68 (1993)
- Unfit for jury service because such service would have conflicted with plans to get married rendering veniremember preoccupied with personal problems—Nichols v. State, 754 S.W.2d 185 (Tex. Crim. App. 1988)
- Commitments to children represented an insurmountable burden to serving on the jury. Rogers v. State, 774 S.W.2d 247 (Tex. Crim. App. 1989), *cert. denied*, 493 U.S. 984, 110 S.Ct. 519, 107 L. Ed. 2d 520 (1989)
- So traumatized by the experience of being called to jury duty that physically shakes, may be properly struck for cause as unfit despite her assurances that she will survive the "crisis." Powell v. State, 897 S.W.2d 307 (Tex. Crim. App. 1994)

The state is allowed to avail itself of each of the challenges available to the defendant because the courts recognize that the state has a duty to see that justice is done in individual cases. Morrow v. State, 910 S.W.2d 471 (Tex. Crim. App. 1995), *cert. denied,* 517 U.S. 1192, 116 S.Ct. 1683, 134 L. Ed. 2d 784 (1996). However, a defendant is not entitled to excuse for cause a veniremember who has a bias against some phase of the law that the state is entitled to rely on because defense counsel has no corresponding duty to see that justice is done. Morrow, (where the defendant challenged a veniremember who wanted to hold the state to a higher burden than beyond a reasonable doubt).

§14:68.1.1 Bias Against Class of Witnesses

Although a veniremember is challengeable for cause if he cannot impartially judge the credibility of witnesses (*see* Hernandez, §14:68.1), he is not challengeable for cause where he would merely be skeptical of the testimony of a certain class of witnesses. The veniremember's testimony overall must show that he has a bias toward that class of witnesses. Jones v. State, 982 S.W.2d 386 (Tex. Crim. App. 1998), *cert. denied,* 120 S.Ct. 444, 145 L. Ed. 2d 362 (1999).

Furthermore, a veniremember is not challengeable for cause simply because he would give certain classes of witnesses a slight edge in terms of credibility; again, the edge in credibility must amount to an extreme or absolute position before the veniremember is challengeable. Ladd v. State, 3 S.W.3d 547 (Tex. Crim. App. 1999).

Where a veniremember's deference to the testimony of a law enforcement officer was not so much to any unfailing honesty he perceived on the part of all policemen so much as his own personal knowledge of their investigatory training and experience, he is not challengeable for cause for failure to fairly evaluate the testimony of a police officer. Gardner v. State, 730 S.W.2d 675 (Tex. Crim. App. 1987), *cert. denied,* 484 U.S. 905, 108 S.Ct. 248, 98 L. Ed. 2d 206 (1987).

§14:68.1.2 Failure to Consider Punishment Range

Both the State and the defense are entitled to jurors who can consider the entire range of punishment for the particular statutory offense—*i.e.,* from the maximum to the minimum and all points in between. Jurors must be able to consider both a situation in which the minimum penalty would be appropriate and a situation in which the maximum penalty would be appropriate. Therefore, both sides may question the panel on the range of punishment and may commit jurors to consider the entire range of punishment for the statutory offense. Cardenas v. State, 325 S.W.3d 179 (Tex. Crim. App. 2010).

A juror who states that he cannot consider the minimum or maximum punishment for a particular statutory offense is subject to a challenge for cause. Cardenas.

The requirement that the juror be able to consider the full punishment range for the offense includes consideration of each statutory variation of the offense, such as the age element in an aggravated sexual assault of a child case. Cardenas (where the offense was aggravated sexual assault of a child under 14).

Where a veniremember would only consider the minimum of the punishment range in a certain narrow circumstance, he is challengeable for cause. This is because the veniremember, in effect, would be creating his own statute concerning the punishment range. Sunday v. State, 745 S.W.2d 436 (Tex.App.—Beaumont 1988, *pet. ref'd*).

A trial court does not commit error in overruling a challenge for cause against a veniremember who is unable to articulate a set of facts meriting a minimum punishment because the inability to articulate such a set of facts does not equate to an inability to consider the full range of punishment. Penry v. State, 903 S.W.2d 715 (Tex. Crim. App. 1995), *cert. denied,* 516 U.S. 977, 116 S.Ct. 480, 133 L. Ed. 2d 408 (1995).

A veniremember is not challengeable as a matter of law if she states that she could consider probation in a proper case. Faulder v. State, 745 S.W.2d 327 (Tex. Crim. App. 1987). A veniremember is not required to state that he could consider probation in a given fact situation. Faulder.

A veniremember is not challengeable as a matter of law if he states that he could consider probation after he had heard all of the evidence. Rische v. State, 834 S.W.2d 942 (Tex.App.—Houston [14th Dist.] 1992, *pet. ref'd*).

A veniremember is not challengeable for cause merely because she will use the facts of the case to determine punishment. Sadler v. State, 977 S.W.2d 140 (Tex. Crim. App. 1998). This is even though a party is allowed to make inquiry of the venire as to whether they would decide the case (especially the punishment issues) any differently based on the status of the victim (where the victim was a nun);

and Maddux v. State, 862 S.W.2d 590 (Tex. Crim. App. 1993)(where the victim was a child).

A veniremember is not challengeable for cause where he is unable to consider the full range of punishment for a particular fact situation where he states that he can consider the full range for the offense as defined by law. Sadler.

A trial court does not err in refusing a challenge for cause for grounds that do not become relevant at trial. Soria v. State, 933 S.W.2d 46 (Tex. Crim. App. 1996) (where the veniremember could not consider the punishment range for the offense of murder but where murder was not raised as a lesser included offense).

§14:68.1.3 Relationship With Party or Witness

A casual acquaintance with a crime victim or with the facts of the case will not disqualify a juror who answers on voir dire that those circumstances will not affect his ability to render a verdict according to the evidence. Little v. State, 758 S.W.2d 551 (Tex. Crim. App. 1988), *cert. denied,* 488 U.S. 934, 109 S.Ct. 328, 102 L. Ed. 2d 346 (1988).

Similarly, a mere acquaintance with the defendant or a state's witness is not a sufficient basis for disqualification. Vaughn v. State, 833 S.W.2d 180 (Tex.App.—Dallas 1992, *pet. ref'd*).

The mere fact that a veniremember had been employed by the District Attorney's office that was prosecuting the case, without more, was not sufficient to disqualify the veniremember. Eubanks v. State, 635 S.W.2d 568 (Tex.App.—Houston [1st Dist.] 1982, *no pet.*).

§14:68.2 Challenges for Cause by Defendant

CCP Art. 35.16(c)(2) permits the defendant to challenge for cause a veniremember on the ground "[t]hat he has a bias or prejudice against any of the law applicable to the case upon which the defendant is entitled to rely, either as a defense to some phase of the offense for which the defendant is being prosecuted or as a mitigation thereof or of the punishment therefor." Cordova v. State, 733 S.W.2d 175 (Tex. Crim. App. 1987), *cert. denied,* 487 U.S. 1240, 108 S.Ct. 2915, 101 L. Ed. 2d 946 (1988).

In addition to the grounds listed in section 14:68.1 above, the following have been recognized as proper areas for defense challenges for cause:

- Inability to afford the defendant his right against self-incrimination—Montoya v. State, 810 S.W.2d 160 (Tex. Crim. App. 1989)
- Inability to consider the law of self-defense—Harris v. State, 784 S.W.2d 5 (Tex. Crim. App. 1989), *cert. denied,* 494 U.S. 1090, 110 S.Ct. 1837, 108 L. Ed. 2d 966 (1990)
- Biased against the defendant—Garcia v. State, 919 S.W.2d 370 (Tex. Crim. App. 1996); Curry v. State, 910 S.W.2d 490 (Tex. Crim. App. 1995)
- Inability to be objective in the case because of knowledge and biases gained from her employment—Sykora v. State, 872 S.W.2d 323 (Tex.App.—Beaumont 1994, *no pet.*)
- Would automatically believe a police officer—Hernandez v. State, 563 S.W.2d 947 (Tex. Crim. App. 1978)
- Related within the third degree of consanguinity or affinity to the injured party or prosecutor—CCP Art. 35.16(c)(1)

The state is allowed to avail itself of each of the challenges available to the defendant because the courts recognize that the state has a duty to see that justice is done in individual cases. Morrow v. State, 910 S.W.2d 471 (Tex. Crim. App. 1995), *cert. denied,* 517 U.S. 1192, 116 S.Ct. 1683, 134 L. Ed. 2d 784 (1996). However, a defendant is not entitled to excuse for cause a veniremember who has a bias against some phase of the law that the state is entitled to rely on because defense counsel has no corresponding duty to see that justice is done. Morrow, (where the defendant challenged a veniremember who wanted to hold the state to a higher burden than beyond a reasonable doubt).

Under Art. 35.16(a)(9) (challenge on the basis of bias or prejudice in favor of or against the defendant), it is not necessary to show a particular bias or prejudice in favor of or against the defendant. It is sufficient that the juror states that he cannot be a fair and impartial juror. Sosa v. State, 769 S.W.2d 909 (Tex. Crim. App.1989).

JURY SELECTION AND VOIR DIRE

§14:68.2.1 Preservation of Error for Denial of Defense Challenges for Cause

In order to preserve error in a trial court's erroneous denial of a defense challenge for cause, the defendant must follow a rigorous predicate including:

- Voir dire of the individual veniremember was recorded and transcribed—Long v. State, 823 S.W.2d 259 (Tex. Crim. App. 1991), *cert. denied*, 505 U.S. 1224, 112 S.Ct. 3042, 120 L. Ed. 2d 910 (1992)
- Counsel asserted a clear and specific challenge for cause clearly articulating the grounds therefore—Miller v. State, 741 S.W.2d 382 (Tex. Crim. App. 1987), *cert. denied,* 486 U.S. 1061, 108 S.Ct. 2835, 100 L. Ed. 2d 935 (1988)
- Counsel used a peremptory challenge on that particular veniremember—Jones v. State, 833 S.W.2d 118 (Tex. Crim. App. 1992), *cert. denied,* 507 U.S. 921, 113 S.Ct. 1285, 122 L. Ed. 2d 678 (1993)
- Defense exhausted all peremptory challenges—Adanandus v. State, 866 S.W.2d 210 (Tex. Crim. App. 1993), *cert. denied,* 510 U.S. 1215, 114 S.Ct. 1338, 127 L. Ed. 2d 686 (1994)
- Trial judge denied request for additional peremptory challenges—Jacobs v. State, 787 S.W.2d 397 (Tex. Crim. App. 1990), *cert. denied,* 496 U.S. 882, 111 S.Ct. 231, 112 L. Ed. 2d 185 (1990)
- Defense was forced to accept an objectionable veniremember on the jury because of the trial court's erroneous actions, *i.e.*, that she would have exercised a peremptory challenge against that veniremember if she had one remaining—Trevino v. State, 991 S.W.2d 849 (Tex. Crim. App. 1999); Green v. State, 840 S.W.2d 394 (Tex. Crim. App. 1992), *cert. denied,* 507 U.S. 1020, 113 S.Ct. 1819, 123 L. Ed. 2d 449 (1993), *disavowed on other grounds.*

PRACTICE TIP: In order to preserve error, recite into the record prior to the jury being seated and sworn, that:

- Defense was forced to use a peremptory challenge on a juror against whom a challenge for cause had been made
- Defense exhausted all allotted peremptory challenges
- Defense requested additional peremptory challenges and that request has been denied (or if additional peremptory challenges were granted, that those also have been exhausted and an additional request has been made and denied); and
- An objectionable juror has been seated and that defense would exercise a peremptory challenge on that juror if afforded an additional peremptory.

Then request an additional peremptory challenge and (presumably) have the request denied.

This harm analysis is the same under Rule 44.2(b) of the Texas Rules of Appellate Procedure. Johnson v. State, 43 S.W.3d 1 (Tex. Crim. App. 2001).

The defendant must demonstrate that he exercised a peremptory challenge on the veniremember upon which he bases his claim. Brosky v. State, 915 S.W.2d 120 (Tex.App.—Fort Worth, *pet. ref'd*), *cert. denied*, 519 U.S. 1020, 117 S.Ct. 537, 136 L. Ed. 2d 422 (1996).

In order to do this, the defendant must generally make the jury strike lists part of the record on appeal. Hernandez v. State, 938 S.W.2d 503 (Tex. App.—Waco 1997, *pet. ref'd*).

The defendant cannot show that he was harmed by the trial court's erroneous denial of his challenge for cause where he uses one of his peremptory challenges on a veniremember out of the "strike zone" and leaves the objectionable juror unchallenged. Comeaux v. State, 445 S.W.3d 745, 751-2 (Tex. Crim. App. 2014).

In order to make a certain claim on appeal, the defendant must have objected on the same ground in the trial court. Trevino v. State, 991 S.W.2d 849 (Tex. Crim. App. 1999); Green v. State, 840 S.W.2d 394 (Tex. Crim. App. 1992), *cert. denied,* 507 U.S.

1020, 113 S.Ct. 1819, 123 L. Ed. 2d 449 (1993), *disavowed on other grounds.*

It is not necessary that the defendant go so far as to explain why the objectionable juror that he has named is, in fact, objectionable. Garcia v. State, 887 S.W.2d 846 (Tex. Crim. App. 1994), *cert. denied,* 514 U.S. 1005, 115 S.Ct. 1317, 131 L. Ed. 2d 198 (1995).

Where the trial court grants two additional peremptory challenges, the defendant must show that the trial court erred in denying his challenge for cause to three prospective jurors. Penry v. State, 903 S.W.2d 715 (Tex. Crim. App. 1995), *cert. denied,* 516 U.S. 977, 116 S.Ct. 480, 133 L. Ed. 2d 408 (1995). The defendant also must have exhausted any additional peremptory challenges granted in order to preserve error for appeal. Penry.

Voir dire error in a non-capital case cannot be error affecting the punishment phase only under CCP Art. 44.29(b); therefore, the defendant has the right to begin a retrial in the guilt-innocence phase. Carson v. State, 6 S.W.3d 536 (Tex. Crim. App. 1999).

§14:68.3 Challenges for Cause by State

CCP Art. 35.16(b)(3) allows the state to challenge for cause veniremembers who have a "bias or prejudice against any phase of the law upon which the state is entitled to rely for conviction or punishment." Unless otherwise noted, the grounds listed below are based on Art. 35.16(b)(3).

In addition to the grounds listed in section §14:68.1, the following have been recognized as valid reasons for a state to challenge a veniremember for cause:

- Holding the state to a higher burden than proof beyond a reasonable doubt—Crane v. State, 786 S.W.2d 338 (Tex. Crim. App. 1990)
- Requiring the state to prove premeditation—Crane.
- Requiring the state to prove motive—Esquivel v. State, 595 S.W.2d 516 (Tex. Crim. App. 1980), *cert. denied,* 449 U.S. 986, 101 S.Ct. 408, 66 L. Ed. 2d 251 (1980)
- Being related to the defendant within the third degree of consanguinity or affinity—Moss v. State, 850 S.W.2d 788 (Tex.App.—Houston [14th Dist.] 1993, *pet. ref'd*). CCP Art. 35.16(b)(2)
- Being unable to consider accomplice testimony. May v. State, 738 S.W.2d 261 (Tex. Crim. App. 1987), *cert. denied,* 484 U.S. 872, 108 S.Ct. 206, 98 L. Ed. 2d 158 (1987)
- Being incapable of convicting in a case without eyewitness testimony—White v. State, 779 S.W.2d 809 (Tex. Crim. App. 1989), *cert. denied,* 495 U.S. 962, 110 S.Ct. 2575, 109 L. Ed. 2d 757 (1990); Marquez v. State, 725 S.W.2d 217 (Tex. Crim. App.1987), *cert. denied*, 484 U.S. 872, 108 S.Ct. 201, 98 L. Ed. 2d 152 (1987)
- Being incapable of convicting in a case on the basis of a confession only. Butler v. State, 872 S.W.2d 227 (Tex. Crim. App. 1994), *cert. denied,* 513 U.S. 1157, 115 S.Ct. 1157, 130 L. Ed. 2d 1079 (1995)
- Requiring the state to prove a specific fact in addition to the elements of the crime before considering the maximum punishment is challengeable for cause—Fuller v. State, 829 S.W.2d 191 (Tex. Crim. App. 1992), *cert. denied,* 508 U.S. 941, 113 S.Ct. 2418, 124 L. Ed. 2d 640 (1993) (where the veniremember stated he would require the state to prove another murder before he could answer the future dangerousness special issue in the affirmative)
- Being unable to consider a defendant's guilt under the law of parties—Nichols v. State, 754 S.W.2d 185 (Tex. Crim. App. 1988), *cert. denied,* 488 U.S. 1019, 109 S.Ct. 819, 102 L. Ed. 2d 808 (1989)
- Being incapable of convicting even if believes one eyewitness beyond a reasonable doubt—Caldwell v. State, 818 S.W.2d 790 (Tex. Crim. App. 1991), *cert. denied,* 503 U.S. 990, 112 S.Ct. 1684, 118 L. Ed. 2d 399 (1992)
- States that without medical testimony to corroborate the complainant, he would not vote to convict even if the complainant's testimony established guilt beyond a reasonable doubt—

Decker v. State, 894 S.W.2d 475 (Tex. App.—Austin 1995, *pet. ref'd*)

- Clearly and unequivocally affirms that she could not clearly and fairly evaluate the testimony of a police officer— Sawyers v. State, 724 S.W.2d 24 (Tex. Crim. App. 1986)
- Being unable to give fair consideration to the maximum of the range of punishment. Cardenas v. State, 325 S.W.3d 179 (Tex. Crim. App. 2010).

TIP TO THE PROSECUTION: A challenge for cause has a greater likelihood of being granted by the trial court and upheld by an appellate court if it is premised upon a veniremember's inability to convict even where he believes the witness, evidence or other scenario beyond a reasonable doubt. Caldwell, supra.

The state is allowed to avail itself of each of the challenges available to the defendant because the courts recognize that the state has a duty to see that justice is done in individual cases. Morrow v. State, 910 S.W.2d 471 (Tex. Crim. App. 1995), *cert. denied,* 517 U.S. 1192, 116 S.Ct. 1683, 134 L. Ed. 2d 784 (1996). However, a defendant is not entitled to excuse for cause a veniremember who has a bias against some phase of the law that the state is entitled to rely on because defense counsel has no corresponding duty to see that justice is done. Morrow (where the defendant challenged a veniremember who wanted to hold the state to a higher burden than beyond a reasonable doubt).

§14:68.3.1 Challenges Where Beyond Reasonable Doubt Not Enough

Where the courts allow exclusion of veniremembers because they would require eyewitness testimony, medical testimony, etc., it is because the veniremember would be, in effect, requiring additional elements in the state's burden of proof. Howard v. State, 941 S.W.2d 102 (Tex. Crim. App. 1996).

However, a venireman who requires a particular type of evidence has not demonstrated an inability to abide by the law if his requirement is predicated upon his personal threshold of reasonable doubt. The state has the burden to show that the venireman's insistence on evidence of a particular type will prevent him from following the law regardless of whether he was otherwise convinced beyond a reasonable doubt, before it can be said it has met its burden to demonstrate the venireman cannot follow the law. Howard; Murphy v. State, 112 S.W.3d 192 (Tex. Crim. App. 2003).

The rationale behind allowing challenges for cause against veniremembers who would require a specific type of evidence before they could convict is that they are raising the state's burden of proof beyond that required by law. As such, they demonstrate a bias against some phase of the law on which the state is entitled to rely (that being the juror's obligation to return a verdict of guilty where the state proves its case beyond a reasonable doubt). Caldwell v. State, 818 S.W.2d 790 (Tex. Crim. App. 1991), *cert. denied,* 503 U.S. 990, 112 S.Ct. 1684, 118 L. Ed. 2d 399 (1992). In other words, factors other than those prescribed by law must not be made absolute prerequisites for imposition of any punishment, including the death penalty. Drew v. State, 743 S.W.2d 207 (Tex. Crim. App. 1987).

Contrast this situation with the classic Garrett situation where a veniremember who needs more than the minimum quantum of evidence (such as more than one witness) before he can find guilt beyond a reasonable doubt is not challengeable for cause. *See,* Garrett v. State, 851 S.W.2d 853 (Tex. Crim. App. 1993).

The difference in the above two situations is that in one situation (Caldwell) the veniremember would not convict even where the case were proven beyond a reasonable doubt, whereas in the second (Garrett) situation the veniremember would not find proof beyond a reasonable doubt.

A juror who says that he will always have a reasonable doubt in a one-witness case is not challengeable for cause on that ground. Zinger v. State, 932 S.W.2d 511 (Tex. Crim. App. 1996). This is because he needs more than the minimum quantum of evidence. *See,* Garrett.

A trial court commits no error in overruling a challenge for cause lodged against a potential juror who believes that a minimum or lesser punishment should be assessed only in a proper case. Fuller v. State, 829 S.W.2d 191 (Tex. Crim. App. 1992), *cert. denied,* 508 U.S. 941, 113 S.Ct. 2418, 124 L. Ed. 2d 640 (1993).

Conversely, a juror who says that even if he believes the one witness beyond a reasonable doubt he cannot convict can be successfully challenged for cause. Coleman v. State, 881 S.W.2d 344 (Tex. Crim. App. 1994), *cert. denied,* 513 U.S. 1096, 115 S.Ct. 763, 130 L. Ed. 2d 660 (1995). This is because the veniremember would be holding the state to a higher burden than proof beyond a reasonable doubt.

A venireman whose definition of a particular term requires a certain type of evidence is not subject to a challenge for cause. Murphy (the venireman's definition of the phrase "criminal acts of violence" required evidence that the defendant committed or attempted to commit other murders before the venireman could answer the future dangerousness special issue in the affirmative in a death penalty case).

The rule that a venire man who cannot convict upon the testimony of a single witness even where he believes that witness beyond a reasonable doubt is challengeable for cause remains in effect after the decision in the Standefer case. Lee v. State, 206 S.W.3d 620 (Tex. Crim. App. 2006).

§14:68.3.2 Preserving Error for Erroneous Granting of State's Challenge for Cause

To show error in the trial court's grant of a State's challenge for cause, a defendant must lodge a timely objection in the trial court. Kemp v. State, 846 S.W.2d 289 (Tex. Crim. App. 1992), *cert. denied,* 508 U.S. 918, 113 S.Ct. 2361, 124 L. Ed. 2d 268 (1993).

The objection is timely where it is lodged at the time of the trial court's ruling and is not abandoned. Zimmerman v. State, 860 S.W.2d 89 (Tex. Crim. App. 1993).

The defendant must next show either that the trial court applied the wrong legal standard in sustaining the challenge or that the trial court abused its discretion in applying the correct legal standard. Vuong v. State, 830 S.W.2d 929, 943 (Tex. Crim. App. 1992), *cert. denied,* 506 U.S. 997, 113 S.Ct. 595, 121 L. Ed. 2d 533 (1992).

Moreover, to obtain a reversal because of the error, a defendant must show that the error actually deprived him of a fair and impartial jury. Jones v. State, 982 S.W.2d 386 (Tex. Crim. App. 1998), *cert. denied,* 120 S.Ct. 444, 145 L. Ed. 2d 362 (1999).

Voir dire error in a non-capital case cannot be error affecting the punishment phase only under CCP Art. 44.29(b); therefore, the defendant has the right to begin a retrial in the guilt-innocence phase. Carson v. State, 6 S.W.3d 536 (Tex. Crim. App. 1999).

§14:70 *Sua Sponte* Excusals

§14:71 Applicable Statute

CCP Art. 35.03. Excuses

Sec. 1. Except as provided by Sections 2 and 3 of this article, the court shall then hear and determine excuses offered for not serving as a juror, including any claim of an exemption or a lack of qualification, and if the court considers the excuse sufficient, the court shall discharge the prospective juror or postpone the prospective juror's service to a date specified by the court, as appropriate.

Sec. 2. Under a plan approved by the commissioners court of the county in the same manner as a plan is approved for jury selection under Section 62.011, Government Code, in a case other than a capital felony case, the court's designee may hear and determine an excuse offered for not serving as a juror, including any claim of an exemption or a lack of qualification. The court's designee may discharge the prospective juror or postpone the prospective juror's service to a date specified by the court's designee, as appropriate, if:

(1) the court's designee considers the excuse sufficient; and

(2) the juror submits to the court's designee a statement of the ground of the exemption or lack of qualification or other excuse.

§14:72 In General

Art. 35.03 affords the trial court wide latitude in determining sufficiency of excuses and discharging veniremembers. Ellason v. State, 815 S.W.2d 656 (Tex. Crim. App. 1991). Pursuant to Art. 35.03, a trial judge has broad discretion in excusing prospective jurors on any proper basis, either with or without the prompting of counsel. Kemp v. State, 846 S.W.2d 289 (Tex. Crim. App. 1992), *cert. denied*, 508 U.S. 918, 113 S.Ct. 2361, 124 L. Ed. 2d 268 (1993).

Article 35.03 provides no enumerated bases for excusing a potential juror; but rather recognizes that there are varying circumstances attendant in each new venire. Butler v. State, 830 S.W.2d 125 (Tex. Crim. App. 1992).

PRACTICE TIP: Where defense counsel opposes the trial court granting an excuse under Art. 35.03, it should be requested that the trial court make findings of fact and conclusions of law on the excuse to preserve the issue for appeal. This also will help prevent the trial court from having unfettered discretion in these matters.

The trial judge is not permitted to excuse and replace a juror after the jury has been sworn (except where there is a qualified alternate available). Gentry v. State, 881 S.W.2d 35 (Tex.App.—Dallas 1994, *pet. ref'd*).

A trial judge has no authority to use Art. 35.03 to excuse a prospective juror who is only subject to a challenge for cause under Art. 35.16. Warren v. State, 768 S.W.2d 300 (Tex. Crim. App.1989); Green v. State, 764 S.W.2d 242 (Tex. Crim. App. 1989).

However, the trial court may on its own motion excuse a prospective juror who is absolutely disqualified pursuant to CCP Art. 35.19. Warren.

Thus, if a prospective juror has been convicted or indicted for theft or any felony or is insane, the trial court has the authority to excuse the juror *sua sponte*. Green.

Also, if the trial court had a proper basis to excuse a veniremember under Art. 35.03, it is immaterial that the court cited Art. 35.16 for its actions. Coleman v. State, 881 S.W.2d 344 (Tex. Crim. App. 1994), *cert. denied,* 513 U.S. 1096, 115 S.Ct. 763, 130 L. Ed. 2d 660 (1995).

The erroneous excusal of a veniremember will call for reversal only if the record shows that the error deprived the defendant of a lawfully constituted jury. The question is whether or not the jurors who actually sat were impartial. Gamboa v. State, 296 S.W.3d 574 (Tex. Crim. App. 2009).

§14:73 Permissible Reasons for Sua Sponte Excusal

The following veniremember excuses have been recognized as valid under Art. 35.03:

- Concern over missing work—Butler v. State, 830 S.W.2d 125 (Tex. Crim. App. 1992)
- Upcoming wedding of the daughter—McFarland v. State, 845 S.W.2d 824 (Tex. Crim. App. 1992), *cert. denied,* 508 U.S. 963, 113 S.Ct. 2937, 124 L. Ed. 2d 686 (1992)
- Starting new job in a different county—Harris v. State, 784 S.W.2d 5 (Tex. Crim. App. 1989), *cert. denied,* 494 U.S. 1090, 110 S.Ct. 1837, 108 L. Ed. 2d 966 (1990)
- Health problems—Ellason v. State, 815 S.W.2d 656 (Tex. Crim. App. 1991)
- Mother's health problems—Leberta v. State, 770 S.W.2d 828 (Tex.App.—Fort Worth 1988, *pet. ref'd*)
- Wife's upcoming surgery—Kemp v. State, 846 S.W.2d 289 (Tex. Crim. App. 1992), *cert. denied*, 508 U.S. 918, 113 S.Ct. 2361, 124 L. Ed. 2d 268 (1993)
- Child care problems—Rousseau v. State, 855 S.W.2d 666 (Tex. Crim. App. 1993), *cert. denied,* 510 U.S. 919, 114 S.Ct. 313, 126 L. Ed. 2d 260 (1993)
- Responsibility to care for grandchildren—Johnson v. State, 773 S.W.2d 322 (Tex. Crim. App. 1989)
- Failure to return timely from a break—Brossette v. State, 885 S.W.2d 841 (Tex.App.—Dallas 1994, *pet. ref'd*)
- Upcoming job performance review. Brossette.
- Discomfort in hearing a murder case coupled with expectation of pressure from neighbors and residents. Murray

v. State, 861 S.W.2d 47 (Tex.App.—Texarkana 1993, *pet. ref'd*)

- Scheduled out of town vacation—Moody v. State, 827 S.W.2d 875 (Tex. Crim. App. 1992), *cert. denied,* 506 U.S. 839, 113 S.Ct. 119, 121 L. Ed. 2d 75 (1992); Crutsinger v. State, 206 S.W.3d 607 (Tex. Crim. App.)
- Where absolutely disqualified pursuant to CCP Art. 35.19. Warren v. State, 768 S.W.2d 300 (Tex. Crim. App. 1989)
- Where veniremember was the only doctor available to treat children at a clinic—Clark v. State, 881 S.W.2d 682 (Tex. Crim. App. 1994)
- Concerned about finances to the point that service would be impaired—Teague v. State, 864 S.W.2d 505 (Tex. Crim. App. 1993), *overruled on other grounds*, Robertson v. State, 871 S.W.2d 701 (Tex. Crim. App. 1993)
- Distracted because of family responsibilities—Saldivar v. State, 980 S.W.2d 475 (Tex.App.—Houston [14th Dist.] 1998, *pet. ref'd*)
- Cannot read and write—Liveoak v. State, 717 S.W.2d 691 (Tex.App.—San Antonio 1986, *pet. ref'd*)
- (Under Art. 35.03) because of ongoing campaign for public office—Narvaiz v. State, 840 S.W.2d 415 (Tex. Crim. App. 1992), *cert. denied,* 507 U.S. 975, 113 S.Ct. 1422, 122 L. Ed. 2d 791 (1993)
- That the juror is hearing impaired—Black v. State, 26 S.W.3d 895 (Tex. Crim. App. 2000)

§14:74 Timing of Sua Sponte Excusal

The power to grant an excusal from jury service pursuant to Art. 35.03 inheres to the trial judge from the first assemblage of the array until the juror is seated and sworn. Butler v. State, 830 S.W.2d 125 (Tex. Crim. App. 1992).

A trial judge may *sua sponte* excuse a veniremember who is absolutely disqualified. Martinez v. State, 621 S.W.2d 797 (Tex. Crim. App. 1981).

The trial judge has the authority to use Art. 35.03 to allow a veniremember to claim an exemption from jury service even after the veniremember has been questioned on voir dire. Rousseau v. State, 855 S.W.2d 666 (Tex. Crim. App. 1993), *cert. denied,* 510 U.S. 919, 114 S.Ct. 313, 126 L. Ed. 2d 260 (1993).

Since the trial court does not need consent of the parties to *sua sponte* excuse a venireman, before the panel is sworn the judge may *sua sponte* excuse a venireman out of the presence of the state and defendant. Wright v. State, 28 S.W.3d 526 (Tex. Crim. App. 2000).

§14:75 Preserving Error for *Sua Sponte* Excusal

Where the trial court erroneously excuses an otherwise qualified veniremember under Art. 35.03, the defendant must make a specific and proper objection and then call the attention of the trial court to the specific complaint to be raised on appeal. Little v. State, 758 S.W.2d 551 (Tex. Crim. App. 1988), *cert. denied*, 488 U.S. 934, 109 S.Ct. 328, 102 L. Ed. 2d 346 (1988); Alvarado v. State, 822 S.W.2d 236 (Tex.App.—Houston [14th Dist.], 1991, *pet. ref'd*).

The defendant also must assert that he has a legitimate objection to the jury chosen. Murray v. State, 861 S.W.2d 47 (Tex.App.—Texarkana 1993, *pet. ref'd*).

Any error in the excusal of a qualified veniremember will not result in reversal unless the defendant shows that he has been injured. Cooks v. State, 844 S.W.2d 697 (Tex. Crim. App. 1992), *cert. denied,* 509 U.S. 927, 113 S.Ct. 3048, 125 L. Ed. 2d 732 (1993).

If a *disqualified* prospective juror (*i.e.*, one who is subject to a challenge for cause, but otherwise qualified) is *sua sponte* excused by the trial court, the defendant must take the following steps to preserve error and establish harm:

- Object to the excusal of the juror
- At the conclusion of the voir dire, claim that he is to be tried by a jury to which he has a legitimate objection (and have a sufficient basis in the record for the complaint)
- Specifically identify the juror or jurors of whom he is complaining
- Exhaust all of peremptory challenges and request additional peremptory challenges (and show that the trial

court denied the request for additional peremptory challenges)

- Green v. State, 764 S.W.2d 242 (Tex. Crim. App. 1989).

PRACTICE TIP: In order to preserve error in the case of veniremembers who were summoned for jury duty but did not appear, the defendant must request writs of attachment for those veniremembers. Coleman v. State, 881 S.W.2d 344 (Tex. Crim. App. 1994), cert. denied, 513 U.S. 1096, 115 S.Ct. 763, 130 L. Ed. 2d 660 (1995). See §14:14.1, §14:14.2 for sample writs of attachment.

If a *qualified* juror is improperly excused *sua sponte*, the defendant can show harm and thus reversible error by establishing that the state exhausted its peremptory challenges. Green, *supra*.

Voir dire error in a non-capital case cannot be error affecting the punishment phase only under CCP Art. 44.29(b); therefore, the defendant has the right to begin a retrial in the guilt-innocence phase. Carson v. State, 6 S.W.3d 536 (Tex. Crim. App. 1999).

§14:80 Trial Court Questioning of Venire

Because the ultimate decision to dismiss potential jurors for cause is a heavy responsibility, the trial judge must be allowed to ask questions to clarify a veniremember's answers and make intelligent and informed decisions. Heiselbetz v. State, 906 S.W.2d 500 (Tex. Crim. App. 1995).

The court may ask questions in order to clarify a juror's position or instruct a juror. Gardner v. State, 730 S.W.2d 675 (Tex. Crim. App. 1987), *cert. denied,* 484 U.S. 905, 108 S.Ct. 248, 98 L. Ed. 2d 206 (1987). Usually such intervention is warranted for purposes of clarification and expedition. Gardner.

If a clear, potential source of bias is evident from the record in the case, the trial court bears the burden of making inquiry to discern whether actual bias exists and whether it exists to such a degree that it requires the excusal of the veniremember. Turner v. State, 671 S.W.2d 679 (Tex.App.—Dallas 1984, *pet. ref'd*).

§14:81 Comments by Trial Court in Front of Venire

§14:81.1 In General

CCP Art. 38.05. Judge Shall Not Discuss Evidence

> *In ruling upon the admissibility of evidence, the judge shall not discuss or comment upon the weight of the same or its bearing in the case, but shall simply decide whether or not it is admissible; nor shall he, at any stage of the proceeding previous to the return of the verdict, make any remark calculated to convey to the jury his opinion of the case.*

As a general rule, the trial court must refrain from commenting on the weight of the evidence in the jury's presence during any stage of the proceeding. CCP Art. 38.05; Livingston v. State, 782 S.W.2d 112 (Tex.App.—Dallas 1989).

A trial court's comments constitute reversible error only where they are reasonably calculated to benefit the state or prejudice the defendant. Livingston; Sharpe v. State, 648 S.W.2d 705 (Tex. Crim. App. 1983).

To determine whether the comment is either reasonably calculated to benefit the State or to prejudice the defendant, an appellate court must first examine whether the trial court's statement was material to the case. Clark v. State, 878 S.W.2d 224 (Tex.App.—Dallas 1994, *no pet.*); Burge v. State, 443 S.W.2d 720 (Tex. Crim. App.1969), *cert. denied*, 396 U.S. 934, 90 S.Ct. 277, 24 L. Ed. 2d 233 (1969).

A statement is material if it:

- Implies approval of the State's argument
- Indicates any disbelief in the defense's position; or
- Diminishes the credibility of the defense's approach to its case

Clark.

Generally, an instruction by the judge to disregard any comment made by him is sufficient to cure any error. Fletcher v. State, 960 S.W.2d 694 (Tex.App.—Tyler 1997); Marks v. State, 617 S.W.2d 250 (Tex. Crim. App. 1981).

TIP TO THE BENCH: Trial judges are advised to be very careful when making any superfluous statement during trial as jurors are prone to seize with alacrity upon any conduct or language of the trial judge which they may interpret as shedding light upon his view of the weight of the evidence, or the merits of the issues involved. Jones v. State, 788 S.W.2d 834 (Tex.App.—Dallas 1990, no pet.).

§14:81.2 Comments That Are Not Error

A trial judge's inadvertent reference to the complainant in the case as "the victim" was not erroneous in a case where the defendant has pled guilty before the jury. Cooper v. State, 910 S.W.2d 605 (Tex.App.—Tyler 1995, *no pet.*).

Where the trial court overruled a defense objection to testimony as hearsay and gave an instruction that, "[t]his testimony is being admitted by the court not for the truth of the statement but for the fact he was so told," the judge was properly explaining the law under Texas Rule of Evidence 103(B) regarding the admission of the statement. Rosales v. Texas, 932 S.W.2d 530 (Tex.App.—Tyler 1995, *pet. ref'd*).

Although it is ill-advised in the presence of the jury, numerous cases have held that when a judge chastises attorneys during a trial for unacceptable conduct it does not violate the rule against court comments. Rosales; Liveoak v. State, 717 S.W.2d 691 (Tex.App.—San Antonio 1986), *pet. ref'd* at 741 S.W.2d 451 (Tex. Crim. App. 1987) ("get on with the case"); Betancourt v. State, 657 S.W.2d 451 (Tex.App.—Corpus Christi 1983, *pet. ref'd*) (arguing with court).

A trial court's comment that, "I don't know if you need to do that anymore for appellate purposes" was not erroneous because it was not calculated to benefit State or prejudice the defendant. Rodela v. State, 829 S.W.2d 845 (Tex.App.—Houston [1st Dist.] 1992, *pet. ref'd*).

It is proper for a trial court to state for the record what he observed in the courtroom if it is done without editorial comment. Rankin v. State, 872 S.W.2d 279 (Tex.App.—Houston [14th Dist.] 1994), *vacated and remanded on other grounds*, 974 S.W.2d 707 (Tex. Crim. App. 1996).

Where a trial judge made comments expressing his dislike of vigorous cross examination of child victims he did not err because, although ill-advised, his remarks were directed at the defense attorney rather than the defendant. Latson v. State, 807 S.W.2d 372 (Tex.App.—Houston [14th Dist.] 1991).

§14:81.3 Comments That Are Error

A trial judge's comments before voir dire of the jury that, "I think that the evidence will show that he [defendant] went to her [victim's] house looking for her daughter and the State's evidence will probably show that Sara Whitehead [victim] was killed somewhere during that time..." were calculated to, and probably did, convey to the jury the court's opinion of the case on a pivotal issue. Graham v. State, 624 S.W.2d 785 (Tex.App.—Fort Worth 1981, *no pet.*).

A trial judge's comments in front of the jury, "[t]hat's fine. You can try that on appeal," were found to be erroneous, although cured by a strong instruction to disregard. Hernandez v. State, 507 S.W.2d 209 (Tex. Crim. App. 1974).

Where the trial judge informed the venire that the indictment alleged that the defendant had two prior convictions, she violated the defendant's right to a fair and impartial trial. Clark v. State, 878 S.W.2d 224 (Tex.App.—Dallas 1994, *no pet.*).

A trial judge committed reversible error at the punishment phase of a trial by instructing the jury to find as a matter of law that the enhancement paragraphs in the indictment were true, where the defendant had entered a plea of not true. Lewis v. State, 814 S.W.2d 513 (Tex.App.—Houston [14th Dist.] 1991, *pet. ref'd*).

A trial court committed error by referring, in the presence of the jury, to the State's expert witness as "a credible witness," but the comment was harmless in light of the court's instruction to disregard. Tennison v. State, 814 S.W.2d 484 (Tex. App.—Waco 1991, *no pet.*).

A trial judge's comment upon admitting evidence that, "I now find that there is evidence of a conspiracy," was reversible error where the defendant was charged with a drug conspiracy offense. Bachus

v. State, 803 S.W.2d 402, (Tex.App.—Dallas 1991, *pet. ref'd*). A trial judge's comment at the time a photo was admitted into evidence that, "I find that the probative value of State's Exhibit 4 greatly outweighs any potential prejudice. I admit 4," is an improper comment. Fletcher v. State, 960 S.W.2d 694 (Tex. App.—Tyler 1997); Marks v. State, 617 S.W.2d 250 (Tex. Crim. App. 1981).

A trial judge's comments to the jury making it clear that he believed that the case would require a punishment hearing was a reversible comment on the weight of the evidence. Jones v. State, 788 S.W.2d 834 (Tex.App.—Dallas 1990, *no pet.*). A trial court's statement that the state's argument was a "reasonable inference from the evidence" constituted reversible error. Dixon v. State, 775 S.W.2d 795 (Tex.App.—El Paso 1989, *pet. ref'd*).

A trial court's comments to the venire to the effect that the defendant had been contemplating the state's plea bargain offer and that defendants may not testify if they are guilty were found to be erroneous even though there was no objection to any of the comments. Blue v. State, 41 S.W.3d 129 (Tex. Crim. App. 2000) (plurality opinion).

A trial court's comment that he would further consider a matter "... as soon as I hear from the defendant ..." is reversible as a comment on the defendant's failure to testify. Bustamante v. State, 48 S.W.3d 761 (Tex. Crim. App. 200).

TIP TO THE BENCH: In carrying out its duties in ruling upon a defendant's objection, a trial court must not embellish the ruling with an unwarranted comment. Smith v. State, 595 S.W.2d 120 (Tex. Crim. App. 1980).

§14:81.4 Complaints About Court's Questions or Comments

In order to preserve error for appeal, the defendant must lodge a timely and specific objection at trial. Ladd v. State, 3 S.W.3d 547 (Tex. Crim. App. 1999); Sattiewhite v. State, 786 S.W.2d 271 (Tex. Crim. App. 1989). The objection must be made at the earliest opportunity. Wheatfall v. State, 882 S.W.2d 829 (Tex. Crim. App. 1994).

As in cases where the defendant is complaining of an improper argument, he should ask that the venire be instructed to disregard the remark. Livingston v. State, 782 S.W.2d 112 (Tex.App.—Dallas 1989). The defendant must show that members of the jury heard the remark. Nelson v. State, 881 S.W.2d 97 (Tex.App.—Houston [1st Dist.] 1994, *pet. ref'd*).

PRACTICE TIP: Where an improper comment is made during individual voir dire, exercise a peremptory challenge on the veniremember who heard the remark. Where the improper comment was made to the entire venire, immediately move to quash the venire. Nelson.

Improper comments made by the trial court to the venire are subject to harm analysis. Unkart v. State, 400 S.W.3d 94, 99 (Tex. Crim. App. 2013). The reviewing court will view the voir dire in its entirety in determining if the defendant has been harmed. Unkart.

Voir dire error in a non-capital case cannot be error affecting the punishment phase only under CCP Art. 44.29(b); therefore, the defendant has the right to begin a retrial in the guilt-innocence phase. Carson v. State, 6 S.W.3d 536 (Tex. Crim. App. 1999).

§14:90 Withholding Of Information By Veniremember

When a juror withholds material information during voir dire that the defense, using due diligence, could not uncover, the parties are denied the opportunity to exercise their challenges, which hinders their selection of an impartial jury. Franklin v. State, 138 S.W.3d 351, 355–56 (Tex. Crim. App. 2004); State v. Gutierrez, 541 S.W.3d 91, 99-100 (Tex. Crim. App. 2017).

A violation, by itself, is insufficient for reversal. The defendant must also have been harmed by that constitutional violation. Franklin, 138 S.W.3d at 358; State v. Gutierrez, 541 S.W.3d at 100;Tex. R. App. P. 44.2(a).

Error occurs where a prejudiced or biased juror is selected without fault or lack of diligence on the part of defense counsel, where defense counsel has acted in good faith on the juror's responses and has no knowledge of their accuracy. Gonzales v. State, 3 S.W.3d 915 (Tex. Crim. App. 1999); Brandon v. State, 599 S.W.2d 567 (Tex. Crim. App. 1979).

A defendant is entitled to a reversal where a juror has withheld information if two criteria are met: (1) the omission is material; and, (2) the defendant has exercised due diligence in eliciting that information. Jones v. State, 596 S.W.2d 134 (Tex. Crim. App. 1980).

Under these circumstances, a reversal is merited because withholding material information denies the defendant the opportunity to knowingly and intelligently exercise peremptory challenges, hence jeopardizing his right to a fair trial before an impartial jury. Salazar v. State, 562 S.W.2d 480 (Tex. Crim. App. 1978).

Where the juror's information is provided by way of a written questionnaire, counsel has a duty to follow up with additional questions to test the accuracy of the written response. Gonzales, *supra.*

§14:91 Material Information

It is not dispositive of the materiality issue that the juror did not intentionally mislead the defendant during voir dire because the good faith of a juror is largely irrelevant when considering the materiality of information withheld. Franklin v. State, 12 S.W.3d 473 (Tex. Crim. App. 2000).

The information need not prove that the juror is actually biased, but it must have a tendency to show bias. Franklin v. State, 138 S.W.3d 351, 355–56 (Tex. Crim. App. 2004).

If the withheld information has a tendency to show bias, an appropriate procedure is to hold a hearing at which evidence should be adduced regarding whether the juror is actually biased. Uranga v. State, 330 S.W.3d 301, 306 (Tex. Crim. App. 2010).

If a trial judge finds that the juror is not actually biased, and that finding is supported by the record, then the defendant has not been harmed by the violation of his constitutional right to an impartial jury. State v. Gutierrez, 541 S.W.3d 91, 100 (Tex. Crim. App. 2017).

If, however, the judge finds that the juror is actually biased, the only remedy is a mistrial. Franklin, 138 S.W.3d at 354.

Appellate courts review the trial court's determination of historical fact for an abuse of discretion (i.e., whether the juror was actually biased), and appellate courts should give almost total deference to the trial court's determination if it is supported by the record. State v. Gutierrez, 541 S.W.3d at 100.

Material information includes information regarding a juror's relationship with any party in a criminal proceeding. Von January v. State, 576 S.W.2d 43 (Tex. Crim. App. 1978). However, mere familiarity with a witness is not necessarily material information. Decker v. State, 717 S.W.2d 903 (Tex. Crim. App. 1986).

Material information also includes the fact that the veniremember has an extensive criminal history. State v. Read, 965 S.W.2d 74 (Tex.App.—Austin 1988, *no pet.*). The defendant should be allowed to pursue questioning of the juror to determine if withheld information is material. Franklin.

§14:92 Defendant's Burden

Defense counsel has an obligation to ask questions calculated to bring out information which might be said to indicate a juror's inability to be impartial and truthful. Jones v. State, 596 S.W.2d 134 (Tex. Crim. App. 1980).

Defense counsel has a duty to follow up on information contained in jury questionnaires; and if he does not, he cannot later complain that a veniremember withheld information or lied on the questionnaire. Gonzales v. State, 3 S.W.3d 915 (Tex. Crim. App. 1999).

Where defense counsel fails to fulfill his obligation to ask questions which will reveal that answers on a questionnaire are incorrect or to otherwise discover material information, there has been a lack of diligence. In this situation, appellate courts will find that the juror did not withhold any information and will not reverse the case. Gonzalez.

Counsel must ask specific questions and not rely on broad ones to satisfy this obligation. Brandon v. State, 599 S.W.2d 567 (Tex. Crim. App. 1979).

The defendant will not be found to have carried his burden where it appears from the record that the veniremember did not understand the question as propounded. Hernandez v. State, 952 S.W.2d 59 (Tex.App.—Austin 1997), *vacated on other grounds*, 957 S.W.2d 851 (Tex. Crim. App.1998). In order for the defendant to carry his burden to show that a veniremember withheld information about a criminal history, he must show that the veniremember knew of the situation. Hernandez.

PRACTICE TIP: Where the failure of a prospective juror to reveal information during voir dire comes to light during trial, ask for an immediate hearing, ask to question the juror on the matter, develop as extensive a record as possible and request a mistrial. See, Salazar v. State, 562 S.W.2d 480 (Tex. Crim. App. 1978).

Where a juror brings new information to light during trial and the trial court does not allow additional questioning of the juror, a defendant preserves error by propounding to the court specific areas of questions that he would ask the juror. Franklin v. State, 12 S.W.3d 473 (Tex. Crim. App. 2000).

TIP TO THE BENCH: If a juror brings new material information to light during a trial, the trial court should allow the defendant to conduct further voir dire examination of the juror to determine if bias exists. See, Franklin.

§14:93 Personal Information About Jurors and Juror Privacy Considerations

Art. 35.29. PERSONAL INFORMATION ABOUT JURORS. (a) Except as provided by Subsections (b) and (c), information collected by the court or by a prosecuting attorney during the jury selection process about a person who serves as a juror, including the juror's home address, home telephone number, social security number, driver's license number, and other personal information, is confidential and may not be disclosed by the court, the prosecuting attorney, the defense counsel, or any court personnel.

(b) On application by a party in the trial, or on application by a bona fide member of the news media acting in such capacity, to the court for the disclosure of information described by Subsection (a), the court shall, on a showing of good cause, permit disclosure of the information sought.

(c) The defense counsel may disclose information described by Subsection (a) to successor counsel representing the same defendant in a proceeding under Article 11.071 without application to the court or a showing of good cause.

§14:100 Peremptory Challenges

A defendant's constitutional rights are not violated when he chooses to use a peremptory challenge against a venireman that the trial court should have excused for cause because peremptory challenges are not of federal constitutional dimension. U.S. v. Martinez-Salazar, 528 U.S. 304, 120 S.Ct. 774, 145 L.Ed.2d 792 (2000).

§14:101 Statutory Law

CCP Art. 35.14. A Peremptory Challenge

A peremptory challenge is made to a juror without assigning any reason therefor.

CCP Art. 35.15. Number of Challenges

(a) In capital cases in which the State seeks the death penalty both the State and defendant shall be entitled to fifteen peremptory challenges. Where two or more defendants are tried together, the State shall be entitled to eight peremptory challenges for each defendant; and each defendant shall be entitled to eight peremptory challenges.

(b) In non-capital felony cases and in capital cases in which the State does not seek the death penalty, the State and defendant shall each be entitled to ten peremptory challenges. If two or more defendants are tried together each defendant shall be entitled to six

peremptory challenges and the State to six for each defendant.

(c) The State and the defendant shall each be entitled to five peremptory challenges in a misdemeanor tried in the district court and to three in the county court, or county court at law. If two or more defendants are tried together, each defendant shall be entitled to three such challenges and the State to three for each defendant in either court.

(d) The State and the defendant shall each be entitled to one peremptory challenge in addition to those otherwise allowed by law if one or two alternate jurors are to be impaneled and two peremptory challenges if three or four alternate jurors are to be impaneled. The additional peremptory challenges provided by this subsection may be used against an alternate juror only, and the other peremptory challenges allowed by law may not be used against an alternate juror.

CCP Art. 35.25. Making Peremptory Challenge

In non-capital cases and in capital cases in which the State's attorney has announced that he will not qualify the jury for, or seek the death penalty, the party desiring to challenge any juror peremptorily shall strike the name of such juror from the list furnished him by the clerk.

§14:102 When Peremptory Challenges Are Made

In non-capital cases, peremptory challenges are made after all the veniremembers have been examined. CCP Art. 35.25. The trial court shall allow adequate time for the making of peremptory challenges. Thomas v. State, 658 S.W.2d 175 (Tex. Crim. App. 1983).

Where an error has been made in the exercise of peremptory challenge or the trial court makes an error in impaneling the jury, it is incumbent on the aggrieved party to object before the jury is sworn or the error is waived. Truong v. State, 782 S.W.2d 904 (Tex.App.—Houston [14th Dist.] 1989, *pet. ref'd*).

A trial court's erroneous denial of a defendant's peremptory challenge to the seating of a juror where all seated jurors are qualified and unbiased, does not require automatic reversal of the defendant's conviction under the Due Process clause. Rivera v. Illinois, 556 U.S. ___, 129 S.Ct. 1446, 173 L.Ed.2d 320 (2009) (trial court had disallowed the defendant's peremptory because of a Batson violation).

§14:103 Forms for Peremptory Challenges

See our companion book *Texas Criminal Forms* (James Publishing) for the following sample forms:

- Form 14-13, Motion for Additional Peremptory Challenges.
- Form 14-15, Peremptory Challenge Tally Form.

§14:110 Batson v. Kentucky Hearings

CCP Art. 35.261. Peremptory Challenges Based on Race Prohibited

(a) After the parties have delivered their lists to the clerk under Article 35.26 of this code and before the court has impaneled the jury, the defendant may request the court to dismiss the array and call a new array in the case. The court shall grant the motion of a defendant for dismissal of the array if the court determines that the defendant is a member of an identifiable racial group, that the attorney representing the state exercised peremptory challenges for the purpose of excluding persons from the jury on the basis of their race, and that the defendant has offered evidence of relevant facts that tend to show that challenges made by the attorney representing the state were made for reasons based on race. If the defendant establishes a prima facie case, the burden then shifts to the attorney

representing the state to give a racially neutral explanation for the challenges. The burden of persuasion remains with the defendant to establish purposeful discrimination.

(b) If the court determines that the attorney representing the state challenged prospective jurors on the basis of race, the court shall call a new array in the case.

United States Constitution Fourteenth Amendment. "... nor shall any State deprive any person of life, liberty, or property, without due process of law, nor deny to any person within its jurisdiction the equal protection of the laws."

§14:111 Introduction and History

More than 115 years ago, the Supreme Court decided in Strauder v. West Virginia, 100 U.S. 303, 25 L.Ed. 664 (1880), that the exclusion of blacks from grand and petit juries in criminal proceedings violated the Equal Protection Clause of the Fourteenth Amendment, but the fact that a particular jury or a series of juries does not statistically reflect the racial composition of the community does not in itself make out an invidious discrimination forbidden by the Clause. Instead, a defendant in a criminal case is entitled to require that the State not deliberately and systematically deny to members of his race the right to participate as jurors in the administration of justice. Alexander v. Louisiana, 405 U.S. 625, 92 S.Ct. 1221, 31 L.Ed.2d 536 (1972).

§14:111.1 Systematic Exclusion Standard

In Swain v. Alabama, 380 U.S. 202, 85 S.Ct. 824, 13 L.Ed.2d 759 (1965), the Supreme Court recognized that a state's purposeful or deliberate denial to blacks of their right to participate as jurors in the administration of justice on the basis of race violates the Equal Protection Clause. Swain stood for the proposition that a black defendant could make out a *prima facie* case of purposeful discrimination by proving that the peremptory challenge system was being perverted by denying blacks the same right and opportunity to participate in the administration of justice enjoyed by the white population. However, at that time the Supreme Court further stated that peremptory challenges remained available to the prosecution in a given case to remove veniremen of a particular race, religion, or nationality for tactical reasons.

In order for a defendant to overcome the Swain presumption that peremptory challenges had not been used in a manner offensive to the Equal Protection Clause, he had to prove that the prosecution systematically used peremptory challenges to remove minority veniremen from service in repeated cases. A number of lower appellate courts interpreted Swain to require a repeated use of peremptory challenges over a number of cases as necessary to establish a violation of the Equal Protection Clause. Hence a "systematic exclusion" was the burden defendants shouldered in order to assert their rights. This burden required an emphasis on the history of jury selection practices by prosecutors in the jurisdiction, rather than a focus on the jury selection factors in the individual case.

§14:111.2 Transitional Cases

Since Swain, the Supreme Court has recognized that a defendant may make a *prima facie* showing of purposeful racial discrimination in the selection of his jury by relying solely on the jury selection practices in his particular case. Alexander v. Louisiana, 405 U.S. 625, 92 S.Ct. 1221, 31 L.Ed.2d 536 (1972). Subsequent cases then began to define the framework for what eventually became the court inquiry of Batson v. Kentucky, *infra*. Especially important to the formulation of the holding in Batson is the presumption that peremptory challenges can constitute a jury selection practice that permits those who are of a mind to discriminate to do so. Avery v. Georgia, 345 U.S. 559, 73 S.Ct. 891, 97 L.Ed.2d 1244 (1953).

The courts have specifically held that racially motivated peremptory challenges do not violate the Sixth Amendment fair cross-section requirements. Holland v. Illinois, 493 U.S. 474, 110 S.Ct. 803, 107 L.Ed.2d 905 (1990); Seubert v. State, 787 S.W.2d 68 (Tex. Crim. App.1990). The fair cross-section requirements of the Sixth Amendment govern only the assembly of a fair venire, not the petit jury itself. Holland and Seubert, *supra*.

§14:112 Batson and Beyond

§14:112.1 Batson Case

On April 30, 1986, the Supreme Court handed down its opinion in Batson v. Kentucky, 476 U.S. 79, 106 S.Ct. 1712, 90 L.Ed.2d 69 (1986). Batson requires trial courts to be sensitive to the racially discriminatory use of peremptory challenges and forces the mandate of equal protection while furthering the ends of justice. The Court reasoned that, due to the heterogeneous population of our nation, public respect for our criminal justice system and the rule of law will be strengthened by ensuring that no citizen is disqualified from jury service because of his race. The significance of the Batson case is that a defendant can now establish a *prima facie* case of purposeful discrimination based solely upon the prosecutor's exercise of peremptory challenges at the defendant's trial. No longer is it necessary to demonstrate any type of pattern or system of challenges outside of the case on trial.

The Batson case does not go so far as to hold that the Equal Protection Clause is violated when racially neutral criteria in the peremptory challenge process results in a disproportionate impact on minority jurors.

Batson further does not limit a party's right to challenge a venireman for cause. Tompkins v. State, 774 S.W.2d 195 (Tex. Crim. App. 1987), affirmed at 490 U.S. 754, 109 S.Ct. 2180, 104 L.Ed.2d 834 (1989).

Batson laid out a framework of inquiry which will be discussed below. The Batson Court did not go beyond this skeletal framework. It did not formulate particular procedures to be followed after a proper objection because of the variety of jury selection practices followed in the state and federal courts. This has, of course, spawned recurrent litigation to establish the practices to be followed in the individual jurisdictions.

§14:112.2 Non-Minority Defendants

In Powers v. Ohio, 499 U.S. 400, 111 S.Ct. 1364, 113 L.Ed.2d 411 (1991), the Supreme Court held that a defendant has standing to assert the equal protection rights of veniremen who are excused as jurors through the discriminatory use of peremptory challenges. Because this rationale does not require racial identity between the defendant and the illegally excused venireman, Powers has the effect of allowing non-minority defendants to object to the prosecution's racially motivated peremptory challenges. This rule was applied to Texas cases through Tex.Code Crim.Proc.Ann. Art. 35.261 (Vernon 1989) in State v. Oliver, 808 S.W.2d 492 (Tex. Crim. App. 1991). *See also*, Mead v. State, 819 S.W.2d 869 (Tex. Crim. App. 1991).

§14:112.3 Any Party

The Supreme Court has further expanded the scope of the Batson decision to prohibit a criminal defendant from engaging in purposeful racial discrimination in the exercise of peremptory challenges. Georgia McCollum, 505 U.S. 42, 112 S.Ct. 2348, 120 L.Ed.2d 33 (1992), on remand 422 S.E.2d 866. The Court found that the harms discussed in Batson are also inflicted by a defendant's racially discriminatory use of peremptory challenges. They found that, because a petit jury is a governmental body, the racially discriminatory use of peremptory challenges by any party invokes the Equal Protection Clause. Thus, the prosecution has third-party standing to challenge a defendant's discriminatory use of peremptory challenges. A prohibition against the discriminatory exercise of peremptory challenges does not violate a criminal defendant's constitutional rights because it is an affront to justice to argue that the right to a fair trial includes the right to discriminate against a group of citizens based upon their race. The only procedural mandate set out in McCollum was a Batson-type inquiry.

§14:112.4 Juvenile Proceedings

The principles of Batson derived through the Equal Protection Clause apply to civil proceedings which include juvenile adjudication proceedings. R.X.F. v. State, 921 S.W.2d 888 (Tex. App.—Waco 1996).

§14:112.5 Gender-Based Discrimination

The Supreme Court has also decided that Batson principles should apply to gender-based, as well as racial, discrimination. *See* J.E.B. v. Alabama ex rel. T.B., 5 11 U.S. 127, 114 S.Ct. 1419, 128 L.Ed.2d 89 (1994), on remand 641 So.2d 821, in which the State of Alabama used 9 of its 10 peremptory challenges to strike men in petitioner's paternity suit.

The Court of Criminal Appeals applied J.E.B., *supra,* to a Texas case in Fritz v. State, 946 S.W.2d 844 (Tex. Crim. App. 1997). The Court found that the prosecution violated the equal protection clause by using seven of its peremptory challenges to remove males.

§14:112.6 Religious Beliefs

Reasoning that "[t]o hold... that a veniremember may not be excluded on account of his religious preference is tantamount to a holding that he may not be struck on account of his beliefs[,]" the Texas Court of Criminal Appeals has declined to extend Batson principles to the use of peremptory challenges based on religious preference. Casarez v. State, 913 S.W.2d 468 (Tex. Crim. App. 1994) (*op. on rehearing*).

Thus, the trial court does not err in failing to grant a new trial where the State singles out Catholics for exclusion from the jury panel. Devoe v. State, 354 S.W.3d 457 (Tex. Crim. App. 2011).

§14:113 Texas Procedure

To codify and implement Batson in Texas, the legislature enacted Tex. Code Crim. Proc. Art. 35.261, which is intended to create uniform procedures and remedies to address claimed constitutional violations during jury selection. State v. Oliver, 808 S.W.2d 492 (Tex. Crim. App. 1991).

A trial court's Batson rulings are reviewed on appeal under the clearly erroneous standard of review. Gibson v. State, 144 S.W.3d 530 (Tex. Crim. App. 2004).

§14:113.1 Timing of Objections

Since the codification of Batson principles in Art. 35.261, the Texas courts have held that an objection to the jury composition must be made prior to the jury being impaneled. Rousseau v. State, 824 S.W.2d 579 (Tex. Crim. App. 1992). A jury is considered "impaneled" when the members have been both selected and sworn. Price v. State, 782 S.W.2d 266 (Tex.App. Beaumont 1989). This principle controls over prior cases which required the objection to also precede discharge of the remaining panel members. Hill v. State, 827 S.W.2d 860 (Tex. Crim. App. 1992). In a capital murder case where individual *voir dire is* being conducted, the objection will be timely when made immediately after the peremptory challenge in question is exercised. Rousseau v. State, *supra.*

§14:113.2 Specificity of Objections

A Batson objection must be reasonably specific in order to merit review. Invoking Batson, Swain, Article 35.261, or mentioning the practice of using peremptory challenges to exclude minorities will usually be sufficient to call for review. Merely objecting that a defendant has a federal and state constitutional right to a cross section of his peers is not sufficient. Rosales v. State, 841 S.W.2d 368 (Tex. Crim. App. 1992).

An objection was held insufficient in Bacy v. State, 827 S.W.2d 91 (Tex.App. Fort Worth 1992 *pet. ref'd*), where the movant stated his objection to exclusion of African-Americans and Hispanics and then on appeal opposed the peremptory challenge of an Asian not mentioned in his trial objection.

PRACTICE TIP: The movant should make sure the following is reflected by the record to properly preserve its Batson challenge:

(1) The racial makeup of the venire, as well as the race of those veniremen peremptorily challenged
(2) The race or ethnicity of the movant
(3) If the crime is interracial this should be placed in the record; see, Gerber v. State, 845 S.W.2d 460 (Tex. App. — Houston [1st Dist.] 1993), and Dewberg v. State, 776 S.W2d 589 (Tex. Cr App. 1989)
(4) Any inconsistent treatment by the challenging party of minority and non-minority veniremembers
(5) If possible, the racial composition of the population eligible for jury service

Keep in mind when making the objection that the race or ethnic origin of a movant or venireman cannot be conclusively proven for purposes of a Batson hearing based solely on the person's surname. Sanchez v. State, 797 S.W.2d 951 (Tex. App.—Dallas 1990). Furthermore, the fact that a veniremember has married a person of a particular ethnicity, and therefore has an ethnic surname, will not automatically categorize that individual as a member of their spouse's ethnicity. Aguilar v. State, 826 S.W.2d 760 (Tex.App. — Fort Worth 1992).

PRACTICE TIP: The easiest and most conclusive method of establishing the race or ethnicity of a person is to have the trial judge take judicial notice of the fact sought to be established. Most trial judges will take judicial notice of the obvious race or ethnicity. If the judge will not take judicial notice as requested, the fact must be proven by an alternate method such as by calling a witness or by stipulation between the parties.

§14:113.2.1 Batson Inapplicable

Appellate courts have refused to extend Batson principles to trial procedures other than peremptory challenges. Ladd v. State, 3 S.W.3d 547 (Tex. Crim. App. 1999) (jury shuffles); Wearren v. State, 877 S.W.2d 545 (Tex.App. — Beaumont 1994, *no pet.*) (jury shuffles).

Also, Batson principles do not extend to the state's non-use of peremptory challenges. Hamel v. State, 803 S.W.2d 878 (Tex.App. — Fort Worth 1991, *pet. ref'd*) (where the defendant argued that the state had acted with racial motivation in not using several peremptory challenges, which would have allowed the process to mathematically reach black veniremembers).

§14:113.3 Burdens of Proof/ Production/ Persuasion

In an opinion clarifying the procedure to be followed in a Batson inquiry, the Texas Court of Criminal Appeals has held that Batson contemplates a scheme of shifting burdens. In Williams v. State, 804 S.W.2d 95 (Tex. Crim. App. 1991), *cert. denied*, 501 U.S. 1239, 111 S.Ct. 2875, 115 L.Ed.2d 1038 (1991), the Court held:

- Movant has the initial burden of proof to establish a *prima facie* case of purposeful discrimination
- Burden (termed a burden of production) then shifts to the challenging party to supply a race-neutral explanation for the peremptory challenge(s)
- Burden (termed a burden of persuasion) next shifts back to the movant to rebut the challenging party's explanations so that it can be rationally inferred that the challenging party engaged in purposeful racial discrimination

§14:113.3.1 Burden of Proof

§14:113.3.1.1 Prima Facie Case Necessary

In order to be entitled to have a Batson or purposeful discrimination claim reviewed by a trial or appellate court, the movant must make out a *prima facie* case of racial discrimination in the challenging party's use of peremptory challenges. A *prima facie* case represents the minimum quantum of evidence necessary to support a rational inference that the allegation of fact is true. The party with the burden of proof must produce at least this much evidence to avoid a finding that the allegation is not true as a matter of law. Tompkins v. State, 774 S.W.2d 195 (Tex. Crim. App. 1987), affirmed at 490 U.S. 754, 109 S.Ct. 2180, 104 L.Ed.2d 834 (1989).

The minimum quantum of evidence necessary to support a rational inference of purposeful racial discrimination (*i.e.*, a *prima facie* case) is any relevant evidence with more than a modicum of probative value. Linscomb v. State, 829 S.W.2d 164 (Tex. Crim. App. 1992). A *prima facie* case is what raises the issue, not what eventually disposes of it. In determining, therefore, whether a *prima facie* case is reflected on the record, courts are not to resolve the question of deliberate racial discrimination on its merits by assessing the probative weight of competing inferences or conflicting evidence. They are simply to decide whether the issue has been raised. Linscomb, *supra.*

A defendant satisfies the requirements of *Batson's* first step by producing evidence sufficient to permit the trial judge to draw an inference that discrimination has occurred; and is not required to make a showing that discrimination occurred more likely than not. Johnson v. California, 545 U.S. 162, 125 S.Ct. 2410, 162 L.Ed.2d 129 (2005).

The following are illustrative of the types of evidence that can be used to raise the inference of discrimination:

- Veniremen peremptorily challenged have no characteristic in common other than race
- Pattern of peremptory challenges against minority jurors on the particular venire
- Past conduct of the challenging party in the use of peremptory challenges
- Type and manner of the challenging party's questions and statements during voir dire
- Type and manner of questions directed to the challenged juror, including a lack of questions, or a lack of meaningful questions
- Disparate treatment of members of the jury venire with the same characteristics, or who answer a question in the same or similar manner
- Disparate examination of members of the venire; *e.g.*, questioning some veniremen in a manner likely to provoke a certain response
- Use of all or most of the peremptory challenges to eliminate minorities from the venire

Keeton v. State, 749 S.W.2d 861 (Tex. Crim. App. 1988).

The mere fact that a party exercised a peremptory against a venireman of a cognizable minority group is not sufficient to meet a movant's *prima facie* burden for purposes of Batson. Staley v. State, 887 S.W.2d 885 (Tex. Crim. App. 1994). The movant must show from the circumstances that the challenging party used its peremptory challenge to exclude the venireman for racial reasons. Chambers v. State, 866 S.W.2d 9 (Tex. Crim. App. 1993).

§14:113.3.1.2 Elements of Prima Facie Case

A movant must demonstrate the following in order to establish a *prima facie* case:

- Challenged venireman was a member of a cognizable minority group
- Challenging party exercised a peremptory challenge to remove that venireman
- Those facts and any other relevant circumstances raise an inference that the challenging party excluded the venireman from the venire on the basis of race

Taylor v. State, 911 S.W.2d 906 (Tex.App.-Fort Worth 1995 *pet. ref'd*).

If the movant is successful in making out a *prima facie* case, it creates a rebuttable presumption that the challenging party engaged in purposeful racial discrimination in the use of its peremptory challenges. Lewis v. State, 779 S.W.2d 449 (Tex. App.Tyler 1989).

Once produced, however, the allegation must be found true unless it is contradicted, impeached, or rebutted by other evidence .... (footnote omitted). Tompkins v. State, 774 S.W.2d 195 (Tex. Crim. App. 1987), affirmed at 490 U.S. 754, 109 S.Ct. 2180, 104 L.Ed.2d 834 (1989).

TIP TO THE BENCH: Batson held that any discrimination, no matter how slight, constituted the prima facie showing necessary to shift the burden of production to the challenging party. In fact, the Texas Court of Criminal Appeals has stated that "the United States Constitution is offended by so much as a single strike exercised on the basis of race." Linscomb v. State, 829 S.W. 2d 164 (Tex. Crim. App. 1992).

§14:113.3.1.3 Cognizable Minorities

The test for whether a particular group is a cognizable racial group is whether it is a recognizable, distinct class singled out for different treatment under laws as written or as applied. U.S. v. Dennis, 804 F.2d 1208 (11th Cir. 1986). Because of the wording of Batson, most courts have not extended its principles to groups outside those which have historically experienced discrimination such as African-Americans, Hispanics, and Native Americans. This limitation draws the line short of threatening the existence and practice of allowing peremptory challenges.

It is axiomatic that African-Americans and Hispanics are cognizable minorities for Batson purposes. Some other groups which have been recognized are:

- An Indian or Pakistani. Bacy v. State, 827 S.W.2d 91 (Tex.App.—Fort Worth 1992, *pet. ref'd*) (where the venireman was described as "an individual of dark complexion, Indian or Pakistani"), and Minard v. State, 836 S.W.2d 287 (Tex. App. — Dallas 1992) ("an Indian who appeared to be from India or of Indian extraction").
- A person of Oriental extraction. Kline v. State, 737 S.W.2d 895 (Tex. App. — Houston [1st Dist.] 1987).
- Native Americans. U.S. v. Roan Eagle, 867 F.2d 436 (8th Cir. 1989), *cert. denied*, 490 U.S. 1028, 109 S.Ct. 1764, 104 L.Ed.2d 199 (1989).

"Race," for purposes of *Batson*, encompasses notions of ancestral line and ethnicity. Discrimination based on such considerations is racial discrimination under *Batson*. Wamget v. State, 67 S.W.3d 851 (Tex. Crim. App. 2001).

The party alleging discrimination based on nationality or ethnicity under *Batson* will not adequately establish the venireperson's ethnicity and cognizable racial group by showing only the country of their birth, and such party will likewise fail to meet its burden of persuasion of race discrimination by showing that the peremptory strike was based only on the country of the venireperson's birth. Wamget, *supra*.

§14:113.3.1.4 Texas Cases

The following Texas cases illustrate where a pattern of peremptory challenges rises to the level of a *prima facie* case:

- Miller-El v. State, 790 S.W.2d 351 (Tex. App.—Dallas 1990), where the prosecutor used five of 10 peremptory challenges to challenge all five remaining African-American veniremen
- Vann v. State, 788 S.W.2d 899 (Tex. App. — Dallas 1990), where the prosecution used six of 10 peremptory challenges to challenge six of nine African-American veniremen
- Salazar v. State, 745 S.W.2d 385 (Tex. App. — Fort Worth 1987), where the prosecutor peremptorily challenged the only Hispanic veniremember, *but see* Staley v. State, 887 S.W.2d 885 (Tex. Crim. App. 1994), where this was found to be insufficient
- Whitsey v. State, 796 S.W.2d 707 (Tex. Crim. App. 1989), where the prosecution peremptorily challenged all six African-American veniremen
- Chambers v. State, 784 S.W.2d 29 (Tex. Crim. App. 1989), where the prosecution peremptorily challenged all three remaining African-American veniremen
- Dewberry v. State, 776 S.W.2d 589 (Tex. Crim. App. 1989), where the prosecution peremptorily challenged five out of six black veniremen (*i.e.*, a disproportionate number of peremptory challenges used against African-Americans)
- Miller-El v. State, 748 S.W.2d 459 (Tex. Crim. App. 1988), where the prosecution used 10 out of 14 peremptory challenges to exclude all but one African-American venireman
- Linscomb v. State, 829 S.W.2d 164 (Tex. Crim. App. 1992), where the defendant established that the prosecutor exercised peremptory challenges against African-American veniremen at more than twice the rate one would expect from random selection

However, *see* Flores v. State, 920 S.W.2d 347 (Tex.App.— San Antonio 1996), where the trial court found that the defendant had not made out a *prima facie* case where the prosecution used five of 12 peremptory challenges (there were two defendants on trial) against Hispanics. The court reasoned that, because there were 14 Hispanics on the venire, four were peremptorily challenged by the defendants, and four were seated on the jury, there was no showing that the peremptory challenges were racially motivated.

Keep in mind that the movant may be able to raise a *prima facie* case merely by their assertions into the record where their assertions are not disputed by the challenging party. For example, in Emerson v. State, 820 S.W.2d 802 (Tex. Crim. App. 1991), the defense made certain assertions from their observations of the venire. The prosecution did not challenge those assertions, so the appellate courts had no choice but to treat the assertions as undisputed fact.

§14:113.3.1.5 Statistical Analysis

The courts also have recognized that a statistical analysis may be used to make out a *prima facie* case. *See* Linscomb v. State, 829 S.W.2d 164 (Tex. Crim. App. 1992), where the court found purposeful discrimination where the prosecution used 40% of its peremptory challenges to challenge members of an identifiable race which only made up 19% of the population. The Court reasoned that the prosecution used strikes against black veniremen at twice the rate one would expect if done by random selection and that, since the U.S. Constitution is offended by so much as a single strike exercised on the basis of race, there was purposeful discrimination.

TIP TO THE CHALLENGING PARTY: In order to argue on appeal that the movant did not make out a prima facie showing requiring the challenging party to go forward with race-neutral explanations, the challenging party must lodge an objection at trial to the trial court's finding of a prima facie case. Chambers v. State 866 S.W.2d 9 (Tex. Crim. App. 1993). Going forward with explanations without any prompting or inquiry by the trial court also will make the preliminary issue of a prima facie case a moot issue. Hill v. State, 827 S.W. 2d 860 (Tex. Crim. App. 1992).

It is difficult for the movant to make out a prima facie case based on statistical analysis alone where there is a small sample size, such as in a misdemeanor case. Hassan v. State, 369 S.W.3d 872, 877 (Tex. Crim. App. 2012).

Once the movant has established a *prima facie* case of purposeful racial discrimination, he is entitled to an adversarial hearing to pursue his claim. Mata v. State, 867 S.W.2d 798 (Tex. App. — El Paso 1993).

If the trial court does not find a *prima facie* case of purposeful discrimination, by implication, Batson ends the inquiry.

§14:113.3.2 Burden of Production

If the trial court finds that the movant has established a *prima facie* case, the challenging party will then be called upon to produce race-neutral explanations for the peremptory challenge(s).

§14:113.3.2.1 Race-Neutral Explanation

A race-neutral explanation is one based on something other than the race of the venireman. Francis v. State, 909 S.W.2d 158 (Tex. App. — Houston [14th Dist.] 1995). An explanation must apply equally to minority and non-minority veniremen in order to be truly race-neutral.

At this step of the inquiry, the issue is the facial validity of the challenging party's explanation. Unless a discriminatory intent is inherent in the explanation, the reason offered will be deemed race-neutral. Hernandez v. New York, 500 U.S. 352,

111 S.Ct. 1859, 114 L.Ed.2d 395 (1991) (plurality opinion).

The emphasis at this phase of the inquiry is whether the explanations are non-discriminatory rather than whether they are persuasive or even plausible. Purkett v. Elem, 115 S.Ct. 1769, 131 L.Ed.2d 834 (1995). What is meant by a "legitimate reason" is not a reason that makes sense, but a reason that does not deny equal protection. Purkett, *supra.*

§14:113.3.2.2 Quantum of Production

The showing required by the challenging party need not rise to the level of proof required for a challenge for cause. Keeton v. State, 749 S.W.2d 861 (Tex. Crim. App. 1988). However, the challenging party must present a clear, specific, and legitimate race-neutral explanation for each peremptory challenge. McGee v. State, 909 S.W.2d 516 (Tex.App. — Tyler 1995).

The challenging party must produce more than a mere assertion that it peremptorily challenged minority veniremen on the assumption, or through intuitive judgment, that they would be partial to the movant because of their shared race. Nor can a challenging party rebut the movant's case merely by denying that it had a discriminatory motive or by affirming good faith in the individual selections. The challenging party must, therefore, articulate a race-neutral explanation related to the particular case on trial. Williams v. State, 804 S.W.2d 95 (Tex. Crim. App. 1991), *cert. denied*, 501 U.S. 1239, 111 S.Ct. 2875, 115 L.Ed. 1038 (1991).

§14:113.3.2.3 Basis of Explanation

The challenging party is not required to ask a specific rubric of questions in order to substantiate its race-neutral explanations. It is sufficient that the *voir dire* establish the veracity of its apprehensions through any means. Chambers v. State, 866 S.W.2d 9 (Tex. Crim. App. 1993).

The race-neutral explanation can be based on the subjective belief of the challenging party. An otherwise legitimate race-neutral explanation will not fail merely because there is conflicting evidence in the record. Varizas v. State, 838 S.W.2d 552 (Tex. Crim. App. 1992) (where the venireman testified that she could not follow the law, then later testified that she could).

The challenging party is allowed to exercise peremptory challenges in the face of conflicting answers where it does not feel the venireman will be a favorable juror for its side or where it considers the venireman disingenuous because of the change of opinion. Mines v. State, 852 S.W.2d 941 (Tex. Crim. App. 1992).

The challenging party may exercise its peremptory challenges on the basis of its legitimate hunches and past experience, so long as racial discrimination is not the motive behind the challenge. Keeton v. State, 749 S.W.2d 861 (Tex. Crim. App. 1988).

The courts have found that intuitive assumptions on the part of the challenging party can be valid race-neutral explanations. However, these types of explanations are more strictly scrutinized on appeal than those corroborated by the record. Branch v. State, 774 S.W.2d 781 (Tex.App.—El Paso 1989, *pet. ref'd*).

The fact that a litigant mentions race in his explanation for a peremptory challenge is indicative, but not conclusive, of purposeful discrimination in the case. However, when the motives behind a challenged peremptory strike are "mixed," *i.e.*, both impermissible (race or gender-based) and permissible (race and gender-neutral), if the striking party shows that he would have struck the juror based solely on the neutral reasons, then the strike does not violate the juror's Fourteenth Amendment right to equal protection of the law. Guzman v. State, 85 S.W.3d 242 (Tex. Crim. App. 2002).

Under this "dual motivation" or "mixed motives" doctrine, if the opponent of a peremptory strike makes a *prima facie* showing of discriminatory purpose, the strike's proponent must demonstrate that he would have exercised the peremptory strike even if the improper factor had not existed or contributed to the decision to strike the prospective juror. The trial court then determines whether the opponent has carried his burden in proving purposeful discrimination. Guzman.

The challenging party must be sure that the explanations are supported by the record and also must be sure that the reason for the challenge does not apply to some non-minority venireman who was not peremptorily challenged. The trial judge has the duty to evaluate the challenging party's explanations in light of the circumstances of the case to determine whether the facially neutral explanations have been invented to mask racial discrimination. Whitsey v. State, 796 S.W.2d 707 (Tex. Crim. App. 1989).

However, the mere fact that the prosecutor struck a minority venireman while not striking a white venireman does not require a finding of discriminatory intent. Gibson v. State, 144 S.W.3d 530 (Tex. Crim. App. 2004).

It is not the correctness, but rather the genuineness of the explanation that is relevant in determining whether the challenge was racially motivated. Jasper v. State, 61 S.W.3d 413 (Tex. Crim. App. 2001).

The Supreme Court has recently said that they have no rule that requires the trial judge to have observed the demeanor cited in the prosecution's race-neutral explanation. Thaler v. Haynes, 175 L.Ed.2d 1003 (2010).

§14:113.3.2.4 Recognized Race-Neutral Explanations

The Texas courts have recognized a lengthy and non-exclusive list of race-neutral explanations for peremptory challenges:

- Relatives or friends in trouble with the law; Earhart v. State, 823 S.W.2d 607 (Tex. Crim. App. 1991), vacated and remanded on other grounds, 113 S.Ct. 3026, 125 L.Ed.2d 715 (1993)
- Tendency to assess minimum punishment; Earhart, *supra*
- Tendency to overspeculate on facts; Earhart, *supra*
- Family member convicted of crime; Wilson v. State, 769 S.W.2d 682 (Tex. App.—Beaumont 1989)
- Lack of steady employment; Johnson v. State, 740 S.W.2d 868 (Tex. App.— Houston [14th Dist.] 1987)
- Lack of ties to the community; Johnson, *supra*
- Rehabilitation a priority at punishment; Salazar v. State, 745 S.W.2d 385 (Tex. App.—Fort Worth 1987)
- Religious affiliation (Seventh Day Adventist); Salazar, *supra*
- Membership in a certain profession (quality control inspector); Salazar, *supra*
- Distrust of prosecutor; Rodgers v. State, 725 S.W.2d 477 (Tex.App.—Houston [1st Dist.] 1987)
- Age and youth; Yarbrough v. State, 732 S.W.2d 86 (Tex.App.—Beaumont 1987)
- No religion; Yarbrough, *supra*
- Prior jury service on a mistried case; Yarbrough, *supra*
- Venireman smiled at defendant; Yarbrough, *supra*
- Body English; Chambers v. State, 724 S.W.2d 440 (Tex. App.—Houston [14th Dist.] 1987)
- Membership in a "fringe" religion; Chambers, *supra*
- Unable to consider full punishment range; Rijo v. State, 721 S.W.2d 562 (Tex.App.—Amarillo 1986)
- Bad attitude toward police credibility; Rasco v. State, 739 S.W.2d 437 (Tex. App.—Houston [14th Dist.] 1987)
- Baptist minister where defense attorney is a minister; Rasco, *supra*
- Opposed to death penalty (in a capital case); Tennard v. State, 802 S.W.2d 678 (Tex. Crim. App. 1990), and Staley v. State, 887 S.W.2d 885 (Tex. Crim. App. 1994)
- Venireman had trouble understanding questions; Tennard, *supra*
- Venireman had reservations about relying on accomplice testimony; Tennard, *supra*
- Venireman had gone to school with defendant and was unable to state her closeness to him; Sims v. State, 768 S.W.2d 863 (Tex.App.—Texarkana 1989)
- Failure to properly fill out jury information form; Catley v. State, 763 S.W.2d 465 (Tex. App.—Houston [14th Dist.] 1988)
- Venireman seemed asleep during *voir dire;* Holman v. State, 772 S.W.2d 530 (Tex.App.—Beaumont 1989)
- Venireman worked at the same place as the defendant; Holton, *supra*
- Poor education; Rice v. State, 746 S.W.2d 356 (Tex.App.—Fort Worth 1988)

- Venireman seemed disinterested and arrogant; Ybarra v. State, 775 S.W.2d 409 (Tex.App.—Waco 1989)
- Marital status of venireman; Crawford v. State, 770 S.W.2d 51 (Tex.App.—Texarkana 1989)
- Venireman would hold prosecution to higher burden of proof than beyond a reasonable doubt; Keeton, *supra*
- An amicable association between the venireman and the defendant's family; Chambers v. State, *supra*
- Where the venireman lists punishment as a low priority in criminal justice system; Yarborough v. State, 868 S.W2d 913 (Tex.App.—Fort Worth 1994)
- Age, lack of employment and religious affiliation; Jack v. State, 867 S.W.2d 942 (Tex.App.—Beaumont 1993)
- Difficulty in being able to consider circumstantial evidence; Tompkins v. State, 774 S.W.2d 195 (Tex. Crim. App. 1987)
- Opposition to law as enacted; Spears v. State, 902 S.W.2d 512 (Tex.App.—Houston [1st Dist.] 1994)
- Venireman's incorrect completion of a blank on a juror information form; Jones v. State, 818 S.W.2d 532 (Tex. App.—Houston [1st Dist.] 1991)
- Prior testimony as a character witness; Gerber v. State, 845 S.W.2d 460 (Tex. App.—Houston [1st Dist.] 1993)
- Where the venireman wore sunglasses during voir dire preventing the prosecutor from being able to tell if his eyes were open; Gerber, *supra*
- Where the venireman was a minister and the prosecutor was concerned about his "ability to forgive"; Gerber, *supra*
- Venireman holds himself out to be a "liberal"; Henderson v. State, 816 S.W.2d 845 (Tex.App.—Fort Worth 1991, *no pet.*)
- A strong religious background; Dixon v. State, 828 S.W.2d 42 (Tex.App.—Tyler, *pet. ref'd*)
- Venireman's employment as a TDC guard; Prosper v. State, 788 S.W.2d 625 (Tex.App.—Houston [14th Dist.] 1990)
- Where the venireman stated that he knew people were sometimes convicted of crimes they did not commit (and prosecutor explained that her "instincts" told her that this venireman would not make a good juror); Chamberlain v. State, 998 S.W.2d 230 (Tex. Crim. App. No. 72,850, June 16, 1999)
- Where the venireman stated that he agreed with the verdict in the O.J. Simpson murder case. Shelling v. State, 52 S.W.3d 213 (Tex.App.—Houston [1st Dist.] 2001, *pet. ref'd*)
- The fact that the venireman "glared at" the prosecutor during voir dire. Nieto v. State, 365 S.W.3d 673 (Tex. Crim. App. 2012).
- The fact that the venireman had the same last name as a known criminal family. Nieto.

In addition to this non-exclusive list, it should be noted that the courts are sympathetic to the challenging party's reasoning that its trial strategy led to the exercise of peremptory challenges in a certain manner. This will not obviate the need for a race-neutral explanation, but will complement such an explanation.

It would also be important for the challenging party to demonstrate that it challenged non-minority veniremen with the same characteristics as the challenged minority veniremen. The challenging party should also demonstrate that it did not use a "pattern" to peremptorily challenge minority jurors. Keeton v. State, 749 S.W.2d 861 (Tex. Crim. App. 1988).

§14:113.3.2.5 Invalid Race-Neutral Explanations

The following are explanations for peremptory challenges of minority veniremen which have been found by the courts to not be race-neutral (*i.e.*, are racially motivated):

- Black veniremen associated with one another and appeared to be "very friendly;" Hill v. State, 775 S.W.2d 754 (Tex.App.—Dallas 1989), affirmed at 827 S.W.2d 860 (Tex. Crim. App. 1992)
- Venireman thought prone to identify with defendant; Hill, *supra*
- No eye contact with prosecutor (where prosecutor did not individually question

venireman); Daniels v. State, 768 S.W.2d 314 (Tex.App.—Tyler 1988)

- Venireman paid more attention to defense attorney; Daniels, *supra*
- Venireman thought to be of low intelligence without asking individual questions; Chivers v. State, 796 S.W.2d 539 (Tex.App.—Dallas 1990)
- Venireman was a member of an organization concerned with the advancement of black person's rights (because the membership of the organization is predominantly black); Somerville v. State, 792 S.W.2d 265 (Tex.App.—Dallas 1990)
- Where prosecution exercised a "sight strike" and felt venireman would not fit with the category of jurors prosecution wanted; Davis v. State, 796 S.W.2d 813 (Tex.App.—Dallas 1990, *pet. ref'd*) (striking party must be able to articulate why he felt the venireman's appearance was unacceptable)
- Where the prosecutor could not recall the reasons that he peremptorily challenged two African-American veniremen; Brooks v. State, 802 S.W.2d 692 (Tex. Crim. App. 1991)
- Where the prosecutor explained that his peremptory challenge was based on a "visceral reaction"; Smith v. State, 790 S.W.2d 794 (Tex.App.—Beaumont 1990)
- Any instance where the challenging party exercises peremptories based upon a shared membership in a minority group; Miller-El v. State, 790 S.W.2d 351 (Tex.App.—Dallas 1990)
- Minority venirewoman indicated that she had been involved in a case where one of the state's medical witnesses had appeared as a witness and further details of her involvement were not pursued; Lewis v. State, 779 S.W.2d 449 (Tex. App.—Tyler 1989)
- Prosecution removed "all males under the age of 30 because of their potential bias or shared identity with appellant"; Fritz v. State, 946 S.W.2d 844 (Tex. Crim. App. 1997)

§14:113.3.3 Burden of Persuasion

After the movant has made a *prima facie* showing of racial discrimination in the use of peremptory challenges and the challenging party has produced explanations for its challenges, the movant has the ultimate burden of proving by a preponderance of the evidence that the peremptory challenges were actually used for a racially discriminatory purpose. Lewis v. State, 815 S.W.2d 560 (Tex. Crim. App. 1991); Marquez v. State, 921 S.W.2d 217 (Tex. Crim. App. 1996).

This burden can be sustained by impeaching or rebutting the challenging party's explanation, for example, by showing that the explanation was merely a sham or a pretext for discrimination. Bryant v. State, 923 S.W.2d 199 (Tex.App.—Waco 1996).

On a Batson challenge the inquiry is limited only to the facial validity of the challenging party's explanation for exercising a peremptory challenge on a minority venireman. Bridges v. State, 909 S.W.2d 151 (Tex.App.—Houston [14th Dist.] 1995).

Where the defendant has proven only that the reason given for the peremptory challenge was incorrect he has not met his burden of persuasion to successfully challenge the state's peremptory strikes at trial. Ford v. State, 1 S.W.3d 691 (Tex. Crim. App. 1999).

The defendant must demonstrate in the trial court that the state's reason for exercising the strike was racially motivated; it is not enough to make this argument on appeal. Ford.

A party's failure to offer any real rebuttal to a proffered race-neutral explanation can be fatal to his claim. Chamberlain v. State, 998 S.W.2d 230 (Tex. Crim. App. 1999).

§14:113.3.3.1 Trial Court's Duty

The trial court has the duty of determining whether the movant has carried its burden of showing purposeful racial discrimination. Francis v. State, 909 S.W.2d 158 (Tex.App.—Houston [14th Dist.] 1995).

The trial judge must assess the entirety of the voir dire on both an objective and subjective basis. Keeton v. State, 749 S.W.2d 861 (Tex. Crim. App. 1988). The court should not accept at face value the race-neutral explanations of the challenging party, but shall review the testimony as a whole to determine if the articulated reasons are merely given to conceal a truly racial motive. Keeton, *supra*.

In determining whether the exercise of a peremptory challenge was racially motivated, the trial judge may reflect upon his own personal experiences with voir dire examinations and compare his observations and assessments of veniremembers with those articulated by the challenging party. The judge also may consider his personal experiences with particular attorneys and any evidence offered by the movant to show a pattern or practice of purposeful discrimination. Ramirez v. State, 862 S.W.2d 648 (Tex.App.—Dallas 1993).

Often the best evidence of whether the movant has carried its burden of persuasion will be the demeanor of the attorney who exercises the challenge. Francis, *supra*.

In evaluating the credibility of the challenging party, the trial court may look to several factors:

- Whether the challenging party failed to question any of the minority veniremen, yet peremptorily challenged them anyway
- If the challenging party peremptorily challenged minority veniremen who gave answers similar to non-minority veniremen who were not challenged
- Whether the challenging party challenged minority veniremen who had the same characteristics professionally, socially, religiously, *etc*., as non-minority veniremen who were not challenged

Young v. State, 848 S.W.2d 203 (Tex.App.—Dallas 1992).

§14:113.3.3.2 Trial Court Considerations

As a general rule, a trial court's resolution of a Batson challenge often involves the weighing of three broad circumstances:

- Strength of the movant's *prima facie* case
- Reason for each peremptory challenge and whether it was contrived to mask a discriminatory purpose
- Overview of the totality of the challenging party's explanations

Woods v. State, 801 S.W.2d 932 (Tex.App.—Austin 1990, *pet. ref'd*).

The trial court can look to the following factors in deciding whether the defendant has met his burden of persuasion: (1) the race-neutral explanations; (2) whether the state's strikes disproportionately impacted minorities; (3) whether the state engaged in disparate questioning; and (4) comparative juror analysis. These factors should be analyzed as a group. No single factor is deserving of more weight than another factor. Watkins v. State, 245 S.W.3d 444 (Tex. Crim. App. 2008).

All the relevant facts and circumstances must be considered by the courts in deciding whether a Batson violation has occurred. These factors can include the State's pattern of striking black prospective jurors in other trials, as well as the disparate questioning of black and white prospective jurors. The inquiry is not whether any one fact alone would require reversal, but whether the peremptory strikes were motivated in substantial part by discriminatory intent. Flowers v. Mississippi, 588 U.S. ___, ___ S.Ct. ___, ___ L.Ed.2d ___ (No. 17-9572, 2019 WL 2552489, June 21, 2019).

Strength of *Prima Facie* Case

In deciding if the movant has sustained its burden of persuasion, the trial (and appellate) court will look to several factors which may already have been examined in deciding if the movant made out a *prima facie* case. These include:

- Whether there were any minority jurors seated on the trial jury
- Percentage of minorities on the jury as contrasted with the percentage on the venire
- Whether a disproportionate number of peremptory challenges were exercised against minority veniremen

Where other members of the challenged venireman's race actually served on the jury, a trial judge may, in appropriate cases, infer that race was not a motive for the peremptory challenge. Jones v. State, 845 S.W.2d 419 (Tex.App.—Houston [1st Dist.] 1992). For example, in Salinas v. State, 888 S.W.2d 93 (Tex.App.—Corpus Christi

1994), the Court found that, even though the defendant had made out a *prima facie* case of racial discrimination, there was not a Batson violation where the prosecution failed to proffer explanations for two of the peremptorily challenged Hispanics on the venire. The appellate court accepted the trial court's conclusion that the prosecution's use of its peremptory challenges was not race-based was supported by other circumstances, *i.e.,* the overwhelming number of Hispanics on the venire and the petit jury.

Strength of Race-Neutral Explanation

Factors to be considered by the trial court during a burden of persuasion analysis to determine whether a peremptory challenge was race-neutral are whether:

- Challenging party's explanation was related to the facts of the case
- There was a lack of meaningful questioning of the challenged venireman
- There was a disparate selection of veniremen, *i.e.,* were veniremen impaneled on the jury with the same or similar characteristics as the challenged veniremen
- There was a disparate examination of a venireman, *i.e.,* questioning of a venireman to evoke a particular response without asking the same questions of other veniremen
- Challenging party's explanation was based on a group bias where the group trait was not shown to apply to the challenged venireman specifically

Whitsey v. State, 796 S.W.2d 707 (Tex. Crim. App. 1989).

Disparate Questioning

The proffering of questions to a challenged venireman designed to provoke a certain response without the proffering of the same or similar question to non-minority veniremen may tend to show racial motivation in the use of peremptory challenges. Another example of disparate questioning recognized in Whitsey, *supra*, is the failure to question a challenged venireman.

Group Bias

If a challenging party makes an assumption about a venireman, but does not question him to verify the assumption, it is some indication that the challenge was not race-neutral. Woods v. State, 801 S.W.2d 932 (Tex. App. Austin 1990, *pet. ref'd*). In this situation, the challenging party is acting upon a group bias which has not been shown to apply to the individual. For example, in Woods the prosecutor exercised a peremptory challenge against a venireman because he wore a punk rock haircut which the prosecutor associated with liberals, radicals and the drug culture. The Court found the challenge racial in motivation because the prosecutor did not question the venireman to verify his assumptions.

Likewise, in Emerson v. State, 851 S.W.2d 269 (Tex. Crim. App. 1993), the state peremptorily challenged a black unemployed college student on grounds that his unemployment and the collegiate environment foment liberalism. The prosecutor asked no individual voir dire questions of the venireman to confirm any of the liberal characteristics he associated with this type of person. Thus, the prosecutor was relying on an improper group bias theory because he did not connect it to the particular venireman through voir dire questioning.

The trial court should not merely accept specific reasoning at face value, but must consider whether the challenging party contrived racially neutral explanations to avoid admitting acts of group discrimination. Miller-El v. State, 790 S.W.2d 351 (Tex.App. Dallas 1990).

While failure to show how a group bias applies directly to a venireman will weigh heavily against legitimacy of race-neutral explanations, this failure does not establish conclusively that the challenging party's reasons were a pretext for racial discrimination. The challenging party may base peremptory challenges on its legitimate hunches and past experiences as long as racial discrimination is not a motive. Frazier v. State, 909 S.W.2d 255 (Tex. App. Houston [14th Dist.] 1995).

Reliance on group bias factors have been upheld in several cases even where not shown to apply directly to the challenged venireman. In Frazier, *supra*, the court upheld the peremptory challenge of a state school employee where, in the opinion of the prosecution, she was the "stereotypical" equivalent of a social worker and possibly too lenient on defendants. In Reese v. State, 905 S.W.2d 631 (Tex.App. Texarkana 1995), the court upheld the prosecution's peremptory challenge of a woman married to a paralegal who worked with a lawyer in a criminal defense practice. In distinguishing the situation from one involving pure group bias, the court reasoned that the prosecution could have feared that the venireman would have been unfavorable to the state because of her presumed familiarity with the system. In Emerson v. State, 851 S.W.2d 269 (Tex. Crim. App. 1993), the court upheld the peremptory challenge of a nurse which was based on her professional status where the prosecution reasoned that she may expect medical testimony in a case where they had none to introduce.

Nonquantifiable Explanations

Race-neutral explanations which are based on nonverbal factors or subjective reasons are not necessarily insufficient to rebut presumption of discrimination, but they merit closer scrutiny than explanations based on objective reasons. Goodwin v. State, 898 S.W.2d 380 (Tex.App. San Antonio 1995). The protection of the constitutional guarantees that Batson recognizes requires the court to scrutinize such elusive, intangible, and easily contrived explanations with a healthy skepticism. Daniels v. State, 768 S.W.2d 314 (Tex.App. Tyler 1988, *pet. ref'd*).

Even if the challenging party was mistaken in some of his subjective beliefs, the trial court could still conclude that the strike was race-neutral if the court finds that the challenging party based the peremptory challenge on an honest belief. Jack v. State, 867 S.W.2d 942 (Tex.App. Beaumont 1993).

Corroboration Requirement

A counsel's statement about an occurrence in the courtroom, which was made for the purposes of the record, recorded by the court reporter, undisputed by the opposing counsel, and unquestioned and unqualified by the judge in whose presence the statement was made, established the occurrence for purposes of the appellate record. Yarborough v. State, 947 S.W.2d 892 (Tex. Crim. App. 1997)

Some courts have previously required that peremptory challenges based on nonquantifiable factors, such as hostility or lack of attentiveness, must have the nonquantifiable factor substantiated in the record by corroboration other than the challenging party's assertion. Roberson v. State, 866 S.W.2d 259 (Tex.App. Fort Worth 1993) (where the prosecutor made a sufficient showing through questioning of the venireman that it had appeared that he had been sleeping during voir dire). *See also*, Hill v. State, 827 S.W.2d 860 (Tex. Crim. App. 1992), *cert. denied*, 113 S.Ct. 297 (1992) (where the prosecutor stated that one of the reasons for a peremptory challenge of a minority venireman was a dislike of the way he answered the prosecutor's questions and the record was silent on specific body language and other nonverbal actions which would have substantiated the prosecutor's belief).

The record will be deemed substantiated where the trial court confirms the challenging party's recitations of courtroom observations. Muhammad v. State, 911 S.W.2d 823 (Tex.App. Texarkana 1995).

Prosecution assumptions which are not verified by questioning of the venireman are some evidence of racial discrimination. Cuestas v. State, 933 S.W.2d 731 (Tex.App. Fort Worth 1996).

PRACTICE TIP: If an assertion made during an objection or hearing is controverted by the opposing party, be sure to present additional evidence to bolster the assertion. For example, in Troff v. State 882 S.W.2d 905 (Tex.App. Houston [1st Dist.] 1994), the defendant made the assertion that two veniremen were Hispanic. The prosecutor challenged this assertion, and the appeals court found that since the assertion was challenged it could not be accepted at face value.

No Corroboration Requirement

Other courts have held that undisputed statements of the challenging party in a Batson hearing constitute "valid proof." Salinas v. State, 888 S.W.2d 93 (Tex.App. Corpus Christi 1994) (where the prosecutor feared that, since the challenged venireman had a business near the offense location, he had information which would affect his opinion), and Moss v. State, 877 S.W.2d

895 (Tex.App. Waco 1995) (where the state asserted that the challenged venireman was not attentive and generally disinterested; an assertion which was not challenged by the defense).

> **PRACTICE TIP:** If the opposing party relies on subjective explanations or courtroom observations which can be refuted by testimony, make a record challenging those subjective beliefs or courtroom observations through the testimony of witnesses who did not observe the asserted factors.

The lack of an explanation by the challenging party, even if based on oversight, represents a failure in the challenging party's burden and constitutes reversible error. Wright v. State, 832 S.W.2d 601 (Tex. Crim. App. 1992).

Race as a Factor

The fact that a litigant mentions race in his explanation for a peremptory challenge is indicative, but not conclusive, of purposeful discrimination in the case. However, when the motives behind a challenged peremptory strike are "mixed," *i.e.*, both impermissible (race or gender-based) and permissible (race and gender-neutral), if the striking party shows that he would have struck the juror based solely on the neutral reasons, then the strike does not violate the juror's Fourteenth Amendment right to equal protection of the law. Guzman v. State, 85 S.W.3d 242 (Tex. Crim. App. 2002).

Under this "dual motivation" or "mixed motives" doctrine, if the opponent of a peremptory strike makes a prima facie showing of discriminatory purpose, the strike's proponent must demonstrate that he would have exercised the peremptory strike even if the improper factor had not existed or contributed to the decision to strike the prospective juror. The trial court then determines whether the opponent has carried his burden in proving purposeful discrimination. Guzman.

Disparate Treatment

If the challenging party is shown by the movant to have peremptorily challenged minority veniremembers with a particular characteristic while not challenging non-minority veniremen with the same or similar characteristic, the court may find that the challenging party has engaged in "disparate" treatment. Whitsey v. State, 796 S.W.2d 707 (Tex. Crim. App. 1989) (opinion on rehearing). A finding of disparate treatment voids the challenging party's race-neutral explanations and results in a finding that there was purposeful discrimination. Whitsey, *supra.*

Evidence of disparate treatment of veniremen weighs heavily against legitimacy of proffered raceneutral explanations given by the challenging party. Miller-El v. State, 790 S.W.2d 351 (Tex.App. Dallas 1990).

Disparate treatment can lead to an imputation of racial bias where the disparate treatment exists as the sole reason or primary reasons stated for the exercise of the peremptory challenge. Esteves v. State, 849 S.W.2d 822 (Tex. Crim. App. 1993).

Examples of Disparate Treatment

Examples of cases in which the challenging party has not peremptorily challenged persons with same or similar characteristics to a challenged minority venireman are as follows:

- Prosecution peremptorily challenged a minority venireman because her brother was in the penitentiary and did not challenge a similarly situated white venireman; Esteves v. State, 849 S.W.2d 822 (Tex. Crim. App. 1993)
- Prosecution peremptorily challenged three minority veniremen for the reason that they had relatives who had been in trouble with the law, while failing to peremptorily challenge seven similarly situated whites; Ramirez v. State, 862 S.W2d 648 (Tex.App. Dallas 1993)
- State peremptorily challenged a minority concluding that he was "more liberal minded" since he had a mustache while not peremptorily challenging a white venireman with a beard; Lewis v. State, 815 S.W.2d 560 (Tex. Crim. App. 1991)
- Black woman was peremptorily challenged for not having kids, but a white juror without kids was not peremptorily challenged; C.E.J. v. State, 788 S.W.2d 849 (Tex. App. — Dallas 1990)

Non-Disparate Treatment

Disparate treatment as such cannot automatically be imputed in every situation where one of the challenging party's reasons for challenging a venireperson would technically apply to another venireperson whom the challenging party found acceptable. McHenry v. State, 823 S.W2d 667 (Tex.App. Dallas 1991). The decision to peremptorily challenge a particular venireperson is not susceptible to rigid quantification, rather, it is a fluid process, often hinging on the interaction of a number of variables and permutations. *See* U.S. v. Lance, 853 E2d 1177 (5th Cir. 1988).

It is unlikely that two venirepersons on one panel will possess the same objectionable attribute or character trait in precisely the same degree. Such qualitative distinctions may cause a challenging party to challenge one venireman and not the other. Roy v. State, 813 S.W.2d 532 (Tex.App. — Dallas 199 1, *pet. ref'd*). For example, in Spears v. State, 902 S.W.2d 512 (Tex.App. Houston [1st Dist.] 1994), the state peremptorily challenged a minority venireman who had a relative who had been convicted of a crime. The state did not peremptorily challenge nonminority veniremen whose relatives had been convicted of a crime. The Court found that the state had not engaged in disparate treatment because the nonminority veniremen had unequivocally stated that their relatives had been treated fairly by the system. *See also*, Copeland v. State, 848 S.W.2d 199 (Tex.App. Corpus Christi 1992, *pet. ref'd*) (where the state peremptorily challenged a black teacher but did not challenge several white teachers; the court found that, since the black teacher had made statements during voir dire which the state took as negative, the challenge was not racially motivated).

In situations where the challenging party has offered more than one plausible reason for striking a venireperson, it is proper for the trial and appellate courts to review these reasons in their entirety in order to assess whether the challenging party's explanation was valid or merely pretextual. When the challenging party has offered numerous race-neutral reasons for its peremptory challenge, the mere fact that there were other acceptable jurors possessing one or more of these objectionable attributes is not sufficient to establish "disparate treatment" by the challenging party in use of its peremptory challenges. Cantu v. State, 842 S.W.2d 667 (Tex. Crim. App. 1992); Adanandus v. State, 866 S.W.2d 210 (Tex. Crim. App. 1993).

Use of Notes to Designate Minorities

One form of disparate treatment that supports an inference that facially valid race-neutral explanations are a sham is the designation in the notes of the challenging party as to which veniremen are minorities. Whitsey v. State, 796 S.W.2d 707 (Tex. Crim. App. 1989).

The use of notes to designate minority members on the panel can suggest that race was a factor in the challenging party's use of peremptory challenges. Francis v. State, 909 S.W.2d 158 (Tex. App. Houston [14th Dist.] 1995) (where the prosecutor's notes contained a circled "B" next to the names of black panel members); Whitsey, *supra*, (where the prosecutor identified black veniremen with the letter "B" written above their names).

§14:120 Death Penalty Case Voir Dire

§14:121 Formation of Venire

§14:121.1 Statutory Law

CCP Art. 34.01. Special Venire

> *A "special venire" is a writ issued in a capital case by order of the district court, commanding the sheriff to summon either verbally or by mail such a number of persons, not less than 50, as the court may order, to appear before the court on a day named in the writ from whom the jury for the trial of such case is to be selected. Where as many as one hundred jurors have been summoned in such county for regular service for the week in which such capital case is set for trial, the judge of the court having jurisdiction of a capital case in which a motion for a special venire has been made, shall grant or refuse such motion for a special venire, and upon such refusal require the case to be tried by regular jurors summoned for service in such county for the week in which such capital case is set for trial and such additional talesmen as may be summoned by the sheriff upon*

order of the court as provided in Article 34.02 of this Code, but the clerk of such court shall furnish the defendant or his counsel a list of the persons summoned as provided in Article 34.04.

CCP Art. 34.05. Mechanical or Electronic Selection Method

A mechanical or electronic method of jury selection as provided by Chapter 62, Government Code, may be used under this chapter.

§14:121.2 Assembling Venire

In a capital case, a venire may be assembled in two alternate manners: (1) as a special venire ordered by the court; or (2) as a "jury panel for the week" if as many as 100 jurors have been summoned in the county for regular service for the week. CCP Art. 34.01.

The district court has the discretion to grant or refuse a defendant's motion for a special venire and to order trial before a jury selected from the regular jury panel for the week where at least 100 jurors have been summoned. CCP Art. 34.01.

A special venire is an order of the court to the sheriff to summon verbally or by mail any number of persons not less than 50 to appear in court on a certain day as prospective jurors. CCP Art. 34.01.

§14:121.3 Summoning Additional Veniremembers

In obtaining additional veniremembers in a capital case, the jury wheel must be resorted to in jury wheel counties; in counties not using jury wheels, the sheriff summons them. CCP Art. 34.02.

Additionally, *see* §14:16.

§14:121.4 Furnishing Defendant With List of Veniremembers

CCP Art. 34.04. Notice of List

No defendant in a capital case in which the state seeks the death penalty shall be brought to trial until he shall have had at least two days (including holidays) a copy of the names of the persons summoned as veniremembers, for the week for which his case is set for trial except where he waives the right or is on bail. When such defendant is on bail, the clerk of the court in which the case is pending shall furnish such a list to the defendant or his counsel at least two days prior to the trial (including holidays) upon timely motion by the defendant or his counsel therefor at the office of such clerk, and the defendant shall not be brought to trial until such list has been furnished defendant or his counsel for at least two days (including holidays). Where the venire is exhausted, by challenges or otherwise, and additional names are drawn, the defendant shall not be entitled to two days service of the names additionally drawn, but the clerk shall compile a list of such names promptly after they are drawn and if the defendant is not on bail, the sheriff shall serve a copy of such list promptly upon the defendant, and if on bail, the clerk shall furnish a copy of such list to the defendant or his counsel upon request, but the proceedings shall not be delayed thereby.

A defendant who is tried for the death penalty and who is in custody is entitled to be furnished a list of the persons summoned at least two days before trial. CCP Art. 34.04. Where the defendant is on bail, he is entitled to the list two days before trial where he timely files a motion therefor. He must pick it up at the clerk's office. CCP Art. 34.04. The two-day requirement in Art. 34.04 is mandatory. Smith v. State, 744 S.W.2d 86 (Tex. Crim. App. 1987).

Service of the jury list does not have to be on the defendant personally. Delivery to his attorney is sufficient. Wyle v. State, 777 S.W.2d 709 (Tex. Crim. App. 1989), *affirmed on remand, at* 836 S.W.2d 796.

It is sufficient to serve the list on the defendant two days before the actual voir dire begins, even though the trial judge gave his introductory remarks to the venire on the same day the list was served. May v. State, 738 S.W.2d 261 (Tex. Crim. App.

1987), *cert. denied*, 484 U.S. 872, 108 S.Ct. 206, 98 L. Ed. 2d 158 (1987).

The defendant is entitled to be served two days before trial with the initial list of veniremembers but not with any list of supplemental veniremembers summoned. Wyle.

§14:121.5 Excusing Veniremembers From Special Venire

In the case of a special venire, the trial court cannot designate others to hear and determine veniremembers' excuses for not serving. Chambers v. State, 903 S.W.2d 21 (Tex. Crim. App. 1995); CCP Art. 35.03. However, this does not prevent others from hearing and determining excuses from veniremembers before they are assigned to the special venire. Chambers.

PRACTICE TIP: In order to preserve error in the case of veniremembers who were summoned for jury duty but did not appear, request writs of attachment for those veniremembers. Coleman v. State, 881 S.W.2d 344 (Tex. Crim. App. 1994), cert. denied, 513 U.S. 1096, 115 S.Ct. 763, 130 L. Ed. 2d 660 (1995).

Additionally, *see* §14:70.

TIP TO THE BENCH: The trial judge is able to conserve trial time and avoid possible error by calling the special venire from a group of veniremembers who have already been summoned and had their excuses heard by the jury room judge. Chambers, supra, allows others to hear excuses from veniremembers before they are assigned to a special venire. See Chambers.

§14:121.6 Forms for Venire Formation

See our companion book *Texas Criminal Forms* (James Publishing) for the following sample forms:

- Form 14-16 Defendant's Motion for Special Venire.
- Form 14-16.2 Defendant's Motion for the Court to Decide Jurors' Exemptions, Excuses and Disqualifications Pursuant to Art. 35.03.
- Form 14-17 Writ to Summon Special Venire.
- Form 14-18 Writ to Serve Defendant Jury List.

§14:130 Mechanics of Capital Voir Dire

CCP Art. 35.17. Voir Dire Examination

> *1. When the court in its discretion so directs, except as provided in Section 2, the state and defendant shall conduct the voir dire examination of prospective jurors in the presence of the entire panel.*
>
> *2. In a capital felony case in which the State seeks the death penalty, the court shall propound to the entire panel of prospective jurors questions concerning the principles, as applicable to the case on trial, of reasonable doubt, burden of proof, return of indictment by grand jury, presumption of innocence, and opinion. Then, on demand of the State or defendant, either is entitled to examine each juror on voir dire individually and apart from the entire panel, and may further question the juror on the principles propounded by the court.*

The trial court may restrict the extent of individual questioning in a death penalty case by requiring counsel to propound general voir dire questions to the venire or a mini-panel as long as questions pertaining specifically to the death penalty are propounded to the veniremembers individually. This procedure satisfies Art. 35.17(2). Martinez v. State, 867 S.W.2d 30 (Tex. Crim. App. 1993), *cert. denied,* 512 U.S. 1246, 114 S.Ct. 2765, 129 L. Ed. 2d 879 (1994).

The use of "mini-panels" in capital cases has been approved by the Court of Criminal Appeals. Butler v. State, 872 S.W.2d 227 (Tex. Crim. App. 1994), *cert. denied,* 513 U.S. 1157, 115 S.Ct. 1157,

130 L. Ed. 2d 1079 (1995); Hall v. State, 661 S.W.2d 113 (Tex. Crim. App. 1983).

In capital cases it is customary for peremptory challenges to be made after each veniremember has been individually questioned. CCP Art. 35.13.

The jury selection system set by the Code of Criminal Procedure requiring death penalty defendants to exercise peremptory challenges following examination of each individual juror, as compared to the non-capital case system in which peremptory challenges are exercised after all prospective jurors have been examined, does not violate state or federal due process or equal protection provisions. Janecka v. State, 739 S.W.2d 813 (Tex. Crim. App. 1987), *reversed on other grounds,* 823 S.W.2d 232 (Tex. Crim. App. 1990).

The practice of withholding peremptory challenges until a qualified pool of veniremembers is established also has been approved. Rousseau v. State, 824 S.W.2d 579 (Tex. Crim. App. 1992), *cert. denied,* 510 U.S. 919, 114 S.Ct. 313, 126 L. Ed. 2d 260 (1993).

However, the trial court does not violate a defendant's Sixth Amendment right to an impartial jury and his Fourteenth Amendment rights to due process and equal protection by denying his motion to postpone the exercise of peremptory challenges until the completion of voir dire. Ladd v. State, 3 S.W.3d 547 (Tex. Crim. App. 1999); Dowthitt v. State, 931 S.W.2d 244 (Tex. Crim. App. 1996).

§14:131 Trial Court Instructions to Capital Veniremembers

As quoted above, CCP Art. 35.17 requires that the trial court propound to the entire venire questions concerning certain aspects of capital murder law. For a sample set of instructions to be propounded by the trial court, *see* §14:131.1.

It is often helpful in death penalty case voir dire to distribute an outline of the law at the first meeting of the venire. The purpose of the outline is to give the veniremembers a reference to study prior to the voir dire interview. The outline should contain explanations of the laws, which will be explained to the veniremembers during the voir dire interview. For a sample voir dire outline for distribution to veniremembers, *see* §14:131.2.

§14:131.1 Form: Sample Instructions for Death Penalty Venire Panel

See our companion book *Texas Criminal Forms* (James Publishing) Form 14-21

§14:131.2 Form: Sample Law Outline for Death Penalty Venire Panel

See our companion book *Texas Criminal Forms* (James Publishing) Form 14-22

§14:132 Refusal to Allow Questioning

The trial court errs where it sustains the state's challenge for cause against a venire member without allowing defense counsel an opportunity to question. This error is subject to harmless error analysis under Rule 44.2(b) and will be found harmless where it is highly unlikely that the defendant would have been able to convince the venireman to agree with the law or that the trial court would have abused its discretion in dismissing the venireman for cause. Simpson v. State, 119 S.W.3d 262 (Tex. Crim. App. 2003).

There must be a contemporaneous objection to preserve error where the trial court has not allowed defense counsel to question a venireman. Ransom v. State, 789 S.W.2d 572 (Tex. Crim. App. 1989).

§14:140 Subject Matter for Capital Voir Dire

Texas Penal Code § 12.31. Capital Felony

> *(a) An individual adjudged guilty of a capital felony in a case in which the state seeks the death penalty shall be punished by imprisonment in the institutional division for life without parole or by death. An individual adjudged guilty of a capital felony in a case in which the state does not seek the death penalty shall be punished by imprisonment in the institutional division for life without parole.*
>
> *(b) In a capital felony trial in which the state seeks the death penalty, prospective jurors shall be informed that a sentence of*

life imprisonment without parole or death is mandatory on conviction of a capital felony. In a capital felony trial in which the state does not seek the death penalty, prospective jurors shall be informed that the state is not seeking the death penalty and that a sentence of life imprisonment without parole is mandatory on conviction of the capital felony.

The right to representation as afforded under Art. I, §10 of the Texas Constitution includes the right to properly question prospective jurors during voir dire in order to effectively exercise peremptory challenges or to establish a predicate for a challenge for cause. Ex parte McKay, 819 S.W.2d 478 (Tex. Crim. App. 1990).

Not all rulings limiting defense counsel's voir dire presentation are constitutional error as a *per se* violation of the right to counsel. Most rulings limiting voir dire will be subject to Rule 44.2(b) harm analysis. However, there may be instances when a judge's limitation on voir dire is so substantial as to warrant labeling the error as constitutional error subject to a Rule 44.2(a) harm analysis. Easley v. State, 424 S.W.3d 535, 538-9 (Tex. Crim. App. 2014).

See our companion book, *Texas Criminal Forms* (James Publishing) Form 14-9.1, for a motion to submit a jury questionnaire.

§14:141 Form: Sample Death Penalty Case Juror Questionnaire Instructions for Juror

See our companion book *Texas Criminal Forms* (James Publishing) Form 14-8 and 14-9.1.

§14:142 Informing Venire of Effect of Answers

The parties are allowed to inform the venire of the effect of their answers to the special issues. Jones v. State, 843 S.W.2d 487 (Tex. Crim. App. 1992), *cert. denied,* 507 U.S. 1035, 113 S.Ct. 1858, 123 L. Ed. 2d 479 (1993). However, CCP Art. 37.071 §2(a) provides that veniremembers not be informed "of the effect of failure of the jury to agree on an issue submitted under th[e] article." Thus, the parties may not inform the venire of the effect of their failure to answer a special issue. Clark v. State, 881 S.W.2d 682 (Tex. Crim. App. 1994); Sattiewhite v. State, 786 S.W.2d 271 (Tex. Crim. App. 1989), *cert. denied*, 498 U.S. 881, 111 S.Ct. 226, 112 L. Ed. 2d 181 (1990).

The error caused by so informing the venire is in large part cured by an appropriate jury charge informing the jurors of their duty under the law to vote according to the evidence on the special issues. Clark.

§14:143 Questioning on Definition of Terms

The trial court has the discretion to prohibit voir dire on a veniremember's understanding of the definition of undefined terms in the charge. Wheatfall v. State, 882 S.W.2d 829 (Tex. Crim. App. 1994) ("deliberate").

A trial court is on firmer ground limiting voir dire on the understanding of undefined terms in capital murder cases than in non-capital cases because in those cases voir dire examination can take an unreasonable length of time. Woolridge v. State, 827 S.W.2d 900 (Tex. Crim. App. 1992). For example, a trial court does not abuse its discretion by refusing to permit counsel to question a veniremember regarding his definition of the term "probability." Lagrone v. State, 942 S.W.2d 602 (Tex. Crim. App. 1997), *cert. denied,* 522 U.S. 917, 118 S.Ct. 305, 139 L. Ed. 2d 235 (1997).

A trial court does not abuse its discretion by refusing voir dire questioning on definitions of the terms "deliberately, probability, and criminal acts of violence" in a capital case. Milton v. State, 599 S.W.2d 824 (Tex. Crim. App. 1980), *cert. denied,* 451 U.S. 1031, 101 S.Ct. 3022, 69 L. Ed. 2d 400 (1981).

A trial court is, however, required under certain circumstances to allow the parties to question the venire as to their comprehension of certain terms as those terms are relevant to the issues in the case. Teague v. State, 864 S.W.2d 505 (Tex. Crim. App. 1993), *overruled on other grounds,* Robertson v. State, 871 S.W.2d 701 (Tex. Crim. App. 1993) (where the issue was the difference between the terms "intentionally" and "deliberately").

This is especially true where a party is making inquiry of the veniremember in an attempt to lay the proper predicate for a challenge for cause. Gardner v. State, 730 S.W.2d 675 (Tex. Crim. App. 1987), *cert. denied,* 484 U.S. 905, 108 S.Ct. 248, 98 L. Ed. 2d 206 (1987).

TIP TO THE BENCH: In situations such as a death penalty case, you can save a great deal of time on voir dire to encourage the parties to agree on a definition for terms not defined by law, which are crucial to a veniremember's function as a juror.

Where terms such as "criminal acts of violence" are not defined for the jury, error in the voir dire examination occurs when the state attempts to limit the venire to a specific definition. Jackson v. State, 822 S.W.2d 18 (Tex. Crim. App. 1990), *cert. denied*, 509 U.S. 921, 113 S.Ct. 3034, 125 L. Ed. 2d 722 (1993). However, a party may suggest a definition to a veniremember, where the party makes it clear that the veniremember will be required to determine for himself what the definition of the term should be. Coble v. State, 871 S.W.2d 192 (Tex. Crim. App. 1993), *cert. denied,* 513 U.S. 829, 115 S.Ct. 101, 130 L. Ed. 2d 50 (1994).

Although the word "society" in the future-dangerousness special issue is not statutorily defined and thus ordinarily should not be defined, the word must be limited to its technical meaning in this particular context in order for the Texas capital murder statute to comply with federal constitutional requirements. Curry v. State, 541 S.W.3d 751 (Tex. Crim. App. 2017), (dissent by Judge Alcala).

§14:144 Questioning About Facts of Case

A party is allowed to attempt to determine if a veniremember could consider, or conceive, that a crime against property can be a crime of violence; but must do so without committing each veniremember to a particular position. Burks v. State, 876 S.W.2d 877 (Tex. Crim. App. 1994), *cert. denied*, 513 U.S. 1114, 115 S.Ct. 909, 130 L. Ed. 2d 791 (1995). The trial court may restrict questions in which counsel attempts to commit a veniremember to a particular resolution based upon facts peculiar to the trial. Coleman v. State, 881 S.W.2d 344 (Tex. Crim. App.1994), *cert. denied*, 513 U.S. 1096, 115 S.Ct. 763, 130 L. Ed. 2d 660 (1995).

§14:145 Questions Regarding Mitigation of Punishment

Whether the veniremember could consider certain types of evidence in mitigation of punishment is a proper area of inquiry. Rhoades v. State, 934 S.W.2d 113 (Tex. Crim. App. 1996).

The trial court may restrict questions in which counsel attempts to commit a veniremember to a particular resolution based upon facts peculiar to the trial. Coleman v. State, 881 S.W.2d 344 (Tex. Crim. App.1994), *cert. denied*, 513 U.S. 1096, 115 S.Ct. 763, 130 L. Ed. 2d 660 (1995).

Counsel improperly committing a veniremember to a particular set of facts occurs where counsel asks a veniremember whether he *believes* a particular type of evidence to be mitigating, rather than asking whether he could *consider* the evidence as a possible mitigating circumstance. Rhoades.

Since a jury will now be instructed in the punishment phase that a defendant must serve a minimum of 40 years before becoming eligible for parole on a capital murder conviction, the trial court will probably not abuse its discretion in permitting questioning of the veniremen about their attitudes on parole. Sells v. State, 121 S.W.3d 748 (Tex. Crim. App. 2003).

§14:146 Questions About Race of Defendant and/or Victim

A capital murder defendant is entitled to have prospective jurors informed of the race of the victim and questioned on the issue of racial bias. Turner v. Murray, 476 U.S. 28, 106 S.Ct. 1683, 90 L. Ed. 2d 27 (1986).

§14:147 Improper Areas

The trial court does not err in preventing counsel from asking questions based on an improper statement of the law. Morrow v. State, 910 S.W.2d 471 (Tex. Crim. App. 1995), *cert. denied,* 517 U.S. 1192, 116 S.Ct. 1683, 134 L. Ed. 2d 784 (1996).

For offenses occurring before September 1, 1999 refusing to allow questioning about parole eligibility is not error in a capital case because this is not a proper area of inquiry. Eldridge v. State, 940 S.W.2d 646 (Tex. Crim. App. 1996).

Effective for offenses committed on or after September 1, 1999 juries are informed in the punishment charge as to the law of parole on a capital life sentence. It follows that counsel will be allowed to question on capital life sentence parole procedures the same as allowed on parole provisions applicable for other offenses.

However, precedent maintaining that parole is not a proper issue for jury consideration remains in effect except to the extent explicitly provided for in Article 37.071 §2(e)(2)(B). Hankins v. State, 132 S.W.3d 380 (Tex. Crim. App. 2004) (defendant sought to voir dire on whether the veniremembers could consider and give full deliberation to the parole board requirements for release.).

Questions which ask veniremembers whether or not he would consider a particular type of evidence as a mitigating factor are objectionable based on the form of the question as an attempt to bind the juror to a particular verdict. Soria v. State, 933 S.W.2d 46 (Tex. Crim. App. 1996).

§14:148 Preserving Error in Denial of Proper Inquiry

In a death penalty prosecution where jurors are examined individually, counsel must exercise a peremptory challenge on the specific veniremember in order to demonstrate harm where the trial court does not permit a proper question and thus denies the intelligent exercise of peremptory challenges. Janecka v. State, 739 S.W.2d 813 (Tex. Crim. App. 1987), *reversed on other grounds,* 823 S.W.2d 232 (Tex. Crim. App. 1990).

Voir dire error in a capital case can be error affecting the punishment phase only under CCP Art. 44.29(c); therefore, depending on the error the retrial could be for a punishment hearing only. Ransom v. State, 920 S.W.2d 288 (Tex. Crim. App. 1994).

§14:150 Challenges for Cause

CCP Art. 35.13. Passing juror for challenge

> *A juror in a capital case in which the state has made it known it will seek the death penalty, held to be qualified, shall be passed for acceptance or challenge first to the state and then to the defendant. Challenges to jurors are either peremptory or for cause.*

For a full discussion of the grounds for challenges for cause *see* §14:60.

§14:151 Excusing Veniremembers for Cause in Capital Cases

Potential jurors must be able to set aside their personal preferences and biases to consider death eligible all those defined as death eligible by §19.03 Penal Code and CCP Art. 37.071. Rachal v. State, 917 S.W.2d 799 (Tex. Crim. App. 1996) (plurality opinion).

A veniremember is challengeable for cause where his views against the death penalty are such that they would prevent or substantially impair the performance of his duties as a juror in accordance with his instructions and oath. Vuong v. State, 830 S.W.2d 929, 943 (Tex. Crim. App. 1992), *cert. denied*, 506 U.S. 997, 113 S.Ct. 595, 121 L. Ed. 2d 533 (1992); Wainwright v. Witt, 469 U.S. 412, 105 S.Ct. 844, 83 L. Ed. 2d 841 (1985). In other words, unless a veniremember is so irrevocably opposed to capital punishment that he could not follow the law or obey the instructions of the trial court, he is not disqualified from capital murder jury service. Riley v. State, 889 S.W.2d 290 (Tex. Crim. App. 1993).

The prosecution has the burden of demonstrating that because of the veniremember's views he will answer the special issues in a way that a life sentence rather than a death penalty will be imposed. Clark v. State, 929 S.W.2d 5 (Tex. Crim. App. 1996).

Veniremembers may not displace the broad legal categories of death eligibility with their personal agendas. Rachal, *supra*. Veniremembers who have stated an opposition to some phase of the law are nonetheless competent to serve as jurors where they state clearly that they are willing to temporarily set aside their own beliefs in deference to the rule of law. Ellis v. State, 726 S.W.2d 39 (Tex. Crim. App. 1986); Lockhart v. McCree, 476 U.S. 162, 106 S.Ct. 1758, 90 L. Ed. 2d 137 (1986). A veniremember may not be excluded from jury service based solely on his opinion of the death penalty when the record clearly demonstrates he is capable of following the law. Riley, *supra*.

If the veniremember equivocates or vacillates in his answers, it is within the sound discretion of the trial court to excuse or not depending on the observations of the court. Brown v. State, 913 S.W.2d 577 (Tex. Crim. App. 1996).

So long as a veniremember consistently affirms that he could in fact answer the special issues in accordance with the evidence, neither the difficulty he may have in doing so, nor the fact that it might violate his conscience, renders him a "vacillating" veniremember in any material sense. Therefore, in this situation a reviewing court will not defer to the findings of the trial court absent an abuse of discretion. Riley.

Where the veniremember states that he will distort his answers to reach a certain result he must be excused because of his inability to follow the law. Clark, *supra*. If a veniremember states that he will not consciously distort his answer to obtain a specific result (or to avoid one) he has not shown an inability to follow the law. Clark.

It is not enough that the veniremember's views on the death penalty might influence his decision making. Vuong, *supra*. Religious scruples against the death penalty in and of themselves are not sufficient to sustain a challenge for cause under the Vuong standard. Clark.

Deliberate failure to report a true verdict is a substantial impairment in any juror, and when supported by the record will authorize sustaining a challenge for cause. Rogers v. State, 774 S.W.2d 247 (Tex. Crim. App. 1989). If a juror is to obey his oath and follow the law, he must be willing not only to accept that in certain circumstances death is an acceptable penalty, but also to be able to answer the statutory questions without conscious distortion or bias. Gunter v. State, 858 S.W.2d 430 (Tex. Crim. App. 1993).

A refusal to take the juror's oath demonstrates that the veniremember's views prevent him from carrying out the duties of a juror. Gunter.

TIP TO THE PROSECUTION: In order to meet the burden under Vuong and Clark, the Court of Criminal Appeals has suggested that the state directly ask the veniremember whether his opposition to the death penalty is such as to cause him to answer one of the special issues in such a way as to ensure a life sentence, regardless of what the facts of the case may be.

A juror who would require more than the minimum quantum of evidence before answering the future dangerous special issue in the affirmative is not subject to a challenge for cause on this ground. Garrett v. State, 851 S.W.2d 853 (Tex. Crim. App. 1993).

§14:152 When to Make Challenge for Cause

A contemporaneous challenge for cause must be asserted against an objectionable veniremember in order to preserve error for appeal. Purtell v. State, 761 S.W.2d 360 (Tex. Crim. App. 1988). The challenge for cause generally must be made before the objectionable veniremember is dismissed and before the questioning of the next veniremember. Barefield v. State, 784 S.W.2d 38 (Tex. Crim. App. 1989).

CCP Art. 35.13 provides that in capital cases, the veniremembers shall be called individually, and upon completion of voir dire by both parties the veniremember is to be passed first to the state for acceptance, challenge for cause or peremptory challenge; and next to the defendant for acceptance, challenge for cause or peremptory challenge. Bigby v. State, 892 S.W.2d 864 (Tex. Crim. App. 1994), *cert. denied,* 515 U.S. 1102, 115 S.Ct. 2617, 132 L. Ed. 2d 860 (1995).

However, requiring the defendant to assert his challenge for cause before the state is required to accept the veniremember or exercise a peremptory challenge is not reversible error because the reversal of the order of challenges has no effect on the selection of jurors. Bigby. Where the challenge system employed ultimately requires the state to exercise its peremptory challenge on a veniremember before the defendant is called upon to exercise his, the defendant has not been harmed. Hughes v. State, 24 S.W.3d 833 (Tex. Crim. App. 2000).

Special circumstances may allow the use of a challenge for cause after the veniremember has been chosen as a juror. Jones v. State, 843 S.W.2d 487 (Tex. Crim. App. 1992), *cert. denied,* 507 U.S. 1035, 113 S.Ct. 1858, 123 L. Ed. 2d 479 (1993). These special circumstances may include that the trial court discovers that the juror may be challengeable for cause, excusable or otherwise disqualified. Draughon v. State, 831 S.W.2d 331 (Tex. Crim. App. 1992), *cert. denied,* 509 U.S. 926, 113 S.Ct. 3045, 125 L. Ed. 2d 730 (1993).

Where the entire jury has not yet been selected and no evidence received in trial of the cause, the judge is permitted general discretion to allow further examination and to entertain additional challenges when it comes to his attention that a previously selected juror may be objectionable for cause, excusable, or otherwise disqualified from jury service. Draughon.

§14:153 Challenges for Cause by Either Party

For an extensive list of grounds for challenges for cause in all types of criminal cases, *see* §14:68.1.

§14:153.1 Grounds Where Challenges Granted

The following have been recognized as proper areas for a challenge for cause by either party in a death penalty case. The defendant would cite CCP Art. 35.16(c)(2), and the state would cite CCP Art. 35.16(b)(1).

- Veniremember would not be able to reconsider the guilt phase evidence independently for purposes of resolving the special issues; Gardner v. State, 730 S.W.2d 675 (Tex. Crim. App. 1987), *cert. denied,* 484 U.S. 905, 108 S.Ct. 248, 98 L. Ed. 2d 206 (1987)
- Veniremember's inability to comprehend the limited function of a juror at the punishment phase of a capital case constitutes such a mental defect as to render him unfit for jury service; Matamoros v. State, 901 S.W.2d 470 (Tex. Crim. App. 1995); Gardner, *supra.*
- Veniremember could never find a murder committed during a robbery to be reasonable as a response to provocation, thus indicating a bias against the law with respect to special issue three; Garcia v. State, 919 S.W.2d 370 (Tex. Crim. App. 1994)
- Veniremember cannot differentiate between the terms "probability" and "possibility," because this renders the veniremember impaired in evaluating the evidence offered to prove future dangerousness; Patrick v. State, 906 S.W.2d 481 (Tex. Crim. App. 1995), *cert. denied,* 517 U.S. 406, 116 S.Ct. 1323, 134 L. Ed. 2d 475 (1996)
- Veniremember would automatically answer the first special issue in the affirmative; Caldwell v. State, 818 S.W.2d 790 (Tex. Crim. App. 1991), *cert. denied,* 503 U.S. 990, 112 S.Ct. 1684, 118 L. Ed. 2d 399 (1992)
- Veniremember would automatically answer the first two special issues in the affirmative, or who would place the burden of proof on the defense; Banda v. State, 890 S.W.2d 42 (Tex. Crim. App.1994), *cert. denied,* 515 U.S. 1105, 115 S.Ct. 2253, 132 L. Ed. 2d 260 (1995)
- Veniremember has a bias or prejudice against one of the special issues; Cumbo v. State, 760 S.W.2d 251 (Tex. Crim. App. 1988)
- A venireperson who says that she cannot answer honestly answer the special issues so that a death penalty results could not judge another person and did not think that she could follow the law in a capital case. Hernandez v. State, 390 S.W.3d 310, 321 (Tex. Crim. App. 2012).

§14:153.2 Grounds Where Challenges Not Granted

A veniremember is not challengeable for cause on the ground that he will not give mitigating effect to particular evidence. Lagrone v. State, 942 S.W.2d 602 (Tex. Crim. App. 1997), *cert. denied,* 522 U.S. 917, 118 S.Ct. 305, 139 L. Ed. 2d 235 (1997); Massey v. State, 933 S.W.2d 141 (Tex. Crim. App. 1996); Morrow v. State, 910 S.W.2d 471 (Tex. Crim. App. 1995), *cert. denied,* 517 U.S. 1192, 116 S.Ct. 1683, 134 L. Ed. 2d 784 (1996).

§14:154 Challenges for Cause by Defendant

CCP Art. 35.16(c)(2) permits the defendant to challenge for cause a veniremember on the ground "[t]hat he has a bias or prejudice against any of the law applicable to the case upon which the defendant is entitled to rely, either as a defense to some phase of the offense for which the defendant is being prosecuted or as a mitigation thereof or of the punishment therefor."

For an extensive list of grounds for challenges for cause by the defendant in all types of criminal cases, *see* §14:68.2.

§14:154.1 Grounds Where Challenges Will Be Granted

The following have been recognized as proper areas for defense challenges for cause in capital cases:

- Veniremember inability to consider the minimum punishment for a lesser included offense; Pierce v. State, 696 S.W.2d 899 (Tex. Crim. App. 1985)
- Veniremember inability to consider a life sentence as a possible punishment for capital murder; Cumbo v. State, 760 S.W.2d 251 (Tex. Crim. App. 1988)
- Veniremember inability to distinguish between deliberate and intentional conduct; Martinez v. State, 763 S.W.2d 413 (Tex. Crim. App. 1988)
- Veniremember inability to disregard parole as a factor in answering the special issues; Felder v. State, 758 S.W.2d 760 (Tex. Crim. App. 1988)
- Veniremember always answers the mitigation special issue in such a way that a death penalty would result; Staley v. State, 887 S.W.2d 885 (Tex. Crim. App. 1994), *cert. denied,* 514 U.S. 1020, 115 S.Ct. 1366, 131 L. Ed. 2d 222 (1995)

§14:154.2 Areas Where Challenges Will Not Be Granted

A veniremember is not challengeable for cause on the ground that he will not give mitigating effect to particular evidence. Lagrone v. State, 942 S.W.2d 602 (Tex. Crim. App. 1997), *cert. denied,* 522 U.S. 917, 118 S.Ct. 305, 139 L. Ed. 2d 235 (1997); Massey v. State, 933 S.W.2d 141 (Tex. Crim. App. 1996); Morrow v. State, 910 S.W.2d 471 (Tex. Crim. App. 1995), *cert. denied,* 517 U.S. 1192, 116 S.Ct. 1683, 134 L. Ed. 2d 784 (1996).

There is no law placing the burden of proof on the state as to the mitigation special issue, so a veniremember is not challengeable for cause simply because he would place the burden of proof on mitigation on the defense. Ladd v. State, 3 S.W.3d 547 (Tex. Crim. App. 1999); Barnes v. State, 876 S.W.2d 316 (Tex. Crim. App. 1994), *cert. denied,* 513 U.S. 861, 115 S.Ct. 174, 130 L. Ed. 2d 110 (1994).

A veniremember is not subject to a challenge for cause merely because he is unable to think of a situation in which he would answer the future dangerousness special issue in the negative. Pierce v. State, 777 S.W.2d 399 (Tex. Crim. App. 1989).

Similarly, a veniremember is not challengeable for cause simply because he cannot immediately envision a scenario in which the minimum punishment would be appropriate. The mere fact that a veniremember cannot envision such a scenario during voir dire does not indicate that he could not consider the minimum punishment if an appropriate scenario presented itself at trial. Ladd.

§14:154.3 Preserving Error for Denial of Defense Challenge

In order to preserve error in a trial court's erroneous denial of a defense challenge for cause, the defendant must follow a rigorous predicate showing that:

- Voir dire of the individual veniremember was recorded and transcribed; Long v. State, 823 S.W.2d 259 (Tex. Crim. App. 1991), *cert. denied,* 505 U.S. 1224, 112 S.Ct. 3042, 120 L. Ed. 2d 910 (1992)
- Defense asserted a clear and specific challenge for cause clearly articulating the grounds therefore; Miller v. State, 741 S.W.2d 382 (Tex. Crim. App. 1987), *cert. denied,* 486 U.S. 1061, 108 S.Ct. 2835, 100 L. Ed. 2d 935 (1988)
- Defense used a peremptory challenge on that particular veniremember; Jones v. State, 833 S.W.2d 118 (Tex. Crim. App. 1992), *cert. denied,* 507 U.S. 921, 113 S.Ct. 1285, 122 L. Ed. 2d 678 (1993)
- Defense exhausted all of his peremptory challenges; Adanandus v. State, 866 S.W.2d 210 (Tex. Crim. App. 1993), *cert. denied,* 510 U.S. 1215, 114 S.Ct. 1338, 127 L. Ed. 2d 686 (1994); Jacobs

v. State, 787 S.W.2d 397 (Tex. Crim. App. 1990), *cert. denied,* 496 U.S. 882, 111 S.Ct. 231, 112 L. Ed. 2d 185 (1990)

- Defense was forced to accept an objectionable veniremember on the jury because of the trial court's erroneous actions, *i.e.*, that he would have exercised a peremptory challenge against that veniremember if he had one remaining; Trevino v. State, 991 S.W.2d 849 (Tex. Crim. App. 1999); Green v. State, 840 S.W.2d 394 (Tex. Crim. App. 1992), *cert. denied,* 507 U.S. 1020, 113 S.Ct. 1819, 123 L. Ed. 2d 449 (1993), *disavowed on other grounds.*

PRACTICE TIP: In order to preserve error, recite into the record prior to the jury being seated and sworn, that:

- Defense was forced to use a peremptory challenge on a juror against whom a challenge for cause had been made
- Defense exhausted all of his peremptory challenges
- Defense has requested additional peremptory challenges and that request has been denied (or if additional peremptory challenges were granted, that those also have been exhausted and an additional request has been made and denied)
- Objectionable juror has been seated and that he would exercise a peremptory challenge on that juror if afforded an additional peremptory. Counsel should then request an additional peremptory challenge and have the request denied

The defendant must demonstrate that he exercised a peremptory challenge on the veniremember upon which he bases his claim. Brosky v. State, 915 S.W.2d 120 (Tex.App.—Fort Worth , *pet. ref'd*), *cert. denied,* 117 S.Ct. 537 (1996)

In order to do this, the defendant bears the burden of including the jury strike lists as part of the record on appeal. Hernandez v. State, 938 S.W.2d 503 (Tex.App.—Waco 1997, *pet. ref'd*).

In order to make a certain claim on appeal, the defendant must have objected on the same ground in the trial court. Trevino v. State, 991 S.W.2d 849 (Tex. Crim. App. 1999); Green v. State, 840 S.W.2d 394 (Tex. Crim. App. 1992), *cert. denied,* 507 U.S. 1020, 113 S.Ct. 1819, 123 L. Ed. 2d 449 (1993), *disavowed on other grounds.* It is not necessary that the defendant go so far as to explain why the objectionable juror that he has named is, in fact, objectionable. Garcia v. State, 887 S.W.2d 846 (Tex. Crim. App. 1994), *cert. denied,* 514 U.S. 1005, 115 S.Ct. 1317, 131 L. Ed. 2d 198 (1995).

Where the trial court grants two additional peremptory challenges, the defendant must show that the trial court erred in denying his challenge for cause to three prospective jurors. Penry v. State, 903 S.W.2d 715 (Tex. Crim. App. 1995), *cert. denied,* 516 U.S. 977, 116 S.Ct. 480, 133 L. Ed. 2d 408 (1995).

Harm from the erroneous denial of a defense challenge occurs: (1) when a defendant exercises a peremptory challenge on a veniremember whom the trial court should have excused for cause at the defendant's request, (2) the defendant uses all of his statutorily allotted peremptory challenges, and (3) the defendant unsuccessfully requests an additional peremptory challenge which he claims he would use on another veniremember whom the defendant identifies as "objectionable" and who actually sits on the jury. When these conditions are met, this harms a defendant because he had to use a peremptory challenge to remove a veniremember who should have been removed for cause which, in effect, wrongfully deprives the defendant of one of his statutory peremptory challenges. Newbury v. State, 135 S.W.3d 22 (Tex. Crim. App. 2004)

Voir dire error in a capital case can be error affecting the punishment phase only under CCP Art. 44.29(c); therefore, depending on the error the retrial could be for a punishment hearing only. Ransom v. State, 920 S.W.2d 288 (Tex. Crim. App. 1994).

§14:155 Challenges for Causes by State in Capital Cases

CCP Art. 35.16(b)(3) allows the state to challenge for cause veniremembers who have a "bias or prejudice against any phase of the law upon which the state is entitled to rely for conviction or punishment."

In addition to the grounds listed here, *see* §14:68.3.

§14:155.1 Grounds Where Challenges Will Be Granted

The following have been recognized as valid reasons for the state to challenge a veniremember for cause in a capital case:

- Veniremember interprets the phrase "criminal acts of violence" to require that the state prove that the defendant has murdered before; Fuller v. State, 829 S.W.2d 191 (Tex. Crim. App. 1992), *cert. denied,* 508 U.S. 941, 113 S.Ct. 2418, 124 L. Ed. 2d 640 (1993); Drew v. State, 743 S.W.2d 207 (Tex. Crim. App. 1987).
- Veniremember would not be able to fairly consider the death penalty as a possible punishment; Long v. State, 823 S.W.2d 259 (Tex. Crim. App. 1991)
- Veniremember would require more than proof beyond a reasonable doubt because the state is seeking the death penalty; Chambers v. State, 866 S.W.2d 9 (Tex. Crim. App. 1993), *cert. denied,* 511 U.S. 1100, 114 S.Ct. 1871, 128 L. Ed. 2d 491 (1994)
- Veniremember is unable to consider the full range of punishment because of the youth of the defendant; Garcia v. State, 919 S.W.2d 370 (Tex. Crim. App. 1994)
- Veniremember is challengeable as having a bias or prejudice against a law upon which the state is entitled to rely if he would always answer the mitigating circumstances punishment issue, Art. 37.071, §2(e), in favor of the defendant; Wolfe v. State, 917 S.W.2d 270 (Tex. Crim. App. 1996)
- Likewise, a veniremember is challengeable under CCP Art. 35.16(b)(3) if he would never answer the future dangerousness issue in favor of the state. Wolfe.
- Veniremember acknowledges that violent property crimes could constitute a continuing threat to society, yet she required proof of violence against people. Such a position indicates that the veniremember would supplant the legal categories of death eligibility with her personal preferences and biases. Howard v. State, 941 S.W.2d 102 (Tex. Crim. App. 1996)
- Veniremember would require that the murder be premeditated before he could vote in such a way that the death penalty be assessed; Patrick v. State, 906 S.W.2d 481 (Tex. Crim. App. 1995), *cert. denied,* 517 U.S. 406, 116 S.Ct. 1323, 134 L. Ed. 2d 475 (1996)
- Veniremember would never vote in such a way that the death penalty would be assessed against a defendant who was a party to a capital murder; Selvage v. State, 680 S.W.2d 17 (Tex. Crim. App. 1984)
- Veniremember who would only consider the death penalty where one of his family members was the victim is not qualified; Fearance v. State, 771 S.W.2d 486 (Tex. Crim. App. 1988), *cert. denied,* 492 U.S. 927, 109 S.Ct. 3266, 106 L. Ed. 2d 611 (1989)
- Veniremember who will only consider the death penalty for a defendant who confessed to the crime is challengeable for cause; Monroe v. Blackburn, 748 F.2d 958 (5th Circ. 1984), *cert. denied,* 476 U.S. 1145, 106 S.Ct. 2261, 90 L. Ed. 2d 706 (1986)
- Veniremember who could only consider the death penalty for a person convicted of a murder for hire is challengeable for cause; Crane v. State, 786 S.W.2d 338 (Tex. Crim. App. 1990)
- Veniremember was properly removed for cause where he acknowledged that he could not resolve his religious conflicts with respect to the death penalty and as a consequence his performance as a juror would be substantially impaired; Cooks v. State, 844 S.W.2d 697 (Tex. Crim. App. 1992), *cert. denied,* 509 U.S. 927, 113 S.Ct. 3048, 125 L. Ed. 2d 732 (1993); Kinnamon v. State, 791

S.W.2d 84 (Tex. Crim. App. 1990), *overruled on other grounds*

- Veniremember ultimately guided by personal beliefs rather than the law and evidence is not qualified to sit on a jury; Castillo v. State, 739 S.W.2d 280 (Tex. Crim. App. 1987), *cert. denied,* 487 U.S. 1228, 108 S.Ct. 2889, 101 L. Ed. 2d 924 (1988)

§14:155.2 Grounds Where Challenges Will Not Be Granted

A veniremember is not subject to a challenge for cause by the state merely because he would require more evidence than the legal minimum in order to answer the future dangerousness special issue in the affirmative. Garrett v. State, 851 S.W.2d 853 (Tex. Crim. App. 1993).

A venireman who requires a particular type of evidence has not demonstrated an inability to abide by the law if his requirement is predicated upon his personal threshold of reasonable doubt. The state has the burden to show that the venireman's insistence on evidence of a particular type will prevent him from honestly answering the special issue regardless of whether he was otherwise convinced beyond a reasonable doubt of future dangerousness, before it can be said it has met its burden to demonstrate the venireman cannot follow the law. Howard v. State, 941 S.W.2d 102 (Tex. Crim. App. 1996); Murphy v. State, 112 S.W.3d 192 (Tex. Crim. App. 2003).

Similarly, a venireman whose definition of a particular term requires a certain type of evidence is not subject to a challenge for cause. Murphy.

It is not permissible for the prosecution to use the language of the Penal Code §12.31(b) oath to disqualify potential jurors; White v. State, 610 S.W.2d 504 (Tex. Crim. App. 1981); Adams v. Texas, 448 U.S. 38, 100 S.Ct. 2521, 65 L. Ed. 2d 581 (1980).

TIP TO THE PROSECUTION: A veniremember may state that he requires specific evidence above and beyond the facts of the case in order to return a death penalty sentence. Before you can excuse the veniremember for cause, it is incumbent on the state to show that the veniremember would refuse to answer the special circumstances questions in any manner in which the death penalty would be imposed, even if the other evidence is sufficient to prove beyond a reasonable doubt that the questions should be answered that way. In other words, the state must show that the veniremember's position is not merely a prediction of his attitude upon hearing the evidence, but is in fact, a categorical refusal to answer "yes" even if other evidence could convince him of the defendant's future dangerousness beyond a reasonable doubt. Howard v. State, 941 S.W.2d 102 (Tex. Crim. App. 1996).

It is the state's burden, as the challenging party, to show that the veniremember's refusal to return a death penalty is predicated upon something other than his understanding of proof beyond a reasonable doubt. Castillo v. State, 913 S.W.2d 529 (Tex. Crim. App. 1995).

§14:155.3 Preserving Error for Improperly Granted State's Challenge

The defendant preserves error in the trial court's improper granting of a state's challenge for cause where he lodges a specific objection before the veniremember is dismissed and before the questioning of the next veniremember begins. Barefield v. State, 784 S.W.2d 38 (Tex. Crim. App. 1989), *cert. denied*, 497 U.S. 1011, 110 S.Ct. 3256, 111 L. Ed. 2d 766 (1990).

An objection is untimely if it is made after that veniremember was excused and questioning begins on the next veniremember. Fuller v. State, 827 S.W.2d 919 (Tex. Crim. App. 1992), *cert. denied,* 509 U.S. 922, 113 S.Ct. 3035, 125 L. Ed. 2d 722 (1993).

In noncapital cases, for a reversal, the defendant must show that he was deprived of a lawfully constituted jury. However, in death penalty cases if a veniremember is wrongfully excused on a state's challenge for cause because of a general opposition to the death penalty, the exclusion of a juror by an unintentional mistake amounts to a constitutional violation requiring reversal. Jones v. State, 982

JURY SELECTION AND VOIR DIRE

S.W.2d 386 (Tex. Crim. App. 1998), *cert. denied,* 120 S.Ct. 444, 145 L. Ed. 2d 362 (1999).

However, where the reason for the improper excusal of the venireman does not implicate *Witherspoon* or *Wainwright* error, the error is harmless. Murphy v. State, 112 S.W.3d 192 (Tex. Crim. App. 2003). (the venireman was improperly excused because her own definition of the phrase "criminal acts of violence" required evidence that the defendant committed or attempted to commit other murders).

Voir dire error in a capital case can be error affecting the punishment phase only under CCP Art. 44.29(c); therefore, depending on the error, the retrial could be for a punishment hearing only. Ransom v. State, 920 S.W.2d 288 (Tex. Crim. App. 1994).

§14:160 Veniremembers Excused by Agreement

CCP Art. 35.05. Excused by Consent

> *One summoned upon a special venire may by consent of both parties be excused from attendance by the court at any time before he is impaneled.*

The court may excuse a special veniremember from attendance by consent of both parties at any time before the veniremember is empaneled. CCP Art. 35.05.

§14:170 Peremptory Challenges in Death Penalty Cases

In capital cases, it is customary for peremptory challenges to be made after each veniremember has been individually questioned. CCP Art. 35.13.

The jury selection system set by the Code of Criminal Procedure requiring death penalty defendants to exercise peremptory challenges following examination of each individual juror, as compared to the noncapital case system in which peremptory challenges are exercised after all prospective jurors have been examined, does not violate state or federal due process or equal protection provisions. Janecka v. State, 739 S.W.2d 813 (Tex. Crim. App. 1987), *reversed on other grounds,* 823 S.W.2d 232 (Tex. Crim. App. 1990).

The procedure controlling the order and timing of the exercise of peremptory challenges is not an absolute requirement. Busby v. State, 990 S.W.2d 263 (Tex. Crim. App. 1999), *cert. denied,* 528 U.S. 1081, 120 S.Ct. 803, 145 L.Ed.2d 676 (2000).

Where the challenge system employed ultimately requires the state to exercise its peremptory challenge on a veniremember before the defendant is called upon to exercise his, the defendant has not been harmed. Hughes v. State, 24 S.W.3d 833 (Tex. Crim. App. 2000).

The practice of withholding peremptory challenges until a qualified pool of veniremembers is established has also been approved. Rousseau v. State, 824 S.W.2d 579 (Tex. Crim. App. 1992), *cert. denied,* 510 U.S. 919, 114 S.Ct. 313, 126 L. Ed. 2d 260 (1993).

However, the trial court does not violate a defendant's Sixth Amendment right to an impartial jury and his Fourteenth Amendment rights to due process and equal protection by denying his motion to postpone the exercise of peremptory challenges until the completion of voir dire. Ladd v. State, 3 S.W.3d 547 (Tex. Crim. App. 1999); Dowthitt v. State, 931 S.W.2d 244 (Tex. Crim. App.1996).

The trial court does not err in denying the defendant's request to make an out-of-time peremptory challenge. Beavers v. State, 856 S.W.2d 429 (Tex. Crim. App. 1993), *cert. denied,* 510 U.S. 951, 114 S.Ct. 399, 126 L. Ed. 2d 346 (1993).

The trial court does not err in allowing the state to use a peremptory challenge against the preceding juror after it has completed its voir dire examination of the succeeding juror, but before the defense has commenced. Barnard v. State, 730 S.W.2d 703 (Tex. Crim. App. 1987), *cert. denied,* 485 U.S. 929, 108 S.Ct. 1098, 99 L. Ed. 2d 261 (1988); *see also*, Franklin v. State, 693 S.W.2d 420 (Tex. Crim. App. 1985), *cert. denied,* 475 U.S. 1031, 106 S.Ct. 1238, 89 L. Ed. 2d 346 (1986).

The defendant must object in a timely fashion in order to preserve error where the state has been allowed to retroactively exercise a peremptory challenge. Fearance v. State, 771 S.W.2d 486 (Tex. Crim. App.1988), *cert. denied*, 492 U.S. 927, 109 S.Ct. 3266, 106 L. Ed. 2d 611 (1989).

A defendant's constitutional rights are not violated when he chooses to use a peremptory challenge against a venireman that the trial court should have excused for cause because peremptory challenges are not of federal constitutional dimension. U.S. v. Martinez-Salazar, 528 U.S. 304, 120 S.Ct. 774, 145 L.Ed.2d 792 (2000).

(This page intentionally left blank.)